Financial Aid for the Disabled and Their Families 2004-2006

RSP FINANCIAL AID DIRECTORIES OF INTEREST TO THE DISABLED AND THEIR FAMILIES

College Student's Guide to Merit and Other No-Need Funding, 2004-2006
More than 1,200 funding opportunities for currently-enrolled or returning college students are described in this directory. 450 pages. ISBN 1-58841-102-8. $32, plus $5 shipping.

Directory of Financial Aids for Women, 2003-2005
Nearly 1,600 funding programs set aside for women are described in this biennial directory, which *School Library Journal* calls "the cream of the crop." 582 pages. ISBN 1-58841-067-6. $45, plus $5 shipping.

Financial Aid for African Americans, 2003-2005
More than 1,400 scholarships, fellowships, loans, grants, and internships open to African Americans are described in this award-winning directory. 538 pages. ISBN 1-58841-068-5. $40, plus $5 shipping.

Financial Aid for Asian Americans, 2003-2005
This is the source to use if you are looking for financial aid for Asian Americans; nearly 1,000 funding opportunities are described. 356 pages. ISBN 1-58841-069-2. $37.50, plus $5 shipping.

Financial Aid for Hispanic Americans, 2003-2005
Nearly 1,300 funding programs open to Americans of Mexican, Puerto Rican, Central American, or other Latin American heritage are described here. 492 pages. ISBN 1-58841-070-6. $40, plus $5 shipping.

Financial Aid for Native Americans, 2003-2005
Detailed information is provided on 1,500 funding opportunities open to American Indians, Native Alaskans, and Native Pacific Islanders. 566 pages. ISBN 1-58841-071-4. $40, plus $5 shipping.

Financial Aid for Research and Creative Activities Abroad, 2004-2006
Described here are 1,100 funding programs (scholarships, fellowships, grants, etc.) available to support research, professional, or creative activities abroad. 348 pages. ISBN 1-58841-107-9. $45, plus $5 shipping.

Financial Aid for Study and Training Abroad, 2004-2006
This directory, which *Children's Bookwatch* calls "invaluable," describes more than 1,000 financial aid opportunities available to support study abroad. 338 pages. ISBN 1-58841-094-3. $39.50, plus $5 shipping.

Financial Aid for the Disabled and Their Families, 2004-2006
Named one of the "Best Reference Books of the Year" by *Library Journal,* this directory describes in detail nearly 1,200 funding opportunities. 502 pages. ISBN 1-58841-096-X. $40, plus $5 shipping.

Financial Aid for Veterans, Military Personnel, and Their Dependents, 2004-2006
According to *Reference Book Review,* this directory (with its 1,100 entries) is "the most comprehensive guide available on the subject." 420 pages. ISBN 1-58841-097-8. $40, plus $5 shipping.

High School Senior's Guide to Merit and Other No-Need Funding, 2004-2006
Here's your guide to 1,100 funding programs that *never* look at income level when making awards to college-bound high school seniors. 410 pages. ISBN 1-58841-100-1. $29.95, plus $5 shipping.

How to Pay for Your Degree in Business & Related Fields, 2004-2006
If you need funding for an undergraduate or graduate degree in business or related fields, this is the directory to use (500+ funding programs described). 300 pages. ISBN 1-58841-103-6. $30, plus $5 shipping.

How to Pay for Your Degree in Education & Related Fields, 2004-2006
Here's hundreds of funding opportunities available to support undergraduate and graduate students preparing for a career in education, guidance, etc. 260 pages. ISBN 1-58841-105-2. $30, plus $5 shipping.

How to Pay for Your Degree in Engineering, 2004-2006
Use this directory to identify the 700 biggest and best funding opportunities available to support undergraduate or graduate studies in engineering. 240 pages. ISBN 1-58841-101-X. $30, plus $5 shipping.

RSP Funding for Nursing Students & Nurses, 2004-2006
Described in detail are 500+ funding opportunities available to nursing students (at any level) and nurses for study, research, professional, or other activities. 198 pages. ISBN 1-58841-095-1. $30, plus $5 shipping.

Financial Aid for the Disabled and Their Families 2004-2006

**Gail Ann Schlachter
R. David Weber**

A List of: Scholarships, Fellowships/Grants, Loans, Forgivable Loans, Grants-in-Aid, and Awards Designed Primarily or Exclusively for Persons with Disabilities and Members of Their Families; Reference Sources on Financial Aid; and a Set of Six Indexes.

Reference Service Press
El Dorado Hills, California
2004

© 2004 by Gail Ann Schlachter

All rights reserved. No part of this publication may be reproduced, stored in a retrieval system, or transmitted, in any form or by any means, electronic, mechanical, photocopying, recording, or otherwise, except for the inclusion of brief quotations in a review, without the prior permission in writing from the publisher.

Library of Congress Cataloging in Publication No.

87-063263

ISBN 1-58841-096-X
ISSN 0898-9222

10 9 8 7 6 5 4 3 2 1

Reference Service Press (RSP) began in 1977 with a single financial aid publication *(Directory of Financial Aids for Women)* and now specializes in the development of financial aid resources in multiple formats, including books, large print books, disks, CD-ROMs, print-on-demand reports, eBooks, and online sources. Long recognized as a leader in the field, RSP has been called, by the *Simba Report on Directory Publishing,* "a true success in the world of independent directory publishers." Both Kaplan Educational Centers and Military.com have hailed RSP as "the leading authority on scholarships."

Reference Service Press
El Dorado Hills Business Park
5000 Windplay Drive, Suite 4
El Dorado Hills, CA 95762
    (916) 939-9620
    Fax: (916) 939-9626
    E-mail: findaid@aol.com
visit our web site: www.rspfunding.com

Manufactured in the United States of America

Price: $40.00, plus $5 shipping.

Contents

Introduction ix

    Why This Directory Is Needed ix
    What's Unique about the Directory ix
    The Extent of Updating in This Edition of the Directory x
    The Arrangement of the Directory x
    Sample Entry xi
    How to Use the Directory xiv
    Plans to Update the Directory xv
    Other Related Publications xv
    Acknowledgements xv
    About the Authors xvi

**Financial Aid Programs for the Disabled
and Their Families** 1

    Visual Disabilities 3
        Scholarships 5
        Fellowships/Grants 39
        Loans 57
        Grants-in-Aid 59
        Awards 81

    Hearing Disabilities 83
        Scholarships 85
        Fellowships/Grants 89
        Grants-in-Aid 94
        Awards 96

    Orthopedic and Developmental Disabilities 99
        Scholarships 101
        Fellowships/Grants 105
        Loans 106
        Grants-in-Aid 107

    Communication/Other Disabilities 119
        Scholarships 121
        Fellowships/Grants 149
        Grants-in-Aid 155
        Awards 165

    Disabilities in General 167
        Scholarships 169
        Fellowships/Grants 210
        Loans 268
        Grants-in-Aid 288
        Awards 335

Families of the Disabled **341**
    Scholarships 343
    Fellowships/Grants 381
    Loans 388
    Grants-in-Aid 390
    Awards 421

Annotated Bibliography of General Financial Aid Directories **423**
    General Directories 425
    Subject/Activity Directories 426
    Directories for Special Groups 428
    Contests and Awards 429
    Internships 429
    Nothing Over $4.95 430
    Cyberspace Sites 432

Indexes **435**
    Program Title Index 437
    Sponsoring Organization Index 461
    Residency Index 471
    Tenability Index 479
    Subject Index 487
    Calendar Index 499

WHY THIS DIRECTORY IS NEEDED

With a total population of 49 million, the disabled constitute America's largest "minority" group. Each year, billions of dollars in financial aid are set aside to assist persons with disabilities and members of their families. But, how can these individuals find out about the available funding?

Traditional financial aid directories don't offer much assistance. Instead, those resources have tended to focus either on a small portion of the total funding or on only one type of funding. For example, the latest edition of *Resources for People with Disabilities* (published by Ferguson) contains more than 8,000 entries, but only one section provides information on funding—and many of the programs covered there are for researchers and organizations working to help the disabled, not for the disabled themselves. Similarly, general financial aid directories have never included more than a few of the programs designed primarily or exclusively for persons with disabilities or their families. The *Scholarship Book* (published by Prentice-Hall) is representative; it describes more than 1,500 diverse funding opportunities, but less than 100 of these are aimed specifically at either disabled persons or members of their family.

As a result, many individuals with disabilities and members of their family (along with the counselors and librarians there to serve them) have been unaware of the vast array of funding opportunities available to them. Now, with the ongoing publication of the award-winning *Financial Aid for the Disabled and Their Families,* all that has changed. Here, in one place, you can now find comprehensive information about the full range of financial aid opportunities set aside specifically for persons with disabilities or members of their family.

WHAT'S UNIQUE ABOUT THE DIRECTORY

In addition to its comprehensive coverage, *Financial Aid for the Disabled and Their Families, 2004-2006* offers several other unique features. Covered here are hundreds of financial aid opportunities not described in any other source. Unlike other funding directories, which generally follow a straight alphabetical arrangement, this one groups entries by both type of disability (e.g., hearing impairments, orthopedic impairments) and type of program (e.g., scholarships, grants-in-aid)—thus facilitating a user's search for appropriate programs. The same convenience is offered in the indexes, where the entries are similarly subdivided by disability and program type. With this organization, users with one set of characteristics (e.g., persons with hearing impairments) will be able to find all programs set aside specifically for them—and not be distracted or have to waste time sorting through descriptions of programs intended for individuals with other types of disabilities. Additionally, a calendar index has been included, so fundseekers working with specific time constraints can pinpoint programs by filing date.

The unique value of *Financial Aid for the Disabled and Their Families* has been well recognized by the reviewers. It was chosen as one of the "best reference books of the year" by *Library Journal* and as one of the "outstanding reference books of the year" by the New York Public Library, which commended Reference Service Press for its "excellent contribution in an area of publishing where quality is at a premium." *Booklist* described the directory as "a well-crafted, easy-to-use, and affordable resource on financial aid." *Disability Resources Monthly* called the directory a "must-have." *College Financial Aid* agrees and, because of its "wealth of information," gave the directory its "four-star" (highest) rating.

American Reference Books Annual predicted that "this directory will assuredly be a major reference tool in most libraries" and labeled it "an essential purchase."

THE EXTENT OF UPDATING IN THE 2004-2006 EDITION OF THE DIRECTORY

The preparation of each new edition of *Financial Aid for the Disabled and Their Families* involves extensive updating and revision. To insure that the information included in the directory is both reliable and current, the editors at Reference Service Press 1) review and update all programs open to persons with disabilities or members of their families currently in our funding database and 2) search exhaustively for new program leads in a variety of sources, including printed directories, news reports, journals, newsletters, house organs, annual reports, and sites on the Internet. Since all program descriptions included in the directory are written directly from information supplied by the sponsoring organization (no information is ever taken from secondary sources), we send up to four data collection letters (followed by up to three telephone inquiries, if necessary) to each sponsor identified in this process. Despite our best efforts, however, some sponsoring organizations still fail to respond and, as a result, their programs are not included in this edition of the directory.

The 2004-2006 edition of the directory completely revises and updates the earlier biennial edition. Programs that have ceased operations have been dropped. Profiles of continuing programs have been rewritten to reflect operations in 2004-2006; more than 80 percent of these programs reported substantive changes in their locations, requirements (particularly application deadline), or benefits since 2002. In addition, more than 400 new entries have been added to the program section of the directory. The resulting listing identifies nearly 1,200 scholarships, fellowships/grants, loans, grants-in-aid, and awards set aside specifically for persons with disabilities and/or members of their families.

THE ARRANGEMENT OF THE DIRECTORY

Financial Aid for the Disabled and Their Families is divided into three separate parts: a descriptive list of financial aid programs designed primarily or exclusively for persons with disabilities and their families; an annotated bibliography of directories listing general financial aid programs; and a set of six indexes.

Financial Aid Programs Available to the Disabled and Their Families. The first part of the directory describes nearly 1,200 financial aid programs designed primarily or exclusively for persons with disabilities and members of their families. The programs described are sponsored by federal and state government agencies, professional organizations, foundations, educational associations, and military/veterans organizations. They are open to applicants at any level (high school through postdoctoral) for such activities as education, research, travel, training, equipment acquisition, career development, or innovative effort. All areas of the sciences, social sciences, and humanities are covered.

Entries in this part are grouped in the following six chapters to facilitate the reader's search for financial aid programs aimed at specific population groups (the list is based on a condensation of the disability categories established in Public Law 94-142, the Education for All Handicapped Children Act).

Visual Disabilities: Programs open to individuals who have visual impairments (are partially sighted or blind), with or without correction.

Hearing Disabilities: Programs open to individuals who have difficulty in receiving linguistic information with or without amplification.

Orthopedic and Developmental Disabilities: Programs open to individuals with 1) a severe orthopedic impairment caused by birth defects (e.g., absence of an extremity), diseases or other causes (e.g., accidents, amputations), or 2) a severe, chronic disability that was manifested before age 22 (including mental retardation).

Communication and Other Disabilities: Programs open to individuals who have a communication disorder (such as stuttering or voice impairment), have a learning disability (including such condi-

INTRODUCTION

SAMPLE ENTRY

(1) **[365]**

(2) **ASTRAZENECA SCHOLARSHIP**

(3) Patient Advocate Foundation
Attn: Executive Vice President of Administrative Operations
753 Thimble Shoals Boulevard, Suite 200
Newport News, VA 23606
(757) 873-6668, ext. 124   Toll-free: (800) 532-5274
Fax: (757) 873-8999
E-mail: info@patientadvocate.org
Web: www.patientadvocate.org

(4) **Summary** To provide financial assistance for college or graduate school to individuals whose studies have been interrupted or delayed by a diagnosis of cancer or other life threatening diseases.

(5) **Eligibility** This program is open to high school seniors, undergraduates, and graduate students whose course of study has been interrupted or delayed by a diagnosis of cancer or other critical or life threatening diseases. Applicants must submit documentation of financial need, high school and/or college transcripts, and at least 2 letters of recommendation. They must be pursuing a course of study that will make them immediately employable after graduation.

(6) **Financial data** The stipend is $5,000 per year.

(7) **Duration** 1 year; may be renewed 1 additional year for an associate or master's degree or 3 additional years for a bachelor's or medical degree. Renewal requires that the recipient maintain a GPA of 3.0 or higher, be enrolled full time, and complete at least 20 hours of community service per year.

(8) **Additional Information** This program is sponsored by AstraZeneca Pharmaceuticals.

(9) **Number awarded** 1 each year.

(10) **Deadline** April of each year.

DEFINITION

(1) **Entry number:** Consecutive number assigned to the references and used to index the entry.

(2) **Program title:** Title of scholarship, fellowship, loan, grant-in-aid, or award.

(3) **Sponsoring organization:** Name, address, telephone number, toll-free number, fax number, e-mail address, and web site (when information was supplied) for organization sponsoring the program.

(4) **Summary:** Identifies the major program requirements; read the rest of the entry for additional detail.

(5) **Eligibility:** Qualifications required of applicants.

(6) **Financial data:** Financial details of the program, including fixed sum, average amount, or range of funds offered, expenses for which funds may and may not be applied, and cash-related benefits supplied (e.g., room and board).

(7) **Duration:** Period for which support is provided; renewal prospects.

(8) **Additional information:** Any unusual (generally nonmonetary) benefits, features, restrictions, or limitations associated with the program.

(9) **Number awarded:** Total number of recipients each year or other specified period.

(10) **Deadline:** The month by which applications must be submitted.

tions as brain injury and dyslexia), are emotionally disturbed, or have other chronic or acute health problems, such as heart condition, tuberculosis, or hemophilia.

Disabilities in General: Programs open to persons with any disability (programs that do not specify or restrict the type of eligible disabilities).

Families of the Disabled: Programs open to the children, stepchildren, adopted children, grandchildren, parents, siblings, and other dependents or family members of persons with disabilities.

Each of these six chapters is further divided (when appropriate) into five type-of-program sections.

Scholarships: Programs that support study or research at the undergraduate level in the United States. Scholarships/loans are covered here as well. Usually no repayment is required, provided stated requirements are met.

Fellowships/Grants: Programs that support graduate or postdoctoral study or research in the United States. Usually no repayment is required, provided stated requirements are met.

Loans: Programs that provide money for a variety of purposes (e.g., education or training, assistive technology, personal assistance) that eventually must be repaid—with or without interest.

Grants-in-Aid: Programs that provide financial assistance for emergency situations, property and income tax liabilities, assistive technology, or the adaptation of housing and vehicles. Usually no repayment is required, provided stated requirements are met.

Awards: Competitions, prizes, and honoraria granted in recognition or support of creative work and public service. Prizes received solely as the result of entering contests are excluded.

Within each of these sections, entries appear alphabetically by program title. A number of programs supply assistance to more than one specific group or supply more than one type of assistance; they are listed in all relevant subsections. For example, since the Charles E. Leonard Memorial Scholarship Fund, sponsored by the Vermont Association for the Blind and Visually Impaired, is open to either blind/visually impaired Vermonters or their children, the program is described in both the Visual Disabilities *and* Families of the Disabled chapters. Similarly, the National Federation of the Blind of Ohio Scholarships are open to blind and visually impaired undergraduate *and* graduate students, so it is included in both the Scholarships *and* Fellowships sections of the Visual Disabilities chapter.

Each program entry has been designed to provide a concise profile that includes information (when available) on program title, organization address, telephone number, fax and toll-free numbers, e-mail address, web site, purpose, eligibility, money awarded, duration, special features, limitations, number of awards, and application deadline. (Refer to the sample on p. ix).

The information reported for each of the programs in this section was supplied in response to questionnaires distributed through the first quarter of 2004. While the listing is intended to cover as comprehensively as possible substantive programs aimed at persons with disabilities and their families, some sponsoring organizations did not respond to the research inquiry and, consequently, are not included in this edition of the directory.

The focus of the directory is on "portable" (noninstitution-specific) programs designed primarily or exclusively for persons with disabilities and their families. Excluded from this list are:

Awards open equally to all segments of the population. See the Annotated Bibliography in this directory for titles of publications that list and describe these unrestricted programs.

Financial aid programs administered by academic institutions solely for the benefit of their currently-enrolled students. Financial aid seekers should write directly to individual schools for this information.

Services, such as training and counseling, that do not involve actual financial assistance to the disabled person. To obtain information on these benefits, check with the appropriate federal, state, local, or private social service agency in your area.

Nonmonetary benefits, such as special license plates for persons with disabilities. To obtain information, check with the appropriate agency in your area.

INTRODUCTION xiii

Indirect aid programs, where funds go to agencies, organizations, researchers, and educational institutions that provide services to persons with disabilities or that study disabilities (rather than directly to the disabled or their families). For information on these programs, consult the various grants directories (such as the *Annual Register of Grant Support,* the *Directory of Research Grants,* or the *Directory of Grants for Organizations Serving Persons with Disabilities)* or conduct a computerized search, using GRANTSELECT or another database.

Money for study or research outside the United States. Since there are comprehensive and up-to-date directories that describe all available funding for study and research abroad (see the Annotated Bibliography section), only programs that support study, research, or other activities in the United States are covered here.

Very restrictive programs, where the funds are generally available only to a limited geographic area (cities or counties), to a very limited membership group (e.g., a local union), or in limited amounts (under $500). To get information on these restrictive programs, contact Reference Service Press directly.

Annotated Bibliography of General Financial Aid Directories. While the directory is the only comprehensive and current listing of financial aid programs designed primarily or exclusively for disabled persons and their families, there are numerous other publications that describe the thousands of resources open equally to all segments of American society. The third part of the directory provides an annotated list of the 40+ key resources that any individual (disabled or not) can use to locate additional financial assistance. The sources are grouped into the following sections: general financial aid directories; subject/activity directories; directories for special groups; contests and awards; internships; nothing over $4.95; and cyberspace sites. Each entry contains bibliographic and order information, as well as an annotation specifying scope, arrangement, publication history, and special features of the listing. If a more comprehensive listing of available directories is required, the reader is directed to the evaluative guide published by Reference Service Press: *How to Find Out About Financial Aid and Funding: A Guide to Print, Electronic, and Internet Resources Listing Scholarships, Fellowships, Loans, Grants, Awards, and Internships.*

Indexes. The directory's six indexes facilitate the search for appropriate financial aid opportunities. Program Title, Sponsoring Organization, Residency, Tenability, Subject, and Calendar Indexes follow a word-by-word alphabetical arrangement and refer the user to the appropriate entry by number.

Program Title Index. This index lists alphabetically all program titles and variant names of the scholarships, fellowships/grants, loans, grants-in-aid, and awards covered in the first section of the directory. Since one program can be listed in more than one section (e.g., a program providing assistance to the disabled *and* to members of the disabled's family at the undergraduate *and* graduate levels is listed in four sections), each entry number in the index has been coded to indicate availability groups (e.g., families of the disabled) and program type (e.g., scholarship, loan, award). By using this coding system, readers can turn directly to the programs that match their financial needs and eligibility characteristics.

Sponsoring Organization Index. This index provides an alphabetical listing of the nearly 700 organizations sponsoring financial aid programs listed in the first part of the directory. As in the Program Title Index, entry numbers have been coded to indicate availability and program type.

Residency Index. This index identifies the residency requirements of the programs listed in the directory. Index entries (state, region, country) are arranged alphabetically (word by word). To facilitate access, the geographic terms in the index are subdivided by recipient group and program type. Use this index when you are looking for money set aside for persons with disabilities and members of their families in a particular geographic area.

Tenability Index. This index identifies the geographic locations where the programs listed in the directory may be used. Index entries (city, county, state, region, country) are arranged alphabetically (word by word) and subdivided by availability group and program type. Use this index when you or your family members are looking for money to support research, study, or other activities in a particular geographic area.

Subject Index. This index allows the reader to use more than 150 subject terms to access the financial aid programs designed primarily or exclusively for persons with disabilities and members of their families listed in the first part of the directory. Extensive "see" and "see also" references facilitate the search for appropriate financial aid programs.

Calendar Index. To assist fundseekers who often must work within specific time constraints, the Calendar Index identifies financial aid programs by filing date. The Calendar Index is arranged by type of program (scholarships, loans, etc.) and divided according to recipient group (hearing impaired, families of the disabled, etc.) and month during which the deadline falls. Filing dates can and quite often do vary from year to year; consequently, this index should be used only as a guide for deadlines beyond 2006. It is important to note that not all sponsoring organizations supplied information on application deadline, so some of the programs described in the directory are not listed here.

HOW TO USE THE DIRECTORY

To Locate Programs Open to Individuals with Various Types of Disabilities. To bring programs with similar eligibility requirements together, the directory is organized into six availability chapters: Visual Disabilities; Hearing Disabilities; Orthopedic and Developmental Disabilities; Communication and Other Disabilities; Disabilities in General; and Families of the Disabled. If you have a disability, be sure to check not only the chapter that covers your specific disability (e.g., Hearing Disabilities chapter) but also the Disabilities in General chapter, where programs that do not specify or restrict the type of eligible disabilities are listed.

To Locate Programs Offering a Particular Type of Assistance. If you are looking for programs offering a particular type of financial aid (e.g., a scholarship for undergraduate courses, an award for outstanding literary achievement), turn to the appropriate chapter in the first part (e.g., Disabilities in General, Families of the Disabled) and read through all the entries in the section that applies (e.g., scholarships, awards). Since programs with multiple purposes are listed in every appropriate location, each of the five type-of-program sections functions as a self-contained entity. In fact, you can browse through any of the sections in the directory without first consulting an index.

To Locate a Particular Financial Aid Program. If you know the name of a particular financial aid program *and* the type of assistance offered by the program (e.g., scholarship) *and* the availability (e.g., visual disabilities, hearing disabilities), then go directly to the appropriate category in the first part of the directory, where you will find the program profiles arranged alphabetically by title. But be careful: program titles can be misleading. the Willard Bernbaum Scholarship is available only to graduate students and therefore is listed under Fellowships/Grants not Scholarships. The Hank Hofstetter Opportunity Grant is, in fact, a scholarship. Consequently, if you are looking for a specific program and do not find it in the subsection you have checked, be sure to refer to the Program Title Index to see if it is covered elsewhere in the directory. To save time, always check the Program Title Index first if you know the name of a specific award but are not sure under which subsection it has been listed.

To Locate Programs Sponsored by a Particular Organization. The Sponsoring Organization Index makes it easy to determine groups that provide financial assistance to persons with disabilities and their families, or to identify specific financial aid programs offered by a particular organization. Each entry number in the index is coded to identify recipient group and program type, enabling users to target appropriate entries.

To Locate Programs Open to Residents of or Tenable in a Particular Area. The Residency Index identifies financial aid programs open to residents of a particular state, region, or country. The Tenability Index shows where the money can be spent. In both indexes, "see" and "see also" references are used liberally, and index entries for a particular geographic area are divided by both type of disability and type of program.

To Locate Financial Aid Programs for Persons with Disabilities and Their Families in a Particular Subject Area. Turn to the Subject Index first if you are interested in identifying financial aid programs for the disabled and their families in a particular field. To facilitate your search, the type of refer-

ence indexed (scholarships, fellowships/grants, loans, grants-in-aid, awards) and the availability group (e.g., hearing disabilities) are clearly identified. Extensive cross-references are provided.

To Locate Financial Aid Programs for Persons with Disabilities and Their Families by Deadline Date. If you are working with specific time constraints and want to weed out the financial aid programs whose filing dates you won't be able to meet, turn first to the Calendar Index and check the program references listed under the program type, appropriate group, and month. Remember, not all sponsoring organizations supplied deadline information, so not all programs are listed in this section. To identify every relevant financial aid program, regardless of filing dates, read through all the entries in each of the program categories (scholarships, loans, etc.) that apply.

To Locate Information on Geographically Restricted or Financially Limited Funding Programs. Only programs aimed at large segments of the population (at least a state) or offering significant awards (nothing under $500) are covered in this directory. To get information on the other, more limited programs, contact Reference Service Press to search its comprehensive database directly.

To Locate Financial Aid Programs Open to All Segments of the Population. Only programs designed with the disabled and their families in mind are listed in this publication. However, there are thousands of other programs that are open equally to all segments of the population. To identify these programs, use the resources described in the second part of the directory, talk to your local librarian, check with your financial aid office on campus, or use a web-based scholarship or grant search service.

PLANS TO UPDATE THE DIRECTORY

This volume, covering 2004-2006, is the ninth biennial edition of *Financial Aid for the Disabled and Their Families.* The next edition will cover the years 2006-2008 and will be released in early 2006.

OTHER RELATED PUBLICATIONS

In addition to *Financial Aid for the Disabled and Their Families,* Reference Service Press publishes several other titles dealing with fundseeking, including the biennially-issued *Money for Graduate Students in the Social & Behavioral Sciences, Directory of Financial Aids for Women,* and *Financial Aid for Veterans, Military Personnel, and Their Dependents.* Since each of these titles focuses on a separate population group, there is little duplication in the listings. In fact, fewer than five percent of the programs described in *Financial Aid for the Disabled and Their Families* can be found in any of RSP's financial aid titles, with one exception. Because veterans constitute such a large portion of the disabled population, there is somewhat more overlap (approximately 15 percent) in the entries included in *Financial Aid for Veterans, Military Personnel and Their Dependents* and *Financial Aid for the Disabled and Their Families.* For more information on these and other related publications, you can 1) write to Reference Service Press' Marketing Department at 5000 Windplay Drive, Suite 4, El Dorado Hills, CA 95762, 2) call us at (916) 939-9620; 3) send us an e-mail message at findaid@aol.com; 4) fax us at (916) 939-9626; or 5) visit our web site: www.rspfunding.com.

ACKNOWLEDGEMENTS

A debt of gratitude is owed all the organizations that contributed information to this edition of *Financial Aid for the Disabled and Their Families.* Their generous cooperation has helped to make this publication an award-winning survey of funding programs.

ABOUT THE AUTHORS

Dr. Gail Schlachter has worked for more than three decades as a library manager, a library educator, and an administrator of library-related publishing companies. Among the reference books to her credit are the biennially-issued *Money for Graduate Students in the Arts & Humanities* and two award-winning bibliographic guides: *Minorities and Women: A Guide to Reference Literature in the Social Sciences* (which was chosen as an "Outstanding Reference Title of the Year" by *Choice*) and *Reference Sources in Library and Information Services* (which won the first Knowledge Industry Publications "Award for Library Literature"). She was the reference book review editor for *RQ* (now *Reference and User Services Quarterly*) for 10 years, is a past president of the American Library Association's Reference and User Services Association (RUSA, formerly RASD), and is a former editor-in-chief of *Reference and User Services Quarterly*. In recognition of her outstanding contributions to reference service, Dr. Schlachter has been awarded both the Isadore Gilbert Mudge Citation and the Louis Shores/Oryx Press Award.

Dr. R. David Weber teaches at economics and history at Harbor College in southern California. He is the author of several critically-acclaimed reference works, including *Dissertations in Urban History* and the three-volume *Energy Information Guide.* With Gail Schlachter, he is the author of Reference Service Press' *College Student's Guide to Merit and Other No-Need Funding,* which was selected by *Choice* as one of the "Outstanding Academic Titles of the Year," and a number of other financial aid titles, including *Financial Aid for African Americans,* which was named the "Editor's Choice" by *Reference Books Bulletin*.

Financial Aid Programs for the Disabled and Their Families

- *Visual Disabilities*
- *Hearing Disabilities*
- *Orthopedic/Developmental Disabilities*
- *Communication/Other Disabilities*
- *Disabilities in General*
- *Families of the Disabled*

Visual Disabilities

- *Scholarships*
- *Fellowships/Grants*
- *Loans*
- *Grants-in-Aid*
- *Awards*

Described here are 263 programs open to individuals who have visual impairments (are partially sighted or blind), with or without correction. Of these, 120 entries cover scholarships (to pursue studies or research on the undergraduate level in the United States); 63 cover fellowships or grants (to pursue graduate or postdoctoral study or research in the United States); 4 cover loans (to provide money that must eventually be repaid, with or without interest); 71 cover grants-in-aid (to support emergency situations, travel, income/property tax liabilities, or the acquisition of assistive technology); and 5 cover awards, competitions, prizes, and honoraria (to recognize or support creative work and public service). If you are looking for a particular program and don't find it in this chapter, be sure to check the Program Title Index to see if it is covered elsewhere in the directory.

Scholarships

[1]
ABRAHAM NEMETH COMMITMENT TO EXCELLENCE SCHOLARSHIP

National Federation of the Blind of Michigan
1212 North Foster
Lansing, MI 48912
(517) 372-8700   E-mail: fjw@attbi.com
Web: www.nfbmi.org

Summary To provide financial assistance for college to Michigan students who are blind.

Eligibility This program is open to legally blind residents of Michigan. Applicants must be enrolled or planning to enroll as a full-time student at a postsecondary institution in the state. They must have a GPA of 2.0 or higher from high school and/or college. Along with their application, they must submit a 1- to 3-page letter in which they describe any situations involving their blindness that they have encountered, their plans for the future, and how this scholarship will help them achieve their academic goals.

Financial data The stipend is $1,000.

Duration 1 year.

Additional Information Information is also available from Melody Lindsey, Scholarship Chair, 2213 Winchell Avenue, Kalamazoo, MI 49008, (269) 388-2686. The winner must attend the convention of the National Federation of the Blind of Michigan. All expenses are paid by the sponsor.

Number awarded 1 each year.

Deadline October of each year.

[2]
ALABAMA COUNCIL OF THE BLIND SCHOLARSHIP FUND

Alabama Council of the Blind
Attn: Scholarship Chair
P.O. Box 1213
Talladega, AL 35161-1213
Toll-free: (888) 545-4222   Fax: (256) 480-1222
E-mail: dart1018@bellsouth.net
Web: www.acb-alabama.org/schol.htm

Summary To provide financial assistance for college to blind residents of Alabama.

Eligibility This program is open to Alabama residents who are legally blind and currently enrolled full time in a college or university. Applicants must submit proof of blindness, a transcript from high school (GPA of 3.0 or higher), 2 letters of recommendation, and a narrative outlining their vocational objectives and the outlook for employment in that area.

Financial data The stipend is $1,000 per year.

Duration 1 year.

Number awarded 1 or more each year.

Deadline May of each year.

[3]
AMERICAN COUNCIL OF THE BLIND OF COLORADO SCHOLARSHIPS

American Council of the Blind
Attn: Coordinator, Scholarship Program
1155 15th Street, N.W., Suite 1004
Washington, DC 20005
(202) 467-5081   Toll-free: (800) 424-8666
Fax: (202) 467-5085   E-mail: info@acb.org
Web: www.acb.org

Summary To provide financial assistance for college to blind students from Colorado.

Eligibility This program is open to legally blind students who are residents of Colorado. In addition to letters of recommendation and copies of academic transcripts, applications must include an autobiographical sketch. A cumulative GPA of 3.3 or higher is generally required. Selection is based on demonstrated academic record, involvement in extracurricular and civic activities, and academic objectives. The severity of the applicant's visual impairment and his/her study methods are also taken into account.

Financial data The stipend is $1,750. In addition, the winners receive a $1,000 cash scholarship from the Kurzweil Foundation and, if appropriate, a Kurzweil-1000 Reading System.

Duration 1 year.

Additional Information These scholarships are sponsored by the American Council of the Blind of Colorado, an affiliate of the American Council of the Blind. Scholarship winners are expected to be present at the council's annual conference; the council will cover all reasonable expenses connected with convention attendance.

Number awarded 2 each year.

Deadline February of each year.

[4]
AMERICAN COUNCIL OF THE BLIND OF MARYLAND SCHOLARSHIP

American Council of the Blind
Attn: Coordinator, Scholarship Program
1155 15th Street, N.W., Suite 1004
Washington, DC 20005
(202) 467-5081   Toll-free: (800) 424-8666
Fax: (202) 467-5085   E-mail: info@acb.org
Web: www.acb.org

Summary To provide financial assistance for college to blind students in Maryland.

Eligibility This program is open to legally blind students who are residents of Maryland and attending a college or university in that state. In addition to letters

of recommendation and copies of academic transcripts, applications must include an autobiographical sketch. A cumulative GPA of 3.3 or higher is generally required. Selection is based on demonstrated academic record, involvement in extracurricular and civic activities, and academic objectives. The severity of the applicant's visual impairment and his/her study methods are also taken into account.

Financial data The stipend is $1,500. In addition, the winner receives a $1,000 cash scholarship from the Kurzweil Foundation and, if appropriate, a Kurzweil-1000 Reading System.

Duration 1 year.

Additional Information This scholarship is sponsored by the American Council of the Blind of Maryland, an affiliate of the American Council of the Blind. Scholarship winners are expected to be present at the council's annual conference; the council will cover all reasonable expenses connected with convention attendance.

Number awarded 1 each year.

Deadline February of each year.

[5]
AMERICAN COUNCIL OF THE BLIND OF MINNESOTA SCHOLARSHIPS

American Council of the Blind of Minnesota
Attn: Scholarship Committee
P.O. Box 7341
Minneapolis, MN 55407
(612) 332-7837
Web: www.acb.org/minnesota/Scholarship.html

Summary To provide financial assistance for college to blind and visually impaired residents of Minnesota.

Eligibility This program is open to residents of Minnesota who are blind or visually impaired. Applicants may be either high school seniors entering their first year of postsecondary study or students in their second year or above of postsecondary work. Along with their application, they must submit information on extracurricular activities, community service involvement, hobbies, and an essay of 500 to 600 words that addresses their goals for the future, how the past has shaped those goals, and the role that their blindness or visual impairment has played in their life.

Financial data The stipend is $750.

Duration 1 year.

Number awarded 2 each year: 1 to a high school senior entering college and 1 to a student already enrolled in a postsecondary educational program.

Deadline June of each year.

[6]
AMERICAN COUNCIL OF THE BLIND OF OREGON GRANT-IN-AID

American Council of the Blind of Oregon
c/o Bev Rushing
4730 Auburn Road, N.E., Space 52
Salem, OR 97301
(503) 362-4151   E-mail: b.rushing@juno.com
Web: www.acboforegon.org/grants.html

Summary To provide financial assistance for college or equipment to blind residents of Oregon.

Eligibility Applicants must either be registered with the Oregon Commission for the Blind or provide proof of legal blindness. If the application is for an education grant, applicants must indicate the name of their institution. If the application is for an equipment grant, applicants must provide an indication of the costs and name of the company from which the equipment is to be purchased.

Financial data The amount of the grant depends on the nature of the application.

Duration 1 year.

Additional Information The American Council of the Blind of Oregon is legally incorporated as the Oregon Council of the Blind, Inc.

Number awarded Varies each year.

Deadline Applications may be submitted at any time; decisions are made quarterly.

[7]
AMERICAN COUNCIL OF THE BLIND OF TEXAS SCHOLARSHIPS

American Council of the Blind of Texas
c/o Chris Prentice, President
109 East Sixth Street
Plainview, TX 79072
(806) 839-2901
E-mail: chris@attorney-prentice.com
Web: www.acbtexas.org/scholarshipinfo.html

Summary To provide financial assistance for college to blind and visually impaired residents of Texas.

Eligibility This program is restricted to legally or totally blind Texas residents (documentation requested). Applicants may be high school seniors, high school graduates, or currently-enrolled college students (including students at technical and vocational institutions of higher learning). All applicants (high school or college) must have a GPA of 3.0 or higher. Required as part of the application process are: a transcript, a copy of the acceptance letter (if not yet attending college), 2 to 3 letters of recommendation not more than 12 months old, and a completed application form signed by a member of the Texas council. Selection is based on academic achievement, community service, and financial need.

Financial data Stipends range from $250 to $1,000 per year. Funds may be used for any educational pur-

pose, including tuition, books, housing, and transportation.
Duration 1 year; recipients may reapply.
Additional Information Recipients do not need to study in a field related to blindness; in general, they may major in any field (although 1 of the scholarships is specifically for a student interested in majoring in food service and another is specifically for a student majoring in business administration). Information is also available from Nolan Dyer, Roy Road, Texarkana, TX 75501, (903) 832-5038.
Number awarded 8 each year: 1 at $1,000; 3 at $500; and 4 at $250.
Deadline April of each year.

[8]
ARIZONA COUNCIL OF THE BLIND SCHOLARSHIP PROGRAM
Arizona Council of the Blind
3124 East Roosevelt Street, Suite 4
Phoenix, AZ 85008-5088
(602) 273-1510   Fax: (602) 938-3748
E-mail: dmmar@uswest.net

Summary To provide financial assistance for undergraduate or graduate studies to legally blind Arizona residents.
Eligibility This program is limited to Arizona residents. Applicants must be legally blind and enrolled or planning to enroll in vocational, technical, graduate, or professional training programs beyond the high school level. For the purposes of this program, legal blindness is defined as visual acuity of 20/200 or less in the better corrected eye and/or 20 degrees or less visual field or visual loss that requires substantial magnification or readers to access print materials. Candidates are interviewed.
Financial data The stipend is $500.
Duration 1 year; recipients may reapply.
Additional Information Of the scholarships awarded, 1 is named the John Van Landingham Scholarship in memory of the founder of the Arizona Council of the Blind. Information is also available from Thomas Belsan, 2550 South Ellsworth Road, Unit 94, Mesa, AZ 85212-2201, (480) 373-8831.
Number awarded 3 each year.
Deadline March of each year.

[9]
ARNOLD SADLER MEMORIAL SCHOLARSHIP
American Council of the Blind
Attn: Coordinator, Scholarship Program
1155 15th Street, N.W., Suite 1004
Washington, DC 20005
(202) 467-5081   Toll-free: (800) 424-8666
Fax: (202) 467-5085   E-mail: info@acb.org
Web: www.acb.org

Summary To provide financial assistance to undergraduate or graduate students who are blind and are interested in studying in a field of service to persons with disabilities.
Eligibility This program is open to students in rehabilitation, education, law, or other fields of service to persons with disabilities. Applicants must be legally blind and U.S. citizens. In addition to letters of recommendation and copies of academic transcripts, applications must include an autobiographical sketch. A cumulative GPA of 3.3 or higher is generally required. Selection is based on demonstrated academic record, involvement in extracurricular and civic activities, and academic objectives. The severity of the applicant's visual impairment and his/her study methods are also taken into account.
Financial data The stipend is $2,000. In addition, the winner receives a $1,000 cash scholarship from the Kurzweil Foundation and, if appropriate, a Kurzweil-1000 Reading System.
Duration 1 year.
Additional Information This scholarship is funded by the Arnold Sadler Memorial Scholarship Fund. Scholarship winners are expected to be present at the council's annual conference; the council will cover all reasonable expenses connected with convention attendance.
Number awarded 1 each year.
Deadline February of each year.

[10]
ARTHUR E. COPELAND SCHOLARSHIP FOR MALES
United States Association of Blind Athletes
Attn: Scholarship Committee
Brown Hall, Suite 015
33 North Institute Street
Colorado Springs, CO 80903
(719) 630-0422   Fax: (719) 630-0616
E-mail: usaba@usa.net
Web: www.usaba.org

Summary To provide financial assistance for undergraduate or graduate study to male members of the United States Association for Blind Athletes (USABA).
Eligibility All legally blind males who have been members of and have participated in USABA activities for the past year are eligible to apply for this scholarship. Applicants must have been admitted to an academic, voca-

tional, technical, professional, or certification program at the postsecondary level. Selection is based on demonstrated academic record, involvement in extracurricular and civic activities, academic goals and objectives, and USABA involvement at various levels.

Financial data The stipend is $500.
Number awarded 1 each year.
Deadline September of each year.

[11]
ASSOCIATION OF BLIND CITIZENS SCHOLARSHIP

Association of Blind Citizens
P.O. Box 246
Holbrook, MA 02343
(781) 961-1023   Fax: (781) 961-0004
E-mail: scholarship@assocofblindcitizens.org
Web: www.assocofblindcitizens.org

Summary To provide financial assistance for college to individuals who are blind or visually impaired.

Eligibility Eligible to apply for this support are high school seniors, high school graduates, and currently-enrolled college students who are blind or visually impaired. They must be interested in working on a college degree. To apply, students must submit a 500-word biography, indicating how the scholarship award would help them achieve their goal of attending college or a recognized vocational program; a high school or college transcript; a certificate of legal blindness or a letter from their ophthalmologist; and 2 letters of reference. The highest ranked applicant receives the Reggie Johnson Memorial Scholarship.

Financial data Stipends are $2,000 or $1,000. Funds may be used to pay for tuition, living expenses, or related expenses resulting from vision impairment.

Duration 1 year.
Number awarded 4 each year: 1 at $2,000 (the Reggie Johnson Memorial Scholarship) and 3 at $1,000.
Deadline April of each year.

[12]
AZ AER STUDENT MERIT SCHOLARSHIP

Association for the Education and Rehabilitation of
  the Blind and Visually Impaired-Arizona Chapter
c/o Vasant Garcia
801 East McKellips Road, Number 24A
Tempe, AZ 85281
(602) 267-0453, ext. 23
Web: www.ed.arizona.edu/azaer

Summary To provide financial assistance for college to residents of Arizona who are visually impaired.

Eligibility This program is open to residents of Arizona who are currently attending a postsecondary educational program or completing their last year of high school. Applicants must be visually impaired, defined as having central acuity of 20/70 or less with best correction or a significant peripheral field loss of 20 degrees or less. Along with their application, they must submit 1) a vitae or resume of their work experience, extracurricular activities, and honors; 2) school transcripts; 3) letters of recommendation, 1 from a current member of the Arizona chapter of the Association for the Education and Rehabilitation of the Blind and Visually Impaired (AZ AER) who will act as the applicant's sponsor and 1 from an academic advisor, teacher, or community leader; and 4) an essay, up to 2 pages, describing the applicant's educational, professional, and personal goals and how this award will help achieve those goals.

Financial data The stipend is $500.
Duration 1 year.
Number awarded 1 each year.
Deadline April of each year.

[13]
BAY STATE COUNCIL OF THE BLIND SCHOLARSHIP

American Council of the Blind
Attn: Coordinator, Scholarship Program
1155 15th Street, N.W., Suite 1004
Washington, DC 20005
(202) 467-5081   Toll-free: (800) 424-8666
Fax: (202) 467-5085   E-mail: info@acb.org
Web: www.acb.org

Summary To provide financial assistance for college to blind students in Massachusetts.

Eligibility This program is open to legally blind students who are residents of Massachusetts. In addition to letters of recommendation and copies of academic transcripts, applications must include an autobiographical sketch. A cumulative GPA of 3.3 or higher is generally required. Selection is based on demonstrated academic record, involvement in extracurricular and civic activities, and academic objectives. The severity of the applicant's visual impairment and his/her study methods are also taken into account. Preference is given to students attending a Massachusetts college or university.

Financial data The stipend is $1,000. In addition, the winner receives a $1,000 cash scholarship from the Kurzweil Foundation and, if appropriate, a Kurzweil-1000 Reading System.

Duration 1 year.

Additional Information This scholarship is sponsored by the Bay State Council of the Blind, an affiliate of the American Council of the Blind. Scholarship winners are expected to be present at the council's annual conference; the council will cover all reasonable expenses connected with convention attendance.

Number awarded 1 each year.
Deadline February of each year.

VISUAL DISABILITIES: SCHOLARSHIPS

[14]
BEVERLY PROWS MEMORIAL SCHOLARSHIP

National Federation of the Blind of Washington
Attn: Scholarship Committee
P.O. Box 2516
Seattle, WA 98111
(206) 624-8007   E-mail: info@nfbw.org
Web: www.nfbw.org

Summary To provide financial assistance for undergraduate or graduate study to blind students in Washington.

Eligibility This program is open to legally blind residents of Washington state who are working on or planning to work on a full-time college or graduate degree. Applicants must submit a letter describing themselves (hobbies, interests, school activities, and future goals), high school and/or college transcripts, and 3 letters of reference.

Financial data The stipend is $3,000.

Duration 1 year.

Additional Information Information is also available from Rita Szantay at (206) 224-7242 (days) or (206) 352-7320 (evenings and weekends). This scholarship was first awarded in 1991. Winners must attend the state convention of the National Federation of the Blind of Washington to accept the award; convention expenses are covered.

Number awarded 1 each year.

Deadline August of each year.

[15]
CALIFORNIA COUNCIL OF THE BLIND SCHOLARSHIPS

California Council of the Blind
578 B Street
Hayward, CA 94541
(510) 537-7877   Toll-free: (800) 221-6359
Fax: (510) 537-7830

Summary To provide financial assistance for undergraduate or graduate study to blind people in California.

Eligibility Applicants must be legally blind residents of California who are enrolled or planning to enroll full time at an accredited college or university at either the undergraduate or graduate level. Selection is based on academic achievement and financial need.

Financial data The amount of the assistance depends on the availability of funds and the needs of the applicant.

Duration 1 year; may be renewed. For graduate students, support is limited to 2 years of work for a master's degree or 3 years for a Ph.D.

Number awarded Varies each year.

Deadline June of each year.

[16]
CHARLES E. LEONARD MEMORIAL SCHOLARSHIP FUND

Vermont Student Assistance Corporation
Champlain Mill
Attn: Scholarship Programs
P.O. Box 2000
Winooski, VT 05404-2601
(802) 654-3798   Toll-free: (800) 642-3177
Fax: (802) 654-3765   TDD: (802) 654-3766
TDD: (800) 281-3341 (within VT)
E-mail: info@vsac.org
Web: www.vsac.org

Summary To provide financial assistance for college to blind or visually impaired Vermonters, their children, or those who intend to pursue a career of service to blind or visually impaired people.

Eligibility Eligible to apply are blind or visually impaired Vermonters; children of blind or visually impaired Vermonters attending a Vermont college or university, an out-of-state school, or a vocational school; and Vermonters attending a Vermont college or university to prepare for a career in the rehabilitation of blind or visually impaired people. Preference is given to blind or visually impaired applicants who plan to study electrical engineering at the University of Vermont, blind or visually impaired applicants who plan to study engineering at any Vermont college or university, or applicants planning other fields of study working with blind and visually impaired people. Selection is based on academic achievement, financial need, and required essays.

Financial data The stipend is $500 per year.

Duration 1 year; recipients may reapply.

Additional Information Information is also available from the Vermont Association for the Blind and Visually Impaired, 37 Elmwood Avenue, Burlington, VT 05401, (802) 863-1358, (800) 639-5861, E-mail: vabvi@aol.com.

Number awarded Approximately 4 each year.

Deadline April of each year.

[17]
CHRISTIAN RECORD SERVICES SCHOLARSHIPS

Christian Record Services
4444 South 52nd Street
P.O. Box 6097
Lincoln, NE 68506-0097
(402) 488-0981   Fax: (402) 488-7582
E-mail: CRSnet@compuserve.com
Web: www.christianrecord.org

Summary To provide financial assistance for college to blind students in the United States and Canada.

Eligibility Applicants must be legally blind and planning to attend college full time on the undergraduate level to secure training that will result in independence and self-support.

Financial data The stipend is $500 per year.
Duration 1 year; may be renewed.
Additional Information Information is also available from the Canadian branch office, 31897 Mercantile Way, Abbotsford, BC, Canada V2T 4C3, (604) 853-6944. Christian Record Services is operated for the benefit of the general public by the General Conference of Seventh-Day Adventists, 6840 Eastern Avenue, N.W., Washington, DC 20012.
Number awarded 10 each year.
Deadline March of each year.

[18]
COLLEGE-BOUND AWARD OF LIGHTHOUSE INTERNATIONAL

Lighthouse International
Attn: Career Incentive Awards Program
111 East 59th Street
New York, NY 10022-1202
(212) 821-9428   Toll-free: (800) 829-0500
Fax: (212) 821-9703   TTY: (212) 821-9713
E-mail: kclark@lighthouse.org
Web: www.lighthouse.org

Summary To provide financial assistance for college to legally blind high school seniors and graduates residing and attending school in selected eastern states.
Eligibility This program is open to legally blind high school seniors or recent high school graduates now planning to begin college. Applicants must be residents of Connecticut, Delaware, Maine, Maryland, Massachusetts, New Hampshire, New Jersey, New York, Pennsylvania, Rhode Island, Vermont, Virginia, or Washington, D.C. and planning to attend school in those states. They must write a 500-word essay, describing their academic achievements and career goals. Candidates are not asked to demonstrate financial need. U.S. citizenship is required.
Financial data The stipend is $5,000.
Duration The award is granted to recipients only once, although they may elect to spend the money over a period of more than 1 year.
Additional Information The recipient must present evidence of enrollment in or acceptance to an educational program before the funds will be released.
Number awarded 1 each year.
Deadline March of each year.

[19]
DALE M. SCHOETTLER SCHOLARSHIP FOR VISUALLY IMPAIRED STUDENTS

California State University
Office of the Chancellor
Attn: Lori Redfearn, Vice President
401 Golden Shore, Sixth Floor
Long Beach, CA 90802-4210
(562) 951-4815   E-mail: lredfearn@calstate.edu
Web: www.calstate.edu

Summary To provide financial assistance to undergraduate and graduate students with visual impairments at campuses of the California State University (CSU) system throughout California.
Eligibility This program is open to undergraduate and graduate students enrolled at CSU campuses who have been declared legally blind. Applicants must have a cumulative GPA of 2.8 or higher.
Financial data The stipend is $5,000 per year.
Duration 1 year.
Number awarded 1 each year.

[20]
DAVID H. NEWMEYER POST-SECONDARY SCHOLARSHIP FOR VISUALLY IMPAIRED STUDENTS

Association for Education and Rehabilitation of the
    Blind and Visually Impaired of Ohio
c/o Anna Pekarski
Cleveland Sight Center
1909 East 101st Street
P.O. Box 1988
Cleveland, OH 44106-1988
(216) 791-8118   Fax: (216) 791-1101
Web: www.aerohio.org

Summary To provide financial assistance for college to visually impaired residents of Ohio.
Eligibility This program is open to residents of Ohio who meet the legal definition of visually impaired. Applicants must be interested in enrolling in academic, vocational, or technical training programs at the postsecondary level. Along with their application, they must submit information on their work experience, a list of their extracurricular activities or special interests, 2 letters of recommendation, proof of acceptance from the school they are attending or planning to attend, and proof of visual impairment.
Financial data The stipend is $500.
Duration 1 year; nonrenewable.
Number awarded 1 each year.
Deadline May of each year.

[21]
DAVID NEWMEYER SCHOLARSHIP

American Council of the Blind of Ohio
Attn: Executive Director
2678 Edgevale Road
P.O. Box 21488
Columbus, OH 43221-0488
(614) 221-6688
Toll-free: (800) 835-2226 (within OH)
Fax: (614) 451-0539   E-mail: kmorlock@gcfn.org
Web: www.acbogcc.org

Summary To provide financial assistance to Ohio undergraduate students who are blind.

Eligibility This program is open to 1) residents of Ohio who are high school seniors or current college students, and 2) students at colleges and universities in Ohio. Applicants must be legally blind and working on or planning to work on an undergraduate degree in any field. Along with their application, they must submit transcripts (must have a GPA of 3.0 or higher), a certificate of legal blindness, and an essay of 250 to 500 words on their career objectives, future plans, personal goals, other academic or personal qualities, and why they believe they are qualified to receive this scholarship.

Financial data A stipend is awarded (amount not specified).

Duration 1 year; recipients may reapply.

Additional Information Information is also available from the scholarship committee, 520 Walnut Street, Perrysburg, OH 43551.

Number awarded 1 each year.

Deadline July of each year.

[22]
DELBERT K. AMAN MEMORIAL SCHOLARSHIP

American Council of the Blind
Attn: Coordinator, Scholarship Program
1155 15th Street, N.W., Suite 1004
Washington, DC 20005
(202) 467-5081   Toll-free: (800) 424-8666
Fax: (202) 467-5085   E-mail: info@acb.org
Web: www.acb.org

Summary To provide financial assistance for college to blind students in South Dakota.

Eligibility This program is open to legally blind students who are either residents of South Dakota or attending a college or university in that state. In addition to letters of recommendation and copies of academic transcripts, applications must include an autobiographical sketch. A cumulative GPA of 3.3 or higher is generally required. Selection is based on demonstrated academic record, involvement in extracurricular and civic activities, and academic objectives. The severity of the applicant's visual impairment and his/her study methods are also taken into account.

Financial data The stipend is $500. In addition, the winner receives a $1,000 cash scholarship from the Kurzweil Foundation and, if appropriate, a Kurzweil-1000 Reading System.

Duration 1 year.

Additional Information This scholarship is sponsored by the South Dakota Association of the Blind, an affiliate of the American Council of the Blind. Scholarship winners are expected to be present at the council's annual conference; the council will cover all reasonable expenses connected with convention attendance.

Number awarded 1 each year.

Deadline February of each year.

[23]
DELTA GAMMA FOUNDATION FLORENCE MARGARET HARVEY MEMORIAL SCHOLARSHIP

American Foundation for the Blind
Attn: Scholarship Committee
11 Penn Plaza, Suite 300
New York, NY 10001
(212) 502-7661   Toll-free: (800) AFB-LINE
Fax: (212) 502-7771   TDD: (212) 502-7662
E-mail: afbinfo@afb.net
Web: www.afb.org/scholarships.asp

Summary To provide financial assistance to blind undergraduate and graduate students who wish to study in the field of rehabilitation and/or education of the blind.

Eligibility This program is open to legally blind juniors, seniors, or graduate students. U.S. citizenship is required. Applicants must be studying in the field of rehabilitation and/or education of visually impaired and blind persons. They must submit a typewritten statement, up to 3 pages in length, describing educational and personal goals, work experience, extracurricular activities, and how scholarship funds will be used. Selection includes consideration of good character and academic excellence.

Financial data The stipend is $1,000.

Duration 1 year.

Additional Information This scholarship is supported by the Delta Gamma Foundation and administered by the American Foundation for the Blind.

Number awarded 1 each year.

Deadline April of each year.

[24]
DES MOINES CHAPTER SCHOLARSHIPS

Iowa Council of the United Blind-Des Moines
  Chapter
c/o President, Dee Clayton
430 Grand Avenue
Des Moines, IA 50309
(515) 282-1275
Web: www.acb.org/iowa/dmchap.htm

Summary To provide financial assistance for college to blind residents of Iowa.
Eligibility This program is open to blind Iowa residents who are attending or planning to attend a college, trade school, or other training program. Applicants must submit a transcript, letter of recommendation, and certification of legal blindness. Selection is based on scholastic achievement, work experience, extracurricular and community activities, and neatness and appropriateness of the completed application form and attachments.
Financial data Stipends range from $500 to $2,000.
Duration 1 year.
Number awarded Varies each year. Recently, 4 of these scholarships were awarded: 1 at $2,000, 1 at $1,500, 1 at $1,000, and 1 at $500.
Deadline April of each year.

[25]
DR. MAE DAVIDOW MEMORIAL SCHOLARSHIP

American Council of the Blind
Attn: Coordinator, Scholarship Program
1155 15th Street, N.W., Suite 1004
Washington, DC 20005
(202) 467-5081   Toll-free: (800) 424-8666
Fax: (202) 467-5085   E-mail: info@acb.org
Web: www.acb.org

Summary To provide financial assistance to blind students entering their freshman year of college.
Eligibility This program is open to entering freshmen in academic programs who are legally blind. They must be U.S. citizens. In addition to letters of recommendation and copies of academic transcripts, applications must include an autobiographical sketch. A cumulative GPA of 3.3 or higher is generally required. Selection is based on demonstrated academic record, involvement in extracurricular and civic activities, and academic objectives. The severity of the applicant's visual impairment and his/her study methods are also taken into account.
Financial data The stipend is $1,500. In addition, the winner receives a $1,000 cash scholarship from the Kurzweil Foundation and, if appropriate, a Kurzweil-1000 Reading System.
Duration 1 year.
Additional Information This scholarship is sponsored by the Pennsylvania Council of the Blind, an affiliate of the American Council of the Blind. Scholarship winners are expected to be present at the council's annual conference; the council will cover all reasonable expenses connected with convention attendance.
Number awarded 1 each year.
Deadline February of each year.

[26]
DR. NICHOLAS S. DICAPRIO SCHOLARSHIP

American Council of the Blind
Attn: Coordinator, Scholarship Program
1155 15th Street, N.W., Suite 1004
Washington, DC 20005
(202) 467-5081   Toll-free: (800) 424-8666
Fax: (202) 467-5085   E-mail: info@acb.org
Web: www.acb.org

Summary To provide financial assistance to outstanding blind undergraduates.
Eligibility Eligible to apply for this scholarship are legally blind U.S. citizens or resident aliens who are undergraduate students. In addition to letters of recommendation and copies of academic transcripts, applications must include an autobiographical sketch. A cumulative GPA of 3.3 or higher is generally required. Selection is based on demonstrated academic record, involvement in extracurricular and civic activities, and academic objectives. The severity of the applicant's visual impairment and his/her study methods are also taken into account.
Financial data The stipend is $2,500. In addition, the winner receives a $1,000 cash scholarship from the Kurzweil Foundation and, if appropriate, a Kurzweil-1000 Reading System.
Duration 1 year.
Additional Information The scholarship winner is expected to be present at the council's annual national convention; the council will cover all reasonable costs connected with convention attendance.
Number awarded 1 each year.
Deadline February of each year.

[27]
DR. S. BRADLEY BURSON MEMORIAL SCHOLARSHIP

American Council of the Blind
Attn: Coordinator, Scholarship Program
1155 15th Street, N.W., Suite 1004
Washington, DC 20005
(202) 467-5081   Toll-free: (800) 424-8666
Fax: (202) 467-5085   E-mail: info@acb.org
Web: www.acb.org

Summary To provide financial assistance to blind students who are undergraduate or graduate students working on a degree in science at an accredited college or university.

Eligibility This program is open to legally blind undergraduate or graduate students majoring in the "hard" sciences (i.e., biology, chemistry, physics, and engineering, but not computer science) in college. They must be U.S. citizens. In addition to letters of recommendation and copies of academic transcripts, applications must include an autobiographical sketch. A cumulative GPA of 3.3 or higher is generally required. Selection is based on demonstrated academic record, involvement in extracurricular and civic activities, and academic objectives. The severity of the applicant's visual impairment and his/her study methods are also taken into account.

Financial data The stipend is $1,000. In addition, the winner receives a $1,000 cash scholarship from the Kurzweil Foundation and, if appropriate, a Kurzweil-1000 Reading System.

Duration 1 year.

Additional Information Scholarship winners are expected to be present at the council's annual conference; the council will cover all reasonable expenses connected with convention attendance.

Number awarded 1 each year.

Deadline February of each year.

[28]
EDUCATOR OF TOMORROW AWARD

National Federation of the Blind
c/o Peggy Elliott
Chair, Scholarship Committee
805 Fifth Avenue
Grinnell, IA 50112
(641) 236-3366
Web: www.nfb.org/sch_intro.htm

Summary To provide financial assistance to blind undergraduate or graduate students who wish to prepare for a career as a teacher.

Eligibility This program is open to legally blind students who are working on or planning to work on a full time undergraduate or graduate degree. Applicants must be preparing for a career in elementary, secondary, or postsecondary teaching. Selection is based on academic excellence, service to the community, and financial need.

Financial data The stipend is $3,000. The Kurzweil Foundation has also provided recipients with an additional $1,000 scholarship and the latest version of the Kurzweil-1000 reading software.

Duration 1 year; recipients may resubmit applications up to 2 additional years.

Additional Information Scholarships are awarded at the federation convention in July. Recipients attend the convention at federation expense; that funding is in addition to the scholarship grant.

Number awarded 1 each year.

Deadline March of each year.

[29]
ELLEN BEACH MACK SCHOLARSHIP

American Council of the Blind of South Carolina
c/o Patsy Jones
1822 Burnham Street
West Columbia, SC 29169
(803) 791-3368
E-mail: jones.patsy@worldnet.att.net
Web: www.acb.org/southcarolina

Summary To provide financial assistance to undergraduate and graduate students with visual impairments in South Carolina.

Eligibility This program is open to residents of South Carolina who are legally blind in both eyes. Applicants must be currently enrolled or accepted at a technical school, college, university, or graduate school. Along with their application, they must submit a letter of recommendation, transcript, and a 2-page autobiographical sketch that describes their goals, strengths, weaknesses, and other pertinent information.

Financial data The stipend is $1,000.

Duration 1 year.

Number awarded 1 or more each year.

Deadline September of each year.

[30]
EMERSON FOULKE MEMORIAL SCHOLARSHIP

National Federation of the Blind of Kentucky
c/o Mrs. Cathy Jackson, President
210 Cambridge Drive
Louisville, KY 40214-2809
(502) 366-2317   E-mail: info@nfbk.org
Web: www.nfbk.org/scholarshipform.html

Summary To provide financial assistance for college to blind residents of Kentucky.

Eligibility This program is open to blind residents of Kentucky who are attending or planning to attend a college or university. Applicants must submit a letter, up to 2 pages in length, describing how the scholarship will help them achieve their career goals; how they are involved in their community, organizations, and other activities; any honors, awards, or special recognition they have received; and how they would like to be involved in the National Federation of the Blind of Kentucky.

Financial data The stipend is $1,000.

Duration 1 year.

Additional Information Information is also available from Lora J. Felty, Scholarship Chair, E-mail: lorajf@aol.com

Number awarded 1 each year.

Deadline July of each year.

[31]
E.U. PARKER SCHOLARSHIP

National Federation of the Blind
c/o Peggy Elliott
Chair, Scholarship Committee
805 Fifth Avenue
Grinnell, IA 50112
(641) 236-3366
Web: www.nfb.org/sch_intro.htm

Summary To provide financial assistance to blind undergraduate and graduate students.

Eligibility This program is open to legally blind students who are working on or planning to work on a full-time undergraduate or graduate degree. Selection is based on academic excellence, service to the community, and financial need.

Financial data The stipend is $3,000. The Kurzweil Foundation has also provided recipients with an additional $1,000 scholarship and the latest version of the Kurzweil-1000 reading software.

Duration 1 year; recipients may resubmit applications up to 2 additional years.

Additional Information Scholarships are awarded at the federation convention in July. Recipients attend the convention at federation expense; that funding is in addition to the scholarship grant.

Number awarded 1 each year.

Deadline March of each year.

[32]
EUNICE FIORITO MEMORIAL SCHOLARSHIP

American Council of the Blind
Attn: Coordinator, Scholarship Program
1155 15th Street, N.W., Suite 1004
Washington, DC 20005
(202) 467-5081   Toll-free: (800) 424-8666
Fax: (202) 467-5085   E-mail: info@acb.org
Web: www.acb.org

Summary To provide financial assistance to outstanding blind undergraduates.

Eligibility Eligible to apply for this scholarship are legally blind U.S. citizens or resident aliens who are undergraduate students. In addition to letters of recommendation and copies of academic transcripts, applications must include an autobiographical sketch. A cumulative GPA of 3.3 or higher is generally required. Selection is based on demonstrated academic record, involvement in extracurricular and civic activities, and academic objectives. The severity of the applicant's visual impairment and his/her study methods are also taken into account.

Financial data A stipend is awarded (amount not specified). In addition, the winner receives a $1,000 cash scholarship from the Kurzweil Foundation and, if appropriate, a Kurzweil-1000 Reading System.

Duration 1 year.

Additional Information The scholarship winner is expected to be present at the council's annual national convention; the council will cover all reasonable costs connected with convention attendance.

Number awarded 1 each year.

Deadline February of each year.

[33]
FERDINAND TORRES SCHOLARSHIP

American Foundation for the Blind
Attn: Scholarship Committee
11 Penn Plaza, Suite 300
New York, NY 10001
(212) 502-7661   Toll-free: (800) AFB-LINE
Fax: (212) 502-7771   TDD: (212) 502-7662
E-mail: afbinfo@afb.net
Web: www.afb.org/scholarships.asp

Summary To provide financial assistance for college to blind students.

Eligibility Applicants must be legally blind and reside in the United States, although U.S. citizenship is not necessary. They must present evidence of economic need, legal blindness, and acceptance into a full-time postsecondary program. Preference is given to residents of New York City. Applicants must submit a typewritten statement of 3 double-spaced pages describing educational and personal goals, work experience, extracurricular activities, and how scholarship funds will be used.

Financial data The stipend is $1,000.

Duration 1 year.

Number awarded 1 each year.

Deadline April of each year.

[34]
FLORIDA COUNCIL OF THE BLIND SCHOLARSHIPS

Florida Council of the Blind
c/o Robert Miller, President
2201 Limerick Drive
Tallahassee, FL 32309
(850) 906-9821   E-mail: easytalk@earthlink.net
Web: www.fcb.org

Summary To provide financial assistance to outstanding blind students from Florida who are interested in pursuing postsecondary education.

Eligibility Applicants must be legally blind; residents of Florida; high school seniors, high school graduates, or college students; and interested in attending college or vocational school. Selection is based on grade and other leadership activity.

Financial data The stipends are $1,500 or $1,000.

Duration 1 year; may be renewed.

Number awarded 3 each year: 2 for $1,500 and 1 for $1,000.

Deadline January of each year.

[35]
FLOYD CALLWARD MEMORIAL SCHOLARSHIP

National Federation of the Blind of New Hampshire
c/o John E. Parker, President
2 Center Street, Apartment 2
Laconia, NH 03246-3737
(603) 528-0107   E-mail: parkerj@worldpath.net

Summary To provide financial assistance to blind students in New Hampshire who wish to work on an undergraduate or graduate degree.

Eligibility This program is open to legally blind and totally blind residents of New Hampshire who are attending or planning to attend college. Applicants must submit 1) a letter describing what they have done to deal with situations involving their blindness, their personal goals and aspirations, and how the scholarship will help them; 2) 2 letters of recommendation; 3) high school or college transcripts; 4) a list of honors and awards; and 5) information on community service and volunteer work. There are no restrictions on level, gender, or field of study. Financial need is not considered.

Financial data The stipend is $1,000. The funds may be used to purchase education-related equipment or services or to defray the costs of tuition, board, and other school fees.

Duration 1 year.

Additional Information This program was established in 1990. Information is also available from Louis Gosselin, c/o New Hampshire State Department of Education, Division of Vocational Rehabilitation, 361 Lincoln Street, Manchester, NH 03103, (603) 669-8733.

Number awarded 1 or more each year.

Deadline September of each year.

[36]
FLOYD QUALLS MEMORIAL SCHOLARSHIPS

American Council of the Blind
Attn: Coordinator, Scholarship Program
1155 15th Street, N.W., Suite 1004
Washington, DC 20005
(202) 467-5081   Toll-free: (800) 424-8666
Fax: (202) 467-5085   E-mail: info@acb.org
Web: www.acb.org

Summary To provide financial assistance to undergraduate and graduate students who are blind.

Eligibility Students who are legally blind may apply for these scholarships. Recipients are selected in each of 4 categories: entering freshmen in academic programs, undergraduates (sophomores, juniors, and seniors) in academic programs, graduate students in academic programs, and vocational school students or students working on an associate's degree from a community college. In addition to letters of recommendation and copies of academic transcripts, applications must include an autobiographical sketch. A cumulative GPA of 3.3 or higher is generally required. Selection is based on demonstrated academic record, involvement in extracurricular and civic activities, and academic objectives. The severity of the applicant's visual impairment and his/her study methods are also taken into account.

Financial data The stipend is $2,500. In addition, the winners receive a $1,000 cash scholarship from the Kurzweil Foundation and, if appropriate, a Kurzweil-1000 Reading System.

Duration 1 year.

Additional Information Scholarship winners are expected to be present at the council's annual conference; the council will cover all reasonable expenses connected with convention attendance.

Number awarded Up to 8 each year: 2 in each of the 4 categories.

Deadline February of each year.

[37]
FLOYD R. CARGILL SCHOLARSHIP

Illinois Council of the Blind
P.O. Box 1336
Springfield, IL 62705
(217) 523-4967   Toll-free: (888) 698-1862
Fax: (217) 523-4302   E-mail: icb@fgi.net

Summary To provide financial assistance for college or professional school to blind students in Illinois.

Eligibility This program is open to students who are legally blind and enrolled in (or applying to) a postsecondary academic, vocational, technical, or professional training program in Illinois. Applicants must submit a 2-page autobiographical sketch; certified transcripts (undergraduates must include high school transcripts and graduate students must include undergraduate transcripts); a letter of recommendation; and proof of acceptance (or a statement that they are under consideration for admission) at a postsecondary school. U.S. citizenship is required.

Financial data The stipend is $750.

Duration 1 year.

Number awarded 1 or more each year.

Deadline June of each year.

[38]
FRED SCHEIGERT SCHOLARSHIPS

Council of Citizens with Low Vision International
c/o Pat Beattie, President
906 North Chambliss Street
Alexandria, VA 22312
Toll-free: (800) 733-2258 Fax: (703) 671-9053
E-mail: bernice@tsoft.net
Web: www.cclvi.org/scholarship.html

Summary To provide financial assistance to undergraduate and graduate students with low vision.

Eligibility Applicants must be certified by an ophthalmologist as having low vision (acuity of 20/70 or worse in the better seeing eye with best correction or side vision with a maximum diameter of no greater than 30 degrees). They may be part-time or full-time entering freshmen, undergraduates, or graduate students. A cumulative GPA of at least 3.0 is required.

Financial data The stipend is $1,000.

Duration 1 year.

Additional Information Information is also available from Janis Stanger, 1239 American Beauty Drive, Salt Lake City, UT 84116.

Number awarded 2 each year.

Deadline April of each year.

[39]
FREEDOM SCIENTIFIC TECHNOLOGY SCHOLARSHIP AWARD PROGRAM

Freedom Scientific Inc.
Attn: Low Vision Group
11800 31st Court North
St. Petersburg, FL 33716
(727) 803-8000, ext. 1044
Toll-free: (800) 444-4443 Fax: (727) 803-8001
E-mail: EricV@freedomscientific.com
Web: www.FreedomScientific.com

Summary To provide financial assistance to blind undergraduate and graduate students in the form of vouchers for the purchase of assistive technology devices.

Eligibility This program is open to legally blind students who are either 1) graduating high school seniors planning to pursue a full-time course of study at a college or university, or 2) college seniors planning to enter graduate school. Applicants must be residents of the United States or Canada. The program is administered through 6 partner organizations: 4 for high school seniors in the United States, 1 for high school seniors in Canada, and 1 for graduate students in the United States and Canada. Selection is based on general guidelines of academic achievement and promise, extracurricular or community service leadership and accomplishments, and demonstrated personal qualities and character. The partner organizations may supplement those general guidelines with their own specific criteria and may also select especially deserving students across all levels of higher education. Students may apply to the partner organization of their choice or, if they have no preference, to the organization assigned for the geographic region in which they live.

Financial data The awards consist of vouchers for $2,500 to be used to purchase Freedom Scientific hardware, software, accessories, training, and/or tutorials.

Duration These are 1-time awards.

Additional Information This program, which began in the 2001-02 school year, is sponsored by Freedom Scientific, maker of technology-based products for people who are blind or vision-impaired. The partner organizations include the National Federation of the Blind, 1800 Johnson Street, Baltimore, MD 21230, (410) 659-9314, Web site: www.nfb.org, which also serves as the regional organization for Connecticut, Delaware, Maine, Maryland, Massachusetts, New Hampshire, New Jersey, New York, Pennsylvania, Puerto Rico, Rhode Island, Vermont, Virginia, Washington, D.C., and West Virginia; the American Foundation for the Blind, Attn: Scholarship Committee, 11 Penn Plaza, Suite 300, New York, NY 10001, (212) 502-7661, (800) AFB-LINE, Fax: (212) 502-7771, TDD: (212) 502-7662, E-mail: afbinfo@afb.net, Web site: www.afb.org/scholarships.asp, which also serves as the regional organization for Alabama, Arkansas, Florida, Georgia, Louisiana, Mississippi, North Carolina, South Carolina, Tennessee, and Texas; the American Council of the Blind, 1155 15th Street, N.W., Suite 1004, Washington, DC 20005, (202) 467-5081, (800) 424-8666, Fax: (202) 467-5085, E-mail: info@acb.org, Web site: www.acb.org, which also serves as the regional organization for Illinois, Indiana, Iowa, Kansas, Kentucky, Michigan, Minnesota, Missouri, Nebraska, Ohio, Oklahoma, and Wisconsin; the Braille Institute of America, 741 North Vermont Avenue, Los Angeles, CA 90029-3594, (323) 663-1111, (800) BRAILLE, Fax: (323) 663-0867, E-mail: info@brailleinstitute.org, Web site: www.braileinstitute.org, which also serves as the regional organization for Alaska, Arizona, California, Colorado, Hawaii, Idaho, Montana, Nevada, New Mexico, North Dakota, Oregon, South Dakota, Utah, Washington, and Wyoming; the Canadian National Institute for the Blind, 1929 Bayview Avenue, Toronto, Ontario M4G 3E8, (416) 486-2500, Web site: www.cnib.ca, which accepts all applications from high school seniors in Canada; and Recording for the Blind and Dyslexic 20 Roszel Road, Princeton, NJ 08540, (609) 452-0606, (800) 221-4792, Web site: www.rfbd.org, which accepts all applications for graduate study in the United States and Canada.

Number awarded 20 each year: 4 from each of the U.S. regional organizations, 2 to Canadian students, and 2 to graduate students.

Deadline Each partner organization sets its own deadline, but most are by March of each year.

[40]
FRIENDS-IN-ART SCHOLARSHIP

Friends-in-Art
c/o Harvey Miller
402 East French Broad Street
Brevard, NC 28712-3410
(828) 862-3412

Summary To provide financial assistance to blind students planning to major or majoring in fields related to the arts.

Eligibility This program is open to blind and visually impaired students who plan to major in music, art, drama, or creative writing or who already are majoring in those fields. Applicants must have a visual acuity of 20/200 or less in the corrected eye and/or 20 degrees or less visual field in the corrected eye. Selection is based on achievement, talent, and excellence in the arts.

Financial data The stipend is $1,000.

Duration 1 year.

Additional Information This program began in 1999.

Number awarded 1 each year.

Deadline April of each year.

[41]
GEORGIA COUNCIL OF THE BLIND SCHOLARSHIPS

Georgia Council of the Blind
c/o Janet Clary, Scholarship Committee Chair
318 Walden Glen Lane
Evans, GA 30809

Summary To provide financial assistance for college or graduate school to students in Georgia who have visual impairments or parents with visual impairments.

Eligibility This program is open to residents of Georgia who are either 1) visually impaired or legally blind or 2) the sighted children of parents who are visually impaired or legally blind. Applicants must be enrolled or accepted for enrollment at a vocational/technical school, a 2-year or 4-year college, or a master's or doctoral program. All fields of study are eligible. Selection is based on academic transcripts, 2 letters of recommendation, a 1-page typed statement of the applicant's educational goals, an audio cassette recording of the applicant reading the goals statement, extracurricular activities, and financial need.

Financial data Stipends up to $1,000 per year are available.

Duration 1 year; recipients may reapply.

Additional Information This program began in 1988.

Number awarded 1 or more each year.

Deadline June of each year.

[42]
GERALD DRAKE MEMORIAL SCHOLARSHIP

National Federation of the Blind of California
Attn: Nancy Burns, President
175 East Olive Avenue, Suite 308
Burbank, CA 91502-1812
(818) 558-6524   Fax: (818) 729-7930
E-mail: dnburns@jps.net
Web: www.nfbcal.org

Summary To provide financial assistance for undergraduate or graduate education to blind students in California.

Eligibility Legally blind full-time students in California may apply for a scholarship, but they must attend the convention of the National Federation of the Blind of California. Applicants must submit an essay in which they describe their educational goals, involvement in the blindness community, and eye condition. High school seniors and college freshmen must submit their high school transcripts; other college students must submit transcripts of all undergraduate and graduate work. Selection is based on academic merit.

Financial data The stipend is $1,500.

Duration 1 year.

Number awarded 1 each year.

Deadline May of each year.

[43]
GLADYS C. ANDERSON MEMORIAL SCHOLARSHIP

American Foundation for the Blind
Attn: Scholarship Committee
11 Penn Plaza, Suite 300
New York, NY 10001
(212) 502-7661   Toll-free: (800) AFB-LINE
Fax: (212) 502-7771   TDD: (212) 502-7662
E-mail: afbinfo@afb.net
Web: www.afb.org/scholarships.asp

Summary To provide financial assistance to legally blind undergraduate women who are studying religious or classical music.

Eligibility This program is open to legally blind women who are U.S. citizens and have been accepted in a college or university program in religious or classical music. Applicants must submit a typewritten statement, up to 2 pages in length, describing educational and career goals, work experience, extracurricular activities, and how scholarship funds will be used. They must also submit a sample performance tape (a voice or instrumental selection).

Financial data The stipend is $1,000.

Duration 1 academic year.

Number awarded 1 each year.

Deadline April of each year.

[44]
HANK HOFSTETTER OPPORTUNITY GRANTS

American Council of the Blind of Indiana
c/o James R. Durst
Indiana School for the Blind
7725 North College Avenue
Indianapolis, IN 46240
Web: www.acb.org/indiana/hofstetter.htm

Summary To provide financial assistance to Indiana residents who are blind and need materials or equipment to continue their education.

Eligibility This fund is open to certified legally blind Indiana residents. They must need funding for materials or equipment to pursue their educational or vocational "opportunities." The following information should be submitted as part of the application: opportunity desired, equipment or supplies needed, a statement on why the applicant should receive the award, a list of other sources/options already explored, and a reference letter.

Financial data The amount awarded varies, depending upon the needs of the recipient. A total of $1,000 is available annually.

Additional Information Information is also available from Donald Koors, 5885 North Central, Indianapolis, IN 46220, (317) 251-2562.

Number awarded 1 or more each year.

Deadline Requests may be submitted at any time but should be received at least 90 days prior to the need.

[45]
HANK LEBONNE SCHOLARSHIP

National Federation of the Blind
c/o Peggy Elliott
Chair, Scholarship Committee
805 Fifth Avenue
Grinnell, IA 50112
(641) 236-3366
Web: www.nfb.org/sch_intro.htm

Summary To provide financial assistance to legally blind students working on an undergraduate or graduate degree.

Eligibility This program is open to legally blind students who are working on or planning to work on a full-time undergraduate or graduate degree. Selection is based on academic excellence, service to the community, and financial need.

Financial data The stipend is $5,000. The Kurzweil Foundation has also provided recipients with an additional $1,000 scholarship and the latest version of the Kurzweil-1000 reading software.

Duration 1 year; recipients may resubmit applications up to 2 additional years.

Additional Information Scholarships are awarded at the federation convention in July. Recipients attend the convention at federation expense; that funding is in addition to the scholarship grant.

Number awarded 1 each year.

Deadline March of each year.

[46]
HARRY LUDWIG MEMORIAL SCHOLARSHIP

Oregon Student Assistance Commission
Attn: Grants and Scholarships Division
1500 Valley River Drive, Suite 100
Eugene, OR 97401-2146
(541) 687-7395
Toll-free: (800) 452-8807, ext. 7395
Fax: (541) 687-7419
Web: www.osac.state.or.us

Summary To provide financial assistance for college or graduate school to residents of Oregon who are visually impaired.

Eligibility This program is open to residents of Oregon who are visually impaired (have residual acuity of 20/70 or less in the better eye with correction, or their visual field is restricted to 20 degrees or less in the better eye). Applicants must be enrolled or planning to enroll as full-time undergraduate or graduate students at a college or university in Oregon.

Financial data Stipends range from $1,000 to $5,000 and average $1,600.

Duration 1 year.

Additional Information This program is administered by the Oregon Student Assistance Commission (OSAC) with funds provided by the Oregon Community Foundation, 1221 S.W. Yamhill, Suite 100, Portland, OR 97205, (503) 227-6846, Fax: (503) 274-7771.

Number awarded Varies each year.

Deadline February of each year.

[47]
HAZEL TEN BROEK MERIT SCHOLARSHIP

National Federation of the Blind of Washington
Attn: Scholarship Committee
P.O. Box 2516
Seattle, WA 98111
(206) 624-8007   E-mail: info@nfbw.org
Web: www.nfbw.org

Summary To provide financial assistance for undergraduate or graduate study to blind students in Washington.

Eligibility This program is open to legally blind residents of Washington state who are working on or planning to work on a full-time college or graduate degree. Applicants must submit a letter describing themselves (hobbies, interests, school activities, and future goals), high school and/or college transcripts, and 3 letters of reference.

Financial data The stipend is $2,000.

Duration 1 year.

VISUAL DISABILITIES: SCHOLARSHIPS

Additional Information Information is also available from Rita Szantay at (206) 224-7242 (days) or (206) 352-7320 (evenings and weekends). This scholarship was first awarded in 1996. Winners must attend the state convention of the National Federation of the Blind of Washington to accept the award; convention expenses are covered.

Number awarded 1 each year.

Deadline August of each year.

[48] HELEN COPELAND SCHOLARSHIP FOR FEMALES

United States Association of Blind Athletes
Attn: Scholarship Committee
Brown Hall, Suite 015
33 North Institute Street
Colorado Springs, CO 80903
(719) 630-0422   Fax: (719) 630-0616
E-mail: usaba@usa.net
Web: www.usaba.org

Summary To provide financial assistance for undergraduate or graduate study to female members of the United States Association for Blind Athletes (USABA).

Eligibility All legally blind females who have been members of and have participated in USABA activities for the past year are eligible to apply for this scholarship. Applicants must have been admitted to an academic, vocational, technical, professional, or certification program at the postsecondary level. Selection is based on demonstrated academic record, involvement in extracurricular and civic activities, academic goals and objectives, and USABA involvement at various levels.

Financial data The stipend is $500.

Number awarded 1 each year.

Deadline September of each year.

[49] HENTGES SCHOLARSHIP

National Federation of the Blind of Missouri
c/o Gary Wunder, President
3910 Tropical Lane
Columbia, MO 65202-6205
(573) 874-1774   Toll-free: (888) 604-1774
E-mail: info@nfbmo.org
Web: www.nfbmo.org

Summary To provide financial assistance for undergraduate or graduate study to blind female students in Missouri.

Eligibility This program is open to legally blind women residents of Missouri who are pursuing or planning to pursue an undergraduate or graduate degree.

Financial data The maximum stipend is $500.

Duration 1 year.

Additional Information Additional information is also available from Chair, Achievement Awards Committee, Sheila Koenig, 634 South National, Apartment 303, Springfield, MO 65804, (417) 869-1078.

Number awarded 1 each year.

Deadline February of each year.

[50] HERMIONE GRANT CALHOUN SCHOLARSHIPS

National Federation of the Blind
c/o Peggy Elliott
Chair, Scholarship Committee
805 Fifth Avenue
Grinnell, IA 50112
(641) 236-3366
Web: www.nfb.org/sch_intro.htm

Summary To provide financial assistance to female blind students interested in working on an undergraduate or graduate degree.

Eligibility This program is open to legally blind women students who are working on or planning to work full time on an undergraduate or graduate degree. Selection is based on academic excellence, service to the community, and financial need.

Financial data The stipend is $3,000. The Kurzweil Foundation has also provided recipients with an additional $1,000 scholarship and the latest version of the Kurzweil-1000 reading software.

Duration 1 year; recipients may resubmit applications up to 2 additional years.

Additional Information Scholarships are awarded at the federation convention in July. Recipients attend the convention at federation expense; that funding is in addition to the scholarship grant.

Number awarded 1 each year.

Deadline March of each year.

[51] HOWARD BROWN RICKARD SCHOLARSHIPS

National Federation of the Blind
c/o Peggy Elliott
Chair, Scholarship Committee
805 Fifth Avenue
Grinnell, IA 50112
(641) 236-3366
Web: www.nfb.org/sch_intro.htm

Summary To provide financial assistance for college or graduate school to blind students studying or planning to study law, medicine, engineering, architecture, or the natural sciences.

Eligibility This program is open to legally blind students who are enrolled in or planning to enroll in a full-time undergraduate or graduate course of study. Applicants must be studying or planning to study law, medi-

cine, engineering, architecture, or the natural sciences. Selection is based on academic excellence, service to the community, and financial need.
Financial data The stipend is $3,000. The Kurzweil Foundation has also provided recipients with an additional $1,000 scholarship and the latest version of the Kurzweil-1000 reading software.
Duration 1 year; recipients may resubmit applications up to 2 additional years.
Additional Information Scholarships are awarded at the federation convention in July. Recipients attend the convention at federation expense; that funding is in addition to the scholarship grant.
Number awarded 1 each year.
Deadline March of each year.

[52]
HOWARD E. MAY MEMORIAL SCHOLARSHIP

National Federation of the Blind of Connecticut
580 Burnside Avenue, Suite 1
East Hartford, CT 06108
(860) 289-1971   E-mail: info@nfbct.org
Web: www.nfbct.org/html/schinfo.htm

Summary To provide financial assistance to blind students pursuing a full-time college education in Connecticut.
Eligibility Applicants must be legally blind and either residents of or full-time college students in Connecticut. Along with their application, they must submit a letter on their career goals and how the scholarship might help them achieve those. Selection is based on academic excellence, extracurricular activities, service to the community, and financial need.
Financial data The stipend is $2,000.
Duration 1 year.
Number awarded 1 each year.
Deadline September of each year.

[53]
IMA DIVERSITY SCHOLARSHIP PROGRAM

Institute of Management Accountants
Attn: Committee on Students
10 Paragon Drive
Montvale, NJ 07645-1760
(201) 573-9000
Toll-free: (800) 638-4427, ext. 1543
Fax: (201) 573-8438   E-mail: students@imanet.org
Web: www.imanet.org

Summary To provide financial assistance to minority and disabled student members of the Institute of Management Accountants (IMA) who are interested in working on an undergraduate or graduate degree in management accounting or financial management.
Eligibility This program is open to undergraduate and graduate students of American Indian/Alaska Native, Asian/Pacific Islander, Black, or Hispanic heritage and students with physical disabilities (defined as hearing impairment, vision impairment, missing extremities, partial paralysis, complete paralysis, or severe distortion of limbs and/or spine). Applicants must be in their sophomore, junior, or senior year or in a graduate program with a major in management accounting, financial management, or information technology. Selection is based on 1) academic merit; 2) quality of their application presentation; 3) demonstrated community leadership; 4) potential for success in expressed career goals in a financial management position; 5) a written statement from applicants expressing their short-term and long-term career goals and objectives, including their participation in the IMA; and 6) letters of recommendation.
Financial data Stipends are $3,000 per year.
Duration 1 year.
Additional Information Up to 15 finalists in each category (including the scholarship winners) receive a scholarship to take 5 parts of the CMA and/or CFM examination within a year of graduation.
Number awarded At least 13 each year.
Deadline February of each year.

[54]
JAMES DOYLE CASE MEMORIAL SCHOLARSHIPS

Mississippi Council of the Blind
2501 North West Street
Jackson, MS 39216
(601) 982-1718
Toll-free: (888) 346-5622 (within MS)
E-mail: mcb@netdoor.com

Summary To provide funding for college to legally blind residents of Mississippi and their children.
Eligibility This program is open to residents of Mississippi who are legally blind or the children of at least 1 legally blind parent. Applicants must be enrolled or accepted for enrollment in an undergraduate or graduate program and carrying or planning to carry at least 12 academic hours. Selection is based on a transcript from the last school or college attended, college entrance examination score, 2 letters of recommendation, and a 300-word biographical essay on the applicant's educational and employment goals. Membership in the sponsoring organization is not required.
Financial data The stipend is $1,000 per year.
Duration 1 year.
Additional Information Information is also available from Rebecca Floyd, President, 131 Red Fox Lane, Madison, MS 39110.
Number awarded 2 each year.
Deadline March of each year.

[55]
JAMES R. CARLOCK SCHOLARSHIP

National Federation of the Blind of Arizona
c/o Ruth Swenson, President
311 West McNair Street
Chandler, AZ 85225-7135
(480) 898-1188
E-mail: rswenson1@mindspring.com
Web: www.nfbarizona.com/SCHOOL.htm

Summary To provide financial assistance for college or professional school to blind students in Arizona.

Eligibility This program is open to legally blind full-time students. Applicants must be residents of Arizona or attending school in Arizona. Selection is based on academic excellence, program quality, service to the community, and financial need.

Financial data The stipend is $750.

Duration 1 year.

Additional Information Information is also available from Marcus Schmidt, Scholarship Chair, 3202 West Murie Drive, Phoenix, AZ 85053, (602) 942-0181, E-mail: marcus.schmidt@pinnaclewest.com.

Number awarded 1 each year.

Deadline May of each year.

[56]
JENNICA FERGUSON ACHIEVEMENT SCHOLARSHIP

National Federation of the Blind of Michigan
1212 North Foster
Lansing, MI 48912
(517) 372-8700   E-mail: fjw@attbi.com
Web: www.nfbmi.org

Summary To provide financial assistance for college to Michigan students who are blind.

Eligibility This program is open to legally blind residents of Michigan. Applicants must be enrolled or planning to enroll full time at a postsecondary institution in the state. They must have a GPA of 2.0 or higher from high school and/or college. Along with their application, they must submit a 1- to 3-page letter in which they describe any situations involving their blindness that they have encountered, their plans for the future, and how this scholarship will help them achieve their academic goals.

Financial data The stipend is $1,000.

Duration 1 year.

Additional Information Information is also available from Melody Lindsey, Scholarship Chair, 2213 Winchell Avenue, Kalamazoo, MI 49008, (269) 388-2686. The winner must attend the convention of the National Federation of the Blind of Michigan. All expenses are paid by the sponsor.

Number awarded 1 each year.

Deadline October of each year.

[57]
JENNICA FERGUSON MEMORIAL SCHOLARSHIP

National Federation of the Blind
c/o Peggy Elliott
Chair, Scholarship Committee
805 Fifth Avenue
Grinnell, IA 50112
(641) 236-3366
Web: www.nfb.org/sch_intro.htm

Summary To provide financial assistance to undergraduate and graduate blind students.

Eligibility This program is open to legally blind students who are working on or planning to work full time on an undergraduate or graduate degree. Selection is based on academic excellence, service to the community, and financial need.

Financial data The stipend is $5,000. The Kurzweil Foundation has also provided recipients with an additional $1,000 scholarship and the latest version of the Kurzweil 1000 reading software.

Duration 1 year; recipients may resubmit applications up to 2 additional years.

Additional Information Scholarships are awarded at the federation convention in July. Recipients attend the convention at federation expense; that funding is in addition to the scholarship grant.

Number awarded 1 each year.

Deadline March of each year.

[58]
JOHN AND RHODA DOWER SCHOLARSHIP

National Federation of the Blind of Missouri
c/o Gary Wunder, President
3910 Tropical Lane
Columbia, MO 65202-6205
(573) 874-1774   Toll-free: (888) 604-1774
E-mail: Info@nfbmo.org
Web: www.nfbmo.org

Summary To provide financial assistance for college to blind students in Missouri.

Eligibility This program is open to legally blind residents of Missouri who are pursuing or planning to pursue an undergraduate or graduate degree.

Financial data The maximum stipend is $1,000.

Duration 1 year.

Additional Information Additional information is also available from the Chair of the Achievement Awards Committee: Sheila Koenig, 634 South National, Apartment 303, Springfield, MO 65804, (417) 869-1078.

Number awarded Up to 3 each year.

Deadline February of each year.

FINANCIAL AID PROGRAMS

[59]
JOHN CAHALL MEMORIAL SCHOLARSHIP FUND

Delaware Council of the Blind and Visually Impaired
c/o Sharon Sutlic, Scholarship Committee
14 Top View Court
Newark, DE 19702
(302) 994-9435
Web: www.dcbvi.org

Summary To provide financial assistance for college to visually impaired Delaware residents.
Eligibility This program is open to blind and visually impaired Delaware residents who are interested in pursuing postsecondary education or training.
Financial data The stipend is $500.
Duration 1 year.
Additional Information This fund was established 1997. Information is also available from the scholarship committee chair at (302) 655-2111.
Number awarded 1 each year.
Deadline March of each year.

[60]
JOHN HEBNER MEMORIAL SCHOLARSHIP

American Council of the Blind
Attn: Coordinator, Scholarship Program
1155 15th Street, N.W., Suite 1004
Washington, DC 20005
(202) 467-5081   Toll-free: (800) 424-8666
Fax: (202) 467-5085   E-mail: info@acb.org
Web: www.acb.org

Summary To provide financial assistance for college to blind or visually impaired students who are also employed full time.
Eligibility This program is open to blind or visually impaired students who are employed full time. Applications must include 1) a personal statement explaining how the scholarship will be beneficial and a description of financial need; 2) a resume, including information about current and previous work experience, educational achievements, community service, etc.; 3) a letter from the applicant's current employer confirming employment status; and 4) a certification of legal blindness. A cumulative GPA of 3.3 or higher is generally required.
Financial data The stipend is $600.
Duration 1 year.
Number awarded 1 each year.
Deadline February of each year.

[61]
JOHN T. MCCRAW SCHOLARSHIP

National Federation of the Blind of Maryland
Attn: Scholarship Committee Chair
9013 Nelson Way
Columbia, MD 21045
(410) 715-9596   E-mail: nfbmd@earthlink.net

Summary To provide financial assistance for college to blind students from Maryland.
Eligibility This program is open to legally blind students who are residents of Maryland or pursuing postsecondary (university, 2- or 4-year college, vocational/technical school) studies in the state. Applicants must submit a completed application form, 2 letters of recommendation, a current transcript, and a statement that summarizes their honors, goals, and plans. Financial need is not considered in the selection process.
Financial data The stipend is either $1,800 or $1,200.
Duration 1 year; recipients may reapply.
Additional Information A special scholarship may be awarded to former McCraw Scholarship recipients. To apply for this special scholarship, former recipients must still meet all of the requirements for the scholarship program and submit a new application. Recipients must attend school on a full-time basis. They must attend the sponsor's annual convention; financial assistance to attend the convention may be provided if the recipient needs and requests it (this is in addition to the scholarship grant).
Number awarded 2 each year.
Deadline May of each year.

[62]
JONATHAN MAY MEMORIAL SCHOLARSHIPS

National Federation of the Blind of Connecticut
580 Burnside Avenue, Suite 1
East Hartford, CT 06108
(860) 289-1971   E-mail: info@nfbct.org
Web: www.nfbct.org/html/schinfo.htm

Summary To provide financial assistance to blind students pursuing a full-time college education in Connecticut.
Eligibility Applicants must be legally blind and either residents of or full-time college students in Connecticut. Along with their application, they must submit a letter on their career goals and how the scholarship might help them achieve those. Selection is based on academic excellence, extracurricular activities, service to the community, and financial need.
Financial data The stipend is $1,000.
Duration 1 year.
Number awarded 1 each year.
Deadline September of each year.

VISUAL DISABILITIES: SCHOLARSHIPS

[63]
KELLIE CANNON MEMORIAL SCHOLARSHIP

American Council of the Blind
Attn: Coordinator, Scholarship Program
1155 15th Street, N.W., Suite 1004
Washington, DC 20005
(202) 467-5081   Toll-free: (800) 424-8666
Fax: (202) 467-5085   E-mail: info@acb.org
Web: www.acb.org

Summary To provide financial assistance to students who are blind and interested in preparing for a career in the computer field.

Eligibility Eligible to apply are high school seniors, high school graduates, and college students who are blind and are interested in majoring in college in computer information systems or data processing. In addition to letters of recommendation and copies of academic transcripts, applications must include an autobiographical sketch. A cumulative GPA of 3.3 or higher is generally required. Selection is based on demonstrated academic record, involvement in extracurricular and civic activities, and academic objectives. The severity of the applicant's visual impairment and his/her study methods are also taken into account.

Financial data The stipend is $2,000. In addition, the winner receives a $1,000 cash scholarship from the Kurzweil Foundation and, if appropriate, a Kurzweil-1000 Reading System.

Duration 1 year.

Additional Information This program is sponsored by Visually Impaired Data Processors International, an affiliate of the American Council of the Blind. The scholarship winner is expected to be present at the council's annual national convention; the council will cover all reasonable costs connected with convention attendance.

Number awarded 1 each year.

Deadline February of each year.

[64]
KENNETH JERNIGAN SCHOLARSHIP

National Federation of the Blind
c/o Peggy Elliott
Chair, Scholarship Committee
805 Fifth Avenue
Grinnell, IA 50112
(641) 236-3366
Web: www.nfb.org/sch_intro.htm

Summary To provide financial assistance to undergraduate and graduate blind students.

Eligibility This program is open to legally blind students who are working on or planning to work full time on an undergraduate or graduate degree. Selection is based on academic excellence, service to the community, and financial need.

Financial data The stipend is $12,000. The Kurzweil Foundation has also provided recipients with an additional $1,000 scholarship and the latest version of the Kurzweil-1000 reading software.

Duration 1 year; recipients may resubmit applications up to 2 additional years.

Additional Information Scholarships are awarded at the federation convention in July. Recipients attend the convention at federation expense; that funding is in addition to the scholarship grant. This scholarship is given by the American Action Fund for Blind Children and Adults, a nonprofit organization that assists blind people.

Number awarded 1 each year.

Deadline March of each year.

[65]
KUCHLER-KILLIAN MEMORIAL SCHOLARSHIP

National Federation of the Blind
c/o Peggy Elliott
Chair, Scholarship Committee
805 Fifth Avenue
Grinnell, IA 50112
(641) 236-3366
Web: www.nfb.org/sch_intro.htm

Summary To provide financial assistance to undergraduate and graduate blind students.

Eligibility This program is open to legally blind students who are working on or planning to work full time on an undergraduate or graduate degree. Selection is based on academic excellence, service to the community, and financial need.

Financial data The stipend is $3,000. The Kurzweil Foundation has also provided recipients with an additional $1,000 scholarship and the latest version of the Kurzweil-1000 reading software.

Duration 1 year; recipients may resubmit applications up to 2 additional years.

Additional Information Scholarships are awarded at the federation convention in July. Recipients attend the convention at federation expense; that funding is in addition to the scholarship grant.

Number awarded 1 each year.

Deadline March of each year.

[66]
LAVYRL JOHNSON MEMORIAL SCHOLARSHIP

National Federation of the Blind of California
Attn: Nancy Burns, President
175 East Olive Avenue, Suite 308
Burbank, CA 91502-1812
(818) 558-6524   Fax: (818) 729-7930
E-mail: dnburns@jps.net
Web: www.nfbcal.org

Summary To provide financial assistance for under-

graduate or graduate education to blind students in California.

Eligibility Legally blind full-time students in California may apply for a scholarship, but they must attend the convention of the National Federation of the Blind of California. Applicants must submit an essay in which they describe their educational goals, involvement in the blindness community, and eye condition. High school seniors and college freshmen must submit their high school transcripts; other college students must submit transcripts of all undergraduate and graduate work. Selection is based on academic merit.

Financial data The stipend is $1,500.
Duration 1 year.
Number awarded 1 each year.
Deadline May of each year.

[67]
LAWRENCE MARCELINO MEMORIAL SCHOLARSHIP

National Federation of the Blind of California
Attn: Nancy Burns, President
175 East Olive Avenue, Suite 308
Burbank, CA 91502-1812
(818) 558-6524   Fax: (818) 729-7930
E-mail: dnburns@jps.net
Web: www.nfbcal.org

Summary To provide financial assistance for graduate or undergraduate education to blind students in California.

Eligibility Legally blind full-time students in California may apply for a scholarship, but they must attend the convention of the National Federation of the Blind of California. Applicants must submit an essay in which they describe their educational goals, involvement in the blindness community, and eye condition. High school seniors and college freshmen must submit their high school transcripts; other college students must submit transcripts of all undergraduate and graduate work. Selection is based on academic merit.

Financial data The stipend is $2,500.
Duration 1 year.
Number awarded 1 each year.
Deadline May of each year.

[68]
LIGHTHOUSE UNDERGRADUATE AWARD FOR RETURNING STUDENTS

Lighthouse International
Attn: Career Incentive Awards Program
111 East 59th Street
New York, NY 10022-1202
(212) 821-9428   Toll-free: (800) 829-0500
Fax: (212) 821-9703   TTY: (212) 821-9713
E-mail: kclark@lighthouse.org
Web: www.lighthouse.org

Summary To provide financial assistance to legally blind undergraduates residing and attending school in designated eastern states who have experienced an interruption in their education.

Eligibility This program is open to legally blind residents of Connecticut, Delaware, Maine, Maryland, Massachusetts, New Hampshire, New Jersey, New York, Pennsylvania, Rhode Island, Vermont, Virginia, or Washington, D.C. Applicants must be working on an undergraduate degree in those states after an absence of 10 years or more. They must write a 500-word essay, describing their academic achievements and career goals. Candidates are not required to demonstrate financial need. U.S. citizenship is required.

Financial data The stipend is $5,000.
Duration The award is granted to recipients only once, although they may elect to spend the money over a period of more than 1 year.
Additional Information The recipient must present evidence of enrollment in or acceptance to an educational program before the funds will be released.
Number awarded 1 each year.
Deadline March of each year.

[69]
LIONS CLUBS SUPPORT SERVICES FOR THE BLIND AND VISUALLY IMPAIRED

Lions Clubs International
Attn: Program Development Department
300 22nd Street
Oak Brook, IL 60523-8842
(630) 571-5466, ext. 316   Fax: (630) 571-1692
E-mail: executiveservices@lionsclubs.org
Web: www.lionsclubs.org

Summary To provide college scholarships and other assistance to blind people.

Eligibility These programs are open to blind people and others involved in service to the blind. Applicants may be seeking support for the following activities: scholarships for the blind and visually impaired, medical research, assistive technology grants, independent mobility, transportation, reading materials and aids, audio products, Braille products, and other aids.

Financial data The amount of this assistance varies.

Additional Information Support is provided by local clubs of Lions Clubs International. Requests send to the international office are referred to the appropriate district governor. If any of the clubs within the district conduct programs for which the applicant might be considered, the governor will advise the particular club to contact the applicant. No funds are available from the office of Lions Clubs International.

[70]
LOUISE RUDE SCHOLARSHIP

Alaska Independent Blind
1561 Nelchima Street, Unit C-1
Anchorage, AK 99501-5577
(907) 563-2525   Toll-free: (800) 478-9998
Fax: (907) 276-0066
Web: www.acb.org/alaska

Summary To provide financial assistance for college to individuals in Alaska whose lives have been dramatically changed by their blindness.

Eligibility Eligible to apply for this assistance are high school seniors and currently-enrolled college students in Alaska who are blind or visually impaired. Their lives must have been dramatically changed by their blindness. To apply, students must submit a completed application form (including a certification of visual status), 2 education and/or employment reference letters, and 2 personal reference letters. Selection is based on scholastic aptitude (60%), volunteer and community service (20%), and employment record (20%).

Financial data Stipends are $2,000, $1,500, or $1,000.

Duration 1 year; recipients may reapply.

Additional Information The scholarship may be used at any accredited college, university, technical school, or vocational institute.

Number awarded 3 each year.

Deadline April of each year.

[71]
MARY MAIN MEMORIAL SCHOLARSHIP

National Federation of the Blind of Connecticut
580 Burnside Avenue, Suite 1
East Hartford, CT 06108
(860) 289-1971   E-mail: info@nfbct.org
Web: www.nfbct.org/html/schinfo.htm

Summary To provide financial assistance to blind students pursuing a full-time college education in Connecticut.

Eligibility Applicants must be legally blind and either residents of or full-time college students in Connecticut. Along with their application, they must submit a letter on their career goals and how the scholarship might help them achieve those. Selection is based on academic excellence, extracurricular activities, service to the community, and financial need.

Financial data The stipend is $1,000.

Duration 1 year.

Number awarded 1 each year.

Deadline September of each year.

[72]
MASSACHUSETTS REHABILITATION COMMISSION OR COMMISSION FOR THE BLIND TUITION WAIVER PROGRAM

Massachusetts Office of Student Financial Assistance
454 Broadway, Suite 200
Revere, MA 02151
(617) 727-9420   Fax: (617) 727-0667
E-mail: osfa@osfa.mass.edu
Web: www.osfa.mass.edu

Summary To provide financial assistance for college to Massachusetts residents who are clients of specified state agencies.

Eligibility Applicants for these scholarships must be certified as clients by the Massachusetts Rehabilitation Commission or Commission for the Blind. They must have been permanent residents of Massachusetts for at least 1 year, must be U.S. citizens or permanent residents, and may not be in default on any federal student loan.

Financial data Eligible clients are exempt from any tuition payments for an undergraduate degree or certificate program at public colleges or universities in Massachusetts.

Duration Up to 4 academic years, for a total of 130 semester hours.

Additional Information Recipients may enroll either part or full time in a Massachusetts publicly-supported institution.

Number awarded Varies each year.

[73]
MAX EDELMAN SCHOLARSHIP

American Council of the Blind of Ohio
Attn: Executive Director
2678 Edgevale Road
P.O. Box 21488
Columbus, OH 43221-0488
(614) 221-6688
Toll-free: (800) 835-2226 (within OH)
Fax: (614) 451-0539   E-mail: kmorlock@gcfn.org
Web: www.acbogcc.org

Summary To provide financial assistance for college to Ohio undergraduate students who are blind.

Eligibility This program is open to 1) residents of Ohio who are high school seniors or current college students, and 2) students at colleges and universities in Ohio.

Applicants must be legally blind and working on or planning to work on an undergraduate degree in any field. Along with their application, they must submit transcripts (must have a GPA of 3.0 or higher), a certificate of legal blindness, and an essay of 250 to 500 words on their career objectives, future plans, personal goals, other academic or personal qualities, and why they believe they are qualified to receive this scholarship.

Financial data A stipend is awarded (amount not specified).

Duration 1 year; recipients may reapply.

Additional Information Information is also available from the scholarship committee, 520 Walnut Street, Perrysburg, OH 43551.

Number awarded 1 each year.

Deadline July of each year.

[74]
MELVA T. OWEN MEMORIAL SCHOLARSHIP

National Federation of the Blind
c/o Peggy Elliott
Chair, Scholarship Committee
805 Fifth Avenue
Grinnell, IA 50112
(641) 236-3366
Web: www.nfb.org/sch_intro.htm

Summary To provide financial assistance to blind undergraduate or graduate students.

Eligibility This program is open to legally blind students who are working on or planning to work full time on an undergraduate or graduate degree. Scholarships, however, will not be awarded for the study of religion or solely to further general or cultural education; the academic program should be directed towards attaining financial independence. Selection is based on academic excellence, service to the community, and financial need.

Financial data The stipend is $10,000. The Kurzweil Foundation has also provided recipients with an additional $1,000 scholarship and the latest version of the Kurzweil-1000 reading software.

Duration 1 year; recipients may resubmit applications up to 2 additional years.

Additional Information Scholarships are awarded at the federation convention in July. Recipients attend the convention at federation expense; that funding is in addition to the scholarship grant.

Number awarded 1 each year.

Deadline March of each year.

[75]
NATIONAL FEDERATION OF THE BLIND COMPUTER SCIENCE SCHOLARSHIP

National Federation of the Blind
c/o Peggy Elliott
Chair, Scholarship Committee
805 Fifth Avenue
Grinnell, IA 50112
(641) 236-3366
Web: www.nfb.org/sch_intro.htm

Summary To provide financial assistance to legally blind undergraduate and graduate students working on a degree in computer science.

Eligibility This program is open to legally blind students who are working on or planning to work full time on an undergraduate or graduate degree in computer science. Selection is based on academic excellence, service to the community, and financial need.

Financial data The stipend is $3,000. The Kurzweil Foundation has also provided recipients with an additional $1,000 scholarship and the latest version of the Kurzweil-1000 reading software.

Duration 1 year; recipients may resubmit applications up to 2 additional years.

Additional Information Scholarships are awarded at the federation convention in July. Recipients attend the convention at federation expense; that funding is in addition to the scholarship grant.

Number awarded 1 each year.

Deadline March of each year.

[76]
NATIONAL FEDERATION OF THE BLIND OF ALABAMA SCHOLARSHIP PROGRAM

National Federation of the Blind of Alabama
Attn: Ben Casey, Scholarship Committee Chair
1705 Armstrong Street, N.W.
Huntsville, AL 35816
(256) 539-1459
Web: www.nfbofalabama.org/scholar.html

Summary To provide financial assistance for college to blind residents of Alabama.

Eligibility This program is open to legally blind residents of Alabama who are attending or planning to attend a college or university in the United States. Applicants must be, or planning to be, either a full-time student or a part-time student working full time. Selection is based on academic excellence, community service, and financial need.

Financial data The stipend is $500.

Duration 1 year; may be renewed.

Additional Information Recipients must attend the sponsor's state convention in order to accept their scholarship.

Number awarded Varies each year.

VISUAL DISABILITIES: SCHOLARSHIPS

Deadline January of each year.

[77]
NATIONAL FEDERATION OF THE BLIND OF ARKANSAS SCHOLARSHIP

National Federation of the Blind of Arkansas
Attn: Chris McKenzie
19 Brooklawn Drive
Little Rock, AR 72205-2304
(501) 228-9751   Toll-free: (800) 680-3087
E-mail: scholarships@nfbark.org
Web: www.nfbark.org/scholarship.shtml

Summary To provide financial assistance for college to blind residents of Arkansas.

Eligibility Eligible to apply for this support are high school seniors and currently-enrolled college students who are blind and residents of Arkansas. To apply, students must submit a completed application, a list of awards and honors, a list of community service activities, a personal statement, a current transcript, and 2 letters of recommendation. A phone interview may be required. Selection is based on academic record, career plans, service to the community, and financial need.

Financial data A stipend is awarded (amount not specified).

Duration 1 year.

Additional Information Information is also available from Daryl Swinson, 1617 Duncan Street, Conway, AR 72032.

Deadline July of each year.

[78]
NATIONAL FEDERATION OF THE BLIND OF CALIFORNIA SCHOLARSHIPS

National Federation of the Blind of California
Attn: Nancy Burns, President
175 East Olive Avenue, Suite 308
Burbank, CA 91502-1812
(818) 558-6524   Fax: (818) 729-7930
E-mail: dnburns@jps.net
Web: www.nfbcal.org

Summary To provide financial assistance for graduate or undergraduate education to blind students in California.

Eligibility Legally blind full-time students in California may apply for a scholarship, but they must attend the convention of the National Federation of the Blind of California. Applicants must submit an essay in which they describe their educational goals, involvement in the blindness community, and eye condition. High school seniors and college freshmen must submit their high school transcripts; other college students must submit transcripts of all undergraduate and graduate work. Selection is based on academic merit.

Financial data The stipend is $1,000.

Duration 1 year.
Number awarded 3 each year.
Deadline May of each year.

[79]
NATIONAL FEDERATION OF THE BLIND OF COLORADO SCHOLARSHIP

National Federation of the Blind of Colorado
c/o Colorado Center for the Blind
2233 West Shepperd Avenue
Littleton, CO 80120-2038
(303) 778-1130   Toll-free: (800) 401-4NFB
Fax: (303) 778-1598
Web: www.nfbco.org/scholarships.html

Summary To provide financial assistance for college to visually impaired students in Colorado.

Eligibility This program is open to legally blind residents of Colorado who are pursuing or planning to pursue a full-time college course of study in the state. At least 1 scholarship is reserved for an applicant who is employed full time and attending or planning to attend a part-time course of study that will result in a new degree and broader opportunities in present or future work. Selection is based on academic record, service to the community, and financial need.

Financial data The stipend depends on the need of the recipient and the availability of funds.

Duration 1 year.

Additional Information Information is also available from Kevan Worley, Chair, Scholarship Committee, 18121-C East Hampden Avenue, PMB 196, Aurora, CO 80013, (303) 306-7122.

Number awarded Varies each year.

Deadline September of each year.

[80]
NATIONAL FEDERATION OF THE BLIND OF FLORIDA SCHOLARSHIPS

National Federation of the Blind of Florida
c/o Dan Hicks, President
4608 West Longfellow Avenue
Tampa, FL 33629-7625
(813) 837-4831   E-mail: president@nfbflorida.org
Web: www.nfbflorida.org/Scholarship.html

Summary To provide financial assistance for college to legally blind residents of Florida.

Eligibility This program is open to high school seniors and college students who are legally blind, are Florida residents, are enrolled or planning to enroll in college, and have a GPA of 2.7 or higher. To apply, students must fill out an application form and send a copy of their current college transcript. Financial need is not considered in the selection process.

Financial data The stipend is $1,000 per year.

Duration 1 year.

Additional Information Information about this program is also available from Kathy Davis, NFBF Scholarship Chair, 121 Deer Lake Circle, Ormond Beach, FL 32174, (386) 677-6886, E-mail: davistk@bellsouth.net. Winners are provided with ground transportation, registration, room, and board at the state federation's annual conference.

Number awarded Varies each year.

Deadline April of each year.

[81]
NATIONAL FEDERATION OF THE BLIND OF IDAHO SCHOLARSHIPS

National Federation of the Blind of Idaho
1301 South Capitol Boulevard, Suite C
Boise, ID 83706-2926
(208) 343-1377
Web: www.nfbidaho.org

Summary To provide financial assistance for college to blind residents of Idaho.

Eligibility This program is open to blind residents of Idaho who are enrolled or planning to enroll in college. Selection is based on academic achievement, community service, and financial need.

Financial data Stipends are either $1,000 or $500.

Duration 1 year

Additional Information Information is also available from Larry Streeter, President, 1375 Hancock Drive, Boise, ID 83706, (208) 343-2328, E-mail: jackstreeter@earthlink.net

Number awarded 3 each year: 1 at $1,000 and 2 at $500.

[82]
NATIONAL FEDERATION OF THE BLIND OF ILLINOIS SCHOLARSHIP

National Federation of the Blind of Illinois
c/o Catherine Horn Randall, President
11 Pitner Place
Jacksonville, IL 62650-2266
(217) 245-7722   E-mail: chr47@mchsi.com
Web: www.nfbillinois.org

Summary To provide financial assistance for college to blind students in Illinois.

Eligibility This program is open to blind students in Illinois who are pursuing a postsecondary education. High school students and currently-enrolled college students are eligible to apply. There is no restriction on subject major.

Financial data Stipends range from $1,500 to $2,000 per year.

Duration 1 year.

Additional Information Information is also available from Debbie Stein, Scholarship Committee, 5817 North Nina Avenue, Chicago, IL 60631, (773) 631-1093, E-mail: dkent@ripco.com.

Number awarded 3 each year.

Deadline March of each year.

[83]
NATIONAL FEDERATION OF THE BLIND OF INDIANA SCHOLARSHIP

National Federation of the Blind of Indiana
c/o Ron Brown, President
6010 Winnpenny Lane
Indianapolis, IN 46220-5253
(317) 205-9226   E-mail: RB15@Iquest.net

Summary To provide financial assistance for college to blind residents of Indiana.

Eligibility An applicant must be blind, an Indiana resident, a high school graduate, and planning to continue on in school. Eligible students are invited to submit a biographical statement that covers their academic record and career plans.

Financial data The stipend ranges from $500 to $1,000.

Duration 1 year.

Number awarded 1 or more each year.

Deadline June of each year.

[84]
NATIONAL FEDERATION OF THE BLIND OF NEBRASKA SCHOLARSHIP

National Federation of the Blind of Nebraska
1033 O Street, Suite 24B
Lincoln, NE 68508-3621
(402) 477-7711   Toll-free: (866) BLIND-IS
E-mail: nfbn@inetnebr.com
Web: nfbn.inebraska.com

Summary To provide financial assistance for college to blind residents of Nebraska.

Eligibility This program is open to residents of Nebraska who are blind and attending or planning to attend a postsecondary institution. Applicants must submit a letter that describes their educational plans, vocational goals, and awards. Their letter should also explain how they deal with situations involving their blindness and how the scholarship will help them.

Financial data The stipend is $1,000 for first place and $500 for second place.

Duration 1 year.

Additional Information Further information is also available from Scholarship Chair, Shane Buresh, 6210 Walker Avenue, Lincoln, NE 68507, (402) 465-5468, E-mail: sburesh@neb.rr.com. The second-place award is sponsored by the Nebraska Association of Blind Students.

Number awarded 2 each year.

VISUAL DISABILITIES: SCHOLARSHIPS

Deadline September of each year.

[85]
NATIONAL FEDERATION OF THE BLIND OF NEW MEXICO SCHOLARSHIP PROGRAM

National Federation of the Blind of New Mexico
c/o James L. Salas
P.O. Box 36032
Albuquerque, NM 87176-6032
(505) 841-8844
Web: www.nfgnm.org

Summary To provide financial assistance to blind students in New Mexico who are interested in attending college.

Eligibility Eligible to apply are blind students in New Mexico who are high school seniors or currently enrolled full time in college. They must be able to demonstrate financial need.

Financial data Stipends up to $1,000 are available.

Duration 1 year.

Number awarded At least 4 each year.

Deadline January of each year.

[86]
NATIONAL FEDERATION OF THE BLIND OF OHIO SCHOLARSHIPS

National Federation of the Blind of Ohio
c/o Barbara Pierce, President
237 Oak Street
Oberlin, OH 44074-1517
(440) 775-2216   Toll-free: (800) 396-NFBO
E-mail: bbpierce@pobox.com
Web: www.nfbohio.org

Summary To provide financial assistance for undergraduate or graduate studies to Ohio residents who are legally blind.

Eligibility Eligible to apply for this support are high school seniors, currently-enrolled college students, and graduate students who reside in Ohio and are legally blind. They must attend or be preparing to attend an accredited institution of higher education on a full-time basis. Selection is based on academic excellence, community service, and financial need.

Financial data The stipend is $1,500 or $1,000.

Duration 1 year.

Additional Information Information is also available from Dr. J. Webster Smith, Chair, Scholarship Committee, 2 Canterbury Street, Athens, OH 45701, (740) 593-4838, E-mail: jsmith1@ohiou.edu. The $1,500 scholarship is named the Jennica Ferguson Memorial Scholarship.

Number awarded 2 each year:1 at $1,500 and 1 at $1,000.

Deadline May of each year.

[87]
NATIONAL FEDERATION OF THE BLIND OF OREGON SCHOLARSHIPS

National Federation of the Blind of Oregon
c/o Carla McQuillan, President
5005 Main Street
Springfield, OR 97478
(541) 726-6924
Toll-free: (800) 422-7093 (within OR)
Fax: (541) 726-5527
Web: www.nfb-or.org/scholarships.htm

Summary To provide financial assistance for college or graduate school to blind residents of Oregon.

Eligibility This program is open to blind residents of Oregon who are working on or planning to work on an undergraduate or graduate degree at a college or university in the state. Applicants must be enrolled full time or enrolled part time and working full time. Selection is based on academic and professional promise as well as potential for leadership in the National Federation of the Blind of Oregon.

Financial data Stipends are either $1,500 or $1,000.

Duration 1 year.

Additional Information Information is also available from Carolyn Brock, Scholarship Chair, (503) 963-1973, E-mail: mmebrock@spiritone.com.

Number awarded 3 each year: 1 at $1,500 and 2 at $1,000.

[88]
NATIONAL FEDERATION OF THE BLIND OF TEXAS SCHOLARSHIPS

National Federation of the Blind of Texas
c/o Tommy Craig, President
6909 Rufus Drive
Austin, TX 78752-3123
(512) 323-5444
E-mail: tommy.craig@nfb-texas.org
Web: www.nfb-texas.org/scholarships.html

Summary To provide financial assistance for college to blind residents of Texas.

Eligibility This program is open to blind residents of Texas who are enrolled or planning to enroll in a college or university. Applicants must submit proof of legal blindness, a current transcript, a 2-page personal letter, and 2 letters of recommendation. Selection is based on merit and financial need.

Financial data Stipends range from $1,000 to $2,000.

Duration 1 year.

Additional Information Information is also available from Elizabeth Campbell, Scholarship Chair, (817) 738-0350, E-mail: scholarship@nfb-texas.org.

Number awarded Varies each year.

Deadline May of each year.

[89]
NATIONAL FEDERATION OF THE BLIND OF UTAH SCHOLARSHIPS

National Federation of the Blind of Utah
c/o Ron Gardner, President
132 West Penman Lane
Bountiful, UT 84010-7634
(801) 292-3000   E-mail: president@nfbutah.org
Web: www.nfbutah.org/utabs/scholarships.html

Summary To provide financial assistance for college or graduate school to blind residents of Utah.

Eligibility This program is open to blind residents of Utah who are working on or planning to work on an undergraduate or graduate degree. Selection is based on academic excellence, community service, and financial need.

Financial data Stipends range from $500 to $1,500.

Duration 1 year.

Number awarded 3 to 5 each year.

Deadline March of each year.

[90]
NATIONAL FEDERATION OF THE BLIND OF VERMONT SCHOLARSHIPS

National Federation of the Blind of Vermont
c/o Brenda Patterson, President
26-B Sibley Avenue
Montpelier, VT 05602-3658
(802) 223-1684   E-mail: nfbvt@nfbvt.org
Web: www.nfbvt.org/scholar.html

Summary To provide financial assistance for college to blind residents of Vermont.

Eligibility This program is open to residents of Vermont who are legally blind or visually impaired. Applicants may be working full or part time on a degree; going to school to improve their skills, upgrade their job, or enter another area of employment; or studying a less traditional area. Special consideration is given to blind single parents and blind persons studying the physical sciences or the arts.

Financial data Stipends range from $300 to $600.

Duration 1 year.

Additional Information Information is also available from Frank Shiner, P.O. Box 1354, Montpelier, VT 05601, (802) 229-0748.

Number awarded Varies each year.

Deadline August of each year.

[91]
NATIONAL FEDERATION OF THE BLIND OF WISCONSIN SCHOLARSHIP

National Federation of the Blind of Wisconsin
Attn: Executive Director
1420 West State Street
Janesville, WI 53546
(608) 758-4800   E-mail: president@nfbwis.org
Web: www.nfbwis.org/scholar.htm

Summary To provide financial assistance for college to blind students in Wisconsin.

Eligibility This program is open to blind residents of Wisconsin who are attending or planning to attend a college or university. Applicants must provide a statement detailing their strengths, personal challenges, goals, and ways of working with their blindness. Selection is based on academic excellence, personal achievement, and community service.

Financial data The stipends are $1,000 or $500. The recipients are also provided with 1) transportation and hotel accommodations to attend the 3-day state convention of the National Federation of the Blind of Wisconsin and 2) transportation, hotel accommodations, and $200 for meals for the week-long national convention.

Duration 1 year.

Additional Information Information is also available from Cheryl Orgas, Scholarship Coordinator, 4222 North Maryland Avenue, Shorewood, WI 53211, (414) 964-7995. The recipient must attend both state and national conventions in their entirety.

Number awarded 2 each year: 1 at $1,000 and 1 at $500.

Deadline March of each year.

[92]
NATIONAL FEDERATION OF THE BLIND SCHOLARSHIPS

National Federation of the Blind
c/o Peggy Elliott
Chair, Scholarship Committee
805 Fifth Avenue
Grinnell, IA 50112
(641) 236-3366
Web: www.nfb.org/sch_intro.htm

Summary To provide financial assistance for college or graduate school to blind students.

Eligibility This program is open to legally blind students who are working on or planning to work on an undergraduate or graduate degree. In general, full-time enrollment is required, although 1 scholarship may be awarded to a part-time student who is working full time. Selection is based on academic excellence, service to the community, and financial need.

Financial data Stipends are $7,000 or $3,000. The Kurzweil Foundation has also provided recipients with an

additional $1,000 scholarship and the latest version of the Kurzweil-1000 reading software.

Duration 1 year; recipients may resubmit applications up to 2 additional years.

Additional Information Scholarships are awarded at the federation convention in July. Recipients attend the convention at federation expense; that funding is in addition to the scholarship grant.

Number awarded 18 each year: 2 at $7,000 and 16 at $3,000.

Deadline March of each year.

[93] NEVADA COUNCIL OF THE BLIND SCHOLARSHIP

Nevada Council of the Blind
c/o Carol Ann Ewing, President
2127 Hallston Street
Las Vegas, NV 89134-5104
(702) 383-0600

Summary To provide financial assistance for college to visually impaired high school seniors in Nevada.

Eligibility Eligible to apply for this scholarship are high school seniors in Nevada who are blind or visually impaired.

Financial data The stipend is either $1,200 or $800 per quarter or semester. Funds must be used for tuition, books, and fees at a college or university in Nevada.

Duration 1 quarter or semester; renewable.

Additional Information Information is also available from Edwin F. Newell, Nevada Council of the Blind President, 1921 Oakleaf Lane, Las Vegas, NV 89146-3003, (702) 871-6890, E-mail: efnewell@lv.rmci.net. Recipients must attend a college or university in Nevada.

Deadline April of each year.

[94] NIB GRANT M. MACK MEMORIAL SCHOLARSHIP

American Council of the Blind
Attn: Coordinator, Scholarship Program
1155 15th Street, N.W., Suite 1004
Washington, DC 20005
(202) 467-5081   Toll-free: (800) 424-8666
Fax: (202) 467-5085   E-mail: info@acb.org
Web: www.acb.org

Summary To provide financial assistance to students who are blind and working on an undergraduate or graduate degree in business or management.

Eligibility All legally blind persons who are majoring in business or management (undergraduate or graduate) and are U.S. citizens or resident aliens are eligible to apply. In addition to letters of recommendation and copies of academic transcripts, applications must include an autobiographical sketch. A cumulative GPA of 3.3 or higher is generally required. Selection is based on demonstrated academic record, involvement in extracurricular and civic activities, and academic objectives. The severity of the applicant's visual impairment and his/her study methods are also taken into account.

Financial data The stipend is $2,000. In addition, the winner receives a $1,000 cash scholarship from the Kurzweil Foundation and, if appropriate, a Kurzweil-1000 Reading System.

Duration 1 year.

Additional Information This scholarship is sponsored by National Industries for the Blind (NIB) in honor of a dedicated leader of the American Council of the Blind. Scholarship winners are expected to be present at the council's annual conference; the council will cover all reasonable expenses connected with convention attendance.

Number awarded 1 each year.

Deadline February of each year.

[95] NORA WEBB-MCKINNEY SCHOLARSHIP

American Council of the Blind of Ohio
Attn: Executive Director
2678 Edgevale Road
P.O. Box 21488
Columbus, OH 43221-0488
(614) 221-6688
Toll-free: (800) 835-2226 (within OH)
Fax: (614) 451-0539   E-mail: kmorlock@gcfn.org
Web: www.acbogcc.org

Summary To provide financial assistance to Ohio students who are interested in working on an undergraduate or graduate degree involving service to blind people.

Eligibility This program is open to 1) residents of Ohio who are high school seniors or current undergraduate or graduate students, and 2) undergraduate and graduate students at colleges and universities in Ohio. Applicants must be interested in working on or planning to work on a degree in a field related to blindness (e.g., special education, rehabilitation teaching or counseling, orientation and mobility, or a concentration on programs serving people who are blind). They may be blind or sighted. Along with their application, they must submit transcripts (must have a GPA of 3.0 or higher) and an essay of 250 to 500 words on their career objectives, future plans, personal goals, other academic or personal qualities, and why they believe they are qualified to receive this scholarship.

Financial data A stipend is awarded (amount not specified).

Duration 1 year; recipients may reapply.

Additional Information Information is also available from the scholarship committee, 520 Walnut Street, Perrysburg, OH 43551.

Number awarded 1 each year.

Deadline July of each year.

[96]
NORTH CAROLINA COUNCIL OF THE BLIND SCHOLARSHIP

North Carolina Council of the Blind
c/o Catherleen Thomas
308 South Peartree Lane
Raleigh, NC 27610
Toll-free: (800) 344-7113 (within NC)
Fax: (336) 562-2625   E-mail: nccb@netpath.net
www.nccounciloftheblind.org

Summary To provide financial assistance for college to blind and visually impaired North Carolina residents.

Eligibility Eligible to apply are blind and visually impaired high school seniors, college students, and vocational school students in North Carolina. Applicants must complete an application form and submit 2 character reference letters, a transcript of courses completed, and a brief biographical statement. Financial need is considered in the selection process.

Financial data The stipend is $1,500.

Duration 1 year.

Additional Information Information is also available from Catherleen Thomas, 308 South Peartree Lane, Raleigh, NC 27610.

Number awarded 1 or more each year.

Deadline April of each year.

[97]
NORTH DAKOTA ASSOCIATION OF THE BLIND SCHOLARSHIPS

North Dakota Association of the Blind
c/o Allan Peterson, President
7009 Horseshoe Bend
Fargo, ND 58104
(701) 282-4644
E-mail: allan_peterson@ndsu.nodak.edu
Web: www.ndab.org/Scholarship.html

Summary To provide financial assistance for college or graduate school to blind students in North Dakota.

Eligibility This program is open to North Dakota residents who are legally blind and attending an institution of higher education in the state. Applicants must be full-time students with a class standing of a sophomore through a graduate student and a GPA of 2.5 or higher. They must submit 2 letters of recommendation, transcripts, a family financial aid statement, and an essay that describes their vocational interests, how the scholarship will help them, their goals and aspirations, and what they have done to deal with situations involving their blindness. Selection is based on academic excellence, financial need, and service to the community.

Financial data Stipends are $1,000 or $500.

Duration 1 year.

Additional Information This program was established in 1990. Information is also available from Ruth Poer, Scholarship Committee Chair, 3315 Broadway #302, Fargo, ND 58102, (701) 235-7007.

Number awarded 3 each year: 1 at $1,000 and 2 at $500.

Deadline March of each year.

[98]
OPPORTUNITIES FOR THE BLIND GRANTS

Opportunities for the Blind, Inc.
Attn: Grant Committee
P.O Box 98
Fairplay, MD 21733
(240) 420-6500   E-mail: OppBlind@yahoo.com
Web: www.opportunitiesfortheblind.org

Summary To provide funding to blind people interested in working on a college degree, establishing or improving their self-employment situation, or obtaining special equipment.

Eligibility This program is open to legally blind U.S. citizens. Applicants must be seeking funding to 1) assist with tuition, books, and supplies for accredited postsecondary education or job training that is not provided by a state agency for the blind; 2) assist with costs related to establishing or improving their self-employment situation; or 3) obtain special equipment that they need for their job. Preference is given to applicants who are already working, or about to begin working, in occupations where the blind are not typically found. Selection is based on the probability of success, but financial need may also be considered.

Financial data Grants normally range from $3,000 to $5,000, and may go as high as $10,000.

Duration This is a 1-time award.

Additional Information This program was established in 1981.

Number awarded Varies each year.

Deadline February, May, August, or October of each year.

[99]
OREGON COUNCIL OF THE BLIND SCHOLARSHIPS

American Council of the Blind
Attn: Coordinator, Scholarship Program
1155 15th Street, N.W., Suite 1004
Washington, DC 20005
(202) 467-5081   Toll-free: (800) 424-8666
Fax: (202) 467-5085   E-mail: info@acb.org
Web: www.acb.org

Summary To provide financial assistance for college to blind students from Oregon.

Eligibility All legally blind persons admitted to undergraduate educational programs who are U.S. citizens

and residents of Oregon are eligible to apply. In addition to letters of recommendation and copies of academic transcripts, applications must include an autobiographical sketch. A cumulative GPA of 3.3 or higher is generally required. Selection is based on demonstrated academic record, involvement in extracurricular and civic activities, their autobiography, and academic objectives. The severity of the applicant's visual impairment and his/her study methods are also taken into account.

Financial data The stipend is $2,500. In addition, the winners receive a $1,000 cash scholarship from the Kurzweil Foundation and, if appropriate, a Kurzweil-1000 Reading System.

Duration 1 year.

Additional Information Funding for this scholarship is provided by the Oregon Council of the Blind, an affiliate of the American Council of the Blind. Scholarship winners are expected to be present at the council's annual conference; the council will cover all reasonable expenses connected with convention attendance.

Number awarded 2 each year.

Deadline February of each year.

[100]
PALMER-MULLIN MEMORIAL SCHOLARSHIP

National Federation of the Blind of Michigan
1212 North Foster
Lansing, MI 48912
(517) 372-8700   E-mail: fjw@attbi.com
Web: www.nfbmi.org

Summary To provide financial assistance to Michigan students who are blind and interested in studying specified subjects in college.

Eligibility This program is open to legally blind residents of Michigan. Applicants must be enrolled or planning to enroll as a full-time student at a postsecondary institution in the state. They must have a GPA of 2.0 or higher from high school and/or college. Along with their application, they must submit a 1- to 3-page letter in which they describe any situations involving their blindness that they have encountered, their plans for the future, and how this scholarship will help them achieve their academic goals. This program is limited to students who are pursuing degrees in the areas of public service, public administration, law, or political science.

Financial data The stipend is $1,000.

Duration 1 year.

Additional Information Information is also available from Melody Lindsey, Scholarship Chair, 2213 Winchell Avenue, Kalamazoo, MI 49008, (269) 388-2686. The winner must attend the convention of the National Federation of the Blind of Michigan. All expenses are paid by the sponsor.

Number awarded 1 each year.

Deadline October of each year.

[101]
PAUL W. RUCKES SCHOLARSHIP

American Foundation for the Blind
Attn: Scholarship Committee
11 Penn Plaza, Suite 300
New York, NY 10001
(212) 502-7661   Toll-free: (800) AFB-LINE
Fax: (212) 502-7771   TDD: (212) 502-7662
E-mail: afbinfo@afb.net
Web: www.afb.org/scholarships.asp

Summary To provide financial assistance to visually impaired students who wish to work on a graduate or undergraduate degree in engineering or computer, physical, or life sciences.

Eligibility This program is open to visually impaired undergraduate or graduate students who are U.S. citizens working on a degree in engineering or the computer, physical, or life sciences. Legal blindness is not required. Applicants must submit a typewritten statement, up to 3 pages in length, describing educational and personal goals, work experience, extracurricular activities, and how scholarship funds will be used.

Financial data The stipend is $2,500.

Duration 1 year.

Number awarded 1 each year.

Deadline April of each year.

[102]
RICHARD BENNET OF MAINE SCHOLARSHIP

American Council of the Blind
Attn: Coordinator, Scholarship Program
1155 15th Street, N.W., Suite 1004
Washington, DC 20005
(202) 467-5081   Toll-free: (800) 424-8666
Fax: (202) 467-5085   E-mail: info@acb.org
Web: www.acb.org

Summary To provide financial assistance for college to blind students from Maine.

Eligibility This program is open to legally blind students who are residents of Maine. In addition to letters of recommendation and copies of academic transcripts, applications must include an autobiographical sketch. A cumulative GPA of 3.3 or higher is generally required. Selection is based on demonstrated academic record, involvement in extracurricular and civic activities, and academic objectives. The severity of the applicant's visual impairment and his/her study methods are also taken into account.

Financial data The stipend is $1,000. In addition, the winner receives a $1,000 cash scholarship from the Kurzweil Foundation and, if appropriate, a Kurzweil-1000 Reading System.

Duration 1 year.

Additional Information This scholarship is sponsored by the American Council of the Blind of Maine, an affiliate of the American Council of the Blind. Scholarship

winners are expected to be present at the council's annual conference; the council will cover all reasonable expenses connected with convention attendance.
Number awarded 1 each year.
Deadline February of each year.

[103]
R.L. GILLETTE SCHOLARSHIPS

American Foundation for the Blind
Attn: Scholarship Committee
11 Penn Plaza, Suite 300
New York, NY 10001
(212) 502-7661   Toll-free: (800) AFB-LINE
Fax: (212) 502-7771   TDD: (212) 502-7662
E-mail: afbinfo@afb.net
Web: www.afb.org/scholarships.asp

Summary To provide financial assistance to legally blind undergraduate women who are studying literature or music.
Eligibility This program is open to women who are legally blind, U.S. citizens, and enrolled in a 4-year baccalaureate degree program in literature or music. Applicants must submit a typewritten statement, up to 3 pages in length, describing educational and personal goals, work experience, extracurricular activities, and how scholarship funds will be used. They must also submit a sample performance tape (not to exceed 30 minutes) or a creative writing sample.
Financial data The stipend is $1,000.
Duration 1 academic year.
Number awarded 2 each year.
Deadline April of each year.

[104]
ROBERT M. STANLEY MEMORIAL SCHOLARSHIP

National Federation of the Blind of North Carolina
c/o Tim Jones, President
128 Summerlea Drive
Charlotte, NC 28214-1324
(704) 391-3204   Fax: (704) 391-3204
E-mail: tjnc2@aol.com
Web: www.nfbofnc.org

Summary To provide financial assistance to blind residents of North Carolina who are interested in pursuing postsecondary education.
Eligibility Legally blind residents of North Carolina are eligible to apply for this program if they are interested in pursuing studies at a college, university, or technical school in the state. Recipients are selected on the basis of academic excellence, service to the community, and financial need.
Financial data The stipend is $1,000. These funds are intended to meet expenses not otherwise covered by public resources.

Duration 1 year.
Number awarded 1 each year.
Deadline April of each year.

[105]
ROSS N. AND PATRICIA PANGERE FOUNDATION SCHOLARSHIPS

American Council of the Blind
Attn: Coordinator, Scholarship Program
1155 15th Street, N.W., Suite 1004
Washington, DC 20005
(202) 467-5081   Toll-free: (800) 424-8666
Fax: (202) 467-5085   E-mail: info@acb.org
Web: www.acb.org

Summary To provide financial assistance for undergraduate or graduate study to outstanding blind students.
Eligibility Eligible to apply for this scholarship are legally blind U.S. citizens or resident aliens who are undergraduate or graduate students. In addition to letters of recommendation and copies of academic transcripts, applications must include an autobiographical sketch. A cumulative GPA of 3.3 or higher is generally required. Selection is based on demonstrated academic record, involvement in extracurricular and civic activities, and academic objectives. The severity of the applicant's visual impairment and his/her study methods are also taken into account.
Financial data A stipend is awarded (amount not specified). In addition, the winner receives a $1,000 cash scholarship from the Kurzweil Foundation and, if appropriate, a Kurzweil-1000 Reading System.
Duration 1 year.
Additional Information The scholarship winner is expected to be present at the council's annual national convention; the council will cover all reasonable costs connected with convention attendance.
Number awarded 2 each year.
Deadline February of each year.

[106]
RUDOLPH DILLMAN MEMORIAL SCHOLARSHIP

American Foundation for the Blind
Attn: Scholarship Committee
11 Penn Plaza, Suite 300
New York, NY 10001
(212) 502-7661   Toll-free: (800) AFB-LINE
Fax: (212) 502-7771   TDD: (212) 502-7662
E-mail: afbinfo@afb.net
Web: www.afb.org/scholarships.asp

Summary To provide financial assistance to legally blind undergraduate or graduate students studying in the field of rehabilitation and/or education of visually impaired and blind persons.

Eligibility Applicants must be able to submit evidence of legal blindness, U.S. citizenship, and acceptance in an accredited undergraduate or graduate training program within the broad field of rehabilitation and/or education of blind and visually impaired persons. They must submit a typewritten statement, up to 3 pages in length, describing educational and personal goals, work experience, extracurricular activities, and how scholarship funds will be used.

Financial data The stipend is $2,500 per year.

Duration 1 academic year; previous recipients may not reapply.

Number awarded 4 each year: 3 without consideration of financial need and 1 to an applicant who can submit evidence of financial need.

Deadline April of each year.

[107]
RUTH BILLOW MEMORIAL EDUCATION FUND

Delta Gamma Foundation
Attn: Director, Service for Sight
3250 Riverside Drive
P.O. Box 21397
Columbus, OH 43221-0397
(614) 481-8169   Fax: (614) 481-0133
E-mail: blbecky@aol.com
Web: www.deltagamma.org

Summary To provide financial assistance to members of Delta Gamma sorority who are visually impaired or preparing for a career in working with the visually impaired.

Eligibility This program is open to undergraduate and graduate members of the sorority who are either 1) blind or visually impaired or 2) pursuing professional training in areas related to working with persons who are blind or visually impaired or in sight preservation. Applicants must be pursuing a program of postsecondary education in the United States or Canada.

Financial data The amount awarded varies, depending upon individual circumstances.

Duration 1 year or more.

Number awarded Varies each year.

Deadline Applications may be submitted at any time.

[108]
SALLY S. JACOBSEN SCHOLARSHIP

National Federation of the Blind
c/o Peggy Elliott
Chair, Scholarship Committee
805 Fifth Avenue
Grinnell, IA 50112
(641) 236-3366
Web: www.nfb.org/sch_intro.htm

Summary To provide financial assistance to blind undergraduate and graduate students working on a degree in the field of education, especially those planning to major in education of disabled youth.

Eligibility This program is open to legally blind students who are working on or planning to work full time on an undergraduate or graduate degree in education. Preference is given to applicants planning to specialize in education of disabled youth. Selection is based on academic excellence, service to the community, and financial need.

Financial data The stipend is $5,000. The Kurzweil Foundation has also provided recipients with an additional $1,000 scholarship and the latest version of the Kurzweil-1000 reading software.

Duration 1 year; recipients may resubmit applications up to 2 additional years.

Additional Information Scholarships are awarded at the federation convention in July. Recipients attend the convention at federation expense; that funding is in addition to the scholarship grant.

Number awarded 1 each year.

Deadline March of each year.

[109]
SIGMA ALPHA IOTA SCHOLARSHIP FOR THE VISUALLY IMPAIRED

Sigma Alpha Iota Philanthropies, Inc.
34 Wall Street, Suite 515
Asheville, NC 28801-2710
(828) 251-0606   Fax: (828) 251-0644
E-mail: philonline@sai-national.org
Web: www.sai-national.org/phil/philschs.html

Summary To provide financial assistance for college or graduate school to visually impaired members of Sigma Alpha Iota (an organization of women musicians) who are working on a degree in music.

Eligibility Members of the organization may apply for these scholarships if they are visually impaired. They must be enrolled in a graduate or undergraduate degree program in music.

Financial data The stipend is $1,000.

Duration 1 year.

Additional Information There is a $25 nonrefundable application fee.

Number awarded 1 or 2 every 3 years.

Deadline April of the year of the awards (2006, 2009, etc.).

[110] SOUTH DAKOTA FREE TUITION FOR VISUALLY IMPAIRED PERSONS

South Dakota Board of Regents
Attn: Scholarship Committee
306 East Capitol Avenue, Suite 200
Pierre, SD 57501-3159
(605) 773-3455   Fax: (605) 773-5320
E-mail: info@ris.sdbor.edu
Web: www.ris.sdbor.edu

Summary To provide financial assistance for college or graduate school to visually impaired residents of South Dakota.

Eligibility Eligible for this program is any visually impaired resident of South Dakota who can meet the entrance requirements for admission to a postsecondary educational institution (including graduate school and medical school) under the supervision of the state board of regents. For purposes of the program, "visual impairment" means that the person cannot, with use of correcting glasses, see sufficiently well to perform ordinary activities for which eyesight is essential. This program does not extend to visually impaired persons who are entitled to receive tuition and fee support from the state's department of vocational rehabilitation.

Financial data Qualified applicants may attend any institution under the supervision of the South Dakota Board of Regents without payment of tuition, library fees, registration fees, or any other fees.

Duration Benefits are provided until the recipient has earned 225 semester hours of credit or the equivalent.

Additional Information Applicants should contact the financial aid director at the South Dakota college or university they plan to attend, not the sponsor. The exemption from charges does not apply if a course is repeated because of unsatisfactory work, unless the problem was caused by illness or some other circumstance for which the student had no responsibility.

Number awarded Varies each year.

[111] SR. HARRIET CHARRON MEMORIAL SCHOLARSHIP

National Federation of the Blind of Maine
c/o Brent Batron
31 Wyndham Street
Portland, ME 04103-1204
(207) 797-8254   E-mail: bbatron@maine.rr.com

Summary To provide financial assistance for college to residents of Maine who are legally blind.

Eligibility All applicants for this scholarship must be 1) legally blind, 2) residents of Maine, and 3) pursuing or planning to pursue a full-time postsecondary course of study. To apply, applicants must submit a personal letter, 1 letter of recommendation, current transcripts, and a letter from a member of the National Federation of the Blind of Maine's board of directors. Selection is based on academic record, service to the community, and financial need.

Financial data The stipend is $500.

Duration The scholarship is offered annually, if sufficient funds are available.

Additional Information The scholarship winners are brought to the National Federation of the Blind of Maine convention at federation expense.

Deadline April of each year.

[112] TEXAS BLIND/DEAF STUDENT EXEMPTION PROGRAM

Texas Higher Education Coordinating Board
Attn: Grants and Special Programs
1200 East Anderson Lane
P.O. Box 12788, Capitol Station
Austin, TX 78711-2788
(512) 427-6101   Toll-free: (800) 242-3062
Fax: (512) 427-6127
E-mail: grantinfo@thecb.state.tx.us
Web: www.collegefortexans.com

Summary To provide a tuition exemption to blind and/or deaf residents of Texas.

Eligibility This program is open to Texas residents who can present certification from the appropriate state vocational rehabilitation agency of their deafness or blindness. Applicants must present to the registrar of a public college or university in Texas a copy of their high school transcript, a letter of recommendation, proof that they have met all admission requirements, and a statement of purpose that indicates the certificate, degree program, or professional enhancement that they intend to pursue.

Financial data Eligible students are exempted from the payment of all dues, fees, and tuition charges at publicly-supported colleges and universities in Texas.

Duration Up to 8 semesters.

Number awarded Varies each year; recently, 2,948 students received support through this program.

[113]
UNDERGRADUATE AWARDS OF LIGHTHOUSE INTERNATIONAL

Lighthouse International
Attn: Career Incentive Awards Program
111 East 59th Street
New York, NY 10022-1202
(212) 821-9428   Toll-free: (800) 829-0500
Fax: (212) 821-9703   TTY: (212) 821-9713
E-mail: kclark@lighthouse.org
Web: www.lighthouse.org

Summary To provide financial assistance to legally blind undergraduate students residing and attending school in designated eastern states.

Eligibility This program is open to legally blind residents of Connecticut, Delaware, Maine, Maryland, Massachusetts, New Hampshire, New Jersey, New York, Pennsylvania, Rhode Island, Vermont, Virginia, or Washington, D.C. Applicants must be attending college (at any level) in those states. They must write a 500-word essay, describing their academic achievements and career goals. Candidates are not required to demonstrate financial need. U.S. citizenship is required.

Financial data The stipend is $5,000.

Duration The award is granted to recipients only once, although they may elect to spend the money over a period of more than 1 year.

Additional Information The recipient must present evidence of enrollment in or acceptance to an educational program before the funds will be released.

Number awarded 1 each year.

Deadline March of each year.

[114]
WALTER YOUNG MEMORIAL SCHOLARSHIP

California Association for Postsecondary Education
  and Disability
Attn: Executive Assistant
71423 Biskra Road
Rancho Mirage, CA 92270
(760) 346-8206   Fax: (760) 340-5275
TTY: (760) 341-4084   E-mail: caped2000@aol.com
Web: www.caped.net/scholarship.html

Summary To provide financial assistance to blind and visually impaired undergraduate and graduate students in California.

Eligibility This program is open to blind and visually impaired students at public and private colleges and universities in California. Undergraduates must have completed at least 6 semester credits and have a GPA of 2.5 or higher. Graduate students must have completed at least 3 semester units and have a GPA of 3.0 or higher. Applicants must submit a 1-page personal letter that demonstrates writing skills; progress toward meeting educational and vocational goals; how they accommodate their disability; involvement in community activities; and any other factor that might strengthen their application. They must also submit a letter of recommendation from a faculty member, verification of disability, official transcripts, proof of current enrollment, and documentation of financial need.

Financial data The stipend is $1,000.

Duration 1 year.

Additional Information Information is also available from Janet Shapiro, Disabled Student Programs and Services, Santa Barbara City College, 721 Cliff Drive, Santa Barbara, CA 93109, (805) 965-0581, ext. 2365, E-mail: shapiro@sbcc.net.

Number awarded 1 each year.

Deadline August of each year.

[115]
WASHINGTON COUNCIL OF THE BLIND SCHOLARSHIPS

Washington Council of the Blind
P.O. Box 6996
Kennewick, WA 99336
Toll-free: (800) 255-1147   E-mail: info@wcbinfo.org
Web: www.wcbinfo.org

Summary To provide financial aid for college or graduate school to blind students in Washington.

Eligibility This program is open to blind residents of Washington state. Applicants must be attending or planning to attend a college or vocational school within the state or a contiguous community as an undergraduate or graduate student. Along with their application, they must submit 2 letters of recommendation, proof of legal blindness, and a 1- to 3-page statement of their reasons for applying for this scholarship and how it will assist them to achieve their goals. The statement should include a brief description of their background, education, work experience, economic status, strengths, weaknesses, and personal goals for the next 5 to 10 years.

Financial data The stipend is at least $2,000 per year.

Duration 1 year.

Additional Information Additional information is available from Denise Colley, Scholarship Committee Chair, 2305 Maxine Street, S.E., Lacey, WA 98503-3451, (360) 438-0072.

Number awarded 1 or more each year.

Deadline July of each year.

[116]
WILLIAM AND DOROTHY FERRELL SCHOLARSHIP AWARD

Association for Education and Rehabilitation of the Blind and Visually Impaired
1703 North Beauregard Street, Suite 440
Alexandria, VA 22311
(703) 671-4500   Fax: (703) 671-6391
E-mail: aer@aerbvi.org
Web: www.aerbvi.org

Summary To provide financial assistance to blind undergraduate and graduate students who wish to study for a career in service to blind and visually impaired people.

Eligibility Applicants for this award must be legally blind, defined as a visual acuity of 20/200 or less in the better corrected eye and/or 20 degrees or less visual field. They must be studying for a career in service to blind and visually impaired people (special education, orientation and mobility, rehabilitation training, etc.) and must submit evidence of enrollment in or acceptance to that program of study.

Financial data The stipend is $500.

Number awarded 2 every other year.

Deadline April of even-numbered years.

[117]
WILLIAM G. COREY MEMORIAL SCHOLARSHIP

American Council of the Blind
Attn: Coordinator, Scholarship Program
1155 15th Street, N.W., Suite 1004
Washington, DC 20005
(202) 467-5081   Toll-free: (800) 424-8666
Fax: (202) 467-5085   E-mail: info@acb.org
Web: www.acb.org

Summary To provide financial assistance to blind students from Pennsylvania who are enrolled in academic, vocational, technical, or professional training programs.

Eligibility All legally blind persons admitted to postsecondary educational programs (undergraduate or graduate) who are U.S. citizens and residents of Pennsylvania are eligible to apply. In addition to letters of recommendation and copies of academic transcripts, applications must include an autobiographical sketch. A cumulative GPA of 3.3 or higher is generally required. Selection is based on demonstrated academic record, involvement in extracurricular and civic activities, the autobiographical sketch, and academic objectives. The severity of the applicant's visual impairment and his/her study methods are also taken into account.

Financial data The stipend is $1,500. In addition, the winner receives a $1,000 cash scholarship from the Kurzweil Foundation and, if appropriate, a Kurzweil-1000 Reading System.

Duration 1 year.

Additional Information Scholarship winners are expected to be present at the council's annual conference; the council will cover all reasonable expenses connected with convention attendance.

Number awarded 1 each year.

Deadline February of each year.

[118]
WILMA H. WRIGHT MEMORIAL SCHOLARSHIP

Delta Gamma Foundation
Attn: Director of Scholarships, Fellowships and Loans
3250 Riverside Drive
P.O. Box 21397
Columbus, OH 43221-0397
(614) 481-8169   Fax: (614) 481-0133
E-mail: kimguirl@hotmail.com
Web: www.deltagamma.org

Summary To provide financial assistance to members of Delta Gamma sorority who are visually impaired or preparing for a career working with the visually impaired.

Eligibility This program is open to initiated members of a collegiate chapter of Delta Gamma in the United States or Canada who have completed 3 semesters or 5 quarters of their college course and have maintained a GPA of 3.0 or higher. Applicants must submit a 1- to 2-page essay in which they introduce themselves, including their career goals, reasons for applying for this scholarship, and the impact Delta Gamma has had on their life. Selection is based on scholastic excellence and participation in chapter, campus, and community leadership activities. Preference is given to candidates who are either 1) blind or visually impaired or 2) pursuing professional training in areas related to working with persons who are blind or visually impaired.

Financial data The stipend is $1,000. Funds are sent directly to the university or college to be used for tuition, books, laboratory fees, room, and board. They may not be used for sorority dues, house fees, or other chapter expenses.

Duration 1 year.

Additional Information Information is also available from Anne Turner, 9315 South Norwood, Tulsa, OK 74136.

Number awarded 1 each year.

Deadline January of each year.

VISUAL DISABILITIES: FELLOWSHIPS/GRANTS

[119]
WISCONSIN COUNCIL OF THE BLIND SCHOLARSHIPS

Wisconsin Council of the Blind
754 Williamson Street
Madison, WI 53703
(608) 255-1166   Toll-free: (800) 783-5213
Fax: (608) 255-3301   E-mail: info@wcblind.org
Web: www.wcblind.org

Summary To provide financial assistance for college to blind students from Wisconsin.

Eligibility This program is open to legally blind residents of Wisconsin who have completed at least 1 year of college or technical schooling. Applicants must be full-time students who have at least a 2.5 GPA.

Financial data The stipend is $1,000.

Duration 1 year.

Number awarded 7 each year.

Deadline September of each year.

[120]
WISCONSIN HEARING AND VISUALLY HANDICAPPED STUDENT GRANT PROGRAM

Wisconsin Higher Educational Aids Board
131 West Wilson Street, Room 902
P.O. Box 7885
Madison, WI 53707-7885
(608) 266-0888   Fax: (608) 267-2808
E-mail: sandy.thomas@heab.state.wi.us
Web: heab.state.wi.us/programs.html

Summary To provide financial support for undergraduate study to Wisconsin residents who are legally deaf or blind.

Eligibility To be eligible for a grant, the student must be a Wisconsin resident, must have financial need as determined by the institution the student attends, must submit evidence of a severe or profound hearing or visual impairment certified by a medical examiner, and must be enrolled in a nonprofit, accredited public or private college, university, or vocational/technical school located in Wisconsin.

Financial data Grants range from $250 to $1,800 per academic year.

Duration 1 year; may be renewed up to 4 additional years.

Additional Information If the disability prevents the student from studying in a Wisconsin institution, he or she may attend an out-of-state institution that specializes in the training of deaf and/or blind students.

Number awarded Varies each year.

Fellowships/Grants

[121]
ALMA MURPHEY MEMORIAL SCHOLARSHIP

American Council of the Blind
Attn: Coordinator, Scholarship Program
1155 15th Street, N.W., Suite 1004
Washington, DC 20005
(202) 467-5081   Toll-free: (800) 424-8666
Fax: (202) 467-5085   E-mail: info@acb.org
Web: www.acb.org

Summary To provide financial assistance for graduate education to students who are blind.

Eligibility This program is open to graduate students in any field of study who are blind. In addition to letters of recommendation and copies of academic transcripts, applications must include an autobiographical sketch. A cumulative GPA of 3.3 or higher is generally required. Selection is based on demonstrated academic record, involvement in extracurricular and civic activities, the autobiographical sketch, and academic objectives. The severity of the applicant's visual impairment and his/her study methods are also taken into account.

Financial data The stipend is $500. In addition, the winner receives a $1,000 cash scholarship from the Kurzweil Foundation and, if appropriate, a Kurzweil-1000 Reading System.

Duration 1 year.

Additional Information Funding for this scholarship is provided by the Braille Revival League of Missouri, an affiliate of the American Council of the Blind. Scholarship winners are expected to be present at the council's annual conference; the council will cover all reasonable expenses connected with convention attendance.

Number awarded 1 each year.

Deadline February of each year.

[122]
ARIZONA COUNCIL OF THE BLIND SCHOLARSHIP PROGRAM

Arizona Council of the Blind
3124 East Roosevelt Street, Suite 4
Phoenix, AZ 85008-5088
(602) 273-1510   Fax: (602) 938-3748
E-mail: dmmar@uswest.net

Summary To provide financial assistance for undergraduate or graduate studies to legally blind Arizona residents.

Eligibility This program is limited to Arizona residents. Applicants must be legally blind and enrolled or planning to enroll in vocational, technical, graduate, or profes-

sional training programs beyond the high school level. For the purposes of this program, legal blindness is defined as visual acuity of 20/200 or less in the better corrected eye and/or 20 degrees or less visual field or visual loss that requires substantial magnification or readers to access print materials. Candidates are interviewed.

Financial data The stipend is $500.

Duration 1 year; recipients may reapply.

Additional Information Of the scholarships awarded, 1 is named the John Van Landingham Scholarship in memory of the founder of the Arizona Council of the Blind. Information is also available from Thomas Belsan, 2550 South Ellsworth Road, Unit 94, Mesa, AZ 85212-2201, (480) 373-8831.

Number awarded 3 each year.

Deadline March of each year.

[123]
ARNOLD SADLER MEMORIAL SCHOLARSHIP

American Council of the Blind
Attn: Coordinator, Scholarship Program
1155 15th Street, N.W., Suite 1004
Washington, DC 20005
(202) 467-5081   Toll-free: (800) 424-8666
Fax: (202) 467-5085   E-mail: info@acb.org
Web: www.acb.org

Summary To provide financial assistance to undergraduate or graduate students who are blind and are interested in studying in a field of service to persons with disabilities.

Eligibility This program is open to students in rehabilitation, education, law, or other fields of service to persons with disabilities. Applicants must be legally blind and U.S. citizens. In addition to letters of recommendation and copies of academic transcripts, applications must include an autobiographical sketch. A cumulative GPA of 3.3 or higher is generally required. Selection is based on demonstrated academic record, involvement in extracurricular and civic activities, and academic objectives. The severity of the applicant's visual impairment and his/her study methods are also taken into account.

Financial data The stipend is $2,000. In addition, the winner receives a $1,000 cash scholarship from the Kurzweil Foundation and, if appropriate, a Kurzweil-1000 Reading System.

Duration 1 year.

Additional Information This scholarship is funded by the Arnold Sadler Memorial Scholarship Fund. Scholarship winners are expected to be present at the council's annual conference; the council will cover all reasonable expenses connected with convention attendance.

Number awarded 1 each year.

Deadline February of each year.

[124]
ARTHUR E. COPELAND SCHOLARSHIP FOR MALES

United States Association of Blind Athletes
Attn: Scholarship Committee
Brown Hall, Suite 015
33 North Institute Street
Colorado Springs, CO 80903
(719) 630-0422   Fax: (719) 630-0616
E-mail: usaba@usa.net
Web: www.usaba.org

Summary To provide financial assistance for undergraduate or graduate study to male members of the United States Association for Blind Athletes (USABA).

Eligibility All legally blind males who have been members of and have participated in USABA activities for the past year are eligible to apply for this scholarship. Applicants must have been admitted to an academic, vocational, technical, professional, or certification program at the postsecondary level. Selection is based on demonstrated academic record, involvement in extracurricular and civic activities, academic goals and objectives, and USABA involvement at various levels.

Financial data The stipend is $500.

Number awarded 1 each year.

Deadline September of each year.

[125]
AZ AER PROFESSIONAL MINI-GRANT

Association for the Education and Rehabilitation of
   the Blind and Visually Impaired-Arizona Chapter
c/o Sandra Stienweis
2213 North 28th Place
Phoenix, AZ 85008
Web: www.ed.arizona.edu/azaer

Summary To provide funding to members of the Arizona Chapter of the Association for the Education and Rehabilitation of the Blind and Visually Impaired (AZ AER) who are interested in pursuing professional growth activities.

Eligibility This program is open to chapter members who are interested in pursuing such activities as attending a workshop or conference, bringing in a speaker to a divisional meeting, developing a newsletter, or purchasing equipment or books. Applicants must submit a complete outline of the proposed use of the funds and the benefit to their division.

Financial data Grants up to $500 are available.

Number awarded 1 or more each year.

[126]
BEVERLY PROWS MEMORIAL SCHOLARSHIP

National Federation of the Blind of Washington
Attn: Scholarship Committee
P.O. Box 2516
Seattle, WA 98111
(206) 624-8007   E-mail: info@nfbw.org
Web: www.nfbw.org

Summary To provide financial assistance for undergraduate or graduate study to blind students in Washington.

Eligibility This program is open to legally blind residents of Washington state who are working on or planning to work on a full-time college or graduate degree. Applicants must submit a letter describing themselves (hobbies, interests, school activities, and future goals), high school and/or college transcripts, and 3 letters of reference.

Financial data The stipend is $3,000.

Duration 1 year.

Additional Information Information is also available from Rita Szantay at (206) 224-7242 (days) or (206) 352-7320 (evenings and weekends). This scholarship was first awarded in 1991. Winners must attend the state convention of the National Federation of the Blind of Washington to accept the award; convention expenses are covered.

Number awarded 1 each year.

Deadline August of each year.

[127]
CALIFORNIA COUNCIL OF THE BLIND SCHOLARSHIPS

California Council of the Blind
578 B Street
Hayward, CA 94541
(510) 537-7877   Toll-free: (800) 221-6359
Fax: (510) 537-7830

Summary To provide financial assistance for undergraduate or graduate study to blind people in California.

Eligibility Applicants must be legally blind residents of California who are enrolled or planning to enroll full time at an accredited college or university at either the undergraduate or graduate level. Selection is based on academic achievement and financial need.

Financial data The amount of the assistance depends on the availability of funds and the needs of the applicant.

Duration 1 year; may be renewed. For graduate students, support is limited to 2 years of work for a master's degree or 3 years for a Ph.D.

Number awarded Varies each year.

Deadline June of each year.

[128]
DALE M. SCHOETTLER SCHOLARSHIP FOR VISUALLY IMPAIRED STUDENTS

California State University
Office of the Chancellor
Attn: Lori Redfearn, Vice President
401 Golden Shore, Sixth Floor
Long Beach, CA 90802-4210
(562) 951-4815   E-mail: lredfearn@calstate.edu
Web: www.calstate.edu

Summary To provide financial assistance to undergraduate and graduate students with visual impairments at campuses of the California State University (CSU) system throughout California.

Eligibility This program is open to undergraduate and graduate students enrolled at CSU campuses who have been declared legally blind. Applicants must have a cumulative GPA of 2.8 or higher.

Financial data The stipend is $5,000 per year.

Duration 1 year.

Number awarded 1 each year.

[129]
DELTA GAMMA FOUNDATION FLORENCE MARGARET HARVEY MEMORIAL SCHOLARSHIP

American Foundation for the Blind
Attn: Scholarship Committee
11 Penn Plaza, Suite 300
New York, NY 10001
(212) 502-7661   Toll-free: (800) AFB-LINE
Fax: (212) 502-7771   TDD: (212) 502-7662
E-mail: afbinfo@afb.net
Web: www.afb.org/scholarships.asp

Summary To provide financial assistance to blind undergraduate and graduate students who wish to study in the field of rehabilitation and/or education of the blind.

Eligibility This program is open to legally blind juniors, seniors, or graduate students. U.S. citizenship is required. Applicants must be studying in the field of rehabilitation and/or education of visually impaired and blind persons. They must submit a typewritten statement, up to 3 pages in length, describing educational and personal goals, work experience, extracurricular activities, and how scholarship funds will be used. Selection includes consideration of good character and academic excellence.

Financial data The stipend is $1,000.

Duration 1 year.

Additional Information This scholarship is supported by the Delta Gamma Foundation and administered by the American Foundation for the Blind.

Number awarded 1 each year.

Deadline April of each year.

[130]
DR. S. BRADLEY BURSON MEMORIAL SCHOLARSHIP

American Council of the Blind
Attn: Coordinator, Scholarship Program
1155 15th Street, N.W., Suite 1004
Washington, DC 20005
(202) 467-5081   Toll-free: (800) 424-8666
Fax: (202) 467-5085   E-mail: info@acb.org
Web: www.acb.org

Summary To provide financial assistance to blind students who are undergraduate or graduate students working on a degree in science at an accredited college or university.

Eligibility This program is open to legally blind undergraduate or graduate students majoring in the "hard" sciences (i.e., biology, chemistry, physics, and engineering, but not computer science) in college. They must be U.S. citizens. In addition to letters of recommendation and copies of academic transcripts, applications must include an autobiographical sketch. A cumulative GPA of 3.3 or higher is generally required. Selection is based on demonstrated academic record, involvement in extracurricular and civic activities, and academic objectives. The severity of the applicant's visual impairment and his/her study methods are also taken into account.

Financial data The stipend is $1,000. In addition, the winner receives a $1,000 cash scholarship from the Kurzweil Foundation and, if appropriate, a Kurzweil-1000 Reading System.

Duration 1 year.

Additional Information Scholarship winners are expected to be present at the council's annual conference; the council will cover all reasonable expenses connected with convention attendance.

Number awarded 1 each year.

Deadline February of each year.

[131]
EDUCATOR OF TOMORROW AWARD

National Federation of the Blind
c/o Peggy Elliott
Chair, Scholarship Committee
805 Fifth Avenue
Grinnell, IA 50112
(641) 236-3366
Web: www.nfb.org/sch_intro.htm

Summary To provide financial assistance to blind undergraduate or graduate students who wish to prepare for a career as a teacher.

Eligibility This program is open to legally blind students who are working on or planning to work on a full-time undergraduate or graduate degree. Applicants must be preparing for a career in elementary, secondary, or postsecondary teaching. Selection is based on academic excellence, service to the community, and financial need.

Financial data The stipend is $3,000. The Kurzweil Foundation has also provided recipients with an additional $1,000 scholarship and the latest version of the Kurzweil-1000 reading software.

Duration 1 year; recipients may resubmit applications up to 2 additional years.

Additional Information Scholarships are awarded at the federation convention in July. Recipients attend the convention at federation expense; that funding is in addition to the scholarship grant.

Number awarded 1 each year.

Deadline March of each year.

[132]
ELLEN BEACH MACK SCHOLARSHIP

American Council of the Blind of South Carolina
c/o Patsy Jones
1822 Burnham Street
West Columbia, SC 29169
(803) 791-3368
E-mail: jones.patsy@worldnet.att.net
Web: www.acb.org/southcarolina

Summary To provide financial assistance to undergraduate and graduate students with visual impairments in South Carolina.

Eligibility This program is open to residents of South Carolina who are legally blind in both eyes. Applicants must be currently enrolled or accepted at a technical school, college, university, or graduate school. Along with their application, they must submit a letter of recommendation, transcript, and a 2-page autobiographical sketch that describes their goals, strengths, weaknesses, and other pertinent information.

Financial data The stipend is $1,000.

Duration 1 year.

Number awarded 1 or more each year.

Deadline September of each year.

[133]
E.U. PARKER SCHOLARSHIP

National Federation of the Blind
c/o Peggy Elliott
Chair, Scholarship Committee
805 Fifth Avenue
Grinnell, IA 50112
(641) 236-3366
Web: www.nfb.org/sch_intro.htm

Summary To provide financial assistance to blind undergraduate and graduate students.

Eligibility This program is open to legally blind students who are working on or planning to work on a full-time undergraduate or graduate degree. Selection is

based on academic excellence, service to the community, and financial need.
Financial data The stipend is $3,000. The Kurzweil Foundation has also provided recipients with an additional $1,000 scholarship and the latest version of the Kurzweil-1000 reading software.
Duration 1 year; recipients may resubmit applications up to 2 additional years.
Additional Information Scholarships are awarded at the federation convention in July. Recipients attend the convention at federation expense; that funding is in addition to the scholarship grant.
Number awarded 1 each year.
Deadline March of each year.

[134]
FLOYD CALLWARD MEMORIAL SCHOLARSHIP
National Federation of the Blind of New Hampshire
c/o John E. Parker, President
2 Center Street, Apartment 2
Laconia, NH 03246-3737
(603) 528-0107   E-mail: parkerj@worldpath.net

Summary To provide financial assistance to blind students in New Hampshire who wish to work on an undergraduate or graduate degree.
Eligibility This program is open to legally blind and totally blind residents of New Hampshire who are attending or planning to attend college. Applicants must submit 1) a letter describing what they have done to deal with situations involving their blindness, their personal goals and aspirations, and how the scholarship will help them; 2) 2 letters of recommendation; 3) high school or college transcripts; 4) a list of honors and awards; and 5) information on community service and volunteer work. There are no restrictions on level, gender, or field of study. Financial need is not considered.
Financial data The stipend is $1,000. The funds may be used to purchase education-related equipment or services or to defray the costs of tuition, board, and other school fees.
Duration 1 year.
Additional Information This program was established in 1990. Information is also available from Louis Gosselin, c/o New Hampshire State Department of Education, Division of Vocational Rehabilitation, 361 Lincoln Street, Manchester, NH 03103, (603) 669-8733.
Number awarded 1 or more each year.
Deadline September of each year.

[135]
FLOYD QUALLS MEMORIAL SCHOLARSHIPS
American Council of the Blind
Attn: Coordinator, Scholarship Program
1155 15th Street, N.W., Suite 1004
Washington, DC 20005
(202) 467-5081   Toll-free: (800) 424-8666
Fax: (202) 467-5085   E-mail: info@acb.org
Web: www.acb.org

Summary To provide financial assistance to undergraduate and graduate students who are blind.
Eligibility Students who are legally blind may apply for these scholarships. Recipients are selected in each of 4 categories: entering freshmen in academic programs, undergraduates (sophomores, juniors, and seniors) in academic programs, graduate students in academic programs, and vocational school students or students working on an associate's degree from a community college. In addition to letters of recommendation and copies of academic transcripts, applications must include an autobiographical sketch. A cumulative GPA of 3.3 or higher is generally required. Selection is based on demonstrated academic record, involvement in extracurricular and civic activities, and academic objectives. The severity of the applicant's visual impairment and his/her study methods are also taken into account.
Financial data The stipend is $2,500. In addition, the winners receive a $1,000 cash scholarship from the Kurzweil Foundation and, if appropriate, a Kurzweil-1000 Reading System.
Duration 1 year.
Additional Information Scholarship winners are expected to be present at the council's annual conference; the council will cover all reasonable expenses connected with convention attendance.
Number awarded Up to 8 each year: 2 in each of the 4 categories.
Deadline February of each year.

[136]
FLOYD R. CARGILL SCHOLARSHIP
Illinois Council of the Blind
P.O. Box 1336
Springfield, IL 62705
(217) 523-4967   Toll-free: (888) 698-1862
Fax: (217) 523-4302   E-mail: icb@tgi.net

Summary To provide financial assistance for college or professional school to blind students in Illinois.
Eligibility This program is open to students who are legally blind and enrolled in (or applying to) a postsecondary academic, vocational, technical, or professional training program in Illinois. Applicants must submit a 2-page autobiographical sketch; certified transcripts (undergraduates must include high school transcripts and graduate students must include undergraduate transcripts); a letter of recommendation; and proof of accep-

tance (or a statement that they are under consideration for admission) at a postsecondary school. U.S. citizenship is required.
Financial data The stipend is $750.
Duration 1 year.
Number awarded 1 or more each year.
Deadline June of each year.

[137]
FRED SCHEIGERT SCHOLARSHIPS

Council of Citizens with Low Vision International
c/o Pat Beattie, President
906 North Chambliss Street
Alexandria, VA 22312
Toll-free: (800) 733-2258 Fax: (703) 671-9053
E-mail: bernice@tsoft.net
Web: www.cclvi.org/scholarship.html

Summary To provide financial assistance to undergraduate and graduate students with low vision.
Eligibility Applicants must be certified by an ophthalmologist as having low vision (acuity of 20/70 or worse in the better seeing eye with best correction or side vision with a maximum diameter of no greater than 30 degrees). They may be part-time or full-time entering freshmen, undergraduates, or graduate students. A cumulative GPA of at least 3.0 is required.
Financial data The stipend is $1,000.
Duration 1 year.
Additional Information Information is also available from Janis Stanger, 1239 American Beauty Drive, Salt Lake City, UT 84116.
Number awarded 2 each year.
Deadline April of each year.

[138]
FREEDOM SCIENTIFIC TECHNOLOGY SCHOLARSHIP AWARD PROGRAM

Freedom Scientific Inc.
Attn: Low Vision Group
11800 31st Court North
St. Petersburg, FL 33716
(727) 803-8000, ext. 1044
Toll-free: (800) 444-4443 Fax: (727) 803-8001
E-mail: EricV@freedomscientific.com
Web: www.FreedomScientific.com

Summary To provide financial assistance to blind undergraduate and graduate students in the form of vouchers for the purchase of assistive technology devices.
Eligibility This program is open to legally blind students who are either 1) graduating high school seniors planning to pursue a full-time course of study at a college or university, or 2) college seniors planning to enter graduate school. Applicants must be residents of the United States or Canada. The program is administered through 6 partner organizations: 4 for high school seniors in the United States, 1 for high school seniors in Canada, and 1 for graduate students in the United States and Canada. Selection is based on general guidelines of academic achievement and promise, extracurricular or community service leadership and accomplishments, and demonstrated personal qualities and character. The partner organizations may supplement those general guidelines with their own specific criteria and may also select especially deserving students across all levels of higher education. Students may apply to the partner organization of their choice or, if they have no preference, to the organization assigned for the geographic region in which they live.
Financial data The awards consist of vouchers for $2,500 to be used to purchase Freedom Scientific hardware, software, accessories, training, and/or tutorials.
Duration These are 1-time awards.
Additional Information This program, which began in the 2001-02 school year, is sponsored by Freedom Scientific, maker of technology-based products for people who are blind or vision-impaired. The partner organizations include the National Federation of the Blind, 1800 Johnson Street, Baltimore, MD 21230, (410) 659-9314, Web site: www.nfb.org, which also serves as the regional organization for Connecticut, Delaware, Maine, Maryland, Massachusetts, New Hampshire, New Jersey, New York, Pennsylvania, Puerto Rico, Rhode Island, Vermont, Virginia, Washington, D.C., and West Virginia; the American Foundation for the Blind, Attn: Scholarship Committee, 11 Penn Plaza, Suite 300, New York, NY 10001, (212) 502-7661, (800) AFB-LINE, Fax: (212) 502-7771, TDD: (212) 502-7662, E-mail: afbinfo@afb.net, Web site: www.afb.org/scholarships.asp, which also serves as the regional organization for Alabama, Arkansas, Florida, Georgia, Louisiana, Mississippi, North Carolina, South Carolina, Tennessee, and Texas; the American Council of the Blind, 1155 15th Street, N.W., Suite 1004, Washington, DC 20005, (202) 467-5081, (800) 424-8666, Fax: (202) 467-5085, E-mail: info@acb.org, Web site: www.acb.org, which also serves as the regional organization for Illinois, Indiana, Iowa, Kansas, Kentucky, Michigan, Minnesota, Missouri, Nebraska, Ohio, Oklahoma, and Wisconsin; the Braille Institute of America, 741 North Vermont Avenue, Los Angeles, CA 90029-3594, (323) 663-1111, (800) BRAILLE, Fax: (323) 663-0867, E-mail: info@brailleinstitute.org, Web site: www.braileinstitute.org, which also serves as the regional organization for Alaska, Arizona, California, Colorado, Hawaii, Idaho, Montana, Nevada, New Mexico, North Dakota, Oregon, South Dakota, Utah, Washington, and Wyoming; the Canadian National Institute for the Blind, 1929 Bayview Avenue, Toronto, Ontario M4G 3E8, (416) 486-2500, Web site: www.cnib.ca, which accepts all applications from high school seniors in Canada; and Recording for the Blind and Dyslexic 20 Roszel Road, Princeton, NJ 08540, (609) 452-0606, (800) 221-4792, Web site: www.rfbd.org, which accepts all applications for graduate study in the United States and Canada.

Number awarded 20 each year: 4 from each of the U.S. regional organizations, 2 to Canadian students, and 2 to graduate students.

Deadline Each partner organization sets its own deadline, but most are by March of each year.

[139]
GEORGIA COUNCIL OF THE BLIND SCHOLARSHIPS

Georgia Council of the Blind
c/o Janet Clary, Scholarship Committee Chair
318 Walden Glen Lane
Evans, GA 30809

Summary To provide financial assistance for college or graduate school to students in Georgia who have visual impairments or parents with visual impairments.

Eligibility This program is open to residents of Georgia who are either 1) visually impaired or legally blind or 2) the sighted children of parents who are visually impaired or legally blind. Applicants must be enrolled or accepted for enrollment at a vocational/technical school, a 2-year or 4-year college, or a master's or doctoral program. All fields of study are eligible. Selection is based on academic transcripts, 2 letters of recommendation, a 1-page typed statement of the applicant's educational goals, an audio cassette recording of the applicant reading the goals statement, extracurricular activities, and financial need.

Financial data Stipends up to $1,000 per year are available.

Duration 1 year; recipients may reapply.

Additional Information This program began in 1988.

Number awarded 1 or more each year.

Deadline June of each year.

[140]
GERALD DRAKE MEMORIAL SCHOLARSHIP

National Federation of the Blind of California
Attn: Nancy Burns, President
175 East Olive Avenue, Suite 308
Burbank, CA 91502-1812
(818) 558-6524   Fax: (818) 729-7930
E-mail: dnburns@jps.net
Web: www.nfbcal.org

Summary To provide financial assistance for undergraduate or graduate education to blind students in California.

Eligibility Legally blind full-time students in California may apply for a scholarship, but they must attend the convention of the National Federation of the Blind of California. Applicants must submit an essay in which they describe their educational goals, involvement in the blindness community, and eye condition. High school seniors and college freshmen must submit their high school transcripts; other college students must submit transcripts of all undergraduate and graduate work. Selection is based on academic merit.

Financial data The stipend is $1,500.

Duration 1 year.

Number awarded 1 each year.

Deadline May of each year.

[141]
GRADUATE AWARD OF LIGHTHOUSE INTERNATIONAL

Lighthouse International
Attn: Career Incentive Awards Program
111 East 59th Street
New York, NY 10022-1202
(212) 821-9428   Toll-free: (800) 829-0500
Fax: (212) 821-9703   TTY: (212) 821-9713
E-mail: kclark@lighthouse.org
Web: www.lighthouse.org

Summary To provide financial assistance to legally blind graduate students residing and attending school in eastern states.

Eligibility This program is open to legally blind graduate students. Applicants must be residing in and pursuing or planning to pursue a graduate-level program in Connecticut, Delaware, Maine, Maryland, Massachusetts, New Hampshire, New Jersey, New York, Pennsylvania, Rhode Island, Vermont, Virginia, or Washington, D.C. They must write a 500-word essay, describing their academic achievements and career goals. Candidates are not required to demonstrate financial need. U.S. citizenship is required.

Financial data The stipend is $5,000.

Duration The award is granted only once, although the recipient may elect to spend the money over a period of more than 1 year.

Additional Information The recipient must present evidence of enrollment in or acceptance to an educational program before the funds will be released.

Number awarded 1 each year.

Deadline March of each year.

[142]
HANK LEBONNE SCHOLARSHIP

National Federation of the Blind
c/o Peggy Elliott
Chair, Scholarship Committee
805 Fifth Avenue
Grinnell, IA 50112
(641) 236-3366
Web: www.nfb.org/sch_intro.htm

Summary To provide financial assistance to legally blind students working on an undergraduate or graduate degree.

Eligibility This program is open to legally blind students who are working on or planning to work on a full-

time undergraduate or graduate degree. Selection is based on academic excellence, service to the community, and financial need.

Financial data The stipend is $5,000. The Kurzweil Foundation has also provided recipients with an additional $1,000 scholarship and the latest version of the Kurzweil-1000 reading software.

Duration 1 year; recipients may resubmit applications up to 2 additional years.

Additional Information Scholarships are awarded at the federation convention in July. Recipients attend the convention at federation expense; that funding is in addition to the scholarship grant.

Number awarded 1 each year.

Deadline March of each year.

[143]
HARRY LUDWIG MEMORIAL SCHOLARSHIP

Oregon Student Assistance Commission
Attn: Grants and Scholarships Division
1500 Valley River Drive, Suite 100
Eugene, OR 97401-2146
(541) 687-7395
Toll-free: (800) 452-8807, ext. 7395
Fax: (541) 687-7419
Web: www.osac.state.or.us

Summary To provide financial assistance for college or graduate school to residents of Oregon who are visually impaired.

Eligibility This program is open to residents of Oregon who are visually impaired (have residual acuity of 20/70 or less in the better eye with correction, or their visual field is restricted to 20 degrees or less in the better eye). Applicants must be enrolled or planning to enroll as full-time undergraduate or graduate students at a college or university in Oregon.

Financial data Stipends range from $1,000 to $5,000 and average $1,600.

Duration 1 year.

Additional Information This program is administered by the Oregon Student Assistance Commission (OSAC) with funds provided by the Oregon Community Foundation, 1221 S.W. Yamhill, Suite 100, Portland, OR 97205, (503) 227-6846, Fax: (503) 274-7771.

Number awarded Varies each year.

Deadline February of each year.

[144]
HAZEL TEN BROEK MERIT SCHOLARSHIP

National Federation of the Blind of Washington
Attn: Scholarship Committee
P.O. Box 2516
Seattle, WA 98111
(206) 624-8007   E-mail: info@nfbw.org
Web: www.nfbw.org

Summary To provide financial assistance for undergraduate or graduate study to blind students in Washington.

Eligibility This program is open to legally blind residents of Washington state who are working on or planning to work on a full-time college or graduate degree. Applicants must submit a letter describing themselves (hobbies, interests, school activities, and future goals), high school and/or college transcripts, and 3 letters of reference.

Financial data The stipend is $2,000.

Duration 1 year.

Additional Information Information is also available from Rita Szantay at (206) 224-7242 (days) or (206) 352-7320 (evenings and weekends). This scholarship was first awarded in 1996. Winners must attend the state convention of the National Federation of the Blind of Washington to accept the award; convention expenses are covered.

Number awarded 1 each year.

Deadline August of each year.

[145]
HELEN COPELAND SCHOLARSHIP FOR FEMALES

United States Association of Blind Athletes
Attn: Scholarship Committee
Brown Hall, Suite 015
33 North Institute Street
Colorado Springs, CO 80903
(719) 630-0422   Fax: (719) 630-0616
E-mail: usaba@usa.net
Web: www.usaba.org

Summary To provide financial assistance for undergraduate or graduate study to female members of the United States Association for Blind Athletes (USABA).

Eligibility All legally blind females who have been members of and have participated in USABA activities for the past year are eligible to apply for this scholarship. Applicants must have been admitted to an academic, vocational, technical, professional, or certification program at the postsecondary level. Selection is based on demonstrated academic record, involvement in extracurricular and civic activities, academic goals and objectives, and USABA involvement at various levels.

Financial data The stipend is $500.

Number awarded 1 each year.

Deadline September of each year.

VISUAL DISABILITIES: FELLOWSHIPS/GRANTS

[146]
HENTGES SCHOLARSHIP

National Federation of the Blind of Missouri
c/o Gary Wunder, President
3910 Tropical Lane
Columbia, MO 65202-6205
(573) 874-1774   Toll-free: (888) 604-1774
E-mail: info@nfbmo.org
Web: www.nfbmo.org

Summary To provide financial assistance for undergraduate or graduate study to blind female students in Missouri.

Eligibility This program is open to legally blind women residents of Missouri who are pursuing or planning to pursue an undergraduate or graduate degree.

Financial data The maximum stipend is $500.

Duration 1 year.

Additional Information Additional information is also available from Chair, Achievement Awards Committee, Sheila Koenig, 634 South National, Apartment 303, Springfield, MO 65804, (417) 869-1078.

Number awarded 1 each year.

Deadline February of each year.

[147]
HERMIONE GRANT CALHOUN SCHOLARSHIPS

National Federation of the Blind
c/o Peggy Elliott
Chair, Scholarship Committee
805 Fifth Avenue
Grinnell, IA 50112
(641) 236-3366
Web: www.nfb.org/sch_intro.htm

Summary To provide financial assistance to female blind students interested in working on an undergraduate or graduate degree.

Eligibility This program is open to legally blind women students who are working on or planning to work full time on an undergraduate or graduate degree. Selection is based on academic excellence, service to the community, and financial need.

Financial data The stipend is $3,000. The Kurzweil Foundation has also provided recipients with an additional $1,000 scholarship and the latest version of the Kurzweil-1000 reading software.

Duration 1 year; recipients may resubmit applications up to 2 additional years.

Additional Information Scholarships are awarded at the federation convention in July. Recipients attend the convention at federation expense; that funding is in addition to the scholarship grant.

Number awarded 1 each year.

Deadline March of each year.

[148]
HOWARD BROWN RICKARD SCHOLARSHIPS

National Federation of the Blind
c/o Peggy Elliott
Chair, Scholarship Committee
805 Fifth Avenue
Grinnell, IA 50112
(641) 236-3366
Web: www.nfb.org/sch_intro.htm

Summary To provide financial assistance for college or graduate school to blind students studying or planning to study law, medicine, engineering, architecture, or the natural sciences.

Eligibility This program is open to legally blind students who are enrolled in or planning to enroll in a full-time undergraduate or graduate course of study. Applicants must be studying or planning to study law, medicine, engineering, architecture, or the natural sciences. Selection is based on academic excellence, service to the community, and financial need.

Financial data The stipend is $3,000. The Kurzweil Foundation has also provided recipients with an additional $1,000 scholarship and the latest version of the Kurzweil-1000 reading software.

Duration 1 year; recipients may resubmit applications up to 2 additional years.

Additional Information Scholarships are awarded at the federation convention in July. Recipients attend the convention at federation expense; that funding is in addition to the scholarship grant.

Number awarded 1 each year.

Deadline March of each year.

[149]
IMA DIVERSITY SCHOLARSHIP PROGRAM

Institute of Management Accountants
Attn: Committee on Students
10 Paragon Drive
Montvale, NJ 07645-1760
(201) 573-9000
Toll-free: (800) 638-4427, ext. 1543
Fax: (201) 573-8438   E-mail: students@imanet.org
Web: www.imanet.org

Summary To provide financial assistance to minority and disabled student members of the Institute of Management Accountants (IMA) who are interested in working on an undergraduate or graduate degree in management accounting or financial management.

Eligibility This program is open to undergraduate and graduate students of American Indian/Alaska Native, Asian/Pacific Islander, Black, or Hispanic heritage and students with physical disabilities (defined as hearing impairment, vision impairment, missing extremities, partial paralysis, complete paralysis, or severe distortion of limbs and/or spine). Applicants must be in their sophomore, junior, or senior year or in a graduate program with

a major in management accounting, financial management, or information technology. Selection is based on 1) academic merit; 2) quality of their application presentation; 3) demonstrated community leadership; 4) potential for success in expressed career goals in a financial management position; 5) a written statement from applicants expressing their short-term and long-term career goals and objectives, including their participation in the IMA; and 6) letters of recommendation.

Financial data Stipends are $3,000 per year.

Duration 1 year.

Additional Information Up to 15 finalists in each category (including the scholarship winners) receive a scholarship to take 5 parts of the CMA and/or CFM examination within a year of graduation.

Number awarded At least 13 each year.

Deadline February of each year.

[150]
JAMES DOYLE CASE MEMORIAL SCHOLARSHIPS

Mississippi Council of the Blind
2501 North West Street
Jackson, MS 39216
(601) 982-1718
Toll-free: (888) 346-5622 (within MS)
E-mail: mcb@netdoor.com

Summary To provide funding for college to legally blind residents of Mississippi and their children.

Eligibility This program is open to residents of Mississippi who are legally blind or the children of at least 1 legally blind parent. Applicants must be enrolled or accepted for enrollment in an undergraduate or graduate program and carrying or planning to carry at least 12 academic hours. Selection is based on a transcript from the last school or college attended, college entrance examination score, 2 letters of recommendation, and a 300-word biographical essay on the applicant's educational and employment goals. Membership in the sponsoring organization is not required.

Financial data The stipend is $1,000 per year.

Duration 1 year.

Additional Information Information is also available from Rebecca Floyd, President, 131 Red Fox Lane, Madison, MS 39110.

Number awarded 2 each year.

Deadline March of each year.

[151]
JAMES R. CARLOCK SCHOLARSHIP

National Federation of the Blind of Arizona
c/o Ruth Swenson, President
311 West McNair Street
Chandler, AZ 85225-7135
(480) 898-1188
E-mail: rswenson1@mindspring.com
Web: www.nfbarizona.com/SCHOOL.htm

Summary To provide financial assistance for college or professional school to blind students in Arizona.

Eligibility This program is open to legally blind full-time students. Applicants must be residents of Arizona or attending school in Arizona. Selection is based on academic excellence, program quality, service to the community, and financial need.

Financial data The stipend is $750.

Duration 1 year.

Additional Information Information is also available from Marcus Schmidt, Scholarship Chair, 3202 West Murie Drive, Phoenix, AZ 85053, (602) 942-0181, E-mail: marcus.schmidt@pinnaclewest.com.

Number awarded 1 each year.

Deadline May of each year.

[152]
JENNICA FERGUSON MEMORIAL SCHOLARSHIP

National Federation of the Blind
c/o Peggy Elliott
Chair, Scholarship Committee
805 Fifth Avenue
Grinnell, IA 50112
(641) 236-3366
Web: www.nfb.org/sch_intro.htm

Summary To provide financial assistance to undergraduate and graduate blind students.

Eligibility This program is open to legally blind students who are working on or planning to work full time on an undergraduate or graduate degree. Selection is based on academic excellence, service to the community, and financial need.

Financial data The stipend is $5,000. The Kurzweil Foundation has also provided recipients with an additional $1,000 scholarship and the latest version of the Kurzweil-1000 reading software.

Duration 1 year; recipients may resubmit applications up to 2 additional years.

Additional Information Scholarships are awarded at the federation convention in July. Recipients attend the convention at federation expense; that funding is in addition to the scholarship grant.

Number awarded 1 each year.

Deadline March of each year.

[153]
JEWISH BRAILLE INSTITUTE OF AMERICA SCHOLARSHIP

Jewish Braille Institute of America, Inc.
110 East 30th Street
New York, NY 10016
(212) 889-2525   Toll-free: (800) 433-1531
Fax: (212) 689-3692   E-mail: admin@jbilibrary.org
Web: www.jewishbraille.org/college.html

Summary To provide financial assistance to blind students working on a graduate degree in Jewish studies.

Eligibility An applicant for this scholarship must be legally blind, must demonstrate financial need, and must intend to utilize the funds for training to enter some field of Jewish community endeavor, including study to become a rabbi, a cantor, or a worker in Jewish communal service and multilingual special education. Financial need is considered in the selection process.

Financial data The amount of the scholarship varies, depending on the recipient's need and the cost of the desired education.

Additional Information No formal application form for this scholarship exists; the Jewish Braille Institute maintains close contact with the applicant, securing information as needed.

Number awarded Awards are made whenever qualified candidates apply.

Deadline Applications may be submitted at any time.

[154]
JOANN FISCHER SCHOLARSHIP

American Council of the Blind of Ohio
Attn: Executive Director
2678 Edgevale Road
P.O. Box 21488
Columbus, OH 43221-0488
(614) 221-6688
Toll-free: (800) 835-2226 (within OH)
Fax: (614) 451-0539   E-mail: kmorlock@gcfn.org
Web: www.acbogcc.org

Summary To provide financial assistance to Ohio graduate students who are blind.

Eligibility This program is open to 1) residents of Ohio who are currently enrolled as graduate students, and 2) graduate students at colleges and universities in Ohio. Applicants must be legally blind and working on or planning to work on a degree in any field. Along with their application, they must submit transcripts (must have a GPA of 3.0 or higher), a certificate of legal blindness, and an essay of 250 to 500 words on their career objectives, future plans, personal goals, other academic or personal qualities, and why they believe they are qualified to receive this scholarship.

Financial data A stipend is awarded (amount not specified).

Duration 1 year; recipients may reapply.

Additional Information Information is also available from the scholarship committee, 520 Walnut Street, Perrysburg, OH 43551.

Number awarded 1 each year.

Deadline July of each year.

[155]
JOHN AND RHODA DOWER SCHOLARSHIP

National Federation of the Blind of Missouri
c/o Gary Wunder, President
3910 Tropical Lane
Columbia, MO 65202-6205
(573) 874-1774   Toll-free: (888) 604-1774
E-mail: info@nfbmo.org
Web: www.nfbmo.org

Summary To provide financial assistance for college to blind students in Missouri.

Eligibility This program is open to legally blind residents of Missouri who are pursuing or planning to pursue an undergraduate or graduate degree.

Financial data The maximum stipend is $1,000.

Duration 1 year.

Additional Information Additional information is also available from the Chair of the Achievement Awards Committee: Sheila Koenig, 634 South National, Apartment 303, Springfield, MO 65804, (417) 869-1078.

Number awarded Up to 3 each year.

Deadline February of each year.

[156]
KAREN D. CARSEL MEMORIAL SCHOLARSHIP

American Foundation for the Blind
Attn: Scholarship Committee
11 Penn Plaza, Suite 300
New York, NY 10001
(212) 502-7661   Toll-free: (800) AFB LINE
Fax: (212) 502-7771   TDD: (212) 502-7662
E-mail: afbinfo@afb.net
Web: www.afb.org/scholarships.asp

Summary To provide financial assistance to legally blind graduate students.

Eligibility Applicants must be legally blind U.S. citizens who have been admitted into a full-time graduate program. They must submit evidence of economic need. Applications must include a typewritten statement, up to 2 pages in length, describing educational and career goals, work experience, extracurricular activities, and how fellowship funds will be used.

Financial data The stipend is $500.

Duration 1 year.

Number awarded 1 each year.

Deadline April of each year.

[157]
KENNETH JERNIGAN SCHOLARSHIP

National Federation of the Blind
c/o Peggy Elliott
Chair, Scholarship Committee
805 Fifth Avenue
Grinnell, IA 50112
(641) 236-3366
Web: www.nfb.org/sch_intro.htm

Summary To provide financial assistance to undergraduate and graduate blind students.

Eligibility This program is open to legally blind students who are working on or planning to work full time on an undergraduate or graduate degree. Selection is based on academic excellence, service to the community, and financial need.

Financial data The stipend is $12,000. The Kurzweil Foundation has also provided recipients with an additional $1,000 scholarship and the latest version of the Kurzweil-1000 reading software.

Duration 1 year; recipients may resubmit applications up to 2 additional years.

Additional Information Scholarships are awarded at the federation convention in July. Recipients attend the convention at federation expense; that funding is in addition to the scholarship grant. This scholarship is given by the American Action Fund for Blind Children and Adults, a nonprofit organization that assists blind people.

Number awarded 1 each year.

Deadline March of each year.

[158]
KUCHLER-KILLIAN MEMORIAL SCHOLARSHIP

National Federation of the Blind
c/o Peggy Elliott
Chair, Scholarship Committee
805 Fifth Avenue
Grinnell, IA 50112
(641) 236-3366
Web: www.nfb.org/sch_intro.htm

Summary To provide financial assistance to undergraduate and graduate blind students.

Eligibility This program is open to legally blind students who are working on or planning to work full time on an undergraduate or graduate degree. Selection is based on academic excellence, service to the community, and financial need.

Financial data The stipend is $3,000. The Kurzweil Foundation has also provided recipients with an additional $1,000 scholarship and the latest version of the Kurzweil-1000 reading software.

Duration 1 year; recipients may resubmit applications up to 2 additional years.

Additional Information Scholarships are awarded at the federation convention in July. Recipients attend the convention at federation expense; that funding is in addition to the scholarship grant.

Number awarded 1 each year.

Deadline March of each year.

[159]
LAVYRL JOHNSON MEMORIAL SCHOLARSHIP

National Federation of the Blind of California
Attn: Nancy Burns, President
175 East Olive Avenue, Suite 308
Burbank, CA 91502-1812
(818) 558-6524   Fax: (818) 729-7930
E-mail: dnburns@jps.net
Web: www.nfbcal.org

Summary To provide financial assistance for undergraduate or graduate education to blind students in California.

Eligibility Legally blind full-time students in California may apply for a scholarship, but they must attend the convention of the National Federation of the Blind of California. Applicants must submit an essay in which they describe their educational goals, involvement in the blindness community, and eye condition. High school seniors and college freshmen must submit their high school transcripts; other college students must submit transcripts of all undergraduate and graduate work. Selection is based on academic merit.

Financial data The stipend is $1,500.

Duration 1 year.

Number awarded 1 each year.

Deadline May of each year.

[160]
LAWRENCE MARCELINO MEMORIAL SCHOLARSHIP

National Federation of the Blind of California
Attn: Nancy Burns, President
175 East Olive Avenue, Suite 308
Burbank, CA 91502-1812
(818) 558-6524   Fax: (818) 729-7930
E-mail: dnburns@jps.net
Web: www.nfbcal.org

Summary To provide financial assistance for graduate or undergraduate education to blind students in California.

Eligibility Legally blind full-time students in California may apply for a scholarship, but they must attend the convention of the National Federation of the Blind of California. Applicants must submit an essay in which they describe their educational goals, involvement in the blindness community, and eye condition. High school seniors and college freshmen must submit their high school transcripts; other college students must submit

transcripts of all undergraduate and graduate work. Selection is based on academic merit.
Financial data The stipend is $2,500.
Duration 1 year.
Number awarded 1 each year.
Deadline May of each year.

[161] LINWOOD WALKER SCHOLARSHIP

American Council of the Blind of Ohio
Attn: Executive Director
2678 Edgevale Road
P.O. Box 21488
Columbus, OH 43221-0488
(614) 221-6688
Toll-free: (800) 835-2226 (within OH)
Fax: (614) 451-0539   E-mail: kmorlock@gcfn.org
Web: www.acbogcc.org

Summary To provide financial assistance to blind Ohio graduate students in service-related fields.
Eligibility This program is open to 1) residents of Ohio who are currently enrolled as graduate students, and 2) graduate students at colleges and universities in Ohio. Applicants must be legally blind and working on or planning to work on a degree in a service-related field (e.g., teaching, health care, public administration). Along with their application, they must submit transcripts (must have a GPA of 3.0 or higher), a certificate of legal blindness, and an essay of 250 to 500 words on their career objectives, future plans, personal goals, other academic or personal qualities, and why they believe they are qualified to receive this scholarship.
Financial data A stipend is awarded (amount not specified).
Duration 1 year; recipients may reapply.
Additional Information Information is also available from the scholarship committee, 520 Walnut Street, Perrysburg, OH 43551.
Number awarded 1 each year.
Deadline July of each year.

[162] LIONS CLUBS SUPPORT SERVICES FOR THE BLIND AND VISUALLY IMPAIRED

Lions Clubs International
Attn: Program Development Department
300 22nd Street
Oak Brook, IL 60523-8842
(630) 571-5466, ext. 316   Fax: (630) 571-1692
E-mail: executiveservices@lionsclubs.org
Web: www.lionsclubs.org

Summary To provide college scholarships and other assistance to blind people.
Eligibility These programs are open to blind people and others involved in service to the blind. Applicants may be seeking support for the following activities: scholarships for the blind and visually impaired, medical research, assistive technology grants, independent mobility, transportation, reading materials and aids, audio products, Braille products, and other aids.
Financial data The amount of this assistance varies.
Additional Information Support is provided by local clubs of Lions Clubs International. Requests send to the international office are referred to the appropriate district governor. If any of the clubs within the district conduct programs for which the applicant might be considered, the governor will advise the particular club to contact the applicant. No funds are available from the office of Lions Clubs International.

[163] MELVA T. OWEN MEMORIAL SCHOLARSHIP

National Federation of the Blind
c/o Peggy Elliott
Chair, Scholarship Committee
805 Fifth Avenue
Grinnell, IA 50112
(641) 236-3366
Web: www.nfb.org/sch_intro.htm

Summary To provide financial assistance to blind undergraduate or graduate students.
Eligibility This program is open to legally blind students who are working on or planning to work full time on an undergraduate or graduate degree. Scholarships, however, will not be awarded for the study of religion or solely to further general or cultural education; the academic program should be directed towards attaining financial independence. Selection is based on academic excellence, service to the community, and financial need.
Financial data The stipend is $10,000. The Kurzweil Foundation has also provided recipients with an additional $1,000 scholarship and the latest version of the Kurzweil-1000 reading software.
Duration 1 year; recipients may resubmit applications up to 2 additional years.
Additional Information Scholarships are awarded at the federation convention in July. Recipients attend the convention at federation expense; that funding is in addition to the scholarship grant.
Number awarded 1 each year.
Deadline March of each year.

[164]
NATIONAL FEDERATION OF THE BLIND COMPUTER SCIENCE SCHOLARSHIP

National Federation of the Blind
c/o Peggy Elliott
Chair, Scholarship Committee
805 Fifth Avenue
Grinnell, IA 50112
(641) 236-3366
Web: www.nfb.org/sch_intro.htm

Summary To provide financial assistance to legally blind undergraduate and graduate students working on a degree in computer science.

Eligibility This program is open to legally blind students who are working on or planning to work full time on an undergraduate or graduate degree in computer science. Selection is based on academic excellence, service to the community, and financial need.

Financial data The stipend is $3,000. The Kurzweil Foundation has also provided recipients with an additional $1,000 scholarship and the latest version of the Kurzweil-1000 reading software.

Duration 1 year; recipients may resubmit applications up to 2 additional years.

Additional Information Scholarships are awarded at the federation convention in July. Recipients attend the convention at federation expense; that funding is in addition to the scholarship grant.

Number awarded 1 each year.

Deadline March of each year.

[165]
NATIONAL FEDERATION OF THE BLIND OF CALIFORNIA SCHOLARSHIPS

National Federation of the Blind of California
Attn: Nancy Burns, President
175 East Olive Avenue, Suite 308
Burbank, CA 91502-1812
(818) 558-6524   Fax: (818) 729-7930
E-mail: dnburns@jps.net
Web: www.nfbcal.org

Summary To provide financial assistance for graduate or undergraduate education to blind students in California.

Eligibility Legally blind full-time students in California may apply for a scholarship, but they must attend the convention of the National Federation of the Blind of California. Applicants must submit an essay in which they describe their educational goals, involvement in the blindness community, and eye condition. High school seniors and college freshmen must submit their high school transcripts; other college students must submit transcripts of all undergraduate and graduate work. Selection is based on academic merit.

Financial data The stipend is $1,000.

Duration 1 year.

Number awarded 3 each year.

Deadline May of each year.

[166]
NATIONAL FEDERATION OF THE BLIND OF OHIO SCHOLARSHIPS

National Federation of the Blind of Ohio
c/o Barbara Pierce, President
237 Oak Street
Oberlin, OH 44074-1517
(440) 775-2216   Toll-free: (800) 396-NFBO
E-mail: bbpierce@pobox.com
Web: www.nfbohio.org

Summary To provide financial assistance for undergraduate or graduate studies to Ohio residents who are legally blind.

Eligibility Eligible to apply for this support are high school seniors, currently-enrolled college students, and graduate students who reside in Ohio and are legally blind. They must attend or be preparing to attend an accredited institution of higher education on a full-time basis. Selection is based on academic excellence, community service, and financial need.

Financial data The stipend is $1,500 or $1,000.

Duration 1 year.

Additional Information Information is also available from Dr. J. Webster Smith, Chair, Scholarship Committee, 2 Canterbury Street, Athens, OH 45701, (740) 593-4838, E-mail: jsmith1@ohiou.edu. The $1,500 scholarship is named the Jennica Ferguson Memorial Scholarship.

Number awarded 2 each year:1 at $1,500 and 1 at $1,000.

Deadline May of each year.

[167]
NATIONAL FEDERATION OF THE BLIND OF OREGON SCHOLARSHIPS

National Federation of the Blind of Oregon
c/o Carla McQuillan, President
5005 Main Street
Springfield, OR 97478
(541) 726-6924
Toll-free: (800) 422-7093 (within OR)
Fax: (541) 726-5527
Web: www.nfb-or.org/scholarships.htm

Summary To provide financial assistance for college or graduate school to blind residents of Oregon.

Eligibility This program is open to blind residents of Oregon who are working on or planning to work on an undergraduate or graduate degree at a college or university in the state. Applicants must be enrolled full time or enrolled part time and working full time. Selection is based on academic and professional promise as well as

potential for leadership in the National Federation of the Blind of Oregon.
Financial data Stipends are either $1,500 or $1,000.
Duration 1 year.
Additional Information Information is also available from Carolyn Brock, Scholarship Chair, (503) 963-1973, E-mail: mmebrock@spiritone.com.
Number awarded 3 each year: 1 at $1,500 and 2 at $1,000.

[168]
NATIONAL FEDERATION OF THE BLIND OF UTAH SCHOLARSHIPS

National Federation of the Blind of Utah
c/o Ron Gardner, President
132 West Penman Lane
Bountiful, UT 84010-7634
(801) 292-3000   E-mail: president@nfbutah.org
Web: www.nfbutah.org/utabs/scholarships.html

Summary To provide financial assistance for college or graduate school to blind residents of Utah.
Eligibility This program is open to blind residents of Utah who are working on or planning to work on an undergraduate or graduate degree. Selection is based on academic excellence, community service, and financial need.
Financial data Stipends range from $500 to $1,500.
Duration 1 year.
Number awarded 3 to 5 each year.
Deadline March of each year.

[169]
NATIONAL FEDERATION OF THE BLIND SCHOLARSHIPS

National Federation of the Blind
c/o Peggy Elliott
Chair, Scholarship Committee
805 Fifth Avenue
Grinnell, IA 50112
(641) 236-3366
Web: www.nfb.org/sch_intro.htm

Summary To provide financial assistance for college or graduate school to blind students.
Eligibility This program is open to legally blind students who are working on or planning to work on an undergraduate or graduate degree. In general, full-time enrollment is required, although 1 scholarship may be awarded to a part-time student who is working full time. Selection is based on academic excellence, service to the community, and financial need.
Financial data Stipends are $7,000 or $3,000. The Kurzweil Foundation has also provided recipients with an additional $1,000 scholarship and the latest version of the Kurzweil-1000 reading software.

Duration 1 year; recipients may resubmit applications up to 2 additional years.
Additional Information Scholarships are awarded at the federation convention in July. Recipients attend the convention at federation expense; that funding is in addition to the scholarship grant.
Number awarded 18 each year: 2 at $7,000 and 16 at $3,000.
Deadline March of each year.

[170]
NIB GRANT M. MACK MEMORIAL SCHOLARSHIP

American Council of the Blind
Attn: Coordinator, Scholarship Program
1155 15th Street, N.W., Suite 1004
Washington, DC 20005
(202) 467-5081   Toll-free: (800) 424-8666
Fax: (202) 467-5085   E-mail: info@acb.org
Web: www.acb.org

Summary To provide financial assistance to students who are blind and working on an undergraduate or graduate degree in business or management.
Eligibility All legally blind persons who are majoring in business or management (undergraduate or graduate) and are U.S. citizens or resident aliens are eligible to apply. In addition to letters of recommendation and copies of academic transcripts, applications must include an autobiographical sketch. A cumulative GPA of 3.3 or higher is generally required. Selection is based on demonstrated academic record, involvement in extracurricular and civic activities, and academic objectives. The severity of the applicant's visual impairment and his/her study methods are also taken into account.
Financial data The stipend is $2,000. In addition, the winner receives a $1,000 cash scholarship from the Kurzweil Foundation and, if appropriate, a Kurzweil-1000 Reading System.
Duration 1 year.
Additional Information This scholarship is sponsored by National Industries for the Blind (NIB) in honor of a dedicated leader of the American Council of the Blind. Scholarship winners are expected to be present at the council's annual conference; the council will cover all reasonable expenses connected with convention attendance.
Number awarded 1 each year.
Deadline February of each year.

[171]
NORA WEBB-MCKINNEY SCHOLARSHIP

American Council of the Blind of Ohio
Attn: Executive Director
2678 Edgevale Road
P.O. Box 21488
Columbus, OH 43221-0488
(614) 221-6688
Toll-free: (800) 835-2226 (within OH)
Fax: (614) 451-0539   E-mail: kmorlock@gcfn.org
Web: www.acbogcc.org

Summary To provide financial assistance to Ohio students who are interested in working on an undergraduate or graduate degree involving service to blind people.

Eligibility This program is open to 1) residents of Ohio who are high school seniors or current undergraduate or graduate students, and 2) undergraduate and graduate students at colleges and universities in Ohio. Applicants must be interested in working on or planning to work on a degree in a field related to blindness (e.g., special education, rehabilitation teaching or counseling, orientation and mobility, or a concentration on programs serving people who are blind). They may be blind or sighted. Along with their application, they must submit transcripts (must have a GPA of 3.0 or higher) and an essay of 250 to 500 words on their career objectives, future plans, personal goals, other academic or personal qualities, and why they believe they are qualified to receive this scholarship.

Financial data A stipend is awarded (amount not specified).

Duration 1 year; recipients may reapply.

Additional Information Information is also available from the scholarship committee, 520 Walnut Street, Perrysburg, OH 43551.

Number awarded 1 each year.

Deadline July of each year.

[172]
NORTH DAKOTA ASSOCIATION OF THE BLIND SCHOLARSHIPS

North Dakota Association of the Blind
c/o Allan Peterson, President
7009 Horseshoe Bend
Fargo, ND 58104
(701) 282-4644
E-mail: allan_peterson@ndsu.nodak.edu
Web: www.ndab.org/Scholarship.html

Summary To provide financial assistance for college or graduate school to blind students in North Dakota.

Eligibility This program is open to North Dakota residents who are legally blind and attending an institution of higher education in the state. Applicants must be full-time students with a class standing of a sophomore through a graduate student and a GPA of 2.5 or higher. They must submit 2 letters of recommendation, transcripts, a family financial aid statement, and an essay that describes their vocational interests, how the scholarship will help them, their goals and aspirations, and what they have done to deal with situations involving their blindness. Selection is based on academic excellence, financial need, and service to the community.

Financial data Stipends are $1,000 or $500.

Duration 1 year.

Additional Information This program was established in 1990. Information is also available from Ruth Poer, Scholarship Committee Chair, 3315 Broadway #302, Fargo, ND 58102, (701) 235-7007.

Number awarded 3 each year: 1 at $1,000 and 2 at $500.

Deadline March of each year.

[173]
PAUL W. RUCKES SCHOLARSHIP

American Foundation for the Blind
Attn: Scholarship Committee
11 Penn Plaza, Suite 300
New York, NY 10001
(212) 502-7661   Toll-free: (800) AFB-LINE
Fax: (212) 502-7771   TDD: (212) 502-7662
E-mail: afbinfo@afb.net
Web: www.afb.org/scholarships.asp

Summary To provide financial assistance to visually impaired students who wish to work on a graduate or undergraduate degree in engineering or computer, physical, or life sciences.

Eligibility This program is open to visually impaired undergraduate or graduate students who are U.S. citizens working on a degree in engineering or the computer, physical, or life sciences. Legal blindness is not required. Applicants must submit a typewritten statement, up to 3 pages in length, describing educational and personal goals, work experience, extracurricular activities, and how scholarship funds will be used.

Financial data The stipend is $2,500.

Duration 1 year.

Number awarded 1 each year.

Deadline April of each year.

[174]
ROSS N. AND PATRICIA PANGERE FOUNDATION SCHOLARSHIPS

American Council of the Blind
Attn: Coordinator, Scholarship Program
1155 15th Street, N.W., Suite 1004
Washington, DC 20005
(202) 467-5081   Toll-free: (800) 424-8666
Fax: (202) 467-5085   E-mail: info@acb.org
Web: www.acb.org

Summary To provide financial assistance for under-

graduate or graduate study to outstanding blind students.

Eligibility Eligible to apply for this scholarship are legally blind U.S. citizens or resident aliens who are undergraduate or graduate students. In addition to letters of recommendation and copies of academic transcripts, applications must include an autobiographical sketch. A cumulative GPA of 3.3 or higher is generally required. Selection is based on demonstrated academic record, involvement in extracurricular and civic activities, and academic objectives. The severity of the applicant's visual impairment and his/her study methods are also taken into account.

Financial data A stipend is awarded (amount not specified). In addition, the winner receives a $1,000 cash scholarship from the Kurzweil Foundation and, if appropriate, a Kurzweil-1000 Reading System.

Duration 1 year.

Additional Information The scholarship winner is expected to be present at the council's annual national convention; the council will cover all reasonable costs connected with convention attendance.

Number awarded 2 each year.

Deadline February of each year.

[175]
RUDOLPH DILLMAN MEMORIAL SCHOLARSHIP

American Foundation for the Blind
Attn: Scholarship Committee
11 Penn Plaza, Suite 300
New York, NY 10001
(212) 502-7661   Toll-free: (800) AFB-LINE
Fax: (212) 502-7771   TDD: (212) 502-7662
E-mail: afbinfo@afb.net
Web: www.afb.org/scholarships.asp

Summary To provide financial assistance to legally blind undergraduate or graduate students studying in the field of rehabilitation and/or education of visually impaired and blind persons.

Eligibility Applicants must be able to submit evidence of legal blindness, U.S. citizenship, and acceptance in an accredited undergraduate or graduate training program within the broad field of rehabilitation and/or education of blind and visually impaired persons. They must submit a typewritten statement, up to 3 pages in length, describing educational and personal goals, work experience, extracurricular activities, and how scholarship funds will be used.

Financial data The stipend is $2,500 per year.

Duration 1 academic year; previous recipients may not reapply.

Number awarded 4 each year: 3 without consideration of financial need and 1 to an applicant who can submit evidence of financial need.

Deadline April of each year.

[176]
RUTH BILLOW MEMORIAL EDUCATION FUND

Delta Gamma Foundation
Attn: Director, Service for Sight
3250 Riverside Drive
P.O. Box 21397
Columbus, OH 43221-0397
(614) 481-8169   Fax: (614) 481-0133
E-mail: blbecky@aol.com
Web: www.deltagamma.org

Summary To provide financial assistance to members of Delta Gamma sorority who are visually impaired or preparing for a career in working with the visually impaired.

Eligibility This program is open to undergraduate and graduate members of the sorority who are either 1) blind or visually impaired or 2) pursuing professional training in areas related to working with persons who are blind or visually impaired or in sight preservation. Applicants must be pursuing a program of postsecondary education in the United States or Canada.

Financial data The amount awarded varies, depending upon individual circumstances.

Duration 1 year or more.

Number awarded Varies each year.

Deadline Applications may be submitted at any time.

[177]
SALLY S. JACOBSEN SCHOLARSHIP

National Federation of the Blind
c/o Peggy Elliott
Chair, Scholarship Committee
805 Fifth Avenue
Grinnell, IA 50112
(641) 236-3366
Web: www.nfb.org/sch_intro.htm

Summary To provide financial assistance to blind undergraduate and graduate students working on a degree in the field of education, especially those planning to major in education of disabled youth.

Eligibility This program is open to legally blind students who are working on or planning to work full time on an undergraduate or graduate degree in education. Preference is given to applicants planning to specialize in education of disabled youth. Selection is based on academic excellence, service to the community, and financial need.

Financial data The stipend is $5,000. The Kurzweil Foundation has also provided recipients with an additional $1,000 scholarship and the latest version of the Kurzweil-1000 reading software.

Duration 1 year; recipients may resubmit applications up to 2 additional years.

Additional Information Scholarships are awarded at the federation convention in July. Recipients attend the

convention at federation expense; that funding is in addition to the scholarship grant.

Number awarded 1 each year.

Deadline March of each year.

[178]
SIGMA ALPHA IOTA SCHOLARSHIP FOR THE VISUALLY IMPAIRED

Sigma Alpha Iota Philanthropies, Inc.
34 Wall Street, Suite 515
Asheville, NC 28801-2710
(828) 251-0606 Fax: (828) 251-0644
E-mail: philonline@sai-national.org
Web: www.sai-national.org/phil/philschs.html

Summary To provide financial assistance for college or graduate school to visually impaired members of Sigma Alpha Iota (an organization of women musicians) who are working on a degree in music.

Eligibility Members of the organization may apply for these scholarships if they are visually impaired. They must be enrolled in a graduate or undergraduate degree program in music.

Financial data The stipend is $1,000.

Duration 1 year.

Additional Information There is a $25 nonrefundable application fee.

Number awarded 1 or 2 every 3 years.

Deadline April of the year of the awards (2006, 2009, etc.).

[179]
SOUTH DAKOTA FREE TUITION FOR VISUALLY IMPAIRED PERSONS

South Dakota Board of Regents
Attn: Scholarship Committee
306 East Capitol Avenue, Suite 200
Pierre, SD 57501-3159
(605) 773-3455 Fax: (605) 773-5320
E-mail: info@ris.sdbor.edu
Web: www.ris.sdbor.edu

Summary To provide financial assistance for college or graduate school to visually impaired residents of South Dakota.

Eligibility Eligible for this program is any visually impaired resident of South Dakota who can meet the entrance requirements for admission to a postsecondary educational institution (including graduate school and medical school) under the supervision of the state board of regents. For purposes of the program, "visual impairment" means that the person cannot, with use of correcting glasses, see sufficiently well to perform ordinary activities for which eyesight is essential. This program does not extend to visually impaired persons who are entitled to receive tuition and fee support from the state's department of vocational rehabilitation.

Financial data Qualified applicants may attend any institution under the supervision of the South Dakota Board of Regents without payment of tuition, library fees, registration fees, or any other fees.

Duration Benefits are provided until the recipient has earned 225 semester hours of credit or the equivalent.

Additional Information Applicants should contact the financial aid director at the South Dakota college or university they plan to attend, not the sponsor. The exemption from charges does not apply if a course is repeated because of unsatisfactory work, unless the problem was caused by illness or some other circumstance for which the student had no responsibility.

Number awarded Varies each year.

[180]
WALTER YOUNG MEMORIAL SCHOLARSHIP

California Association for Postsecondary Education and Disability
Attn: Executive Assistant
71423 Biskra Road
Rancho Mirage, CA 92270
(760) 346-8206 Fax: (760) 340-5275
TTY: (760) 341-4084 E-mail: caped2000@aol.com
Web: www.caped.net/scholarship.html

Summary To provide financial assistance to blind and visually impaired undergraduate and graduate students in California.

Eligibility This program is open to blind and visually impaired students at public and private colleges and universities in California. Undergraduates must have completed at least 6 semester credits and have a GPA of 2.5 or higher. Graduate students must have completed at least 3 semester units and have a GPA of 3.0 or higher. Applicants must submit a 1-page personal letter that demonstrates writing skills; progress toward meeting educational and vocational goals; how they accommodate their disability; involvement in community activities; and any other factor that might strengthen their application. They must also submit a letter of recommendation from a faculty member, verification of disability, official transcripts, proof of current enrollment, and documentation of financial need.

Financial data The stipend is $1,000.

Duration 1 year.

Additional Information Information is also available from Janet Shapiro, Disabled Student Programs and Services, Santa Barbara City College, 721 Cliff Drive, Santa Barbara, CA 93109, (805) 965-0581, ext. 2365, E-mail: shapiro@sbcc.net.

Number awarded 1 each year.

Deadline August of each year.

[181]
WASHINGTON COUNCIL OF THE BLIND SCHOLARSHIPS

Washington Council of the Blind
P.O. Box 6996
Kennewick, WA 99336
Toll-free: (800) 255-1147   E-mail: info@wcbinfo.org
Web: www.wcbinfo.org

Summary To provide financial aid for college or graduate school to blind students in Washington.

Eligibility This program is open to blind residents of Washington state. Applicants must be attending or planning to attend a college or vocational school within the state or a contiguous community as an undergraduate or graduate student. Along with their application, they must submit 2 letters of recommendation, proof of legal blindness, and a 1- to 3-page statement of their reasons for applying for this scholarship and how it will assist them to achieve their goals. The statement should include a brief description of their background, education, work experience, economic status, strengths, weaknesses, and personal goals for the next 5 to 10 years.

Financial data The stipend is at least $2,000 per year.

Duration 1 year.

Additional Information Additional information is available from Denise Colley, Scholarship Committee Chair, 2305 Maxine Street, S.E., Lacey, WA 98503-3451, (360) 438-0072.

Number awarded 1 or more each year.

Deadline July of each year.

[182]
WILLIAM AND DOROTHY FERRELL SCHOLARSHIP AWARD

Association for Education and Rehabilitation of the Blind and Visually Impaired
1703 North Beauregard Street, Suite 440
Alexandria, VA 22311
(703) 671-4500   Fax: (703) 671-6391
E-mail: aer@aerbvi.org
Web: www.aerbvi.org

Summary To provide financial assistance to blind undergraduate and graduate students who wish to study for a career in service to blind and visually impaired people.

Eligibility Applicants for this award must be legally blind, defined as a visual acuity of 20/200 or less in the better corrected eye and/or 20 degrees or less visual field. They must be studying for a career in service to blind and visually impaired people (special education, orientation and mobility, rehabilitation training, etc.) and must submit evidence of enrollment in or acceptance to that program of study.

Financial data The stipend is $500.

Number awarded 2 every other year.

Deadline April of even-numbered years.

[183]
WILLIAM G. COREY MEMORIAL SCHOLARSHIP

American Council of the Blind
Attn: Coordinator, Scholarship Program
1155 15th Street, N.W., Suite 1004
Washington, DC 20005
(202) 467-5081   Toll-free: (800) 424-8666
Fax: (202) 467-5085   E-mail: info@acb.org
Web: www.acb.org

Summary To provide financial assistance to blind students from Pennsylvania who are enrolled in academic, vocational, technical, or professional training programs.

Eligibility All legally blind persons admitted to postsecondary educational programs (undergraduate or graduate) who are U.S. citizens and residents of Pennsylvania are eligible to apply. In addition to letters of recommendation and copies of academic transcripts, applications must include an autobiographical sketch. A cumulative GPA of 3.3 or higher is generally required. Selection is based on demonstrated academic record, involvement in extracurricular and civic activities, the autobiographical sketch, and academic objectives. The severity of the applicant's visual impairment and his/her study methods are also taken into account.

Financial data The stipend is $1,500. In addition, the winner receives a $1,000 cash scholarship from the Kurzweil Foundation and, if appropriate, a Kurzweil-1000 Reading System.

Duration 1 year.

Additional Information Scholarship winners are expected to be present at the council's annual conference; the council will cover all reasonable expenses connected with convention attendance.

Number awarded 1 each year.

Deadline February of each year.

Loans

[184]
CALIFORNIA COUNCIL OF THE BLIND LOANS

California Council of the Blind
578 B Street
Hayward, CA 94541
(510) 537-7877   Toll-free: (800) 221-6359
Fax: (510) 537-7830

Summary To provide low-interest equipment loans to

blind people in California so they can obtain special equipment and become better employed.

Eligibility Applicants must be blind residents of California who need to borrow money to purchase special job-related adaptive equipment. They must have been denied funding for the same or similar equipment by their employer or the State Department of Rehabilitation. The purchases may include Braille typewriters, talking calculators, voice-output computers, or other devices that permit a blind employee to perform tasks that formerly required sight.

Financial data The amount of the loan depends on the cost of the desired equipment, ranging from $1,000 to $9,000. Recipients pay a 1-time 5% service fee.

Duration Loans must be repaid in 1 to 3 years, depending on the size of the loan.

Number awarded Varies each year.

Deadline Applications may be submitted at any time.

[185]
NATIONAL FEDERATION OF THE BLIND LOANS FOR ASSISTIVE TECHNOLOGY

National Federation of the Blind
Attn: Committee on Assistive Technology
1800 Johnson Street
Baltimore, MD 21230
(410) 659-9314   Fax: (410) 685-5653
Web: www.nfb.org

Summary To provide financial assistance to the visually impaired who are interested in purchasing assistive technology.

Eligibility Eligible to apply are blind individuals who need assistive technology to improve their employment possibilities or to improve the quality of their daily lives. Such technology might include computers, screen reading hardware/software, electronic note-takers, Braille embossers, optical character recognition (OCR) systems, refreshable Braille devices, or speech synthesizers.

Financial data The maximum loan is generally $3,000. Interest rates may be as low as 1.6%. Borrowers normally should be able to repay at least $50 per month.

Duration Loan terms are usually 1 to 4 years.

Additional Information This program was established in 1991. Information is also available from Curtis Chong, 300 Grand Avenue, Apartment 916, Des Moines, IA 50312, (515) 277-1288.

Number awarded Varies each year.

[186]
SPECIALLY ADAPTED HOMES FOR DISABLED VETERANS

Department of Veterans Affairs
810 Vermont Avenue, N.W.
Washington, DC 20420
(202) 418-4343   Toll-free: (800) 827-1000
Web: www.va.gov

Summary To provide funding to certain disabled veterans for a home specially adapted to their needs.

Eligibility Grants (also referred to as $48,000 grants) are available to veterans who are entitled to compensation for permanent and total service-connected disability due to: 1) the loss or loss of use of both lower extremities, such as to preclude locomotion without the aid of braces, crutches, canes, or a wheelchair; or 2) blindness in both eyes, having only light perception, plus loss or loss of use of 1 lower extremity; or 3) a loss or loss of use of 1 lower extremity together with residuals of organic disease or injury or the loss or loss of use of 1 upper extremity, such as to preclude locomotion without resort to braces, canes, crutches, or a wheelchair. Grants (also referred to as $9,250 grants) are available to who are entitled to compensation for permanent and total service-connected disability due to 1) blindness in both eyes with 5/200 visual acuity or less, or 2) anatomical loss or loss of use of both hands.

Financial data The U.S. Department of Veterans Affairs (VA) may approve a grant of not more than 50% of the cost of building, buying, or remodeling homes for eligible veterans, or paying indebtedness of such homes already acquired, up to a maximum grant of $48,000. Eligible veterans with available loan guarantee entitlements may also obtain a guaranteed loan or a direct loan from the VA to supplement the grant to acquire a specially adapted home. Grants up to $9,250 are available for adaptations to a veteran's residence that are determined by the VA to be reasonably necessary. Those grants may also be used to assist veterans to acquire a residence that already has been adapted with special features for the veteran's disability.

Duration This is a 1-time grant.

Additional Information Veterans who receive a specially adapted housing grant may be eligible for Veterans Mortgage Life Insurance.

Number awarded Varies each year.

Deadline Applications are accepted at any time.

[187]
WISCONSIN COUNCIL OF THE BLIND LOANS

Wisconsin Council of the Blind
754 Williamson Street
Madison, WI 53703
(608) 255-1166   Toll-free: (800) 783-5213
Fax: (608) 255-3301   E-mail: info@wcblind.org
Web: www.wcblind.org

Summary To provide low-interest loans to blind residents of Wisconsin.

Eligibility This program is open to legally blind residents of Wisconsin who are seeking funding for any of 5 categories: business, home improvement, personal, technology, or parent/child technology. Special consideration is given to loan requests that will increase the borrower's net income.

Financial data The amount of the loan depends on the nature of the request. Since this program began, more than $8 million has been loaned.

Number awarded Varies each year.

Deadline Applications may be submitted at any time.

Grants-in-Aid

[188]
ALABAMA COUNTY HOMESTEAD EXEMPTIONS

Alabama Department of Revenue
Attn: Property Tax Division
Gordon Persons Building
50 North Ripley Street, Room 4126
P.O. Box 327210
Montgomery, AL 36132-7210
(334) 242-1525
Web: www.ador.state.al.us

Summary To exempt disabled, blind, and elderly residents of Alabama from ad valorem property taxes imposed by counties.

Eligibility Residents of Alabama are eligible to apply if they are over the age of 65 and have a net annual income of $12,000 or less for income tax purposes for the preceding year; or are retired due to permanent and total disability, regardless of age; or are blind, regardless of age or retirement status.

Financial data Qualifying residents are exempt from ad valorem property taxes levied by counties, including taxes levied for school districts, to a maximum of $5,000 in assessed value, or 160 acres in area.

Duration 1 year; this exemption will be granted as long as the resident continues to meet the eligibility requirements.

Number awarded Varies each year.

[189]
ALABAMA STATE HOMESTEAD EXEMPTIONS

Alabama Department of Revenue
Attn: Property Tax Division
Gordon Persons Building
50 North Ripley Street, Room 4126
P.O. Box 327210
Montgomery, AL 36132-7210
(334) 242-1525
Web: www.ador.state.al.us

Summary To exempt disabled, blind, and elderly residents of Alabama from ad valorem property taxes imposed by the state.

Eligibility Residents of Alabama are eligible to apply if they are 1) over the age of 65; 2) retired due to permanent and total disability, regardless of age; or 3) blind, regardless of age or retirement status.

Financial data Qualifying residents are exempt from all ad valorem property taxes levied by the state, up to 160 acres in area.

Duration 1 year; this exemption will be granted as long as the resident continues to meet the eligibility requirements.

Number awarded Varies each year.

[190]
AMERICAN COUNCIL OF THE BLIND OF OREGON GRANT-IN-AID

American Council of the Blind of Oregon
c/o Bev Rushing
4730 Auburn Road, N.E., Space 52
Salem, OR 97301
(503) 362-4151   E-mail: b.rushing@juno.com
Web: www.acboforegon.org/grants.html

Summary To provide financial assistance for college or equipment to blind residents of Oregon.

Eligibility Applicants must either be registered with the Oregon Commission for the Blind or provide proof of legal blindness. If the application is for an education grant, applicants must indicate the name of their institution. If the application is for an equipment grant, applicants must provide an indication of the costs and name of the company from which the equipment is to be purchased.

Financial data The amount of the grant depends on the nature of the application.

Duration 1 year.

Additional Information The American Council of the Blind of Oregon is legally incorporated as the Oregon Council of the Blind, Inc.

Number awarded Varies each year.

Deadline Applications may be submitted at any time; decisions are made quarterly.

[191]
ARIZONA INCOME TAX EXEMPTION FOR THE BLIND

Arizona Department of Revenue
1600 West Monroe Street
Phoenix, AZ 85007-2650
(602) 542-3572
Toll-free: (800) 352-4090 (within AZ)
Web: www.revenue.state.az.us

Summary To exempt a portion of the income of blind people from state income taxes in Arizona.
Eligibility This exemption is available to blind residents of Arizona who meet a legal definition of blindness.
Financial data Exempt from state income taxation is $1,500 of the income of blind people.
Duration The exemption continues as long as the recipient resides in Arizona.

[192]
ARKANSAS DISABLED VETERANS PROPERTY TAX EXEMPTION

Arkansas Assessment Coordination Department
1614 West Third Street
Little Rock, AR 72201-1815
(501) 324-9240   Fax: (501) 324-9242
E-mail: dasbury@acd.state.ar.us
Web: www.accessarkansas.org/acd

Summary To exempt from taxation the property owned by veterans with disabilities, surviving spouses, and minor dependent children in Arkansas.
Eligibility To qualify, the disabled veteran must have been awarded a special monthly compensation from the Department of Veterans Affairs for the loss of, or the loss of use of 1 or more limbs, or total blindness in 1 or both eyes, or a 100% total and permanent service-connected disability. This exemption also extends to the veteran's unremarried surviving spouse and the veteran's minor children.
Financial data Qualifying veterans (or their unremarried widows or dependent children) are exempt from payment of all state taxes on their homestead and personal property.
Duration This exemption continues as long as the qualifying veteran (or dependent) resides in Arkansas.
Number awarded Varies each year.
Deadline Applications may be submitted at any time.

[193]
ASSOCIATION OF BLIND CITIZENS ASSISTIVE TECHNOLOGY FUND

Association of Blind Citizens
P.O. Box 246
Holbrook, MA 02343
(781) 961-1023   Fax: (781) 961-0004
E-mail: atf@assocofblindcitizens.org
Web: www.assocofblindcitizens.org

Summary To provide funding to blind people interested in purchasing adaptive devices or software.
Eligibility This program is open to legally blind residents of the United States. Applicants must be interested in purchasing a technology product that will improve their employment opportunities, increase their level of independence, and enhance their overall quality of life. They must have a family income of less than $50,000 per year and cash assets of less than $20,000. The products covered by this program must retail for at least $200 but no more than $6,000. The request form must include a 500-word description of the device and how it will help the applicant achieve employment or increase their independence.
Financial data Grants cover 50% of the retail price of adaptive devices or software.
Duration These are 1-time grants.
Number awarded Varies each year.
Deadline June, September, or December of each year.

[194]
AUTOMOBILE ASSISTANCE FOR DISABLED VETERANS

Department of Veterans Affairs
810 Vermont Avenue, N.W.
Washington, DC 20420
(202) 418-4343   Toll-free: (800) 827-1000
Web: www.va.gov

Summary To supply funding for certain disabled veterans and current service personnel who require specially adapted automobiles.
Eligibility To be eligible for a grant for an automobile, a veteran or current service member must have a service-connected loss or permanent loss of use of 1 or both hands or feet or permanent impairment of vision of both eyes to a prescribed degree. For adaptive equipment eligibility only, veterans entitled to compensation for ankylosis of 1 or both knees, or 1 or both hips, also qualify.
Financial data The grant consists of a payment by the Department of Veterans Affairs (VA) of up to $9,000 toward the purchase of an automobile or other conveyance. The VA will also pay for the adaptive equipment, its repair, and the replacement or reinstallation required for the safe operation of the vehicle purchased with VA

assistance or for a previously or subsequently acquired vehicle.
Duration This is a 1-time grant.
Number awarded Varies each year.
Deadline Applications may be submitted at any time.

[195]
AZ AER CONSUMER GRANT

Association for the Education and Rehabilitation of the Blind and Visually Impaired-Arizona Chapter
c/o Sandra Stienweis
2213 North 28th Place
Phoenix, AZ 85008
Web: www.ed.arizona.edu/azaer

Summary To provide funding to members of the Arizona Chapter of the Association for the Education and Rehabilitation of the Blind and Visually Impaired (AZ AER) who need assistance in pursuing an activity.
Eligibility This program is open to chapter members who need assistance for such activities as attendance at a workshop or conference, a class, or a trip. Applicants must submit a complete outline of the proposed use of the funds and the benefit to them.
Financial data Grants up to $500 are available.
Number awarded 1 or more each year.

[196]
CALIFORNIA DISABLED VETERAN EXEMPTION FROM THE IN LIEU TAX FEE FOR A MANUFACTURED HOME OR MOBILEHOME

Department of Housing and Community Development
Attn: Registration and Titling
1800 Third Street
P.O. Box 2111
Sacramento, CA 95812-2111
(916) 323-9224   Toll-free: (800) 952-8356
Web: www.hcd.ca.gov

Summary To provide a special property tax exemption to disabled California veterans and/or their spouses who own and occupy a mobile home.
Eligibility This program is open to disabled veterans and/or their spouses in California who have a manufactured home or mobilehome as their principal place of residence. Veterans must be disabled as a result of injury or disease incurred in military service and have been a resident of California 1) at the time of entry into the service and be blind, or have lost the use of 1 or more limbs, or be totally disabled; 2) on November 7, 1972 and be blind in both eyes, or have lost the use of 2 or more limbs; or 3) on January 1, 1975 and be totally disabled. The spouses and unmarried surviving spouses of those disabled veterans are also eligible.

Financial data The exemption applies to the first $20,000 of the assessed market value of the manufactured home or mobilehome. Veterans and/or spouses whose income falls below a specified level are entitled to an additional $10,000 exemption. The amount of the exemption is 100% if the home is owned by a veteran only, a veteran and spouse, or a spouse only; 50% if owned by a veteran and another person other than a spouse or by a spouse and another person other than the veteran; 67% if owned by a veteran, the spouse, and another person; 34% if owned by a veteran and 2 other people other than a spouse or by a spouse and 2 other people; 50% if owned by a veteran, the spouse, and 2 other people; or 25% if owned by a veteran and 3 other people or by a spouse and 3 other people.
Duration The exemption is available annually as long as the applicant meets all requirements.
Number awarded Varies each year.

[197]
CALIFORNIA PROPERTY TAX POSTPONEMENT FOR SENIOR CITIZENS, BLIND, OR DISABLED CITIZENS

State Controller's Office
Attn: Property Tax Postponement Program
P.O. Box 942850
Sacramento, CA 94250-5880
(916) 327-5587   Toll-free: (800) 952-5661
TDD: (916) 323-3504
E-mail: postponement@sco.ca.gov
Web: www.sco.ca.gov

Summary To allow blind, disabled, and elderly California residents to postpone their property taxes.
Eligibility Applicants for this program (and all other recorded owners except spouses and direct-line relatives) must be blind, disabled, or 62 years of age or older as of December 31 of the first year of application; must have owned and occupied as their principal place of residence on December 31 of that year the property for which property taxes are to be postponed; must have a total household income of $24,000 or less ($34,000 for those who filed and qualified for tax postponement in 1983); must have at least a combined 20% equity interest in the home at the time a postponement lien is filed; and must receive a secured property tax bill.
Financial data Qualified homeowners may postpone payment of part or all of the property taxes on their home by having the state pay their property taxes for them. Since the state is in effect lending the money to the homeowner, it obtains a Property Tax Postponement Lien on the home and charges simple interest. Interest rates are set in July of each year, and that rate applies to that particular year's postponed taxes; currently, the rate is 3%. A total of $8 million in property tax is postponed each year.
Duration 1 year; may be renewed upon reapplication each year. The lien and interest are not due until the

homeowner moves from the qualified property, sells or otherwise conveys title to the home, dies and does not have a spouse or other qualified individual who continues to reside in the home, or allows future property taxes or other senior liens to become delinquent.

Number awarded Varies each year; currently, more than 14,000 California residents participate in the program.

Deadline The filing period is from July through December of each year.

[198]
CONNECTICUT TAX RELIEF PROGRAM FOR BLIND PEOPLE

Office of Policy and Management
Attn: Intergovernmental Policy Division
450 Capitol Avenue
Hartford, CT 06106-1308
(860) 418-6322
Toll-free: (800) 286-2214 (within CT)
Fax: (860) 418-6493   TDD: (860) 418-6456
E-mail: ronald.madrid@po.state.ct.us
Web: www.opm.state.ct.us/igp/grants/dtotdis.htm

Summary To exempt blind residents of Connecticut from a portion of their personal property taxes.

Eligibility Eligible to apply for this exemption are Connecticut residents who are blind. An additional exemption may be available to blind residents whose total adjusted gross income is less than $24,500 if unmarried or $30,000 if married.

Financial data The basic state exemption is $3,000 of assessed valuation. Municipalities may elect to provide an additional exemption of $3,000 to blind residents whose income is less than the qualifying level.

Duration 1 year; exemptions continue as long as the eligible resident lives in Connecticut.

Number awarded Varies each year.

Deadline Applications for the additional municipality exemption must be submitted to the assessor's office of the town or residence by September of every other year.

[199]
DELAWARE INCOME TAX DEDUCTION FOR BLIND AND ELDERLY PERSONS

Division of Revenue
Carvel State Office Building
820 North French Street
P.O. Box 8763
Wilmington, DE 19899-8763
(302) 577-3300
Web: www.state.de.us/revenue

Summary To provide a deduction from state income taxation to blind people and those over the age of 65 in Delaware.

Eligibility This deduction is available to residents of Delaware who are 1) 65 years of age or older or 2) blind.

Financial data Taxpayers are entitled to an additional standard deduction of $2,500 if they are blind or older than 65. For blind people older than 65, the additional standard deduction is $5,000.

Duration The deduction continues as long as the recipient remains a resident of Delaware for state income tax purposes.

Number awarded Varies each year.

[200]
FEDERAL INCOME TAX DEDUCTION FOR THE BLIND AND ELDERLY

Internal Revenue Service
c/o Western Area Distribution Center
Rancho Cordova, CA 95743-0001
Toll-free: (800) TAX-FORM   Fax: (703) 368-9694
Web: www.irs.gov

Summary To exempt a portion of the income of blind and elderly citizens from federal income tax liability.

Eligibility Eligible for these deduction are tax filers who are legally blind and/or over the age of 65, or whose spouses are legally blind and/or over the age of 65. The deductions are in addition to the standard deductions for taxpayers who do not itemize their deductions. Taxpayers who itemize deductions do not qualify for these additional deductions.

Financial data Each deduction is $1,150 for taxpayers filing as single or head of household; for married taxpayers (whether filing jointly or separately) and qualifying widow(er)s, each deduction is $900; 1 deduction is allowed for each individual who is either blind and/or over the age of 65.

Duration 1 year; must reapply each year.

Additional Information The address above is for taxpayers in the western states; for taxpayers in the central states, the address is c/o Central Area Distribution Center, P.O. Box 8903, Bloomington, IL 61702-8903; for taxpayers in the eastern states, the address if c/o Eastern Area Distribution Center, P.O. Box 85074, Richmond, VA 23261-5074.

Number awarded Varies each year.

Deadline This deduction is taken on the qualifying tax filers' federal income tax return, which is due in April of each year.

VISUAL DISABILITIES: GRANTS-IN-AID

[201]
FLORIDA HOMESTEAD EXEMPTION FOR DISABLED VETERANS

Florida Department of Veterans' Affairs
Mary Grizzle Building, Room 311-K
11351 Ulmerton Road
Largo, FL 33778-1630
(727) 518-3202   Fax: (727) 518-3217
E-mail: cohenm@vba.va.gov
Web: www.floridavets.org/benefits/hmsted.html

Summary To exempt the real estate owned by disabled veterans and their surviving spouses in Florida from taxation.

Eligibility An exemption is available to the following classes of Florida residents: 1) honorably discharged veterans who have a service-connected permanent and total disability; 2) the spouses or surviving spouses of such veterans; 3) veterans who are paraplegic, are hemiplegic, are permanently and totally disabled, must use a wheelchair for mobility, or are legally blind and have a gross annual household income less than the adjusted maximum; and 4) veterans with service connected disabilities of 10% or more. Applicants must reside in the property for which they are applying for an exemption.

Financial data Veterans who are permanently and totally disabled, their surviving unremarried spouses, and veterans with specified disabilities and income less than the qualifying limit are entitled to exemption of all real estate taxes on property they use and own as a homestead. Veterans with disabilities of at least 10% are entitled to a $5,000 property tax exemption.

Duration The exemption is available as long as the veteran or surviving spouse resides in Florida.

Number awarded Varies each year.

[202]
FREEDOM SCIENTIFIC TECHNOLOGY SCHOLARSHIP AWARD PROGRAM

Freedom Scientific Inc.
Attn: Low Vision Group
11800 31st Court North
St. Petersburg, FL 33716
(727) 803-8000, ext. 1044
Toll-free: (800) 444-4443   Fax: (727) 803-8001
E-mail: EricV@freedomscientific.com
Web: www.FreedomScientific.com

Summary To provide financial assistance to blind undergraduate and graduate students in the form of vouchers for the purchase of assistive technology devices.

Eligibility This program is open to legally blind students who are either 1) graduating high school seniors planning to pursue a full-time course of study at a college or university, or 2) college seniors planning to enter graduate school. Applicants must be residents of the United States or Canada. The program is administered through 6 partner organizations: 4 for high school seniors in the United States, 1 for high school seniors in Canada, and 1 for graduate students in the United States and Canada. Selection is based on general guidelines of academic achievement and promise, extracurricular or community service leadership and accomplishments, and demonstrated personal qualities and character. The partner organizations may supplement those general guidelines with their own specific criteria and may also select especially deserving students across all levels of higher education. Students may apply to the partner organization of their choice or, if they have no preference, to the organization assigned for the geographic region in which they live.

Financial data The awards consist of vouchers for $2,500 to be used to purchase Freedom Scientific hardware, software, accessories, training, and/or tutorials.

Duration These are 1-time awards.

Additional Information This program, which began in the 2001-02 school year, is sponsored by Freedom Scientific, maker of technology-based products for people who are blind or vision-impaired. The partner organizations include the National Federation of the Blind, 1800 Johnson Street, Baltimore, MD 21230, (410) 659-9314, Web site: www.nfb.org, which also serves as the regional organization for Connecticut, Delaware, Maine, Maryland, Massachusetts, New Hampshire, New Jersey, New York, Pennsylvania, Puerto Rico, Rhode Island, Vermont, Virginia, Washington, D.C., and West Virginia; the American Foundation for the Blind, Attn: Scholarship Committee, 11 Penn Plaza, Suite 300, New York, NY 10001, (212) 502-7661, (800) AFB-LINE, Fax: (212) 502-7771, TDD: (212) 502-7662, E-mail: afbinfo@afb.net, Web site: www.afb.org/scholarships.asp, which also serves as the regional organization for Alabama, Arkansas, Florida, Georgia, Louisiana, Mississippi, North Carolina, South Carolina, Tennessee, and Texas; the American Council of the Blind, 1155 15th Street, N.W., Suite 1004, Washington, DC 20005, (202) 467-5081, (800) 424-8666, Fax: (202) 467-5085, E-mail: info@acb.org, Web site: www.acb.org, which also serves as the regional organization for Illinois, Indiana, Iowa, Kansas, Kentucky, Michigan, Minnesota, Missouri, Nebraska, Ohio, Oklahoma, and Wisconsin; the Braille Institute of America, 741 North Vermont Avenue, Los Angeles, CA 90029-3594, (323) 663-1111, (800) BRAILLE, Fax: (323) 663-0867, E-mail: info@brailleinstitute.org, Web site: www.brailleinstitute.org, which also serves as the regional organization for Alaska, Arizona, California, Colorado, Hawaii, Idaho, Montana, Nevada, New Mexico, North Dakota, Oregon, South Dakota, Utah, Washington, and Wyoming; the Canadian National Institute for the Blind, 1929 Bayview Avenue, Toronto, Ontario M4G 3E8, (416) 486-2500, Web site: www.cnib.ca, which accepts all applications from high school seniors in Canada; and Recording for the Blind and Dyslexic 20 Roszel Road, Princeton, NJ 08540, (609) 452-0606, (800) 221-4792, Web site: www.rfbd.org, which accepts all applications for graduate study in the United States and Canada.

[203]
GEORGIA INCOME TAX DEDUCTION FOR THE BLIND

Georgia Department of Revenue
Attn: Income Tax Division
1800 Century Center Boulevard, N.E.
Atlanta, GA 30345-3205
(404) 417-4477   Toll-free: (877) 602-8477
E-mail: inctax@rev.state.ga.us
Web: www2.state.ga.us

Summary To provide a deduction from state income taxation to blind people in Georgia.

Eligibility Eligible are persons classified as residents of Georgia for the purpose of state income taxation who are blind.

Financial data Qualified blind residents are entitled to a deduction of $1,300 from their state income taxation.

Duration The deduction continues as long as the recipient resides in Georgia.

[204]
HAWAII INCOME TAX EXEMPTION FOR DISABLED RESIDENTS

Department of Taxation
Attn: Taxpayer Services Branch
425 Queen Street
P.O. Box 259
Honolulu, HI 96809-0259
(808) 587-4242   Toll-free: (800) 222-3229
Fax: (808) 587-1488   TDD: (808) 587-1418
Web: www.hawaii.gov/tax/tax.html

Summary To exempt a portion of the income of disabled residents from state income tax in Hawaii.

Eligibility Eligible for this exemption are 1) blind residents whose central visual acuity does not exceed 20/200 in the better eye with corrective lenses or whose visual acuity is greater than 20/200 but is accompanied by a limitation in the field of vision such that the widest diameter of the visual field subtends an angle no greater than 20 degrees; 2) deaf residents whose average loss in the speech frequencies in the better ear is 82 decibels A.S.A. or worse; or 3) totally disabled residents (physically or mentally) who are unable to engage in any substantial gainful business or occupation (a person whose gross income exceeds $30,000 per year is assumed to be engaged in a substantial gainful business or occupation).

Financial data The maximum exemptions from state income tax are as follows: single disabled resident, $7,000; disabled husband and wife, $14,000; disabled husband or wife, with non-disabled spouse under 65, $8,040; disabled husband or wife, with non-disabled spouse age 65 or over, $9,080.

Duration The exemption continues as long as the recipient resides in Hawaii.

Additional Information Residents who claim this special exemption are not eligible to claim additional exemptions for their children or other dependents.

[205]
IDAHO CIRCUIT BREAKER PROPERTY TAX REDUCTION

Idaho State Tax Commission
Attn: Public Information Office
800 Park Boulevard, Plaza IV
P.O. Box 36
Boise, ID 83722-0410
(208) 334-7736   Toll-free: (800) 972-7660
TDD: (800) 377-3529
Web: www.state.id.us/tax/home.html

Summary To reduce a portion of the property tax of disabled and other veterans and other disabled or elderly residents of Idaho.

Eligibility Eligible for this property tax reduction are residents of Idaho who own and live in a primary residence in the state and have an annual income of $21,290 or less (after deducting designated forms of income, including compensation received by a veteran from the U.S. Department of Veterans Affairs for a 40% to 100% service-connected disability). Applicants must be in 1 or more of the following categories: disabled (as recognized by an appropriate federal agency), blind, former prisoner of war or hostage, veteran with at least 10% service-connected disability or receiving VA pension for a nonservice-connected disability, 65 years of age or older, widow(er) of any age, or fatherless or motherless child under 18 years of age.

Financial data The maximum amount of reduction is the lesser of $1,200 or the actual taxes on the recipient's qualifying home. The minimum reduction is the lesser of $100 or the actual taxes on the home.

Duration Applications for this reduction must be submitted each year.

Additional Information All recipients of this reduction automatically receive Idaho's Homeowner's Exemption, which reduces the taxable value of the home (excluding land) by 50% or $50,000, whichever is less. Solid waste, irrigation, or other fees charged by some counties are not taxes and cannot be reduced by this program.

Number awarded Varies each year.

Deadline April of each year.

(From previous entry:)

Number awarded 20 each year: 4 from each of the U.S. regional organizations, 2 to Canadian students, and 2 to graduate students.

Deadline Each partner organization sets its own deadline, but most are by March of each year.

[206]
IDAHO INCOME TAX DEDUCTION FOR THE BLIND AND THEIR WIDOW(ER)S

Idaho State Tax Commission
Attn: Public Information Office
800 Park Boulevard, Plaza IV
P.O. Box 36
Boise, ID 83722-0410
(208) 334-7660   Toll-free: (800) 972-7660
TDD: (800) 377-3529
Web: www.state.id.us/tax/home.html

Summary To exempt a portion of the income of blind or elderly residents from state income tax in Idaho.

Eligibility Eligible for this deduction are blind residents of Idaho and residents over the age of 65.

Financial data Single individuals and heads of households who are blind or elderly receive an additional $1,150 standard deduction; married individuals who are blind or elderly receive an additional $900 standard deduction.

Duration 1 year; must reapply each year.

Number awarded Varies each year.

Deadline April of each year.

[207]
ILLINOIS GRANTS FOR SPECIALLY ADAPTED HOUSING

Illinois Department of Veterans' Affairs
833 South Spring Street
P.O. Box 19432
Springfield, IL 62794-9432
(217) 782-6641
Toll-free: (800) 437-9824 (within IL)
Fax: (217) 782-4161   TDD: (217) 524-4645
E-mail: webmail@dva.state.il.us
Web: www.state.il.us/agency/dva

Summary To provide financial assistance to service-connected disabled veterans who need to purchase or adapt a suitable primary residence in Illinois.

Eligibility Eligible Illinois veterans must have total and permanent service-connected disabilities caused by 1) the loss, or loss of use, of both lower extremities, such as to preclude locomotion without the aid of braces, crutches, canes, or a wheelchair; or 2) disability that includes blindness in both eyes, having only light perception, plus loss or loss of use of 1 lower extremity; or 3) a loss or loss of use of 1 lower extremity together with residuals of organic disease or injury, or the loss or loss of use of 1 upper extremity that so affects the functions of balance or propulsion as to preclude locomotion without resort to braces, canes, crutches, or a wheelchair. Veterans may also qualify if they have a service-connected disability that is not totally disabling but involves visual impairment or loss, or loss of use, of both hands.

Financial data Totally and permanently disabled veterans who qualify for a grant of $35,500 from the U.S. Department of Veterans Affairs (VA) for the construction of specially adapted housing also qualify for a grant of $12,000 from the state of Illinois. Illinois veterans who are not totally disabled but otherwise qualify for a grant of $6,000 from the VA for remodeling specially adapted housing also qualify for a grant of $2,000 from the state of Illinois.

Duration This is a 1-time grant.

Number awarded Varies each year.

Deadline Applications for grants may be submitted at any time.

[208]
ILLINOIS INCOME TAX EXEMPTION FOR THE BLIND

Illinois Department of Revenue
101 West Jefferson Street
P.O. Box 19044
Springfield, IL 62794-9044
(217) 782-9337   Toll-free: (800) 732-8866
Web: www.revenue.state.il.us

Summary To provide an income tax deduction to blind people in Illinois.

Eligibility Legally blind residents of Illinois are entitled to take this deduction from their state income tax.

Financial data The deduction is $1,000.

Duration The deduction continues as long as the recipient resides in Illinois.

[209]
INDIANA INCOME TAX EXEMPTION FOR THE BLIND

Indiana Department of Revenue
Attn: Taxpayer Services Division
Indiana Government Center North
100 North Senate Avenue
Indianapolis, IN 46204-2253
(317) 232-2240   TDD: (317) 232-4952
E-mail: pfrequest@dor.state.in.us
Web: www.state.in.us/dor

Summary To exempt a portion of the income of blind people from state taxation in Indiana.

Eligibility Eligible are residents of Indiana who are legally blind.

Financial data An additional exemption of $1,000 from the income for state income taxation in Indiana is allowed.

Duration The exemption continues as long as the recipient resides in Indiana.

[210]
INDIANA PROPERTY TAX DEDUCTION FOR BLIND OR DISABLED PERSONS

Department of Local Government Finance
Indiana Government Center North, Room 1058
100 North Senate Avenue
Indianapolis, IN 46201
(317) 232-3777   Fax: (317) 232-8779
E-mail: taxboard@tcb.state.in.us
Web: www.in.gov/dlgf

Summary To exempt Indiana residents who are blind or disabled from a portion of their property tax.

Eligibility Eligible for this program are Indiana residents who are blind or disabled and receive less than $17,000 in annual taxable income. A blind person is defined as an individual who has vision in the better eye with correcting glasses of 20/200 or less, or a disqualifying visual field defect as determined upon examination by a designated ophthalmologist or optometrist. A disabled person is defined as an individual unable to engage in any substantial gainful activity by reason of a medically determinable physical or mental impairment that can be expected to result in death or has lasted and can be expected to last for at least 12 continuous months.

Financial data The property tax deduction is $6,000.

Duration This deduction may be taken annually, as long as the Indiana resident meets the requirements of the program.

Additional Information Property taxes are administered by individual counties in Indiana. For further information, contact your county tax assessor.

Number awarded Varies each year.

Deadline Applications must be filed during the 12 months before May of each year for which the individual wishes to obtain the deduction.

[211]
KANSAS HOMESTEAD TAX REFUND

Kansas Department of Revenue
Attn: Taxpayer Assistance Center
Robert B. Docking State Office Building
915 S.W. Harrison Street
Topeka, KS 66612-1712
(785) 368-8222   Toll-free: (877) 526-7738
Fax: (785) 291-3614   TTY: (785) 296-6461
Web: www.ksrevenue.org

Summary To provide a property tax refund to disabled and other residents of Kansas.

Eligibility To be eligible, residents of Kansas must meet 1 of the following requirements: 1) have been permanently and totally disabled or blind during all of the taxable year; 2) be 55 years of age or older on the first of the year; or 3) have had 1 or more dependent children under the age of 18 living with them the entire year. Total household income may not have exceeded $25,000 and the applicant must have owned, or rented, and occupied the homestead, or lived in a nursing home upon which general property taxes were assessed; the applicant must not owe any delinquent taxes on the homestead and the property tax or rent paid must not have been paid from public funds.

Financial data The size of the refund depends on the applicant's total household income and either the amount paid as property tax by homeowners or 20% of rent paid for occupancy by renters; the maximum refund is $600.

Duration The refund is payable annually as long as the disabled or other applicant resides in Kansas.

Number awarded Varies each year.

Deadline Claims must be filed by April of each year.

[212]
KANSAS INTANGIBLES TAX SENIOR CITIZEN OR DISABILITY EXEMPTION

Kansas Department of Revenue
Attn: Taxpayer Assistance Center
Robert B. Docking State Office Building
915 S.W. Harrison Street
Topeka, KS 66612-1712
(785) 368-8222   Toll-free: (877) 526-7738
Fax: (785) 291-3614   TTY: (785) 296-6461
Web: www.ksrevenue.org

Summary To exempt a portion of the income received by senior citizens and disabled residents in Kansas from the intangibles tax.

Eligibility This exemption applies to residents of local areas in Kansas that levy an intangibles tax on gross earnings received from such property as savings accounts, stocks, bonds, accounts receivable, and mortgages. Applicants must 1) be disabled, blind, or 60 years of age or older and 2) have a household income of $20,000 or less.

Financial data Qualified residents are entitled to exempt from their intangibles income an amount that depends on their income. If total household income is $15,000 or less, the exemption is $5,000. For incomes between $15,000 and $20,000, the exemption is calculated as the difference between $5,000 and the amount of the income over $15,000.

Duration This benefit continues as long as the recipient remains a resident of the Kansas locality that imposes an intangibles tax.

Number awarded Varies each year.

VISUAL DISABILITIES: GRANTS-IN-AID

[213]
KANSAS STATE DEAF-BLIND FUND

Kansas State Department of Education
Student Support Services
Attn: Kansas Project for Children and Young Adults Who Are Deaf-Blind
120 Southeast 10th Avenue
Topeka, KS 66612-1182
(785) 296-0917   Toll-free: (800) 203-9462
Fax: (785) 296-4944

Summary To provide supplementary financial assistance to deaf-blind or severely disabled students in Kansas.

Eligibility Applications may be submitted by school personnel for students in Kansas (up to the age of 21) who are deaf-blind and/or have severe multiple disabilities. Approval for funding is granted on a first-come, first-served basis, when the costs for educational technology, equipment, consultation, or evaluation exceed the amount local education agencies are able to provide out of federal, state, or local funds. Priority candidates are deaf-blind children from birth through 2 years of age, students who are exiting state hospital schools and returning to their home district, students who have a suspected vision loss and documented hearing loss and are in need of an evaluation, and students who have a suspected hearing loss and documented vision loss who are in need of an evaluation.

Financial data Eligible students are awarded up to $3,000 per year. Funds must be used for educational technology, equipment, consultation, or evaluation.

Duration 1 year; may be renewed.

Number awarded Varies each year.

Deadline January of each year.

[214]
LIONS CLUBS SUPPORT SERVICES FOR THE BLIND AND VISUALLY IMPAIRED

Lions Clubs International
Attn: Program Development Department
300 22nd Street
Oak Brook, IL 60523-8842
(630) 571-5466, ext. 316   Fax: (630) 571-1692
E-mail: executiveservices@lionsclubs.org
Web: www.lionsclubs.org

Summary To provide college scholarships and other assistance to blind people.

Eligibility These programs are open to blind people and others involved in service to the blind. Applicants may be seeking support for the following activities: scholarships for the blind and visually impaired, medical research, assistive technology grants, independent mobility, transportation, reading materials and aids, audio products, Braille products, and other aids.

Financial data The amount of this assistance varies.

Additional Information Support is provided by local clubs of Lions Clubs International. Requests send to the international office are referred to the appropriate district governor. If any of the clubs within the district conduct programs for which the applicant might be considered, the governor will advise the particular club to contact the applicant. No funds are available from the office of Lions Clubs International.

[215]
MAINE INCOME TAX DEDUCTION FOR THE BLIND

Maine Revenue Services
Attn: Income/Estate Tax Division
24 State House Station
Augusta, ME 04333-0024
(207) 626-8475   Fax: (207) 626-9694
E-mail: Income.tax@maine.gove
Web: www.maine.gov

Summary To deduct of portion of the income of blind Maine residents from income taxation.

Eligibility Eligible for this deduction are inhabitants of Maine who are legally blind as determined by the Department of Human Services.

Financial data The deduction is $900.

Duration Eligible blind residents qualify for this exemption as long as they reside in Maine.

Number awarded Varies each year.

Deadline The deduction is included along with the state income tax forms, filed in April of each year.

[216]
MAINE PROPERTY TAX EXEMPTION FOR THE BLIND

Maine Revenue Services
Attn: Property Tax Division
P.O. Box 9106
Augusta, ME 04332-9106
(207) 287-2011   Fax: (207) 287-6396
E-mail: prop.tax@maine.gov
Web: www.maine.gov

Summary To exempt the estates of blind Maine residents from property taxation.

Eligibility Eligible for this program are inhabitants of Maine who are legally blind as determined by the Department of Human Services.

Financial data The exemption is equal to $4,000 times the certified ratio.

Duration Eligible blind residents qualify for this exemption as long as they own residential property in Maine.

Number awarded Varies each year.

Deadline When an eligible person first submits an application, the proof of entitlement must reach the assessors of the local municipality prior to the end of

March. Once eligibility has been established, notification need not be repeated in subsequent years.

[217]
MARYLAND INCOME TAX EXEMPTION FOR BLIND AND ELDERLY RESIDENTS

Comptroller of Maryland
Attn: Revenue Administration Division
80 Calvert Street
Annapolis, MD 21411
(410) 260-7980
Toll-free: (800) MD-TAXES (within MD)
Fax: (410) 974-3456   TDD: (410) 260-7157
E-mail: taxhelp@comp.state.md.us
Web: individuals.marylandtaxes.com

Summary To provide a supplemental income tax exemption to blind and senior residents of Maryland.

Eligibility Eligible are Maryland residents who are either blind or 65 years of age or older.

Financial data Eligible Maryland residents are entitled to an additional exemption of $1,000 (in addition to the regular $2,400 personal exemption) from their income for state income tax purposes.

Duration The exemption continues as long as the recipient resides in Maryland.

[218]
MARYLAND INCOME TAX EXEMPTION FOR READERS FOR BLIND RESIDENTS

Comptroller of Maryland
Attn: Revenue Administration Division
80 Calvert Street
Annapolis, MD 21411
(410) 260-7980
Toll-free: (800) MD-TAXES (within MD)
Fax: (410) 974-3456   TDD: (410) 260-7157
E-mail: taxhelp@comp.state.md.us
Web: individuals.marylandtaxes.com

Summary To exempt from state income taxation in Maryland a portion of the expenses incurred by blind people for a reader.

Eligibility Eligible are Maryland residents who 1) are blind and who pay for the use of a reader, and 2) are employers and pay for a reader for a blind employee.

Financial data Blind people may exclude up to $5,000 of expenses incurred for a reader from state income taxation. Employers may exclude up to $1,000 of expenses incurred for a reader for a blind employee.

Duration The exclusion continues as long as the recipient resides in Maryland and utilizes the services of a reader.

[219]
MARYLAND REAL PROPERTY TAX EXEMPTION FOR BLIND PERSONS

State Department of Assessments and Taxation
Attn: Tax Credit Program
301 West Preston Street, Room 900
Baltimore, MD 21201-2395
(410) 767-1184
Toll-free: (888) 246-5941 (within MD)
TTY: (800) 735-2258
E-mail: taxcredits@dat.state.md.us
Web: www.dat.state.md.us

Summary To exempt the homes of blind people and their surviving spouses from a portion of property taxation in Maryland.

Eligibility This program is open to Maryland residents who are legally blind. Also eligible are their surviving spouses.

Financial data The first $6,000 of assessment on the dwelling houses owned by qualifying blind people is exempt from real property taxes in Maryland.

Duration This exemption continues as long as the qualifying blind person resides in Maryland and owns his or her home.

[220]
MASSACHUSETTS INCOME TAX EXEMPTION FOR BLIND PEOPLE

Massachusetts Department of Revenue
Attn: Customer Service Bureau
200 Arlington Street
Chelsea, MA 02150-2375
(617) 887-MDOR
Toll-free: (800) 392-6089 (within MA)
Fax: (617) 887-1900
Web: www.dor.state.ma.us

Summary To exempt a portion of the income received by blind people from state income taxation in Massachusetts.

Eligibility Eligible for this exemption are residents of Massachusetts who are classified as legally blind.

Financial data Blind persons in Massachusetts are entitled to exempt $2,200 from their income for purposes of state income taxation.

Duration The benefit continues as long as the recipient remains a resident of Massachusetts for state income tax purposes.

Number awarded Varies each year.

[221]
MASSACHUSETTS PROPERTY TAX EXEMPTION

Department of Veterans' Services
239 Causeway Street, Suite 100
Boston, MA 02114
(617) 727-3578 Toll-free: (888) 844-2383
Fax: (617) 727-5903
E-mail: mdvs@vet.state.ma.us
Web: www.state.ma.us/veterans

Summary To provide a property tax exemption to disabled and other veterans (and their families) in Massachusetts.

Eligibility This program is open to veterans who are residents of Massachusetts, were residents for at least 6 months prior to entering the service, have been residents for at least 5 consecutive years, and are occupying property as their domicile. The program is open to several categories of qualified veterans and their families: 1) veterans who have a disability rating of 10% or more as a result of wartime service; veterans who served in the Spanish war, the Philippine insurrection, or the Chinese Relief Expedition; veterans who have been awarded the Purple Heart; unremarried surviving spouses of veterans who served in the armed forces between April 6, 1917 and November 11, 1918 and whose estate is worth less than $20,000; and mothers and fathers of military personnel who lost their lives in wartime service; 2) veterans who have a loss or permanent loss of use of 1 foot at or above the ankle; have a loss or permanent loss of use of 1 hand at or above the wrist; have a loss or permanent loss of sight of 1 eye; or have been awarded the Medal of Honor, the Distinguished Service Cross, the Navy Cross, or the Air Force Cross; 3) veterans who have a loss or permanent loss of use of both feet at or above the ankle, a loss or permanent loss of use of both hands at or above the wrist, a loss or permanent loss of use of 1 foot at or above the ankle and 1 hand at or above the wrist, or a loss or permanent loss of use of both eyes; 4) veterans who have a permanent and total disability as a result of a service-connected injury and have received assistance from the U.S. Department of Veterans Affairs in acquiring "special adapted housing;" 5) unremarried surviving spouses of veterans who died in combat as members of the armed forces in military action at the islands of Quemoy and Matsu in the Pacific; 6) veterans who have a disability rating of 100% as a result of injury in wartime service and in the line of duty and who are incapable of working; and 7) paraplegic veterans with service-related injuries. Surviving spouses (including those who have remarried) of all veterans in the second, third, fourth, sixth, and seventh categories are also eligible for these exemptions.

Financial data The annual exemption is $250 or $2,000 of assessed taxable value of property for the first and fifth categories; $425 or $4,000 of assessed taxable value of property for the second category; $775 or $8,000 of assessed taxable value of property for the third category; $950 or $10,000 of assessed taxable value of property for the fourth category; or $600 or $6,000 of assessed taxable value of property for the sixth category. Veterans and spouses in the seventh category are exempt from all property taxes on their domiciles.

Duration The exemptions are provided each year that the veteran or unremarried surviving spouse lives in Massachusetts and owns the property as a domicile.

Additional Information Applications are available from local assessor's offices.

Number awarded Varies each year.

[222]
MICHIGAN HOMESTEAD PROPERTY TAX CREDIT FOR VETERANS AND BLIND PEOPLE

Michigan Department of Treasury
Attn: Homestead Exemption
Treasury Building
430 West Allegan Street
Lansing, MI 48922
(517) 373-3200 Toll-free: (800) 487-7000
TTY: (517) 636-4999
E-mail: treasPtd2@michigan.gov
Web: www.michigan.gov/treasury

Summary To provide a property tax credit to veterans, military personnel, their spouses, blind people, and their surviving spouses in Michigan.

Eligibility Eligible to apply are residents of Michigan who are 1) blind and own their homestead; 2) a veteran with a service-connected disability or his/her surviving spouse; 3) a surviving spouse of a veteran deceased in service; 4) a veteran of wars before World War I, a pensioned veteran, a surviving spouse of those veterans, or an active military member whose household income is less than $7,500; or 5) a surviving spouse of a non-disabled or non-pensioned veteran of the Korean War, World War II, and World War I whose household income is less than $7,500. All applicants must own or rent a home in Michigan, have been a Michigan resident for at least 6 months during the year in which application is made, and fall within qualifying income levels (up to $82,650 in household income).

Financial data The maximum credit is $1,200. The exact amount varies. For homeowners, the credit depends on the state equalized value of the homestead and on an allowance for filing category. For renters, 20% of the rent is considered property tax eligible for credit.

Duration 1 year; eligibility must be established each year.

Number awarded Varies each year.

Deadline December of each year.

[223]
MICHIGAN INCOME TAX EXEMPTION FOR PEOPLE WITH DISABILITIES

Michigan Department of Treasury
Attn: Income Tax
Treasury Building
430 West Allegan Street
Lansing, MI 48922
(517) 373-3200   Toll-free: (800) 827-4000
TTY: (517) 636-4999
E-mail: treasIndTax@michigan.gov
Web: www.michigan.gov/treasury

Summary To exempt a portion of the income of deaf, blind, and disabled residents of Michigan from state income taxation.

Eligibility Eligible for this exemption are residents of Michigan who 1) receive messages through a sense other than hearing, such as lip reading or sign language; 2) have vision in their better eye of 20/200 or less with corrective lenses or peripheral field of vision of 20 degrees or less; or 3) are hemiplegic, paraplegic, quadriplegic, or totally and permanently disabled.

Financial data Qualifying people with disabilities receive an exemption of $1,900 from their adjusted gross income for purposes of state taxation.

Duration The exemption continues as long as the recipient resides in Michigan.

[224]
MISSISSIPPI HOMESTEAD TAX EXEMPTION FOR THE DISABLED

Mississippi State Tax Commission
Attn: Property Tax Division
P.O. Box 1033
Jackson, MS 39215-1033
(601) 923-7631   Fax: (601) 923-7637
E-mail: property@mstc.state.ms.us
Web: www.mstc.state.ms.us

Summary To exempt from property taxes a portion of the value of homesteads owned by people with disabilities and blind people in Mississippi.

Eligibility Eligible for this exemption are residents of Mississippi who are totally disabled or legally blind and own a homestead that they occupy as a home. Disability and blindness are defined according to federal Social Security regulations.

Financial data The exemption covers the first $7,500 of assessed value of the property.

Duration The exemption continues as long as the disabled person resides in Mississippi.

Number awarded Varies each year.

Deadline For the first time that an exemption is requested, it must be submitted before the end of March of that year. Subsequently, most Mississippi counties do not require renewal filing unless the homestead of applicant's status changes.

[225]
MISSISSIPPI TAX EXEMPTION FOR THE BLIND

Mississippi State Tax Commission
Attn: Individual Income Tax Division
P.O. Box 1033
Jackson, MS 39215-1033
(601) 923-7089   Fax: (601) 923-7039
Web: www.mstc.state.ms.us

Summary To exempt a portion of the income of blind people and their spouses from state income tax liability in Mississippi.

Eligibility Eligible for this exemption are residents of Mississippi who have been declared legally blind and their spouses.

Financial data The exemption is $1,500.

Duration The exemption continues as long as the blind person resides in Mississippi.

Number awarded Varies each year.

Deadline The exemption must be requested on the resident's state income tax return, which is due in April.

[226]
MISSOURI BLIND PENSION

Missouri Department of Social Services
Attn: Division of Family Services
221 West High Street
P.O. Box 1527
Jefferson City, MO 65102-1527
(573) 751-4815   Fax: (800) 735-2966

Summary To provide assistance to blind residents of Missouri who are not eligible for other support.

Eligibility This program is open to blind (vision less than 5/200) residents of Missouri who are 18 years of age or older; do not own real or personal property worth more than $20,000 (excluding the value of the home used as a resident); have not given away, sold, or transferred real or personal property in order to be eligible; are of good moral character; have no sighted spouse living in Missouri who can provide support; do not publicly solicit alms; are not residents of a public, private, or endowed institution except a public medical institution; are willing to have medical treatment or an operation to cure blindness (unless 75 years of age or older); and are ineligible for federal Supplemental Security Income and Missouri Supplemental Aid to the Blind.

Financial data Eligible individuals receive a monthly cash grant of up to $423. and Medicaid.

Duration Qualified blind people are eligible for this assistance as long as they reside in Missouri.

Number awarded Varies each year.

[227]
MISSOURI COUNCIL OF THE BLIND SPECIAL SERVICE PROGRAM

Missouri Council of the Blind
5453 Chippewa Street
St. Louis, MO 63109-1635
(314) 832-7172
Toll-free: (800) 342-5632 (within MO)
Fax: (314) 832-7796
E-mail: moblind@mindspring.com
Web: www.acb.org/missouri

Summary To provide funding for emergency purposes to blind residents of Missouri.

Eligibility This program is open to residents of Missouri who are legally blind and need emergency funds. Applicants need not be members of the Missouri Council of the Blind.

Financial data Grants normally are limited to $300, although in extreme cases grants up to $500 may be approved.

Duration This is a 1-time payment.

Additional Information Information is also available from Phyllis Zirkle, Special Services Chair, 11695 S.W. Rogers Road, Stewartsville, MO 64490, (816) 667-5884.

Number awarded Varies each year.

Deadline Applications may be submitted at any time.

[228]
MISSOURI SUPPLEMENTAL AID TO THE BLIND

Missouri Department of Social Services
221 West High Street
P.O. Box 1527
Jefferson City, MO 65102-1527
(573) 751-4815   Fax: (800) 735-2966

Summary To provide supplemental income to blind residents of Missouri.

Eligibility This program is open to blind (vision less than 5/200) residents of Missouri who are 18 years of age or older; are single and do not own real and personal property worth more than $2,000, or, if married and living with a spouse, do not own real and personal property worth more than $4,000 (the residence, clothing, furniture, household equipment, personal jewelry, or any property used directly by the blind person in earning a living are not included in that valuation); do not have parents living in Missouri or a sighted spouse who can provide support; do not publicly solicit alms; are not residents of a public, private, or endowed institution except a public medical institution; are in need of assistance because of insufficient income to meet basic needs; and are required to apply for federal Supplemental Security Income.

Financial data Eligible individuals receive a monthly cash grant of up to $423 and Medicaid.

Duration Qualified blind people are eligible for this assistance as long as they reside in Missouri.

Number awarded Varies each year.

[229]
MONTANA INCOME TAX EXEMPTION FOR THE BLIND

Montana Department of Revenue
Attn: Individual Income Tax
125 North Roberts, Third Floor
P.O. Box 5805
Helena, MT 59604-5805
(406) 444-6900   Fax: (406) 444-1505
TDD: (406) 444-2830
Web: www.state.mt.us/revenue

Summary To provide a state income tax exemption to blind residents of Montana and their spouses.

Eligibility Eligible are all persons considered Montana residents for purposes of state income taxation who are blind or whose spouse is blind.

Financial data Blind people and their spouses may claim an additional exemption of $1,740 from their income for state taxation purposes.

Duration The exemption continues as long as the recipient resides in Montana.

[230]
NEW HAMPSHIRE PROPERTY TAX EXEMPTION FOR CERTAIN DISABLED SERVICEMEN

New Hampshire Department of Revenue
  Administration
45 Chenell Drive
P.O. Box 457
Concord, NH 03302-0457
(603) 271-2687   TDD: (800) 735-2964

Summary To exempt from taxation certain property owned by New Hampshire disabled veterans or their surviving spouses.

Eligibility Eligible for this exemption are New Hampshire residents who are honorably discharged veterans with a total and permanent service-connected disability that involves double amputation of the upper or lower extremities or any combination thereof, paraplegia, or blindness of both eyes with visual acuity of 5/200 or less. Applicants or their surviving spouses must own a specially adapted homestead that has been acquired with the assistance of the U.S. Department of Veterans Affairs.

Financial data Qualifying disabled veterans and surviving spouses are exempt from all taxation on such specially adapted homestead.

Duration 1 year; once the credit has been approved, it is automatically renewed as long as the qualifying person owns the same residence in New Hampshire.

Number awarded Varies each year.

Deadline The original application for a permanent tax credit must be submitted by April.

[231]
NEW HAMPSHIRE REAL ESTATE EXEMPTION FOR THE BLIND

New Hampshire Department of Revenue
　Administration
45 Chenell Drive
P.O. Box 457
Concord, NH 03302-0457
(603) 271-2687　　　　TDD: (800) 735-2964

Summary To provide a partial exemption from real estate taxes for blind residents of New Hampshire.

Eligibility Residents of New Hampshire are covered by this program if they are blind, own and occupy their primary residence in New Hampshire, and live in a municipality that has chosen through a referendum vote to grant an exemption to the legally blind.

Financial data $15,000 of the value of the residential real estate is exempted from taxation for qualifying residents. Towns may exempt any amount they determine is appropriate to address significant increases in property values.

Duration 1 year; this exemption will be continued as long as the recipient meets the eligibility requirements.

Number awarded Varies each year.

[232]
NEW JERSEY HOMESTEAD REBATE

New Jersey Division of Taxation
Attn: Office of Information and Publications
50 Barrack Street
P.O. Box 281
Trenton, NJ 08695-0281
(609) 292-6400
Toll-free: (800) 323-4400 (within selected states)
TTY: (800) 286-6613 (within selected states)
E-mail: taxation@tax.state.nj.us
Web: www.state.nj.us/treasury/taxation

Summary To refund a portion of property taxes paid by residents of New Jersey, especially those who are blind, disabled, or elderly.

Eligibility This rebate is available to all residents of New Jersey, but separate provisions apply to those who are 1) blind, 2) permanently and totally disabled, or 3) aged 65 or older. Applicants must 1) either own the home in which they reside or rent a dwelling with its own separate kitchen and bath facilities; and 2) have an income of $100,000 or less (for other residents, the income threshold is $40,000).

Financial data The rebate depends on 1) whether the applicant is a homeowner or a tenant; 2) the filing status (single, married filing separate return, married filing joint return, head of household, qualifying widow or widower); and 3) the applicant's income. It ranges from $90 to $775. (For residents under 65 years of age and not blind or disabled, the maximum rebate is $100.)

Duration The rebate is available as long as the person remains a New Jersey resident.

Number awarded Varies each year.

Deadline The rebate is claimed as part of the annual income tax return, due in April of each year.

[233]
NEW JERSEY INCOME TAX EXEMPTIONS FOR THE BLIND AND DISABLED

New Jersey Division of Taxation
Attn: Office of Information and Publications
50 Barrack Street
P.O. Box 281
Trenton, NJ 08695-0281
(609) 292-6400
Toll-free: (800) 323-4400 (within selected states)
TTY: (800) 286-6613 (within selected states)
E-mail: taxation@tax.state.nj.us
Web: www.state.nj.us/treasury/taxation

Summary To provide an income tax exemption in New Jersey to blind and disabled people.

Eligibility Residents of New Jersey who are blind or disabled are entitled to this exemption.

Financial data Each blind or disabled person is entitled to an exemption of $1,000 from income for taxation purposes.

Duration The exemption continues as long as the qualifying condition persists and the person remains a New Jersey resident.

Number awarded Varies each year.

[234]
NEW JERSEY PARTIAL EXEMPTION FROM REALTY TRANSFER FEE FOR SENIOR CITIZENS OR DISABLED PERSONS

New Jersey Division of Taxation
Attn: Office of Information and Publications
50 Barrack Street
P.O. Box 281
Trenton, NJ 08695-0281
(609) 292-6400
Toll-free: (800) 323-4400 (within selected states)
TTY: (800) 286-6613 (within selected states)
E-mail: taxation@tax.state.nj.us
Web: www.state.nj.us/treasury/taxation

Summary To provide an exemption from realty transfer fees paid by senior citizens, persons with disabilities, and blind people in New Jersey.

Eligibility Eligible for these exemptions are persons aged 62 and older, permanently and totally disabled individuals, and blind people who are legal residents of New

Jersey for 1 year immediately preceding October 1 of the year before the year for which the exemption is requested, and purchasers of certain residential property during the year.

Financial data The standard realty transfer fee is $2.00 per $500 for the first $150,000 of the sales price, $3.35 per $500 for sales prices from $150,000 to $200,000, or $3.90 per $500 for sales prices in excess of $200,000. For persons who qualify for this reduction, the fee is $0.50 per $500 for the first $150,000 of the sales price or $1.25 per $500 for sales prices in excess of $150,000.

Duration The exemption applies whenever a qualified purchaser buys a new residence.

Number awarded Varies each year.

[235]
NEW JERSEY PROPERTY TAX DEDUCTION

New Jersey Division of Taxation
Attn: Office of Information and Publications
50 Barrack Street
P.O. Box 281
Trenton, NJ 08695-0281
(609) 292-6400
Toll-free: (800) 323-4400 (within selected states)
TTY: (800) 286-6613 (within selected states)
E-mail: taxation@tax.state.nj.us
Web: www.state.nj.us/treasury/taxation

Summary To exclude from income taxation a portion of the property taxes paid by residents of New Jersey.

Eligibility This deduction is available to residents of New Jersey whose income is greater than $20,000 (or $10,000 if single or married filing separately). It is also available to residents, regardless of income who are 1) blind, 2) permanently and totally disabled, or 3) aged 65 or older. Applicants must either own the home in which they reside or rent a dwelling with its own separate kitchen and bath facilities.

Financial data Qualified residents are entitled to deduct from their income (for state taxation purposes) 100% of their property taxes, to a maximum of $10,000. For renters, 18% of their rent is considered the equivalent of property taxes and may be deducted, to a maximum of $10,000.

Duration The deduction continues as long as the person remains a New Jersey resident.

Additional Information This program began in 1996. Taxpayers may not claim both the property tax deduction and the property tax credit; they may claim whichever is most beneficial, but only the deduction or the credit.

Number awarded Varies each year.

Deadline The deduction is claimed as part of the annual income tax return, due in April of each year.

[236]
NEW JERSEY VETERANS AND SPOUSES CATASTROPHIC ENTITLEMENTS

New Jersey Department of Military and Veterans Affairs
Attn: Division of Veterans Programs
101 Eggert Crossing Road
P.O. Box 340
Trenton, NJ 08625-0340
(609) 530-7045
Toll-free: (800) 624-0508 (within NJ)
Fax: (609) 530-7075
Web: www.state.nj.us

Summary To supplement the compensation benefits paid by the U.S. Department of Veterans Affairs (VA) to disabled New Jersey veterans or their surviving spouses.

Eligibility Eligible for this benefit are veterans who are receiving VA compensation benefits for 100% disability ratings and who have the following disabilities: loss of sight; amputation of both hands, both feet, or 1 hand and 1 foot; hemiplegia and permanent paralysis of 1 leg and 1 arm on either side of the body; paraplegia and permanent paralysis of both legs and lowers parts of the body; osteochondritis and permanent loss of use of both legs; multiple sclerosis and the loss of use of both feet or both legs; and quadriplegia. Service must have been during wartime and the veteran must have been a resident of New Jersey at the time of entry into the military and be so currently. Surviving spouses of disabled veterans are also eligible.

Financial data Eligible veterans or survivors receive $750 a year, paid in monthly installments.

Duration This benefit is payable for the life of the veteran or spouse.

Number awarded Varies each year.

[237]
NEW MEXICO TAX EXEMPTION FOR THE BLIND AND ELDERLY

New Mexico Taxation and Revenue Department
Attn: Tax Information and Policy Office
1100 South St. Francis Drive
P.O. Box 630
Santa Fe, NM 87504-0630
(505) 827-2523
Web: www.state.nm.us/tax

Summary To exempt a portion of the income of New Mexico residents who are blind or over the age of 65 from state income tax liability.

Eligibility This program is open to residents of New Mexico who are 65 years of age or older or who are blind.

Financial data The income exemption ranges from $1,000 to $8,000, depending on filing status and income. The maximum income that still qualifies for an exemption is $25,500 for married individuals filing separate returns, $51,000 for heads of household, surviving spouses, and

married individuals filing joint returns, or $28,500 for single individuals.
Duration The exemption continues as long as the qualifying resident remains in the state.
Number awarded Varies each year.
Deadline The qualifying resident claims the exemption on the New Mexico state income tax return, which is due in April.

[238]
NEW YORK STATE BLIND ANNUITY

New York State Division of Veterans' Affairs
5 Empire State Plaza, Suite 2836
Albany, NY 12223-1551
(518) 474-6114
Toll-free: (888) VETS-NYS (within NY)
Fax: (518) 473-0379
E-mail: info@veterans.state.ny.us
Web: www.veterans.state.ny.us

Summary To provide an annuity to blind wartime veterans and their surviving spouses in New York.
Eligibility This benefit is available to veterans who served on active duty during World War I, World War II, the Korean War, the Vietnam Conflict, or the Persian Gulf, and to veterans who received an expeditionary medal for service in Lebanon, Grenada, or Panama. Applicants must 1) meet the New York State standards of blindness; 2) have received an honorable or general discharge, or a discharge other than for dishonorable service; and 3) be now, and continue to be, residents of and continuously domiciled in New York State. The annuity is also payable to unremarried spouses of deceased veterans who were receiving annuity payments (or were eligible to do so) at the time of their death, and are residents of and continuously domiciled in New York State.
Financial data The annuity is $1,000 per year.
Number awarded Varies each year.

[239]
NORTH CAROLINA INCOME TAX EXEMPTION FOR THE AGED AND BLIND

North Carolina Department of Revenue
Attn: Individual Income Tax
501 North Wilmington Street
P.O. Box 25000
Raleigh, NC 27640-0640
(919) 733-4684
Web: www.dor.state.nc.us

Summary To deduct a portion of the income of blind and elderly residents from state income taxation in North Carolina.
Eligibility This deduction is available to residents of North Carolina who are blind or 65 years of age or older (and/or whose spouse is blind or 65 years of age or older and a joint return is filed).
Financial data The deduction depends on the filing status of the taxpayer; it is $750 for single and head of household, or $600 for married filing jointly, married filing separately, or qualifying widow(er).
Duration The deduction is available as long as the recipient resides in North Carolina.
Number awarded Varies each year.

[240]
NORTH DAKOTA PROPERTY TAX EXEMPTION FOR THE BLIND

Office of State Tax Commissioner
State Capitol Building
600 East Boulevard Avenue, Department 127
Bismarck, ND 58505-0599
(701) 328-2770   Toll-free: (800) 638-2901
Fax: (701) 328-3700   TTY: (800) 366-6888
E-mail: taxinfo@state.nd.us
Web: www.ndtaxdepartment.com

Summary To provide partial tax exemption in North Dakota to blind persons and their spouses.
Eligibility Blind persons are defined as those who are totally blind, who have visual acuity of not more than 20/200 in the better eye with correction, or whose vision is limited in field so that the widest diameter subtends an angle no greater than 20 degrees. Eligible for this exemption is property that is owned by a blind person, by the spouse of a blind person, or jointly by a blind person and a spouse. The property that is exempt includes the entire building classified as residential, and owned and occupied as a residence by a person who qualifies, as long as the building contains no more than 2 apartments or rental units that are leased.
Financial data The exemption applies to all or any part of fixtures, building, and improvements upon any nonfarmland up to a taxable valuation of $5,000.
Duration The exemption continues as long as the blind person resides in the home in North Dakota.
Number awarded Varies each year.

[241]
OKLAHOMA INCOME TAX EXEMPTION FOR THE BLIND

Oklahoma Tax Commission
Attn: Income Tax
2501 North Lincoln Boulevard
Oklahoma City, OK 73194-0009
(405) 521-3160
Toll-free: (800) 522-8165 (within OK)
Fax: (405) 522-0063
E-mail: otcmaster@oktax.state.ok.us
Web: www.oktax.state.ok.us

Summary To exempt a portion of the income of blind people and their spouses in Oklahoma from state taxation.

Eligibility This exemption is available to residents of Oklahoma and their spouses who are legally blind.

Financial data Each qualifying resident is entitled to claim an additional exemption of $1,000.

Duration The exemption is available as long as the recipient resides in Oklahoma.

[242]
OPPORTUNITIES FOR THE BLIND GRANTS

Opportunities for the Blind, Inc.
Attn: Grant Committee
P.O Box 98
Fairplay, MD 21733
(240) 420-6500   E-mail: OppBlind@yahoo.com
Web: www.opportunitiesfortheblind.org

Summary To provide funding to blind people interested in working on a college degree, establishing or improving their self-employment situation, or obtaining special equipment.

Eligibility This program is open to legally blind U.S. citizens. Applicants must be seeking funding to 1) assist with tuition, books, and supplies for accredited postsecondary education or job training that is not provided by a state agency for the blind; 2) assist with costs related to establishing or improving their self-employment situation; or 3) obtain special equipment that they need for their job. Preference is given to applicants who are already working, or about to begin working, in occupations where the blind are not typically found. Selection is based on the probability of success, but financial need may also be considered.

Financial data Grants normally range from $3,000 to $5,000, and may go as high as $10,000.

Duration This is a 1-time award.

Additional Information This program was established in 1981.

Number awarded Varies each year.

Deadline February, May, August, or October of each year.

[243]
OREGON INCOME TAX DEDUCTION FOR THE BLIND

Oregon Department of Revenue
Revenue Building
955 Center Street, N.E.
Salem, OR 97310-2551
(503) 378-4988
Toll-free: (800) 356-4222 (within OR)
TTY: (800) 886-7204 (within OR)
Web: www.dor.state.or.us

Summary To enable blind residents of Oregon to deduct a portion of their income from state taxation.

Eligibility This deduction is available to blind taxpayers in Oregon.

Financial data The additional deduction is $1,200 for single people and heads of households. It is $1,000 for married people filing jointly or separately and for qualifying widow(er)s.

Duration The deduction continues as long as the recipient resides in Oregon.

Deadline Deductions are filed with state income tax returns in April of each year.

[244]
OREGON LIONS PATIENT CARE PROGRAM

Oregon Lions Sight & Hearing Foundation
Attn: Patient Care Coordinator
1410 S.W. Morrison Street, Suite 760
Portland, OR 97205
(503) 827-6952, ext. 23
Toll-free: (800) 635-4667, ext. 23
Fax: (503) 827-6958   E-mail: info@orlions.org
Web: www.orlions.org

Summary To provide funding to needy Oregon residents who require eye or ear surgery.

Eligibility Applicants must have been residents of Oregon for at least 6 months and be sponsored by a local Lions, Lioness, Leo, or Lions Auxiliary Club. They must require treatment for vision (e.g., cataract surgery, cornea transplant, enucleation, ocular prosthetic, treatment of macular degeneration) or hearing (e.g., tympanoplasty, cochlear implant, nasal septoplasty, treatment of diabetic retinopathy, vitrectomy) but be unable to afford the procedure. Their income must be less than 150% of the federal poverty level and they must be without other resources (private insurance, Medicare, or the Oregon Health Plan) to pay for the treatment.

Financial data Grants provide approximately one-third of the total regular cost for the procedure.

Duration These are 1-time grants.

Number awarded Approximately 50 each year.

Deadline Applications may be submitted at any time.

FINANCIAL AID PROGRAMS

[245]
OREGON PROPERTY TAX DEFERRAL FOR DISABLED AND SENIOR CITIZENS

Oregon Department of Revenue
Attn: Property Tax Division
Revenue Building
955 Center Street, N.E.
Salem, OR 97310-2551
(503) 378-4988
Toll-free: (800) 356-4222 (within OR)
TDD: (800) 886-7204 (within OR)
Web: www.dor.state.or.us

Summary To enable disabled and senior Oregon residents to defer payment of their property taxes.

Eligibility This program is open to residents of Oregon who are 1) determined to be eligible to receive or be receiving federal Society Security disability benefits due to disability or blindness, or 2) 62 years of age or older. Applicants must own a residence and have a total household income less than $32,500.

Financial data The state pays all taxes on the property to the county but places a lien on the property and charges 6% per year on the deferred taxes. The lien and interest become due and payable when the disabled person or senior citizen sells the property or changes its ownership, moves permanently from the property (unless for medical reasons), or dies.

Duration 1 year; the deferment is automatically renewed as long as the property owner lives in the residence.

Number awarded Varies each year.

Deadline Applications for new deferrals must be filed in the appropriate county assessor's office by April of each year.

[246]
PEARLE VISION FOUNDATION INDIVIDUAL GRANT

Pearle Vision Foundation
Attn: Administrator
2465 Joe Field Road
Dallas, TX 75229
(972) 277-6191   Fax: (972) 277-6422
Web: www.pearlevision.com

Summary To award grants to individuals who demonstrate financial hardship and are in need of low vision aids or equipment.

Eligibility This program is open to persons of low vision who need aids or equipment. Applications must be submitted prior to the purchase, sponsored by a second party (e.g., an eye care professional, member of the clergy, or social worker) who can verify the applicant's vision condition and financial need, and include both evidence of financial hardship (e.g., payroll stubs, tax records, letters of denial from insurance) and estimated total cost of the low vision aid or equipment to be purchased. The attending physician must complete a "physician's statement" and attach a copy of the applicant's most current medical records.

Financial data The amount awarded depends upon the applicant's needs.

Duration Recipients may reapply.

Number awarded Varies each year.

Deadline Applications must be submitted by January, April, July, or October of each year.

[247]
PENNSYLVANIA BLIND VETERANS PENSION

Bureau for Veterans Affairs
Fort Indiantown Gap
Annville, PA 17003-5002
(717) 865-8911
Toll-free: (800) 54 PA VET (within PA)
Fax: (717) 865-8589   E-mail: jdavison@state.pa.us
Web: sites.state.pa.us

Summary To provide financial assistance to blind residents of Pennsylvania who lost their sight while serving in the U.S. armed forces.

Eligibility Persons who have 3/60 or 10/200 or less normal vision are eligible if they are honorably discharged veterans and were residents of Pennsylvania when they joined the U.S. armed forces. Their blindness must have resulted from a service-connected injury or disease.

Financial data The pension is $150 per month.

Duration The pension is awarded for the life of the veteran.

Number awarded Varies each year.

Deadline Applications may be submitted at any time.

[248]
PENNSYLVANIA REAL ESTATE TAX EXEMPTION

Bureau for Veterans Affairs
Fort Indiantown Gap
Annville, PA 17003-5002
(717) 865-8907
Toll-free: (800) 54 PA VET (within PA)
Fax: (717) 865-8589   E-mail: jdavison@state.pa.us
Web: sites.state.pa.us

Summary To exempt Pennsylvania veterans with disabilities and their unremarried surviving spouses from all state real estate taxes.

Eligibility Eligible to apply for this exemption are honorably discharged veterans who are residents of Pennsylvania and who are blind, paraplegic, or 100% disabled from a service-connected disability sustained during wartime military service. The dwelling must be owned by the veteran solely or jointly with a spouse, and the need for the exemption must be determined by the State Veterans' Commission. Upon the death of the veteran,

the tax exemption passes on to the veteran's unremarried surviving spouse.
Financial data This program exempts the principal residence (and the land on which it stands) from all real estate taxes.
Duration The exemption continues as long as the eligible veteran or unremarried widow resides in Pennsylvania.
Number awarded Varies each year.

[249]
SALLY PRENTICE MEMORIAL PERSONAL ADVANCEMENT AWARD

National Federation of the Blind of Connecticut
580 Burnside Avenue, Suite 1
East Hartford, CT 06108
(860) 289-1971   E-mail: info@nfbct.org
Web: www.nfbct.org/html/schinfo.htm

Summary To enable blind people in Connecticut to carry out a program of personal advancement.
Eligibility Applicants must be legally blind residents of Connecticut who have developed a personal advancement program that they wish to implement. Along with their application, they must submit a letter describing the personal advancement program they have designed for themselves and how the award will help them carry out that program. Selection is based on program quality, service to the community, and financial need. Applicants need not be members of the National Federation of the Blind.
Financial data This award is $1,000.
Duration The award is presented annually.
Additional Information This award is presented in memory of Sally Prentice, a long-time member of the National Federation of the Blind and a dedicated leader in Connecticut.
Number awarded 2 each year.
Deadline September of each year.

[250]
SOCIAL SECURITY DISABILITY INSURANCE (SSDI) BENEFITS

Social Security Administration
6401 Security Boulevard
Baltimore, MD 21235-0001
(410) 594-1234   Toll-free: (800) 772-1213
TTY: (800) 325-0778
Web: www.ssa.gov

Summary To provide monthly benefits to workers and their families if the worker becomes disabled or blind.
Eligibility This program defines disabled people as those who are unable to do any kind of work for which they are suited and whose disability has lasted or is expected to last for at least a year or to result in death. Blind people qualify if their vision cannot be corrected to better than 20/200 in their better eye or if their visual field is 20 degrees or less, even with corrective lens. Family members who are eligible include 1) unmarried children, including adopted children and, in some cases, stepchildren and grandchildren who are under 18 years of age (19 if still in high school full time); 2) unmarried children, over 18 years of age, if they have a disability that started before age 22; and 3) spouses who are 62 years of age or older, or of any age if caring for a child of the disabled worker who is under 16 years of age or disabled. For deceased workers, disabled widow(er)s 50 years of age or older are also eligible. Applicants must also have worked long enough and recently enough under Social Security in order to qualify. Workers who become disabled before the age of 24 need 6 credits in the 3-year period ending when the disability begins; workers who become disabled between the ages of 24 and 31 must have credit for having worked half the time between the age of 21 and the date of disability; workers 31 years of age or older at the time of disability must have earned as many total credits as needed for retirement (from 20 credits if disabled at age 31 through 42 to 40 credits if disabled at age 62 or older) and must have earned at least 20 of the credits in the 10 years immediately before becoming disabled. An exception applies to blind workers who need no recent credit but may have earned the required credit any time after 1936.
Financial data The amount of the monthly benefit depends on several factors, including the worker's age at the time of disability, the number of dependents, and the amount of earnings on which Social Security taxes have been paid. Recently, the average monthly benefit for disabled workers was $839; for spouses of disabled workers it was $214; and for children of disabled workers it was $246.
Duration For a disabled or blind person, whether a worker, widow, widower, surviving divorced spouse, or person over the age of 18 who became disabled before the age of 22, monthly benefits continue until the person is no longer disabled or dies. For a dependent spouse, benefits are paid until the worker is no longer disabled or dies. For a dependent child, the benefits continue until the child marries or reaches the age of 18 (19 if still enrolled as a full-time high school student).
Additional Information Disabled workers may test their ability to return to work for a trial work period of up to 9 months, during which time they receive full SSDI benefits. At the end of that period, a decision is made as to whether or not they are able to engage in substantial gainful activity. Persons who find that they cannot continue substantial gainful employment continue to receive SSDI benefits without interruption. Persons who can engage in substantial gainful activity receive benefits for an additional 3 months after which payments cease. Several factors are considered to determine if the person can engage in substantial gainful employment, but the most important is income.
Number awarded Varies; recently, approximately 5.7 million persons were receiving SSDI monthly benefits.

Annual benefits paid were approximately $4.8 billion. Another 1.7 million dependents (including 150,000 spouses and 1,550,000 children) were receiving $400 million in annual benefits.

[251]
SOUTH CAROLINA HOMESTEAD EXEMPTION PROGRAM

South Carolina Comptroller General
Attn: Local Government Division
305 Wade Hampton Office Building
P.O. Box 11228
Columbia, SC 29211
(803) 734-2121   Fax: (803) 734-2064
E-mail: cgoffice@cg.state.sc.us
Web: www.cg.state.sc.us

Summary To establish a homestead exemption for South Carolina residents who are elderly, disabled, or blind, and their widow(er)s.

Eligibility Legal residents of South Carolina who own a house or mobile home are eligible for this exemption if they are aged 65 or older, totally and permanently disabled, or legally blind. Spouses of deceased persons who were eligible also qualify to receive the exemption if they were at least 50 years of age when their spouse died.

Financial data The first $50,000 of the fair market value of the qualified applicant's home is exempted from property taxes. The exemption is from county, municipal, school, and special assessment real estate property taxes.

Duration The exemption continues as long as the homeowners live in their primary residence in South Carolina.

Additional Information This program is administered by county auditors.

Number awarded Varies each year.

Deadline Persons applying for this exemption for the first time must do so prior to July of each year; subsequently, no re-application is necessary unless the title or use of the property changes.

[252]
SOUTH CAROLINA SPECIALLY ADAPTED HOUSING TAX EXEMPTION

South Carolina Office of Veterans Affairs
1205 Pendleton Street, Room 477
Columbia, SC 29201-3789
(803) 734-0200   Fax: (803) 734-0197
E-mail: va@govoepp.state.sc.us
Web: www.govoepp.state.sc.us/vetaff.htm

Summary To provide for the exemption of taxes on specially adapted housing in South Carolina that was acquired from the U.S. Department of Veterans Affairs (VA).

Eligibility Veterans having service-connected disabilities resulting in the loss or loss of use of lower extremities (requiring braces, crutches, or wheelchairs for locomotion) as well as blinded veterans who have loss of use of a lower extremity qualify for specially adapted housing from the VA. Disabled veterans who are residents of South Carolina and who have acquired such housing with financial assistance from the VA are eligible for this exemption; if the eligible veteran is deceased, the spouse, dependent children, or dependent parents are eligible for the exemption.

Financial data The exemption extends to state, county, and municipal taxes on any real estate acquired as specially adapted housing.

Duration The exemption continues as long as an eligible veteran or a qualified dependent owns and occupies the property.

Number awarded Varies each year.

Deadline Applications may be submitted at any time.

[253]
SPECIALLY ADAPTED HOMES FOR DISABLED VETERANS

Department of Veterans Affairs
810 Vermont Avenue, N.W.
Washington, DC 20420
(202) 418-4343   Toll-free: (800) 827-1000
Web: www.va.gov

Summary To provide funding to certain disabled veterans for a home specially adapted to their needs.

Eligibility Grants (also referred to as $48,000 grants) are available to veterans who are entitled to compensation for permanent and total service-connected disability due to: 1) the loss or loss of use of both lower extremities, such as to preclude locomotion without the aid of braces, crutches, canes, or a wheelchair; or 2) blindness in both eyes, having only light perception, plus loss or loss of use of 1 lower extremity; or 3) a loss or loss of use of 1 lower extremity together with residuals of organic disease or injury or the loss or loss of use of 1 upper extremity, such as to preclude locomotion without resort to braces, canes, crutches, or a wheelchair. Grants (also referred to as $9,250 grants) are available to who are entitled to compensation for permanent and total service-connected disability due to 1) blindness in both eyes with 5/200 visual acuity or less, or 2) anatomical loss or loss of use of both hands.

Financial data The U.S. Department of Veterans Affairs (VA) may approve a grant of not more than 50% of the cost of building, buying, or remodeling homes for eligible veterans, or paying indebtedness of such homes already acquired, up to a maximum grant of $48,000. Eligible veterans with available loan guarantee entitlements may also obtain a guaranteed loan or a direct loan from the VA to supplement the grant to acquire a specially adapted home. Grants up to $9,250 are available for adaptations to a veteran's residence that are determined

by the VA to be reasonably necessary. Those grants may also be used to assist veterans to acquire a residence that already has been adapted with special features for the veteran's disability.

Duration This is a 1-time grant.

Additional Information Veterans who receive a specially adapted housing grant may be eligible for Veterans Mortgage Life Insurance.

Number awarded Varies each year.

Deadline Applications are accepted at any time.

[254]
SUPPLEMENTAL SECURITY INCOME (SSI)

Social Security Administration
6401 Security Boulevard
Baltimore, MD 21235-0001
(410) 594-1234   Toll-free: (800) 772-1213
TTY: (800) 325-0778
Web: www.ssa.gov

Summary To provide monthly payments to disabled, blind, and elderly people who have limited income and resources.

Eligibility A person 18 years of age or older is considered disabled if a physical or mental impairment prevents him or her from doing any substantial gainful work and is expected to last for at least 12 months or to result in death. Children under the age of 18 are considered disabled if they have a physical or mental impairment that is comparable in severity to a disability that would prevent an adult from working and is expected to last at least 12 months or result in death. Children with certain conditions are automatically disabled and eligible for these benefits; the conditions include HIV infection, blindness, deafness, cerebral palsy, Down syndrome, muscular dystrophy, significant mental deficiency, diabetes (with amputation of 1 foot), amputation of 2 limbs, or amputation of leg at the hip. Regardless of age, a person whose vision is no better than 20/200 or who has a limited visual field of 20 degrees or less with the best corrective eyeglasses is considered blind; individuals with visual impairments not severe enough to meet the definition of blindness still may qualify as disabled persons. People over the age of 65 are also eligible. All applicants must be United States citizens, nationals, or permanent residents with limited resources (less than $2,000 for an individual or $3,000 for a couple); items excluded from resources include the home used as a principal place of residence, personal and household goods, life insurance with face value of $1,500 or less, a car, burial plots for individuals and immediate family members, and burial funds up to $1,500. Eligible earned income generally must be less than $800 a month. Unearned income (as from other welfare benefits, pensions, rent, or annuities) may not exceed $572 per month for single people or $840 per month for couples.

Financial data The basic monthly payment is $552 for an eligible individual or $829 for an eligible individual with an eligible spouse. Many states add money to that basic payment. SSI recipients may also be eligible for food stamps and other nutrition programs.

Duration Assistance is provided as long as the recipient remains blind or disabled and in financial need.

Additional Information Although SSI is administered through the Social Security Administration, it is not financed by Social Security taxes. Financing of SSI is provided through general funds of the U.S. Treasury. Recipients of SSI need not have been employed or paid Social Security taxes, but they may be eligible for both SSI and Social Security. Disabled and blind applicants for SSI are referred to their state vocational rehabilitation agency to determine their eligibility for a program of vocational rehabilitation. Disabled drug addicts or alcoholics are referred for appropriate treatment if it is available at an approved facility or institution.

Number awarded Recently, the number of SSI blind and disabled recipients was approximately 5,650,000. Another 941,000 children under 18 years of age were also receiving benefits.

[255]
TENNESSEE INCOME TAX EXEMPTION FOR BLIND RESIDENTS

Tennessee Department of Revenue
Andrew Jackson State Office Building
500 Deaderick Street
Nashville, TN 37242-1099
(615) 253-0600
Toll-free: (800) 342-1003 (within TN)
Fax: (615) 253-3580
E-mail: tn.revenue@state.tn.us
Web: www.tennessee.gov/revenue

Summary To exempt from state taxation the dividend and interest income of blind residents of Tennessee.

Eligibility This exemption applies to income received by blind residents of Tennessee as 1) dividends from stock, investment trusts, and mutual funds; and 2) interest from bonds, notes, and mortgages. As defined by this program, blindness means that vision does not exceed 20/200 in the better eye with correcting lenses or that the widest diameter of the visual field subtends an angle no greater than 20 degrees.

Financial data All dividend and interest income is exempt from taxation if the recipient meets the definition of blindness. However, when taxable interest/dividend income is received jointly by a blind person and a sighted spouse, only one half of the jointly received income is exempted from taxation. The sighted spouse is entitled only to a $1,250 exemption.

Duration The exemption continues as long as the recipient meets the definition of blindness and resides in Tennessee.

[256]
TENNESSEE PROPERTY TAX RELIEF FOR DISABLED VETERANS AND THEIR SPOUSES

Tennessee Comptroller of the Treasury
Attn: Property Tax Relief Program
James K. Polk State Office Building
505 Deaderick Street, Room 1600
Nashville, TN 37243-0278
(615) 747-8871   Fax: (615) 532-3866
E-mail: Kim.Darden@state.tn.us
Web: www.comptroller.state.tn.us/pa/patxrvet.htm

Summary To provide property tax relief for veterans with disabilities and their spouses in Tennessee.

Eligibility This exemption is offered to veterans or their surviving unremarried spouses who are residents of Tennessee and own and live in their home in the state. The veteran must have served in the U.S. armed forces and 1) have acquired, as a result of such service, a disability from paraplegia, or permanent paralysis of both legs and lower part of the body resulting from traumatic injury, or disease to the spinal cord or brain, or from total blindness, or from loss or loss of use of both legs or arms from any service-connected cause; 2) have been rated by the U.S. Department of Veterans Affairs (VA) as 100% permanently disabled as a result of service as a prisoner of war for at least 5 months; or 3) have been rated by the VA as 100% permanently and totally disabled from any other service-connected combat-related cause. Veterans who experience total blindness are also eligible. The relief does not extend to any person who was dishonorably discharged from any of the armed services.

Financial data The amount of the relief depends on the property assessment and the tax rate in the city or county where the beneficiary lives.

Duration 1 year; may be renewed as long as the eligible veteran or surviving unremarried spouse owns and occupies the primary residence.

Number awarded Varies each year.

[257]
TEXAS PROPERTY TAX EXEMPTION FOR DISABLED VETERANS AND THEIR FAMILIES

Texas Veterans Commission
P.O. Box 12277
Austin, TX 78711-2277
(512) 463-5538   Fax: (512) 475-2395
E-mail: info@tvc.state.tx.us
Web: www.tvc.state.tx.us

Summary To extend property tax exemptions on the appraised value of their property to disabled and other Texas veterans and their surviving family members.

Eligibility Eligible veterans must be Texas residents rated at least 10% service-connected disabled. Surviving spouses and children of eligible veterans are also covered by this program.

Financial data For veterans in Texas whose disability is rated as 10 through 30%, the first $5,000 of the appraised property value is exempt from taxation; veterans rated as 31 through 50% disabled are exempt from the first $7,500 of appraised value; those with a 51 through 70% disability are exempt from the first $10,000 of appraised value; the exemption applies to the first $12,000 of appraised value for veterans with disabilities rated as 71% or more. A veteran whose disability is 10% or more and who is 65 years or older is entitled to exemption of the first $12,000 of appraised property value. A veteran whose disability consists of the loss of use of 1 or more limbs, total blindness in 1 or both eyes, or paraplegia is exempt from the first $12,000 of the appraised value. The unremarried surviving spouse of a deceased veteran who, at the time of death had a compensable disability and was entitled to an exemption, is entitled to the same exemption. The surviving spouse of a person who died on active duty is entitled to exemption of the first $5,000 of appraised value of the spouse's property. A surviving child of a person who dies on active duty is entitled to exemption of the first $5,000 of appraised value of the child's property as long as the child is unmarried and under 21 years of age.

Duration 1 year; may be renewed as long as the eligible veteran (or unremarried surviving spouse or child) owns and occupies the primary residence in Texas.

Additional Information This program is administered at the local level by the various taxing authorities.

Number awarded Varies each year.

Deadline April of each year.

[258]
THERESA C. HERRON MEMORIAL SCHOLARSHIP

National Federation of the Blind of New Hampshire
c/o John E. Parker, President
2 Center Street, Apartment 2
Laconia, NH 03246-3737
(603) 528-0107   E-mail: parkerj@worldpath.net

Summary To provide assistance to visually impaired high school students in New Hampshire.

Eligibility This program is open to high school students in New Hampshire who are either legally blind or totally blind. Applicants must submit a current transcript, a statement of their vocational goals, a list of awards and honors received, and information on their community service and volunteer work. There are no restrictions on level or field of study.

Financial data The grant-in-aid is $500. The funds are to be used to pay for vision-impaired expenses incurred by high school students in New Hampshire, including readers and special equipment.

Duration 1 year; may be renewed.

Additional Information Information is also available from Louis Gosselin, New Hampshire State Department

of Education, Division of Vocational Rehabilitation, 361 Lincoln Street, Manchester, NH 03103, (603) 669-8733.
Number awarded 1 or more each year.
Deadline September of each year.

Awards

[259]
APH INSIGHTS

American Printing House for the Blind, Inc.
1839 Frankfort Avenue
Louisville, KY 40206-3152
(502) 895-2405 Toll-free: (800) 223-1839, ext. 357
Fax: (502) 899-2363   E-mail: rwilliams@aph.org
Web: www.aph.org

Summary To recognize and reward outstanding art work by individuals who are blind or visually impaired.
Eligibility Any person who meets the legal definition of blindness is eligible to submit art work to be considered for the InSights exhibition. The definition of blindness is: corrected visual acuity of 20/200 or less in the better eye, or a visual field limited to 20 degrees or less. Both 2- and 3-dimensional works may be submitted. The types of work may include, but are not limited to, painting, drawing, printmaking, and crafts such as pottery, metal work, fiber, etc. Participants may not enter more than 1 piece of art work. Artists may not have received help in the execution of their art (although they may have received advice in selecting materials and colors). The work of students in preschool through 12th grade is judged in grade placement categories; the work of adult artists is judged in categories according to medium. Selection is based on originality of concept, expressive use of media, and artistic excellence.
Financial data Award winners receive a cash prize and a ribbon.
Duration The competition is held annually.
Additional Information Work not selected for the InSights exhibition is returned. Award winners are invited to come to Louisville to receive their awards; stipends are available to assist with travel expenses. This competition was first held in 1992.
Number awarded Varies each year; recently, 17 of these awards were presented.
Deadline Preschool through high school entries must be receive by mid-April of each year. Adult entries must be received by the end of April.

[260]
BLIND EDUCATOR OF THE YEAR AWARD

National Federation of the Blind
Attn: Director or Community Relations
1800 Johnson Street
Baltimore, MD 21230
(410) 659-9314, ext. 272   Fax: (410) 685-5653
E-mail: CommunityRelations@nfb.org
Web: www.nfb.org

Summary To recognize and reward outstanding blind educators.
Eligibility Candidates for this award must be not only distinguished educators but individuals who have contributed to the nation. All candidates must be blind. The recipient is chosen to symbolize the best in teaching and the best in service to the blind.
Financial data The award is $1,000.
Duration The award is presented annually.
Additional Information This award was established in 1986. Nominations should be sent to Steve Benson, 7020 North Tahoma, Chicago, IL 60646. Honorees must be present at the annual convention of the National Federation of the Blind.
Number awarded 1 each year.
Deadline Nominations must be submitted by May of each year.

[261]
HINDA HONIGMAN AWARD FOR THE BLIND

National Federation of Music Clubs
1336 North Delaware Street
Indianapolis, IN 46202-2481
(317) 638-4003   Fax: (317) 638-0503
E-mail: info@nfmc-music.org
Web: www.nfmc-music.org

Summary To recognize and reward the accomplishments of blind musical students who are members of the National Federation of Music Clubs (NFMC).
Eligibility This program is open to blind students between 16 and 26 years of age who are U.S. citizens and student members of the federation. Both instrumentalists and vocalists are eligible. Applications must include a letter of recommendation from the entrant's teacher, an affidavit from an attending ophthalmologist certifying that the applicant is officially blind (with 20/200 or less vision after correction), and a tape recording with 3 selections performed by the applicant.
Financial data The first-place winner receives $650 and the second-place winner $350. Funds are to be used for further study.
Duration The awards are presented annually.
Additional Information Information on this award is also available from Norma Alexander, 1219 Forsyth Street, Winston-Salem, NC 27101-2403; information on all scholarships is available from Chair, Competitions

and Awards Board, Mrs. Lamoine M. Hall, Jr., 4137 Whitfield Avenue, Fort Worth, TX 76109-5432.

Number awarded 2 each year.

Deadline January of each year.

[262]
MARY P. OENSLAGER SCHOLASTIC ACHIEVEMENT AWARDS

Recording for the Blind and Dyslexic
Attn: Public Affairs Department
Anne T. Macdonald Center
20 Roszel Road
Princeton, NJ 08540
(609) 452-0606   Toll-free: (866) RFBD-585
E-mail: custserv@rfbd.org
Web: www.rfbd.org/applications_awards.htm

Summary To recognize and reward the outstanding academic achievements of blind college seniors.

Eligibility To be eligible for this award, candidates must 1) be legally blind; 2) have received, or will receive, a bachelor's degree from a 4-year accredited college or university in the United States or its territories during the year the award is given; 3) have an overall academic average of 3.0 or more on a 4.0 scale; and 4) be registered borrowers from Recording for the Blind and Dyslexic. Selection is based on evidence of leadership, enterprise, and service to others.

Financial data Scholastic Achievement winners receive $6,000 each, Special Honors winners $3,000 each, and Honors winners $1,000 each.

Duration The awards are presented annually.

Number awarded 9 each year: 3 Scholastic Achievement winners, 3 Special Honors winners, and 3 Honors winners.

Additional Information These awards are named for the founder of the program who established it in 1959 and endowed it with a gift of $1 million in 1990.

Deadline February of each year.

[263]
VIVIAN MENEES NELSON MUSIC AWARD FOR THE DISABLED AND VISUALLY IMPAIRED

National Federation of Music Clubs
1336 North Delaware Street
Indianapolis, IN 46202-2481
(317) 638-4003   Fax: (317) 638-0503
E-mail: info@nfmc-music.org
Web: www.nfmc-music.org

Summary To recognize and reward disabled or blind instrumentalists and vocalists who are members of the National Federation of Music Clubs.

Eligibility Applicants must be between 25 and 34 years of age, U.S. citizens, members of the federation, and disabled or visually impaired. Applications must include a letter of recommendation from a teacher, an affidavit from a medical doctor stating the nature of the applicant's disability, and a 15-minute tape recording (no disc or stereo accepted) performed or sung by the applicant.

Financial data The award is $1,000.

Duration The award is presented annually.

Additional Information Applications and further information are also available from Mrs. Wendell Heiny, 300 South Clinton Street, Denver, CO 80231, (303) 340-2960; information on all federation scholarships and awards is available from Chair, Competitions and Awards Board, Mrs. Lamoine M. Hall, Jr., 4137 Whitfield Avenue, Fort Worth, TX 76109-5432. There is a $5 entry fee.

Number awarded 1 each year.

Deadline January of each year.

Hearing Disabilities

- *Scholarships*
- *Fellowships/Grants*
- *Grants-in-Aid*
- *Awards*

Described here are 36 programs open to individuals who have difficulty in receiving linguistic information, with or without amplification. Of these, 15 entries cover scholarships (to pursue studies or research on the undergraduate level in the United States); 12 cover fellowships/grants (to pursue graduate or postdoctoral study or research in the United States); 7 cover grants-in-aid (to support emergency situations, travel, income/property tax liabilities, or the acquisition of assistive technology); and 2 cover awards, competitions, prizes, and honoraria (to recognize or support creative work and public service). If you are looking for a particular program and don't find it in this chapter, be sure to check the Program Title Index to see if it is covered elsewhere in the directory.

Scholarships

[264]
ALEXANDER GRAHAM BELL ASSOCIATION COLLEGE SCHOLARSHIP AWARDS

Alexander Graham Bell Association for the Deaf
Attn: Financial Aid Coordinator
3417 Volta Place, N.W.
Washington, DC 20007-2778
(202) 337-5220   Fax: (202) 337-8314
TTY: (202) 337-5221
E-mail: financialaid@agbell.org
Web: www.agbell.org/financialaid.cfm

Summary To provide financial assistance to undergraduate and graduate students with moderate to profound hearing loss.

Eligibility This program is open to undergraduate and graduate students who have had a hearing loss since birth or before acquiring language with a 60 dB or greater loss in the better ear in the speech frequencies of 500, 1000, and 2000 Hz. Applicants must use speech and residual hearing and/or speechreading (lipreading) as their primary and preferred mode of communication. They must be accepted by or already attending full time a college or university that primarily enrolls students with normal hearing. Preference is given to undergraduates. Financial need is considered in the selection process.

Financial data Stipends range from $250 to $2,000.

Duration 1 year; may be renewed 1 additional year.

Additional Information In past years, individual awards have been designated as the Allie Raney Hunt Memorial Scholarship Award, the David Von Hagen Scholarship Award, the Elsie Bell Grosvenor Scholarship Awards, the Franklin and Henrietta Dickman Memorial Scholarship Awards, the Herbert P. Feibelman Jr. (PS) Scholarship Award, the Lucille A. Abt Scholarship Awards, the Maude Winkler Scholarship Awards, the Oral Hearing-Impaired Section Scholarship Award, the Robert H. Weitbrecht Scholarship Awards, the Second Century Fund Awards, and the Volta Scholarship Award. Some of those awards included additional eligibility requirements. Only the first 500 requests for applications are accepted.

Number awarded Varies each year; recently, 22 of these scholarships were awarded.

Deadline Applications must be requested between September and December of each year and submitted by February of each year.

[265]
ARTS AND SCIENCES AWARDS

Alexander Graham Bell Association for the Deaf
Attn: Financial Aid Coordinator
3417 Volta Place, N.W.
Washington, DC 20007-2778
(202) 337-5220   Fax: (202) 337-8314
TTY: (202) 337-5221
E-mail: financialaid@agbell.org
Web: www.agbell.org/financialaid.cfm

Summary To provide financial aid to hearing impaired students who are participating in extracurricular activities in arts and sciences.

Eligibility Applicants must be diagnosed as having a moderate to profound hearing loss (55 dB or greater loss in the better ear in the speech frequencies of 500, 1000, and 2000 Hz) and must use speech, residual hearing, and/or speechreading as their primary form of communication. They must be between 6 and 19 years of age and enrolled in an art or science program as an extracurricular activity during after-school time, summer, or weekends. Recreational summer camps, sports camps or sports, and travel and study abroad programs that do not have an explicit arts or science focus are not eligible.

Financial data The amount of the award varies, depending upon the cost of the program in which the recipient is enrolled.

Duration 1 year; may be renewed upon reapplication.

Number awarded Varies each year.

Deadline Applications must be requested between December and February of each year and submitted by May of each year.

[266]
BRIAN MCCARTNEY MEMORIAL SCHOLARSHIP

Michigan Association for Deaf, Hearing and Speech Services
Attn: Executive Director
2929 Convington Court, Suite 200
Lansing, MI 48912-4939
(517) 487-0066   Toll-free: (800) YOUR-EAR
Fax: (517) 487-2586   TTY: (517) 487-0202
E-mail: yourear@pilot.msu.edu

Summary To provide college aid to high school seniors in Michigan with hearing or speech impairments.

Eligibility This program is open to high school seniors in Michigan who are hard of hearing, speech and/or language impaired, or deaf. They must be U.S. citizens, intend to further their education at a 2- or 4-year college or university (including trade or technical schools), have a GPA of 2.5 or higher, be of good character, provide at least 3 letters of recommendation, and submit an essay on 1) their community service experiences or activities that demonstrate leadership, 2) their career goals, and 3) how they plan to use the scholarship if they receive it. Priority is given to applicants who have not

been awarded other scholarships or educational financial grants.
Financial data The stipend is $500.
Duration 1 year.
Additional Information This program started in 1992.
Number awarded 2 each year.
Deadline February of each year.

[267]
ETHNIC MISSIONS SCHOLARSHIP PROGRAM

Baptist General Convention of Texas
State Missions Commission
Attn: Ethnic Missions
333 North Washington
Dallas, TX 75246-1798
(214) 828-5342   Toll-free: (800) 352-5342
Fax: (214) 828-5284   E-mail: munoz@bgct.org
Web: www.bgct.org/ethnic_missions

Summary To provide financial assistance for college or seminary education to ethnic and deaf students in Texas who are members of Texas Baptist ethnic congregations.
Eligibility This program is open to members of Texas Baptist congregations who are Asian, Hispanic, or deaf and have a "sense of call" as a lay person or minister. Applicants must be U.S. citizens or permanent residents, have resided in Texas for at least 1 year, demonstrate financial need, and plan to attend or be attending a Texas Baptist university or the Southwestern Baptist Theological Seminary. Students still in high school must have a GPA of at least 3.0; students previously enrolled in a college or seminary must have at least a 2.0 GPA. Applicants must submit brief essays on what they, as a Baptist, believe about God, Jesus, sin, salvation, church membership, and baptism. They must also explain how they became a Christian, why they are seeking a Christian university education, and what they plan to do following graduation.
Financial data The grant for full-time students is $800 per year or $400 per semester. Part-time students receive $27 per credit hour.
Duration 1 year; may be renewed.
Additional Information The scholarships are funded through the Week of Prayer and the Mary Hill Davis Offering for state missions sponsored annually by Women's Missionary Union of Texas.

[268]
HEARING IMPAIRED CHURCH MULTIPLICATION TEAM SCHOLARSHIPS

Southern Baptist Convention
North American Mission Board
Attn: Church Multiplication Team
4200 North Point Parkway
Alpharetta, GA 30022-4176
(770) 410-6235   Fax: (770) 410-6012
E-mail: jdoyle@namb.net
Web: www.namb.net

Summary To provide financial assistance to Baptists who are deaf and interested in religious vocations.
Eligibility This program is open to U.S. citizens who are hearing impaired and involved in some type of approved Baptist ministry. Applicants must be able to demonstrate financial need. Only students in accredited institutions working toward a basic college (bachelor's) or seminary (M.Div.) degree are eligible. As part of the selection process, applicants must submit an essay describing their interest in and commitment to a Christian vocation.
Financial data The maximum grants are $500 per year for students attending accredited colleges, $600 per year for students in non-Southern Baptist Convention seminaries, and $850 per year for students at 1 of the 6 Southern Baptist Convention seminaries.
Duration 1 year; renewable.
Additional Information The 6 Southern Baptist seminaries are Golden Gate Baptist Theological Seminary (Mill Valley, California), Midwestern Baptist Theological Seminary (Kansas City, Missouri), New Orleans Baptist Theological Seminary (New Orleans, Louisiana), Southeastern Baptist Theological Seminary (Wake Forest, North Carolina), Southern Baptist Theological Seminary (Louisville, Kentucky), and Southwestern Baptist Theological Seminary (Fort Worth, Texas).
Number awarded Varies each year.
Deadline Applications may be submitted at any time, but they must be received at least 1 month (preferably sooner) before the student enrolls in a school.

[269]
HENRY AND ANNA PLAPINGER ENDOWMENT AWARD

Jewish Deaf Congress
c/o Dr. Alexander Fleischman, President Emeritus
4960 East Sabal Palm Boulevard, Apartment 207
Tamarac, FL 33319-2629
(305) 977-7887

Summary To provide financial assistance to deaf rabbinical candidates attending a seminary.
Eligibility This program is open to rabbinical candidates at a seminary who are deaf.
Financial data The amount of the award depends on the need of the candidate and the availability of funds.

Number awarded Awards are presented whenever a suitable candidate applies. The program has been dormant for several years because of a lack of applicants, but the award is still available.

[270]
IMA DIVERSITY SCHOLARSHIP PROGRAM

Institute of Management Accountants
Attn: Committee on Students
10 Paragon Drive
Montvale, NJ 07645-1760
(201) 573-9000
Toll-free: (800) 638-4427, ext. 1543
Fax: (201) 573-8438   E-mail: students@imanet.org
Web: www.imanet.org

Summary To provide financial assistance to minority and disabled student members of the Institute of Management Accountants (IMA) who are interested in working on an undergraduate or graduate degree in management accounting or financial management.

Eligibility This program is open to undergraduate and graduate students of American Indian/Alaska Native, Asian/Pacific Islander, Black, or Hispanic heritage and students with physical disabilities (defined as hearing impairment, vision impairment, missing extremities, partial paralysis, complete paralysis, or severe distortion of limbs and/or spine). Applicants must be in their sophomore, junior, or senior year or in a graduate program with a major in management accounting, financial management, or information technology. Selection is based on 1) academic merit; 2) quality of their application presentation; 3) demonstrated community leadership; 4) potential for success in expressed career goals in a financial management position; 5) a written statement from applicants expressing their short-term and long-term career goals and objectives, including their participation in the IMA; and 6) letters of recommendation.

Financial data Stipends are $3,000 per year.

Duration 1 year.

Additional Information Up to 15 finalists in each category (including the scholarship winners) receive a scholarship to take 5 parts of the CMA and/or CFM examination within a year of graduation.

Number awarded At least 13 each year.

Deadline February of each year.

[271]
KATHERINE VAZ SCHOLARSHIP

Luso-American Education Foundation
Attn: Administrative Director
7080 Donlon Way, Suite 202
P.O. Box 2967
Dublin, CA 94568
(925) 828-3883   Fax: (925) 828-3883
Web: www.luso-american.org/laef

Summary To provide financial assistance for undergraduate study to members of the Luso-American community who are deaf or interested in studying writing.

Eligibility This program is open to college and high school students with a connection to the Portuguese community in America. Applicants must be either deaf or interested in studying writing.

Financial data The stipend is $1,000.

Duration 1 year; renewable.

Number awarded 1 each year.

Deadline February of each year.

[272]
MINNIE PEARL SCHOLARSHIP PROGRAM

EAR Foundation
c/o Baptist Hospital
1817 Patterson Street
Nashville, TN 37203-2110
(615) 329-7807   Toll-free: (800) 545-HEAR
Fax: (615) 329-7935   TDD: (800) 545-HEAR
Fax: earfound@earfoundation.org
Web: www.earfoundation.com/minnie.html

Summary To provide financial assistance to hearing impaired students who want to attend college.

Eligibility Applicants must be mainstreamed high school seniors with severe to profound bilateral hearing loss. Their primary means of communication may be manual or oral. They must have earned a GPA of 3.0 or higher; plan to attend a junior college, university, or technical school on a full-time basis; and be U.S. citizens. Along with their application, they must submit brief essays on how they feel about mainstreaming, their goals after graduating from college, and why they are a good candidate for this scholarship.

Financial data The stipend is $2,500 per year.

Duration 1 year; may be renewed up to 3 additional years if the recipient maintains a GPA of 3.0 or higher.

Additional Information This program was established in 1986.

Number awarded Varies each year; recently, 16 of these scholarships were awarded.

Deadline February of each year.

[273]
NATIONAL FRATERNAL SOCIETY OF THE DEAF SCHOLARSHIPS

National Fraternal Society of the Deaf
1118 South Sixth Street
Springfield, IL 62703
(217) 789-7429 Fax: (217) 789-7489
TTY: (217) 789-7438 E-mail: thefrat@nfsd.com
Web: www.nfsd.com

Summary To provide financial assistance for college to members of the National Fraternal Society of the Deaf.

Eligibility Deaf, hard of hearing, or hearing persons who are enrolled in or accepted at a postsecondary educational institution are eligible to apply if they have been members of the society for at least 1 year prior to application.

Financial data The stipend is $1,000.

Duration 1 year; may be renewed 1 additional year.

Number awarded 10 each year.

Deadline June of each year.

[274]
SCHOLARSHIP TRUST FOR THE DEAF AND NEAR DEAF

Travelers Protective Association of America
Attn: TPA Scholarship Trust for the Deaf and Near Deaf
3755 Lindell Boulevard
St. Louis, MO 63108-3476
(314) 371-0533 Fax: (314) 371-0537
E-mail: tpanathq@freewwweb.com
Web: www.travelersprotectiveasn.com

Summary To provide assistance to deaf and hearing impaired persons who need funds to obtain additional education, mechanical devices, specialized medical treatment, or other treatments.

Eligibility The only requirement for aid is that applicants must be U.S. citizens who are deaf or hearing impaired.

Financial data Varies each year; since the fund was established, more than $800,000 has been awarded. Money may be used for mechanical devices, tuition at schools that specialize in educating the deaf (e.g., Gallaudet University, Rochester Institute of Technology, Central Institute for the Deaf), note takers and interpreters in classes in regular schools that do not provide those services to the deaf, speech and language therapy (especially for those who have had the Cochlear Implant), medical or other specialized treatments, and computer programs that assist deaf and their families learn and apply skills presented in the classroom.

Duration 1 year; recipients may reapply.

Additional Information This fund was established in 1975. Funds have been awarded to children as young as 2 months and to adults as old as 82 years.

Number awarded Varies each year; since the trust was established, it has distributed nearly $1 million to more than 1,800 recipients.

Deadline February of each year.

[275]
SCHOOL-AGE FINANCIAL AID AWARDS

Alexander Graham Bell Association for the Deaf
Attn: Financial Aid Coordinator
3417 Volta Place, N.W.
Washington, DC 20007-2778
(202) 337-5220 Fax: (202) 337-8314
TTY: (202) 337-5221
E-mail: financialaid@agbell.org
Web: www.agbell.org

Summary To provide financial aid to students at independent or parochial elementary, junior high, or high schools who have a moderate to profound hearing loss.

Eligibility To be eligible, applicants must meet the following requirements: 1) be enrolled in or accepted by a nondiscriminatory independent or parochial elementary, junior high, or high school for students with normal hearing (college students are not eligible); 2) have been moderately to profoundly hearing impaired (55 dB or greater loss in the speech frequencies of 500, 1000, and 2000 Hz) since birth or prelinguistically; 3) use speech, residual hearing, and/or speechreading as their primary form of communication; and 4) be at least 6 but less than 21 years of age. The family must be able to demonstrate financial need.

Financial data The amount of the award depends on the needs of the child; generally, awards range from $300 to $1,000 per year.

Duration 1 year; may be renewed upon reapplication.

Number awarded Varies each year.

Deadline Applications must be requested between January and March of each year.

[276]
SERTOMA SCHOLARSHIPS FOR HEARING-IMPAIRED STUDENTS

Sertoma International
Attn: Sponsorships Department
1912 East Meyer Boulevard
Kansas City, MO 64132-1174
(816) 333-8300 Fax: (816) 333-4320
TTY: (816) 333-8300 E-mail: cneely@sertoma.org
Web: www.sertoma.org

Summary To provide financial assistance for college to hearing impaired students.

Eligibility This program is open to students who have a clinically significant bilateral hearing loss and are interested in working on a bachelor's degree at a 4-year college or university. Students working on a community college degree, associate degree, or vocational program

degree are ineligible. Applicants must be able to document their hearing loss. They must be entering or continuing undergraduate studies on a full-time basis in the United States or Canada. A GPA of at least 3.2 is required. Selection is based on past academic performance, goals, a statement of purpose, and overall merit. Financial need is not considered.

Financial data The stipend is $1,000 per year.

Duration 1 year; may be renewed up to 4 times.

Additional Information Sertoma, which stands for SERvice TO MAnkind, is a volunteer service organization with 25,000 members in 800 clubs across North America. Funding for this program is provided by Oticon, Phonic Ear, Starkey, the Lenexa Kansas Sertoma Club, and the Sertoma Foundation. To request an application, students must send a self-addressed, stamped envelope.

Number awarded 20 each year.

Deadline April of each year.

[277]
TEXAS BLIND/DEAF STUDENT EXEMPTION PROGRAM

Texas Higher Education Coordinating Board
Attn: Grants and Special Programs
1200 East Anderson Lane
P.O. Box 12788, Capitol Station
Austin, TX 78711-2788
(512) 427-6101   Toll-free: (800) 242-3062
Fax: (512) 427-6127
E-mail: grantinfo@thecb.state.tx.us
Web: www.collegefortexans.com

Summary To provide a tuition exemption to blind and/or deaf residents of Texas.

Eligibility This program is open to Texas residents who can present certification from the appropriate state vocational rehabilitation agency of their deafness or blindness. Applicants must present to the registrar of a public college or university in Texas a copy of their high school transcript, a letter of recommendation, proof that they have met all admission requirements, and a statement of purpose that indicates the certificate, degree program, or professional enhancement that they intend to pursue.

Financial data Eligible students are exempted from the payment of all dues, fees, and tuition charges at publicly-supported colleges and universities in Texas.

Duration Up to 8 semesters.

Number awarded Varies each year; recently, 2,948 students received support through this program.

[278]
WISCONSIN HEARING AND VISUALLY HANDICAPPED STUDENT GRANT PROGRAM

Wisconsin Higher Educational Aids Board
131 West Wilson Street, Room 902
P.O. Box 7885
Madison, WI 53707-7885
(608) 266-0888   Fax: (608) 267-2808
E-mail: sandy.thomas@heab.state.wi.us
Web: heab.state.wi.us/programs.html

Summary To provide financial support for undergraduate study to Wisconsin residents who are legally deaf or blind.

Eligibility To be eligible for a grant, the student must be a Wisconsin resident, must have financial need as determined by the institution the student attends, must submit evidence of a severe or profound hearing or visual impairment certified by a medical examiner, and must be enrolled in a nonprofit, accredited public or private college, university, or vocational/technical school located in Wisconsin.

Financial data Grants range from $250 to $1,800 per academic year.

Duration 1 year; may be renewed up to 4 additional years.

Additional Information If the disability prevents the student from studying in a Wisconsin institution, he or she may attend an out-of-state institution that specializes in the training of deaf and/or blind students.

Number awarded Varies each year.

Fellowships/Grants

[279]
ALAN B., '32, AND FLORENCE B., '35, CRAMMATTE FELLOWSHIP

Gallaudet University Alumni Association
Attn: Graduate Fellowship Fund Committee
Peikoff Alumni House
Gallaudet University
800 Florida Avenue, N.E.
Washington, DC 20002-3695
(202) 651-5060   Fax: (202) 651-5062
TTY: (202) 651-5060
E-mail: alumni.relations@gallaudet.edu
Web: www.gallaudet.edu

Summary To provide financial assistance to deaf students who wish to work on a graduate degree in a field related to business at universities for people who hear normally.

Eligibility This program is open to deaf and hard of hearing graduates of Gallaudet University or other

accredited academic institutions who have been accepted for graduate study in a business-related field at colleges or universities for people who hear normally. Applicants must be working on a doctorate or other terminal degree. Financial need is considered in the selection process.

Financial data The amount awarded varies, depending upon the needs of the recipient and the availability of funds.

Duration 1 year; may be renewed.

Additional Information This fund is 1 of 11 designated funds included in the Graduate Fellowship Fund of the Gallaudet University Alumni Association. Recipients must carry a full-time semester load.

Number awarded Up to 1 each year.

Deadline April of each year.

[280]
ALEXANDER GRAHAM BELL ASSOCIATION COLLEGE SCHOLARSHIP AWARDS

Alexander Graham Bell Association for the Deaf
Attn: Financial Aid Coordinator
3417 Volta Place, N.W.
Washington, DC 20007-2778
(202) 337-5220   Fax: (202) 337-8314
TTY: (202) 337-5221
E-mail: financialaid@agbell.org
Web: www.agbell.org/financialaid.cfm

Summary To provide financial assistance to undergraduate and graduate students with moderate to profound hearing loss.

Eligibility This program is open to undergraduate and graduate students who have had a hearing loss since birth or before acquiring language with a 60 dB or greater loss in the better ear in the speech frequencies of 500, 1000, and 2000 Hz. Applicants must use speech and residual hearing and/or speechreading (lipreading) as their primary and preferred mode of communication. They must be accepted by or already attending full time a college or university that primarily enrolls students with normal hearing. Preference is given to undergraduates. Financial need is considered in the selection process.

Financial data Stipends range from $250 to $2,000.

Duration 1 year; may be renewed 1 additional year.

Additional Information In past years, individual awards have been designated as the Allie Raney Hunt Memorial Scholarship Award, the David Von Hagen Scholarship Award, the Elsie Bell Grosvenor Scholarship Awards, the Franklin and Henrietta Dickman Memorial Scholarship Awards, the Herbert P. Feibelman Jr. (PS) Scholarship Award, the Lucille A. Abt Scholarship Awards, the Maude Winkler Scholarship Awards, the Oral Hearing-Impaired Section Scholarship Award, the Robert H. Weitbrecht Scholarship Awards, the Second Century Fund Awards, and the Volta Scholarship Award. Some of those awards included additional eligibility requirements. Only the first 500 requests for applications are accepted.

Number awarded Varies each year; recently, 22 of these scholarships were awarded.

Deadline Applications must be requested between September and December of each year and submitted by February of each year.

[281]
ALPHA SIGMA PI FRATERNITY FELLOWSHIP

Gallaudet University Alumni Association
Attn: Graduate Fellowship Fund Committee
Peikoff Alumni House
Gallaudet University
800 Florida Avenue, N.E.
Washington, DC 20002-3695
(202) 651-5060   Fax: (202) 651-5062
TTY: (202) 651-5060
E-mail: alumni.relations@gallaudet.edu
Web: www.gallaudet.edu

Summary To provide financial assistance to deaf students who wish to work on a doctoral degree at universities for people who hear normally.

Eligibility This program is open to deaf and hard of hearing graduates of Gallaudet University or other accredited colleges or universities who have been accepted for graduate study at academic institutions for people who hear normally. Applicants must be working on a doctorate or other terminal degree. Preference is given to alumni members of Alpha Sigma Pi Fraternity. Financial need is considered in the selection process.

Financial data The amount awarded varies, depending upon the needs of the recipient and the availability of funds.

Duration 1 year; may be renewed.

Additional Information This program was established in 2001 as 1 of 11 designated funds within the Graduate Fellowship Fund of the Gallaudet University Alumni Association. Recipients must carry a full-time load.

Number awarded Up to 1 each year.

Deadline April of each year.

[282]
DORIS B. ORMAN, '25, FELLOWSHIP

Gallaudet University Alumni Association
Attn: Graduate Fellowship Fund Committee
Peikoff Alumni House
Gallaudet University
800 Florida Avenue, N.E.
Washington, DC 20002-3695
(202) 651-5060   Fax: (202) 651-5062
TTY: (202) 651-5060
E-mail: alumni.relations@gallaudet.edu
Web: www.gallaudet.edu

Summary To provide financial assistance to deaf women who wish to work on a graduate degree at universities for people who hear normally.

Eligibility This program is open to deaf or hard of hearing women graduates of Gallaudet University or other accredited academic institutions who have been accepted for graduate study at colleges or universities for people who hear normally. Applicants must be working on a doctorate or other terminal degree. They must have a particular interest in the arts, the humanities, and community leadership. Financial need is considered in the selection process.

Financial data The amount awarded varies, depending upon the needs of the recipient and the availability of funds.

Duration 1 year; may be renewed.

Additional Information This program is 1 of 11 designated funds within the Graduate Fellowship Fund of the Gallaudet University Alumni Association. Recipients must carry a full-time semester load.

Number awarded Up to 1 each year.

Deadline April of each year.

[283]
GALLAUDET UNIVERSITY PRESIDENT'S FELLOWSHIP PROGRAM

Gallaudet University
Attn: Dean of the College of Liberal Arts, Sciences, and Technologies
SAC 2220
800 Florida Avenue, N.E.
Washington, DC 20002
(202) 651-5801   Fax: (202) 651-5759
TTY: (202) 651-5682
E-mail: eileen.matthews@gallaudet.edu
Web: www.gallaudet.edu

Summary To provide support to hearing impaired doctoral students interested in a teaching assistantship at Gallaudet University while they complete work on their degree.

Eligibility This program is open to deaf and hard of hearing full-time graduate students working on a Ph.D. or other terminal degree at a university in the United States other than Gallaudet. Applicants must be able and willing to serve as a teaching assistant at Gallaudet while they complete work on their degree. They must already possess sign skills at an appropriate level and aspire to a teaching and research career. Fields of study vary each year; recently, they were biology, chemistry, communication studies, English, government, mathematics, psychology (personality or developmental), and social work.

Financial data Grants provide up to $12,000 per year for tuition; a stipend in return for teaching duties; academic privileges, such as library, WLRC, and e-mail access; and some travel support for professional conferences.

Duration 1 year; may be renewed up to 4 additional years.

Additional Information This program was established in 2003. The program does not guarantee future employment at Gallaudet, but does require a 2-year commitment to teaching at the university if a faculty vacancy occurs. During their tenure at Gallaudet, fellows are expected to 1) serve as teaching assistants in appropriate departments and teach up to 2 courses per semester; 2) attend faculty development mentoring activities; 3) maintain good standing in their graduate program; and 4) make timely progress toward their degree.

Number awarded Up to 5 each year.

Deadline May of each year.

[284]
GUAA GRADUATE FELLOWSHIP FUND

Gallaudet University Alumni Association
Attn: Graduate Fellowship Fund Committee
Peikoff Alumni House
Gallaudet University
800 Florida Avenue, N.E.
Washington, DC 20002-3695
(202) 651-5060   Fax: (202) 651-5062
TTY: (202) 651-5060
E-mail: alumni.relations@gallaudet.edu
Web: www.gallaudet.edu

Summary To provide financial assistance to deaf students who wish to work on a graduate degree at universities for people who hear normally.

Eligibility This program is open to deaf and hard of hearing graduates of Gallaudet University or other accredited academic institutions who have been accepted for graduate study at colleges or universities for people who hear normally. Applicants must be working on a doctoral or other terminal degree. Financial need is considered in the selection process.

Financial data The amount awarded varies, depending upon the number of qualified candidates applying for assistance, the availability of funds, and the needs of individual applicants.

Duration 1 year; may be renewed.

Additional Information This program includes the following named fellowships: the Boyce R. Williams, '32, Fellowship, the David Peikoff, '29, Fellowship, the James N. Orman, '23, Fellowship, the John A. Trundle, 1885, Fellowship, the Old Dominion Foundation Fellowship, and the Waldo T., '49 and Jean Kelsch, '51, Cordano Fellowship. Recipients must carry a full-time semester load.

Number awarded Varies each year; recently, 9 of these fellowships were awarded.

Deadline April of each year.

[285]
HEARING IMPAIRED CHURCH MULTIPLICATION TEAM SCHOLARSHIPS

Southern Baptist Convention
North American Mission Board
Attn: Church Multiplication Team
4200 North Point Parkway
Alpharetta, GA 30022-4176
(770) 410-6235   Fax: (770) 410-6012
E-mail: jdoyle@namb.net
Web: www.namb.net

Summary To provide financial assistance to Baptists who are deaf and interested in religious vocations.

Eligibility This program is open to U.S. citizens who are hearing impaired and involved in some type of approved Baptist ministry. Applicants must be able to demonstrate financial need. Only students in accredited institutions working toward a basic college (bachelor's) or seminary (M.Div.) degree are eligible. As part of the selection process, applicants must submit an essay describing their interest in and commitment to a Christian vocation.

Financial data The maximum grants are $500 per year for students attending accredited colleges, $600 per year for students in non-Southern Baptist Convention seminaries, and $850 per year for students at 1 of the 6 Southern Baptist Convention seminaries.

Duration 1 year; renewable.

Additional Information The 6 Southern Baptist seminaries are Golden Gate Baptist Theological Seminary (Mill Valley, California), Midwestern Baptist Theological Seminary (Kansas City, Missouri), New Orleans Baptist Theological Seminary (New Orleans, Louisiana), Southeastern Baptist Theological Seminary (Wake Forest, North Carolina), Southern Baptist Theological Seminary (Louisville, Kentucky), and Southwestern Baptist Theological Seminary (Fort Worth, Texas).

Number awarded Varies each year.

Deadline Applications may be submitted at any time, but they must be received at least 1 month (preferably sooner) before the student enrolls in a school.

[286]
HENRY SYLE MEMORIAL FELLOWSHIP FOR SEMINARY STUDIES

Gallaudet University Alumni Association
Attn: Graduate Fellowship Fund Committee
Peikoff Alumni House
Gallaudet University
800 Florida Avenue, N.E.
Washington, DC 20002-3695
(202) 651-5060   Fax: (202) 651-5062
TTY: (202) 651-5060
E-mail: alumni.relations@gallaudet.edu
Web: www.gallaudet.edu

Summary To provide financial assistance to deaf students who wish to pursue seminary studies at universities for people who hear normally.

Eligibility This program is open to deaf and hard of hearing graduates of Gallaudet University or other accredited academic institutions who have been accepted for graduate seminary study at colleges or universities for people who hear normally. Applicants must be working on a doctoral or other terminal degree. Financial need is considered in the selection process.

Financial data The amount awarded varies, depending upon the needs of the recipient and the availability of funds.

Duration 1 year; may be renewed.

Additional Information When this fund becomes fully endowed, it will be 1 of 11 designated funds within the Graduate Fellowship Fund of the Gallaudet University Alumni Association. Recipients must carry a full-time semester load.

Number awarded Up to 1 each year.

Deadline April of each year.

[287]
IADES FELLOWSHIP AWARD

International Alumnae of Delta Epsilon Sorority
c/o Virginia Borgaard
2453 Bear Den Road
Frederick, MD 21701
E-mail: vborgaard@juno.com

Summary To provide financial assistance to deaf women who are working on a graduate degree.

Eligibility Eligible to apply are deaf women who have completed 12 or more units in a doctoral-level program with a GPA of 3.0 or more. They need not be members of Delta Epsilon. Along with their application, they must submit official transcripts, a recent copy of their audiogram, and 2 letters of recommendation.

Financial data The stipend is $1,000.

Duration 1 year.

Additional Information This program was established in 1989.

Number awarded 1 or more each year.

Deadline August of each year.

[288]
IMA DIVERSITY SCHOLARSHIP PROGRAM

Institute of Management Accountants
Attn: Committee on Students
10 Paragon Drive
Montvale, NJ 07645-1760
(201) 573-9000
Toll-free: (800) 638-4427, ext. 1543
Fax: (201) 573-8438   E-mail: students@imanet.org
Web: www.imanet.org

Summary To provide financial assistance to minority and disabled student members of the Institute of Management Accountants (IMA) who are interested in working on an undergraduate or graduate degree in management accounting or financial management.

Eligibility This program is open to undergraduate and graduate students of American Indian/Alaska Native, Asian/Pacific Islander, Black, or Hispanic heritage and students with physical disabilities (defined as hearing impairment, vision impairment, missing extremities, partial paralysis, complete paralysis, or severe distortion of limbs and/or spine). Applicants must be in their sophomore, junior, or senior year or in a graduate program with a major in management accounting, financial management, or information technology. Selection is based on 1) academic merit; 2) quality of their application presentation; 3) demonstrated community leadership; 4) potential for success in expressed career goals in a financial management position; 5) a written statement from applicants expressing their short-term and long-term career goals and objectives, including their participation in the IMA; and 6) letters of recommendation.

Financial data Stipends are $3,000 per year.

Duration 1 year.

Additional Information Up to 15 finalists in each category (including the scholarship winners) receive a scholarship to take 5 parts of the CMA and/or CFM examination within a year of graduation.

Number awarded At least 13 each year.

Deadline February of each year.

[289]
REGINA OLSON HUGHES, '18, FELLOWSHIP

Gallaudet University Alumni Association
Attn: Graduate Fellowship Fund Committee
Peikoff Alumni House
Gallaudet University
800 Florida Avenue, N.E.
Washington, DC 20002-3695
(202) 651-5060   Fax: (202) 651-5062
TTY: (202) 651-5060
E-mail: alumni.relations@gallaudet.edu
Web: www.gallaudet.edu

Summary To provide financial assistance to deaf students who wish to work on a graduate degree in fine arts at universities for people who hear normally.

Eligibility This program is open to deaf and hard of hearing graduates of Gallaudet University or other accredited academic institutions who have been accepted for graduate study in fine arts at colleges or universities for people who hear normally. Applicants must be working on a doctoral or other terminal degree. Financial need is considered in the selection process.

Financial data The amount awarded varies, depending upon the needs of the recipient and the availability of funds.

Duration 1 year; may be renewed.

Additional Information This program, established in 1995, is 1 of 11 designated funds within the Graduate Fellowship Fund of the Gallaudet University Alumni Association. Recipients must carry a full-time semester load.

Number awarded Up to 1 each year.

Deadline April of each year.

[290]
WILLIAM C. STOKOE SCHOLARSHIP

National Association of the Deaf
814 Thayer Avenue
Silver Spring, MD 20910-4500
(301) 587-1788   Fax: (301) 587-1791
TTY: (301) 587-1789   E-mail: nadinfo@nad.org
Web: www.nad.org

Summary To provide financial assistance to deaf graduate students who are pursuing studies or conducting research in a field related to sign language.

Eligibility This program is open to deaf students who have graduated from a 4-year college program and are currently enrolled in a master's or doctoral degree program in a field related to sign language or the deaf community. Applicants may also be developing a special project on 1 of those topics.

Financial data The stipend is $2,000.

Duration 1 year.

Additional Information Most of the money for the scholarship comes from the sales of a book, *Sign Language and the Deaf Community: Essays in Honor of Wil-*

liam C. Stokoe. The editors and authors of the book, published in 1980 by the National Association of the Deaf, donated all their royalties to the scholarship fund. The holder of the scholarship must create and finish, within a year, a project that relates to sign language or the deaf community. The recipient must prepare a brief report (either written or videotaped) at the end of the project, which normally but not always relates to the student's work in school.

Number awarded 1 each year.
Deadline March of each year.

Grants-in-Aid

[291]
GM MOBILITY REIMBURSEMENT PROGRAM

General Motors
100 Renaissance Drive
Mail Code: 482-A25-D35
P.O. Box 100
Detroit, MI 48265-1000
(313) 667-8547   Toll-free: (800) 323-9935
Fax: (313) 667-8950   TDD: (800) TDD-9935
Web: www.gmmobility.com

Summary To provide a cash reimbursement for the cost of installing adaptive driving aids on new purchases from General Motors.

Eligibility Eligible for this rebate are purchasers or lessors of new General Motors cars, trucks, or vans that require adaptive driving aids or conversion equipment for users with disabilities. The equipment may be an "alerting device" that assists deaf or hard of hearing drivers with emergency vehicle siren detectors and enhanced turn signal reminders.

Financial data Up to $1,000 is reimbursed.

Additional Information Applications for reimbursement are submitted through the dealer from whom the vehicle was originally purchased. Only retail purchases or leases of new General Motors vehicles qualify for this program. The reimbursement applies only to equipment installed by converters in the after market, not to factory installed equipment of any kind.

Deadline The conversion process must be completed within 9 months of vehicle delivery and the claim form must be submitted within 90 days after the completion of the conversion.

[292]
HAWAII INCOME TAX EXEMPTION FOR DISABLED RESIDENTS

Department of Taxation
Attn: Taxpayer Services Branch
425 Queen Street
P.O. Box 259
Honolulu, HI 96809-0259
(808) 587-4242   Toll-free: (800) 222-3229
Fax: (808) 587-1488   TDD: (808) 587-1418
Web: www.hawaii.gov/tax/tax.html

Summary To exempt a portion of the income of disabled residents from state income tax in Hawaii.

Eligibility Eligible for this exemption are 1) blind residents whose central visual acuity does not exceed 20/200 in the better eye with corrective lenses or whose visual acuity is greater than 20/200 but is accompanied by a limitation in the field of vision such that the widest diameter of the visual field subtends an angle no greater than 20 degrees; 2) deaf residents whose average loss in the speech frequencies in the better ear is 82 decibels A.S.A. or worse; or 3) totally disabled residents (physically or mentally) who are unable to engage in any substantial gainful business or occupation (a person whose gross income exceeds $30,000 per year is assumed to be engaged in a substantial gainful business or occupation).

Financial data The maximum exemptions from state income tax are as follows: single disabled resident, $7,000; disabled husband and wife, $14,000; disabled husband or wife, with non-disabled spouse under 65, $8,040; disabled husband or wife, with non-disabled spouse age 65 or over, $9,080.

Duration The exemption continues as long as the recipient resides in Hawaii.

Additional Information Residents who claim this special exemption are not eligible to claim additional exemptions for their children or other dependents.

[293]
KANSAS STATE DEAF-BLIND FUND

Kansas State Department of Education
Student Support Services
Attn: Kansas Project for Children and Young Adults
  Who Are Deaf-Blind
120 Southeast 10th Avenue
Topeka, KS 66612-1182
(785) 296-0917   Toll-free: (800) 203-9462
Fax: (785) 296-4944

Summary To provide supplementary financial assistance to deaf-blind or severely disabled students in Kansas.

Eligibility Applications may be submitted by school personnel for students in Kansas (up to the age of 21) who are deaf-blind and/or have severe multiple disabilities. Approval for funding is granted on a first-come, first-served basis, when the costs for educational tech-

nology, equipment, consultation, or evaluation exceed the amount local education agencies are able to provide out of federal, state, or local funds. Priority candidates are deaf-blind children from birth through 2 years of age, students who are exiting state hospital schools and returning to their home district, students who have a suspected vision loss and documented hearing loss and are in need of an evaluation, and students who have a suspected hearing loss and documented vision loss who are in need of an evaluation.

Financial data Eligible students are awarded up to $3,000 per year. Funds must be used for educational technology, equipment, consultation, or evaluation.

Duration 1 year; may be renewed.

Number awarded Varies each year.

Deadline January of each year.

[294]
MICHIGAN INCOME TAX EXEMPTION FOR PEOPLE WITH DISABILITIES

Michigan Department of Treasury
Attn: Income Tax
Treasury Building
430 West Allegan Street
Lansing, MI 48922
(517) 373-3200   Toll-free: (800) 827-4000
TTY: (517) 636-4999
E-mail: treasIndTax@michigan.gov
Web: www.michigan.gov/treasury

Summary To exempt a portion of the income of deaf, blind, and disabled residents of Michigan from state income taxation.

Eligibility Eligible for this exemption are residents of Michigan who 1) receive messages through a sense other than hearing, such as lip reading or sign language; 2) have vision in their better eye of 20/200 or less with corrective lenses or peripheral field of vision of 20 degrees or less; or 3) are hemiplegic, paraplegic, quadriplegic, or totally and permanently disabled.

Financial data Qualifying people with disabilities receive an exemption of $1,900 from their adjusted gross income for purposes of state taxation.

Duration The exemption continues as long as the recipient resides in Michigan.

[295]
OREGON LIONS PATIENT CARE PROGRAM

Oregon Lions Sight & Hearing Foundation
Attn: Patient Care Coordinator
1410 S.W. Morrison Street, Suite 760
Portland, OR 97205
(503) 827-6952, ext. 23
Toll-free: (800) 635-4667, ext. 23
Fax: (503) 827-6958   E-mail: info@orlions.org
Web: www.orlions.org

Summary To provide funding to needy Oregon residents who require eye or ear surgery.

Eligibility Applicants must have been residents of Oregon for at least 6 months and be sponsored by a local Lions, Lioness, Leo, or Lions Auxiliary Club. They must require treatment for vision (e.g., cataract surgery, cornea transplant, enucleation, ocular prosthetic, treatment of macular degeneration) or hearing (e.g., tympanoplasty, cochlear implant, nasal septoplasy, treatment of diabetic retinopathy, vitrectomy) but be unable to afford the procedure. Their income must be less than 150% of the federal poverty level and they must be without other resources (private insurance, Medicare, or the Oregon Health Plan) to pay for the treatment.

Financial data Grants provide approximately one-third of the total regular cost for the procedure.

Duration These are 1-time grants.

Number awarded Approximately 50 each year.

Deadline Applications may be submitted at any time.

[296]
PARENT-INFANT/PRESCHOOL SERVICES FINANCIAL AID PROGRAM

Alexander Graham Bell Association for the Deaf
Attn: Financial Aid Coordinator
3417 Volta Place, N.W.
Washington, DC 20007-2778
(202) 337-5220   Fax: (202) 337-8314
TTY: (202) 337-5221
E-mail: financialaid@agbell.org
Web: www.agbell.org

Summary To provide financial aid to the parents of infants and preschool children with moderate to profound hearing loss who need assistance to cover expenses associated with early intervention services.

Eligibility Applicants must be parents or guardians of children less than 6 years of age who have been diagnosed as having a moderate to profound hearing loss (55 dB or greater loss in the speech frequencies of 500, 1000, and 2000 Hz). The parent or guardian must be committed to an oral approach for education of their child, including the development of the child's listening, speech, oral communication, and cognitive skills. The family must be able to demonstrate financial need.

Financial data The amount awarded depends on the needs of the child; most awards range from $300 to $1,000 per year.
Duration 1 year; may be renewed upon reapplication, but preference is given to new applicants who are just enrolling their child in preschool.
Number awarded Varies each year.
Deadline Applications must be requested between June and August of each year.

[297]
SCHOLARSHIP TRUST FOR THE DEAF AND NEAR DEAF

Travelers Protective Association of America
Attn: TPA Scholarship Trust for the Deaf and Near Deaf
3755 Lindell Boulevard
St. Louis, MO 63108-3476
(314) 371-0533 Fax: (314) 371-0537
E-mail: tpanathq@freewwweb.com
Web: www.travelersprotectiveasn.com

Summary To provide assistance to deaf and hearing impaired persons who need funds to obtain additional education, mechanical devices, specialized medical treatment, or other treatments.
Eligibility The only requirement for aid is that applicants must be U.S. citizens who are deaf or hearing impaired.
Financial data Varies each year; since the fund was established, more than $800,000 has been awarded. Money may be used for mechanical devices, tuition at schools that specialize in educating the deaf (e.g., Gallaudet University, Rochester Institute of Technology, Central Institute for the Deaf), note takers and interpreters in classes in regular schools that do not provide those services to the deaf, speech and language therapy (especially for those who have had the Cochlear Implant), medical or other specialized treatments, and computer programs that assist deaf and their families learn and apply skills presented in the classroom.
Duration 1 year; recipients may reapply.
Additional Information This fund was established in 1975. Funds have been awarded to children as young as 2 months and to adults as old as 82 years.
Number awarded Varies each year; since the trust was established, it has distributed nearly $1 million to more than 1,800 recipients.
Deadline February of each year.

Awards

[298]
MISS DEAF AMERICA PAGEANT AWARDS

National Association of the Deaf
814 Thayer Avenue
Silver Spring, MD 20910-4500
(301) 587-1788 Fax: (301) 587-1791
TTY: (301) 587-1789 E-mail: nadinfo@nad.org
Web: www.nad.org/mda/index.html

Summary To recognize and reward outstanding young deaf women.
Eligibility This is a 2-tiered competition. Young deaf women between the ages of 18 and 28 compete first on the state level; winners take part in the national pageant. Winners are selected on the basis of talent, community service, academics, current events, deaf culture, and more.
Financial data The amounts awarded vary. For example, state winners receive an all expense-paid trip to the national competition and a cash award (generally in the $200 range). The national winner and runners-up receive larger cash awards.
Duration The competition is held biennially, during the summer of even-numbered years, in conjunction with the National Association of the Deaf conventions.
Deadline The deadline dates of the state competitions vary; check with the sponsor in your area.

[299]
OPTIMIST INTERNATIONAL COMMUNICATION CONTEST FOR THE DEAF AND HARD OF HEARING

Optimist International
Attn: Programs Department
4494 Lindell Boulevard
St. Louis, MO 63108
(314) 371-6000 Toll-free: (800) 500-8130, ext. 224
Fax: (314) 371-6006
E-mail: programs@optimist.org
Web: www.optimist.org

Summary To recognize and reward outstanding presentations made by deaf high school students.
Eligibility All students in public, private, or parochial elementary, junior high, and senior high schools in the United States, Canada, or the Caribbean who are identified by their school as having a hearing loss or impairment may enter. They are invited to make a presentation from 4 to 5 minutes on a topic that changes annually; a recent topic was "United We Stand in Optimism." Competition is first conducted at the level of individual

clubs, with winners advancing to zone and then district competitions. Selection is based on material organization (40 points), delivery and presentation (30 points), and overall effectiveness (30 points).

Financial data Each district winner receives a $1,500 college scholarship, payable to an educational institution of the recipient's choice, subject to the approval of Optimist International.

Duration The competition is held annually.

Additional Information Entry information is available only from local Optimist Clubs.

Number awarded Nearly 500 Optimist International clubs and 45 districts participate in this program. Each participating district offers 1 scholarship; some districts may offer a second award with separate competitions for signing and oral competitors, or for male and female entrants.

Deadline Each club sets its own deadline. The district deadline is the end of September of each year.

Orthopedic/Developmental Disabilities

- *Scholarships*
- *Fellowships/Grants*
- *Loans*
- *Grants-in-Aid*

Described here are 57 programs open to individuals with 1) a severe orthopedic impairment caused by birth defects (e.g., absence of an extremity), diseases, or other causes (e.g., accidents, amputations), or 2) a severe, chronic disability that was manifested before age 22 (including mental retardation). In all, 14 entries cover scholarships (to pursue studies or research on the undergraduate level in the United States); 3 cover fellowships/grants (to pursue graduate or postdoctoral education or research in the United States); 3 cover loans(to provide money that must eventually be repaid, with or without interest); and 37 cover grants-in-aid (to support emergency situations, travel, income/property tax liabilities, or the acquisition of assistive technology). If you are looking for a particular program and don't find it in this chapter, be sure to check the Program Title Index to see if it is covered elsewhere in the directory.

Scholarships

[300]
BLANCHE FISCHER FOUNDATION GRANTS

Blanche Fischer Foundation
Attn: Executive Director
1509 S.W. Sunset Boulevard, Suite 1-B
Portland, OR 97239-2689
(503) 819-8205   Fax: (503) 246-4941
E-mail: bff@bff.org
Web: www.bff.org

Summary To provide financial assistance to disabled or physically handicapped persons in Oregon.

Eligibility This support is available to Oregon residents who have a disability of a physical nature. Assistance is not available to individuals with mental problems. Applicants must be able to demonstrate financial need. They may be seeking funding for education, special equipment, or for any other purpose the sponsor considers appropriate.

Financial data The amount awarded varies, depending upon the needs of the recipient. All grants are paid to the vendor or provider of services, not directly to the applicant.

Duration These are generally 1-time awards.

Additional Information This foundation was established in 1981.

Number awarded Varies each year; recently, 65 individuals received grants worth approximately $35,000.

Deadline Applications may be submitted at any time.

[301]
CHAIRSCHOLARS FOUNDATION NATIONAL SCHOLARSHIPS

ChairScholars Foundation, Inc.
16101 Carencia Lane
Odessa, FL 33556-3278
(813) 920-2737   E-mail: info@chairscholars.org
Web: www.chairscholars.org

Summary To provide financial assistance for college to physically challenged students.

Eligibility This program is open to high school seniors and college freshmen who are physically challenged. Applicants should be chair confined, although this is not a requirement. They should be able to demonstrate financial need, have a record of satisfactory academic performance (at least a "B+" average), and show some form of community service or social contribution in the past. Along with their application, they must submit an essay of 300 to 500 words on how they became physically challenged, how their situation has affected them and their family, and their goals and aspirations for the future. Graduate students and all students over 21 years of age are not eligible.

Financial data Stipends are $5,000 or $3,000 per year. Funds are to be used for tuition and school expenses.

Duration Up to 4 years for high school seniors; up to 3 years for college freshmen.

Number awarded 10 each year.

Deadline February of each year.

[302]
EAGA SCHOLARSHIP AWARD

Eastern Amputee Golf Association
Attn: Bob Buck, Executive Director
2015 Amherst Drive
Bethlehem, PA 18015-5606
Toll-free: (888) 868-0992   Fax: (610) 867-9295
E-mail: info@eaga.org
Web: www.eaga.org

Summary To provide financial assistance for college to members of the Eastern Amputee Golf Association (EAGA) and their families.

Eligibility This program is open to students who are 1) residents of and/or 2) currently enrolled or accepted for enrollment at a college or university in designated eastern states (Connecticut, Delaware, District of Columbia, Maine, Maryland, Massachusetts, New Hampshire, New Jersey, New York, Pennsylvania, Rhode Island, Vermont, Virginia, or West Virginia). Applicants must be amputee members of the association (those who have experienced the loss of 1 or more extremities at a major joint due to amputation or birth defect) or members of their families. Financial need is considered in the selection process.

Financial data The stipend is $1,000.

Duration 1 year; may be renewed if the recipient maintains a GPA of 2.0 or higher and continues to demonstrate financial need.

Additional Information The EAGA was incorporated in 1987. It welcomes 2 types of members: amputee members and associate members (non-amputees who are interested in the organization and support its work but are not eligible for these scholarships). This program includes the following named scholarships: the Paul DesChamps Scholarship Award, the JFK Rehab/EAGA Scholarship, the Ray Froncillo Scholarship, and the Northeastern Amputee Class Scholarship.

Number awarded 5 each year.

Deadline June of each year.

[303]
EVELYN BARTY SCHOLARSHIP AWARDS PROGRAM

Billy Barty Foundation
10222 Crosby Road
Harrison, OH 45030
(513) 738-4428   Fax: (513) 738-4428

Summary To provide financial assistance for college to people of short stature and members of their families.

Eligibility This program is open to high school seniors, high school graduates, and students currently enrolled in a 4-year college or university who are less than 4 feet 10 inches tall. Their parents and siblings are also eligible. Selection is based on scholarship, leadership, and financial need.

Financial data The amount of the scholarship varies.

Duration 1 year; recipients may reapply.

Additional Information These scholarships were named in honor of the average-sized sister of Billy Barty after her recent death. She had devoted many hours of volunteer time to the foundation.

Number awarded Up to 5 each year.

Deadline October of each year.

[304]
FORWARD FACE SCHOLARSHIPS

Forward Face
Attn: Scholarship Committee
317 East 34th Street, Suite 901A
New York, NY 10016
(212) 684-5860   Fax: (212) 684-5864
E-mail: camille@forwardface.org
Web: www.forwardface.org

Summary To provide financial assistance for educational purposes to students with craniofacial conditions.

Eligibility This program is open to students who are 13 years of age or older and have a craniofacial condition. Applicants must write essays on how a particular teacher or faculty member has made a positive impact on them, the impact of their craniofacial condition on their educational experiences, the personal qualities and abilities that make them the best candidate for the scholarship, a description of themselves that enables the readers to get to know them as persons, and where they see themselves in 10 years. Selection is based on personal qualities, goals, and recommendations. Financial need is not a consideration.

Financial data The scholarship is $1,000. Funds must be used for educational purposes.

Duration 1 year; nonrenewable.

Number awarded 1 or more each year.

Deadline January of each year.

[305]
FOUR-YEAR SBAA EDUCATIONAL SCHOLARSHIP FUND

Spina Bifida Association of America
Attn: Scholarship Committee
4590 MacArthur Boulevard, N.W., Suite 250
Washington, DC 20007-4226
(202) 944-3285, ext. 19   Toll-free: (800) 621-3141
Fax: (202) 944-3295   E-mail: sbaa@sbaa.org
Web: www.sbaa.org/html/sbaa_scholarships.html

Summary To provide financial assistance for college to members of the Spina Bifida Association of America (SPAA).

Eligibility Eligible to apply for these scholarships are persons born with spina bifida who are current members of the association. Applicants must be high school juniors entering their senior year at the time of application. Selection is based on academic record, other efforts shown in school, financial need, work history, community service, leadership, and commitment to personal goals.

Financial data The stipend is $5,000 per year.

Duration 4 years.

Additional Information This program was established in 1998.

Number awarded 1 each year.

Deadline February of each year.

[306]
IMA DIVERSITY SCHOLARSHIP PROGRAM

Institute of Management Accountants
Attn: Committee on Students
10 Paragon Drive
Montvale, NJ 07645-1760
(201) 573-9000
Toll-free: (800) 638-4427, ext. 1543
Fax: (201) 573-8438   E-mail: students@imanet.org
Web: www.imanet.org

Summary To provide financial assistance to minority and disabled student members of the Institute of Management Accountants (IMA) who are interested in working on an undergraduate or graduate degree in management accounting or financial management.

Eligibility This program is open to undergraduate and graduate students of American Indian/Alaska Native, Asian/Pacific Islander, Black, or Hispanic heritage and students with physical disabilities (defined as hearing impairment, vision impairment, missing extremities, partial paralysis, complete paralysis, or severe distortion of limbs and/or spine). Applicants must be in their sophomore, junior, or senior year or in a graduate program with a major in management accounting, financial management, or information technology. Selection is based on 1) academic merit; 2) quality of their application presentation; 3) demonstrated community leadership; 4) potential for success in expressed career goals in a financial

management position; 5) a written statement from applicants expressing their short-term and long-term career goals and objectives, including their participation in the IMA; and 6) letters of recommendation.

Financial data Stipends are $3,000 per year.

Duration 1 year.

Additional Information Up to 15 finalists in each category (including the scholarship winners) receive a scholarship to take 5 parts of the CMA and/or CFM examination within a year of graduation.

Number awarded At least 13 each year.

Deadline February of each year.

[307]
MAYS MISSION FOR THE HANDICAPPED SCHOLARSHIP

Mays Mission for the Handicapped
604 Colonial Drive
Herber Springs, AR 72545
(501) 362-7526   Fax: (501) 362-7529
E-mail: info@maysmission.org
Web: www.maysmission.org/school.html

Summary To provide financial assistance to college students who have a mental or physical disability.

Eligibility Eligible to apply are students who are able to document a significant mental or physical disability, score 18 or better on the ACT or 870 or higher on the SAT, and are working full time on a bachelor's degree (must provide proof of enrollment). An interview may be required. Selection is based on financial need, personality, academic goals, character, and ability.

Financial data A stipend is awarded (amount not specified).

Duration 1 semester; may be renewed.

Additional Information Recipients must attend school full time, maintain a GPA of 2.3 or higher, and write monthly "update letters" about their grades, struggles, triumphs, and campus life.

Number awarded Varies each year; recently of these scholarships were awarded.

Deadline June of each year for the fall semester; October of each year for the spring semester.

[308]
NATIONAL AMPUTEE GOLF ASSOCIATION SCHOLARSHIP

National Amputee Golf Association
Attn: Executive Director
11 Walnut Hill Road
Amherst, NH 03031
(603) 672-6444   Toll-free: (800) 633-NAGA
Fax: (603) 672-2987   E-mail: info@nagagolf.org
Web: www.nagagolf.org/scholarship.htm

Summary To provide financial assistance for college to members of the National Amputee Golf Association and their dependents.

Eligibility This program is open to amputee members in good standing in the association and their dependents. Applicants must submit information on their scholastic background (GPA in high school and college, courses of study); type of amputation and cause (if applicable), a cover letter describing their plans for the future; and documentation of financial need. They need not be competitive golfers. Selection is based on academic record, financial need, involvement in extracurricular or community activities, and area of study.

Financial data The stipend is up to $1,000 per year, depending on need.

Duration Up to 4 years, provided the recipient maintains at least half-time enrollment and a GPA of 2.0 or higher and continues to demonstrate financial need.

Number awarded 1 or more each year.

Deadline July of each year.

[309]
NFED MEMORIAL SCHOLARSHIP PROGRAM

National Foundation for Ectodermal Dysplasias
410 East Main Street
P.O. Box 114
Mascoutah, IL 62258-0114
(618) 566-2020   Fax: (618) 566-4718
E-mail: info@nfed.org
Web: www.nfed.org/scholar.htm

Summary To provide financial assistance for college to students with ectodermal dysplasia.

Eligibility This program is open to individuals who are affected by ectodermal dysplasia and are attending or planning to attend a college, university, trade school, or junior college. Selection is based on demonstrated academic ability, a written essay (topic changes annually), extracurricular activities, community involvement, employment, and financial need.

Financial data A stipend is awarded; the exact amount depends upon the needs of the recipient. Funds are sent to the recipient's school.

Duration 1 year.

Number awarded 1 or more each year. A total of $10,000 is available for scholarships each year.

Deadline April of each year.

[310]
NORTH CAROLINA NATIONAL GUARD ASSOCIATION SPECIAL POPULATION SCHOLARSHIP

North Carolina National Guard Association
Attn: Educational Foundation, Inc.
7410 Chapel Hill Road
Raleigh, NC 27607-5047
(919) 851-3390
Toll-free: (800) 821-6159 (within NC)
Fax: (919) 859-4990   E-mail: ncnga@bellsouth.net
Web: www.ncnga.org/education/index.asp

Summary To provide financial assistance for college to members and dependents of members of the North Carolina National Guard Association who have a disability.

Eligibility This program is open to active and associate members of the association as well as the spouses, children, grandchildren, and legal dependents of active, retired, or deceased members. Applicants must be learning disabled and/or physically disabled. They may be high school seniors, high school graduates, or currently-enrolled college students. Selection is based on financial need, academic achievement, citizenship, leadership, and other application information.

Financial data Stipends are $950, $750, or $350.

Duration 1 year; may be renewed.

Number awarded Varies each year.

Deadline January of each year for high school graduates and college students; February of each year for high school seniors.

[311]
ROBERT DOLE SCHOLARSHIP FUND FOR DISABLED STUDENTS

United Negro College Fund
Attn: Director, Educational Services
8260 Willow Oaks Corporate Drive
P.O. Box 10444
Fairfax, VA 22031-8044
(703) 205-3466   Toll-free: (866) 671-7237
Fax: (703) 205-3574
Web: www.uncf.org

Summary To provide financial assistance to physically and mentally-challenged students at UNCF-member colleges and universities who have unmet financial need.

Eligibility To apply, students must be attending a UNCF-member college or university, have a physical or learning disability, and have at least a 2.5 GPA. Applicants must submit a completed application form, a 500-word essay on the challenges of their disability, and a photograph. Financial need is considered in the selection process.

Financial data The stipend is $3,500.

Duration 1 year.

Deadline October of each year.

[312]
SBAA EDUCATIONAL SCHOLARSHIP FUND

Spina Bifida Association of America
Attn: Scholarship Committee
4590 MacArthur Boulevard, N.W., Suite 250
Washington, DC 20007-4226
(202) 944-3285, ext. 19   Toll-free: (800) 621-3141
Fax: (202) 944-3295   E-mail: sbaa@sbaa.org
Web: www.sbaa.org/html/sbaa_scholarships.html

Summary To provide financial assistance for college or graduate school to members of the Spina Bifida Association of America (SPAA).

Eligibility Eligible to apply for these scholarships are persons of any age born with spina bifida who are current members of the association. Applicants must 1) be a high school graduate or possess a GED, and 2) be enrolled in or accepted by a college, junior college, graduate program, or approved trade, vocational, or business school. Selection is based on academic record, other efforts shown in school, financial need, work history, community service, leadership, and commitment to personal goals.

Financial data The amount of the award depends on the need of the recipient and the availability of funds.

Duration 1 year.

Additional Information This program, established in 1988, includes the Joseph DiStefano Annual Scholarship.

Number awarded Varies each year; recently, a total of $10,000 was available for this program.

Deadline February of each year.

[313]
SBAC SCHOLARSHIP

Spina Bifida Association of Connecticut, Inc.
Attn: Allocations Committee
P.O. Box 2545
Hartford, CT 06146
Toll-free: (800) 574-6274   E-mail: sbac@sbac.org
Web: www.sbac.org

Summary To provide financial assistance for college to residents of Connecticut who have spina bifida.

Eligibility This program is open to people with spina bifida whose parent or guardian has been a member of the Spina Bifida Association of Connecticut (SBAC) for at least 2 years. Applicants must be attending or planning to attend an institution of higher education. Along with their application, they must submit an essay (1 to 2 pages) on their educational objectives and goals. Selection is based on the essay, academic record, involvement in community service, leadership qualities, and financial need. Active family and/or individual member participation in SBAC events and activities receives additional consideration.

Financial data The stipend is $1,000. Funds are paid directly to the recipient's school.

Duration 1 year.
Number awarded 1 or more each year.
Deadline July of each year.

Fellowships/Grants

[314]
BLANCHE FISCHER FOUNDATION GRANTS

Blanche Fischer Foundation
Attn: Executive Director
1509 S.W. Sunset Boulevard, Suite 1-B
Portland, OR 97239-2689
(503) 819-8205   Fax: (503) 246-4941
E-mail: bff@bff.org
Web: www.bff.org

Summary To provide financial assistance to disabled or physically handicapped persons in Oregon.
Eligibility This support is available to Oregon residents who have a disability of a physical nature. Assistance is not available to individuals with mental problems. Applicants must be able to demonstrate financial need. They may be seeking funding for education, special equipment, or for any other purpose the sponsor considers appropriate.
Financial data The amount awarded varies, depending upon the needs of the recipient. All grants are paid to the vendor or provider of services, not directly to the applicant.
Duration These are generally 1-time awards.
Additional Information This foundation was established in 1981.
Number awarded Varies each year; recently, 65 individuals received grants worth approximately $35,000.
Deadline Applications may be submitted at any time.

[315]
IMA DIVERSITY SCHOLARSHIP PROGRAM

Institute of Management Accountants
Attn: Committee on Students
10 Paragon Drive
Montvale, NJ 07645-1760
(201) 573-9000
Toll-free: (800) 638-4427, ext. 1543
Fax: (201) 573-8438   E-mail: students@imanet.org
Web: www.imanet.org

Summary To provide financial assistance to minority and disabled student members of the Institute of Management Accountants (IMA) who are interested in working on an undergraduate or graduate degree in management accounting or financial management.
Eligibility This program is open to undergraduate and graduate students of American Indian/Alaska Native, Asian/Pacific Islander, Black, or Hispanic heritage and students with physical disabilities (defined as hearing impairment, vision impairment, missing extremities, partial paralysis, complete paralysis, or severe distortion of limbs and/or spine). Applicants must be in their sophomore, junior, or senior year or in a graduate program with a major in management accounting, financial management, or information technology. Selection is based on 1) academic merit; 2) quality of their application presentation; 3) demonstrated community leadership; 4) potential for success in expressed career goals in a financial management position; 5) a written statement from applicants expressing their short-term and long-term career goals and objectives, including their participation in the IMA; and 6) letters of recommendation.
Financial data Stipends are $3,000 per year.
Duration 1 year.
Additional Information Up to 15 finalists in each category (including the scholarship winners) receive a scholarship to take 5 parts of the CMA and/or CFM examination within a year of graduation.
Number awarded At least 13 each year.
Deadline February of each year.

[316]
SBAA EDUCATIONAL SCHOLARSHIP FUND

Spina Bifida Association of America
Attn: Scholarship Committee
4590 MacArthur Boulevard, N.W., Suite 250
Washington, DC 20007-4226
(202) 944-3285, ext. 19   Toll-free: (800) 621-3141
Fax: (202) 944-3295   E-mail: sbaa@sbaa.org
Web: www.sbaa.org/html/sbaa_scholarships.html

Summary To provide financial assistance for college or graduate school to members of the Spina Bifida Association of America (SPAA).
Eligibility Eligible to apply for these scholarships are persons of any age born with spina bifida who are current members of the association. Applicants must 1) be a high school graduate or possess a GED, and 2) be enrolled in or accepted by a college, junior college, graduate program, or approved trade, vocational, or business school. Selection is based on academic record, other efforts shown in school, financial need, work history, community service, leadership, and commitment to personal goals.
Financial data The amount of the award depends on the need of the recipient and the availability of funds.
Duration 1 year.
Additional Information This program, established in 1988, includes the Joseph DiStefano Annual Scholarship.
Number awarded Varies each year; recently, a total of $10,000 was available for this program.

Deadline February of each year.

Loans

[317]
MASSADVANTAGE PURCHASE AND REHABILITATION LOANS

Massachusetts Housing Finance Agency
One Beacon Street
Boston, MA 02108-3110
(617) 854-1020   Fax: (617) 854-1029
TDD: (617) 854-1025
Web: www.mhfa.com

Summary To provide low-interest loans to residents of Massachusetts to purchase homes that require improvements, including making the home more accessible to persons with disabilities.

Eligibility This program is open to Massachusetts residents whose family income is below certain income levels that vary in different parts of the state but range from $72,400 (in most of the state) to $88,800 (in Boston) for families of 1 or 2 persons and from $83,200 (in most of the state) to $101,000 (in Boston) for families of 3 or more people. Applicants must be first-time homebuyers interested in purchasing a home in need of major repair. The home must be a 1- to 4-family home (excluding condominiums) located in Massachusetts. Loans may be used to purchase the home and make alterations, renovations, additions, repairs, or improvements that will preserve or improve the home's basic livability, safety, utility, or accessibility for persons with a permanent physical disability. Licensed contractors must complete all rehabilitation work.

Financial data Loans range from a minimum of $7,500 to a maximum of 97% of the lesser of the sales price plus rehabilitation cost or the estimated appraised value after rehabilitation, as long as that does not exceed the maximum Acquisition Cost Limit (which depends on the type of home and area of the state and ranges from $130,300 for an existing single-family home in Franklin County to $542,500 for an existing 4-family home in Boston). Interest rates vary but are below conventional market levels.

Additional Information Loans may not be used for Title 5 repairs, assessments for public improvements, recreation or entertainment facilities, or the purchase of personal property.

Number awarded Varies each year.

Deadline Applications may be submitted at any time.

[318]
MHFA HOME IMPROVEMENT LOAN PROGRAM

Massachusetts Housing Finance Agency
One Beacon Street
Boston, MA 02108-3110
(617) 854-1020   Fax: (617) 854-1029
TDD: (617) 854-1025
Web: www.mhfa.com

Summary To provide low-interest loans to residents of Massachusetts to make home improvements, including making their homes more accessible to persons with physical disabilities.

Eligibility Homeowners in Massachusetts may qualify for these loans if their family income is below certain income levels that vary in different parts of the state but range from $72,400 (in most of the state) to $88,800 (in Boston) for families of 1 or 2 persons and from $83,200 (in most of the state) to $101,000 (in Boston) for families of 3 or more people. Eligible property must be a 1- to 4-family home or residential condominium located in Massachusetts that has been used by the borrower as the principal residence for at least 1 year. Mixed-use properties are ineligible. Loans may be used to make alterations, renovations, additions, repairs, or improvements that will preserve or improve the home's basic livability, safety, utility, or accessibility for persons with a permanent physical disability. Applicants must have a good credit record, stable income, and less than 50% of net monthly income committed as debt.

Financial data Loans range from $10,000 to $50,000. The maximum loan-to-value is 100% of the assessed or appraised value. Interest rates vary; recently, they were 4.25% on most loans or 4.5% on 20-year loans.

Duration Loan terms are 5, 10, 15, or 20 years.

Additional Information Loans may not be used for work started before loan closing.

Number awarded Varies each year.

Deadline Applications may be submitted at any time.

[319]
SPECIALLY ADAPTED HOMES FOR DISABLED VETERANS

Department of Veterans Affairs
810 Vermont Avenue, N.W.
Washington, DC 20420
(202) 418-4343   Toll-free: (800) 827-1000
Web: www.va.gov

Summary To provide funding to certain disabled veterans for a home specially adapted to their needs.

Eligibility Grants (also referred to as $48,000 grants) are available to veterans who are entitled to compensation for permanent and total service-connected disability due to: 1) the loss or loss of use of both lower extremities, such as to preclude locomotion without the aid of braces, crutches, canes, or a wheelchair; or 2) blindness

in both eyes, having only light perception, plus loss or loss of use of 1 lower extremity; or 3) a loss or loss of use of 1 lower extremity together with residuals of organic disease or injury or the loss or loss of use of 1 upper extremity, such as to preclude locomotion without resort to braces, canes, crutches, or a wheelchair. Grants (also referred to as $9,250 grants) are available to who are entitled to compensation for permanent and total service-connected disability due to 1) blindness in both eyes with 5/200 visual acuity or less, or 2) anatomical loss or loss of use of both hands.

Financial data The U.S. Department of Veterans Affairs (VA) may approve a grant of not more than 50% of the cost of building, buying, or remodeling homes for eligible veterans, or paying indebtedness of such homes already acquired, up to a maximum grant of $48,000. Eligible veterans with available loan guarantee entitlements may also obtain a guaranteed loan or a direct loan from the VA to supplement the grant to acquire a specially adapted home. Grants up to $9,250 are available for adaptations to a veteran's residence that are determined by the VA to be reasonably necessary. Those grants may also be used to assist veterans to acquire a residence that already has been adapted with special features for the veteran's disability.

Duration This is a 1-time grant.

Additional Information Veterans who receive a specially adapted housing grant may be eligible for Veterans Mortgage Life Insurance.

Number awarded Varies each year.

Deadline Applications are accepted at any time.

Grants-in-Aid

[320]
ALTERNATIVES IN MOTION GRANTS

Alternatives in Motion
1916 Breton Road, S.E.
Grand Rapids, MI 49506
(616) 493-2620   Toll-free: (877) 468-9335
Fax: (616) 493-2621
Web: www.alternativesinmotion.org

Summary To provide funding to people who need assistance to purchase a wheelchair.

Eligibility This program is open to people who can demonstrate a medical necessity for a wheelchair but do not have financial resources to purchase it. Interested parties must visit a local wheelchair vendor and determine their exact mobility needs in consultation with rehabilitation and seating specialists. They must submit that information (including estimates of the cost of the wheelchair), a letter of medical necessity from their physician, documentation of ineligibility for private insurance or Medicare/Medicaid, and a copy of their most recent federal tax return.

Financial data Grants cover the full cost of wheelchairs as verified by the vendor and medical experts.

Duration These are 1-time grants.

Additional Information This foundation was established in 1995.

Number awarded Varies each year; recently, the foundation provided 32 wheelchairs at a cost of $190,675 in cash and $35,272 worth of in-kind donations.

Deadline Applications may be submitted at any time.

[321]
ARKANSAS DISABLED VETERANS PROPERTY TAX EXEMPTION

Arkansas Assessment Coordination Department
1614 West Third Street
Little Rock, AR 72201-1815
(501) 324-9240   Fax: (501) 324-9242
E-mail: dasbury@acd.state.ar.us
Web: www.accessarkansas.org/acd

Summary To exempt from taxation the property owned by veterans with disabilities, surviving spouses, and minor dependent children in Arkansas.

Eligibility To qualify, the disabled veteran must have been awarded a special monthly compensation from the Department of Veterans Affairs for the loss of, or the loss of use of 1 or more limbs, or total blindness in 1 or both eyes, or a 100% total and permanent service-connected disability. This exemption also extends to the veteran's unremarried surviving spouse and the veteran's minor children.

Financial data Qualifying veterans (or their unremarried widows or dependent children) are exempt from payment of all state taxes on their homestead and personal property.

Duration This exemption continues as long as the qualifying veteran (or dependent) resides in Arkansas.

Number awarded Varies each year.

Deadline Applications may be submitted at any time.

[322]
AUTOMOBILE ASSISTANCE FOR DISABLED VETERANS

Department of Veterans Affairs
810 Vermont Avenue, N.W.
Washington, DC 20420
(202) 418-4343   Toll-free: (800) 827-1000
Web: www.va.gov

Summary To supply funding for certain disabled veterans and current service personnel who require specially adapted automobiles.

Eligibility To be eligible for a grant for an automobile, a veteran or current service member must have a ser-

vice-connected loss or permanent loss of use of 1 or both hands or feet or permanent impairment of vision of both eyes to a prescribed degree. For adaptive equipment eligibility only, veterans entitled to compensation for ankylosis of 1 or both knees, or 1 or both hips, also qualify.
Financial data The grant consists of a payment by the Department of Veterans Affairs (VA) of up to $9,000 toward the purchase of an automobile or other conveyance. The VA will also pay for the adaptive equipment, its repair, and the replacement or reinstallation required for the safe operation of the vehicle purchased with VA assistance or for a previously or subsequently acquired vehicle.
Duration This is a 1-time grant.
Number awarded Varies each year.
Deadline Applications may be submitted at any time.

[323]
BARR UNITED AMPUTEE ASSISTANCE FUND
United Amputee Services Association, Inc.
P.O. Box 4277
Winter Park, FL 32793-4277
(407) 359-5500   Fax: (407) 359-8855
Web: www.oandp.com

Summary To provide funding to amputees who require assistance for prosthetic care.
Eligibility This program is open to amputees who cannot afford limbs or other maintenance costs of prosthetic care. Applicants must be able to submit proof of denial of all other funding resources, although bilateral amputees are not eligible unless another source of funding from an individual or organization is also available. Requests for applications must be submitted by a board-certified or state-licensed prosthetist.
Financial data Grants provide reimbursement for materials and maintenance costs to prosthetists.
Duration These are 1-time grants.
Additional Information This program was established in 1995 with funding from the Barr Foundation of Boca Raton, Florida The application fee is $25.
Number awarded Varies each year.
Deadline Requests for applications may be submitted at any time.

[324]
BLANCHE FISCHER FOUNDATION GRANTS
Blanche Fischer Foundation
Attn: Executive Director
1509 S.W. Sunset Boulevard, Suite 1-B
Portland, OR 97239-2689
(503) 819-8205   Fax: (503) 246-4941
E-mail: bff@bff.org
Web: www.bff.org

Summary To provide financial assistance to disabled or physically handicapped persons in Oregon.
Eligibility This support is available to Oregon residents who have a disability of a physical nature. Assistance is not available to individuals with mental problems. Applicants must be able to demonstrate financial need. They may be seeking funding for education, special equipment, or for any other purpose the sponsor considers appropriate.
Financial data The amount awarded varies, depending upon the needs of the recipient. All grants are paid to the vendor or provider of services, not directly to the applicant.
Duration These are generally 1-time awards.
Additional Information This foundation was established in 1981.
Number awarded Varies each year; recently, 65 individuals received grants worth approximately $35,000.
Deadline Applications may be submitted at any time.

[325]
CALIFORNIA DISABLED VETERAN EXEMPTION FROM THE IN LIEU TAX FEE FOR A MANUFACTURED HOME OR MOBILEHOME
Department of Housing and Community
  Development
Attn: Registration and Titling
1800 Third Street
P.O. Box 2111
Sacramento, CA 95812-2111
(916) 323-9224   Toll-free: (800) 952-8356
Web: www.hcd.ca.gov

Summary To provide a special property tax exemption to disabled California veterans and/or their spouses who own and occupy a mobile home.
Eligibility This program is open to disabled veterans and/or their spouses in California who have a manufactured home or mobilehome as their principal place of residence. Veterans must be disabled as a result of injury or disease incurred in military service and have been a resident of California 1) at the time of entry into the service and be blind, or have lost the use of 1 or more limbs, or be totally disabled; 2) on November 7, 1972 and be blind in both eyes, or have lost the use of 2 or more limbs; or 3) on January 1, 1975 and be totally disabled.

The spouses and unmarried surviving spouses of those disabled veterans are also eligible.

Financial data The exemption applies to the first $20,000 of the assessed market value of the manufactured home or mobilehome. Veterans and/or spouses whose income falls below a specified level are entitled to an additional $10,000 exemption. The amount of the exemption is 100% if the home is owned by a veteran only, a veteran and spouse, or a spouse only; 50% if owned by a veteran and another person other than a spouse or by a spouse and another person other than the veteran; 67% if owned by a veteran, the spouse, and another person; 34% if owned by a veteran and 2 other people other than a spouse or by a spouse and 2 other people; 50% if owned by a veteran, the spouse, and 2 other people; or 25% if owned by a veteran and 3 other people or by a spouse and 3 other people.

Duration The exemption is available annually as long as the applicant meets all requirements.

Number awarded Varies each year.

[326]
DELAWARE PENSION BENEFITS FOR PARAPLEGIC VETERANS

Delaware Commission of Veterans Affairs
Robbins Building
802 Silver Lake Boulevard, Suite 100
Dover, DE 19904
(302) 739-2792
Toll-free: (800) 344-9900 (within DE)
Fax: (302) 739-2794 E-mail: adavila@state.de.us
Web: www.state.de.us/veteran/index.htm

Summary To provide a monthly pension to paraplegic veterans in Delaware.

Eligibility Eligible for this benefit are Delaware residents who are paraplegic as a result of service in the armed forces of the United States while it was officially at war or during a period when the United States was engaged in hostilities with another nation as a member of the United Nations. Applicants must be listed on the rolls of the U.S. Department of Veterans Affairs as totally disabled.

Financial data The pension is $3,000 per year.

Duration Recipients remain eligible for this pension as long as they reside in Delaware.

[327]
FLORIDA HOMESTEAD EXEMPTION FOR DISABLED VETERANS

Florida Department of Veterans' Affairs
Mary Grizzle Building, Room 311-K
11351 Ulmerton Road
Largo, FL 33778-1630
(727) 518-3202 Fax: (727) 518-3217
E-mail: cohenm@vba.va.gov
Web: www.floridavets.org/benefits/hmsted.html

Summary To exempt the real estate owned by disabled veterans and their surviving spouses in Florida from taxation.

Eligibility An exemption is available to the following classes of Florida residents: 1) honorably discharged veterans who have a service-connected permanent and total disability; 2) the spouses or surviving spouses of such veterans; 3) veterans who are paraplegic, are hemiplegic, are permanently and totally disabled, must use a wheelchair for mobility, or are legally blind and have a gross annual household income less than the adjusted maximum; and 4) veterans with service-connected disabilities of 10% or more. Applicants must reside in the property for which they are applying for an exemption.

Financial data Veterans who are permanently and totally disabled, their surviving unremarried spouses, and veterans with specified disabilities and income less than the qualifying limit are entitled to exemption of all real estate taxes on property they use and own as a homestead. Veterans with disabilities of at least 10% are entitled to a $5,000 property tax exemption.

Duration The exemption is available as long as the veteran or surviving spouse resides in Florida.

Number awarded Varies each year.

[328]
FORD MOBILITY MOTORING PROGRAM

Ford Motor Company
Attn: Mobility Program
500 Hulet Drive
P.O. Box 529
Bloomfield Hills, MI 48303
Toll-free: (800) 952-2248, ext. 111
TDD: (800) 833-0312 Fax: (248) 333-0300
Web: www.mobilitymotoringprogram.com

Summary To provide a cash reimbursement for the cost of installing adaptive driving aids on new vehicles from Ford or Lincoln-Mercury.

Eligibility Eligible for this rebate are people who purchase or lease new Ford, Lincoln, or Mercury vehicles that require adaptive driving aids or conversion equipment for users with disabilities.

Financial data Up to $1,000 is reimbursed for adaptive equipment or up to $200 for alerting devices, lumbar support, or running boards.

Additional Information The program also provides 24-hour roadside assistance.
Number awarded Varies each year.
Deadline Applicants have 12 months from the date or purchase or lease to initiate the adaptive work and 1 year from that date to process their claim.

[329]
GIVETECH GRANTS

GiveTech.org
4630 Geary Boulevard, Suite 101
San Francisco, CA 94118
(415) 750-2576   Fax: (415) 387-1516
E-mail: info@givetech.org
Web: www.givetech.org

Summary To provide funding for the purchase of computer equipment to people with severe physical disabilities.
Eligibility This program is open to people with severe physical disabilities that leave them physically unable to use a computer through normal means (e.g., mouse and/or keyboard) but who remain lucid. Applicants must lack the financial ability to purchase the necessary computer input technology to allow them to use a computer. They must demonstrate that their lives would be greatly improved by the ability to use a computer.
Financial data Grants provide for full or partial support for purchase of hardware, software, or peripherals.
Duration These are 1-time grants.
Number awarded Varies each year.
Deadline Applications may be submitted at any time.

[330]
GM MOBILITY REIMBURSEMENT PROGRAM

General Motors
100 Renaissance Drive
Mail Code: 482-A25-D35
P.O. Box 100
Detroit, MI 48265-1000
(313) 667-8547   Toll-free: (800) 323-9935
Fax: (313) 667-8950   TDD: (800) TDD-9935
Web: www.gmmobility.com

Summary To provide a cash reimbursement for the cost of installing adaptive driving aids on new purchases from General Motors.
Eligibility Eligible for this rebate are purchasers or lessors of new General Motors cars, trucks, or vans that require adaptive driving aids or conversion equipment for users with disabilities. The equipment may be an "alerting device" that assists deaf or hard of hearing drivers with emergency vehicle siren detectors and enhanced turn signal reminders.
Financial data Up to $1,000 is reimbursed.
Additional Information Applications for reimbursement are submitted through the dealer from whom the vehicle was originally purchased. Only retail purchases or leases of new General Motors vehicles qualify for this program. The reimbursement applies only to equipment installed by converters in the after market, not to factory installed equipment of any kind.
Deadline The conversion process must be completed within 9 months of vehicle delivery and the claim form must be submitted within 90 days after the completion of the conversion.

[331]
ILLINOIS GRANTS FOR SPECIALLY ADAPTED HOUSING

Illinois Department of Veterans' Affairs
833 South Spring Street
P.O. Box 19432
Springfield, IL 62794-9432
(217) 782-6641
Toll-free: (800) 437-9824 (within IL)
Fax: (217) 782-4161   TDD: (217) 524-4645
E-mail: webmail@dva.state.il.us
Web: www.state.il.us/agency/dva

Summary To provide financial assistance to service-connected disabled veterans who need to purchase or adapt a suitable primary residence in Illinois.
Eligibility Eligible Illinois veterans must have total and permanent service-connected disabilities caused by 1) the loss, or loss of use, of both lower extremities, such as to preclude locomotion without the aid of braces, crutches, canes, or a wheelchair; or 2) disability that includes blindness in both eyes, having only light perception, plus loss or loss of use of 1 lower extremity; or 3) a loss or loss of use of 1 lower extremity together with residuals of organic disease or injury, or the loss or loss of use of 1 upper extremity that so affects the functions of balance or propulsion as to preclude locomotion without resort to braces, canes, crutches, or a wheelchair. Veterans may also qualify if they have a service-connected disability that is not totally disabling but involves visual impairment or loss, or loss of use, of both hands.
Financial data Totally and permanently disabled veterans who qualify for a grant of $35,500 from the U.S. Department of Veterans Affairs (VA) for the construction of specially adapted housing also qualify for a grant of $12,000 from the state of Illinois. Illinois veterans who are not totally disabled but otherwise qualify for a grant of $6,000 from the VA for remodeling specially adapted housing also qualify for a grant of $2,000 from the state of Illinois.
Duration This is a 1-time grant.
Number awarded Varies each year.
Deadline Applications for grants may be submitted at any time.

ORTHOPEDIC/DEVELOPMENTAL: GRANTS-IN-AID

[332]
LIMBS FOR LIFE PROTHESIS FUND

Limbs for Life Foundation
5929 North May, Suite 511
Oklahoma City, OK 73112
(405) 843-5174   Fax: (405) 843-5123
Toll-free: (888) 235-5462
E-mail: admin@limbsforlife.org
Web: www.limbsforlife.org/programs.htm

Summary To provide funding to amputees who lack financial resources to obtain adequate prosthetic care.

Eligibility This program is open to amputees who can demonstrate that their financial resources are inadequate to obtain prosthetic care. Applicants should write a letter (telephone calls and e-mails are not accepted) explaining their circumstances and need.

Financial data Grants provide partial or complete funding for an advanced prothesis and fitting.

Duration These are 1-time grants.

Additional Information The foundation was established in 1995.

Number awarded Varies each year; since the foundation was established, it has provided assistance to more than 75 amputees.

Deadline Applications may be submitted at any time.

[333]
MAINE TAX EXEMPTION FOR SPECIALLY ADAPTED HOUSING UNITS

Maine Revenue Services
Attn: Property Tax Division
P.O. Box 9106
Augusta, ME 04332-9106
(207) 287-2011   Fax: (207) 287-6396
E-mail: prop.tax@maine.gove
Web: www.maine.gov

Summary To exempt the specially adapted housing units of Maine veterans with disabilities or their surviving spouses from taxation.

Eligibility Veterans who served in the U.S. armed forces during any federally-recognized war period, are legal residents of Maine, are paraplegic veterans within the meaning of U.S. statutes, and have received a grant from the U.S. government for specially adapted housing are eligible. The exemption also applies to property held in joint tenancy with the veteran's spouse and to the specially adapted housing of unremarried widow(er)s of eligible veterans.

Financial data Estates of paraplegic veterans are exempt up to $47,500 of just valuation for a specially adapted housing unit.

Duration The exemption is valid for the lifetime of the paraplegic veteran or unremarried widow(er).

Number awarded Varies each year.

Deadline When an eligible person first submits an application, the proof of entitlement must reach the assessors of the local municipality prior to the end of March. Once eligibility has been established, notification need not be repeated in subsequent years.

[334]
MICHIGAN INCOME TAX EXEMPTION FOR PEOPLE WITH DISABILITIES

Michigan Department of Treasury
Attn: Income Tax
Treasury Building
430 West Allegan Street
Lansing, MI 48922
(517) 373-3200   Toll-free: (800) 827-4000
TTY: (517) 636-4999
E-mail: treasIndTax@michigan.gov
Web: www.michigan.gov/treasury

Summary To exempt a portion of the income of deaf, blind, and disabled residents of Michigan from state income taxation.

Eligibility Eligible for this exemption are residents of Michigan who 1) receive messages through a sense other than hearing, such as lip reading or sign language; 2) have vision in their better eye of 20/200 or less with corrective lenses or peripheral field of vision of 20 degrees or less; or 3) are hemiplegic, paraplegic, quadriplegic, or totally and permanently disabled.

Financial data Qualifying people with disabilities receive an exemption of $1,900 from their adjusted gross income for purposes of state taxation.

Duration The exemption continues as long as the recipient resides in Michigan.

[335]
NATIONAL CRANIOFACIAL ASSOCIATION TRAVEL GRANTS-IN-AID

FACES: The National Craniofacial Association
P.O. Box 11082
Chattanooga, TN 37401
(423) 266-1632   Toll-free: (800) 3-FACES-3
Fax: (423) 267-3124
E-mail: faces@faces-cranio.org
Web: www.faces-cranio.org

Summary To provide funding for travel expenses for persons with severe facial deformities who travel to comprehensive medical centers for reconstructive facial surgery.

Eligibility Persons with craniofacial deformities resulting from birth defects, injury, or disease are eligible to apply for these grants-in-aid if they need to travel to comprehensive medical centers to undergo reconstructive facial surgery and/or evaluation.

Financial data Funds are available for transportation, food, lodging, parking, and tolls related to securing or undergoing treatment. No medical costs are covered. Grants also provide for 1 accompanying person for each trip.

Additional Information FACES: The National Craniofacial Association was founded in 1969 as the Debbie Fox Foundation. It changed its name because it no longer serves only Debbie.

Number awarded Varies each year.

Deadline Applications may be submitted at any time.

[336] NATIONAL TRANSPLANT ASSISTANCE FUND GRANTS

National Transplant Assistance Fund
3475 West Chester Pike, Suite 230
Newtown Square, PA 19073
Toll-free: (800) 642-8399 Fax: (610) 353-1616
Web: www.transplantfund.org

Summary To provide funding to transplant and spinal cord injury patients.

Eligibility This program is open to transplant and spinal cord injury patients who need funding to pay expenses not covered by insurance.

Financial data Grants provide direct financial assistance for medically-related transplant expenses not covered by insurance.

Duration These are 1-time grants.

Additional Information In addition to these grants, the sponsor assists patients in their own fundraising activities. It provides guidance in campaign planning and implementation, support materials and procedures (including banners, flyers, pins, organ donor ribbons, and bumper stickers), publicity expertise and materials, and a link to the sponsor's web site.

Number awarded Varies each year.

Deadline Applications may be submitted at any time.

[337] NEW HAMPSHIRE PROPERTY TAX EXEMPTION FOR CERTAIN DISABLED SERVICEMEN

New Hampshire Department of Revenue
  Administration
45 Chenell Drive
P.O. Box 457
Concord, NH 03302-0457
(603) 271-2687 TDD: (800) 735-2964

Summary To exempt from taxation certain property owned by New Hampshire disabled veterans or their surviving spouses.

Eligibility Eligible for this exemption are New Hampshire residents who are honorably discharged veterans with a total and permanent service-connected disability that involves double amputation of the upper or lower extremities or any combination thereof, paraplegia, or blindness of both eyes with visual acuity of 5/200 or less. Applicants or their surviving spouses must own a specially adapted homestead that has been acquired with the assistance of the U.S. Department of Veterans Affairs.

Financial data Qualifying disabled veterans and surviving spouses are exempt from all taxation on such specially adapted homestead.

Duration 1 year; once the credit has been approved, it is automatically renewed as long as the qualifying person owns the same residence in New Hampshire.

Number awarded Varies each year.

Deadline The original application for a permanent tax credit must be submitted by April.

[338] NEW HAMPSHIRE SERVICE-CONNECTED TOTAL DISABILITY TAX CREDIT

New Hampshire Department of Revenue
  Administration
45 Chenell Drive
P.O. Box 457
Concord, NH 03302-0457
(603) 271-2687 TDD: (800) 735-2964

Summary To provide property tax credits in New Hampshire to disabled veterans or their surviving spouses.

Eligibility Eligible for this tax credit are New Hampshire residents who are honorably discharged veterans and who 1) have a total and permanent service-connected disability, or 2) are a double amputee or paraplegic because of a service-connected disability. Unremarried surviving spouses of qualified veterans are also eligible.

Financial data Qualifying disabled veterans and surviving spouses receive an annual credit of $700 for property taxes on residential property. In addition, individual towns in New Hampshire may adopt a local option to double the dollar amount credited to disabled veterans, from $700 to $1,400.

Duration 1 year; once the credit has been approved, it is automatically renewed for as long as the qualifying person owns the same residence in New Hampshire.

Number awarded Varies each year.

Deadline The original application for a permanent tax credit must be submitted by April.

ORTHOPEDIC/DEVELOPMENTAL: GRANTS-IN-AID

[339]
NEW JERSEY VETERANS AND SPOUSES CATASTROPHIC ENTITLEMENTS

New Jersey Department of Military and Veterans Affairs
Attn: Division of Veterans Programs
101 Eggert Crossing Road
P.O. Box 340
Trenton, NJ 08625-0340
(609) 530-7045
Toll-free: (800) 624-0508 (within NJ)
Fax: (609) 530-7075
Web: www.state.nj.us

Summary To supplement the compensation benefits paid by the U.S. Department of Veterans Affairs (VA) to disabled New Jersey veterans or their surviving spouses.

Eligibility Eligible for this benefit are veterans who are receiving VA compensation benefits for 100% disability ratings and who have the following disabilities: loss of sight; amputation of both hands, both feet, or 1 hand and 1 foot; hemiplegia and permanent paralysis of 1 leg and 1 arm on either side of the body; paraplegia and permanent paralysis of both legs and lowers parts of the body; osteochondritis and permanent loss of use of both legs; multiple sclerosis and the loss of use of both feet or both legs; and quadriplegia. Service must have been during wartime and the veteran must have been a resident of New Jersey at the time of entry into the military and be so currently. Surviving spouses of disabled veterans are also eligible.

Financial data Eligible veterans or survivors receive $750 a year, paid in monthly installments.

Duration This benefit is payable for the life of the veteran or spouse.

Number awarded Varies each year.

[340]
NEW YORK "ELIGIBLE FUNDS" PROPERTY TAX EXEMPTIONS FOR VETERANS

New York State Division of Veterans' Affairs
5 Empire State Plaza, Suite 2836
Albany, NY 12223-1551
(518) 474-6114
Toll-free: (888) VETS-NYS (within NY)
Fax: (518) 473-0379
E-mail: info@veterans.state.ny.us
Web: www.veterans.state.ny.us

Summary To provide a partial exemption from property taxes for veterans and their surviving spouses who are residents of New York.

Eligibility This program is open to veterans who have purchased properties in New York with pension, bonus, or insurance money (referred to as "eligible funds"). Specially adapted homes of paraplegics, or the homes of their widowed spouses, are also covered.

Financial data This exemption reduces the property's assessed value to the extent that "eligible funds" were used in the purchase, generally to a maximum of $5,000. It is applicable to general municipal taxes but not to school taxes or special district levies.

Duration This exemption is available annually.

Number awarded Varies each year.

Deadline Applications must be filed with the local assessor by "taxable status date;" in most towns, that is the end of February.

[341]
NFED TREATMENT FUND

National Foundation for Ectodermal Dysplasias
410 East Main Street
P.O. Box 114
Mascoutah, IL 62258-0114
(618) 566-2020   Fax: (618) 566-4718
E-mail: info@nfed.org
Web: www.nfed.org/treatme.htm

Summary To provide funding for medical and dental care to people with ectodermal dysplasia (ED).

Eligibility This program is open to all people with an ED syndrome who need assistance for dental or medical care. Typical care includes, but is not limited to, dentures, wigs, plastic surgery, dental implants, air conditioners, and personal cooling equipment. All care for which payment is sought must be related to ectodermal dysplasia. Selection is based on treatment needs, family income, extenuating circumstances, and the number of members of the family who are affected by an ED syndrome.

Financial data The amount of assistance depends on the need of the recipient and the availability of funds.

Duration Individuals receiving funding for dental care or wigs can reapply after 18 months have passed.

Additional Information This program was established in 1987.

Number awarded Varies each year; recently, a total of $140,000 was available for this program.

Deadline March, June, September, or December of each year.

[342]
NORTH DAKOTA PROPERTY TAX EXEMPTION FOR THE DISABLED

Office of State Tax Commissioner
State Capitol Building
600 East Boulevard Avenue, Department 127
Bismarck, ND 58505-0599
(701) 328-2770   Toll-free: (800) 638-2901
Fax: (701) 328-3700   TTY: (800) 366-6888
E-mail: taxinfo@state.nd.us
Web: www.ndtaxdepartment.com

Summary To provide partial tax exemption in North Dakota to persons permanently confined to the use of a wheelchair and their spouses.

Eligibility Persons permanently confined to the use of a wheelchair are those who cannot walk with the assistance of crutches or any other device and will never be able to do so; this must be certified by a physician selected by a local governing board. The property must be owned and occupied as a homestead according to state law. The homestead may be owned by the spouse or jointly owned by the disabled person and spouse provided both reside on the homestead. Qualified residents and, if deceased, their unremarried surviving spouses are entitled to this exemption. Income is not considered in determining eligibility for the exemption.

Financial data The maximum benefit may not exceed $3,600 taxable value, because a homestead is limited to $80,000 market value.

Duration The exemption continues as long as the homestead in North Dakota is owned by the disabled person and/or the spouse.

Additional Information The exemption does not apply to special assessments levied upon the homestead.

Number awarded Varies each year.

[343]
NORTH DAKOTA PROPERTY TAX EXEMPTIONS FOR DISABLED VETERANS

Office of State Tax Commissioner
State Capitol Building
600 East Boulevard Avenue, Department 127
Bismarck, ND 58505-0599
(701) 328-2770   Toll-free: (800) 638-2901
Fax: (701) 328-3700   TTY: (800) 366-6888
E-mail: taxinfo@state.nd.us
Web: www.ndtaxdepartment.com

Summary To provide disabled North Dakota veterans and their spouses or widow(er)s with property tax exemptions.

Eligibility Veterans with disabilities who qualify for tax exemptions fall into 2 categories: 1) paraplegics, including those whose disability is not service-connected, regardless of income, and 2) honorably discharged veterans with more than a 50% service-connected disability whose income is less than $14,000. The property must be owned and occupied as a homestead according to state law. Spouses and unremarried widow(er)s are also eligible.

Financial data The maximum benefit may not exceed $3,600 taxable value, because a homestead is limited to $80,000 market value.

Duration 1 year; renewable as long as qualified individuals continue to reside in North Dakota and live in their homes.

Number awarded Varies each year.

Deadline Applications may be submitted to the county auditor at any time.

[344]
OREGON INCOME TAX DEDUCTION FOR THE SEVERELY DISABLED

Oregon Department of Revenue
Revenue Building
955 Center Street, N.E.
Salem, OR 97310-2551
(503) 378-4988
Toll-free: (800) 356-4222 (within OR)
TTY: (800) 886-7204 (within OR)
Web: www.dor.state.or.us

Summary To enable residents of Oregon who have a severe disability to deduct a portion of their income from state taxation.

Eligibility This deduction is available to taxpayers in Oregon who have a severe disability, defined to include permanent loss of use of 1 or both feet, permanent loss of use of both hands, permanent blindness, or permanent condition that, without special equipment or help, limits the ability to earn a living, maintain a household, or transport oneself.

Financial data The additional deduction is $1,200 for single people and heads of households. It is $1,000 for married people filing jointly or separately and for qualifying widow(er)s.

Duration The deduction continues as long as the recipient resides in Oregon.

Deadline Deductions are filed with state income tax returns in April of each year.

[345]
PENNSYLVANIA PARALYZED VETERANS PENSION

Bureau for Veterans Affairs
Fort Indiantown Gap
Annville, PA 17003-5002
(717) 865-8911
Toll-free: (800) 54 PA VET (within PA)
Fax: (717) 865-8589   E-mail: jdavison@state.pa.us
Web: sites.state.pa.us

Summary To provide financial assistance to Pennsylvania veterans who became disabled while serving in the U.S. armed forces.

Eligibility Applicants must be current residents of Pennsylvania who suffered an injury or disease resulting in loss or loss of use of 2 or more extremities while serving in the U.S. armed forces during an established period of war or armed conflict or as a result of hostilities during combat-related activities in peacetime. At the time of entry into military service, applicants must have been residents of Pennsylvania.

Financial data The pension is $150 per month.

Duration The pension is awarded for the life of the veteran.

Number awarded Varies each year.

Deadline Applications may be submitted at any time.

[346]
PENNSYLVANIA REAL ESTATE TAX EXEMPTION

Bureau for Veterans Affairs
Fort Indiantown Gap
Annville, PA 17003-5002
(717) 865-8907
Toll-free: (800) 54 PA VET (within PA)
Fax: (717) 865-8589   E-mail: jdavison@state.pa.us
Web: sites.state.pa.us

Summary To exempt Pennsylvania veterans with disabilities and their unremarried surviving spouses from all state real estate taxes.

Eligibility Eligible to apply for this exemption are honorably discharged veterans who are residents of Pennsylvania and who are blind, paraplegic, or 100% disabled from a service-connected disability sustained during wartime military service. The dwelling must be owned by the veteran solely or jointly with a spouse, and the need for the exemption must be determined by the State Veterans' Commission. Upon the death of the veteran, the tax exemption passes on to the veteran's unremarried surviving spouse.

Financial data This program exempts the principal residence (and the land on which it stands) from all real estate taxes.

Duration The exemption continues as long as the eligible veteran or unremarried widow resides in Pennsylvania.

Number awarded Varies each year.

[347]
SATURN MOBILITY PROGRAM FOR PERSONS WITH DISABILITIES

Saturn Corporation
Attn: Customer Assistance Center
100 Saturn Parkway
P.O. Box 1500
Spring Hill, TN 37174-1500
Toll-free: (800) 553-6000   Fax: (615) 486-7970
TTY: (800) 833-6000

Summary To provide a cash reimbursement for the cost of installing adaptive driving aids on new purchases of Saturn vehicles.

Eligibility Eligible for this rebate are purchasers or lessors of new Saturn vehicles that require adaptive driving aids or conversion equipment for users with disabilities. Mobility adaptations include wheelchair and scooter lifts, hand controls for throttle and brake, steering devices and extensions, lower effort steering aids, lower effort brakes, modified vehicle switches, wheelchair tie-downs, custom pedal extensions, and other adaptive conversions; alerting devices (emergency vehicle siren detectors) for drivers with a hearing loss of 30 dB in any part of the frequency range also qualify. Some adaptations require proof of physician's prescription.

Financial data The maximum reimbursement for driver or passenger mobility equipment is $1,000. For driver or passenger alerting devices, the maximum reimbursement is $200. If the user requires both mobility aids and alerting devices, the maximum reimbursement is $1,000 ($200 for alerting devices and the remaining portion of up to $800 for mobility aids).

Additional Information Applications for reimbursement are submitted through the dealer from whom the vehicle was originally purchased. Only retail purchases or leases of new Saturn vehicles qualify for this program. The reimbursement applies only to equipment installed by converters in the after market, not to factory installed equipment of any kind.

Deadline The conversion process for mobility adaptations must be completed within 12 months of vehicle purchase. Alerting devices must be installed within 60 days from the date of purchase and the claim form must be submitted within 30 days after the completion of the installation.

[348]
SOUTH CAROLINA DISABLED PERSON PROPERTY TAX EXEMPTION

South Carolina Department of Revenue
Attn: Property Division
301 Gervais Street
P.O. Box 125
Columbia, SC 29214
(803) 898-5480   Fax: (803) 898-5822
Web: www.sctax.org

Summary To exempt the home of disabled residents of South Carolina and their unremarried widow(er)s from property taxation.

Eligibility Eligible for this exemption are residents of South Carolina who are defined as paraplegic or hemiplegic and own a dwelling house that is their domicile. Surviving spouses are also eligible as long as they do not remarry, reside in the dwelling, and obtain the fee or life estate in the dwelling.

Financial data The exemption applies to all taxes on 1 house and a lot (not to exceed 1 acre).

Duration The exemption extends as long as the person with a disability resides in the house, or as long as the surviving spouse remains unremarried and resides in the house.

Number awarded Varies each year.

Deadline Applications may be submitted at any time.

[349]
SOUTH CAROLINA SPECIALLY ADAPTED HOUSING TAX EXEMPTION

South Carolina Office of Veterans Affairs
1205 Pendleton Street, Room 477
Columbia, SC 29201-3789
(803) 734-0200 Fax: (803) 734-0197
E-mail: va@govoepp.state.sc.us
Web: www.govoepp.state.sc.us/vetaff.htm

Summary To provide for the exemption of taxes on specially adapted housing in South Carolina that was acquired from the U.S. Department of Veterans Affairs (VA).

Eligibility Veterans having service-connected disabilities resulting in the loss or loss of use of lower extremities (requiring braces, crutches, or wheelchairs for locomotion) as well as blinded veterans who have loss of use of a lower extremity qualify for specially adapted housing from the VA. Disabled veterans who are residents of South Carolina and who have acquired such housing with financial assistance from the VA are eligible for this exemption; if the eligible veteran is deceased, the spouse, dependent children, or dependent parents are eligible for the exemption.

Financial data The exemption extends to state, county, and municipal taxes on any real estate acquired as specially adapted housing.

Duration The exemption continues as long as an eligible veteran or a qualified dependent owns and occupies the property.

Number awarded Varies each year.

Deadline Applications may be submitted at any time.

[350]
SOUTH DAKOTA PROPERTY TAX EXEMPTION FOR VETERANS AND THEIR WIDOWS OR WIDOWERS

South Dakota Department of Revenue
Attn: Property Tax Division
445 East Capitol Avenue
Pierre, SD 57501-3185
(605) 773-5120 Toll-free: (800) 829-9188
Fax: (605) 773-6729
E-mail: PropTaxIn@state.sd.us
Web: www.state.sd.us

Summary To exempt from property taxation the homes of disabled veterans in South Dakota and their widow(er)s.

Eligibility This program applies to dwellings or parts of multiple family dwellings in South Dakota that are specifically designed for use by paraplegics as wheelchair homes and that are owned and occupied by veterans who have lost or lost the use of both lower extremities. The unremarried widow or widower of such a veteran is also eligible. The dwelling must be owned and occupied by the veteran for 1 full calendar year before the exemption becomes effective. For purposes of this program, the term "dwelling" generally includes the real estate up to 1 acre on which the building is located.

Financial data Qualified dwellings are exempt from property taxation in South Dakota.

Duration The exemption applies as long as the dwelling is owned and occupied by the disabled veteran or widow(er).

Number awarded Varies each year.

[351]
SPECIALLY ADAPTED HOMES FOR DISABLED VETERANS

Department of Veterans Affairs
810 Vermont Avenue, N.W.
Washington, DC 20420
(202) 418-4343 Toll-free: (800) 827-1000
Web: www.va.gov

Summary To provide funding to certain disabled veterans for a home specially adapted to their needs.

Eligibility Grants (also referred to as $48,000 grants) are available to veterans who are entitled to compensation for permanent and total service-connected disability due to: 1) the loss or loss of use of both lower extremities, such as to preclude locomotion without the aid of braces, crutches, canes, or a wheelchair; or 2) blindness in both eyes, having only light perception, plus loss or loss of use of 1 lower extremity; or 3) a loss or loss of use of 1 lower extremity together with residuals of organic disease or injury or the loss or loss of use of 1 upper extremity, such as to preclude locomotion without resort to braces, canes, crutches, or a wheelchair. Grants (also referred to as $9,250 grants) are available to who are entitled to compensation for permanent and total service-connected disability due to 1) blindness in both eyes with 5/200 visual acuity or less, or 2) anatomical loss or loss of use of both hands.

Financial data The U.S. Department of Veterans Affairs (VA) may approve a grant of not more than 50% of the cost of building, buying, or remodeling homes for eligible veterans, or paying indebtedness of such homes already acquired, up to a maximum grant of $48,000. Eligible veterans with available loan guarantee entitlements may also obtain a guaranteed loan or a direct loan from the VA to supplement the grant to acquire a specially adapted home. Grants up to $9,250 are available for adaptations to a veteran's residence that are determined by the VA to be reasonably necessary. Those grants may also be used to assist veterans to acquire a residence that already has been adapted with special features for the veteran's disability.

Duration This is a 1-time grant.

Additional Information Veterans who receive a specially adapted housing grant may be eligible for Veterans Mortgage Life Insurance.

Number awarded Varies each year.

Deadline Applications are accepted at any time.

ORTHOPEDIC/DEVELOPMENTAL: GRANTS-IN-AID

[352]
SPINA BIFIDA ALLOWANCE FOR CHILDREN OF VIETNAM VETERANS

Department of Veterans Affairs
810 Vermont Avenue, N.W.
Washington, DC 20420
(202) 418-4343   Toll-free: (800) 827-1000
Web: www.va.gov

Summary To provide support to children of Vietnam veterans who have spina bifida.

Eligibility This program is open to spina bifida patients whose veteran parent performed active military, naval, or air service in the Republic of Vietnam during the Vietnam era. Children may be of any age or marital status, but they must have been conceived after the date on which the veteran first served in Vietnam. The monthly allowance is set at 3 levels, depending upon the degree of disability suffered by the child. The levels are based on neurological manifestations that define the severity of disability: impairment of the functioning of the extremities, impairment of bowel or bladder function, and impairment of intellectual functioning.

Financial data Support depends on the degree of disability. The monthly rate for children at the first level is $232, at the second level $804, or at the third level $1,373.

Additional Information Applications are available from the nearest VA medical center. Recipients are also entitled to vocational training and medical treatment.

Number awarded Varies each year.

Deadline Applications are accepted at any time.

[353]
TENNESSEE INCOME TAX EXEMPTION FOR QUADRIPLEGICS

Tennessee Department of Revenue
Andrew Jackson State Office Building
500 Deaderick Street
Nashville, TN 37242-1099
(615) 253-0600
Toll-free: (800) 342-1003 (within TN)
Fax: (615) 253-3580
E-mail: tn.revenue@state.tn.us
Web: www.tennessee.gov/revenue

Summary To exempt from state taxation the dividend and interest income of quadriplegic residents of Tennessee.

Eligibility This exemption is provided to residents of Tennessee who are certified by a medical doctor to be quadriplegic and who have taxable income that is from 1) dividends from stock, investment trusts, and mutual funds; and 2) interest from bonds, notes, and mortgages. The income must be derived from circumstances resulting in the individual's becoming a quadriplegic.

Financial data All income is exempt from taxation if the income is derived from circumstances resulting in the applicant's becoming a quadriplegic. However, when taxable interest/dividend income is received jointly by a quadriplegic and a spouse who is not a quadriplegic or who is quadriplegic but the taxable income was not derived from circumstances resulting in the spouse's becoming quadriplegic, only one half of the jointly received income is exempted from taxation. The spouse who is not quadriplegic or whose quadriplegic condition did not result in the income is entitled only to a $1,250 exemption.

Duration The exemption continues as long as the recipient resides in Tennessee.

[354]
TENNESSEE PROPERTY TAX RELIEF FOR DISABLED VETERANS AND THEIR SPOUSES

Tennessee Comptroller of the Treasury
Attn: Property Tax Relief Program
James K. Polk State Office Building
505 Deaderick Street, Room 1600
Nashville, TN 37243-0278
(615) 747-8871   Fax: (615) 532-3866
E-mail: Kim.Darden@state.tn.us
Web: www.comptroller.state.tn.us/pa/patxrvet.htm

Summary To provide property tax relief for veterans with disabilities and their spouses in Tennessee.

Eligibility This exemption is offered to veterans or their surviving unremarried spouses who are residents of Tennessee and own and live in their home in the state. The veteran must have served in the U.S. armed forces and 1) have acquired, as a result of such service, a disability from paraplegia, or permanent paralysis of both legs and lower part of the body resulting from traumatic injury, or disease to the spinal cord or brain, or from total blindness, or from loss or loss of use of both legs or arms from any service-connected cause; 2) have been rated by the U.S. Department of Veterans Affairs (VA) as 100% permanently disabled as a result of service as a prisoner of war for at least 5 months; or 3) have been rated by the VA as 100% permanently and totally disabled from any other service-connected combat-related cause. Veterans who experience total blindness are also eligible. The relief does not extend to any person who was dishonorably discharged from any of the armed services.

Financial data The amount of the relief depends on the property assessment and the tax rate in the city or county where the beneficiary lives.

Duration 1 year; may be renewed as long as the eligible veteran or surviving unremarried spouse owns and occupies the primary residence.

Number awarded Varies each year.

[355]
TEXAS PROPERTY TAX EXEMPTION FOR DISABLED VETERANS AND THEIR FAMILIES

Texas Veterans Commission
P.O. Box 12277
Austin, TX 78711-2277
(512) 463-5538   Fax: (512) 475-2395
E-mail: info@tvc.state.tx.us
Web: www.tvc.state.tx.us

Summary To extend property tax exemptions on the appraised value of their property to disabled and other Texas veterans and their surviving family members.

Eligibility Eligible veterans must be Texas residents rated at least 10% service-connected disabled. Surviving spouses and children of eligible veterans are also covered by this program.

Financial data For veterans in Texas whose disability is rated as 10 through 30%, the first $5,000 of the appraised property value is exempt from taxation; veterans rated as 31 through 50% disabled are exempt from the first $7,500 of appraised value; those with a 51 through 70% disability are exempt from the first $10,000 of appraised value; the exemption applies to the first $12,000 of appraised value for veterans with disabilities rated as 71% or more. A veteran whose disability is 10% or more and who is 65 years or older is entitled to exemption of the first $12,000 of appraised property value. A veteran whose disability consists of the loss of use of 1 or more limbs, total blindness in 1 or both eyes, or paraplegia is exempt from the first $12,000 of the appraised value. The unremarried surviving spouse of a deceased veteran who, at the time of death had a compensable disability and was entitled to an exemption, is entitled to the same exemption. The surviving spouse of a person who died on active duty is entitled to exemption of the first $5,000 of appraised value of the spouse's property. A surviving child of a person who dies on active duty is entitled to exemption of the first $5,000 of appraised value of the child's property as long as the child is unmarried and under 21 years of age.

Duration 1 year; may be renewed as long as the eligible veteran (or unremarried surviving spouse or child) owns and occupies the primary residence in Texas.

Additional Information This program is administered at the local level by the various taxing authorities.

Number awarded Varies each year.

Deadline April of each year.

[356]
TRAVIS ROY FOUNDATION GRANTS

Travis Roy Foundation
c/o Palmer & Dodge LLP
111 Huntington Avenue at Prudential Center
Boston, MA 02199-7613
(617) 239-0100   Fax: (617) 227-4420
E-mail: Administrator@travisroyfoundation.org
Web: www.travisroyfoundation.org

Summary To provide funding to paraplegics and quadriplegics for purchase of equipment or modifications to improve their daily life.

Eligibility This program is open to paraplegics and quadriplegics who reside in the United States or Canada. Applicants must be paralyzed due to a spinal cord injury; individuals with paralysis due to other causes, such as multiple sclerosis or spina bifida, are not eligible. Grant funds must be sought for equipment or modifications, including upgrade and maintenance of wheelchairs, assistance in van purchases, vehicle modifications (e.g., hand controls or lifts), home modifications (e.g., ramp and elevator installation), exercise equipment, or other adaptive equipment. Financial need must be demonstrated.

Financial data Grants range from $4,000 to $7,500. Funds are distributed directly to suppliers of the desired equipment or modification.

Duration These are 1-time grants.

Additional Information This foundation was established in 1997.

Number awarded Varies each year.

Deadline Applications may be submitted at any time.

Communication/Other Disabilities

Scholarships •
Fellowships/Grants •
Grants-in-Aid •
Awards •

Described here are 154 programs open to individuals who have a communication disorder (such as stuttering or voice impairment), have a learning disability (including such conditions as brain injury and dyslexia), are emotionally disturbed, or have other chronic or acute health problems, such as heart condition, tuberculosis, or hemophilia. Of these, 97 entries cover scholarships (to pursue studies or research on the undergraduate level in the United States); 20 cover fellowships/grants (to pursue graduate or postdoctoral study or research in the United States); 33 cover grants-in-aid (to support emergency situations, travel, income/property tax liabilities, or the acquisition of assistive technology); and 4 cover awards, competitions, prizes, and honoraria (to recognize or support creative work and public service). If you are looking for a particular program and don't find it in this chapter, be sure to check the Program Title Index to see if it is covered elsewhere in the directory.

Scholarships

[357] AGSD SCHOLARSHIP

Association for Glycogen Storage Disease
P.O. Box 896
Durant, IA 52747-9769
(563) 785-6038   Fax: (563) 785-6038
E-mail: maryc@agsdus.org
Web: www.agsdus.org

Summary To provide financial aid to college students with Glycogen Storage Disease.

Eligibility This program is open to currently-enrolled college students who are affected by Glycogen Storage Disease. Applicants must be members of the association (or their parents must be members).

Financial data The amount awarded varies each year.

Duration 1 year.

Number awarded 1 each year.

Deadline June of each year.

[358] AIR FORCE OFFICERS' WIVES' CLUB OF WASHINGTON, D.C. SCHOLARSHIPS

Air Force Officers' Wives' Club of Washington, D.C.
Attn: AFOWC Scholarship Committee
50 Theisen Street
Bolling Air Force Base
Washington, DC 20032-5411

Summary To provide financial assistance for undergraduate or graduate education to the dependents of Air Force members in the Washington, D.C. area.

Eligibility This program is open to the children and/or non-military spouses of active-duty, retired, or deceased Air Force members in the Washington D.C. area. The children may be either college-bound high school seniors or high school seniors enrolled in a learning disability program who will continue in a higher education program; the spouses may be working on a postsecondary or advanced degree. Selection is based on academic and citizenship achievements; financial need is not considered. Applicants who receive an appointment to a service academy are not eligible.

Financial data Stipends are at least $1,000 per year. Funds may be used only for payment of tuition or academic fees.

Duration 1 year.

Number awarded Varies each year.

Deadline February of each year.

[359] AMERICAN CANCER SOCIETY SCHOLARSHIP

Patient Advocate Foundation
Attn: Executive Vice President of Administrative Operations
753 Thimble Shoals Boulevard, Suite 200
Newport News, VA 23606
(757) 873-6668, ext. 124   Toll-free: (800) 532-5274
Fax: (757) 873-8999
E-mail: info@patientadvocate.org
Web: www.patientadvocate.org

Summary To provide financial assistance for college or graduate school to individuals whose studies have been interrupted or delayed by a diagnosis of cancer or other life threatening diseases.

Eligibility This program is open to high school seniors, undergraduates, and graduate students whose course of study has been interrupted or delayed by a diagnosis of cancer or other critical or life threatening diseases. Applicants must submit documentation of financial need, high school and/or college transcripts, and at least 2 letters of recommendation. They must be pursuing a course of study that will make them immediately employable after graduation.

Financial data The stipend is $5,000 per year.

Duration 1 year; may be renewed 1 additional year for an associate or master's degree or 3 additional years for a bachelor's or medical degree. Renewal requires that the recipient maintain a GPA of 3.0 or higher, be enrolled full time, and complete at least 20 hours of community service per year.

Number awarded 1 each year.

Deadline April of each year.

[360] AMGEN SCHOLARSHIP

Patient Advocate Foundation
Attn: Executive Vice President of Administrative Operations
753 Thimble Shoals Boulevard, Suite 200
Newport News, VA 23606
(757) 873-6668, ext. 124   Toll-free: (800) 532-5274
Fax: (757) 873-8999
E-mail: info@patientadvocate.org
Web: www.patientadvocate.org

Summary To provide financial assistance for college or graduate school to individuals whose studies have been interrupted or delayed by a diagnosis of cancer or other life threatening diseases.

Eligibility This program is open to high school seniors, undergraduates, and graduate students whose course of study has been interrupted or delayed by a diagnosis of cancer or other critical or life threatening diseases. Applicants must submit documentation of financial need, high school and/or college transcripts, and at least 2 letters of recommendation. They must be pursuing a course of

study that will make them immediately employable after graduation.

Financial data The stipend is $5,000 per year.

Duration 1 year; may be renewed 1 additional year for an associate or master's degree or 3 additional years for a bachelor's or medical degree. Renewal requires that the recipient maintain a GPA of 3.0 or higher, be enrolled full time, and complete at least 20 hours of community service per year.

Additional Information This program is sponsored by Amgen, Inc.

Number awarded 1 each year.

Deadline April of each year.

[361]
ANDREW CRAIG MEMORIAL SCHOLARSHIP

PKU of Illinois
P.O. Box 102
Palatine, IL 60078-0102
(630) 415-2219   Fax: (208) 978-8963
E-mail: info@pkuil.org
Web: www.pkuil.org

Summary To provide financial assistance for college to Illinois residents who have been diagnosed with phenylketonuria (PKU).

Eligibility This program is open to residents of Illinois who have been diagnosed with either classic or variant PKU. Applicants must be 17 years of age or older and either 1) entering college or vocational school, or 2) returning to school for a degree. Recipients are selected by a random drawing from among qualified applicants.

Financial data The stipend is $1,000 per year.

Duration 1 year; recipients may reapply but not in successive years.

Additional Information This program was established in 1997. Information is also available from Kate Chovanec, 4205 Larkspur Lane, Lane in the Hills, IL 60102, (847) 854-4778, E-mail: KMChov@msn.com.

Number awarded 2 each year.

Deadline October of each year.

[362]
ANNE AND MATT HARBISON SCHOLARSHIP

P. Buckley Moss Society
601 Shenandoah Village Drive, Box 1C
Waynesboro, VA 22980
(540) 943-5678   Fax: (540) 949-8408
E-mail: society@mosssociety.org
Web: www.mosssociety.org

Summary To provide financial assistance for college to high school seniors with language-related learning disabilities.

Eligibility Eligible to be nominated for this scholarship are high school seniors with language-related learning disabilities. Nominations may be submitted by society members only. The nomination packet must include verification of a language-related learning disability from a counselor or case manager, high school transcript, 2 letters of recommendation, and 4 essays by the nominees: on themselves; their learning disability and its effect on their lives; their extracurricular, community, work, and church accomplishments; and their plans for next year.

Financial data The stipend is $1,000. Funds are paid to the recipient's college or university.

Duration 1 year; may be renewed for up to 3 additional years.

Number awarded 1 each year.

Deadline March of each year.

[363]
ANNE FORD SCHOLARSHIP

National Center for Learning Disabilities
Attn: Scholarship
381 Park Avenue South, Suite 1401
New York NY 10016-8806
(212) 545-7510   Fax: (212) 545-9665
E-mail: AFScholarship@ncld.org
Web: www.ld.org

Summary To provide financial assistance for college to high school seniors with learning disabilities.

Eligibility This program is open to high school seniors with learning disabilities who plan to work on a university degree. Applicants must submit an essay (750 to 1,000 words in length) describing their learning disability and how it has affected their life, including scholastic development, relationships with family and friends, community involvement, and future aspirations. They should specify their positive and negative experiences with a learning disability, and elaborate on how they have coped with the negative aspects. Their essay should demonstrate how they meet the program's goal of supporting "a person who has faced the challenges of having a learning disability and who, through hard work and perseverance, has created a life of purpose and achievement." If they prefer, they may submit a video or audio tape (up to 15 minutes in length) with accompanying script or outline that describes their experiences with a learning disability. Other required submissions include high school transcripts, portfolios (if applicable), 3 letters of recommendation, a financial statement (financial need is strongly considered in the selection process), and SAT and/or ACT scores. U.S. citizenship is required. Minorities and women are encouraged to apply.

Financial data The stipend is $2,500 per year.

Duration 4 years, provided the recipient submits annual reports (written or in video format) detailing their progress in school and describing their insights about their personal growth.

Additional Information This program was established in 2002.

Number awarded 1 each year.
Deadline December of each year.

[364]
ARTHUR B. KANE MEMORIAL SCHOLARSHIPS

Aventis Behring
Attn: Choice Member Support Center
1020 First Avenue
P.O. Box 61501
King of Prussia, PA 19406
(610) 878-4000   Toll-free: (888) 508-6978
Fax: (610) 878-4009
E-mail: AventisBehringChoice@AventisBehring.com
Web: www.aventisbehring.com

Summary To provide financial assistance for college to students with bleeding disorders who are members of the Aventis Behring Choice program.

Eligibility This program is open to participants in the program who are attending or planning to attend a college, university, or vocational/trade school. Applicants must have hemophilia A or B or von Willebrand's disease.

Financial data The stipend is $6,250 per year.

Duration Up to 4 years, provided the recipient maintains full-time enrollment and satisfactory progress towards a degree.

Additional Information This program, offered by a pharmaceutical manufacturer, provides the largest scholarship awards available to the bleeding disorders community. Recipients must spend 2 to 4 hours each year mentoring teenagers with bleeding disorders and encouraging them in their pursuit of higher education.

Number awarded At least 4 each year.
Deadline March of each year.

[365]
ASTRAZENECA SCHOLARSHIP

Patient Advocate Foundation
Attn: Executive Vice President of Administrative Operations
753 Thimble Shoals Boulevard, Suite 200
Newport News, VA 23606
(757) 873-6668, ext. 124   Toll-free: (800) 532-5274
Fax: (757) 873-8999
E-mail: info@patientadvocate.org
Web: www.patientadvocate.org

Summary To provide financial assistance for college or graduate school to individuals whose studies have been interrupted or delayed by a diagnosis of cancer or other life threatening diseases.

Eligibility This program is open to high school seniors, undergraduates, and graduate students whose course of study has been interrupted or delayed by a diagnosis of cancer or other critical or life threatening diseases. Applicants must submit documentation of financial need, high school and/or college transcripts, and at least 2 letters of recommendation. They must be pursuing a course of study that will make them immediately employable after graduation.

Financial data The stipend is $5,000 per year.

Duration 1 year; may be renewed 1 additional year for an associate or master's degree or 3 additional years for a bachelor's or medical degree. Renewal requires that the recipient maintain a GPA of 3.0 or higher, be enrolled full time, and complete at least 20 hours of community service per year.

Additional Information This program is sponsored by AstraZeneca Pharmaceuticals.

Number awarded 1 each year.
Deadline April of each year.

[366]
AWARD OF EXCELLENCE ASTHMA SCHOLARSHIPS

American Academy of Allergy, Asthma & Immunology
611 East Wells Street
Milwaukee, WI 53202-3889
(414) 272-6071   Toll-free: (800) 822-2762
Fax: (414) 272-6070   E-mail: info@aaaai.org
Web: www.aaaai.org

Summary To provide financial assistance for college to high school seniors who have asthma.

Eligibility This program is open to U.S. citizens who are graduating high school seniors with asthma. Applicants must submit a high school transcript, a letter of recommendation from a principal or guidance counselor, and a 1-page essay on how they have achieved their educational goals while coping with asthma. Selection is based on academic achievement, extracurricular activities, and community service.

Financial data The scholarship stipend is $1,000 per year. Merit awards are $100.

Duration 1 year; nonrenewable.

Additional Information This program, established in 1982, includes 1 scholarship designated as the Tanner McQuiston Memorial Scholarship.

Number awarded At least 23 scholarships and 30 merit awards are presented each year.

Deadline December of each year.

[367]
BANTA COLLEGE-TO-WORK SCHOLARSHIP
Wisconsin Foundation for Independent Colleges, Inc.
735 North Water Street, Suite 800
Milwaukee, WI 53202-4100
(414) 273-5980   Fax: (414) 273-5995
E-mail: info@wficweb.org
Web: www.wficweb.org/documents/coll_work.htm

Summary To provide financial assistance and work experience to students (especially those with learning disabilities) majoring in fields related to business and engineering at private colleges in Wisconsin.

Eligibility This program is open to full-time juniors and seniors at the 20 independent colleges or universities in Wisconsin. Students with learning disabilities are encouraged to apply. Applicants may be majoring in any liberal arts field, they must be preparing for a career in accounting, production management, marketing, human resources, information technology, computer sciences, graphic design, or mechanical, electrical or industrial engineering. They must have a GPA of 3.0 or higher (waived for students with learning disabilities) and be interested in an internship at a Banta Corporation location, including Chicago and Menasha, Wisconsin. Along with their application, they must submit a 1-page autobiography, transcripts, a list of campus involvement and academic honors, a resume including 3 references, and 2 letters of recommendation.

Financial data The stipends are $3,500 for the scholarship and $1,500 for the internship.

Duration 1 year for the scholarship; 10 weeks during the summer for the internship.

Additional Information The participating schools are Alverno College, Beloit College, Cardinal Stritch University, Carroll College, Carthage College, Concordia University of Wisconsin, Edgewood College, Lakeland College, Lawrence University, Marian College, Marquette University, Milwaukee Institute of Art & Design, Milwaukee School of Engineering, Mount Mary College, Northland College, Ripon College, St. Norbert College, Silver Lake College, Viterbo University, and Wisconsin Lutheran College. This program is sponsored by Banta Corporation (www.banta.com).

Number awarded 2 each year.

Deadline January of each year.

[368]
BETH CAREW MEMORIAL SCHOLARSHIPS
AHF, Inc.
31 Moody Road
P.O. Box 985
Enfield, CT 06083-0985
Toll-free: (800) 243-4621   Fax: (860) 763-7022
E-mail: info@ahfinfo.com
Web: www.ahfinfo.com

Summary To provide financial assistance for college to students who have a bleeding disorder.

Eligibility This program is open to high school seniors and college freshmen, sophomores, and juniors who have hemophilia, von Willebrand Disease, or another related inherited bleeding disorder. Applicants must be attending or planning to attend an accredited college or university in the United States as a full-time student. As part of their application, they must submit essays on their academic goals, why they would be a good choice for this scholarship, their participation in extracurricular activities and community volunteerism, their greatest challenge as a person living with a bleeding disorder, examples of choices they have made that demonstrate good and bad judgement on their part, and other financial assistance they are or may be receiving.

Financial data The stipend is $2,000.

Duration 1 year.

Additional Information This program was established in 2002 to honor Beth Carew, who died in 1994 as 1 of the very few women to have hemophilia A.

Number awarded 5 each year.

Deadline April of each year.

[369]
BILL MCADAM SCHOLARSHIP FUND
Hemophilia Foundation of Michigan
c/o Cathy McAdam
22226 Doxtator
Dearborn, MI 48128
(313) 563-0515   Fax: (313) 563-1412
E-mail: mcmcadam@comcast.net

Summary To provide financial assistance for college to students with a bleeding disorder or members of their families.

Eligibility This program is open to 1) students with a hereditary bleeding disorder (hemophilia, von Willebrand, etc.) or 2) members of their families (spouse, partner, child, sibling). Applicants must be U.S. citizens and enrolled or planning to enroll at an accredited 2- or 4-year college, trade or technical school, or other certification program. Along with their application, they must submit 2 letters of recommendation and 3 essays: 1) their short- and long-term goals and who or what influenced the shaping of their goals; 2) how the emerging disability culture impacts the bleeding disorder community; and 3) the definition of peace.

Financial data The stipend is $2,000.
Duration 1 year.
Number awarded 1 each year.
Deadline May of each year.

[370]
BOOMER ESIASON FOUNDATION SCHOLARSHIP PROGRAM

Boomer Esiason Foundation
c/o Giacomo Picco
452 Fifth Avenue, Tower 22
New York, NY 10018
(212) 525-7777   Fax: (212) 525-0777
E-mail: gpicco@esiason.org
Web: www.esiason.org

Summary To provide financial assistance to undergraduate and graduate students who have cystic fibrosis (CF).

Eligibility This program is open to CF patients who are working on an undergraduate or graduate degree. Applicants must submit a letter from a social worker describing their needs, a detailed breakdown of tuition costs from their academic institution, transcripts, and a 1-page essay on their post-graduation goals. Selection is based on academic ability, character, leadership potential, service to the community, and financial need. Finalists are interviewed by telephone.

Financial data Stipends range from $500 to $2,000. Funds are paid directly to the academic institution to assist in covering the cost of tuition and fees.

Duration 1 year; nonrenewable.

Additional Information Recipients must be willing to participate in the sponsor's CF Ambassador Program by speaking once a year at a designated CF event to help education the general public about CF.

Number awarded 10 to 15 each year.

[371]
BRIAN CSIKOS MEMORIAL SCHOLARSHIP

Hemophilia Association of New Jersey
Attn: Scholarship Committee
197 Route 18 South, Suite 206 North
East Brunswick, NJ 08816
(732) 249-6000   Fax: (732) 249-7999
E-mail: mailbox@hanj.org
Web: www.hanj.org

Summary To provide financial assistance for an undergraduate degree to New Jersey residents with a bleeding disorder.

Eligibility This program is open to New Jersey residents with a bleeding disorder (Hemophilia A or B, von Willebrand Disease, or a similar blood coagulation disorder) who are planning to attend or are currently attending an accredited college or university. Membership in the Hemophilia Association of New Jersey is required. To apply, students must have at least a 2.5 GPA, have been actively involved in extracurricular activities, and be able to demonstrate financial need. They must submit a formal application, a family financial profile, official transcripts, and a brief essay (up to 2 pages) on how they meet the eligibility criteria.

Financial data The stipend is $1,000 per year.

Duration 1 year; may be renewed for up to 3 additional years, provided the recipient maintains at least a 2.25 GPA and funding is available.

Number awarded 1 new award each year.

Deadline April of each year.

[372]
BRIAN MCCARTNEY MEMORIAL SCHOLARSHIP

Michigan Association for Deaf, Hearing and Speech Services
Attn: Executive Director
2929 Convington Court, Suite 200
Lansing, MI 48912-4939
(517) 487-0066   Toll-free: (800) YOUR-EAR
Fax: (517) 487-2586   TTY: (517) 487-0202
E-mail: yourear@pilot.msu.edu

Summary To provide college aid to high school seniors in Michigan with hearing or speech impairments.

Eligibility This program is open to high school seniors in Michigan who are hard of hearing, speech and/or language impaired, or deaf. They must be U.S. citizens, intend to further their education at a 2- or 4-year college or university (including trade or technical schools), have a GPA of 2.5 or higher, be of good character, provide at least 3 letters of recommendation, and submit an essay on 1) their community service experiences or activities that demonstrate leadership, 2) their career goals, and 3) how they plan to use the scholarship if they receive it. Priority is given to applicants who have not been awarded other scholarships or educational financial grants.

Financial data The stipend is $500.

Duration 1 year.

Additional Information This program started in 1992.

Number awarded 2 each year.

Deadline February of each year.

[373]
BRISTOL-MYERS SQUIBB ONCOLOGY/IMMUNOLOGY SCHOLARSHIP

Patient Advocate Foundation
Attn: Executive Vice President of Administrative Operations
753 Thimble Shoals Boulevard, Suite 200
Newport News, VA 23606
(757) 873-6668, ext. 124   Toll-free: (800) 532-5274
Fax: (757) 873-8999
E-mail: info@patientadvocate.org
Web: www.patientadvocate.org

Summary   To provide financial assistance for college or graduate school to individuals who are cancer survivors or are living with AIDS/HIV.

Eligibility   This program is open to high school seniors, undergraduates, and graduate students whose course of study has been interrupted or delayed because of cancer or AIDS/HIV. Applicants must submit documentation of financial need, high school and/or college transcripts, and at least 2 letters of recommendation. They must be pursuing a course of study that will make them immediately employable after graduation.

Financial data   The stipend is $5,000 per year.

Duration   1 year; may be renewed 1 additional year for an associate or master's degree or 3 additional years for a bachelor's or medical degree. Renewal requires that the recipient maintain a GPA of 3.0 or higher, be enrolled full time, and complete at least 20 hours of community service per year.

Additional Information   This program is sponsored by Bristol Myers-Squibb Oncology.

Number awarded   1 each year.

Deadline   April of each year.

[374]
CALIFORNIA YOUNG CANCER SURVIVOR SCHOLARSHIP PROGRAM

American Cancer Society-California Division
1710 Webster Street
Oakland, CA 94612
(510) 893-7900   Toll-free: (800) 877-1710, ext. 146
Fax: (510) 835-8656
E-mail: tony.daquipa@cancer.org
Web: www.cancer.org

Summary   To provide financial assistance for college to residents of California who have been diagnosed as having cancer.

Eligibility   This program is open to residents of California who were diagnosed with cancer before the age of 18. Applicants must be currently younger than 25 years of age and attending or planning to attend an accredited 2-year or 4-year institution of higher education in California. Along with their application, they must submit 3 essays (250 words each) on their goals, life experiences, and community service. Selection is based on financial need; determination, motivation, and educational goals; GPA (2.5 or higher); and community service.

Financial data   Stipends range up to $5,000 per year, depending on the need of the recipient. Funds are paid directly to the recipient's institution.

Duration   1 year.

Number awarded   Varies each year; recently, 45 of these scholarships were awarded.

Deadline   April of each year

[375]
CALVIN DAWSON MEMORIAL SCHOLARSHIP

Hemophilia Foundation of Greater Florida
1320 North Orange Avenue, Suite 227
Winter Park, FL 32789
Toll-free: (800) 293-6527
E-mail: hfgf@hemophiliaflorida.org
Web: www.hemophiliaflorida.org

Summary   To provide financial assistance for college to residents of Florida with bleeding disorders and to members of their families.

Eligibility   This program is open to residents of Florida who have hemophilia or other related hereditary bleeding disorder. Applicants may be graduating high school senior or students already enrolled at a college, technical or trade school, or other certification program.

Financial data   Stipends range up to $1,000.

Duration   1 year.

Number awarded   Varies 5 each year.

Deadline   April of each year.

[376]
CANCER SURVIVORS' SCHOLARSHIP

Cancer Survivors' Fund
P.O. Box 792
Missouri City, TX 77459
(281) 437-7142   Fax: (281) 437-9568
E-mail: info@cancersurvivorsfund.org
Web: www.cancersurvivorsfund.org

Summary   To provide financial assistance for undergraduate or graduate study to residents of Texas who have had cancer.

Eligibility   This program is open to Texas residents who are enrolled in or accepted for enrollment in an accredited undergraduate or graduate school. Applicants must be a cancer survivor or currently diagnosed with cancer; they do not have to be receiving treatment to qualify. They must submit an essay, from 500 to 1,200 words in length, on how their experience with cancer has impacted their life values and career goals. Selection is based on the applicant's personal hardship and financial need.

Financial data   A stipend is awarded (amount not specified).

Duration 1 year.
Additional Information Recipients must agree to do volunteer work to use their cancer experience to help other young cancer patients and survivors cope with a life-threatening or life-altering event.
Number awarded 1 or more each year.
Deadline May of each year.

[377]
CHERYL GRIMMEL AWARD

Patient Advocate Foundation
Attn: Executive Vice President of Administrative Operations
753 Thimble Shoals Boulevard, Suite 200
Newport News, VA 23606
(757) 873-6668, ext. 124 Toll-free: (800) 532-5274
Fax: (757) 873-8999
E-mail: info@patientadvocate.org
Web: www.patientadvocate.org

Summary To provide financial assistance for college or graduate school to individuals whose studies have been interrupted or delayed by a diagnosis of cancer or other life threatening diseases.
Eligibility This program is open to high school seniors, undergraduates, and graduate students whose course of study has been interrupted or delayed by a diagnosis of cancer or other critical or life threatening diseases. Applicants must submit documentation of financial need, high school and/or college transcripts, and at least 2 letters of recommendation. They must be pursuing a course of study that will make them immediately employable after graduation.
Financial data The stipend is $5,000 per year.
Duration 1 year; may be renewed 1 additional year for an associate or master's degree or 3 additional years for a bachelor's or medical degree. Renewal requires that the recipient maintain a GPA of 3.0 or higher, be enrolled full time, and complete at least 20 hours of community service per year.
Number awarded 1 each year.
Deadline April of each year.

[378]
CONCERTA "I SEE SUCCESS" ADHD SCHOLARSHIP CONTEST

McNeil Consumer & Specialty Pharmaceuticals
7050 Camp Hill Road
Fort Washington, PA 19034
Web: www.concerta.net

Summary To provide college scholarships to children between 6 and 18 years of age who are diagnosed with ADHD.
Eligibility In order to enter a child with ADHD in this competition, an adult must write a nomination letter (250 words or less), describing how and why the child has been able to cope with the disorder and how he or she has improved and succeeded in academics, personal interactions, and/or extracurricular activities. The nominator must be a U.S. resident. The essay must be in English, be original, and not have been previously published or submitted to any other competition. Modification of an existing work does not qualify as original. Nominees must fall into 1 of these age groups: 6 through 9, 10 though 13, or 14 through 18. Selection is based on description of nominee's challenges brought about by ADHD, description of steps taken to help the nominee overcome these challenges, description of nominee's progress or growth in academics, self-esteem, interpersonal skills, relationships, and/or extracurricular activities. At least 1 First Prize winner is selected from each of the 50 states and Washington, D.C.
Financial data For First Prize winners, $1,000 will be placed in a Upromise account, to be used for their education. From that group, 6 Grand Prizes will be awarded; for each Grand Prize winner, $10,000 will be placed in a Upromise account, to be used for their college education. Several Bonus Prizes are also awarded. The value of all awards totals $279,000.
Additional Information Nominations must be sent to CONCERTA Scholarship Contest, P.O. Box 14024, Bridgeport, CT 06673-4024.
Number awarded 210 First Prize winners (70 in each age group), 6 Grand Prize winners (2 in each age group), and 9 Bonus Prizes (3 in each age group) are awarded each year.
Deadline November of each year.

[379]
CREON FAMILY SCHOLARSHIP PROGRAM

Solvay Pharmaceuticals, Inc.
Attn: Creon Family Scholarship Program
901 Sawyer Road
Marietta, GA 30062
(770) 578-5898
Toll-free: (800) 354-0026, ext. 5898
Fax: (770) 578-5597
Web: www.solvaypharmaceuticals-us.com

Summary To provide financial assistance for college to students with Cystic Fibrosis (CF).
Eligibility This program is open to high school seniors, vocational school students, and college students with CF. U.S. citizenship is required. Students must submit a completed application with a photograph, an official school transcript, all requested financial information, and a letter of reference, along with a creative representation (essay, poem, photograph, etc.) of their choice; no materials are returned. Selection is based academic achievement, leadership qualities, the ability to serve as a role model to others with CF, and financial need.
Financial data The stipend is $2,000 per year.
Duration Up to 4 years.

Additional Information This program started in 1992. Winners, upon mailing in a prescription from their prescribers, also receive a 1-year supply of CREON MINIMICROSPHERES (Pancrelipase Delayed-Release Capsules, USP) Brand pancreatic enzymes.
Number awarded 20 each year.
Deadline May of each year.

[380]
CYSTIC FIBROSIS SCHOLARSHIPS

Cystic Fibrosis Scholarship Foundation
2814 Grant Street
Evanston, IL 60201
(847) 328-0127   Fax: (847) 328-0127
E-mail: MKBCFSF@aol.com
Web: cfscholarship.org

Summary To provide financial assistance to undergraduate students who have cystic fibrosis.
Eligibility This program is open to students enrolled or planning to enroll in college (either a 2-year or a 4-year program) or vocational school. Applicants must have cystic fibrosis. Selection is based on academic achievement, leadership, and financial need.
Financial data The stipend is $1,000. Funds are sent directly to the student's institution to be used for tuition, books, room, and board.
Duration 1 year; recipients may reapply.
Additional Information These scholarships were first awarded for 2002.
Deadline March of each year.

[381]
DEBE BIRZER HALL OF FAME SCHOLARSHIP

Kansas Federation of Business & Professional
  Women's Clubs, Inc.
Attn: Kansas BPW Educational Foundation
c/o Barb Gibson, President
703 West 19th
Ottawa, KS 66067
E-mail: jhawk80@weblink2000.net
Web: www.geocities.com/ksbpwfound

Summary To provide financial assistance for college to residents of Kansas who have a learning disability.
Eligibility This program is open to Kansas residents (men and women) who are at least a high school senior, have a diagnosed learning disability, and will be taking at least 3 credit hours of postsecondary education. Applicants must submit 1) proof of disability, and 2) a 3-page personal biography in which they express their career goals, the direction they want to take in the future, their proposed field of study, their reason for selecting that field, the institutions they plan to attend and why, their circumstances for reentering school (if a factor), and what makes them uniquely qualified for this scholarship.

They must also be able to document financial need. Applications must be submitted through a local unit of the sponsor.
Financial data The stipend is $500.
Duration 1 year.
Number awarded 1 or more each year.
Deadline January of each year.

[382]
DONNELLY AWARDS

World Team Tennis, Inc.
Attn: Billie Jean King WTT Charities
250 Park Avenue South, Ninth Floor
New York, NY 20003
(212) 979-0202   Fax: (212) 253-3490
Web: www.wtt.com/charities/donnelly.asp

Summary To provide financial assistance to young tennis players who have diabetes.
Eligibility This program is open to scholar/athletes between 14 and 21 years of age who play tennis competitively either on a school team or as a ranked tournament player and have type I diabetes. Awards are presented to students from the 10 World Team Tennis (WTT) communities as well as nationally. Applicants must submit a short essay on the significance of diabetes in their lives. Selection is based on values, commitment, sportsmanship, community involvement, and financial need.
Financial data The award is a $5,000 college scholarship.
Duration 1 year.
Additional Information This program was established in 1998 by the Billie Jean King Foundation in cooperation with the American Diabetes Association. The 10 WTT communities are Hartford (Connecticut), Kansas City (Missouri), Newport Beach (California), Philadelphia (Pennsylvania), Sacramento (California), Schenectady (New York), Springfield (Missouri), St. Louis (Missouri), Westchester (New York), and Wilmington (Delaware). Information is also available from Billie Jean King WTT Charities, Inc., Attn: Anne Guerrant, 569 North Acacia Drive, Gilbert, AZ 85233-4122, (602) 740-5622, E-mail: aguerrant@wtt.com.
Number awarded 11 each year: 1 in each of the WTT communities plus 1 from anywhere in the United States.
Deadline November of each year.

COMMUNICATION/OTHER DISABILITIES: SCHOLARSHIPS

[383]
DUGDALE/VAN EYS SCHOLARSHIP AWARD

Tennessee Hemophilia and Bleeding Disorders
    Foundation
7003 Chadwick Drive, Suite 269
Brentwood, TN 37027
(615) 373-0351
Web: www.thbdf.org

Summary To provide financial assistance for college to students with hemophilia or to related individuals in Tennessee.

Eligibility This program is open to Tennessee consumers and those receiving care at a Tennessee HTC. Applicants must be 1) persons with hemophilia, or 2) their children, spouses, or caregivers. Financial need is considered in the selection process.

Financial data A stipend is provided; the amount varies but is usually around $2,000.

Duration 1 year; recipients may reapply.

Number awarded 1 or more each year.

Deadline May of each year.

[384]
EDEN SERVICES CHARLES H. HOENS, JR. SCHOLARS PROGRAM

Autism Society of America
Attn: Awards and Scholarships
7910 Woodmont Avenue, Suite 300
Bethesda, MD 20814-3015
(301) 657-0881   Toll-free: (800) 3-AUTISM
Fax: (301) 657-0869
E-mail: info@autism-society.org
Web: www.autism-society.org

Summary To provide financial assistance for college to high school seniors or graduates with autism.

Eligibility This program is open to high school seniors or graduates who have been accepted to or are already enrolled in an accredited postsecondary school (college, trade school, etc.) and who have autism. Applicants must submit 3 copies of 1) documentation of their status as an individual with autism; 2) secondary school transcripts; 3) documentation of acceptance into an accredited postsecondary educational or vocational program of study; 4) 2 letters of recommendation; and 5) a 500-word statement outlining their qualifications and proposed plan of study. A telephone interview may be required.

Financial data The stipend is $1,000.

Duration 1 year.

Additional Information This program was formerly known as the Ann M. Martin Scholarship.

Number awarded 1 each year.

Deadline February of each year.

[385]
EPILEPSY FOUNDATION OF MASSACHUSETTS & RHODE ISLAND SCHOLARSHIPS

Epilepsy Foundation of Massachusetts & Rhode
    Island
540 Gallivan Boulevard, Second Floor
Boston, MA 02124-5401
(617) 506-6041   Toll-free: (888) 576-9996
Web: www.epilepsyfoundation.org/local/massri

Summary To provide financial assistance for college or graduate school to people who have epilepsy and live in Massachusetts or Rhode Island.

Eligibility This program is open to residents of Massachusetts or Rhode Island who have been diagnosed with epilepsy (seizure disorder). Applicants must be accepted or enrolled in a postsecondary educational or vocational program as an undergraduate or graduate student. As part of the application process, students must include an essay (up to 220 words in length) on their academic and career goals and how having epilepsy has affected or influenced those goals and their work towards achieving them.

Financial data The stipend is $1,000.

Duration 1 year; may be renewed.

Additional Information This program includes the following named scholarships: the James Lyons Scholarship, the Dr. George F. Howard III Scholarship, the George Hauser/Novartis Scholarship, and the Shannon McDermott Scholarship.

Number awarded 1 each year.

Deadline June of each year.

[386]
EPILEPSY FOUNDATION OF NEW JERSEY SCHOLARSHIP PROGRAM

Epilepsy Foundation of New Jersey
429 River View Plaza
Trenton, NJ 08611
(609) 392-4900   Fax: (609) 392-5621
E-mail: efnj@efnj.com
Web: www.efnj.com

Summary To provide financial assistance for college to high school seniors with epilepsy in New Jersey.

Eligibility This program is open to high school seniors who are residents of New Jersey and have epilepsy. Applicants must submit a brief personal statement explaining their academic and career goals. Selection is based on financial need, academic record, extracurricular activities, and extent of disability.

Financial data The stipend is $1,000 per year. Funds are paid directly to the recipient.

Duration 1 year.

Additional Information Recipients may attend college in any state. Information is also available from the

EFNJ Scholarship Program, Lions Head Office Park, 33 Beaverson Boulevard, Suite 8A, Brick, NJ 08723.

Number awarded Up to 4 each year.

Deadline May of each year.

[387]
ERIC DELSON MEMORIAL SCHOLARSHIP

Eric Delson Memorial Scholarship Program
Attn: Heather Post
1826 Orange Tree Lane
Redlands, CA 92374
Toll-free: (800) 225-5967
Web: www.caremark.com

Summary To provide financial assistance for college or graduate school to students with hemophilia.

Eligibility Students diagnosed with clinical hemophilia are eligible to apply for this program if they are 1) high school seniors, high school graduates, college students, or graduate students currently enrolled or planning to enroll in an accredited 2-year or 4-year college, university, vocational/technical school, or graduate school; or 2) students entering grades 7-12 at a private secondary school in the United States. This program is not open to students with related blood disorders (e.g., von Willebrand Disease). Selection is based on academic record, potential to succeed, leadership, participation in school and community activities, honors, work experience, statement of educational and career goals, recommendations, and unusual personal or family circumstances.

Financial data The stipend is $2,500. Funds are paid in 2 equal installments directly to the recipient.

Duration 1 year; may be renewed for up to 3 additional years, provided the recipient maintains a 3.0 GPA.

Additional Information This program is funded by Caremark Therapeutic Services.

Number awarded Up to 3 each year.

Deadline June of each year.

[388]
ERIC DOSTIE MEMORIAL COLLEGE SCHOLARSHIP

LA Kelley Communications
68 East Main Street, Suite 102
Georgetown, MA 01833-2112
(978) 352-7657   Toll-free: (800) 249-7977
Fax: (978) 352-6254   E-mail: info@kelleycom.com
Web: www.kelleycom.com/finaid/finaid.html

Summary To provide financial assistance for college to students with hemophilia or members of their families.

Eligibility This program is open to 1) students with hemophilia or a related bleeding disorder or 2) members of their families. Applicants must be U.S. citizens and enrolled or planning to enroll full time in an accredited 2- or 4-year college program. They must have a GPA of 2.5 or higher. Along with their application, they must submit a 400-word essay that explains what motivates them to pursue a higher education, what subjects they plan to study, what major forces or obstacles in their life has led to that path of study, what they plan to do with their education after school, and how that may be of benefit to humankind. Financial need is also considered in the selection process.

Financial data The stipend is $1,000.

Duration 1 year.

Number awarded 8 each year.

Deadline February of each year.

[389]
FLORIDA DIVISION COLLEGE SCHOLARSHIPS

American Cancer Society-Florida Division
3709 West Jetton Avenue
Tampa, FL 33629-5146
(813) 253-0541, ext. 405
Toll-free: (800) 444-1410, ext. 405 (within FL)
Fax: (813) 254-5857
E-mail: marilyn.westley@cancer.org
Web: www.cancer.org

Summary To provide financial assistance for college to students diagnosed with cancer in Florida.

Eligibility This program is open to Florida residents who have been diagnosed with cancer before the age of 21, are under 21 at the time of application, are high school seniors or graduates, and have been accepted to an accredited 2-year or 4-year college or university in Florida. Consideration is also given to students planning to enroll in a regionally-accredited vocational/technical school. Applicants must submit a completed application form, 3 letters of recommendation (including 1 from a physician), their financial aid form, an official transcript, their standardized test scores, and a 500-word essay on their philosophical, educational, and occupational goals. Selection is based on financial need, academic record, leadership ability, and community service.

Financial data Stipends provide up to $2,000 per year for tuition plus $300 per year for textbooks.

Duration Scholarships are limited to a maximum of 130 semester hours.

Additional Information This program was established in 1992. It is Florida's first and only college scholarship exclusively for students with a history of cancer.

Number awarded Varies each year; recently, 154 of these scholarships were awarded.

Deadline April of each year.

COMMUNICATION/OTHER DISABILITIES: SCHOLARSHIPS

[390]
GLAXOSMITHKLINE SCHOLARSHIP

Patient Advocate Foundation
Attn: Executive Vice President of Administrative Operations
753 Thimble Shoals Boulevard, Suite 200
Newport News, VA 23606
(757) 873-6668, ext. 124   Toll-free: (800) 532-5274
Fax: (757) 873-8999
E-mail: info@patientadvocate.org
Web: www.patientadvocate.org

Summary To provide financial assistance for college or graduate school to individuals whose studies have been interrupted or delayed by a diagnosis of cancer or other life threatening diseases.

Eligibility This program is open to high school seniors, undergraduates, and graduate students whose course of study has been interrupted or delayed by a diagnosis of cancer or other critical or life threatening diseases. Applicants must submit documentation of financial need, high school and/or college transcripts, and at least 2 letters of recommendation. They must be pursuing a course of study that will make them immediately employable after graduation.

Financial data The stipend is $5,000 per year.

Duration 1 year; may be renewed 1 additional year for an associate or master's degree or 3 additional years for a bachelor's or medical degree. Renewal requires that the recipient maintain a GPA of 3.0 or higher, be enrolled full time, and complete at least 20 hours of community service per year.

Additional Information This program is sponsored by GlaxoSmithKline.

Number awarded 1 each year.

Deadline April of each year.

[391]
GREAT LAKES DIVISION COLLEGE SCHOLARSHIP

American Cancer Society-Great Lakes Division
Attn: College Scholarship Program
1755 Abbey Road
East Lansing, MI 48823-1907
(517) 332-2222   Toll-free: (800) 723-0360
Fax: (517) 333-4656
Web: www.gl.cancer.org

Summary To provide financial assistance for college to students from Michigan and Indiana who have a history of cancer.

Eligibility This program is open to Michigan and Indiana residents who are U.S. citizens and have had a diagnosis of cancer before age 21. Applicants must be attending an accredited college or university in either of the 2 states. Along with their application, they must submit a 500-word essay on their philosophical, educational, and occupational goals. Selection is based on the essay, 2 letters of recommendation, grades, and financial need.

Financial data The stipend is $1,000. Funds must be used for tuition.

Duration 1 year; recipients may reapply.

Additional Information This program was established in 1997.

Number awarded Varies each year; recently, 71 of these scholarships were awarded.

Deadline April of each year.

[392]
GREAT LAKES HEMOPHILIA FOUNDATION EDUCATION AND TRAINING ASSISTANCE SCHOLARSHIPS

Great Lakes Hemophilia Foundation
638 North 18th Street, Suite 108
P.O. Box 704
Milwaukee, WI 53201-0704
(414) 257-0200   Toll-free: (888) 797-GLHF
Fax: (414) 257-1225   E-mail: info@glhf.org
Web: www.glhf.org/scholar.htm

Summary To provide financial assistance for college to Wisconsin residents with a bleeding disorder and their families.

Eligibility This program is open to residents of Wisconsin who have a bleeding disorder and their parents, spouses, children, and siblings. Applicants must be attending or planning to attend college, vocational school, technical school, or a certification program. Adults who require retraining because they can no longer function in their chosen field as a result of health complications from bleeding disorders are also eligible.

Financial data Stipends range from $500 to $2,000.

Duration 1 year.

Number awarded Several each year.

Deadline April of each year.

[393]
GREGORY W. GILE MEMORIAL SCHOLARSHIP

Epilepsy Foundation of Idaho
310 West Idaho Street
Boise, ID 83702
(208) 344-4340
Toll-free: (800) 237-6676 (within ID)
E-mail: efid@epilepsyidaho.org
Web: www.epilepsyidaho.org/gile-scholar.htm

Summary To provide financial assistance for college and the purchase of medical drugs to Idaho residents who have epilepsy.

Eligibility To apply for this program, students must have graduated from a high school in Idaho, be entering or continuing in college, be an Idaho resident and U.S. citizen or permanent resident, have been diagnosed with

epilepsy, and agree to enroll in at least 12 credits per term. Preference is given to applicants planning to attend an Idaho institution. Selection is based on career plans, recommendations, how the applicant has faced the challenges due to epilepsy, and financial need.
Financial data The stipend is $1,000.
Duration 1 year.
Additional Information This program was established in 1988. The Epilepsy Foundation of Idaho also provides Limited Emergency Financial Assistance for anti-epileptic drug purchases.
Number awarded 1 each year.
Deadline March of each year.

[394]
HAWAI'I CHILDREN'S CANCER FOUNDATION SCHOLARSHIPS

Hawai'i Community Foundation
Attn: Scholarship Department
1164 Bishop Street, Suite 800
Honolulu, HI 96813
(808) 537-6333   Toll-free: (888) 731-3863
Fax: (808) 521-6286
E-mail: scholarships@hcf-hawaii.org
Web: www.hawaiicommunityfoundation.org

Summary To provide financial assistance for college to residents of Hawaii who have had cancer.
Eligibility This program is open to residents of Hawaii who are survivors of childhood cancer attending or planning to attend a postsecondary education program. Applicants must be able to demonstrate academic achievement (GPA of 2.7 or higher), good moral character, and financial need.
Financial data Funds are provided in the form of reimbursement for the purchase of books, supplies, or equipment for education.
Duration 1 year.
Additional Information Information is also available from the Hawai'i Children's Cancer Foundation, 1814 Liliha Street, Honolulu, HI 96817, (808) 528-5161.
Number awarded 1 or more each year.
Deadline June of each year.

[395]
HEMOPHILIA EDUCATION FUND

American Red Cross
c/o Scholarship America
Attn: Scholarship Management Services
1505 Riverview Road
P.O. Box 297
St. Peter, MN 56082
(507) 931-1682   Toll-free: (800) 537-4180
Fax: (507) 931-9168   E-mail: smsinfo@csfa.org

Summary To provide financial assistance for college to persons with hemophilia and their children.
Eligibility To be eligible, candidates must be high school seniors, high school graduates, or students already enrolled in full-time study. Applicants must either be receiving treatment for hemophilia or have a parent receiving treatment for hemophilia A. They must be planning to enroll full time at an accredited 2- or 4-year college, university, or vocational/technical school. Selection is based on academic performance, leadership, participation in school and community activities, work experience, career goals, and personal and family financial circumstances.
Financial data Up to $5,000 per year, payable in 2 equal installments. The award is paid directly to the recipient, but the check is made out jointly to the recipient and the recipient's school. Funds may be used for tuition, living expenses, and books. The amount awarded cannot exceed the verified cost of tuition, fees, books, and room and board.
Duration 1 year; may be renewed 1 additional year.
Additional Information This program is managed by Scholarship America and sponsored by the American Red Cross. Recipients must attend an accredited college or university in the continental United States. Scholarships are awarded for undergraduate study only.
Number awarded 3 each year: 2 to students with hemophilia and 1 to the child of a parent with hemophilia.
Deadline January of each year.

[396]
HEMOPHILIA FEDERATION OF AMERICA SCHOLARSHIP PROGRAM

Hemophilia Federation of America
Attn: Mary Beth Carrier, Program Director
102-B Westmark Boulevard
Lafayette, LA 70506
(337) 991-0067   Toll-free: (800) 230-9797
Fax: (337) 991-0087
E-mail: mb.carrier@cox-internet.com
Web: www.hemophiliafed.org

Summary To provide financial assistance for college to students who have a bleeding disorder.
Eligibility This program is open to high school seniors and current college students who have hemophilia or von Willebrand Disease. Applicants must be attending or planning to attend an accredited 2-year or 4-year college, university, or vocational/technical school in the United States.
Financial data The stipend is $1,500 per year.
Duration 1 year.
Number awarded Up to 3 each year.
Deadline December of each year.

[397]
HEMOPHILIA FOUNDATION OF MICHIGAN ACADEMIC SCHOLARSHIPS

Hemophilia Foundation of Michigan
Attn: Client Services Coordinator
905 West Eisenhower Circle
Ann Arbor, MI 48103
(734) 332-4226   Toll-free: (800) 482-3041
Fax: (734) 332-4204   E-mail: colleen@hfmich.org
Web: www.hfmich.org/support_scholarships.cfm

Summary To provide financial assistance for college to Michigan residents with hemophilia and their families.

Eligibility High school seniors, high school graduates, and currently-enrolled college students are eligible to apply if they are Michigan residents and have hemophilia or another bleeding disorder. Family members of people with bleeding disorders and family members of people who have died from the complications of a bleeding disorder are also eligible. Applicants are required to submit a completed application form, a transcript, and a letter of recommendation.

Financial data Stipends range from $500 to $1,500.

Duration 1 year.

Number awarded Varies each year.

Deadline April of each year.

[398]
HEMOPHILIA HEALTH SERVICES MEMORIAL SCHOLARSHIPS

Hemophilia Health Services
Attn: Scholarship Committee
6820 Charlotte Pike, Suite 100
Nashville, TN 37209-4234
(615) 850-5175
Toll-free: (800) 800-6606, ext. 5175
Fax: (615) 352-2588
E-mail: Scholarship@HemophiliaHealth.com
Web: www.accredohealth.net

Summary To provide financial assistance for college or graduate school to people with hemophilia or other bleeding disorders.

Eligibility This program is open to individuals with hemophilia, von Willebrand Disease, or other bleeding disorders. Applicants must be 1) high school seniors; 2) college freshmen, sophomores, or juniors; or 3) college seniors planning to attend graduate school or students already enrolled in graduate school. They must submit an essay, up to 250 words, on the following topic: "What has been your personal challenge in living with a bleeding disorder?" U.S. citizenship is required. Selection is based on academic achievement in relation to tested ability, involvement in extracurricular and community activities, and financial need.

Financial data The stipend is at least $1,000. Funds are paid directly to the recipient.

Duration 1 year; recipients may reapply.

Additional Information This program, which started in 1995, includes the following named scholarships: the Tim Haas Scholarship, the Ricky Hobson Scholarship, and the Jim Stineback Scholarship. It is administered by Scholarship Program Administrators, Inc., 1201 Eighth Avenue South, P.O. Box 23737, Nashville, TN 27202-3737, (615) 320-3149, Fax: (615) 320-3151, E-mail: info@spaprog.com. Recipients must enroll full time.

Number awarded Several each year.

Deadline April of each year.

[399]
HEMOPHILIA OF IOWA SCHOLARSHIP

Hemophilia of Iowa, Inc.
c/o Lisa Wolterman, President
404 East Washington Street
Lake City, IA 51449
E-mail: lwol@iowatelecom.net
Web: wwww.hemophiliaofiowa.org

Summary To provide financial assistance for college to members of Hemophilia of Iowa, Inc.

Eligibility Applicants must be members of the sponsoring organization, must either have hemophilia (or a related bleeding disorder) or be the immediate family members (parents, siblings) of someone who has hemophilia or a related bleeding disorder. They may be graduating high school seniors or currently in college.

Financial data The stipend is $750 if the recipient is enrolled full time or $250 if the recipient is enrolled part time. Funds are paid directly to the recipient.

Duration 1 semester; recipients may reapply.

Number awarded 6 each year: 3 to full-time students and 3 to part-time students.

Deadline May of each year.

[400]
HEMOPHILIA RESOURCES OF AMERICA SCHOLARSHIPS

Hemophilia Resources of America
Attn: Scholarships
45 Route 46 East, Suite 609
P.O. Box 2011
Pine Brook, NJ 07058
(973) 276-0254   Toll-free: (800) 549-2654
Fax: (973) 276-0998   E-mail: hra@hrahemo.com
Web: www.hrahemo.com/about/scholarship.html

Summary To provide financial assistance for college to 1) persons with a bleeding disorder or 2) their dependents.

Eligibility Eligible to apply for this program are persons with hemophilia or von Willebrand disease and their children. They must be interested in working on a college degree at a 2-year or 4-year institution (including vocational/technical school). Selection is based on an essay on future goals and aspirations; school, work, commu-

nity, and volunteer activities; 2 letters of recommendation; and financial need.
Financial data Most stipends are $1,000; the Todd M. Richardson Memorial Scholarship is $2,500.
Duration 1 year.
Additional Information This program began in 1995.
Number awarded Varies each year. Recently, this program awarded 28 scholarships at $1,000 plus 1 Todd M. Richardson Memorial Scholarship at $2,500.
Deadline April of each year.

[401]
HERB SCHLAUGHENHOUPT, JR. MEMORIAL SCHOLARSHIP

Kentucky Hemophilia Foundation
982 Eastern Parkway
Louisville, KY 40217
(502) 634-8161   Toll-free: (800) 582-CURE
Fax: (502) 634-9995   E-mail: info@kyhemo.org
Web: www.kyhemo.org/scholarships.htm

Summary To provide financial assistance for college to students in Kentucky who have a bleeding disorder and to members of their families.
Eligibility This program is open to residents of Kentucky who have hemophilia or a related inherited bleeding disorder. Also eligible are their immediate family members. Applicants must be interested in attending a university, college, trade, or vocational school.
Financial data The stipend is $500. Funds must be used for tuition, room, board, and related educational expenses.
Duration 1 year.
Number awarded 2 each year.
Deadline Applications must be submitted by January or July of each year.

[402]
HYDROCEPHALUS ASSOCIATION SCHOLARSHIPS

Hydrocephalus Association
870 Market Street, Suite 705
San Francisco, CA 94102
(415) 732-7040   Toll-free: (888) 598-3789
Fax: (415) 732-7044   E-mail: hydroassoc@aol.com
Web: www.hydroassoc.org

Summary To provide financial assistance for college or graduate school to young adults with hydrocephalus.
Eligibility This program is open to individuals between the ages of 17 and 30 who have hydrocephalus. The scholarship must be used for an educational purpose, including but not limited to a 4-year or junior college, a high school postgraduate year, a technical or trade school, an accredited employment training program, or a graduate program. Applicants may be in the process of applying to a program or university, or already be enrolled. They must include essays on their hobbies, interests, and activities; their educational and career goals; how having hydrocephalus has impacted their life; how they would help others with hydrocephalus; and how the scholarship will help them. Financial need is not considered in the selection process.
Financial data The stipend is $500. Funds may be used for tuition, books, housing, or any other educationally-related expense.
Duration 1 year.
Additional Information This program consists of 3 named scholarships: the Gerald S. Fudge Scholarship, established in 1993, the Morris L. Ziskind Memorial Scholarship, established in 2002, and the Anthony Abbene Scholarship, established in 2003.
Number awarded 3 each year.
Deadline March of each year.

[403]
I.H. MCLENDON MEMORIAL SCHOLARSHIP

Sickle Cell Disease Association of America-
  Connecticut Chapter
Attn: Garey E. Coleman
114 Woodland Street, Suite 2101
Hartford, CT 06105-1299
(860) 714-5540   Fax: (860) 714-8007
E-mail: scdaa@iconn.net
Web: www.sicklecellct.org

Summary To provide financial assistance for college to high school seniors in Connecticut who have sickle cell disease.
Eligibility This program is open to Connecticut residents who have sickle cell disease. Applicants must be graduating high school seniors, have a GPA of 3.0 or higher, be in the top third of their class, and be interested in attending a 2- or 4-year college or university. Along with their application, they must submit a statement outlining their personal and career goals and how the scholarship will help them achieve those goals, 3 letters of recommendation, and a letter from their physician attesting to existence of sickle cell disease. Finalists are interviewed.
Financial data The stipend is $1,000.
Duration 1 year.
Number awarded 1 each year.
Deadline April of each year.

[404]
IMMUNE DEFICIENCY FOUNDATION SCHOLARSHIP

Immune Deficiency Foundation
Attn: Scholarship/Medical Programs
40 West Chesapeake Avenue, Suite 308
Towson, MD 21204-4803
(410) 321-6647   Toll-free: (800) 296-4433, ext. 211
Fax: (410) 321-9165
E-mail: tb@primaryimmune.org
Web: www.primaryimmune.org

Summary To provide financial assistance for undergraduate education to students with a primary immune deficiency disease.

Eligibility Eligible to apply for these scholarships are students at a college, university, or community college who have a primary immune deficiency disease. Applicants must submit an autobiographical statement, 2 letters of recommendation, a family financial statement, and a letter of verification from their immunologist. Financial need is the main factor considered in selecting the recipients and the size of the award.

Financial data Stipends are either $1,000 or $750, depending on the recipient's financial need.

Duration 1 year; may be renewed.

Additional Information This program, established in 1986, is administered by the Immune Deficiency Foundation (IDF) with funding from the American Red Cross, Aventis Behring, Baxter Healthcare Corporation, Bayer Corporation, FFF Enterprise, Inc., and ZLB Bioplasma Inc. Additional support is provided through the Eric C. Marder Memorial Scholarship Program.

Number awarded Varies each year. Recently, 34 of these scholarships were awarded: 3 at $1,000 and 31 at $750.

Deadline March of each year.

[405]
INA BRUDNICK SCHOLARSHIP AWARD

Great Comebacks Award Program
P.O. Box 9922
Rancho Santa Fe, CA 92067
Web: www.greatcomebacks.com/us/scholar.htm

Summary To provide financial assistance to college students with Crohn's disease or other related physical conditions.

Eligibility This program is open to people under 24 years of age who have Crohn's disease, colitis, or an ostomy. Applicants must be able to demonstrate financial need. Along with their application, they must submit statements on how their life has been changed or affected by IBD or their ostomy, who or what helped them most in getting through their physical and emotional struggle, what advice they would give to someone struggling with IBD and/or facing ostomy surgery, and their dreams of what they want to accomplish in the future.

Financial data The stipend is $2,500.

Duration 1 year.

Additional Information This scholarship is provided by ConvaTec, a Bristol-Myers Squibb Company.

Number awarded 1 or more each year.

Deadline October of each year.

[406]
JAMES A. GIRARD SCHOLARSHIP

Epilepsy Foundation of Vermont
P.O. Box 6292
Rutland, VT 05702
(802) 775-1686   Toll-free: (800) 565-0972
E-mail: epilepsy@sover.net
Web: www.sover.net/~epilepsy/default.htm

Summary To provide financial assistance for college to high school seniors in Vermont who have epilepsy.

Eligibility This program is open to high school seniors in Vermont who have epilepsy. Applicants must be planning to go on to higher education after graduation.

Financial data The stipend is $1,000.

Duration 1 year.

Number awarded 1 each year.

[407]
JAY'S WORLD COLLEGE SCHOLARSHIP PROGRAM

Jay's World Childhood Cancer Foundation
c/o Napolitano
5 Knoll Lane
Glen Head, NY 11545
(516) 671-7410
Web: www.jaysworld.org/jaysworld/scholar.htm

Summary To provide financial assistance for college to residents of New York who have had childhood cancer.

Eligibility This program is open to New York residents who have been cured of cancer, are in remission, or are able to attend college while undergoing treatment for cancer. Applicants must submit a brief paper describing what it was like to be a child with cancer; how it affected their family, friends, and school life; and what the experience has taught them and how it can benefit their life. Financial need is considered in the selection process.

Financial data A stipend is awarded (amount not specified).

Duration 1 year.

Additional Information The sponsoring foundation was founded in 1997.

Number awarded 1 or more each year.

Deadline April of each year.

[408]
JEAN SPINELLI MEMORIAL SCHOLARSHIP

Vermont Student Assistance Corporation
Champlain Mill
Attn: Scholarship Programs
P.O. Box 2000
Winooski, VT 05404-2601
(802) 654-3798   Toll-free: (800) 642-3177
Fax: (802) 654-3765   TDD: (802) 654-3766
TDD: (800) 281-3341 (within VT)
E-mail: info@vsac.org
Web: www.vsac.org

Summary To provide financial assistance to Vermont residents who are upper-division or graduate students and cancer survivors or caregivers to someone with cancer.

Eligibility This scholarship is available to residents of Vermont who are juniors or seniors in college or currently enrolled in graduate school. Applicants must be a cancer survivor or be (or have been) the primary caregiver to someone afflicted with cancer. They must be able to demonstrate 1) the spirit to live a productive, meaningful life while afflicted with cancer, or 2) selfless devoted care-giving to a friend or family member afflicted with cancer. Selection is based on required essays, a letter of recommendation, and financial need.

Financial data The stipend is $500.

Duration 1 year; recipients may reapply.

Number awarded 1 each year.

Deadline June of each year.

[409]
JOHN ARENA MEMORIAL SCHOLARSHIP FUND

Learning Disabilities Association of California
c/o State Office
P.O. Box 601067
Sacramento, CA 95860-1067
(916) 725-7881   Toll-free: (866) LDA-of-CA
Fax: (916) 725-8786   E-mail: office@ldaca.org
Web: www.ldaca.org

Summary To provide funding for young adults with learning disabilities who are interested in pursuing postsecondary education in California.

Eligibility This program is open to adults 18 years of age or older who have documented learning disabilities and wish to attend an accredited community college, 4-year college or university, technical or vocational school, or school of the arts in any state. In the case of a tie, preference is given to members or family of members of the Learning Disabilities Association of California. Financial need is not considered in the selection process.

Financial data The stipend is $500; funds may be used for tuition, books, materials, supplies, and/or learning aids.

Duration 1 year.

Additional Information Information is also available from Joyce Riley, Chair, Awards and Scholarships, (949) 673-5981.

Number awarded 1 or more each year.

Deadline June of each year.

[410]
JOHN YOUTSEY MEMORIAL SCHOLARSHIP FUND

Hemophilia of Georgia
8800 Roswell Road, Suite 170
Atlanta, GA 30350
(770) 518-8272   E-mail: mail@hog.org
Web: www.hog.org/scholarships.htm

Summary To provide financial assistance for college to residents of Georgia who have a bleeding disorder or have lost a parent because of the disorder.

Eligibility This program is open to permanent residents of Georgia who have hemophilia or related bleeding disorders and to children who have lost a parent to complications from a bleeding disorder. They may be graduating high school seniors or currently-enrolled college students. Selection is based on academic record, financial need, and personal goals.

Financial data A stipend is awarded (amount not specified).

Duration 1 year.

Additional Information Funds may be used for either a college or a vocational education.

[411]
JUVENILE ARTHRITIS SCHOLARSHIPS

Arthritis Foundation-Southern New England Chapter
Attn: Scholarship Chair
35 Cold Spring Road, Suite 411
Rocky Hill, CT 06067
(860) 563-1177   Toll-free: (800) 541-8350
Fax: (860) 563-6018   E-mail: info.sne@arthritis.org
Web: www.arthritis.org

Summary To provide financial assistance for college to high school seniors from Connecticut and Rhode Island who have arthritis or rheumatic disease.

Eligibility This program is open to seniors graduating from high schools in Connecticut and Rhode Island who have arthritis or rheumatic disease. Applicants must be interested in attending a college or university. Selection is based on academic record and financial need.

Financial data The stipend is $500.

Duration 1 year.

Number awarded 3 to 5 each year.

Deadline April of each year.

[412]
KERMIT B. NASH ACADEMIC SCHOLARSHIP

Sickle Cell Disease Association of America
Attn: Scholarship Committee
200 Corporate Pointe, Suite 495
Culver City, CA 90230-8727
(310) 216-6363   Toll-free: (800) 421-8453
Fax: (310) 215-3722
E-mail: scdaa@sicklecelldisease.org
Web: www.sicklecelldisease.org/nash_scholar.htm

Summary To provide financial assistance for college to graduating high school seniors who have sickle cell disease.

Eligibility This program is open to graduating high school seniors who have sickle cell disease (not the trait). Applicants must have a GPA of 3.0 or higher and be U.S. citizens or permanent residents planning to attend an accredited 4-year college or university as a full-time student. They must submit a personal essay, up to 1,000 words, on an aspect of the impact of the disease on their lives or on society. Selection is based on GPA, general academic achievement and promise, SAT scores, leadership and community service, severity of academic challenges and obstacles posed by sickle cell disease, and the quality of their essay.

Financial data The stipend is $5,000 per year.

Duration Up to 4 years.

Additional Information The Sickle Cell Disease Association of America (SCDAA) was formerly the National Association for Sickle Cell Disease. It established this program in 1999. Requests for applications must be submitted in writing; telephone requests are not honored.

Number awarded 1 each year.

[413]
KEVIN CHILD SCHOLARSHIP

National Hemophilia Foundation
Attn: Department of Finance, Administration & MIS
116 West 32nd Street, 11th Floor
New York, NY 10001-3212
(212) 328-3700
Toll-free: (800) 42-HANDI, ext. 3700
Fax: (212) 328-3777   E-mail: info@hemophilia.org
Web: www.hemophilia.org/about/scholarships.htm

Summary To provide financial assistance for college to students with hemophilia.

Eligibility This program is open to students entering their first year of undergraduate study as well as those currently enrolled in college. Applicants must have hemophilia or another bleeding disorder. Selection is based on academic performance, participation in school and community activities, and an essay on educational and career goals.

Financial data The stipend is $1,000.

Duration 1 year.

Additional Information The program was established by the Child family after the death of 21-year old Kevin in 1989. Information is also available from Mary Child Smoot, (203) 968-2776, E-mail: Smooter@aol.com

Number awarded 1 each year.

Deadline June of each year.

[414]
LARRY SMOCK SCHOLARSHIP

National Kidney Foundation of Indiana, Inc.
Attn: Program Coordinator
911 East 86th Street, Suite 100
Indianapolis, IN 46204-1840
(317) 722-5640   Toll-free: (800) 382-9971
Fax: (317) 722-5650   E-mail: nkfi@myvine.com
Web: www.kidneyindiana.org

Summary To provide financial assistance to kidney patients in Indiana who are interested in pursuing higher education in an academic or monitored occupational setting.

Eligibility Eligible to apply for this award are Indiana residents who have at least a high school diploma or its equivalent and who have received a kidney transplant or are on dialysis. Applicants must be interested in attending college, trade school, or vocational school to work on an academic or occupational degree. Finalists are interviewed. Letters of reference (not from the applicant's family) are required. Financial need is considered in the selection process.

Financial data The amount awarded depends upon the needs of the recipient. Funds are paid directly to the recipient's school.

Duration 1 year; may be renewed.

Additional Information This fund was established in 1992.

Number awarded Several each year.

Deadline February of each year.

[415]
LILLY REINTEGRATION SCHOLARSHIPS

The Center for Reintegration, Inc.
Attn: Lilly Secretariat
734 North LaSalle Street
PMB 1167
Chicago, IL 60610
Toll-free: (800) 809-8202   Fax: (312) 664-5454
E-mail: lillyscholarships@reintegration.com
Web: www.reintegration.com

Summary To provide financial assistance to undergraduate and graduate students diagnosed with schizophrenia.

Eligibility This program is open to students diagnosed with schizophrenia, schizophreniform, or schizoaffective disorder who are receiving medical treatment for the disease and are actively involved in rehabilitative or reinte-

grative efforts. They must be interested in pursuing postsecondary education, including trade or vocational school programs, high school equivalency programs, associate degrees, bachelor's degrees, and graduate programs. As part of the application process, students must write an essay describing their skills, interests, and personal and professional goals.

Financial data The amount awarded varies, depending upon the specific needs of the recipient. Funds may be used to pay for tuition and related expenses, such as textbooks and laboratory fees.

Duration 1 year.

Additional Information This program, established in 1998, is funded by Eli Lilly and Company.

Number awarded Varies each year; recently, more than 80 of these scholarships were awarded.

Deadline February of each year.

[416]
LITTLE PEOPLE OF AMERICA SCHOLARSHIPS

Little People of America
National Headquarters
P.O. Box 65030
Lubbock, TX 79464-5030
(806) 687-1840   Toll-free: (888) LPA-2001
Fax: (806) 687-6237
E-mail: LPADatabase@juno.com
Web: www.lpaonline.org

Summary To provide financial assistance for college to members of the Little People of America.

Eligibility Membership in Little People of America is open to people who, for medical reasons, are 4 feet 10 inches or under in height. Members are eligible to apply for these scholarships if they are high school seniors or students attending college or trade school. Applicants must submit transcripts, 3 letters of recommendation, documentation of financial need, and a personal statement that explains their reasons for applying for a scholarship, their plans for the future, and any other relevant information.

Financial data The amount awarded varies, depending upon the needs of the recipients and the availability of funds. Generally, the stipend is $500.

Duration 1 year; may be renewed.

Additional Information Information is also available from Lois Gerage-Lamb, 6511 Lake Circle Drive, Dallas, TX 75214-3416, (214) 826-6284, E-mail: littlelogl@aol.com.

Number awarded Varies; generally between 5 and 10 each year.

Deadline March of each year.

[417]
MARION HUBER LEARNING THROUGH LISTENING AWARDS

Recording for the Blind and Dyslexic
Attn: Public Affairs Department
Anne T. Macdonald Center
20 Roszel Road
Princeton, NJ 08540
(609) 452-0606   Toll-free: (866) RFBD-585
E-mail: custserv@rfbd.org
Web: www.rfbd.org/applications_awards.htm

Summary To provide financial assistance to outstanding high school students with learning disabilities who plan to continue their education.

Eligibility The recipients are chosen from learning disabled students who are graduating seniors in public or private high schools in the United States or its territories and planning to continue their education at a 2-year or 4-year college or vocational school. They must be registered Recording for the Blind and Dyslexic borrowers and have earned a GPA of 3.0 or higher in grades 10-12. Selection is based on outstanding scholastic achievement, leadership, enterprise, and service to others.

Financial data Stipends are $6,000 or $2,000.

Duration 1 year.

Additional Information This program was established in 1992.

Number awarded 6 each year: 3 at $6,000 and 3 at $2,000.

Deadline February of each year.

[418]
MARK REAMES MEMORIAL SCHOLARSHIPS

Hemophilia Society of Colorado
Attn: Scholarship Committee
10020 East Girard, Suite 100
Denver, CO 80231
(303) 750-6990   Toll-free: (888) 687-CLOT
Fax: (303) 750-7035   E-mail: info@cohemo.org
Web: www.cohemo.org

Summary To provide financial assistance for college to students from Colorado who have a bleeding disorder and to members of their families.

Eligibility This program is open to residents of Colorado who have hemophilia or a related inherited bleeding disorder and their immediate family members. Applicants must submit proof of enrollment at an institution of higher education (4-year college or university, 2-year college, professional trade school); an essay on how their varied interests, life experiences, and/or community involvement led to their current career goals; high school and (if applicable) college transcripts; documentation of financial need; and 2 letters of recommendation.

Financial data The stipend is $1,000. Funds must be used for tuition, room, board, and related educational expenses.

Duration 1 year.
Number awarded 2 each year.
Deadline June of each year.

[419]
MARK RICHARD MUSIC MEMORIAL SCHOLARSHIP

Epilepsy Foundation of Idaho
310 West Idaho Street
Boise, ID 83702
(208) 344-4340
Toll-free: (800) 237-6676 (within ID)
E-mail: efid@epilepsyidaho.org
Web: www.epilepsyidaho.org/music-scholar.htm

Summary To provide financial assistance for college to Idaho residents who have epilepsy.
Eligibility To apply for this program, students must have graduated from a high school in Idaho, be entering or continuing in college, be an Idaho resident and U.S. citizen or permanent resident, have been diagnosed with epilepsy, and agree to enroll in at least 12 credits per term. Preference is given to applicants planning to attend an Idaho institution. Selection is based on career plans, recommendations, how the applicant has faced the challenges due to epilepsy, and financial need.
Financial data The stipend is $500.
Duration 1 year.
Additional Information This program was established in 1999. The Epilepsy Foundation of Idaho also provides Limited Emergency Financial Assistance for anti-epileptic drug purchases.
Number awarded 1 each year.
Deadline March of each year.

[420]
MATT STAUFFER MEMORIAL SCHOLARSHIPS

Ulman Cancer Fund for Young Adults
4725 Dorsey Hall Drive, Suite A
PMB 505
Ellicott City, MD 21042
(410) 964-0202   Toll-free: (888) 393-FUND
E-mail: scholarship@ulmanfund.org
Web: www.ulmanfund.org

Summary To provide financial assistance for college to young adults who have had cancer.
Eligibility This program is open to college students who are battling, or have overcome, cancer. Applicants must be able to demonstrate financial need.
Financial data The stipend is $1,000.
Duration 1 year.
Number awarded Varies each year; recently, 7 of these scholarships were awarded.

[421]
MAYS MISSION FOR THE HANDICAPPED SCHOLARSHIP

Mays Mission for the Handicapped
604 Colonial Drive
Herber Springs, AR 72545
(501) 362-7526   Fax: (501) 362-7529
E-mail: info@maysmission.org
Web: www.maysmission.org/school.html

Summary To provide financial assistance to college students who have a mental or physical disability.
Eligibility Eligible to apply are students who are able to document a significant mental or physical disability, score 18 or better on the ACT or 870 or higher on the SAT, and are working full time on a bachelor's degree (must provide proof of enrollment). An interview may be required. Selection is based on financial need, personality, academic goals, character, and ability.
Financial data A stipend is awarded (amount not specified).
Duration 1 semester; may be renewed.
Additional Information Recipients must attend school full time, maintain a GPA of 2.3 or higher, and write monthly "update letters" about their grades, struggles, triumphs, and campus life.
Number awarded Varies each year; recently 6 of these scholarships were awarded.
Deadline June of each year for the fall semester; October of each year for the spring semester.

[422]
MID-SOUTH DIVISION COLLEGE SCHOLARSHIPS

American Cancer Society-Mid-South Division
1100 Ireland Way, Suite 300
Birmingham, AL 35205-7014
(205) 930-8860   Toll-free: (800) ACS-2345
Fax: (205) 930-8877
Web: www.cancer.org

Summary To provide financial assistance for college to residents of designated southern states who have been diagnosed as having cancer.
Eligibility This program is open to residents of Alabama, Arkansas, Kentucky, Louisiana, Mississippi, and Tennessee. Applicants must be younger than 25 years of age, have had a cancer diagnosis before age 21, have a GPA of 2.5 or higher, and have been accepted to an accredited school. Selection is based on academic achievement, leadership, community service, and financial need.
Financial data The stipend is $1,000.
Duration 1 year.
Number awarded Varies each year; recently, 197 of these scholarships were awarded.

[423]
MIDWEST DIVISION YOUTH SCHOLARSHIP PROGRAM

American Cancer Society-Midwest Division
8364 Hickman Road, Suite D
Des Moines, IA 50325
(515) 253-0147   Fax: (515) 253-0806
Web: www.cancer.org

Summary To provide financial assistance for college to residents of selected Midwestern states who have been diagnosed as having cancer.

Eligibility This program is open to residents (for at least 1 year) of Iowa, Minnesota, South Dakota, and Wisconsin who were diagnosed with cancer before the age of 21 and are currently younger than 21 years of age. Applicants must have maintained a GPA above the average level and be attending or planning to attend an accredited 2- or 4-year college or university or a vocational/technical school. Along with their application, they must submit an essay on how cancer has impacted their life and how they plan to use that experience in their future. Selection is based on their commitment to academic or vocational goals, leadership and community service, and financial need.

Financial data The stipend is $1,000. Funds are paid directly to the recipient's institution.

Duration 1 year.

Additional Information Information is also available from the Youth Scholarship Program, P.O. Box 902, Pewaukee, WI 53072-0902, (262) 523-5572.

Number awarded Varies each year; recently, 40 of these scholarships were awarded.

Deadline March of each year.

[424]
MIKE CONLEY MEMORIAL SCHOLARSHIPS

Hemophilia Society of Colorado
Attn: Scholarship Committee
10020 East Girard, Suite 100
Denver, CO 80231
(303) 750-6990   Toll-free: (888) 687-CLOT
Fax: (303) 750-7035   E-mail: info@cohemo.org
Web: www.cohemo.org

Summary To provide financial assistance for college to students from Colorado who have a bleeding disorder.

Eligibility This program is open to residents of Colorado who have hemophilia or a related inherited bleeding disorder. Applicants must submit proof of acceptance or enrollment at a college or university, an essay on why they think they should receive this scholarship and how it might affect their future goals, transcripts, documentation of financial need, and 2 letters of recommendation.

Financial data The stipend is $1,000. Funds must be used for tuition, room, board, and related educational expenses.

Duration 1 year.

Number awarded Varies each year; recently, 3 of these scholarships were awarded.

Deadline June of each year.

[425]
MIKE HYLTON & RON NIEDERMAN SCHOLARSHIP

Factor Support Network Pharmacy
Attn: Scholarship Committee
900 Avenida Acaso, Suite A
Camarillo, CA 93012-8749
(805) 388-9336   Toll-free: (877) FSN-4-YOU
Fax: (805) 482-6324
Web: www.factorsupport.com/scholarships.htm

Summary To provide financial assistance to persons with hemophilia and to their immediate families.

Eligibility This program is open to people with bleeding disorders, their spouses, and their children. Applicants must be attending or planning to attend a postsecondary institution, including trade and technical schools. They must submit 3 short essays, on their career goals, their involvement in the hemophilia or bleeding disorder community, and how a bleeding disorder has affected their life.

Financial data The stipend is $1,000. Funds are paid directly to the recipient.

Duration 1 year.

Additional Information This program was established in 1999.

Number awarded 10 each year.

Deadline April of each year.

[426]
MONICA BAILES AWARD

Patient Advocate Foundation
Attn: Executive Vice President of Administrative Operations
753 Thimble Shoals Boulevard, Suite 200
Newport News, VA 23606
(757) 873-6668, ext. 124 Toll-free: (800) 532-5274
Fax: (757) 873-8999
E-mail: info@patientadvocate.org
Web: www.patientadvocate.org

Summary To provide financial assistance for college or graduate school to individuals whose studies have been interrupted or delayed by a diagnosis of cancer or other life threatening diseases.

Eligibility This program is open to high school seniors, undergraduates, and graduate students whose course of study has been interrupted or delayed by a diagnosis of cancer or other critical or life threatening diseases. Applicants must submit documentation of financial need, high school and/or college transcripts, and at least 2 letters of recommendation. They must be pursuing a course of

study that will make them immediately employable after graduation.

Financial data The stipend is $5,000 per year.

Duration 1 year; may be renewed 1 additional year for an associate or master's degree or 3 additional years for a bachelor's or medical degree. Renewal requires that the recipient maintain a GPA of 3.0 or higher, be enrolled full time, and complete at least 20 hours of community service per year.

Number awarded 1 each year.

Deadline April of each year.

[427] NATIONAL KIDNEY FOUNDATION OF CONNECTICUT SCHOLARSHIP PROGRAM

National Kidney Foundation of Connecticut
2139 Silas Deane Highway
Rocky Hill, CT 06067
(860) 257-3770   Fax: (860) 257-3429
E-mail: info@kidneyct.org
Web: www.kidneyct.org/how.html

Summary To provide financial assistance for college to residents of Connecticut who have kidney or urological problems or their dependents.

Eligibility This program is open to dialysis and kidney transplant patients in Connecticut and their dependents, as well as people with Childhood Nephrotic Syndrome. Applicants may be entering college as freshmen, continuing students, or older students returning to school. They must have a GPA of 2.5 or higher. Selection is based on academic performance, financial need, and history of community service.

Financial data Stipends up to $1,000 per year are available.

Duration 1 year; may be renewed.

Number awarded Varies each year.

Deadline June of each year.

[428] NATIONAL KIDNEY FOUNDATION OF MASSACHUSETTS, RHODE ISLAND, NEW HAMPSHIRE, AND VERMONT ACADEMIC AWARDS

National Kidney Foundation of Massachusetts,
   Rhode Island, New Hampshire, and Vermont, Inc.
Attn: Academic Awards Committee
129 Morgan Drive
Norwood, MA 02062
(781) 278-0222   Toll-free: (800) 542-4001
Fax: (781) 278-0333
E-mail: sdean@kidneyhealth.org
Web: www.kidneyhealth.org

Summary To provide financial assistance for college to high school seniors and graduates from selected Northeastern states who have kidney disease or to their family members.

Eligibility This program is open to students from Massachusetts, Rhode Island, New Hampshire, and Vermont, who are high school seniors or graduates pursuing postsecondary education. Applicants must have active and current kidney disease or be an immediate relative (parent, sibling, child, legal guardian) of a person with active and current kidney disease. The kidney disease must have a significant impact on the applicant's life. A kidney condition that is not progressive or does not impede the person's lifestyle in any way will not be considered. Applicants must submit a 1-page essay describing how the presence of kidney disease in their family has affected their life and career goals, discussing the major they plan to pursue, and including how their experience may have affected their decisions regarding this plan of study and/or particular school. Selection is based on academic achievement and financial need.

Financial data The stipend is $700 per year, paid in 2 installments at the beginning of each semester.

Duration 1 year.

Number awarded 13 each year.

Deadline March of each year.

[429] NEW ENGLAND CHAPTER SCHOLARSHIPS

Asthma and Allergy Foundation of America-New
   England Chapter
220 Boylston Street
Chestnut Hill, MA 02467
(617) 965-7771   Toll-free: (877) 2-ASTHMA
Fax: (617) 965-8886
E-mail: info@asthmaandallergies.org
Web: www.asthmaandallergies.org

Summary To provide financial assistance for college to high school students from New England who suffer from asthma and significant allergies.

Eligibility This program is open to juniors and seniors at high schools in New England who plan to begin higher education after graduating from high school. Applicants must suffer from asthma or significant allergies and must submit an essay on what they would suggest to make their school or community more asthma and allergy friendly. Selection is based on the essay, academic record, extracurricular activities, community service, work experience, and academic honors and achievements.

Financial data The stipend is $500.

Duration 1 year.

Additional Information Recipients are expected to serve as a role model to other teens who suffer from asthma and significant allergies by appearing at 2 events and speaking to the press.

Number awarded 2 each year.

Deadline January of each year.

[430]
NEW HORIZONS SCHOLARSHIPS

New Horizons Scholars Program
55 Second Street, 15th Floor
San Francisco, CA 94105-3491
Toll-free: (866) 3-HORIZON
Web: www.hsf.net/DOC-PDF/NewHorizons.pdf

Summary To provide financial assistance for college to Hispanic and African American high school seniors who are infected with Hepatitis C or who are dependents of someone with Hepatitis C.

Eligibility This program is open to high school seniors planning to enroll full time at a 4-year college or university in the following fall. Applicants must be of African American heritage or of Hispanic heritage (each parent half Hispanic or 1 parent fully Hispanic) and have a high school GPA of 3.0 or higher. Along with their application, they must submit 1) verification by a physician that they have Hepatitis C or are the dependent of a person with Hepatitis C; 2) transcripts; 3) a letter of recommendation; 4) documentation of financial need; and 5) a personal statement that addresses the following topics: heritage and family background, personal and academic achievements, academic plans and career goals, efforts toward making a difference in the community, and financial need.

Financial data A stipend is awarded (amount not specified).

Duration 1 year.

Additional Information This program began in 2003 as the result of a partnership of the Thurgood Marshall Scholarship Fund and the Hispanic Scholarship Fund, with support from the Roche Foundation.

Number awarded 1 or more each year.

Deadline February of each year.

[431]
NORTH CAROLINA NATIONAL GUARD ASSOCIATION SPECIAL POPULATION SCHOLARSHIP

North Carolina National Guard Association
Attn: Educational Foundation, Inc.
7410 Chapel Hill Road
Raleigh, NC 27607-5047
(919) 851-3390
Toll-free: (800) 821-6159 (within NC)
Fax: (919) 859-4990 E-mail: ncnga@bellsouth.net
Web: www.ncnga.org/education/index.asp

Summary To provide financial assistance for college to members and dependents of members of the North Carolina National Guard Association who have a disability.

Eligibility This program is open to active and associate members of the association as well as the spouses, children, grandchildren, and legal dependents of active, retired, or deceased members. Applicants must be learning disabled and/or physically disabled. They may be high school seniors, high school graduates, or currently-enrolled college students. Selection is based on financial need, academic achievement, citizenship, leadership, and other application information.

Financial data Stipends are $950, $750, or $350.

Duration 1 year; may be renewed.

Number awarded Varies each year.

Deadline January of each year for high school graduates and college students; February of each year for high school seniors.

[432]
NOVARTIS ONCOLOGY SCHOLARSHIP

Patient Advocate Foundation
Attn: Executive Vice President of Administrative Operations
753 Thimble Shoals Boulevard, Suite 200
Newport News, VA 23606
(757) 873-6668, ext. 124 Toll-free: (800) 532-5274
Fax: (757) 873-8999
E-mail: info@patientadvocate.org
Web: www.patientadvocate.org

Summary To provide financial assistance for college or graduate school to individuals whose studies have been interrupted or delayed by a diagnosis of cancer or other life threatening diseases.

Eligibility This program is open to high school seniors, undergraduates, and graduate students whose course of study has been interrupted or delayed by a diagnosis of cancer or other critical or life threatening diseases. Applicants must submit documentation of financial need, high school and/or college transcripts, and at least 2 letters of recommendation. They must be pursuing a course of study that will make them immediately employable after graduation.

Financial data The stipend is $5,000 per year.

Duration 1 year; may be renewed 1 additional year for an associate or master's degree or 3 additional years for a bachelor's or medical degree. Renewal requires that the recipient maintain a GPA of 3.0 or higher, be enrolled full time, and complete at least 20 hours of community service per year.

Additional Information This program is sponsored by Novartis Oncology.

Number awarded 1 each year.

Deadline April of each year.

[433]
OHIO SCHOLARSHIPS FOR YOUNG CANCER SURVIVORS

American Cancer Society-Ohio Division
Survivor Scholarship Review Committee
5555 Frantz Road
Dublin, OH 43017
(614) 889-9565   Fax: (614) 889-6578
Toll-free: (888) ACS-OHIO
E-mail: OhioACS@cancer.org
Web: www.cancer.org

Summary To provide financial assistance for college to residents of Ohio who have been diagnosed as having cancer.

Eligibility This program is open to residents of Ohio who were diagnosed with cancer before the age of 21. Applicants must be U.S. citizens, currently younger than 25 years of age, who plan to attend an accredited university or community college in the United States. Along with their application, they must submit an essay on how cancer has impacted their live and how they plan to use that experience in their future. Selection is based on academic performance, community service, and leadership.

Financial data The stipend is $1,000 per year.

Duration 1 year; recipients are encouraged to reapply.

Number awarded Approximately 100 each year.

Deadline February of each year.

[434]
PATIENT ADVOCATE FOUNDATION SCHOLARSHIPS FOR SURVIVORS

Patient Advocate Foundation
Attn: Vice President of Administrative Operations
700 Thimble Shoals Boulevard, Suite 200
Newport News, VA 23606
Toll-free: (800) 532-5274   Fax: (757) 873-8999
E-mail: help@patientadvocate.org
Web: www.patientadvocate.org

Summary To provide financial assistance for college or graduate school to students seeking to initiate or complete a course of study that has been interrupted or delayed by a diagnosis of cancer or other life threatening disease.

Eligibility This program is open to undergraduates working on an associate or bachelor's degree, master's degree students, and medical school students. The college or graduate education of applicants must have been interrupted or delayed by a diagnosis of cancer or other life threatening disease. Along with their application, they must submit a 1,000-word essay on why they have chosen to further their education, how the illness has affected their family and their decision to continue their education, and how they feel they can help others by earning their degree. Financial need is also considered in the selection process.

Financial data The stipend is $5,000. Funds are paid directly to the college or university to help cover tuition and other fee costs. The cost of books is not included.

Duration 1 year; may be renewed 1 additional year for an associate or master's degree or 3 additional years for a bachelor's or medical degree. Renewal depends on the recipient's maintaining an overall GPA of 3.0 or higher and full-time enrollment.

Additional Information This program includes the following programs named in honor of sustaining partners: the Cheryl Grimmel Award, the Monica Bailes Award, the American Cancer Society Scholarship, the AMGEN, Inc. Scholarship, the AstraZeneca Scholarship, the Bristol Myers-Squibb Oncology/Immunology Scholarship (limited to a cancer survivor or someone living with AIDS/HIV), the GlaxoSmithKline Scholarship, and the Novartis Oncology Scholarship. Students must complete 20 hours of community service during each year they receive support.

Number awarded 8 each year.

Deadline April of each year.

[435]
PETER AND BRUCE BIDSTRUP SCHOLARSHIP FUND

Arizona Kidney Foundation
Attn: Patient Services Director
4203 East Indian School Road, Suite 140
Phoenix, AZ 85018
(602) 840-1644   Fax: (602) 840-2360
E-mail: glennas@azkidney.org
Web: www.azkidney.org

Summary To provide financial assistance for college to kidney patients in Arizona.

Eligibility This program is open to students in Arizona who are undergoing dialysis treatment or have received kidney transplants. Applicants must be attending or planning to attend a college, community college, or technical school in Arizona. Financial need is considered in the selection process.

Financial data This scholarship pays the tuition fees at schools in Arizona.

Additional Information This scholarship fund was established in 1985 to honor Peter and Bruce Bidstrup, who did not survive kidney disease. Its selection committee is chaired by their mother, Carol Bidstrup. Recipients must attend school in Arizona.

Number awarded Varies each year.

[436]
PFIZER EPILEPSY SCHOLARSHIP AWARD

Pfizer Inc.
c/o Eden Communications Group
515 Valley Street, Suite 200
Maplewood, NJ 07040
(973) 275-6500 Toll-free: (800) AWARD-PF
Fax: (973) 275-9792
E-mail: info@epilepsy-scholarship.com
Web: www.epilepsy-scholarship.com

Summary To provide financial assistance for undergraduate or graduate study to individuals with epilepsy.

Eligibility Applicants must be under a physician's care for epilepsy (and taking prescribed medication) and must submit an application with 2 letters of recommendation (1 from the physician) and verification of academic status. They must be high school seniors entering college in the fall; college freshmen, sophomores, or juniors continuing in the fall; or college seniors planning to enter graduate school in the fall. Along with their application, they must submit a 250-word essay on something of direct personal importance to them as a person with epilepsy. Selection is based on demonstrated achievement in academic and extracurricular activities; financial need is not considered.

Financial data The stipend is $3,000.

Duration 1 year; nonrenewable.

Number awarded 16 each year.

Deadline February of each year.

[437]
ROBERT DOLE SCHOLARSHIP FUND FOR DISABLED STUDENTS

United Negro College Fund
Attn: Director, Educational Services
8260 Willow Oaks Corporate Drive
P.O. Box 10444
Fairfax, VA 22031-8044
(703) 205-3466 Toll-free: (866) 671-7237
Fax: (703) 205-3574
Web: www.uncf.org

Summary To provide financial assistance to physically and mentally-challenged students at UNCF-member colleges and universities who have unmet financial need.

Eligibility To apply, students must be attending a UNCF-member college or university, have a physical or learning disability, and have at least a 2.5 GPA. Applicants must submit a completed application form, a 500-word essay on the challenges of their disability, and a photograph. Financial need is considered in the selection process.

Financial data The stipend is $3,500.

Duration 1 year.

Deadline October of each year.

[438]
ROBERT GUTHRIE PKU SCHOLARSHIP

National PKU News
6869 Woodlawn Avenue, N.E., Suite 116
Seattle, WA 98115-5469
E-mail: schuett@pkunews.org
Web: www.pkunews.org

Summary To provide financial assistance for college to students with phenylketonuria (PKU).

Eligibility This program is open to college-age people with PKU who are on the required diet. Applicants must be accepted to an accredited college or technical school before the scholarship is awarded, but they may apply before acceptance is confirmed. Residents of all countries are eligible to apply. Selection is based on academic achievement and financial need.

Financial data Stipends vary but recently have been $2,000.

Duration 1 year.

Number awarded Varies each year; recently, 2 of these scholarships were awarded.

Deadline October of each year.

[439]
ROBERT J. AND DENNIS R. KELLY MEMORIAL SCHOLARSHIP

Hemophilia Association of New Jersey
Attn: Scholarship Committee
197 Route 18 South, Suite 206 North
East Brunswick, NJ 08816
(732) 249-6000 Fax: (732) 249-7999
E-mail: mailbox@hanj.org
Web: www.hanj.org

Summary To provide financial assistance for an undergraduate degree to New Jersey residents with a bleeding disorder.

Eligibility This program is open to New Jersey residents with a bleeding disorder (Hemophilia A or B, von Willebrand Disease, or a similar blood coagulation disorder) who are planning to attend or are currently attending an accredited college or university. Membership in the Hemophilia Association of New Jersey is required. To apply, students must have at least a 2.5 GPA, have been actively involved in athletics during their high school years as a participant or in a coaching capacity, and be able to demonstrate financial need. They must submit a formal application, a family financial profile, official transcripts, and a brief essay (up to 2 pages) on how they meet the eligibility criteria.

Financial data The stipend is $1,000 per year.

Duration 1 year; may be renewed for up to 3 additional years, provided the recipient maintains at least a 2.25 GPA and funding is available.

Additional Information Recipients are expected to continue their involvement in school sports.

Number awarded 1 new award each year.

Deadline April of each year.

[440]
ROBIN ROMANO MEMORIAL SCHOLARSHIP

Robin Romano Memorial Fund
c/o Ken Fratus
Boston Globe Sports
P.O. Box 2378
Boston, MA 02107-2378
(617) 929-2848   Fax: (617) 929-2872

Summary To provide financial assistance for college to high school seniors and graduates who are cancer survivors.

Eligibility Eligible to apply for this support are high school seniors, high school graduates, and currently-enrolled college students who are cancer survivors.

Financial data The stipend is $7,500.

Duration Up to 4 years.

Additional Information Partial scholarships are often awarded to other students. This program was started in 2000. Since then, the fund has raised nearly $150,000 and has awarded full or partial scholarships to 10 students.

Number awarded 1 or more each year.

[441]
ROCKY MOUNTAIN DIVISION COLLEGE SCHOLARSHIP PROGRAM

American Cancer Society-Rocky Mountain Division
2255 South Oneida
Denver, CO 80224
(303) 758-2030 Toll-free: (800) 892-9455, ext. 491
Fax: (303) 758-7006
E-mail: kimberly.spencer@cancer.org
Web: www.cancer.org

Summary To provide financial assistance for college to high school seniors in selected western states who have been diagnosed as having cancer.

Eligibility This program is open to U.S. citizens who are graduating from high schools in Colorado, Idaho, North Dakota, Utah, and Wyoming. Applicants must have had a diagnosis of cancer and have been accepted to an accredited 2- or 4-year college, university, or vocational/technical school. Selection is based on academic performance, community service, leadership, and financial need.

Financial data The stipend is $1,000.

Duration 1 year.

Number awarded Varies each year.

[442]
SCOTT TARBELL SCHOLARSHIPS

Hemophilia Health Services
Attn: Scholarship Committee
6820 Charlotte Pike, Suite 100
Nashville, TN 37209-4234
(615) 850-5175
Toll-free: (800) 800-6606, ext. 5175
Fax: (615) 352-2588
E-mail: Scholarship@HemophiliaHealth.com
Web: www.accredohealth.net

Summary To provide financial assistance to high school seniors and current college students who have hemophilia and are interested in working on a degree or certification in computer science and/or mathematics.

Eligibility This program is open to high school seniors and college freshmen, sophomores, and juniors who have hemophilia A or B severe. Applicants must be interested in working on a degree or certification in computer science and/or mathematics. Along with their application, they must submit an essay, up to 250 words, on the following topic: "Upon receiving your education in math and/or computer science, how will you use the new technologies (i.e., computer, internet, etc.) to better mankind and what ethical issues will you need to address?" U.S. citizenship is required. Selection is based on academic achievement in relation to tested ability, involvement in extracurricular and community activities, and financial need.

Financial data The maximum stipend is $2,000. Funds are paid directly to the recipient.

Duration 1 year; recipients may reapply.

Additional Information This program, which started in 2003, is administered by Scholarship Program Administrators, Inc., 1201 Eighth Avenue South, P.O. Box 23737, Nashville, TN 27202-3737, (615) 320-3149, Fax: (615) 320-3151, E-mail: info@spaprog.com.

Number awarded Varies each year, depending on the availability of funds.

Deadline April of each year.

[443]
SHANNON O'DANIEL MEMORIAL SCHOLARSHIP

Epilepsy Foundation of Kentuckiana
501 East Broadway, Suite 110
Louisville, KY 40202
(502) 584-8817   Toll-free: (866) 275-1078
Web: www.efky.org/scholarship.asp

Summary To provide financial assistance for college to high school seniors in Kentucky who have epilepsy.

Eligibility This program is open to college-bound high school seniors in Kentucky who have epilepsy. Applicants must submit a description of their participation in extracurricular activities, 2 letters of recommendation, their current transcript, and an essay (up to 250 words)

on something of direct personal importance to them as a person with epilepsy.
Financial data The stipend is $1,000.
Duration 1 year.
Additional Information This program was established in 2001.
Number awarded 1 each year.
Deadline April of each year.

[444]
SOOZIE COURTER SHARING A BRIGHTER TOMORROW HEMOPHILIA SCHOLARSHIPS

Wyeth Pharmaceuticals
Attn: Scholarships
P.O. Box 8299
Philadelphia, PA 19101-8299
Toll-free: (888) 322-6010
Web: www.hemophiliavillage.com

Summary To provide financial assistance for college or graduate school to students who have hemophilia.
Eligibility This program is open to high school students, GED recipients, undergraduates, and graduate students. Applicants must have either hemophilia A or B and be enrolled or planning to enroll in an accredited college, university, community college, or vocational school.
Financial data The stipend is $5,000 per year for undergraduate or graduate students or $1,000 per year for vocational school students.
Duration 1 year.
Additional Information This program began in 1998. It was given its current name in 2000 to honor Soozie Courter, "a valued and respected friend of the hemophilia community who passed away in 1999."
Number awarded 17 each year: 12 to undergraduates, 2 to graduate students, and 3 to vocational school students.

[445]
SOUTHEAST DIVISION COLLEGE SCHOLARSHIPS

American Cancer Society-Southeast Division
2200 Lake Boulevard
Atlanta, GA 30319
(404) 816-7800 Fax: (404) 816-9443
Toll-free: (800) 282-4914
Web: www.cancer.org

Summary To provide financial assistance for undergraduate or graduate study to residents of selected southern states who have been diagnosed as having cancer.
Eligibility This program is open to residents of Georgia, North Carolina, and South Carolina who have been diagnosed with cancer before 21 years of age. Applicants must be attending or planning to attend an accredited 2- or 4-year college or university, vocational/technical school, or graduate program. Selection is based on leadership, community service, and financial need.
Financial data The stipend is $1,000.
Duration 1 year.
Additional Information This program began in 1999.
Number awarded Varies each year; since the program began, scholarships have been awarded to 129 residents of Georgia, 130 residents of North Carolina, and 70 residents of South Carolina.

[446]
STEPHEN T. MARCHELLO SCHOLARSHIP

Stephen T. Marchello Scholarship Foundation
1170 East Long Place
Centennial, CO 80122
(303) 886-5018 E-mail: fmarchello@earthlink.net
Web: www.stmfoundation.org

Summary To provide financial assistance for college to students from Colorado who have survived childhood cancer.
Eligibility This program is open to high school seniors who either live in or were treated for cancer in Colorado. They may also have attended Camp Rainbow in Arizona. Applicants must submit essays on 2 topics: 1) their academic and professional goals, why they have chosen to pursue those goals, and how this scholarship will help them obtain their goals; and 2) an event in world history that has made a significant positive effect and their reasons why they feel this was important. In addition to those 2 essays, selection is based on high school GPA; SAT or ACT scores; information provided by the doctor, clinic, or hospital where they were treated; and 2 letters of reference.
Financial data The stipend is $2,500 per year.
Duration Up to 4 years.
Additional Information This foundation was established by the family of Stephen T. Marchello who died of cancer in 1999. It awarded its first scholarship in 2000. Steve was a counselor at Camp Rainbow for several years.
Number awarded 1 or more each year.
Deadline March of each year.

[447]
SUSAN BUNCH MEMORIAL SCHOLARSHIP

California Association for Postsecondary Education and Disability
Attn: Executive Assistant
71423 Biskra Road
Rancho Mirage, CA 92270
(760) 346-8206   Fax: (760) 340-5275
TTY: (760) 341-4084   E-mail: caped2000@aol.com
Web: www.caped.net/scholarship.html

Summary To provide financial assistance to undergraduate and graduate students in California who have a learning disability.

Eligibility This program is open to students at public and private colleges and universities in California who have a learning disability. Undergraduates must have completed at least 6 semester credits and have a GPA of 2.5 or higher. Graduate students must have completed at least 3 semester units and have a GPA of 3.0 or higher. Applicants must submit a 1-page personal letter that demonstrates writing skills; progress toward meeting educational and vocational goals; how they accommodate their disability; involvement in community activities; and any other factor that might strengthen their application. They must also submit a letter of recommendation from a faculty member, verification of disability, official transcripts, proof of current enrollment, and documentation of financial need.

Financial data The stipend is $1,000.

Duration 1 year.

Additional Information Information is also available from Janet Shapiro, Disabled Student Programs and Services, Santa Barbara City College, 721 Cliff Drive, Santa Barbara, CA 93109, (805) 965-0581, ext. 2365, E-mail: shapiro@sbcc.net.

Number awarded 1 each year.

Deadline August of each year.

[448]
SYBIL FONG SAM SCHOLARSHIPS

Sickle Cell Disease Association of America-Connecticut Chapter
Attn: Garey E. Coleman
114 Woodland Street, Suite 2101
Hartford, CT 06105-1299
(860) 714-5540   Fax: (860) 714-8007
E-mail: scdaa@iconn.net
Web: www.sicklecellct.org

Summary To provide financial assistance for college to high school seniors in Connecticut who have sickle cell disease.

Eligibility This program is open to Connecticut residents who have sickle cell disease. Applicants must be graduating high school seniors, have a GPA of 3.0 or higher, be in the top third of their class, and be interested in attending a 2- or 4-year college or university. As part of the application process, they must submit a statement outlining their personal and career goals and how the scholarship will help them achieve those goals. Selection is based on that essay, 3 letters of recommendation, and an interview.

Financial data Stipends are $500, $300, or $200.

Duration 1 year.

Number awarded 3 each year: 1 each at $500, $300, and $200.

Deadline March of each year.

[449]
TERRY ZAHN SCHOLARSHIPS

American Cancer Society-Mid-Atlantic Division
8219 Town Center Drive
Baltimore, MD 21236-0026
(410) 931-6850   Toll-free: (888) 227-6333
Fax: (410) 931-6879
Web: www.cancer.org

Summary To provide financial assistance for college to residents of designated mid-Atlantic states who have been diagnosed as having cancer.

Eligibility This program is open to U.S. citizens who are residents of Delaware, the District of Columbia, Maryland, Virginia, and West Virginia. Applicants must be younger than 25 years of age and have had a cancer diagnosis before the age of 21. They must be attending or planning to attend an accredited institution of higher education.

Financial data The stipend is $1,000.

Duration 1 year.

Number awarded Varies each year; recently, 52 of these scholarships were awarded.

Deadline March of each year.

[450]
TIM & TOM GULLIKSON FOUNDATION COLLEGE SCHOLARSHIPS

Tim & Tom Gullikson Foundation
Attn: Executive Director
175 North Main Street
Branford, CT 06405
Toll-free: (888) GULLIKSON
Web: www.gullikson.com

Summary To provide financial assistance for college to patients/survivors and/or children of patients or survivors of brain tumors.

Eligibility This program is open to high school seniors, high school graduates, and currently-enrolled or returning college students. Applicants must be brain tumor patients/survivors and/or children of brain tumor patients or survivors. Special consideration is given to applicants who have a connection to the tennis community. Financial need is considered in the selection process.

Financial data The sponsor awards a maximum of $25,000 in scholarships annually. The amounts of the individual scholarships are not specified. Funds are paid directly to the recipient's school and may be used for tuition, fees, books, room, and board.
Duration 1 year. Recipients may reapply up to 3 additional years; however, the total money awarded to each recipient cannot exceed $20,000.
Number awarded Varies each year.
Deadline March of each year.

[451]
UTAH HEMOPHILIA FOUNDATION SCHOLARSHIPS

Utah Hemophilia Foundation
880 East 3375 South
Salt Lake City, UT 84106
(801) 484-0325   Toll-free: (866) 504-4366
Fax: (801) 484-4177
E-mail: info@hemophiliautah.org
Web: www.hemophiliautah.org

Summary To provide financial assistance for college to residents of Utah with bleeding disorders and their caregivers.
Eligibility This program is open to people in Utah with bleeding disorders and to caregivers of people with bleeding disorders. Applicants must be attending or planning to attend a college or university.
Financial data Stipends are $1,500 or $500.
Duration 1 year.
Additional Information This program includes the Choice Source Therapeutics Scholarships (sponsored by Choice Source Therapeutics) and the Chris Townsend Memorial Scholarship.
Number awarded Varies each year, Recently, 7 of these scholarships were awarded: 5 at $1,500 and 2 at $500.

[452]
WALTER HAMILTON SCHOLARSHIP

Hemophilia Association of New Jersey
Attn: Scholarship Committee
197 Route 18 South, Suite 206 North
East Brunswick, NJ 08816
(732) 249-6000   Fax: (732) 249-7999
E-mail: mailbox@hanj.org
Web: www.hanj.org

Summary To provide financial assistance for undergraduate or graduate studies to New Jersey residents with a bleeding disorder.
Eligibility This program is open to New Jersey residents with a bleeding disorder (Hemophilia A or B, von Willebrand Disease, or a similar blood coagulation disorder) who are planning to attend or are currently attending an accredited college or university as an undergraduate or graduate student. Undergraduate applicants must be attending school on a full-time basis; graduate school applicants may be enrolled on a full-time or part-time basis. Membership in the Hemophilia Association of New Jersey is required. Students must submit a formal application, a family financial profile, official transcripts, and a brief essay (up to 2 pages) on how they meet the eligibility criteria. Selection is based on academic ability and financial need.
Financial data The undergraduate scholarship is $1,000 per year. The fellowship for full-time graduate students (12 credits per semester for 2 semesters) is $1,000 per year; the fellowship for part-time graduate students (6 credit hours per semester for 2 semesters) is $500 per year.
Duration Undergraduate scholarship: 1 year, renewable for up to 3 additional years provided the recipient maintains a GPA of 2.25 or higher. Full-time graduate student fellowship: 1 year, renewable for 1 additional year provided the recipient maintains a GPA of 3.0 or higher. Part-time graduate student fellowship: 1 year, renewable for up to 3 additional years provided the recipient maintains a GPA of 3.0 or higher. All renewals are subject to the availability of funding.
Number awarded 2 each year.
Deadline April of each year.

[453]
YOUTH OPPORTUNITY SCHOLARSHIPS

Delaware Community Foundation
100 West 10th Street, Suite 115
P.O. Box 1636
Wilmington, DE 19899
(302) 571-8004   Fax: (302) 571-1553
E-mail: rgentsch@delcf.org
Web: www.delcf.org

Summary To provide financial assistance for college to Delaware residents who have experienced a chronic illness.
Eligibility This program is open to students and former students of Delaware schools who have experienced a chronic illness, lasting 6 months or longer, that has impaired their ability to pursue their education. Priority is given to students of the First State School. Selection is based on financial need, demonstrated academic promise, and potential for success. Applicants must be interested in pursuing academic or vocational education at an institution in Delaware or any other state.
Financial data The program provides tuition assistance at academic or vocational qualified institutions of higher education.
Duration 1 year; recipients may reapply.
Number awarded 1 or more each year.

Fellowships/Grants

[454]
AIR FORCE OFFICERS' WIVES' CLUB OF WASHINGTON, D.C. SCHOLARSHIPS

Air Force Officers' Wives' Club of Washington, D.C.
Attn: AFOWC Scholarship Committee
50 Theisen Street
Bolling Air Force Base
Washington, DC 20032-5411

Summary To provide financial assistance for undergraduate or graduate education to the dependents of Air Force members in the Washington, D.C. area.

Eligibility This program is open to the children and/or non-military spouses of active-duty, retired, or deceased Air Force members in the Washington D.C. area. The children may be either college-bound high school seniors or high school seniors enrolled in a learning disability program who will continue in a higher education program; the spouses may be working on a postsecondary or advanced degree. Selection is based on academic and citizenship achievements; financial need is not considered. Applicants who receive an appointment to a service academy are not eligible.

Financial data Stipends are at least $1,000 per year. Funds may be used only for payment of tuition or academic fees.

Duration 1 year.

Number awarded Varies each year.

Deadline February of each year.

[455]
AMGEN SCHOLARSHIP

Patient Advocate Foundation
Attn: Executive Vice President of Administrative Operations
753 Thimble Shoals Boulevard, Suite 200
Newport News, VA 23606
(757) 873-6668, ext. 124   Toll-free: (800) 532-5274
Fax: (757) 873-8999
E-mail: info@patientadvocate.org
Web: www.patientadvocate.org

Summary To provide financial assistance for college or graduate school to individuals whose studies have been interrupted or delayed by a diagnosis of cancer or other life threatening diseases.

Eligibility This program is open to high school seniors, undergraduates, and graduate students whose course of study has been interrupted or delayed by a diagnosis of cancer or other critical or life threatening diseases. Applicants must submit documentation of financial need, high school and/or college transcripts, and at least 2 letters of recommendation. They must be pursuing a course of study that will make them immediately employable after graduation.

Financial data The stipend is $5,000 per year.

Duration 1 year; may be renewed 1 additional year for an associate or master's degree or 3 additional years for a bachelor's or medical degree. Renewal requires that the recipient maintain a GPA of 3.0 or higher, be enrolled full time, and complete at least 20 hours of community service per year.

Additional Information This program is sponsored by Amgen, Inc.

Number awarded 1 each year.

Deadline April of each year.

[456]
BOOMER ESIASON FOUNDATION SCHOLARSHIP PROGRAM

Boomer Esiason Foundation
c/o Giacomo Picco
452 Fifth Avenue, Tower 22
New York, NY 10018
(212) 525-7777   Fax: (212) 525-0777
E-mail: gpicco@esiason.org
Web: www.esiason.org

Summary To provide financial assistance to undergraduate and graduate students who have cystic fibrosis (CF).

Eligibility This program is open to CF patients who are working on an undergraduate or graduate degree. Applicants must submit a letter from a social worker describing their needs, a detailed breakdown of tuition costs from their academic institution, transcripts, and a 1-page essay on their post-graduation goals. Selection is based on academic ability, character, leadership potential, service to the community, and financial need. Finalists are interviewed by telephone.

Financial data Stipends range from $500 to $2,000. Funds are paid directly to the academic institution to assist in covering the cost of tuition and fees.

Duration 1 year; nonrenewable.

Additional Information Recipients must be willing to participate in the sponsor's CF Ambassador Program by speaking once a year at a designated CF event to help education the general public about CF.

Number awarded 10 to 15 each year.

[457]
BRISTOL-MYERS SQUIBB ONCOLOGY/IMMUNOLOGY SCHOLARSHIP

Patient Advocate Foundation
Attn: Executive Vice President of Administrative Operations
753 Thimble Shoals Boulevard, Suite 200
Newport News, VA 23606
(757) 873-6668, ext. 124 Toll-free: (800) 532-5274
Fax: (757) 873-8999
E-mail: info@patientadvocate.org
Web: www.patientadvocate.org

Summary To provide financial assistance for college or graduate school to individuals who are cancer survivors or are living with AIDS/HIV.

Eligibility This program is open to high school seniors, undergraduates, and graduate students whose course of study has been interrupted or delayed because of cancer or AIDS/HIV. Applicants must submit documentation of financial need, high school and/or college transcripts, and at least 2 letters of recommendation. They must be pursuing a course of study that will make them immediately employable after graduation.

Financial data The stipend is $5,000 per year.

Duration 1 year; may be renewed 1 additional year for an associate or master's degree or 3 additional years for a bachelor's or medical degree. Renewal requires that the recipient maintain a GPA of 3.0 or higher, be enrolled full time, and complete at least 20 hours of community service per year.

Additional Information This program is sponsored by Bristol Myers-Squibb Oncology.

Number awarded 1 each year.

Deadline April of each year.

[458]
CANCER SURVIVORS' SCHOLARSHIP

Cancer Survivors' Fund
P.O. Box 792
Missouri City, TX 77459
(281) 437-7142   Fax: (281) 437-9568
E-mail: info@cancersurvivorsfund.org
Web: www.cancersurvivorsfund.org

Summary To provide financial assistance for undergraduate or graduate study to residents of Texas who have had cancer.

Eligibility This program is open to Texas residents who are enrolled in or accepted for enrollment in an accredited undergraduate or graduate school. Applicants must be a cancer survivor or currently diagnosed with cancer; they do not have to be receiving treatment to qualify. They must submit an essay, from 500 to 1,200 words in length, on how their experience with cancer has impacted their life values and career goals. Selection is based on the applicant's personal hardship and financial need.

Financial data A stipend is awarded (amount not specified).

Duration 1 year.

Additional Information Recipients must agree to do volunteer work to use their cancer experience to help other young cancer patients and survivors cope with a life-threatening or life-altering event.

Number awarded 1 or more each year.

Deadline May of each year.

[459]
DIVERSITY COALITION FELLOWSHIPS

American Association of Museums
Attn: Professional Education Fellowships
1575 Eye Street, N.W., Suite 400
Washington, DC 20005
(202) 289-9114   Fax: (202) 289-6578
E-mail: seminars@aam-us.org
Web: www.aam-us.org

Summary To provide funding to museum professionals from diverse backgrounds who are interested in participating in a seminar or the annual meeting of the American Association of Museums (AAM).

Eligibility This program is open to AAM members who work at a museum in the United States. Applicants must be full-time, paid museum professionals or full-time graduate students engaged in a museum-related course of study. They must represent a diverse constituency, defined as people of all ethnic and racial backgrounds, gender, sexual orientation, religious affiliation, and physical abilities, including people living with HIV/AIDS. As part of their application, they must submit an essay explaining why they wish to attend the professional education program, how the subject matter and general experience of attending the program will assist them in their current position and overall professional development, what they will contribute to the program, and what they would do to increase and support diversity in museums. Selection is based on the comprehensiveness and relevance of the essay answers, importance of the professional development opportunity to the applicant's career goals, demonstrated financial need, quality of reference letters, ability to meet all application requirements, and clarity and completeness of the application.

Financial data The grant is $500.

Duration The grants are presented annually.

Additional Information The Diversity Coalition was originally organized in 1998 as the AAM Ethnic Coalition by the AAM Asian Pacific American Professional Interest Committee (PIC), the AAM Latino Network PIC, the AAM Native Americans and Museums Collaboration PIC, and the Association of African American Museums. In 2000, it expanded to include other diverse groups and was renamed the Diversity Coalition.

Number awarded Varies each year.

Deadline Applications may be submitted at any time, but they must be received at least 6 weeks prior to the seminar date.

[460]
DOROTHY WEIGNER AWARD

Vermont Studio Center
80 Pearl Street
P.O. Box 613
Johnson, VT 05656
(802) 635-2727   Fax: (802) 635-2730
E-mail: info@vscvt.org
Web: www.vermontstudiocenter.org

Summary To provide funding to women artists who are cancer survivors and interested in a residency at the Vermont Studio Center in Johnson, Vermont.
Eligibility Eligible to apply for this support are painters, sculptors, printmakers, and photographers who are cancer survivors. Applicants must be interested in a residency at the studio in Johnson, Vermont. Selection is based on artistic merit.
Financial data The residency fee of $3,500 covers studio space, room, board, lectures, and studio visits. The fellowship pays all residency fees.
Duration 4 weeks.
Additional Information The application fee is $25.
Number awarded 1 each year.
Deadline June of each year.

[461]
EPILEPSY FOUNDATION OF MASSACHUSETTS & RHODE ISLAND SCHOLARSHIPS

Epilepsy Foundation of Massachusetts & Rhode Island
540 Gallivan Boulevard, Second Floor
Boston, MA 02124-5401
(617) 506-6041   Toll-free: (888) 576-9996
Web: www.epilepsyfoundation.org/local/massri

Summary To provide financial assistance for college or graduate school to people who have epilepsy and live in Massachusetts or Rhode Island.
Eligibility This program is open to residents of Massachusetts or Rhode Island who have been diagnosed with epilepsy (seizure disorder). Applicants must be accepted or enrolled in a postsecondary educational or vocational program as an undergraduate or graduate student. As part of the application process, students must include an essay (up to 220 words in length) on their academic and career goals and how having epilepsy has affected or influenced those goals and their work towards achieving them.
Financial data The stipend is $1,000.
Duration 1 year; may be renewed.

Additional Information This program includes the following named scholarships: the James Lyons Scholarship, the Dr. George F. Howard III Scholarship, the George Hauser/Novartis Scholarship, and the Shannon McDermott Scholarship.
Number awarded 1 each year.
Deadline June of each year.

[462]
ERIC DELSON MEMORIAL SCHOLARSHIP

Eric Delson Memorial Scholarship Program
Attn: Heather Post
1826 Orange Tree Lane
Redlands, CA 92374
Toll-free: (800) 225-5967
Web: www.caremark.com

Summary To provide financial assistance for college or graduate school to students with hemophilia.
Eligibility Students diagnosed with clinical hemophilia are eligible to apply for this program if they are 1) high school seniors, high school graduates, college students, or graduate students currently enrolled or planning to enroll in an accredited 2-year or 4-year college, university, vocational/technical school, or graduate school; or 2) students entering grades 7-12 at a private secondary school in the United States. This program is not open to students with related blood disorders (e.g., von Willebrand Disease). Selection is based on academic record, potential to succeed, leadership, participation in school and community activities, honors, work experience, statement of educational and career goals, recommendations, and unusual personal or family circumstances.
Financial data The stipend is $2,500. Funds are paid in 2 equal installments directly to the recipient.
Duration 1 year; may be renewed for up to 3 additional years, provided the recipient maintains a 3.0 GPA.
Additional Information This program is funded by Caremark Therapeutic Services.
Number awarded Up to 3 each year.
Deadline June of each year.

[463]
HEMOPHILIA HEALTH SERVICES MEMORIAL SCHOLARSHIPS

Hemophilia Health Services
Attn: Scholarship Committee
6820 Charlotte Pike, Suite 100
Nashville, TN 37209-4234
(615) 850-5175
Toll-free: (800) 800-6606, ext. 5175
Fax: (615) 352-2588
E-mail: Scholarship@HemophiliaHealth.com
Web: www.accredohealth.net

Summary To provide financial assistance for college

or graduate school to people with hemophilia or other bleeding disorders.

Eligibility This program is open to individuals with hemophilia, von Willebrand Disease, or other bleeding disorders. Applicants must be 1) high school seniors; 2) college freshmen, sophomores, or juniors; or 3) college seniors planning to attend graduate school or students already enrolled in graduate school. They must submit an essay, up to 250 words, on the following topic: "What has been your personal challenge in living with a bleeding disorder?" U.S. citizenship is required. Selection is based on academic achievement in relation to tested ability, involvement in extracurricular and community activities, and financial need.

Financial data The stipend is at least $1,000. Funds are paid directly to the recipient.

Duration 1 year; recipients may reapply.

Additional Information This program, which started in 1995, includes the following named scholarships: the Tim Haas Scholarship, the Ricky Hobson Scholarship, and the Jim Stineback Scholarship. It is administered by Scholarship Program Administrators, Inc., 1201 Eighth Avenue South, P.O. Box 23737, Nashville, TN 27202-3737, (615) 320-3149, Fax: (615) 320-3151, E-mail: info@spaprog.com. Recipients must enroll full time.

Number awarded Several each year.

Deadline April of each year.

[464] HYDROCEPHALUS ASSOCIATION SCHOLARSHIPS

Hydrocephalus Association
870 Market Street, Suite 705
San Francisco, CA 94102
(415) 732-7040   Toll-free: (888) 598-3789
Fax: (415) 732-7044   E-mail: hydroassoc@aol.com
Web: www.hydroassoc.org

Summary To provide financial assistance for college or graduate school to young adults with hydrocephalus.

Eligibility This program is open to individuals between the ages of 17 and 30 who have hydrocephalus. The scholarship must be used for an educational purpose, including but not limited to a 4-year or junior college, a high school postgraduate year, a technical or trade school, an accredited employment training program, or a graduate program. Applicants may be in the process of applying to a program or university, or already be enrolled. They must include essays on their hobbies, interests, and activities; their educational and career goals; how having hydrocephalus has impacted their life; how they would help others with hydrocephalus; and how the scholarship will help them. Financial need is not considered in the selection process.

Financial data The stipend is $500. Funds may be used for tuition, books, housing, or any other educationally-related expense.

Duration 1 year.

Additional Information This program consists of 3 named scholarships: the Gerald S. Fudge Scholarship, established in 1993, the Morris L. Ziskind Memorial Scholarship, established in 2002, and the Anthony Abbene Scholarship, established in 2003.

Number awarded 3 each year.

Deadline March of each year.

[465] JEAN SPINELLI MEMORIAL SCHOLARSHIP

Vermont Student Assistance Corporation
Champlain Mill
Attn: Scholarship Programs
P.O. Box 2000
Winooski, VT 05404-2601
(802) 654-3798   Toll-free: (800) 642-3177
Fax: (802) 654-3765   TDD: (802) 654-3766
TDD: (800) 281-3341 (within VT)
E-mail: info@vsac.org
Web: www.vsac.org

Summary To provide financial assistance to Vermont residents who are upper-division or graduate students and cancer survivors or caregivers to someone with cancer.

Eligibility This scholarship is available to residents of Vermont who are juniors or seniors in college or currently enrolled in graduate school. Applicants must be a cancer survivor or be (or have been) the primary caregiver to someone afflicted with cancer. They must be able to demonstrate 1) the spirit to live a productive, meaningful life while afflicted with cancer, or 2) selfless devoted care-giving to a friend or family member afflicted with cancer. Selection is based on required essays, a letter of recommendation, and financial need.

Financial data The stipend is $500.

Duration 1 year; recipients may reapply.

Number awarded 1 each year.

Deadline June of each year.

[466] LILLY REINTEGRATION SCHOLARSHIPS

The Center for Reintegration, Inc.
Attn: Lilly Secretariat
734 North LaSalle Street
PMB 1167
Chicago, IL 60610
Toll-free: (800) 809-8202   Fax: (312) 664-5454
E-mail: lillyscholarships@reintegration.com
Web: www.reintegration.com

Summary To provide financial assistance to undergraduate and graduate students diagnosed with schizophrenia.

Eligibility This program is open to students diagnosed with schizophrenia, schizophreniform, or schizoaffective

disorder who are receiving medical treatment for the disease and are actively involved in rehabilitative or reintegrative efforts. They must be interested in pursuing postsecondary education, including trade or vocational school programs, high school equivalency programs, associate degrees, bachelor's degrees, and graduate programs. As part of the application process, students must write an essay describing their skills, interests, and personal and professional goals.

Financial data The amount awarded varies, depending upon the specific needs of the recipient. Funds may be used to pay for tuition and related expenses, such as textbooks and laboratory fees.

Duration 1 year.

Additional Information This program, established in 1998, is funded by Eli Lilly and Company.

Number awarded Varies each year; recently, more than 80 of these scholarships were awarded.

Deadline February of each year.

[467]
PATIENT ADVOCATE FOUNDATION SCHOLARSHIPS FOR SURVIVORS

Patient Advocate Foundation
Attn: Vice President of Administrative Operations
700 Thimble Shoals Boulevard, Suite 200
Newport News, VA 23606
Toll-free: (800) 532-5274 Fax: (757) 873-8999
E-mail: help@patientadvocate.org
Web: www.patientadvocate.org

Summary To provide financial assistance for college or graduate school to students seeking to initiate or complete a course of study that has been interrupted or delayed by a diagnosis of cancer or other life threatening disease.

Eligibility This program is open to undergraduates working on an associate or bachelor's degree, master's degree students, and medical school students. The college or graduate education of applicants must have been interrupted or delayed by a diagnosis of cancer or other life threatening disease. Along with their application, they must submit a 1,000-word essay on why they have chosen to further their education, how the illness has affected their family and their decision to continue their education, and how they feel they can help others by earning their degree. Financial need is also considered in the selection process.

Financial data The stipend is $5,000. Funds are paid directly to the college or university to help cover tuition and other fee costs. The cost of books is not included.

Duration 1 year; may be renewed 1 additional year for an associate or master's degree or 3 additional years for a bachelor's or medical degree. Renewal depends on the recipient's maintaining an overall GPA of 3.0 or higher and full-time enrollment.

Additional Information This program includes the following programs named in honor of sustaining partners: the Cheryl Grimmel Award, the Monica Bailes Award, the American Cancer Society Scholarship, the AMGEN, Inc. Scholarship, the AstraZeneca Scholarship, the Bristol Myers-Squibb Oncology/Immunology Scholarship (limited to a cancer survivor or someone living with AIDS/HIV), the GlaxoSmithKline Scholarship, and the Novartis Oncology Scholarship. Students must complete 20 hours of community service during each year they receive support.

Number awarded 8 each year.

Deadline April of each year.

[468]
PFIZER EPILEPSY SCHOLARSHIP AWARD

Pfizer Inc.
c/o Eden Communications Group
515 Valley Street, Suite 200
Maplewood, NJ 07040
(973) 275-6500 Toll-free: (800) AWARD PF
Fax: (973) 275-9792
E-mail: info@epilepsy-scholarship.com
Web: www.epilepsy-scholarship.com

Summary To provide financial assistance for undergraduate or graduate study to individuals with epilepsy.

Eligibility Applicants must be under a physician's care for epilepsy (and taking prescribed medication) and must submit an application with 2 letters of recommendation (1 from the physician) and verification of academic status. They must be high school seniors entering college in the fall; college freshmen, sophomores, or juniors continuing in the fall; or college seniors planning to enter graduate school in the fall. Along with their application, they must submit a 250-word essay on something of direct personal importance to them as a person with epilepsy. Selection is based on demonstrated achievement in academic and extracurricular activities; financial need is not considered.

Financial data The stipend is $3,000.

Duration 1 year; nonrenewable.

Number awarded 16 each year.

Deadline February of each year.

[469]
SOOZIE COURTER SHARING A BRIGHTER TOMORROW HEMOPHILIA SCHOLARSHIPS

Wyeth Pharmaceuticals
Attn: Scholarships
P.O. Box 8299
Philadelphia, PA 19101-8299
Toll-free: (888) 322-6010
Web: www.hemophiliavillage.com

Summary To provide financial assistance for college or graduate school to students who have hemophilia.

Eligibility This program is open to high school students, GED recipients, undergraduates, and graduate students. Applicants must have either hemophilia A or B and be enrolled or planning to enroll in an accredited college, university, community college, or vocational school.

Financial data The stipend is $5,000 per year for undergraduate or graduate students or $1,000 per year for vocational school students.

Duration 1 year.

Additional Information This program began in 1998. It was given its current name in 2000 to honor Soozie Courter, "a valued and respected friend of the hemophilia community who passed away in 1999."

Number awarded 17 each year: 12 to undergraduates, 2 to graduate students, and 3 to vocational school students.

[470]
SOUTHEAST DIVISION COLLEGE SCHOLARSHIPS

American Cancer Society-Southeast Division
2200 Lake Boulevard
Atlanta, GA 30319
(404) 816-7800   Fax: (404) 816-9443
Toll-free: (800) 282-4914
Web: www.cancer.org

Summary To provide financial assistance for undergraduate or graduate study to residents of selected southern states who have been diagnosed as having cancer.

Eligibility This program is open to residents of Georgia, North Carolina, and South Carolina who have been diagnosed with cancer before 21 years of age. Applicants must be attending or planning to attend an accredited 2- or 4-year college or university, vocational/technical school, or graduate program. Selection is based on leadership, community service, and financial need.

Financial data The stipend is $1,000.

Duration 1 year.

Additional Information This program began in 1999.

Number awarded Varies each year; since the program began, scholarships have been awarded to 129 residents of Georgia, 130 residents of North Carolina, and 70 residents of South Carolina.

[471]
SUSAN BUNCH MEMORIAL SCHOLARSHIP

California Association for Postsecondary Education
   and Disability
Attn: Executive Assistant
71423 Biskra Road
Rancho Mirage, CA 92270
(760) 346-8206   Fax: (760) 340-5275
TTY: (760) 341-4084   E-mail: caped2000@aol.com
Web: www.caped.net/scholarship.html

Summary To provide financial assistance to undergraduate and graduate students in California who have a learning disability.

Eligibility This program is open to students at public and private colleges and universities in California who have a learning disability. Undergraduates must have completed at least 6 semester credits and have a GPA of 2.5 or higher. Graduate students must have completed at least 3 semester units and have a GPA of 3.0 or higher. Applicants must submit a 1-page personal letter that demonstrates writing skills; progress toward meeting educational and vocational goals; how they accommodate their disability; involvement in community activities; and any other factor that might strengthen their application. They must also submit a letter of recommendation from a faculty member, verification of disability, official transcripts, proof of current enrollment, and documentation of financial need.

Financial data The stipend is $1,000.

Duration 1 year.

Additional Information Information is also available from Janet Shapiro, Disabled Student Programs and Services, Santa Barbara City College, 721 Cliff Drive, Santa Barbara, CA 93109, (805) 965-0581, ext. 2365, E-mail: shapiro@sbcc.net.

Number awarded 1 each year.

Deadline August of each year.

[472]
WALTER HAMILTON SCHOLARSHIP

Hemophilia Association of New Jersey
Attn: Scholarship Committee
197 Route 18 South, Suite 206 North
East Brunswick, NJ 08816
(732) 249-6000   Fax: (732) 249-7999
E-mail: mailbox@hanj.org
Web: www.hanj.org

Summary To provide financial assistance for undergraduate or graduate studies to New Jersey residents with a bleeding disorder.

Eligibility This program is open to New Jersey residents with a bleeding disorder (Hemophilia A or B, von Willebrand Disease, or a similar blood coagulation disorder) who are planning to attend or are currently attending an accredited college or university as an undergraduate or graduate student. Undergraduate applicants must be

attending school on a full-time basis; graduate school applicants may be enrolled on a full-time or part-time basis. Membership in the Hemophilia Association of New Jersey is required. Students must submit a formal application, a family financial profile, official transcripts, and a brief essay (up to 2 pages) on how they meet the eligibility criteria. Selection is based on academic ability and financial need.

Financial data The undergraduate scholarship is $1,000 per year. The fellowship for full-time graduate students (12 credits per semester for 2 semesters) is $1,000 per year; the fellowship for part-time graduate students (6 credit hours per semester for 2 semesters) is $500 per year.

Duration Undergraduate scholarship: 1 year, renewable for up to 3 additional years provided the recipient maintains a GPA of 2.25 or higher. Full-time graduate student fellowship: 1 year, renewable for 1 additional year provided the recipient maintains a GPA of 3.0 or higher. Part-time graduate student fellowship: 1 year, renewable for up to 3 additional years provided the recipient maintains a GPA of 3.0 or higher. All renewals are subject to the availability of funding.

Number awarded 2 each year.

Deadline April of each year.

[473]
WILLARD BERNBAUM SCHOLARSHIP

Cystic Fibrosis Foundation
Attn: President
6931 Arlington Road, Suite 200
Bethesda, MD 20814
(301) 951-4422   Toll-free: (800) FIGHT CF
Fax: (301) 951-6378
Web: www.cysticfibrosis.com

Summary To provide financial assistance to graduate students who have cystic fibrosis (CF).

Eligibility This program is open to graduate students who have CF. Applicants must submit a 1-page letter describing their educational program and financial need.

Financial data The stipend is $1,000.

Duration 1 year.

Number awarded 1 or more each year.

Grants-in-Aid

[474]
AGMA EMERGENCY RELIEF FUND

American Guild of Musical Artists
Attn: National Executive Secretary
1430 Broadway
New York, NY 10018
(212) 265-3687   Toll-free: (800) 543-2462
Fax: (212) 262-9088
E-mail: agma@MusicalArtists.org
Web: www.MusicalArtists.org

Summary To provide emergency assistance to members of the American Guild of Musical Artists (AGMA) who are dealing with accidents, illness, or other traumatic events.

Eligibility This assistance is available to members of the guild who are classical performing artists of opera, concert, and dance, and the stage managers, directors, and choreographers of opera and dance. Applicants may include young performers faced with unexpected injury or illness, artists living with AIDS, or mature performers in need of medical assistance.

Financial data The amount of the assistance varies.

Number awarded Varies each year.

Deadline Applications may be submitted at any time.

[475]
ALZHEIMER'S FAMILY RELIEF PROGRAM

American Health Assistance Foundation
Attn: AFRP Manager
22512 Gateway Center Drive
Clarksburg, MD 20871
(301) 948-3244   Toll-free: (800) 437-AHAF
Fax: (301) 258-9454   E-mail: jwilson@ahaf.org
Web: www.ahaf.org/afrp/afrp_body.htm

Summary To provide funding to Alzheimer's Disease patients and their families for emergency needs.

Eligibility This program is open to patients who have been diagnosed by a physician as suffering from Alzheimer's Disease, probable Alzheimer's Disease, or dementia of the Alzheimer's type. Their caregivers are also eligible to apply. Liquid assets (including cash, checking and savings accounts, money market accounts, stocks, bonds, and mutual funds) of the patient (or patient and caregiver if the patient is the caregiver's dependent) may not exceed $10,000. Liquid assets do not include the patient's car or house, but all of the assets are taken into account in determining the urgency of need. Applications are accepted for such expenses as short-term nursing care, home health care,

respite care, adult day care, medications, medical or personal hygiene supplies, transportation, and other expenses related to care for the patient with Alzheimer's Disease. Patients residing in a nursing home are not eligible. First-time applicants receive priority consideration.
Financial data Grants up to $500 are available, depending on the need of the recipient.
Duration Grants may be renewed.
Number awarded Varies each year, depending on the availability of funds. Since this program was created in 1988, it has provided more than $1.9 million in emergency financial assistance to Alzheimer's patients and caregivers in need.
Deadline Applications may be submitted at any time; grants are awarded on a first-come, first-served basis.

[476]
AMGEN GRANTS
Cancer Care, Inc.
Attn: Director, Social Services
275 Seventh Avenue
New York, NY 10001
(212) 712-8080   Toll-free: (800) 813-HOPE
Fax: (212) 712-8495   E-mail: info@cancercare.org
Web: www.cancercare.org

Summary To provide financial assistance for transportation to individuals who have cancer.
Eligibility This assistance is available to individuals fighting cancer. Applicants must provide the sponsoring organization's social workers and/or case managers with information about their source of income, monthly income and expenses, and (in some cases) invoices for the cost of services.
Financial data Grants provide limited assistance to help cover transportation costs. Funds are not for basic living expenses, such as rent, mortgages, utility payments, or food.
Duration This is a 1-time award.
Additional Information Funding for this program is provided by Amgen.
Number awarded Varies each year.
Deadline Applications may be submitted at any time.

[477]
ARIZONA KIDNEY FOUNDATION ASSISTANCE PROGRAMS
Arizona Kidney Foundation
Attn: Patient Services Director
4203 East Indian School Road, Suite 140
Phoenix, AZ 85018
(602) 840-1644   Fax: (602) 840-2360
E-mail: glennas@azkidney.org
Web: www.azkidney.org

Summary To provide financial assistance for special needs to kidney patients in Arizona.

Eligibility This program is open to residents in Arizona who are undergoing dialysis treatment or have received kidney transplants. Applicants must have exhausted other sources of financial aid. The following forms of assistance are available: 1) dental program provides limited dental treatment delivered to eliminate dental caries and/or alleviate pain, infection, swelling, and/or injury, but not cosmetic, orthodontic, or prosthetic services; 2) food, requested through the patient's social worker; 3) medication, for anti-ulcer, antibiotics, anti-hypertensive meds, anti-rejection meds, phoslo, or renagel; 4) nutritional supplements, as requested by dietitian or nephrologist; 5) rent or mortgage payments; 6) utilities; and 7) transportation to and from dialysis or to and from pre- or post-transplant medical appointments.
Financial data The amount provided depends on the nature of the assistance: 1) for the dental program, selected dentists in Arizona have agreed to accept the fees offered by the sponsor as payment in full, minus a co-payment by the patient of $10 per visit; 2) the food program is limited to $120 per patient per year; 3) the full cost of generic medication is provided, minus a $7.50 co-payment per prescription; 4) the full cost of designated nutritional supplements is provided; 5) rent or mortgage payments depend on the circumstances of each individual case; 6) utilities assistance is limited to $200 per patient per request; and 7) transportation assistance is limited to $100 per patient per month.
Duration Most of the assistance programs are provided as long as the patient can document need. Nutritional supplements are limited to 6 months per year. Transportation assistance is limited to 3 weeks a month.
Number awarded Varies each year.

[478]
AVONCARES PROGRAM FOR MEDICALLY UNDERSERVED WOMEN
Cancer Care, Inc.
Attn: Director, Social Services
275 Seventh Avenue
New York, NY 10001
(212) 712-8080   Toll-free: (800) 813-HOPE
Fax: (212) 712-8495   E-mail: info@cancercare.org
Web: www.cancercare.org

Summary To provide financial assistance to women who have cancer.
Eligibility This assistance is available to women with breast or cervical cancer. Applicants must demonstrate limited income and resources for diagnostic services and/or treatment for cancer. They must be under- or uninsured and underserved.
Financial data Limited financial assistance is provided for transportation, child care, and escort services. Funding is also available to help pay the costs of diagnostic (post-screening) services. Grants do not cover basic living expenses, such as rent, mortgages, utility payments, or food.

Duration This is a 1-time award.
Additional Information Funding for this program is provided by a grant from Avon.
Number awarded Varies each year.
Deadline Applications may be submitted at any time.

[479]
BEF LUNG TRANSPLANT GRANT PROGRAM
Boomer Esiason Foundation
c/o Giacomo Picco
452 Fifth Avenue, Tower 22
New York, NY 10018
(212) 525-7777   Fax: (212) 525-0777
E-mail: gpicco@esiason.org
Web: www.esiason.org

Summary To provide funding for travel and relocation costs during lung transplants to families of patients who have cystic fibrosis (CF).
Eligibility This program is open to families of CF patients who have lung transplants. Applicants must need funds to pay for expenses not covered by their insurance, including, but not limited to, 1) patient and family transportation costs for evaluation, surgery, an clinic visits after transplant; and 2) housing, food, and living expenses associated with relocation to the transplant site. Along with their application, they must provide a letter from a social worker verifying that the patient has CF and needs assistance and a detailed cost breakdown specifying how the requested funds will be allocated.
Financial data Grants cover qualified expenses.
Duration These are 1-time grants.
Number awarded Varies each year.
Deadline Applications may be submitted at any time.

[480]
BRISTOL-MYERS GRANTS
Cancer Care, Inc.
Attn: Director, Social Services
275 Seventh Avenue
New York, NY 10001
(212) 712-8080   Toll-free: (800) 813-HOPE
Fax: (212) 712-8495   E-mail: info@cancercare.org
Web: www.cancercare.org

Summary To provide financial assistance to individuals who have lung cancer.
Eligibility This assistance is available to individuals fighting lung cancer. Applicants must provide the sponsoring organization's social workers and/or case managers with information about their source of income, monthly income and expenses, and (in some cases) invoices for the cost of services.
Financial data Grants are provided to help cover, over a period of weeks, transportation to treatments, pain medication, child care, and home care. Funds are not for basic living expenses, such as rent, mortgages, utility payments, or food.
Duration This is a 1-time award.
Additional Information Funding for this program is provided by Bristol-Myers Squibb Company.
Number awarded Varies each year.
Deadline Applications may be submitted at any time.

[481]
CANCER CARE FINANCIAL ASSISTANCE
Cancer Care, Inc.
Attn: Director, Social Services
275 Seventh Avenue
New York, NY 10001
(212) 712-8080   Toll-free: (800) 813-HOPE
Fax: (212) 711-8495   E-mail: info@cancercare.org
Web: www.cancercare.org

Summary To provide financial assistance to the residents of New York, New Jersey, and Connecticut who have cancer and need financial assistance to cover treatment-related costs.
Eligibility This program is open to residents of New York, New Jersey, and Connecticut who are suffering from cancer. Applicants must provide the sponsoring organization's social workers and/or case managers with information about their source of income, monthly income and expenses, and (in some cases) invoices for the cost of services. Patients who are Medicaid-eligible, in the process of applying for Medicaid homemaker/home attendant service, or Medicaid pending are eligible automatically.
Financial data Funds are available to cover the costs of home care, child care for cancer patients and their families, pain medication, and transportation to chemotherapy or radiation treatments. Grants do not cover living expenses, such as rent, mortgages, utility payments, or food.
Additional Information Financial assistance is reassessed every 3 months, to determine if there are any changes in the patient or family's needs.
Number awarded Varies each year.
Deadline Applications may be submitted at any time.

[482]
CARE PROGRAM
National Gaucher Foundation, Inc.
Attn: Program Director
5410 Edson Lane, Suite 260
Rockville, MD 20852-3130
(301) 816-1515, ext. 519 Toll-free: (800) 925-8885
Fax: (301) 816-1516
E-mail: ngf@gaucherdisease.org
Web: www.gaucherdisease.org/support.htm

Summary To assist Gaucher patients who need help with paying their insurance premiums.

Eligibility To be eligible, a patient must be diagnosed with Type I Gaucher Disease, have a physician's prescription for enzyme replacement therapy, be eligible for insurance, be able to demonstrate extraordinary financial hardship, and need financial assistance to pay insurance premium payments.

Financial data This program provides funds to subsidize, or purchase in full, a health insurance policy that includes coverage for enzyme replacement therapy.

Duration The time period varies, depending on each individual case. Patients who receive grants are required to reapply on an annual basis or at the end of the designated grant period.

Additional Information There are 6 genetic diseases that are prevalent in the Jewish population. Only 1 is treatable—Gaucher Disease, which is caused by a genetic mutation resulting in low levels of a key enzyme called glucocerebrosidase, important in breaking down a fatty substance in cells.

Number awarded Varies each year.

Deadline Applications may be submitted at any time and are considered on a quarterly basis.

[483]
CARE+PLUS PROGRAM

National Gaucher Foundation, Inc.
Attn: Program Director
5410 Edson Lane, Suite 260
Rockville, MD 20852-3130
(301) 816-1515, ext. 519 Toll-free: (800) 925-8885
Fax: (301) 816-1516
E-mail: ngf@gaucherdisease.org
Web: www.gaucherdisease.org/support.htm

Summary To provide assistance to needy Gaucher patients for a variety of Gaucher-related expenses, such as diagnostic tests, infusion charges, travel expenses, etc.

Eligibility To be eligible, a patient must be diagnosed with Type I Gaucher Disease, have a physician's prescription for enzyme replacement therapy, be eligible for insurance, and be able to demonstrate extraordinary financial hardship.

Financial data This program provides funds to pay for diagnostic tests and other ancillary medical expenses for Gaucher Disease not covered by insurance; infusion charges for enzyme replacement therapy not covered by insurance; membership fees for organizations that provide access to insurance for Gaucher patients; travel expenses to and from office/hospital for enzyme replacement therapy or a Gaucher medical evaluation; day care expenses for Gaucher patient's family members while the patient receives enzyme replacement therapy or a Gaucher medical evaluation; and over-the-counter medications that are prescribed for Gaucher patients.

Duration The time period varies, depending on each individual case. Patients who receive grants are required to reapply on an annual basis or at the end of the designated grant period.

Additional Information There are 6 genetic diseases that are prevalent in the Jewish population. Only 1 is treatable—Gaucher Disease, which is caused by a genetic mutation resulting in low levels of a key enzyme called glucocerebrosidase, important in breaking down a fatty substance in cells.

Number awarded Varies each year.

Deadline Applications may be submitted at any time and are considered on a quarterly basis.

[484]
COAL MINERS BLACK LUNG BENEFITS

Department of Labor
Employment Standards Administration
Office of Workers' Compensation Programs
Attn: Division of Coal Mine Workers' Compensation
200 Constitution Avenue, N.W., Room C3520
Washington, DC 20210
(202) 219-6795 Toll-free: (800) 347-2502
TDD: (800) 326-2577
Web: www.dol.gov/esa/public/owcp_org.htm

Summary To provide monthly benefits to coal miners who are disabled because of pneumoconiosis (black lung disease) and to their surviving dependents.

Eligibility Present and former coal miners (including certain transportation and construction workers who were exposed to coal mine dust) and their surviving dependents, including surviving spouses, orphaned children, and totally dependent parents, brothers, and sisters, may file claims if they are totally disabled.

Financial data Benefit amounts vary; recently; the basic monthly benefit was $534 for a single totally disabled miner or surviving spouse, $801 per month for a claimant with 1 dependent, $935 per month for a claimant with 2 dependents, or $1,069 per month for a claimant with 3 or more dependents. Benefit payments are reduced by the amounts received for pneumoconiosis under state workers' compensation awards and by excess earnings.

Duration Benefits are paid as long as the miner is unable to work in the mines or until the miner dies.

Number awarded Varies; approximately 50,000 miners and eligible surviving dependents currently receive nearly $400 million per year in benefits from this program.

COMMUNICATION/OTHER DISABILITIES: GRANTS-IN-AID

[485]
EPILEPSY FOUNDATION OF KANSAS AND WESTERN MISSOURI MEDICATION ASSISTANCE

Epilepsy Foundation of Kansas and Western Missouri
6550 Troost, Suite B
Kansas City, MO 64131
(816) 444-2800   Toll-free: (800) 972-5163
E-mail: info@efha.org
Web: www.efha.org

Summary To provide funding to low-income residents of Kansas and western Missouri who need assistance for the purchase of anti-epilepsy medication.

Eligibility This program is open to low-income residents of Kansas and western Missouri who have epilepsy. Applicants must be able to demonstrate that they need assistance for the purchase of anti-epilepsy medication. They may be seeking emergency assistance or ongoing assistance.

Financial data Emergency assistance provides a supply of medication that the foundation purchases for the consumer. Consumers determined eligible for ongoing assistance receive a membership card that they can use for a 50% discount on the cost of medication that they purchase at a participating pharmacy.

Duration Emergency assistance provides a 1-time, 1-month supply. Ongoing assistance cards are valid for 1 year but may be renewed.

Additional Information This program began in 1960.

Number awarded Varies each year; recently, it provided 152 emergency medication prescriptions at a cost of $20,770.90 and 580 ongoing prescriptions at a cost of $51,528.74 (this figure includes the amount paid by consumers).

Deadline Applications may be submitted at any time.

[486]
FUND FOR WRITERS AND EDITORS WITH AIDS

PEN American Center
Attn: Coordinator, Writers Fund
568 Broadway, Suite 401
New York, NY 10012-3225
(212) 334-1660, ext. 101   Fax: (212) 334-2181
E-mail: pen@pen.org
Web: www.pen.org/writfund.html

Summary To provide financial assistance to published writers, produced playwrights, and editors with Acquired Immune Deficiency Syndrome (AIDS).

Eligibility Professional authors and editors with AIDS are eligible to apply if they are in need of emergency financial assistance. They must be U.S. residents and have had their works published or produced (applicants will be asked to submit samples of their work). Applicants need not be members of PEN, however. Funding is not provided to pay for research activities, to enable the completion of writing projects, or to cover publication or education expenses.

Financial data Grants up to $1,000 are available; most awards average between $300 and $700.

Duration Grants may be requested as often as they are needed.

Number awarded Varies each year.

Deadline Applications may be submitted at any time; they are reviewed every 6 to 8 weeks.

[487]
GREGORY W. GILE MEMORIAL SCHOLARSHIP

Epilepsy Foundation of Idaho
310 West Idaho Street
Boise, ID 83702
(208) 344-4340
Toll-free: (800) 237-6676 (within ID)
E-mail: efid@epilepsyidaho.org
Web: www.epilepsyidaho.org/gile-scholar.htm

Summary To provide financial assistance for college and the purchase of medical drugs to Idaho residents who have epilepsy.

Eligibility To apply for this program, students must have graduated from a high school in Idaho, be entering or continuing in college, be an Idaho resident and U.S. citizen or permanent resident, have been diagnosed with epilepsy, and agree to enroll in at least 12 credits per term. Preference is given to applicants planning to attend an Idaho institution. Selection is based on career plans, recommendations, how the applicant has faced the challenges due to epilepsy, and financial need.

Financial data The stipend is $1,000.

Duration 1 year.

Additional Information This program was established in 1988. The Epilepsy Foundation of Idaho also provides Limited Emergency Financial Assistance for anti-epileptic drug purchases.

Number awarded 1 each year.

Deadline March of each year.

[488]
HAWAII INCOME TAX EXCLUSION FOR PATIENTS WITH HANSEN'S DISEASE

Department of Taxation
Attn: Taxpayer Services Branch
425 Queen Street
P.O. Box 259
Honolulu, HI 96809-0259
(808) 587-4242   Toll-free: (800) 222-3229
Fax: (808) 587-1488   TDD: (808) 587-1418
Web: www.hawaii.gov/tax/tax.html

Summary To exempt payments to patients with Hansen's Disease from state income taxation in Hawaii.

Eligibility Compensation paid by the state of Hawaii or the United States to a patient affected with Hansen's Disease (also known as leprosy) is subject to this exclusion.
Financial data All compensation is excluded from income for purposes of state taxation.
Duration The exclusion continues as long as the recipient resides in Hawaii.

[489]
HEMOPHILIA FOUNDATION OF MICHIGAN EMERGENCY FINANCIAL ASSISTANCE PROGRAM

Hemophilia Foundation of Michigan
Attn: Client Services Coordinator
905 West Eisenhower Circle
Ann Arbor, MI 48103
(734) 332-4226   Toll-free: (800) 482-3041
Fax: (734) 332-4204   E-mail: colleen@hfmich.org
Web: www.hfmich.org/support_financialaid.cfm

Summary To provide financial assistance for emergency needs to Michigan residents with hemophilia.
Eligibility This program is open to residents of Michigan who have a bleeding disorder and have a temporary financial emergency. The need may be for food, utility bills, rent, or car repair for individuals whose bleeding disorder impacts their income. Selection is based on severity of the need and the ability of applicants to change their financial standing. Requests may come directly from applicants or their hemophilia treatment center.
Financial data Grants depend on the availability of funds and the need of the recipient.
Duration Recipients may obtain these funds only once in each 12-month period.
Number awarded Varies each year.
Deadline Applications may be submitted at any time.

[490]
HIRSHBERG FUND

Cancer Care, Inc.
Attn: Director, Social Services
275 Seventh Avenue
New York, NY 10001
(212) 712-8080   Toll-free: (800) 813-HOPE
Fax: (212) 712-8495   E-mail: info@cancercare.org
Web: www.cancercare.org

Summary To provide financial assistance to individuals who have pancreatic cancer.
Eligibility This assistance is available to individuals fighting pancreatic cancer. Applicants must provide the sponsoring organization's social workers and/or case managers with information about their source of income, monthly income and expenses, and (in some cases) invoices for the cost of services.

Financial data Grants are provided to help cover, over a period of weeks, transportation to treatments, homecare, child care, medication, chemotherapy, or radiation therapy treatments. Funds are not for basic living expenses, such as rent, mortgages, utility payments, or food.
Duration This is a 1-time award.
Number awarded Varies each year.
Deadline Applications may be submitted at any time.

[491]
IDAHO INCOME TAX EXEMPTION FOR MAINTAINING A HOME FOR THE DEVELOPMENTALLY DISABLED

Idaho State Tax Commission
Attn: Public Information Office
800 Park Boulevard, Plaza IV
P.O. Box 36
Boise, ID 83722-0410
(208) 334-7660   Toll-free: (800) 972-7660
TDD: (800) 377-3529
Web: www.state.id.us/tax/home.html

Summary To exempt from state taxation a portion of the income of residents of Idaho who maintain a home for a family member, including themselves and their spouses, who is developmentally disabled.
Eligibility Individuals in Idaho who maintain a household that includes a developmentally disabled person (of any age) are eligible for this program if they provide at least half of the support of the developmentally disabled family member. The taxpayer and spouse may be included as a member of the family. Developmental disability is defined as a chronic disability that 1) is attributable to an impairment such as mental retardation, cerebral palsy, epilepsy, autism, or related condition; 2) results in substantial functional limitation in 3 or more of the following areas of life activity: self-care, receptive and expressive language, learning, mobility, self-direction, capacity for independent living, or economic self-sufficiency; and 3) reflects the need for a combination and sequence of special, interdisciplinary or generic care, treatment, or other services that are of lifelong or extended duration and individually planned and coordinated.
Financial data The amount of the deduction is $1,000 for each developmentally disabled family member, up to a maximum of $3,000.
Duration Application for the deduction must be submitted each year.
Additional Information This deduction also applies to taxpayers maintaining a home for a family member who is age 65 or older. Taxpayers who do not claim the $1,000 deduction may be able to claim a tax credit of $100 for each member of the family who is developmentally disabled or elderly, to a maximum of 3 members.
Number awarded Varies each year.

Deadline April of each year.

[492]
MARY KAY ASH CHARITABLE FOUNDATION GRANTS

Cancer Care, Inc.
Attn: Director, Social Services
275 Seventh Avenue
New York, NY 10001
(212) 712-8080   Toll-free: (800) 813-HOPE
Fax: (212) 712-8495   E-mail: info@cancercare.org
Web: www.cancercare.org

Summary To provide financial assistance to women who have cancer.

Eligibility This assistance is available to women who have any type of cancer. Applicants must provide the sponsoring organization's social workers and/or case managers with information about their source of income, monthly income and expenses, and (in some cases) invoices for the cost of services.

Financial data Limited financial assistance is provided for transportation, home care, and child care services. Grants do not cover basic living expenses, such as rent, mortgages, utility payments, or food.

Duration This is a 1-time award.

Additional Information This program is sponsored by the Mary Kay Ash Charitable Foundation.

Number awarded Varies each year.

Deadline Applications may be submitted at any time.

[493]
MUSCULAR DYSTROPHY ASSOCIATION DIRECT SERVICES

Muscular Dystrophy Association
3300 East Sunrise Drive
Tucson, AZ 85718-3208
(520) 529-2000   Toll-free: (800) 572-1717
Fax: (520) 529-5454   E-mail: mda@mdausa.org
Web: www.mdausa.org

Summary To provide financial assistance for purchase and repair of equipment that will enhance the mobility and independent living of persons with muscular dystrophy.

Eligibility This program is open to individuals with muscular dystrophy, regardless of their age, education, or employment status. Applicants must have a medical prescription for a wheelchair, leg braces, or communication device issued by the local Muscular Dystrophy Association (MDA) clinic physician.

Financial data The maximum allowable assistance is established by the MDA annually. In addition, the association may help to pay for the cost of repairs or modifications to wheelchairs and leg braces and may provide, when available, good-condition recycled wheelchairs and other durable medical equipment.

Number awarded Varies each year.

Deadline Applications may be submitted to local chapters or field offices at any time.

[494]
NATIONAL KIDNEY FOUNDATION OF ARKANSAS EMERGENCY GRANTS

National Kidney Foundation of Arkansas
#1 Lile Court, Suite 201
Little Rock, AR 72205
(501) 664-4343   Fax: (501) 664-7145
E-mail: nkfa@aristotle.net
Web: www.kidneyar.com/patient_services.htm

Summary To provide funding for emergency needs to kidney patients in Arkansas.

Eligibility This program is open to residents of Arkansas who have kidney disease. Applicants must need assistance to meet emergency financial problems. Requests must be submitted through a clinic or dialysis unit social worker.

Financial data The amount of the grant depends on the need of the recipient and the availability of funds.

Duration These are 1-time grants.

Number awarded Varies each year.

Deadline Applications may be submitted at any time.

[495]
NATIONAL KIDNEY FOUNDATION OF COLORADO, IDAHO, MONTANA AND WYOMING PATIENT EMERGENCY ASSISTANCE GRANTS

National Kidney Foundation of Colorado, Idaho,
  Montana and Wyoming, Inc.
3151 South Vaughn Way, Suite 505
Aurora, CO 80014-3514
(720) 748-9991   Toll-free: (800) 263-4005
Fax: (720) 748-1263
E-mail: rleone@kidneycimw.org
Web: www.kidneycimw.org

Summary To provide financial assistance to patients with kidney or urinary tract diseases who live in Colorado, Idaho, Montana, and Wyoming.

Eligibility These programs are open patients with kidney or urinary tract diseases who reside in Colorado, Idaho, Montana, or Wyoming. In general, they should be referred by a social worker because they are in need of funds to supplement the cost of medications, treatment supplies, dental needs, and transportation expenses.

Financial data The amount awarded varies, depending upon the needs of the recipient.

Duration Funds are provided as needed.

Number awarded Varies each year.

Deadline Applications may be submitted at any time.

[496]
NATIONAL KIDNEY FOUNDATION OF CONNECTICUT PATIENT EMERGENCY ASSISTANCE FUND

National Kidney Foundation of Connecticut
2139 Silas Deane Highway
Rocky Hill, CT 06067
(860) 257-3770   Fax: (860) 257-3429
E-mail: info@kidneyct.org
Web: www.kidneyct.org/how.html

Summary To provide emergency financial assistance to individuals in Connecticut who have kidney or urological problems.

Eligibility This assistance is available to pre-dialysis, dialysis, pre-transplant, and post-transplant patients in Connecticut who are referred by a social worker. Applicants should be people who would be at medical risk without assistance.

Financial data The amount awarded varies, depending upon the needs of the recipient. Funds may be used to help pay utilities, pharmacy bills, transportation, groceries, rent, and related expenses.

Duration In general, these are 1-time funds.

Number awarded Varies each year.

Deadline Applications may be submitted at any time.

[497]
NATIONAL KIDNEY FOUNDATION OF INDIANA EMERGENCY FINANCIAL AID

National Kidney Foundation of Indiana, Inc.
Attn: Program Coordinator
911 East 86th Street, Suite 100
Indianapolis, IN 46204-1840
(317) 722-5640   Toll-free: (800) 382-9971
Fax: (317) 722-5650   E-mail: nkfi@myvine.com
Web: www.kidneyindiana.org

Summary To provide emergency financial assistance to individuals in Indiana who have kidney or urinary tract diseases.

Eligibility This assistance is available to patients in Indiana who have kidney or urinary tract diseases and are referred by a social worker.

Financial data The amount awarded varies, depending upon the needs of the recipient.

Duration In general, these are 1-time funds.

Number awarded Varies each year.

Deadline Applications may be submitted at any time.

[498]
NATIONAL KIDNEY FOUNDATION OF IOWA PATIENT SPECIAL NEEDS FUND

National Kidney Foundation of Iowa, Inc.
c/o Mercy Medical Center
701 Tenth Street, S.E., Suite 5618
P.O. Box 1364
Cedar Rapids, IA 52406-1364
(319) 369-4474   Toll-free: (800) 369-3619
Fax: (319) 369-4419
E-mail: NKFofiowa@msn.com
Web: www.kidneyia.org/programs.html

Summary To provide funding for special needs to individuals in Iowa who have kidney or urinary tract diseases.

Eligibility This assistance is available to dialysis and transplant patients in Iowa who are referred by a social worker. Applicants must have special needs that other funding does not cover.

Financial data Grants up to $500 per patient are available.

Duration In general, these are 1-time funds.

Number awarded Varies each year.

Deadline Applications may be submitted at any time.

[499]
NATIONAL KIDNEY FOUNDATION OF KENTUCKY EMERGENCY FINANCIAL ASSISTANCE

National Kidney Foundation of Kentucky, Inc.
250 East Liberty Street, Suite 710
Louisville, KY 40202
(502) 585-5433   Toll-free: (800) 737-LIFE
Fax: (502) 585-1445   E-mail: nkfk@nkfk.org
Web: www.nkfk.org/programs.htm

Summary To provide emergency financial assistance to individuals in Kentucky who have kidney or urinary tract diseases.

Eligibility This assistance is available to dialysis and transplant patients in Kentucky who are referred by a social worker.

Financial data The amount of emergency money awarded varies, depending upon the needs of the recipient. Funds are to be used for transportation, medicine, housing, food supplements, or other immediate needs (e.g., glasses, dentures, utilities).

Duration In general, these are 1-time funds.

Number awarded Varies each year.

Deadline Applications may be submitted at any time.

[500]
NATIONAL KIDNEY FOUNDATION OF MIDDLE TENNESSEE EMERGENCY FINANCIAL ASSISTANCE

National Kidney Foundation of Middle Tennessee, Inc.
2120 Crestmoor Road
Nashville, TN 37215-2613
(615) 383-3887   Toll-free: (800) 380-3887
Fax: (615) 383-2647   E-mail: nkfmdtn@aol.com
Web: www.nkfmdtn.org/Patient.htm

Summary To provide emergency financial assistance to individuals in Tennessee who have kidney or urinary tract diseases.

Eligibility This assistance is available to dialysis and transplant patients in Tennessee who are referred by a social worker.

Financial data The amount of emergency money awarded varies, depending upon the needs of the recipient. Funds are to be used for transportation, medicine, medical equipment, rent, food supplements, or other immediate needs (e.g., glasses, dentures, utilities).

Duration In general, these are 1-time funds.

Number awarded Varies each year. Recently, 304 patients received this assistance.

Deadline Applications may be submitted at any time.

[501]
NATIONAL KIDNEY FOUNDATION OF THE VIRGINIAS PATIENT ASSISTANCE GRANTS

National Kidney Foundation of the Virginias, Inc.
2601 Willard Road, Suite 103
Richmond, VA 23294
(804) 288-8342   Toll-free: (888) KIDNEY-8
Fax: (804) 282-7835
E-mail: welcome@kidneyva.org
Web: www.kidneyva.org/services/index.html

Summary To provide emergency financial assistance to individuals in Virginia and parts of West Virginia who have kidney or urinary tract diseases.

Eligibility This assistance is available to residents of Virginia and parts of West Virginia with chronic renal disease or urological disorders. Applicants must be under the care of a nephrologist, dialysis center, or urologist. Small grants are available for crisis situations (i.e., housing, utilities, insurance, nutritional supplements, transportation, etc.). Large grants are for specific treatment-related expenses: dental care, transportation costs, and medications. Patients must submit applications jointly with a social worker.

Financial data Small grants range up to $100. Large grants range from $101 to $500.

Duration In general, these are 1-time funds.

Number awarded Varies each year. The sponsor attempts to budget $54,000 for small grants and $24,000 for large grants each year and to spend the money in equal monthly installments.

Deadline Applications may be submitted at any time.

[502]
NATIONAL TRANSPLANT ASSISTANCE FUND GRANTS

National Transplant Assistance Fund
3475 West Chester Pike, Suite 230
Newtown Square, PA 19073
Toll-free: (800) 642-8399   Fax: (610) 353-1616
Web: www.transplantfund.org

Summary To provide funding to transplant and spinal cord injury patients.

Eligibility This program is open to transplant and spinal cord injury patients who need funding to pay expenses not covered by insurance.

Financial data Grants provide direct financial assistance for medically-related transplant expenses not covered by insurance.

Duration These are 1-time grants.

Additional Information In addition to these grants, the sponsor assists patients in their own fundraising activities. It provides guidance in campaign planning and implementation, support materials and procedures (including banners, flyers, pins, organ donor ribbons, and bumper stickers), publicity expertise and materials, and a link to the sponsor's web site.

Number awarded Varies each year.

Deadline Applications may be submitted at any time.

[503]
PATIENT AID PROGRAM

Bone Marrow Foundation
337 East 88th Street, Suite 1B
New York, NY 10128
(212) 838-3029   Toll-free: (800) 365-1336
E-mail: info@bonemarrow.org
Web: www.bonemarrow.org

Summary To provide financial assistance to bone marrow transplant patients and their families.

Eligibility This program is open to both children and adult bone marrow transplant patients. Patients must be affiliated with a certified transplant center that is associated with the Bone Marrow Foundation (for a list, write to the foundation). They must have a social worker and physician at the transplant center each complete a part of the application form.

Financial data Each patient is eligible for up to $1,000. Funds are to be used to cover the costs of support services (e.g., donor searches, compatibility testing, bone marrow harvesting, medications, home care services, child care services, medical equipment, transportation, sperm baking, cord blood banking, and housing expenses associated with the transplant). This funding

cannot not be used to pay for outstanding medical bills or any other pre-existing bills associated with the transplant.
Duration This is generally a 1-time award, although occasionally recipients can reapply.
Additional Information This program was started in 1992. Currently, it operates in 70 certified transplant centers across the country. As funding increases, patients nationwide will be able to benefit.
Number awarded Varies each year.
Deadline Applications may be submitted at any time.

[504]
QUALITY OF LIFE PATIENT GRANTS

Aventis Behring
Attn: Choice Member Support Center
1020 First Avenue
P.O. Box 61501
King of Prussia, PA 19406
(610) 878-4000   Toll-free: (888) 508-6978
Fax: (610) 878-4009
E-mail: AventisBehringChoice@AventisBehring.com
Web: www.aventisbehring.com

Summary To provide funding to members of the Aventis Behring Choice program who need assistance paying for expenses not covered by insurance.
Eligibility This program is open to participants in the program who have hemophilia A or B or von Willebrand Disease. Applicants must be seeking funding for travel, child care, dental care, medical devices, or other expenses not covered by insurance. They must be able to demonstrate financial need.
Financial data Grants up to $500 are available.
Additional Information This is the only program of its kind offered by a pharmaceutical manufacturer and available to members of the bleeding disorders community.
Number awarded Varies each year.
Deadline Applications may be submitted at any time.

[505]
SANOFI GRANTS

Cancer Care, Inc.
Attn: Director, Social Services
275 Seventh Avenue
New York, NY 10001
(212) 712-8080   Toll-free: (800) 813-HOPE
Fax: (212) 712-8495   E-mail: info@cancercare.org
Web: www.cancercare.org

Summary To provide financial assistance to individuals who have colon cancer.
Eligibility This assistance is available to individuals fighting colon cancer. Applicants must provide the sponsoring organization's social workers and/or case managers with information about their source of income, monthly income and expenses, and (in some cases) invoices for the cost of services.
Financial data Grants are provided to help cover, over a period of weeks, transportation to treatments, pain medication, child care, home care, and colostomy supplies. Funds are not for basic living expenses, such as rent, mortgages, utility payments, or food.
Duration This is a 1-time award.
Number awarded Varies each year.
Deadline Applications may be submitted at any time.

[506]
VFW LADIES AUXILIARY CANCER AID GRANTS

Ladies Auxiliary to the Veterans of Foreign Wars
c/o National Headquarters
406 West 34th Street
Kansas City, MO 64111
(816) 561-8655, ext. 29   Fax: (816) 931-4753
E-mail: info@ladiesauxvfw.com
Web: www.ladiesauxvfw.com/cancer.html

Summary To provide financial assistance to members of the Ladies Auxiliary to the Veterans of Foreign Wars (VFW) who have cancer.
Eligibility This program is open to auxiliary members who have paid their current dues and have cancer. Applicants must have been an auxiliary member for a full year before having surgery or treatment for cancer.
Financial data Grants normally range from $300 to $500.
Duration Once a grant has been awarded, the recipient must wait 12 months before applying for another. Only 2 grants will be awarded to each member.
Number awarded Varies each year; recently, 6,040 of these grants were awarded.
Deadline Applications may be submitted at any time.

Awards

[507]
HOW I LIVE WITH MANAGED ASTHMA POSTER CONTEST

American Academy of Allergy, Asthma & Immunology
Attn: AAAAI/AAP Poster Contest
611 East Wells Street
Milwaukee, WI 53202-3889
(414) 272-6071   Fax: (414) 272-6070
E-mail: postercontest@aaaai.org
Web: www.aaaai.org

Summary To recognize and reward elementary school children who submit posters illustrating how they manage asthma in their everyday life.

Eligibility This program is open to students in 3 grade categories: first and second, third through fifth, and sixth through eighth. Applicants draw posters that illustrate how they manage asthma in their everyday life. Entries may use any medium (paint, markers, crayons, or colored pencils) and must be on a plain white sheet of paper that is 8 1/2" x 11" or larger.

Financial data In each grade category, the first-place winner receives a $500 U.S. savings bond and a $200 gift certificate from selected retailers, the second-place winner receives a $250 U.S. savings bond and a $100 gift certificate, and the third-place winner receives a $100 U.S. savings bond and a $50 gift certificate. Each winner's school receives a free supply of asthma education materials.

Duration The competition is held annually.

Additional Information This program is cosponsored by the American Academy of Pediatrics.

Number awarded 9 awards are presented each year: 3 in each of the 3 grade categories.

Deadline December of each year.

[508]
MAKING A DIFFERENCE AWARD

Epilepsy Foundation
Attn: Eva Pagano
4351 Garden City Drive
Landover, MD 20785-7223
(301) 459-3700   Toll-free: (800) EFA-1000
Fax: (301) 577-2684   TDD: (800) 332-2070
E-mail: epagano@efa.org
Web: www.epilepsyfoundation.org

Summary To recognize and reward women with epilepsy who have inspired and changed the lives of others.

Eligibility This program is open to women from all backgrounds who are at least 18 years of age and have epilepsy. Nominees should have contributed in a significant way to support and advance the quality of life for women with epilepsy, inspire people with epilepsy and those with other chronic disabilities, or enhance public understanding of epilepsy and its impact on women. Nominations are accepted from all parties, including the nominee herself. Selection is based on the significant or positive differences already made in the lives of others (70%) and any ongoing activities designed to achieve positive change (30%).

Financial data The award consists of $1,500 plus travel and expenses to attend the awards presentation ceremonies during the EFA annual national conference.

Duration The awards are presented annually.

Additional Information This award, first presented in 2001, is sponsored by GlaxoSmithKline.

Number awarded 1 each year.

Deadline June of each year.

[509]
THE MANY COLORS OF ADHD CALENDAR CONTEST

Shire US Inc.
7900 Tanners Gate Drive
Florence, KY 41042
(859) 282-2100   Toll-free: (866) DRAW-ADHD
Fax: (859) 282-1794
Web: www.shire.com

Summary To recognize and reward outstanding art and writings by children under the age of 17 who have attention deficit/hyperactivity disorder (ADHD).

Eligibility This is a nationwide calendar art and writing contest designed to give children with ADHD an opportunity to express their feelings about how the disorder. Entrants must be between the ages of 6 and 16. They must submit artwork, a short essay, or a poem that portrays how in some way ADHD affects their lives.

Financial data Winning students receive a $1,000 gift certificate and publication of their entry in a special full-color calendar featuring the words and art of children with ADHD.

Duration The competition is held annually.

Number awarded 15 each year.

Deadline January of each year.

[510]
OUTSTANDING INDIVIDUAL WITH AUTISM OF THE YEAR AWARD

Autism Society of America
Attn: Awards and Scholarships
7910 Woodmont Avenue, Suite 300
Bethesda, MD 20814-3015
(301) 657-0881   Toll-free: (800) 3-AUTISM
Fax: (301) 657-0869
E-mail: info@autism-society.org
Web: www.autism-society.org

Summary To recognize and reward people with autism who have excelled in an area of human activity.

Eligibility This award is presented for a demonstration of exceptional dedication or effort on the part of an individual with autism who has excelled in 1 or more areas of life experiences or contributions. Achievement may include, but is not limited to, academics, the arts, athletics, community service, employment, extracurricular activities, transitions, or independent living skills.

Financial data The awardee receives complimentary registration to the annual conference, a special commemorative plaque, and a cash award of $1,000.

Duration The award is presented annually.

Number awarded 1 each year.

Deadline February of each year.

Disabilities in General

Scholarships •
Fellowships/Grants •
Loans •
Grants-in-Aid •
Awards •

Described here are 446 programs that do not specify or restrict the type of eligible disability. Of these, 108 entries cover scholarships (to pursue studies or research on the undergraduate level in the United States); 132 cover fellowships/grants (to pursue graduate or postdoctoral education or research in the United States); 50 cover loans (to provide money that eventually must be repaid, with or without interest); 142 cover grants-in-aid (to support emergency situations, travel, income/property liabilities, or the acquisition of assistive technology); and 14 cover awards, competitions, prizes, and honoraria (to recognize or support creative work and public service). If you are looking for a particular program and don't find it in this chapter, be sure to check the Program Title Index to see if it is covered elsewhere in the directory.

Scholarships

[511] AEROSPACE ILLINOIS SPACE GRANT CONSORTIUM PROGRAM

Aerospace Illinois Space Grant Consortium
c/o University of Illinois at Urbana-Champaign
Department of Aeronautical and Astronomical Engineering
308 Talbot Lab
104 South Wright Street
Urbana, IL 61801-2935
(217) 244-8048   Fax: (217) 244-0720
E-mail: dejeffer@uiuc.edu
Web: www.aae.uiuc.edu/Aeroill/index.html

Summary To provide financial support to faculty, staff, and students at Aerospace Illinois member institutions who are interested in pursuing space related academic activities.

Eligibility Aerospace Illinois has established 4 program elements: 1) undergraduate/high school teaching and research, to attract undergraduates and secondary school students to aerospace science and engineering; 2) training in graduate research, through research experiences focused on aerospace science and engineering; 3) outreach and public service, to employ the region's extensive existing public educational information networks and outreach programs to attract the highest quality student populations, especially underrepresented minorities, women, and persons with disabilities; and 4) fellowships with industry, to add substantially to the national aerospace science and engineering pool. Aerospace Illinois is a component of the U.S. National Aeronautics and Space Administration which encourages applications from women, minorities, and persons with disabilities.

Financial data Awards depend on the availability of funds and the nature of the proposal.

Duration Depends on the program.

Additional Information Aerospace Illinois includes 4 member institutions: the University of Illinois at Urbana-Champaign (UIUC), the University of Chicago (UC), Illinois Institute of Technology (IIT), and Northwestern University (NU). It also includes 3 affiliate institutions: Southern Illinois University (SIU), Western Illinois University (WIU), and the University of Illinois at Chicago. This program is funded by NASA. Recently, undergraduate/high school teaching and research projects included the aerodynamic facilities tour at IIT, the high school summer research program at NU, K-12 education programs at SIU, Motivation through Aviation and Space at WIU, Camp 21st at UIUC, Illinois Aerospace Institute at UIUC, and the WYSE summer program at UIUC. Training in graduate research projects included control of jet screech noise at IIT, electronic component cooling at IIT, high lift airfoils at IIT, high reynolds number turbulent boundary layers at IIT, investigation of incipient stall at IIT, non-equilibrium turbulent layers at IIT, independent research at NU, experiments in high energy astrophysics research support at UC, and the chemical laser lab at UIUC. Outreach and public service projects included the interprofessional project at IIT, Dearborn Observatory open house at NU, NASA College Research Program at NU, and the design lab at UIUC. Fellowships with industry included the NASA space grant fellowship at IIT, the NASA space grant minority scholarship at IIT, the NASA college summer research program at NU, graduate fellowships at UC, undergraduate scholarships at UC, Aerospace Illinois scholarships at UIUC, Engineering of the Future at UIUC, NASA Academy at UIUC, space grant/industry fellowships at UIUC, and women in engineering scholarships at UIUC.

Number awarded Varies each year.

[512] AIMR 11 SEPTEMBER MEMORIAL SCHOLARSHIP FUND

Association for Investment Management and Research
Attn: Research Foundation of AIMR
560 Ray C. Hunt Drive
P.O. Box 3668
Charlottesville, VA 22903-0668
(434) 951-5391   Toll-free: (800) 247-8132
Fax: (434) 951-5370
E-mail: 11septemberfund@aimr.org
Web: www.aimr.org

Summary To provide financial assistance for college study in fields related to business to disabled victims of the September 11, 2001 terrorist attack and the family members of victims.

Eligibility This program is open to 1) victims of the September 11, 2001 terrorist attacks who are permanently disabled, and 2) children, spouses, and domestic partners of persons who died or were permanently disabled as a direct result of the attacks. Applicants must be planning undergraduate or vocational school study of finance, economics, accounting, or business ethics at an accredited institution. They may come from any country and may study at any qualifying college or university in the world. Selection is based on financial need, academic record, and demonstrated commitment to high levels of professional ethics.

Financial data The stipend is $5,000 per year.

Duration 1 year; may be renewed up to 4 additional years.

Additional Information This program is administered by Scholarship Management Services of Scholarship America, 1505 Riverview Road, P.O. Box 297, St. Peter, MN 56082, (507) 931-1682, (800) 537-4180, Fax: (507) 931-9168, E-mail: smsinfo@csfa.org.

Number awarded Varies each year.

Deadline May of each year.

[513]
AMERICAN METEOROLOGICAL SOCIETY UNDERGRADUATE SCHOLARSHIPS

American Meteorological Society
Attn: Fellowship/Scholarship Coordinator
45 Beacon Street
Boston, MA 02108-3693
(617) 227-2426, ext. 246   Fax: (617) 742-8718
E-mail: amsinfo@ametsoc.org
Web: www.ametsoc.org

Summary To provide financial assistance to undergraduates majoring in meteorology or some aspect of atmospheric sciences.

Eligibility This program is open to undergraduate students entering their final year of study and majoring in meteorology or some aspect of the atmospheric or related oceanic and hydrologic sciences. Applicants must intend to make atmospheric or related sciences their career. They must be U.S. citizens or permanent residents, be enrolled full time in an accredited U.S. institution, and have a cumulative GPA of 3.0 or higher. Along with their application, they must submit a 100-word essay on their most important achievements that qualify them for this scholarship and a 500-word essay on their career goals in the atmospheric or related oceanic or hydrologic fields. Selection is based on academic excellence and achievement; financial need is not considered. The sponsor specifically encourages applications from women, minorities, and students with disabilities who are traditionally underrepresented in the atmospheric and related oceanic sciences.

Financial data Stipends range from $700 to $5,000 per year.

Duration 1 year.

Additional Information This program includes the following named scholarships: the Howard H. Hanks, Jr. Scholarship in Meteorology ($700), the AMS 75th Anniversary Scholarship ($2,000), the Ethan and Allan Murphy Memorial Scholarship ($2,000), the Howard T. Orville Scholarship in Meteorology ($2,000), the Dr. Pedro Grau Undergraduate Scholarship ($2,500, 2 awarded), the Guillermo Salazar Rodriguez Scholarship ($2,500, 2 awarded), the John R. Hope Scholarship ($2,500), the Richard and Helen Hagemeyer Scholarship ($3,000), and the Werner A. Baum Undergraduate Scholarship ($5,000). Requests for an application must be accompanied by a self-addressed stamped envelope.

Number awarded 11 each year.

Deadline February of each year.

[514]
ARKANSAS GOVERNOR'S COMMISSION ON PEOPLE WITH DISABILITIES SCHOLARSHIPS

Arkansas Governor's Commission on People with Disabilities
1616 Brookwood Drive
P.O. Box 3781
Little Rock, AR 72203
(501) 296-1626   Fax: (501) 296-1627
TDD: (501) 296-1623

Summary To provide financial assistance for undergraduate education to Arkansas students with disabilities.

Eligibility Disabled Arkansas high school seniors, high school graduates, and college students who are planning to pursue postsecondary education are eligible to apply. Previous winners may also submit an application. Letters of recommendation are required but may not be written by relatives. Selection is based upon academic achievement, severity of disability and resulting functional limitations, desire for further education, contributions to the community, and financial need.

Financial data The stipend varies, up to $500 per year.

Duration 1 year; recipients may reapply.

Additional Information Recipients may attend colleges, universities, or vocational/technical schools. Schools need not be located in Arkansas.

Number awarded Varies each year.

Deadline January of each year.

[515]
BANK OF AMERICA ADA ABILITIES SCHOLARSHIP PROGRAM

The Center for Scholarship Administration, Inc.
Attn: Bank of America ADA Abilities Scholarship Program
P.O. Box 1465
Taylors, SC 29687-1465
(864) 268-3363   Fax: (864) 268-7160
E-mail: cfsainc@bellsouth.net
Web: www.scholarshipprograms.org

Summary To provide financial assistance to disabled high school seniors or college students from selected states who are interested in preparing for a career with a banking institution.

Eligibility This program is open to high school seniors, high school graduates, and currently-enrolled college students who have a disability (must have written documentation from an appropriate provider that the candidate meets the definition of disabled in the Americans with Disabilities Act). Applicants must be U.S. citizens and permanent residents of 1 of the following states: Arizona, Arkansas, California, Florida, Georgia, Idaho, Illinois, Iowa, Kansas, Maryland, Missouri, Nevada, New Mexico, North Carolina, Oklahoma, Oregon, South Caro-

lina, Tennessee, Texas, Virginia, Washington, or the District of the Columbia. They must 1) have a cumulative GPA of 3.0 or higher; 2) be majoring in finance, business, or computer systems; 3) be younger than 40 years of age; and 4) be planning a career with a banking institution.

Financial data The maximum stipend is $5,000, depending on financial need, the annual cost of the recipient's institution, and any other financial aid (excluding loans) received by the student.

Duration 1 year.

Additional Information This program is administered by The Center for Scholarship Administration on behalf of the Bank of America Foundation.

Number awarded Varies each year.

Deadline February of each year.

[516]
BUFFETT FOUNDATION SCHOLARSHIP PROGRAM

Buffett Foundation
Attn: Scholarship Office
P.O. Box 4508
Decatur, IL 62525
(402) 451-6011   E-mail: buffettfound@aol.com
Web: www.BuffettScholarships.org

Summary To provide financial assistance to entering or currently-enrolled college students in Nebraska.

Eligibility This program is open to U.S. citizens who are Nebraska residents. Applicants must be entering or currently enrolled in a state school, community college, or trade school in Nebraska. They must be in financial need, be the only family member presently receiving a grant from the foundation, have at least a 2.5 GPA, and have applied for federal financial aid. Selection is based on academic performance and financial need. Preference is given to minority students, students with disabilities, and married or unmarried students with dependents.

Financial data The maximum stipend is $2,500 per semester. Funds are sent directly to the recipient's school and must be used to pay tuition and fees; they may not be used to pay for books or other expenses.

Duration Up to 5 years for a 4-year college, or up to 3 years for a 2-year school. Students on scholarship may not drop out for a period of time and be reinstated as a scholarship recipient; they must reapply along with first-time students.

Additional Information Students on a 12-month program or the quarter system may use the scholarship for summer tuition; students on the semester system may not use funds for summer school. Students who are not working must enroll in at least 12 credit hours; students who are working must enroll in at least 9 credit hours.

Deadline April of each year.

[517]
BUILDING RURAL INITIATIVE FOR DISABLED THROUGH GROUP EFFORT (B.R.I.D.G.E.) ENDOWMENT FUND SCHOLARSHIPS

National FFA Organization
Attn: Scholarship Office
6060 FFA Drive
P.O. Box 68960
Indianapolis, IN 46268-0960
(317) 802-4321   Fax: (317) 802-5321
E-mail: scholarships@ffa.org
Web: www.ffa.org

Summary To provide financial assistance to FFA members with disabilities who are interested in studying agriculture in college.

Eligibility This program is open to members with physical disabilities who are graduating high school seniors planning to enroll full time in college. Applicants must be interested in working on a 2-year or 4-year degree in agriculture. Selection is based on academic achievement (10 points for GPA, 10 points for SAT or ACT score, 10 points for class rank), leadership in FFA activities (30 points), leadership in community activities (10 points), and participation in the Supervised Agricultural Experience (SAE) program (30 points). U.S. citizenship is required.

Financial data A stipend is awarded (amount not specified). Funds are paid directly to the recipient.

Duration 1 year; nonrenewable.

Number awarded 1 or more each year.

Deadline February of each year.

[518]
CALIFORNIA ASSOCIATION FOR POSTSECONDARY EDUCATION AND DISABILITY SCHOLARSHIPS

California Association for Postsecondary Education and Disability
Attn: Executive Assistant
71423 Biskra Road
Rancho Mirage, CA 92270
(760) 346-8206   Fax: (760) 340-5275
TTY: (760) 341-4084 E-mail: caped2000@aol.com
Web: www.caped.net/scholarship.html

Summary To provide financial assistance to undergraduate and graduate students in California who have a disability.

Eligibility This program is open to students at public and private colleges and universities in California who have a disability. Undergraduates must have completed at least 6 semester credits and have a GPA of 2.5 or higher. Graduate students must have completed at least 3 semester units and have a GPA of 3.0 or higher. Applicants must submit a 1-page personal letter that demonstrates writing skills; progress toward meeting educational and vocational goals; how they accommodate their disability; involvement in community activities; and

any other personal factor that might strengthen their application. They must also submit a letter of recommendation from a faculty person, verification of disability, official transcripts, proof of current enrollment, and documentation of financial need.

Financial data The stipend is $1,000.

Duration 1 year.

Additional Information Information is also available from Janet Shapiro, Disabled Student Programs and Services, Santa Barbara City College, 721 Cliff Drive, Santa Barbara, CA 93109, (805) 965-0581, ext. 2365, E-mail: shapiro@sbcc.net. This program includes the following named scholarships: the California Association for Postsecondary Education and Disability Conference Scholarship, the California Association for Postsecondary Education and Disability Past Presidents' Scholarship, and the William May Memorial Scholarship.

Number awarded 3 each year.

Deadline August of each year.

[519]
CALIFORNIA REAL ESTATE ENDOWMENT FUND SCHOLARSHIP PROGRAM

California Community Colleges
Attn: Student Financial Assistance Programs
1102 Q Street
Sacramento, CA 95814-6511
(916) 324-0925   E-mail: rquintan@cccco.edu
Web: www.cccco.edu

Summary To provide financial assistance to disadvantaged California community college students who are studying real estate.

Eligibility This program is open to students at community colleges in California who are majoring in real estate or (if their college does not offer a real estate major) business administration with a concentration in real estate. Applicants must have completed at least a 3-unit college course in real estate with a grade of "C" or better and must be enrolled in at least 6 semester units of real estate for the semester of the scholarship. Students must meet 1 of the following financial need criteria: 1) have completed the Free Application for Federal Student Aid (FAFSA) and been determined by their college to have financial need; 2) come from a family with an income less than $12,885 for 1 person, $17,415 for 2 persons, $21,945 for 3 persons, $26,475 for 4 persons, or an additional $4,530 for each additional family member; or 3) come from a family with an income less than $50,000 and be from a disadvantaged group (have low economic status and/or have been denied opportunities in society for reasons of gender, race, ethnicity, economics, language, education, physical disabilities, or other mitigating factors). Scholarships are awarded on a first-come, first-served basis.

Financial data Awards up to $400 per semester are available.

Duration 1 semester; may be renewed if the student remains enrolled in at least 6 units of real estate with a GPA of 2.0 or higher.

Additional Information Students apply to their community college, not to the sponsoring organization.

Number awarded From 75 to 90 each year; approximately $60,000 per year is available for this program.

Deadline April of each year.

[520]
CALIFORNIA-HAWAII ELKS MAJOR PROJECT UNDERGRADUATE SCHOLARSHIP FOR STUDENTS WITH DISABILITIES

California-Hawaii Elks Association
Attn: Scholarship Committee
5450 East Lamona Avenue
Fresno, CA 93727-2224
(559) 255-4531   Fax: (559) 456-2659
Web: www.chea-elks.org/uspsd.html

Summary To provide financial assistance for college to residents of California and Hawaii with disabilities.

Eligibility This program is open to residents of California or Hawaii who have a physical impairment, neurological impairment, visual impairment, hearing impairment, and/or speech/language disorder. Applicants must be a senior in high school, be a high school graduate, or have passed the GED test. U.S. citizenship is required. Selection is based on financial need, GPA, severity of disability, seriousness of purpose, and depth of character. Applications are available from an Elks Lodge in California or Hawaii; students must first request an interview with the lodge's scholarship chairman or Exalted Ruler.

Financial data The annual stipend is $1,000 for community colleges and vocational schools or $2,000 per year for 4-year colleges or universities.

Duration 1 year; may be renewed for up to 3 additional years.

Number awarded 20 to 30 each year.

Deadline March of each year.

[521]
CAPED GENERAL EXCELLENCE SCHOLARSHIP

California Association for Postsecondary Education
  and Disability
Attn: Executive Assistant
71423 Biskra Road
Rancho Mirage, CA 92270
(760) 346-8206   Fax: (760) 340-5275
TTY: (760) 341-4084   E-mail: caped2000@aol.com
Web: www.caped.net/scholarship.html

Summary To provide financial assistance to undergraduate and graduate students in California who have a disability and can demonstrate academic achievement and involvement in community and campus activities.

Eligibility This program is open to students at public and private colleges and universities in California who have a disability. Undergraduates must have completed at least 6 semester credits and have a GPA of 2.5 or higher. Graduate students must have completed at least 3 semester units and have a GPA of 3.0 or higher. Applicants must submit a 1-page personal letter that demonstrates writing skills; progress toward meeting educational and vocational goals; how they accommodate their disability; involvement in community activities; and any other factor that might strengthen their application. They must also submit a letter of recommendation from a faculty member, verification of disability, official transcripts, proof of current enrollment, and documentation of financial need. This award is presented to the applicant who demonstrates the highest level of academic achievement and involvement in community and campus life.

Financial data The stipend is $1,500.

Duration 1 year.

Additional Information Information is also available from Janet Shapiro, Disabled Student Programs and Services, Santa Barbara City College, 721 Cliff Drive, Santa Barbara, CA 93109, (805) 965-0581, ext. 2365, E-mail: shapiro@sbcc.net.

Number awarded 1 each year.

Deadline August of each year.

[522]
CARVER SCHOLARS PROGRAM

Roy J. Carver Charitable Trust
202 Iowa Avenue
Muscatine, IA 52761-3733
(563) 263-4010   Fax: (563) 263-1547
E-mail: info@carvertrust.org
Web: www.carvertrust.org

Summary To provide financial assistance for college to students in Iowa who have overcome significant obstacles to attend college.

Eligibility This program is open to students attending the 3 public universities in Iowa, the 24 participating private 4-year colleges and universities in the state, or a community college in Iowa and planning to transfer to 1 of those 4-year institutions. Applicants must be sophomores seeking support for their junior year. They must present evidence of unusual social and/or other barriers to attending college full time; examples include, but are not limited to, students who 1) are from 1-parent families; 2) are attending college while working full time; 3) have social, mental, or physical disabilities; and 4) have families to support. They must have graduated from a high school in Iowa or have been residents of the state for at least 5 consecutive years immediately prior to applying, be full-time students, have at least a 2.8 GPA, be U.S. citizens, and submit a financial profile indicating insufficient personal, family, and institutional resources to pay full-time college tuition. A particular goal of the program is to assist students "who fall between the cracks of other financial aid programs." Applications must be submitted to the financial aid office at the Iowa college or university the applicant attends.

Financial data Stipends generally average $5,200 at public universities or $7,600 at private colleges in Iowa.

Duration 1 year; may be renewed 1 additional year.

Additional Information This program was established in 1988.

Number awarded Varies each year; since the program's establishment, it has awarded more than 1,300 scholarships worth more than $8 million.

Deadline April of each year.

[523]
CENTRAL INTELLIGENCE AGENCY UNDERGRADUATE SCHOLARSHIP PROGRAM

Central Intelligence Agency
Attn: Recruitment Center
P.O. Box 4090
Reston, VA 20195
Toll-free: (800) 368-3886
Web: www.cia.gov/employment/student.html

Summary To provide scholarship/loans and work experience to high school seniors and college sophomores, especially minorities and people with disabilities, who are interested in working for the Central Intelligence Agency (CIA) after graduation from college.

Eligibility This program is open to U.S. citizens who are either high school seniors or college sophomores. Seniors must be at least 18 years of age by April of the year they apply and have minimum scores of 1000 on the SAT or 21 on the ACT. College sophomores must have a GPA of 3.0 or higher. All applicants must be able to demonstrate financial need (household income of $70,000 or less for a family of 4 or $80,000 or less for a family of 5 or more) and be able to meet the same employment standards as permanent employees of the CIA. An explicit goal of the program is to attract minorities and students with disabilities to a career with the CIA.

Financial data Scholars are provided a salary and up to $18,000 per year for tuition, fees, books, and supplies. They must agree to continue employment with the CIA after college graduation for a period 1.5 times the length of their college support.

Duration 1 year; may be renewed if the student maintains a GPA of 3.0 or higher and full-time enrollment in a 4- or 5-year college program.

Additional Information Scholars work each summer at a CIA facility. In addition to a salary, they receive the cost of transportation between school and the Washington, D.C. area and a housing allowance.

Number awarded Varies each year.

Deadline October of each year.

[524]
CHIEF MASTER SERGEANTS OF THE AIR FORCE SCHOLARSHIPS

Air Force Sergeants Association
Attn: Scholarship Program
P.O. Box 50
Temple Hills, MD 20757
(301) 899-3500   Toll-free: (800) 638-0594
Fax: (301) 899-8136   E-mail: staff@amf.org
Web: www.afsahq.org/body_education01.htm

Summary To provide financial assistance for college to the dependent children of enlisted Air Force personnel.

Eligibility Applicants must be the unmarried dependent children (including stepchildren and legally adopted children), under the age of 23, of enlisted personnel serving in the U.S. Air Force, Air National Guard, or Air Force Reserves, whether on active duty or retired. Selection is based on academic ability (SAT score of 1000 or higher and GPA of 3.5 or higher), character, leadership, writing ability, and potential for success; financial need is not a consideration. A unique aspect of these scholarships is that applicants may supply additional information regarding circumstances that entitle them to special consideration; examples of such circumstances include student disabilities, financial hardships, parent disabled and unable to work, parent missing in action/killed in action/prisoner of war, or other unusual extenuating circumstances.

Financial data Stipends are $3,000, $2,000, or $1,000; funds may be used for tuition, room and board, fees, books, supplies, and transportation.

Duration 1 year; may be renewed if the recipient maintains full-time enrollment.

Additional Information The Air Force Sergeants Association administers this program on behalf of the Airmen Memorial Foundation. It was established in 1987 and named in honor of CMSAF Richard D. Kisling, the late third Chief Master Sergeant of the Air Force. In 1997, following the deaths of CMSAF's (Retired) Andrews and Harlow, it was given its current name. Requests for applications must be accompanied by a stamped self-addressed envelope.

Number awarded 11 each year: 1 at $3,000, 2 at $2,000, and 8 at $1,000. Since this program began, it has awarded 135 scholarships worth $200,000.

Deadline March of each year.

[525]
CHRISTIAN A. HERTER MEMORIAL SCHOLARSHIP

Massachusetts Office of Student Financial
  Assistance
454 Broadway, Suite 200
Revere, MA 02151
(617) 727-9420   Fax: (617) 727-0667
E-mail: osfa@osfa.mass.edu
Web: www.osfa.mass.edu

Summary To provide financial assistance for college to Massachusetts residents who overcome major adversities.

Eligibility Applicants for these scholarships must have been permanent legal residents of Massachusetts for at least 1 year, must be attending a secondary school in the 10th or 11th grade, must have a cumulative GPA of 2.5 or higher, and must be planning to pursue undergraduate education at an accredited degree-granting institution in the United States. They must have overcome a major adversity in their lives (e.g., physical or mental abuse, catastrophic illness) or other personal obstacles or hardships of a societal, geographic, mental, or physical nature.

Financial data Awards cover up to 50% of the student's unmet financial need, to a maximum of $15,000 per year.

Duration 4 or 5 years.

Number awarded 25 each year.

Deadline March

[526]
CINDY KOLB MEMORIAL SCHOLARSHIP

California Association for Postsecondary Education
  and Disability
Attn: Executive Assistant
71423 Biskra Road
Rancho Mirage, CA 92270
(760) 346-8206   Fax: (760) 340-5275
TTY: (760) 341-4084   E-mail: caped2000@aol.com
Web: www.caped.net/scholarship.html

Summary To provide financial assistance to 4-year college and universities students in California who have a disability.

Eligibility This program is open to students at 4-year colleges and universities in California who have a disability. Applicants must have completed at least 6 semester credits with a GPA of 2.5 or higher. They must submit a 1-page personal letter that demonstrates writing skills; progress toward meeting educational and vocational goals; how they accommodate their disability; involvement in community activities; and any other factor that might strengthen their application. They must also submit a letter of recommendation from a faculty member, verification of disability, official transcripts, proof of current enrollment, and documentation of financial need.

Financial data The stipend is $1,000.

Duration 1 year.

Additional Information Information is also available from Janet Shapiro, Disabled Student Programs and Services, Santa Barbara City College, 721 Cliff Drive, Santa Barbara, CA 93109, (805) 965-0581, ext. 2365, E-mail: shapiro@sbcc.net.

Number awarded 1 each year.

Deadline August of each year.

[527]
CONNECTICUT SPACE GRANT COLLEGE CONSORTIUM STUDENT PROJECT GRANTS

Connecticut Space Grant College Consortium
c/o University of Hartford
UT 219
200 Bloomfield Avenue
West Hartford, CT 06117-1599
(860) 768-4813 Fax: (860) 768-5073
E-mail: ctspgrant@hartford.edu
Web: uhaweb.hartford.edu/ctspgrant

Summary To provide funding to undergraduate students at member institutions of the Connecticut Space Grant College Consortium who need to purchase supplies or equipment for space-related projects.

Eligibility This program is open to undergraduate students at member institutions of the Connecticut Space Grant College Consortium. Applicants must be proposing to conduct a project in aerospace science and engineering in areas normally funded by the U.S. National Aeronautics and Space Administration (NASA). U.S. citizenship is required. A faculty member must agree to serve as project advisor. The program actively encourages women, underrepresented minorities, and those with disabilities to apply.

Financial data The maximum grant is $500. Funds may be used for supplies and materials only, not for travel, entertainment, entry fees, tuition, salaries, fringe benefits, or indirect costs.

Duration 1 semester or 1 year.

Additional Information Member institutions are the University of Connecticut, University of Hartford, University of New Haven, and Trinity College. This program is funded by NASA.

Number awarded 1 or more each year.

Deadline October or May of each year.

[528]
CONNECTICUT SPACE GRANT COLLEGE CONSORTIUM TRAVEL GRANTS

Connecticut Space Grant College Consortium
c/o University of Hartford
UT 219
200 Bloomfield Avenue
West Hartford, CT 06117-1599
(860) 768-4813 Fax: (860) 768-5073
E-mail: ctspgrant@hartford.edu
Web: uhaweb.hartford.edu/ctspgrant

Summary To provide funding for travel to students and faculty at member institutions of the Connecticut Space Grant College Consortium.

Eligibility This program is open to students and faculty at member institutions of the Connecticut Space Grant College Consortium. Applicants normally must be proposing to collaborate with researchers of the U.S. National Aeronautics and Space Administration (NASA), to present their aerospace-related research at conferences, to use specialized equipment at NASA facilities, or to visit NASA centers to establish research contacts. Travel is normally limited to destinations within the United States. The program actively encourages women, underrepresented minorities, and those with disabilities to apply.

Financial data Grants cover expenses up to $1,000 per trip.

Additional Information Member institutions are the University of Connecticut, University of Hartford, University of New Haven, and Trinity College. This program is funded by NASA.

Number awarded Varies each year; recently, a total of $7,500 was available for student travel and $2,600 for faculty travel.

Deadline May of each year.

[529]
CONNECTICUT SPACE GRANT COLLEGE CONSORTIUM UNDERGRADUATE STUDENT FELLOWSHIPS

Connecticut Space Grant College Consortium
c/o University of Hartford
UT 219
200 Bloomfield Avenue
West Hartford, CT 06117-1599
(860) 768-4813 Fax: (860) 768-5073
E-mail: ctspgrant@hartford.edu
Web: uhaweb.hartford.edu/ctspgrant

Summary To enable undergraduate students at member institutions of the Connecticut Space Grant College Consortium to work on space-related projects under the guidance of a faculty member.

Eligibility This program is open to full-time undergraduate students at member institutions of the Connecticut Space Grant College Consortium. Applicants must be proposing to conduct a senior project, honors research,

or other educational project in aerospace science and engineering in areas normally funded by the U.S. National Aeronautics and Space Administration (NASA). U.S. citizenship is required. The program actively encourages women, underrepresented minorities, and those with disabilities to apply.

Financial data Grants are $2,500.

Duration 1 semester or 1 year.

Additional Information Member institutions are the University of Connecticut, University of Hartford, University of New Haven, and Trinity College. This program is funded by NASA.

Number awarded 10 each year.

Deadline October or May of each year.

[530]
DESGC UNDERGRADUATE TUITION SCHOLARSHIPS

Delaware Space Grant Consortium
c/o University of Delaware
Bartol Research Institute
104 Center Mall, #217
Newark, DE 19716-4793
(302) 831-1094   Fax: (302) 831-1843
E-mail: desgc@bartol.udel.edu
Web: www.delspace.org

Summary To provide financial support to undergraduate students in Delaware and Pennsylvania involved in space-related studies.

Eligibility This program is open to undergraduate students in aerospace engineering and space science-related fields studying at institutions belonging to the Delaware Valley Space Grant College (DVSGC) Consortium. U.S. citizenship is required. As a component of the U.S. National Aeronautics and Space Administration (NASA) Space Grant program, this program encourages applications from women, minorities, and persons with disabilities.

Financial data This program provides tuition assistance up to $4,000 per year.

Duration 1 year; may be renewed.

Additional Information This program, established in 1996, is funded by NASA. Members of the consortium include Delaware State University (Dover, Delaware), Delaware Technical and Community College (Dover, Georgetown, Newark, and Wilmington, Delaware), Franklin and Marshall College (Lancaster, Pennsylvania), Gettysburg College (Gettysburg, Pennsylvania), Lehigh University (Bethlehem, Pennsylvania), Swarthmore College (Swarthmore, Pennsylvania), University of Delaware (Newark, Delaware), Villanova University (Villanova, Pennsylvania), and Wilmington College (New Castle, Delaware).

Number awarded Varies each year; recently, 8 of these scholarships were awarded.

Deadline February of each year.

[531]
DISTRICT OF COLUMBIA SPACE GRANT CONSORTIUM AWARDS

District of Columbia Space Grant Consortium
c/o American University
Department of Physics
McKinley Building, Suite 106
4400 Massachusetts Avenue, N.W.
Washington, DC 20016-8058
(202) 885-2780   Fax: (202) 885-2723
E-mail: SpaceGrant@aol.com
Web: www.DCSpaceGrant.org

Summary To provide financial assistance to undergraduate and graduate students studying space-related fields at member institutions of the District of Columbia Space Grant Consortium.

Eligibility This program is open to students at member institutions of the consortium. Each participating university conducts its own program. The consortium is a component of the Space Grant program of the U.S. National Aeronautics and Space Administration (NASA), which encourages participation by women, underrepresented minorities, and persons with disabilities.

Financial data Each university determines the amount of the awards.

Additional Information Institutions participating in the consortium include American University, Gallaudet University, George Washington University, Howard University, and the University of the District of Columbia. Funding for this program is provided by NASA.

Number awarded Varies each year.

[532]
EARL AND EUGENIA QUIRK SCHOLARSHIP

VSA Arts of Wisconsin
4785 Hayes Road, Suite 102
Madison, WI 53704
(608) 241-2131   Fax: (608) 241-1982
TTY: (608) 241-2131   E-mail: vsawis@vsawis.org
Web: www.vsawis.org

Summary To provide financial assistance to residents of Wisconsin who have a disability and are interested in studying the arts in college.

Eligibility This program is open to Wisconsin residents who have a physical, cognitive, learning, emotional, or behavioral disability. Applicants must have a GPA of 2.5 or higher and have been accepted at or be attending an accredited college or university program of fine arts or a closely related arts-oriented field. Along with their application, they must submit 3 letters of recommendation and photographs or visual artwork or video/audio tapes of performance art. Selection is based on demonstrated leadership or participation in community or school service groups, involvement in extracurricular activities, awards or recognition received for involvement in the arts, and financial need.

Financial data The stipend is $750.

Duration 1 year; recipients may reapply (and are given priority).
Number awarded 3 each year; at least 1 is reserved for a graduating high school senior.
Deadline March of each year.

[533]
EDWARD T. CONROY MEMORIAL SCHOLARSHIP PROGRAM

Maryland Higher Education Commission
Attn: Office of Student Financial Assistance
839 Bestgate Road, Suite 400
Annapolis, MD 21401-3013
(410) 260-4565   Toll-free: (800) 974-1024
Fax: (410) 974-5376   TTY: (800) 735-2258
E-mail: osfamall@mhec.state.md.us
Web: www.mhec.state.md.us/SSA/CONROY.htm

Summary To provide financial assistance for college or graduate school to specified categories of veterans, public safety employees, and their children in Maryland.

Eligibility This program is open to undergraduate and graduate students in the following categories: 1) children and unremarried surviving spouses of state or local public safety employees or volunteers who died in the line of duty; 2) children of armed forces members whose death or 100% disability was directly caused by military service; 3) POW/MIA veterans of the Vietnam Conflict and their children; 4) children and surviving spouses of victims of the September 11, 2001 terrorist attacks who died in the World Trade Center in New York City, the Pentagon in Virginia, or United Airlines Flight 93 in Pennsylvania; 5) veterans who have, as a direct result of military service, a disability of 25% or greater and have exhausted or are no longer eligible for federal veterans' educational benefits; and 6) state or local public safety officers or volunteers who were 100% disabled in the line of duty. The parent, veteran, POW, or public safety officer or volunteer must have been a resident of Maryland at the time of death or when declared disabled. Financial need is not considered.

Financial data The amount of the award is equal to tuition and fees at a Maryland postsecondary institution, to a maximum of $14,200 for children and spouses of the September 11 terrorist attacks or $6,178 for all other recipients.

Duration Up to 5 years of full-time study or 8 years of part-time study.

Additional Information Recipients must enroll at a 2-year or 4-year Maryland college or university as a full-time or part-time degree-seeking undergraduate or graduate student or attend a private career school.

Number awarded Varies each year.

Deadline July of each year.

[534]
FACILITATION AWARDS FOR SCIENTISTS AND ENGINEERS WITH DISABILITIES

National Science Foundation
Directorate for Education and Human Resources
Attn: Coordinator, Facilitation Awards for Scientists and Engineers with Disabilities
4201 Wilson Boulevard, Room 815
Arlington, VA 22230
(703) 292-4684   TDD: (703) 292-5090
Web: www.ehr.nsf.gov

Summary To provide supplemental financing to individuals with disabilities who wish to pursue careers in science and engineering and who are working on projects supported by the National Science Foundation (NSF).

Eligibility This program is open to individuals with disabilities who are principal investigators, other senior professionals, or graduate and undergraduate students participating in a specific project supported by the foundation. Requests for special equipment or assistance necessary to enable an individual with a disability to participate in a specific NSF-supported project may be included in the original proposal submitted to a NSF program or submitted as a separate request for supplemental funding for an existing NSF grant.

Financial data Funds may be requested to purchase special equipment, modify equipment, or provide services required specifically for the work to be undertaken. No maximum amount has been set for requests, but it is expected that the cost (including equipment adaptation and installation) will not be a major proportion of the total proposed budget for the project.

Additional Information Examples of specific equipment for which funds may be requested include prosthetic devices to manipulate a particular apparatus; equipment to convert sound to visual signals, or vice versa, for a particular experiment; access to a special site or to a mode of transportation; a reader or interpreter with special technical competence related to the project; or other special-purpose equipment or assistance needed to conduct a particular project. Items that compensate in a general way for the disabling condition are not eligible; examples include standard wheelchairs, general prosthetics, hearing aids, TTY/TDD devices, general readers for the blind, or ramps, elevators, or other structural modifications of research facilities.

Number awarded Varies each year.

Deadline Applications may be submitted at any time.

[535]
FAMILIES OF FREEDOM SCHOLARSHIP FUND

Scholarship America
Attn: Scholarship Management Services
1505 Riverview Road
P.O. Box 297
St. Peter, MN 56082
(507) 931-1682   Toll-free: (877) 862-0136
Fax: (507) 931-9168
E-mail: familiesoffreedom@csfa.org
Web: www.familiesoffreedom.org

Summary To provide college scholarships to financially-needy individuals and the families of individuals who were victims of the terrorist attacks on September 11, 2001.

Eligibility This program is open to the individuals who were disabled as a result of the terrorist attacks on September 11, 2001 and to the relatives of those individuals who were killed or permanently disabled during the attacks. Primarily, the fund will benefit dependents (including spouses and children) of the following groups: airplane crew and passengers; World Trade Center workers and visitors; Pentagon workers and visitors; and rescue workers, including fire fighters, emergency medical personnel, and law enforcement personnel. Applicants must be enrolled or planning to enroll in an accredited 2- or 4-year college, university, or vocational/technical school in the United States. They must be able to demonstrate financial need.

Financial data Stipends range from $1,000 to $28,000 per year, depending upon the need of the recipient. Recently, awards averaged $13,100 per academic year. Funds are distributed annually, in 2 equal installments. Checks are made payable jointly to the student and the student's school.

Duration 1 year; may be renewed.

Additional Information This program was established on September 17, 2001. The fundraising goal of $100 million was reached on September 4, 2002. The fund will operate until December 31, 2030.

Number awarded This is an entitlement program; all eligible students will receive funding. In its first year of operation, it distributed approximately $925,000 to 125 students.

Deadline Applications may be submitted at any time.

[536]
FLORIDA SPACE GRANT CONSORTIUM UNDERGRADUATE SPACE RESEARCH PARTICIPATION PROGRAM

Florida Space Grant Consortium
c/o Center for Space Education
Building M6-306, Room 7010
Mail Stop: FSGC
Kennedy Space Center, FL 32899
(321) 452-4301   Fax: (321) 449-0739
E-mail: fsgc@mail.ufl.edu
Web: fsgc.engr.ucf.edu

Summary To provide funding to undergraduate students at universities participating in the Florida Space Grant Consortium (FSGC) who wish to work on a summer research project.

Eligibility This program is open to juniors and seniors at colleges and universities that are members of the consortium. Students must be nominated by a faculty member at a consortium institution or by a researcher in a Florida industrial facility who proposes to mentor the student on a summer research project. Students are particularly encouraged to participate at an institution other than their own. Nominees must be enrolled in a space-related field of study, broadly defined to include aeronautics, astronautics, remote sensing, atmospheric sciences, and other fundamental sciences and technologies relying on and/or directly impacting space technological resources. Included within that definition are space science; earth observing science; space life sciences; space medicine; space policy, law, and engineering; space facilities and applications; and space education. The program particularly solicits nominations of women, minorities, and students with disabilities.

Financial data The grant is $3,000, to be used as a student stipend. The sponsoring university or industry may provide additional funds for the student stipend but may not charge for overhead or indirect costs.

Duration 10 weeks, during the summer.

Additional Information This program is funded by the U.S. National Aeronautics and Space Administration (NASA). The consortium member universities are Bethune-Cookman College, Eckerd College, Embry-Riddle Aeronautical University, Florida A&M University, Florida Atlantic University, Florida Community Colleges, Florida Gulf Coast University, Florida Institute of Technology, Florida International University, Florida Southern College, Florida State University, University of Central Florida, University of Florida, University of Miami, University of North Florida, University of South Florida, and University of West Florida.

Number awarded 15 each year.

Deadline Notices of intent must be submitted by January of each year. Completed proposals are due in March.

[537]
GEOLOGICAL SOCIETY OF AMERICA UNDERGRADUATE STUDENT RESEARCH GRANTS

Geological Society of America
Attn: Program Officer Grants, Awards and Medals
3300 Penrose Place
P.O. Box 9140
Boulder, CO 80301-9140
(303) 357-1037   Fax: (303) 447-1133
E-mail: lcarter@geosociety.org
Web: www.geosociety.org

Summary To provide support to undergraduate student members of the Geological Society of America (GSA) interested in conducting research at universities in designated sections of the United States.

Eligibility This program is open to undergraduate students who are majoring in geology at universities in 4 GSA sections: north-central, northeastern, south-central, and southeastern. Applicants must be Student Associates of the GSA. Applications from women, minorities, and persons with disabilities are strongly encouraged.

Financial data Grant amounts vary.

Duration 1 year.

Additional Information Within the 4 participating sections, information is available from the secretary. For the name and address of the 4 section secretaries, contact the sponsor.

Number awarded 1 or more each year in each of the 4 sections.

Deadline January of each year.

[538]
GEORGIA SPACE GRANT CONSORTIUM FELLOWSHIPS

Georgia Space Grant Consortium
c/o Georgia Institute of Technology
Aerospace Engineering
Paul Weber Space Science and Technology Building, Room 210
Atlanta, GA 30332-0150
(404) 894-0521   Fax: (404) 894-9313
E-mail: wanda.pierson@aerospace.gatech.edu
Web: www.ae.gatech.edu/research/gsgc

Summary To provide financial assistance for undergraduate and graduate study of space-related fields to students at member institutions of the Georgia Space Grant Consortium (GSGC).

Eligibility This program is open to U.S. citizens who are undergraduate and graduate students at member institutions of the GSGC. Applicants must be working on a degree in mathematics, science, engineering, computer science, or a technical discipline related to space. Selection is based on transcripts, 3 letters of reference, and an essay of 100 to 500 words on the applicant's professional interests and objectives and their relationship to the field of aerospace. Awards are provided as part of the Space Grant program of the U.S. National Aeronautics and Space Administration, which encourages participation by women, minorities, and people with disabilities.

Financial data A stipend is awarded (amount not specified).

Additional Information Institutions that are members of the GSGC include Albany State University, Clark Atlanta University, Columbus State University, Fort Valley State University, Georgia Institute of Technology, Kennesaw State University, Mercer University, Morehouse College, Spelman College, State University of West Georgia, and the University of Georgia. This program is funded by NASA.

Number awarded 1 each year.

[539]
HAL CONNOLLY SCHOLAR-ATHLETE AWARD

California Governor's Committee on Employment of People with Disabilities
Employment Development Department
Attn: Scholar-Athlete Awards Program
800 Capitol Mall, MIC 41
Sacramento, CA 95814
(916) 654-8055   Toll-free: (800) 695-0350
Fax: (916) 654-9821   TTY: (916) 654-9820
E-mail: rnagle@edd.ca.gov
Web: www.disabilityemployment.org

Summary To provide supplemental financial assistance to potential college freshmen in California who have participated in athletics although disabled.

Eligibility Applicants must be high school seniors with disabilities, no more than 19 years of age on January 1 of the year of application, who have competed in California high school athletics at a varsity or equivalent level and possess academic and athletic records that demonstrate qualities of leadership and accomplishment. They must have completed high school with a GPA of 2.8 or better and plan to attend an accredited college or university in California, but they do not have to intend to participate formally in collegiate athletic activities. Selection is based on cumulative GPA (15%), cumulative GPA as it relates to the nature of the student's disability (15%), athletic accomplishments as they relate to the student's disability (30%), an essay on "How Sports Participation Has Affected My Life at School and in the Community As a Person with a Disability" (25%), and overall personal achievement (15%). The top finalists may be interviewed before selections are made. Male and female students compete separately.

Financial data The awards are $1,000, contingent upon the winners' acceptance at an accredited California college or university. Funds may be used for tuition, books, supplies, and other educational expenses. Exceptions are granted to students who choose to

attend schools out of state primarily to accommodate their disability.
Duration Awards are granted annually.
Number awarded Up to 6 each year: 3 are set aside for females and 3 for males.
Deadline January of each year.

[540]
HARRY ALAN GREGG FOUNDATION GRANTS
Harry Alan Gregg Foundation
One Verney Drive
Greenfield, NH 03047
(603) 547-3311, ext. 401   Fax: (603) 547-6212
E-mail: hag@cmf.org
Web: www.cmf.org/greggfoundationinfo.htm

Summary To provide financial assistance to children and adults in New Hampshire who have physical, emotional, or intellectual disabilities.
Eligibility This program is open to New Hampshire residents who have physical, intellectual, or emotional disabilities. Funds may be requested for broad purposes but must specifically benefit the applicant. Examples of acceptable purposes include, but are not limited to: the costs of nonreimbursed medical, dental, vision, hearing, or therapy treatments; specialty equipment, services, or supplies; modifications to living area, work site, or vehicle; respite services for the recipient or care givers; recreational functions, such as camperships or other activities; and vocational, educational, or driver training tuition assistance. Selection is based on demonstrated need, ability of the foundation to measurably affect the quality of life of the recipient, and financial need of the applicant.
Financial data Grants range from $100 to $1,000 and average between $400 and $500.
Additional Information If the foundation has declined a request, the applicant may reapply 6 months after the original request was submitted. Recipients may receive a maximum of 4 grants (no more than 2 in any year).
Number awarded Varies each year.
Deadline Applications may be submitted at any time.

[541]
IDAHO MINORITY AND "AT RISK" STUDENT SCHOLARSHIP
Idaho State Board of Education
Len B. Jordan Office Building
650 West State Street, Room 307
P.O. Box 83720
Boise, ID 83720-0037
(208) 334-2270   Fax: (208) 334-2632
E-mail: board@osbe.state.id.us
Web: www.idahoboardofed.org

Summary To provide financial assistance for college to disabled and other "at risk" high school seniors in Idaho.
Eligibility This program focuses on talented students who may be at risk of failing to meet their ambitions because of physical, economic, or cultural limitations. Applicants must be high school graduates, be Idaho residents, and meet at least 3 of the following 5 requirements: 1) have a disability; 2) be a member of an ethnic minority group historically underrepresented in higher education; 3) have substantial financial need; 4) be a first-generation college student; 5) be a migrant farm worker or a dependent of a farm worker.
Financial data The maximum stipend is $3,000 per year.
Duration 1 year; may be renewed for up to 3 additional years.
Additional Information This program was established in 1991 by the Idaho state legislature. Information is also available from high school counselors and financial aid offices of colleges and universities in Idaho. Recipients must plan to attend or be attending 1 of 8 participating postsecondary institutions in the state on a full-time basis. For a list of those schools, write to the State of Idaho Board of Education.
Number awarded Approximately 40 each year.

[542]
IDAHO SPACE GRANT CONSORTIUM GRADUATE FELLOWSHIPS
Idaho Space Grant Consortium
c/o University of Idaho
College of Engineering
P.O. Box 441011
Moscow, ID 83844-1011
(208) 885-6438   Fax: (208) 885-6645
E-mail: isgc@uidaho.edu
Web: ivc.uidaho.edu/isgc/fellow.html

Summary To provide funding for research in space-related fields to graduate students at institutions belonging to the Idaho Space Grant Consortium (ISGC).
Eligibility This program is open to graduate students at ISGC member institutions. Applicants may be majoring in engineering, mathematics, science, or science/math education, but they must be interested in conducting research in an area of focus of the National Aeronautics and Space Administration (NASA). An undergraduate and current GPA of 3.0 or higher and U.S. citizenship are required. As a component of the NASA Space Grant program, ISGC encourages participation by women, underrepresented minorities, and persons with disabilities.
Financial data The stipend is $6,000 per year.
Duration 1 year; may be renewed.
Additional Information Members of the consortium include Albertson College of Idaho, Boise State University, College of Southern Idaho, Idaho State University,

Lewis Clark State College, North Idaho College, Northwest Nazarene College, Brigham Young University of Idaho, and the University of Idaho. This program is funded by NASA.

Number awarded Varies each year.

Deadline February of each year.

[543]
IDAHO SPACE GRANT CONSORTIUM SCHOLARSHIP PROGRAM

Idaho Space Grant Consortium
c/o University of Idaho
College of Engineering
P.O. Box 441011
Moscow, ID 83844-1011
(208) 885-6438   Fax: (208) 885-6645
E-mail: isgc@uidaho.edu
Web: ivc.uidaho.edu/isgc/fellow.html

Summary To provide financial assistance for study in space-related fields to undergraduate students at institutions belonging to the Idaho Space Grant Consortium (ISGC).

Eligibility This program is open to undergraduate students at ISGC member institutions. Applicants must be majoring in engineering, mathematics, science, or science/math education and have a cumulative GPA of 3.0 or higher. They should be planning to pursue a 4-year degree in a space-related field. Along with their application, they must submit a 500-word essay on their future career and educational goals and why they believe the U.S. National Aeronautics and Space Administration (NASA) should support their education. U.S. citizenship is required. As a component of the NASA Space Grant program, the ISGC encourages participation by women, underrepresented minorities, and persons with disabilities.

Financial data The stipend is $1,000 per year.

Duration 1 year; may be renewed.

Additional Information Members of the consortium include Albertson College of Idaho, Boise State University, College of Southern Idaho, Idaho State University, Lewis Clark State College, North Idaho College, Northwest Nazarene College, Brigham Young University of Idaho, and the University of Idaho. This program is funded by NASA.

Number awarded Varies each year.

Deadline February of each year.

[544]
ILLINOIS MIA/POW SCHOLARSHIP

Illinois Department of Veterans' Affairs
833 South Spring Street
P.O. Box 19432
Springfield, IL 62794-9432
(217) 782-6641
Toll-free: (800) 437-9824 (within IL)
Fax: (217) 782-4161   TDD: (217) 524-4645
E-mail: webmail@dva.state.il.us
Web: www.state.il.us/agency/dva

Summary To provide financial assistance for 1) the undergraduate education of Illinois dependents of disabled or deceased veterans or those listed as prisoners of war or missing in action and 2) the rehabilitation or education of disabled dependents of those veterans.

Eligibility To be eligible, applicants must be the spouses, natural children, legally adopted children, or stepchildren of a veteran or service member who 1) has been declared by the U.S. Department of Defense or the U.S. Department of Veterans Affairs to be permanently disabled from service-connected causes with 100% disability, deceased as the result of a service-connected disability, a prisoner of war, or missing in action, and 2) at the time of entering service was an Illinois resident or was an Illinois resident within 6 months of entering such service. Special support is available for dependents who are disabled.

Financial data An eligible dependent is entitled to full payment of tuition and certain fees at any Illinois state-supported college, university, or community college. In lieu of that benefit, an eligible dependent who has a physical, mental, or developmental disability is entitled to receive a grant to be used to cover the cost of treating the disability at 1 or more appropriate therapeutic, rehabilitative, or educational facilities. For disabled dependents, the total benefit cannot exceed the cost equivalent of 4 calendar years of full-time enrollment, including summer terms, at the University of Illinois.

Duration This scholarship may be used for a period equivalent to 4 calendar years, including summer terms. Dependents have 12 years from the initial term of study to complete the equivalent of 4 calendar years. Disabled dependents who elect to use the grant for rehabilitative purposes may do so as long as the total benefit does not exceed the cost equivalent of 4 calendar years of full-time enrollment at the University of Illinois.

Additional Information An eligible child must begin using the scholarship prior to his or her 26th birthday. An eligible spouse must begin using the scholarship prior to 10 years from the effective date of eligibility (e.g., prior to August 12, 1989 or 10 years from date of disability or death).

Number awarded Varies each year.

[545]
INDIANA SPACE GRANT CONSORTIUM UNDERGRADUATE SCHOLARSHIPS

Indiana Space Grant Consortium
c/o Purdue University
School of Industrial Engineering
1287 Grissom Hall
West Lafayette, IN 47907-1287
(765) 494-5873   Fax: (765) 496-3449
E-mail: bcaldwel@ecn.purdue.edu
Web: www.insgc.org

Summary To provide funding to undergraduate students at member institutions of the Indiana Space Grant Consortium (INSGC) interested in conducting research related to space.

Eligibility This program is open to undergraduate students enrolled full time at institutions that are members of the INSGC. Applicants must be interested in conducting research related to 1 of the strategic enterprise areas of the U.S. National Aeronautics and Space Administration (NASA): space science, earth science, biological and physical research, human exploration and development of space, and aerospace technology. U.S. citizenship is required. The program encourages representation of women, underrepresented minorities, and persons with disabilities.

Financial data The maximum grant is $1,500 per year.

Duration 1 year; may be renewed.

Additional Information This program is funded by NASA. The academic member institutions of the INSGC are Purdue University, Ball State University, Indiana University, Indiana University-Purdue University at Indianapolis, Purdue University at Calumet, Taylor University, University of Evansville, University of Notre Dame, and Valparaiso University.

Number awarded Varies each year. Approximately $60,000 is available for undergraduate scholarships and graduate fellowships.

Deadline February of each year.

[546]
INDUSTRY UNDERGRADUATE SCHOLARSHIPS

American Meteorological Society
Attn: Fellowship/Scholarship Coordinator
45 Beacon Street
Boston, MA 02108-3693
(617) 227-2426, ext. 246   Fax: (617) 742-8718
E-mail: amsinfo@ametsoc.org
Web: www.ametsoc.org

Summary To encourage outstanding undergraduate students to pursue careers in the atmospheric and related oceanic and hydrologic sciences.

Eligibility This program is open to full-time students entering their junior year who are either 1) enrolled or planning to enroll in a course of study leading to a bachelor's degree in the atmospheric or related oceanic or hydrologic sciences, or 2) enrolled in a program leading to a bachelor's degree in science or engineering who have demonstrated a clear intent to pursue a career in the atmospheric or related oceanic or hydrologic sciences following completion of appropriate specialized education at the graduate level. Applicants must have a GPA of 3.0 or higher and be U.S. citizens or permanent residents. Along with their application, they must submit 2 essays of 100 words or less: 1 on their career goals in the atmospheric or related oceanographic or hydrologic fields and 1 on their most important achievements that qualify them for this scholarship. The sponsor specifically encourages applications from women, minorities, and students with disabilities who are traditionally underrepresented in the atmospheric and related oceanic sciences. Selection is based on merit and potential for accomplishment in the field.

Financial data The stipend is $2,000 per academic year.

Duration 1 year; may be renewed for the final year of college study.

Additional Information Requests for an application must be accompanied by a self-addressed stamped envelope.

Number awarded Varies each year; recently, 9 of these scholarships were awarded.

Deadline February of each year.

[547]
KANSAS SPACE GRANT CONSORTIUM PROGRAM

Kansas Space Grant Consortium
c/o University of Kansas
135 Nichols Hall
2335 Irving Hill Road
Lawrence, KS 66045-7612
(785) 864-7401   Fax: (785) 864-3361
E-mail: ksgc@ukans.edu
Web: www.ksgc.org

Summary To provide funding for space-related activities to students and faculty at member institutions of the Kansas Space Grant Consortium.

Eligibility This program is open to faculty and students at member institutions. Support is provided for undergraduate research scholarships, graduate research assistantships, undergraduate and graduate student participation in activities sponsored by the U.S. National Aeronautics and Space Administration (NASA), faculty participation in NASA research projects, and other activities in fields of interest to NASA. The consortium is a component of NASA's Space Grant program, which encourages participation by women, underrepresented minorities, and persons with disabilities.

Financial data Each participating institution determines the amounts of its awards.

Additional Information The member institutions of the consortium are Emporia State University, Fort Hayes State University, Haskell Indian Nations University, Kansas State University, Pittsburgh State University, University of Kansas, and Wichita State University. Funding for this program is provided by NASA.

Number awarded Varies each year.

Deadline Each participating institution establishes its own deadlines.

[548]
LESTER WALLS III SCHOLARSHIP

Landscape Architecture Foundation
Attn: Scholarship Program
636 Eye Street, N.W.
Washington, DC 20001-3736
(202) 216-2356   Fax: (202) 898-1185
E-mail: msippel@asla.org
Web: www.laprofession.org

Summary To provide financial assistance to students with disabilities interested in working on a degree in landscape architecture or any student interested in working on a barrier-free design project.

Eligibility Eligible to apply are either 1) students with disabilities working on a degree in landscape architecture or 2) any student in landscape architecture who wishes to conduct a research project on barrier-free design. Applicants must submit a 2-page autobiography and statement of professional and personal goals, including a brief description of the disability, and samples of work completed to date or planned, either as slides or drawings of plans, sections, elevations, sketches, models, or completed projects. Selection is based on professional experience, community involvement, extracurricular activities, and financial need.

Financial data This award is $500.

Additional Information This scholarship was established in memory of an alumnus of California Polytechnic State University and founder of his own landscape architecture firm.

Number awarded 1 each year.

Deadline March of each year.

[549]
LOUISE C. NACCA MEMORIAL SCHOLARSHIP

Cerebral Palsy of New Jersey
Attn: Scholarship Coordinator
7 Sanford Avenue
Belleville, NJ 07109
(973) 751-0200, ext. 203

Summary To provide financial assistance for college to students with disabilities in New Jersey.

Eligibility This program is open to high school seniors, high school graduates, and currently-enrolled college students who reside in New Jersey and have a permanent disability. There is no restriction on the type of disability. Applicants must be between 18 and 45 years of age and interested in pursuing education and/or training that leads to a career, profession, or occupation.

Financial data Stipends range from $1,300 to $10,000 per year.

Duration 1 year.

Additional Information Recipients may attend any type of school or educational facility beyond the secondary school level (including college, university, professional school, or trade school) in any state.

Number awarded Varies each year; recently, 56 of these scholarships were awarded.

Deadline January of each year.

[550]
LYNN M. SMITH MEMORIAL SCHOLARSHIP

California Association for Postsecondary Education
  and Disability
Attn: Executive Assistant
71423 Biskra Road
Rancho Mirage, CA 92270
(760) 346-8206   Fax: (760) 340-5275
TTY: (760) 341-4084 E-mail: caped2000@aol.com
Web: www.caped.net/scholarship.html

Summary To provide financial assistance to community college students in California who have a disability.

Eligibility This program is open to students at community colleges in California who have a disability. Applicants must be preparing for a vocational career and have completed at least 6 semester credits with a GPA of 2.5 or higher. They must submit a 1-page personal letter that demonstrates writing skills; progress toward meeting educational and vocational goals; how they accommodate their disability; involvement in community activities; and any other personal information that might strengthen their application. They must also submit a letter of recommendation from a faculty member, verification of disability, official transcripts, proof of current enrollment, and documentation of financial need.

Financial data The stipend is $1,000.

Duration 1 year.

Additional Information Information is also available from Janet Shapiro, Disabled Student Programs and Services, Santa Barbara City College, 721 Cliff Drive, Santa Barbara, CA 93109, (805) 965-0581, ext. 2365, E-mail: shapiro@sbcc.net.

Number awarded 1 each year.

Deadline August of each year.

[551]
MARK J. SCHROEDER SCHOLARSHIP IN METEOROLOGY

American Meteorological Society
Attn: Fellowship/Scholarship Coordinator
45 Beacon Street
Boston, MA 02108-3693
(617) 227-2426, ext. 246   Fax: (617) 742-8718
E-mail: amsinfo@ametsoc.org
Web: www.ametsoc.org

Summary To provide financial assistance to students majoring in meteorology or some aspect of atmospheric sciences who demonstrate financial need.

Eligibility This program is open to undergraduate students entering their final year of study and majoring in meteorology or some aspect of the atmospheric or related oceanic and hydrologic sciences. Applicants must intend to make atmospheric or related sciences their career. They must be U.S. citizens or permanent residents, be enrolled full time in an accredited U.S. institution, and have a cumulative GPA of 3.0 or higher. Along with their application, they must submit a 100-word essay on their most important achievements that qualify them for this scholarship and a 500-word essay on their career goals in the atmospheric or related oceanic or hydrologic fields. Selection is based on academic achievement and financial need. The sponsor specifically encourages applications from women, minorities, and students with disabilities who are traditionally underrepresented in the atmospheric and related oceanic sciences.

Financial data The stipend is $5,000.

Duration 1 year.

Additional Information This scholarship was established in 1995. Requests for an application must be accompanied by a self-addressed stamped envelope.

Number awarded 1 each year.

Deadline February of each year.

[552]
MARYLAND SPACE SCHOLARS PROGRAM

Maryland Space Grant Consortium
c/o Johns Hopkins University
Bloomberg Center for Physics and Astronomy
3400 North Charles Street, Room 207
Baltimore, MD 21218-2686
(410) 516-7106   Fax: (410) 516-4109
E-mail: henry@pha.jhu.edu
Web: www.mdspacegrant.org/scholars_about.html

Summary To provide financial assistance to undergraduates who are interested in studying space-related fields at selected universities in Maryland that are members of the Maryland Space Grant Consortium.

Eligibility This program is open to residents of Maryland and graduates of Maryland high schools who are enrolled full time at a member institution. Applicants must be interested in majoring in a field related to space, including (but not limited to) astronomy, the biological and life sciences, chemistry, computer science, engineering, geological sciences, or physics. U.S. citizenship is required. This program is a component of the U.S. National Aeronautics and Space Administration (NASA) Space Grant program, which encourages participation by women, underrepresented minorities, and persons with disabilities.

Financial data Scholars receive partial payment of tuition at the participating university they attend.

Duration 1 year; may be renewed if the recipient maintains a GPA of 3.0 or higher.

Additional Information The participating universities are Hagerstown Community College, Johns Hopkins University, Morgan State University, Towson University, the University of Maryland at College Park, and Washington College. Funding for this program is provided by NASA.

Number awarded Varies each year; recently 21 of these scholarships were awarded (3 at Johns Hopkins University, 5 at Morgan State University, 3 at Hagerstown Community College, 2 at Towson University, and 8 at the University of Maryland at College Park).

Deadline August of each year.

[553]
MASSACHUSETTS REHABILITATION COMMISSION OR COMMISSION FOR THE BLIND TUITION WAIVER PROGRAM

Massachusetts Office of Student Financial Assistance
454 Broadway, Suite 200
Revere, MA 02151
(617) 727-9420   Fax: (617) 727-0667
E-mail: osfa@osfa.mass.edu
Web: www.osfa.mass.edu

Summary To provide financial assistance for college to Massachusetts residents who are clients of specified state agencies.

Eligibility Applicants for these scholarships must be certified as clients by the Massachusetts Rehabilitation Commission or Commission for the Blind. They must have been permanent residents of Massachusetts for at least 1 year, must be U.S. citizens or permanent residents, and may not be in default on any federal student loan.

Financial data Eligible clients are exempt from any tuition payments for an undergraduate degree or certificate program at public colleges or universities in Massachusetts.

Duration Up to 4 academic years, for a total of 130 semester hours.

Additional Information Recipients may enroll either part or full time in a Massachusetts publicly-supported institution.

Number awarded Varies each year.

[554]
MASSACHUSETTS SPACE GRANT CONSORTIUM UNDERGRADUATE RESEARCH OPPORTUNITY PROGRAM

Massachusetts Space Grant Consortium
c/o Massachusetts Institute of Technology
Building 33, Room 208
77 Massachusetts Avenue
Cambridge, MA 02139
(617) 258-5546   Fax: (617) 253-0823
E-mail: halaris@mit.edu
Web: www.mit.edu

Summary To provide funding to undergraduates in Massachusetts who are interested in conducting research in space science or engineering.

Eligibility This program is open to undergraduate students at institutions that are members of the Massachusetts Space Grant Consortium (MASGC). Applicants must be proposing to conduct research related to space science and/or space engineering with faculty or at nearby laboratories. U.S. citizenship is required. MASGC is a component of the U.S. National Aeronautics and Space Administration (NASA) Space Grant program, which encourages participation by women, underrepresented minorities, and persons with disabilities.

Financial data The amount of the award depends on the availability of funding and the nature of the proposal.

Duration 1 semester.

Additional Information Undergraduate member institutions of the MASGC are Boston University, College of the Holy Cross, the Five College Astronomy Department, Harvard University, Massachusetts Institute of Technology, Northeastern University, Tufts University, University of Massachusetts, Williams College, Wellesley College, and Worcester Polytechnic Institute. This program is funded by NASA.

Number awarded Varies each year.

Deadline December of each year.

[555]
MICHIGAN SPACE GRANT CONSORTIUM FELLOWSHIPS

Michigan Space Grant Consortium
c/o University of Michigan
2106 Space Physics Research Laboratory
2455 Hayward Avenue
Ann Arbor, MI 48109-2143
(734) 764-9508   Fax: (734) 764-4585
E-mail: blbryant@umich.edu
Web: www.umich.edu/~msgc

Summary To provide funding to students at member institutions of the Michigan Space Grant Consortium who wish to conduct space-related research.

Eligibility This program is open to undergraduate and graduate students at affiliates of the Michigan consortium who are proposing to conduct research in aerospace, space science, earth system science, and other related fields in science, engineering, or mathematics; students working on educational research topics in mathematics, science, or technology are also eligible. Applicants must identify a mentor in the faculty research, education, or public service communities with whom they intend to work and who is available to write a letter of recommendation for the student. U.S. citizenship is required. Women, underrepresented minorities, and persons with disabilities are especially encouraged to apply.

Financial data The maximum grant is $2,500 for undergraduates or $5,000 for graduate students.

Additional Information The consortium consists of Eastern Michigan University, Grand Valley State University, Hope College, Michigan State University, Michigan Technological University, Oakland University, Saginaw Valley State University, University of Michigan, Wayne State University, and Western Michigan University. This program is supported by the U.S. National Aeronautics and Space Administration (NASA).

Number awarded Varies; a total of $125,000 is available for these fellowships each year.

Deadline November of each year.

[556]
MINNESOTA SPACE GRANT CONSORTIUM SCHOLARSHIPS AND FELLOWSHIPS

Minnesota Space Grant Consortium
c/o University of Minnesota
Department of Aerospace Engineering and
  Mechanics
107 Akerman Hall
110 Union Street S.E.
Minneapolis, MN 55455
(612) 626-9295   Fax: (612) 626-1558
E-mail: mnsgc@aem.umn.edu
Web: www.aem.umn.edu

Summary To provide financial assistance for space-related science and engineering studies to undergraduate and graduate students in Minnesota.

Eligibility This program is open to graduate and undergraduate full-time students at institutions that are affiliates of the Minnesota Space Grant Consortium. U.S. citizenship and a GPA of 3.2 or higher are required. Eligible fields of study include the physical sciences (astronomy, astrophysics, chemistry, computer science, mathematics, physics, planetary geoscience, and planetary science), life sciences (biology, biochemistry, botany, health science/nutrition, medicine, molecular/cellular biology, and zoology), social sciences (anthropology, architecture, art, economics, education, history, philosophy, political science/public policy, and psychology), earth sciences (atmospheric science, climatology/meteorology, environmental science, geography,

geology, geophysics, and oceanography), and engineering (agricultural, aeronautical, aerospace, architectural, bioengineering, chemical, civil, computer, electrical, electronic, environmental, industrial, materials science, mechanical, mining, nuclear, petroleum, engineering science, and engineering mechanics). The Minnesota Space Grant Consortium is a component of the U.S. National Aeronautics and Space Administration (NASA) Space Grant program, which encourages participation by women, underrepresented minorities, and persons with disabilities.

Financial data This program awards approximately $125,000 in undergraduate scholarships and $25,000 in graduate fellowships each year. The amounts of the awards are set by each of the participating institutions, which augment funding from this program with institutional resources.

Duration 1 year; renewable.

Additional Information This program is funded by NASA. The member institutions are: Augsburg College, Bethel College, Bemidji State University, College of St. Catherine, Carleton College, Concordia College, Fond du Lac Community College, Itasca Community College, Leech Lake Tribal College, Macalaster College, Normandale Community College, Southwest State University, University of Minnesota at Duluth, University of Minnesota at Twin Cities, and University of St. Thomas.

Number awarded 8 to 12 undergraduate scholarships and 2 to 3 graduate fellowships are awarded each year.

Deadline March of each year.

[557]
MINNESOTA VETERANS EDUCATIONAL ASSISTANCE

Minnesota Department of Veterans Affairs
Veterans Service Building
20 West 12th Street, Second Floor
St. Paul, MN 55155-2079
(651) 296-6728   Fax: (651) 296-3954
E-mail: paula.plum@mdva.state.mn.us
Web: www.mdva.state.mn.us

Summary To provide financial assistance for college to disabled and other Minnesota veterans.

Eligibility To be eligible for this benefit, veterans must have been residents of Minnesota at the time they entered the armed forces and for the preceding 6 months, must have been separated under honorable conditions after having served on active duty for at least 181 consecutive days, must be U.S. citizens, and must have completely exhausted all federal benefits. Disabled veterans who served less than 181 days are also eligible if they were released because of their disability.

Financial data This program provides educational assistance for tuition at schools in Minnesota, up to a maximum of $750.

Duration This assistance is available on a 1-time only basis. Veterans may carry portions of the tuition benefit into future periods of schooling, but when the $750 has been exhausted, the benefit is complete.

Number awarded Varies each year.

[558]
MISSISSIPPI SPACE GRANT CONSORTIUM CAMPUS ACTIVITIES

Mississippi Space Grant Consortium
c/o University of Mississippi
217 Vardaman Hall
P.O. Box 1848
University, MS 38677-1848
(662) 915-1187   Fax: (662) 915-3927
E-mail: arandle@olemiss.edu
Web: www.olemiss.edu

Summary To provide funding to undergraduate and graduate students for space-related activities at colleges and universities that are members of the Mississippi Space Grant Consortium.

Eligibility This program is open to undergraduate and graduate students at member institutions of the Mississippi consortium. Each participating college or university establishes its own program and criteria for admission, but all activities are in engineering, mathematics, and science fields of interest to the U.S. National Aeronautics and Space Administration (NASA). U.S. citizenship is required. The consortium is a component of NASA's Space Grant program, which encourages participation by women, underrepresented minorities, and persons with disabilities.

Financial data Each participating institution establishes the amounts of the awards. Recently, the average undergraduate award was $1,308 and the average graduate award was $2,975. A total of $96,350 was awarded.

Additional Information Consortium members include Alcorn State University, Coahoma Community College, Delta State University, Hinds Community College (Utica Campus), Itawamba Community College, Jackson State University, Meridian Community College, Mississippi Delta Community College, Mississippi Gulf Coast Community College (Jackson County Campus), Mississippi State University, Mississippi University for Women, Mississippi Valley State University, Northeast Mississippi Community College, Pearl River Community College, the University of Mississippi, and the University of Southern Mississippi. This program is funded by NASA.

Number awarded Varies each year; recently, a total of 66 students received support through this program.

[559]
MONTANA SPACE GRANT CONSORTIUM UNDERGRADUATE SCHOLARSHIPS

Montana Space Grant Consortium
c/o Montana State University
261 EPS Building
P.O. Box 173835
Bozeman, MT 59717-3835
(406) 994-4223   Fax: (406) 994-4452
E-mail: msgc@montana.edu
Web: www.montana.edu

Summary To provide financial assistance to students in Montana who are interested in working on an undergraduate degree in the space sciences and/or engineering.

Eligibility This program is open to full-time undergraduate students at member institutions of the Montana Space Grant Consortium (MSGC) majoring in fields related to space sciences and engineering. Those fields include, but are not limited to, astronomy, biological and life sciences, chemical engineering, chemistry, civil engineering, computer sciences, electrical engineering, geological sciences, mechanical engineering, and physics. Priority is given to students who have been involved in aerospace-related research. U.S. citizenship is required. The MSGC is a component of the U.S. National Aeronautics and Space Administration (NASA) Space Grant program, which encourages participation by women, underrepresented minorities, and persons with disabilities. Financial need is not considered in the selection process.

Financial data The stipend is $1,000 per year.

Duration 1 year; may be renewed.

Additional Information The MSGC member institutions are Blackfeet Community College, Carroll College, Chief Dull Knife College, Fort Belknap College, Fort Peck Community College, Little Big Horn College, Montana State University at Billings, Montana State University at Bozeman, Montana State University-Northern, Montana Tech, Rocky Mountain College, Salish Kootenai College, Stone Child College, the University of Montana, and the University of Montana-Western.

Additional Information Funding for this program is provided by NASA.

Number awarded Varies each year; recently, 26 of these scholarships were awarded.

Deadline March of each year.

[560]
MVSNA STUDENT SCHOLARSHIP

Missouri Vocational Special Need Association
c/o Cindy Grizzell, Awards Chair
Waynesville Technical Academy
810 Roosevelt
Waynesville, MO 65583
(573) 774-6106
E-mail: cgrizzell@waynesville.k12.mo.us

Summary To provide financial assistance to vocational/technical students in Missouri who are members of designated special populations.

Eligibility This program is open to Missouri vocational/technical students who are members of special populations, defined as individuals who are academically or economically disadvantaged, have limited English proficiency, or are nontraditional, disabled, pregnant teenagers, single/teen parents, or foster children. Applicants must submit brief essays on their professional or career goals; the challenges they have had to overcome to reach their educational goals; how they have received help from their school, teachers, or community; and how the award will help them in pursuing continued education. Selection is based on realism of career goal, financial need, unusual circumstances, and personal references.

Financial data A stipend is awarded (amount not specified).

Duration 1 year.

Number awarded 1 each year.

Deadline April of each year.

[561]
NAVESNP/PINEY MOUNTAIN PRESS STUDENT AWARD

National Association of Vocational Education
  Special Needs Personnel
c/o Zipura Matias, Awards Chair
Swann Special Care Center
109 Kenwood Road
Champaign, IL 61821-2905
(217) 356-5164   E-mail: zipuram@yahoo.com
Web: www.navesnp.org/awards.htm

Summary To provide financial assistance to vocational/technical students who are members of a special population.

Eligibility This program is open to vocational/technical students who are members of a special population, defined to include those who are academically or economically disadvantaged, limited English proficient, nontraditional, disabled, pregnant teenagers, single/teen parents, or foster children. Applicants must demonstrate how they have overcome barriers to achieve their highest potential for success. Selection is based on their choice of a realistic career goal, financial need, unusual circumstances, and letters of reference.

Financial data The stipend is $1,000.
Duration 1 year.
Additional Information Piney Mountain Press supports half the stipend.
Number awarded 1 each year.
Deadline October of each year.

[562]
NEBRASKA SPACE GRANT STATEWIDE SCHOLARSHIP COMPETITION

Nebraska Space Grant Consortium
c/o University of Nebraska at Omaha
Allwine Hall 422
6001 Dodge Street
Omaha, NE 68182-0406
(402) 554-3772
Toll-free: (800) 858-8648, ext. 4-3772 (within NE)
Fax: (402) 554-3781   E-mail: nasa@unomaha.edu
Web: www.unomaha.edu/~nasa/funding/ssc.html

Summary To provide financial assistance to undergraduate and graduate students in Nebraska interested in aerospace-related study or research.
Eligibility This program is open to undergraduate and graduate students at schools that are members of the Nebraska Space Grant Consortium. Applicants must be U.S. citizens participating in approved aviation or aerospace-related research or course work. Selection is based primarily on past academic performance in the classroom. Special attention is given to applications submitted by women, underrepresented minorities, and persons with disabilities.
Financial data Maximum awards are $500 per semester for undergraduate or graduate course work, $750 per semester for undergraduate research, or $2,500 per semester for graduate research.
Duration 1 semester; may be renewed if the recipient maintains a GPA of 3.0 or higher.
Additional Information The following schools are members of the Nebraska Space Grant Consortium: University of Nebraska at Omaha, University of Nebraska at Lincoln, University of Nebraska at Kearney, University of Nebraska Medical Center, Creighton University, Western Nebraska Community College, Chadron State College, College of St. Mary, Metropolitan Community College, Grace University, Hastings College, Little Priest Tribal College, and Nebraska Indian Community College. Funding for this program is provided by the National Aeronautics and Space Administration.
Deadline April of each year.

[563]
NEVADA SPACE GRANT CONSORTIUM UNDERGRADUATE SCHOLARSHIP PROGRAM

Nevada Space Grant Consortium
c/o University of Nevada at Reno
1664 North Virginia Street
MS/172
Reno, NV 89557-0138
(775) 784-6261   Fax: (775) 327-2235
E-mail: nvsg@mines.unr.edu
Web: www.unr.edu/spacegrant

Summary To provide financial assistance for space-related study to undergraduate students at institutions that are members of the Nevada Space Grant Consortium (NSGC).
Eligibility This program is open to undergraduate students at NSGC member institutions. Applicants must be pursuing a degree in an aerospace-related field (including the behavioral sciences, biological sciences, business, communications, computer science, economics, education, engineering, international affairs, law, natural sciences, physical sciences, publication administration, and sociology) that is concerned with or likely to improve the understanding, assessment, development, and utilization of space. They must be U.S. citizens and enrolled full time. This program is part of the Space Grant program of the U.S. National Aeronautics and Space Administration (NASA), which encourages participation by members of underrepresented groups (African Americans, Hispanics, American Indians, Pacific Islanders, physically disabled people, and women of all races).
Financial data The stipend is $2,500 per year. Funds may be used for tuition or registration fees. Funds may not be regarded as payment for research work or any other work.
Duration 1 year; may be renewed.
Additional Information Members of the NSGC include all state institutes of higher learned in Nevada: 2 Ph.D.-granting universities (the University of Nevada at Las Vegas and the University of Nevada at Reno), 4 community colleges (Southern Nevada, Great Basin, Truckee Meadows, and Western Nevada), and the system's research organization, the Desert Research Institute. Funding for this program is provided by NASA.
Number awarded Varies each year.
Deadline March of each year.

[564]
NEW HAMPSHIRE CHARITABLE FOUNDATION STATEWIDE STUDENT AID PROGRAM

New Hampshire Charitable Foundation
37 Pleasant Street
Concord, NH 03301-4005
(603) 225-6641   Toll-free: (800) 464-6641
Fax: (603) 225-1700   E-mail: info@nhcf.org
Web: www.nhcf.org

Summary To provide scholarships and loans for undergraduate or graduate study to New Hampshire residents.

Eligibility This program is open to New Hampshire residents who are graduating high school seniors or undergraduate students between 17 and 23 years of age or graduate students of any age. Applicants must be enrolled in or planning to enroll in an accredited 2- or 4-year college, university, or vocational school on at least a half-time basis. The school may be in New Hampshire or another state. Selection is based on financial need, academic merit, community service, school activities, and work experience. Priority is given to students with the fewest financial resources and to vocational/technical school students.

Financial data Awards range from $500 to $2,500 and average $1,800. Most are made in the form of grants (recently, 82% of all awards) or no-interest or low-interest loans (recently 18% of all awards).

Duration 1 year; approximately one third of the awards are renewable.

Additional Information Through this program, students submit a single application for more than 250 different scholarship and loan funds. Many of the funds have additional requirements, covering such elements as the field of study; residency in region, county, city, or town; graduation from designated high schools; and special attributes (of Belgian descent, employee of designated firms, customer of Granite State Telephone Company, disabled, suffering from a life-threatening or serious chronic illness, of Lithuanian descent, dependent of a New Hampshire police officer, dependent of a New Hampshire Episcopal minister, of Polish descent, former Sea Cadet or Naval Junior ROTC, or employed in the tourism industry). The Citizens' Scholarship Foundation of America reviews all applications; recipients are selected by the New Hampshire Charitable Foundation. A $15 application fee is required.

Number awarded Varies each year; recently, a total of $2.3 million was awarded.

Deadline April of each year.

[565]
NEW HAMPSHIRE SPACE GRANT CONSORTIUM PROJECT SUPPORT

New Hampshire Space Grant Consortium
c/o University of New Hampshire
Institute for the Study of Earth, Oceans, and Space
Morse Hall
39 College Road
Durham, NH 03824-3525
(603) 862-0094   Fax: (603) 862-1915
E-mail: nhspacegrant@unh.edu
Web: www.nhsgc.sr.unh.edu

Summary To provide financial assistance to students at member institutions of the New Hampshire Space Grant Consortium (NHSGC) who are interested in participating in space-related activities.

Eligibility This program is open to students at member institutions of the NHSGC. Applicants must be studying space physics, astrophysics, astronomy, or aspects of computer science, engineering, earth sciences, ocean sciences, atmospheric sciences, or life sciences that utilize space technology and/or adopt a planetary view of the global environment. U.S. citizenship is required. The New Hampshire Space Grant Consortium is a component of the U.S. National Aeronautics and Space Administration (NASA) Space Grant program, which encourages participation by women, underrepresented minorities, and persons with disabilities.

Financial data The amount of the award depends on the nature of the project.

Duration From 1 quarter to 1 year.

Additional Information This program is funded by NASA. Currently, projects operating through this program include space grant fellowships at the University of New Hampshire, Agnes M. Lindsay Trust/NASA Challenge Scholars Initiative at the New Hampshire Community Technical College System, Presidential Scholars Research Assistantships at Dartmouth College, and Women in Science Internships at Dartmouth.

Number awarded Varies each year.

Deadline Each participating college or university sets its own deadline.

[566]
NEW JERSEY UTILITIES ASSOCIATION SCHOLARSHIPS

New Jersey Utilities Association
50 West State Street, Suite 1006
Trenton, NJ 08608
(609) 392-1000   Fax: (609) 396-4231
Web: www.njua.org

Summary To provide financial assistance to minority, female, and disabled high school seniors in New Jersey interested in majoring in selected subjects in college.

Eligibility Eligible to apply for this scholarship are women, minorities (Black, Hispanic, American Indi-

an/Alaska Native, or Asian American/Pacific Islander), and persons with disabilities who are high school seniors in New Jersey. They must be able to demonstrate financial need, be planning to enroll on a full-time basis at an institute of higher education, and be planning to work on a bachelor's degree in engineering, environmental science, chemistry, biology, business administration, or accounting. Children of employees of any New Jersey Utilities Association-member company are ineligible. Selection is based on overall academic excellence and demonstrated financial need.

Financial data The stipend is $1,500 per year.
Duration 4 years.
Number awarded 2 each year.

[567]
NORTH DAKOTA SPACE GRANT PROGRAM FELLOWSHIPS

North Dakota Space Grant Program
c/o University of North Dakota
Department of Space Studies
Clifford Hall, Fifth Floor
P.O. Box 9008
University Avenue and Tulane
Grand Forks, ND 58202-9008
(701) 777-4856   Toll-free: (800) 828-4274
Fax: (701) 777-3711   E-mail: bieri@space.edu
Web: www.space.edu/spacegrant/fellowinfo.html

Summary To provide funding for space-related research to undergraduate and graduate students at specified academic institutions affiliated with the North Dakota Space Grant Program (NDSGP).

Eligibility This program is open to undergraduate and graduate students at specified NDSGP universities who are studying in fields related to space and are paired with an advisor for a research project. U.S. citizenship is required. Other qualifying criteria are set by each participating institution. The NDSGP is a component of the U.S. National Aeronautics and Space Administration (NASA) Space Grant program, which encourages the participation of women, underrepresented minorities, and persons with disabilities.

Financial data The stipend is $2,000.

Additional Information Participating NDSCP members are the University of North Dakota and North Dakota State University. This program is funded by NASA.

Number awarded Varies each year.

[568]
NORTH DAKOTA SPACE GRANT PROGRAM SCHOLARSHIPS

North Dakota Space Grant Program
c/o University of North Dakota
Department of Space Studies
Clifford Hall, Fifth Floor
P.O. Box 9008
University Avenue and Tulane
Grand Forks, ND 58202-9008
(701) 777-4856   Toll-free: (800) 828-4274
Fax: (701) 777-3711   E-mail: bieri@space.edu
Web: www.space.edu/spacegrant/fellowinfo.html

Summary To provide financial assistance for space-related study to undergraduates at academic institutions affiliated with the North Dakota Space Grant Program (NDSGP).

Eligibility This program is open to undergraduate students at NDSGP associate colleges and universities who are studying in fields related to space. U.S. citizenship is required. Other qualifying criteria are set by each participating institution. The NDSGP is a component of the U.S. National Aeronautics and Space Administration (NASA) Space Grant program, which encourages the participation of women, underrepresented minorities, and persons with disabilities.

Financial data Stipends are $500 at 2-year public and tribal colleges or $750 at 4-year public state universities.

Additional Information Associate NDSCP members are Bismarck State College, Cankdeska Cikana Community (Little Hoop Community College), Dickinson State University, Fort Berthold Community College, Lake Region State College, Mayville State University, Minot State University, Minot State University-Bottineau Campus, North Dakota State College of Science, Sitting Bull College, Turtle Mountain Community College, Valley City State University, and Williston State College. This program is funded by NASA.

Number awarded 39 each year: 3 at each participating college and university.

[569]
OHIO SPACE GRANT CONSORTIUM COMMUNITY COLLEGE SCHOLARSHIP

Ohio Space Grant Consortium
c/o Ohio Aerospace Institute
22800 Cedar Point Road
Cleveland, OH 44142
(440) 962-3032   Toll-free: (800) 828-OSGC
Fax: (440) 962-3057   E-mail: osgc@oai.org
Web: www.osgc.org/Scholarship.html

Summary To provide financial assistance to students at selected community colleges in Ohio who are interested in continuing their studies at a 4-year university in the state that is a member of the Ohio Space Grant Consortium (OSGC).

Eligibility This program is open to U.S. citizens who are students at designated community colleges in Ohio, normally enrolled full time in their freshman year (although applications are accepted from part-time students demonstrating academic merit and from students at any stage of their college career). Applicants must be enrolled in a program that includes course work related to an understanding of or interest in technological fields supporting aerospace, e.g. associate degrees related to mathematics, science, and such advanced technology fields as engineering, computers, electronics, and industrial technology. They must also have a GPA of 3.0 or higher and plans to continue their education in a 4-year program at an OSGC-member university. Along with their application, they must submit college transcripts, 2 letters of recommendation, and a brief resume of their education, significant accomplishments, work experience, educational and professional goals, and any other relevant information. Women, underrepresented minorities, and persons with disabilities are particularly encouraged to apply.

Financial data The stipend is $1,000.

Duration 1 year; nonrenewable.

Additional Information These scholarships are funded through the National Space Grant College and Fellowship Program administered by the National Aeronautics and Space Administration (NASA), with matching funds provided by the member colleges, the Ohio Aerospace Institute, and private industry. The participating institutions include Columbus State Community College, Cuyahoga Community College, Lorain County Community College, Owens Community College, Lakeland Community College, and Terra Community College. OSGC member institutions include the University of Akron, Case Western Reserve University, Cedarville University, Central State University, University of Cincinnati, Cleveland State University, University of Dayton, Marietta College (petroleum engineering), Miami University (manufacturing engineering), Ohio Northern University, Ohio State University, Ohio University, University of Toledo, Wilberforce University, Wright State University, and Youngstown State University.

Number awarded 1 or more each year.

[570]
OHIO SPACE GRANT CONSORTIUM JUNIOR SCHOLARSHIPS

Ohio Space Grant Consortium
c/o Ohio Aerospace Institute
22800 Cedar Point Road
Cleveland, OH 44142
(440) 962-3032   Toll-free: (800) 828-OSGC
Fax: (440) 962-3057   E-mail: osgc@oai.org
Web: www.osgc.org/Scholarship.html

Summary To provide financial assistance to students in their junior year at selected universities in Ohio who wish to working on a bachelor's degree in an aerospace-related field.

Eligibility These scholarships are available to U.S. citizens who expect to complete within 2 years the requirements for a bachelor of science degree in an aerospace-related discipline (aeronautical engineering, aerospace engineering, astronomy, biology, chemical engineering, chemistry, civil engineering, computer engineering and science, control engineering, electrical engineering, engineering mechanics, geography, geology, industrial engineering, manufacturing engineering, materials science and engineering, mathematics, mechanical engineering, petroleum engineering, physics, and systems engineering). Applicants must be attending 1 of the participating universities in Ohio. They must propose and initiate a research project on campus under the guidance of a faculty member. Women, underrepresented minorities, and physically challenged persons are particularly encouraged to apply. Selection is based on academic record, recommendations, and a personal statement of career goals, anticipated benefits from the Space Grant program, and plans for their research laboratory experience.

Financial data The stipend is $2,000.

Duration 1 year; recipients may apply for a senior scholarship if they maintain satisfactory academic performance and good progress on their research project.

Additional Information These scholarships are funded through the National Space Grant College and Fellowship Program administered by the National Aeronautics and Space Administration (NASA), with matching funds provided by the member universities, the Ohio Aerospace Institute, and private industry. The participating institutions include the University of Akron, Case Western Reserve University, Cedarville University, Central State University, University of Cincinnati, Cleveland State University, University of Dayton, Marietta College (petroleum engineering), Miami University (manufacturing engineering), Ohio Northern University, Ohio State University, Ohio University, University of Toledo, Wilberforce University, Wright State University, and Youngstown State University.

Number awarded Varies each year; recently, 20 of these scholarships were awarded.

Deadline February of each year.

[571]
OHIO SPACE GRANT CONSORTIUM SENIOR SCHOLARSHIP

Ohio Space Grant Consortium
c/o Ohio Aerospace Institute
22800 Cedar Point Road
Cleveland, OH 44142
(440) 962-3032　　　　Toll-free: (800) 828-OSGC
Fax: (440) 962-3057　　　E-mail: osgc@oai.org
Web: www.osgc.org/Scholarship.html

Summary To provide financial assistance to students in their senior year at designated universities in Ohio who wish to conduct research while working on a baccalaureate degree in an aerospace-related field.

Eligibility These scholarships are available to U.S. citizens who expect to complete the requirements for a bachelor's degree in an aerospace-related discipline (aeronautical engineering, aerospace engineering, astronomy, biology, chemical engineering, chemistry, civil engineering, computer engineering and science, control engineering, electrical engineering, engineering mechanics, geography, geology, industrial engineering, manufacturing engineering, materials science and engineering, mathematics, mechanical engineering, petroleum engineering, physics, and systems engineering) within 1 year. They must be attending 1 of the participating universities in Ohio. Women, underrepresented minorities, and physically challenged persons are particularly encouraged to apply. Applicants must propose a research project to be conducted during the scholarship period in a campus laboratory. Selection is based on academic record, recommendations, the proposed research project, and a personal statement of career goals and anticipated benefits from the Space Grant program.

Financial data The grant is $3,000.

Duration 1 year.

Additional Information These scholarships are funded through the National Space Grant College and Fellowship Program administered by the National Aeronautics and Space Administration (NASA), with matching funds provided by the member universities, the Ohio Aerospace Institute, and private industry. The participating institutions are the University of Akron, Case Western Reserve University, Cedarville University, Central State University, University of Cincinnati, Cleveland State University, University of Dayton, Marietta College (petroleum engineering), Miami University (Manufacturing engineering), Ohio Northern University, Ohio State University, Ohio University, University of Toledo, Wilberforce University, Wright State University, and Youngstown State University. Scholars are required to describe their research at an annual spring research symposium sponsored by the consortium.

Number awarded Varies each year; recently, 31 of these scholarships were awarded.

Deadline February of each year.

[572]
OREGON SPACE GRANT UNDERGRADUATE SCHOLAR PROGRAM

Oregon Space Grant
c/o Oregon State University
Department of Nuclear Engineering
130 Radiation Center
Corvallis, OR 97331-5902
(541) 737-2414　　　　Fax: (541) 737-0480
E-mail: kleina@ne.orst.edu
Web: www.ne.orst.edu

Summary To provide financial assistance for study in space-related fields to undergraduate students at colleges and universities that are members of Oregon Space Grant (OSG).

Eligibility This program is open to undergraduate students at member institutions who are enrolled full time in science and engineering fields related to the mission of the U.S. National Aeronautics and Space Administration (NASA). U.S. citizenship is required. Selection is based on scholastic achievement, career goals, a 500-word essay on a space-related topic, and 2 letters of recommendation. Applications are especially encouraged from women, underrepresented minorities, and people with disabilities.

Financial data The stipend is $1,000.

Duration 1 year.

Additional Information Institutions that are members of OSG include Oregon State University, Portland State University, the University of Oregon, Southern Oregon University, Eastern Oregon University, and Oregon Institute of Technology. This program is funded by NASA.

Number awarded 10 each year.

Deadline October of each year.

[573]
OSGC EDUCATION PROGRAM

Oklahoma NASA Space Grant Consortium
c/o University of Oklahoma
College of Geosciences
710 Asp Avenue, Suite 5
Norman, Oklahoma 73069
(405) 447-8483　　　　Fax: (405) 447-8455
E-mail: vduca@ou.edu
Web: www.okspacegrant.ou.edu

Summary To provide financial assistance to students in Oklahoma who are enrolled in aerospace-related studies at the undergraduate and graduate level.

Eligibility This program is open to undergraduate and graduate students at member and affiliate institutions of the Oklahoma Space Grant Consortium (OSGC). U.S. citizenship is required. The OSGC is a component of the U.S. National Aeronautics and Space Administration (NASA) Space Grant program, which encourages participation by women, underrepresented minorities, and persons with disabilities.

Financial data Financing depends on the availability of funds.

Additional Information Members of OSGC are Oklahoma State University, the University of Oklahoma, Cameron University, and Langston University. Write to the sponsor for information on the program at each participating university. This program is funded by NASA.

[574]
OUTSTANDING SECONDARY SPECIAL POPULATIONS CAREER AND TECHNICAL EDUCATION STUDENT AWARD

Vocational Foundation of Nebraska
P.O. Box 22607
Lincoln, NE 68542-2607
(402) 423-6786

Summary To recognize and reward, with scholarships, career and technical students in Nebraska who are members of groups defined as "special populations."

Eligibility This program is open to students who are currently enrolled in career and technical education in Nebraska or have been enrolled within the past 12 months. Students must be members of a "special populations" group, including individuals with disabilities. They must be nominated by a teacher who 1) describes how they have demonstrated a high level of competence in the program through class activities, work experience, laboratory training, related projects, or extracurricular activities, and 2) explains what distinguishes them from others in terms of capability, motivation, achievements, performances, and contributions. Nominees must also complete an application in which they describe how they will apply their career and technical education to their future plans and list projects or experiences that have seemed most interesting or important to them and school and community activities.

Financial data The award is a $1,000 scholarship. Funds must be used for attendance at a Nebraska postsecondary institution.

Duration The award is presented annually.

Number awarded 1 each year.

Deadline Nominations must be submitted no later than March of each year.

[575]
PENNSYLVANIA SPACE GRANT CONSORTIUM SCHOLARSHIPS

Pennsylvania Space Grant Consortium
c/o Pennsylvania State University
2217 Earth-Engineering Sciences Building
University Park, PA 16802
(814) 863-7687   Fax: (814) 863-8286
E-mail: spacegrant@psu.edu
Web: www.psu.edu

Summary To provide financial assistance for space-related study to undergraduate students at universities affiliated with the Pennsylvania Space Grant Consortium.

Eligibility This program is open to full-time undergraduate students at participating universities. Applicants must be studying a field that does, or can, promote the understanding, assessment, and utilization of space, including aerospace, earth science, or space science. U.S. citizenship is required. Students from underrepresented groups (women, minorities, rural populations, and those with disabilities) are especially encouraged to apply.

Financial data The stipend is set by each participating university. At Pennsylvania State University, for instance, it is $4,000 per year.

Duration 1 year.

Additional Information Participating institutions include Carnegie Mellon University, Clarion University, Pennsylvania State University, University of Pittsburgh, Susquehanna University, Lincoln University, Temple University, West Chester University, and Pennsylvania State University at Abington. At Pennsylvania State University, the award is designated as the Sylvia Stein Memorial Space Grant Scholarship. This program is sponsored by the U.S. National Aeronautics and Space Administration (NASA).

Number awarded Varies each year.

Deadline Each participating university sets its own deadline.

[576]
P.O. PISTILLI SCHOLARSHIPS

Design Automation Conference
c/o Cherrice Traver
Union College
ECE Department
Schenectady, NY 12308
(518) 388-6326   Fax: (518) 388-6789
E-mail: traverc@union.edu
Web: doc.union.edu/acsee.html

Summary To provide financial assistance to female, minority, or disabled high school seniors who are interested in preparing for a career in computer science or electrical engineering.

Eligibility Eligible to apply are "underrepresented" high school seniors: women, African Americans, Hispanic Americans, Native Americans, and persons with disabilities. Applicants must be interested in preparing for a career in electrical engineering, computer engineering, or computer science. They must have at least a 3.0 GPA, have demonstrated high achievements in math and science courses, and be able to demonstrate significant financial need. U.S. citizenship is not required, but applicants must be U.S. residents when they apply and must plan to attend an accredited U.S. college or university. They must submit a completed application form, 3 letters of recommendation, official transcripts, ACT/SAT and/or PSAT scores, a personal statement outlining future

goals, a copy of their latest income tax return, and a copy of the FAFSA form they submitted.

Financial data Stipends are $4,000 per year. Awards are paid each year in 2 equal installments.

Duration 1 year; renewable for up to 4 additional years.

Additional Information This program is funded by the Design Automation Conference and the IEEE Circuits and System Society. It is directed by the Association for Computing Machinery's Special Interest Group on Design Automation.

Number awarded 2 to 7 each year.

Deadline January of each year.

[577]
PORAC SCHOLARSHIPS

Peace Officers Research Association of California
Attn: Peace Officers Research and Education Foundation
2495 Natomas Park Drive, Suite 555
Sacramento, CA 95833-2935
(916) 921-0660   Toll-free: (800) 937-6722
Fax: (916) 614-1875   E-mail: gracer@porac.org
Web: porac.org/scholarship.html

Summary To provide financial assistance for college to relatives of members of the Peace Officers Research Association of California (PORAC) and to members who are medically retired.

Eligibility This program is open to California residents who are 1) family members of law enforcement officers who have died in the line of duty; 2) dependents whose parent or legal guardian is an active PORAC member; 3) spouses and dependents of deceased PORAC members; and 4) PORAC members who have medically retired. Applicants must submit a composition, up to 750 words, on "My goals, present and future: why I am applying for this scholarship and its importance to me." They may be interested in scholastic or vocational study, but they are encouraged to consider law enforcement as a career. Selection is based on the essay, academic achievement (GPA of 2.0 or higher for dependents), school activities, community service, and financial need.

Financial data The stipend is $1,000.

Duration 1 year.

Additional Information Recipients must enroll full time.

Number awarded Varies each year; recently, 16 of these scholarships were awarded.

Deadline March of each year.

[578]
RESEARCH SUPPLEMENTS FOR UNDERGRADUATE STUDENTS WITH DISABILITIES

National Institutes of Health
Division of Extramural Outreach and Information Resources
Attn: GrantsInfo
6701 Rockledge Drive, Suite 6095
Bethesda, MD 20892-7910
(301) 435-0714   Fax: (301) 480-8443
E-mail: GrantsInfo@nih.gov
Web: www.nih.gov

Summary To provide support to undergraduate students with disabilities who are interested in participating in an ongoing research project funded by the National Institutes of Health (NIH).

Eligibility This program is open to undergraduate students who meet the definition of disabled in the Americans with Disabilities Act: an individual who "has a physical or mental impairment that substantially limits one or more major life activities." A list of disabilities that might confer eligibility for supplemental awards under this program includes, but is not limited to, the following: total deafness in both ears, visual acuity less than 20/200 with corrective lenses, speech impairment, missing extremities, partial paralysis, complete paralysis, convulsive disorders, mental or emotional illness, learning disabilities, kidney dialysis, and severe distortion of the limbs and/or spine. In all cases, undergraduate students supported under this supplement must, with reasonable assistance, be able to contribute to the research supported by the parent grant. Any principal investigator at a domestic institution holding an eligible parent grant (funded by the NIH) is eligible—in cooperation with the disabled undergraduate student—to submit a request for a supplement to support the candidate with a disability. The student must currently be enrolled at an academic institution (that may be, but does not need to be, the institution with the parent grant) and be interested in biomedical, behavioral, clinical, or social science research. The proposed project must be separate and apart from any requirement of the regular academic program. Selection is based on 1) the qualifications of the student, including career goals, prior research training, research potential, and relevant experience; 2) the plan for the proposed research experience in the supplemental request and its relationship to the parent grant; 3) the appropriateness of the proposed accommodations for the student; 4) evidence from the principal investigator that the experience will enhance the research potential, knowledge, and/or skills of the student, and that adequate mentorship will be provided; 5) evidence from the principal investigator that the activities of the student will be an integral part of the project; and 6) evidence of the student's educational achievement and interest in science.

Financial data The disabled undergraduate student receives a salary that is consistent with the institution's policy, up to $8 per hour, plus $200 per month for sup-

plies and travel. Funds may also be requested to permit accommodation to the research environment. That may include research equipment, but only if it is directly related to the project and to accommodating the disabilities of the individual. Some types of accommodations that might be provided under this program include: specialized equipment, assistive devices, and personnel, such as readers, interpreters, or assistants.

Duration Students are expected to devote an equivalent of at least 3 months of full-time effort to the research project and related activities in and 1 year, and in most cases, the period of support should last at least 2 years.

Number awarded Usually, each parent grant may have only 1 supplement for a person with a disability.

Deadline Principal investigators—in cooperation with the disabled student—are encouraged to submit an application no later than 3 months before the anniversary date of the last 2 years remaining on the parent grant.

[579]
RHODE ISLAND EDUCATIONAL BENEFITS FOR DISABLED AMERICAN VETERANS

Division of Veterans' Affairs
480 Metacom Avenue
Bristol, RI 02809-0689
(401) 253-8000   Fax: (401) 254-2320
TDD: (401) 254-1345
E-mail: dfoehr@gw.dhs.state.ri.us
Web: www.dhs.state.ri.us

Summary To provide assistance to disabled veterans in Rhode Island who wish to pursue higher education at a public institution in the state.

Eligibility This program is open to permanent residents of Rhode Island who have been verified by the Department of Veterans Affairs (DVA) as having a disability of at least 10% resulting from military service.

Financial data Eligible veterans are entitled to take courses at any public institution of higher education in Rhode Island without the payment of tuition, exclusive of other fees and charges.

Number awarded Varies each year.

[580]
RHODE ISLAND SPACE GRANT UNDERGRADUATE SCHOLARSHIP PROGRAM

Rhode Island Space Grant
c/o Brown University
Lincoln Field Building
Box 1846
Providence, RI 02912-1846
(401) 863-2889   Fax: (401) 863-1292
E-mail: RISpaceGrant@brown.edu
Web: www.planetary.brown.edu/RI_Space_Grant

Summary To provide financial assistance to undergraduate students at institutions that are members of the Rhode Island Space Grant Consortium (RISGC) who are interested in a career in a space-related field of science, mathematics, or engineering.

Eligibility This program is open to undergraduate students at RISGC-member universities. Applicants must be studying in science, mathematics, or engineering fields of interest to the National Aeronautics and Space Administration (NASA). U.S. citizenship is required. The sponsor is a component of NASA's Space Grant program, which encourages participation by women, underrepresented minorities, and persons with disabilities.

Financial data A stipend is provided (amount not specified).

Duration 1 year.

Additional Information Members of the RISGC are Bryant College, Community College of Rhode Island, Providence College, Roger Williams University, Rhode Island College, Rhode Island School of Design, Salve Regina University, University of Rhode Island, and Wheaton College. This program is funded by NASA. Scholars are required to devote 75% of their time to their studies and 25% of their time to science education outreach activities organized and coordinated by Rhode Island Space Grant.

Number awarded Varies each year; recently, 9 of these scholarships were awarded.

[581]
ROCKY MOUNTAIN NASA SPACE GRANT CONSORTIUM UNDERGRADUATE SCHOLARSHIPS

Rocky Mountain NASA Space Grant Consortium
c/o Utah State University
EL Building, Room 302
Logan, UT 84322-4140
(435) 797-4042   Fax: (435) 797-4044
E-mail: rmc@sdl.usu.edu
Web: www.rmc.sdl.usu.edu

Summary To provide financial support to undergraduate students at designated universities in Utah or Colorado who are working on a degree in fields of interest to the National Aeronautics and Space Administration (NASA).

Eligibility This program is open to undergraduate students at member institutions of the Rocky Mountain NASA Space Grant Consortium who are studying engineering, science, medicine, or technology. U.S. citizenship is required. Selection is based on academic performance to date and potential for the future, with emphasis on space-related research interests. This program is part of the NASA Space Grant program, which encourages participation by women, underrepresented minorities, and persons with disabilities.

Financial data The amount of the awards depends on the availability of funds.

Additional Information Members of the consortium are Utah State University, the University of Utah, Brig-

ham Young University, University of Denver, Weber State University, Snow College, and Southern Utah University. This program is funded by NASA.

Number awarded Varies each year.

[582]
SARA CONLON MEMORIAL SCHOLARSHIP

Council for Exceptional Children
Attn: Yes I Can! Foundation for Exceptional Children
1110 North Glebe Road, Suite 300
Arlington, VA 22201-5704
(703) 620-3660   Toll-free: (800) 224-6830, ext. 462
Fax: (703) 264-9494   TTY: (866) 915-5000
E-mail: yesican@cec.sped.org
Web: yesican.sped.org

Summary To provide financial assistance for college to students with disabilities who are committed to majoring in special education.

Eligibility This program is open to full-time students with disabilities who are majoring or planning to major in special education. Applicants must submit a 200-word statement of their philosophical, educational, and occupational goals. Selection is based on academic achievement, ability, promise, and financial need.

Financial data The stipend is $500.

Duration 1 year; may not be renewed.

Additional Information This program began in 2004.

Number awarded 1 each year.

Deadline January of each year.

[583]
SOUTH CAROLINA SPACE GRANT CONSORTIUM UNDERGRADUATE SCHOLARSHIP PROGRAM

South Carolina Space Grant Consortium
c/o College of Charleston
Department of Geology
58 Coming Street
Charleston, SC 29424
(843) 953-5463   Fax: (843) 953-5446
E-mail: baughmant@cofc.edu
Web: www.cofc.edu/~scsgrant

Summary To provide financial assistance for space-related study to undergraduate students in South Carolina.

Eligibility This program is open to undergraduate students at member institutions of the South Carolina Space Grant Consortium. Applicants should be rising juniors or seniors majoring in space-related studies, although students from the basic sciences, astronomy, science education, planetary science, environmental studies, engineering, fine arts, and journalism are also eligible to apply. U.S. citizenship is required. Selection is based on academic qualifications of the applicant; 2 letters of recommendation; a description of past activities, current interests, and future plans concerning an aerospace-related field; and faculty sponsorship. The South Carolina Space Grant Consortium is a component of the U.S. National Aeronautics and Space Administration (NASA) Space Grant program, which encourages the participation of women, underrepresented minorities, and persons with disabilities.

Financial data The stipend is $1,500 per year.

Duration 1 year.

Additional Information Members of the consortium are Benedict College, The Citadel, College of Charleston, Clemson University, Coastal Carolina University, Furman University, University of South Carolina, Wofford College, South Carolina State University, The Medical University of South Carolina, and University of the Virgin Islands. This program is funded by NASA.

Number awarded Varies each year.

Deadline January of each year.

[584]
SOUTH DAKOTA FREE TUITION FOR VETERANS AND OTHERS WHO PERFORMED WAR SERVICE

South Dakota Board of Regents
Attn: Scholarship Committee
306 East Capitol Avenue, Suite 200
Pierre, SD 57501-3159
(605) 773-3455   Fax: (605) 773-5320
E-mail: info@ris.sdbor.edu
Web: www.ris.sdbor.edu

Summary To provide free tuition at South Dakota public colleges and universities to certain veterans.

Eligibility This program is open to current residents of South Dakota who have been discharged from the military forces of the United States under honorable conditions. Applicants must meet 1 of the following criteria: 1) served on active duty at any time between August 2, 1990 and March 3, 1991; 2) received an Armed Forces Expeditionary Medal, Southwest Asia Service Medal, or other U.S. campaign or service medal for participation in combat operations against hostile forces outside the boundaries of the United States: or 3) have a service-connected disability rating of at least 10%. They may not be eligible for any other educational assistance from the U.S. government. Qualifying veterans must apply for this benefit within 20 years after the date proclaimed for the cassation of hostilities or within 6 years from and after the date of their discharge from military service, whichever is later.

Financial data Eligible veterans are entitled to attend any South Dakota state-supported institution of higher education or state-supported technical or vocational school free of tuition and mandatory fees.

Duration Eligible veterans are entitled to receive 1 month of free tuition for each month of qualifying service, from a minimum of 1 year to a maximum of 4 years.

Number awarded Varies each year.

[585]
S.P.I.N. SCHOLARSHIPS

Special People in Need
500 West Madison Street, Suite 3700
Chicago, IL 60661-2511
(312) 715-5235   E-mail: ipeter@wilvaine.com

Summary To provide funding to individuals with disabilities who are interested in working on a college degree.

Eligibility This program is open to people with disabilities who are enrolled or planning to enroll at a college or university. Students who are not disabled but who have had to overcome extremely difficult circumstances may also be eligible. Applicants must submit transcripts, a letter of recommendation from an educator, evidence of financial need, and a letter from their educational institution agreeing to serve as the administrator of the scholarship. Support is not provided to international or graduate students.

Financial data Grants range from $2,000 to $4,000. Funds are dispersed directly to the institution.

Duration 1 year; may be renewed if the recipient provides evidence of satisfactory performance and continues to use the funds only for the purpose for which they were originally granted.

Number awarded Varies each year.

Deadline April of each a year.

[586]
STAN BECK FELLOWSHIP

Entomological Society of America
Attn: Entomological Foundation
9301 Annapolis Road, Suite 210
Lanham, MD 20706-3115
(301) 459-9082   Fax: (301) 459-9084
E-mail: melodie@entfdn.org
Web: www.entfdn.org/beck.html

Summary To assist "needy" students working on an undergraduate or graduate degree in science who are nominated by members of the Entomological Society of America (ESA).

Eligibility Candidates for this fellowship must be nominated by members of the society. Nominees may be studying science on any level. However, they must be "needy" students. For the purposes of this program, need may be based on physical limitations, or economic, minority, or environmental conditions.

Financial data The stipend varies each year.

Duration 1 year; may be renewed up to 3 additional years.

Additional Information Recipients are expected to be present at the society's annual meeting, where the award will be presented.

Number awarded 1 or more each year.

Deadline August of each year.

[587]
STANLEY E. JACKSON SCHOLARSHIP AWARD FOR ETHNIC MINORITY GIFTED/TALENTED STUDENTS WITH DISABILITIES

Council for Exceptional Children
Attn: Yes I Can! Foundation for Exceptional Children
1110 North Glebe Road, Suite 300
Arlington, VA 22201-5704
(703) 620-3660 Toll-free: (800) 224-6830, ext. 462
Fax: (703) 264-9494   TTY: (866) 915-5000
E-mail: yesican@cec.sped.org
Web: yesican.sped.org

Summary To provide financial assistance for college to gifted minority students with disabilities.

Eligibility Applicants must be gifted or talented in 1 or more of the following categories: general intellectual ability, specific academic aptitude, creativity, leadership, or visual or performing arts. They must be disabled, financially needy, ready to begin college, and a member of an ethnic minority group (e.g., Asian, African American, Hispanic, or Native American). Candidates must submit a 200 word statement of philosophical, educational, and occupational goals as part of the application process. Selection is based on academic achievement, ability, promise, and financial need. U.S. citizenship is required.

Financial data The stipend is $500.

Duration 1 year; nonrenewable.

Additional Information Scholarships may be used for 2- or 4-year college programs or for vocational, technical, or fine arts training programs. Recipients must enroll full time.

Number awarded 1 or more each year.

Deadline January of each year.

[588]
STANLEY E. JACKSON SCHOLARSHIP AWARD FOR ETHNIC MINORITY STUDENTS WITH DISABILITIES

Council for Exceptional Children
Attn: Yes I Can! Foundation for Exceptional Children
1110 North Glebe Road, Suite 300
Arlington, VA 22201-5704
(703) 620-3660 Toll-free: (800) 224-6830, ext. 462
Fax: (703) 264-9494   TTY: (866) 915-5000
E-mail: yesican@cec.sped.org
Web: yesican.sped.org

Summary To provide financial assistance for college to minority students with disabilities.

Eligibility Applicants must be students with disabilities who intend to enroll for the first time on a full-time

basis in a college, university, vocational/technical school, or fine arts institute and are able to document financial need. Only minority (African American, Asian, Native American, or Hispanic) students are eligible for the award. Candidates must submit a 200-word statement of philosophical, educational, and occupational goals as part of the application process. Selection is based on academic achievement, ability, promise, and financial need. U.S. citizenship is required.

Financial data The stipend is $500.

Duration 1 year; nonrenewable.

Additional Information Scholarships may be used for 2- or 4-year college programs or for vocational, technical, or fine arts training programs. Recipients must enroll full time.

Number awarded 1 or more each year.

Deadline January of each year.

[589]
STANLEY E. JACKSON SCHOLARSHIP AWARD FOR GIFTED/TALENTED STUDENTS WITH DISABILITIES

Council for Exceptional Children
Attn: Yes I Can! Foundation for Exceptional Children
1110 North Glebe Road, Suite 300
Arlington, VA 22201-5704
(703) 620-3660 Toll-free: (800) 224-6830, ext. 462
Fax: (703) 264-9494   TTY: (866) 915-5000
E-mail: yesican@cec.sped.org
Web: yesican.sped.org

Summary To provide financial assistance for college to gifted students with educationally handicapping disabilities.

Eligibility Applicants must be disabled and have also demonstrated gifted and/or talented abilities in any 1 or more of the following categories: general intellectual ability, specific academic aptitude, creativity, leadership, or visual or performing arts. They must 1) have not yet begun college and 2) be able to document financial need. Candidates must submit a 200-word statement of philosophical, educational, and occupational goals as part of the application process. Selection is based on academic achievement, ability, promise, and financial need. U.S. citizenship is required.

Financial data The stipend is $500.

Duration 1 year; nonrenewable.

Additional Information Scholarships may be used for 2- or 4-year college programs or for vocational, technical, or fine arts training programs. Recipients must enroll full time.

Number awarded 1 or more each year.

Deadline January of each year.

[590]
STANLEY E. JACKSON SCHOLARSHIP AWARD FOR STUDENTS WITH DISABILITIES

Council for Exceptional Children
Attn: Yes I Can! Foundation for Exceptional Children
1110 North Glebe Road, Suite 300
Arlington, VA 22201-5704
(703) 620-3660 Toll-free: (800) 224-6830, ext. 462
Fax: (703) 264-9494   TTY: (866) 915-5000
E-mail: yesican@cec.sped.org
Web: yesican.sped.org

Summary To provide financial assistance for college to students with disabilities.

Eligibility Applicants must be disabled, have not yet begun college, and be able to document financial need. They must submit a 200-word statement of philosophical, educational, and occupational goals as part of the application process. Selection is based on academic achievement, ability, promise, and financial need. U.S. citizenship is required.

Financial data The stipend is $500.

Duration 1 year; nonrenewable.

Additional Information Scholarships may be used for 2- or 4-year college programs or for vocational, technical, or fine arts training programs. Recipients must enroll full time.

Number awarded 1 or more each year.

Deadline January of each year.

[591]
STATE VOCATIONAL REHABILITATION SERVICES PROGRAM

Department of Education
Office of Special Education and Rehabilitative Services
Attn: Rehabilitation Services Administration
400 Maryland Avenue, S.W., Room 3329, MES
Washington, DC 20202-2551
(202) 205-4829   Fax: (202) 205-9340
E-mail: roseann_ashby@ed.gov
Web: www.ed.gov

Summary To provide financial assistance for undergraduate or graduate study to individuals with disabilities as part of their program of vocational rehabilitation.

Eligibility To be eligible for vocational rehabilitation services, an individual must 1) have a physical or mental impairment that is a substantial impediment to employment; 2) be able to benefit in terms of employment from vocational rehabilitation services; and 3) require vocational rehabilitation services to prepare for, enter, engage in, or retain gainful employment. Priority is given to applicants with the most significant disabilities. Persons accepted for vocational rehabilitation develop an Individualized Written Rehabilitation Program (IWRP) in consultation with a counselor for the vocational rehabilitation agency in the state in which they live. The IWRP may

include a program of postsecondary education if the disabled person and counselor agree that such a program will fulfill the goals of vocational rehabilitation. In most cases, the IWRP will provide for postsecondary education only to a level at which the disabled person will become employable, but that may include graduate education if the approved occupation requires an advanced degree as a minimum condition of entry. Students accepted to a program of postsecondary education as part of their IWRP must apply for all available federal, state, and private financial aid.

Financial data Funding for this program is provided by the federal government through grants to state vocational rehabilitation agencies. Grants under the basic support program currently total nearly $2.5 billion per year. States must supplement federal funding with matching funds of 21.3%. Persons who are accepted for vocational rehabilitation by the appropriate state agency receive financial assistance based on the cost of their education and other funds available to them, including their own or family contribution and other sources of financial aid. Allowable costs in most states include tuition, fees, books, supplies, room, board, transportation, personal expenses, child care, and expenses related to disability (special equipment, readers, attendants, interpreters, or notetakers).

Duration Assistance is provided until the disabled person achieves an educational level necessary for employment as provided in the IWRP.

Additional Information You will need to contact your state vocational rehabilitation agency to apply for this program.

Number awarded Varies each year. Recently, more than 1.2 million (of whom more than 80% have significant disabilities) were participating in this program.

[592]
STRATTON/TIPTON SCHOLARSHIP FOR ADULT RETURNING STUDENTS

Kentucky Association of Vocational Education
  Special Needs Personnel
c/o Donna Ledden
Boone County High School
7056 Burlington Pike
Florence, KY 41042
(859) 282-5655
E-mail: dledden1@boone.k12.ky.us
Web: www.kavesnp.org/scholar.htm

Summary To provide financial assistance to adults with special needs enrolled at a college or university in Kentucky.

Eligibility This program is open to adults in Kentucky who are studying for 1) an associate degree or certificate/diploma through the Kentucky Community and Technical College System (KCTCS), or 2) an associate or bachelor's degree from a Kentucky college or university. Applicants must meet the definition of a special needs student: persons with disabilities, educationally and economically disadvantaged people, foster children, individuals preparing for nontraditional employment, single parents (including single pregnant women), displaced homemakers, individuals of limited English language proficiency, individuals in a correctional institution, and individuals with other barriers to educational achievement. They must have earned a GPA of 2.5 or higher in their most recently completed semester of course work at a KCTCS institution or a Kentucky college or university. Selection is based on academic achievement, letters of reference, and career potential.

Financial data The stipend is $500.

Duration 1 year; nonrenewable.

Number awarded 1 each year.

Deadline March of each year.

[593]
STRATTON/TIPTON SCHOLARSHIP FOR HIGH SCHOOL SENIORS

Kentucky Association of Vocational Education
  Special Needs Personnel
c/o Donna Ledden
Boone County High School
7056 Burlington Pike
Florence, KY 41042
(859) 282-5655
E-mail: dledden1@boone.k12.ky.us
Web: www.kavesnp.org/scholar.htm

Summary To provide financial assistance for college to high school seniors with special needs in Kentucky.

Eligibility This program is open to seniors at high schools in Kentucky who are planning to 1) enroll in a certificate/diploma program or associate degree program at an institution that is part of the Kentucky Community and Technical College System (KCTCS), or 2) work on an associate or bachelor's degree at a college or university. Applicants must meet the definition of a special needs student: persons with disabilities, educationally and economically disadvantaged people, foster children, individuals preparing for nontraditional employment, single parents (including single pregnant women), displaced homemakers, individuals of limited English language proficiency, individuals in a correctional institution, and individuals with other barriers to educational achievement. They must have a cumulative GPA of 2.5 or higher for grades 9-12. Selection is based on academic achievement, letters of reference, and career potential.

Financial data The stipend is $500.

Duration 1 year; nonrenewable.

Number awarded 1 each year.

Deadline March of each year.

[594]
SUPREME EMBLEM CLUB OF THE UNITED STATES OF AMERICA GRANT-IN-AID AWARDS

Supreme Emblem Club of the United States of America
c/o Cheryl White, Supreme Corresponding Secretary
7326 SR 19, 1807
Mt. Gilead, OH 43338
(419) 946-1559   Fax: (419) 747-6647
E-mail: cherylw56@redbird.net
Web: www.emblemclub.com

Summary To provide financial aid for college to members or the children of members of the Supreme Emblem Club of the United States of America who have a physically challenging condition.

Eligibility This program is open to high school graduates or those already in college. Applicants must be sponsored by the Emblem Club in which the student or the student's mother or grandmother is a member. They must be serious about continuing their education but, because of a physically challenging situation, are unable to meet the high criteria applied to the Emblem Club's Scholarship Program.

Financial data The amount awarded varies each year. Funds must be used for tuition, books, or fees.

Duration 1 year.

Additional Information The sponsoring Emblem Club must be a current contributor to the regular scholarship fund for the applicant to be considered for an award.

Number awarded Varies each year.

Deadline March of each year.

[595]
SURVIVORS' AND DEPENDENTS' EDUCATIONAL ASSISTANCE PROGRAM

Department of Veterans Affairs
810 Vermont Avenue, N.W.
Washington, DC 20420
(202) 418-4343   Toll-free: (888) GI-BILL1
Web: www.gibill.va.gov

Summary To provide financial assistance for undergraduate or graduate study to children and spouses of deceased and disabled veterans, MIAs, and POWs.

Eligibility Eligible for this assistance are spouses and children of 1) veterans who died or are permanently and totally disabled as the result of a disability arising from active service in the armed forces; 2) veterans who died from any cause while rated permanently and totally disabled from a service-connected disability; 3) servicemembers listed for more than 90 days as currently missing in action or captured in the line of duty by a hostile force; and 4) servicemembers listed for more than 90 days as presently detained or interned by a foreign government or power. Children must be between 18 and 26 years of age, although extensions may be granted. Spouses and children over 14 years of age with physical or mental disabilities are also eligible.

Financial data Monthly stipends from this program are $695 for full-time study at an academic institution, $522 for three-quarter time, or $347 for half-time. For farm cooperative work, the monthly stipends are $561 for full-time, $421 for three-quarter time, or $281 for half-time. For an apprenticeship or on-the-job training, the monthly stipend is $506 for the first 6 months, $378 for the second 6 months, $251 for the third 6 months, and $127 for the remainder of the program.

Duration Up to 45 months (or the equivalent in part-time training). Spouses must complete their training within 10 years of the date they are first found eligible.

Additional Information Benefits may be used to work on associate, bachelor, or graduate degrees at colleges and universities, including independent study, cooperative training, and study abroad programs. Courses leading to a certificate or diploma from business, technical, or vocational schools may also be taken. Other eligible programs include apprenticeships, on-job training programs, farm cooperative courses, correspondence courses (for spouses only), secondary school programs (for recipients who are not high school graduates), tutorial assistance, remedial deficiency and refresher training, or work-study (for recipients who are enrolled at least three-quarter time). Eligible children who are handicapped by a physical or mental disability that prevents pursuit of an educational program may receive special restorative training that includes language retraining, lip reading, auditory training, Braille reading and writing, and similar programs. Eligible spouses and children over 14 years of age who are handicapped by a physical or mental disability that prevents pursuit of an educational program may receive specialized vocational training that includes specialized courses, alone or in combination with other courses, leading to a vocational objective that is suitable for the person and required by reason of physical or mental handicap. Ineligible courses include bartending or personality development courses; correspondence courses by dependent or surviving children; non-accredited independent study courses; any course given by radio; self-improvement courses, such as reading, speaking, woodworking, basic seamanship, and English as a second language; audited courses; any course that is avocational or recreational in character; courses not leading to an educational, professional, or vocational objective; courses taken and successfully completed previously; courses taken by a federal government employee and paid for under the Government Employees' Training Act; and courses taken while in receipt of benefits for the same program from the Office of Workers' Compensation Programs.

Number awarded Varies each year.

Deadline Applications may be submitted at any time.

[596]
TEXAS EXEMPTION FOR PEACE OFFICERS DISABLED IN THE LINE OF DUTY

Texas Higher Education Coordinating Board
Attn: Grants and Special Programs
1200 East Anderson Lane
P.O. Box 12788, Capitol Station
Austin, TX 78711-2788
(512) 427-6101   Toll-free: (800) 242-3062
Fax: (512) 427-6127
E-mail: grantinfo@thecb.state.tx.us
Web: www.collegefortexans.com

Summary To provide educational assistance to disabled Texas peace officers.

Eligibility This program is open to Texas residents permanently disabled as a result of an injury suffered as a peace officer who are unable to continue employment as a peace officer because of the disability. Applicants must be planning to attend a publicly-supported college or university in Texas as an undergraduate student.

Financial data Eligible students are exempted from the payment of all dues, fees, and tuition charges at publicly-supported colleges and universities in Texas.

Duration Up to 12 semesters.

Additional Information For more information, students should contact the admission office at the institution they plan to attend.

Number awarded Varies each year; recently, 5 of these exemptions were awarded.

[597]
TEXAS SPACE GRANT CONSORTIUM UNDERGRADUATE SCHOLARSHIPS

Texas Space Grant Consortium
Attn: Administrative Assistant
3925 West Braker Lane, Suite 200
Austin, TX 78759
(512) 471-3583   Toll-free: (800) 248-8742
Fax: (512) 471-3585
E-mail: jurgens@tsgc.utexas.edu
Web: www.tsgc.utexas.edu/grants

Summary To provide financial assistance to undergraduate students at Texas universities working on degrees in the fields of space science and engineering.

Eligibility Applicants must be U.S. citizens, eligible for financial assistance, and registered for full-time study as juniors or seniors in an undergraduate program at 1 of the participating universities. Students apply to their university representative; each representative then submits up to 3 candidates into the statewide selection process. Fields of study have included aerospace engineering, biology, chemical engineering, chemistry, electrical engineering, geology, industrial engineering, mathematics, mechanical engineering, and physics. The program encourages participation by members of groups underrepresented in science and engineering (persons with disabilities, women, African Americans, Hispanic Americans, Native Americans, and Pacific Islanders). Scholarships are awarded competitively, on the basis of above-average performance in academics, participation in space education projects, participation in research projects, and exhibited leadership qualities.

Financial data The stipend is $1,000.

Duration 1 year; nonrenewable.

Additional Information The participating universities are Baylor University, Lamar University, Prairie View A&M University, Rice University, San Jacinto College, Southern Methodist University, Sul Ross State University, Texas A&M University (including Kingsville and Corpus Christi campuses), Texas Christian University, Texas Southern University, Texas Tech University, Trinity University, University of Houston (including Clear Lake and Downtown campuses), University of Texas at Arlington, University of Texas at Austin, University of Texas at Dallas, University of Texas at El Paso, University of Texas at San Antonio, and University of Texas/Pan American. This program is funded by the National Aeronautics and Space Administration (NASA).

Number awarded Varies each year; recently, 29 of these scholarships were awarded.

Deadline March of each year.

[598]
TEXAS 4-H COURAGEOUS HEART SCHOLARSHIPS

Texas 4-H Foundation
Attn: Executive Director
Texas A&M University
7606 Eastmark Drive, Suite 101
Box 4-H
College Station, TX 77843-2473
(979) 845-1213   Fax: (979) 845-6495
E-mail: p-pearce@tamu.edu
Web: texas4-h.tamu.edu

Summary To provide financial assistance to 4-H members in Texas who plan to work on a baccalaureate degree, associate degree, or technical certification at an institution in the state but who would have difficulty winning other scholarships because of such obstacles as a disability.

Eligibility This program is open to graduating seniors at high schools in Texas who have been actively participating in 4-H and plan to attend an institution in the state to work on a baccalaureate degree, associate degree, or technical certification. Applicants must have passed all sections of the TAAS/TASP/TAKS test and be able to demonstrate that because they have faced obstacles, they are not competitive for other Texas 4-H scholarships. Such obstacles may include significant disability(ies), devastating personal or family catastrophe or illness, or unusually restrictive socioeconomic conditions. Selection is based on a consideration of the obstacles overcome, GPA, test scores, 4-H experience, financial

need, and a personal interview. Some scholarships require a major in agriculture; others are unrestricted.
Financial data Stipends range from $500 to $15,000, depending on the contributions from various donors.
Duration 1 year.
Additional Information Students submit 1 application. The foundation determines the scholarships for which they are eligible, based on the specific requirements established by particular sponsors. Students who apply to the Texas FFA Association or the Texas chapter of Family, Career and Community Leaders of America (FCCLA) for a scholarship will have their 4-H application voided.
Number awarded Varies each year; recently, Texas 4-H awarded 156 scholarships with a total value of more than $1,000,000.
Deadline Students submit their applications to their county extension office, which must forward them to the district extension office by February of each year.

[599]
THEODORE R. AND VIVIAN M. JOHNSON SCHOLARSHIP PROGRAM

State University System of Florida
Attn: Office of Academic and Student Affairs
325 West Gaines Street, Suite 1501
Tallahassee, FL 32399-1950
(850) 245-0467   Fax: (850) 245-9667
E-mail: we're.listening@fldoe.org
Web: www.fldoe.org

Summary To provide financial assistance to Florida undergraduate students with disabilities.
Eligibility This program is open to students with disabilities enrolled at a State University System of Florida institution. Applicants must submit an official transcript (with GPA of 2.0 or higher); documentation of the nature and/or extent of their disability, which may be in 1 or more of the following classifications: hearing impairment, physical impairment, specific learning disability, speech/language impairment, visual impairment, or other impairment; and documentation of financial need.
Financial data The stipend depends on the availability of funds.
Duration 1 year; may be renewed if recipient maintains a GPA of 2.0 or higher and enrolls in at least 18 credits each academic year.
Additional Information This program is administered by the equal opportunity program at each of the 11 State University System of Florida 4-year institutions. Contact that office for further information. Funding is provided by the Theodore R. and Vivian M. Johnson Foundation with matching funding from the Florida Legislature.
Number awarded Several each year.
Deadline May of each year.

[600]
TROY BARBOZA EDUCATION FUND

Hawai'i Community Foundation
Attn: Scholarship Department
1164 Bishop Street, Suite 800
Honolulu, HI 96813
(808) 537-6333   Toll-free: (888) 731-3863
Fax: (808) 521-6286
E-mail: scholarships@hcf-hawaii.org
Web: www.hawaiicommunityfoundation.org

Summary To provide financial assistance for college to disabled public employees in Hawaii or their dependents.
Eligibility This program is open to 1) disabled public employees in Hawaii who were injured in the line of duty or 2) dependents or other immediate family members of public employees in Hawaii who were disabled or killed in the line of duty. The public employee must work or have worked in a job where lives are risked for the protection and safety of others. The injury must have left the employee incapacitated or incapable or continuing in his or her profession and must have occurred after October 22, 1977. Also eligible are private citizens who have performed a heroic act for the protection and welfare of others.
Financial data The amount awarded varies, depending upon the needs of the recipient and the funds available.
Duration 1 year.
Number awarded 1 or more each year.
Deadline February of each year.

[601]
USA FUNDS ACCESS TO EDUCATION SCHOLARSHIPS

Scholarship America
Attn: Scholarship Management Services
1505 Riverview Road
P.O. Box 297
St. Peter, MN 56082
(507) 931-1682   Toll-free: (800) 537-4180
Fax: (507) 931-9168
E-mail: scholarship@usafunds.org
Web: www.usafunds.org

Summary To provide financial assistance to undergraduate and graduate students, especially those who are members of ethnic minority groups or have physical disabilities.
Eligibility This program is open to high school seniors and graduates who plan to enroll or are already enrolled undergraduate or graduate course work at an accredited 2- or 4-year college, university, or vocational/technical school. Half-time undergraduate students are also eligible. Up to 50% of the awards are targeted at students who have a documented physical disability or are a member of an ethnic minority group, including but not limited to Native Hawaiian, Alaskan Native, Black/African

American, Asian, Pacific Islander, American Indian, or Hispanic/Latino. Residents of all 50 states, the District of Columbia, Puerto Rico, Guam, the U.S. Virgin Islands, and all U.S. territories and commonwealths are eligible. Preference is given to applicants from the following areas: Arizona, Hawaii and the Pacific Islands, Indiana, Kansas, Maryland, Mississippi, Nevada, and Wyoming. Applicants must also be U.S. citizens or eligible noncitizens and come from a family with an annual adjusted gross income of $35,000 or less. In addition to financial need, selection is based on past academic performance and future potential, leadership and participation in school and community, work experience, career and educational aspirations and goals, and references.

Financial data The stipend is $1,500 per year for full-time undergraduate or graduate students or $750 per year for half-time undergraduate students. Funds are paid jointly to the student and the school.

Duration 1 year; may be renewed until the student receives a final degree or certificate or until the total award to a student reaches $6,000, whichever comes first. Renewal requires the recipient to maintain a GPA of 2.5 or higher.

Additional Information This program, established in 2000, is sponsored by USA Funds which serves as the education loan guarantor and administrator in the 8 states and the Pacific Islands where the program gives preference.

Number awarded Varies each year; recently, 2,519 of these scholarships were awarded.

Deadline April of each year.

[602]
UTAH ELKS ASSOCIATION HANDICAPPED STUDENT SCHOLARSHIP AWARD

Utah Elks Association
c/o Phillip Johnson
1402 West Green Avenue
Provo, UT 84604
(801) 375-5149   E-mail: phgun@aol.com
Web: www.inovion.com

Summary To provide financial assistance for college to high school seniors in Utah who are disabled.

Eligibility Eligible to apply for this award are high school seniors in Utah who have a physical disability that impedes or restricts normal progress. As part of the application process, students must submit a total of 4 to 5 letters of recommendation; a support letter from a doctor stating the continuing nature of the disability; official high school transcripts; and a personal statement (300 words or less) on their goals and how past, present, and future activities make the realization of the goals probable. The local Elks lodge must endorse the application. Financial need must be documented.

Financial data A stipend is awarded (amount not specified).

Duration 1 year.

Number awarded Varies each year, depending upon the funds available.

[603]
VERMONT SPACE GRANT UNDERGRADUATE SCHOLARSHIPS

Vermont Space Grant Consortium
c/o University of Vermont
College of Engineering and Mathematics
Votey Building, Room 209
12 Colchester Avenue
Burlington, VT 05405-0156
(802) 656-1429   Fax: (802) 656-8802
E-mail: zeno@emba.uvm.edu
Web: www.emba.uvm.edu/VSGC/awards.html

Summary To provide financial assistance for undergraduate study in space-related fields to students in Vermont.

Eligibility This program is open to Vermont residents who are 1) enrolled in an undergraduate degree program at a Vermont institution of higher education with a GPA of 3.0 or higher or 2) seniors graduating from a high school in Vermont. Applicants must be planning to pursue a professional career that has direct relevance to the U.S. aerospace industry and the goal of the National Aeronautics and Space Administration (NASA), such as astronomy, biology, engineering, mathematics, physics, and other basic sciences (including earth sciences and medicine). They must submit an essay, up to 3 pages in length, on their career plans and the relationship of those plans to areas of interest to NASA. U.S. citizenship is required. Selection is based on academic standing, letters of recommendation, and the essay. The Vermont Space Grant Consortium (VSGC) is a component of the NASA Space Grant program, which encourages participation by women, underrepresented minorities, and persons with disabilities.

Financial data The stipend is $1,500 per year.

Duration 1 year; may be renewed upon reapplication.

Additional Information This program is funded by NASA. Participating institutions are the College of Engineering and Mathematics at the University of Vermont, St. Michael's College, Norwich University, Vermont Technical College, the Vermont State Mathematics Coalition, and Aviation Technology School/Burlington Technical Center.

Number awarded Up to 10 each year.

Deadline February of each year.

[604]
VIRGINIA SPACE GRANT AEROSPACE UNDERGRADUATE RESEARCH SCHOLARSHIPS

Virginia Space Grant Consortium
Attn: Fellowship Coordinator
Old Dominion University Peninsula Center
600 Butler Farm Road
Hampton, VA 23666
(757) 766-5210   Fax: (757) 766-5205
E-mail: vsgc@pen.k12.va.us
Web: www.vsgc.odu.edu/html/fellowships.htm

Summary To provide financial assistance for research in space-related fields to undergraduate students in Virginia.

Eligibility This program is open to undergraduate students who will be enrolled in a program of full-time study in an aerospace-related discipline at 1 of the Virginia Space Grant Consortium (VSGC) Colleges. Applicants must be U.S. citizens who have completed at least 2 years of an undergraduate program with a GPA of 3.0 or higher. They must be proposing to participate in an active, identified research activity that has aerospace applications. The research must be supervised by a faculty mentor and may be conducted on the home campus or at an industrial or government facility. It should be continuous and may be conducted any time during the academic year, summer, or both. Since an important purpose of this program is to increase the participation of underrepresented minorities, females, and persons with disabilities in aerospace-related careers, the VSGC especially encourages applications from those students.

Financial data Grants provide a student stipend of $3,000 during the academic year and a $3,500 stipend during the summer (either before or after the academic year). Recipients may request an additional $1,000 research allocation for materials and travel to support research activities conducted during the academic year and/or a $1,000 research allocation during the summer. The maximum award per year cannot exceed $8,500.

Duration 1 year; renewable.

Additional Information The VSGC colleges are College of William and Mary, Hampton University, Old Dominion University, the University of Virginia, and Virginia Polytechnic Institute and State University. This program is funded by the U.S. National Aeronautics and Space Administration (NASA). Awardees are required to participate in the VSGC annual student research conference in late March or early April.

Number awarded Varies each year.

Deadline February of each year.

[605]
VIRGINIA SPACE GRANT COMMUNITY COLLEGE SCHOLARSHIP PROGRAM

Virginia Space Grant Consortium
Attn: Fellowship Coordinator
Old Dominion University Peninsula Center
600 Butler Farm Road
Hampton, VA 23666
(757) 766-5210   Fax: (757) 766-5205
E-mail: vsgc@pen.k12.va.us
Web: www.vsgc.odu.edu/html/fellowships.htm

Summary To provide financial assistance to students who are interested in pursuing space-related studies at community colleges in Virginia.

Eligibility This program is open to students currently enrolled in a Virginia community college who are U.S. citizens and have completed at least the first semester of their program with a GPA of 3.0 or higher. Awards are generally made to full-time students, but part-time students demonstrating academic merit are also eligible. Applicants can be enrolled in any program that includes course work related to an understanding of or interest in technological fields supporting aerospace. A particular goal of the program is to increase the participation of underrepresented minorities, women, and persons with disabilities in aerospace-related, high technology careers.

Financial data The maximum stipend is $1,500.

Duration 1 year; nonrenewable.

Additional Information This program is funded by the U.S. National Aeronautics and Space Administration (NASA).

Number awarded Approximately 10 each year.

Deadline February of each year.

[606]
VIRGINIA SPACE GRANT TEACHER EDUCATION SCHOLARSHIP PROGRAM

Virginia Space Grant Consortium
Attn: Fellowship Coordinator
Old Dominion University Peninsula Center
600 Butler Farm Road
Hampton, VA 23666
(757) 766-5210   Fax: (757) 766-5205
E-mail: vsgc@pen.k12.va.us
Web: www.vsgc.odu.edu/html/fellowships.htm

Summary To provide financial assistance for college to students in Virginia planning a career as science, mathematics, or technology educators.

Eligibility This program is open to full-time undergraduate students at 1 of the Virginia Space Grant Consortium (VSGC) Colleges in a track that will qualify them to teach in a pre-college setting. Priority is given to those majoring in technology education, mathematics, or science, particularly earth/space/environmental science. Applicants may apply while seniors in high school or

sophomores in a community college, with the award contingent on their matriculation at a VSGC college and entrance into a teacher certification program. They must submit a statement of academic goals and plan of study, explaining their reasons for desiring to enter the teaching profession, specifically the fields of science, mathematics, or technology education. Students currently enrolled in a VSGC college can apply when they declare their intent to enter the teacher certification program. Students enrolled in a career transition program leading to a degree in education are also eligible to apply. Applicants must be U.S. citizens with a GPA of 3.0 or higher. Since an important purpose of this program is to increase the participation of underrepresented minorities, women, and persons with disabilities in science, mathematics, and technology education, the VSGC especially encourages applications from those students.

Financial data The maximum stipend is $1,000.

Duration 1 year; nonrenewable.

Additional Information The VSGC colleges are College of William and Mary, Hampton University, Old Dominion University, the University of Virginia, and Virginia Polytechnic Institute and State University. This program is funded by the U.S. National Aeronautics and Space Administration (NASA).

Number awarded Approximately 10 each year.

Deadline February of each year.

[607]
VOCATIONAL REHABILITATION FOR DISABLED VETERANS

Department of Veterans Affairs
810 Vermont Avenue, N.W.
Washington, DC 20420
(202) 418-4343   Toll-free: (800) 827-1000
Web: www.va.gov

Summary To provide vocational rehabilitation to certain categories of veterans with disabilities.

Eligibility This program is open to veterans who have a service-connected disability of at least 10% and a serious employment handicap or 20% and an employment handicap. They must have been discharged or released from military service under other than dishonorable conditions. The Department of Veterans Affairs (VA) must determine that they would benefit from a training program that would help them prepare for, find, and keep suitable employment. The program may be 1) institutional training at a certificate, 2-year college, 4-year college or university, or technical program; 2) unpaid on-the-job training in a federal, state, or local agency or a federally-recognized Indian tribal agency, training in a home, vocational course in a rehabilitation facility or sheltered workshop, independent instruction, or institutional non-farm cooperative; or 3) paid training through a farm cooperative, apprenticeship, on-the-job training, or on-the-job non-farm cooperative.

Financial data While in training and for 2 months after, eligible disabled veterans may receive subsistence allowances in addition to their disability compensation or retirement pay. For institutional training, the full-time monthly rate is $454.96 with no dependents, $564.34 with 1 dependent, $665.03 with 2 dependents, and $48.48 for each additional dependent; the three-quarter time monthly rate is $341.85 for no dependents, $423.87 with 1 dependent, $497.21 with 2 dependents, and $37.28 for each additional dependent; the half-time monthly rate is $228.74 for no dependents, $283.41 with 1 dependent, $333.13 with 2 dependents, and $24.87 for each additional dependent. For unpaid on-the-job training, the monthly rate is $454.96 for no dependents, $564.34 with 1 dependent, $665.03 with 2 dependents, and $48.48 for each additional dependent. For paid training, the monthly rate is based on the wage received, to a maximum of $397.79 for no dependents, $481.05 with 1 dependent, $554.39 with 2 dependents, and $36.06 for each additional dependent. The VA also pays the costs of tuition, books, fees, supplies, and equipment; it may also pay for special supportive services, such as tutorial assistance, prosthetic devices, lipreading training, and signing for the deaf. If during training or employment services the veteran's disabilities cause transportation expenses that would not be incurred by nondisabled persons, the VA will pay for at least a portion of those expenses. If the veteran encounters financial difficulty during training, the VA may provide an advance against future benefit payments.

Duration Up to 48 months of full-time training or its equivalent in part-time training. If a veteran with a serious disability receives services under an extended evaluation to improve training potential, the total of the extended evaluation and the training phases of the rehabilitation program may exceed 48 months. Usually, the veteran must complete a rehabilitation program within 12 years from the date of notification of entitlement to compensation by the VA. Following completion of the training portion of a rehabilitation program, a veteran may receive counseling and job search and adjustment services for 18 months.

Additional Information The program may also provide employment assistance, self-employment assistance, training in a rehabilitation facility, or college and other training. Veterans who are seriously disabled may receive services and assistance to improve their ability to live more independently in their community. After completion of the training phase, the VA will assist the veteran to find and hold a suitable job.

Number awarded Varies each year.

Deadline Applications are accepted at any time.

[608]
WEST VIRGINIA SPACE GRANT CONSORTIUM UNDERGRADUATE NASA SPACE GRANT FELLOWSHIPS

West Virginia Space Grant Consortium
c/o West Virginia University
College of Engineering and Mineral Resources
G-68 Engineering Sciences Building
P.O. Box 6070
Morgantown, WV 26506-6070
(304) 293-4099   Fax: (304) 293-4970
E-mail: nasa@cemr.wvu.edu
Web: www.cemr.wvu.edu/~wwwnasa

Summary To provide financial assistance to high school seniors who wish to attend academic institutions affiliated with the West Virginia Space Grant Consortium to prepare for a career in space-related science or engineering.

Eligibility This program is open to high school seniors in West Virginia who are planning to attend a college or university that is a member of the West Virginia Space Grant Consortium. U.S. citizenship is required. Selection is based on academic record and desire to pursue a career in science or engineering. The consortium is a component of the Space Grant program of the U.S. National Aeronautics and Space Administration (NASA), which encourages participation by women, underrepresented minorities, and persons with disabilities.

Financial data The program provides payment of full tuition, fees, room, and board.

Duration 4 years.

Additional Information Funding for this program is provided by NASA. During the summers, some recipients work at a NASA center on a project under the supervision of a NASA advisor; others work with researchers at their respective colleges. The consortium includes Bethany College, Fairmont State College, Marshall University, Salem International University, Shepherd College, West Liberty State College, West Virginia Institute of Technology, West Virginia State College, West Virginia University, West Virginia Wesleyan College, and Wheeling-Jesuit University.

Number awarded Varies each year.

Deadline Each participating college or university establishes its own deadline.

[609]
WEST VIRGINIA SPACE GRANT CONSORTIUM UNDERGRADUATE SCHOLARSHIP PROGRAM

West Virginia Space Grant Consortium
c/o West Virginia University
College of Engineering and Mineral Resources
G-68 Engineering Sciences Building
P.O. Box 6070
Morgantown, WV 26506-6070
(304) 293-4099   Fax: (304) 293-4970
E-mail: nasa@cemr.wvu.edu
Web: www.cemr.wvu.edu/~wwwnasa

Summary To provide financial assistance to undergraduates at academic institutions affiliated with the West Virginia Space Grant Consortium who wish to prepare for a career in space-related science or engineering.

Eligibility This program is open to undergraduates at member institutions of the consortium. Applicants must be U.S. citizens and West Virginia residents. Selection is based on academic record and desire to pursue a career in science or engineering. The consortium is a component of the Space Grant program of the U.S. National Aeronautics and Space Administration (NASA), which encourages participation by women, underrepresented minorities, and persons with disabilities.

Financial data Stipends are either $2,000 or $1,000.

Duration 1 year.

Additional Information Funding for this program is provided by NASA. In addition to their class work, recipients either work with faculty members in their major department on a research project or participate in the Consortium Challenge Program by working with elementary students on their science projects. The consortium members are Bethany College, Fairmont State College, Marshall University, Salem International University, Shepherd College, West Liberty State College, West Virginia Institute of Technology, West Virginia State College, West Virginia University, West Virginia Wesleyan College, and Wheeling-Jesuit University.

Number awarded Varies each year.

Deadline Each participating college or university establishes its own deadline.

[610]
WISCONSIN PART-TIME STUDY GRANTS FOR VETERANS AND THEIR DEPENDENTS

Wisconsin Department of Veterans Affairs
30 West Mifflin Street
P.O. Box 7843
Madison, WI 53707-7843
(608) 266-1311   Toll-free: (800) WIS-VETS
Fax: (608) 267-0403
E-mail: wdvaweb@dva.state.wi.us
Web: dva.state.wi.us/ben_education.asp

Summary To provide financial assistance for part-time undergraduate or graduate education to 1) Wisconsin veterans or 2) the widow(er)s or dependent children of deceased veterans.

Eligibility Applicants for these grants must be veterans (must have served on active duty for at least 2 consecutive years or for at least 90 days during specified wartime periods) and residents of Wisconsin at the time of making the application. They must also have been Wisconsin residents either at the time of entry into active duty or for at least 5 consecutive years after completing service on active duty. Unremarried widow(er)s and minor or dependent children of deceased veterans who would qualify if the veteran were alive today are also eligible for these grants, as long as they are Wisconsin residents. Students who have not yet completed a bachelor's degree are eligible for these grants even if they are also receiving Montgomery GI Bill benefits from the U.S. Department of Veterans Affairs. Recipients must enroll in part-time study (11 credits or less if they do not have a bachelor's degree or 8 credits or less if they do). They may enroll at any accredited college, university, or vocational technical school in Wisconsin, whether state-supported or private; they may also attend out-of-state schools that are within 50 miles of the Wisconsin border if the course is not offered at a Wisconsin school within 50 miles of their residence. Qualifying programs include undergraduate study, graduate study if the student has only a bachelor's degree, correspondence courses, on-the-job training, apprenticeships, internships, and any other study related to the student's occupational, professional, or educational goals. Graduate students are not eligible if 1) they have already received a master's degree, doctor's degree, or equivalent; or 2) they are still entitled to U.S. Department of Veterans Affairs educational benefits. Students with a current gross annual income greater than $47,500 (plus $500 for each dependent in excess of 2) are not eligible.

Financial data Eligible applicants are entitled to reimbursement of up to 85% of the costs of tuition and fees. Veterans with a service-connected disability that is rated 30% or higher may be reimbursed for up to 100% of tuition and fees. Students must pay the costs when they register and then obtain reimbursement after completion of the course of study.

Duration Applicants may receive no more than 4 of these grants during a 12-month period.

Number awarded Varies each year.

Deadline Applications may be submitted at any time, but they must be received within 60 days following completion of the course.

[611]
WISCONSIN SPACE GRANT CONSORTIUM UNDERGRADUATE RESEARCH AWARDS

Wisconsin Space Grant Consortium
c/o University of Wisconsin at Madison
Space Science and Engineering Center
1225 West Dayton Street, Room 251
Madison, WI 53706-1280
(608) 263-4206   Fax: (608) 263-5974
E-mail: toma@ssec.wisc.edu
Web: www.uwgb.edu/wsgc

Summary To provide funding to undergraduate students at colleges and universities participating in the Wisconsin Space Grant Consortium (WSGC) who are interested in conducting space-related research.

Eligibility This program is open to undergraduate students enrolled at 1 of the institutions participating in the WSGC. Applicants must be U.S. citizens; be enrolled full time in an undergraduate program related to space science, aerospace, or interdisciplinary space studies; and have a GPA of 3.0 or higher. They must be proposing to create and implement a small research project of their own design as academic year, summer, or part-time employment that is directly related to their interests and career objectives in space science, aerospace, or space-related studies. Students must request a faculty or research staff member on their campus to act as an advisor; the consortium locates a scientist or engineer from 1 of the research-intensive universities to serve as a second mentor for successful applicants. The consortium especially encourages applications from students pursuing interdisciplinary space studies (e.g., engineering, the sciences, architecture, law, business, and medicine), underrepresented minorities, women, and persons with disabilities. Selection is based on academic performance and space-related promise.

Financial data Stipends up to $3,500 per year or summer session are available. An additional $500 may be awarded for exceptional expenses, such as high travel costs.

Duration 1 academic year or summer.

Additional Information Funding for this program is provided by the U.S. National Aeronautics and Space Administration. The schools participating in the consortium include the University of Wisconsin campuses at Green Bay, La Crosse, Madison, Milwaukee, Oshkosh, Parkside, and Whitewater; College of the Menominee Nation; Marquette University; Carroll College; Lawrence University; Milwaukee School of Engineering; Ripon College; and Medical College of Wisconsin.

Number awarded Varies each year; recently, 9 of these grants were awarded.

Deadline February of each year.

[612]
WISCONSIN SPACE GRANT CONSORTIUM UNDERGRADUATE SCHOLARSHIPS

Wisconsin Space Grant Consortium
c/o University of Wisconsin at Green Bay
Natural and Applied Sciences
2420 Nicolet Drive
Green Bay, WI 54311-7001
(920) 465-2941   Fax: (920) 465-2376
E-mail: brandts@uwgb.edu
Web: www.uwgb.edu/wsgc

Summary To provide financial support to undergraduate students at universities participating in the Wisconsin Space Grant Consortium (WSGC).

Eligibility This program is open to undergraduate students enrolled at 1 of the universities participating in the WSGC. Applicants must be U.S. citizens; be working full time on a bachelor's degree in space science, aerospace, or interdisciplinary space studies (including, but not limited to, engineering, the sciences, architecture, law, business, and medicine); and have a GPA of 3.0 or higher. The consortium especially encourages applications from underrepresented minorities, women, and students with disabilities. Selection is based on academic performance and potential for success.

Financial data Stipends up to $1,500 per year are available.

Duration 1 academic year.

Additional Information Funding for this program is provided by the U.S. National Aeronautics and Space Administration. The schools participating in the consortium include the University of Wisconsin campuses at Green Bay, La Crosse, Madison, Milwaukee, Oshkosh, Parkside, and Whitewater; College of the Menominee Nation; Marquette University; Carroll College; Lawrence University; Milwaukee School of Engineering; Ripon College; and Medical College of Wisconsin.

Number awarded Varies each year; recently, 21 of these scholarships were awarded.

Deadline February of each year.

[613]
WISCONSIN TALENT INCENTIVE PROGRAM (TIP) GRANTS

Wisconsin Higher Educational Aids Board
131 West Wilson Street, Room 902
P.O. Box 7885
Madison, WI 53707-7885
(608) 266-1665   Fax: (608) 267-2808
E-mail: john.whitt@heab.state.wi.us
Web: heab.state.wi.us/programs.html

Summary To provide financial assistance for college to needy and educationally disadvantaged students in Wisconsin.

Eligibility This program is open to residents of Wisconsin entering a college or university in the state who meet requirements of both financial need and educational disadvantage. Financial need qualifications include 1) family contribution (a dependent student whose expected parent contribution is $200 or less, an independent student with dependents whose academic year contribution is $200 or less, or an independent student with no dependents whose maximum contribution is $1,200 or less); 2) AFDC benefits (a dependent student whose family is receiving AFDC benefits or an independent student who is receiving AFDC benefits); or 3) unemployment (a dependent student whose parents are ineligible for unemployment compensation and have no current income from employment, or an independent student and spouse, if married, who are ineligible for unemployment compensation and have no current income from employment). Educational disadvantage qualifications include students who are 1) minorities (African American, Native American, Hispanic, or southeast Asian); 2) enrolled in a special academic support program due to insufficient academic preparation; 3) a first-generation college student (neither parent graduated from a 4-year college or university); 4) disabled according to the Department of Workforce Development, Division of Vocational Rehabilitation; 5) currently or formerly incarcerated in a correctional institution; or 6) from an environmental and academic background that deters the pursuit of educational plans. Students already in college are not eligible.

Financial data Grants range up to $1,800 per year.

Duration 1 year; may be renewed up to 4 additional years provided the recipient continues to be a Wisconsin resident enrolled at least half time in a degree or certificate program, makes satisfactory academic progress, demonstrates financial need, and remains enrolled continuously from semester to semester and from year to year. If recipients withdraw from school or cease to attend classes for any reason (other than medical necessity), they may not reapply.

Number awarded Varies each year.

[614]
WISCONSIN TUITION AND FEE REIMBURSEMENT GRANTS

Wisconsin Department of Veterans Affairs
30 West Mifflin Street
P.O. Box 7843
Madison, WI 53707-7843
(608) 266-1311   Toll-free: (800) WIS-VETS
Fax: (608) 267-0403
E-mail: wdvaweb@dva.state.wi.us
Web: dva.state.wi.us/ben_education.asp

Summary To provide financial assistance for undergraduate education to Wisconsin veterans.

Eligibility This program is open to veterans (must have served on active duty for at least 2 years or for the

full period of their initial service obligation, whichever is less) who are current residents of Wisconsin and were also residents of Wisconsin either at the time of entry into service or for 5 consecutive years after completing active duty. Students may attend any institution, center, or school within the University of Wisconsin System or the Wisconsin Technical College System as part-time or full-time undergraduates. Any applicant with a current gross annual income greater than $47,500 (plus $500 for each dependent in excess of 2) does not qualify.

Financial data This program provides reimbursement of up to 85% of the costs of tuition and fees. Veterans with a service-connected disability that is rated 30% or higher may be reimbursed for up to 100% of tuition and fees.

Duration These grants are available for courses taken within 10 years of separation from active-duty military service. Veterans may receive reimbursement for up to 120 credits of part-time study or 8 semesters of full-time study.

Number awarded Varies each year.

Deadline Applications may be submitted at any time, but no later than 60 days after the ending date of the semester for which reimbursement is sought.

[615]
WSTLA PRESIDENTS' SCHOLARSHIP

Washington State Trial Lawyers Association
1809 Seventh Avenue, Suite 1500
Seattle, WA 98101-1328
(206) 464-1011   Fax: (206) 464-0703
E-mail: wstla@wstla.org
Web: www.wstla.org

Summary To provide financial assistance for college to Washington residents who have a disability or have been a victim of injury.

Eligibility This program is open to seniors at high schools in Washington who are planning to work on a bachelor's degree at an institution of higher education in the state. Applicants must be able to demonstrate 1) financial need; 2) a history of achievement despite having been a victim of injury or overcoming a disability, handicap, or similar challenge; 3) a record of serving others; and 4) a commitment to apply their education toward helping others.

Financial data Stipends average $2,500. Funds are paid directly to the recipient's chosen institution of higher learning to be used for tuition, room, board, and fees.

Duration 1 year.

Additional Information This fund was established in 1991.

Number awarded 1 or more each year.

Deadline March of each year.

[616]
WYOMING SPACE GRANT CONSORTIUM UNDERGRADUATE RESEARCH FELLOWSHIPS

Wyoming Space Grant Consortium
c/o University of Wyoming
Physical Sciences Building, Room 210
P.O. Box 3905
Laramie, WY 82071-3905
(307) 766-2862   Fax: (307) 766-2652
E-mail: wy.spacegrant@uwyo.edu
Web: wyomingspacegrant.uwyo.edu

Summary To provide funding for space-related research to undergraduate students in Wyoming.

Eligibility This program is currently open to undergraduate students at the University of Wyoming and all community colleges in Wyoming. Applicants must be U.S. citizens who are interested in conducting a space-related research project under the mentorship of a faculty member. A major in science or engineering is not required, because the program assumes that even non-science majors broaden their educations with a research experience. The faculty mentor must have active status and/or plan to be on site and readily available to the student. Selection is based on the scientific merit of the proposed project, the pedagogical benefits to the student as a result of the overall research experience, and the quality of the proposal and recommendations. Wyoming Space Grant is a component of the Space Grant program of the U.S. National Aeronautics and Space Administration (NASA), which encourages participation by women, underrepresented minorities, and persons with disabilities.

Financial data Grants range up to $5,000. Funds may be used only for undergraduate salary support, at the rate of $7.75 per hour. Tuition is not provided for the student's home institution, special institutes, or off-campus programs. Other expenditures not usually supported include travel, page charges, equipment, and supplies; applicants are encouraged to seek matching funds to cover those expenditures, and proposals that include matching by nonfederal funds are given priority.

Duration Research may be conducted during the academic year or summer.

Additional Information This program is funded by NASA. Recipients are expected to keep the program informed of their progress, submit a final report in a timely manner, participate in publications of research results, and present a colloquium on their research.

Number awarded 4 to 6 each year.

Deadline February of each year.

[617]
YELLOW RIBBON SCHOLARSHIP

National Tourism Foundation
Attn: Scholarships
546 East Main Street
Lexington, KY 40508-2342
(859) 226-4444 Toll-free: (800) 682-8886
Fax: (859) 226-4437 E-mail: ntf@ntastaff.com
Web: www.ntfonline.org

Summary To provide financial assistance for college to students with disabilities who are planning a career in the travel and tourism industry.

Eligibility This program is open to students with a physical or sensory disability (verified by an accredited physician) who are seeking an education at any level beyond high school. Both high school seniors and currently-enrolled college students may apply; high school applicants must have at least a 3.0 GPA and college applicants must have at least a 2.5 GPA. Applicants must be residents of and studying in North America, be planning a career in the travel or tourism industry (e.g., hotel management, restaurant management, tourism), and submit an essay on how they intend to use their education in the field. They must also submit 2 letters of recommendation, 1 from a faculty member and 1 from a professional in the travel industry.

Financial data The stipend is $6,000.

Duration 1 year.

Additional Information Award winners also receive complimentary registration and an all-expense paid trip (valued at more than $3,000) to the association's annual convention, as well as a 1-year subscription to *Courier* magazine, *Tuesday* newsletter, and *NTF Headlines* newsletter. In any 1 year, applicants may receive only 1 award from the association.

Number awarded 1 each year.

Deadline April of each year.

[618]
11 SEPTEMBER MEMORIAL SCHOLARSHIP

Association of Investment Professionals
Attn: 11 September Memorial Scholarship Fund
P.O. Box 3668
Charlottesville, VA 22903-0668
(434) 951-5344 Toll-free: (800) 237-8132
E-mail: rich.wyler@aimr.org
Web: www.aimr.org

Summary To provide financial assistance for selected majors in college to individuals disabled in the September 11 terrorist attacks or to the relatives of individuals injured or killed in the attacks.

Eligibility College scholarships are offered to those who meet the following 2 criteria: 1) they were permanently disabled in the attacks, or were the spouses, domestic partners, or dependents of anyone killed or permanently disabled in the attacks, and 2) they will be pursuing a college-level education in finance, economics, or related fields. Applicants may be residents of any state or country.

Financial data Annual stipends range up to $25,000.

Duration 1 year; renewable up to 3 additional years.

Additional Information Association for Investment Management and Research (AIMR) lost at least 56 of its members and Chartered Financial Analyst candidates in the terrorist attacks of 11 September.

Deadline Applications may be submitted at any time.

Fellowships/Grants

[619]
AAAS/NIH SCIENCE POLICY FELLOWSHIPS

American Association for the Advancement of Science
Attn: Science and Technology Policy Fellowship Programs
1200 New York Avenue, N.W.
Washington, DC 20005-3920
(202) 326-6700 Fax: (202) 289-4950
E-mail: fellowships@aaas.org
Web: fellowships.aaas.org/nih

Summary To provide postdoctoral and mid-career scientists and engineers with an opportunity to work at the National Institutes of Health (NIH) in Bethesda, Maryland.

Eligibility Applicants must have a Ph.D., M.D. or equivalent doctoral-level degree at the time of application in a physical, biological, or behavioral science; medicine; any field of engineering; or any relevant interdisciplinary field. They must 1) be critical thinkers who are articulate, adaptable, and able to work with a variety of people with different professional backgrounds; 2) demonstrate exceptional competence in a specific area of science; 3) be cognizant of and demonstrate sensitivity toward policy issues; and 4) have a strong interest in applying their professional knowledge toward the development of health policy. U.S. citizenship is required; federal employees are not eligible. Underrepresented minorities and persons with disabilities are encouraged to apply.

Financial data The stipend ranges from $60,000 to $75,000, depending on the fellow's education and experience. Also provided are allowances for health insurance, relocation, and professional travel.

Duration 1 year, beginning in September; may be renewed 1 additional year.

Additional Information Fellows work at 1 of the NIH institutes or centers, the Office of Science Policy, or the Office of the Director. Responsibilities may include the

following: collect and analyze scientific and technical information pertinent to the preparation of reports and other documents regarding a broad range of NIH research policy and planning issues; participate in the evaluation of scientific opportunities, funding implications, and impact of federal policies on the conduct of biomedical research; initiate scholarly activities and coordinate analytic approaches to evaluate and interpret the economic impact of biomedical research on public health and society; participate in activities that consider and advance safeguards of research on human subjects; coordinate and organize planning and policy activities in response to Congressional actions and recommendations of external advisors and the NIH leadership; promote policies and planning that enhance the interactions among public and private research sectors with the goals of fostering collaboration and improved efficiency in the transfer of scientific knowledge and technologies to benefit the health of the nation; and advise on the development of policies to promote and advance the public awareness of, and interest in, biomedical research and health benefits to society.

Number awarded Up to 2 each year.

Deadline January of each year.

[620]
AAAS/NSF FELLOWSHIP PROGRAM

American Association for the Advancement of Science
Attn: Science and Technology Policy Fellowship Programs
1200 New York Avenue, N.W.
Washington, DC 20005-3920
(202) 326-6700   Fax: (202) 289-4950
E-mail: fellowships@aaas.org
Web: fellowships.aaas.org/research

Summary To provide postdoctoral and mid-career scientists and engineers with an opportunity to work at the National Science Foundation (NSF) in Arlington, Virginia.

Eligibility Applicants must have a Ph.D. or equivalent doctoral-level degree at the time of application in a physical, biological, or social science or any field of engineering; persons with a master's degree in engineering and at least 3 years of post-degree experience are also eligible. They must be interested in working at the NSF. Candidates must demonstrate exceptional competence in some area of science or engineering directly related to the focus of the program; they should be critical thinkers who are articulate, adaptable, and adept at working with a variety of people from differing professional backgrounds, including decision makers and others outside of the scientific and engineering community. U.S. citizenship is required; federal employees are not eligible. Underrepresented minorities and persons with disabilities are especially encouraged to apply.

Financial data The stipend ranges from $60,000 to $74,000, plus allowances for health insurance, relocation, and professional travel.

Duration 1 year, beginning in September.

Additional Information Fellows work at the NSF, learning how it funds science and providing scientific, engineering, and educational input on issues relating to its mission. They are placed in offices throughout the NSF, working on projects of mutual interest to the fellows and the host directorate or office. Fellows work with staff involved in planning, development, and oversight of agency programs in all fields of fundamental scientific and engineering research as well as technology, education, and public, legal, and legislative affairs.

Number awarded Approximately 3 each year.

Deadline January of each year.

[621]
AAAS/NTI FELLOWSHIPS IN GLOBAL SECURITY

American Association for the Advancement of Science
Attn: Science and Technology Policy Fellowship Programs
1200 New York Avenue, N.W.
Washington, DC 20005-3920
(202) 326-6700   Fax: (202) 289-4950
E-mail: fellowships@aaas.org
Web: fellowships.aaas.org/nti

Summary To provide postdoctoral and mid-career biomedical and public health experts with an opportunity to work in Congressional offices in the area of biological threats.

Eligibility Applicants must have a Dr.P.H., D.V.M., M.D., or Ph.D. in the biological sciences, public health, or a related field at the time of the application. They must be able to write clearly; be able to articulate scientific concepts for non-scientific audiences; have the ability to work productively in an interdisciplinary setting with policy-makers and others outside the public health and medical/bioscience communities; have an interest in applying public health, medical, and scientific knowledge to national security and foreign policy issues; have an appreciation of political, social, and economic issues; and have a strong desire to reduce the global threat of bioweapon use. International experience is desirable but not required. U.S. citizenship is required; federal employees are not eligible. Underrepresented minorities and persons with disabilities are encouraged to apply.

Financial data The stipend is $60,000, plus allowances for health insurance, relocation, and professional travel.

Duration 1 year, beginning in September; may be renewed 1 additional year.

Additional Information Fellows work in collaboration with the Nuclear Threat Initiative (NTI), established in 2001 by Ted Turner and former U.S. Senator Sam Nunn,

to reduce global threats from nuclear, biological, and chemical weapons. Fellows work to bring public health and medical expertise to bear on issues related to biological weapons, bioterrorism nonproliferation, and federal-response planning efforts. Information is also available from NTI, 1747 Pennsylvania Avenue, N.W., Seventh Floor, Washington, D.C. 20006, (202) 296-4810, (202) 296-4811.

Number awarded At least 1 each year.
Deadline January of each year.

[622]
ABC TALENT DEVELOPMENT SCHOLARSHIP-GRANT PROGRAM

ABC Entertainment
Attn: Talent Development Programs
500 South Buena Vista Street
Burbank, CA 91521-4390
(818) 460-7770 E-mail: abc.fellowships@abc.com
Web: www.abctalendevelopment.com

Summary To provide funding to emerging artists (including high school, college, and graduate students) from diverse backgrounds in selected cities who are interested in completing a creative project.

Eligibility This program is open to high school, college, and graduate students from Chicago, Houston, Los Angeles, Minneapolis, New York, Raleigh-Durham, and Washington, D.C. Applications must be submitted through participating sponsors (high schools, colleges, universities, or civic, social service, or professional organizations) in those communities. Emerging artists who are members of sponsoring organizations are also eligible to apply. Many of the designated sponsors focus on service to minorities and students with disabilities, because a goal of the program is to discover, develop, and encourage creative talent from diverse backgrounds. Applicants must be proposing to complete an existing creative project. They must submit a work resume, personal bio, essay of 500 to 800 words on their career goals and interest in the field, and samples of the proposed project. If the project involves a screenplay or television script, submissions must include a treatment, 10 pages of proposed story idea, and a detailed budget. If the project involves a video, submissions must include a sample reel of a previously completed film or video project, a proposal, and a detailed budget. Material that may not be submitted in support of an application includes published material (e.g., short stories), scripts adapted from other material not indicative of writing for television or film, sequels to motion pictures, plays, magazine articles, drawings, projects that have been fully executed creatively (i.e., polished scripts or videos needing post production only), or projects that have been previously entered into a competition or festival.

Financial data Individuals receive grants of $20,000 to help finance the development of their project. Sponsoring organizations with winning submissions receive $10,000 grants to further develop their creative programs.

Duration 1 year.

Additional Information Selected participants are paired with a mentor at Walt Disney Studios or ABC Entertainment. The program concludes with a 3-day workshop in Los Angeles. Recently, the sponsoring organizations included the International Latino Cultural Center of Chicago, the Mille Lacs Band of Ojibwe, American Indian Artists, Inc, the International Agency for Minority Artist Affairs, National Hispanic Foundation for the Arts, National Asian American Telecommunications Association, National Association for the Advancement of Colored People, and the Media Access Office of the California Governor's Committee on Employment of People with Disabilities. This program began in 2001.

Number awarded Varies each year; recently, 16 of these grants were awarded.

Deadline December of each year.

[623]
ACADEMY OF NATURAL SCIENCES RESEARCH EXPERIENCES FOR UNDERGRADUATES FELLOWSHIPS

Academy of Natural Sciences of Philadelphia
Attn: REU Coordinator
1900 Benjamin Franklin Parkway
Philadelphia, PA 19103-1195
(215) 299-1000   Fax: (215) 299-1028
E-mail: reucoordinator@acnatsci.org
Web: www.acnatsci.org/research/reu.html

Summary To provide undergraduate students with an opportunity to conduct summer research in botany, entomology, ichthyology, malacology, ornithology, or paleontology at the Academy of Natural Sciences of Philadelphia.

Eligibility This program is open to U.S. citizens and permanent residents who are entering their sophomore, junior, or senior year at a college or university. Applicants must be interested in working on a research project under the mentorship of an academy scientist in systematics, natural history, evolutionary biology, and ecology. Their proposals should draw upon the academy's collections in botany, entomology, ichthyology, malacology, ornithology, and paleontology, as well as the library and archives. Applications are particularly encouraged from women, minorities, and students with disabilities.

Financial data The program provides travel to and from Philadelphia; housing; expenses for supplies, field trips, and research; and a stipend of $300 per week.

Duration 10 weeks, beginning in June.

Number awarded Varies each year.

Deadline February of each year.

[624]
ADVANCE FELLOWS AWARDS

National Science Foundation
Attn: ADVANCE Program
4201 Wilson Boulevard
Arlington, VA 22230
(703) 292-5111   TDD: (703) 292-5090
E-mail: ahogan@nsf.gov
Web: www.nsf.gov/home/crssprgm/advance

Summary To provide funding to women scholars who are entering or reentering an academic career and wish to undertake research and other projects in science and engineering fields supported by the National Science Foundation (NSF).

Eligibility This program is open to women who are affiliated or plan to affiliate with an institution of higher learning in the United States, its territories or possessions, or the Commonwealth of Puerto Rico. Applicants must hold a Ph.D. in a field of science or engineering supported by NSF; be a U.S. citizen, national, or permanent resident; and be establishing a full-time independent academic research and education career. They must 1) have received their first doctoral degree in science or engineering from 1 to 4 years previously, be in a postdoctoral or equivalent status, have never held a tenure-track or tenured position, and have not served as a principal investigator on any NSF award with the exception of doctoral dissertation, postdoctoral fellowship, or research-planning grants; or 2) be out of the full-time science and engineering workforce and have been out of that workforce for 2 to 8 years to attend to family responsibilities; or 3) either have resigned from a full-time academic science or engineering appointment because of relocation of a spouse in the preceding 24 months and not hold a tenure-track or tenured position or be planning to leave a full-time academic science or engineering appointment because of relocation of a spouse to occur in the 12 months following the proposal due date. All applications must include a career development component that describes plans for career-enhancing research and education activities. Applicants who already hold an academic affiliation must describe the facilities at their institution that are available for them to carry out their career development plan; applicants who are not currently affiliated must identify the institutional resources necessary for the proposed activities and describe plans for affiliating with a host institution. Members of underrepresented minority groups and individuals with disabilities are especially encouraged to apply.

Financial data Awards provide annual salary support of up to $60,000 plus applicable fringe benefits and a career development allotment of up to $25,000 per year (to be used for activities directly related to the proposed research and education activities in the fellow's career development plan, such as computing, travel to professional workshops, materials and supplies, publication charges, technical support, student support, and related needs). Indirect costs may be included at the host or home institution's standard rate.

Duration Up to 3 years.

Additional Information Information is available from coordinators in each of the NSF directorates; for a list of their names and telephone numbers, contact the sponsor. If the recipient does not currently hold an academic appointment, the award will commence only when she affiliates with a host institution that agrees to provide resources necessary to support the proposed career-development plan.

Number awarded 20 to 40 each year.

Deadline June of each year.

[625]
AEROSPACE ILLINOIS SPACE GRANT CONSORTIUM PROGRAM

Aerospace Illinois Space Grant Consortium
c/o University of Illinois at Urbana-Champaign
Department of Aeronautical and Astronomical
   Engineering
308 Talbot Lab
104 South Wright Street
Urbana, IL 61801-2935
(217) 244-8048   Fax: (217) 244-0720
E-mail: dejeffer@uiuc.edu
Web: www.aae.uiuc.edu/Aeroill/index.html

Summary To provide financial support to faculty, staff, and students at Aerospace Illinois member institutions who are interested in pursuing space-related academic activities.

Eligibility Aerospace Illinois has established 4 program elements: 1) undergraduate/high school teaching and research, to attract undergraduates and secondary school students to aerospace science and engineering; 2) training in graduate research, through research experiences focused on aerospace science and engineering; 3) outreach and public service, to employ the region's extensive existing public educational information networks and outreach programs to attract the highest quality student populations, especially underrepresented minorities, women, and persons with disabilities; and 4) fellowships with industry, to add substantially to the national aerospace science and engineering pool. Aerospace Illinois is a component of the U.S. National Aeronautics and Space Administration which encourages applications from women, minorities, and persons with disabilities.

Financial data Awards depend on the availability of funds and the nature of the proposal.

Duration Depends on the program.

Additional Information Aerospace Illinois includes 4 member institutions: the University of Illinois at Urbana-Champaign (UIUC), the University of Chicago (UC), Illinois Institute of Technology (IIT), and Northwestern University (NU). It also includes 3 affiliate institutions: Southern Illinois University (SIU), Western Illinois University

(WIU), and the University of Illinois at Chicago. This program is funded by NASA. Recently, undergraduate/high school teaching and research projects included the aerodynamic facilities tour at IIT, the high school summer research program at NU, K-12 education programs at SIU, Motivation through Aviation and Space at WIU, Camp 21st at UIUC, Illinois Aerospace Institute at UIUC, and the WYSE summer program at UIUC. Training in graduate research projects included control of jet screech noise at IIT, electronic component cooling at IIT, high lift airfoils at IIT, high reynolds number turbulent boundary layers at IIT, investigation of incipient stall at IIT, non-equilibrium turbulent layers at IIT, independent research at NU, experiments in high energy astrophysics research support at UC, and the chemical laser lab at UIUC. Outreach and public service projects included the interprofessional project at IIT, Dearborn Observatory open house at NU, NASA College Research Program at NU, and the design lab at UIUC. Fellowships with industry included the NASA space grant fellowship at IIT, the NASA space grant minority scholarship at IIT, the NASA college summer research program at NU, graduate fellowships at UC, undergraduate scholarships at UC, Aerospace Illinois scholarships at UIUC, Engineering of the Future at UIUC, NASA Academy at UIUC, space grant/industry fellowships at UIUC, and women in engineering scholarships at UIUC.

Number awarded Varies each year.

[626]
AFRICAN AMERICAN STUDIES PROGRAM VISITING SCHOLARS

University of Houston
African American Studies Program
Attn: Visiting Scholars Program
315 Agnes Arnold Hall
Houston, TX 77204-3047
(713) 743-2811   Fax: (713) 743-2818
E-mail: jconyers@uh.edu
Web: www.hfac.uh.edu/aas/visitgrad.html

Summary To provide support to junior scholars who are interested in conducting research on the African American community while affiliated with the University of Houston's African American Studies Program.

Eligibility Applications are sought from junior scholars in social sciences, humanities, or African American studies who completed their Ph.D. within the past 6 years. They must be interested in conducting research on the African American community while affiliated with the University of Houston's African American Studies Program and in assuming a tenured or tenure-track position there after their residency as a Visiting Scholar is completed. Applicants proposing to conduct research on the African American community in Houston and the state of Texas are given priority. Interested applicants should submit a current curriculum vitae, a 2-page description of the proposed research, 3 letters of recommendation, and a syllabus of the undergraduate course to be taught. Minorities, women, veterans, and persons with disabilities are specifically encouraged to apply.

Financial data Visiting Scholars receive a salary appropriate to their rank.

Duration 1 academic year.

Additional Information Visiting Scholars are assigned a research assistant, if needed, and are provided administrative support. Recipients must teach 1 class related to African American studies. They are required to be in residence at the university for the entire academic year and must make 2 presentations on their research. In addition, they must acknowledge the sponsor's support in any publication that results from their tenure at the university.

Number awarded 1 each year.

Deadline December of each year.

[627]
AHRQ HEALTH SERVICES RESEARCH GRANTS

Agency for Healthcare Research and Quality
Attn: Division of Grants Management
2101 East Jefferson Street, Suite 601
Rockville, MD 20852-4908
(301) 594-1844   Fax: (301) 594-3210
E-mail: mlam@ahrq.gov
Web: www.ahrq.gov

Summary To provide funding to scholars interested in conducting research that is designed to improve the outcomes, quality, cost, and utilization of health care services.

Eligibility This program is open to investigators at domestic and foreign, nonprofit, public and private organizations, including universities, clinics, units of state and local governments, nonprofit firms, and nonprofit foundations. Applicants must be proposing research in 1 of the priority areas of the Agency for Healthcare Research and Quality (AHRQ): 1) support improvements in health outcomes; 2) strengthen quality measurement and improvement; and 3) identify strategies to improve access, foster appropriate use, and reduce unnecessary expenditures. Research should also focus on population groups that are particularly vulnerable to impaired access to and suboptimal quality of care: low-income groups, racial and ethnic minority groups, women, children, the elderly, individuals with special health needs (such as individuals with disabilities and those who need chronic care and end-of-life health care), and individuals living in inner-city, rural, and frontier areas. The agency especially encourages women, members of minority groups, and persons with disabilities to apply as principal investigators.

Financial data The amount of the award depends on the nature of the proposal. Applications for more than $500,000 per year in direct costs must have prior approval from the agency before they will be accepted.

Duration Up to 2 years.

Number awarded Varies each year.
Deadline Applications may be submitted at any time.

[628]
AHRQ INDEPENDENT SCIENTIST AWARD

Agency for Healthcare Research and Quality
Attn: Office of Research Review, Education and Policy
2101 East Jefferson Street, Suite 400
Rockville, MD 20852-4908
(301) 594-1449   E-mail: training@ahrq.gov
Web: www.ahrq.gov

Summary To provide funding to newly independent scientists interested in conducting research to improve the outcomes, effectiveness, quality, cost, and utilization of health care services.

Eligibility This program is open to U.S. citizens or permanent residents who have a clinical (e.g., M.D., D.O., D.D.S.) or research (e.g., Ph.D., Sc.D.) doctoral degree and are no more than 5 years beyond their latest research training experience. Applicants must be interested in conducting health services research designed to 1) support improvements in health outcomes at both the clinical and systems levels; 2) strengthen quality measurement and improvement including the use of evidence-based practice information and tools; 3) identify strategies to improve access, foster appropriate use, and reduce unnecessary expenditures, including research on the organization, financing, and delivery of health care and the characteristics of primary care practices; 4) advance methodologies in health services research, especially cost-effectiveness analysis; and 5) focus on ethical issues across the spectrum of health care delivery. Special attention is paid to applications that focus on developing the careers of investigators who will study minority, child, and older adult health services research; some awards are made specifically to applications that foster the research careers of investigators studying those populations. Awards are also made specifically to individual investigators from predominantly minority institutions. Applications are especially encouraged from women, minorities, and individuals with disabilities.

Financial data Grants provide salary up to $75,000 annually plus associated fringe benefits. Applicants may request additional funding to offset the cost of tuition, fees, books, and travel related to career development. Indirect costs are reimbursed at 8% of modified total direct costs.

Duration 3 to 5 years; nonrenewable.

Additional Information >At least 75% of the recipient's full-time professional effort must be devoted to the program and the remainder devoted to other research-related and/or teaching pursuits consistent with the objectives of the award.

Number awarded Varies each year.

[629]
AHRQ MENTORED CLINICAL SCIENTIST DEVELOPMENT AWARD

Agency for Healthcare Research and Quality
Attn: Office of Research Review, Education and Policy
2101 East Jefferson Street, Suite 400
Rockville, MD 20852-4908
(301) 594-1452   E-mail: training@ahrq.gov
Web: www.ahrq.gov

Summary To provide funding to postdoctorates interested in pursuing additional research training to enable them to become independent investigators in health services research.

Eligibility This program is open to U.S. citizens or permanent residents who have received a clinical doctoral degree (M.D., D.O., D.C., O.D., D.D.S., Pharm.D., or doctorally-prepared nurses). Applicants must have identified a mentor with extensive research experience and be willing to spend at least 75% of full-time professional effort conducting research and developing a research career to improve the outcomes, effectiveness, quality, access to, and cost and utilization of health care services. Special attention is paid to applications that focus on developing the careers of investigators who will study minority, child, and older adult health services research; some awards are made specifically to applications that foster the research careers of investigators studying those populations. Awards are also made specifically to individual investigators from predominantly minority institutions. Applications are especially encouraged from women, minorities, and individuals with disabilities.

Financial data Grants provide salary up to $75,000 annually plus associated fringe benefits. Also available are up to $25,000 per year for research development support (tuition, fees, and books related to career development; research expenses, including supplies, equipment, and technical personnel; travel to research meetings or training; and statistical services, including personnel and computer time) and reimbursement of indirect costs at 8% of modified total direct costs.

Duration 3 to 5 years.

Number awarded Varies each year.

Deadline January, May, or September of each year.

[630]
AHRQ SMALL RESEARCH GRANT PROGRAM

Agency for Healthcare Research and Quality
Attn: Division of Grants Management
2101 East Jefferson Street, Suite 601
Rockville, MD 20852-4908
(301) 594-1840   Fax: (301) 594-3210
E-mail: mburr@ahrq.gov
Web: www.ahrq.gov

Summary To provide funding for small research projects designed to improve the quality, appropriateness,

and effectiveness of health care services and access to those services.
Eligibility This program is open to investigators at domestic, nonprofit, public and private organizations, including universities, clinics, units of state and local governments, nonprofit firms, and nonprofit foundations. Applicants must be proposing projects for promoting improvements in clinical practice and in the organization, financing, and delivery of health care services. Proposals may be for research, evaluation, demonstrations, or pilot studies. The Agency for Healthcare Research and Quality (AHRQ) especially encourages women, members of minority racial and ethnic groups, and persons with disabilities to apply as principal investigators.
Financial data Total direct costs may not exceed $100,000.
Duration Up to 2 years.
Additional Information Funding from this program may not be used for dissertation research.
Number awarded Varies each year.
Deadline March, July, or November of each year.

[631]
AMERICAN METEOROLOGICAL SOCIETY GRADUATE FELLOWSHIP IN THE HISTORY OF SCIENCE

American Meteorological Society
Attn: Fellowship/Scholarship Coordinator
45 Beacon Street
Boston, MA 02108-3693
(617) 227-2426, ext. 246   Fax: (617) 742-8718
E-mail: amsinfo@ametsoc.org
Web: www.ametsoc.org

Summary To provide financial assistance to graduate students interested in conducting dissertation research on the history of meteorology.
Eligibility This program is open to graduate students who are planning to complete a dissertation on the history of the atmospheric or related oceanic or hydrologic sciences. Fellowships may be used to support research at a location away from the student's institution, provided the plan is approved by the student's thesis advisor. In such an instance, an effort is made to place the student into a mentoring relationship with a member of the society at an appropriate institution. The sponsor specifically encourages applications from women, minorities, and students with disabilities who are traditionally underrepresented in the atmospheric and related oceanic sciences.
Financial data The stipend is $15,000 per year.
Duration 1 year.
Number awarded 1 each year.
Deadline February of each year.

[632]
ANDREW W. MELLON POSTDOCTORAL RESEARCH FELLOWSHIP AT OMOHUNDRO INSTITUTE

Omohundro Institute of Early American History and Culture
P.O. Box 8781
Williamsburg, VA 23187-8781
(757) 221-1115   Fax: (757) 221-1047
E-mail: ieahc1@wm.edu
Web: www.wm.edu/oieach/fello.html

Summary To provide funding to scholars in American studies who wish to revise their first book manuscript in residence at the Omohundro Institute of Early American History and Culture in Williamsburg, Virginia.
Eligibility Applicants must have received a Ph.D. at least 12 months previously in a field that encompasses an aspect of the lives of North America's indigenous and immigrant peoples during the colonial, Revolutionary, and early national periods of the United States and the related histories of Canada, the Caribbean, Latin America, the British Isles, Europe, and Africa, from the 16th century to approximately 1815. They must submit a completed book-length manuscript that they wish to revise for publication while in residence at the institute. The manuscript must not be under contract to another publisher, because the institute will hold the rights to publish the revised study. Applicants may not have previously published a book or have a book under contract. Members of underrepresented groups (including people of color, persons with disabilities, Vietnam veterans, and women) are specifically encouraged to apply.
Financial data The fellowship includes a stipend of $45,000, a comprehensive benefits package, funds for travel to conferences and research centers, and access to office, research, and computer facilities at the institute.
Duration 1 year.
Additional Information Funding for this program is provided by the Andrew W. Mellon Foundation.
Number awarded 1 each year.
Deadline October of each year.

[633]
ARCTIC RESEARCH OPPORTUNITIES

National Science Foundation
Attn: Office of Polar Programs
4201 Wilson Boulevard, Room 755S
Arlington, VA 22230
(703) 292-8029   Fax: (703) 292-9082
TDD: (703) 292-5090
Web: www.nsf.gov/od/opp

Summary To provide funding for research related to the Arctic.
Eligibility This program is open to investigators affiliated with U.S. universities, research institutions, or other

organizations, including local or state governments. Applicants must be proposing to conduct research in the 3 program areas of Arctic Natural Sciences (including atmospheric sciences, biological sciences, earth sciences, glaciology, and ocean sciences); Arctic Social Sciences (including anthropology, archaeology, economics, geography, linguistics, political science, psychology, science and technology studies, sociology, traditional knowledge, and related subjects); and Arctic System Science (encompassing 3 components: 1) how do human activities interact with changes in the Arctic to affect the sustainability of ecosystems and societies? 2) what are the limits of Arctic system predictability? and 3) how will changes in Arctic cycles and feedbacks affect Arctic and global systems?). Proposals should involve field studies in the Arctic, although projects outside the Arctic but directly related to Arctic science and engineering are also considered, as are related laboratory and theoretical studies. The program particularly encourages proposals from women, minorities, and persons with disabilities.

Financial data The amounts of the awards depend on the nature of the proposal and the availability of funds.

Number awarded Varies each year. Recently, this program planned to award 130 to 160 grants worth approximately $66 million.

Deadline August or February of each year.

[634]
ARKANSAS GOVERNOR'S COMMISSION ON PEOPLE WITH DISABILITIES FELLOWSHIPS

Arkansas Governor's Commission on People with Disabilities
1616 Brookwood Drive
P.O. Box 3781
Little Rock, AR 72203
(501) 296-1626   Fax: (501) 296-1627
TDD: (501) 296-1623

Summary To provide financial assistance for graduate education to Arkansas students with disabilities.

Eligibility Disabled Arkansas college seniors, college graduates, and graduate students who are planning to pursue graduate education are eligible to apply. Previous winners may also submit an application. Letters of recommendation are required but may not be written by relatives. Selection is based upon academic achievement, severity of disability and resulting functional limitations, desire for further education, contributions to the community, and financial need.

Financial data The stipend varies, up to $500 per year.

Duration 1 year; recipients may reapply.

Additional Information Schools attended by the recipients need not be located in Arkansas.

Number awarded 20 each year.

Deadline January of each year.

[635]
ARKANSAS SPACE GRANT CONSORTIUM COLLABORATIVE RESEARCH GRANTS

Arkansas Space Grant Consortium
c/o University of Arkansas at Little Rock
Graduate Institute of Technology
2801 South University Avenue
Little Rock, AR 72204
(501) 569-8212   Fax: (501) 569-8039
E-mail: asgc@ualr.edu
Web: asgc.ualr.edu/spacegrant

Summary To provide funding to faculty at member universities of the Arkansas Space Grant Consortium (ASGC) for research that involves collaboration with students and faculty at other institutions in Arkansas.

Eligibility This program is open to faculty at institutions that are members of the ASGC. Applicants must be seeking funding for research projects in fields of interest to the National Aeronautics and Space Administration (NASA), including astronomy, biochemistry, biology, chemistry, computer science, earth science, engineering, engineering technology, instrumentation, materials science, mathematics, physics, psychology, and space medicine. Inclusion of faculty and students at other Arkansas institutions of higher education are favorably considered; at least 1 faculty member and 1 student at 1 or more institutions must be funded. Inclusion of women, minorities, and people with disabilities is given special consideration.

Financial data The maximum grant is $15,000 per year. At least $3,000 should be budgeted for activities by faculty and students at the collaborating institutions. No more than $3,000 can be budgeted for the purchase of new equipment.

Duration 1 year. May be renewed for a second year if the grantee submits a proposal for external funding by the end of the first year. May be renewed for a third year if the grantee submits a proposal to at least 2 sources of external funding by the end of the second year.

Additional Information ASGC member institutions are Arkansas State University, University, Arkansas Tech University, Harding University, Henderson State University, Hendrix College, Lyon College, Ouachita Baptist University, University of Central Arkansas, University of Arkansas at Fayetteville, University of Arkansas at Little Rock, University of Arkansas at Montecito, University of Arkansas at Pine Bluff, University of Arkansas for Medical Sciences, and University of the Ozarks. This program is funded by NASA.

Number awarded Varies each year.

[636]
ARKANSAS SPACE GRANT CONSORTIUM RESEARCH INFRASTRUCTURE GRANTS

Arkansas Space Grant Consortium
c/o University of Arkansas at Little Rock
Graduate Institute of Technology
2801 South University Avenue
Little Rock, AR 72204
(501) 569-8212 Fax: (501) 569-8039
E-mail: asgc@ualr.edu
Web: asgc.ualr.edu/spacegrant

Summary To provide research funding to faculty at member universities of the Arkansas Space Grant Consortium (ASGC).

Eligibility This program is open to faculty at institutions that are members of the ASGC. Applicants must be seeking research starter grants for projects that seem likely to receive support from the U.S. National Aeronautics and Space Administration (NASA) and be willing to mentor student scholarship and fellowship research. Fields of study include astronomy, biochemistry, biology, chemistry, computer science, earth science, engineering, engineering technology, instrumentation, materials science, mathematics, physics, psychology, and space medicine. The consortium is a component of NASA's Space Grant program, which encourages participation by underrepresented minorities, women, and persons with disabilities.

Financial data The funding depends on the nature of the proposal.

Duration Up to 3 years.

Additional Information ASGC member institutions are Arkansas State University, University, Arkansas Tech University, Harding University, Henderson State University, Hendrix College, Lyon College, Ouachita Baptist University, University of Central Arkansas, University of Arkansas at Fayetteville, University of Arkansas at Little Rock, University of Arkansas at Montecito, University of Arkansas at Pine Bluff, University of Arkansas for Medical Sciences, and University of the Ozarks. This program is funded by NASA.

Number awarded Varies each year; since this program began in 1990, it has awarded approximately 300 of these grants.

[637]
ASTRONOMY AND ASTROPHYSICS POSTDOCTORAL FELLOWSHIPS

National Science Foundation
Directorate for Mathematical and Physical Sciences
Attn: Division of Astronomical Sciences
4201 Wilson Boulevard, Room 1045
Arlington, VA 22230
(703) 292-4895 TDD: (703) 292-5090
E-mail: efriel@nsf.gov
Web: www.nsf.gov/mps.general.htm

Summary To provide funding to recent doctoral recipients in astronomy or astrophysics who are interested in pursuing a program of research and education.

Eligibility This program is open to U.S. citizens, nationals, and permanent residents who completed a Ph.D. in astronomy or astrophysics during the previous 3 years. Applicants must be interested in a program of research of an observational, instrumental, or theoretical nature, especially research that is particularly facilitated or enabled by new ground-based capability in radio, optical/IR, or solar astrophysics. The proposal must include a coherent program of educational activities, such as teaching a course each year at the host institution or an academic institution with ties to the host institution, or engaging in a significant, coordinated program of outreach or general education. Women, underrepresented minorities, and persons with disabilities are strongly encouraged to apply.

Financial data Grants up to $60,000 per year are available, including stipends of $45,000 per year, a research allowance of $10,000 per year, and an institutional allowance of $5,000 per year.

Duration Up to 3 years.

Number awarded Up to 10 each year.

Deadline October of each year.

[638]
BIUNNO SCHOLARSHIP FOR LAW STUDENTS WITH DISABILITIES

Essex County Bar Association
Attn: Rights of Persons with Disabilities Committee
One Riverfront Plaza, Seventh Floor
Newark, NJ 07102-5497
(973) 622-6207 Fax: (973) 622-4341
Web: www.EssexBar.com

Summary To provide financial assistance to students with disabilities from New Jersey who are interested in attending law school.

Eligibility Applicants must be able to demonstrate a present and permanent physical or mental disability that substantially limits 1 or more of the major life activities (medical documentation is required); be residents of New Jersey, with preference given to Essex County residents; be attending or accepted at a law school; and have earned a GPA of 3.0 or higher as an undergraduate student (if an incoming law student) or in law school. Pri-

ority is given to applicants who are planning a career in the field of advocacy for persons with disabilities. Intent may be demonstrated by completion of a course in disability law, work in a disability or disability-related clinic, or prior job experience in an advocacy field or with a public interest organization. Financial need must be demonstrated.

Financial data Stipends range from $3,000 to $6,000. Funds are paid directly to the recipient's school or to a company providing equipment for the disabled student.

Duration 1 year.

Deadline April of each year.

[639]
BYRD FELLOWSHIP PROGRAM

Ohio State University
Byrd Polar Research Center
Attn: Fellowship Committee
Scott Hall Room 108
1090 Carmack Road
Columbus, OH 43210-1002
(614) 292-0531   Fax: (614) 292-4097
Web: www-bprc.mps.ohio-state.edu

Summary To provide funding to postdoctorates interested in conducting research on the Arctic or Antarctic areas at Ohio State University.

Eligibility This program is open to postdoctorates of superior academic background who are interested in pursuing advanced research on either Arctic or Antarctic problems at the Byrd Polar Research Center at Ohio State University. Applicants must have received their doctorates within the past 5 years. Each application should include a statement of general research interest, a description of the specific research to be conducting during the fellowship, and a curriculum vitae. Women, minorities, Vietnam-era veterans, disabled veterans, and individuals with disabilities are particularly encouraged to apply.

Financial data The stipend is $35,000 per year; an allowance of $3,000 for research and travel is also provided.

Duration 18 months.

Additional Information This program was established by a major gift from the Byrd Foundation in memory of Rear Admiral Richard Evelyn Byrd and Marie Ames Byrd, his wife. Except for field work or other research activities requiring absence from campus, fellows are expected to be in residence at the university for the duration of the program.

Deadline April of each year.

[640]
CALIFORNIA ASSOCIATION FOR POSTSECONDARY EDUCATION AND DISABILITY SCHOLARSHIPS

California Association for Postsecondary Education and Disability
Attn: Executive Assistant
71423 Biskra Road
Rancho Mirage, CA 92270
(760) 346-8206   Fax: (760) 340-5275
TTY: (760) 341-4084   E-mail: caped2000@aol.com
Web: www.caped.net/scholarship.html

Summary To provide financial assistance to undergraduate and graduate students in California who have a disability.

Eligibility This program is open to students at public and private colleges and universities in California who have a disability. Undergraduates must have completed at least 6 semester credits and have a GPA of 2.5 or higher. Graduate students must have completed at least 3 semester units and have a GPA of 3.0 or higher. Applicants must submit a 1-page personal letter that demonstrates writing skills; progress toward meeting educational and vocational goals; how they accommodate their disability; involvement in community activities; and any other personal factor that might strengthen their application. They must also submit a letter of recommendation from a faculty person, verification of disability, official transcripts, proof of current enrollment, and documentation of financial need.

Financial data The stipend is $1,000.

Duration 1 year.

Additional Information Information is also available from Janet Shapiro, Disabled Student Programs and Services, Santa Barbara City College, 721 Cliff Drive, Santa Barbara, CA 93109, (805) 965-0581, ext. 2365, E-mail: shapiro@sbcc.net. This program includes the following named scholarships: the California Association for Postsecondary Education and Disability Conference Scholarship, the California Association for Postsecondary Education and Disability Past Presidents' Scholarship, and the William May Memorial Scholarship.

Number awarded 3 each year.

Deadline August of each year.

[641]
CALIFORNIA SPACE GRANT GRADUATE STUDENT PROGRAM

California Space Grant Consortium
c/o University of California at San Diego
California Space Institute
9500 Gilman Drive, Department 0524
La Jolla, CA 92093
(858) 822-1597　　　　　　Fax: (858) 534-7840
E-mail: spacegrant@ucsd.edu
Web: calspace.ucsd.edu

Summary To provide financial assistance for graduate study and research in space-related science, engineering, or technology at the 8 branches of the University of California.

Eligibility This program is open to graduate students in space-related science, engineering, and technology at the 8 campuses of the UC system. Most programs include research components. U.S. citizenship is required. As the California element of the Space Grant program of the U.S. National Aeronautics and Space Administration (NASA), this program encourages applications from underrepresented ethnic or gender groups and by persons with disabilities.

Financial data Each campus sets its own stipend.

Duration 1 year.

Additional Information This program is funded by NASA.

Number awarded Varies each year.

Deadline Each of the participating UC campuses sets its own deadline.

[642]
CAPED GENERAL EXCELLENCE SCHOLARSHIP

California Association for Postsecondary Education and Disability
Attn: Executive Assistant
71423 Biskra Road
Rancho Mirage, CA 92270
(760) 346-8206　　　　　　Fax: (760) 340-5275
TTY: (760) 341-4084　　E-mail: caped2000@aol.com
Web: www.caped.net/scholarship.html

Summary To provide financial assistance to undergraduate and graduate students in California who have a disability and can demonstrate academic achievement and involvement in community and campus activities.

Eligibility This program is open to students at public and private colleges and universities in California who have a disability. Undergraduates must have completed at least 6 semester credits and have a GPA of 2.5 or higher. Graduate students must have completed at least 3 semester units and have a GPA of 3.0 or higher. Applicants must submit a 1-page personal letter that demonstrates writing skills; progress toward meeting educational and vocational goals; how they accommodate their disability; involvement in community activities; and any other factor that might strengthen their application. They must also submit a letter of recommendation from a faculty member, verification of disability, official transcripts, proof of current enrollment, and documentation of financial need. This award is presented to the applicant who demonstrates the highest level of academic achievement and involvement in community and campus life.

Financial data The stipend is $1,500.

Duration 1 year.

Additional Information Information is also available from Janet Shapiro, Disabled Student Programs and Services, Santa Barbara City College, 721 Cliff Drive, Santa Barbara, CA 93109, (805) 965-0581, ext. 2365, E-mail: shapiro@sbcc.net.

Number awarded 1 each year.

Deadline August of each year.

[643]
CENTURY SCHOLARSHIP

American Library Association
Attn: Association of Specialized and Cooperative
　Library Agencies
50 East Huron Street
Chicago, IL 60611-2795
(312) 280-4396
Toll-free: (800) 545-2433, ext. 4396
Fax: (312) 944-8085　　　　TDD: (312) 944-7298
TDD: (888) 814-7692　　　　E-mail: ascla@ala.org
Web: www.ala.org/ascla/centuryscholarship.html

Summary To provide financial assistance to library science students with disabilities.

Eligibility This program is open to graduate students with disabilities who have been admitted to a library school accredited by the American Library Association. Applicants must submit medical documentation of their disability or disabilities and a description of the services and/or accommodations they require for their studies. U.S. or Canadian citizenship is required. Selection is based on academic excellence, leadership, professional goals, and financial need.

Financial data The stipend is $2,500; funds are to be used for services or accommodations not provided by law or by the university.

Duration 1 year.

Additional Information This scholarship was first offered in 2000.

Number awarded 1 or more each year.

Deadline April of each year.

[644]
CHRISTOPHER REEVE PARALYSIS FOUNDATION FELLOWSHIPS

Vermont Studio Center
80 Pearl Street
P.O. Box 613
Johnson, VT 05656
(802) 635-2727   Fax: (802) 635-2730
E-mail: info@vscvt.org
Web: www.vermontstudiocenter.org

Summary To provide funding to artists and writers with disabilities interested in a residency at the Vermont Studio Center in Johnson, Vermont.

Eligibility Eligible to apply for this support are painters, sculptors, printmakers, photographers, writers, and poets who have a disability. Applicants must be interested in a residency at the studio in Johnson, Vermont. Selection is based on artistic merit.

Financial data The residency fee of $3,500 covers studio space, room, board, lectures, and studio visits. The fellowship pays all residency fees.

Duration 4 weeks.

Additional Information This program is sponsored by the Christopher Reeve Paralysis Foundation.

Number awarded 3 each year.

Deadline September of each year.

[645]
CONGRESSIONAL FELLOWSHIPS

American Association for the Advancement of Science
Attn: Science and Technology Policy Fellowship Programs
1200 New York Avenue, N.W.
Washington, DC 20005-3920
(202) 326-6700   Fax: (202) 289-4950
E-mail: fellowships@aaas.org
Web: fellowships.aaas.org/congressional

Summary To provide postdoctoral and mid-career scientists and engineers with an opportunity to work as special legislative assistants on the staffs of members of Congress or congressional committees.

Eligibility Applicants must have a Ph.D. or equivalent doctoral-level degree at the time of application in a physical, biological, or social science or any field of engineering; persons with a master's degree in engineering and at least 3 years of post-degree experience are also eligible. Candidates must demonstrate exceptional competence in some area of science or engineering; have a good scientific and technical background; be cognizant of many matters in nonscientific areas; demonstrate sensitivity toward political and social issues; have a strong interest and some experience in applying personal knowledge toward the solution of societal problems; and be interested in working as special legislative assistants for Congress. U.S. citizenship is required; federal employees are not eligible. Underrepresented minorities and persons with disabilities are especially encouraged to apply.

Financial data The stipend is $60,000, plus allowances for health insurance and relocation

Duration 1 year, beginning in September.

Additional Information The program includes an orientation on congressional and executive branch operations and a year-long seminar program on issues involving science and public policy. Approximately 30 other national science and engineering societies sponsor fellows in collaboration with this program; for a list of all of those, contact the sponsor.

Number awarded 2 each year.

Deadline January of each year.

[646]
CONNECTICUT SPACE GRANT COLLEGE CONSORTIUM GRADUATE STUDENT FELLOWSHIPS

Connecticut Space Grant College Consortium
c/o University of Hartford
UT 219
200 Bloomfield Avenue
West Hartford, CT 06117-1599
(860) 768-4813   Fax: (860) 768-5073
E-mail: ctspgrant@hartford.edu
Web: uhaweb.hartford.edu/ctspgrant

Summary To provide funding to graduate students at member institutions of the Connecticut Space Grant College Consortium interested in working on space-related projects under the guidance of a faculty member.

Eligibility This program is open to full-time graduate students at member institutions of the Connecticut Space Grant College Consortium. Applicants must be proposing to conduct research in aerospace science and engineering in areas normally funded by the U.S. National Aeronautics and Space Administration (NASA). U.S. citizenship is required. The program actively encourages women, underrepresented minorities, and those with disabilities to apply.

Financial data The grant is $6,250.

Duration 1 semester or 1 year.

Additional Information Member institutions are the University of Connecticut, University of Hartford, University of New Haven, and Trinity College. This program is funded by NASA.

Number awarded 4 each year.

Deadline October or May of each year.

[647]
CONNECTICUT SPACE GRANT COLLEGE CONSORTIUM TRAVEL GRANTS

Connecticut Space Grant College Consortium
c/o University of Hartford
UT 219
200 Bloomfield Avenue
West Hartford, CT 06117-1599
(860) 768-4813   Fax: (860) 768-5073
E-mail: ctspgrant@hartford.edu
Web: uhaweb.hartford.edu/ctspgrant

Summary To provide funding for travel to students and faculty at member institutions of the Connecticut Space Grant College Consortium.

Eligibility This program is open to students and faculty at member institutions of the Connecticut Space Grant College Consortium. Applicants normally must be proposing to collaborate with researchers of the U.S. National Aeronautics and Space Administration (NASA), to present their aerospace-related research at conferences, to use specialized equipment at NASA facilities, or to visit NASA centers to establish research contacts. Travel is normally limited to destinations within the United States. The program actively encourages women, underrepresented minorities, and those with disabilities to apply.

Financial data Grants cover expenses up to $1,000 per trip.

Additional Information Member institutions are the University of Connecticut, University of Hartford, University of New Haven, and Trinity College. This program is funded by NASA.

Number awarded Varies each year; recently, a total of $7,500 was available for student travel and $2,600 for faculty travel.

Deadline May of each year.

[648]
CULTURAL ANTHROPOLOGY GRANTS FOR HIGH RISK EXPLORATORY RESEARCH

National Science Foundation
Directorate for Social, Behavioral, and Economic Sciences
Attn: Division of Behavioral and Cognitive Sciences
4201 Wilson Boulevard, Room 995
Arlington, VA 22230
(703) 292-8758   TDD: (703) 292-9068
E-mail: splattne@nsf.gov
Web: www.nsf.gov/sbe/bcs/anthro/highrisk.htm

Summary To provide funding to scholars interested in conducting high-risk research in cultural anthropology.

Eligibility This program is open to scholars interested in conducting research projects in anthropology that might be considered too risky for normal review procedures. A project is considered risky if the data may not be obtainable in spite of all reasonable preparation on the researcher's part. Proposals for extremely urgent research where access to the data may not be available in the normal review schedule, even with all reasonable preparation by the researcher, are also appropriate for this program. Graduate students are not eligible to apply. Women, minorities, and persons with disabilities are strongly encouraged to participate in this program.

Financial data Grants up to $25,000, including indirect costs, are available.

Number awarded Varies each year, depending on the availability of funds.

Deadline Applications may be submitted at any time.

[649]
CULTURAL ANTHROPOLOGY RESEARCH EXPERIENCE FOR GRADUATES SUPPLEMENTS

National Science Foundation
Directorate for Social, Behavioral, and Economic Sciences
Attn: Division of Behavioral and Cognitive Sciences
4201 Wilson Boulevard, Room 995
Arlington, VA 22230
(703) 292-8758   TDD: (703) 292-9068
E-mail: splattne@nsf.gov
Web: www.nsf.gov/sbe/sber/anthro

Summary To provide funding to graduate students interested in conducting dissertation research in cultural anthropology.

Eligibility Applications may be submitted through regular university channels by dissertation advisors on behalf of graduate students in cultural anthropology. The faculty member must be currently a principal investigator on a research award from the National Science Foundation. The application must be for supplemental funds for a doctoral student's closely mentored but independent research experience. The student's research should be a creative project, not a clerk or assistant's task. Selection is based on the appropriateness and value of the educational experience for the student participant, particularly the independence and theoretical significance of the student's activities and the quality of the supervision. Each principal investigator normally may seek funding for only 1 graduate student; exceptions are considered for training additional qualified students who are members of underrepresented groups. Women, minorities, and persons with disabilities are strongly encouraged to participate in this program.

Financial data Supplemental grants up to $5,000 are available. Institutions are encouraged to treat these supplements like dissertation research grants (which incur no indirect costs).

Duration 1 year.

Number awarded Varies each year, depending on the availability of funds.

Deadline January of each year.

[650]
DEFENSE POLICY FELLOWSHIPS

American Association for the Advancement of Science
Attn: Science and Technology Policy Fellowship Programs
1200 New York Avenue, N.W.
Washington, DC 20005-3920
(202) 326-6700   Fax: (202) 289-4950
E-mail: fellowships@aaas.org
Web: fellowships.aaas.org/defense

Summary To provide postdoctoral and mid-career scientists and engineers with an opportunity to supply current technical knowledge to U.S. Department of Defense (DoD) programs.

Eligibility Prospective fellows must have a Ph.D. or equivalent doctoral-level degree in a physical, biological, or social science, any field of engineering, or any relevant interdisciplinary field; persons with a master's degree in engineering and at least 3 years of post-degree experience are also eligible. Candidates must demonstrate exceptional competence in some area of science or engineering; communicate and work effectively with decision makers and others outside of the scientific and engineering community; exhibit willingness and flexibility to tackle problems in a number of nonscientific areas; demonstrate sensitivity toward political, economic, and technological issues; and have some experience and/or strong interest in integrating modern science, technology, and business practices in the area of defense. Applicants must be U.S. citizens and must obtain a security clearance; federal employees are not eligible. Underrepresented minorities and persons with disabilities are especially encouraged to apply.

Financial data The stipend is $60,000, plus allowances for health insurance and professional travel.

Duration 1 year, beginning in September; may be renewed for 1 additional year.

Additional Information Fellows work in 1 of the following offices: the Office of the Under Secretary of Defense for Acquisition, Technology and Logistics; the Missile Defense Agency; the Office of Naval Research; the U.S. Army's Research Office; or the Defense Threat Reduction Agency. Assignments may involve significant interagency, congressional, or international activity. The program includes a 2-week orientation on international affairs and executive branch and congressional operations.

Number awarded 3 or more each year.

Deadline January of each year.

[651]
DIPLOMACY FELLOWSHIPS

American Association for the Advancement of Science
Attn: Science and Technology Policy Fellowship Programs
1200 New York Avenue, N.W.
Washington, DC 20005-3920
(202) 326-6700   Fax: (202) 289-4950
E-mail: fellowships@aaas.org
Web: fellowships.aaas.org/diplomacy

Summary To provide postdoctoral and mid-career scientists and engineers with an opportunity to work with various federal agencies in areas that involve international affairs, foreign policy, or international development.

Eligibility Prospective fellows must have a Ph.D. or equivalent doctoral-level degree in a physical, biological, or social science, any field of engineering, or any relevant interdisciplinary field; persons with a master's degree in engineering and at least 3 years of post-degree experience are also eligible. Candidates must demonstrate exceptional competence in some area of science or engineering; be cognizant of the ways in which science and technology affect a broad range of international development and foreign policy issues; communicate and work effectively with decision makers and others outside of the scientific and engineering communities; exhibit willingness and flexibility to tackle problems in a number of nonscientific areas; demonstrate sensitivity toward political, economic, and social issues; and have some experience and/or strong interest in applying knowledge toward the solution of problems in the area of foreign affairs or international development. Applicants must be U.S. citizens and must obtain a security clearance; federal employees are not eligible. Underrepresented minorities and persons with disabilities are especially encouraged to apply.

Financial data The stipend ranges from $60,000 to $75,000, plus allowances for health insurance and professional travel.

Duration 1 year, beginning in September; may be renewed for 1 additional year.

Additional Information Assignments are available at: 1) the U.S. Agency for International Development (USAID), where fellows work on matters related to sustainable development, especially in economic growth, the environment, population and health, democratization, humanitarian assistance, and education; 2) the Department of State where fellows may be assigned to the Bureau of Oceans and International Environmental and Scientific Affairs; the Bureau of Democracy, Human Rights and Labor; the Bureau of Economic and Business Affairs; any of the 4 bureaus that report to the Under Secretary for Arms Control and International Security Affairs; or any of the 6 regional bureaus of State; or 3) the Fogarty International Center of the National Institutes of Health (NIH) where they work with a community of

researchers, administrators, and policy-makers to advance medical research through international cooperation. All and Extension Service of the U.S. Department of Agriculture (USDA), where they work with program specialists and national program leaders to help develop activities that support international project objectives in Armenia. All fellowship assignments provide international travel opportunities. At the State Department, that program is known as the Parker-Gentry Fellowship. At NIH, the program is designated the Sheldon M. Wolff, M.D. Fellowship on International Health.

Number awarded 15 or more each year: 10 or more at USAID, 1 or more at the State Department, and 1 at NIH.

Deadline January of each year.

[652]
DISABLED INVESTIGATORS DEVELOPING INDEPENDENT RESEARCH CAREERS RESEARCH SUPPLEMENTS

National Institutes of Health
Division of Extramural Outreach and Information Resources
Attn: GrantsInfo
6701 Rockledge Drive, Suite 6095
Bethesda, MD 20892-7910
(301) 435-0714   Fax: (301) 480-8443
E-mail: GrantsInfo@nih.gov
Web: www.nih.gov

Summary To provide funding to staff or faculty members with disabilities who are interested in developing independent careers in the biomedical, behavioral, clinical, or social sciences.

Eligibility Investigators with disabilities must be affiliated with an academic institution, have a doctoral degree, be beyond the level of a research trainee, be a member of the staff or faculty, and have at least 1 year of postdoctoral experience. Candidates must be interested in conducting research in the biomedical, behavioral, clinical, or social sciences. They may have received prior research or research training support from the National Institutes of Health (NIH) or support under the Minority Biomedical Research Support Program (MBRS), Minority-Research Infrastructure Support Program (M-RISP), Minority Access to Research Careers Program (MARC), Career Opportunities in Research Education and Training (COR), small grants, or Academic Research Enhancement Award (AREA) program. But, an individual who has received independent research support as a principal investigator on a regular research grant or as a project leader on a program project or center grant, or as a principal investigator on an individual research career award, is not eligible for support under this program. Selection is based on 1) the qualifications of the candidate, including career goals, prior research training, research potential, and relevant experience; 2) the plan for the proposed research experience in the supplemental request and its relationship to the parent grant; 3) the appropriateness of the proposed accommodations for the candidate; 4) evidence from the principal investigator that the experience will enhance the research potential, knowledge, and/or skills of the candidate, and that adequate mentorship will be provided; and 5) evidence from the principal investigator that the activities of the candidate will be an integral part of the project.

Financial data The requested salary and fringe benefits must be in accordance with the salary structure of the grantee institution, consistent with the level of effort. Additional funds up to $10,000 may be requested for supplies and travel. Funds may be requested to permit accommodation to the research environment. That may include research equipment, but only if it is directly related to the project and to accommodating the disabilities of the individual. Some types of accommodations that might be provided under this program include: specialized equipment, assistive devices, and personnel, such as readers, interpreters, or assistants.

Duration There are 2 types of support. The short-term investigator research supplement provides short-term support for staff or faculty members to conduct full-time research for 3 to 5 months each year, during the summer or another portion of the academic year, over a maximum period of 4 years. The long-term investigator research supplement provides long-term research support for up to 4 years at a minimum of 30% effort during each 12-month period.

[653]
DISTRICT OF COLUMBIA SPACE GRANT CONSORTIUM AWARDS

District of Columbia Space Grant Consortium
c/o American University
Department of Physics
McKinley Building, Suite 106
4400 Massachusetts Avenue, N.W.
Washington, DC 20016-8058
(202) 885-2780   Fax: (202) 885-2723
E-mail: SpaceGrant@aol.com
Web: www.DCSpaceGrant.org

Summary To provide financial assistance to undergraduate and graduate students studying space-related fields at member institutions of the District of Columbia Space Grant Consortium.

Eligibility This program is open to students at member institutions of the consortium. Each participating university conducts its own program. The consortium is a component of the Space Grant program of the U.S. National Aeronautics and Space Administration (NASA), which encourages participation by women, underrepresented minorities, and persons with disabilities.

Financial data Each university determines the amount of the awards.

Additional Information Institutions participating in the consortium include American University, Gallaudet University, George Washington University, Howard Uni-

versity, and the University of the District of Columbia. Funding for this program is provided by NASA.

Number awarded Varies each year.

[654]
DIVERSITY COALITION FELLOWSHIPS

American Association of Museums
Attn: Professional Education Fellowships
1575 Eye Street, N.W., Suite 400
Washington, DC 20005
(202) 289-9114   Fax: (202) 289-6578
E-mail: seminars@aam-us.org
Web: www.aam-us.org

Summary To provide funding to museum professionals from diverse backgrounds who are interested in participating in a seminar or the annual meeting of the American Association of Museums (AAM).

Eligibility This program is open to AAM members who work at a museum in the United States. Applicants must be full-time, paid museum professionals or full-time graduate students engaged in a museum-related course of study. They must represent a diverse constituency, defined as people of all ethnic and racial backgrounds, gender, sexual orientation, religious affiliation, and physical abilities, including people living with HIV/AIDS. As part of their application, they must submit an essay explaining why they wish to attend the professional education program, how the subject matter and general experience of attending the program will assist them in their current position and overall professional development, what they will contribute to the program, and what they would do to increase and support diversity in museums. Selection is based on the comprehensiveness and relevance of the essay answers, importance of the professional development opportunity to the applicant's career goals, demonstrated financial need, quality of reference letters, ability to meet all application requirements, and clarity and completeness of the application.

Financial data The grant is $500.

Duration The grants are presented annually.

Additional Information The Diversity Coalition was originally organized in 1998 as the AAM Ethnic Coalition by the AAM Asian Pacific American Professional Interest Committee (PIC), the AAM Latino Network PIC, the AAM Native Americans and Museums Collaboration PIC, and the Association of African American Museums. In 2000, it expanded to include other diverse groups and was renamed the Diversity Coalition.

Number awarded Varies each year.

Deadline Applications may be submitted at any time, but they must be received at least 6 weeks prior to the seminar date.

[655]
DOCTORAL DISSERTATION IMPROVEMENT GRANTS IN THE DIRECTORATE FOR BIOLOGICAL SCIENCES

National Science Foundation
Directorate for Biological Sciences
Attn: Division of Environmental Biology
4201 Wilson Boulevard
Arlington, VA 22230
(703) 292-8480   TDD: (703) 292-5090
E-mail: ddig-deb@nsf.gov
Web: www.nsf.gov/bio

Summary To provide partial support for dissertation research in selected areas supported by the National Science Foundation (NSF) Directorate for Biological Sciences (DBS).

Eligibility Applications may be submitted through regular university channels by dissertation advisors on behalf of graduate students who have advanced to candidacy and have begun or are about to begin dissertation research. Students must be enrolled at U.S. institutions but need not be U.S. citizens. Proposals should focus on the ecology, ecosystems, systematics, or population biology programs in the DBS Division of Environmental Biology, or the animal behavior or ecological and evolutionary physiology programs in the DBS Division of Integrative Biology and Neuroscience. Women, minorities, and persons with disabilities are strongly encouraged to apply.

Financial data Grants range up to $12,000; funds may be used for travel to specialized facilities or field research locations, specialized research equipment, purchase of supplies and services not otherwise available, fees for computerized or other forms of data, and rental of environmental chambers or other research facilities. Funding is not provided for stipends, tuition, textbooks, journals, allowances for dependents, travel to scientific meetings, publication costs, dissertation preparation or reproduction, or indirect costs.

Duration Normally 2 years.

Additional Information Information on programs in the Division of Environmental Biology is available at the address and telephone number above; information from the Division of Integrative Biology and Neuroscience is available at (703) 292-7875, E-mail: ddig-ibm@nsf.gov.

Number awarded 90 each year; approximately $900,000 is available for this program each year.

Deadline November of each year.

[656]
DOCTORAL DISSERTATION RESEARCH IMPROVEMENT GRANTS IN THE DIRECTORATE FOR SOCIAL, BEHAVIORAL, AND ECONOMIC SCIENCES

National Science Foundation
Directorate for Social, Behavioral, and Economic Sciences
Attn: Division of Social and Economic Sciences
4201 Wilson Boulevard
Arlington, VA 22230
(703) 292-8670   TDD: (703) 292-5090
E-mail: sesfl@nsf.gov
Web: www.nsf.gov/sbe/docdiss

Summary To provide partial support to doctoral candidates conducting dissertation research in selected areas of the social, behavioral, and economic sciences.

Eligibility Applications may be submitted through regular university channels by dissertation advisors on behalf of graduate students who have advanced to candidacy and have begun or are about to begin dissertation research. Students must be enrolled at U.S. institutions but need not be U.S. citizens. Programs that have been most active in supporting dissertation research include archaeology; cognitive neuroscience; cultural anthropology; decision, risk, and management science; geography and regional science; law and social science; linguistics; physical anthropology; political science; science and technology studies; sociology; and societal dimensions of engineering, science, and technology. Other disciplines that receive support if appropriate include economics; human cognition and perception; and methodology, measurement, and statistics. Budget requests may be submitted for such dissertation research-related expenses as data collection and sample survey costs, microfilms and other forms of specialized data, payments to subjects or informants, specialized research equipment, analysis and services not otherwise available, supplies and travel to specialized facilities or field research locations, and partial living expenses for conducting necessary research away from the student's university. Women, minorities, and persons with disabilities are strongly encouraged to apply.

Financial data Grants have the limited purpose of providing funds to enhance the quality of dissertation research. They are to be used exclusively for necessary expenses incurred in the actual conduct of the dissertation research. Funding is not provided for stipends, tuition, textbooks, journals, allowances for dependents, travel to scientific meetings, publication costs, dissertation preparation or reproduction, or indirect costs.

Duration Up to 2 years.

Additional Information Information is also available from the Division of Behavioral and Cognitive Sciences, (703) 292-8740.

Number awarded 200 to 300 each year. Approximately $2.5 million is available for this program annually.

Deadline Deadline dates for the submission of dissertation improvement grant proposals differ by program within the Division of Social and Economic Science and the Division of Behavioral and Cognitive Sciences; applicants should obtain information regarding target dates for proposals from the relevant program.

[657]
DONALD D. HAMMILL FOUNDATION RESEARCH SCHOLARSHIPS

Donald D. Hammill Foundation
8700 Shoal Creek Boulevard
Austin, TX 78757
(512) 451-0784   Fax: (512) 451-8542
E-mail: DDHFound@aol.com

Summary To provide financial assistance to doctoral students who need to complete a dissertation that pertains to characteristics, services, or issues related to disability areas.

Eligibility Applicants requesting financial aid to complete their dissertation must be 1) admitted to candidacy; 2) conducting a study pertaining to characteristics, services, or issues related to a disability area; and 3) planning to complete their study by the end of the award period. Selection is based on the perceived importance of the study, the academic background of the applicant, and the need for financial assistance. Preference is given to applicants who have a disability or who are experiencing serious financial distress.

Financial data Grants up to $5,000 are awarded. Funds must be used for living expenses, materials, child care, data collections, clerical services, and other related activities.

Duration Up to 1 year.

Additional Information Recipients must provide a brief progress report midway through the study and submit a copy of their dissertation upon completion. Publications that result from the funded research must acknowledge support of the foundation.

Number awarded 1 or more each year.

Deadline June of each year.

[658]
EDWARD T. CONROY MEMORIAL SCHOLARSHIP PROGRAM

Maryland Higher Education Commission
Attn: Office of Student Financial Assistance
839 Bestgate Road, Suite 400
Annapolis, MD 21401-3013
(410) 260-4565   Toll-free: (800) 974-1024
Fax: (410) 974-5376   TTY: (800) 735-2258
E-mail: osfamail@mhec.state.md.us
Web: www.mhec.state.md.us/SSA/CONROY.htm

Summary To provide financial assistance for college or graduate school to specified categories of veterans, public safety employees, and their children in Maryland.

Eligibility This program is open to undergraduate and graduate students in the following categories: 1) children and unremarried surviving spouses of state or local public safety employees or volunteers who died in the line of duty; 2) children of armed forces members whose death or 100% disability was directly caused by military service; 3) POW/MIA veterans of the Vietnam Conflict and their children; 4) children and surviving spouses of victims of the September 11, 2001 terrorist attacks who died in the World Trade Center in New York City, the Pentagon in Virginia, or United Airlines Flight 93 in Pennsylvania; 5) veterans who have, as a direct result of military service, a disability of 25% or greater and have exhausted or are no longer eligible for federal veterans' educational benefits; and 6) state or local public safety officers or volunteers who were 100% disabled in the line of duty. The parent, veteran, POW, or public safety officer or volunteer must have been a resident of Maryland at the time of death or when declared disabled. Financial need is not considered.

Financial data The amount of the award is equal to tuition and fees at a Maryland postsecondary institution, to a maximum of $14,200 for children and spouses of the September 11 terrorist attacks or $6,178 for all other recipients.

Duration Up to 5 years of full-time study or 8 years of part-time study.

Additional Information Recipients must enroll at a 2-year or 4-year Maryland college or university as a full-time or part-time degree-seeking undergraduate or graduate student or attend a private career school.

Number awarded Varies each year.

Deadline July of each year.

[659]
ELA FOUNDATION SCHOLARSHIPS

Ethel Louise Armstrong Foundation
Attn: Executive Director
2460 North Lake Avenue
PMB 128
Altadena, CA 91001
(626) 398-8840   Fax: (626) 398 8843
E-mail: executivedirector@ela.org
Web: www.ela.org

Summary To provide financial assistance for graduate school to women with disabilities.

Eligibility This program is open to women with disabilities who are currently enrolled in or actively applying to a graduate program at an accredited college or university in the United States. Applicants must be active in a local, state, or national disability organization, either in person or electronically, that is providing services or advocacy for people with disabilities. Along with their application, they must submit a 1,000-word essay on "How I will change the face of disability on the planet." Selection is based on academic and leadership merit.

Financial data The stipend ranges from $1,000 to $2,000 per year.

Duration 1 year.

Additional Information The sponsoring foundation was founded in 1994 by Margaret Staton, who was disabled by a spinal cord tumor at 2 years of age. Recipients must agree to 1) network with the sponsor's board of directors and current and alumni scholarship recipients, and 2) update the sponsor on their progress in their academic and working career.

Number awarded Varies each year.

Deadline May of each year.

[660]
ENVIRONMENTAL FELLOWSHIPS

American Association for the Advancement of Science
Attn: Science and Technology Policy Fellowship Programs
1200 New York Avenue, N.W.
Washington, DC 20005-3920
(202) 326-6700   Fax: (202) 289-4950
E-mail: fellowships@aaas.org
Web: fellowships.aaas.org/environmental

Summary To provide postdoctoral and mid-career scientists and engineers with an opportunity to work with the U.S. Environmental Protection Agency (EPA) on projects relating to science, policy, and the environment.

Eligibility Prospective fellows must have a Ph.D. at the time of application and must show exceptional competence in some area of science or engineering related to the environment; have an excellent scientific and technical background; have a strong interest and some experience in applying scientific or other professional knowledge toward the identification and assessment of future environmental problems. Applications are invited from individuals in a physical, biological, or social science, any field of engineering, or any relevant interdisciplinary field. Persons with a master's degree in engineering and at least 3 years of post-degree experience are also eligible. U.S. citizenship is required; federal employees are not eligible. Underrepresented minorities and persons with disabilities are especially encouraged to apply.

Financial data The stipend is $60,000, plus allowances for health insurance, relocation, and professional travel.

Duration 1 year, beginning in September; may be renewed 1 additional year.

Additional Information Fellows work on ecosystem health, pollution prevention, sustainability, community based solutions, human and environmental risk assessment, environmental socioeconomic concerns, hazardous air pollutants, global environmental hazards, pesticides (including biologicals), municipal waste water, drinking water, management and control of hazardous substances, chemical testing and assessment, radiation,

and innovative technologies (such as green technologies).
Number awarded Approximately 10 each year.
Deadline January of each year.

[661]
FACILITATION AWARDS FOR SCIENTISTS AND ENGINEERS WITH DISABILITIES

National Science Foundation
Directorate for Education and Human Resources
Attn: Coordinator, Facilitation Awards for Scientists and Engineers with Disabilities
4201 Wilson Boulevard, Room 815
Arlington, VA 22230
(703) 292-4684   TDD: (703) 292-5090
Web: www.ehr.nsf.gov

Summary To provide supplemental financing to individuals with disabilities who wish to pursue careers in science and engineering and who are working on projects supported by the National Science Foundation (NSF).

Eligibility This program is open to individuals with disabilities who are principal investigators, other senior professionals, or graduate and undergraduate students participating in a specific project supported by the foundation. Requests for special equipment or assistance necessary to enable an individual with a disability to participate in a specific NSF-supported project may be included in the original proposal submitted to a NSF program or submitted as a separate request for supplemental funding for an existing NSF grant.

Financial data Funds may be requested to purchase special equipment, modify equipment, or provide services required specifically for the work to be undertaken. No maximum amount has been set for requests, but it is expected that the cost (including equipment adaptation and installation) will not be a major proportion of the total proposed budget for the project.

Additional Information Examples of specific equipment for which funds may be requested include prosthetic devices to manipulate a particular apparatus; equipment to convert sound to visual signals, or vice versa, for a particular experiment; access to a special site or to a mode of transportation; a reader or interpreter with special technical competence related to the project; or other special-purpose equipment or assistance needed to conduct a particular project. Items that compensate in a general way for the disabling condition are not eligible; examples include standard wheelchairs, general prosthetics, hearing aids, TTY/TDD devices, general readers for the blind, or ramps, elevators, or other structural modifications of research facilities.

Number awarded Varies each year.
Deadline Applications may be submitted at any time.

[662]
FACULTY EARLY CAREER DEVELOPMENT PROGRAM

National Science Foundation
Directorate for Education and Human Resources
Attn: Senior Staff Associate for Cross Directorate Programs
4201 Wilson Boulevard, Room 805
Arlington, VA 22230
(703) 292-8600   TDD: (703) 292-5090
Web: www.nsf.gov/career

Summary To provide support for science and engineering research to outstanding new faculty who intend to develop academic careers involving both research and education.

Eligibility This program, identified as the CAREER program, is open to faculty members who meet all of the following requirements: 1) be employed in a tenure-track (or equivalent) position at an institution in the United States, its territories or possessions, or the Commonwealth of Puerto Rico which awards a baccalaureate or advanced degree in a field supported by the National Science Foundation (NSF); 2) hold a doctoral degree in a field of science or engineering supported by NSF: 3) not have competed more than 2 times in this program; 4) be untenured; and 5) not be a current or former recipient of a Presidential Early Career Award for Scientists and Engineers (PECASE) or CAREER award. Applicants must be U.S. citizens, nationals, or permanent residents. They must submit a career development plan that indicates 1) the objectives and significance of the proposed integrated research and education activities; 2) the relationship of the research to the current state of knowledge in the field, and of the education activities to the current state of knowledge on effective teaching and learning in the field of study; 3) an outline of the plan of work, describing the methods and procedures to be used, including evaluation of the education activities; 4) the relation of the plan to the applicants' career goals and job responsibilities, and to the goals of their department or organization; and 5) a summary of prior research and educational accomplishments. Proposals from women, underrepresented minorities, and persons with disabilities are especially encouraged.

Financial data The total grant is $400,000 (or $500,000 for the Directorate of Biological Sciences) over the full period of the award.

Duration 5 years.

Additional Information This program is operated by various disciplinary divisions within the NSF; for a list of the participating divisions and their telephone numbers, contact the sponsor. Outstanding recipients of these grants are nominated for the NSF component of the PECASE awards, which are awarded to 20 recipients of these grants as an honorary award.

Number awarded 300 to 350 each year. Approximately $60 million is budgeted to support this program annually.

Deadline July of each year.

[663]
FLORIDA SPACE GRANT CONSORTIUM FELLOWSHIP PROGRAM

Florida Space Grant Consortium
c/o Center for Space Education
Building M6-306, Room 7010
Mail Stop: FSGC
Kennedy Space Center, FL 32899
(321) 452-4301   Fax: (321) 449-0739
E-mail: fsgc@mail.ufl.edu
Web: fsgc.engr.ucf.edu

Summary To provide financial assistance to graduate students in space studies at universities participating in the Florida Space Grant Consortium (FSGC).

Eligibility Eligible to be nominated for this program are U.S. citizens who are enrolled full time in master's or doctoral programs at universities participating in the consortium. Nominees must be enrolled in a space-related field of study, broadly defined to include aeronautics, astronautics, remote sensing, atmospheric sciences, and other fundamental sciences and technologies relying on and/or directly impacting space technological resources. Included within that definition are space science; earth observing science; space life sciences; space medicine; space policy, law, and engineering; astronomy and astrophysics; space facilities and applications; and space education. Their undergraduate GPA should be at least 3.5. The program particularly solicits nominations of women, minorities, and students with disabilities.

Financial data The maximum stipend is $20,000 per year for doctoral candidates or $12,000 per year for master's degree students.

Duration 1 year; may be renewed up to 2 additional years for doctoral candidates or 1 additional year for master's degree students, provided the recipient maintains a GPA of 3.5 or higher.

Additional Information This program is funded by the U.S. National Aeronautics and Space Administration (NASA). The consortium member universities are Bethune-Cookman College, Eckerd College, Embry-Riddle Aeronautical University, Florida A&M University, Florida Atlantic University, Florida Community Colleges, Florida Gulf Coast University, Florida Institute of Technology, Florida International University, Florida Southern College, Florida State University, University of Central Florida, University of Florida, University of Miami, University of North Florida, University of South Florida, and University of West Florida.

Number awarded 3 or 4 each year.

Deadline Notices of intent must be submitted by January of each year. Completed proposals are due in April.

[664]
GEOLOGICAL SOCIETY OF AMERICA GENERAL RESEARCH GRANTS PROGRAM

Geological Society of America
Attn: Program Officer Grants, Awards and Medals
3300 Penrose Place
P.O. Box 9140
Boulder, CO 80301-9140
(303) 357-1037   Fax: (303) 447-1133
E-mail: lcarter@geosociety.org
Web: www.geosociety.org

Summary To provide support to graduate student members of the Geological Society of America (GSA) interested in conducting research at universities in the United States, Canada, Mexico, or Central America.

Eligibility This program is open to GSA members working on a master's or doctoral degree at a university in the United States, Canada, Mexico, or Central America. Applicants must be interested in conducting research on geology. Applications from minorities, women, and persons with disabilities are strongly encouraged.

Financial data The proposed budget may include the cost of travel, room and board in the field, materials and supplies, and other expenses directly related to the fulfillment of the research contract. Expenses requested for equipment or rental of equipment, film, some supplies, computer time, software, thin sections, and in-house charges for analytical instruments usually provided by a university must be fully justified. Funds cannot be used for the purchase of ordinary field equipment, for maintenance of the families of the grantees and their assistants, as reimbursement for work already accomplished, to attend professional meetings, for thesis preparation, to defray the costs of tuition, or for the employment of persons to conduct research.

Duration 1 year.

Additional Information In addition to general grants, GSA awards a number of specialized grants: the Gretchen L. Blechschmidt Award for women (especially in the fields of biostratigraphy and/or paleooceanography); the John T. Dillon Alaska Research Award for earth science problems particular to Alaska, the Robert K. Fahnestock Memorial Award for the field of sediment transport or related aspects of fluvial geomorphology; the Lipman Research Award for volcanology and petrology; the Bruce L. "Biff" Reed Award for studies in the tectonic and magmatic evolution of Alaska; the Alexander Sisson Award for studies in Alaska and the Caribbean; the Harold T. Stearns Fellowship Award for work on the geology of the Pacific Islands and the circum-Pacific region; and the John Montagne Fund Award for research in the field of quaternary geomorphology. Furthermore, 9 of the 14 GSA divisions (geophysics, hydrogeology, sedimentary geology, structural geology and tectonics, archaeological geology, coal geology, planetary geology, quaternary geology and geomorphology, and engineering geology) also offer divisional

grants. Some of those awards are named: the Allan V. Cox Award of the Geophysics Division, the Claude C. Albritton, Jr. Scholarship of the Archaeological Geology Division, the Antoinette Lierman Medlin Scholarships of the Coal Geology Division, the J. Hoover Mackin Research Grants and the Arthur D. Howard Research Grants of the Quaternary Geology and Geomorphology Division, and the Roy J. Shlemon Scholarship Awards of the Engineering Geology Division. In addition, 4 of the 6 geographic sections (south-central, north-central, southeastern, and northeastern) offer grants to graduate students at universities within their section.

Number awarded Varies each year; recently, the society awarded 224 grants worth more than $400,000 through this and all of its specialized programs.

Deadline January of each year.

[665]
GEORGIA SPACE GRANT CONSORTIUM FELLOWSHIPS

Georgia Space Grant Consortium
c/o Georgia Institute of Technology
Aerospace Engineering
Paul Weber Space Science and Technology
  Building, Room 210
Atlanta, GA 30332-0150
(404) 894-0521   Fax: (404) 894-9313
E-mail: wanda.pierson@aerospace.gatech.edu
Web: www.ae.gatech.edu/research/gsgc

Summary To provide financial assistance for undergraduate and graduate study of space-related fields to students at member institutions of the Georgia Space Grant Consortium (GSGC).

Eligibility This program is open to U.S. citizens who are undergraduate and graduate students at member institutions of the GSGC. Applicants must be working on a degree in mathematics, science, engineering, computer science, or a technical discipline related to space. Selection is based on transcripts, 3 letters of reference, and an essay of 100 to 500 words on the applicant's professional interests and objectives and their relationship to the field of aerospace. Awards are provided as part of the Space Grant program of the U.S. National Aeronautics and Space Administration, which encourages participation by women, minorities, and people with disabilities.

Financial data A stipend is awarded (amount not specified).

Additional Information Institutions that are members of the GSGC include Albany State University, Clark Atlanta University, Columbus State University, Fort Valley State University, Georgia Institute of Technology, Kennesaw State University, Mercer University, Morehouse College, Spelman College, State University of West Georgia, and the University of Georgia. This program is funded by NASA.

Number awarded 1 each year.

[666]
GERALDINE R. DODGE FOUNDATION FELLOWSHIP

College Art Association of America
Attn: Fellowship Program
275 Seventh Avenue
New York, NY 10001-6798
(212) 691-1051, ext. 242   Fax: (212) 627-2381
E-mail: fellowship@collegeart.org
Web: www.collegeart.org

Summary To provide financial assistance and work experience to art historians from culturally diverse backgrounds who are completing graduate degrees and are interested in working in New Jersey.

Eligibility This program is open to art historians who have been underrepresented in the field because of their race, religion, gender, age, national origin, sexual orientation, disability, or history of economic disadvantage. Applicants must be U.S. citizens or permanent residents and able to demonstrate financial need. They must expect to receive the M.F.A. or Ph.D. degree in the year following application and then be interested in working at a cultural institution in New Jersey.

Financial data The stipend is $5,000.

Duration 1 year: the final year of the degree program.

Additional Information In addition to providing a stipend for the terminal year of their degree program, the College Art Association (CAA) helps fellows search for employment at a museum, art center, college, or university in New Jersey. Upon securing a position, CAA provides a $10,000 subsidy to the employer as part of the fellow's salary. Participating organizations must match this 2:1. In addition to administrative and/or teaching responsibilities, all fellows' positions must include a curatorial or public service component. Salary or stipend, position description, and term of employment will vary and are determined in consultation with individual fellows and their potential employers. This program began in 1993. Funding is provided by the Milton & Sally Avery Arts Foundation, Geraldine R. Dodge Foundation, National Endowment for the Arts, National Endowment for the Humanities, and Terra Foundation for the Arts.

Number awarded 1 each year.

Deadline January of each year.

[667]
GOALI FACULTY IN INDUSTRY AWARDS

National Science Foundation
Attn: Directorate for Engineering GOALI Coordinator
4201 Wilson Boulevard
Arlington, VA 22230
(703) 292-8300   TDD: (703) 292-5090
E-mail: lejohnso@nsf.gov
Web: www.eng.nsf.gov

Summary To provide funding to science and engineering faculty who wish to conduct research as part of the Grant Opportunities for Academic Liaison with Indus-

try (GOALI) program of the National Science Foundation (NSF).

Eligibility This program is open to full-time faculty members at U.S. colleges and universities in science and engineering fields of interest to NSF. Applicants must present a plan for collaboration between their institution and industry, with a description of the facilities and resources that will be available at the industrial site to support the proposed research. The program encourages participation by women and underrepresented minority engineers and scientists as well as those with disabilities.

Financial data Awards range from $25,000 to $50,000, including 50% of the faculty member's salary and fringe benefits during the industrial residency period. Up to 20% of the total requested amount may be used for travel and research expenses for the faculty and his/her students, including materials but excluding equipment; up to 10% of the total direct cost may be allocated for administrative expenses in lieu of indirect costs. The industrial partner must commit to support the other 50% of the faculty salary and fringe benefits.

Duration 1 year.

Number awarded Varies each year.

[668] GOALI POSTDOCTORAL INDUSTRIAL FELLOWSHIPS

National Science Foundation
Attn: Directorate for Engineering GOALI Coordinator
4201 Wilson Boulevard
Arlington, VA 22230
(703) 292-8300   TDD: (703) 292-5090
E-mail: lejohnso@nsf.gov
Web: www.eng.nsf.gov

Summary To provide an opportunity for recent postdoctorates to work in industry as part of the Grant Opportunities for Academic Liaison with Industry (GOALI) program of the National Science Foundation (NSF).

Eligibility Applicants for these fellowships must have held a Ph.D. degree in a science or engineering field of interest to NSF for no more than 3 years. They must submit a plan for full-time work in industry under the guidance of an academic adviser and an industrial mentor. The program encourages participation by women and underrepresented minority engineers and scientists as well as those with disabilities.

Financial data Awards range up to $42,000, including 67% of the stipend for the fellow and transportation and moving expenses up to $3,000. Up to 10% of the total budget allowance may be used by the faculty adviser for research-related expenses. Up to 10% of the total direct cost may be allocated for administrative expenses in lieu of indirect costs. The industrial partner must commit to support the other 33% of the fellow's stipend.

Duration 1 or 2 years.

Number awarded Varies each year.

[669] GRANT PROGRAM FOR STUDENTS WITH DISABILITIES IN GRADUATE SCIENCE DEGREE PROGRAMS

Foundation for Science and Disability, Inc.
c/o Dr. Richard Mankin
Chair, Science Student Grant Committee
503 N.W. 89th Street
Gainesville, FL 32607-1400
(352) 374-5774   Fax: (352) 374-5781
E-mail: rmankin@gainesville.usda.ufl.edu
Web: www.as.wvu.edu/~scidis/organizations

Summary To provide supplemental grants to graduate students with disabilities who are interested in studying science, mathematics, medicine, computer science, or engineering.

Eligibility Eligible to apply are college seniors (who have been accepted to graduate or professional school) and graduate students who have some type of physical disability and are interested in working on a degree in an area of computer science, engineering, mathematics, medicine, or science. Applications must include an essay (about 250 words) describing professional goals and objectives, as well as the specific purpose for which the grant would be used. Also included must be 2 letters of recommendation from faculty members, 1 of whom must be the student's academic research advisor. Selection is based on financial need, sincerity of purpose, and scholarship and/or research ability.

Financial data The award is $1,000. Funds may be used for an assistive device or instrument, as financial support to work with a professor on an individual research project, or for some other special need.

Duration The award is granted annually.

Additional Information The Foundation for Science and Disability, Inc. is an affiliate society of the American Association for the Advancement of Science. This award is made only to students who are beginning or continuing a graduate degree.

Number awarded Varies each year.

Deadline November of each year.

[670]
HARRIETT G. JENKINS PREDOCTORAL FELLOWSHIP PROGRAM

United Negro College Fund Special Programs Corporation
2750 Prosperity Avenue, Suite 600
Fairfax, VA 22031
(703) 205-7656　　　　Toll-free: (800) 231-9155
Fax: (703) 205-7645
E-mail: hgjfellows@uncfsp.org
Web: www.uncfsp.org/nasa.asp

Summary To provide financial assistance to women, minorities, and people with disabilities working on a graduate degree in a field of interest to the National Aeronautics and Space Administration (NASA).

Eligibility This program is open to members of groups underrepresented in mathematics, science, technology, and engineering—women, minorities, and people with disabilities. Applicants must be full-time graduate students in a program leading to a master's or doctoral degree in a NASA-related discipline (aeronautics, aerospace, astronomy, bioengineering, biology, chemistry, computer science, earth sciences, engineering, environmental sciences, life sciences, materials sciences, mathematics, meteorology, physical sciences, physics/health physics, and science education). They must be U.S. citizens with a GPA of 3.0 or higher. Priority is given to 1) applicants who have previously participated in NASA undergraduate programs; 2) applicants who have received their undergraduate degree from minority institutions; and 3) undergraduate minority, women, and disabled applicants from majority institutions.

Financial data The stipend is $22,000 per year for doctoral fellows or $16,000 for master's degree students. Fellows who are also awarded a research mini-grant at a NASA Center or the Jet Propulsion Laboratory receive an additional $6,000 stipend, $700 housing allowance, and $700 travel allowance.

Duration 3 years.

Additional Information This program, established in 2001, is funded by NASA and administered by the United Negro College Fund Special Programs Corporation. Fellows may also compete for a research mini-grant to engage in a NASA research experience that is closely aligned with the research conducted at the fellow's institution. The participating NASA facilities are Ames Research Center (Moffett Field, California), Jet Propulsion Laboratory (Pasadena, California), Dryden Flight Research Center (Edwards, California), Johnson Space Center (Houston, Texas), Stennis Space Center (Stennis Space Center, Mississippi), Marshall Space Flight Center (Marshall Space Flight Center, Alabama), Glenn Research Center (Cleveland, Ohio), Kennedy Space Center (Kennedy Space Center, Florida), Langley Research Center (Hampton, Virginia), and Goddard Space Flight Center (Greenbelt, Maryland).

Number awarded Up to 20 each year.

Deadline January of each year.

[671]
HOMELAND SECURITY FELLOWSHIPS

American Association for the Advancement of Science
Attn: Science and Technology Policy Fellowship Programs
1200 New York Avenue, N.W.
Washington, DC 20005-3920
(202) 326-6700　　　　Fax: (202) 289-4950
E-mail: fellowships@aaas.org
Web: fellowships.aaas.org/dhs

Summary To provide postdoctoral and mid-career scientists and engineers with an opportunity to work on scientific and engineering issues within the U.S. Department of Homeland Security.

Eligibility Prospective fellows must have a Dr.P.H., D.V.M., M.D., Ph.D. or equivalent doctoral-level degree in a physical, biological, or social science or engineering at the time of application; persons with a master's degree in engineering and at least 3 years of post-degree experience are also eligible. Applicants must demonstrate exceptional competence in some area of science or engineering, have a good scientific and technical background, have excellent written and oral communication skills, have the ability to work in an interdisciplinary setting with policy-makers and other non-scientific partners, be cognizant of and demonstrate sensitivity toward political and social issues, and have a strong interest and some experience in applying personal knowledge toward the solution of societal problems. U.S. citizenship is required; federal employees are not eligible. Underrepresented minorities and persons with disabilities are especially encouraged to apply.

Financial data The stipend ranges from $60,000 to $75,000, depending on the fellow's education, experience, and salary history. Also provided are allowances for health insurance, relocation, and professional travel.

Duration 1 year, beginning in September; may be renewed for 1 additional year.

Additional Information Fellows are assigned to the Office of Research and Development of the Department of Homeland Security. Projects may involve building homeland security programs to defend against weapons of mass destruction, incorporating the research and development capability of the national and federal laboratories into homeland defense, developing counter terrorism measures, managing operational test and evaluation at secure sites, establishing standards programs, or helping develop a Homeland Security Advanced Research Projects Agency.

Number awarded Up to 3 each year.

Deadline January of each year.

[672]
IDAHO SPACE GRANT CONSORTIUM GRADUATE FELLOWSHIPS

Idaho Space Grant Consortium
c/o University of Idaho
College of Engineering
P.O. Box 441011
Moscow, ID 83844-1011
(208) 885-6438　　　　Fax: (208) 885-6645
E-mail: isgc@uidaho.edu
Web: ivc.uidaho.edu/isgc/fellow.html

Summary To provide funding for research in space-related fields to graduate students at institutions belonging to the Idaho Space Grant Consortium (ISGC).

Eligibility This program is open to graduate students at ISGC member institutions. Applicants may be majoring in engineering, mathematics, science, or science/math education, but they must be interested in conducting research in an area of focus of the National Aeronautics and Space Administration (NASA). An undergraduate and current GPA of 3.0 or higher and U.S. citizenship are required. As a component of the NASA Space Grant program, ISGC encourages participation by women, underrepresented minorities, and persons with disabilities.

Financial data The stipend is $6,000 per year.

Duration 1 year; may be renewed.

Additional Information Members of the consortium include Albertson College of Idaho, Boise State University, College of Southern Idaho, Idaho State University, Lewis Clark State College, North Idaho College, Northwest Nazarene College, Brigham Young University of Idaho, and the University of Idaho. This program is funded by NASA.

Number awarded Varies each year.

Deadline February of each year.

[673]
IDAHO SPACE GRANT CONSORTIUM RESEARCH INITIATION GRANTS

Idaho Space Grant Consortium
c/o University of Idaho
College of Engineering
P.O. Box 441011
Moscow, ID 83844-1011
(208) 885-7303　　　　Fax: (208) 885-6645
E-mail: isgc@uidaho.edu
Web: ivc.uidaho.edu/isgc

Summary To provide funding for research in space-related fields to faculty members at institutions belonging to the Idaho Space Grant Consortium (ISGC).

Eligibility This program is open to faculty members in aeronautics, space, and related fields at institutions affiliated with ISGC. Applicants must be seeking funding for research programs that will result in proposals to the U.S. National Aeronautics and Space Administration (NASA) and other federal, state, and private organizations for further funding and continued program development. Travel to a NASA center or enterprise is strongly encouraged. U.S. citizenship is required. As a component of the NASA Space Grant program, ISGC encourages participation by women, underrepresented minorities, and persons with disabilities. Selection is based on the relevance of the proposal to ISGC and NASA goals, relevance to aerospace and space sciences, collaboration plan with a NASA center or enterprise, involvement of undergraduate students in the research, technical merit, potential for continued external funding, and the proposed budget.

Financial data Grants up to $10,000 are provided but require an equal matching amount from the recipient's university, college, or department. Salaries may be used as a source of the required match.

Duration Projects must be completed within 1 year.

Additional Information Members of the consortium include Albertson College of Idaho, Boise State University, College of Southern Idaho, Idaho State University, Lewis Clark State College, North Idaho College, Northwest Nazarene College, Brigham Young University of Idaho, and the University of Idaho. This program is funded by NASA.

Number awarded Varies each year.

Deadline January of each year.

[674]
IDAHO SPACE GRANT CONSORTIUM TRAVEL STIPENDS

Idaho Space Grant Consortium
c/o University of Idaho
College of Engineering
P.O. Box 441011
Moscow, ID 83844-1011
(208) 885-4934　　　　Fax: (208) 885-6645
E-mail: isgc@uidaho.edu
Web: ivc.uidaho.edu/isgc

Summary To provide funding to faculty and students at member institutions of the Idaho Space Grant Consortium (ISGC) who are interested in traveling to meetings or conferences.

Eligibility This program is open to faculty members and students at institutions affiliated with ISGC. Applicants must be interested in traveling to a field center of the U.S. National Aeronautics and Space Administration (NASA) or a NASA-related meeting or conference. Students may travel to summer internships at NASA centers; faculty may travel to establish contacts with out-of-state scientists or researchers. International travel is not supported. U.S. citizenship is required. As a component of the NASA Space Grant program, ISGC encourages participation by women, underrepresented minorities, and persons with disabilities.

Financial data Matching grants up to $1,500 are available. Funds may cover up to half the cost of the travel.

Additional Information Members of the consortium include Albertson College of Idaho, Boise State University, College of Southern Idaho, Idaho State University, Lewis Clark State College, North Idaho College, Northwest Nazarene College, Brigham Young University of Idaho, and the University of Idaho. This program is funded by NASA.

Number awarded Varies each year.

Deadline Applications may be submitted at any time.

[675]
INDIANA SPACE GRANT CONSORTIUM GRADUATE FELLOWSHIPS

Indiana Space Grant Consortium
c/o Purdue University
School of Industrial Engineering
1287 Grissom Hall
West Lafayette, IN 47907-1287
(765) 494-5873   Fax: (765) 496-3449
E-mail: bcaldwel@ecn.purdue.edu
Web: www.insgc.org

Summary To provide funding to graduate students at member institutions of the Indiana Space Grant Consortium (INSGC) interested in conducting research related to space.

Eligibility This program is open to graduate students enrolled full time at institutions that are members of the INSGC. Applicants must be interested in conducting research related to 1 of the strategic enterprise areas of the U.S. National Aeronautics and Space Administration (NASA): space science, earth science, biological and physical research, human exploration and development of space, and aerospace technology. U.S. citizenship is required. The program encourages representation of women, underrepresented minorities, and persons with disabilities.

Financial data The maximum grant is $5,000 per year for master's degree students or $10,000 for doctoral students.

Duration 1 year; students may not receive an award in consecutive years.

Additional Information This program is funded by NASA. The academic member institutions of the INSGC are Purdue University, Ball State University, Indiana University, Indiana University-Purdue University at Indianapolis, Purdue University at Calumet, Taylor University, University of Evansville, University of Notre Dame, and Valparaiso University.

Number awarded Varies each year. Approximately $60,000 is available for undergraduate scholarships and graduate fellowships.

Deadline February of each year.

[676]
INDIVIDUALS WITH DISABILITIES IN POSTDOCTORAL TRAINING RESEARCH SUPPLEMENTS

National Institutes of Health
Division of Extramural Outreach and Information Resources
Attn: GrantsInfo
6701 Rockledge Drive, Suite 6095
Bethesda, MD 20892-7910
(301) 435-0714   Fax: (301) 480-8443
E-mail: GrantsInfo@nih.gov
Web: www.nih.gov

Summary To provide support to postdoctorates with disabilities who are interested in participating in an ongoing research project funded by the National Institutes of Health (NIH).

Eligibility This program is open to postdoctorates who meet the definition of disabled in the Americans with Disabilities Act: an individual who "has a physical or mental impairment that substantially limits 1 or more major life activities." A list of disabilities that might confer eligibility for supplemental awards under this program includes, but is not limited to, the following: total deafness in both ears, visual acuity less than 20/200 with corrective lenses, speech impairment, missing extremities, partial paralysis, complete paralysis, convulsive disorders, mental or emotional illness, learning disabilities, kidney dialysis, and severe distortion of the limbs and/or spine. In all cases, postdoctorates supported under this supplement must, with reasonable assistance, be able to contribute to the research supported by the parent grant. Any principal investigator at a domestic institution holding an eligible parent grant (funded by the NIH) is eligible—in cooperation with the disabled postdoctorate—to submit a request for a supplement to support a disabled candidate. The candidates must have completed all requirements for a doctoral degree and be interested in biomedical or behavioral research. They may be affiliated with either the applicant institution or another institution. Only under extraordinary circumstances is it acceptable for candidates to continue working with their former predoctoral mentors. Selection is based on 1) the qualifications of the candidate, including career goals, prior research training, research potential, and relevant experience; 2) the plan for the proposed research experience in the supplemental request and its relationship to the parent grant; 3) the appropriateness of the proposed accommodations for the candidate; 4) evidence from the principal investigator that the experience will enhance the research potential, knowledge, and/or skills of the candidate, and that adequate mentorship will be provided; and 5) evidence from the principal investigator that the activities of the candidate will be an integral part of the project.

Financial data The salary and fringe benefits must be in accordance with the salary structure of the grantee institution, consistent with the level of effort, to a maximum of $40,000 per year. Additional funds up to $6,000

may be requested for supplies and travel. Funds may also be requested to permit accommodation to the research environment. That may include research equipment, but only if it is directly related to the project and to accommodating the disabilities of the individual.

Duration Fellows are expected to devote an equivalent of at least 3 months full-time effort to the research project and related activities in any 1 year, and in most cases the period of support should last at least 2 years.

Number awarded Usually, each parent grant may have only 1 supplement for a person with a disability.

Deadline Principal investigators—in cooperation with the disabled candidate—are encouraged to submit an application no later than 3 months before the anniversary date of the last 2 years remaining on the parent grant.

[677]
INDUSTRY-BASED GRADUATE RESEARCH ASSISTANTSHIPS AND COOPERATIVE FELLOWSHIPS IN THE MATHEMATICAL SCIENCES

National Science Foundation
Directorate for Mathematical and Physical Sciences
Attn: Division of Mathematical Sciences
4201 Wilson Boulevard, Room 1025
Arlington, VA 22230
(703) 292-4862   TDD: (703) 292-5090
E-mail: ldouglas@nsf.gov
Web: www.nsf.gov/mps/general.htm

Summary To provide financial assistance to graduate students in mathematics who wish to gain experience in industrial settings.

Eligibility This program is open to graduate students in mathematics who are U.S. citizens, nationals, or permanent residents. Applicants may propose either 1) a research assistantship, in which they conduct research for a master's thesis or doctoral dissertation under the joint supervision of a university faculty member and an industrial scientist, spending part time at the industrial site on a regular basis and the remainder in the classroom or in other campus-based activities; or 2) a cooperative fellowship, in which they work full time as an intern in an industrial setting. Applications are especially encouraged from women, underrepresented minorities, and persons with disabilities.

Financial data The program provides up to 50% (with an upper limit of $20,000) of the total support for each student. The university faculty member involved in the joint supervision of these students may request up to $6,000 as a faculty research allowance.

Duration Up to 1 year.

Number awarded Varies each year.

Deadline November of each year.

[678]
INDUSTRY/GOVERNMENT GRADUATE FELLOWSHIPS

American Meteorological Society
Attn: Fellowship/Scholarship Coordinator
45 Beacon Street
Boston, MA 02108-3693
(617) 227-2426, ext. 246   Fax: (617) 742-8718
E-mail: amsinfo@ametsoc.org
Web: www.ametsoc.org

Summary To encourage students entering their first year of graduate school to work on an advanced degree in the atmospheric and related oceanic and hydrologic sciences.

Eligibility This program is open to students entering their first year of graduate study who wish to pursue advanced degrees in the atmospheric or related oceanic or hydrologic sciences. Students currently studying chemistry, computer sciences, engineering, environmental sciences, mathematics, or physics who intend to pursue careers in the atmospheric or related oceanic or hydrologic sciences are also eligible to apply. Applicants must be U.S. citizens or permanent residents and have a GPA of 3.0 or higher. Along with their application, they must submit 2 essays of 100 words or less: 1 on their career goals in the atmospheric or related oceanographic or hydrologic fields and 1 on their most important achievements that qualify them for this scholarship. The sponsor specifically encourages applications from women, minorities, and students with disabilities who are traditionally underrepresented in the atmospheric and related oceanic sciences. Selection is based on academic performance as an undergraduate and plans to pursue a career in the atmospheric or related oceanic and hydrologic sciences.

Financial data The stipend is $15,000 per academic year.

Duration 9 months.

Additional Information This program was initiated in 1991. It is funded by high-technology firms and government agencies. Requests for an application must be accompanied by a self-addressed stamped envelope.

Number awarded Varies each year; recently, 16 of these scholarships were awarded.

Deadline February of each year.

[679]
INFORMATION TECHNOLOGY RESEARCH GRANTS

National Science Foundation
Attn: Information Technology Research Program
4201 Wilson Boulevard
Arlington, VA 22230
(703) 292-5111　　　　　　　TDD: (703) 292-5090
E-mail: itr@nsf.gov
Web: www.itr.nsf.gov

Summary To provide funding to investigators interested in conducting research related to information technology.

Eligibility This program is open to investigators at U.S. academic institutions and nonprofit research institutions. Collaborations with international researchers, for-profit corporations, and national laboratories are encouraged, but the proposal must be submitted through a U.S. institution. Applicants must be interested in conducting research on computers and computation; networking and communication; information and data storage, manipulation, and presentation; new applications of information technology in all science and engineering disciplines; new science and engineering research that is facilitated by information technology and by collaboration with computer scientists; and uses of this knowledge and technology to advance social, educational, scientific, and engineering goals. Fundamental research that contributes to national security, including new models for information and network security, new information technology for emergency response, and new information technology for prevention, detection, remediation, and attribution of terrorist attacks, is especially encouraged. Proposals may be for small projects, medium projects, or large projects. Proposals from women, underrepresented minorities, and persons with disabilities are especially encouraged.

Financial data Small project grants may have a total budget up to $500,000, not to exceed $180,000 in each year; medium project grants may have a total budget from $500,000 to $4 million, not to exceed $1 million in each year; large project grants may have a total budget from $4 million to $15 million, not to exceed $3 million in each year.

Duration 3 years for small projects; 5 years for medium and large projects.

Additional Information This program, which began in 2000, is operated by various disciplinary divisions within the NSF; for a list of the participating divisions and their telephone numbers, contact the sponsor.

Number awarded Varies each year, depending on the availability of funds. Recently, the program expected to award 60 to 90 small project grants, 40 to 50 medium project grants, and 3 to 4 large project grants. The total allocated to this program recently was $145 million. Normally, 30% of total funding is spent on small projects, 40 to 60% on medium projects, and 10 to 20% to large projects.

Deadline For small project, pre-proposals are not required and full proposals are due in December of each year. For medium projects, pre-proposals are not required and full proposals are due in February of each year. For large projects, pre-proposals must be submitted in November and full proposals are due the following March.

[680]
KANSAS SPACE GRANT CONSORTIUM PROGRAM

Kansas Space Grant Consortium
c/o University of Kansas
135 Nichols Hall
2335 Irving Hill Road
Lawrence, KS 66045-7612
(785) 864-7401　　　　　　Fax: (785) 864-3361
E-mail: ksgc@ukans.edu
Web: www.ksgc.org

Summary To provide funding for space-related activities to students and faculty at member institutions of the Kansas Space Grant Consortium.

Eligibility This program is open to faculty and students at member institutions. Support is provided for undergraduate research scholarships, graduate research assistantships, undergraduate and graduate student participation in activities sponsored by the U.S. National Aeronautics and Space Administration (NASA), faculty participation in NASA research projects, and other activities in fields of interest to NASA. The consortium is a component of NASA's Space Grant program, which encourages participation by women, underrepresented minorities, and persons with disabilities.

Financial data Each participating institution determines the amounts of its awards.

Additional Information The member institutions of the consortium are Emporia State University, Fort Hayes State University, Haskell Indian Nations University, Kansas State University, Pittsburgh State University, University of Kansas, and Wichita State University. Funding for this program is provided by NASA.

Number awarded Varies each year.

Deadline Each participating institution establishes its own deadlines.

[681]
KENTUCKY SPACE GRANT CONSORTIUM RESEARCH GRANTS

Kentucky Space Grant Consortium
c/o Western Kentucky University
Department of Physics and Astronomy, TCCW 246
Hardin Planetarium and Astrophysical Observatory
One Big Red Way
Bowling Green, KY 42101-3576
(270) 745-4156 Fax: (270) 745-4255
E-mail: Richard.Hackney@wku.edu
Web: www.wku.edu/KSGC

Summary To provide financial assistance to faculty members at designated institutions in Kentucky who are interested in conducting space-related research.

Eligibility This program is open to faculty members at member institutions of the Kentucky Space Grant Consortium. Applicants must be interested in conducting research that will enhance their competitiveness for future funding. Preference is given to proposals that involve students in the research. Investigators are encouraged to develop projects related to strategic enterprises of the U.S. National Aeronautics and Space Administration (NASA), to collaborate with NASA field centers, or to utilize NASA data. The Kentucky Space Grant Consortium is a component of the NASA Space Grant program, which encourages participation by women, underrepresented minorities, and persons with disabilities.

Financial data Awards up to $5,000 require a 1:1 institutional match; awards up to $10,000 require a 2:1 match.

Duration 1 year; may be renewed.

Additional Information This program is funded by NASA. The KSGC member institutions are Centre College, Eastern Kentucky University, Kentucky State University, Morehead State University, Murray State University, Northern Kentucky University, Transylvania University, University of Kentucky, University of Louisville, and Western Kentucky University. The institution must provide adequate faculty time and any indirect costs.

Number awarded Varies each year.

Deadline April of each year.

[682]
LASPACE FELLOWSHIPS

Louisiana Space Consortium
c/o Louisiana State University
Physics and Astronomy
371 Nicholson Hall
Baton Rouge, LA 70803-4001
(225) 578-8697 Fax: (225) 578-1222
E-mail: wefel@phunds.phys.lsu.edu
Web: phacts.phys.lsu.edu

Summary To provide financial assistance to students working on a graduate degree in an aerospace-related discipline at a college or university belonging to the Louisiana Space Consortium (LaSPACE).

Eligibility This program is open to U.S. citizens working on a master's or doctoral degree in a space- or aerospace-related field as a full-time student at 1 of the LaSPACE member schools. LaSPACE is a component of the U.S. National Aeronautics and Space Administration (NASA) Space Grant program, which encourages participation by members of groups underrepresented in science, mathematics, and engineering (women, minorities, and persons with disabilities).

Financial data The stipend is $17,500 per year for students working on a master's degree or $20,000 per year for students working on a doctorate.

Duration 1 year; renewable for up to 2 additional years for master's degree students and up to 4 additional years for Ph.D. students.

Additional Information Fellows work with an established aerospace researcher at 1 of the LaSPACE member institutions: Dillard University, Grambling State University, L.S.U. Agricultural Center, Louisiana State University and A&M College, Louisiana Tech University, Loyola University, McNeese State University, Nicholls State University, Northwestern State University of Louisiana, Southeastern Louisiana University, Southern University and A&M College, Southern University at New Orleans, Southern University at Shreveport-Bossier City, Tulane University, University of New Orleans, University of Louisiana at Lafayette, University of Louisiana at Monroe, and Xavier University of Louisiana. Funding for this program is provided by NASA. Fellows are expected to describe the work in a yearly written report and in seminars presented to various audiences.

Number awarded 1 to 3 each year.

Deadline October of each year.

[683]
LESLIE ISENBERG FUND SCHOLARSHIP

American Speech-Language-Hearing Foundation
Attn: Graduate Student Scholarship Competition
10801 Rockville Pike
Rockville, MD 20852-3279
(301) 897-5700 Toll-free: (800) 498-2071
Fax: (301) 571-0457 TTY: (800) 498-2071
E-mail: foundation@asha.org
Web: www.ashfoundation.org

Summary To provide financial assistance to persons with disabilities and others who are interested in studying communication sciences or related programs in graduate school.

Eligibility Applicants must be accepted for full-time graduate study in an accredited communication sciences and disorders program. Priority is given to students with disabilities. Selection is based on academic and personal merit. Students who have received a prior scholarship from the American Speech-Language-Hearing Foundation are not eligible.

Financial data The stipend ranges from $2,000 to $4,000. Funds must be used for educational support (e.g., tuition, books, school-related living expenses), not for personal or conference travel.
Duration 1 year.
Number awarded 1 each year.
Deadline June of each year.

[684] LESTER WALLS III SCHOLARSHIP

Landscape Architecture Foundation
Attn: Scholarship Program
636 Eye Street, N.W.
Washington, DC 20001-3736
(202) 216-2356   Fax: (202) 898-1185
E-mail: msippel@asla.org
Web: www.laprofession.org

Summary To provide financial assistance to students with disabilities interested in working on a degree in landscape architecture or any student interested in working on a barrier-free design project.
Eligibility Eligible to apply are either 1) students with disabilities working on a degree in landscape architecture or 2) any student in landscape architecture who wishes to conduct a research project on barrier-free design. Applicants must submit a 2-page autobiography and statement of professional and personal goals, including a brief description of the disability, and samples of work completed to date or planned, either as slides or drawings of plans, sections, elevations, sketches, models, or completed projects. Selection is based on professional experience, community involvement, extracurricular activities, and financial need.
Financial data This award is $500.
Additional Information This scholarship was established in memory of an alumnus of California Polytechnic State University and founder of his own landscape architecture firm.
Number awarded 1 each year.
Deadline March of each year.

[685] MASSACHUSETTS SPACE GRANT CONSORTIUM GRADUATE FELLOWSHIPS

Massachusetts Space Grant Consortium
c/o Massachusetts Institute of Technology
Building 33, Room 208
77 Massachusetts Avenue
Cambridge, MA 02139
(617) 258-5546   Fax: (617) 253-0823
E-mail: halaris@mit.edu
Web: www.mit.edu

Summary To provide funding to first-year graduate students for space-related research or study at institutions in Massachusetts.
Eligibility This program is open to first-year graduate students at institutions that are members of the Massachusetts Space Grant Consortium (MASGC). Applicants must be pursuing research or study in space-related science or engineering fields. U.S. citizenship is required. Selection is based on academic achievement and interest in space science or space engineering. MASGC is a component of the U.S. National Aeronautics and Space Administration (NASA) Space Grant program, which encourages participation by women, underrepresented minorities, and persons with disabilities.
Financial data The fellowships provide full tuition plus a stipend.
Duration 1 academic year.
Additional Information Graduate member institutions of the MASGC are Boston University, the Five College Astronomy Department, Harvard University, Massachusetts Institute of Technology, Tufts University, University of Massachusetts, Wellesley College, and Worcester Polytechnic Institute. This program is funded by NASA.
Number awarded Varies each year.
Deadline February of each year.

[686] MATHEMATICAL SCIENCES POSTDOCTORAL RESEARCH FELLOWSHIPS

National Science Foundation
Directorate for Mathematical and Physical Sciences
Attn: Division of Mathematical Sciences
4201 Wilson Boulevard, Room 1025
Arlington, VA 22230
(703) 292-4862   TDD: (703) 292-5090
E-mail: msprf@nsf.gov
Web: www.nsf.gov/mps.general.htm

Summary To provide financial assistance to postdoctorates interested in pursuing research training in mathematics.
Eligibility Applicants for these fellowships must 1) be U.S. citizens, nationals, or permanent residents; 2) have earned a Ph.D. in a mathematical science or have had equivalent research training and experience; 3) have held the Ph.D. for no more than 2 years; and 4) have not previously held any other postdoctoral fellowship from the National Science Foundation (NSF). They must be proposing to conduct a program of postdoctoral research training at an appropriate nonprofit U.S. institution, including government laboratories, national laboratories, and privately sponsored nonprofit institutes, as well as institutions of higher education. Occasionally, research may be conducted at a foreign institution. A senior scientist at the institution must indicate availability for consultation and agreement to work with the fellow. Women, underrepresented minorities, and persons with disabilities are strongly encouraged to apply.
Financial data The total award is $108,000, consisting of 3 components: 1) a monthly stipend of $4,000 for

full-time support or $2,000 for half-time support, paid directly to the fellow; 2) a research allowance of $7,500, also paid directly to the fellow; and 3) an institutional allowance of $4,500, paid to the host institution for fringe benefits (including health insurance payments for the fellow) and expenses incurred in support of the fellow, such as space, equipment, and general purpose supplies.

Duration The program provides ongoing support for 2 9-month academic years and 6 summer months, for a total of 24 months of support, within a 48-month period. Fellows have 2 options for the academic years' stipend: 1) full-time support for any 18 academic-year months in a 3-year period, in intervals not shorter than 3 consecutive months, or 2) a combination of full-time and half-time support over a period of 3 academic years, usually 1 academic year full-time and 2 academic years half-time. Not more than 2 summer months' support may be received in any calendar year.

Additional Information Under certain circumstances, it may be desirable for portions of the work to be done at foreign institutions. Approval to do so must be obtained in advance from both the sponsoring senior scientist and the NSF. Information is also available from the American Mathematical Society, 210 Charles Street, P.O. Box 6248, Providence, RI 02940, (401) 455-4105, Fax: (401) 455-4004, E-mail: nsfpostdocs@ams.org.

Number awarded 30 to 35 each year.

Deadline October of each year.

[687]
MATHEMATICAL SCIENCES UNIVERSITY–INDUSTRY POSTDOCTORAL RESEARCH FELLOWSHIPS

National Science Foundation
Directorate for Mathematical and Physical Sciences
Attn: Division of Mathematical Sciences
4201 Wilson Boulevard, Room 1025
Arlington, VA 22230
(703) 292-4862   TDD: (703) 292-5090
E-mail: ldouglas@nsf.gov
Web: www.nsf.gov/mps/general.htm

Summary To provide financial assistance to recent doctoral recipients in mathematics who wish to broaden their knowledge, experience, and research perspectives in an industrial environment.

Eligibility To become fellows, candidates must 1) be U.S. citizens, nationals, or permanent residents; 2) be eligible to be appointed as a research associate or assistant professor at the institution submitting the proposal; 3) have earned a Ph.D. in a mathematical science or have had equivalent research training and experience; 4) have held the Ph.D. for no more than 7 years; 5) have not held a tenured position at any academic institution; and 6) have not previously held any other postdoctoral fellowship from the National Science Foundation (NSF). Applications must be submitted by a university principal investigator who will serve as scientific mentor to a fellow with an industrial sponsor. The proposal may either identify the prospective postdoctoral fellow or present a plan for recruiting the fellows. Principal investigators are encouraged to submit proposals that include women, underrepresented minorities, and persons with disabilities as postdoctoral fellows. Selection is based on the quality of the proposed research to be conducted at both the academic and industrial sites, the qualifications of and commitment by both the faculty mentor and the industrial sponsor, the appropriateness of the academic/industrial interaction, and the impact of the proposed training on the professional development of the postdoctoral fellow.

Financial data The total award is $111,000, of which $71,000 is provided by the National Science Foundation and $40,000 by the industrial sponsor. The award includes a stipend allowance for the fellow of $80,000 ($40,000 per year) plus a fringe benefit allowance of $16,000 ($8,000 per year), an allowance of $4,500 for the sponsoring institution in lieu of indirect costs, a research allowance of $4,500 for the fellow to be used for travel, publication costs, and other research-related expenses, and an allowance of $6,000 for the faculty mentor for research expenses related to the industrial partnership.

Duration 2 years.

Number awarded Varies each year.

Deadline November of each year.

[688]
MATHEMATICAL SCIENCES UNIVERSITY–INDUSTRY SENIOR RESEARCH FELLOWSHIPS

National Science Foundation
Directorate for Mathematical and Physical Sciences
Attn: Division of Mathematical Sciences
4201 Wilson Boulevard, Room 1025
Arlington, VA 22230
(703) 292-4862   TDD: (703) 292-5090
E-mail: ldouglas@nsf.gov
Web: www.nsf.gov/mps/general.htm

Summary To provide financial assistance to senior scholars in mathematics who wish to broaden their knowledge, experience, and research perspectives by exposure to industrial environments, and to industrial researchers who wish to experience and participate in the full range of university research environments.

Eligibility This program is open to faculty members and industrial scientists who are U.S. citizens, nationals, or permanent residents and who have earned a Ph.D. in a mathematical science or have had research training and experience equivalent to that represented by such a degree. Faculty members must be proposing to conduct research in an industrial setting, and industrial scientists must be proposing to conduct research in a university environment. All applicants must make a commitment to return to the home institution for a minimum of 1 year following the fellowship tenure. Applications are

especially encouraged from women, underrepresented minorities, and persons with disabilities.

Financial data The program provides a salary equivalent to the fellow's regular 6-month full-time salary (to a maximum of $50,000, or $60,000 including fringe benefits), a research allowance of $10,000, and an institutional allowance, in lieu of indirect costs, of $10,000.

Duration Normally 12 months.

Additional Information Faculty fellows are usually expected to participate in this program during a sabbatical leave.

Number awarded Varies each year.

Deadline November of each year.

[689]
MICHIGAN SPACE GRANT CONSORTIUM FELLOWSHIPS

Michigan Space Grant Consortium
c/o University of Michigan
2106 Space Physics Research Laboratory
2455 Hayward Avenue
Ann Arbor, MI 48109-2143
(734) 764-9508   Fax: (734) 764-4585
E-mail: blbryant@umich.edu
Web: www.umich.edu/~msgc

Summary To provide funding to students at member institutions of the Michigan Space Grant Consortium who wish to conduct space-related research.

Eligibility This program is open to undergraduate and graduate students at affiliates of the Michigan consortium who are proposing to conduct research in aerospace, space science, earth system science, and other related fields in science, engineering, or mathematics; students working on educational research topics in mathematics, science, or technology are also eligible. Applicants must identify a mentor in the faculty research, education, or public service communities with whom they intend to work and who is available to write a letter of recommendation for the student. U.S. citizenship is required. Women, underrepresented minorities, and persons with disabilities are especially encouraged to apply.

Financial data The maximum grant is $2,500 for undergraduates or $5,000 for graduate students.

Additional Information The consortium consists of Eastern Michigan University, Grand Valley State University, Hope College, Michigan State University, Michigan Technological University, Oakland University, Saginaw Valley State University, University of Michigan, Wayne State University, and Western Michigan University. This program is supported by the U.S. National Aeronautics and Space Administration (NASA).

Number awarded Varies; a total of $125,000 is available for these fellowships each year.

Deadline November of each year.

[690]
MICHIGAN SPACE GRANT CONSORTIUM RESEARCH SEED GRANTS

Michigan Space Grant Consortium
c/o University of Michigan
2106 Space Physics Research Laboratory
2455 Hayward Avenue
Ann Arbor, MI 48109-2143
(734) 764-9508   Fax: (734) 764-4585
E-mail: blbryant@umich.edu
Web: www.umich.edu/~msgc

Summary To provide funding to faculty at member institutions of the Michigan Space Grant Consortium (MSGC) who are interested in conducting space-related research.

Eligibility This program is open to faculty (research and professorial) at affiliates of the MSGC. Applicants must be interested in conducting a research project in engineering, science, mathematics, life sciences, or related educational areas. Preference is given to projects focusing on aerospace, space, or earth system science, although awards are not strictly limited to those topics. Initiation of a new area of research is preferred over efforts to continue an existing project or study. Women, underrepresented minorities, and persons with disabilities are encouraged to apply.

Financial data Grants up to $5,000 are available. At least 1:1 cost matching (cash contributions or in-kind support) with nonfederal funds is required.

Additional Information The consortium consists of Eastern Michigan University, Grand Valley State University, Hope College, Michigan State University, Michigan Technological University, Oakland University, Saginaw Valley State University, University of Michigan, Wayne State University, and Western Michigan University. This program is supported by the U.S. National Aeronautics and Space Administration (NASA).

Number awarded Varies each year.

Deadline November of each year.

[691]
MINNESOTA SPACE GRANT CONSORTIUM SCHOLARSHIPS AND FELLOWSHIPS

Minnesota Space Grant Consortium
c/o University of Minnesota
Department of Aerospace Engineering and
  Mechanics
107 Akerman Hall
110 Union Street S.E.
Minneapolis, MN 55455
(612) 626-9295   Fax: (612) 626-1558
E-mail: mnsgc@aem.umn.edu
Web: www.aem.umn.edu

Summary To provide financial assistance for space-related science and engineering studies to undergraduate and graduate students in Minnesota.

Eligibility This program is open to graduate and undergraduate full-time students at institutions that are affiliates of the Minnesota Space Grant Consortium. U.S. citizenship and a GPA of 3.2 or higher are required. Eligible fields of study include the physical sciences (astronomy, astrophysics, chemistry, computer science, mathematics, physics, planetary geoscience, and planetary science), life sciences (biology, biochemistry, botany, health science/nutrition, medicine, molecular/cellular biology, and zoology), social sciences (anthropology, architecture, art, economics, education, history, philosophy, political science/public policy, and psychology), earth sciences (atmospheric science, climatology/meteorology, environmental science, geography, geology, geophysics, and oceanography), and engineering (agricultural, aeronautical, aerospace, architectural, bioengineering, chemical, civil, computer, electrical, electronic, environmental, industrial, materials science, mechanical, mining, nuclear, petroleum, engineering science, and engineering mechanics). The Minnesota Space Grant Consortium is a component of the U.S. National Aeronautics and Space Administration (NASA) Space Grant program, which encourages participation by women, underrepresented minorities, and persons with disabilities.

Financial data This program awards approximately $125,000 in undergraduate scholarships and $25,000 in graduate fellowships each year. The amounts of the awards are set by each of the participating institutions, which augment funding from this program with institutional resources.

Duration 1 year; renewable.

Additional Information This program is funded by NASA. The member institutions are: Augsburg College, Bethel College, Bemidji State University, College of St. Catherine, Carleton College, Concordia College, Fond du Lac Community College, Itasca Community College, Leech Lake Tribal College, Macalaster College, Normandale Community College, Southwest State University, University of Minnesota at Duluth, University of Minnesota at Twin Cities, and University of St. Thomas.

Number awarded 8 to 12 undergraduate scholarships and 2 to 3 graduate fellowships are awarded each year.

Deadline March of each year.

[692]
MISSISSIPPI SPACE GRANT CONSORTIUM CAMPUS ACTIVITIES

Mississippi Space Grant Consortium
c/o University of Mississippi
217 Vardaman Hall
P.O. Box 1848
University, MS 38677-1848
(662) 915-1187   Fax: (662) 915-3927
E-mail: arandle@olemiss.edu
Web: www.olemiss.edu

Summary To provide funding to undergraduate and graduate students for space-related activities at colleges and universities that are members of the Mississippi Space Grant Consortium.

Eligibility This program is open to undergraduate and graduate students at member institutions of the Mississippi consortium. Each participating college or university establishes its own program and criteria for admission, but all activities are in engineering, mathematics, and science fields of interest to the U.S. National Aeronautics and Space Administration (NASA). U.S. citizenship is required. The consortium is a component of NASA's Space Grant program, which encourages participation by women, underrepresented minorities, and persons with disabilities.

Financial data Each participating institution establishes the amounts of the awards. Recently, the average undergraduate award was $1,308 and the average graduate award was $2,975. A total of $96,350 was awarded.

Additional Information Consortium members include Alcorn State University, Coahoma Community College, Delta State University, Hinds Community College (Utica Campus), Itawamba Community College, Jackson State University, Meridian Community College, Mississippi Delta Community College, Mississippi Gulf Coast Community College (Jackson County Campus), Mississippi State University, Mississippi University for Women, Mississippi Valley State University, Northeast Mississippi Community College, Pearl River Community College, the University of Mississippi, and the University of Southern Mississippi. This program is funded by NASA.

Number awarded Varies each year; recently, a total of 66 students received support through this program.

[693]
MONTANA SPACE GRANT CONSORTIUM GRADUATE FELLOWSHIPS

Montana Space Grant Consortium
c/o Montana State University
261 EPS Building
P.O. Box 173835
Bozeman, MT 59717-3835
(406) 994-4223 Fax: (406) 994-4452
E-mail: msgc@montana.edu
Web: www.montana.edu

Summary To provide financial assistance to students in Montana who are interested in working on a graduate degree in the space sciences and/or engineering.

Eligibility This program is open to full-time graduate students in Montana working on degrees in fields related to space sciences and engineering; those fields include, but are not limited to, astronomy, biological and life sciences, chemical engineering, chemistry, civil engineering, computer sciences, electrical engineering, geological sciences, mechanical engineering, and physics. Priority is given to students who have been involved in aerospace-related research. U.S. citizenship is required. The Montana Space Grant Consortium is a component of the U.S. National Aeronautics and Space Administration (NASA) Space Grant program, which encourages participation by women, underrepresented minorities, and persons with disabilities. Financial need is not considered in the selection process.

Financial data The fellowships provide payment of tuition and fees plus a stipend of $15,000 per year.

Duration 1 year; may be renewed.

Additional Information Funding for this program is provided by NASA.

Number awarded Varies each year; recently, 5 of these fellowships were awarded.

Deadline March of each year.

[694]
MONTANA SPACE GRANT CONSORTIUM RESEARCH INITIATION GRANTS

Montana Space Grant Consortium
c/o Montana State University
261 EPS Building
P.O. Box 173835
Bozeman, MT 59717-3835
(406) 994-4223 Fax: (406) 994-4452
E-mail: msgc@montana.edu
Web: www.montana.edu

Summary To provide seed money for research related to space sciences and engineering.

Eligibility This program is open to individuals in Montana (most of the awards go to full-time graduate students) who need support to conduct research related to space sciences and/or engineering. This program is part of the U.S. National Aeronautics and Space Administration (NASA) Space Grant program, which encourages participation by women, underrepresented minorities, and persons with disabilities.

Financial data These grants provide "seed money" only.

Duration 1 year; generally nonrenewable.

Additional Information Awardees are required to submit a follow-on proposal to NASA for regular research funding during the year of the grant.

Number awarded Varies each year; recently, 4 of these grants were awarded.

[695]
NASA EARTH SYSTEM SCIENCE FELLOWSHIP PROGRAM

National Aeronautics and Space Administration
Attn: NASA Peer Review Services, Code Y
500 E Street, S.W., Suite 200
Washington, DC 20024-2760
(202) 358-0855 E-mail: acrouch@hq.nasa.gov
Web: research.hq.nasa.gov/research.cfm

Summary To provide financial assistance to graduate students in earth system science.

Eligibility This program is open to students accepted or enrolled in a full-time M.Sc. and/or Ph.D. program at accredited U.S. universities. Applicants must be interested in conducting interdisciplinary research involving the study of the earth as a system. Both basic science and applied research are supported. Basic science topics fall into 5 categories: 1) how is the global earth system changing? 2) what are the primary forcings of the earth system? 3) how does the earth system respond to natural and human-induced changes? 4) what are the consequences of change in the earth system for human civilization? and 5) how well can we predict future changes in the earth system? Applied research themes are organized around the following: biology and biogeochemistry of ecosystems and the global carbon cycle; atmospheric chemistry, aerosols, and solar radiation; global water and energy cycle; oceans and ice in the earth system; and solid earth science. Applications are accepted for research in atmospheric chemistry and physics, ocean biology and physics, ecosystem dynamics, hydrology, cryospheric processes, geology, geophysics, or information science and engineering; research in paleo-climate, paleo-ecology, and paleo-hydrology is discouraged. U.S. citizens and permanent residents are given preference, although the program is not restricted to them. Students with disabilities and from underrepresented minority groups (African Americans, Native Americans, Alaskan Natives, Mexican Americans, Puerto Ricans, and Native Pacific Islanders) are especially urged to apply.

Financial data The award is $24,000 per year, to be used to cover the recipient's stipend ($18,000); travel expenses to scientific conferences and seminars, health

insurance, books, and other items ($3,000); and tuition and fees, payable as a university allowance ($3,000).

Duration 1 year; may be renewed for up to 2 additional years.

Additional Information This program was established in 1990. Beginning in 1996, the National Aeronautics and Space Administration (NASA) combined the earth science portion of its Graduate Student Researchers Program (GSRP), supported by the NASA Education Division, and the Graduate Student Fellowship in Global Change Research, supported by the Office of Earth Science, to establish this program.

Number awarded Up to 50 each year.

Deadline March of each year for new applications; May of each year for renewal applications.

[696]
NASA GRADUATE STUDENT RESEARCHERS PROGRAM

National Aeronautics and Space Administration
Attn: Office of Human Resources and Education
Code FE
Washington, DC 20546-0001
(202) 358-0402   Fax: (202) 358-3032
E-mail: kblanding@mail.hq.nasa.gov
Web: fellowships.hq.nasa.gov/gsrp

Summary To provide funding to graduate students interested in conducting research in fields of interest to the U.S. National Aeronautics and Space Administration (NASA).

Eligibility This program is open to full-time students enrolled or planning to enroll in an accredited graduate program at a U.S. college or university. Applicants must be citizens of the United States, sponsored by a faculty advisor or department chair, and interested in conducting research in space sciences at their home university or at NASA field centers. Selection is based on academic qualifications, quality of the proposed research and its relevance to NASA's program, the student's proposed utilization of center research facilities (except for NASA headquarters), and ability of the student to accomplish the defined research. African Americans, Native Americans, Alaskan Natives, Mexican Americans, Puerto Ricans, Native Pacific Islanders, women, and persons with disabilities are strongly urged to apply.

Financial data The program provides a $18,000 student stipend, a $3,000 student expense allowance, and a $3,000 university allowance.

Duration 1 year; may be renewed for up to 2 additional years.

Additional Information This program was established in 1980. Awards for NASA Headquarters are sponsored by the Office of Space Science (OSS), the Office of Biological and Physical Research (OBPR), and the Office of Earth Science (OES). The areas of interest include structure/evolution of the universe, origins/planetary systems, solar system exploration, sun-earth connection, information systems, microgravity science and applications, life sciences, and earth sciences. Fellows selected by NASA Headquarters conduct research at their respective universities. Other awards are distributed through NASA field centers, each of which has its own research agenda and facilities. These centers include Ames Research Center (Moffett Field, California), Dryden Flight Research Facility (Edwards, California), Goddard Space Flight Center (Greenbelt, Maryland), Jet Propulsion Laboratory (Pasadena, California), Johnson Space Center (Houston, Texas), Kennedy Space Center (Kennedy Space Center, Florida), Langley Research Center (Hampton, Virginia), Glenn Research Center (Cleveland, Ohio), Marshall Space Flight Center (Huntsville, Alabama), and Stennis Space Center (Stennis Space Center, Mississippi). Fellows spend some period of time in residence at the center, taking advantage of the unique research facilities of the installation and working with center personnel. Travel outside the United States is allowed if it is essential to the research effort and charged to a grant.

Number awarded This program supports approximately 300 graduate students each year.

Deadline January of each year.

[697]
NASA-DESGC GRADUATE STUDENT FELLOWSHIPS

Delaware Space Grant Consortium
c/o University of Delaware
Bartol Research Institute
104 Center Mall, #217
Newark, DE 19716-4793
(302) 831-1094   Fax: (302) 831-1843
E-mail: desgc@bartol.udel.edu
Web: www.delspace.org

Summary To provide financial support to graduate students in Delaware and Pennsylvania involved in space-related studies.

Eligibility This program is open to graduate students at member institutions of the Delaware Space Grant Consortium (DESGC) embarking on or involved in aerospace-related research, technology, or design. Fields of interest have included astronomy, chemical engineering, geography, marine studies, materials science, mechanical engineering, and physics. U.S. citizenship is required. The DESGC is a component of the U.S. National Aeronautics and Space Administration (NASA) Space Grant program, which encourages applications from women, minorities, and persons with disabilities.

Financial data This program provides tuition and stipends.

Duration 1 year; may be renewed.

Additional Information This program, established in 1991, is funded by NASA. Members of the consortium include Delaware State University (Dover, Delaware), Delaware Technical and Community College (Dover,

Georgetown, Newark, and Wilmington, Delaware), Franklin and Marshall College (Lancaster, Pennsylvania), Gettysburg College (Gettysburg, Pennsylvania), Lehigh University (Bethlehem, Pennsylvania), Swarthmore College (Swarthmore, Pennsylvania), University of Delaware (Newark, Delaware), Villanova University (Villanova, Pennsylvania), and Wilmington College (New Castle, Delaware).

Number awarded Varies each year; since this program was established, it has awarded 45 fellowships to 27 graduate students.

Deadline February of each year.

[698]
NATIONAL DEFENSE SCIENCE AND ENGINEERING GRADUATE FELLOWSHIP PROGRAM

American Society for Engineering Education
Attn: NDSEG Fellowship Program
1818 N Street, N.W., Suite 600
Washington, DC 20036-2479
(202) 331-3516   Fax: (202) 265-8504
E-mail: ndseg@asee.org
Web: www.asee.org/ndseg

Summary To provide financial assistance to doctoral students in areas of science and engineering that are of military importance.

Eligibility Graduate students in the following specialties are eligible: aeronautical and astronautical engineering; biosciences, including toxicology; chemical engineering; chemistry; cognitive, neural, and behavioral sciences; computer science; electrical engineering; geosciences, including terrain, water, and air; materials science and engineering; mathematics; mechanical engineering; naval architecture and ocean engineering; oceanography; and physics, including optics. Applicants must be U.S. citizens or nationals at or near the beginning of their graduate study planning to pursue a doctoral degree in 1 of the indicated specialties. Applications are particularly encouraged from women, underrepresented minorities (American Indians, African Americans, Hispanics, Native Alaskans, and Pacific Islanders), and persons with disabilities. Selection is based on all available evidence of ability, including academic records, letters of recommendation, and GRE scores.

Financial data The annual stipend is $23,500 for the first year, $24,500 for the second year; and $25,500 for the third year; the program also pays the recipient's institution full tuition and required fees (not to include room and board). An additional allowance may be considered for a student with a disability.

Duration 3 years, as long as satisfactory academic progress is maintained.

Additional Information This program is sponsored by the Army Research Office, the Air Force Office of Scientific Research, and the Office of Naval Research. Recipients do not incur any military or other service obligation.

Number awarded Varies each year; recently, 170 of these fellowships were awarded. Recipients must attend school on a full-time basis.

Deadline January of each year.

[699]
NATIONAL SCIENCE FOUNDATION RESEARCH OPPORTUNITY AWARDS

National Science Foundation
Directorate for Education and Human Resources
Attn: Senior Staff Associate for Cross Directorate
  Programs
4201 Wilson Boulevard, Room 805
Arlington, VA 22230
(703) 292-8600   TDD: (703) 292-5090
Web: www.ehr.nsf.gov/crssprgm/rui/start.shtm

Summary To enable faculty members at predominantly undergraduate institutions to conduct research as visiting scientists on projects of investigators who are supported by the National Science Foundation (NSF).

Eligibility Participants must be citizens or nationals of the United States teaching at predominantly undergraduate institutions, defined as U.S. 2-year, 4-year, master's-level, and small doctoral colleges and universities that 1) grant baccalaureate degrees in NSF-supported fields or provide programs of instruction for students pursuing such degrees after transferring; 2) have undergraduate enrollment exceeding graduate enrollment; and 3) award no more than an average of 10 Ph.D. and/or D.Sc. degrees per year in all disciplines that NSF supports. Applicants must be teaching in a department that offers courses that qualify for bachelor's degree credit in NSF-supportable fields and may offer master's degrees but may not award a doctorate or offer doctoral courses and supervise doctoral research. Applications must be submitted by an NSF-supported investigator at another institution who wishes to employ the proposed visiting researcher under a Research Opportunity Award (ROA) collaboration. Individuals interested in becoming visiting researchers make their own contacts with investigators who currently have or are applying for NSF research grants. A principal investigator may also initiate the collaboration. Applications may be submitted as part of a new NSF proposal, as a supplement to an ongoing NSF award, or by rearranging the project budget in an ongoing award without requesting supplemental funding from NSF. Selection is based on the capability of the investigators, the technical soundness of the proposed effort, the contribution of the ROA activity to the ongoing research project, and its potential impact upon the ROA visitor and the visitor's institution. The NSF strongly encourages women, minorities, and persons with disabilities to participate in this program.

Financial data Funding is usually provided as a supplement to an ongoing NSF research grant. It may be

covered by rebudgeting funds already awarded or by inclusion in the original proposal to NSF. Most NSF programs limit support to moderate amounts, frequently including only the direct costs of participation (e.g., salary and fringe benefits for the visitor, travel costs, and essential supplies).

Duration Support generally ranges from 2 to 12 months. Most ROA activities are summer experiences, although partial support of sabbaticals is occasionally provided.

Additional Information This program operates through the various disciplinary divisions within the NSF; for a list of the respective telephone numbers, contact the Senior Staff Associate for Cross Directorate Programs.

Number awarded Depends on the number of grant applications that seek the use of a visiting researcher.

Deadline Applications for supplemental funding may be submitted at any time, but they must be received at least 3 months before the funds are needed.

[700]
NEBRASKA SPACE GRANT STATEWIDE SCHOLARSHIP COMPETITION

Nebraska Space Grant Consortium
c/o University of Nebraska at Omaha
Allwine Hall 422
6001 Dodge Street
Omaha, NE 68182-0406
(402) 554-3772
Toll-free: (800) 858-8648, ext. 4-3772 (within NE)
Fax: (402) 554-3781   E-mail: nasa@unomaha.edu
Web: www.unomaha.edu/~nasa/funding/ssc.html

Summary To provide financial assistance to undergraduate and graduate students in Nebraska interested in aerospace-related study or research.

Eligibility This program is open to undergraduate and graduate students at schools that are members of the Nebraska Space Grant Consortium. Applicants must be U.S. citizens participating in approved aviation or aerospace-related research or course work. Selection is based primarily on past academic performance in the classroom. Special attention is given to applications submitted by women, underrepresented minorities, and persons with disabilities.

Financial data Maximum awards are $500 per semester for undergraduate or graduate course work, $750 per semester for undergraduate research, or $2,500 per semester for graduate research.

Duration 1 semester; may be renewed if the recipient maintains a GPA of 3.0 or higher.

Additional Information The following schools are members of the Nebraska Space Grant Consortium: University of Nebraska at Omaha, University of Nebraska at Lincoln, University of Nebraska at Kearney, University of Nebraska Medical Center, Creighton University, Western Nebraska Community College, Chadron State College, College of St. Mary, Metropolitan Community College, Grace University, Hastings College, Little Priest Tribal College, and Nebraska Indian Community College. Funding for this program is provided by the National Aeronautics and Space Administration.

Deadline April of each year.

[701]
NEVADA SPACE GRANT CONSORTIUM GRADUATE FELLOWSHIP PROGRAM

Nevada Space Grant Consortium
c/o University of Nevada at Reno
1664 North Virginia Street
MS/172
Reno, NV 89557-0138
(775) 784-6261   Fax: (775) 327-2235
E-mail: nvsg@mines.unr.edu
Web: www.unr.edu/spacegrant

Summary To provide financial assistance for space-related study to graduate students at institutions that are members of the Nevada Space Grant Consortium (NSGC).

Eligibility This program is open to graduate students at NSGC member institutions. Applicants must be working on a degree in an aerospace-related field (including the behavioral sciences, biological sciences, business, communications, computer science, economics, education, engineering, international affairs, law, natural sciences, physical sciences, public administration, and sociology) that is concerned with or likely to improve the understanding, assessment, development, and utilization of space. They must be U.S. citizens, be enrolled full time (or accepted for full-time study), present a proposed research or activity plan related to space, include in the research or activity plan an extramural experience at a field center of the U.S. National Aeronautics and Space Administration (NASA), plan to be involved in NSGC outreach activities, not receive other federal funds, and intend to pursue a career in a field of interest to NASA. Members of underrepresented groups (African Americans, Hispanics, American Indians, Pacific Islanders, physically disabled people, and women of all races) who have an interest in aerospace fields are encouraged to apply.

Financial data The grant is $22,500, including $16,000 as a stipend for the student and $6,500 for tuition and a student research and travel allowance.

Duration 12 months; may be renewed up to 24 additional months.

Additional Information Members of the NSGC include all state institutes of higher learned in Nevada: 2 Ph.D.-granting universities (the University of Nevada at Las Vegas and the University of Nevada at Reno), 4 community colleges (Southern Nevada, Great Basin, Truckee Meadows, and Western Nevada), and the system's research organization, the Desert Research Institute. Funding for this program is provided by NASA.

Number awarded Varies each year; recently, 13 of these awards were granted.
Deadline March of each year.

[702]
NEW HAMPSHIRE CHARITABLE FOUNDATION STATEWIDE STUDENT AID PROGRAM

New Hampshire Charitable Foundation
37 Pleasant Street
Concord, NH 03301-4005
(603) 225-6641   Toll-free: (800) 464-6641
Fax: (603) 225-1700   E-mail: info@nhcf.org
Web: www.nhcf.org

Summary To provide scholarships and loans for undergraduate or graduate study to New Hampshire residents.

Eligibility This program is open to New Hampshire residents who are graduating high school seniors or undergraduate students between 17 and 23 years of age or graduate students of any age. Applicants must be enrolled in or planning to enroll in an accredited 2- or 4-year college, university, or vocational school on at least a half-time basis. The school may be in New Hampshire or another state. Selection is based on financial need, academic merit, community service, school activities, and work experience. Priority is given to students with the fewest financial resources and to vocational/technical school students.

Financial data Awards range from $500 to $2,500 and average $1,800. Most are made in the form of grants (recently, 82% of all awards) or no-interest or low-interest loans (recently 18% of all awards).

Duration 1 year; approximately one third of the awards are renewable.

Additional Information Through this program, students submit a single application for more than 250 different scholarship and loan funds. Many of the funds have additional requirements, covering such elements as the field of study; residency in region, county, city, or town; graduation from designated high schools; and special attributes (of Belgian descent, employee of designated firms, customer of Granite State Telephone Company, disabled, suffering from a life-threatening or serious chronic illness, of Lithuanian descent, dependent of a New Hampshire police officer, dependent of a New Hampshire Episcopal minister, of Polish descent, former Sea Cadet or Naval Junior ROTC, or employed in the tourism industry). The Citizens' Scholarship Foundation of America reviews all applications; recipients are selected by the New Hampshire Charitable Foundation. A $15 application fee is required.

Number awarded Varies each year; recently, a total of $2.3 million was awarded.

Deadline April of each year.

[703]
NEW HAMPSHIRE SPACE GRANT CONSORTIUM PROJECT SUPPORT

New Hampshire Space Grant Consortium
c/o University of New Hampshire
Institute for the Study of Earth, Oceans, and Space
Morse Hall
39 College Road
Durham, NH 03824-3525
(603) 862-0094   Fax: (603) 862-1915
E-mail: nhspacegrant@unh.edu
Web: www.nhsgc.sr.unh.edu

Summary To provide financial assistance to students at member institutions of the New Hampshire Space Grant Consortium (NHSGC) who are interested in participating in space-related activities.

Eligibility This program is open to students at member institutions of the NHSGC. Applicants must be studying space physics, astrophysics, astronomy, or aspects of computer science, engineering, earth sciences, ocean sciences, atmospheric sciences, or life sciences that utilize space technology and/or adopt a planetary view of the global environment. U.S. citizenship is required. The New Hampshire Space Grant Consortium is a component of the U.S. National Aeronautics and Space Administration (NASA) Space Grant program, which encourages participation by women, underrepresented minorities, and persons with disabilities.

Financial data The amount of the award depends on the nature of the project.

Duration From 1 quarter to 1 year.

Additional Information This program is funded by NASA. Currently, projects operating through this program include space grant fellowships at the University of New Hampshire, Agnes M. Lindsay Trust/NASA Challenge Scholars Initiative at the New Hampshire Community Technical College System, Presidential Scholars Research Assistantships at Dartmouth College, and Women in Science Internships at Dartmouth.

Number awarded Varies each year.

Deadline Each participating college or university sets its own deadline.

[704]
NIAMS SMALL GRANT PROGRAM FOR NEW INVESTIGATORS

National Institute of Arthritis and Musculoskeletal
  and Skin Diseases
Attn: Chief, Review Branch
45 Center Drive, Room 5A25U
Bethesda, MD 20892-6500
(301) 594-4953   Fax: (301) 480-4543
E-mail: jf43z@nih.gov
Web: www.niams.nih.gov

Summary To provide support to new investigators in scientific areas of interest to the National Institute of

Arthritis and Musculoskeletal and Skin Diseases (NIAMS).

Eligibility This program is open to investigators at U.S. for-profit and nonprofit organizations, public and private, such as universities, colleges, hospitals, laboratories, units of state and local government, and eligible agencies of the federal government. Racial/ethnic minority individuals, women, and persons with disabilities are specifically encouraged to apply as principal investigators. Applications are also encouraged from new investigators who hold a faculty position at an Historically Black College or University (HBCU) or other institution that has a student population consisting predominantly of individuals from racial or ethnic groups that are underrepresented in science. The proposal should be for pilot research that is likely to lead to a subsequent individual research project grant. Areas of research include rheumatic diseases, muscle biology, musculoskeletal diseases, and skin diseases. Support provided through this program may not be used for thesis or dissertation research.

Financial data Grants range up to $50,000 per year in direct costs.

Duration Up to 3 years.

Number awarded Varies each year; recently, approximately $1.5 million was available for this program to support 15 to 20 new grants.

Deadline February, June, or October of each year.

[705]
NORTH DAKOTA SPACE GRANT PROGRAM FELLOWSHIPS

North Dakota Space Grant Program
c/o University of North Dakota
Department of Space Studies
Clifford Hall, Fifth Floor
P.O. Box 9008
University Avenue and Tulane
Grand Forks, ND 58202-9008
(701) 777-4856   Toll-free: (800) 828-4274
Fax: (701) 777-3711   E-mail: bieri@space.edu
Web: www.space.edu/spacegrant/fellowinfo.html

Summary To provide funding for space-related research to undergraduate and graduate students at specified academic institutions affiliated with the North Dakota Space Grant Program (NDSGP).

Eligibility This program is open to undergraduate and graduate students at specified NDSGP universities who are studying in fields related to space and are paired with an advisor for a research project. U.S. citizenship is required. Other qualifying criteria are set by each participating institution. The NDSGP is a component of the U.S. National Aeronautics and Space Administration (NASA) Space Grant program, which encourages the participation of women, underrepresented minorities, and persons with disabilities.

Financial data The stipend is $2,000.

Additional Information Participating NDSCP members are the University of North Dakota and North Dakota State University. This program is funded by NASA.

Number awarded Varies each year.

[706]
NSF DIRECTOR'S AWARD FOR DISTINGUISHED TEACHING SCHOLARS

National Science Foundation
Directorate for Education and Human Resources
Attn: Division of Undergraduate Education
4201 Wilson Boulevard, Room 835N
Arlington, VA 22230
(703) 292-4627   Fax: (703) 292-9015
TDD: (703) 292-5090   E-mail: hlevitan@nsf.gov
Web: www.ehr.nsf.gov

Summary To recognize and reward, with funding for additional research, scholars affiliated with institutions of higher education who have contributed to the teaching of science, technology, engineering, and mathematics (STEM) at the K-12 and undergraduate level.

Eligibility This program is open to teaching-scholars affiliated with institutions of higher education who are nominated by their president, chief academic officer, or other independent researcher. Nominees should have integrated research and education and approached both education and research in a scholarly manner. They should have demonstrated leadership in their respective fields as well as innovativeness and effectiveness in facilitating K-12 and undergraduate student learning in STEM disciplines. Consideration is given to faculty who have 1) generated partnerships between their university and K-12 educators that apply higher education resources in serving K-12 needs; 2) distinguished themselves as scholars in their research discipline and as educators of undergraduates; 3) encouraged scholars to explore ways of integrating education and research; 4) disseminated exemplary experiences of scholars in education; 5) supported scholars to serve as mentors for other faculty who are trying to balance and integrate their scholarly contributions to STEM education; or 6) supported faculty who have a scholarly approach to both research and education. Based on letters of nomination, selected scholars are invited to submit applications for support of their continuing efforts to integrate education and research. Nominations of women, underrepresented minorities, and persons with disabilities are especially encouraged.

Financial data The maximum grant is $300,000 for the life of the project.

Duration 4 years.

Number awarded Approximately 6 each year.

Deadline Preliminary proposals are due in November of each year; full applications must be submitted in February.

[707]
NSF SCHOLAR-IN-RESIDENCE AT NIH PROGRAM

National Science Foundation
Directorate for Engineering
4201 Wilson Boulevard
Arlington, VA 22230
(703) 292-8300   TDD: (703) 292-5090
E-mail: rkhosla@nsf.gov
Web: www.eng.nsf.gov

Summary To provide an opportunity for science and engineering faculty to conduct research in laboratories of the National Institutes of Health (NIH).

Eligibility This program is open to full-time faculty members at U.S. colleges and universities in mathematics, physical science, and engineering fields of interest to the National Science Foundation (NSF). Applicants must be proposing to conduct research at the intramural laboratories of the NIH that focuses on the interaction between their field and the medical and biological sciences and biomedical engineering. Women, minorities, and persons with disabilities are strongly encouraged to apply.

Financial data The NSF provides summer salary, travel, and per diem costs for the visiting scholar while on the NIH campus, as well as travel costs associated with short-term visits to the NIH campus by students working with the scholar at his/her home institution. The home institution of the scholar is expected to provide cost sharing through sabbatical salary or other resources. NIH provides office space, research facilities, research costs in the form of expendable and minor equipment purchases to the host laboratory, and the time of its research staff.

Duration 6 months to 1 year, either consecutively or staggered within an 18-month time frame.

Additional Information This program is offered through 2 NSF directorates: engineering (see above for contact information) and mathematical and physical sciences, (703) 292-8800, E-mail: dcaldwel@nsf.gov.

Number awarded Up to 10 each year.

Deadline Applications may be submitted at any time.

[708]
NSF SMALL BUSINESS INNOVATION RESEARCH GRANTS

National Science Foundation
Directorate for Engineering
Attn: Division of Design, Manufacture, and Industrial Innovation
4201 Wilson Boulevard, Room 550
Arlington, VA 22230
(703) 292-8330   TDD: (703) 292-5090
E-mail: sbir@nsf.gov
Web: www.eng.nsf.gov/sbir

Summary To provide funding to small and creative engineering, science, education, and technology-related firms to conduct innovative, high-risk research on scientific and technical problems.

Eligibility For the purposes of this program, a "small business" is any organization that is independently owned and operated for profit, not dominant in the field in which it is operating, and meets the size standard of 500 employees or less. The primary employment of the principal investigator must be with the firm at the time of award and during the conduct of the proposed project. Members of minority racial and ethnic groups, women, and persons with disabilities are particularly encouraged to apply as principal investigators. Preference is given to women-owned small business concerns and to socially and economically disadvantaged small business concerns. Women-owned small business concerns are at least 51% owned by a woman or women who also control and operate them. Socially and economically disadvantaged small business concerns are at least 51% owned by an Indian tribe, Native Hawaiian organization, or 1 or more socially and economically disadvantaged individuals (Black Americans, Hispanic Americans, Native Americans, Asian Pacific Americans, or subcontinent Asian Americans). The project must be performed in the United States. Current priorities for critical technology areas of national importance include advanced materials and manufacturing systems, information-based technologies, biotechnology, and electronics.

Financial data Support is offered in 2 phases. In phase 1, awards normally may not exceed $100,000 (for both direct and indirect costs); in phase 2, awards normally may not exceed $500,000 (including both direct and indirect costs).

Duration Phase 1 awards may extend up to 6 months; phase 2 awards may extend up to 2 years.

Number awarded Depends on the availability of funds; the National Science Foundation (NSF) plans to award 200 phase 1 grants each year. Recently, $20 million was budgeted for this program

Deadline June of each year for proposals in advanced materials and manufacturing systems and in information-based technologies; January of each year for biotechnology and electronics.

[709]
NSF STANDARD AND CONTINUING GRANTS

National Science Foundation
4201 Wilson Boulevard
Arlington, VA 22230
(703) 292-5111   TDD: (703) 292-5090
E-mail: info@nsf.gov
Web: www.nsf.gov

Summary To provide financial support for research in broad areas of science and engineering.

Eligibility The National Science Foundation (NSF) supports research through its Directorates of Biological Sciences; Computer and Information Science and Engi-

neering; Education and Human Resources; Engineering; Geosciences; Mathematical and Physical Sciences; and Social, Behavioral, and Economic Sciences. Within those general areas of science and engineering, NSF awards 2 types of grants: 1) standard grants, in which NSF agrees to provide a specific level of support for a specified period of time with no statement of NSF intent to provide additional future support without submission of another proposal; and 2) continuing grants, in which NSF agrees to provide a specific level of support for an initial specified period of time with a statement of intent to provide additional support of the project for additional periods, provided funds are available and the results achieved warrant further support. Although NSF often solicits proposals for support of targeted areas through issuance of specific program solicitations, it also accepts unsolicited proposals. Scientists, engineers, and educators usually act as the principal investigator and initiate proposals that are officially submitted by their employing organization. Most employing organizations are universities, colleges, and nonprofit nonacademic organizations (such as museums, observatories, research laboratories, and professional societies). Certain programs are open to for-profit organizations, state and local governments, or unaffiliated individuals. Principal investigators usually must be U.S. citizens, nationals, or permanent residents. NSF particularly encourages members of racial and ethnic minority groups, women, and persons with disabilities to apply as principal investigators.

Financial data Funding levels vary, depending on the nature of the project and the availability of funds. Awards resulting from unsolicited research proposals are subject to statutory cost-sharing.

Duration Standard grants specify the period of time, usually up to 1 year; continuing grants normally specify 1 year as the initial period of time, with support to continue for additional periods.

Additional Information Researchers interested in support from NSF should contact the address above to obtain further information on areas of support and programs operating within the respective directorates. They should consult with a program officer before submitting an application. Information on programs is available on the NSF home page. NSF does not normally support technical assistance, pilot plant efforts, research requiring security classification, the development of products for commercial marketing, or market research for a particular project or invention. Bioscience research with disease-related goals, including work on the etiology, diagnosis, or treatment of physical or mental disease, abnormality, or malfunction in human beings or animals, is normally not supported.

Number awarded Approximately 10,000 new awards are issued each year.

Deadline Many programs accept proposals at any time. Other programs establish target dates or deadlines; those target dates and deadlines are published in the *NSF Bulletin* and in specific program announcements/solicitations.

[710] NUTRITION ACTION FELLOWSHIP

Center for Science in the Public Interest
Attn: Executive Director
1875 Connecticut Avenue, N.W., Suite 300
Washington, DC 20009-5728
(202) 332-9110   Fax: (202) 265-4954
E-mail: cspi@cspinet.org
Web: www.cspinet.org/job/nutrition_fellow.html

Summary To provide funding to postdoctorates interested in serving as a nutrition advocate at the Center for Science in the Public Interest

Eligibility This program is open to recent graduates with a Ph.D. or M.D. who are interested in serving as a nutrition advocate at the center. Applicants should have demonstrated interest in public interest advocacy and nutrition science, food safety, or health policy. They should also be able to demonstrate academic achievement and writing ability. Minorities, women, and persons with disabilities are particularly encouraged to apply.

Financial data The stipend is $35,000. A generous and comprehensive benefits package is also provided.

Duration 1 year, preferably starting in summer.

Additional Information Fellows work in the center's Washington office on nutrition science policy and/or food safety issues.

Number awarded 1 each year.

Deadline Applications may be submitted at any time.

[711] OFFICE OF NAVAL RESEARCH HISTORICALLY BLACK ENGINEERING COLLEGES FUTURE ENGINEERING FACULTY FELLOWSHIP PROGRAM

Office of Naval Research
c/o North Carolina A&T State University
College of Engineering
551 McNair Hall
Greensboro, NC 27411
(336) 334-7760   E-mail: jck@ncat.edu
Web: www.onr.navy.mil

Summary To provide financial assistance for graduate education to students interested in becoming faculty members in engineering at Historically Black Colleges and Universities (HBCUs).

Eligibility This program is open to U.S. citizens and nationals who intend to work on a Ph.D. in designated fields of engineering and, in return for the support, agree to join the engineering faculty of an HBCU. Applicants should be at or near the beginning of doctoral study. The designated fields of study include aerospace, chemical, civil, electrical, manufacturing, mechanical, and ocean

engineering. Women, underrepresented minorities, and persons with disabilities are especially encouraged to apply. Selection is based on academic achievement, area of study, a personal statement, letters of recommendation, and conditions of appointment.

Financial data The program provides full payment of tuition and required fees and a competitive stipend that varies each year. Recently, stipends were $17,500 for the first year, $18,500 for the second year, and $19,500 for the third year. A travel allowance of $1,000 is also provided.

Duration 3 years.

Additional Information This program is administered by North Carolina A&T State University on behalf of the Office of Naval Research (ONR). Information is also available from ONR 353, 800 North Quincy Street, Arlington, VA 22217-5660, (703) 696-4224, E-mail: 363_HBCU@onr.navy.mil.

Number awarded 3 each year.

Deadline March of each year.

[712]
OHIO SPACE GRANT CONSORTIUM DOCTORAL FELLOWSHIP

Ohio Space Grant Consortium
c/o Ohio Aerospace Institute
22800 Cedar Point Road
Cleveland, OH 44142
(440) 962-3032   Toll-free: (800) 828-OSGC
Fax: (440) 962-3057   E-mail: osgc@oai.org
Web: www.osgc.org/Fellowship.html

Summary To provide financial assistance to graduate students working on a doctoral degree in an aerospace-related discipline at major universities in Ohio.

Eligibility These fellowships are available to U.S. citizens enrolled full time in a doctoral program in an aerospace-related discipline (aeronautical engineering, aerospace engineering, astronomy, biology, chemical engineering, chemistry, civil engineering, computer engineering and science, control engineering, electrical engineering, engineering mechanics, geology, industrial engineering, manufacturing engineering, materials science and engineering, mathematics, mechanical engineering, petroleum engineering, physics, and systems engineering) at 1 of the participating universities in Ohio. Applicants must have completed a master's degree or 2 years of graduate study. Women, underrepresented minorities, and physically challenged persons are particularly encouraged to apply. Selection is based on academic achievement, recommendations, academic background, and the relevance of the applicant's research interests and experience.

Financial data The stipend is $18,000 per year plus tuition at the university attended.

Duration Up to 3 years.

Additional Information These fellowships are funded through the National Space Grant College and Fellowship Program administered by the National Aeronautics and Space Administration (NASA), with matching funds provided by the member universities, the Ohio Aerospace Institute, and private industry. The participating universities include: Air Force Institute of Technology, University of Akron, Case Western Reserve University, University of Cincinnati, Cleveland State University, University of Dayton, Ohio State University, Ohio University, University of Toledo, Wright State University, and Youngstown State University. Recipients are required to conduct a significant portion of their doctoral research in residence at NASA Glenn Research Center/Ohio Aerospace Institute or at another approved NASA center.

Number awarded 2 each year.

Deadline February of each year.

[713]
OHIO SPACE GRANT CONSORTIUM MASTER'S FELLOWSHIP

Ohio Space Grant Consortium
c/o Ohio Aerospace Institute
22800 Cedar Point Road
Cleveland, OH 44142
(440) 962-3032   Toll-free: (800) 828-OSGC
Fax: (440) 962-3057   E-mail: osgc@oai.org
Web: www.osgc.org/Fellowship.html

Summary To provide financial assistance to graduate students who wish to work on a master's degree in an aerospace-related discipline at major universities in Ohio.

Eligibility These fellowships are available to U.S. citizens enrolled full time in a master's degree program in an aerospace-related discipline (aeronautical engineering, aerospace engineering, astronomy, biology, chemical engineering, chemistry, civil engineering, computer engineering and science, control engineering, electrical engineering, engineering mechanics, geology, industrial engineering, manufacturing engineering, materials science and engineering, mathematics, mechanical engineering, petroleum engineering, physics, and systems engineering) at 1 of the participating universities in Ohio. Women, underrepresented minorities, and physically challenged persons are particularly encouraged to apply. Selection is based on academic achievement, recommendations, academic background, and the relevance of the applicant's research interests and experience.

Financial data The stipend is $14,000 per academic year plus tuition at the university attended.

Duration Up to 18 months; may be renewed for an additional 12 months.

Additional Information These fellowships are funded through the National Space Grant College and Fellowship Program administered by the National Aeronautics and Space Administration (NASA), with matching funds provided by the member universities, the Ohio Aero-

space Institute, and private industry. The participating universities include: Air Force Institute of Technology, University of Akron, Case Western Reserve University, University of Cincinnati, Cleveland State University, University of Dayton, Ohio State University, Ohio University, University of Toledo, Wright State University, and Youngstown State University.

Number awarded 4 each year.

Deadline February of each year.

[714]
OMOHUNDRO INSTITUTE POSTDOCTORAL NEH FELLOWSHIP

Omohundro Institute of Early American History and Culture
P.O. Box 8781
Williamsburg, VA 23187-8781
(757) 221-1110   Fax: (757) 221-1047
E-mail: ieahc1@wm.edu
Web: www.wm.edu/oieach/fello.html

Summary To provide funding to scholars in American studies who wish to revise their dissertation or other manuscript in residence at the Omohundro Institute of Early American History and Culture in Williamsburg, Virginia.

Eligibility Applicants must have completed a Ph.D. in a field that encompasses all aspects of the lives of North America's indigenous and immigrant peoples during the colonial, Revolutionary, and early national periods of the United States and the related histories of Canada, the Caribbean, Latin America, the British Isles, Europe, and Africa, from the 16th century to approximately 1815. They must be U.S. citizens or have lived in the United States for the 3 previous years. The proposed fellowship project must not be under contract to another publisher. The revisions must be made at the Omohundro Institute. Applicants may not have previously published a book or have entered into a contract for the publication of a scholarly monograph. Members of underrepresented groups (including people of color, persons with disabilities, Vietnam veterans, and women) are particularly encouraged to apply. Selection is based on the potential of the candidate's dissertation or other manuscript to make a distinguished, book length contribution to scholarship.

Financial data The fellowship includes a stipend of $40,000 per year in the first year, funds for travel to conferences and research centers, and access to office, research, and computer facilities at the Institute.

Duration 2 years.

Additional Information Funding for this program is provided by the National Endowment for the Humanities (NFH). Fellows hold concurrent appointment as assistant professor in the appropriate department at the College of William and Mary and teach a total of 6 semester hours during the 2-year term.

Number awarded 1 each year.

Deadline October of each year.

[715]
OSGC EDUCATION PROGRAM

Oklahoma NASA Space Grant Consortium
c/o University of Oklahoma
College of Geosciences
710 Asp Avenue, Suite 5
Norman, Oklahoma 73069
(405) 447-8483   Fax: (405) 447-8455
E-mail: vduca@ou.edu
Web: www.okspacegrant.ou.edu

Summary To provide financial assistance to students in Oklahoma who are enrolled in aerospace-related studies at the undergraduate and graduate level.

Eligibility This program is open to undergraduate and graduate students at member and affiliate institutions of the Oklahoma Space Grant Consortium (OSGC). U.S. citizenship is required. The OSGC is a component of the U.S. National Aeronautics and Space Administration (NASA) Space Grant program, which encourages participation by women, underrepresented minorities, and persons with disabilities.

Financial data Financing depends on the availability of funds.

Additional Information Members of OSGC are Oklahoma State University, the University of Oklahoma, Cameron University, and Langston University. Write to the sponsor for information on the program at each participating university. This program is funded by NASA.

[716]
OSGC RESEARCH PROGRAM

Oklahoma NASA Space Grant Consortium
c/o University of Oklahoma
College of Geosciences
710 Asp Avenue, Suite 5
Norman, Oklahoma 73069
(405) 447-8483   Fax: (405) 447-8455
E-mail: vduca@ou.edu
Web: www.okspacegrant.ou.edu

Summary To provide funding to faculty and staff at member institutions of the Oklahoma Space Grant Consortium (OSGC) who are interested in conducting research related to the mission of the U.S. National Aeronautics and Space Administration (NASA).

Eligibility This program provides support for space-related research activities at member and affiliate institutions of the OSGC. Proposals may be submitted by faculty and staff of those institutions 1) to foster multi-disciplinary and multi-university research through special conferences, programs, and correspondence; and 2) to enhance the support infrastructure for faculty to facilitate the pursuit of NASA-related research, including both administrative support and marginal funds for travel and critical equipment or supplies. The OSGC is a compo-

nent of the NASA Space Grant program, which encourages participation by women, minorities, and persons with disabilities.

Financial data Financing depends on the availability of funds.

Additional Information Members of OSGC are Oklahoma State University, the University of Oklahoma, Cameron University, and Langston University. This program is funded by NASA.

[717]
PENNSYLVANIA SPACE GRANT CONSORTIUM FELLOWSHIPS

Pennsylvania Space Grant Consortium
c/o Pennsylvania State University
2217 Earth-Engineering Sciences Building
University Park, PA 16802
(814) 863-7687   Fax: (814) 863-8286
E-mail: spacegrant@psu.edu
Web: www.psu.edu

Summary To provide financial assistance for space-related study to graduate students at universities affiliated with the Pennsylvania Space Grant Consortium.

Eligibility This program is open to graduate students at participating universities. Applicants must be studying a field that does, or can, promote the understanding, assessment, and utilization of space, including aerospace, earth science, or space science. U.S. citizenship is required. Students from underrepresented groups (women, minorities, rural populations, and those with disabilities) are especially encouraged to apply.

Financial data The stipend is $5,000 per year.

Duration 2 years.

Additional Information Participating institutions include Pennsylvania State University, Carnegie-Mellon University, Temple University, and the University of Pittsburgh. This program is sponsored by the U.S. National Aeronautics and Space Administration (NASA).

Number awarded Varies each year.

Deadline February of each year.

[718]
POST-BACCALAUREATE AND POST-MASTER'S DEGREE STUDENTS WITH DISABILITIES RESEARCH SUPPLEMENTS

National Institutes of Health
Division of Extramural Outreach and Information Resources
Attn: GrantsInfo
6701 Rockledge Drive, Suite 6095
Bethesda, MD 20892-7910
(301) 435-0714   Fax: (301) 480-8443
E-mail: GrantsInfo@nih.gov
Web: www.nih.gov

Summary To provide support to recent graduates with disabilities who are interested in participating in an ongoing research project funded by the National Institutes of Health (NIH) to gain experience before applying to medical or graduate school.

Eligibility This program is open to recent baccalaureate and master's degree graduates who meet the definition of disabled in the Americans with Disabilities Act: an individual who "has a physical or mental impairment that substantially limits one or more major life activities." A list of disabilities that might confer eligibility for supplemental awards under this program includes, but is not limited to, the following: total deafness in both ears, visual acuity less than 20/200 with corrective lenses, speech impairment, missing extremities, partial paralysis, complete paralysis, convulsive disorders, mental or emotional illness, learning disabilities, kidney dialysis, and severe distortion of the limbs and/or spine. In all cases, candidates supported under this supplement must, with reasonable assistance, be able to contribute to the research supported by the parent grant. Any principal investigator at a domestic institution holding an eligible parent grant (funded by the NIH) is eligible—in cooperation with the disabled candidate—to submit a request for a supplement to support the candidate with a disability. The candidate must be interested in gaining experience in health-related science research while applying for medical, dental, or other professional school. Selection is based on 1) the qualifications of the candidate, including career goals, prior research training, research potential, and relevant experience; 2) the plan for the proposed research experience in the supplemental request and its relationship to the parent grant; 3) the appropriateness of the proposed accommodations for the candidate; 4) evidence from the principal investigator that the experience will enhance the research potential, knowledge, and/or skills of the candidate, and that adequate mentorship will be provided; 5) evidence from the principal investigator that the activities of the candidate will be an integral part of the project; and 6) evidence of the candidate's educational achievement and interest in science.

Financial data The salary must be reasonable and consistent with the institutional salary policies. It may not exceed the amount allowed for graduate students. Additional funds up to $3,000 per year may be requested for

salary and supplies. Funds may also be requested to permit accommodation to the research environment. That may include research equipment, but only if it is directly related to the project and to accommodating the disabilities of the individual. Some types of accommodations that might be provided under this program include: specialized equipment, assistive devices, and personnel, such as readers, interpreters, or assistants.

Duration Normally 1 year; may be extended up to 1 additional year if evidence is provided to show that the candidate is actively pursuing entry into graduate or health profession school.

Number awarded Varies. Usually, each parent grant may have only 1 supplement for a person with a disability.

Deadline Principal investigators—in cooperation with the disabled candidate—are encouraged to submit an application no later than 3 months before the anniversary date of the last 2 years remaining on the parent grant.

[719]
POSTDOCTORAL RESEARCH FELLOWSHIPS IN BIOLOGICAL INFORMATICS

National Science Foundation
Directorate for Biological Sciences
Attn: Division of Biological Infrastructure
4201 Wilson Boulevard, Room 615
Arlington, VA 22230
(703) 292-8470   TDD: (703) 292-5090
E-mail: ckimsey@nsf.gov
Web: www.nsf.gov/bio

Summary To provide opportunities for junior doctoral-level scientists to conduct research and acquire training either in the United States or abroad in biological fields that overlap with the informational, computational, mathematical, and statistical sciences.

Eligibility This program is open to persons who are citizens, nationals, or permanent residents of the United States at the time of application. Applicants must have earned a Ph.D. no earlier than 2 years preceding the deadline date and have not been a principal investigator or co-principal investigator on a federal research grant of more than $20,000. Applicants must be proposing a research and training plan in biological informatics at an appropriate nonprofit U.S. or foreign host institution (colleges and universities, government and national laboratories and facilities, and privately-sponsored nonprofit institutes and museums). Preference is given to applicants who choose foreign locations or those moving to new institutions and research environments with which they have not had prior affiliation. The fellowship may not be held at the same institution as where the applicant's doctorate was earned. Applications are strongly encouraged from women, minorities, and persons with disabilities.

Financial data The grant is $50,000 per year; that includes an annual stipend of $36,000; a research allowance of $9,000 per year paid to the fellow for materials and supplies, subscription fees, and recovery costs for databases, travel, and publication expenses; and an institutional allowance of $5,000 per year for fringe benefits and expenses incurred in support of the fellow.

Duration 2 years; may be renewed for 1 additional year at a U.S. institution if the first 2 years are at a foreign institution.

Number awarded Approximately 20 each year.

Deadline November of each year.

[720]
POSTDOCTORAL RESEARCH FELLOWSHIPS IN MICROBIAL BIOLOGY

National Science Foundation
Directorate for Biological Sciences
Attn: Division of Biological Infrastructure
4201 Wilson Boulevard, Room 615
Arlington, VA 22230
(703) 292-8470   TDD: (703) 292-5090
E-mail: ckimsey@nsf.gov
Web: www.nsf.gov/bio

Summary To provide opportunities for junior doctoral-level scientists to conduct research and acquire training either in the United States or abroad in microbial biology.

Eligibility This program is open to persons who are citizens, nationals, or permanent residents of the United States at the time of application. Applicants must have earned a Ph.D. no earlier than 18 months preceding the deadline date and have not received a federal research grant previously. They must be proposing a research and training plan in microbial biology (including systematics, ecology, physiology, biochemistry, and genetics) at an appropriate nonprofit U.S. or foreign host institution (colleges and universities, government and national laboratories and facilities, and privately-sponsored nonprofit institutes and museums). Preference is given to applicants who choose foreign locations or those moving to new institutions and research environments with which they have not had prior affiliation. The fellowship may not be held at the same institution as where the applicant's doctorate was earned. Applications are strongly encouraged from women, minorities, and persons with disabilities.

Financial data The grant is $50,000 per year; that includes an annual stipend of $36,000; a research allowance of $9,000 per year paid to the fellow for materials and supplies, subscription fees, and recovery costs for databases, travel, and publication expenses; and an institutional allowance of $5,000 per year for fringe benefits and expenses incurred in support of the fellow.

Duration 2 or 3 years. Fellows are encouraged to spend at least part of that time at a foreign host institution.

Number awarded 20 each year. Approximately $2 million is available for this program each year.

Deadline September of each year.

[721]
PREDOCTORAL FELLOWSHIP AWARDS FOR STUDENTS WITH DISABILITIES

National Institutes of Health
Division of Extramural Outreach and Information Resources
Attn: GrantsInfo
6701 Rockledge Drive, Suite 6095
Bethesda, MD 20892-7910
(301) 435-0714   Fax: (301) 480-8443
E-mail: GrantsInfo@nih.gov
Web: www.nih.gov

Summary To provide financial assistance to students with disabilities interested in working on a graduate degree and preparing for a career in biomedical and behavioral research.

Eligibility This program is open to individuals with disabilities who are 1) citizens, nationals, or permanent residents of the United States and 2) enrolled for research training leading to the Ph.D. or equivalent research degree, the combined M.D./Ph.D. degree, or other combined professional doctorate/research Ph.D. degrees in the biomedical or behavioral sciences. Support is not available for individuals enrolled in medical or other professional schools unless they are enrolled in a combined professional doctorate/Ph.D. degree program in biomedical or behavioral research. A person with disabilities is defined according to the Americans with Disabilities Act as an individual who "has a physical or mental impairment that substantially limits 1 or more major life activities, a record of such impairment, or who is regarded as having such an impairment." Qualified students with disabilities are those who, with reasonable accommodation for their disability, are capable of pursuing a research career after appropriate education, training, and experience. A list of disabilities that might confer eligibility for awards under this program includes, but is not limited to, the following: total deafness in both ears, visual acuity less than 20/200 with corrective lenses, speech impairment, missing extremities, partial paralysis, complete paralysis, convulsive disorders, mental or emotional illness, learning disabilities, kidney dialysis, and severe distortion of limbs and/or spine. In all cases, individuals supported under this program must, with reasonable assistance, be able to complete the requirements for the degree program in which they are enrolled.

Financial data The fellowship provides an annual stipend of $19,968, a tuition and fee allowance (100% of all costs up to $3,000 and 60% of costs above $3,000), and an institutional allowance of $2,500 for travel to scientific meetings and for laboratory and other training expenses. Additional funds may be requested to make changes or adjustments in the academic or research environment, to make it possible for the individual to perform the work necessary to meet the requirements of the degree program.

Duration Up to 5 years.

Additional Information These fellowships are offered by most components of the National Institutes of Health (NIH). Write for a list of names and telephone numbers of responsible officers at each component.

Number awarded Varies each year.

Deadline April or November of each year.

[722]
PROFESSIONAL DEVELOPMENT FELLOWSHIPS FOR DOCTORAL CANDIDATES IN ART HISTORY

College Art Association of America
Attn: Fellowship Program
275 Seventh Avenue
New York, NY 10001-6798
(212) 691-1051, ext. 248   Fax: (212) 627-2381
E-mail: fellowship@collegeart.org
Web: www.collegeart.org

Summary To provide financial assistance to doctoral candidates from socially and economically diverse backgrounds who are completing a Ph.D. degree in art history.

Eligibility This program is open to Ph.D. candidates in art history who have been underrepresented in the field because of their race, religion, gender, age, national origin, sexual orientation, disability, or financial status. Applicants must be U.S. citizens or permanent residents and able to demonstrate financial need. They must expect to receive the Ph.D. degree in the year following application.

Financial data The stipend is $5,000.

Duration 1 year: the final year of the degree program.

Additional Information In addition to providing a stipend for the terminal year of their degree program, the College Art Association (CAA) helps fellows search for employment at a museum, art center, college, or university. Upon securing a position, CAA provides a $10,000 subsidy to the employer as part of the fellow's salary. Participating organizations must match this 2:1. In addition to administrative and/or teaching responsibilities, all fellows' positions must include a curatorial or public service component. Salary or stipend, position description, and term of employment will vary and are determined in consultation with individual fellows and their potential employers. This program began in 1993. Funding is provided by the Milton & Sally Avery Arts Foundation, Geraldine R. Dodge Foundation, National Endowment for the Arts, National Endowment for the Humanities, and Terra Foundation for the Arts.

Number awarded 1 each year.

Deadline January of each year.

[723]
PROFESSIONAL DEVELOPMENT FELLOWSHIPS FOR MASTER OF FINE ARTS CANDIDATES

College Art Association of America
Attn: Fellowship Program
275 Seventh Avenue
New York, NY 10001-6798
(212) 691-1051, ext. 248   Fax: (212) 627-2381
E-mail: fellowship@collegeart.org
Web: www.collegeart.org

Summary To provide financial assistance to graduate students from socially and economically diverse backgrounds who are completing an M.F.A. degree in art history.

Eligibility This program is open to M.F.A. candidates in art history who have been underrepresented in the field because of their race, religion, gender, age, national origin, sexual orientation, disability, or financial status. Applicants must be U.S. citizens or permanent residents and able to demonstrate financial need. They must expect to receive the M.F.A. degree in the year following application.

Financial data The stipend is $5,000.

Duration 1 year: the final year of the degree program.

Additional Information In addition to providing a stipend for the terminal year of their degree program, the College Art Association (CAA) helps fellows search for employment at a museum, art center, college, or university. Upon securing a position, CAA provides a $10,000 subsidy to the employer as part of the fellow's salary. Participating organizations must match this 2:1. In addition to administrative and/or teaching responsibilities, all fellows' positions must include a curatorial or public service component. Salary or stipend, position description, and term of employment will vary and are determined in consultation with individual fellows and their potential employers. This program began in 1993. Funding is provided by the Milton & Sally Avery Arts Foundation, Geraldine R. Dodge Foundation, National Endowment for the Arts, National Endowment for the Humanities, and Terra Foundation for the Arts.

Number awarded 1 each year.

Deadline January of each year.

[724]
RESEARCH FELLOWSHIPS OF THE NATIONAL INSTITUTE ON DISABILITY AND REHABILITATION RESEARCH

Department of Education
Office of Special Education and Rehabilitative Services
Attn: National Institute on Disability and Rehabilitation Research
400 Maryland Avenue, S.W., Room 3427
Washington, DC 20202-2500
(202) 205-9800   Fax: (202) 205-8515
E-mail: ellen.blaisiotti@ed.gov
Web: www.ed.gov

Summary To provide funding to graduate students and experienced scholars interested in conducting research related to disabilities and rehabilitation.

Eligibility This program is open to graduate students and experienced researchers, including individuals with disabilities. Distinguished fellowships are available to individuals who hold a doctorate or comparable academic status and have 7 or more years of experience relevant to rehabilitation research. Merit fellowships are open to persons who have either advanced professional training or experience in independent study in an area that is directly related to disability and rehabilitation. Selection is based on the quality and level of formal education, previous work experience, and recommendations of present or former supervisors or colleagues that include an indication of the applicant's ability to work creatively in scientific research; the quality of a research proposal; the importance of the problem to be investigated to the mission of the National Institute on Disability and Rehabilitation Research; the research hypothesis or related objectives and the methodology and design to be followed; assurance of the availability of any necessary data resources, equipment, or institutional support, including technical consultation and support where appropriate, required to carry out the proposed activity.

Financial data Distinguished fellowships are $55,000 per year; merit fellowships are $45,000 per year.

Duration 1 year.

Additional Information These awards are also known as the Mary E. Switzer Memorial Fellowships.

Number awarded 10 each year, including both distinguished and merit fellowships.

Deadline October of each year.

[725]
RESEARCH SUPPLEMENTS FOR GRADUATE STUDENTS WITH DISABILITIES

National Institutes of Health
Division of Extramural Outreach and Information Resources
Attn: GrantsInfo
6701 Rockledge Drive, Suite 6095
Bethesda, MD 20892-7910
(301) 435-0714　　　　　　　Fax: (301) 480-8443
E-mail: GrantsInfo@nih.gov
Web: www.nih.gov

Summary To provide support to graduate students with disabilities who are interested in participating in an ongoing research project funded by the National Institutes of Health (NIH).

Eligibility This program is open to graduate students who meet the definition of disabled in the Americans with Disabilities Act: an individual who "has a physical or mental impairment that substantially limits 1 or more major life activities." A list of disabilities that might confer eligibility for supplemental awards under this program includes, but is not limited to, the following: total deafness in both ears, visual acuity less than 20/200 with corrective lenses, speech impairment, missing extremities, partial paralysis, complete paralysis, convulsive disorders, mental or emotional illness, learning disabilities, kidney dialysis, and severe distortion of the limbs and/or spine. In all cases, graduate students supported under this supplement must, with reasonable assistance, be able to contribute to the research supported by the parent grant. Any principal investigator at a domestic institution holding an eligible parent grant (funded by the NIH) is eligible—in cooperation with the disabled graduate student—to submit a request for a supplement to support the student with a disability. The student must currently be enrolled at an academic institution in a master's or doctoral program in biomedical, behavioral, clinical, or social sciences. Selection is based on 1) the qualifications of the student, including career goals, prior research training, research potential, and relevant experience; 2) the plan for the proposed research experience in the supplemental request and its relationship to the parent grant; 3) the appropriateness of the proposed accommodations for the student; 4) evidence from the principal investigator that the experience will enhance the research potential, knowledge, and/or skills of the student, and that adequate mentorship will be provided; 5) evidence from the principal investigator that the activities of the student will be an integral part of the project; and 6) evidence of the student's educational achievement and interest in science.

Financial data Salary support is established by the institution at any level that is reasonable, in accordance with the salary structure of the grantee institution, and consistent with the level of effort. Additional funds up to $4,000 per year may be requested for supplies and travel. Funds may also be requested to permit accommodation to the research environment. That may include research equipment, but only if it is directly related to the project and to accommodating the disabilities of the individual. Some types of accommodations that might be provided under this program include: specialized equipment, assistive devices, and personnel, such as readers, interpreters, or assistants.

Duration 1 academic year or 3 months during the summer.

Number awarded Varies. Usually, each parent grant may have only 1 supplement for a person with a disability.

Deadline Principal investigators—in cooperation with the disabled student—are encouraged to submit an application no later than 3 months before the anniversary date of the last 2 years remaining on the parent grant.

[726]
RHODE ISLAND SPACE GRANT GRADUATE FELLOWSHIP PROGRAM

Rhode Island Space Grant
c/o Brown University
Lincoln Field Building
Box 1846
Providence, RI 02912-1846
(401) 863-2889　　　　　　　Fax: (401) 863-1292
E-mail: RISpaceGrant@brown.edu
Web: www.planetary.brown.edu/RI_Space_Grant

Summary To provide financial assistance to graduate students at institutions that are members of the Rhode Island Space Grant Consortium (RISGC) who wish to pursue studies and space-related research in science, mathematics, or engineering.

Eligibility This program is open to graduate students at RISGC-member universities. Applicants must be studying in science, mathematics, or engineering fields of interest to the National Aeronautics and Space Administration (NASA). U.S. citizenship is required. The sponsor is a component of NASA's Space Grant program, which encourages participation by women, underrepresented minorities, and persons with disabilities.

Financial data A stipend is provided (amount not specified).

Duration 1 year.

Additional Information Members of the RISGC are Bryant College, Community College of Rhode Island, Providence College, Roger Williams University, Rhode Island College, Rhode Island School of Design, Salve Regina University, University of Rhode Island, and Wheaton College. This program is funded by NASA. Fellows are required to devote 75% of their time to their studies and research and 25% of their time to science education outreach activities organized and coordinated by Rhode Island Space Grant.

Number awarded Varies each year; recently, 4 of these fellowships were awarded.

[727]
RIDGE 2000 POSTDOCTORAL FELLOWSHIP PROGRAM

National Science Foundation
Directorate for Geosciences
Attn: Division of Ocean Sciences
4201 Wilson Boulevard, Room 725
Arlington, VA 22230
(703) 292-8582   TDD: (703) 292-9085
E-mail: depp@nsf.gov
Web: www.geo.nsf.gov

Summary To provide opportunities for young scientists to conduct geological research on the mid-ocean ridge system as part of the Ridge Inter-Disciplinary Global Experiments (RIDGE) 2000 Initiative.

Eligibility Eligible are U.S. citizens, nationals, or permanent resident aliens who will have earned a doctoral degree within 2 years of taking up the award and who have arranged to conduct research under a senior scientist at an appropriate U.S. nonprofit institution (government laboratory, privately-sponsored nonprofit institution, national laboratory, or institution of higher education). The institution may not be the same as where the applicant received the doctorate, and the senior scientist's area of expertise should be different from that acquired by the applicant in previous research training. The proposed research must attempt to understand the geological processes of planetary renewal that occur along the mid-oceanic plate boundary and the chemical and biological processes that sustain life, in the absence of sunlight, in the deep ocean. Currently, the program has identified 3 sites as the focus of research: 9-10 degrees North segment of the East Pacific Rise, East or Central Lau Spreading Center, and Endeavor segment of the Juan de Fuca Ridge. Selection is based on ability as evidenced by past research work; suitability and availability of the sponsoring senior scientist and other associated colleagues; suitability of the host institution for the proposed research; likely impact on the future scientific development of the applicant; scientific quality of the research likely to emerge; and the potential impact of the research on the RIDGE 2000 Initiative. Women, minorities, and persons with disabilities are particularly encouraged to apply.

Financial data Fellowships provide a salary and benefits consistent with normal institutional practice for postdoctoral fellows; an institutional allowance (in lieu of indirect costs) of $300 per month for partial reimbursement of expenses incurred in support of the research (such as space, equipment, secretarial assistance, and general purpose supplies); and a special research allowance of $5,000 per year, expendable at the fellow's discretion and intended to be used for scientific equipment and supplies, travel, publication expenses, and other research-related costs.

Duration 2 years; may be renewed for 1 additional year.

Additional Information Additional information is available from the RIDGE 2000 office, Pennsylvania State University, 221 Mueller Lab, University Park, PA 16802, (814) 865-7434, E-mail: RIDGE2000@psu.edu.

Number awarded 1 or more each year.

Deadline February or August of each year.

[728]
RISK POLICY FELLOWSHIPS IN HEALTH, SAFETY AND THE ENVIRONMENT

American Association for the Advancement of Science
Attn: Science and Technology Policy Fellowship Programs
1200 New York Avenue, N.W.
Washington, DC 20005-3920
(202) 326-6700   Fax: (202) 289-4950
E-mail: fellowships@aaas.org
Web: fellowships.aaas.org/risk

Summary To provide postdoctoral and mid-career scientists and engineers with an opportunity to offer scientific and technical input on issues of human health, economic, and environmental aspects of risk assessment or risk management.

Eligibility Applicants must have a Ph.D. or equivalent doctoral degree in a physical, biological, or social science, any field of engineering, or any relevant interdisciplinary field; holders of a D.V.M., M.D., or Ph.D. in the natural sciences or economics are especially encouraged to apply. Persons with a master's degree in engineering and at least 3 years of post-degree professional experience are eligible. Candidates must demonstrate exceptional competence in some area of science or engineering and an interest in applying their expertise to the economic and technical assessment of problems related to human health or the environment. U.S. citizenship is required; federal employees are not eligible. Underrepresented minorities and persons with disabilities are especially encouraged to apply.

Financial data The stipend is $60,000, plus allowances for health insurance, relocation, and professional travel.

Duration 1 year, beginning in September.

Additional Information Fellows provide scientific and technical input on issues relating to human health, economic, and environmental aspects of risk assessment or risk management in areas of relevance to the U.S. Food and Drug Administration (FDA), the U.S. Department of Agriculture (USDA), or the Environmental Protection Agency (EPA). Fellows working with the FDA are assigned to its Center for Food Safety and Applied Nutrition, which focuses on risk assessment to ensure that balanced scientific conclusions are drawn regarding adverse human health effects resulting from exposure to foodborne chemical and microbiological hazards. Fellows assigned to USDA work in the Office of Risk Assessment and Cost-Benefit Analysis, the Food Safety

Inspection Service, or the Animal and Plant Health Inspection Service; assignments involve working on domestic and international aspects of food safety and food security, providing guidance and technical assistance throughout the risk analysis process, analyzing proposed USDA regulations, and coordinating risk assessment work within the department and with other agencies. Fellows working at the EPA are assigned to the National Center for Environmental Assessment, where the emphasis is on human health and ecological risk assessment and risk management policy.

Number awarded Approximately 5 each year.
Deadline January of each year.

[729] ROBERT A. DANNELS MEMORIAL SCHOLARSHIP

American Nuclear Society
Attn: Scholarship Coordinator
555 North Kensington Avenue
La Grange Park, IL 60526-5592
(708) 352-6611   Fax: (708) 352-0499
E-mail: outreach@ans.org
Web: www2.ans.org/honors/scholarships

Summary To provide financial assistance to disabled or other students who are interested in pursuing graduate studies in nuclear science or engineering.
Eligibility This program is open to full-time graduate students in programs leading to an advanced degree in nuclear science, nuclear engineering, or other nuclear-related field at an accredited institution in the United States. Applicants must be U.S. citizens or permanent residents and must be sponsored by an organization within the American Nuclear Society (ANS). Nomination of students with disabilities is particularly encouraged.
Financial data The stipend is $3,500.
Duration 1 year.
Additional Information Requests for applications must be accompanied by a self-addressed stamped envelope.
Number awarded 1 each year.
Deadline January of each year.

[730] ROCKY MOUNTAIN NASA SPACE GRANT CONSORTIUM GRADUATE RESEARCH FELLOWSHIPS

Rocky Mountain NASA Space Grant Consortium
c/o Utah State University
EL Building, Room 302
Logan, UT 84322-4140
(435) 797-4042   Fax: (435) 797-4044
E-mail: rmc@sdl.usu.edu
Web: www.rmc.sdl.usu.edu

Summary To provide financial support for research and study to graduate students at designated universities in Utah or Colorado who are working on a degree in fields of interest to the National Aeronautics and Space Administration (NASA).
Eligibility This program is open to graduate students at member institutions of the Rocky Mountain NASA Space Grant Consortium who are studying engineering, science, medicine, or technology. U.S. citizenship is required. Selection is based on academic performance to date and potential for the future, with emphasis on space-related research interests. This program is part of the NASA Space Grant program, which encourages participation by women, underrepresented minorities, and persons with disabilities.
Financial data The amount of the awards depends on the availability of funds.
Additional Information Members of the consortium are Utah State University, the University of Utah, Brigham Young University, and the University of Denver. This program is funded by NASA.
Number awarded Varies each year.

[731] ROGER REVELLE FELLOWSHIP IN GLOBAL STEWARDSHIP

American Association for the Advancement of Science
Attn: Science and Technology Policy Fellowship Programs
1200 New York Avenue, N.W.
Washington, DC 20005-3920
(202) 326-6700   Fax: (202) 289-4950
E-mail: fellowships@aaas.org
Web: fellowships.aaas.org/revelle

Summary To provide postdoctoral and mid-career scientists and engineers with an opportunity to work in the Washington, D.C. policy community on domestic or international environmental issues.
Eligibility Prospective fellows must have a Ph.D. or equivalent doctoral-level degree and at least 3 years of post-degree experience; persons with a master's degree in engineering and at least 6 years of post-degree experience are also eligible. Candidates must be interested in an assignment in the Washington, D.C. policy community; demonstrate exceptional competence in some area

of science or engineering; have a good scientific and technical background; be cognizant of and demonstrate sensitivity toward political and social issues; and have a strong interest and some experience applying personal knowledge toward the solution of societal problems. They must be interested in a program that focuses on human interaction with ecosystems, including population, sustainable development, food, oceans, global climate change, and related environmental concerns. U.S. citizenship is required; federal employees are not eligible. Underrepresented minorities and persons with disabilities are especially encouraged to apply.

Financial data The stipend is $60,000, plus allowances for health insurance, relocation, and professional travel.

Duration 1 year, beginning in September.

Additional Information Fellows work in Congress, an executive branch agency, or a non-governmental organization within the environmental policy community. The program includes an orientation on executive branch and congressional operations.

Number awarded 1 each year.

Deadline January of each year.

[732]
RUI FACULTY RESEARCH PROJECTS

National Science Foundation
Directorate for Education and Human Resources
Attn: Senior Staff Associate for Cross Directorate
  Programs
4201 Wilson Boulevard, Room 805
Arlington, VA 22230
(703) 292-8600   TDD: (703) 292-5090
Web: www.ehr.nsf.gov/crssprgm/rui/start.shtm

Summary To provide support to faculty at predominantly undergraduate institutions who are interested in conducting science or engineering research.

Eligibility This program is open to faculty members in all fields of science and engineering supported by the National Science Foundation (NSF) who are teaching at predominantly undergraduate institutions, defined as U.S. 2-year, 4-year, masters-level, and small doctoral colleges and universities that 1) grant baccalaureate degrees in NSF-supported fields or provide programs of instruction for students pursuing such degrees after transferring; 2) have undergraduate enrollment exceeding graduate enrollment; and 3) award no more than an average of 10 Ph.D. and/or D.Sc. degrees per year in all disciplines that NSF supports. Applicants must be teaching in a department that offers courses that qualify for bachelor's degree credit in NSF-supportable fields and may offer master's degrees but may not award a doctorate or offer doctoral courses and supervise doctoral research. Proposals may be for research at the home institution (including work in the field) and/or away from the home institution at a research university or a government or industrial laboratory. Applications are especially encouraged from women, minorities, and persons with disabilities.

Financial data Awards range from $10,000 to more than $100,000. Funding may cover salaries and wages, research assistantships (focused upon undergraduate students), fringe benefits, travel, materials and supplies, publication costs and page charges, consultant services, equipment needed for individual research projects with a single research focus, field work, research at other institutions, and indirect costs.

Duration 1 to 3 years.

Additional Information This program is part of the NSF Research in Undergraduate Institutions (RUI) program; it is operated by various disciplinary divisions within the NSF; for a list of the participating divisions and their telephone numbers, contact the Senior Staff Associate for Cross Directorate Programs.

Deadline Deadlines are established by the respective participating NSF disciplinary divisions.

[733]
SOUTH CAROLINA SPACE GRANT CONSORTIUM GRADUATE FELLOWSHIPS

South Carolina Space Grant Consortium
c/o College of Charleston
Department of Geology
58 Coming Street
Charleston, SC 29424
(843) 953-5463   Fax: (843) 953-5446
E-mail: baughmant@cofc.edu
Web: www.cofc.edu/~scsgrant

Summary To provide financial assistance for space-related study to graduate students in South Carolina.

Eligibility This program is open to graduate students at member institutions of the South Carolina Space Grant Consortium. Applicants must be interested in space-related studies, although the program has accepted students with interests ranging from remote sensing and engineering to astrophysics. U.S. citizenship is required. Selection is based on academic qualifications of the applicant; 2 letters of recommendation; a description of past activities, current interests, and future plans concerning an aerospace-related field; and faculty sponsorship. The South Carolina Space Grant Consortium is a component of the U.S. National Aeronautics and Space Administration (NASA) Space Grant program, which encourages the participation of women, underrepresented minorities, and persons with disabilities.

Financial data The stipend is $3,000 per year.

Duration 1 year.

Additional Information Members of the consortium are Benedict College, The Citadel, College of Charleston, Clemson University, Coastal Carolina University, Furman University, University of South Carolina, Wofford College, South Carolina State University, The Medical University of South Carolina, and University of the Virgin Islands. This program is funded by NASA.

Number awarded Varies each year.
Deadline February of each year.

[734]
SOUTH CAROLINA SPACE GRANT CONSORTIUM RESEARCH GRANTS

South Carolina Space Grant Consortium
c/o College of Charleston
Department of Geology
58 Coming Street
Charleston, SC 29424
(843) 953-5463   Fax: (843) 953-5446
E-mail: baughmant@cofc.edu
Web: www.cofc.edu/~scsgrant

Summary To provide funding for space-related research to faculty at institutional members of the South Carolina Space Grant Consortium.

Eligibility This program is open to tenured or tenure-track faculty at member institutions of the South Carolina Space Grant Consortium. Applicants must be proposing to conduct research in earth science, space science, aeronautics, or the human exploration and development of space. Priority is given to researchers who wish to conduct research at a center of the U.S. National Aeronautics and Space Administration (NASA). Selection is based on scientific merit of the proposed project, relevancy to NASA strategic plans, project personnel, and reasonableness of budget. The South Carolina Space Grant Consortium is a component of the NASA Space Grant program, which encourages the participation of women, underrepresented minorities, and persons with disabilities.

Financial data Grants range up to $25,000. Grants must be matched on a 1:1 basis with nonfederal funds.

Duration 1 year.

Additional Information Members of the consortium are Benedict College, The Citadel, College of Charleston, Clemson University, Coastal Carolina University, Furman University, University of South Carolina, Wofford College, South Carolina State University, The Medical University of South Carolina, and University of the Virgin Islands. This program is funded by NASA.

Number awarded Varies each year; a total of $100,000 is available for this program each year.

Deadline Letters of intent must be submitted by May of each year. Final proposals are due in June.

[735]
S.P.I.N. GRANTS

Special People in Need
500 West Madison Street, Suite 3700
Chicago, IL 60661-2511
(312) 715-5235   E-mail: ipeter@wilvaine.com

Summary To provide funding to individuals with disabilities, so they can engage in productive activities.

Eligibility This program is open to people with disabilities who are working with a fiscal agent qualified to receive and administer grant funds. Applicants must submit a letter describing the need for which they are seeking support, specific financial information regarding the intended use of the grant, a letter from the fiscal agent confirming the nature of the need and the correctness of the facts in the applicant's letter, biographical data or other information, and documentation of financial need. Selection is based on evidence that the applicant is well suited to effectuate the purposes of the grant by engaging in productive activity in which they could not otherwise engage.

Financial data Grants normally range from $2,000 to $3,000.

Duration These are generally 1-time awards.

Number awarded A small number each year.

Deadline April of each a year.

[736]
STAN BECK FELLOWSHIP

Entomological Society of America
Attn: Entomological Foundation
9301 Annapolis Road, Suite 210
Lanham, MD 20706-3115
(301) 459-9082   Fax: (301) 459-9084
E-mail: melodie@entfdn.org
Web: www.entfdn.org/beck.html

Summary To assist "needy" students working on an undergraduate or graduate degree in science who are nominated by members of the Entomological Society of America (ESA).

Eligibility Candidates for this fellowship must be nominated by members of the society. Nominees may be studying science on any level. However, they must be "needy" students. For the purposes of this program, need may be based on physical limitations, or economic, minority, or environmental conditions.

Financial data The stipend varies each year.

Duration 1 year; may be renewed up to 3 additional years.

Additional Information Recipients are expected to be present at the society's annual meeting, where the award will be presented.

Number awarded 1 or more each year.

Deadline August of each year.

[737]
STATE VOCATIONAL REHABILITATION SERVICES PROGRAM

Department of Education
Office of Special Education and Rehabilitative Services
Attn: Rehabilitation Services Administration
400 Maryland Avenue, S.W., Room 3329, MES
Washington, DC 20202-2551
(202) 205-4829   Fax: (202) 205-9340
E-mail: roseann_ashby@ed.gov
Web: www.ed.gov

Summary To provide financial assistance for undergraduate or graduate study to individuals with disabilities as part of their program of vocational rehabilitation.

Eligibility To be eligible for vocational rehabilitation services, an individual must 1) have a physical or mental impairment that is a substantial impediment to employment; 2) be able to benefit in terms of employment from vocational rehabilitation services; and 3) require vocational rehabilitation services to prepare for, enter, engage in, or retain gainful employment. Priority is given to applicants with the most significant disabilities. Persons accepted for vocational rehabilitation develop an Individualized Written Rehabilitation Program (IWRP) in consultation with a counselor for the vocational rehabilitation agency in the state in which they live. The IWRP may include a program of postsecondary education if the disabled person and counselor agree that such a program will fulfill the goals of vocational rehabilitation. In most cases, the IWRP will provide for postsecondary education only to a level at which the disabled person will become employable, but that may include graduate education if the approved occupation requires an advanced degree as a minimum condition of entry. Students accepted to a program of postsecondary education as part of their IWRP must apply for all available federal, state, and private financial aid.

Financial data Funding for this program is provided by the federal government through grants to state vocational rehabilitation agencies. Grants under the basic support program currently total nearly $2.5 billion per year. States must supplement federal funding with matching funds of 21.3%. Persons who are accepted for vocational rehabilitation by the appropriate state agency receive financial assistance based on the cost of their education and other funds available to them, including their own or family contribution and other sources of financial aid. Allowable costs in most states include tuition, fees, books, supplies, room, board, transportation, personal expenses, child care, and expenses related to disability (special equipment, readers, attendants, interpreters, or notetakers).

Duration Assistance is provided until the disabled person achieves an educational level necessary for employment as provided in the IWRP.

Additional Information You will need to contact your state vocational rehabilitation agency to apply for this program.

Number awarded Varies each year. Recently, more than 1.2 million (of whom more than 80% have significant disabilities) were participating in this program.

[738]
SUPPLEMENTS FOR ESTABLISHED INVESTIGATORS WHO BECOME DISABLED

National Institutes of Health
Division of Extramural Outreach and Information Resources
Attn: GrantsInfo
6701 Rockledge Drive, Suite 6095
Bethesda, MD 20892-7910
(301) 435-0714   Fax: (301) 480-8443
E-mail: GrantsInfo@nih.gov
Web: www.nih.gov

Summary To provide assistance to established research investigators with grants from the National Institutes of Health (NIH) who become disabled.

Eligibility Established investigators on NIH research, program project, or center grants who become disabled during the current project period are eligible to request assistance in completing the currently-funded research project in biomedical or behavioral sciences. Selection is based on 1) the appropriateness of the proposed accommodations for the established investigator regarding his or her role on the research project and the nature of the disability; and 2) the appropriateness of the cost of the proposed accommodations to be paid from the supplement in relationship to the total direct cost of the parent project.

Financial data Support is available for items that will permit the investigator to complete the remaining years of a currently-funded research project. These may include: salary support for an individual who can assist the established investigator in meeting the goals of the research project, specialized equipment (e.g., computers), or modifications of the investigator's working environment. The requested support must be consistent with the type of disability and the nature of the approved research.

Duration This support is available for the remaining years of the currently-funded project.

Additional Information In future competing applications, funds for continuation of the accommodations provided under this program must be requested in the parent grant application and may not be requested as a research supplement.

Number awarded Varies each year.

Deadline Applications may be submitted at any time.

[739]
SURVIVORS' AND DEPENDENTS' EDUCATIONAL ASSISTANCE PROGRAM

Department of Veterans Affairs
810 Vermont Avenue, N.W.
Washington, DC 20420
(202) 418-4343   Toll-free: (888) GI-BILL1
Web: www.gibill.va.gov

Summary To provide financial assistance for undergraduate or graduate study to children and spouses of deceased and disabled veterans, MIAs, and POWs.

Eligibility Eligible for this assistance are spouses and children of 1) veterans who died or are permanently and totally disabled as the result of a disability arising from active service in the armed forces; 2) veterans who died from any cause while rated permanently and totally disabled from a service-connected disability; 3) servicemembers listed for more than 90 days as currently missing in action or captured in the line of duty by a hostile force; and 4) servicemembers listed for more than 90 days as presently detained or interned by a foreign government or power. Children must be between 18 and 26 years of age, although extensions may be granted. Spouses and children over 14 years of age with physical or mental disabilities are also eligible.

Financial data Monthly stipends from this program are $695 for full-time study at an academic institution, $522 for three-quarter time, or $347 for half-time. For farm cooperative work, the monthly stipends are $561 for full-time, $421 for three-quarter time, or $281 for half-time. For an apprenticeship or on-the-job training, the monthly stipend is $506 for the first 6 months, $378 for the second 6 months, $251 for the third 6 months, and $127 for the remainder of the program.

Duration Up to 45 months (or the equivalent in part-time training). Spouses must complete their training within 10 years of the date they are first found eligible.

Additional Information Benefits may be used to work on associate, bachelor, or graduate degrees at colleges and universities, including independent study, cooperative training, and study abroad programs. Courses leading to a certificate or diploma from business, technical, or vocational schools may also be taken. Other eligible programs include apprenticeships, on-job training programs, farm cooperative courses, correspondence courses (for spouses only), secondary school programs (for recipients who are not high school graduates), tutorial assistance, remedial deficiency and refresher training, or work-study (for recipients who are enrolled at least three-quarter time). Eligible children who are handicapped by a physical or mental disability that prevents pursuit of an educational program may receive special restorative training that includes language retraining, lip reading, auditory training, Braille reading and writing, and similar programs. Eligible spouses and children over 14 years of age who are handicapped by a physical or mental disability that prevents pursuit of an educational program may receive specialized vocational training that includes specialized courses, alone or in combination with other courses, leading to a vocational objective that is suitable for the person and required by reason of physical or mental handicap. Ineligible courses include bartending or personality development courses; correspondence courses by dependent or surviving children; non-accredited independent study courses; any course given by radio; self-improvement courses, such as reading, speaking, woodworking, basic seamanship, and English as a second language; audited courses; any course that is avocational or recreational in character; courses not leading to an educational, professional, or vocational objective; courses taken and successfully completed previously; courses taken by a federal government employee and paid for under the Government Employees' Training Act; and courses taken while in receipt of benefits for the same program from the Office of Workers' Compensation Programs.

Number awarded Varies each year.

Deadline Applications may be submitted at any time.

[740]
TED SCRIPPS FELLOWSHIPS IN ENVIRONMENTAL JOURNALISM

University of Colorado at Boulder
Attn: Center for Environmental Journalism
1511 University Avenue
Campus Box 478
Boulder, CO 80309-0478
(303) 492-4114   E-mail: cej@colorado.edu
Web: www.colorado.edu/journalism/cej

Summary To provide journalists with an opportunity to gain more knowledge about environmental issues at the University of Colorado at Boulder.

Eligibility This program is open to full-time U.S. print and broadcast journalists who have at least 5 years' professional experience and have completed an undergraduate degree. Applicants may be general assignment reporters, editors, producers, environmental reporters, or full-time freelancers. Prior experience in covering the environment is not required. Professionals in such related fields as teaching, public relations, or advertising are not eligible. Applicants must be interested in a program at the university that includes classes, weekly seminars, and field trips. They also must engage in independent study expected to lead to a significant piece of journalistic work. Applications are especially encouraged from women, ethnic minorities, disabled persons, and veterans (particularly veterans of the Vietnam era).

Financial data The program covers tuition and fees and pays a $41,000 stipend. Employers are strongly encouraged to continue benefits, including health insurance.

Duration 9 months.

Additional Information This is a non-degree program. Fellows must obtain a leave of absence from their

regular employment and must return to their job following the fellowship.

Number awarded 5 each year.

Deadline February of each year.

[741]
TEXAS SPACE GRANT CONSORTIUM GRADUATE FELLOWSHIPS

Texas Space Grant Consortium
Attn: Administrative Assistant
3925 West Braker Lane, Suite 200
Austin, TX 78759
(512) 471-3583   Toll-free: (800) 248-8742
Fax: (512) 471-3585
E-mail: jurgens@tsgc.utexas.edu
Web: www.tsgc.utexas.edu/grants

Summary To provide financial assistance to graduate students at Texas universities working on degrees in the fields of space science and engineering.

Eligibility Applicants must be U.S. citizens, eligible for financial assistance, and registered for full-time study in a graduate program at 1 of the participating universities. Students apply to their respective university representative; each representative then submits up to 3 candidates into the statewide selection process. Fields of study have included aerospace engineering, astronomy, biology, computer science and engineering, electrical engineering, materials science and engineering, medicine, physics, and physiology. Applications from women and underrepresented students (persons with disabilities, African Americans, Hispanic Americans, Native Americans, and Pacific Islanders) are encouraged. Fellowships are awarded competitively, on the basis of GPA, Graduate Record Examination scores, interest in space, and recommendations from the applicant's university.

Financial data The stipend is $5,000 per year, to be used to supplement half-time graduate support (or a fellowship) offered by the home institution.

Duration 1 year; may be renewed for up to a maximum of 3 years, provided the recipient spends no more than 2 of those years as a master's degree candidate.

Additional Information The participating universities are Baylor University, Lamar University, Prairie View A&M University, Rice University, San Jacinto College, Southern Methodist University, Sul Ross State University, Texas A&M University (including Kingsville and Corpus Christi campuses), Texas Christian University, Texas Southern University, Texas Tech University, Trinity University, University of Houston (including Clear Lake and Downtown campuses), University of Texas at Arlington, University of Texas at Austin, University of Texas at Dallas, University of Texas at El Paso, University of Texas at San Antonio, University of Texas Health Science Center at Houston, University of Texas Health Science Center at San Antonio, University of Texas Medical Branch at Galveston, University of Texas/Pan American, and University of Texas Southwestern Medical Center. This program is funded by the National Aeronautics and Space Administration (NASA).

Number awarded Varies each year; recently, 20 of these fellowships were awarded.

Deadline February of each year.

[742]
USA FUNDS ACCESS TO EDUCATION SCHOLARSHIPS

Scholarship America
Attn: Scholarship Management Services
1505 Riverview Road
P.O. Box 297
St. Peter, MN 56082
(507) 931-1682   Toll-free: (800) 537-4180
Fax: (507) 931-9168
E-mail: scholarship@usafunds.org
Web: www.usafunds.org

Summary To provide financial assistance to undergraduate and graduate students, especially those who are members of ethnic minority groups or have physical disabilities.

Eligibility This program is open to high school seniors and graduates who plan to enroll or are already enrolled undergraduate or graduate course work at an accredited 2- or 4-year college, university, or vocational/technical school. Half-time undergraduate students are also eligible. Up to 50% of the awards are targeted at students who have a documented physical disability or are a member of an ethnic minority group, including but not limited to Native Hawaiian, Alaskan Native, Black/African American, Asian, Pacific Islander, American Indian, or Hispanic/Latino. Residents of all 50 states, the District of Columbia, Puerto Rico, Guam, the U.S. Virgin Islands, and all U.S. territories and commonwealths are eligible. Preference is given to applicants from the following areas: Arizona, Hawaii and the Pacific Islands, Indiana, Kansas, Maryland, Mississippi, Nevada, and Wyoming. Applicants must also be U.S. citizens or eligible non-citizens and come from a family with an annual adjusted gross income of $35,000 or less. In addition to financial need, selection is based on past academic performance and future potential, leadership and participation in school and community, work experience, career and educational aspirations and goals, and references.

Financial data The stipend is $1,500 per year for full-time undergraduate or graduate students or $750 per year for half-time undergraduate students. Funds are paid jointly to the student and the school.

Duration 1 year; may be renewed until the student receives a final degree or certificate or until the total award to a student reaches $6,000, whichever comes first. Renewal requires the recipient to maintain a GPA of 2.5 or higher.

Additional Information This program, established in 2000, is sponsored by USA Funds which serves as the

education loan guarantor and administrator in the 8 states and the Pacific Islands where the program gives preference.
Number awarded Varies each year; recently, 2,519 of these scholarships were awarded.
Deadline April of each year.

[743]
VIRGINIA SPACE GRANT AEROSPACE GRADUATE RESEARCH FELLOWSHIPS

Virginia Space Grant Consortium
Attn: Fellowship Coordinator
Old Dominion University Peninsula Center
600 Butler Farm Road
Hampton, VA 23666
(757) 766-5210   Fax: (757) 766-5205
E-mail: vsgc@pen.k12.va.us
Web: www.vsgc.odu.edu/html/fellowships.htm

Summary To provide financial assistance for research in space-related fields to graduate students in Virginia.
Eligibility This program is open to graduate students who will be enrolled in a program of full-time study in an aerospace-related discipline at 1 of the Virginia Space Grant Consortium (VSGC) Colleges. Applicants must be U.S. citizens with a GPA of 3.0 or higher. They must submit a proposed research and plan of study that includes its key elements, what the applicant intends to accomplish, and the aerospace application of the proposed research activity. Selection is based on the applicants' academic qualifications, the quality of their proposed research plan, and its relevance to this program. Since an important purpose of this program is to increase the participation of underrepresented minorities, females, and persons with disabilities in aerospace-related careers, the VSGC especially encourages applications from those students.
Financial data The grant is $5,000. Funds are add-on awards, designed to supplement and enhance such basic graduate research support as research assistantships, teaching assistantships, and nonfederal scholarships and fellowships.
Duration 1 year; may be renewed up to 2 additional years.
Additional Information The VSGC colleges are College of William and Mary, Hampton University, Old Dominion University, the University of Virginia, and Virginia Polytechnic Institute and State University. This program is funded by the U.S. National Aeronautics and Space Administration (NASA). Awardees are required to certify through their academic department that basic research support of at least $5,000 is being provided before receipt of Space Grant funds.
Number awarded At least 5 each year.
Deadline February of each year.

[744]
VOCATIONAL REHABILITATION FOR DISABLED VETERANS

Department of Veterans Affairs
810 Vermont Avenue, N.W.
Washington, DC 20420
(202) 418-4343   Toll-free: (800) 827-1000
Web: www.va.gov

Summary To provide vocational rehabilitation to certain categories of veterans with disabilities.
Eligibility This program is open to veterans who have a service-connected disability of at least 10% and a serious employment handicap or 20% and an employment handicap. They must have been discharged or released from military service under other than dishonorable conditions. The Department of Veterans Affairs (VA) must determine that they would benefit from a training program that would help them prepare for, find, and keep suitable employment. The program may be 1) institutional training at a certificate, 2-year college, 4-year college or university, or technical program; 2) unpaid on-the-job training in a federal, state, or local agency or a federally-recognized Indian tribal agency, training in a home, vocational course in a rehabilitation facility or sheltered workshop, independent instruction, or institutional non-farm cooperative; or 3) paid training through a farm cooperative, apprenticeship, on-the-job training, or on-the-job non-farm cooperative.
Financial data While in training and for 2 months after, eligible disabled veterans may receive subsistence allowances in addition to their disability compensation or retirement pay. For institutional training, the full-time monthly rate is $454.96 with no dependents, $564.34 with 1 dependent, $665.03 with 2 dependents, and $48.48 for each additional dependent; the three-quarter time monthly rate is $341.85 for no dependents, $423.87 with 1 dependent, $497.21 with 2 dependents, and $37.28 for each additional dependent; the half-time monthly rate is $228.74 for no dependents, $283.41 with 1 dependent, $333.13 with 2 dependents, and $24.87 for each additional dependent. For unpaid on-the-job training, the monthly rate is $454.96 for no dependents, $564.34 with 1 dependent, $665.03 with 2 dependents, and $48.48 for each additional dependent. For paid training, the monthly rate is based on the wage received, to a maximum of $397.79 for no dependents, $481.05 with 1 dependent, $554.39 with 2 dependents, and $36.06 for each additional dependent. The VA also pays the costs of tuition, books, fees, supplies, and equipment; it may also pay for special supportive services, such as tutorial assistance, prosthetic devices, lipreading training, and signing for the deaf. If during training or employment services the veteran's disabilities cause transportation expenses that would not be incurred by nondisabled persons, the VA will pay for at least a portion of those expenses. If the veteran encounters financial difficulty during training, the VA may provide an advance against future benefit payments.

Duration Up to 48 months of full-time training or its equivalent in part-time training. If a veteran with a serious disability receives services under an extended evaluation to improve training potential, the total of the extended evaluation and the training phases of the rehabilitation program may exceed 48 months. Usually, the veteran must complete a rehabilitation program within 12 years from the date of notification of entitlement to compensation by the VA. Following completion of the training portion of a rehabilitation program, a veteran may receive counseling and job search and adjustment services for 18 months.

Additional Information The program may also provide employment assistance, self-employment assistance, training in a rehabilitation facility, or college and other training. Veterans who are seriously disabled may receive services and assistance to improve their ability to live more independently in their community. After completion of the training phase, the VA will assist the veteran to find and hold a suitable job.

Number awarded Varies each year.

Deadline Applications are accepted at any time.

[745]
WEST VIRGINIA SPACE GRANT CONSORTIUM GRADUATE FELLOWSHIP PROGRAM

West Virginia Space Grant Consortium
c/o West Virginia University
College of Engineering and Mineral Resources
G-68 Engineering Sciences Building
P.O. Box 6070
Morgantown, WV 26506-6070
(304) 293-4099   Fax: (304) 293-4970
E-mail: nasa@cemr.wvu.edu
Web: www.cemr.wvu.edu/~wwwnasa

Summary To provide financial assistance to graduate students at designated academic institutions affiliated with the West Virginia Space Grant Consortium who wish to conduct research on space-related science or engineering topics.

Eligibility This program is open to graduate students at participating member institutions of the consortium. Applicants must be interested in working on a research project with a faculty member who has received a West Virginia Space Grant Consortium Research Initiation Grant. U.S. citizenship is required. The consortium is a component of the Space Grant program of the U.S. National Aeronautics and Space Administration (NASA), which encourages participation by women, underrepresented minorities, and persons with disabilities.

Financial data The amount of the award for the graduate student depends on the amount of the research grant that the faculty member has received.

Duration 1 year.

Additional Information Funding for this program is provided by NASA. The participating consortium members are Marshall University, West Virginia Institute of Technology, West Virginia University, and Wheeling-Jesuit University.

Number awarded Varies each year.

[746]
WEST VIRGINIA SPACE GRANT CONSORTIUM RESEARCH CAPABILITY ENHANCEMENT MINI-GRANTS

West Virginia Space Grant Consortium
c/o West Virginia University
College of Engineering and Mineral Resources
G-68 Engineering Sciences Building
P.O. Box 6070
Morgantown, WV 26506-6070
(304) 293-4099   Fax: (304) 293-4970
E-mail: nasa@cemr.wvu.edu
Web: www.comr.wvu.edu/~wwwnasa

Summary To provide funding to faculty at academic institutions affiliated with the West Virginia Space Grant Consortium for support of space-related activities.

Eligibility This program is open to faculty members at colleges and universities that are members of the West Virginia Space Grant Consortium. Applicants must be seeking funding for such activities as trips to centers of the U.S. National Aeronautics and Space Administration (NASA) to develop research collaborations or attendance at conferences to present research findings. The consortium is a component of NASA's Space Grant program, which encourages participation by women, underrepresented minorities, and persons with disabilities.

Financial data Grants range up to $1,000.

Additional Information Funding for this program is provided by NASA. The consortium includes Bethany College, Fairmont State College, Marshall University, Salem International University, Shepherd College, West Liberty State College, West Virginia Institute of Technology, West Virginia State College, West Virginia University, West Virginia Wesleyan College, and Wheeling-Jesuit University.

Number awarded 15 to 20 each year.

[747]
WEST VIRGINIA SPACE GRANT CONSORTIUM RESEARCH INITIATION GRANTS

West Virginia Space Grant Consortium
c/o West Virginia University
College of Engineering and Mineral Resources
G-68 Engineering Sciences Building
P.O. Box 6070
Morgantown, WV 26506-6070
(304) 293-4099   Fax: (304) 293-4970
E-mail: nasa@cemr.wvu.edu
Web: www.cemr.wvu.edu/~wwwnasa

Summary To provide funding for space-related research to faculty at academic institutions affiliated with the West Virginia Space Grant Consortium.

Eligibility This program is open to junior faculty members at colleges and universities that are members of the West Virginia Space Grant Consortium. Applicants must be seeking to pursue research in areas of interest to the U.S. National Aeronautics and Space Administration (NASA) and to establish long-term relationships with NASA researchers. U.S. citizenship is required. The consortium is a component of NASA's Space Grant program, which encourages participation by women, underrepresented minorities, and persons with disabilities.

Financial data Grants range from $5,000 to $20,000. At least 35% of the award must be allocated for a graduate student research assistant.

Duration 1 year.

Additional Information Funding for this program is provided by NASA. The consortium includes Bethany College, Fairmont State College, Marshall University, Salem International University, Shepherd College, West Liberty State College, West Virginia Institute of Technology, West Virginia State College, West Virginia University, West Virginia Wesleyan College, and Wheeling-Jesuit University.

Number awarded 4 to 6 each year.

[748]
WISCONSIN PART-TIME STUDY GRANTS FOR VETERANS AND THEIR DEPENDENTS

Wisconsin Department of Veterans Affairs
30 West Mifflin Street
P.O. Box 7843
Madison, WI 53707-7843
(608) 266-1311   Toll-free: (800) WIS-VETS
Fax: (608) 267-0403
E-mail: wdvaweb@dva.state.wi.us
Web: dva.state.wi.us/ben_education.asp

Summary To provide financial assistance for part-time undergraduate or graduate education to 1) Wisconsin veterans or 2) the widow(er)s or dependent children of deceased veterans.

Eligibility Applicants for these grants must be veterans (must have served on active duty for at least 2 consecutive years or for at least 90 days during specified wartime periods) and residents of Wisconsin at the time of making the application. They must also have been Wisconsin residents either at the time of entry into active duty or for at least 5 consecutive years after completing service on active duty. Unremarried widow(er)s and minor or dependent children of deceased veterans who would qualify if the veteran were alive today are also eligible for these grants, as long as they are Wisconsin residents. Students who have not yet completed a bachelor's degree are eligible for these grants even if they are also receiving Montgomery GI Bill benefits from the U.S. Department of Veterans Affairs. Recipients must enroll in part-time study (11 credits or less if they do not have a bachelor's degree or 8 credits or less if they do). They may enroll at any accredited college, university, or vocational technical school in Wisconsin, whether state-supported or private; they may also attend out-of-state schools that are within 50 miles of the Wisconsin border if the course is not offered at a Wisconsin school within 50 miles of their residence. Qualifying programs include undergraduate study, graduate study if the student has only a bachelor's degree, correspondence courses, on-the-job training, apprenticeships, internships, and any other study related to the student's occupational, professional, or educational goals. Graduate students are not eligible if 1) they have already received a master's degree, doctor's degree, or equivalent; or 2) they are still entitled to U.S. Department of Veterans Affairs educational benefits. Students with a current gross annual income greater than $47,500 (plus $500 for each dependent in excess of 2) are not eligible.

Financial data Eligible applicants are entitled to reimbursement of up to 85% of the costs of tuition and fees. Veterans with a service-connected disability that is rated 30% or higher may be reimbursed for up to 100% of tuition and fees. Students must pay the costs when they register and then obtain reimbursement after completion of the course of study.

Duration Applicants may receive no more than 4 of these grants during a 12-month period.

Number awarded Varies each year.

Deadline Applications may be submitted at any time, but they must be received within 60 days following completion of the course.

[749]
WISCONSIN SPACE GRANT CONSORTIUM GRADUATE FELLOWSHIPS

Wisconsin Space Grant Consortium
c/o University of Wisconsin at Green Bay
Natural and Applied Sciences
2420 Nicolet Drive
Green Bay, WI 54311-7001
(920) 465-2941   Fax: (920) 465-2376
E-mail: brandts@uwgb.edu
Web: www.uwgb.edu/wsgc

Summary To provide financial assistance to graduate students at member institutions of the Wisconsin Space Grant Consortium (WSGC) who are interested in conducting aerospace, space science, or other interdisciplinary aerospace-related research.

Eligibility This program is open to graduate students enrolled at the universities participating in the WSGC. Applicants must be U.S. citizens; be enrolled full time in a master's or Ph.D. program related to space science, aerospace, or interdisciplinary aerospace studies (including, but not limited to, engineering, the sciences, architecture, law, business, and medicine); have a GPA of 3.0 or higher; and be interested in conducting space-related research. The consortium especially encourages applications from underrepresented minorities, women, persons with disabilities, and those pursuing interdisciplinary aerospace studies. Selection is based on academic performance and space-related promise.

Financial data Grants up to $5,000 per year are provided.

Duration 1 academic year.

Additional Information Funding for this program is provided by the U.S. National Aeronautics and Space Administration. The schools participating in the consortium include the University of Wisconsin campuses at Green Bay, La Crosse, Madison, Milwaukee, Oshkosh, Parkside, and Whitewater; College of the Menominee Nation; Marquette University; Carroll College; Lawrence University; Milwaukee School of Engineering; Ripon College; and Medical College of Wisconsin.

Number awarded Varies each year; recently, 7 of these fellowships were awarded.

Deadline February of each year.

[750]
WISCONSIN SPACE GRANT CONSORTIUM RESEARCH INFRASTRUCTURE PROGRAM

Wisconsin Space Grant Consortium
c/o University of Wisconsin at Madison
Space Science and Engineering Center
1225 West Dayton Street, Room 251
Madison, WI 53706-1280
(608) 263-4206   Fax: (608) 263-5974
E-mail: toma@ssec.wisc.edu
Web: www.uwgb.edu/wsgc

Summary To provide funding to staff at academic and industrial affiliates of the Wisconsin Space Grant Consortium (WSGC) who are interested in developing space-related research infrastructure.

Eligibility This program is open to faculty and research staff at the WSGC universities and colleges and staff at WSGC industrial affiliates. Applicants must be interested in establishing a space-related research program. Faculty and staff on university/industry teams in all areas of research are considered, but research initiatives must focus on activities related to the mission of the U.S. National Aeronautics and Space Administration (NASA). Those activities include earth and atmospheric sciences, astronautics, aeronautics, space sciences, and other space-related fields (e.g., agriculture, business, law, medicine, nursing, social and behavioral sciences, and space architecture). Grants are made in 2 categories: 1) faculty research seed grants and/or faculty proposal writing grants; and 2) other research initiatives, such as seminars, workshops, and/or travel to NASA centers. Preference is given to applications that emphasize new lines of space-related research, establishing collaborations among faculty from liberal arts colleges with faculty from research-intensive doctoral universities, linking academic and industrial affiliates, coordinated efforts with other NASA programs, increasing research capability, building research infrastructure, establishing research collaborations, and initiating research opportunities in line with the NASA Strategic Enterprises, especially by women, underrepresented minorities, and persons with disabilities. Selection is based on the proposal topic, quality, credentials of the investigator(s), and probability of success in developing space-related research infrastructure.

Financial data For faculty research seed grants and proposal writing grants, most awards range up to $5,000, although 1 grant of $10,000 is available. For other research initiatives, the maximum grant is $1,000.

Duration 1 year. Proposals for 2-year projects may be considered if they include a 2-year budget and justification of why the project requires a 2-year effort.

Additional Information Funding for this program is provided by NASA. Academic members of WSGC include the University of Wisconsin campuses at Green Bay, La Crosse, Madison, Milwaukee, Oshkosh, Parkside, and Whitewater; College of the Menominee Nation; Marquette University; Carroll College; Lawrence Univer-

sity; Milwaukee School of Engineering; Ripon College; and Medical College of Wisconsin. Industrial affiliates include Astronautics Corporation of America, Orbital Technologies Corporation, Space Explorers, Inc., Wisconsin Association of CESA Administrators, Wisconsin Department of Public Instruction, Wisconsin Department of Transportation, and Wisconsin Space Business Roundtable.

Number awarded Varies each year; recently, 4 of these grants were awarded.

Deadline February of each year.

Loans

[751]
ABILITY LOAN PROGRAM

Alabama Department of Rehabilitation Services
Attn: Statewide Technology Access and Response (STAR) System
2129 East South Boulevard
Montgomery, AL 36116-2455
(334) 281-8780   Toll-free: (800) 441-7607
Fax: (334) 281-1973   TTY: (800) 499-1816
Web: www.rehab.state.al.us/star

Summary To provide low-interest loans to persons with disabilities in Alabama interested in purchasing adaptive equipment and services.

Eligibility Eligible to apply for this assistance are persons in Alabama who have a disability or a family member with a disability. A disability is defined to include any medical, developmental, learning, or psychological impairment that substantially limits 1 or more major life activities (e.g., ability to walk, communicate, see, hear, learn, secure and maintain employment). Applicants must be interested in purchasing adaptive equipment, including telecommunications devices, closed circuit televisions, computer adaptive access or output, Braille machines, environmental control units, augmentative or alternative communication devices, wheelchairs, adaptive driving controls, power lifts, ramps, roll-in showers, or any other device or related service.

Financial data This program offers low-interest, extended term loans up to $10,000 to persons in Alabama who have a disability or a family member with a disability. The amount loaned depends on the cost of the adaptive equipment needed and the applicant's demonstrated ability to repay the loans.

Additional Information This program is offered jointly by the Southern Disability Foundation and SouthTrust Bank of Alabama. The program is also supported by the Alabama Department of Rehabilitation Services through its Statewide Technology Access and Response (STAR) system.

Number awarded Varies each year.

Deadline Applications may be submitted at any time.

[752]
ARIZONA LOANS FOR ASSISTIVE TECHNOLOGY

Arizona Technology Access Program
c/o Northern Arizona University
Institute for Human Development
4105 North 20th Street, Suite 260
Phoenix, AZ 85016
(602) 776-4670   Toll-free: (800) 477-9921
TTY: (602) 728-9536
E-mail: Pamela.Alcala@nau.edu
Web: www.azlat.org

Summary To provide low-interest loans for the purchase of assistive technology to residents of Arizona who have a disability.

Eligibility This program is open to residents of Arizona who wish to borrow money to purchase assistive technology for a person with a disability. The proposed purchase may involve any device or service that improves independence or quality of life for a person with a disability. Examples include hearing aids, wheelchairs, Braille note takers, safety rails in the bathroom, and specialized computer keyboards. Purchase of vehicles is not covered, although such modifications to vehicles as lifts or hand controls are included. Applicants must include an itemized price quote from vendors; home modifications in excess of $1,000 require submission of 3 bids from licensed contractors. They must be able to demonstrate ability to repay the loans and have an existing relationship with a financial institution (or be willing to open an account) so that monthly loan payments can be automatically withdrawn in a direct debit from the account.

Financial data Loans range from $500 to $3,000. The interest rate is equal to the prime rate plus 3 points or 9%, whichever is greater.

Duration Loans must be repaid within 60 months.

Additional Information This program is managed by the Arizona Technology Access Program (a program of the Institute for Human Development at Northern Arizona University), the Arizona MultiBank Community Development Corporation (an initiative of the Arizona Bankers Association established in 1992), and the Arizona Community Foundation. Additional support is provided by a grant from the National Institute for Disability Rehabilitation and Research (NIDRR) of the U.S. Department of Education's Office of Special Education and Rehabilitative Services and the Nina Mason Pulliam Charitable Trust.

Number awarded Varies each year.

Deadline Applications may be submitted at any time.

[753]
ARKANSAS TECHNOLOGY REVOLVING LOAN FUND

Arkansas Rehabilitation Services
Attn: Financial Management
1616 Brookwood Drive
Little Rock, AR 72202
(501) 296-1619   Toll-free: (800) 828-2799
E-mail: lmwalker@ars.state.ar.us
Web: www.arkansas-ican.org

Summary To provide low-interest loans for the purchase of assistive technology to residents of Arkansas who have a disability.

Eligibility This program is open to people with disabilities who are residents of Arkansas. Applicants must be interested in borrowing money to purchase adaptive equipment and related services to enable people with disabilities to live independently in their homes, go to school, work, and have access to the community. Businesses and nonprofit organizations may also apply to improve access to their buildings and services that will be used by persons with disabilities. Examples include walkers, wheelchairs, scooters, vehicle modifications or adaptations, hearing aids, TTYs, flashing alarms, CCTVs, specialized computers, home modifications, assistive animals, adapted toys or recreational equipment, levered door handles, ramps, power doors, and accessible elevators that make a business, work site, or public facility barrier free. Applicants must show that they can pay back the loan and that the adaptive equipment will benefit 1 or more persons with a disability.

Financial data The maximum loan is $10,000.

Duration Loans must be repaid within 5 years.

Additional Information This program was established by legislation passed in 1993 and 1995.

Number awarded Varies each year.

Deadline Applications may be submitted at any time.

[754]
ASSISTIVE TECHNOLOGY LOAN GUARANTEE PROGRAM

California Assistive Technology System
660 J Street, Suite 270
Sacramento, CA 95814-2495
(916) 325-1690   Fax: (916) 325-1699
TTY: (916) 325-1695   E-mail: info@atnet.org
Web: www.atnet.org/resources/loan.html

Summary To guarantee loans made by private banks to California residents with disabilities (or their employers) who are interested in purchasing assistive technology equipment.

Eligibility This program is open to residents of California who have disabilities and their employers. Applicants must be interested in purchasing durable equipment, adaptive aids, and/or assistive devices to maintain employment or live more independently. They must be ineligible for Vocational Rehabilitation Services, be unable to obtain the needed equipment through Medi-Care or other funding sources, be able to make the loan payments, and be interested in equipment that is appropriate or best-suited to the applicant's disability.

Financial data Under this program, loans are made by private banks but with a 100% guarantee by the California Department of Rehabilitation. No down payment is required of the borrower. Banks are asked to consider charging more favorable interest rates and extending the time period during which the loan is to be repaid. Some loans have been made with a 1% discount. If default occurs, the bank is refunded the remaining balance on principal and its expenses incurred in collecting and reselling the equipment from the loan guarantee fund.

Additional Information This program was established in 1981. Information is also available from the California Department of Rehabilitation, (916) 263-8687, TTY: (916) 263-8944, E-mail: atinfo@dor.ca.gov.

Number awarded Varies each year.

Deadline Applications may be submitted at any time.

[755]
ASSISTIVE TECHNOLOGY OF MINNESOTA FINANCIAL LOAN PROGRAM

Assistive Technology of Minnesota
Attn: Executive Director
1800 Pioneer Creek Center
P.O. Box 310
Maple Plain, MN 55359-0310
(763) 479-8239   Toll-free: (866) 535-8239
Fax: (763) 479-8243   TDD: (800) 627-3529
Web: www.atmn.org/micro_loan_info.htm

Summary To provide low-interest loans for the purchase of assistive technology to residents of Minnesota who have a disability.

Eligibility This program is open to residents of Minnesota who have a disability and wish to acquire assistive technology. Applicants must be able to demonstrate that the service or device they wish to acquire will help them to become more independent, obtain employment, improve their employment situation, or receive training to prepare then for employment. Loan qualification criteria are generally lower than for conventional loans.

Financial data The amount of the loan depends on the nature of the assistive technology to be acquired. The sponsoring organization pays down the interest rate to make loans more affordable.

Additional Information This program operates in conjunction with its banking partner, Firstar Bank.

Number awarded Varies each year.

Deadline Applications may be submitted at any time.

[756]
ASSISTIVE TECHNOLOGY OF OHIO LOW INTEREST LOAN PROGRAM

Assistive Technology of Ohio
J.L. Camera Center, Ninth Floor
2050 Kenny Road
Columbus, OH 43221
(614) 292-2426
Toll-free: (800) 784-3425 (within OH)
TTY: (614) 292-6132   E-mail: spetka.1@osu.edu
Web: www.atohio.org/low_cost_loan.htm

Summary To provide low-interest loans for the purchase of assistive technology to residents of Ohio who have a disability.

Eligibility This program is open to residents of Ohio with disabilities who wish to borrow money to purchase assistive technology devices and/or services. Examples include, but are not limited to, manual and power wheelchairs, AAC devices, Braille writers, home modifications, wheelchair lifts, and vehicle modifications.

Financial data Loans with low interest rates are offered for the purchases.

Additional Information This program, established in 1992, operates in partnership with Fifth Third Bank.

Number awarded Varies each year.

Deadline Applications may be submitted at any time.

[757]
ATLFA LOANS

Assistive Technology Loan Fund Authority
P.O. Box K091
Richmond, VA 23288-0300
(804) 662-9000   Fax: (804) 662-9533
TTY: (804) 662-9000
Web: www.atlfa.org

Summary To provide low-interest loans for the purchase of assistive technology to residents of Virginia who have a disability.

Eligibility This program is open to Virginians with disabilities and their family members. Applicants must be interested in borrowing money for 3 categories: 1) home improvement loans, to facilitate independence related to a specific disability (e.g., ramps, roll-in showers, environmental controls); many relatively small home improvement loans are unsecured, but for more substantial modifications these loans are secured with a second deed of trust; 2) automobile loans, to enable a person with a disability to purchase a van or car and to make necessary accommodations; loans are made for vehicles that are modified to accommodate a specific disability (e.g., wheelchair lifts, hand controls) and are secured by the vehicle; and 3) unsecured loans, for the purchase of such equipment as wheelchairs, electronic scooters, computers with voice input and output, hearing aids, low vision aids, communication devices, and other equipment; these loans are generally unsecured. The Assistive Technology Loan Fund Authority (ATLFA) makes loans up to $4,000 directly to qualified applicants. Other loans are made by SunTrust Bank. Applicants must demonstrate that the proposed purchase of assistive technology will help an individual with a disability to become more independent.

Financial data SunTrust Bank lends up to 100% of the value of the home on equity loans for home improvements and up to 100% of the cost of a vehicle. Unsecured loans (whether made by SunTrust or directly by ATLFA) depend on the cost of the equipment. For loans made by SunTrust, ATLFA buys down the interest rate 4% below the rate the bank charges to other lenders. The interest rate on direct ATLFA loans is 5%.

Duration Loan terms are up to 240 months for home improvement equity loans, up to 72 months for used vehicles less than 3 years old, up to 60 months for older used vehicles, up to 72 months for new vehicles (up to 78 months with an additional 1/2% interest rate), up to 48 months for unsecured loans under $5,000, or up to 60 months for unsecured loans over $5,000. Direct loans from ATLFA are for 48 months.

Additional Information If an applicant does not meet SunTrust's normal credit standards, ATLFA may guarantee the loan.

Number awarded Varies each year.

Deadline Applications may be submitted at any time.

[758]
ATTAIN-A-LOAN

Assistive Technology Through Action in INdiana
Symphony Center Building
32 East Washington Street, Suite 1400
Indianapolis, IN 46204
(317) 486-8808   Toll-free: (800) 528-8246
Fax: (317) 486-8809   TDD: (800) 743-3333
E-mail: attaininfo@attaininc.org
Web: www.attaininc.org

Summary To provide loans to residents of Indiana who have disabilities that require the purchase of assistive technology.

Eligibility This program is open to Indiana residents who have a disability, have a family member with a disability, or are the guardian of a person with a disability. Applicants must be seeking to borrow money to purchase an assistive technology device that will maintain or improve their independence or quality of life.

Financial data Loans range from $500 to $2,000. Low interest rates are charged.

Additional Information This program operates in partnership with Fifth Third Bank.

Number awarded Varies each year.

Deadline Applications may be submitted at any time.

[759]
CAL-VET LOAN PROGRAM

California Department of Veterans Affairs
Attn: Division of Farm and Home Purchases
1227 O Street, Room 200
P.O. Box 942895
Sacramento, CA 94295-0001
(916) 653-2525
Toll-free: (800) 952-LOAN (within CA)
Fax: (916) 653-2401   TDD: (800) 324-5966
E-mail: Kenn.Capps@cdva.ca.gov
Web: www.cdva.ca.gov/calvet/bestloan.htm

Summary To provide low-cost and low-interest financing to California servicemembers, veterans, and their spouses who are interested in purchasing homes, farms, or mobile homes for use as their primary residence.

Eligibility This program is open to veterans and servicemembers who are currently residents of California, regardless of where they were born or where they resided when they entered active military service. Applicants must have been released or discharged from active duty under honorable conditions or be currently serving on active duty. They must have served at least 90 days on active duty unless 1) discharged sooner due to service-connected disability, 2) eligible to receive a U.S. campaign or expeditionary medal, or 3) called to active duty from the Reserve or National Guard due to Presidential Order. Depending on the source of loan funds, additional requirements apply. For use of general obligation bond funds, applicants must be veterans who served on active duty prior to January 1, 1977, who apply within 30 years from their release from active duty, and who served at least 1 day during a specified war period of World War II (December 7, 1941 through December 31, 1946), the Korean period (June 27, 1950 through January 31, 1955), the Vietnam era (August 5, 1964 through May 7, 1975), or the Persian Gulf War (August 2, 1990 through a date yet to be determined); there are no purchase price limitations on the properties that can be purchased with these funds nor are there any income limitations on the veteran borrower, but unremarried spouses of veterans are not eligible to be funded with general obligation bond proceeds; funds may be used to purchase homes (including individual units in condominiums and planned unit developments), farms, mobile homes on land owned by the applicant, and mobile homes in mobile home parks. Borrowers using revenue bond funding may be veterans or servicemembers who served either during wartime or peacetime; unremarried spouses of veterans are also eligible; all applicants, however, must qualify either as a first-time homebuyer or as a purchaser in a targeted area of the state defined as an area of low income or chronic economic distress; the properties must qualify under purchase price limitations that vary throughout the state and the applicants must qualify under income limitations that also vary in different areas of the state; revenue bond loans are available only on single-family residences (including individual units in condominiums and planned unit developments) and mobile homes on land owned by the applicant. Veterans who do not qualify for either general obligation or revenue bond loans may be eligible for the unrestricted bond program, but they must meet the wartime service requirement.

Financial data The maximum loan on single family homes (including condominiums, townhouses, and mobile homes affixed to land owned by the borrower) is $322,700 (or $240,000 for loans guaranteed by the U.S. Department of Veterans Affairs); on mobile homes in approved mobile home parks, it is $70,000. The funding fee ranges from 1.25% to 3%, but is waived for veterans with disability ratings of 10% or higher. The loan origination fee is 1% of the loan amount. Interest rates recently were 4.5% on revenue bond loans, 4.25% on general obligation bond loans (5.25% for mobile homes in parks), or 4.5% on unrestricted fund loans.

Duration Loans are typically for 30 years, although shorter periods are available.

Additional Information Veteran contract purchasers who move from the Cal-Vet financed property may qualify to have their Cal-Vet loan transferred to another property or may qualify for a second loan contract. Loans that have been repaid or assigned to an ex-spouse in a divorce action may be obtained again. Information on current purchase price and family income limitations for revenue bond loans is available from the Department of Veterans Affairs state headquarters or local district sales offices. The veteran or a member of the veteran's immediate family must occupy the property within 60 days after signing a Cal-Vet loan contract and must continue to reside on the property as the principal place of residence until the loan is paid in full. Acceptance of a bonus or benefit from another state for the qualifying period of military service disqualifies the veteran from Cal-Vet benefits.

Number awarded Varies each year.

Deadline Applications may be submitted at any time.

[760]
CENTRAL INTELLIGENCE AGENCY UNDERGRADUATE SCHOLARSHIP PROGRAM

Central Intelligence Agency
Attn: Recruitment Center
P.O. Box 4090
Reston, VA 20195
Toll-free: (800) 368-3886
Web: www.cia.gov/employment/student.html

Summary To provide scholarship/loans and work experience to high school seniors and college sophomores, especially minorities and people with disabilities, who are interested in working for the Central Intelligence Agency (CIA) after graduation from college.

Eligibility This program is open to U.S. citizens who are either high school seniors or college sophomores.

Seniors must be at least 18 years of age by April of the year they apply and have minimum scores of 1000 on the SAT or 21 on the ACT. College sophomores must have a GPA of 3.0 or higher. All applicants must be able to demonstrate financial need (household income of $70,000 or less for a family of 4 or $80,000 or less for a family of 5 or more) and be able to meet the same employment standards as permanent employees of the CIA. An explicit goal of the program is to attract minorities and students with disabilities to a career with the CIA.

Financial data Scholars are provided a salary and up to $18,000 per year for tuition, fees, books, and supplies. They must agree to continue employment with the CIA after college graduation for a period 1.5 times the length of their college support.

Duration 1 year; may be renewed if the student maintains a GPA of 3.0 or higher and full-time enrollment in a 4- or 5-year college program.

Additional Information Scholars work each summer at a CIA facility. In addition to a salary, they receive the cost of transportation between school and the Washington, D.C. area and a housing allowance.

Number awarded Varies each year.

Deadline October of each year.

[761]
CTTAP ASSISTIVE TECHNOLOGY LOAN PROGRAM

Connecticut Tech Act Project
c/o Connecticut Department of Social Services
Bureau of Rehabilitation Services
25 Sigourney Street, 11th Floor
Hartford, CT 06106-5033
(860) 424-4871   Toll-free: (800) 537-2549
Fax: (860) 424-4850   TDD: (800) 537-2549
E-mail: cttap@aol.com
Web: www.techactproject.com/loan/index.htm

Summary To provide low-interest loans to residents of Connecticut who have a disability that requires the use of assistive technology.

Eligibility This program is open to residents of Connecticut who have 1) a physical or mental impairment that substantially limits at least 1 major daily activity and 2) either an income at or below 100% of the state median or an income above 100% of the state median level but an inability to meet conventional loan standards. Applicants must be seeking to purchase a tool, device, or piece of equipment designed to help them develop, maintain, or improve their ability to function daily. Examples of qualifying items include kitchen gadgets, vans adapted with special controls, hearing aids, motorized wheelchairs, computers controlled by voice or other special switches, or augmentative alternative communications tools. Construction on part of a building to make use of the device possible also qualifies.

Financial data The amount of the loan depends on the price of the equipment and the financial status of the applicant. Loans are provided by People's Bank at special low interest rates.

Additional Information This program, established in 1994, is sponsored by the Connecticut Department of Social Services, Bureau of Rehabilitation Services in partnership with People's Bank. Funding is provided by a grant from the National Institute on Disability and Rehabilitation Research (NIDRR) of the U.S. Department of Education, Office of Special Education and Rehabilitative Services.

Number awarded Varies each year.

Deadline Applications may be submitted at any time.

[762]
DAKOTALINK LOW INTEREST LOAN PROGRAM

DakotaLink
1925 Plaza Boulevard
Rapid City, SD 57702
(605) 394-1876
Toll-free: (800) 645-0673 (within SD)
Fax: (605) 394-5315   TDD: (800) 645-0673
E-mail: atinfo@tie.net
Web: dakotalink.tie.net/loantxt.html

Summary To provide loans to persons with disabilities in South Dakota who need to purchase equipment to become more independent.

Eligibility This program is open to South Dakota residents who have a disability (physical or mental) or a family member with a disability. The disability must substantially limit 1 or more major life activities (which include but are not limited to walking, talking, seeing, hearing, working, or the ability to care for oneself). Applicants must have been denied full or partial funding for assistive technology equipment.

Financial data Loans range between $250 and $10,000. Funds may be used to obtain assistive devices, such as hearing aids, TDDs, speech access computers, closed circuit televisions, wheelchairs, or vans with power lifts. A low interest rate is charged on these loans.

Duration Recipients have up to 8 years to repay the loan.

Additional Information This program, which began in 1997, is sponsored jointly by DakotaLink and Wells Fargo Bank. Information from the bank is also available at (605) 394-3800 or (800) 321-4141.

Number awarded Varies each year.

Deadline Applications may be submitted at any time.

[763]
DCU ACCESS LOANS

Digital Federal Credit Union
Attn: Access Loans
220 Donald Lynch Boulevard
P.O. Box 9130
Marlborough, MA 01752-9130
Toll-free: (800) 328-8797   Fax: (508) 263-6392
TTY: (800) 395-5146   E-mail: dcu@duc.org
Web: www.dcu.org/prodserv/loans/access.html

Summary To provide loans to members of the Digital Federal Credit Union (DCU) who wish to purchase assistive technology devices.

Eligibility These loans are available for the purchase of a product, device, or building modification designed to assist someone with a disability. The borrower need not be the beneficiary of the purchase. Applicants must be DCU members with a good credit rating. Membership in DCU is open to employees of many companies and to members of the American Association of People with Disabilities (AAPD). Qualified purchases include, but are not limited to, powered non-vehicle transportation (scooters, power wheelchairs, stair-climbing power chairs, all-terrain wheelchairs), manual transportation (standard manual wheelchairs, custom sport wheelchairs, specialized hand cycles), adaptive computer and communications equipment (air tube systems for spinal cord injuries, voice systems for the blind, educational and rehabilitation systems for children and adults), durable medical equipment (slings for lifting paraplegics and quadriplegics, breathing systems, specialized beds), rehabilitative equipment, or building modifications.

Financial data Loans are available for 100% of the purchase amount, from $1,500 to $25,000. Interest rates depend on personal credit history, but may be as low as 7.3% for 5-year loans or 8.8% for 6-year loans.

Duration Borrowers may have up to 6 years to repay the loans.

Number awarded Varies each year.

Deadline Applications may be submitted at any time.

[764]
DCU MOBILITY VEHICLE LOANS

Digital Federal Credit Union
Attn: Access Loans
220 Donald Lynch Boulevard
P.O. Box 9130
Marlborough, MA 01752-9130
Toll-free: (800) 328-8797   Fax: (508) 263-6392
TTY: (800) 395-5146   E-mail: dcu@duc.org
Web: www.dcu.org/prodserv/loans/mobility.html

Summary To provide loans to members of the Digital Federal Credit Union (DCU) who wish to purchase vehicles modified for people with disabilities.

Eligibility These loans are available for the expense of modifying a vehicle to provide mobility to a person with a disability (as with lift equipment or hand controls). The borrower need not be the beneficiary of the purchase. Applicants must be DCU members with a good credit rating. Membership in DCU is open to employees of many companies and to members of the American Association of People with Disabilities (AAPD).

Financial data Loans are available for 120% of the purchase amount (to cover sales tax, filing fees, etc.), from $5,000 to $100,000. Interest rates depend on personal credit history, but may be as low as 4.49% for 5-year loans, 5.99% for 7-year loans, or 6.59% for 10-year loans.

Duration Borrowers may have up to 10 years to repay the loans.

Number awarded Varies each year.

Deadline Applications may be submitted at any time.

[765]
DRAMATISTS GUILD FUND GRANTS

Dramatists Guild Fund, Inc.
1501 Broadway, Suite 701
New York, NY 10036-5501
(212) 391-8384   Fax: (212) 944-0420

Summary To provide loans to dramatists who are experiencing illness or other emergency.

Eligibility Published or produced dramatists are eligible to apply if they are U.S. citizens, in financial need, and experiencing illness or another emergency that requires assistance.

Financial data Interest-free loans, averaging $1,000, are offered.

Duration Recipients may reapply, if the need arises.

Additional Information This fund cannot provide grants-in-aid or other long-range career assistance.

Number awarded Varies each year.

Deadline Applications may be submitted at any time.

[766]
EDUCATIONAL LOANS TO ASSIST RETRAINING OF CERTAIN DISABLED INDIVIDUALS

American Dental Association
Attn: ADA Endowment and Assistance Fund
211 East Chicago Avenue, Suite 820
Chicago, IL 60611-2678
(312) 440-2567   Fax: (312) 440-2822
Web: www.ada.org

Summary To provide loans to dentists who require retraining because of a disability.

Eligibility This program is open to dentists who require retraining due to a disabling accident or illness. Applicants must 1) verify that they suffer from a disability that requires retraining to resume their dental practice career; 2) verify that the disability precludes reentry into their dental practice career; 3) submit a physician's statement attesting to the extent of the disability and that

it precludes reentry into a dental practice career; 4) submit an estimate of the cost of books, tuition, and institutional fees; and 5) show that the disability has caused an impairment in their ability to continue a dental practice career and that other sources of adequate funding are not available.
Financial data Loan amounts are based on the need of the recipient but do not exceed $10,000. Funds are paid directly to the educational institution for the cost of retraining.
Duration The maximum loan is for 2 years.
Number awarded Up to 5 each year.
Deadline Applications may be submitted at any time.

[767]
ENABLE LOAN PROGRAM
Vermont State Housing Authority
One Prospect Street
Montpelier, VT 05602-3556
(802) 828-3295 Fax: (802) 828-3248
TTY: (800) 798-3118
Web: www.vsha.org

Summary To provide loans for home modifications that will make a dwelling better suited for Vermont elders or people with disabilities.
Eligibility Any resident can apply for a loan to modify a dwelling for the elderly or disabled in Vermont. Loans may be requested for the following home modifications: accessible parking spaces, bathroom modifications, entry ramps, kitchen modifications, stair handrails, visual smoke detectors and doorbells, wider doorways, and stair lifts.
Financial data Low-interest loans up to $5,000 are available.
Duration The terms of the loan are flexible, ranging between 6 months and 10 years.
Number awarded Varies each year. The program relies on a revolving fund of approximately $120,000.
Deadline Applications may be submitted at any time.

[768]
EQUIPMENT LOAN FUND FOR THE DISABLED
New York State Office of Children and Family Services
Attn: Commission for the Blind & Visually Handicapped
South Building, Room 201
52 Washington Street
Rensselaer, NY 12144
(518) 474-0197
Toll-free: (800) 342-3009 (within NY)
E-mail: cfspio@dfa.state.ny.us
Web: www.dfa.state.ny.us

Summary To provide low-interest loans for the purchase of necessary equipment to persons with disabilities in New York.
Eligibility This program is open to individuals with mental or physical disabilities who are residents of New York and need equipment to overcome barriers in daily living or employment. Examples include wheelchairs, van lifts for wheelchairs, ramps, communication devices for the deaf, hearing impaired prosthetic devices, and devices that allow people who are blind or visually impaired to discern printed material. Applicants must be unable to obtain funding from any other source.
Financial data Between $500 and $4,000 can be loaned on this program. The current interest rate charged is 8%. Money is loaned either directly to the disabled person or to another person responsible for that individual.
Duration Recipients have up to 8 years to repay.
Number awarded Varies each year.
Deadline Applications may be submitted at any time.

[769]
FAAST ALTERNATIVE FINANCING PROGRAM
Florida Alliance for Assistive Services and Technology, Inc.
325 John Knox Road, Building B
Tallahassee, FL 32303-4151
(850) 487-3278 Toll-free: (888) 788-9216
Fax: (850) 487-2805 TDD: (850) 922-5951
E-mail: faast@faast.org
Web: faast.org/financing_program.htm

Summary To provide low-interest loans for the purchase of assistive technology to residents of Florida who have a disability.
Eligibility This program is open to residents of Florida who have a physical or mental impairment that substantially limits 1 or more of the major activities, have a record of such impairment, or are regarded as having such impairment. Applicants must be interested in purchasing assistive technology or accessibility for assistive technology and have the ability to repay a loan. Funds may be used to purchase assistive technology equipment that will help Floridians with disabilities become

more independent or more productive members of the community. Acquisition of automobiles, trucks, or vans that do not require modifications (such as hand controls, ramps, or wheelchair lifts) or computers that do not include modifications (voice input/output, large print/Braille output) are not eligible.

Financial data Loans range from $500 to $20,000.

Duration Loans from $500 to $2,999 must be repaid in 24 months, from $3,000 to $6,999 in 60 months, and from $7,000 to $20,000 in 72 months.

Additional Information This program was established in 2001. Loans are issued by AmSouth Bank and guaranteed by the Florida Alliance for Assistive Services and Technology (FAAST). Loans include a $75 processing fee.

Number awarded Varies each year.

Deadline Applications may be submitted at any time.

[770]
HAWAII ASSISTIVE TECHNOLOGY LOAN PROGRAM

Assistive Technology Resource Centers of Hawaii
414 Kuwili Street, Suite 104
Honolulu, HI 96817
(808) 532-7110
Toll-free: (800) 645-3007 (within HI)
Fax: (808) 532-7120
TTY: (800) 645-3007 (within HI)
E-mail: atrc@atrc.org
Web: www.atrc.org/Funding/HAT%20loan

Summary To offer Hawaii residents low-interest loans to acquire assistive technology devices.

Eligibility Any Hawaii resident, disabled or not, may apply for this funding as long as the device or service purchased with the funds benefits 1 or more persons with a disability and promotes their independence and productivity in the community. Assistive technology devices can be anything from prosthetics to medical equipment, computers, specialized furniture, home modifications, vehicles, or lifts. Applicants may also be seeking funding for assistive technology training, repair, or maintenance.

Financial data Loans range from $500 to $30,000. Interest rates are 1.5 percentage points lower than other loans of the same type.

Additional Information Loans are offered through American Savings Bank and guaranteed by this program.

Number awarded Varies each year.

Deadline Applications may be submitted at any time.

[771]
IDAHO ASSISTIVE TECHNOLOGY LOW INTEREST LOAN PROGRAM

Idaho Assistive Technology Project
Attn: Sue House
129 West Third Street
Moscow, ID 83843-4401
(208) 885-3573   Toll-free: (800) IDA-TECH
Fax: (208) 885-3628   TTY: (800) IDA-TECH
Web: www.educ.uidaho.edu

Summary To provide loans for assistive technology to Idaho residents.

Eligibility This program is open to Idaho residents who have a disability or are acting on behalf of a person with a disability. Applicants must be seeking to borrow money in order to purchase an assistive technology device; the program interprets that term broadly and has approved loans for the purchase of many different items that may be used by the person with the disability to increase, maintain, or improve functional capabilities. The program does not provide for the purchase of vehicles, although modifications to the vehicle for assistive purposes can be covered by the loan program.

Financial data Loans up to $10,000 are available. The interest rate is the prime rate at the time the loan is made.

Duration Loans for as long as 5 years are available.

Additional Information This program, which began in 1994, is supported by Zions Bank N.A., KeyBank, N.A., and the Idaho Community Foundation.

Number awarded Varies each year. A total of $56,000 has been loaned to date.

Deadline Applications may be submitted at any time.

[772]
IOWA ABLE LOAN PROGRAM

Iowa COMPASS
c/o Center for Disabilities and Development
100 Hawkins Drive, Room S295
Iowa City, IA 52242-1011
(319) 353-8777   Toll-free: (800) 779-2001
TTY: (877) 686-0032
E-mail: jennifer-britton@uiowa.edu
Web: www.uiowa.edu/infotech/IowaAble.htm

Summary To provide low-interest loans for the purchase of assistive technology to residents of Iowa who have a disability.

Eligibility This program is open to individuals with disabilities and their families who live in Iowa. Applicants must be interested in purchasing assistive technology or making adaptations to enhance the independence of people with disabilities in their homes, at work, or in their communities. Loans may be used to adapt a vehicle but not to purchase the vehicle.

Financial data Loans range from $1,000 to $5,000. The interest rate is 9.5%.

Duration The maximum repayment period is 60 months.
Additional Information This program is a collaborative effort of U.S. Bank, InfoTech (a service of the Iowa Program for Assistive Technology), and the Iowa Able Foundation.
Number awarded Varies each year.
Deadline Applications may be submitted at any time.

[773]
KATCO FLEXIBLE TERM LOAN PROGRAM

Kansas Assistive Technology Cooperative
625 Merchant, Suite 210
Emporia, KS 66801
(620) 341-9002   Toll-free: (866) 465-2826
Fax: (620) 342-6400   TTY: (620) 341-9002
E-mail: katcomail@sbcglobal.net
Web: www.katco.net

Summary To provide low-interest loans for the purchase of assistive technology to residents of Kansas who have a disability.
Eligibility This program is open to residents of Kansas who have a disability, are a parent of a minor with a disability, or are the guardian of a person with a disability. Applicants must be interested in borrowing money to purchase assistive technology, defined as an "item, piece of equipment, or product system, whether acquired commercially off the shelf, modified or customized, that is used to increase, maintain or improve functional capabilities of individuals with disabilities." Examples include wheelchairs, scooters, other mobility aids, Braille equipment, scanners, hearing aids and other assistive listening systems, computers and adaptive computer peripherals, environmental control units, building modifications for accessibility, motor vehicle modifications for accessibility, and motor vehicles requiring modifications for accessibility (if the value of the vehicle is greater than the cost of the modifications). Applicants must have a good credit history and be able to repay the loan.
Financial data The amount of the loan depends on the cost of the assistive technology to be purchased. Interest rates are lower than on conventional loans.
Duration Loans must be repaid within 10 years.
Additional Information The Kansas Assistive Technology Cooperative (KATCO), established in 2000, operates this program in cooperation with Alliance Bank.
Number awarded Varies each year.
Deadline Applications may be submitted at any time.

[774]
KENTUCKY ASSISTIVE TECHNOLOGY LOANS

Kentucky Assistive Technology Loan Corporation
Attn: Program Director
P.O. Box 12231
Lexington, KY 40581-2231
Toll-free: (877) 675-0195   Fax: (859) 246-2124
E-mail: nancye.hansen@mail.state.ky.us
Web: www.kyatloan.org

Summary To provide low-interest loans for the purchase of assistive technology to residents of Kentucky who have a disability.
Eligibility This program is open to people who have been residents of Kentucky for at least 6 consecutive months and either have a disability that permanently affects a major life activity or are a parent, guardian, or caretaker of a person with a disability. Applicants must be interested in borrowing money to purchase assistive technology to be used by the person with a disability. Assistive technology includes items, pieces of equipment, and devices that enable an individual with a disability to improve his or her independence and quality of life. Examples include hearing aids, computers, augmentative communication devices, wheelchair ramps, and van lifts. Loans for those devices are issued by Fifth Third Bank of Kentucky. Low- to moderate-income individuals may qualify for loans from the Kentucky Housing Corporation for home modifications or environmental control devices.
Financial data Loans range from $500 to $25,000. The interest rate on loans issued by Fifth Third Bank is 5%. The interest rate on loans issued by the Kentucky Housing Corporation for home modifications and environmental control devices is 4%.
Duration Loans must be repaid in 5 years.
Additional Information The Kentucky legislature established this program in 1996. It operates jointly with Fifth Third Bank of Kentucky and the Kentucky Housing Corporation.
Number awarded Varies each year.
Deadline Applications may be submitted at any time.

[775]
LATAN ASSISTIVE TECHNOLOGY LOAN PROGRAM

Louisiana Assistive Technology Access Network
Attn: Assistive Technology Loan Program Director
3042 Old Forge Drive
Baton Rouge, LA 70808
(225) 925-9500   Toll-free: (800) 270-6185
Fax: (225) 925-9560   E-mail: kbrunet@latan.org
Web: www.latan.org/at_loans.html

Summary To provide low-interest loans for the purchase of assistive technology to residents of Louisiana who have a disability.

Eligibility This program is open to residents of Louisiana who have a disability. A family member, guardian, or curator may apply on behalf of the person with a disability. The applicant must be older than 18 years of age or have a cosigner over 18. They must be able to demonstrate that the proposed purchase of assistive technology will improve or maintain their level of independence, increase or maintain their productivity, or improve their quality of life. Examples of devices and services that may be obtained with loan funds include computers with adaptive input or output devices, new and used vehicle loans for vehicles that will be modified, loan refinancing for late model vehicles that have been modified, vehicle modifications, augmentative or alternative communication devices, assistive devices for the deaf or speech impaired, closed circuit TV or brailling machines for the sight impaired, adaptive driving controls, adaptive home modifications (including ramps and power lifts), prosthetics and/or orthotics, environmental control units, wheelchairs (power and manual), adaptive mobility products, any other item or device that improves or maintains the independence of a person, or any service to support the device (including assessments, training on the device, or extended warranties).

Financial data Loans range from $1,500 to $50,000, depending on the cost of the adaptive equipment and the borrower's demonstrated ability to repay the debt. Funding may cover up to 100% of the equipment. Interest rates are fixed and lower than on conventional loans.

Duration These are extended-term loans.

Additional Information Loans of this program are issued by Union Planters Bank.

Number awarded Varies each year.

Deadline Applications may be submitted at any time.

[776]
LOANS FOR ACCESSIBILITY

Corporation for Independent Living
30 Jordan Lane
Wethersfield, CT 06109-1258
(860) 563-6011, ext. 221   Fax: (860) 563-2562
E-mail: cil@cilhomes.com
Web: www.cilhomes.com

Summary To provide below-market interest rate loans to low- or moderate-income people with physical disabilities and others to modify their existing housing in Connecticut.

Eligibility Eligible to participate in this program are Connecticut residents who have a physical disability (including people in wheelchairs, the deaf or hearing impaired, the blind or visually impaired, and people who have multiple sclerosis, cerebral palsy, traumatic brain injury, or any other physical disability), own their homes, and have total household income at or below 150% of median income. Also eligible are homeowner parents of a child with a physical disability and landlords of a person with a physical disability whose total household income is at or below 100% of the median. Loan funds may be used to purchase and install fixtures and improvements required to improve accessibility and/or usability of a residential dwelling in Connecticut.

Financial data Loan amounts range from $1,000 to $20,000 at an annual interest rate of up to 7% repayable within a maximum term of 30 years.

Additional Information Funding for this program is provided by the Connecticut Department of Economic and Community Development.

Number awarded Varies each year.

Deadline Applications may be submitted at any time.

[777]
MAKING HOMES ACCESSIBLE (MHA) LOAN PROGRAM

Nebraska Assistive Technology Partnership
5143 South 48th Street, Suite C
Lincoln, NE 68516-2204
(402) 471-0734   Toll-free: (888) 806-6287
Fax: (402) 471-6052   E-mail: atp@atp.state.ne.us
Web: www.nde.state.ne.us/ATP

Summary To make forgivable loans to Nebraska residents with disabilities who are interested in modifying their homes to make them accessible.

Eligibility This program is open to Nebraska residents who 1) have a physical or mental impairment that limits their ability to live independently, 2) own a home that they want to add on to or modify to help them live independently, and 3) have an income that does not exceed 100% of the median income for the county in which they live. The requested modification must be related to the applicants' disability and assist them to live independently. Examples of possible home modifications include installing a ramp to allow access in and out of the house, remodeling a bathroom, or remodeling a kitchen.

Financial data Loans range from $1,000 to $14,999. These are deferred loans that are conditional grants with liens placed against the property. Loans up to $4,999 are forgiven after 5 years. Loans of $5,000 and over are forgiven after 10 years. If the house is sold before those times, a prorated pay back is required.

Additional Information These loans are made in cooperation with the Nebraska Department of Economic Development and other state agencies.

Number awarded Varies each year.

Deadline Applications may be submitted at any time.

[778]
MARYLAND ASSISTIVE TECHNOLOGY GUARANTEED LOAN PROGRAM

Maryland Technology Assistance Program
Attn: Project Director
2301 Argonne Drive, Room T-17
Baltimore, MD 21218-1696
(410) 554-9233   Toll-free: (800) 832-4827
Fax: (410) 554-9237   TTY: (410) 554-9233
TTY: (800) 832-4827   E-mail: loans@mdtap.org
Web: www.mdtap.org

Summary To provide low-interest loans to disabled Maryland residents who need to obtain assistive devices.

Eligibility This program is open to anyone who wishes to borrow money to buy assistive technology for a Maryland resident with a disability. People with disabilities, family members, and friends are all eligible to apply. The equipment may include any device that helps a person with a disability live more independently and productively. Funds are also available to pay for training to use equipment, insurance, extended warranties, and maintenance plans. Loans are made only to credit-worthy borrowers, but the criteria for credit-worthiness are less stringent than those at banks.

Financial data The amount loaned varies, depending upon the needs of the recipient, from $500 to $30,000. Interest rates vary but are generally below the prime rate. For borrowers who qualify for loans without guarantees, the rates are higher.

Number awarded Varies each year.

Deadline Applications may be submitted at any time.

[779]
MICHIGAN ASSISTIVE TECHNOLOGY LOAN FUND

Michigan Disability Rights Coalition
c/o UCP Michigan
3401 East Saginaw, Suite 216
Lansing, MI 48912
(517) 203-1200   Toll-free: (800) 828-2714
E-mail: miatloanfund@aol.com
Web: www.mi-atlf.org

Summary To provide low-interest loans for the purchase of assistive technology to residents of Michigan who have a disability.

Eligibility This program is open to residents of Michigan who either have a disability or are an older person who needs assistive technology. Family members may apply on behalf of children or other family members with the disability. Applicants must be a member of the Michigan Disability Rights Coalition (MDRC) and deposit 1 share ($5) to open an account at the Financial Health Credit Union. They must be interested in borrowing money to purchase assistive technology devices and services, including modifications of vehicles and homes. Loans may also cover cost of training, warranties, and service agreements. The proposed purchase of assistive technology must provide the person with a disability greater access, increased mobility, enhanced communication, or job opportunities.

Financial data The maximum loan is $20,000. The interest rate is established by the Financial Health Credit Union at the time the loan is approved and is fixed for the life of the loan.

Duration Repayment terms are based on the expected useful life on the assistive technology device.

Additional Information The Michigan Disability Rights Coalition established this program with support from UCP Michigan, the Financial Health Credit Union, and Centers for Independent Living

Number awarded Varies each year.

Deadline Applications may be submitted at any time.

[780]
MONTANA ASSISTIVE TECHNOLOGY LOAN PROGRAM

Rural Institute on Disabilities
Attn: MonTECH Program
634 Eddy Avenue
Missoula, MT 59812
(406) 243-5676   Toll-free: (800) 732-0323
E-mail: montech@selway.umt.edu
Web: montech.ruralinstitute.umt.edu

Summary To provide low-interest loans for the purchase of assistive technology to residents of Montana who have a disability.

Eligibility This program is open to Montana residents with disabilities who can benefit from the use of assistive technology devices. Qualifying equipment includes any device that will allow a person with a disability to maintain or enhance their independent functioning or participation in family, community, school, work, or recreational activities. Examples include, but are not limited to, hearing aids, augmentative communication devices, text telephones, environmental control devices, computers equipped with hardware and software adaptations, vision aids, wheelchairs, and vehicle modifications.

Financial data The maximum loan is $10,000. The interest rate is fixed at the prime rate in effect when the loan is made. Up to 75% of the loan is guaranteed by the MonTECH Program.

Duration Loans must be repaid within a maximum of 60 months. The average term is 36 months.

Additional Information This program operates in cooperation with First Security Bank of Missoula. A loan fee of $50 is added to the amount financed.

Number awarded Varies each year. First Security Bank has allocated $100,000 to the loan program for lending to credit-worthy applicants and the MonTECH Program has contributed approximately $120,000 to serve as guarantee funds for individuals who would not otherwise qualify for a loan.

Deadline Applications may be submitted at any time.

[781]
MPOWER ADAPTIVE EQUIPMENT LOAN PROGRAM

Alpha One
127 Main Street
South Portland, ME 04106
(207) 767-2189   Fax: (207) 799-8346
Toll-free: (800) 640-7200   TTY: (207) 767-5387
TTY: (866) 906-5375
E-mail: info@mpowermaine.org
Web: www.alpha-one.org

Summary To provide low-interest loans for the purchase of assistive technology to residents of Maine who have a disability.

Eligibility Loan applications may be submitted by individuals with disabilities, non-disabled individuals, businesses, or community organizations in Maine, as long as the loan is to purchase adaptive equipment that assists 1 or more persons with a disability to improve their independence or quality of life, or to become more productive members of the community. Examples of equipment that may be purchased with these loans include wheelchairs, hearing aids, TTYs, assistive animals, adaptive toys, recreational equipment, home modifications, new home access features, visual fire alarms, prosthetics, adapted vehicles or boats, stair lifts, computer technology, ramps, large print readers, or orthotics, communication devices for non-verbal people, and assistive animals. Loans are also available to business in Maine to acquire such items as elevators and lifts, building modifications (entrances, bathrooms, common areas), worksite adaptations for employees, and accessible transit vehicles.

Financial data Individuals may borrow from $250 to $100,000, depending on ability to repay and credit history. Businesses and nonprofit organizations may borrow up to $100,000 of their costs, based on credit worthiness and ability to repay. The interest rate ranges from zero to the prime rate in Boston.

Additional Information This program is administered by Alpha One (which processes loans for individuals) and the Finance Authority of Maine (which processes loans for businesses). It was formerly known as the Kim D. Wallace Adaptive Equipment Loan Program.

Number awarded Varies each year. This is a revolving loan fund; a total of $5 million is available for loans, which can be made as soon as existing loans are repaid.

Deadline Applications may be submitted at any time.

[782]
NATIONAL INSTITUTES OF HEALTH UNDERGRADUATE SCHOLARSHIP PROGRAM

National Institutes of Health
Attn: Office of Loan Repayment and Scholarship
2 Center Drive, Room 2E30
Bethesda, MD 20892-0230
Toll-free: (800) 528-7689   Fax: (301) 480-3123
TTY: (888) 352-3001   E-mail: ugsp@nih.gov
Web: ugsp.info.nih.gov

Summary To provide loans-for-service for undergraduate education in the life sciences to students from disadvantaged backgrounds.

Eligibility This program is open to U.S. citizens, nationals, and permanent residents who are enrolled or accepted for enrollment as full-time students at accredited institutions of higher education and committed to careers in biomedical, behavioral, and social science health-related research. Applicants must come from a family that meets federal standards of low income, currently defined as a family with an annual income below $17,960 for a 1-person family, ranging to below $61,920 for families of 8 or more. Applicants must have a GPA of 3.5 or higher or be in the top 5% of their class. They are ranked according to the following priorities: first, juniors and seniors who have completed 2 years of undergraduate course work; second, other undergraduates who have completed 4 core science courses in biology, chemistry, physics, and calculus; third, freshmen and sophomores at accredited undergraduate institutions; and fourth, high school seniors who have been accepted for enrollment as full-time students at accredited undergraduate institutions. The sponsor especially encourages applications from underrepresented minorities, women, and individuals with disabilities.

Financial data Stipends are available up to $20,000 per year, to be used for tuition, educational expenses (such as books and lab fees), and qualified living expenses while attending a college or university. Recipients incur a service obligation to work as an employee of the National Institutes of Health (NIH) in Bethesda, Maryland for 10 consecutive weeks (during the summer) during the sponsored year and, upon graduation, for 52 weeks for each academic year of scholarship support. The NIH 52-week employment obligation may be deferred if the recipient goes to graduate or medical school.

Duration 1 year; may be renewed for up to 3 additional years.

Number awarded 15 each year.

Deadline February of each year.

[783]
NEBRASKA HOMECHOICE MORTGAGE LOAN PROGRAM

Nebraska Assistive Technology Partnership
5143 South 48th Street, Suite C
Lincoln, NE 68516-2204
(402) 471-0734   Toll-free: (888) 806-6287
Fax: (402) 471-6052   E-mail: atp@atp.state.ne.us
Web: www.nde.state.ne.us/ATP

Summary To make loans to Nebraska residents with disabilities and their families who are interested in purchasing a home.

Eligibility This program is open to Nebraska residents who 1) are disabled as defined by the Americans with Disabilities Act of 1990 or handicapped as defined by the Fair Housing Amendments Act of 1988, and 2) live in a low- (below 50% of local median income) to moderate-income (below 100% of local median income) household. Loans are available to people with disabilities or who have family members with disabilities living with them. Applicants must be seeking to purchase a single-family home.

Financial data Loans available to borrowers provide the following benefits: lower down payment requirements (depending on income, this ranges from $250 up to 2% of the sale price or appraised value of the home); qualifying and underwriting standards that look at personal budgets and do not rely solely on debt-to-income ratios; use of nontraditional credit histories; and support from other agencies to help a borrower be a successful homeowner.

Additional Information This program was developed by Fannie Mae and the Nebraska Home Of Your Own Coalition, (888) 806-6287.

Number awarded Varies each year.

Deadline Applications may be submitted at any time.

[784]
NEVADA ASSISTIVE TECHNOLOGY LOAN FUND

Nevada Community Enrichment Program
Attn: Assistive Technology Center
2820 West Charleston Boulevard, Suite D-37
Las Vegas, NV 89102
(702) 259-1903   Toll-free: (888) 214-2557
Fax: (702) 259-1240

Summary To provide loans to residents of Nevada with disabilities who require assistance in purchasing assistive technology devices.

Eligibility This program is open to Nevada residents with a physical or mental impairment that substantially limits 1 or more major life activities. Guardians, parents, or other immediate family members may also submit applications on behalf of the person with a disability. Applicants must be seeking funding to purchase an item, device, piece of equipment, or product system (whether acquired commercially off the shelf, modified, or customized) that is used to increase, maintain, or improve functional capabilities of people with disabilities. Loans are not available to people whose income is in excess of 500% of the federal poverty level.

Financial data Maximum loans are $25,000 for home modification, $20,000 for an electric wheelchair, $15,000 for vehicle modifications, or $10,000 for assistive technology. A preferred interest rate, based on the Wall Street Journal prime rate, is charged.

Duration Loans must be repaid within 10 years (or 20 years for home modification).

Additional Information This program was established in 1991 as the result of an agreement among the Nevada Division of Rehabilitation, the Assistive Technology Center at Nevada Community Enrichment Program, and Bank of America (which issues the loans with guarantees from the Division of Rehabilitation).

Number awarded Varies each year.

Deadline Applications may be submitted at any time.

[785]
NEW HAMPSHIRE CHARITABLE FOUNDATION STATEWIDE STUDENT AID PROGRAM

New Hampshire Charitable Foundation
37 Pleasant Street
Concord, NH 03301-4005
(603) 225-6641   Toll-free: (800) 464-6641
Fax: (603) 225-1700   E-mail: info@nhcf.org
Web: www.nhcf.org

Summary To provide scholarships and loans for undergraduate or graduate study to New Hampshire residents.

Eligibility This program is open to New Hampshire residents who are graduating high school seniors or undergraduate students between 17 and 23 years of age or graduate students of any age. Applicants must be enrolled in or planning to enroll in an accredited 2- or 4-year college, university, or vocational school on at least a half-time basis. The school may be in New Hampshire or another state. Selection is based on financial need, academic merit, community service, school activities, and work experience. Priority is given to students with the fewest financial resources and to vocational/technical school students.

Financial data Awards range from $500 to $2,500 and average $1,800. Most are made in the form of grants (recently, 82% of all awards) or no-interest or low-interest loans (recently 18% of all awards).

Duration 1 year; approximately one third of the awards are renewable.

Additional Information Through this program, students submit a single application for more than 250 different scholarship and loan funds. Many of the funds have additional requirements, covering such elements as the field of study; residency in region, county, city, or

town; graduation from designated high schools; and special attributes (of Belgian descent, employee of designated firms, customer of Granite State Telephone Company, disabled, suffering from a life-threatening or serious chronic illness, of Lithuanian descent, dependent of a New Hampshire police officer, dependent of a New Hampshire Episcopal minister, of Polish descent, former Sea Cadet or Naval Junior ROTC, or employed in the tourism industry). The Citizens' Scholarship Foundation of America reviews all applications; recipients are selected by the New Hampshire Charitable Foundation. A $15 application fee is required.

Number awarded Varies each year; recently, a total of $2.3 million was awarded.

Deadline April of each year.

[786]
NEW HAMPSHIRE GUARANTEED COLLATERAL LOAN FUND

New Hampshire Assistive Technology Partnership Project
Attn: Project Director
University of New Hampshire, Institute on Disability
The Concord Center, Unit 14
10 Ferry Street
Concord, NH 03301
(603) 228-2084
Toll-free: (800) 238-2048 (within NH)
Fax: (603) 228-3270

Summary To provide loans for the purchase of assistive technology to residents of New Hampshire with disabilities.

Eligibility This program is open to residents of New Hampshire who have a disability. Applicants must be interested in obtaining funding for the purchase of assistive technology devices and services. They may not be eligible for any other source of funding.

Financial data Loans range from $1,000 to $5,000. Interest rates are set at the prevailing passbook rate, or approximately 2.5%.

Additional Information This program was established in 1994 through the Institute on Disability at the University of New Hampshire. Funding is provided by the Bank of New Hampshire.

Number awarded Varies each year.

Deadline Applications may be submitted at any time.

[787]
NMTAP FINANCIAL LOAN PROGRAM

New Mexico Technology Assistance Program
435 St. Michael's Drive, Building D
Santa Fe, NM 87505
Toll-free: (800) 866-2253   TTY: (800) 659-4915
E-mail: ccadena@state.nm.us
Web: www.nmtap.com/finloan.html

Summary To provide loans to individuals with disabilities in New Mexico who wish to become more independent.

Eligibility These loans are available to residents of New Mexico who have a disability and wish to purchase assistive devices or equipment (wheelchairs, hearing aids, scooters, augmentative communication devices, lifts for automobiles, or adapted motor vehicles). Applicants must submit information on the type of assistive technology they need, the type of benefits to which they currently have access, medical records indicating their disability, and documentation of financial need.

Financial data The maximum loan is $25,000. For loans with terms of 60 months or less, the interest rate is equal to the Wall Street Journal (WSJ) prime rate in effect at the time the loan is made. For loan terms longer than 60 months, the interest rate is 1% above the WSJ prime rate.

Additional Information The New Mexico Technology Assistance Program (NMTAP) has joined with Wells Fargo Bank to offer these loans.

Number awarded Varies each year.

Deadline Applications may be submitted at any time.

[788]
NORTH DAKOTA ASSISTIVE TECHNOLOGY FINANCIAL LOAN PROGRAM

North Dakota Interagency Program for Assistive Technology
c/o Connie Rawls, Support Staff
200 Bjornson Drive
P.O. Box 743
Cavalier, ND 58220
(701) 265-4807   Toll-free: (800) 265-IPAT
Fax: (701) 265-3150   TTY: (800) 265-IPAT
E-mail: crawls@polarcomm.com
Web: www.ndipat.org

Summary To make unsecured loans to North Dakota residents for the purchase of assistive technology.

Eligibility This program is open to North Dakota residents who have (or are a family member of someone who has) a physical or mental impairment that substantially limits 1 or more major life activities. There are no minimum or maximum income eligibility requirements; however, applicants must demonstrate their ability to repay the loan. They must be seeking funding to purchase assistive technology devices needed to increase their independence and level of participation.

Financial data The amount loaned varies, depending upon the needs of the recipient.

Additional Information This program is also sponsored by the North Dakota Association for the Disabled, (701) 775-5577. Loans are made through First National Bank. As loans are repaid, funds become available to lend to others.

Number awarded Varies each year.

Deadline Applications may be submitted at any time.

[789]
OREGON VETERANS HOME LOAN PROGRAM

Oregon Department of Veterans' Affairs
Attn: Veterans' Home Loan Program
700 Summer Street N.E., Suite 100
Salem, OR 97310-1285
(503) 373-2005
Toll-free: (888) ORE-VETS (within OR)
Fax: (503) 373-2393   TDD: (503) 373-2217
E-mail: orvetshomeloans@odva.state.or.us
Web: www.odva.state.or.us

Summary To help disabled and other Oregon veterans or the surviving spouses of certain veterans buy homes.

Eligibility This program is open to veterans who served honorably on active duty for not less than 210 consecutive days (unless released earlier because of a service-connected disability). Applicants must either have entered military service prior to 1977 or served in a theater of operations for which a campaign or expeditionary ribbon or medal is authorized by the United States (including Grenada, Libya, Panama, Somalia, Haiti, El Salvador, the Persian Gulf, the Balkans, Kosovo, Afghanistan, or Iraq). They must be Oregon residents at the time of application for the loan. Spouses who are eligible must be Oregon residents who have not remarried and whose spouses either died while on active duty or are listed as prisoners of war or missing in action. The eligibility of a veteran ends 30 years after the last date of separation from service; the eligibility of a spouse expires 30 years after notification of the veteran's death, capture, or disappearance, or upon remarriage. Applicants must demonstrate sufficient income to make loan repayments and be good credit risks. Loans may be used only to finance owner-occupied, single-family residential housing for qualified eligible veterans or their spouses. The purchase of vacation homes, the refinancing of existing loans, or the purchase of income properties, such as farms and rentals, cannot be financed.

Financial data Insured loans are made up to 95% of the net appraised value on homes that are real property (to a current maximum of $322,700) or to 85% of the net appraised value on homes that are not real property. For farms that are real property, loans are made up to 90% of the net appraised value, to a maximum of $185,000. Interest rates vary and depend on the service record of the veteran and the amount of the origination fee. Recently, for veterans who entered military service prior to 1977, the rate was 4.99% with a 1.5% origination fee or 5.25% with a 1% origination fee. For veterans who earned a campaign medal or ribbon after 1977, the rate was 5.125% with a 1.5% origination fee or 5.25% with a 1% origination fee.

Duration The maximum loan term is 30 years and the minimum is 15 years. Normally, veterans may receive only 2 loans. If they are rated by the U.S. Department of Veterans Affairs or a branch of the U.S. armed forces as at least 50% disabled, they may assume more than 2 loans if they must acquired a different principal residence for compelling medical reasons, they are transferred by an employer for employment reasons, or their spouse is transferred by an employer for employment reasons and the spouse provides more than 50% of the household income.

Additional Information Recipients must live on the property and use it as their primary home within 90 days after the loan has closed.

Number awarded Varies each year.

Deadline Applications may be submitted at any time.

[790]
PENNSYLVANIA ASSISTIVE TECHNOLOGY FINANCING PROGRAM

Pennsylvania Assistive Technology Foundation
102 Pickering Avenue, Suite 200
Exton, PA 19341
Toll-free: (888) 744-1938   Fax: (484) 875-0982
TTY: (877) 693-7271
E-mail: patf@amexcenters.com
Web: www.assistive-technology4pa.org

Summary To provide low-interest loans to Pennsylvanians with disabilities who wish to purchase assistive technology.

Eligibility Any Pennsylvania resident with a disability or any older Pennsylvanian may apply. Family members may also apply, even if they do not live with the individual with disabilities. Advocates, service providers, guardians, and authorized representatives may also apply as long as the assistive technical will be used by an individual with disabilities. A disability is defined, for the purposes of this program, as any physical or mental impairment that substantially limits 1 or more of the major life activities (such as walking, speaking, reading, or hearing). Loans will be made only for the purchase of assistive technology devices and services, including modified vehicles and home modifications.

Financial data Loans range from $1,000 to $25,000. Interest rates vary, based on the prime rate of interest that is in effect on the day the lending institution receives an application.

Duration Repayment terms depend on the expected useful life of the assistive technology that the recipient wishes to purchase; e.g., loans for computers and

related devices need to be repaid in 3 years and loans for home modifications in 10 years.

Additional Information This program has operated since 1998, with loans issued by First Union National Bank and guaranteed by the Pennsylvania Department of Community and Economic Development Applications are first submitted to 1 of 10 regional disability organizations within Pennsylvania. Those organizations assist applicants in filling out all forms and then forward them to the foundation for processing and loan approval. For the name and address of the disability organization in your area, contact the foundation.

Number awarded Varies each year. Since the program began, more than 70 loans, worth more than $560,000, have been issued.

Deadline Applications may be submitted at any time.

[791]
PREQUALIFICATION PILOT LOAN PROGRAM

Small Business Administration
Attn: Office of Business Development
409 Third Street, S.W.
Washington, DC 20416
(202) 205-6673   Toll-free: (800) 8-ASK-SBA
Fax: (202) 205-7064   TDD: (703) 344-6640
Web: www.sba.gov/financing/frprequal.html

Summary To provide loan guarantees to businesses whose owners meet specified eligibility standards.

Eligibility This program targets business owners who qualify as low moderate income, new market customers, disabled, new and emerging businesses, veterans, exporters, rural, and specialized businesses. Applicants must be seeking guaranteed loans for working capital or for real estate and equipment.

Financial data The maximum loan is $250,000. The SBA guarantees up to 85% of loans of $150,000 and less and up to 75% of loans above $150,000. Interest rates are negotiated between borrowers and lenders but may not exceed specified rates pegged to the Prime Rate. Fixed rate loans of $50,000 or more may not exceed Prime plus 2.25% if the maturity is less than 7 years or Prime plus 2.75% if the maturity is 7 years or more. For loans between $25,000 and $50,000, maximum rates may not exceed Prime plus 3.25% if the maturity is less than 7 years or Prime plus 3.75% if the maturity is 7 years or more. For loans of $25,000 or less, maximum rates may not exceed Prime plus 4.25% if the maturity is less than 7 years or Prime plus 4.75% if the maturity is 7 years or more. Variable rate loans may be pegged to either the lowest prime rate or the SBA optional peg rate, calculated quarterly and published in the Federal Register.

Duration Maximum loan maturities are generally 7 years for working capital or 25 years for real estate and equipment.

Additional Information A key feature of this program is the use of nonprofit (usually Small Business Development Center) or for-profit organizations as intermediaries to assist prospective borrowers in developing a viable loan application package. That application can be submitted directly to the SBA for expedited consideration of a loan prequalification. On approval, the intermediary can assist the applicant in locating a competitive lender. Small Business Development Centers serving as intermediaries do not charge a fee for loan packaging but for-profit organizations charge a fee.

Number awarded Varies each year.

Deadline Loan applications may be submitted at any time.

[792]
SHOW ME LOANS

Missouri Assistive Technology
c/o Missouri Department of Labor and Industrial Relations
3315 West Truman Boulevard, Room 213
P.O. Box 504
Jefferson City, MO 65102-0504
(573) 751-4091   Toll-free: (800) 647-8557
Fax: (573) 751-4135   E-mail: mexline@swbell.net
Web: www.dolir.state.mo.us

Summary To provide low-interest loans for the purchase of assistive technology to residents of Missouri who have a disability.

Eligibility This program is open to residents of Missouri who have a disability and their family members. Applicants must be interested in borrowing money to purchase assistive technology that will enable 1 or more individuals with a disability to become more independent. Loans may be used to purchase equipment (wheelchairs, electric scooters, hearing aids, computers, augmentative communication devices, electronic print enlarging devices, or other equipment made for people with disabilities), assistive technology services (such as an evaluation or training to learn how to use a device), home modifications (wheelchair ramps, stairway lifts, widening doorways, or bathroom modifications), or vehicle modifications (such as wheelchair lifts, ramps, or hand controls). The applicant's annual adjusted gross income must be less than $60,000 for an individual or an individual plus a second exemption, spouse, or dependent; for each additional dependent claimed, maximum income may be an additional $5,000.

Financial data Loans range from $500 to $10,000. The interest rate depends on the borrower's income, to a maximum of 1% below the prime interest rate.

Duration The maximum loan term is 60 months.

Number awarded Varies each year.

Deadline Applications may be submitted at any time.

[793]
TECHCONNECT LOW INTEREST LOAN PROGRAM

Illinois Assistive Technology Project
1 West Old State Capitol Plaza, Suite 100
Springfield, IL 62701
(217) 522-7985
Toll-free: (800) 852-5110 (within IL)
Fax: (217) 522-8067   TTY: (217) 522-9966
E-mail: techconnect@iltech.org
Web: www.iltech.org

Summary To provide low-interest loans for the purchase of assistive technology to residents of Illinois who have a disability.

Eligibility This program is open to residents of Illinois who have a disability or are a family member or authorized representative of a person with a disability. Applicants must be able to demonstrate that having assistive technology equipment or services would improve the life of the person with a disability and that their annual income is below specified levels (recently, $44,300 for a family of 1, rising to $148,650 for a family of 8). Eligible assistive technology includes, but is not limited to, hearing aids and assistive listening devices, communication systems, computers and disability-related software, environmental control units, Braille equipment, CCTVs and other low vision devices, manual or motorized wheelchairs and scooters, home modifications, and motor vehicle modifications.

Financial data Loans range from $500 to $40,000, with an interest rate of 3.5%.

Additional Information This program is provided by the Illinois Department of Human Services, Office of Rehabilitation Services, together with the Illinois Assistive Technology Project, the Coalition of Citizens with Disabilities in Illinois, the Illinois Network of Centers for Independent Living, the Statewide Independent Living Council, and the Centers for Independent Living. Loans are issued by Security Bank of Springfield.

Number awarded Varies each year.

Deadline Applications may be submitted at any time.

[794]
TEXAS VETERANS HOME IMPROVEMENT PROGRAM

Texas Veterans Land Board
Stephen F. Austin Building
1700 North Congress Avenue, Room 700
P.O. Box 12873
Austin, TX 78711-2873
(512) 463-5060
Toll-free: (800) 252-VETS (within TX)
TDD: (512) 463-5330
E-mail: vlbinfo@glo.state.tx.us
Web: www.glo.state.tx.us/vlb/vhip/index.html

Summary To assist Texas veterans, National Guard members, and unremarried surviving spouses who wish to maintain older homes but who cannot qualify for the high interest rates of conventional home improvement loans.

Eligibility This program is open to 1) veterans who served for at least 90 consecutive days of active duty after September 16, 1940 in the Army, Navy, Air Force, Marines, Coast Guard, U.S. Public Health Service, or a reserve component of those services; 2) members of the Texas National Guard who have enlisted or received an appointment and have completed all Initial Active Duty for Training (IADT) requirements; and 3) members of reserve components who have completed 20 years of service and are eligible for retirement. Applicants may not have been dishonorably discharged and must have listed Texas as their home of record at the time of entry into the military or have been a resident of Texas for at least 1 year prior to filing an application. The unremarried surviving spouses of Texas veterans who are missing in action, died in the line of duty, or died from a service-connected cause may be eligible to participate in the program. Applicants must be interested in making alterations, repairs, and improvements to, or in connection with, their existing residence if, and only if, repairs will 1) substantially protect or improve the basic livability or energy efficiency of the property; 2) correct damage resulting from a natural disaster; or 3) correct conditions that are hazardous to health or safety. Examples of eligible improvements include carpeting, fencing, room additions, patios, driveways, and garages. Examples of ineligible improvements include exterior spas, saunas, whirlpools, tree surgery, tennis courts, swimming pools, and barbecue pits. The home must be in Texas and the veteran's primary residence. In addition to single family dwellings, condominiums, duplexes, triplexes, and fourplexes are eligible as long as 1 of the units is the veteran's primary residence. Duplexes, triplexes, and fourplexes must be at least 5 years old. Modular or manufactured homes that are on a permanent foundation and are a part of the real estate may also be eligible. Interest rate incentives are available to Texas veterans who 1) entered the armed services before January 1, 1977 and have been discharged from active duty for less than 30 years; 2) have a service-connected disability of 10% or greater as verified by the U.S. Department of Veterans Affairs; 3) are currently teaching or willing to teach full time in a primary or secondary school in Texas (the Troops to Teachers Program); or 4) choose Greenbuilding features when making home improvements.

Financial data The maximum loan on a single family residence is $25,000. The maximum loan on a manufactured or modular home is $17,500. Loans over $10,000 are for 2 to 20 years; those for $10,000 or less are for 2 to 10 years. Interest rates recently were 5.66%. Interest rate reductions include 1.21 percentage points for qualified service era (prior to January 1, 1977) veterans, 0.5 percentage points for the Troops to Teachers program, 0.5 percentage points for the Veterans with Disabilities program, 0.3 percentage points for the Greenbuilding program, and 0.25 percentage points for loans

with a term of 15 or fewer years. The maximum combined interest rate reduction for the Troops to Teachers program, the Veterans with Disabilities program, and/or the Greenbuilding program is 0.75 percentage points.

Number awarded Varies each year.

Deadline Applications may be submitted at any time.

[795]
TEXAS VETERANS HOUSING ASSISTANCE PROGRAM

Texas Veterans Land Board
Stephen F. Austin Building
1700 North Congress Avenue, Room 700
P.O. Box 12873
Austin, TX 78711-2873
(512) 463-5060
Toll-free: (800) 252-VETS (within TX)
TDD: (512) 463-5330
E-mail: vlbinfo@glo.state.tx.us
Web: www.glo.state.tx.us/vlb/vhap/index.html

Summary To provide low-interest loans to assist Texas veterans, National Guard members, and unremarried surviving spouses in purchasing their own homes.

Eligibility This program is open to 1) veterans who served for at least 90 consecutive days of active duty after September 16, 1940 in the Army, Navy, Air Force, Marines, Coast Guard, U.S. Public Health Service, or a reserve component of those services; 2) members of the Texas National Guard who have enlisted or received an appointment and have completed all Initial Active Duty for Training (IADT) requirements; and 3) members of reserve components who have completed 20 years of service and are eligible for retirement. Applicants may not have been dishonorably discharged and must have listed Texas as their home of record at the time of entry into the military or have been a resident of Texas for at least 1 year prior to filing an application. The unremarried surviving spouses of Texas veterans who are missing in action, died in the line of duty, or died from a service-connected cause may be eligible to participate in the program. Applicants must be interested in purchasing a new or existing home, including a duplex, triplex, or fourplex if the structure is more than 5 years old, or a modular or manufactured home if it is on a permanent foundation and meets loan guidelines established by the Federal National Mortgage Association or the Federal Home Loan Mortgage Corporation and has an economic life of at least 30 years. Any home purchased with funds from this program must be the primary residence of the veteran for at least 3 years. Interest rate incentives are available to Texas veterans who 1) entered the armed services before January 1, 1977 and have been discharged from active duty for less than 30 years; 2) have a service-connected disability of 10% or greater as verified by the U.S. Department of Veterans Affairs; 3) are currently teaching or willing to teach full time in a primary or secondary school in Texas (the Troops to Teachers Program); or 4) choose Greenbuilding features in new home construction.

Financial data The maximum loan available through this program is $200,000. Loans for $45,000 or less may be requested directly from the Texas Veterans Land Board (VLB) and may cover up to 85% of the home's appraised value. Loans over $45,000 are originated through a VLB participating lender. The price of the home may exceed $200,000, but loans in excess of that amount must be a "2-note loan" made in conjunction with a conventional, FHA, or VA loan. No fees are charged on direct loans; loans available through a VLB-approved lender require an origination fee up to 1% and a participation fee up to 1%. Interest rates recently were 5.66%. Interest rate reductions include 1.21 percentage points for qualified service era (prior to January 1, 1977) veterans, 0.5 percentage points for the Troops to Teachers program, 0.5 percentage points for the Veterans with Disabilities program, 0.3 percentage points for the Greenbuilding program, and 0.25 percentage points for loans with a term of 15 or fewer years. The maximum combined interest rate reduction for the Troops to Teachers program, the Veterans with Disabilities program, and/or the Greenbuilding program is 0.75 percentage points.

Duration Loans are available with 15, 20, 25, or 30 year terms.

Number awarded Varies each year.

Deadline Applications may be submitted at any time.

[796]
TRANSPORTATION LOAN GUARANTEE PROGRAM

California Assistive Technology System
660 J Street, Suite 270
Sacramento, CA 95814-2495
(916) 325-1690   Fax: (916) 325-1699
TTY: (916) 325-1695   E-mail: info@atnet.org
Web: www.atnet.org/resources/loan.html

Summary To make it easier for residents of California whose children have a disability and use a wheelchair to finance the purchase of vehicles and/or specially adapted equipment.

Eligibility Parents or legal guardians of wheelchair bound children are eligible to apply if they need to purchase and/or modify a vehicle to provide transportation for their child. Similarly, persons with disabilities who require a modified vehicle for mobility in order to maintain employment are also eligible for this program. Household income may not exceed the levels for low-income or moderate-income families in the county. The applicant must demonstrate an ability to repay the loan and have been steadily employed for a minimum of 1 year prior to the date of the loan request (or have income from some other source). Applicants must demonstrate that they could not get payment support from any other

source. Clients of the California Department of Rehabilitation are excluded from participating in this program.

Financial data The loan guarantee is limited to a maximum of $35,000. No down payment is required of the borrower. Banks are asked to consider charging more favorable interest rates. Some loans have been made with a 1% discount. If default occurs, the bank is refunded the remaining balance on the principal and any expenses incurred in collecting and reselling the vehicle from the loan guarantee fund.

Additional Information Occasionally, the California Department of Rehabilitation actually buys down the bank's market interest rate in order to make the monthly payments more affordable to the applicants. In some cases, the department may decide to subsidize the price of the product as well. Information is also available from the California Department of Rehabilitation, (916) 263-8687, TTY: (916) 263-8944, E-mail: atinfo@dor.ca.gov.

Number awarded Varies each year.

Deadline Applications may be submitted at any time.

[797]
ULS ASSISTIVE TECHNOLOGY LOAN PROGRAM

University Legal Services
Attn: Assistive Technology Program
220 I Street, N.E., Suite 130
Washington, DC 20002
(202) 547-0198   Fax: (202) 547-2662
TTY: (202) 547-2657   E-mail: atpdc@uls-dc.com
Web: www.atpdc.org/loanpro.htm

Summary To provide loans for the purchase of assistive technology to residents of the District of Columbia who have a disability and their families.

Eligibility This program is open to District of Columbia residents with a disability and their family members or legal guardians. Applicants must be interested in obtaining assistive technology devices and services, including assessments/evaluation, wheelchairs or scooters, computers, hearing aids, low vision aids, communication devices, environmental control systems, or other equipment.

Financial data Loans range from $500 to $5,000. The interest rate is 5%.

Duration Loans must be repaid in 5 years.

Additional Information This program is sponsored by University Legal Services/Assistive Technology Program (ULS/ATP) and City First Bank of DC.

Number awarded Varies each year.

Deadline Applications may be submitted at any time.

[798]
UTAH ASSISTIVE TECHNOLOGY FOUNDATION LOAN PROGRAM

Utah Assistive Technology Foundation
6835 Old Main Hill
Logan, UT 84322-6835
(435) 797-3811   Toll-free: (800) 524-5152
Fax: (435) 797-2355   E-mail: uatf@cpd2.usu.edu
Web: www.uatf.org

Summary To provide low- and no-interest loans to residents of Utah who have disabilities and need assistance in purchasing assistive technology.

Eligibility This program is open to residents of Utah with disabilities who require such devices as wheelchairs, scooters, van lifts, computers, computer interface equipment and software, page turners, flashing doorbells, speech synthesizers, communication boards, Braille typewriters, scanners, and other devices designed to help people gain, maintain, or regain independence. The devices may be intended to assist people at work, in school, at home, and in recreation and leisure activities. Signature loans are available and do not require a down payment.

Financial data Loans are available to cover the cost of the assistive technology, or the portion of the cost that is not covered by insurance. The maximum loan for modified vans and automobiles is $2,300. No interest is charged on loans for devices; interest rates for adapted vans vary from 0% to 3%. Zions Bank actually makes the loans, and the foundation pays the bank the difference between the rate charged to the borrower (0%) and the Wall Street Journal Prime Interest Rate.

Duration Loans for vehicles must be repaid in 5 years; loans for other devices must be repaid in 3 years.

Additional Information The foundation was organized in 1991.

Number awarded Varies each year.

Deadline Applications may be submitted at any time.

[799]
VA HOME LOAN GUARANTIES

Department of Veterans Affairs
810 Vermont Avenue, N.W.
Washington, DC 20420
(202) 418-4343   Toll-free: (800) 827-1000
Web: www.va.gov

Summary To assist disabled and other veterans, certain military personnel, and their unremarried surviving spouses in the purchase of residences.

Eligibility Veterans who are eligible for this program include those who served on active duty at any time since September 16, 1940 and were discharged or separated under other than dishonorable conditions. Unless discharged earlier for a service-connected disability, veterans must have served on active duty continuously for 90 days, if any part of their service occurred during

World War II, the Korean conflict, or the Vietnam era; veterans who served in peacetime between those wars, or who served as an enlistee prior to September 8, 1980 or as an officer prior to October 17, 1981, must have performed at least 181 days of continuous active duty; veterans separated from enlisted service that began after September 7, 1980, or service as an officer that began after October 16, 1981, must have completed 24 months of continuous active duty unless discharged earlier under specified conditions. Service personnel who have not served at least 181 continuous days in active-duty status are eligible if not discharged, while their service continues without a break. Veterans, including members of the Reserves or National Guard, who served at least 90 days of active duty during the Persian Gulf War are also eligible. Members of the Selected Reserve are eligible if they have completed at least 6 years in the Reserves or National Guard or were discharged because of a service-connected disability. Unremarried surviving spouses of veterans who served after September 16, 1940 and who died as a result of service-connected disabilities, and spouses of service personnel on active duty who are officially listed as missing in action or prisoners of war and who have been in such status for more than 90 days are also eligible. Eligibility also extends to U.S. citizens who served in the armed forces of a U.S. ally in World War II and members of organizations with recognized contributions to the U.S. World War II effort.

Financial data The Department of Veterans Affairs (VA) does not lend money; the actual loan must come from a commercial lender. The loan may be for any amount, and the VA will guarantee payment on loans for the purchase of homes, farm homes, condominium units, or refinancing of existing loans up to 50% of loans up to $45,000 (or up to $22,500), from 40 to 50% on loans from $45,001 to $56,250 (or $22,500), to 40% on loans from $56,251 to $144,000 (or up to $36,000) and to 25% on loans over $144,000 (up to $60,000). On manufactured homes and/or lot loans, the amount of guaranty is 40% of the loan, not to exceed $20,000. Interest rates vary with market conditions but are fixed for the life of the loan, which may be as long as 30 years and 32 days. No down payments are prescribed by VA. A funding fee must be paid to VA, although it may be included in the loan amount; the amount of the fee varies, depending on the type of loan and whether the borrower is a veteran or a reservist, but ranges from 0.5% to 3% of the amount of the loan. The funding fee is waived for disabled veterans and unremarried surviving spouses of veterans who died as a result of service.

Additional Information In addition to the purchase of a new home, VA Loans may be used to buy a residential condominium; to build a home; to repair, alter, or improve a home; to refinance an existing home loan; to buy a manufactured home with or without a lot; to buy and improve a manufactured home lot; to install a solar heating and/or cooling system or other weatherization improvements; to purchase and improve simultaneously a home with energy conserving measures; to refinance an existing VA Loan to reduce the interest rate; or to refinance a manufactured home loan to acquire a lot. Mortgages guaranteed by VA usually offer an interest rate lower than conventional mortgage rates, require no down payment, provide a long repayment period, allow the VA to appraise the property and inspect it to ensure that it conforms to the plans and specifications, and permit early prepayment without premium or penalty. The VA does not have legal authority to act as an architect, supervise construction of the home, guarantee that the home is free of defects, or act as an attorney if the veteran encounters legal difficulties in buying or constructing a home. Veterans must certify that they intend to live in the home they are buying or building with a VA Loan. Veterans who wish to refinance or improve a home must certify that they are actually in residence at the time of application.

Number awarded Varies each year.

Deadline Applications may be submitted at any time.

[800]
VERMONT ADAPTIVE EQUIPMENT REVOLVING LOAN FUND

Vermont Assistive Technology Project
Attn: Project Director
103 South Main Street
Waterbury, VT 05671-2305
(802) 241-2672
Toll-free: (800) 750-6355 (within VT)
Fax: (802) 241-2174   TTY: (802) 241-1464
E-mail: jtucker@dad.state.vt.us
Web: www.dad.state.vt.us/atp/funding/index.htm

Summary To provide loans to Vermont residents who have disabilities and wish to purchase assistive technology.

Eligibility Any Vermonter with a disability, family member or legal guardian, and nonprofit organization or partnership can apply for a loan to purchase assistive technology. For the purposes of this program, assistive technology is "any device or related service that improves a person's ability to be more independent at home, work, school, or play." This includes, but is not limited to, home equipment and modifications, adapted vehicles, wheelchairs and scooters, employment equipment, and hearing and visual aids. Persons who do not qualify for regular bank loans may qualify for these loans, which offer special payment rates. Borrowers must demonstrate the relationship between the equipment to be purchased and their disability. Credit history and current income/expense records are reviewed in the selection process.

Financial data Loans range from $1,000 to $25,000. Loan terms are based on an applicant's ability to repay, the anticipated useful life of the equipment, and the availability of funds.

Duration Loans for this program, established in 1990, are made by the Vermont Development Credit Union, 18

Pearl Street, Burlington, VT 05401, (802) 865-3404, (800) 865-8328.

Number awarded Varies each year.

Deadline Applications may be submitted at any time.

Grants-in-Aid

[801]
ADA RELIEF FUND GRANTS

American Dental Association
Attn: ADA Endowment and Assistance Fund
211 East Chicago Avenue, Suite 820
Chicago, IL 60611-2678
(312) 440-2567   Fax: (312) 440-2822
Web: www.ada.org

Summary To provide relief grants to dentists and their dependents who, because of accidental injury, a medical condition, or advanced age, are not self-supporting.

Eligibility This program is open to dentists, their spouses, and their children under 18 years of age. Dependents of deceased dentists are also eligible. Membership in the American Dental Association (ADA) is not required and members receive no special consideration in awarding of grants. Applicants must be seeking assistance because an accidental injury, advanced age, physically-debilitating illness, or medically-related condition prevents them from gainful employment and results in an inability to be wholly self-sustaining. They must apply through their component or constituent dental society, which forwards the application to the trustees of this fund.

Financial data The amount of the grant depends on the particular circumstances of each applicant, including financial need, age and physical condition, opportunity for assistance from immediate family members, financial assets, and all other relevant factors.

Duration Initial grants are for 6 months. Renewal grants are for an additional 12 months. Emergency grants are 1-time awards.

Additional Information The ADA has been making relief grants to needy dentists since 1906.

Number awarded Varies each year.

Deadline Applications may be submitted at any time.

[802]
ALABAMA AD VALOREM TAX EXEMPTION FOR SPECIALLY ADAPTED HOUSES

Alabama Department of Revenue
Attn: Property Tax Division
Gordon Persons Building
50 North Ripley Street, Room 4126
P.O. Box 327210
Montgomery, AL 36132-7210
(334) 242-1525
Web: www.ador.state.al.us

Summary To provide a property tax exemption to the owners of specially adapted housing (housing adapted for disabled veterans) in Alabama.

Eligibility The home of any veteran which is or was acquired pursuant to the provisions of Public Law 702, 80th Congress (specially adapted housing grant for veterans) as amended (38 USC) will be exempted from ad valorem taxation if the house is owned and occupied by the veteran or the veteran's unremarried widow(er).

Financial data Qualifying houses are exempt from all ad valorem taxation.

Duration This exemption continues as long as the qualifying veteran or the unremarried widow(er) resides in the house.

Number awarded Varies each year.

[803]
ALABAMA COUNTY HOMESTEAD EXEMPTIONS

Alabama Department of Revenue
Attn: Property Tax Division
Gordon Persons Building
50 North Ripley Street, Room 4126
P.O. Box 327210
Montgomery, AL 36132-7210
(334) 242-1525
Web: www.ador.state.al.us

Summary To exempt disabled, blind, and elderly residents of Alabama from ad valorem property taxes imposed by counties.

Eligibility Residents of Alabama are eligible to apply if they are over the age of 65 and have a net annual income of $12,000 or less for income tax purposes for the preceding year; or are retired due to permanent and total disability, regardless of age; or are blind, regardless of age or retirement status.

Financial data Qualifying residents are exempt from ad valorem property taxes levied by counties, including taxes levied for school districts, to a maximum of $5,000 in assessed value, or 160 acres in area.

Duration 1 year; this exemption will be granted as long as the resident continues to meet the eligibility requirements.

Number awarded Varies each year.

[804]
ALABAMA MILITARY RETIREE INCOME TAX EXEMPTION

Alabama Department of Revenue
Attn: Income Tax Division
Gordon Persons Building
50 North Ripley Street, Room 4212
P.O. Box 327410
Montgomery, AL 36132-7410
(334) 242-1105   Fax: (334) 242-0064
E-mail: erohelpdesk@revenue.state.al.us
Web: www.ador.state.al.us

Summary To exempt a portion of the income of veterans and their survivors from taxation in Alabama.

Eligibility Eligible are Alabama recipients of regular military retired pay or military survivors benefits. Recipients of benefits paid by the U.S. Department of Veterans Affairs (including disability retirement payments) are also eligible for this exemption.

Financial data All income received as military retired pay, veterans' disability payment, or military survivors benefits is exempt from state, county, or municipal income taxation.

Duration The exemption continues as long as the recipient resides in Alabama.

[805]
ALABAMA PRINCIPAL RESIDENCE EXEMPTION

Alabama Department of Revenue
Attn: Property Tax Division
Gordon Persons Building
50 North Ripley Street, Room 4126
P.O. Box 327210
Montgomery, AL 36132-7210
(334) 242-1525
Web: www.ador.state.al.us

Summary To exempt disabled and elderly residents of Alabama from ad valorem property taxes imposed by the state.

Eligibility Residents of Alabama are eligible to apply if they are over the age of 65 and have a net annual income of $7,500 or less for income tax purposes for the preceding year; or are totally disabled. They must own and occupy as their principal residence a single-family home with up to 160 adjacent acres.

Financial data Qualifying residents are exempt from all ad valorem property taxes levied by the state on their principal residence.

Duration 1 year; this exemption will be granted as long as the resident continues to meet the eligibility requirements.

Number awarded Varies each year.

[806]
ALABAMA STATE HOMESTEAD EXEMPTIONS

Alabama Department of Revenue
Attn: Property Tax Division
Gordon Persons Building
50 North Ripley Street, Room 4126
P.O. Box 327210
Montgomery, AL 36132-7210
(334) 242-1525
Web: www.ador.state.al.us

Summary To exempt disabled, blind, and elderly residents of Alabama from ad valorem property taxes imposed by the state.

Eligibility Residents of Alabama are eligible to apply if they are 1) over the age of 65; 2) retired due to permanent and total disability, regardless of age; or 3) blind, regardless of age or retirement status.

Financial data Qualifying residents are exempt from all ad valorem property taxes levied by the state, up to 160 acres in area.

Duration 1 year; this exemption will be granted as long as the resident continues to meet the eligibility requirements.

Number awarded Varies each year.

[807]
ALASKA PROPERTY TAX EXEMPTION

Department of Community and Economic Development
Attn: Office of the State Assessor
550 West Seventh Avenue, Suite 1790
Anchorage, AK 99501-3510
(907) 269-4580   Fax: (907) 269-4539
E-mail: steve_vansant@dced.state.ak.us
Web: www.dced.state.ak.us

Summary To exempt from taxation the property owned by veterans with disabilities in Alaska.

Eligibility Eligible for this exemption are veterans with disabilities in Alaska whose disability was incurred or aggravated in the line of duty and whose disability has been rated as 50% or more by the military service or the U.S. Department of Veterans Affairs. Senior citizens who are 65 years of age or older are also eligible for this exemption.

Financial data Qualified veterans are exempt from taxation on the first $150,000 of assessed valuation on real property owned and occupied as their primary and permanent residence.

Duration The exemption continues as long as the veteran with a disability resides in Alaska.

Additional Information Applications may be obtained from the local assessor's office. Since 1986, the cost of this program has exceeded the funding available for it. Recipients are granted a prorated level of payments.

Number awarded Varies each year. Recently, a total of 18,435 disabled veterans and senior citizens received an average exemption of $1,764 on their property.
Deadline Applications may be submitted at any time.

[808]
AMTRAK DISABLED TRAVELERS DISCOUNT

National Railroad Passenger Corporation
Attn: Office of Amtrak Access
60 Massachusetts Avenue, N.E.
Washington, DC 20002
Toll-free: (800) USA-RAIL   TTY: (800) 523-6590
Web: www.amtrak.com

Summary To provide financial assistance to citizens with disabilities who travel by rail.
Eligibility Travelers with disabilities are eligible for a discount if they present appropriate identification, which may be in the form of a card issued by a handicapped organization, such as the American Foundation for the Blind, or a local, state, or federal government agency. A letter from a physician certifying that the passenger has an impairment that limits ability to use Amtrak services is also acceptable.
Financial data Travelers with disabilities are entitled to 15% off the lowest available fare (regular, discounted, 1-way, round-trip). Children (aged 2 through 11) with disabilities pay one half of the disabled adult fare. Any adult companion may accompany a passenger with a mobility impairment at 15% off the regular fare. Passengers with mobility impairments may reserve accessible bedrooms at 30% off the standard bedroom rate and have priority in reserving accessible bedrooms up to 14 days prior to travel.
Additional Information The discounted fares have no holiday or length of stay restrictions. Information on other special services provided for disabled rail travelers is also available from Amtrak's Office of Customer Relations,. No discount is provided on club car seats or sleeping space charges.
Number awarded There is no limit; all eligible travelers are granted discounts.

[809]
ARKANSAS DISABLED VETERANS PROPERTY TAX EXEMPTION

Arkansas Assessment Coordination Department
1614 West Third Street
Little Rock, AR 72201-1815
(501) 324-9240   Fax: (501) 324-9242
E-mail: dasbury@acd.state.ar.us
Web: www.accessarkansas.org/acd

Summary To exempt from taxation the property owned by veterans with disabilities, surviving spouses, and minor dependent children in Arkansas.
Eligibility To qualify, the disabled veteran must have been awarded a special monthly compensation from the Department of Veterans Affairs for the loss of, or the loss of use of 1 or more limbs, or total blindness in 1 or both eyes, or a 100% total and permanent service-connected disability. This exemption also extends to the veteran's unremarried surviving spouse and the veteran's minor children.
Financial data Qualifying veterans (or their unremarried widows or dependent children) are exempt from payment of all state taxes on their homestead and personal property.
Duration This exemption continues as long as the qualifying veteran (or dependent) resides in Arkansas.
Number awarded Varies each year.
Deadline Applications may be submitted at any time.

[810]
ARKANSAS INCOME TAX EXEMPTIONS FOR MILITARY COMPENSATION AND DISABILITY PAY

Arkansas Department of Finance and Administration
Attn: Revenue Division, Individual Income Tax
    Section
Joel Ledbetter Building, Room 110
1800 Seventh Street
P.O. Box 3628
Little Rock, AR 72203-3628
(501) 682-7225   Fax: (501) 682-7691
E-mail: Individual.Income@rev.state.ar.us
Web: www.state.ar.us/dfa

Summary To exempt a portion of the income of military personnel and disabled veterans from state income taxes in Arkansas.
Eligibility Eligible are residents of Arkansas receiving military compensation or military disability income.
Financial data The first $6,000 of U.S. military compensation pay or military disability income is exempt from state income taxation.
Duration The exemptions continue as long as the recipient resides in Arkansas.

[811]
ARKANSAS INCOME TAX EXEMPTIONS FOR RETIREMENT AND DISABILITY PAY

Arkansas Department of Finance and Administration
Attn: Revenue Division, Individual Income Tax
    Section
Joel Ledbetter Building, Room 110
1800 Seventh Street
P.O. Box 3628
Little Rock, AR 72203-3628
(501) 682-7225   Fax: (501) 682-7691
E-mail: Individual.Income@rev.state.ar.us
Web: www.state.ar.us/dfa

Summary To exempt a portion of the income from

retirement or disability plans from state income taxes in Arkansas.

Eligibility Eligible are residents of Arkansas receiving income from retirement or disability plans. Surviving spouses also qualify for the exemption.

Financial data Exempt from state income taxation is the first $6,000 in disability pay, retired pay, or survivors benefits. Any resident who receives both military retirement or disability pay and other retirement or disability benefits is entitled to only a single $6,000 deduction. Surviving spouses are also limited to a single $6,000 exemption. Military retirees may adjust their figures if the payment includes survivor's benefit payments; the amount of adjustment must be listed on the income statement, and supporting documentation must be submitted with the return.

Duration The exemption continues as long as the recipient resides in Arkansas.

[812]
ARKANSAS SALES TAX EXEMPTION FOR ADAPTIVE MEDICAL EQUIPMENT

Arkansas Department of Finance and Administration
Attn: Revenue Division, Sales and Use Tax Section
Joel Ledbetter Building, Room 1340
1800 Seventh Street
P.O. Box 1272
Little Rock, AR 72203-1272
(501) 682-7104   Fax: (501) 682-7904
E-mail: sales.tax@rev.state.ar.us
Web: www.state.ar.us/dfa

Summary To exempt adaptive equipment from sales tax in Arkansas.

Eligibility Rental, sale, or repair of adaptive and disposable medical equipment in Arkansas qualifies for this exemption. Adaptive equipment includes wheelchairs, leg braces, raised toilet seats, wheelchair batteries, grab bars and hand rails, automobile hand controls, Braille writers, hearing aids, and other equipment used by people with disabilities.

Financial data Qualified equipment is exempt from payment of all sales tax.

Additional Information This exemption does not apply to equipment purchased by physicians, hospitals, nursing homes, or long-term care facilities for use by their patients or residents.

[813]
ARTISTS' FELLOWSHIP AID PROGRAM

Artists' Fellowship, Inc.
c/o Salmagundi Club
47 Fifth Avenue
New York, NY 10003
(646) 230-9833

Summary To provide emergency financial aid to artists and their families who are in financial distress because of physical and/or mental disabilities.

Eligibility Professional painters, graphic artists, or sculptors (or members of their families) who are in financial distress because of disability or age, which has interrupted or ended a self-supporting income, are eligible to apply for this assistance.

Financial data The amount awarded varies, depending upon the needs of the recipient. Grants generally range from $900 to $8,000. More than $50,000 is distributed each year.

Duration This is a 1-time grant, presented in response to an emergency situation.

Additional Information No restrictions apply to the use of the money, and aid is given with no expectation of repayment. Applicants need not be members of the foundation. This is not a scholarship fund or grant-giving foundation to aid promising young artists. Only emergency aid to artists with disabilities is available.

Number awarded Generally more than 20 each year.

Deadline Applications may be submitted at any time.

[814]
CALIFORNIA DISABLED VETERAN EXEMPTION FROM THE IN LIEU TAX FEE FOR A MANUFACTURED HOME OR MOBILEHOME

Department of Housing and Community
   Development
Attn: Registration and Titling
1800 Third Street
P.O. Box 2111
Sacramento, CA 95812-2111
(916) 323-9224   Toll-free: (800) 952-8356
Web: www.hcd.ca.gov

Summary To provide a special property tax exemption to disabled California veterans and/or their spouses who own and occupy a mobile home.

Eligibility This program is open to disabled veterans and/or their spouses in California who have a manufactured home or mobilehome as their principal place of residence. Veterans must be disabled as a result of injury or disease incurred in military service and have been a resident of California 1) at the time of entry into the service and be blind, or have lost the use of 1 or more limbs, or be totally disabled; 2) on November 7, 1972 and be blind in both eyes, or have lost the use of 2 or more limbs; or 3) on January 1, 1975 and be totally disabled. The spouses and unmarried surviving spouses of those disabled veterans are also eligible.

Financial data The exemption applies to the first $20,000 of the assessed market value of the manufactured home or mobilehome. Veterans and/or spouses whose income falls below a specified level are entitled to an additional $10,000 exemption. The amount of the exemption is 100% if the home is owned by a veteran only, a veteran and spouse, or a spouse only; 50% if

owned by a veteran and another person other than a spouse or by a spouse and another person other than the veteran; 67% if owned by a veteran, the spouse, and another person; 34% if owned by a veteran and 2 other people other than a spouse or by a spouse and 2 other people; 50% if owned by a veteran, the spouse, and 2 other people; or 25% if owned by a veteran and 3 other people or by a spouse and 3 other people.

Duration The exemption is available annually as long as the applicant meets all requirements.

Number awarded Varies each year.

[815]
CALIFORNIA PROPERTY TAX POSTPONEMENT FOR SENIOR CITIZENS, BLIND, OR DISABLED CITIZENS

State Controller's Office
Attn: Property Tax Postponement Program
P.O. Box 942850
Sacramento, CA 94250-5880
(916) 327-5587   Toll-free: (800) 952-5661
TDD: (916) 323-3504
E-mail: postponement@sco.ca.gov
Web: www.sco.ca.gov

Summary To allow blind, disabled, and elderly California residents to postpone their property taxes.

Eligibility Applicants for this program (and all other recorded owners except spouses and direct-line relatives) must be blind, disabled, or 62 years of age or older as of December 31 of the first year of application; must have owned and occupied as their principal place of residence on December 31 of that year the property for which property taxes are to be postponed; must have a total household income of $24,000 or less ($34,000 for those who filed and qualified for tax postponement in 1983); must have at least a combined 20% equity interest in the home at the time a postponement lien is filed; and must receive a secured property tax bill.

Financial data Qualified homeowners may postpone payment of part or all of the property taxes on their home by having the state pay their property taxes for them. Since the state is in effect lending the money to the homeowner, it obtains a Property Tax Postponement Lien on the home and charges simple interest. Interest rates are set in July of each year, and that rate applies to that particular year's postponed taxes; currently, the rate is 3%. A total of $8 million in property tax is postponed each year.

Duration 1 year; may be renewed upon reapplication each year. The lien and interest are not due until the homeowner moves from the qualified property, sells or otherwise conveys title to the home, dies and does not have a spouse or other qualified individual who continues to reside in the home, or allows future property taxes or other senior liens to become delinquent.

Number awarded Varies each year; currently, more than 14,000 California residents participate in the program.

Deadline The filing period is from July through December of each year.

[816]
CHALLENGED ATHLETES GRANTS

Challenged Athletes Foundation
Attn: Assistant Director
2148 Jimmy Durante Boulevard, Suite B
Del Mar, CA 92014
(858) 793-9293   Fax: (858) 793-9291
E-mail: execdir@challengedathletes.org
Web: www.challengedathletes.org

Summary To provide funding to disabled athletes for travel, coaching, or equipment.

Eligibility This program is open to athletes of any age with a permanent physical disability that is recognized by the International Paralympic Committee. Applicants must need funding for sport-specific training, competitions (including travel), or athletic equipment. Along with their application, they must submit information on their short- and long-term goals in the sport of their choice, how this grant will help them reach their goal, their motto or words to live by, a list of their volunteer or community service work, and documentation of financial need. Applicants for handcycles, sports chairs, or prosthetic feet are eligible for 2-year grants.

Financial data Grants for 1 year are limited to $1,500; 2-year grants average between $200 and $3,500.

Duration 1 or 2 years. Recipients may reapply.

Additional Information This foundation is the off shoot of an event held in 1994 to raise funds for triathlete Jim MacLaren, who became a quadriplegic while competing.

Number awarded Varies each year; since the program began, it has awarded more than $2.7 million to 875 athletes.

Deadline November of each year.

[817]
CHILDREN OF WOMEN VIETNAM VETERANS ALLOWANCE

Department of Veterans Affairs
810 Vermont Avenue, N.W.
Washington, DC 20420
(202) 418-4343   Toll-free: (800) 827-1000
Web: www.va.gov

Summary To provide support to children of women Vietnam veterans who have birth defects.

Eligibility This program is open to biological children of women veterans who served in the Republic of Vietnam and were conceived after the date the veteran first served, which must have been between February 28,

1961 and May 7, 1975. Applicants must have certain birth defects identified as resulting in permanent physical or mental disability. Conditions that are a familial disorder, a birth-related injury, or a fetal or neonatal infirmity with well-established causes are not included.

Financial data Support depends on the degree of disability. The monthly rate for children at the first level is $105, at the second level $232, at the third level $804, or at the fourth level $1,373.

Additional Information Applications are available from the nearest VA medical center. Recipients are also entitled to vocational training and medical treatment.

Number awarded Varies each year.

Deadline Applications are accepted at any time.

[818]
CLOTHING ALLOWANCE FOR DISABLED VETERANS

Department of Veterans Affairs
810 Vermont Avenue, N.W.
Washington, DC 20420
(202) 418-4343 Toll-free: (800) 827-1000
Web: www.va.gov

Summary To provide financial aid to disabled veterans who have unusual needs for clothing because of their disabilities.

Eligibility Veterans are entitled to receive this benefit if they have a service-connected disability for which they must wear or use prosthetic or orthopedic appliances (including a wheelchair) that the Department of Veterans Affairs (VA) determines tend to wear out or tear clothing. The allowance is also available to a veteran whose service-connected skin condition requires prescribed medication that irreparably damages the veteran's outer garments.

Financial data Varies; recently, the clothing allowance was $528 per year.

Duration The allowance is granted annually.

Number awarded Varies each year.

Deadline Applications may be submitted at any time.

[819]
COLORADO PENSION SUBTRACTION

Colorado Department of Revenue
Attn: Taxpayer Service Division
1375 Sherman Street, Room 242A
Denver, CO 80261-0005
(303) 232-2446 Toll-free: (800) 811-0172
Web: www.revenue.state.co.us

Summary To exempt a portion of the income of disabled and other persons over the age of 55 from state income taxation in Colorado.

Eligibility This exemption is available to taxpayers over the age of 55 who are classified as Colorado residents for purposes of state income taxation, and to beneficiaries such as a widowed spouse or orphan child who are receiving a pension or annuity because of the death of the person who earned the pension. To qualify, the payment must be a retirement benefit that arose from an employer/employee relationship, service in the uniformed services of the United States, or contributions to a retirement plan that are deductible for federal income tax purposes. Disability retirement payments received by persons 55 years of age or older also qualify.

Financial data For retirees who are at least 65 years of age, up to $24,000 of qualified pension or retirement income may be excluded from income for purposes of Colorado state taxation. For persons who are at least 55 but under 65 years of age, up to $20,000 of qualified pension or retirement income may be excluded.

Duration The exclusion continues as long as the recipient resides in Colorado.

Additional Information Disability retirement payments received by persons under 55 years of age do not qualify for the pension exclusion.

[820]
COLORADO PROPERTY TAX REBATE

Colorado Department of Revenue
Attn: Taxpayer Service Division
1375 Sherman Street, Room 242A
Denver, CO 80261-0005
(303) 232-2446 Toll-free: (800) 811-0172
Web: www.revenue.state.co.us

Summary To provide a property tax credit to elderly or disabled residents of Colorado.

Eligibility This program is open to Colorado residents who were not claimed as a dependent on any other person's federal income tax return and are 65 or older, or a surviving spouse at least 58 years of age, or disabled. Applicants must own and occupy their own home, townhome, condominium, or mobile home and have an income of less than $11,000 if single or $14,700 if married.

Financial data The credit depends on income and filing status, to a maximum of $600.

Duration The exemption continues as long as the recipient resides in Colorado.

[821]
COLORADO RENT REBATE

Colorado Department of Revenue
Attn: Taxpayer Service Division
1375 Sherman Street, Room 242A
Denver, CO 80261-0005
(303) 232-2446 Toll-free: (800) 811-0172
Web: www.revenue.state.co.us

Summary To provide a tax credit to elderly or disabled renters in Colorado.

Eligibility This program is open to Colorado residents who were not claimed as a dependent on any other person's federal income tax return and are 65 or older, or a surviving spouse at least 58 years of age, or disabled. Applicants must rent their living quarters or mobile home space and have an income of less than $11,000 if single or $14,700 if married.

Financial data The credit depends on income and filing status, to a maximum of $600.

Duration The exemption continues as long as the recipient resides in Colorado.

Additional Information Payments made to nursing homes or for apartments in a building that is exempt from local property tax may not be used for the rent credit.

[822]
CONNECTICUT DISABLED TAX RELIEF PROGRAM

Office of Policy and Management
Attn: Intergovernmental Policy Division
450 Capitol Avenue
Hartford, CT 06106-1308
(860) 418-6322
Toll-free: (800) 286-2214 (within CT)
Fax: (860) 418-6493   TDD: (860) 418-6456
E-mail: ronald.madrid@po.state.ct.us
Web: www.opm.state.ct.us/igp/grants/dtotdis.htm

Summary To exempt disabled residents of Connecticut from a portion of their personal property taxes.

Eligibility Eligible to apply for this exemption are Connecticut residents who are rated as totally and permanently disabled by the U.S. Social Security Administration. If they never engaged in employment covered by Social Security, they are also eligible if they have become qualified for permanent and total disability benefits under any federal, state, or local government retirement or disability plan. An additional exemption may be available to residents whose total adjusted gross income is less than $25,400 if unmarried or $31,100 if married.

Financial data The basic state exemption is $1,000 of assessed valuation. Municipalities may elect to provide an additional exemption of $1,000 to residents whose income is less than the qualifying level.

Duration 1 year; exemptions continue as long as the eligible resident lives in Connecticut.

Number awarded Varies each year; recently, a total of 11,970 residents received property tax exemptions through this program.

Deadline Applications for the additional municipality exemption must be submitted to the assessor's office of the town or residence by September of every other year.

[823]
CONNECTICUT ELDERLY AND DISABLED HOMEOWNERS TAX RELIEF PROGRAM

Office of Policy and Management
Attn: Intergovernmental Policy Division
450 Capitol Avenue
Hartford, CT 06106-1308
(860) 418-6322
Toll-free: (800) 286-2214 (within CT)
Fax: (860) 418-6493   TDD: (860) 418-6456
E-mail: ronald.madrid@po.state.ct.us
Web: www.opm.state.ct.us/igp/grants/circuitb.htm

Summary To provide a credit to elderly and disabled residents of Connecticut for a portion of their real property taxes.

Eligibility Eligible to apply for this relief are Connecticut residents who are 1) over 65 years of age, or 2) rated as totally and permanently disabled by the U.S. Social Security Administration. If they never engaged in employment covered by Social Security, they are also eligible if they have become qualified for permanent and total disability benefits under any federal, state, or local government retirement or disability plan. Applicants must have total adjusted gross income less than $25,400 if unmarried or $31,100 if married. The credit applies to property owned by the applicant and located on a "standard building lot," including residences, mobile homes, life care facilities, modular homes, condominiums, and dwellings on leased land.

Financial data The credit depends on the income of the recipient, to a maximum of $1,250 for married homeowners or $1,000 for unmarried homeowners.

Duration 1 year; the credit is available as long as the eligible homeowner lives in Connecticut.

Number awarded Varies each year; recently, a total of 40,481 homeowners received property tax credits through this program.

Deadline Applications must be submitted to the assessor's office of the town or residence by May of every other year.

[824]
CONNECTICUT ELDERLY AND DISABLED RENTERS REBATE PROGRAM

Office of Policy and Management
Attn: Intergovernmental Policy Division
450 Capitol Avenue
Hartford, CT 06106-1308
(860) 418-6322
Toll-free: (800) 286-2214 (within CT)
Fax: (860) 418-6493   TDD: (860) 418-6456
E-mail: ronald.madrid@po.state.ct.us
Web: www.opm.state.ct.us/igp/grants/renters.htm

Summary To provide a partial reimbursement of rent and utility bills paid by elderly and disabled residents of Connecticut.

Eligibility Applicants must have resided in Connecticut for more than 1 year and be 1) over 65 years of age; 2) over 50 years of age and the surviving spouse of a renter who at the time of death had qualified and was receiving this relief or, 3) rated as totally and permanently disabled by the U.S. Social Security Administration. If they never engaged in employment covered by Social Security, they are also eligible if they have become qualified for permanent and total disability benefits under any federal, state, or local government retirement or disability plan. Applicants must have total adjusted gross income less than $25,400 if unmarried or $31,100 if married. They must be renting the property where they live; rental units are defined to include apartments, cooperatives, land lease for mobile home, condominiums, hotel/motel rooms, boarding houses, nursing homes, and convalescent hospitals.

Financial data The rebate depends on the income of the recipient and the amount they paid in rent and utility bills during the preceding year, to a maximum of $900 for married renters or $700 for unmarried renters.

Duration 1 year; the rebate is available as long as the eligible renter lives in Connecticut.

Number awarded Varies each year; recently, a total of 29,464 renters received rebates through this program.

Deadline Applications must be submitted to the assessor's office of the town or residence by September of each year.

[825]
CONNECTICUT PERSONAL PROPERTY TAX EXEMPTION FOR DISABLED VETERANS

Office of Policy and Management
Attn: Intergovernmental Policy Division
450 Capitol Avenue
Hartford, CT 06106-1308
(860) 418-6322
Toll-free: (800) 286-2214 (within CT)
Fax: (860) 418-6493 TDD: (860) 418-6456
E-mail: ronald.madrid@po.state.ct.us
Web: www.opm.state.ct.us/igp/grants/addvet.htm

Summary To exempt disabled veterans and their surviving spouses who are residents of Connecticut from a portion of their personal property taxes.

Eligibility Eligible to apply for this exemption are Connecticut veterans who are rated as disabled by the U.S. Department of Veterans Affairs (VA). Unremarried surviving spouses of qualified veterans are also eligible. An additional exemption may be available to veterans and spouses whose total adjusted gross income is less than $25,400 if unmarried or $31,100 if married. If the veteran is rated as 100% disabled by the U.S. Department of Veterans Affairs (VA), the maximum income levels are $18,000 if unmarried or $21,000 if married.

Financial data The amount of the exemption depends on the level of the VA disability rating: for 10 to 25%, it is $1,500; for more than 25 to 50%, $2,000; for more than 50 to 75%, $2,500; for more than 75% and for veterans older than 65 years of age with any level of disability, $3,000. Municipalities may elect to provide an additional exemption, equal to twice the amount provided, to veterans and spouses whose income is less than the qualifying level. For veterans and spouses who do not meet the income requirement, the additional exemption from participating municipalities is equal to 50% of the basic state exemption.

Duration 1 year; exemptions continue as long as the eligible resident lives in Connecticut.

Number awarded Varies each year; recently, a total of 208,538 veterans received property tax exemptions through this and other programs in Connecticut.

Deadline Applications for the additional municipality exemption must be submitted to the assessor's office of the town or residence by September of every other year.

[826]
CONNECTICUT REAL ESTATE TAX EXEMPTION FOR DISABLED VETERANS

Office of Policy and Management
Attn: Intergovernmental Policy Division
450 Capitol Avenue
Hartford, CT 06106-1308
(860) 418-6322
Toll-free: (800) 286-2214 (within CT)
Fax: (860) 418-6493 TDD: (860) 418-6456
E-mail: ronald.madrid@po.state.ct.us
Web: www.opm.state.ct.us/igp/grants/addvet.htm

Summary To exempt Connecticut veterans with disabilities and their surviving spouses from the payment of a portion of their local property taxes.

Eligibility There are 2 categories of Connecticut veterans who qualify for exemptions from their dwelling house and the lot on which it is located: 1) those with major service-connected disabilities (paraplegia or osteochondritis resulting in permanent loss of the use of both legs or permanent paralysis of both legs and lower parts of the body; hemiplegia with permanent paralysis of 1 leg and 1 arm or either side of the body resulting from injury to the spinal cord, skeletal structure, or brain, or from disease of the spinal cord not resulting from syphilis; total blindness; amputation of both arms, both legs, both hands or both feet, or the combination of a hand and a foot; sustained through enemy action or resulting from an accident occurring or disease contracted in such active service) and 2) those with less severe disabilities (loss of use of 1 arm or 1 leg because of service-connected injuries). Surviving unremarried spouses of eligible deceased veterans are entitled to the same exemption as would have been granted to the veteran, as long as they continue to be the legal owner/occupier of the exempted residence. An additional exemption is available to veterans and spouses whose total adjusted gross income is less than $25,400 if unmarried or

$31,100 if married. If the veteran is rated as 100% disabled by the U.S. Department of Veterans Affairs (VA), the maximum income levels are $18,000 if unmarried or $21,000 if married.

Financial data Veterans in the first category receive an exemption from local property taxation of $10,000 of assessed valuation. Veterans in the second category receive exemptions of $5,000 of assessed valuation. For veterans whose income is less than the specified levels, additional exemptions of $20,000 for the first category or $10,000 for the second category are available from municipalities that choose to participate. For veterans whose income exceeds the specified levels, the additional exemption from participating municipalities is $5,000 for the first category or $2,500 for the second category. Connecticut municipalities may also elect to exempt from taxation specially adapted housing acquired or modified by a veteran under the provisions of Section 801 of Title 38 of the United States Code.

Duration 1 year; exemptions continue as long as the eligible resident (or surviving spouse) owns/occupies the primary residence and lives in Connecticut.

Number awarded Varies each year; recently, a total of 208,538 veterans received property tax exemptions through this and other programs in Connecticut.

Deadline Applications for the additional municipality exemption must be submitted to the assessor's office of the town or residence by September of every other year.

[827]
CONNECTICUT SOLDIERS', SAILORS' AND MARINES' FUND

Connecticut Department of Veterans' Affairs
Attn: Soldiers', Sailors' and Marines' Fund
101 South Street
West Hartford, CT 06110-1962
(860) 953-4345
Toll-free: (800) 491-4941 (within CT)
Fax: (860) 953-4317
Web: www.state.ct.us/ssmf

Summary To provide temporary financial assistance to needy Connecticut veterans.

Eligibility This program is open to veterans who were honorably discharged after at least 90 days of service during wartime (World War I, World War II, Korea, Vietnam, Lebanon, Grenada, Operation Ernest Will, Panama, or the Persian Gulf) and are currently residents of Connecticut. Applicants must be able to demonstrate need for the following types of assistance: medical care and doctor office visits; emergency dental care needs; prescription medication and purchase of eyeglasses; hearing aid evaluation and hearing aids; assistance with rental payments, mortgage payments, and utilities (including gas, water, electric, and fuel oil); funeral expenses; home health aide and visiting nurse association homemaker services; prosthetic devices; and orthopedic shoes and appliances. Support is not provided for payment of taxes, payment of insurance premiums (except hospital and medical insurance), loans, payments of principal on mortgages, purchase of real estate, purchase of business stock, alimony or child support payments, assistance with the payments on past-due bills or loans, or purchase of furniture, automobiles, or other capital goods.

Financial data The fund provides payments in the form of 1-time grants.

Duration The funds are provided for emergency situations only; the program does not assist ongoing financial needs.

Additional Information This program is subsidized by the state of Connecticut but administered by the American Legion of Connecticut.

Number awarded Varies each year.

Deadline Applications may be submitted at any time.

[828]
COVAD BROADBAND ENTREPRENEUR AWARD

Association for Enterprise Opportunity
1601 North Kent Street, Suite 1101
Arlington, VA 22209
(703) 841-7760   Fax: (703) 841-7748
E-mail: aeo@assoceo.org
Web: www.microenterpriseworks.org

Summary To provide funding to entrepreneurs (especially women, minorities, and people with disabilities) who are interested in obtaining broadband access to the Internet.

Eligibility This program is open to low- and moderate-income entrepreneurs who have 5 or fewer employees, $35,000 or less cash on hand, and no access to traditional bank loans. Preference is given to entrepreneurs who are women, minorities, or people with disabilities. Applicants must be based in and/or serve clients within the service area of Covad Communications Group, Inc. in the following states: Arizona, California, Illinois, Massachusetts, Michigan, New Mexico, Pennsylvania, or Tennessee. They must own or have regular access to a computer and be able to implement installation of broadband within 30 days of the grant award. It is not necessary that entrepreneurs have existing access to the Internet or an e-mail address as long as they intend to use the grant funds to set up Internet and e-mail service. They must submit a cover letter and business plan that demonstrate how broadband access will improve and strengthen their business.

Financial data Grants provide a $500 cash award (which may be used for purchase of a new computer) and free Covad broadband installation and service for 1 year. The total value of the grant is more than $2,500.

Duration These are 1-time grants.

DISABILITIES IN GENERAL: GRANTS-IN-AID

Additional Information Covad Communications Group, Inc. established this program in 2003 and selected the Association for Enterprise Opportunity (AEO) to administer it. Information is available from 10 local partners selected by AEO to process and forward applications. Those 10 local organizations are CHARO Community Development Corporation of Los Angeles, Community Business Network of Boston, Detroit Entrepreneurship Institute, Inc. of Detroit, New Mexico Community Development Loan Fund of Albuquerque, Renaissance Entrepreneurship Center of San Francisco, Self-Employment Loan Fund of Phoenix, Start Up of East Palo Alto, California, The Abilities Fund of Centerville, Iowa, Women's Opportunities Resource Center of Philadelphia, and Women's Self-Employment Project of Chicago.

Number awarded Up to 144 each year.

Deadline Each of the 10 local partners sets its own deadline date.

[829]
DAIMLERCHRYSLER AUTOMOBILITY PROGRAM

DaimlerChrysler Corporation
Attn: Automobility Program
P.O. Box 5080
Troy, MI 48007-5080
Toll-free: (800) 255-9877   Fax: (248) 925-3053
TTY: (800) 922-3826
Web: www.automobility.daimlerchrysler.com

Summary To provide a cash reimbursement for the cost of installing adaptive driving aids on new purchases from DaimlerChrysler Motors.

Eligibility Eligible for this rebate are purchasers of new DaimlerChrysler Motors cars, trucks, or vans that require adaptive driving aids or conversion equipment for users with disabilities.

Financial data Conversions to Dodge Ram Vans, Ram Conversion Vans, Ram Wagons, Dodge Caravans, Grand Caravans, Chrysler Voyagers, and Chrysler Town & Country models are reimbursed up to $1,000. The maximum reimbursement on all other DaimlerChrysler vehicle models is $750. Running boards qualify for maximum reimbursement of $400 and alerting devices for $200.

Additional Information Applications for reimbursement are submitted through the dealer from whom the vehicle was originally purchased. Only retail purchases and leases of new DaimlerChrysler Motors vehicles qualify for this program. The reimbursement applies only to equipment installed by converters in the after market, not to factory installed equipment of any kind.

Deadline The conversion process must be completed within 6 months of vehicle purchase or lease. Reimbursement claims must be submitted within 60 days after completion of the conversion.

[830]
DELAWARE INCOME TAX EXCLUSION FOR DISABLED AND ELDERLY PERSONS

Division of Revenue
Carvel State Office Building
820 North French Street
P.O. Box 8763
Wilmington, DE 19899-8763
(302) 577-3300
Web: www.state.de.us/revenue

Summary To provide a partial exemption from state income taxation to people with disabilities and those over the age of 60 in Delaware.

Eligibility This exemption is available to residents of Delaware who are 60 years of age or over or totally and permanently disabled. Married applicants filing a joint return must have a combined earned income of less than $5,000 and total gross income less than $20,000; applicants who are single or married and filing a separate return must have earned income of less than $2,500 and total gross income less than $10,000.

Financial data Married residents filing a joint return are entitled to exempt $4,000 from their gross income for purposes of state income taxation; single residents and married residents filing a separate return are entitled to exclude $2,000 from their gross income.

Duration The exemption continues as long as the recipient remains a resident of Delaware for state income tax purposes.

Number awarded Varies each year.

[831]
DISABLED AMERICAN VETERANS DISASTER RELIEF FUND

Disabled American Veterans
P.O. Box 14301
Cincinnati, OH 45250-0301
(859) 441-7300   Fax: (859) 441-1416
E-mail: ahdav@onc.nct
Web: www.dav.org

Summary To identify and assist needy disabled veterans who have survived a natural calamity.

Eligibility At times of natural disaster—flood, earthquake, tornado, or other calamity—representatives of the Disabled American Veterans (DAV) will search out disabled veterans who need assistance.

Financial data The amount of assistance depends on the nature of the disasters and the needs of veterans; recently, an annual total of $393,823 was dispersed to help disabled veterans secure temporary lodging, food, and other necessities.

Duration These funds are granted to relieve emergency situations only; they are not available on an ongoing basis.

Additional Information Disabled veterans need not be DAV members to receive aid through this program.

Since this program began in 1968, it has dispersed more than $4.2 million. DAV formerly operated a separate Emergency Relief Fund, but incorporated that into this program.
Number awarded Varies each year.
Deadline Funds are made available as soon as the need arises.

[832]
DISABLED CHILDREN'S RELIEF FUND GRANTS

Disabled Children's Relief Fund
402 Pennsylvania Avenue
P.O. Box 7420
Freeport, NY 11520
(516) 377-1605
Web: www.dcrf.com

Summary To provide funding for assistive devices or other services that benefit children with disabilities.
Eligibility This program provides support for blind, deaf, and amputee children and children with cerebral palsy, muscular dystrophy, spastic quadriplegia, encephalitis, rheumatoid arthritis, spina bifida, Down's Syndrome, or other disabilities. Grants may be sought to obtain wheelchairs, orthopedic braces, walkers, lifts, hearing aids, eyeglasses, medical equipment, physical therapy, or surgery. Applications may be submitted by families (parent or guardian) for an individual child or by a nonprofit organization for a small group of children. Preference is given to children who do not have adequate health insurance, especially the physically challenged.
Financial data Modest awards are provided.
Duration These are 1-time grants.
Number awarded Varies each year.
Deadline September of each year.

[833]
EAGLES MEMORIAL FOUNDATION MEDICAL ASSISTANCE

Fraternal Order of Eagles
Attn: Eagles Memorial Foundation
4710 14th Street West
Bradenton, FL 34207
(941) 758-5456   Fax: (941) 758-4042
Web: www.foe.com

Summary To provide medical assistance for the children of deceased members of the Fraternal Order of Eagles who died in action.
Eligibility Applicants must be the minor (under 18 years of age), unmarried children of a deceased parent who was a member of the Fraternal Order of Eagles or its Ladies Auxiliary at the time of death; the member must have died from injuries or diseases incurred or aggravated in the line of duty while serving 1) in the armed forces of the United States or Canada; 2) as volunteer law enforcement officers in the United States; 3) as volunteer fire fighters; or 4) as volunteer emergency medical service officers.
Financial data Benefits up to $10,000 are provided to eligible recipients for doctor, dentist, and hospital bills; the cost of eyeglasses, drugs, and medical and dental devices (including orthodontia); and psychiatric care.
Duration The total benefit is a lifetime payment to each recipient.
Additional Information Benefits are not paid for any injury or illness resulting from the unlawful use of drugs, the excessive use of alcohol, the commission or attempt to commit a crime, or any self-inflicted injury.
Number awarded Varies each year.

[834]
ELSIE S. BELLOWS FUND GRANTS

United Cerebral Palsy
Attn: Bellows Fund
1660 L Street, N.W., Suite 700
Washington, DC 20036-5602
(202) 776-0406   Toll-free: (800) USA-5UCP
Fax: (202) 776-0414   TTY: (202) 973-7197
Web: www.ucp.org

Summary To provide funding to individuals with disabilities interested in purchasing assistive technology equipment.
Eligibility This program is open to individuals with disabilities who are represented by a local affiliate of United Cerebral Palsy (UCP). Applicants must be interested in purchasing assistive technology devices, such as wheelchairs (manual or electric), augmentative communication devices, environmental controls, computer equipment, lifts, or hearing aids. Funding is not available for automobiles, evaluations or other assistive technology services, or furniture and appliances that are not adapted. The individuals must have exhausted all governmental and personal financial resources available to them. Applications must be submitted on their behalf by a local UCP affiliate.
Financial data Grants depend on the availability of funds and the cost of the proposed assistive technology purchase.
Duration These are 1-time grants.
Additional Information Information is also available from Jack Schillinger, Administrator, 1225 N.E. 93rd Street, Miami Shores, FL 33138-2940, (305) 757-8989, Fax: (305) 759-1305, E-mail: jschill497@aol.com.
Number awarded Varies each year; recently, approximately $273,000 was available for these grants.
Deadline Applications may be submitted at any time.

[835]
FEDERAL INCOME TAX CREDIT FOR THE ELDERLY OR THE DISABLED

Internal Revenue Service
c/o Western Area Distribution Center
Rancho Cordova, CA 95743-0001
Toll-free: (800) TAX-FORM   Fax: (703) 368-9694
Web: www.irs.gov

Summary To provide a federal income tax credit for certain elderly and disabled citizens.

Eligibility Eligible for this credit are U.S. citizens or residents who are either 1) 65 years of age or older or 2) under 65 and retired on permanent and total disability, not yet of mandatory retirement age, and receiving taxable disability benefits. Beneficiaries of this credit must also have adjusted gross income below certain levels depending on their filing status: $17,500 for single, head of household, or qualifying widow(er) with dependent child filers; $20,000 for married taxpayers filing a joint return if only 1 spouse is elderly or disabled; $25,000 for married taxpayers filing a joint return if both spouses qualify as elderly or disabled; or $12,500 for married taxpayers filing a separate return who did not live with their spouse at any time during the year. Alternatively, taxpayers also qualify if the total of their nontaxable Social Security and other nontaxable pension(s) is less than $5,000 for single, head of household, or qualifying widow(er) with dependent child filers; $5,000 for married taxpayers filing a joint return if only 1 spouse is elderly or disabled; $7,500 for married taxpayers filing a joint return if both spouses qualify as elderly or disabled; or $3,750 for married taxpayers filing a separate return who did not live with their spouse at any time during the year.

Financial data The amount of this credit is calculated on the basis of the filing status and income of the recipient, up to a maximum of $1,125 per year.

Duration 1 year; must reapply each year.

Additional Information The address above is for taxpayers in the western states; for taxpayers in the central states, the address is c/o Central Area Distribution Center, P.O. Box 8903, Bloomington, IL 61702-8903; for taxpayers in the eastern states, the address if c/o Eastern Area Distribution Center, P.O. Box 85074, Richmond, VA 23261-5074.

Number awarded Varies each year.

Deadline This credit is applied to the qualifying tax filers' federal income tax return, which is due in April of each year.

[836]
FIRST HAND GRANTS

First Hand Foundation
c/o Cerner Corporation
2800 Rockcreek Parkway
Kansas City, MO 64117
(816) 201-1569   Fax: (816) 201-7569
E-mail: firstha@firsthandfoundation.org
Web: www.firsthandfoundation.org/grants.asp

Summary To provide funding to meet special needs of children with disabilities.

Eligibility Any person (family member, friend, social worker, health provider) may submit an application on behalf of a child with a special need anywhere in the world. Requests are accepted for 3 categories of assistance: 1) clinical expenses associated with such procedures and treatments as prescriptions, therapy, prostheses, specialized infant formula, organ transplants, craniofacial reconstruction, or dental work clinically relevant to the child's well-being and health; 2) durable medical goods, such as wheelchairs, assistive technology equipment, specialized transportation, van lifts, and other forms of physical equipment that are clinically relevant to the child's well-being and health; or 3) displacement expenses associated with families of seriously ill children who must relocate during treatment so the child can be with a family member. Funds are available to children whose cases involve craniofacial abnormalities, cleft lip and palate repair, kidney dialysis and transplant, cancer treatment, genetic testing, prosthetic limbs, sleep apnea research, prescription drugs, language therapy, dental rehabilitation, nursing equipment, and reconstructive surgery. Children must be younger than 17 years of age (or 20 years of age if the child is in a childlike mental state). The case must involve a specific child with a specific need and be in a proactive stage. The family may have no other financial net, such as Medicaid or private insurance. Funding is not provided for construction or home modification projects; alternative and/or experimental drugs, treatment, or therapy where there is significant controversy in the medical community as to appropriateness or therapeutic benefits; requests for research funding, mass population grants, or other nonprofit organizational grants; or requests for debt reduction.

Financial data Grants depend on the nature of the assistance to be provided. The sponsor requests doctors, hospitals, and equipment providers to cooperate by discounting their services below listed prices.

Duration These are 1-time grants.

Additional Information Cerner Corporation established this foundation in 1995.

Number awarded Varies each year.

Deadline Applications may be submitted at any time. They are reviewed on the first Wednesday of each month.

[837]
FLORIDA HOMESTEAD EXEMPTION FOR DISABLED VETERANS

Florida Department of Veterans' Affairs
Mary Grizzle Building, Room 311-K
11351 Ulmerton Road
Largo, FL 33778-1630
(727) 518-3202   Fax: (727) 518-3217
E-mail: cohenm@vba.va.gov
Web: www.floridavets.org/benefits/hmsted.html

Summary To exempt the real estate owned by disabled veterans and their surviving spouses in Florida from taxation.

Eligibility An exemption is available to the following classes of Florida residents: 1) honorably discharged veterans who have a service-connected permanent and total disability; 2) the spouses or surviving spouses of such veterans; 3) veterans who are paraplegic, are hemiplegic, are permanently and totally disabled, must use a wheelchair for mobility, or are legally blind and have a gross annual household income less than the adjusted maximum; and 4) veterans with service-connected disabilities of 10% or more. Applicants must reside in the property for which they are applying for an exemption.

Financial data Veterans who are permanently and totally disabled, their surviving unremarried spouses, and veterans with specified disabilities and income less than the qualifying limit are entitled to exemption of all real estate taxes on property they use and own as a homestead. Veterans with disabilities of at least 10% are entitled to a $5,000 property tax exemption.

Duration The exemption is available as long as the veteran or surviving spouse resides in Florida.

Number awarded Varies each year.

[838]
GEORGIA HOMESTEAD TAX EXEMPTION FOR DISABLED VETERANS

Georgia Department of Revenue
Attn: Property Tax Division
4245 International Parkway, Suite A
Hapeville, GA 30354-3918
(404) 968-0707   Fax: (404) 968-0778
E-mail: griggers@gw.rev.state.ga.us
Web: www2.state.ga.us

Summary To exempt from property taxation a portion of the value of homesteads owned by disabled veterans in Georgia and their families.

Eligibility This program is open to residents of Georgia who qualify as a 100% disabled veteran under any of several provisions of state law. Surviving spouses and minor children are also eligible. Applicants must actually occupy a homestead and use it as their legal residence for all purposes.

Financial data The first $43,000 of assessed valuation of the homestead owned by disabled veterans or their family members is exempt from property taxes for state, county, municipal, and school purposes.

Duration The exemption remains in effect as long as the veteran or family member owns and resides in the homestead.

Number awarded Varies each year.

Deadline The deadline for filing the exemption the first time is the end of May in most Georgia counties. In counties with installment billings, the deadline is at the end of April; in counties with a population of 81,300 to 89,000, the due date is at the end of February.

[839]
GEORGIA INCOME TAX EXEMPTION FOR DISABLED PERSONS

Georgia Department of Revenue
Attn: Income Tax Division
1800 Century Center Boulevard, N.E.
Atlanta, GA 30345-3205
(404) 417-4477   Toll-free: (877) 602-8477
E-mail: inctax@rev.state.ga.us
Web: www2.state.ga.us

Summary To exempt a portion of the retirement income of the elderly and persons with disabilities from state income taxation in Georgia.

Eligibility Eligible are persons classified as residents of Georgia for the purpose of state income taxation who are either 62 years of age or older or permanently and totally disabled.

Financial data Up to $14,500 of retirement income received by people with disabilities or the elderly is exempt from state income taxation.

Duration The exemption continues as long as the recipient resides in Georgia.

[840]
GOTTLIEB FOUNDATION EMERGENCY GRANTS

Adolph and Esther Gottlieb Foundation, Inc.
Attn: Grants Manager
380 West Broadway
New York, NY 10012-5115
(212) 226-0581   Fax: (212) 226-0584
E-mail: sross@gottliebfoundation.org
Web: www.GottliebFoundation.org

Summary To provide emergency financial assistance to artists.

Eligibility This program is open to painters, sculptors, and printmakers who have been working at their art in a mature phase for at least 10 years. Applicants must be facing financial need due to an imminent and unforeseen catastrophic situation, as from a fire, flood, or medical emergency. The program does not consider requests for dental work, chronic situations, capital

improvements, projects of any kind, or situations resulting from general indebtedness or lack of employment.
Financial data Grants to the artists range from $1,000 to $10,000; the average award is $4,000.
Duration These are 1-time grants.
Number awarded Varies each year.
Deadline Applications may be submitted at any time.

[841]
GRANTS FOR ACCESSIBILITY

Corporation for Independent Living
30 Jordan Lane
Wethersfield, CT 06109-1258
(860) 563-6011, ext. 221   Fax: (860) 563-2562
E-mail: cil@cilhomes.com
Web: www.cilhomes.com

Summary To provide grants to low- or moderate-income people with physical disabilities and need to modify their existing housing in Connecticut.
Eligibility Eligible to participate in this program are Connecticut residents who have a physical disability (including people in wheelchairs, the deaf or hearing impaired, the blind or visually impaired, and people who have multiple sclerosis, cerebral palsy, traumatic brain injury, or any other physical disability), own their homes, and have a total household income at or below 80% of median income. Also eligible are homeowner parents of a child who is physically disabled and tenants who have the landlord's written consent to make accessibility renovations. Grant funds may be used to purchase and install fixtures and improvements required to improve accessibility and/or usability of a residential dwelling in Connecticut.
Financial data Grants range from $1,000 to $20,000. Initially, a full lien is placed against the recipient's home. Total lien amounts are reduced automatically by 10% every year. At the end of 10 years, the grant is forgiven in full and the lien is removed.
Additional Information Funding for this program is provided by the Connecticut Department of Economic and Community Development.
Number awarded Varies each year.
Deadline Applications may be submitted at any time.

[842]
GREYHOUND SERVICES FOR CUSTOMERS WITH DISABILITIES

Greyhound Lines, Inc.
Attn: ADA Coordinator
P.O. Box 660362
Dallas, TX 75266-0362
(972) 789-7690   Toll-free: (800) 752-4841
Fax: (972) 789-7699   TTY: (800) 345-3109
E-mail: jpierso@greyhound.com
Web: www.greyhound.com/services/ada.shtml

Summary To underwrite the cost of companions or assistants who accompany persons with disabilities traveling on Greyhound buses.
Eligibility This program is available to any person with a disability who requires assistance with personal hygiene, eating, medications, or while the bus is in motion. Proof of disability is not required.
Financial data A passenger with a disability may request a free ticket for a personal care attendant.
Duration The benefits of this program continue as long as the person with a disability needs a companion for physical assistance in bus travel.
Additional Information Greyhound carries all wheelchairs, including battery operated ones, and certain other aids and devices for travelers with disabilities as baggage without cost. It also provides priority boarding, assistance with connections, special terminal seating, and any other required assistance. Travelers with disabilities who wish to travel alone must make arrangements with Greyhound at least 48 hours in advance of departure for any special assistance they will require on route. The traveler with a disability and companion must stay together the entire trip and the companion must assist the disabled person enroute and in boarding and alighting.
Number awarded There is no limit; all eligible travelers are granted fares for companions without additional cost.

[843]
HARRY ALAN GREGG FOUNDATION GRANTS

Harry Alan Gregg Foundation
One Verney Drive
Greenfield, NH 03047
(603) 547-3311, ext. 401   Fax: (603) 547-6212
E-mail: hag@cmt.org
Web: www.cmf.org/greggfoundationinfo.htm

Summary To provide financial assistance to children and adults in New Hampshire who have physical, emotional, or intellectual disabilities.
Eligibility This program is open to New Hampshire residents who have physical, intellectual, or emotional disabilities. Funds may be requested for broad purposes but must specifically benefit the applicant. Examples of acceptable purposes include, but are not limited to: the costs of nonreimbursed medical, dental, vision, hearing,

or therapy treatments; specialty equipment, services, or supplies; modifications to living area, work site, or vehicle; respite services for the recipient or care givers; recreational functions, such as camperships or other activities; and vocational, educational, or driver training tuition assistance. Selection is based on demonstrated need, ability of the foundation to measurably affect the quality of life of the recipient, and financial need of the applicant.

Financial data Grants range from $100 to $1,000 and average between $400 and $500.

Additional Information If the foundation has declined a request, the applicant may reapply 6 months after the original request was submitted. Recipients may receive a maximum of 4 grants (no more than 2 in any year).

Number awarded Varies each year.

Deadline Applications may be submitted at any time.

[844]
HAWAII GRANTS FOR SPECIAL HOUSING FOR DISABLED VETERANS

Office of Veterans Services
Attn: Veterans Services Coordinator
459 Patterson Road
E-Wing, Room 1-A103
Honolulu, HI 96819-1522
(808) 433-0426   Fax: (808) 433-0385
E-mail: ovs@dod.state.hi.us
Web: www.dod.state.hi.us/ovs/benefits.html

Summary To provide grants to disabled veterans in Hawaii for purchasing or remodeling a home.

Eligibility This program is open to totally disabled veterans in Hawaii. Applicants must be proposing to purchase or remodel a home to improve handicapped accessibility.

Financial data Grants up to $5,000 are available.

Duration These are 1-time grants.

[845]
HAWAII INCOME TAX EXEMPTION FOR DISABLED RESIDENTS

Department of Taxation
Attn: Taxpayer Services Branch
425 Queen Street
P.O. Box 259
Honolulu, HI 96809-0259
(808) 587-4242   Toll-free: (800) 222-3229
Fax: (808) 587-1488   TDD: (808) 587-1418
Web: www.hawaii.gov/tax/tax.html

Summary To exempt a portion of the income of disabled residents from state income tax in Hawaii.

Eligibility Eligible for this exemption are 1) blind residents whose central visual acuity does not exceed 20/200 in the better eye with corrective lenses or whose visual acuity is greater than 20/200 but is accompanied by a limitation in the field of vision such that the widest diameter of the visual field subtends an angle no greater than 20 degrees; 2) deaf residents whose average loss in the speech frequencies in the better ear is 82 decibels A.S.A. or worse; or 3) totally disabled residents (physically or mentally) who are unable to engage in any substantial gainful business or occupation (a person whose gross income exceeds $30,000 per year is assumed to be engaged in a substantial gainful business or occupation).

Financial data The maximum exemptions from state income tax are as follows: single disabled resident, $7,000; disabled husband and wife, $14,000; disabled husband or wife, with non-disabled spouse under 65, $8,040; disabled husband or wife, with non-disabled spouse age 65 or over, $9,080.

Duration The exemption continues as long as the recipient resides in Hawaii.

Additional Information Residents who claim this special exemption are not eligible to claim additional exemptions for their children or other dependents.

[846]
HAWAII PROPERTY TAX EXEMPTIONS FOR DISABLED VETERANS

Office of Veterans Services
Attn: Veterans Services Coordinator
459 Patterson Road
E-Wing, Room 1-A103
Honolulu, HI 96819-1522
(808) 433-0426   Fax: (808) 433-0385
E-mail: ovs@dod.state.hi.us
Web: www.dod.state.hi.us/ovs/benefits.html

Summary To exempt the homes of disabled veterans and surviving spouses in Hawaii from real estate taxation.

Eligibility This program is open to totally disabled veterans in Hawaii and their surviving spouses.

Financial data The real property owned and occupied as a home is exempt from taxation.

Duration The exemption applies as long as the disabled veteran or his/her widow(er) resides in Hawaii.

[847]
HOME IMPROVEMENTS AND STRUCTURAL ALTERATIONS FOR DISABLED VETERANS

Department of Veterans Affairs
810 Vermont Avenue, N.W.
Washington, DC 20420
(202) 418-4343   Toll-free: (800) 827-1000
Web: www.va.gov

Summary To provide funding to disabled veterans who require disability access to their home.

Eligibility This program is open to veterans eligible for disability benefits from the U.S. Department of Veterans

Affairs (VA). Applicants must need help in paying for home improvements necessary for the continuation of treatment or providing disability access to their home and essential lavatory and sanitary facilities.

Financial data The maximum grant is $4,100 for veterans with service-connected disabilities or $1,200 for veterans with nonservice-connected disabilities.

Duration This is a 1-time grant.

Additional Information Applications are available from the nearest VA medical center.

Number awarded Varies each year.

Deadline Applications are accepted at any time.

[848]
IDAHO CIRCUIT BREAKER PROPERTY TAX REDUCTION

Idaho State Tax Commission
Attn: Public Information Office
800 Park Boulevard, Plaza IV
P.O. Box 36
Boise, ID 83722-0410
(208) 334-7736   Toll-free: (800) 972-7660
TDD: (800) 377-3529
Web: www.state.id.us/tax/home.html

Summary To reduce a portion of the property tax of disabled and other veterans and other disabled or elderly residents of Idaho.

Eligibility Eligible for this property tax reduction are residents of Idaho who own and live in a primary residence in the state and have an annual income of $21,290 or less (after deducting designated forms of income, including compensation received by a veteran from the U.S. Department of Veterans Affairs for a 40% to 100% service-connected disability). Applicants must be in 1 or more of the following categories: disabled (as recognized by an appropriate federal agency), blind, former prisoner of war or hostage, veteran with at least 10% service connected disability or receiving VA pension for a nonservice-connected disability, 65 years of age or older, widow(er) of any age, or fatherless or motherless child under 18 years of age.

Financial data The maximum amount of reduction is the lesser of $1,200 or the actual taxes on the recipient's qualifying home. The minimum reduction is the lesser of $100 or the actual taxes on the home.

Duration Applications for this reduction must be submitted each year.

Additional Information All recipients of this reduction automatically receive Idaho's Homeowner's Exemption, which reduces the taxable value of the home (excluding land) by 50% or $50,000, whichever is less. Solid waste, irrigation, or other fees charged by some counties are not taxes and cannot be reduced by this program.

Number awarded Varies each year.

Deadline April of each year.

[849]
IDAHO INCOME TAX DEDUCTION FOR RETIREMENT BENEFITS

Idaho State Tax Commission
Attn: Public Information Office
800 Park Boulevard, Plaza IV
P.O. Box 36
Boise, ID 83722-0410
(208) 334-7660   Toll-free: (800) 972-7660
TDD: (800) 377-3529
Web: www.state.id.us/tax/home.html

Summary To deduct the retirement and disability income of certain residents from state income tax in Idaho.

Eligibility Eligible for this deduction are full-year residents of Idaho who are age 65 or older, or disabled and age 62 and older, and who are receiving the following annuities and benefits: 1) retirement annuities paid by the United States to a retired civil service employee or the unremarried widow of the employee; 2) retirement benefits paid from the firemen's retirement fund of the state of Idaho to a retired fireman or the unremarried widow of a retired fireman; 3) retirement benefits paid from the policeman's retirement fund of a city within Idaho to a retired policeman or the unremarried widow of a retired policeman; or 4) retirement benefits paid by the United States to a retired member of the U.S. military service or the unremarried widow of those veterans.

Financial data The amount of retirement or disability benefits may be deducted from taxable state income in Idaho, to a maximum deduction of $31,338 for married couples or $20,892 for single persons.

Duration 1 year; must reapply each year.

Number awarded Varies each year.

Deadline April of each year.

[850]
IDAHO VETERANS TEMPORARY EMERGENCY GRANT PROGRAM

Idaho Division of Veterans Services
Attn: Office of Veterans Advocacy
805 West Franklin Street, Room 201
Boise, ID 83702-5560
(208) 334-1245   Fax: (208) 334-4753
Web: www.idvs.state.id.us/idvsserv.html

Summary To provide emergency assistance to disabled veterans, wartime veterans, and their families in Idaho.

Eligibility Eligible for these grants are disabled veterans, wartime veterans, and surviving dependents who are residents of Idaho. Applicants must be in need of assistance for food, fuel, shelter, and other necessities of daily living.

Financial data The maximum amount available under this program is $1,000, issued in small incremental grants.

Duration The limit of $1,000 applies for the lifetime of each veteran or his/her family.

Additional Information This program was established by the Idaho legislature in lieu of granting a wartime bonus to Idaho veterans.

Number awarded Varies each year.

[851]
ILLINOIS HOUSING TAX EXEMPTION

Illinois Department of Veterans' Affairs
833 South Spring Street
P.O. Box 19432
Springfield, IL 62794-9432
(217) 782-6641
Toll-free: (800) 437-9824 (within IL)
Fax: (217) 782-4161   TDD: (217) 524-4645
E-mail: webmail@dva.state.il.us
Web: www.state.il.us/agency/dva

Summary To provide an exemption on the assessed value of specially adapted housing to Illinois veterans with disabilities and their spouses.

Eligibility Specially adapted housing units for disabled veterans that have been purchased or constructed with federal funds are eligible for this exemption. The exemption is extended to the veteran, the spouse, or the unremarried surviving spouse.

Financial data Under this program, an exemption is allowed on the assessed value of eligible real property, up to a maximum of $47,500 of assessed valuation.

Duration 1 year; renewable as long as the veteran, or spouse, or unremarried surviving spouse resides in the specially adapted housing in Illinois.

Number awarded Varies each year.

Deadline Applications for the exemption may be submitted at any time.

[852]
ILLINOIS INCOME TAX SUBTRACTION FOR GOVERNMENT RETIREES

Illinois Department of Revenue
101 West Jefferson Street
P.O. Box 19044
Springfield, IL 62794-9044
(217) 782-9337   Toll-free: (800) 732-8866
Web: www.revenue.state.il.us

Summary To exempt the retirement income of veterans and other government employees from state taxation in Illinois.

Eligibility This exemption applies to the income received from government retirement and disability plans, including military plans.

Financial data All government retirement and disability income of eligible residents is exempt from state income taxation.

Duration The exemption continues as long as the recipient resides in Illinois.

[853]
IMPROVED DEATH PENSION FOR SURVIVORS

Department of Veterans Affairs
810 Vermont Avenue, N.W.
Washington, DC 20420
(202) 418-4343   Toll-free: (800) 827-1000
Web: www.va.gov

Summary To provide pensions to disabled and other spouses and children of deceased veterans with wartime service.

Eligibility This program is open to surviving spouses and unmarried children of veterans who were discharged under conditions other than dishonorable and who had at least 90 days of active military service, at least 1 day of which was during a period of war, or a service-connected disability. If the veteran died in service but not in the line of duty, benefits may be payable if the veteran had completed at least 2 years of honorable service. Spouses may not have remarried and children must be under 18 years of age, or 23 if attending a VA-approved school. Children who became incapable of self-support because of a disability before age 18 may be eligible for a pension as long as the condition exists, unless the child marries or the child's income exceeds the applicable limit.

Financial data The pension program provides the following annual rates, payable monthly: surviving spouse without dependent children, $6,497; surviving spouse with 1 dependent child, $8,507; surviving spouse in need of regular aid and attendance without dependent children, $10,387; surviving spouse in need of regular aid and attendance with 1 dependent child, $12,393; surviving spouse permanently housebound without dependent children, $7,942; surviving spouse permanently housebound with 1 dependent child, $9,948; increase for each additional dependent child, $1,653. Surviving children who are living alone receive $1,586 annually. The payment is reduced by the annual income from other sources, such as Social Security.

Duration For surviving spouse: until remarriage. For surviving unmarried child: until the age of 18, or 23 if attending a VA-approved school. For surviving child with disability: as long as the condition exists or until marriage.

Additional Information Pensions are not payable to those whose estates are so large that it is reasonable for them to look to the estates for maintenance.

Number awarded Varies each year.

Deadline Applications may be submitted at any time.

[854]
IMPROVED DISABILITY PENSION PROGRAM FOR VETERANS

Department of Veterans Affairs
810 Vermont Avenue, N.W.
Washington, DC 20420
(202) 418-4343   Toll-free: (800) 827-1000
Web: www.va.gov

Summary To provide a pension for disabled or elderly veterans who served during wartime but whose disabilities are not service connected.

Eligibility In order to qualify for a pension under this program, veterans must be permanently and totally disabled for reasons not traceable to service nor due to willful misconduct or vicious habits. Veterans 65 years of age or older and not working are considered permanently and totally disabled. The discharge must have been under conditions other than dishonorable, and service must include at least 90 days (unless separated earlier because of a service-connected disability) during wartime in the Mexican Border Period, World War I, World War II, the Korean Conflict, the Vietnam Era, or the Persian Gulf Campaign. A pension is not payable to those who have estates that can provide adequate maintenance.

Financial data The pension program provides for the following annual rates, payable monthly: veteran without dependent spouse or child, $9,690; veteran with 1 dependent, $12,692; veteran in need of regular aid and attendance without dependents, $16,169; veteran in need of regular aid and attendance with 1 dependent, $19,167; veteran permanently housebound without dependents, $11,843; veteran permanently housebound with 1 dependent, $14,844; 2 veterans married to each other if both meet disability and service requirements, $12,692; veterans of World War I and the Mexican Border Period, an additional $2,197; for each additional dependent child, $1,653. The annual payment is reduced by the amount of the annual countable income of the veteran and, if applicable, a spouse and dependent child. If a veteran without a spouse or child is being provided with nursing home or domiciliary care by the Department of Veterans Affairs, the pension is reduced by up to $90 per month after 3 full calendar months of care.

Duration The pension is paid for the life of the recipient.

Number awarded Varies each year.

Deadline Applications are accepted at any time.

[855]
INDIANA DISABILITY RETIREMENT INCOME TAX DEDUCTION

Indiana Department of Revenue
Attn: Taxpayer Services Division
Indiana Government Center North
100 North Senate Avenue
Indianapolis, IN 46204-2253
(317) 232-2240   TDD: (317) 232-4952
E-mail: pfrequest@dor.state.in.us
Web: www.state.in.us/dor

Summary To exempt a portion of the disability income of residents of Indiana from state taxation.

Eligibility This exclusion is available to residents of Indiana who are retired as a result of permanent and total disability.

Financial data Up to $5,200 per year of disability pay may be excluded from income for purposes of state taxation. The amount of the exclusion is reduced by the excess of the person's federal adjusted gross income over $15,000.

Duration The exclusion is available as long as the recipient resides in Indiana.

[856]
INDIANA PROPERTY TAX DEDUCTION FOR BLIND OR DISABLED PERSONS

Department of Local Government Finance
Indiana Government Center North, Room 1058
100 North Senate Avenue
Indianapolis, IN 46201
(317) 232-3777   Fax: (317) 232-8779
E-mail: taxboard@tcb.state.in.us
Web: www.in.gov/dlgf

Summary To exempt Indiana residents who are blind or disabled from a portion of their property tax.

Eligibility Eligible for this program are Indiana residents who are blind or disabled and receive less than $17,000 in annual taxable income. A blind person is defined as an individual who has vision in the better eye with correcting glasses of 20/200 or less, or a disqualifying visual field detect as determined upon examination by a designated ophthalmologist or optometrist. A disabled person is defined as an individual unable to engage in any substantial gainful activity by reason of a medically determinable physical or mental impairment that can be expected to result in death or has lasted and can be expected to last for at least 12 continuous months.

Financial data The property tax deduction is $6,000.

Duration This deduction may be taken annually, as long as the Indiana resident meets the requirements of the program.

Additional Information Property taxes are administered by individual counties in Indiana. For further information, contact your county tax assessor.

Number awarded Varies each year.

Deadline Applications must be filed during the 12 months before May of each year for which the individual wishes to obtain the deduction.

[857]
INDIANA PROPERTY TAX DEDUCTIONS FOR DISABLED VETERANS

Department of Local Government Finance
Indiana Government Center North, Room 1058
100 North Senate Avenue
Indianapolis, IN 46201
(317) 232-3777 Fax: (317) 232-8779
E-mail: taxboard@tcb.state.in.us
Web: www.in.gov/dlgf

Summary To exempt disabled Indiana veterans and their spouses from a portion of their property taxes.

Eligibility This program is open to the following categories of veterans who are residents of Indiana: 1) served honorably at least 90 days and are either totally disabled (the disability does not need to be service-connected) or are at least 62 years old and have at least a 10% service-connected disability; 2) served honorably during wartime and have at least a 10% service connected disability; or 3) served during World War I and are disabled. A statutory disability rating for pulmonary tuberculosis does not qualify. A disability incurred during Initial Active Duty for Training (IADT) with the National Guard or Reserves is eligible only if the disability occurred from an event during the period of active duty and that duty was performed during wartime. Surviving spouses of those 3 categories of veterans are also eligible.

Financial data Property tax deductions are $6,000 for veterans and spouses in the first category (only if the assessed value of the real property owned by the veteran or spouse does not exceed $113,000), $12,000 in the second category, or $9,000 in the third category (only if the assessed value of the real property owned by the veteran does not exceed $163,000; there is no limit on the value of the property owned by a surviving spouse).

Duration 1 year; may be renewed as long as the eligible veteran or surviving unremarried spouse owns and occupies the primary residence in Indiana.

Number awarded Varies each year.

Deadline Applications must be submitted no later than May of each year.

[858]
IOWA PENSION/RETIREMENT INCOME EXCLUSION

Iowa Department of Revenue
Attn: Taxpayer Services
Hoover State Office Building
1305 East Walnut
P.O. Box 10457
Des Moines, IA 50306-0457
(515) 281-3114
Toll-free: (800) 367-3388 (within IA)
Fax: (515) 242-6487 E-mail: idrf@idrf.state.ia.us
Web: www.state.ia.us/tax

Summary To exempt a portion of the income received by military and other retirees in Iowa from state taxation.

Eligibility This exemption applies to the retirement income of residents of Iowa who are 1) 55 years of age or older, 2) disabled, or 3) a surviving spouse or a survivor having an insurable interest in an individual who would have qualified from the exclusion on the basis of age or disability.

Financial data For joint filers, the exclusion is the lesser of $12,000 or the taxable amount of the retirement income; for all other statuses of filers, each eligible taxpayer can claim as an exemption the lesser of $6,000 or the taxable amount of the retirement income.

Duration The exemption continues as long as the recipient remains a resident of Iowa for state income tax purposes.

Number awarded Varies each year.

[859]
IOWA PROPERTY TAX CREDIT FOR DISABLED AND ELDERLY RESIDENTS

Iowa Department of Revenue
Attn: Property Tax Division
Hoover State Office Building
1305 East Walnut
P.O. Box 10457
Des Moines, IA 50306-0457
(515) 281-4040
Toll-free: (800) 367-3388 (within IA)
Fax: (515) 242-6487 E-mail: idrf@idrf.state.ia.us
Web: www.state.ia.us/tax

Summary To provide a property tax credit to residents of Iowa who have a disability or are elderly.

Eligibility This credit is available to residents of Iowa who are either totally disabled and over 18 years of age or 65 years of age or older. Applicants must have household income less than $17.589 per year.

Financial data Eligible residents receive a percentage credit on their property taxes that depends on their household income: from $0.00 to $9,060.99: 100%; from $9,061 to $10,126.99: 85%; from $10,127 to $11,192.99: 70%; from $11,193 to $13,324.99: 50%; from $13,325 to $15,456.99: 35%; from $15,457 to $17,588.99: 25%.

Duration The credit continues as long as the recipient remains a resident of Iowa and owns a homestead subject to property taxation.

Number awarded Varies each year. Recently, the total value of credits extended through this program was more than $16 million.

Deadline Claims must be filed with the county treasurer by the end of May of each year. The treasurer may extend the filing deadline to the end of September, or the Director of Revenue may extend the filing deadline to the end of December.

[860]
KANSAS DISABLED ACCESS INCOME TAX CREDIT

Kansas Department of Revenue
Attn: Taxpayer Assistance Center
Robert B. Docking State Office Building
915 S.W. Harrison Street
Topeka, KS 66612-1712
(785) 368-8222   Toll-free: (877) 526-7738
Fax: (785) 291-3614   TTY: (785) 296-6461
Web: www.ksrevenue.org

Summary To provide an income tax credit to individual and business taxpayers in Kansas who incur certain expenditures to make their property accessible to people with disabilities.

Eligibility This credit is available to state income taxpayers in Kansas who make buildings or facilities accessible and usable by persons with disabilities in conformity with the Americans with Disabilities Act of 1990. The credit applies to the taxpayer's principal dwelling or the principal dwelling of a lineal ascendant or descendant, including construction of a small barrier-free living unit attached to the principal dwelling. The only expenditures that qualify for this credit are those that are specifically intended to 1) make an existing facility accessible to people with disabilities; 2) remove existing architectural barriers; or 3) modify or adapt an existing facility or piece of equipment in order to employ people with disabilities.

Financial data For individuals, the amount of the credit depends on adjusted gross income and the amount of the expenditure, ranging from 100% of the expenditure for incomes less than $25,000, to 50% for incomes greater than $45,000 but less than $55,000; persons with incomes greater than $55,000 do not qualify for the credit; the maximum individual credit is $9,000. For businesses, the credit is 50% of the amount of the expenditure, to a maximum of $10,000.

Duration This is a 1-time credit.

Number awarded Varies each year.

Deadline Claims are filed with the state income tax return, due in April.

[861]
KANSAS HOMESTEAD TAX REFUND

Kansas Department of Revenue
Attn: Taxpayer Assistance Center
Robert B. Docking State Office Building
915 S.W. Harrison Street
Topeka, KS 66612-1712
(785) 368-8222   Toll-free: (877) 526-7738
Fax: (785) 291-3614   TTY: (785) 296-6461
Web: www.ksrevenue.org

Summary To provide a property tax refund to disabled and other residents of Kansas.

Eligibility To be eligible, residents of Kansas must meet 1 of the following requirements: 1) have been permanently and totally disabled or blind during all of the taxable year; 2) be 55 years of age or older on the first of the year; or 3) have had 1 or more dependent children under the age of 18 living with them the entire year. Total household income may not have exceeded $25,000 and the applicant must have owned, or rented, and occupied the homestead, or lived in a nursing home upon which general property taxes were assessed; the applicant must not owe any delinquent taxes on the homestead and the property tax or rent paid must not have been paid from public funds.

Financial data The size of the refund depends on the applicant's total household income and either the amount paid as property tax by homeowners or 20% of rent paid for occupancy by renters; the maximum refund is $600.

Duration The refund is payable annually as long as the disabled or other applicant resides in Kansas.

Number awarded Varies each year.

Deadline Claims must be filed by April of each year.

[862]
KANSAS INTANGIBLES TAX SENIOR CITIZEN OR DISABILITY EXEMPTION

Kansas Department of Revenue
Attn: Taxpayer Assistance Center
Robert B. Docking State Office Building
915 S.W. Harrison Street
Topeka, KS 66612-1712
(785) 368-8222   Toll-free: (877) 526-7738
Fax: (785) 291-3614   TTY: (785) 296-6461
Web: www.ksrevenue.org

Summary To exempt a portion of the income received by senior citizens and disabled residents in Kansas from the intangibles tax.

Eligibility This exemption applies to residents of local areas in Kansas that levy an intangibles tax on gross earnings received from such property as savings accounts, stocks, bonds, accounts receivable, and mortgages. Applicants must 1) be disabled, blind, or 60 years of age or older and 2) have a household income of $20,000 or less.

Financial data Qualified residents are entitled to exempt from their intangibles income an amount that depends on their income. If total household income is $15,000 or less, the exemption is $5,000. For incomes between $15,000 and $20,000, the exemption is calculated as the difference between $5,000 and the amount of the income over $15,000.

Duration This benefit continues as long as the recipient remains a resident of the Kansas locality that imposes an intangibles tax.

Number awarded Varies each year.

[863]
KANSAS STATE DEAF-BLIND FUND

Kansas State Department of Education
Student Support Services
Attn: Kansas Project for Children and Young Adults Who Are Deaf-Blind
120 Southeast 10th Avenue
Topeka, KS 66612-1182
(785) 296-0917 Toll-free: (800) 203-9462
Fax: (785) 296-4944

Summary To provide supplementary financial assistance to deaf-blind or severely disabled students in Kansas.

Eligibility Applications may be submitted by school personnel for students in Kansas (up to the age of 21) who are deaf-blind and/or have severe multiple disabilities. Approval for funding is granted on a first-come, first-served basis, when the costs for educational technology, equipment, consultation, or evaluation exceed the amount local education agencies are able to provide out of federal, state, or local funds. Priority candidates are deaf-blind children from birth through 2 years of age, students who are exiting state hospital schools and returning to their home district, students who have a suspected vision loss and documented hearing loss and are in need of an evaluation, and students who have a suspected hearing loss and documented vision loss who are in need of an evaluation.

Financial data Eligible students are awarded up to $3,000 per year. Funds must be used for educational technology, equipment, consultation, or evaluation.

Duration 1 year; may be renewed.

Number awarded Varies each year.

Deadline January of each year.

[864]
KENTUCKY HOMESTEAD EXEMPTION FOR THE DISABLED

Kentucky Revenue Cabinet
Attn: Department of Property Valuation
200 Fair Oaks Lane, Fourth Floor
Frankfort, KY 40620
(502) 564-8338 Fax: (502) 564-8368
E-mail: thomas.crawford@mail.state.ky.us
Web: revenue.state.ky.us

Summary To exempt the homestead of totally disabled and elderly Kentucky residents from property taxation.

Eligibility Applicants must be classified as 1) totally disabled under a program authorized by the U.S. government or by the Railroad Retirement System, or 2) 65 years of age or older on January 1 of the year in which application is made.

Financial data Up to $26,800 of the assessed valuation of the property is exempt from taxation.

Duration This exemption continues as long as the recipient resides in Kentucky and is certified as disabled. Until age 65, however, eligible disabled recipients must apply for the exemption on an annual basis.

Additional Information Applicants for this exemption must own and reside in the property.

Number awarded Varies each year.

[865]
LENOX BAKER SPECIAL ASSISTANCE PROGRAM

United Cerebral Palsy of North Carolina, Inc.
Attn: Director, Outreach Services
620 North West Street, Suite 103
P.O. Box 27707
Raleigh, NC 27611-7707
(919) 832-3787, ext. 119 Toll-free: (800) 868-3787
Fax: (919) 832-5928 E-mail: SONeal@ucpnc.com
Web: www.ucp.org/main.cfm/124

Summary To assist disabled residents of North Carolina and South Carolina with their special financial needs.

Eligibility This funding is available to disabled residents of North Carolina and South Carolina who need financial assistance to pay for equipment, medical treatment, medication, or transportation (excluding maintenance of personal vehicles). All other sources of payment must have been explored and denied (or only partial funding made). No on-going requests for financial assistance will be considered, nor will any requests for daily living expenses (e.g., utilities, premium payments).

Financial data This fund is quite limited; the largest amount granted is $750 and most grants are smaller than that. The exact amount awarded varies, depending upon the needs of the individual; however, only partial funding can be offered.

DISABILITIES IN GENERAL: GRANTS-IN-AID

Duration Individuals may not receive this assistance more than 1 time per year.

Additional Information If the applicant is covered by Medicaid or Medicare, it is necessary to submit a prior authorization form to the appropriate Medicaid office to determine if all or part of the cost will be covered.

Number awarded Varies each year.

Deadline Applications may be submitted at any time.

[866]
LLEWELLYN MILLER FUND

American Society of Journalists and Authors
Attn: Charitable Trust
1501 Broadway, Suite 302
New York, NY 10036
(212) 997-0947   Fax: (212) 768-7414
Web: www.asja.org/miller.php

Summary To assist professional freelance writers who are in financial need because of a disability or other causes.

Eligibility Applicants need not be members of the American Society of Journalists and Authors, but they must establish a record of past professional freelance writing over a sustained period of years. Preference is given to nonfiction writers. The writers who may apply are those in financial need because of 1) age (60 or older); 2) a disability; or 3) illness. In certain circumstances, professional freelancers undergoing an "extraordinary professional crisis" may also be eligible.

Financial data The maximum award is $3,500.

Duration A recipient may apply for an additional grant at the end of a 12-month period.

Additional Information Applications may be submitted by either the applicant or a nominator on the applicant's behalf. Grants are not available to beginning freelancers seeking funds for writing projects nor for works-in-progress of any kind.

Number awarded Varies each year.

Deadline Applications may be submitted at any time.

[867]
LONGSHORE AND HARBOR WORKERS' COMPENSATION PROGRAM

Department of Labor
Employment Standards Administration
Office of Workers' Compensation Programs
Attn: Division of Longshore and Harbor Workers' Compensation
200 Constitution Avenue, N.W., Room C4315
Washington, DC 20210
(202) 693-0038   Fax: (202) 693-1380
TDD: (800) 326-2577
Web: www.dol.gov/esa/public/owcp_org.htm

Summary To provide benefits to maritime workers disabled or killed during the course of employment and to their spouses.

Eligibility This program is open to longshoremen, harbor workers, and other maritime workers who are injured during the course of employment; by extension, various other classes of private industry workers (including workers engaged in the extraction of natural resources on the outer continental shelf, employees of defense contractors overseas, and employees at post exchanges on military bases) are also eligible if they become disabled for work-related causes. In addition, survivor benefits are provided if the work-related injury causes the employee's death.

Financial data The compensation for disability is 66 2/3% of the employee's average weekly wage, with a minimum of 50% of the national average weekly wage (NAWW) and a maximum of 200% of the NAWW. In a recent year, the Department of Labor calculated the NAWW as $466.91, so the minimum weekly disability payment was $233.46 and the maximum was $933.82. Death benefits are equivalent to the average weekly wage of the deceased employee, with a minimum equivalent to 100% of the NAWW and a maximum equivalent to 200% of the NAWW.

Duration Benefits are paid as long as the worker remains disabled; death benefits are paid for the life of the qualified survivor.

Additional Information This program also provides medical benefits and rehabilitation services to qualifying longshoremen, harbor workers, and other workers.

Number awarded Varies; nearly 15,000 maritime workers recently received compensation and medical benefits through this program.

[868]
MAINE TAX EXEMPTIONS FOR VETERANS

Maine Revenue Services
Attn: Property Tax Division
P.O. Box 9106
Augusta, ME 04332-9106
(207) 287-2011   Fax: (207) 287-6396
E-mail: prop.tax@maine.gove
Web: www.maine.gov

Summary To exempt the estates of disabled Maine veterans and selected family members from property taxation.

Eligibility Eligible for this program are veterans who served in wartime during World War I, World War II, the Korean campaign, the Vietnam war, or the Persian Gulf war, are legal residents of Maine, and are either older than 62 years or are receiving a pension or compensation from the U.S. government for total disability (whether service connected or not). Vietnam veterans must have served 180 days on active duty unless discharged earlier for a service-connected disability. The exemption also includes 1) property held in joint tenancy with the veterans' spouses, and 2) property of unremar-

ried widow(er)s, minor children, and mothers of deceased veterans if those dependents are receiving a pension or compensation from the U.S. government.

Financial data Estates of disabled veterans and eligible dependents, including both real and personal property, are exempt up to $5,000 of just valuation. For veterans and dependents who served in wartime prior to World War II, the estates up to $7,000 are exempt.

Duration Veterans, spouses, unremarried widow(er)s, and mothers are eligible for this exemption throughout their lifetimes; minor children of veterans are eligible until they reach the age of 18.

Number awarded Varies each year.

Deadline When an eligible person first submits an application, the proof of entitlement must reach the assessors of the local municipality prior to the end of March. Once eligibility has been established, notification need not be repeated in subsequent years.

[869]
MARYLAND INCOME TAX EXEMPTION FOR DISABLED AND ELDERLY RESIDENTS

Comptroller of Maryland
Attn: Revenue Administration Division
80 Calvert Street
Annapolis, MD 21411
(410) 260-7980
Toll-free: (800) MD-TAXES (within MD)
Fax: (410) 974-3456   TDD: (410) 260-7157
E-mail: taxhelp@comp.state.md.us
Web: individuals.marylandtaxes.com

Summary To exempt a portion of the income of disabled and elderly residents (and selected spouses) from state income taxation in Maryland.

Eligibility Eligible are Maryland residents who receive income from a pension, annuity, or endowment from an employee retirement system and who are at least 65 years of age or classified as totally disabled; spouses of disabled persons also qualify. The disability must be a mental or physical impairment that prevents the person from engaging in gainful activity and that is expected to be of long, continuing, or indefinite duration (or to result in death).

Financial data Persons with disabilities, who have a spouse who is totally disabled, or who are aged 65 or older may exclude from state income taxation up to $18,500 of income received as a pension, annuity, or endowment.

Duration The exemption continues as long as the recipient resides in Maryland.

[870]
MARYLAND REAL PROPERTY TAX EXEMPTION FOR DISABLED VETERANS

State Department of Assessments and Taxation
Attn: Tax Credit Program
301 West Preston Street, Room 900
Baltimore, MD 21201-2395
(410) 767-1184
Toll-free: (888) 246-5941 (within MD)
TTY: (800) 735-2258
E-mail: taxcredits@dat.state.md.us
Web: www.dat.state.md.us

Summary To exempt the homes of disabled veterans and their spouses from property taxation in Maryland.

Eligibility This program is open to Maryland residents who are veterans with a 100% service-connected permanent disability and their surviving spouses.

Financial data The dwelling houses owned by qualifying disabled veterans and their spouses are exempt from real property taxes in Maryland.

Duration This exemption continues as long as the qualifying disabled veterans or spouses reside in Maryland and own their home.

[871]
MARYLAND RENTERS' TAX CREDITS

State Department of Assessments and Taxation
Attn: Renters' Tax Credit Program
301 West Preston Street, Room 900
Baltimore, MD 21201-2395
(410) 767-4433
Toll-free: (800) 944-7403 (within MD)
TTY: (800) 735-2258
E-mail: taxcredits@dat.state.md.us
Web: www.dat.state.md.us

Summary To provide a tax credit to elderly and disabled residents of Maryland who rent their homes.

Eligibility This program is open to Maryland residents who are renters and either older than 60 years of age or 100% disabled. Applicants must pay minimum amounts for rent that are based on their income; e.g., renters with income less than $5,000 per year must pay at least $14 per month for rent, while renters with income of $30,000 per year must pay at least $1,044 per month for rent.

Financial data The program establishes a tax limit based on income (e.g., for an income of $5,000 the tax limit is $25, for an income of $20,000 the tax limit is $980) and assumes that 15% of the rent goes to property tax. The amount that the property tax portion of the rent exceeds the tax limit is provided as a tax credit, to a maximum of $600 per year.

Duration This credit is available annually as long as the qualifying renters reside in Maryland and rent their homes.

Additional Information Elderly and disabled Maryland residents who believe they may qualify for this credit are encouraged to submit information on their income and the amount they spend on rent. The State Department of Assessments and Taxation will determine if they are eligible and, if so, the exact amount of their credit.

Deadline Applications must be submitted by August of each year.

[872]
MASSACHUSETTS PROPERTY TAX EXEMPTION

Department of Veterans' Services
239 Causeway Street, Suite 100
Boston, MA 02114
(617) 727-3578   Toll-free: (888) 844-2383
Fax: (617) 727-5903
E-mail: mdvs@vet.state.ma.us
Web: www.state.ma.us/veterans

Summary To provide a property tax exemption to disabled and other veterans (and their families) in Massachusetts.

Eligibility This program is open to veterans who are residents of Massachusetts, were residents for at least 6 months prior to entering the service, have been residents for at least 5 consecutive years, and are occupying property as their domicile. The program is open to several categories of qualified veterans and their families: 1) veterans who have a disability rating of 10% or more as a result of wartime service; veterans who served in the Spanish war, the Philippine insurrection, or the Chinese Relief Expedition; veterans who have been awarded the Purple Heart; unremarried surviving spouses of veterans who served in the armed forces between April 6, 1917 and November 11, 1918 and whose estate is worth less than $20,000; and mothers and fathers of military personnel who lost their lives in wartime service; 2) veterans who have a loss or permanent loss of use of 1 foot at or above the ankle; have a loss or permanent loss of use of 1 hand at or above the wrist; have a loss or permanent loss of sight of 1 eye; or have been awarded the Medal of Honor, the Distinguished Service Cross, the Navy Cross, or the Air Force Cross; 3) veterans who have a loss or permanent loss of use of both feet at or above the ankle, a loss or permanent loss of use of both hands at or above the wrist, a loss or permanent loss of use of 1 foot at or above the ankle and 1 hand at or above the wrist, or a loss or permanent loss of use of both eyes; 4) veterans who have a permanent and total disability as a result of a service-connected injury and have received assistance from the U.S. Department of Veterans Affairs in acquiring "special adapted housing;" 5) unremarried surviving spouses of veterans who died in combat as members of the armed forces in military action at the islands of Quemoy and Matsu in the Pacific; 6) veterans who have a disability rating of 100% as a result of injury in wartime service and in the line of duty and who are incapable of working; and 7) paraplegic veterans with service-related injuries. Surviving spouses (including those who have remarried) of all veterans in the second, third, fourth, sixth, and seventh categories are also eligible for these exemptions.

Financial data The annual exemption is $250 or $2,000 of assessed taxable value of property for the first and fifth categories; $425 or $4,000 of assessed taxable value of property for the second category; $775 or $8,000 of assessed taxable value of property for the third category; $950 or $10,000 of assessed taxable value of property for the fourth category; or $600 or $6,000 of assessed taxable value of property for the sixth category. Veterans and spouses in the seventh category are exempt from all property taxes on their domiciles.

Duration The exemptions are provided each year that the veteran or unremarried surviving spouse lives in Massachusetts and owns the property as a domicile.

Additional Information Applications are available from local assessor's offices.

Number awarded Varies each year.

[873]
MASSACHUSETTS VETERANS ANNUITY PROGRAM

Department of Veterans' Services
239 Causeway Street, Suite 100
Boston, MA 02114
(617) 727-3578   Toll-free: (888) 844-2383
Fax: (617) 727-5903
E-mail: mdvs@vet.state.ma.us
Web: www.state.ma.us/veterans/annuity.htm

Summary To provide an annuity to disabled veterans from Massachusetts and to the parents and spouses of deceased military personnel.

Eligibility This program is open to 1) veterans who have a 100% service-connected disability, 2) the parents of military personnel who died in service; and 3) the unremarried spouses of military personnel who died in service. Veterans must have been residents of Massachusetts at the time of entry into military service who served during specified wartime periods and have received other than a dishonorable discharge. All applicants must currently be residents of Massachusetts.

Financial data Recipients are entitled to an annuity of $1,500 per year.

Duration The annuity is paid as long as the recipient continues to reside in Massachusetts.

[874]
MEDICARE DME PROGRAM
Centers for Medicare & Medicaid Services
Attn: Medicare
7500 Security Boulevard
Baltimore, MD 21244-1850
Toll-free: (800) 772-1213   TTY: (800) 325-0778
Web: www.medicare.gov

Summary To enable Medicare recipients to acquire durable medical equipment (DME), such as wheelchairs, walkers, hospital beds, and oxygen equipment prescribed for home use by a doctor.

Eligibility People are eligible for Medicare if they or a spouse worked for at least 40 quarters in Medicare-covered employment, are at least 65 years old, and are U.S. citizens or permanent residents. Part A helps pay for care in a hospital, a skilled nursing facility, or home and hospice care (including DME). Part B helps pay for doctors, outpatient hospital care, and other medical services (such as DME).

Financial data Most people do not pay a monthly Part A premium because they or a spouse has 40 or more quarters of Medicare-covered employment. To participate in Part B, a monthly premium (currently $58.70). is required, as are a $100 annual deductible and a 20% coinsurance rate. Medicare carriers do not pay the entire bill for DME. Instead, they determine an allowable charge (based on the actual charge) and the prevailing charge in a geographic area. The regional Medicare carrier pays 80% of the allowable amount; the remainder is paid by the beneficiary or another third party.

Additional Information DME is defined as medical equipment that is ordered by a doctor for use in the home. These items must be reuseable.

Number awarded Varies each year.

Deadline Applications may be submitted at any time.

[875]
MICHIGAN ELKS ASSOCIATION CHARITABLE GRANT FUND SCHOLARSHIP
Michigan Elks Association
c/o Franz A. Brenner, Secretary-Treasurer
43904 Leeann Lane
Canton, MI 48187

Summary To provide financial assistance for college to "special needs" students in Michigan.

Eligibility This program is open to "special needs" students who are Michigan residents. For the purposes of this program, "special needs" students are defined as those who have physical impairments, visual impairments, hearing impairments, speech impairments, or other disabilities. Applicants must be high school seniors and planning to attend an accredited college, university, trade school, or vocational school. Financial need is considered.

Financial data The stipend is $2,000 per year.

Duration 1 year; may be renewed upon to 3 additional years.

Additional Information Funds may not be used for graduate study.

Number awarded Varies each year.

[876]
MICHIGAN HOMESTEAD PROPERTY TAX CREDIT FOR VETERANS AND BLIND PEOPLE
Michigan Department of Treasury
Attn: Homestead Exemption
Treasury Building
430 West Allegan Street
Lansing, MI 48922
(517) 373-3200   Toll-free: (800) 487-7000
TTY: (517) 636-4999
E-mail: treasPtd2@michigan.gov
Web: www.michigan.gov/treasury

Summary To provide a property tax credit to veterans, military personnel, their spouses, blind people, and their surviving spouses in Michigan.

Eligibility Eligible to apply are residents of Michigan who are 1) blind and own their homestead; 2) a veteran with a service-connected disability or his/her surviving spouse; 3) a surviving spouse of a veteran deceased in service; 4) a veteran of wars before World War I, a pensioned veteran, a surviving spouse of those veterans, or an active military member whose household income is less than $7,500; or 5) a surviving spouse of a non-disabled or non-pensioned veteran of the Korean War, World War II, and World War I whose household income is less than $7,500. All applicants must own or rent a home in Michigan, have been a Michigan resident for at least 6 months during the year in which application is made, and fall within qualifying income levels (up to $82,650 in household income).

Financial data The maximum credit is $1,200. The exact amount varies. For homeowners, the credit depends on the state equalized value of the homestead and on an allowance for filing category. For renters, 20% of the rent is considered property tax eligible for credit.

Duration 1 year; eligibility must be established each year.

Number awarded Varies each year.

Deadline December of each year.

DISABILITIES IN GENERAL: GRANTS-IN-AID

[877]
MICHIGAN INCOME TAX EXEMPTION FOR PEOPLE WITH DISABILITIES

Michigan Department of Treasury
Attn: Income Tax
Treasury Building
430 West Allegan Street
Lansing, MI 48922
(517) 373-3200   Toll-free: (800) 827-4000
TTY: (517) 636-4999
E-mail: treasIndTax@michigan.gov
Web: www.michigan.gov/treasury

Summary To exempt a portion of the income of deaf, blind, and disabled residents of Michigan from state income taxation.

Eligibility Eligible for this exemption are residents of Michigan who 1) receive messages through a sense other than hearing, such as lip reading or sign language; 2) have vision in their better eye of 20/200 or less with corrective lenses or peripheral field of vision of 20 degrees or less; or 3) are hemiplegic, paraplegic, quadriplegic, or totally and permanently disabled.

Financial data Qualifying people with disabilities receive an exemption of $1,900 from their adjusted gross income for purposes of state taxation.

Duration The exemption continues as long as the recipient resides in Michigan.

[878]
MICHIGAN VETERANS TRUST FUND EMERGENCY GRANTS

Department of Military and Veterans Affairs
Attn: Michigan Veterans Trust Fund
2500 South Washington Avenue
Lansing, MI 48913-5101
(517) 483-5469   E-mail: paocmn@michigan.gov
Web: www.michigan.gov/dmva

Summary To provide temporary financial assistance to disabled and other Michigan veterans and their families, if they are facing personal emergencies.

Eligibility Eligible for this assistance are veterans and their families residing in Michigan who are temporarily unable to provide the basic necessities of life. Support is not provided for long-term problems or chronic financial difficulties. The qualifying veteran must have been discharged under honorable conditions with at least 180 days of active wartime service or have been separated as a result of a physical or mental disability incurred in the line of duty.

Financial data No statutory limit exists on the amount of assistance that may be provided; a local board in each Michigan county determines if the applicant is genuinely needy and the amount of assistance to be awarded.

Duration This assistance is provided to meet temporary needs only.

Number awarded Varies each year.

Deadline Applications may be submitted at any time.

[879]
MINNESOTA STATE SOLDIERS ASSISTANCE FUND

Minnesota Department of Veterans Affairs
Veterans Service Building
20 West 12th Street, Second Floor
St. Paul, MN 55155-2079
(651) 296-6728   Fax: (651) 296-3954
E-mail: paula.plum@mdva.state.mn.us
Web: www.mdva.state.mn.us

Summary To provide emergency financial assistance to disabled veterans and their families in Minnesota.

Eligibility This program is open to veterans who are temporarily disabled (from service-connected or other causes) to the extent that normal employment is not possible. Their dependents and survivors are also eligible. Applicants must also meet income and asset guidelines and must be residents of Minnesota.

Financial data Limited emergency assistance is available. The funds may be used to pay for food and shelter, utility bills, and emergency medical treatment (including optical and dental benefits).

Duration This is a short-term program, with benefits payable up to 6 months only. If the veteran's disability is expected to be long term in nature or permanent, the department may continue to provide assistance while application is made for long-term benefits, such as Social Security disability or retirement benefits.

Number awarded Varies each year.

Deadline Applications may be submitted at any time.

[880]
MISSISSIPPI AD VALOREM TAX EXEMPTION FOR DISABLED VETERANS

Mississippi State Veterans Affairs Board
3460 Highway 80 East
P.O. Box 5947
Pearl, MS 39288-5947
(601) 576-4850   Fax: (601) 576-4868
Web: www.vab.state.ms.us

Summary To exempt the property of disabled veterans from ad valorem taxation in Mississippi.

Eligibility This exemption applies to homesteads owned by American veterans in Mississippi who were honorably discharged. Applicants must have a 100% permanent service-connected disability.

Financial data All qualifying homesteads of $6,000 or less in assessed value are exempt from ad valorem taxation.

Duration This exemption applies as long as the disabled veteran owns the homestead in Mississippi.

Number awarded Varies each year.

[881]
MISSISSIPPI HOMESTEAD TAX EXEMPTION FOR THE DISABLED

Mississippi State Tax Commission
Attn: Property Tax Division
P.O. Box 1033
Jackson, MS 39215-1033
(601) 923-7631   Fax: (601) 923-7637
E-mail: property@mstc.state.ms.us
Web: www.mstc.state.ms.us

Summary To exempt from property taxes a portion of the value of homesteads owned by people with disabilities and blind people in Mississippi.

Eligibility Eligible for this exemption are residents of Mississippi who are totally disabled or legally blind and own a homestead that they occupy as a home. Disability and blindness are defined according to federal Social Security regulations.

Financial data The exemption covers the first $7,500 of assessed value of the property.

Duration The exemption continues as long as the disabled person resides in Mississippi.

Number awarded Varies each year.

Deadline For the first time that an exemption is requested, it must be submitted before the end of March of that year. Subsequently, most Mississippi counties do not require renewal filing unless the homestead of applicant's status changes.

[882]
MISSOURI SENIOR CITIZEN, DISABLED VETERAN, AND DISABLED PERSON PROPERTY TAX CREDIT CLAIM

Missouri Department of Revenue
Attn: Division of Taxation and Collection
301 West High Street, Room 330
P.O. Box 2800
Jefferson City, MO 65105-2800
(573) 751-3505   Toll-free: (800) 877-6881
TDD: (800) 735-2966
E-mail: PropertyTaxCredit@mail.state.mo.us
Web: www.state.mo.us/dor/tax

Summary To provide a property tax credit to low-income disabled veterans, senior citizens, and other persons with disabilities or their spouses in Missouri.

Eligibility This program is open to residents of Missouri (or their spouses) who are low-income (up to $27,000 per year for married filing combined or $25,000 per year for all other claimants) and have paid property tax or rent on their homestead during the tax year. Applicants must be 1) 65 years of age or older, 2) classified by the U.S. Department of Veterans Affairs as a 100% service-connected disabled veteran, 3) 60 years of age or older and receiving surviving spouse Society Security benefits, or 4) 100% disabled.

Financial data The tax credit depends on the claimant's income and amount paid in property taxes or rent, up to a maximum of $750 per year.

Duration The tax credit is available annually.

Number awarded Varies each year.

Deadline Eligible veterans, people with disabilities, and senior citizens may claim this credit when they file their state income tax return, in April of each year.

[883]
MONTANA DISABILITY INCOME EXCLUSION

Montana Department of Revenue
Attn: Individual Income Tax
125 North Roberts, Third Floor
P.O. Box 5805
Helena, MT 59604-5805
(406) 444-6900   Fax: (406) 444-1505
TDD: (406) 444-2830
Web: www.state.mt.us/revenue

Summary To provide a state income tax exclusion to residents of Montana who receive disability payments.

Eligibility Eligible are all persons considered Montana residents for purposes of state income taxation who are receiving disability payments.

Financial data Eligible residents may exclude up to $5,200 a year of disability payments.

Duration The exclusion continues as long as the recipient resides in Montana and receives disability payments.

[884]
MONTANA REAL PROPERTY TAX RELIEF

Montana Veterans Affairs Division
1900 Williams Street
P.O. Box 5715
Helena, MT 59604
(406) 324-3741   Fax: (406) 324-3145
E-mail: jjacobsen@state.mt.us
Web: www.state.mt.us

Summary To exempt from taxation the real property of disabled or deceased veterans and their widow(er)s in Montana.

Eligibility This exemption applies to residential property in Montana that is owned and occupied by an honorably discharged veteran who is rated as 100% disabled or is being paid at the 100% disabled rate by the U.S. Department of Veterans Affairs (USDVA). Also eligible are unmarried spouses of veterans who own and occupy a residence in Montana. Spouses must obtain documentation from the USDVA that the veteran was rated as 100% disabled or was being paid at the 100% disabled rate at the time of death, or that the veteran died while on active duty.

Financial data Eligible veterans or spouses are entitled to real property tax relief that depends on their

income. Single veterans with an income of $30,000 or less are exempt from all property taxes; if their income is $30,001 to $33,000, they pay 20% of the regular tax; those with income from $33,000 to $36,000 pay 30% of the regular tax; and those with income from $36,001 to $39,000 pay 50% of the regular tax. Married veterans with an income of $36,000 or less are exempt from all property taxes; if their income is $36,001 to $39,000, they pay 20% of the regular tax; those with income from $39,001 to $42,000 pay 30% of the regular tax; and those with income from $42,001 to $45,000 pay 50% of the regular tax. Surviving spouses with an income of $25,000 or less are exempt from all property taxes; if their income is $25,001 to $28,000, they pay 20% of the regular tax; those with income from $28,001 to $31,000 pay 30% of the regular tax; and those with income from $31,000 to $34,000 pay 50% of the regular tax.

Duration The exemption continues as long as the residence in Montana is owned and occupied by the disabled veteran, or, if deceased, by the veteran's unremarried spouse.

Number awarded Varies each year.

[885]
MUSICIANS FOUNDATION FINANCIAL ASSISTANCE

Musicians Foundation, Inc.
875 Sixth Avenue, Suite 2303
New York, NY 10001
(212) 239-9137   Fax: (212) 239-9138
E-mail: info@musiciansfoundation.org
Web: www.musiciansfoundation.org

Summary To provide emergency assistance to professional musicians who need assistance for living, medical, or related expenses.

Eligibility Eligible to apply for this assistance are professional musicians who are working in the United States, regardless of their genre. Applicants must need financial assistance because of their age, illness, disability, or other misfortune. Their family members may also apply.

Financial data The amount awarded varies, depending upon the needs of the recipient. Funds are to be used to meet current living, medical, and related costs.

Duration These are generally 1-time awards.

Additional Information The foundation does not award scholarships, loans, or composition grants.

Number awarded Varies each year.

Deadline Applications may be submitted at any time.

[886]
NATIONAL VACCINE INJURY COMPENSATION PROGRAM

Health Resources and Services Administration
Bureau of Health Professions
Attn: Division of Vaccine Injury Compensation
5600 Fishers Lane, Room 16C-17
Rockville, MD 20857
(301) 443-2703   Toll-free: (800) 338-2382
Fax: (301) 443-3354   E-mail: jceresa@hrsa.gov
Web: www.hrsa.gov/bhpr/vicp

Summary To provide a no-fault system to compensate those who became injured or died as a result of adverse vaccine or toxoid reactions for vaccines administered after October 1, 1988.

Eligibility The vaccines and toxoids covered under the compensation law are: diphtheria and tetanus toxoids and pertussis vaccine (DTP); measles, mumps, and rubella (MMR); oral poliovirus vaccine (OPV) and inactivated poliovirus vaccine (IPV); hepatitis B vaccine; haemophilus influenza type b vaccine; varicella vaccine; rotavirus vaccine; and pneumococcal conjugate vaccines. No petition may be filed under this program if a civil action is pending for damages related to the vaccine injury or if damages were awarded by a court or in a settlement of a civil action against the vaccine manufacturer or administrator. Applicants must file a petition with the U.S. Court of Federal Claims. In the case of an injury, the effects must have continued at least 6 months after vaccine administration and the claim must be filed within 36 months after the first symptoms appeared. In the case of a death, the claim must be filed within 24 months of the death and within 48 months after the onset of the vaccine-related injury from which the death occurred. Medical documentation must be provided. The court will make a decision based on the individual's health status prior to administering the vaccine, the type of vaccine and the date given, and the date of onset and extent of injury occurring after receiving the vaccine.

Financial data For vaccine-related injury, the program provides reasonable compensation for past and future unreimbursable medical, custodial care, and/or rehabilitation costs; $250,000 maximum for actual and projected pain and suffering and/or emotional distress; lost earnings; and reasonable attorneys' fees and costs. For vaccine-related death, the program provides $250,000 compensation to the estate of the deceased and reasonable attorneys' fees and costs.

Duration Benefits can be awarded for the lifetime of the recipient.

Additional Information This program, established in 1988, is jointly administered by the U.S. Department of Health and Human Services, the U.S. Court of Federal Claims, and the U.S. Department of Justice. Information on the rules of the court, including requirements for filing a petition, is available from U.S. Court of Federal Claims, Attn: Clerk, 717 Madison Place, N.W., Washington, DC 20005, (202) 219-9657. The deadline has passed for fil-

ing claims for conditions that resulted from a vaccine administered prior to October 1, 1988 (the effective date of the National Childhood Vaccine Injury Act).

Number awarded Varies each year.

Deadline In the case of a disability/injury, the residual effects or complications must have continued for at least 6 months after the vaccine was administered before a petition can be filed. In addition, in the case of a disability/injury, the claim must be filed within 36 months after the first symptoms appear. In the case of death, the claim must be filed within 24 months of the death and within 48 months after the appearance of the first symptoms of the disability/injury from which the death occurred.

[887]
NEVADA DISABLED VETERAN'S TAX EXEMPTION

Nevada Office of Veterans' Services
Attn: Executive Director
1201 Terminal Way, Room 108
Reno, NV 89520
(775) 688-1653   Fax: (775) 688-1656
Web: www.state.nv.us/veterans/benefits.html

Summary To exempt from taxation in Nevada a portion of the property owned by disabled veterans or their surviving spouses.

Eligibility This program is open to veterans who are residents of Nevada and have incurred a service-connected disability of 60% or more. Applicants must have received an honorable separation from military service. The widow(er) of a disabled veteran, who was eligible at the time of death, may also be eligible for this benefit.

Financial data Veterans and widow(er)s are entitled to exempt from taxation the portion of their property's assessed value that depends on the extent of the disability. For disabilities from 60 to 79%, the exemption is on the first $10,000 assessed valuation; for disabilities from 80 to 99%, the exemption is on the first $15,000 assessed valuation; for disabilities of 100%, the exemption is on the first $20,000 assessed valuation.

Duration Disabled veterans and their widow(er)s are entitled to this exemption as long as they live in Nevada.

Additional Information Disabled veterans and widow(er)s are able to split their exemption between vehicle taxes and/or property taxes. Further information is available at local county assessors' offices.

Number awarded Varies each year.

[888]
NEW HAMPSHIRE REAL ESTATE EXEMPTION FOR THE DISABLED

New Hampshire Department of Revenue
  Administration
45 Chenell Drive
P.O. Box 457
Concord, NH 03302-0457
(603) 271-2687   TDD: (800) 735-2964

Summary To provide a partial exemption from real estate taxes for disabled residents of New Hampshire.

Eligibility Residents of New Hampshire are covered by this program if they are eligible for benefits to the disabled from the U.S. Social Security Administration, own and occupy their primary residence in New Hampshire, and live in a municipality that has chosen through a referendum vote to grant an exemption to the disabled. Their income and assets may not exceed specified limits.

Financial data The amount of the exemption (and the allowable level of income and assets) is determined by a vote of the municipality.

Duration 1 year; this exemption will be continued as long as the recipient meets the eligibility requirements.

Number awarded Varies each year.

[889]
NEW HAMPSHIRE SERVICE-CONNECTED TOTAL DISABILITY TAX CREDIT

New Hampshire Department of Revenue
  Administration
45 Chenell Drive
P.O. Box 457
Concord, NH 03302-0457
(603) 271-2687   TDD: (800) 735-2964

Summary To provide property tax credits in New Hampshire to disabled veterans or their surviving spouses.

Eligibility Eligible for this tax credit are New Hampshire residents who are honorably discharged veterans and who 1) have a total and permanent service-connected disability, or 2) are a double amputee or paraplegic because of a service-connected disability. Unremarried surviving spouses of qualified veterans are also eligible.

Financial data Qualifying disabled veterans and surviving spouses receive an annual credit of $700 for property taxes on residential property. In addition, individual towns in New Hampshire may adopt a local option to double the dollar amount credited to disabled veterans, from $700 to $1,400.

Duration 1 year; once the credit has been approved, it is automatically renewed for as long as the qualifying person owns the same residence in New Hampshire.

Number awarded Varies each year.

Deadline The original application for a permanent tax credit must be submitted by April.

[890]
NEW JERSEY HOMESTEAD REBATE

New Jersey Division of Taxation
Attn: Office of Information and Publications
50 Barrack Street
P.O. Box 281
Trenton, NJ 08695-0281
(609) 292-6400
Toll-free: (800) 323-4400 (within selected states)
TTY: (800) 286-6613 (within selected states)
E-mail: taxation@tax.state.nj.us
Web: www.state.nj.us/treasury/taxation

Summary To refund a portion of property taxes paid by residents of New Jersey, especially those who are blind, disabled, or elderly.

Eligibility This rebate is available to all residents of New Jersey, but separate provisions apply to those who are 1) blind, 2) permanently and totally disabled, or 3) aged 65 or older. Applicants must 1) either own the home in which they reside or rent a dwelling with its own separate kitchen and bath facilities; and 2) have an income of $100,000 or less (for other residents, the income threshold is $40,000).

Financial data The rebate depends on 1) whether the applicant is a homeowner or a tenant; 2) the filing status (single, married filing separate return, married filing joint return, head of household, qualifying widow or widower); and 3) the applicant's income. It ranges from $90 to $775. (For residents under 65 years of age and not blind or disabled, the maximum rebate is $100.)

Duration The rebate is available as long as the person remains a New Jersey resident.

Number awarded Varies each year.

Deadline The rebate is claimed as part of the annual income tax return, due in April of each year.

[891]
NEW JERSEY INCOME TAX EXCLUSIONS FOR PERSONS WITH DISABILITIES

New Jersey Division of Taxation
Attn: Office of Information and Publications
50 Barrack Street
P.O. Box 281
Trenton, NJ 08695-0281
(609) 292-6400
Toll-free: (800) 323-4400 (within selected states)
TTY: (800) 286-6613 (within selected states)
E-mail: taxation@tax.state.nj.us
Web: www.state.nj.us/treasury/taxation

Summary To exclude from income taxation in New Jersey certain benefits received by veterans and other persons with disabilities.

Eligibility Residents of New Jersey with disabilities are entitled to this exclusion if they are receiving benefits from public agencies, including compensation from the U.S. Department of Veterans Affairs for permanent and total disability or from the state of New Jersey for temporary disability.

Financial data Disability payments are excluded from income for state taxation purposes.

Duration The exclusion applies as long as the individual receives qualifying disability payments.

Number awarded Varies each year.

[892]
NEW JERSEY INCOME TAX EXEMPTIONS FOR THE BLIND AND DISABLED

New Jersey Division of Taxation
Attn: Office of Information and Publications
50 Barrack Street
P.O. Box 281
Trenton, NJ 08695-0281
(609) 292-6400
Toll-free: (800) 323-4400 (within selected states)
TTY: (800) 286-6613 (within selected states)
E-mail: taxation@tax.state.nj.us
Web: www.state.nj.us/treasury/taxation

Summary To provide an income tax exemption in New Jersey to blind and disabled people.

Eligibility Residents of New Jersey who are blind or disabled are entitled to this exemption.

Financial data Each blind or disabled person is entitled to an exemption of $1,000 from income for taxation purposes.

Duration The exemption continues as long as the qualifying condition persists and the person remains a New Jersey resident.

Number awarded Varies each year.

[893]
NEW JERSEY PARTIAL EXEMPTION FROM REALTY TRANSFER FEE FOR SENIOR CITIZENS OR DISABLED PERSONS

New Jersey Division of Taxation
Attn: Office of Information and Publications
50 Barrack Street
P.O. Box 281
Trenton, NJ 08695-0281
(609) 292-6400
Toll-free: (800) 323-4400 (within selected states)
TTY: (800) 286-6613 (within selected states)
E-mail: taxation@tax.state.nj.us
Web: www.state.nj.us/treasury/taxation

Summary To provide an exemption from realty transfer fees paid by senior citizens, persons with disabilities, and blind people in New Jersey.

Eligibility Eligible for these exemptions are persons aged 62 and older, permanently and totally disabled individuals, and blind people who are legal residents of New Jersey for 1 year immediately preceding October 1 of the year before the year for which the exemption is requested, and purchasers of certain residential property during the year.

Financial data The standard realty transfer fee is $2.00 per $500 for the first $150,000 of the sales price, $3.35 per $500 for sales prices from $150,000 to $200,000, or $3.90 per $500 for sales prices in excess of $200,000. For persons who qualify for this reduction, the fee is $0.50 per $500 for the first $150,000 of the sales price or $1.25 per $500 for sales prices in excess of $150,000.

Duration The exemption applies whenever a qualified purchaser buys a new residence.

Number awarded Varies each year.

[894]
NEW JERSEY PENSION EXCLUSION

New Jersey Division of Taxation
Attn: Office of Information and Publications
50 Barrack Street
P.O. Box 281
Trenton, NJ 08695-0281
(609) 292-6400
Toll-free: (800) 323-4400 (within selected states)
TTY: (800) 286-6613 (within selected states)
E-mail: taxation@tax.state.nj.us
Web: www.state.nj.us/treasury/taxation

Summary To exclude from taxation a portion of the retirement income of elderly and disabled residents of New Jersey.

Eligibility Residents of New Jersey who are permanently and totally disabled or aged 62 or older may exclude all or a portion of pension and annuity income from taxable income.

Financial data The annual exclusion is $17,500 for a married couple filing jointly, $8,750 for a married person filing separately, or $13,125 for a single individual, head of household, or qualifying widow(er).

Duration The exclusion continues as long as the person remains a New Jersey resident.

Number awarded Varies each year.

[895]
NEW JERSEY PROPERTY TAX DEDUCTION

New Jersey Division of Taxation
Attn: Office of Information and Publications
50 Barrack Street
P.O. Box 281
Trenton, NJ 08695-0281
(609) 292-6400
Toll-free: (800) 323-4400 (within selected states)
TTY: (800) 286-6613 (within selected states)
E-mail: taxation@tax.state.nj.us
Web: www.state.nj.us/treasury/taxation

Summary To exclude from income taxation a portion of the property taxes paid by residents of New Jersey.

Eligibility This deduction is available to residents of New Jersey whose income is greater than $20,000 (or $10,000 if single or married filing separately). It is also available to residents, regardless of income who are 1) blind, 2) permanently and totally disabled, or 3) aged 65 or older. Applicants must either own the home in which they reside or rent a dwelling with its own separate kitchen and bath facilities.

Financial data Qualified residents are entitled to deduct from their income (for state taxation purposes) 100% of their property taxes, to a maximum of $10,000. For renters, 18% of their rent is considered the equivalent of property taxes and may be deducted, to a maximum of $10,000.

Duration The deduction continues as long as the person remains a New Jersey resident.

Additional Information This program began in 1996. Taxpayers may not claim both the property tax deduction and the property tax credit; they may claim whichever is most beneficial, but only the deduction or the credit.

Number awarded Varies each year.

Deadline The deduction is claimed as part of the annual income tax return, due in April of each year.

[896]
NEW JERSEY PROPERTY TAX EXEMPTION FOR DISABLED VETERANS OR SURVIVING SPOUSES

New Jersey Division of Taxation
Attn: Office of Information and Publications
50 Barrack Street
P.O. Box 281
Trenton, NJ 08695-0281
(609) 292-6400
Toll-free: (800) 323-4400 (within selected states)
TTY: (800) 286-6613 (within selected states)
E-mail: taxation@tax.state.nj.us
Web: www.state.nj.us/treasury/taxation

Summary To provide a real estate tax exemption to New Jersey veterans with disabilities and certain surviving widow(er)s.

Eligibility This exemption is available to New Jersey residents who have been honorably discharged with active wartime service in the U.S. armed forces and have been certified by the U.S. Department of Veterans Affairs as totally and permanently disabled as a result of wartime service-connected conditions. Unremarried surviving spouses of eligible disabled veterans or of certain wartime servicepersons who died on active duty are also entitled to this exemption. Applicants must be the full owner of and a permanent resident in the dwelling house for which the exemption is claimed.

Financial data A 100% exemption from locally-levied real estate taxes is provided.

Duration 1 year; the exemption continues as long as the eligible veteran remains a resident of New Jersey.

Additional Information This program is administered by the local tax assessor or collector. Veterans who are denied exemptions have the right to appeal the decision to their county and state governments.

Number awarded Varies each year.

Deadline Applications may be submitted at any time.

[897]
NEW JERSEY PROPERTY TAX REIMBURSEMENT

New Jersey Division of Taxation
Attn: Office of Information and Publications
50 Barrack Street
P.O. Box 281
Trenton, NJ 08695-0281
(609) 292-6400
Toll-free: (800) 323-4400 (within selected states)
TTY: (800) 286-6613 (within selected states)
E-mail: taxation@tax.state.nj.us
Web: www.state.nj.us/treasury/taxation

Summary To reimburse residents of New Jersey who are disabled or elderly for the increase in property taxes due on their home.

Eligibility This reimbursement is available to residents of New Jersey who are either 1) 65 years of age or older, or 2) receiving federal Social Security disability benefits. Applicants must have lived in New Jersey continuously since before January 1, 1992 and have owned and lived in their home (or have leased a site in a mobile home park on which they have placed a manufactured or mobile home that they own) since before January 1, 1999. Their annual income must be below $39,475 if single or $48,404 if married. They must have paid the full amount of property taxes due on their home for the past 2 years.

Financial data Qualifying homeowners are entitled to reimbursement of all property taxes they have paid in excess of the base year (the first year in which they met all the eligibility requirements).

Duration The reimbursement is available as long as the person remains a New Jersey resident and meets eligibility requirements.

Number awarded Varies each year.

Deadline May of each year.

[898]
NEW MEXICO DISABLED VETERAN PROPERTY TAX EXEMPTION

New Mexico Department of Veterans' Services
P.O. Box 2324
Santa Fe, NM 87504-2324
(505) 827-6300 Fax: (505) 827-6372
E-mail: nmdvs@state.nm.us
Web: www.state.nm.us

Summary To exempt disabled veterans and their spouses from payment of property taxes in New Mexico.

Eligibility This exemption is available to veterans who are rated 100% service-connected disabled by the U.S. Department of Veterans Affairs, are residents of New Mexico, and own a primary residence in the state. Also eligible are qualifying veterans' unremarried surviving spouses, if they are New Mexico residents and continue to own the residence.

Financial data Veterans and surviving spouses are exempt from payment of property taxes in New Mexico.

Duration 1 year; continues until the qualifying veteran or spouse no longer live in the residence.

Number awarded Varies each year.

[899]
NEW YORK ALTERNATIVE PROPERTY TAX EXEMPTIONS FOR VETERANS

New York State Division of Veterans' Affairs
5 Empire State Plaza, Suite 2836
Albany, NY 12223-1551
(518) 474-6114
Toll-free: (888) VETS-NYS (within NY)
Fax: (518) 473-0379
E-mail: info@veterans.state.ny.us
Web: www.veterans.state.ny.us

Summary To provide wartime veterans and their spouses who are residents of New York with a partial exemption from property taxes.

Eligibility This program is open to veterans who served during the Spanish-American War, the Mexican Border Period, World War I, World War II, the Korean War, Vietnam, or the Persian Gulf Conflict, or who received the expeditionary medal for service in Lebanon, Grenada, or Panama. Applicants must have been discharged under honorable conditions; additional benefits are available to those who served in a combat zone and to those who have a service-connected disability. The legal title to the property must be in the name of the veteran or the spouse of the veteran or both, or the unremarried surviving spouse of the veteran. The property must be used exclusively for residential purposes. This program is only available in counties, cities, towns, and villages in New York that have opted to participate.

Financial data This program provides an exemption of 15% of the assessed valuation of the property, to a basic maximum of $12,000 per year; local governments may opt for a reduced maximum of $9,000 or $6,000, or for an increased maximum of $15,000, $18,000, $21,000, $24,000, or $27,000. For combat-zone veterans, an additional 10% of the assessed valuation is exempt, to a basic maximum of $8,000 per year; local governments may opt for a reduced maximum of $6,000 or $4,000, or for an increased maximum of $10,000, $12,000, $14,000, $16,000, or $18,000. For disabled veterans, the exemption is the percentage of assessed value equal to half of the service-connected disability rating, to a basic maximum of $40,000 per year; local governments may opt for a reduced maximum of $30,000 or $20,000, or for an increased maximum of $50,000, $60,000, $70,000, $80,000, or $90,000. At its option, New York City may use the following increased maximum exemptions: war veteran, $45,000; combat-zone veteran, $30,000; disabled veteran, $150,000.

Duration This exemption is available annually.

Number awarded Varies each year.

Deadline Applications must be filed with the local assessor by "taxable status date;" in most towns, that is the end of February.

[900]
NEW YORK STATE DISABILITY INCOME EXCLUSION

New York State Department of Taxation and Finance
W.A. Harriman Campus
Tax and Finance Building
Albany, NY 12227-0001
(518) 438-8581
Toll-free: (800) 225-5829 (within NY)
Web: www.nystax.gov

Summary To exclude disability pay from state income taxation in New York.

Eligibility Eligible are persons who are considered residents of New York for state income taxation purposes and who are receiving any form of disability retirement pay. Applicants must be permanently and totally disabled and not yet 65 years of age.

Financial data Eligible residents may exclude either their actual weekly disability pay or $100 per week ($5,200 per year), whichever is less. The amount of the exclusion is reduced by the amount that the applicant's federal adjusted gross income exceeds $15,000, so no exclusion is available if that exceeds $20,200 and 1 person could take the exclusion or $25,400 if both spouses could take the exclusions.

Duration The exclusion is provided as long as the recipient remains a resident of New York.

Number awarded Varies each year.

[901]
NORTH CAROLINA PROPERTY TAX RELIEF FOR DISABLED VETERANS

North Carolina Department of Revenue
Attn: Property Tax Division
501 North Wilmington Street
P.O. Box 25000
Raleigh, NC 27640-0640
(919) 733-7711
Web: www.dor.state.nc.us

Summary To provide property tax relief to disabled North Carolina veterans.

Eligibility Disabled veterans who are residents of North Carolina are eligible for these programs.

Financial data Any vehicle owned by a disabled veteran that is altered with special equipment to accommodate a service-connected disability is exempt from personal property taxes. In addition, disabled veterans who receive assistance from the U.S. Department of Veterans Affairs (VA) for the acquisition of specially adapted housing are eligible for an exemption on the first $38,000 in assessed value of the housing and land that is owned and used as a residence by the disabled veteran.

Duration The exemptions continue as long as the eligible veteran is a resident of North Carolina.

Number awarded Varies each year.

[902]
NORTH CAROLINA PROPERTY TAX RELIEF FOR ELDERLY AND PERMANENTLY DISABLED PERSONS

North Carolina Department of Revenue
Attn: Property Tax Division
501 North Wilmington Street
P.O. Box 25000
Raleigh, NC 27640-0640
(919) 733-7711
Web: www.dor.state.nc.us

Summary To provide property tax relief to elderly and disabled North Carolina residents.

Eligibility This program is open to residents of North Carolina who 1) are permanently and totally disabled or at least 65 years of age, and 2) have an income of less than $18,500. Applicants must own and occupy real property as their permanent residence.

Financial data Qualified owners are exempt from taxation on 50% of the appraised value of their property or $20,000, whichever is greater.

Duration The exemptions continue as long as the eligible property owner is a resident of North Carolina.

Number awarded Varies each year.

Deadline Applications must be submitted by May of each year.

DISABILITIES IN GENERAL: GRANTS-IN-AID

[903]
NORTH DAKOTA PROPERTY TAX CREDIT FOR SENIOR CITIZENS OR DISABLED PERSONS

Office of State Tax Commissioner
State Capitol Building
600 East Boulevard Avenue, Department 127
Bismarck, ND 58505-0599
(701) 328-2770 Toll-free: (800) 638-2901
Fax: (701) 328-3700 TTY: (800) 366-6888
E-mail: taxinfo@state.nd.us
Web: www.ndtaxdepartment.com

Summary To provide property tax credits for disabled or senior citizen residents of North Dakota.

Eligibility To qualify for this program, applicants must be residents of North Dakota and either totally and permanently disabled (regardless of age) or at least 65 years of age. For husbands and wives who are living together, only 1 can apply for the credit. Applicants must reside in the property for which the credit is claimed. Their income cannot exceed $14,000 and their aggregate assets cannot exceed $50,000 (excluding the first unencumbered $80,000 of market value of their homestead).

Financial data The credit provided ranges from 20% (up to $400) to 100% (up to $2,000) of the property's taxable value, depending upon the recipient's income.

Duration Once approved, the deduction continues as long as the recipient meets the qualification requirements.

Additional Information No person whose homestead is a farm structure exempt from taxation can qualify to receive this property tax credit.

Number awarded Varies each year.

Deadline Applications must be submitted in January of the year for which the property tax credit is requested.

[904]
NORTH DAKOTA PROPERTY TAX EXEMPTIONS FOR DISABLED VETERANS

Office of State Tax Commissioner
State Capitol Building
600 East Boulevard Avenue, Department 127
Bismarck, ND 58505-0599
(701) 328-2770 Toll-free: (800) 638-2901
Fax: (701) 328-3700 TTY: (800) 366-6888
E-mail: taxinfo@state.nd.us
Web: www.ndtaxdepartment.com

Summary To provide disabled North Dakota veterans and their spouses or widow(er)s with property tax exemptions.

Eligibility Veterans with disabilities who qualify for tax exemptions fall into 2 categories: 1) paraplegics, including those whose disability is not service-connected, regardless of income, and 2) honorably discharged veterans with more than a 50% service-connected disability whose income is less than $14,000. The property must be owned and occupied as a homestead according to state law. Spouses and unremarried widow(er)s are also eligible.

Financial data The maximum benefit may not exceed $3,600 taxable value, because a homestead is limited to $80,000 market value.

Duration 1 year; renewable as long as qualified individuals continue to reside in North Dakota and live in their homes.

Number awarded Varies each year.

Deadline Applications may be submitted to the county auditor at any time.

[905]
NURSES HOUSE FINANCIAL ASSISTANCE

Nurses House, Inc.
c/o Veronica M. Driscoll Center for Nursing
2113 Western Avenue, Suite 2
Guilderland, NY 12084-9559
(518) 456-7858 Fax: (518) 452-3760
E-mail: mail@NursesHouse.org
Web: www.NursesHouse.org

Summary To provide temporary financial assistance to nurses who are unable to meet current living expenses because of disability or other causes.

Eligibility Assistance is provided to registered nurses who need temporary financial assistance because of disability, illness, unemployment, or other causes. Applicants must need funding for rent or mortgage payments, food, utilities, telephone, health insurance, etc. Requests for assistance can be made by the nurse, a colleague, a friend, or other source.

Financial data The amount of assistance offered depends on need of the recipient.

Duration These are intended as short-term grants to tide the nurse over a temporary crisis or need.

Additional Information Nurses House was established in 1922 when Emily Bourne donated $300,000 to purchase a 10-acre estate on Long Island to serve as a rest home for nurses. In 1959, the property was sold and proceeds were invested to provide income for the services of Nurses House. The name has been retained and nurses receiving assistance are still called guests.

Number awarded Varies each year; recently, more than $100,000 is grants were awarded.

Deadline Applications may be submitted at any time.

[906]
OHIO EMERGENCY RELIEF AID

Governor's Office of Veterans' Affairs
77 South High Street, 30th Floor
Columbus, OH 43215-6117
(614) 644-0892   Fax: (614) 466-9354
Web: www.state.oh.us/gova

Summary To provide emergency aid to Ohio war veterans or their dependents who, because of disability or disaster, are in financial need.

Eligibility Eligible to apply for this aid are disabled and other veterans, their spouses, widow(er)s, children, or parents who require emergency financial relief because of sickness, accident, or destitution. The veteran must have served during World War I, World War II, the Korean conflict, or the Vietnam era. All applicants must be Ohio residents.

Financial data The amount granted varies, depending on the needs of the recipient.

Duration These are emergency funds only and are not designed to be a recurring source of income.

Additional Information These grants are made by the various county veterans services offices in Ohio.

Number awarded Varies each year.

Deadline Applications may be submitted at any time.

[907]
OHIO INCOME TAX DEDUCTION FOR DISABILITY BENEFITS

Ohio Department of Taxation
Attn: Income Tax Audit Division
30 East Broad Street
P.O. Box 182847
Columbus, OH 43218-2847
(614) 433-5817
Toll-free: (800) 282-1780 (within OH)
Fax: (614) 433-7771
Web: www.state.oh.us/tax

Summary To deduct disability benefits from state income taxation in Ohio.

Eligibility This deduction is available to residents of Ohio who are receiving benefits from an employee's disability plan paid as the result of a permanent physical or mental disability. Payments that otherwise qualify as retirement or pension benefits, temporary wage continuation plans, and payments for temporary illnesses or injuries do not qualify.

Financial data All payments for permanent disability are excluded from income for purposes of Ohio state taxation.

Duration The exclusion is available as long as the recipient resides in Ohio and receives eligible disability payments.

Number awarded Varies each year.

[908]
OKLAHOMA DISABILITY DEDUCTION

Oklahoma Tax Commission
Attn: Income Tax
2501 North Lincoln Boulevard
Oklahoma City, OK 73194-0009
(405) 521-3160
Toll-free: (800) 522-8165 (within OK)
Fax: (405) 522-0063
E-mail: otcmaster@oktax.state.ok.us
Web: www.oktax.state.ok.us

Summary To provide an income tax deduction to Oklahoma residents with disabilities who incur expenses for modifying facilities.

Eligibility This deduction is available to Oklahoma residents who have a physical disability that constitutes a substantial handicap to employment. Applicants must have incurred expenses to modify a motor vehicle, home, or work place necessary to compensate for the disability.

Financial data All expenses allowed by the Social Security Administration may be deducted from income for purposes of Oklahoma taxation.

Duration The deduction may be taken in any year when qualifying expenses are incurred.

Deadline Income tax returns must be filed by April of each year.

[909]
OKLAHOMA FINANCIAL ASSISTANCE PROGRAM

Oklahoma Department of Veterans Affairs
Veterans Memorial Building
2311 North Central Avenue
Oklahoma City, OK 73150
(405) 521-3684   Fax: (405) 521-6533
E-mail: scylmer@odva.state.ok.us
Web: www.odva.state.ok.us

Summary To provide emergency aid to Oklahoma veterans and their families who, because of disability or disaster, are in financial need.

Eligibility This program is open to veterans with at least 90 days of wartime service and an honorable discharge who are current residents of Oklahoma and have resided in Oklahoma for at least 1 year immediately preceding the date of application. Applicants must be seeking funds for rent or mortgage payments, food, and/or utilities as the result of a loss from a disaster such as flood, storm, or fire, or from an injury or illness that has interrupted the veteran's ability to work and caused him or her to become delinquent in the above payments. Widow(er)s and minor children may also qualify for the benefit.

Financial data The amount of the grant depends on the need of the recipient.

Duration The grant is available only on a 1-time basis.

DISABILITIES IN GENERAL: GRANTS-IN-AID

Additional Information No financial assistance will be granted when regular monetary benefits are being received from other state agencies. The funds cannot be used for old debts, car payments, or medical expenses.

Number awarded Varies each year.

Deadline Applications must be submitted to the local post or chapter of a veterans services organization for initial approval or disapproval. They may be submitted at any time during the year.

[910] OREGON PROPERTY TAX DEFERRAL FOR DISABLED AND SENIOR CITIZENS

Oregon Department of Revenue
Attn: Property Tax Division
Revenue Building
955 Center Street, N.E.
Salem, OR 97310-2551
(503) 378-4988
Toll-free: (800) 356-4222 (within OR)
TDD: (800) 886-7204 (within OR)
Web: www.dor.state.or.us

Summary To enable disabled and senior Oregon residents to defer payment of their property taxes.

Eligibility This program is open to residents of Oregon who are 1) determined to be eligible to receive or be receiving federal Society Security disability benefits due to disability or blindness, or 2) 62 years of age or older. Applicants must own a residence and have a total household income less than $32,500.

Financial data The state pays all taxes on the property to the county but places a lien on the property and charges 6% per year on the deferred taxes. The lien and interest become due and payable when the disabled person or senior citizen sells the property or changes its ownership, moves permanently from the property (unless for medical reasons), or dies.

Duration 1 year; the deferment is automatically renewed as long as the property owner lives in the residence.

Number awarded Varies each year.

Deadline Applications for new deferrals must be filed in the appropriate county assessor's office by April of each year.

[911] OREGON PROPERTY TAX EXEMPTION FOR VETERANS WITH DISABILITIES AND THEIR SPOUSES

Oregon Department of Revenue
Attn: Property Tax Division
Revenue Building
955 Center Street, N.E.
Salem, OR 97310-2551
(503) 378-4988
Toll-free: (800) 356-4222 (within OR)
TDD: (800) 886-7204 (within OR)
Web: www.dor.state.or.us

Summary To exempt disabled Oregon veterans and their spouses from a portion of their property taxes.

Eligibility Qualifying veterans are those who received a discharge or release under honorable conditions after service of either 1) 90 consecutive days during World War I, World War II, or the Korean conflict; or 2) 210 consecutive days after January 31, 1955. Eligible individuals must meet 1 of these conditions: 1) a war veteran who is officially certified by the U.S. Department of Veterans Affairs (VA) or any branch of the U.S. armed forces as having disabilities of 40% or more; 2) a war veteran who is certified each year by a licensed physician as being 40% or more disabled and has total gross income that is less than $8,778 with no dependents, $11,497 with 1 dependent, or an amount that increases by $1,496 for each additional dependent; or 3) a war veteran's surviving spouse who has not remarried, even if the veteran's spouse was not disabled or did not take advantage of the exemption if disabled. Recipients of this exemption must own and live on the property in Oregon.

Financial data The exemption is $9,860 of the homestead property's real market value.

Duration 1 year; may be renewed as long as the eligible veteran or surviving unremarried spouse owns and occupies the primary residence.

Number awarded Varies each year.

Deadline This exemption is not automatic. Applications must be submitted by March of each year.

[912] OREGON PROPERTY TAX EXEMPTION FOR VETERANS WITH SERVICE-CONNECTED DISABILITIES AND THEIR SPOUSES

Oregon Department of Revenue
Attn: Property Tax Division
Revenue Building
955 Center Street, N.E.
Salem, OR 97310-2551
(503) 378-4988
Toll-free: (800) 356-4222 (within OR)
TDD: (800) 886-7204 (within OR)
Web: www.dor.state.or.us

Summary To exempt disabled Oregon veterans and their spouses from a portion of their property taxes.

Eligibility Qualifying veterans are those who received a discharge or release under honorable conditions after service of either 1) 90 consecutive days during World War I, World War II, or the Korean conflict; or 2) 210 consecutive days after January 31, 1955. Eligible individuals must meet 1 of these conditions: 1) a war veteran who has been certified within the last 3 years by the U.S. Department of Veterans Affairs (VA) or any branch of the U.S. armed forces as having service-connected disabilities of 40% or more; or 2) a surviving spouse of a war veteran who died because of service-connected injury or illness or who received at least 1 year of this exemption. Recipients of this exemption must own and live on the property in Oregon.

Financial data The exemption is $13,130 of the homestead property's real market value.

Duration 1 year; may be renewed as long as the eligible veterans or surviving spouse owns and occupies the primary residence.

Number awarded Varies each year.

Deadline This exemption is not automatic. Applications must be submitted by March of each year.

[913]
OTTO SUSSMAN TRUST GRANTS

Otto Sussman Trust
P.O. Box 1374
Trainsmeadow Station
Flushing, NY 11370-9998

Summary To provide financial assistance to individuals residing in selected states who are suffering from illness.

Eligibility Eligible to apply are residents of New York, New Jersey, Oklahoma, or Pennsylvania who are experiencing financial need because of illness or death in the family. Applications are considered only if validated by and submitted through social service agencies or, if appropriate, the financial aid officer of a college or university.

Financial data The amount awarded varies, depending upon the needs of the recipient. The average grant is $2,500. Each year, more than $100,000 is distributed.

Duration This is a 1-time grant.

Number awarded Varies; generally, at least 40 each year.

Deadline Applications may be submitted at any time.

[914]
PENNSYLVANIA PROPERTY TAX AND RENT REBATE PROGRAM

Pennsylvania Department of Revenue
Attn: Property Tax or Rent Rebate Program
Department 280503
Harrisburg, PA 17128-0503
(717) 787-8201   Toll-free: (888) 222-9190
Fax: (717) 787-2391   TTY: (800) 447-3020
E-mail: parev@revenue.state.pa.us
Web: www.revenue.state.pa.us

Summary To provide a partial rebate of property taxes or rent paid by disabled and elderly residents of Pennsylvania.

Eligibility This rebate is available to Pennsylvania residents who are 1) permanently disabled, 18 years of age or older, and unable to work because of a medically determined physical or mental disability; 2) 65 years of age or older; or 3) a widow or widower and 50 years of age or older. Claimants must have total household income of $15,000 or less and either owned and occupied a home or rented and occupied a home, apartment, nursing home, boarding home, or similar residence in Pennsylvania.

Financial data Qualifying claimants are reimbursed up to $500 per year for the amount they paid in property taxes or rent.

Duration The rebate is paid annually.

Additional Information This program was established in 1971.

Number awarded Varies each year.

Deadline June of each year.

Duration The rebate is paid annually.

[915]
PENNSYLVANIA REAL ESTATE TAX EXEMPTION

Bureau for Veterans Affairs
Fort Indiantown Gap
Annville, PA 17003-5002
(717) 865-8907
Toll-free: (800) 54 PA VET (within PA)
Fax: (717) 865-8589   E-mail: jdavison@state.pa.us
Web: sites.state.pa.us

Summary To exempt Pennsylvania veterans with disabilities and their unremarried surviving spouses from all state real estate taxes.

Eligibility Eligible to apply for this exemption are honorably discharged veterans who are residents of Pennsylvania and who are blind, paraplegic, or 100% disabled from a service-connected disability sustained during wartime military service. The dwelling must be owned by the veteran solely or jointly with a spouse, and the need for the exemption must be determined by the State Veterans' Commission. Upon the death of the veteran,

the tax exemption passes on to the veteran's unremarried surviving spouse.

Financial data This program exempts the principal residence (and the land on which it stands) from all real estate taxes.

Duration The exemption continues as long as the eligible veteran or unremarried widow resides in Pennsylvania.

Number awarded Varies each year.

[916]
PENNSYLVANIA VETERANS EMERGENCY ASSISTANCE

Bureau for Veterans Affairs
Fort Indiantown Gap
Annville, PA 17003-5002
(717) 865-8905
Toll-free: (800) 54 PA VET (within PA)
Fax: (717) 865-8589   E-mail: jdavison@state.pa.us
Web: sites.state.pa.us

Summary To provide financial aid on an emergency and temporary basis to Pennsylvania veterans (or their dependents) who are disabled, sick, or without means.

Eligibility Eligible to apply for this assistance are honorably discharged veterans who served in the U.S. armed forces during wartime and are now disabled, sick, or in financial need. Widow(er)s or orphan children of recently deceased veterans are also eligible if the veteran would have qualified prior to death. Applicants must have been residents of Pennsylvania for 1 year prior to the date of application.

Financial data Financial aid for the necessities of life (food, dairy, shelter, fuel, and clothing) is provided; the amount varies, depending upon the needs of the recipient.

Duration Aid is provided on a temporary basis only, not to exceed 3 months in a 12-month period.

Number awarded Varies each year.

Deadline Applications may be submitted at any time, but the factors that caused the emergency must have occurred within 180 days prior to the application.

[917]
PHARMACEUTICAL ASSISTANCE TO THE AGED AND DISABLED (PAAD) PROGRAM

New Jersey Department of Health and Senior
   Services
Attn: PAAD, Lifeline and Special Benefit Programs
P.O. Box 715
Trenton, NJ 08625-0715
(609) 588-7048   Toll-free: (800) 792-9745
Fax: (609) 588-7122   TTY: (609) 588-7180
Web: www.state.nj.us

Summary To provide financial support to disabled and other residents of New Jersey who use prescription drugs.

Eligibility This program is open to residents of New Jersey who are either at least 18 years of age and receiving Social Security disability benefits or over 65 years of age. Applicants must need funds to purchase prescription drugs, insulin and insulin needles, certain diabetic testing materials, and syringes and needles for injectable medicines used for the treatment of multiple sclerosis. They must have an annual income of less than $20,437 if single or $25,058 if married.

Financial data Eligible residents are entitled to purchase drugs for $5 per prescription. The state of New Jersey collects any payments due to the beneficiary from any other assistance program, insurance, or retirement benefits that cover prescription drugs.

Duration Initial prescriptions are limited to a 34-day supply; subsequent refills are allowed for a 34-day supply or 100-unit doses, whichever is greater, if this amount is medically necessary and prescribed by a physician.

Number awarded Varies each year.

Deadline Applications may be submitted at any time.

[918]
PROFESSIONAL DEVELOPMENT ASSISTANCE FOR ARTISTS WITH DISABILITIES

Ohio Arts Council
Attn: Individual Artists Coordinator
727 East Main Street
Columbus, OH 43205-1796
(614) 466-2613   Fax: (614) 466-4494
TDD: (800) 750-0750
E-mail: ken.emerick@oac.state.oh.us
Web: www.oac.state.oh.us

Summary To provide funding to emerging Ohio artists with disabilities who are interested in engaging in professional development activities.

Eligibility Applicants must have been residents of Ohio for at least 1 year and must have exhibited, performed, or published work in the past 3 years. They may not be enrolled in a certificate- or degree-granting program. Artists with any type of disability are eligible, but preference is given to those with hearing, mobility, or visual impairments.

Financial data The grant is $500. Funds may be used for such purposes as matting and framing work for an exhibition; making slides, photos or videos; documenting artwork; hiring interpreters; or purchasing assistive devices or supplies.

Duration 1 year; applicants who are funded for 2 consecutive years must wait 1 year before they apply again.

Number awarded Only a few each year.

Deadline Applications may be submitted at any time; awards are made on a first-come, first-served basis.

[919]
RAILROAD RETIREMENT DISABILITY ANNUITY

Railroad Retirement Board
Attn: Office of Public Affairs
844 North Rush Street
Chicago, IL 60611-2092
(312) 751-4777   Fax: (312) 751-7154
Web: www.rrb.gov

Summary To provide an annuity to railroad workers with disabilities and their families.

Eligibility The Railroad Retirement Board provides annuities for 2 types of disabilities. Eligible for total disability are regular employees of companies covered by the Railroad Retirement Act (railroads engaged in interstate commerce and certain of their subsidiaries, railroad associations, and national railway labor organizations) who are totally disabled for all regular work and have at least 10 years of creditable railroad service; credit for a month of railroad service is given for every month in which an employee had some compensated service for at least 1 day, but the required 120 service months need not be consecutive. The other type of disability, occupational disability, is available to employees who have at least 20 years of service, or who are aged 60 or older and have at least 10 years of service, and are permanently disabled from their regular railroad occupation. Survivor benefits are available to widows, widowers, unmarried children, and, in certain cases, parents, remarried widow(er)s, grandchildren, and surviving divorced spouses. For widow(er)s of workers with disabilities, annuities are payable at the age of 60; widow(er)s who are permanently and totally disabled are eligible if they are between the ages of 50 and 59 and the disability began within 7 years after the employee's death; widow(er)s of any age are eligible if they are caring for a child of the deceased employee under the age of 18 or a child with a disability of any age who became disabled before age 22. Unmarried children (or grandchildren if both parents are deceased) are eligible for survivor benefits if they are under the age of 18, or still enrolled full time in an elementary or secondary school, or disabled if they became totally and permanently disabled before age 22. Parents over the age of 60 who were dependent on the employee for at least half of the parent's support also qualify for survivor benefits. Surviving divorced spouses qualify if they were married to the employee for at least 10 years and are 60 or older (50 or older if disabled), or if they are still caring for a child of the employee under the age of 16 or disabled. Remarried widow(er)s retain eligibility if they remarry after age 60 (after age 50 if disabled).

Financial data Benefits are based on months of service and earnings credits. Recently, the average monthly annuity paid to employees over 65 years of age with disabilities was $1,410, for those under 65 years of age with disabilities it was $1,884, for spouses and divorced spouses it was $595, for disabled widows and widowers it was $976, for widowed mothers and fathers it was $1,261, for remarried widows and widowers it was $646, for divorced widows and widowers it was $646, and for children it was $742.

Duration Disability annuities are paid until the employee dies or recovers from the disability; survivor annuities are paid until death or, in the case of able-bodied children, until age 18 or graduation from high school.

Additional Information Employees who are disabled from their regular railroad occupation may work in another job and earn up to $400 per month or $4,800 per year without loss of any railroad retirement disability benefits. A 5-month waiting period beginning with the month after the month of the onset of disability is required before disability annuity payments can begin.

Number awarded Varies each year; recently, the number of employees over 65 years of age with disabilities receiving benefits was 36,100, under 65 years of age with disabilities was 46,200, and disabled widows and widowers was 5,236.

[920]
SALLIE MAE 911 EDUCATION FUND LOAN RELIEF PROGRAM

Sallie Mae 911 Education Fund
c/o The Community Foundation for the National Capital Region
Attn: Kenny Emson
1201 15th Street, N.W., Suite 420
Washington, DC 20005-2842
(202) 955-5890   Toll-free: (800) 441-4043
Web: www.salliemae.com

Summary To enable spouses, same-sex partners, and co-borrowers of those killed or totally and permanently disabled in the terrorist attacks of September 11, 2001 to pay off the student loans that are owned or serviced by Sallie Mae.

Eligibility The following individuals are eligible for this program: 1) spouses of those killed or declared totally and permanently disabled in the terrorist attacks of September 11, 2001 who are the borrowers on a) an eligible student loan owned or serviced by Sallie Mae; or b) a Sallie Mae spousal consolidated FFELP student loan; 2) same-sex partners of those killed or declared totally and permanently disabled in the attacks who are the borrowers on an eligible student loan owned or serviced by Sallie Mae; 3) co-borrowers of those killed or declared totally and permanently disabled in the attacks who are the borrowers on an eligible student loan owned or serviced by Sallie Mae; 4) individuals who were totally and permanently disabled in the terrorist attacks and hold a private education student loan owned or serviced by Sallie Mae; and 5) estate administrators or similar individuals who were killed in the attack and who held a private education student loan owned or serviced by Sallie Mae.

Financial data This fund will pay off the student loans of eligible applicants that are owned or serviced by Sallie Mae.

Duration All eligible applicants will receive a check for the amount of their eligible student loan owned or serviced by Sallie Mae from the Community Foundation for the National Capital Region within approximately 60 days from the date the application was received.

Additional Information Individuals who either lost their lives or were totally and permanently disabled in the terrorist attacks and held Sallie Mae FFELP student loans will have their loans discharged in the FFELP program and therefore are not included in this loan relief program.

Deadline Applications for loan relief may be submitted at any time.

[921]
SENIOR GOLD PRESCRIPTION DISCOUNT PROGRAM

New Jersey Department of Health and Senior Services
Attn: Senior Gold Prescription Discount Program
P.O. Box 724
Trenton, NJ 08625-0724
(609) 588-7048   Toll-free: (800) 792-9745
Fax: (609) 588-7122   TTY: (609) 588-7180
Web: www.state.nj.us

Summary To provide financial support to elderly and disabled residents of New Jersey who use prescription drugs.

Eligibility This program is open to residents of New Jersey who are either at least 65 years of age or receiving Social Security Title II disability benefits. Applicants must need funds to purchase prescription drugs, insulin, insulin supplies, or diabetic testing materials. They must have an annual income between $20,437 and $30,437 if single or between $25,058 and $35,058 if married.

Financial data Eligible residents are entitled to purchase drugs for $15 plus 50% of the remaining cost of the prescription. After they have paid annual out-of-pocket expenses of $2,000 if single or $3,000 if married, they need only make the $15 copayment.

Duration Initial prescriptions are limited to a 34-day supply; subsequent refills are allowed for a 34-day supply or 100-unit doses, whichever is greater, if this amount is medically necessary and prescribed by a physician.

Number awarded Varies each year.

Deadline Applications may be submitted at any time.

[922]
SINGERS' ASSISTANCE

Society of Singers
6500 Wilshire Boulevard, Suite 640
Los Angeles, CA 90048
(323) 653-7672   Toll-free: (866) 767-7671
Fax: (323) 653-7675   E-mail: help@singers.org
Web: www.singers.org/pages/assist.htm

Summary To provide assistance to professional singers who are facing medical or other crises.

Eligibility This program is open to professional singers who have derived their primary income from singing for 5 years or more. Applicants must have financial needs resulting from medical, personal, or family crises. They must submit 5 years of career documentation, copies of bills for which help is needed, diagnosis letter and treatment plan from primary physicians or dentists with costs estimates or bills, and documentation of financial need.

Financial data Grants are paid directly to creditors to provide for such needs as rent, utilities, medical and/or dental expenses, substance abuse rehabilitation, psychotherapy, or HIV/AIDS treatment. Support is not provided for credit card debts, tax debts, loans, voice lessons, demos, head-shots, or other music projects.

Duration These are 1-time grants.

Number awarded Varies each year.

Deadline Applications may be submitted at any time.

[923]
SOCIAL SECURITY DISABILITY INSURANCE (SSDI) BENEFITS

Social Security Administration
6401 Security Boulevard
Baltimore, MD 21235-0001
(410) 594-1234   Toll-free: (800) 772-1213
TTY: (800) 325-0778
Web: www.ssa.gov

Summary To provide monthly benefits to workers and their families if the worker becomes disabled or blind.

Eligibility This program defines disabled people as those who are unable to do any kind of work for which they are suited and whose disability has lasted or is expected to last for at least a year or to result in death. Blind people qualify if their vision cannot be corrected to better than 20/200 in their better eye or if their visual field is 20 degrees or less, even with corrective lens. Family members who are eligible include 1) unmarried children, including adopted children and, in some cases, stepchildren and grandchildren who are under 18 years of age (19 if still in high school full time); 2) unmarried children, over 18 years of age, if they have a disability that started before age 22; and 3) spouses who are 62 years of age or older, or of any age if caring for a child of the disabled worker who is under 16 years of age or disabled. For deceased workers, disabled widow(er)s 50 years of age or older are also eligible. Applicants must

also have worked long enough and recently enough under Social Security in order to qualify. Workers who become disabled before the age of 24 need 6 credits in the 3-year period ending when the disability begins; workers who become disabled between the ages of 24 and 31 must have credit for having worked half the time between the age of 21 and the date of disability; workers 31 years of age or older at the time of disability must have earned as many total credits as needed for retirement (from 20 credits if disabled at age 31 through 42 to 40 credits if disabled at age 62 or older) and must have earned at least 20 of the credits in the 10 years immediately before becoming disabled. An exception applies to blind workers who need no recent credit but may have earned the required credit any time after 1936.

Financial data The amount of the monthly benefit depends on several factors, including the worker's age at the time of disability, the number of dependents, and the amount of earnings on which Social Security taxes have been paid. Recently, the average monthly benefit for disabled workers was $839; for spouses of disabled workers it was $214; and for children of disabled workers it was $246.

Duration For a disabled or blind person, whether a worker, widow, widower, surviving divorced spouse, or person over the age of 18 who became disabled before the age of 22, monthly benefits continue until the person is no longer disabled or dies. For a dependent spouse, benefits are paid until the worker is no longer disabled or dies. For a dependent child, the benefits continue until the child marries or reaches the age of 18 (19 if still enrolled as a full-time high school student).

Additional Information Disabled workers may test their ability to return to work for a trial work period of up to 9 months, during which time they receive full SSDI benefits. At the end of that period, a decision is made as to whether or not they are able to engage in substantial gainful activity. Persons who find that they cannot continue substantial gainful employment continue to receive SSDI benefits without interruption. Persons who can engage in substantial gainful activity receive benefits for an additional 3 months after which payments cease. Several factors are considered to determine if the person can engage in substantial gainful employment, but the most important is income.

Number awarded Varies; recently, approximately 5.7 million persons were receiving SSDI monthly benefits. Annual benefits paid were approximately $4.8 billion. Another 1.7 million dependents (including 150,000 spouses and 1,550,000 children) were receiving $400 million in annual benefits.

[924]
SOUTH CAROLINA DISABLED VETERANS PROPERTY TAX EXEMPTION

South Carolina Department of Revenue
Attn: Property Division
301 Gervais Street
P.O. Box 125
Columbia, SC 29214
(803) 898-5480   Fax: (803) 898-5822
Web: www.sctax.org

Summary To exempt the residence of disabled South Carolina veterans, their unremarried widow(er)s, and others from property taxation.

Eligibility Eligible for this exemption are veterans in South Carolina who are 100% permanently and totally disabled from service-connected causes. The exemption is also available to unremarried widow(er)s of 1) disabled veterans who have died; 2) servicemembers killed in the line of duty; and 3) law enforcement officers killed in the line of duty. Surviving spouses must have owned the lot and dwelling house in fee or for life, or jointly with the spouse. They remain eligible if they dispose of the exempt dwelling and acquire another residence in South Carolina for use as a residence with a value no greater than 150% of the fair market value of the exempt dwelling, but no subsequent house of a surviving spouse is eligible for exemption.

Financial data The exemption applies to all taxes on 1 house and a lot (not to exceed 1 acre).

Duration The exemption extends as long as the veteran resides in the house, or as long as the spouse of a deceased veteran, servicemember, or law enforcement officer remains unremarried and resides in the original house or a single new dwelling.

Number awarded Varies each year.

Deadline Applications may be submitted at any time.

[925]
SOUTH CAROLINA HOMESTEAD EXEMPTION PROGRAM

South Carolina Comptroller General
Attn: Local Government Division
305 Wade Hampton Office Building
P.O. Box 11228
Columbia, SC 29211
(803) 734-2121   Fax: (803) 734-2064
E-mail: cgoffice@cg.state.sc.us
Web: www.cg.state.sc.us

Summary To establish a homestead exemption for South Carolina residents who are elderly, disabled, or blind, and their widow(er)s.

Eligibility Legal residents of South Carolina who own a house or mobile home are eligible for this exemption if they are aged 65 or older, totally and permanently disabled, or legally blind. Spouses of deceased persons who were eligible also qualify to receive the exemption

if they were at least 50 years of age when their spouse died.

Financial data The first $50,000 of the fair market value of the qualified applicant's home is exempted from property taxes. The exemption is from county, municipal, school, and special assessment real estate property taxes.

Duration The exemption continues as long as the homeowners live in their primary residence in South Carolina.

Additional Information This program is administered by county auditors.

Number awarded Varies each year.

Deadline Persons applying for this exemption for the first time must do so prior to July of each year; subsequently, no re-application is necessary unless the title or use of the property changes.

[926]
SOUTH CAROLINA PERMANENT DISABILITY RETIREMENT INCOME TAX EXCLUSION

South Carolina Department of Revenue
301 Gervais Street
P.O. Box 125
Columbia, SC 29214
(803) 898-5000   Toll-free: (800) 763-1295
Fax: (803) 898-5822
Web: www.sctax.org

Summary To exempt the retirement income received by people with total and permanent disabilities from state taxation in South Carolina.

Eligibility This exemption is available to residents of South Carolina who are permanently and totally disabled and who are also unable to be gainfully employed. People who are receiving disability income from 1 job but are able to perform another job are not eligible for this exclusion.

Financial data Qualified permanent disability retirement income is exempt from state income taxation in South Carolina.

Duration The exemption continues as long as the recipient resides in South Carolina and receives the specified disability retirement income.

Number awarded Varies each year.

[927]
SOUTH CAROLINA TAX EXEMPTION FOR COMPENSATION, PENSION, DISABILITY RETIREMENT PAY, AND VETERANS ADMINISTRATION PAYMENTS

South Carolina Office of Veterans Affairs
1205 Pendleton Street, Room 477
Columbia, SC 29201-3789
(803) 734-0200   Fax: (803) 734-0197
E-mail: va@govoepp.state.sc.us
Web: www.govoepp.state.sc.us/vetaff.htm

Summary To exempt from taxes the income received by veterans in South Carolina from certain sources.

Eligibility Eligible for this exemption are veterans in South Carolina who are receiving pension, compensation, or disability retirement pay from the armed forces, or educational assistance or other benefits from the U.S. Department of Veterans Affairs.

Financial data Income received by eligible veterans is not subject to state taxation.

Duration The exemption continues as long as the eligible veteran resides in South Carolina and receives the specified income.

Number awarded Varies each year.

Deadline Applications may be submitted at any time.

[928]
SOUTH DAKOTA PROPERTY TAX REFUND FOR SENIOR CITIZENS AND CITIZENS WITH DISABILITIES

South Dakota Department of Revenue
Attn: Tax Refund Office
445 East Capitol Avenue
Pierre, SD 57501-3100
(605) 773-3311   Toll-free: (800) 829-9188
Fax: (605) 773-5129
Web: www.state.sd.us

Summary To provide a partial refund of property taxes to elderly and disabled residents (including disabled veterans) and their surviving spouses in South Dakota.

Eligibility This program is open to residents of South Dakota who either have a qualified disability or are 65 years of age or older. Applicants must live alone and have a yearly income of less than $9,750 or live in a household whose members' combined income is less than $12,750. They must have owned the house in which they are now living for at least 3 years or, if they have owned the house for fewer than 3 years, have been residents of South Dakota for 5 years or longer. Veterans must have a disability of 60% or greater. Other people with disabilities must have been qualified to receive Social Security disability benefits or Supplemental Security Income disability benefits. Widows and widowers are eligible even if they do not meet the requirements as long as their spouse received a property tax refund in the year before death and the widow or widower has

continued to live in the same house and has remained unmarried.

Financial data Qualified residents are entitled to a refund of a portion of the property taxes they paid during the preceding calendar year.

Duration Residents of South Dakota are entitled to this refund annually.

Additional Information This program has been in effect since 1974. South Dakotans are not entitled to both a sales tax refund and a property tax refund in the same year. The state will calculate both refunds and pay the amount that is greater.

Number awarded Varies each year.

Deadline June of each year.

[929]
SOUTH DAKOTA SALES TAX REFUND FOR SENIOR CITIZENS AND CITIZENS WITH DISABILITIES

South Dakota Department of Revenue
Attn: Tax Refund Office
445 East Capitol Avenue
Pierre, SD 57501-3100
(605) 773-3311   Toll-free: (800) 829-9188
Fax: (605) 773-5129
Web: www.state.sd.us

Summary To provide a partial refund of sales taxes to elderly and disabled residents (including disabled veterans) in South Dakota.

Eligibility This program is open to residents of South Dakota who either have a qualified disability or are 65 years of age or older. Applicants must live alone and have a yearly income of less than $9,750 or live in a household whose members' combined income is less than $12,750. Veterans must have a disability of 60% or greater. Other people with disabilities must have been qualified to receive Social Security disability benefits or Supplemental Security Income disability benefits.

Financial data Qualified residents are entitled to a refund of a portion of the sales taxes they paid during the preceding calendar year.

Duration Residents of South Dakota are entitled to this refund annually.

Additional Information This program has been in effect since 1974. South Dakotans are not entitled to both a sales tax refund and a property tax refund in the same year. The state will calculate both refunds and pay the amount that is greater.

Number awarded Varies each year.

Deadline June of each year.

[930]
SUPPLEMENTAL AND EMERGENCY GRANT PROGRAM FOR INDIVIDUALS

Able Trust
Attn: Grant Proposal
106 East College Avenue, Suite 820
Tallahassee, FL 32301
(850) 224-4493
Toll-free: (888) 838-ABLE (within FL)
Fax: (850) 224-4496   TDD: (850) 224-4493
E-mail: info@abletrust.org
Web: www.abletrust.org

Summary To provide emergency and other financial assistance related to employment to Florida citizens with disabilities.

Eligibility Individual applicants must be Florida residents who have a documented disability recognized under the Americans with Disabilities Act (or be a legal guardian applying on behalf of such an individual). Proposals are considered for emergency situations or as a supplement to an individual plan developed by an agency of the state of Florida. These proposals must be for assistance that cannot be provided by the state and that relate to the immediate employment of the applicant. An emergency situation is defined as 1 in which the individual applicant "will incur the loss of an opportunity to secure or maintain employment if assistance cannot be provided within 60 days." Proposals are not accepted if they include funds for salaries or expenses already provided for; request the purchase of a vehicle; request the purchase of computer equipment for individuals without a direct employment outcome; include requests for an individual's tuition costs if federal and/or state financial aid is available; include requests for fellowships, scholarships, or travel grants; or include a request for the purchase of real property or building improvements.

Financial data The maximum grant is $10,000 per year; the average ranges from $2,000 to $3,000 for equipment purchase or an on-the-job accommodation.

Duration 1 year; recipients may reapply.

Additional Information The Able Trust also makes grants to Florida not-for-profit agencies serving citizens with disabilities in the state. It is also designated as the Florida Governor's Alliance for the Employment of Citizens with Disabilities. Not more than 1 proposal from the same individual will be considered at any 1 time.

Number awarded Varies each year. Recently, 14 individuals received grants from this agency.

Deadline Proposals may be submitted at any time.

DISABILITIES IN GENERAL: GRANTS-IN-AID

[931]
SUPPLEMENTAL SECURITY INCOME (SSI)

Social Security Administration
6401 Security Boulevard
Baltimore, MD 21235-0001
(410) 594-1234   Toll-free: (800) 772-1213
TTY: (800) 325-0778
Web: www.ssa.gov

Summary To provide monthly payments to disabled, blind, and elderly people who have limited income and resources.

Eligibility A person 18 years of age or older is considered disabled if a physical or mental impairment prevents him or her from doing any substantial gainful work and is expected to last for at least 12 months or to result in death. Children under the age of 18 are considered disabled if they have a physical or mental impairment that is comparable in severity to a disability that would prevent an adult from working and is expected to last at least 12 months or result in death. Children with certain conditions are automatically disabled and eligible for these benefits; the conditions include HIV infection, blindness, deafness, cerebral palsy, Down syndrome, muscular dystrophy, significant mental deficiency, diabetes (with amputation of 1 foot), amputation of 2 limbs, or amputation of leg at the hip. Regardless of age, a person whose vision is no better than 20/200 or who has a limited visual field of 20 degrees or less with the best corrective eyeglasses is considered blind; individuals with visual impairments not severe enough to meet the definition of blindness still may qualify as disabled persons. People over the age of 65 are also eligible. All applicants must be United States citizens, nationals, or permanent residents with limited resources (less than $2,000 for an individual or $3,000 for a couple); items excluded from resources include the home used as a principal place of residence, personal and household goods, life insurance with face value of $1,500 or less, a car, burial plots for individuals and immediate family members, and burial funds up to $1,500. Eligible earned income generally must be less than $800 a month. Unearned income (as from other welfare benefits, pensions, rent, or annuities) may not exceed $572 per month for single people or $840 per month for couples.

Financial data The basic monthly payment is $552 for an eligible individual or $829 for an eligible individual with an eligible spouse. Many states add money to that basic payment. SSI recipients may also be eligible for food stamps and other nutrition programs.

Duration Assistance is provided as long as the recipient remains blind or disabled and in financial need.

Additional Information Although SSI is administered through the Social Security Administration, it is not financed by Social Security taxes. Financing of SSI is provided through general funds of the U.S. Treasury. Recipients of SSI need not have been employed or paid Social Security taxes, but they may be eligible for both SSI and Social Security. Disabled and blind applicants for SSI are referred to their state vocational rehabilitation agency to determine their eligibility for a program of vocational rehabilitation. Disabled drug addicts or alcoholics are referred for appropriate treatment if it is available at an approved facility or institution.

Number awarded Recently, the number of SSI blind and disabled recipients was approximately 5,650,000. Another 941,000 children under 18 years of age were also receiving benefits.

[932]
TENNESSEE PROPERTY TAX RELIEF FOR DISABLED AND ELDERLY HOMEOWNERS

Tennessee Comptroller of the Treasury
Attn: Property Tax Relief Program
James K. Polk State Office Building
505 Deaderick Street, Room 1600
Nashville, TN 37243-0278
(615) 747-8871   Fax: (615) 532-3866
Web: www.comptroller.state.tn.us/pa/patxreld.htm

Summary To provide property tax relief for elderly and disabled home owners in Tennessee.

Eligibility This exemption is offered to residents of Tennessee who own and live in their home and are either 1) 65 years of age or older, or 2) totally and permanently disabled as rated by the Social Security Administration. To qualify, the combined income of all owners of the property cannot exceed $12,210.

Financial data The amount of the relief depends on the property assessment and the tax rate in the city or county where the beneficiary lives.

Duration 1 year; may be renewed as long as the qualified Tennessee resident owns and occupies the primary residence.

Number awarded Varies each year.

[933]
TENNESSEE PROPERTY TAX RELIEF FOR DISABLED VETERANS AND THEIR SPOUSES

Tennessee Comptroller of the Treasury
Attn: Property Tax Relief Program
James K. Polk State Office Building
505 Deaderick Street, Room 1600
Nashville, TN 37243-0278
(615) 747-8871   Fax: (615) 532-3866
E-mail: Kim.Darden@state.tn.us
Web: www.comptroller.state.tn.us/pa/patxrvet.htm

Summary To provide property tax relief for veterans with disabilities and their spouses in Tennessee.

Eligibility This exemption is offered to veterans or their surviving unremarried spouses who are residents of Tennessee and own and live in their home in the state. The veteran must have served in the U.S. armed forces and 1) have acquired, as a result of such service, a disability from paraplegia, or permanent paralysis of both legs and lower part of the body resulting from traumatic

injury, or disease to the spinal cord or brain, or from total blindness, or from loss or loss of use of both legs or arms from any service-connected cause; 2) have been rated by the U.S. Department of Veterans Affairs (VA) as 100% permanently disabled as a result of service as a prisoner of war for at least 5 months; or 3) have been rated by the VA as 100% permanently and totally disabled from any other service-connected combat-related cause. Veterans who experience total blindness are also eligible. The relief does not extend to any person who was dishonorably discharged from any of the armed services.

Financial data The amount of the relief depends on the property assessment and the tax rate in the city or county where the beneficiary lives.

Duration 1 year; may be renewed as long as the eligible veteran or surviving unremarried spouse owns and occupies the primary residence.

Number awarded Varies each year.

[934]
TEXAS PROPERTY TAX EXEMPTION FOR DISABLED VETERANS AND THEIR FAMILIES

Texas Veterans Commission
P.O. Box 12277
Austin, TX 78711-2277
(512) 463-5538   Fax: (512) 475-2395
E-mail: info@tvc.state.tx.us
Web: www.tvc.state.tx.us

Summary To extend property tax exemptions on the appraised value of their property to disabled and other Texas veterans and their surviving family members.

Eligibility Eligible veterans must be Texas residents rated at least 10% service-connected disabled. Surviving spouses and children of eligible veterans are also covered by this program.

Financial data For veterans in Texas whose disability is rated as 10 through 30%, the first $5,000 of the appraised property value is exempt from taxation; veterans rated as 31 through 50% disabled are exempt from the first $7,500 of appraised value; those with a 51 through 70% disability are exempt from the first $10,000 of appraised value; the exemption applies to the first $12,000 of appraised value for veterans with disabilities rated as 71% or more. A veteran whose disability is 10% or more and who is 65 years or older is entitled to exemption of the first $12,000 of appraised property value. A veteran whose disability consists of the loss of use of 1 or more limbs, total blindness in 1 or both eyes, or paraplegia is exempt from the first $12,000 of the appraised value. The unremarried surviving spouse of a deceased veteran who, at the time of death had a compensable disability and was entitled to an exemption, is entitled to the same exemption. The surviving spouse of a person who died on active duty is entitled to exemption of the first $5,000 of appraised value of the spouse's property. A surviving child of a person who dies on active duty is entitled to exemption of the first $5,000 of appraised value of the child's property as long as the child is unmarried and under 21 years of age.

Duration 1 year; may be renewed as long as the eligible veteran (or unremarried surviving spouse or child) owns and occupies the primary residence in Texas.

Additional Information This program is administered at the local level by the various taxing authorities.

Number awarded Varies each year.

Deadline April of each year.

[935]
UTAH PROPERTY TAX EXEMPTION FOR DISABLED VETERANS

Utah Office of Veterans Affairs
Attn: Director
550 Foothill Boulevard, Room 206
Salt Lake City, UT 84108
(801) 326-2372
Toll-free: (800) 894-9497 (within UT)
Fax: (801) 326-2369   E-mail: tschow@utah.gov
Web: www.ut.ngb.army.mil/veterans/exempt.htm

Summary To exempt a portion of the property of disabled veterans and their families in Utah from taxation.

Eligibility This program is available to residents of Utah who are disabled veterans or their unremarried widow(er)s or minor orphans. The disability must be at least 10% and incurred as the result of injuries in the line of duty.

Financial data The exemption is equivalent to the disability rating of the veteran.

Duration This benefit is available as long as the disabled veteran or family members reside in Utah.

Deadline Tax exemption applications must be filed with the county government of residence by August of each year.

[936]
VERMONT PROPERTY TAX EXEMPTION FOR DISABLED VETERANS

Office of Veterans Affairs
118 State Street
Drawer 20
Montpelier, VT 05620-4401
(802) 828-3379   Toll-free: (888) 666-9844
Fax: (802) 828-5932
E-mail: llefevre@va.state.vt.us
Web: www.va.state.vt.us

Summary To exempt disabled Vermont veterans and their dependents from the payment of at least a portion of the state's property tax.

Eligibility Entitled to a property tax exemption are veterans of any war (or their spouses, widow(er)s, or children) who are receiving wartime disability compensation for at least a 50% disability, wartime death compensa-

tion, wartime dependence and indemnity compensation, or pension for disability paid through any military department or the Department of Veterans Affairs. Unremarried widow(er)s of previously qualified veterans are also entitled to the exemption whether or not they are receiving government compensation or a pension.

Financial data Up to $10,000 of the assessed value of real and personal property belonging to eligible veterans or their unremarried widow(er)s is exempt from taxation; individual towns may increase the exemption to as much as $20,000.

Duration 1 year; may be renewed as long as the eligible veteran or widow(er) continues to be the owner/occupant of the residence and lives in Vermont.

Additional Information Only 1 exemption may be allowed on a property.

Number awarded Varies each year.

Deadline April of each year.

[937]
VETERANS DISABILITY COMPENSATION

Department of Veterans Affairs
810 Vermont Avenue, N.W.
Washington, DC 20420
(202) 418-4343   Toll-free: (800) 827-1000
Web: www.va.gov

Summary To provide monthly compensation to veterans who have a disability that occurred or was made worse during military service.

Eligibility Disabled persons who are eligible for compensation under this program are those whose disability resulted from injury or disease incurred or aggravated during active service in the U.S. armed forces in the line of duty during wartime or peacetime service. They must have been discharged or separated under other than dishonorable conditions.

Financial data Disabled veterans who are found to be eligible for disability compensation are entitled to monthly payments, depending on the degree of disability as determined by the Department of Veterans Affairs. Recent rates are: 10% disability, $104 per month; 20%, $201; 30%, $310; 40%, $445; 50%, $633; 60%, $801; 70%, $1,008; 80%, $1,171; 90%, $1,317; 100%, $2,193. Veterans whose service-connected disabilities are rated at 30% or more are entitled to additional allowances for dependents; the additional amount is determined according to the number of dependents and the degree of disability and ranges from $37 to $125 for a spouse and from $19 to $64 for each additional child. In lieu of the additional compensation payable to a veteran with a spouse, a veteran whose disability is rated at 30% or more and who is in need of the aid and attendance of another person may receive an additional amount.

Duration Compensation continues as long as the veteran remains disabled.

Additional Information In addition to monthly compensation under this program, disabled veterans may also be entitled to prosthetic appliances if they are receiving treatment in a facility under the direct jurisdiction of the Department of Veterans Affairs (VA), or outpatient care under certain specified conditions. Blind veterans are eligible for various aids and services, including adjustment to blindness training, home improvements and structural alterations, low vision aids and training in their use, guide dogs, and material for the blind from the Library of Congress. Former prisoners of war who were incarcerated for at least 30 days are entitled to a presumption of service connection for disabilities resulting from certain diseases if manifested to a degree of 10% at any time after active service. Persian Gulf veterans who suffer from chronic disabilities resulting from undiagnosed illnesses may receive disability compensation. VA rating boards determine the degree of disability of each veteran, based on an estimate of the extent to which certain disabilities reduce the typical veteran's ability to earn a living. If a veteran has 2 or more disabilities, the rating board will determine a combined rating and base compensation on that figure.

Number awarded Varies each year.

Deadline Applications are accepted at any time.

[938]
VOCATIONAL REHABILITATION FOR DISABLED VETERANS

Department of Veterans Affairs
810 Vermont Avenue, N.W.
Washington, DC 20420
(202) 418-4343   Toll-free: (800) 827-1000
Web: www.va.gov

Summary To provide vocational rehabilitation to certain categories of veterans with disabilities.

Eligibility This program is open to veterans who have a service-connected disability of at least 10% and a serious employment handicap or 20% and an employment handicap. They must have been discharged or released from military service under other than dishonorable conditions. The Department of Veterans Affairs (VA) must determine that they would benefit from a training program that would help them prepare for, find, and keep suitable employment. The program may be 1) institutional training at a certificate, 2-year college, 4-year college or university, or technical program; 2) unpaid on-the-job training in a federal, state, or local agency or a federally-recognized Indian tribal agency, training in a home, vocational course in a rehabilitation facility or sheltered workshop, independent instruction, or institutional non-farm cooperative; or 3) paid training through a farm cooperative, apprenticeship, on-the-job training, or on-the-job non-farm cooperative.

Financial data While in training and for 2 months after, eligible disabled veterans may receive subsistence allowances in addition to their disability compensation

or retirement pay. For institutional training, the full-time monthly rate is $454.96 with no dependents, $564.34 with 1 dependent, $665.03 with 2 dependents, and $48.48 for each additional dependent; the three-quarter time monthly rate is $341.85 for no dependents, $423.87 with 1 dependent, $497.21 with 2 dependents, and $37.28 for each additional dependent; the half-time monthly rate is $228.74 for no dependents, $283.41 with 1 dependent, $333.13 with 2 dependents, and $24.87 for each additional dependent. For unpaid on-the-job training, the monthly rate is $454.96 for no dependents, $564.34 with 1 dependent, $665.03 with 2 dependents, and $48.48 for each additional dependent. For paid training, the monthly rate is based on the wage received, to a maximum of $397.79 for no dependents, $481.05 with 1 dependent, $554.39 with 2 dependents, and $36.06 for each additional dependent. The VA also pays the costs of tuition, books, fees, supplies, and equipment; it may also pay for special supportive services, such as tutorial assistance, prosthetic devices, lipreading training, and signing for the deaf. If during training or employment services the veteran's disabilities cause transportation expenses that would not be incurred by nondisabled persons, the VA will pay for at least a portion of those expenses. If the veteran encounters financial difficulty during training, the VA may provide an advance against future benefit payments.

Duration Up to 48 months of full-time training or its equivalent in part-time training. If a veteran with a serious disability receives services under an extended evaluation to improve training potential, the total of the extended evaluation and the training phases of the rehabilitation program may exceed 48 months. Usually, the veteran must complete a rehabilitation program within 12 years from the date of notification of entitlement to compensation by the VA. Following completion of the training portion of a rehabilitation program, a veteran may receive counseling and job search and adjustment services for 18 months.

Additional Information The program may also provide employment assistance, self-employment assistance, training in a rehabilitation facility, or college and other training. Veterans who are seriously disabled may receive services and assistance to improve their ability to live more independently in their community. After completion of the training phase, the VA will assist the veteran to find and hold a suitable job.

Number awarded Varies each year.

Deadline Applications are accepted at any time.

[939]
WEST VIRGINIA HOMESTEAD EXEMPTION

West Virginia State Tax Department
Attn: Taxpayer Services Division
P.O. Box 3784
Charleston, WV 25337-3784
(304) 558-3333
Toll-free: (800) 982-8297 (within WV)
Fax: (304) 558-3269   TDD: (800) 282-9833
Web: www.state.wv.us/taxdiv

Summary To provide a partial exemption of property taxes on residences owned by disabled or elderly persons and retired veterans in West Virginia.

Eligibility Eligible for this exemption are single-family residences owned and occupied by any person who is permanently and totally disabled or at least 65 years old. Applicants must have been West Virginia residents for 2 consecutive calendar years prior to the tax year to which the exemption relates. Members of the U.S. military forces who maintain West Virginia as their state of residence throughout military service and return to the state to purchase a homestead upon retirement or separation from the military because of permanent and total disability are considered to meet the residency requirement and also qualify for this exemption.

Financial data The exemption applies to the first $20,000 of the total assessed value of eligible property.

Duration The exemption continues as long as the eligible property is owned and occupied by the qualifying person in West Virginia.

Number awarded Varies each year.

Deadline Individuals with disabilities apply for this exemption during July, August, or September of any year. Once they have filed for the exemption, they do not need to refile in subsequent years if they sign a statement that they will notify the assessor within 30 days if they cease to be eligible for the exemption on the basis of disability.

Additional Information Applications for this program are submitted to the office of the county assessor in each West Virginia county.

[940]
WEST VIRGINIA SENIOR CITIZEN OR DISABILITY INCOME TAX DEDUCTION

West Virginia State Tax Department
Attn: Taxpayer Services Division
P.O. Box 3784
Charleston, WV 25337-3784
(304) 558-3333
Toll-free: (800) 982-8297 (within WV)
Fax: (304) 558-3269   TDD: (800) 282-9833
Web: www.state.wv.us/taxdiv

Summary To provide income tax exemptions for West Virginia residents with disabilities and their surviving spouses.

Eligibility Residents of West Virginia who are totally and permanently disabled (or 65 years of age or older) are eligible for this income tax exemption. Surviving spouses of eligible residents are also entitled to the exemption.

Financial data Up to $8,000 of income is exempt from taxation.

Duration The exemption continues as long as the eligible resident (or his/her spouse) remains a resident of West Virginia.

[941] WISCONSIN DISABILITY INCOME EXCLUSION

Wisconsin Department of Revenue
Attn: Division of Income, Sales and Excise Tax
P.O. Box 8933
Madison, WI 53708-8933
(608) 266-1911   Fax: (608) 261-6240
Web: www.dor.state.wi.us

Summary To exclude from state income taxation a portion of the disability income received by residents of Wisconsin.

Eligibility This exclusion is available to residents of Wisconsin who are younger than 65 years of age but who are retired on permanent and total disability.

Financial data Up to $5,200 per year may be excluded from income for purposes of state taxation.

Duration The exclusion is available as long as the recipient resides in Wisconsin.

Number awarded Varies each year.

[942] WISCONSIN VETERANS' SUBSISTENCE AID GRANTS

Wisconsin Department of Veterans Affairs
30 West Mifflin Street
P.O. Box 7843
Madison, WI 53707-7843
(608) 266-1311   Toll-free: (800) WIS-VETS
Fax: (608) 267-0403
E-mail: wdvaweb@dva.state.wi.us
Web: dva.state.wi.us/Ben_subsistencegrants.asp

Summary To provide temporary, emergency financial aid to disabled and other Wisconsin veterans or their dependents.

Eligibility This program is open to veterans (must have served on active duty for at least 2 consecutive years or for at least 90 days during specified wartime periods) who are current residents of Wisconsin and were also residents of Wisconsin either at the time of entry into service or for 5 consecutive years after completing service on active duty. Unremarried widow(er)s and minor or dependent children are also eligible if the deceased veteran's spouse or parent would have been eligible if still living, and if the surviving dependent is also a Wisconsin resident. Applicants must have suffered a loss of income because of illness, disability, or death and be seeking temporary, emergency financial aid.

Financial data The grant equals the amount of lost income or whatever is necessary to pay basic subsistence costs, whichever is less. Basic subsistence costs include essentials such as food, rent or mortgage payments, utilities, and basic transportation costs, although in some cases health insurance premiums, child support payments, property taxes, homeowners insurance, prescribed medications, and other items are covered. In cases of natural disaster, aid may be given to replace such essential items as clothing, food, and utensils.

Duration Assistance is provided on a temporary basis only, up to a maximum of 3 months of subsistence aid within a 12-month period. If the disability or other factor causing loss of income continues beyond that time, the applicant must rely on help from the permanent programs sponsored by the U.S. Department of Veterans Affairs, Social Security, or other agencies.

Additional Information The grant does not normally cover credit card, car, or other debt payments, life insurance premiums, car repairs, long distance phone calls, or religious or entertainment expenses.

Number awarded Varies each year.

Deadline Applications may be submitted at any time.

Awards

[943] CHRISTOPHER REEVE ACTING SCHOLARSHIP

California Governor's Committee on Employment of
  People with Disabilities
Attn: Media Access Office
4640 Lankershim Boulevard, Suite 305
North Hollywood, CA 91602
(818) 752-1196   Fax: (818) 753-3426
TTY: (818) 753-3427
E-mail: gcastane@edd.ca.gov
Web: www.disabilityemployment.org

Summary To recognize and reward adult actors with disabilities in California who are interested in developing their skills.

Eligibility This competition is open to residents of California who are actors/actresses 18 years of age and older with a disability. Applicants must submit a headshot, 250-word bio, and letter of intent (up to 250 words) on what they will do with the scholarship if they win. They must prepare a scene (with a partner of their choice) from 3 to 5 minutes in length.

Financial data The award is $5,000.

Duration The competition is held annually.
Additional Information This program began in 1997. Scenes are presented at a public performance in Hollywood.
Number awarded 1 each year.
Deadline September of each year.

[944]
DISNEY YOUNG PERFORMER'S SCHOLARSHIP

California Governor's Committee on Employment of
   People with Disabilities
Attn: Media Access Office
4640 Lankershim Boulevard, Suite 305
North Hollywood, CA 91602
(818) 752-1196   Fax: (818) 753-3426
TTY: (818) 753-3427
E-mail: gcastane@edd.ca.gov
Web: www.disabilityemployment.org

Summary To recognize and reward young actors with disabilities in California who are interested in developing their skills.
Eligibility This competition is open to residents of California who are actors/actresses younger than 18 years of age with a disability. Applicants must submit a headshot, 250-word bio, and letter of intent (up to 250 words) on what they will do with the award if they win. They must prepare a scene (with a partner of their choice) from 1 to 3 minutes in length.
Financial data The award is $1,000.
Duration The competition is held annually.
Additional Information Scenes are presented at a public performance in Hollywood.
Number awarded 1 each year.
Deadline September of each year.

[945]
INTERNATIONAL ART SHOW BY ARTISTS WITH DISABILITIES

Sister Kenny Rehabilitation Institute
c/o Abbott Northwestern Hospital
800 East 28th Street
Minneapolis, MN 55407-3799
(612) 863-4463
E-mail: Kathleen.Schultz@allina.com
Web: www.allina.com

Summary To recognize and reward the creative talents of artists with disabilities.
Eligibility Any artist with a physical or mental impairment that substantially limits 1 or more major life activities (such as caring for oneself, performing manual tasks, walking, seeing, hearing, breathing, learning, or working) is eligible. All forms of art may be entered, but works are judged in 6 categories: 1) watercolor, 2) oils and acrylics, 3) graphic (including printmaking, charcoal, ink, computer design, pastels, and colored pencil), 4) sculpture (including relief, ceramics, woodcarving, metal, clay, and stone), 5) photography. (including black and white and color), and 6) mixed media. All work must be original and have been created within the past 5 years. Works that are heavier than 20 pounds or that exceed 36 inches in any direction are not accepted. Entries are limited to 2 works per artist. Previous show submissions may not be reentered.
Financial data In each category, first prize is $100, second prize is $75, third prize is $50, and honorable mention is $25. The work chosen as "Best of Show" receives a $500 cash award. Other prizes and encouragement awards are also presented. Recently, more than $8,000 in prizes was awarded.
Duration The competition is held annually.
Additional Information The show is sponsored by the Abbott Northwestern Sister Kenny Auxiliary and Sister Kenny Rehabilitation Institute (a division of Abbott Northwestern Hospital). Entrants may designate their artwork for sale or not for sale. The auxiliary retains 25% of the selling price of each artwork sold to help defray the expenses of the show.
Number awarded At least 25 cash prizes are awarded each year: 1 "Best of Show" and 4 in each of the 6 categories.
Deadline Artwork may be sent at any time but must be received before the end of March. The show runs from late April through late May.

[946]
JOYCE WALSH JUNIOR DISABILITY AWARD

National Federation of Music Clubs
1336 North Delaware Street
Indianapolis, IN 46202-2481
(317) 638-4003   Fax: (317) 638-0503
E-mail: info@nfmc-music.org
Web: www.nfmc-music.org

Summary To provide financial assistance to young instrumentalists and vocalists with disabilities who are members of the National Federation of Music Clubs (NFMC).
Eligibility This program is open to disabled musicians (instrumentalists or vocalists) who are between 12 and 19 years of age, U.S. citizens, and junior members of the federation. Applicants must submit a cassette tape, up to 10 minutes in length, of their performance of 2 selections from contrasting style periods.
Financial data The awards are $2,500 for first place and $1,500 for second place. In addition, awards of $500 are given to the winner in each of the 4 NFMC regions. All awards must be used for musical study.
Duration The awards are presented annually.
Additional Information These awards are funded by the T-Shirt Project Endowment. Applications and further information are also available from Mrs. B.E. Walsh, 905

Dial Drive, Kennett, MO 63857-2015, (573) 888-3347; information on all federation scholarships and awards is also available from Chair, Competitions and Awards Board, Mrs. Lamoine M. Hall, Jr., 4137 Whitfield Avenue, Fort Worth, TX 76109-5432. There is a $2 entry fee.

Number awarded 14 each year.

Deadline January of each year.

[947]
LIFE PRESIDENTIAL UNSUNG HERO AWARD

Leaders in Furthering Education
6274 Linton Boulevard, Suite 103
Delray Beach, FL 33484
(561) 865-0955   Fax: (561) 865-0938
E-mail: life@life-edu.org
Web: www.life-edu.org/unsung.html

Summary To recognize and reward outstanding disabled veterans.

Eligibility This award seeks to honor "an outstanding veteran who has demonstrated heroic efforts in surmounting disability and whose contribution to the community serves as an inspiration to others."

Financial data The award is $50,000.

Duration The award is presented annually.

Additional Information This award was first presented in 1997.

Number awarded 1 each year.

[948]
NATIONAL BASS CHAMPIONSHIP FOR THE PHYSICALLY CHALLENGED

Turning P.O.I.N.T.
403 Pacific Avenue
Terrell, TX 75160
(972) 524-4231   Fax: (972) 551-4231
E-mail: pointntl@aol.com
Web: www.turningpointtexas.org

Summary To recognize and reward outstanding fishing skills among persons with disabilities.

Eligibility Any individual with a disability (from the United States or abroad) interested in fishing is eligible to compete in either of 2 categories: children under the age of 18 and adults.

Financial data In the adult category, the prize is a Honda 4-wheeler motorcycle worth $4,000. In the children's category, the prize is a $2,000 wheelchair. Some smaller prizes are also awarded.

Duration The competition is held annually.

Additional Information The location of the contest changes annually. The competition has been held annually since 1985. Currently, about 200 participate in the competition. There is a $100 entry fee.

Number awarded At least 10 prizes are awarded each year.

Deadline The competition is generally held in April or May.

[949]
NORMAN G. BROOKS STAND-UP COMEDY COMPETITION SCHOLARSHIP

California Governor's Committee on Employment of People with Disabilities
Attn: Media Access Office
4640 Lankershim Boulevard, Suite 305
North Hollywood, CA 91602
(818) 752-1196   Fax: (818) 753-3426
TTY: (818) 753-3427
E-mail: gcastane@edd.ca.gov
Web: www.disabilityemployment.org

Summary To recognize and reward comedians with disabilities in California who are interested in developing their skills.

Eligibility This competition is open to residents of California who are comedians with a disability. Applicants must submit a head-shot, bio, and letter of intent (up to 200 words) on how they plan to use the award to further their comedic career. They must prepare and present a 3-minute stand-up routine. Celebrity judges select the winner.

Financial data The award is $1,500.

Duration The competition is held annually.

Additional Information This program began in 2000. Routines are presented at a public performance in Hollywood.

Number awarded 1 each year.

Deadline June of each year.

[950]
PANASONIC YOUNG SOLOISTS AWARD

VSA Arts
Attn: Education Office
1300 Connecticut Avenue, N.W., Suite 700
Washington, DC 20036
(202) 628-2800   Toll-free: (800) 933-8721
Fax: (202) 737-0725   TTY: (202) 737-0645
E-mail: soloists@vsarts.org
Web: www.vsarts.org

Summary To provide recognition and financial assistance to performing musicians who are physically or mentally challenged.

Eligibility Contestants must be vocalists or instrumentalists under 25 years of age who have a disability and are interested in pursuing personal or professional studies in music. They are required to submit an audition tape and a 1-page biography that describes why they should be selected to receive this award. Tapes are evaluated on the basis of technique, tone, intonation, rhythm, and interpretation.

Financial data The winners receive up to $2,500 for the purpose of broadening their musical experience or training and a $500 award.
Duration The competition is held annually.
Additional Information Applications must first be submitted to the respective state organization of Very Special Arts (VSA). Funding for these awards is provided by Panasonic Consumer Electronics Company. This program did not operate in 2004 because of the International VSA Arts Festival in June of that year. It will resume in 2005.
Number awarded 2 each year.
Deadline October of each year.

[951]
PAUL G. HEARNE/AAPD LEADERSHIP AWARDS
American Association of People with Disabilities
1629 H Street, N.W., Suite 503
Washington, DC 20006
(202) 457-0046   Toll-free: (800) 840-8844
Fax: (202) 457-0473   TTY: (202) 457-0046
E-mail: aapd@aol.com
Web: www.aapd-dc.org

Summary To recognize and reward people with disabilities who provide outstanding leadership in their communities.
Eligibility These awards are presented to emerging leaders with disabilities who demonstrate outstanding leadership while having a positive impact on the community of people with disabilities. Applicants must submit a 700-word essay on the most serious barriers for people with disabilities and how they have addressed those barriers in pursuing their leadership goals.
Financial data The award is $10,000. Funds are intended to enable recipients to continue their leadership activities.
Duration The awards are presented annually.
Additional Information This program, established in 1999, is sponsored by the American Association of People with Disabilities (AAPD) and funded by the Milbank Foundation for Rehabilitation, Mitsubishi Electric America Foundation, Bodman Foundation, Seth Sprague Educational and Charitable Foundation, and other businesses and individuals. Recipients are paired with a nationally-recognized leader in the disability community who supports them through mentoring.
Number awarded Up to 3 each year.
Deadline September of each year.

[952]
PAVESNP LIFE/WORK CHALLENGE AWARDS
Pennsylvania Association of Vocational Education Special Needs Personnel
c/o Vocational Education Services in Pennsylvania
Penn State McKeesport
4000 University Drive
101 Ostermayer
McKeesport, PA 15132
(412) 675-9065
Web: www.pavesnp.org

Summary To recognize and reward outstanding vocational education students in Pennsylvania who have special needs.
Eligibility Nominations for these awards may be submitted by professionals or paraprofessionals who are members of the Pennsylvania Association of Vocational Education Special Needs Personnel (PAVESNP). Nominees must be enrolled in an approved career and technical program in the current or previous school year and be receiving services from a special needs program (disabled, disadvantaged, or limited-English proficient). They must demonstrate evidence of a personal commitment to maximizing individual potential, social skills that enhance employability, strong personal work ethic, and occupational competence.
Financial data Awards are $500 for first place, $300 for second, and $100 for third.
Duration Awards are presented annually.
Additional Information Information is also available from Marjorie Eckman, Pittsburgh Public Schools, 1398 Page Street, Pittsburgh, PA 15233.
Number awarded 3 each year.
Deadline February of each year.

[953]
PIKE PRIZE
Boston University School of Law
Attn: Pike Institute on Law and Disability
765 Commonwealth Avenue
Boston, MA 02215
(617) 353-2904   Fax: (617) 353-2906
TTY: (617) 353-2904   E-mail: pikeinst@bu.edu
Web: www.bu.edu/law/pike/prize.html

Summary To recognize and reward outstanding persons with disabilities and other individuals and organizations concerned with disability law.
Eligibility Only nominations are accepted. Eligible to be nominated for this prize are individuals with disabilities whose accomplishments have been especially noteworthy. Also eligible are 1) agencies, institutions, associations, programs, and organizations that have made an especially noteworthy contribution to promoting a greater understanding of disability law; and 2) persons without a disability whose accomplishments in promot-

ing a greater understanding of disability law have been especially noteworthy.

Financial data The successful nominee receives a sizeable monetary award and a trip to Boston to accept the prize.

Duration The prize is awarded annually.

Additional Information This prize is named for N. Neal Pike, who was blind since childhood, graduated from the Boston University School of Law in 1937, has practiced law in Massachusetts for more than 50 years, and established the N. Neal Pike Institute on Law and Disability in 1983 for further study, research, development, teaching, and advocacy of disability law.

Number awarded 1 each year.

Deadline August of each year.

[954]
PLAYWRIGHT DISCOVERY AWARD

VSA Arts
Attn: Education Office
1300 Connecticut Avenue, N.W., Suite 700
Washington, DC 20036
(202) 628-2800   Toll-free: (800) 933-8721
Fax: (202) 737-0725   TTY: (202) 737-0645
E-mail: playwright@vsarts.org
Web: www.vsarts.org

Summary To recognize and reward young playwrights who submit scripts that deal with disabilities.

Eligibility This program is open to U.S. citizens and permanent residents in grades 6-12 who submit an original, unproduced, and unpublished script for a 1-act play (less than 40 pages in length) that addresses the issue of disability. Applicants are not required to have a disability, but their script must examine how disability affects their lives and the lives of others. They may write from their own experience or about an experience in the life of another person or fictional character. Plays are intended for an audience of middle through high school students and adults and must be appropriate in language and subject matter for that age group.

Financial data Awardees receive a cash award of $1,000, a trip to Washington, D.C. to attend the award presentation and see a professional production or staged reading of their play at the John F. Kennedy Center for the Performing Arts, a mentoring luncheon with distinguished members of the selection committee, and press opportunities.

Duration The competition is held annually.

Additional Information The sponsor, VSA Arts, was formerly known as Very Special Arts.

Number awarded 2 each year.

Deadline April of each year.

[955]
RICARDO MONTALBAN/NOSOTROS ACTING SCHOLARSHIP

California Governor's Committee on Employment of People with Disabilities
Attn: Media Access Office
4640 Lankershim Boulevard, Suite 305
North Hollywood, CA 91602
(818) 752-1196   Fax: (818) 753-3426
TTY: (818) 753-3427
E-mail: gcastane@edd.ca.gov
Web: www.disabilityemployment.org

Summary To recognize and reward adult actors with disabilities in California who are interested in developing their skills.

Eligibility This competition is open to residents of California who are actors/actresses 18 years of age and older with a disability. Applicants must submit a headshot, 250-word bio, and letter of intent (up to 250 words) on what they will do with the award if they win. They must prepare a scene (with a partner of their choice) from 3 to 5 minutes in length.

Financial data The award is $2,000.

Duration The competition is held annually.

Additional Information Scenes are presented at a public performance in Hollywood.

Number awarded 1 each year.

Deadline September of each year.

[956]
VIVIAN MENEES NELSON MUSIC AWARD FOR THE DISABLED AND VISUALLY IMPAIRED

National Federation of Music Clubs
1336 North Delaware Street
Indianapolis, IN 46202-2481
(317) 638-4003   Fax: (317) 638-0503
E-mail: info@nfmc-music.org
Web: www.nfmc-music.org

Summary To recognize and reward disabled or blind instrumentalists and vocalists who are members of the National Federation of Music Clubs.

Eligibility Applicants must be between 25 and 34 years of age, U.S. citizens, members of the federation, and disabled or visually impaired. Applications must include a letter of recommendation from a teacher, an affidavit from a medical doctor stating the nature of the applicant's disability, and a 15-minute tape recording (no disc or stereo accepted) performed or sung by the applicant.

Financial data The award is $1,000.

Duration The award is presented annually.

Additional Information Applications and further information are also available from Mrs. Wendell Heiny, 300 South Clinton Street, Denver, CO 80231, (303) 340-2960; information on all federation scholarships and

awards is available from Chair, Competitions and Awards Board, Mrs. Lamoine M. Hall, Jr., 4137 Whitfield Avenue, Fort Worth, TX 76109-5432. There is a $5 entry fee.

Number awarded 1 each year.
Deadline January of each year.

Families of the Disabled

- *Scholarships*
- *Fellowships/Grants*
- *Loans*
- *Grants-in-Aid*
- *Awards*

Described here are 235 programs open to the children, stepchildren, adopted children, grandchildren, parents, siblings, or other dependents or family members of the disabled. Of these, 120 entries cover scholarships (to pursue studies or research on the undergraduate level in the United States); 18 cover fellowships/grants (to pursue graduate or postdoctoral study or research in the United States); 6 cover loans (to provide money that must eventually be repaid, with or without interest); 90 cover grants-in-aids (to support emergency situations, travel, income/property tax liabilities, or the acquisition of assistive technology); and 1 covers awards, competitions, prizes, and honoraria (to recognize or support creative work and public service). If you are looking for a particular program and don't find it in this chapter, be sure to check the Program Title Index to see if it is covered elsewhere in the directory.

Scholarships

[957]
AIMR 11 SEPTEMBER MEMORIAL SCHOLARSHIP FUND

Association for Investment Management and Research
Attn: Research Foundation of AIMR
560 Ray C. Hunt Drive
P.O. Box 3668
Charlottesville, VA 22903-0668
(434) 951-5391   Toll-free: (800) 247-8132
Fax: (434) 951-5370
E-mail: 11septemberfund@aimr.org
Web: www.aimr.org

Summary To provide financial assistance for college study in fields related to business to disabled victims of the September 11, 2001 terrorist attack and the family members of victims.
Eligibility This program is open to 1) victims of the September 11, 2001 terrorist attacks who are permanently disabled, and 2) children, spouses, and domestic partners of persons who died or were permanently disabled as a direct result of the attacks. Applicants must be planning undergraduate or vocational school study of finance, economics, accounting, or business ethics at an accredited institution. They may come from any country and may study at any qualifying college or university in the world. Selection is based on financial need, academic record, and demonstrated commitment to high levels of professional ethics.
Financial data The stipend is $5,000 per year.
Duration 1 year; may be renewed up to 4 additional years.
Additional Information This program is administered by Scholarship Management Services of Scholarship America, 1505 Riverview Road, P.O. Box 297, St. Peter, MN 56082, (507) 931-1682, (800) 537-4180, Fax: (507) 931-9168, E-mail: smsinfo@csfa.org.
Number awarded Varies each year.
Deadline May of each year.

[958]
AIR LINE PILOTS ASSOCIATION SCHOLARSHIP PROGRAM

Air Line Pilots Association
Attn: Jan Redden
1625 Massachusetts Avenue, N.W.
Washington, DC 20036
(202) 797-4059   E-mail: ReddenJ@alpa.org
Web: www.alpa.org

Summary To provide financial assistance for college to the children of disabled or deceased members of the Air Line Pilots Association.
Eligibility Sons and daughters of medically retired, disabled, or deceased members of the Air Line Pilots Association are eligible to apply. Although the program envisions selection of students enrolling as college freshman, eligible individuals who are already enrolled in college may also apply. Selection is based on a number of factors, including academic record and financial need.
Financial data The stipend is $3,000 per year.
Duration 1 year; may be renewed up to 3 additional years, if the student maintains a GPA of 3.0 or higher.
Number awarded Each year the association grants 1 new award and continues 3 previously-made awards.
Deadline March of each year.

[959]
ALABAMA G.I. DEPENDENTS' SCHOLARSHIP PROGRAM

Alabama Department of Veterans Affairs
770 Washington Avenue, Suite 530
P.O. Box 1509
Montgomery, AL 36102-1509
(334) 242-5077   Fax: (334) 242-5102
E-mail: wmoore@va.state.al.us
Web: www.va.state.al.us/scholarship.htm

Summary To provide educational benefits to the dependents of disabled, deceased, and other Alabama veterans.
Eligibility Eligible are spouses, children, stepchildren, and unremarried widow(er)s of veterans who served honorably for 90 days or more and 1) are currently rated as 20% or more service-connected disabled or were so rated at time of death; 2) were a former prisoner of war; 3) have been declared missing in action; 4) died as the result of a service-connected disability; or 5) died while on active military duty in the line of duty. The veteran must have been a permanent civilian resident of Alabama for at least 1 year prior to entering active military service; veterans who were not Alabama residents at the time of entering active military service may also qualify if they have a 100% disability and were permanent residents of Alabama for at least 5 years prior to filing the application for this program or prior to death, if deceased. Children and stepchildren must be under the age of 26, but spouses and unremarried widow(er)s may be of any age.
Financial data Eligible dependents may attend any Alabama institution of higher learning or enroll in a prescribed course of study at any Alabama state-supported trade school without payment of any tuition, book fees, or laboratory charges.
Duration This is an entitlement program for 4 years of full-time undergraduate or graduate study or part-time equivalent. Spouses and unremarried widow(er)s whose veteran spouse is rated between 20 and 90% disabled,

or 100% disabled but not permanently so, may attend only 2 standard academic years.

Additional Information Benefits for children, spouses, and unremarried widow(er)s are available in addition to federal government benefits. Assistance is not provided for noncredit courses, placement testing, GED preparation, continuing educational courses, pre-technical courses, or state board examinations.

Number awarded Varies each year.

Deadline Applications may be submitted at any time.

[960]
ALABAMA SCHOLARSHIPS FOR DEPENDENTS OF BLIND PARENTS

Alabama Department of Rehabilitation Services
Attn: Don Sims, Rehabilitation Specialist
2129 East South Boulevard
Montgomery, AL 36116-2455
(334) 613-2248
Web: www.rehab.state.al.us

Summary To provide financial assistance for college to students whose blind parents are residents of Alabama.

Eligibility Eligible to apply are seniors or recent graduates of Alabama high schools whose family head of household is blind and whose annual family income is limited (less than $9,000 for a family with 1 child, $12,000 with 2 children, $15,000 with 3 children, or $18,000 with 4 or more children). Applicants must 1) have been permanent residents of Alabama for at least 5 years, 2) apply within 2 years after graduation from high school, and 3) be under 23 years of age.

Financial data Eligible students receive free tuition, waiver of fees, and necessary textbooks at any Alabama state-supported postsecondary institution.

Duration Up to 36 months at an institution of higher education, or for the period required to complete a course of study at a trade school.

Additional Information Recipients must complete their course of study within 5 years (unless interrupted by military service), but at least prior to the age of 30.

Number awarded Varies each year.

[961]
ARKANSAS LAW ENFORCEMENT OFFICERS' DEPENDENTS' SCHOLARSHIPS

Arkansas Department of Higher Education
Attn: Financial Aid Division
114 East Capitol Avenue
Little Rock, AR 72201-3818
(501) 371-2050   Toll-free: (800) 54-STUDY
Fax: (501) 371-2001
E-mail: finaid@adhe.arknet.edu
Web: www.arscholarships.com

Summary To provide financial assistance for undergraduate education to the dependents of deceased or disabled Arkansas law enforcement officers, fire fighters, or other designated public employees.

Eligibility This program is open to the spouses and/or children (natural, adopted, or step) of Arkansas residents who were killed or permanently disabled in the line of duty as law enforcement officers, municipal police officers, sheriffs and deputy sheriffs, constables, state correction employees, game wardens, state park employees who are commissioned law enforcement officers or emergency response employees, full-time or volunteer fire fighters, state forestry employees engaged in fighting forest fires, certain Arkansas Highway and Transportation Department employees, and public school teachers. Children must be less than 23 years of age. Spouses may not have remarried. All applicants must have been Arkansas residents for at least 6 months.

Financial data The scholarship covers tuition, on-campus room charges, and fees (but not books, school supplies, food, materials, or dues for extracurricular activities) at any state-supported college or university in Arkansas.

Duration Up to 8 semesters, as long as the student is pursuing a baccalaureate or associate degree.

Number awarded Varies each year.

Deadline July of each year for fall term, November of each year for spring or winter term, April of each year for first summer session, or June of each year for second summer session.

[962]
ASSISTANCE FOR SURVIVING CHILDREN OF NAVAL PERSONNEL DECEASED AFTER RETIREMENT (CDR)

Navy-Marine Corps Relief Society
Attn: Education Division
4015 Wilson Boulevard, Tenth Floor
Arlington, VA 22203
(703) 696-4960   Fax: (703) 696-0144
E-mail: education@hq.nmcrs.org
Web: www.nmcrs.org/education.html

Summary To provide financial assistance for college to the children of Navy or Marine Corps personnel who died as a result of disabilities or length of service.

Eligibility Eligible for this assistance are the unmarried, dependent children, stepchildren, or legally adopted children under the age of 23 of members of the Navy or Marine Corps who died after retirement due to disability or length of service.

Financial data Grants up to $2,000 per year are available.

Additional Information This program is limited to undergraduate studies and vocational training.

Number awarded Varies each year.

Deadline February of each year.

[963]
BEACON BRIGHTER TOMORROWS SCHOLARSHIP

Rhode Island Foundation
Attn: Scholarship Coordinator
One Union Station
Providence, RI 02903
(401) 274-4564   Fax: (401) 331-8085
E-mail: libbym@rifoundation.org
Web: www.rifoundation.org

Summary To provide financial assistance for college to spouses and dependents of workers insured by Beacon Mutual Insurance Company who were killed or permanently disabled in industrial accidents.

Eligibility This program is open to spouses and/or legal dependents of workers insured by the company who were killed or permanently disabled in an industrial accident. Applicants must have been accepted into an accredited postsecondary institution on a full- or part-time basis. The must submit an essay (up to 300 words) on what they hope they will be doing in their professional life 10 years from now. Financial need is considered in the selection process.

Financial data Stipends range from $1,000 to $2,000.

Number awarded 1 to 2 each year.

Deadline May of each year.

[964]
BILL MCADAM SCHOLARSHIP FUND

Hemophilia Foundation of Michigan
c/o Cathy McAdam
22226 Doxtator
Dearborn, MI 48128
(313) 563-0515   Fax: (313) 563-1412
E-mail: mcmcadam@comcast.net

Summary To provide financial assistance for college to students with a bleeding disorder or members of their families.

Eligibility This program is open to 1) students with a hereditary bleeding disorder (hemophilia, von Willebrand, etc.) or 2) members of their families (spouse, partner, child, sibling). Applicants must be U.S. citizens and enrolled or planning to enroll at an accredited 2- or 4-year college, trade or technical school, or other certification program. Along with their application, they must submit 2 letters of recommendation and 3 essays: 1) their short- and long-term goals and who or what influenced the shaping of their goals; 2) how the emerging disability culture impacts the bleeding disorder community; and 3) the definition of peace.

Financial data The stipend is $2,000.

Duration 1 year.

Number awarded 1 each year.

Deadline May of each year.

[965]
BLACKHORSE ASSOCIATION SCHOLARSHIPS

Blackhorse Association
c/o Chairperson, Scholarship Committee
P.O. Box 10423
Fort Irwin, CA 92310
E-mail: jorge@whiprush.org
Web: www.11thacr-bha.org

Summary To provide financial assistance for college to children of former members of the 11th Armored Cavalry (Blackhorse) Regiment.

Eligibility This program is open to children and stepchildren of former members of the regiment (including the 58th CE and 409th RR). Applicants must be enrolled or planning to enroll in an accredited college or university at the undergraduate level. Preference is given to 1) children of deceased members, 2) children of members who were wounded or otherwise incapacitated while serving the regiment, and 3) applicants who demonstrate financial need.

Financial data The stipend is $1,500 per year.

Duration 4 years.

Number awarded Varies each year.

Deadline March of each year.

[966]
BRIDGE TO TOMORROW GRANT PROGRAM

Jack Kent Cooke Foundation
44115 Woodridge Parkway, Suite 200
Lansdowne, VA 20176
(703) 723-8000
E-mail: jkc@jackkentcookefoundation.org
Web: www.jackkentcookefoundation.org

Summary To provide financial assistance for college to family members of those directly affected by the events of September 11, 2001.

Eligibility This program is open to 1) dependents and spouses of people killed aboard United Airlines Flight 93, American Airlines Flight 77, American Airlines Flight 11, or United Airlines Flight 175, and 2) dependents or spouses of people killed, missing, or permanently disabled at the Pentagon or World Trade Center on Sep-

tember 11, 2001. Applicants must be pursuing undergraduate study at a 2-year, 4-year, technical, or trade school in the United States. Along with their application, they must submit a cost of attendance worksheet; a copy of the institution's billing statement; and a brief statement that covers the amount and percentage of family income lost, the impact on their educational expenses obligation, amount and status of any issued or pending life insurance proceeds in any form for the direct and indirect benefit of the applicant, and the amount and status of any issue or pending funds from other charitable sources for the direct or indirect benefit of the applicant.

Financial data Grants up to $15,000 per semester are available to help cover tuition, required fees, books, room, board, and additional expenses.

Duration 1 semester. Recipients must reapply each school term.

Additional Information This program was first offered in 2002. Information is also available from the Jack Kent Cooke Foundation, Bridge to Tomorrow Grant Program, 2255 North Dubuque Road, P.O Box 4030, Iowa City, IA 52243, (800) 498-6478, E-mail: jkc@act.org. Recipients must attend school on a full-time basis.

Number awarded A total of $1 million was set aside for this program. Grants are awarded on a first-come, first-served basis until all funds have been disbursed.

[967]
CALIFORNIA FEE WAIVER PROGRAM FOR CHILDREN OF VETERANS

California Department of Veterans Affairs
Attn: Division of Veterans Services
1227 O Street, Room 101
Sacramento, CA 95814
(916) 503-8397
Toll-free: (800) 952-LOAN (within CA)
Fax: (916) 653-2563 TDD: (800) 324-5966
E-mail: ruckergl@cdva.ca.gov
Web: www.cdva.ca.gov/service/feewaiver.asp

Summary To provide financial assistance for college to the children of disabled or deceased veterans in California.

Eligibility Eligible for this program are the children of veterans who either died of a service-connected disability or have a service-connected disability of any level of severity. The applicants must plan to attend a California postsecondary school. California veteran status is not required for this program, although the applicant's income, including the value of support received from the parents, cannot exceed the national poverty level. Dependents in college who are eligible to receive federal education benefits from the U.S. Department of Veterans Affairs are not eligible for these fee waivers.

Financial data This program provides for waiver of registration fees to students attending any publicly-supported community or state college or university in California.

Duration 1 year; may be renewed.

Number awarded Varies each year.

[968]
CALIFORNIA FEE WAIVER PROGRAM FOR DEPENDENTS OF DECEASED OR DISABLED NATIONAL GUARD MEMBERS

California Department of Veterans Affairs
Attn: Division of Veterans Services
1227 O Street, Room 101
Sacramento, CA 95814
(916) 503-8397
Toll-free: (800) 952-LOAN (within CA)
Fax: (916) 653-2563 TDD: (800) 324-5966
E-mail: ruckergl@cdva.ca.gov
Web: www.cdva.ca.gov/service/feewaiver.asp

Summary To provide financial assistance for college to dependents of disabled and deceased members of the California National Guard.

Eligibility Eligible for this program are spouses, children, and unremarried widow(er)s of members of the California National Guard who, in the line of duty and in the active service of the state, were killed, died of a disability, or became permanently disabled.

Financial data Full-time college students receive a waiver of tuition and registration fees at any publicly-supported community or state college or university in California.

Duration 1 year; may be renewed.

Number awarded Varies each year.

[969]
CALIFORNIA FEE WAIVER PROGRAM FOR DEPENDENTS OF TOTALLY DISABLED VETERANS

California Department of Veterans Affairs
Attn: Division of Veterans Services
1227 O Street, Room 101
Sacramento, CA 95814
(916) 503-8397
Toll-free: (800) 952-LOAN (within CA)
Fax: (916) 653-2563 TDD: (800) 324-5966
E-mail: ruckergl@cdva.ca.gov
Web: www.cdva.ca.gov/service/feewaiver.asp

Summary To provide financial assistance for college to dependents of disabled and other California veterans.

Eligibility Eligible for this program are spouses, children, and unremarried widow(er)s of veterans who are currently totally service-connected disabled (or are being compensated for a service-connected disability at a rate of 100%) or who died of a service-connected cause or disability. The veteran parent must have served during a qualifying war period and must have been discharged

or released from military service under honorable conditions. The child cannot be over 27 years of age (extended to 30 if the student was in the military); there are no age limitations for spouses or surviving spouses. This program does not have an income limit. Dependents in college are not eligible if they are qualified to receive educational benefits from the U.S. Department of Veterans Affairs.

Financial data Full-time college students receive a waiver of tuition and registration fees at any publicly-supported community or state college or university in California.

Duration Children of eligible veterans may receive postsecondary benefits until the needed training is completed or until the dependent reaches 27 years of age (extended to 30 if the dependent serves in the armed forces). Widow(er)s and spouses are limited to a maximum of 48 months' full-time training or the equivalent in part-time training.

Number awarded Varies each year.

[970]
CALIFORNIA LAW ENFORCEMENT PERSONNEL DEPENDENTS GRANT PROGRAM

California Student Aid Commission
Attn: Specialized Programs
10811 International Drive
P.O. Box 419029
Rancho Cordova, CA 95741-9029
(916) 526-8276   Toll-free: (888) CA-GRANT
Fax: (916) 526-7977
E-mail: specialized@csac.ca.gov
Web: www.csac.ca.gov

Summary To provide financial assistance for college to the dependents of California law enforcement officers who have been totally disabled or killed in the line of duty.

Eligibility To be eligible, an applicant must be the natural child, adopted child, or spouse of a California peace officer (Highway Patrol, marshal, sheriff, police officer), employee of the Department of Corrections or Youth Authority, or fire fighter whose total disability or death was the result of an accident or injury caused by external violence or physical force incurred in the performance of duty. Applicants must be enrolled in a minimum of 6 units at a California postsecondary institution accredited by the Western Association of Schools and Colleges and be able to demonstrate financial need.

Financial data The amount of the award depends on the need of the recipient, to a maximum of $9,708 at independent schools and colleges in California, $3,429 at branches of the University of California, or $1,428 at branches of the California State University system.

Duration 1 academic year; may be renewed for up to 5 additional years at 4-year colleges and universities or up to 3 additional years at community colleges.

Additional Information If the student receives other scholarships or grants, the award may be adjusted or withdrawn, depending upon financial need. Acceptance of work-study, loans, or employment will generally not affect the amount of money offered through this program.

Number awarded Varies; generally, 7 each year.

Deadline Applications may be submitted at any time.

[971]
CHARLES ADLER SCIENCE MATH SCHOLARSHIP

American Legion
Attn: Department of Maryland
War Memorial Building
101 North Gay Street, Room E
Baltimore, MD 21202
(410) 752-3104   Fax: (410) 752-3822
E-mail: mdlegion@clark.net
Web: www.mdlegion.org

Summary To provide financial assistance for college to Maryland residents who are the children of veterans and who wish to study science or mathematics in college.

Eligibility Maryland residents may apply for these scholarships if they are the children of veterans and between 16 and 19 years of age. Applicants must be interested in majoring in mathematics or 1 of the sciences on a full-time basis in college. Special consideration is given to applicants whose veteran parent is disabled or whose family demonstrates financial need.

Financial data The stipend is $500.

Duration 1 year.

Number awarded 1 each year.

Deadline March of each year.

[972]
CHARLES E. LEONARD MEMORIAL SCHOLARSHIP FUND

Vermont Student Assistance Corporation
Champlain Mill
Attn: Scholarship Programs
P.O. Box 2000
Winooski, VT 05404-2601
(802) 654-3798   Toll-free: (800) 642-3177
Fax: (802) 654-3766   TDD: (802) 654-3766
TDD: (800) 281-3341 (within VT)
E-mail: info@vsac.org
Web: www.vsac.org

Summary To provide financial assistance for college to blind or visually impaired Vermonters, their children, or those who intend to pursue a career of service to blind or visually impaired people.

Eligibility Eligible to apply are blind or visually impaired Vermonters; children of blind or visually

impaired Vermonters attending a Vermont college or university, an out-of-state school, or a vocational school; and Vermonters attending a Vermont college or university to prepare for a career in the rehabilitation of blind or visually impaired people. Preference is given to blind or visually impaired applicants who plan to study electrical engineering at the University of Vermont, blind or visually impaired applicants who plan to study engineering at any Vermont college or university, or applicants planning other fields of study working with blind and visually impaired people. Selection is based on academic achievement, financial need, and required essays.

Financial data The stipend is $500 per year.

Duration 1 year; recipients may reapply.

Additional Information Information is also available from the Vermont Association for the Blind and Visually Impaired, 37 Elmwood Avenue, Burlington, VT 05401, (802) 863-1358, (800) 639-5861, E-mail: vabvi@aol.com.

Number awarded Approximately 4 each year.

Deadline April of each year.

[973]
CHIEF MASTER SERGEANTS OF THE AIR FORCE SCHOLARSHIPS

Air Force Sergeants Association
Attn: Scholarship Program
P.O. Box 50
Temple Hills, MD 20757
(301) 899-3500   Toll-free: (800) 638-0594
Fax: (301) 899-8136   E-mail: staff@amf.org
Web: www.afsahq.org/body_education01.htm

Summary To provide financial assistance for college to the dependent children of enlisted Air Force personnel.

Eligibility Applicants must be the unmarried dependent children (including stepchildren and legally adopted children), under the age of 23, of enlisted personnel serving in the U.S. Air Force, Air National Guard, or Air Force Reserves, whether on active duty or retired. Selection is based on academic ability (SAT score of 1000 or higher and GPA of 3.5 or higher), character, leadership, writing ability, and potential for success; financial need is not a consideration. A unique aspect of these scholarships is that applicants may supply additional information regarding circumstances that entitle them to special consideration; examples of such circumstances include student disabilities, financial hardships, parent disabled and unable to work, parent missing in action/killed in action/prisoner of war, or other unusual extenuating circumstances.

Financial data Stipends are $3,000, $2,000, or $1,000; funds may be used for tuition, room and board, fees, books, supplies, and transportation.

Duration 1 year; may be renewed if the recipient maintains full-time enrollment.

Additional Information The Air Force Sergeants Association administers this program on behalf of the Airmen Memorial Foundation. It was established in 1987 and named in honor of CMSAF Richard D. Kisling, the late third Chief Master Sergeant of the Air Force. In 1997, following the deaths of CMSAF's (Retired) Andrews and Harlow, it was given its current name. Requests for applications must be accompanied by a stamped self-addressed envelope.

Number awarded 11 each year: 1 at $3,000, 2 at $2,000, and 8 at $1,000. Since this program began, it has awarded 135 scholarships worth $200,000.

Deadline March of each year.

[974]
COLORADO DEPENDENTS TUITION ASSISTANCE PROGRAM

Colorado Commission on Higher Education
1380 Lawrence Street, Suite 1200
Denver, CO 80204
(303) 866-2723   Fax: (303) 866-4266
E-mail: cche@state.co.us
Web: www.state.co.us/cche_dir/hecche.html

Summary To provide financial assistance for college to the dependents of disabled or deceased Colorado National Guardsmen, law enforcement officers, and fire fighters.

Eligibility Eligible for the program are dependents of Colorado law enforcement officers, fire fighters, and National Guardsmen disabled or killed in the line of duty, as well as dependents of prisoners of war or service personnel listed as missing in action. Students must be Colorado residents enrolled at a school participating in the program. Dependents of disabled personnel must demonstrate financial need.

Financial data Eligible students receive free tuition at Colorado public institutions of higher education. If the recipient wishes to attend a private college, university, or proprietary school, the award is limited to the amount of tuition at a comparable state-supported institution.

Duration Up to 8 academic semesters or 12 academic quarters, provided the recipient maintains a GPA of 2.5 or higher.

Additional Information Recipients must attend accredited postsecondary institutions in Colorado.

Number awarded Varies each year.

[975]
DISABLED WORKERS COMMITTEE SCHOLARSHIP

Disabled Workers Committee
Attn: Barbara Shepard
Gold Star Park
489 Gold Star Highway, Suite 110
Groton, CT 06340

Summary To provide financial assistance for college to children of people with disabilities in Connecticut.
Eligibility This program is open to seniors graduating from high schools in Connecticut who are the children of totally and permanently disabled persons, injured in the workplace. Selection is based on academic achievement and financial need.
Financial data The stipend is $2,500 per year.
Duration 1 year; may be renewed for up to 3 additional years.
Number awarded 1 each year.
Deadline March of each year.

[976]
DUGDALE/VAN EYS SCHOLARSHIP AWARD

Tennessee Hemophilia and Bleeding Disorders Foundation
7003 Chadwick Drive, Suite 269
Brentwood, TN 37027
(615) 373-0351
Web: www.thbdf.org

Summary To provide financial assistance for college to students with hemophilia or to related individuals in Tennessee.
Eligibility This program is open to Tennessee consumers and those receiving care at a Tennessee HTC. Applicants must be 1) persons with hemophilia, or 2) their children, spouses, or caregivers. Financial need is considered in the selection process.
Financial data A stipend is provided; the amount varies but is usually around $2,000.
Duration 1 year; recipients may reapply.
Number awarded 1 or more each year.
Deadline May of each year.

[977]
EAGA SCHOLARSHIP AWARD

Eastern Amputee Golf Association
Attn: Bob Buck, Executive Director
2015 Amherst Drive
Bethlehem, PA 18015-5606
Toll-free: (888) 868-0992   Fax: (610) 867-9295
E-mail: info@eaga.org
Web: www.eaga.org

Summary To provide financial assistance for college to members of the Eastern Amputee Golf Association (EAGA) and their families.
Eligibility This program is open to students who are 1) residents of and/or 2) currently enrolled or accepted for enrollment at a college or university in designated eastern states (Connecticut, Delaware, District of Columbia, Maine, Maryland, Massachusetts, New Hampshire, New Jersey, New York, Pennsylvania, Rhode Island, Vermont, Virginia, or West Virginia). Applicants must be amputee members of the association (those who have experienced the loss of 1 or more extremities at a major joint due to amputation or birth defect) or members of their families. Financial need is considered in the selection process.
Financial data The stipend is $1,000.
Duration 1 year; may be renewed if the recipient maintains a GPA of 2.0 or higher and continues to demonstrate financial need.
Additional information The EAGA was incorporated in 1987. It welcomes 2 types of members: amputee members and associate members (non-amputees who are interested in the organization and support its work but are not eligible for these scholarships). This program includes the following named scholarships: the Paul DesChamps Scholarship Award, the JFK Rehab/EAGA Scholarship, the Ray Froncillo Scholarship, and the Northeastern Amputee Class Scholarship.
Number awarded 5 each year.
Deadline June of each year.

[978]
EDWARD T. CONROY MEMORIAL SCHOLARSHIP PROGRAM

Maryland Higher Education Commission
Attn: Office of Student Financial Assistance
839 Bestgate Road, Suite 400
Annapolis, MD 21401-3013
(410) 260-4565   Toll-free: (800) 974-1024
Fax: (410) 974-5376   TTY: (800) 735-2258
E-mail: osfamail@mhec.state.md.us
Web: www.mhec.state.md.us/SSA/CONROY.htm

Summary To provide financial assistance for college or graduate school to specified categories of veterans, public safety employees, and their children in Maryland.
Eligibility This program is open to undergraduate and graduate students in the following categories: 1) children and unremarried surviving spouses of state or local public safety employees or volunteers who died in the line of duty; 2) children of armed forces members whose death or 100% disability was directly caused by military service; 3) POW/MIA veterans of the Vietnam Conflict and their children; 4) children and surviving spouses of victims of the September 11, 2001 terrorist attacks who died in the World Trade Center in New York City, the Pentagon in Virginia, or United Airlines Flight 93 in Pennsylvania; 5) veterans who have, as a direct result of military service, a disability of 25% or greater and have

exhausted or are no longer eligible for federal veterans' educational benefits; and 6) state or local public safety officers or volunteers who were 100% disabled in the line of duty. The parent, veteran, POW, or public safety officer or volunteer must have been a resident of Maryland at the time of death or when declared disabled. Financial need is not considered.

Financial data The amount of the award is equal to tuition and fees at a Maryland postsecondary institution, to a maximum of $14,200 for children and spouses of the September 11 terrorist attacks or $6,178 for all other recipients.

Duration Up to 5 years of full-time study or 8 years of part-time study.

Additional Information Recipients must enroll at a 2-year or 4-year Maryland college or university as a full-time or part-time degree-seeking undergraduate or graduate student or attend a private career school.

Number awarded Varies each year.

Deadline July of each year.

[979]
ELKS NATIONAL FOUNDATION EMERGENCY EDUCATIONAL FUND GRANTS

Elks National Foundation
Attn: Scholarship Department
2750 North Lake View Avenue
Chicago, IL 60614-1889
(773) 755-4732   Fax: (773) 755-4729
E-mail: scholarship@elks.org
Web: www.elks.org/enf

Summary To provide emergency financial assistance to college students who are children of deceased or disabled members of B.P.O. Elks.

Eligibility This program is open to children of Elks who have died or are totally disabled. Applicants must be unmarried, under 23 years of age, able to demonstrate financial need, and attending a college or university in the United States as a full-time undergraduate student. The student's parent must have been a member in good standing at the time of death or, if disabled, have been a member in good standing before he or she became incapacitated and must continue to be an Elk in good standing when the application for assistance is submitted. Applications must give the B.P.O. Elks Lodge affiliation of the Elk parent.

Financial data The amount of the assistance depends on the need of the applicant but normally ranges up to $3,000 per year.

Duration 1 year; may be renewed up to 3 additional years.

Number awarded Varies each year.

Deadline December of each year for new applications; October of each year for renewal applications.

[980]
ERIC DOSTIE MEMORIAL COLLEGE SCHOLARSHIP

LA Kelley Communications
68 East Main Street, Suite 102
Georgetown, MA 01833-2112
(978) 352-7657   Toll-free: (800) 249-7977
Fax: (978) 352-6254   E-mail: info@kelleycom.com
Web: www.kelleycom.com/finaid/finaid.html

Summary To provide financial assistance for college to students with hemophilia or members of their families.

Eligibility This program is open to 1) students with hemophilia or a related bleeding disorder or 2) members of their families. Applicants must be U.S. citizens and enrolled or planning to enroll full time in an accredited 2- or 4-year college program. They must have a GPA of 2.5 or higher. Along with their application, they must submit a 400-word essay that explains what motivates them to pursue a higher education, what subjects they plan to study, what major forces or obstacles in their life has led to that path of study, what they plan to do with their education after school, and how that may be of benefit to humankind. Financial need is also considered in the selection process.

Financial data The stipend is $1,000.

Duration 1 year.

Number awarded 8 each year.

Deadline February of each year.

[981]
EVELYN BARTY SCHOLARSHIP AWARDS PROGRAM

Billy Barty Foundation
10222 Crosby Road
Harrison, OH 45030
(513) 738-4428   Fax: (513) 738-4428

Summary To provide financial assistance for college to people of short stature and members of their families.

Eligibility This program is open to high school seniors, high school graduates, and students currently enrolled in a 4-year college or university who are less than 4 feet 10 inches tall. Their parents and siblings are also eligible. Selection is based on scholarship, leadership, and financial need.

Financial data The amount of the scholarship varies.

Duration 1 year; recipients may reapply.

Additional Information These scholarships were named in honor of the average-sized sister of Billy Barty after her recent death. She had devoted many hours of volunteer time to the foundation.

Number awarded Up to 5 each year.

Deadline October of each year.

FAMILIES OF DISABLED: SCHOLARSHIPS

[982]
FAMILIES OF FREEDOM SCHOLARSHIP FUND

Scholarship America
Attn: Scholarship Management Services
1505 Riverview Road
P.O. Box 297
St. Peter, MN 56082
(507) 931-1682 Toll-free: (877) 862-0136
Fax: (507) 931-9168
E-mail: familiesoffreedom@csfa.org
Web: www.familiesoffreedom.org

Summary To provide college scholarships to financially-needy individuals and the families of individuals who were victims of the terrorist attacks on September 11, 2001.

Eligibility This program is open to the individuals who were disabled as a result of the terrorist attacks on September 11, 2001 and to the relatives of those individuals who were killed or permanently disabled during the attacks. Primarily, the fund will benefit dependents (including spouses and children) of the following groups: airplane crew and passengers; World Trade Center workers and visitors; Pentagon workers and visitors; and rescue workers, including fire fighters, emergency medical personnel, and law enforcement personnel. Applicants must be enrolled or planning to enroll in an accredited 2- or 4-year college, university, or vocational/technical school in the United States. They must be able to demonstrate financial need.

Financial data Stipends range from $1,000 to $28,000 per year, depending upon the need of the recipient. Recently, awards averaged $13,100 per academic year. Funds are distributed annually, in 2 equal installments. Checks are made payable jointly to the student and the student's school.

Duration 1 year; may be renewed.

Additional Information This program was established on September 17, 2001. The fundraising goal of $100 million was reached on September 4, 2002. The fund will operate until December 31, 2030.

Number awarded This is an entitlement program; all eligible students will receive funding. In its first year of operation, it distributed approximately $925,000 to 125 students.

Deadline Applications may be submitted at any time.

[983]
FIRST CAVALRY DIVISION ASSOCIATION SCHOLARSHIPS

First Cavalry Division Association
302 North Main Street
Copperas Cove, TX 76522-1799
(254) 547-6537 E-mail: FirstCav@vvm.com
Web: www.vvm.com/~firstcav

Summary To provide financial assistance for the undergraduate education of dependents of disabled and deceased veterans of the First Cavalry Division.

Eligibility Eligible to apply are: children of soldiers who died or have been declared totally and permanently disabled from injuries incurred while serving with the First Cavalry Division during any armed conflict; children of soldiers who died while serving in the First Cavalry Division during peacetime; and children of soldiers of the First Cavalry Division, USAF Forward Air Controllers, A1E pilots, or war correspondents who were involved in the battles of the Ia Drang valley from November 3 through 19, 1965. Students who meet 1 of those qualifications may apply for these scholarships if they have previously registered with the First Cavalry Division Association.

Financial data The award is currently $800 per year, or a maximum of $3,200 for 4 years. The checks are made out jointly to the student and the school and may be used for whatever the student needs, including tuition, books, and clothing.

Duration 1 year; may be renewed up to 3 additional years.

Additional Information Requests for applications must be accompanied by a self-addressed stamped envelope.

Number awarded Varies each year.

Deadline May of each year.

[984]
FIRST MARINE DIVISION ASSOCIATION SCHOLARSHIPS

First Marine Division Association
14325 Willard Road, Suite 107
Chantilly, VA 20151-2110
(703) 803-3195 Fax: (703) 803-7114
E-mail: oldbreed@aol.com

Summary To provide financial assistance for undergraduate education to dependents of veterans of the First Marine Division.

Eligibility This program is open to dependents of veterans who are honorably discharged, totally and permanently disabled, or deceased from any cause and who served in the First Marine Division or in a unit attached to that Division. Applicants must be attending or planning to attend an accredited college, university, or trade school as a full-time undergraduate student.

Financial data The amounts of the awards vary; payments are made directly to the educational institution.

Duration 1 year; may be renewed up to 3 additional years.

Additional Information Award winners who marry before completing the course or who drop out for non-scholastic reasons must submit a new application before benefits can be resumed.

Number awarded Varies each year.

[985]
FLORIDA SCHOLARSHIPS FOR CHILDREN OF DECEASED OR DISABLED VETERANS

Florida Department of Education
Attn: Office of Student Financial Assistance
1940 North Monroe Street, Suite 70
Tallahassee, FL 32303-4759
(850) 410-5185   Toll-free: (888) 827-2004
Fax: (850) 488-3612   E-mail: osfa@fldoe.org
Web: www.floridastudentfinancialaid.org

Summary To provide financial assistance for college to the children of Florida veterans who are disabled, deceased, or officially classified as prisoners of war or missing in action.

Eligibility Eligible for these scholarships are residents of Florida between 16 and 22 years of age who are the dependent children of 100% disabled or deceased wartime veterans or of servicemen officially classified as prisoners of war or missing in action. Veteran parents who served in the Newfoundland air tragedy, Vietnam, Korea, World War II, or World War I must have been residents of Florida when they entered the armed forces. Veteran parents who died or became disabled in the Iranian Rescue Mission, the Lebanon and Grenada military arenas, the *USS Stark* attack, Operation Just Cause in Panama, the Persian Gulf War, or Operating Enduring Freedom must have been Florida residents during the dates of those activities. In addition, veteran parents who served in Vietnam, Korea, World War II, or World War I must have been Florida residents for 5 years prior to the student's application.

Financial data Qualified students who attend a Florida public institution of higher education receive payment of tuition and fees. Students who attend an eligible nonpublic Florida institution of higher education receive an award equal to the amount they would be required to pay for the average tuition and fees at a public institution at the comparable level.

Duration 1 quarter or semester; may be renewed for up to 11 additional quarters or 7 additional semesters as long as the student maintains a GPA of 2.0 or higher and full-time enrollment.

Number awarded Varies each year; recently, this program provided 215 awards.

Deadline March of each year.

[986]
FRANCIS P. MATTHEWS AND JOHN E. SWIFT EDUCATIONAL TRUST SCHOLARSHIPS

Knights of Columbus
Attn: Director of Scholarship Aid
P.O. Box 1670
New Haven, CT 06507-0901
(203) 772-2130, ext. 332   Fax: (203) 773-3000

Summary To provide financial assistance at Catholic colleges or universities to children of disabled or deceased veterans, law enforcement officers, or firemen who are/were also Knights of Columbus members.

Eligibility Eligible are children of members of the sponsoring organization who were either totally and permanently disabled or killed as a result of military service during World War II, the Korean conflict, the Vietnam War, or the Persian Gulf War; of full-time law enforcement officers who became disabled or lost their lives as a result of criminal violence; or of firemen who became disabled or were killed in the line of duty. For the children of veterans, the death or disability must have occurred during a period of conflict or within 10 years of its official termination. Students must be high school seniors at the time of application.

Financial data The amounts of the awards vary but are designed to cover tuition, room and board, books, and required fees at the Catholic college or university of the recipient's choice.

Duration 1 year; may be renewed up to 3 additional years.

Additional Information Recipients must attend Catholic colleges.

Number awarded Varies each year.

Deadline April of each year.

[987]
FREE TUITION FOR DEPENDENTS OF DISABLED OR DECEASED SOUTH DAKOTA NATIONAL GUARD MEMBERS

South Dakota Board of Regents
Attn: Scholarship Committee
306 East Capitol Avenue, Suite 200
Pierre, SD 57501-3159
(605) 773-3455   Fax: (605) 773-5320
E-mail: info@ris.sdbor.edu
Web: www.ris.sdbor.edu

Summary To provide financial assistance for college to the dependents of disabled and deceased members of the South Dakota National Guard.

Eligibility This program is open to the spouses and children of members of the South Dakota Army or Air National Guard who died or sustained a total and permanent disability while on state active duty or any authorized duty training. Applicants must be younger than 25 years of age and proposing to work on an undergraduate degree at a public institution of higher education in South Dakota.

Financial data Qualifying applicants are eligible for a 100% reduction in tuition at any state-supported postsecondary institution in South Dakota.

Duration 8 semesters or 12 quarters of either full- or part-time study.

Number awarded Varies each year.

FAMILIES OF DISABLED: SCHOLARSHIPS

[988]
GENERAL HENRY H. ARNOLD EDUCATION GRANT PROGRAM

Air Force Aid Society
Attn: Education Assistance Department
1745 Jefferson Davis Highway, Suite 202
Arlington, VA 22202-3410
(703) 607-3072, ext. 51   Toll-free: (800) 429-9475
Web: www.afas.org

Summary To provide financial assistance for college to dependents of active-duty, retired, or deceased Air Force personnel.

Eligibility This program is open to 1) dependent children of Air Force personnel who are either active duty, reservists on extended active duty, retired due to length of active-duty service or disability, or deceased while on active duty or in retired status; 2) spouses of active-duty Air Force members and reservists on extended active duty; and 3) surviving spouses of Air Force members who died while on active duty or in retired status. Applicants must be enrolled or planning to enroll as full-time undergraduate students in an accredited college, university, or vocational/trade school. Spouses must be attending school within the 48 contiguous states. Selection is based on family income and education costs.

Financial data The stipend is $1,500.

Duration 1 year; may be renewed if the recipient maintains a GPA of 2.0 or higher.

Additional Information Since this program was established in the 1988-89 academic year, it has awarded more than 63,000 grants.

Number awarded Varies each year.

Deadline April of each year.

[989]
GEORGIA COUNCIL OF THE BLIND SCHOLARSHIPS

Georgia Council of the Blind
c/o Janet Clary, Scholarship Committee Chair
318 Walden Glen Lane
Evans, GA 30809

Summary To provide financial assistance for college or graduate school to students in Georgia who have visual impairments or parents with visual impairments.

Eligibility This program is open to residents of Georgia who are either 1) visually impaired or legally blind or 2) the sighted children of parents who are visually impaired or legally blind. Applicants must be enrolled or accepted for enrollment at a vocational/technical school, a 2-year or 4-year college, or a master's or doctoral program. All fields of study are eligible. Selection is based on academic transcripts, 2 letters of recommendation, a 1-page typed statement of the applicant's educational goals, an audio cassette recording of the applicant reading the goals statement, extracurricular activities, and financial need.

Financial data Stipends up to $1,000 per year are available.

Duration 1 year; recipients may reapply.

Additional Information This program began in 1988.

Number awarded 1 or more each year.

Deadline June of each year.

[990]
GEORGIA LAW ENFORCEMENT PERSONNEL DEPENDENTS GRANT

Georgia Student Finance Commission
Attn: Scholarships and Grants Division
2082 East Exchange Place, Suite 200
Tucker, GA 30084-5305
(770) 724-9000   Toll-free: (800) 505-GSFC
Fax: (770) 724-9089
E-mail: info@mail.gsfc.state.ga.us
Web: www.gsfc.org/GSFC/grants/dsp_glepd.cfm

Summary To provide financial assistance for college to children of disabled or deceased Georgia law enforcement officers, fire fighters, and prison guards.

Eligibility Eligible to apply are dependent children of law enforcement officers, fire fighters, and prison guards in Georgia who have been permanently disabled or killed in the line of duty. Applicants must be enrolled as full-time undergraduate students in a Georgia private or public college, university, or technical institution. U.S. citizenship or permanent resident status and compliance with the Georgia Drug-Free Postsecondary Education Act are required.

Financial data The grant is $2,000 per academic year, not to exceed $8,000 during an entire program of study.

Duration 1 year; may be renewed (if satisfactory progress is maintained) for up to 3 additional years.

Number awarded Varies each year; recently, 38 of these grants were awarded.

Deadline July of each year.

[991]
GEORGIA PUBLIC SAFETY MEMORIAL GRANT

Georgia Student Finance Commission
Attn: Scholarships and Grants Division
2082 East Exchange Place, Suite 200
Tucker, GA 30084-5305
(770) 724-9000   Toll-free: (800) 505-GSFC
Fax: (770) 724-9089
E-mail: info@mail.gsfc.state.ga.us
Web: www.gsfc.org/GSFC/grants/dsp_gps.cfm

Summary To provide financial assistance for college to the children of Georgia public safety officers who have been permanently disabled or killed in the line of duty.

Eligibility This program is open to dependent children of Georgia law enforcement officers, fire fighters, EMT, correction officers, or prison guards who have been per-

manently disabled or killed in the line of duty. Applicants must be enrolled or accepted as full-time undergraduate students in a Georgia public college, university, or technical institution and be in compliance with the Georgia Drug-Free Postsecondary Education Act. U.S. citizenship or permanent resident status is required.

Financial data The award covers the cost of attendance at a public postsecondary school in Georgia, minus any other aid received.

Duration 1 year; may be renewed (if satisfactory progress is maintained) for up to 3 additional years.

Additional Information This program began in 1994.

Number awarded Varies each year; recently, 30 of these grants were awarded.

Deadline July of each year.

[992]
GREAT LAKES HEMOPHILIA FOUNDATION EDUCATION AND TRAINING ASSISTANCE SCHOLARSHIPS

Great Lakes Hemophilia Foundation
638 North 18th Street, Suite 108
P.O. Box 704
Milwaukee, WI 53201-0704
(414) 257-0200   Toll-free: (888) 797-GLHF
Fax: (414) 257-1225   E-mail: info@glhf.org
Web: www.glhf.org/scholar.htm

Summary To provide financial assistance for college to Wisconsin residents with a bleeding disorder and their families.

Eligibility This program is open to residents of Wisconsin who have a bleeding disorder and their parents, spouses, children, and siblings. Applicants must be attending or planning to attend college, vocational school, technical school, or a certification program. Adults who require retraining because they can no longer function in their chosen field as a result of health complications from bleeding disorders are also eligible.

Financial data Stipends range from $500 to $2,000.

Duration 1 year.

Number awarded Several each year.

Deadline April of each year.

[993]
HEMOPHILIA EDUCATION FUND

American Red Cross
c/o Scholarship America
Attn: Scholarship Management Services
1505 Riverview Road
P.O. Box 297
St. Peter, MN 56082
(507) 931-1682   Toll-free: (800) 537-4180
Fax: (507) 931-9168   E-mail: smsinfo@csfa.org

Summary To provide financial assistance for college to persons with hemophilia and their children.

Eligibility To be eligible, candidates must be high school seniors, high school graduates, or students already enrolled in full-time study. Applicants must either be receiving treatment for hemophilia or have a parent receiving treatment for hemophilia A. They must be planning to enroll full time at an accredited 2- or 4-year college, university, or vocational/technical school. Selection is based on academic performance, leadership, participation in school and community activities, work experience, career goals, and personal and family financial circumstances.

Financial data Up to $5,000 per year, payable in 2 equal installments. The award is paid directly to the recipient, but the check is made out jointly to the recipient and the recipient's school. Funds may be used for tuition, living expenses, and books. The amount awarded cannot exceed the verified cost of tuition, fees, books, and room and board.

Duration 1 year; may be renewed 1 additional year.

Additional Information This program is managed by Scholarship America and sponsored by the American Red Cross. Recipients must attend an accredited college or university in the continental United States. Scholarships are awarded for undergraduate study only.

Number awarded 3 each year: 2 to students with hemophilia and 1 to the child of a parent with hemophilia.

Deadline January of each year.

[994]
HEMOPHILIA FOUNDATION OF MICHIGAN ACADEMIC SCHOLARSHIPS

Hemophilia Foundation of Michigan
Attn: Client Services Coordinator
905 West Eisenhower Circle
Ann Arbor, MI 48103
(734) 332-4226   Toll-free: (800) 482-3041
Fax: (734) 332-4204   E-mail: colleen@hfmich.org
Web: www.hfmich.org/support_scholarships.cfm

Summary To provide financial assistance for college to Michigan residents with hemophilia and their families.

Eligibility High school seniors, high school graduates, and currently-enrolled college students are eligible to apply if they are Michigan residents and have hemophilia or another bleeding disorder. Family members of people with bleeding disorders and family members of people who have died from the complications of a bleeding disorder are also eligible. Applicants are required to submit a completed application form, a transcript, and a letter of recommendation.

Financial data Stipends range from $500 to $1,500.

Duration 1 year.

Number awarded Varies each year.

Deadline April of each year.

[995]
HEMOPHILIA OF IOWA SCHOLARSHIP

Hemophilia of Iowa, Inc.
c/o Lisa Wolterman, President
404 East Washington Street
Lake City, IA 51449
E-mail: lwol@iowatelecom.net
Web: wwww.hemophiliaofiowa.org

Summary To provide financial assistance for college to members of Hemophilia of Iowa, Inc.

Eligibility Applicants must be members of the sponsoring organization, must either have hemophilia (or a related bleeding disorder) or be the immediate family members (parents, siblings) of someone who has hemophilia or a related bleeding disorder. They may be graduating high school seniors or currently in college.

Financial data The stipend is $750 if the recipient is enrolled full time or $250 if the recipient is enrolled part time. Funds are paid directly to the recipient.

Duration 1 semester; recipients may reapply.

Number awarded 6 each year: 3 to full-time students and 3 to part-time students.

Deadline May of each year.

[996]
HEMOPHILIA RESOURCES OF AMERICA SCHOLARSHIPS

Hemophilia Resources of America
Attn: Scholarships
45 Route 46 East, Suite 609
P.O. Box 2011
Pine Brook, NJ 07058
(973) 276-0254   Toll-free: (800) 549-2654
Fax: (973) 276-0998   E-mail: hra@hrahemo.com
Web: www.hrahemo.com/about/scholarship.html

Summary To provide financial assistance for college to 1) persons with a bleeding disorder or 2) their dependents.

Eligibility Eligible to apply for this program are persons with hemophilia or von Willebrand disease and their children. They must be interested in working on a college degree at a 2-year or 4-year institution (including vocational/technical school). Selection is based on an essay on future goals and aspirations; school, work, community, and volunteer activities; 2 letters of recommendation; and financial need.

Financial data Most stipends are $1,000; the Todd M. Richardson Memorial Scholarship is $2,500.

Duration 1 year.

Additional Information This program began in 1995.

Number awarded Varies each year. Recently, this program awarded 28 scholarships at $1,000 plus 1 Todd M. Richardson Memorial Scholarship at $2,500.

Deadline April of each year.

[997]
HERB SCHLAUGHENHOUPT, JR. MEMORIAL SCHOLARSHIP

Kentucky Hemophilia Foundation
982 Eastern Parkway
Louisville, KY 40217
(502) 634-8161   Toll-free: (800) 582-CURE
Fax: (502) 634-9995   E-mail: info@kyhemo.org
Web: www.kyhemo.org/scholarships.htm

Summary To provide financial assistance for college to students in Kentucky who have a bleeding disorder and to members of their families.

Eligibility This program is open to residents of Kentucky who have hemophilia or a related inherited bleeding disorder. Also eligible are their immediate family members. Applicants must be interested in attending a university, college, trade, or vocational school.

Financial data The stipend is $500. Funds must be used for tuition, room, board, and related educational expenses.

Duration 1 year.

Number awarded 2 each year.

Deadline Applications must be submitted by January or July of each year.

[998]
HORIZON SCHOLARSHIPS

Maine Employers' Mutual Insurance Company
Attn: MEMIC Education Fund
261 Commercial Street
P.O. Box 11409
Portland, ME 04104
(207) 791-3300   Toll-free: (800) 660-1306
Fax: (207) 791-3335
E-mail: mbourque@memic.com
Web: www.memic.com

Summary To provide financial assistance for college or graduate school to Maine residents whose parent or spouse was killed or permanently disabled in a work-related accident.

Eligibility This program is open to Maine residents who are the child or spouse of a worker killed or permanently disabled as the result of a work-related injury. The worker must have been insured through the sponsor at the time of the workplace injury. Applicants must be attending or planning to attend an accredited college or university as an undergraduate or graduate student. They must submit a personal statement of 500 words or less on their aspirations and how their educational plans relate to them. Selection is based on financial need, academic performance, community involvement, and other life experiences.

Financial data Stipends range up to $5,000, depending on the need of the recipient. Funds are paid directly to the recipient's institution.

Duration 1 year; may be renewed.

Additional Information The Maine Employers' Mutual Insurance Company (MEMIC) was established in 1993 as the result of reforms in Maine's workers' compensation laws. It is currently the largest workers' compensation insurance company in the state.

Number awarded Varies each year; recently, 3 of these scholarships were awarded.

Deadline April of each year.

[999] IDAHO PUBLIC SAFETY OFFICER DEPENDENT SCHOLARSHIP

Idaho State Board of Education
Len B. Jordan Office Building
650 West State Street, Room 307
P.O. Box 83720
Boise, ID 83720-0037
(208) 334-2270   Fax: (208) 334-2632
E-mail: board@osbe.state.id.us
Web: www.idahoboardofed.org

Summary To provide financial assistance for college to dependents of disabled or deceased Idaho public safety officers.

Eligibility Eligible for these scholarships are dependents of full-time Idaho public safety officers employed in the state who were killed or disabled in the line of duty.

Financial data Each scholarship provides a full waiver of tuition and fees at public institutions of higher education or public vocational schools within Idaho, an allowance of $500 per semester for books, and on-campus housing and a campus meal plan.

Duration Benefits are available for a maximum of 36 months.

Number awarded Varies each year; recently, 4 of these scholarships were awarded.

[1000] ILLINOIS GRANT PROGRAM FOR DEPENDENTS OF CORRECTIONAL OFFICERS

Illinois Student Assistance Commission
Attn: Scholarship and Grant Services
1755 Lake Cook Road
Deerfield, IL 60015-5209
(847) 948-8550   Toll-free: (800) 899-ISAC
Fax: (847) 831-8549
TDD: (847) 831-8326, ext. 2822
E-mail: cssupport@isac.org
Web: www.isac1.org/ilaid/depcorof.html

Summary To provide financial assistance for college or graduate school to the children or spouses of disabled or deceased Illinois correctional workers.

Eligibility This program is open to the spouses and children of Illinois correctional officers who were at least 90% disabled or killed in the line of duty. Applicants must be enrolled on at least a half-time basis as an undergraduate at an approved Illinois public or private 2-year or 4-year college, university, or hospital school. They need not be Illinois residents at the time of application.

Financial data The grants provide funds for tuition and mandatory fees.

Duration Up to 8 academic semesters or 12 academic quarters of study.

Number awarded Varies each year.

[1001] ILLINOIS GRANT PROGRAM FOR DEPENDENTS OF POLICE OR FIRE OFFICERS

Illinois Student Assistance Commission
Attn: Scholarship and Grant Services
1755 Lake Cook Road
Deerfield, IL 60015-5209
(847) 948-8550   Toll-free: (800) 899-ISAC
Fax: (847) 831-8549
TDD: (847) 831-8326, ext. 2822
E-mail: cssupport@isac.org
Web: www.isac1.org/ilaid/polfirgt.html

Summary To provide financial assistance for college to the children or spouses of disabled or deceased Illinois police or fire officers.

Eligibility This program is open to the spouses and children of Illinois police and fire officers who were at least 90% disabled or killed in the line of duty. Applicants must be enrolled on at least a half-time basis in either undergraduate or graduate study at an approved Illinois public or private 2-year or 4-year college, university, or hospital school. They need not be Illinois residents at the time of application.

Financial data The grants provide funds for tuition and mandatory fees.

Duration Up to 8 academic semesters or 12 academic quarters of study.

Number awarded Varies each year.

[1002] ILLINOIS HONORARY SCHOLARSHIPS

Illinois Department of Veterans' Affairs
833 South Spring Street
P.O. Box 19432
Springfield, IL 62794-9432
(217) 782-6641
Toll-free: (800) 437-9824 (within IL)
Fax: (217) 782-4161   TDD: (217) 524-4645
E-mail: webmail@dva.state.il.us
Web: www.state.il.us/agency/dva

Summary To provide financial assistance for college to the children of Illinois veterans (with preference given to the children of disabled or deceased veterans).

Eligibility Each county in the state is entitled to award an honorary scholarship to the child of a veteran of World War I, World War II, the Korean Conflict, or the Vietnam Conflict. Preference is given to children of disabled or deceased veterans.

Financial data Students selected for this program receive free tuition at any branch of the University of Illinois.

Duration Up to 4 years.

Number awarded Each county in Illinois is entitled to award 1 scholarship. The Board of Trustees of the university may, from time to time, add to the number of honorary scholarships (when such additions will not create an unnecessary financial burden on the university).

[1003] ILLINOIS MIA/POW SCHOLARSHIP

Illinois Department of Veterans' Affairs
833 South Spring Street
P.O. Box 19432
Springfield, IL 62794-9432
(217) 782-6641
Toll-free: (800) 437-9824 (within IL)
Fax: (217) 782-4161   TDD: (217) 524-4645
E-mail: webmail@dva.state.il.us
Web: www.state.il.us/agency/dva

Summary To provide financial assistance for 1) the undergraduate education of Illinois dependents of disabled or deceased veterans or those listed as prisoners of war or missing in action and 2) the rehabilitation or education of disabled dependents of those veterans.

Eligibility To be eligible, applicants must be the spouses, natural children, legally adopted children, or stepchildren of a veteran or service member who 1) has been declared by the U.S. Department of Defense or the U.S. Department of Veterans Affairs to be permanently disabled from service-connected causes with 100% disability, deceased as the result of a service-connected disability, a prisoner of war, or missing in action, and 2) at the time of entering service was an Illinois resident or was an Illinois resident within 6 months of entering such service. Special support is available for dependents who are disabled.

Financial data An eligible dependent is entitled to full payment of tuition and certain fees at any Illinois state-supported college, university, or community college. In lieu of that benefit, an eligible dependent who has a physical, mental, or developmental disability is entitled to receive a grant to be used to cover the cost of treating the disability at 1 or more appropriate therapeutic, rehabilitative, or educational facilities. For disabled dependents, the total benefit cannot exceed the cost equivalent of 4 calendar years of full-time enrollment, including summer terms, at the University of Illinois.

Duration This scholarship may be used for a period equivalent to 4 calendar years, including summer terms. Dependents have 12 years from the initial term of study to complete the equivalent of 4 calendar years. Disabled dependents who elect to use the grant for rehabilitative purposes may do so as long as the total benefit does not exceed the cost equivalent of 4 calendar years of full-time enrollment at the University of Illinois.

Additional Information An eligible child must begin using the scholarship prior to his or her 26th birthday. An eligible spouse must begin using the scholarship prior to 10 years from the effective date of eligibility (e.g., prior to August 12, 1989 or 10 years from date of disability or death).

Number awarded Varies each year.

[1004] INDIANA CHILD OF VETERAN AND PUBLIC SAFETY OFFICER SUPPLEMENTAL GRANT PROGRAM

State Student Assistance Commission of Indiana
ISTA Center Building
150 West Market Street, Suite 500
Indianapolis, IN 46204-2811
(317) 232-2350
Toll-free: (888) 528-4719 (within IN)
Fax: (317) 232-3260
E-mail: grants@ssaci.state.in.us
Web: www.in.gov/ssaci/programs/cvo.html

Summary To provide financial assistance for undergraduate or graduate education to students in Indiana who are 1) the children of disabled or other veterans, and 2) the children and spouses of certain deceased or disabled public safety officers.

Eligibility The veterans portion of this program is open to Indiana residents who are the natural or adopted children of veterans who served in the active-duty U.S. armed forces during a period of wartime. Applicants may be of any age; parents must have lived in Indiana for at least 3 years during their lifetime. The veteran parent must also 1) have a service-connected disability as determined by the U.S. Department of Veterans Affairs or the Department of Defense; 2) have received a Purple Heart Medal; or 3) have been a resident of Indiana at the time of entry into the service and declared a POW or MIA after January 1, 1960. Students at the Indiana Soldiers' and Sailors' Children's Home are also eligible. The public safety officer portion of this program is open to 1) the children and spouses of police officers, fire fighters, and emergency medical technicians killed in the line of duty, and 2) the children and spouses of Indiana state policy troopers permanently and totally disabled in the line of duty. Children must be younger than 23 years of age and enrolled full time in an undergraduate or graduate degree program. Spouses must be enrolled in an undergraduate program and must have been married to the covered public safety officer at the time of death or disability.

Financial data Qualified applicants receive a 100% remission of tuition and all mandatory fees for under-

graduate or graduate work at state-supported postsecondary schools and universities in Indiana.

Duration Up to 124 semester hours of study.

Additional Information The veterans portion of this program is administered by the Indiana Department of Veterans' Affairs, 302 West Washington Street, Room E-120, Indianapolis, IN 46204-2738, (317) 232-3910, (800) 400-4520, Fax: (317) 232-7721, E-mail: jkiser@dva.state.in.us, Web site: www.in.gov/veteran.

Number awarded Varies each year.

Deadline Applications must be submitted at least 30 days before the start of the college term.

[1005]
JAMES DOYLE CASE MEMORIAL SCHOLARSHIPS

Mississippi Council of the Blind
2501 North West Street
Jackson, MS 39216
(601) 982-1718
Toll-free: (888) 346-5622 (within MS)
E-mail: mcb@netdoor.com

Summary To provide funding for college to legally blind residents of Mississippi and their children.

Eligibility This program is open to residents of Mississippi who are legally blind or the children of at least 1 legally blind parent. Applicants must be enrolled or accepted for enrollment in an undergraduate or graduate program and carrying or planning to carry at least 12 academic hours. Selection is based on a transcript from the last school or college attended, college entrance examination score, 2 letters of recommendation, and a 300-word biographical essay on the applicant's educational and employment goals. Membership in the sponsoring organization is not required.

Financial data The stipend is $1,000 per year.

Duration 1 year.

Additional Information Information is also available from Rebecca Floyd, President, 131 Red Fox Lane, Madison, MS 39110.

Number awarded 2 each year.

Deadline March of each year.

[1006]
JEAN SPINELLI MEMORIAL SCHOLARSHIP

Vermont Student Assistance Corporation
Champlain Mill
Attn: Scholarship Programs
P.O. Box 2000
Winooski, VT 05404-2601
(802) 654-3798   Toll-free: (800) 642-3177
Fax: (802) 654-3765   TDD: (802) 654-3766
TDD: (800) 281-3341 (within VT)
E-mail: info@vsac.org
Web: www.vsac.org

Summary To provide financial assistance to Vermont residents who are upper-division or graduate students and cancer survivors or caregivers to someone with cancer.

Eligibility This scholarship is available to residents of Vermont who are juniors or seniors in college or currently enrolled in graduate school. Applicants must be a cancer survivor or be (or have been) the primary caregiver to someone afflicted with cancer. They must be able to demonstrate 1) the spirit to live a productive, meaningful life while afflicted with cancer, or 2) selfless devoted care-giving to a friend or family member afflicted with cancer. Selection is based on required essays, a letter of recommendation, and financial need.

Financial data The stipend is $500.

Duration 1 year; recipients may reapply.

Number awarded 1 each year.

Deadline June of each year.

[1007]
JOHN YOUTSEY MEMORIAL SCHOLARSHIP FUND

Hemophilia of Georgia
8800 Roswell Road, Suite 170
Atlanta, GA 30350
(770) 518-8272   E-mail: mail@hog.org
Web: www.hog.org/scholarships.htm

Summary To provide financial assistance for college to residents of Georgia who have a bleeding disorder or have lost a parent because of the disorder.

Eligibility This program is open to permanent residents of Georgia who have hemophilia or related bleeding disorders and to children who have lost a parent to complications from a bleeding disorder. They may be graduating high school seniors or currently-enrolled college students. Selection is based on academic record, financial need, and personal goals.

Financial data A stipend is awarded (amount not specified).

Duration 1 year.

Additional Information Funds may be used for either a college or a vocational education.

[1008]
KATHERN F. GRUBER SCHOLARSHIPS

Blinded Veterans Association
477 H Street, N.W.
Washington, DC 20001-2694
(202) 371-8880   Toll-free: (800) 669-7079
Fax: (202) 371-8258   E-mail: bva@bva.org
Web: www.bva.org/services.html

Summary To provide financial assistance for undergraduate or graduate study to spouses and children of blinded veterans.

Eligibility This program is open to dependent children and spouses of blinded veterans of the U.S. armed forces. The veteran need not be a member of the Blinded Veterans Association. The veteran's blindness may be either service connected or nonservice connected, but it must meet the following definition: central visual acuity of 20/200 or less in the better eye with corrective glasses, or central visual acuity of more than 20/200 if there is a field defect in which the peripheral field has contracted to such an extent that the widest diameter of visual field subtends an angular distance no greater than 20 degrees in the better eye. The applicant must have been accepted or be currently enrolled as a full-time student in an undergraduate or graduate program at an accredited institution of higher learning. Selection is based on high school and/or college transcripts, 3 letters of recommendation, and a 300-word essay on the applicant's career goals and aspirations.

Financial data The stipends are $2,000 or $1,000 and are intended to be used to cover the student's expenses, including tuition, other academic fees, books, dormitory fees, and cafeteria fees. Funds are paid directly to the recipient's school.

Duration 1 year; recipients may reapply.

Additional Information Scholarships may be used for only 1 degree (vocational, bachelor's, or graduate) or nongraduate certificate (e.g., nursing, secretarial).

Number awarded 16 each year: 8 at $2,000 and 8 at $1,000.

Deadline April of each year.

[1009]
KENTUCKY DECEASED OR DISABLED LAW ENFORCEMENT OFFICER AND FIRE FIGHTER DEPENDENT TUITION WAIVER

Kentucky Fire Commission
Attn: Executive Director
2750 Research Park Drive—Barn Annex
P.O. Box 14092
Lexington, KY 40512-4092
(859) 246-3483   Toll-free: (800) 782-6823
Fax: (859) 246-3484   E-mail: ronnie.day@kctcs.net
Web: www.kctcs.net/kyfirecommission/index.htm

Summary To provide financial assistance for college to the children and spouses of Kentucky police officers or fire fighters deceased or disabled in the line of duty.

Eligibility This program is open to spouses, widow(er)s, and children of Kentucky residents who became a law enforcement officer, fire fighter, or volunteer fire fighter and who 1) was killed while in active service or training for active service; 2) died as a result of a service-connected disability; or 3) became permanently and totally disabled as a result of active service or training for active service. Children must be younger than 23 years of age; spouses and widow(er)s may be of any age.

Financial data Recipients are entitled to a waiver of tuition at state-supported universities, community colleges, and technical training institutions in Kentucky.

Duration 1 year; may be renewed up to a maximum total of 36 months.

Number awarded Varies each year; all qualified applicants are entitled to this aid.

[1010]
KENTUCKY VETERANS TUITION WAIVER PROGRAM

Kentucky Department of Veterans Affairs
Attn: Division of Field Operations
545 South Third Street, Room 123
Louisville, KY 40202
(502) 595-4447
Toll-free: (800) 928-4012 (within KY)
Fax: (502) 595-4448
Web: www.kdva.net

Summary To provide financial assistance for college to the children, spouses, or unremarried widow(er)s of disabled or deceased Kentucky veterans.

Eligibility This program is open to the children, stepchildren, adopted children, spouses, and unremarried widow(er)s of veterans who are residents of Kentucky (or were residents at the time of their death). The qualifying veteran must meet 1 of the following conditions: 1) died on active duty; 2) died as a direct result of a service-connected disability (as determined by the U.S. Department of Veterans Affairs); 3) has a 100% service-connected disability; 4) is totally disabled from a non-service connected cause but has wartime service; 5) died after service during a wartime period; or 6) was a prisoner of war or declared missing in action. The military service may have been as a member of the U.S. armed forces, the Kentucky National Guard while on state active duty, or a Reserve component on active duty. Children of veterans must be between 17 and 23 years of age; no age limit applies to spouses or unremarried widow(er)s. All applicants must be attending or planning to attend a 2-year, 4-year, or vocational technical school operated and funded by the Kentucky Department of Education.

Financial data Eligible dependents and survivors are exempt from tuition and matriculation fees at any state-supported institution of higher education in Kentucky.

Duration Tuition is waived until the recipient completes 36 months of training, receives a college degree, or (in the case of children of veterans) reaches 23 years of age, whichever comes first. Spouses and unremarried widow(er)s are not subject to the age limitation.
Number awarded Varies each year.

[1011]
KIDS' CHANCE OF ARIZONA SCHOLARSHIPS

Kids' Chance of Arizona
P.O. Box 36753
Phoenix, AZ 85067-6753
(602) 253-4360
Web: kidschance.org/arizona.htm

Summary To provide financial assistance for college to Arizona residents whose parent was killed or permanently disabled in an employment-related accident.
Eligibility This program is open to Arizona residents between 16 and 25 years of age whose parent was killed or disabled in an employment-related accident. Applicants must be attending or planning to attend a college, university, or trade school. They must submit high school transcripts, letters of recommendation, verification of school attendance, and a 1-page letter explaining their educational goals and need for financial assistance.
Financial data A stipend is awarded (amount not specified).
Duration 1 year; may be renewed.
Additional Information Information is also available from Marilyn Kinnier, scholarship vice president, (480) 251-5002, or Cheryl Altman, co-scholarship vice president, (602) 541-9863.
Number awarded Varies each year.

[1012]
KIDS' CHANCE OF ARKANSAS SCHOLARSHIPS

Kids' Chance of Arkansas
P.O. Box 950
Little Rock, AR 72203
(866) 880-8444
Web: www.awcc.state.ar.us

Summary To provide financial assistance for college to Arkansas residents whose parent was killed or permanently disabled in an employment-related accident.
Eligibility This program is open to children of workers who have been killed or become permanently and totally disabled from a compensable Arkansas Workers' Compensation injury or accident. Applicants must be between 16 and 22 years of age; be able to demonstrate good academic achievement and aptitude; and be attending or planning to attend an accredited vocational/technical school, college, or university. The injury or death of their parent must have resulted in a decrease in family earnings that creates an obstacle to the continuation of their education.
Financial data The stipend depends on the financial need of the recipient.
Duration 1 year.
Additional Information This program was established in 2002.
Number awarded Varies each year; recently, 3 of these scholarships were awarded.
Deadline May of each year.

[1013]
KIDS' CHANCE OF INDIANA SCHOLARSHIP PROGRAM

Kids' Chance of Indiana, Inc.
6612 East 75th Street, Suite 105
Indianapolis, IN 46250
Toll-free: (877) 261-8977
Web: www.kidschancein.org

Summary To provide financial assistance for college or graduate school to Indiana residents whose parent was killed or permanently disabled in a work-related accident.
Eligibility This program is open to Indiana residents between 16 and 25 years of age who are the children of workers fatally or catastrophically injured as a result of a work-related accident or occupational disease. The death or injury must be compensable by the Workers' Compensation Board of the state of Indiana and must have resulted in a substantial decline in the family's income that is likely to impede the student's pursuit of his or her educational objectives. Applicants must be attending or planning to attend a trade/vocational school, junior/community college, undergraduate college or university, or graduate school. Financial need is considered in the selection process.
Financial data Stipends range from $500 to $3,000 per year. Funds may be used for tuition and fees, books, room and board, and utilities.
Duration 1 year; may be renewed.
Additional Information Recipients may attend a public or private educational institution in any state. Information is also available from Marg Hamilton, Scholarship Application Coordinator, (317) 570-9502, Fax: (317) 570-9572.
Number awarded Varies each year.

FAMILIES OF DISABLED: SCHOLARSHIPS 361

[1014]
KIDS' CHANCE OF IOWA SCHOLARSHIPS

Kids' Chance of Iowa
c/o Ted Holglam
34 South First Avenue
Marshalltown, IA 50158
(515) 753-5549
Web: www.kidschanceiowa.org

Summary To provide financial assistance for college to Iowa residents whose parent was killed or permanently disabled in an employment-related accident.

Eligibility This program is open to Iowa residents between 17 and 25 years of age who have had a parent permanently or catastrophically injured or killed in an employment-related accident. Applicants must be attending or planning to attend an accredited college or technical school. The parent's death or injury must have resulted in a substantial decline in the family income.

Financial data The stipend depends on the financial need of the recipient. Funding is intended to cover tuition and books, but it may also include housing and meals.

Duration 1 year; may be renewed if the recipient maintains acceptable grades.

Additional Information This program was established in 1997. Information is also available from Patricia L. McCollom, Chair, 114 N.W. Fifth Street, P.O. Box 95, Ankeny, IA 50021, (515) 964-3868, Fax: (515) 965-1286, E-mail: IALCP@aol.com.

Number awarded Varies each year.

[1015]
KIDS' CHANCE OF LOUISIANA SCHOLARSHIPS

Kids' Chance of Louisiana
c/o The Louisiana Bar Foundation
601 St. Charles Avenue, Third Floor
New Orleans, LA 70130
(504) 561-1046   Fax: (504) 566-1926
E-mail: kidschance@raisingthebar.org
Web: www.raisingthebar.org

Summary To provide financial assistance for college to Louisiana residents whose parent was killed or permanently disabled in an employment-related accident.

Eligibility This program is open to Louisiana residents between 16 and 25 years of age who are the dependent of a worker killed or permanently and totally disabled in an accident that is compensable under a state or federal Workers' Compensation Act or law. Applicants must be attending or planning to attend an accredited Louisiana university; community, technical, or vocational college; or state-approved proprietary school. Financial need is considered in the selection process.

Financial data Stipends range from $500 to $3,000. Funds, paid directly to the school where the child is enrolled, may be used for tuition, books, fees, room, and general living expenses.

Duration 1 year; recipients may reapply as long as they maintain a "C" average or higher.

Additional Information Kids' Chance was founded in 1988 by the Workers' Compensation Section of the Georgia Bar Association. The program in Louisiana is administered by the Louisiana Bar Foundation.

Number awarded Varies each year.

Deadline May of each year.

[1016]
KIDS' CHANCE OF MARYLAND SCHOLARSHIPS

Kids' Chance of Maryland, Inc.
P.O. Box 20262
Baltimore, MD 21284
(410) 832-4702   Fax: (410) 832-4726
E-mail: info@kidschance-md.org
Web: www.kidschance-md.org

Summary To provide financial assistance for college to Maryland residents whose parent was killed or permanently disabled in an employment-related accident.

Eligibility This program is open to Maryland residents between 16 and 25 years of age who had a parent permanently or catastrophically injured or killed in an employment related accident compensable under the Maryland Workers' Compensation Act. Applicants must be attending or planning to attend college or technical school. Financial need is considered in the selection process.

Financial data Stipends depend on the need of the students. Funds are intended to cover tuition and books but may also including housing and meals.

Duration 1 year; recipients may reapply.

Number awarded Varies each year.

[1017]
KIDS' CHANCE OF MISSISSIPPI SCHOLARSHIP FUND

Mississippi Bar Foundation
Attn: Administrative Law and Workers'
   Compensation Section
643 North State Street
P.O. Box 2168
Jackson, MS 39225-2168
(601) 948-4471   Fax: (601) 355-8635
Web: www.msbar.org/kidchance.html

Summary To provide financial assistance for college to Mississippi residents whose parent was killed or disabled on the job.

Eligibility This program is open to Mississippi residents between 17 and 23 years of age who have had a parent killed or permanently and totally disabled in an accident that is compensable under the Mississippi Workers' Compensation Act. Applicants must demonstrate substantial financial need.

Financial data A stipend is awarded (amount not specified).
Duration 1 year; may be renewed.
Number awarded Varies each year.
Deadline April of each year.

[1018]
KIDS' CHANCE OF MISSOURI SCHOLARSHIPS

Kids' Chance Inc. of Missouri
Attn: Scholarship Committee
P.O. Box 410384
St. Louis, MO 63141
(314) 997-3390   Toll-free: (800) 484-5733
E-mail: susgrp@charter.net
Web: www.mokidschance.org

Summary To provide financial assistance for college to Missouri residents whose parent was killed or permanently disabled in a work-related accident.
Eligibility This program is open to Missouri residents whose parent sustained a serious injury or fatality in a Missouri work-related accident covered by workers' compensation. Applicants must be attending or planning to attend an accredited vocational school or college within the United States. They must be able to demonstrate financial need.
Financial data Stipends depend on the need of the recipient. Funds may be used to cover tuition, books, supplies, housing, meals, and other expenses not covered by other grants and/or scholarships.
Duration 1 year; may be renewed.
Additional Information This program was established in 1996.
Number awarded Varies each year.
Deadline April or October of each year.

[1019]
KIDS' CHANCE OF PENNSYLVANIA SCHOLARSHIPS

Kids' Chance of Pennsylvania
P.O. Box 543
Pottstown, PA 19464
(484) 945-2104   Fax: (610) 970-7520
E-mail: info@kidschanceofpa.org
Web: www.kidschanceofpa.org

Summary To provide financial assistance for college to Pennsylvania residents whose parent was killed or permanently disabled in a work-related accident.
Eligibility This program is open to Pennsylvania residents between 16 and 25 years of age who have been accepted by an accredited postsecondary educational institution anywhere in the United States. At least 1 parent must have been killed or seriously injured as a result of a work-related accident covered under the Pennsylvania Workers' Compensation Act. Financial need is considered in the selection process.
Financial data Regardless of the state where the recipient attends school, the stipend may not exceed the annual cost of tuition and books at the most expensive public postsecondary educational institution in Pennsylvania.
Duration 1 year; may be renewed.
Number awarded Varies each year; recently, 27 students were receiving support through this program.
Deadline April of each year.

[1020]
KIDS' CHANCE OF SOUTH CAROLINA SCHOLARSHIPS

Kids' Chance of South Carolina
1135 Dixie Red Road
Leesville, SC 29070
(803) 532-0608   Fax: (803) 532-9892
Web: www.kidschancesc.org

Summary To provide financial assistance for college or graduate school to South Carolina residents whose parent was killed or permanently disabled in a work-related accident.
Eligibility This program is open to South Carolina residents between 16 and 25 years of age who are the children of workers fatally or catastrophically injured as a result of a work-related accident or occupational disease. Applicants must be attending or planning to attend a trade school, vocational school, community or junior college, undergraduate college or university, or graduate school. The work-related injury or occupational disease from which their parent suffers or died must be compensable by the Workers' Compensation Board of South Carolina and must have resulted in a substantial decline in the family's income that is likely to interfere with the student's pursuit of his or her educational objectives.
Financial data Stipends range from $500 to $3,000 per year. Funds may be used for tuition and fees, books, room and board, and utilities.
Duration 1 year; may be renewed.
Additional Information Recipients may attend school in any state.
Number awarded Varies each year.

[1021]
KIDS' CHANCE OF WEST VIRGINIA SCHOLARSHIPS

Greater Kanawha Valley Foundation
Attn: Scholarship Coordinator
One Huntington Square, 16th Floor
900 Lee Street, East
P.O. Box 3041
Charleston, WV 25331-3041
(304) 346-3620   Fax: (304) 346-3640
E-mail: tgkvf@tgkvf.com
Web: www.tgkvf.com/scholarship.html

Summary To provide financial assistance for college to students whose parents were injured in a West Virginia work-related accident.

Eligibility This program is open to children between the ages of 16 and 25 whose parents were seriously injured in a West Virginia work-related accident. Applicants may reside in any state and be pursuing any field of study at an accredited trade or vocational school, college, or university. They must have at least a 2.5 GPA and demonstrate good moral character. Preference is given to applicants who can demonstrate financial need, academic excellence, leadership abilities, and contributions to school and community.

Financial data The stipend is $1,000 per year.

Duration 1 year; may be renewed.

Additional Information This program is sponsored by Kids' Chance of West Virginia, Inc.

Number awarded 3 each year.

Deadline February of each year.

[1022]
KIDS' CHANCE SCHOLARSHIP FUND

Alabama Law Foundation
415 Dexter Avenue
P.O. Box 671
Montgomery, AL 36101
(334) 269-1515   E-mail: info@alfinc.org
Web: www.alfinc.org/kids.html

Summary To provide financial assistance for college to Alabama residents whose parent was killed or disabled on the job.

Eligibility This program is open to high school seniors and college students (including students at technical colleges) in Alabama whose parent was killed or permanently and totally disabled in an on-the-job accident. Financial need is considered in the selection process.

Financial data Stipends range from $500 to $3,000 but do not exceed the cost of tuition and books at the most expensive public university in Alabama.

Additional Information This program was established in 1992 by the Workers' Compensation Section of the Alabama State Bar and is currently administered by the Alabama Law Foundation.

Number awarded Varies each year; recently, 17 of these scholarships were awarded, including 2 at $2,000, 3 at $1,500, 3 at $1,000, 3 at $750, and 6 at $500.

Deadline April of each year.

[1023]
KIDS' CHANCE SCHOLARSHIPS

Kids' Chance, Inc.
P.O. Box 623
Valdosta, GA 31603
(229) 244-0153   Fax: (229) 245-0413
E-mail: kids300@bellsouth.net
Web: kidschance.org

Summary To provide financial assistance for college to Georgia residents whose parent was killed or permanently disabled in an employment-related accident.

Eligibility This program is open to Georgia residents between 16 and 25 years of age who parent's on-the-job death or injury resulted in a substantial decline in family income. Applicants must be attending or planning to attend college or technical school.

Financial data The stipend depends on the financial need of the recipient, to a maximum of $5,333. Funds may be used for tuition, books, housing, meals, transportation, and/or as a supplement to the income of the family to compensate for money the student would earn by dropping out of school.

Duration 1 year; may be renewed if the recipient maintains satisfactory academic progress.

Additional Information This program was established by the Workers' Compensation Section of the Georgia Bar in 1988. It has served as a model for comparable programs that currently operate in 23 other states.

Number awarded Varies each year; recently, 49 students were receiving $110,205 in support through this program.

[1024]
LOUISIANA VETERANS STATE AID PROGRAM

Louisiana Department of Veterans Affairs
1885 Wooddale Boulevard, Room 1013
P.O. Box 94095, Capitol Station
Baton Rouge, LA 70804-9095
(225) 922-0500   Fax: (225) 922-0511
E-mail: dperkins@vetaffairs.com
Web: www.ldva.org/benefits.html

Summary To provide financial assistance for college to children and surviving spouses of certain disabled or deceased Louisiana veterans.

Eligibility Eligible under this program are children (between 16 and 25 years of age) of veterans who served during World War I, World War II, the Korean war, or the Vietnam conflict and either died or sustained a disability

rated as 90% or more by the U.S. Department of Veterans Affairs. Deceased veterans must have resided in Louisiana for at least 12 months prior to entry into service. Living disabled veterans must have resided in Louisiana for at least 24 months prior to the child's admission into the program. Also eligible are surviving spouses (of any age) of veterans who had been residents of Louisiana for at least 1 year preceding entry into service and who died in war service in the line of duty or from an established wartime service-connected disability subsequently.

Financial data Eligible persons accepted as full-time students at Louisiana state-supported colleges, universities, trade schools, or vocational/technical schools will be admitted free and are exempt from payment of all tuition, laboratory, athletic, medical, and other special fees. Free registration does not cover books, supplies, room and board, or fees assessed by the student body on themselves (such as yearbooks and weekly papers).

Duration Tuition, fee exemption, and possible payment of cash subsistence allowance are provided for a maximum of 4 school years to be completed in not more than 5 years from date of original entry.

Additional Information Attendance must be on a full-time basis. Surviving spouses must remain unmarried and must take advantage of the benefit within 10 years after eligibility is established.

Number awarded Varies each year.

Deadline Applications must be received no later than 3 months prior to the beginning of a semester.

[1025]
MAINE VETERANS DEPENDENTS EDUCATIONAL BENEFITS

Bureau of Maine Veterans' Services
117 State House Station
Augusta, ME 04333-0117
(207) 626-4464
Toll-free: (800) 345-0116 (within ME)
Fax: (207) 626-4471
E-mail: mvs@me.ngb.army.mil
Web: www.state.me.us/va/defense/vb.htm

Summary To provide financial assistance for undergraduate or graduate education to dependents of disabled and other Maine veterans.

Eligibility Applicants for these benefits must be children (high school seniors or graduates under 25 years of age), non-divorced spouses, or unremarried widow(er)s of veterans who meet 1 or more of the following requirements: 1) living and determined to have a total permanent disability resulting from a service-connected disability; 2) killed in action; 3) died from a service-connected disability; 4) died while totally and permanently disabled due to a service-connected disability but whose death was not related to the service-connected disability; or 5) a member of the armed forces on active duty who has been listed for more than 90 days as missing in action, captured, forcibly detained, or interned in the line of duty by a foreign government or power. The veteran parent must have been a resident of Maine at the time of entry into service or a resident of Maine for 5 years preceding application for these benefits. Children may be seeking no higher than a bachelor's degree. Spouses, widows, and widowers may work on an advanced degree if they already have a bachelor's degree at the time of enrollment into this program.

Financial data Recipients are entitled to free tuition at institutions of higher education supported by the state of Maine.

Duration Benefits extend for a maximum of 8 semesters. Recipients have 6 consecutive academic years to complete their education.

Additional Information College preparatory schooling and correspondence courses do not qualify under this program.

Number awarded Varies each year.

[1026]
MARGARET FUNDS SCHOLARSHIPS

Woman's Missionary Union
Attn: WMU Foundation
P.O. Box 11346
Birmingham, AL 35202-1346
(205) 408-5525   Toll-free: (877) 482-4483
Fax: (205) 408-5508
E-mail: wmufoundation@wmu.org
Web: www.wmufoundation.com

Summary To provide financial assistance for undergraduate or graduate study to the dependent children of appointed missionaries and missionary associates, provided both parents are under North American Mission Board (NAMB) appointment.

Eligibility Students who are dependents of NAMB missionaries and were born prior to or during missionary service are eligible, provided 1) the missionaries or missionary associates are on active status with NAMB and have served a minimum of 4 years or 2) the missionary or missionary associate died or became totally disabled while in missionary service. Missionaries and missionary associates who are placed on reserve status and have served on active status for at least 10 years are also eligible, as are missionaries and missionary associates who have served at least 10 years with NAMB and have resigned to serve in another church or denominational work-related vocation. Married students may not apply.

Financial data Benefits are based on credit hours and years of mission service completed. For undergraduates, stipends range from $21 per credit hour (for 4 years of mission service completed) to $42 per credit hour (for 10 or more years of mission service completed). For graduate students, benefits are paid according to the following: 1) balance of unused undergraduate scholarship; 2) for seminary study, up to 50% of undergraduate benefits. For students who attend technical or professional

schools not associated with accredited colleges, payment is made on total hours of training. For missionary or missionary associates retired or placed on reserve status, benefits are based on financial need. All benefits are paid in 4 equal installments to the recipient's college or seminary and cannot exceed the cost of the training.

Duration 1 academic term; may be renewed.

Additional Information This program includes several named awards with additional requirements. Students who are graduating college seniors, have maintained at least a 3.0 GPA in college, and have demonstrated scholarship, leadership, and character while in college are eligible to apply for the Elizabeth Lowndes Award of $400. The Julia C. Pugh Scholarship stipulates that the recipient must have significant financial need and not qualify for regular scholarships. The Mattie J.C. Russell Scholarship is limited to the children of home missionaries. The Mary B. Rhodes Medical Scholarship is for medical students who are the children of foreign missionaries. Endowment Fund Scholarships of $400 are given to former Margaret Fund students appointed as missionaries and $200 scholarships are given to former students of Baptist mission boards appointed as regular missionaries, missionary associates, missionary journeymen, or US 2 missionaries. Undergraduates must begin their studies within 5 years and complete them within 10 years; graduate students must begin within 3 years and complete within 5 years.

Number awarded Varies each year.

[1027]
MARILYN YETSO MEMORIAL SCHOLARSHIP
Ulman Cancer Fund for Young Adults
4725 Dorsey Hall Drive, Suite A
PMB 505
Ellicott City, MD 21042
(410) 964-0202   Toll-free: (888) 393-FUND
E-mail: scholarship@ulmanfund.org
Web: www.ulmanfund.org

Summary To provide financial assistance to college students who have a parent with cancer.

Eligibility This program is open to college students who have or have lost a parent to cancer. Applicants must be able to demonstrate financial need.

Financial data The stipend is $1,000.

Duration 1 year.

Number awarded 1 each year.

[1028]
MARK REAMES MEMORIAL SCHOLARSHIPS
Hemophilia Society of Colorado
Attn: Scholarship Committee
10020 East Girard, Suite 100
Denver, CO 80231
(303) 750-6990   Toll-free: (888) 687-CLOT
Fax: (303) 750-7035   E-mail: info@cohemo.org
Web: www.cohemo.org

Summary To provide financial assistance for college to students from Colorado who have a bleeding disorder and to members of their families.

Eligibility This program is open to residents of Colorado who have hemophilia or a related inherited bleeding disorder and their immediate family members. Applicants must submit proof of enrollment at an institution of higher education (4-year college or university, 2-year college, professional trade school); an essay on how their varied interests, life experiences, and/or community involvement led to their current career goals; high school and (if applicable) college transcripts; documentation of financial need; and 2 letters of recommendation.

Financial data The stipend is $1,000. Funds must be used for tuition, room, board, and related educational expenses.

Duration 1 year.

Number awarded 2 each year.

Deadline June of each year.

[1029]
MARYLAND LEGION SCHOLARSHIPS
American Legion
Attn: Department of Maryland
War Memorial Building
101 North Gay Street, Room E
Baltimore, MD 21202
(410) 752-1405   Fax: (410) 752-3822
E-mail: mdlegion@clark.net
Web: www.mdlegion.org

Summary To provide financial assistance for college to Maryland residents who are the children of veterans, particularly veterans with disabilities.

Eligibility Maryland residents may apply for these scholarships if they are the children of veterans and have not reached their 20th birthday by January 1 of the calendar year the application is filed. Applicants must intend to enroll as full-time college students. Special consideration is given to applicants whose veteran parent is disabled or whose family demonstrates financial need.

Financial data The stipend is $500.

Duration 1 year.

Number awarded Up to 11 each year.

Deadline March of each year.

[1030]
MICHIGAN VETERANS TRUST FUND TUITION GRANTS

Department of Military and Veterans Affairs
Attn: Michigan Veterans Trust Fund
2500 South Washington Avenue
Lansing, MI 48913-5101
(517) 483-5469　　E-mail: paocmn@michigan.gov
Web: www.michigan.gov/dmva

Summary To provide financial assistance for college to the children of Michigan veterans who are totally disabled or deceased as a result of service-connected causes.

Eligibility This program is open to children of Michigan veterans who are totally disabled as a result of wartime service, or died from service-connected conditions, or were killed in action, or are listed as missing in action. Applicants must be between 16 and 26 years of age and must have lived in Michigan at least 12 months prior to the date of application. They must be or plan to become a full-time undergraduate student at a public institution of higher education in Michigan.

Financial data Recipients are exempt from payment of the first $2,800 per year of tuition or any other fee that takes the place of tuition.

Duration 1 year; may be renewed if the recipient maintains full-time enrollment and a GPA of 2.25 or higher.

Number awarded Varies each year.

[1031]
MIKE HYLTON & RON NIEDERMAN SCHOLARSHIP

Factor Support Network Pharmacy
Attn: Scholarship Committee
900 Avenida Acaso, Suite A
Camarillo, CA 93012-8749
(805) 388-9336　　Toll-free: (877) FSN-4-YOU
Fax: (805) 482-6324
Web: www.factorsupport.com/scholarships.htm

Summary To provide financial assistance to persons with hemophilia and to their immediate families.

Eligibility This program is open to people with bleeding disorders, their spouses, and their children. Applicants must be attending or planning to attend a postsecondary institution, including trade and technical schools. They must submit 3 short essays, on their career goals, their involvement in the hemophilia or bleeding disorder community, and how a bleeding disorder has affected their life.

Financial data The stipend is $1,000. Funds are paid directly to the recipient.

Duration 1 year.

Additional Information This program was established in 1999.

Number awarded 10 each year.

Deadline April of each year.

[1032]
MILLIE BROTHER SCHOLARSHIP

CODA International
P.O. Box 30715
Santa Barbara, CA 93130-0715
E-mail: coda@coda-international.org
Web: coda-international.org/scholar.html

Summary To provide financial assistance for college to the children of deaf parents.

Eligibility This program is open to the hearing children of deaf parents who are high school seniors or graduates. Applicants must submit a 2-page essay on their experience as the child of deaf parents, how it has shaped them as individuals, and their future career aspirations; essays are judged on organization, content, creativity, and sense of purpose. In addition to the essay, selection is based on a high school transcript and 2 letters of recommendation.

Financial data The stipend is $2,000.

Duration 1 year.

Additional Information Winning essays are published in the *CODA Connection*, the newsletter of Children of Deaf Adults (CODA) International. Information is also available from Dr. Robert Hoffmeister, Chair, Scholarship Committee, Boston University, Programs in Deaf Studies, 605 Commonwealth Avenue, Boston, MA 02215, (617) 353-3205, TTY: (617) 353-3205.

Number awarded 2 each year.

Deadline May of each year.

[1033]
MISSISSIPPI LAW ENFORCEMENT OFFICERS AND FIREMEN SCHOLARSHIP PROGRAM

Mississippi Office of Student Financial Aid
3825 Ridgewood Road
Jackson, MS 39211-6453
(601) 432-6997
Toll-free: (800) 327-2980 (within MS)
Fax: (601) 432-6527　　E-mail: sfa@ihl.state.ms.us
Web: www.ihl.state.ms.us

Summary To provide financial assistance for college to the spouses and children of disabled or deceased Mississippi law enforcement officers and fire fighters.

Eligibility This program is open to children and spouses of full-time law enforcement officers and fire fighters who became permanently and totally disabled or who died in the line of duty and were Mississippi residents at the time of death or injury. Applicants must be high school seniors or graduates interested in attending a state-supported postsecondary institution in Mississippi on a full-time basis. Children may be natural, adopted, or stepchildren up to 23 years of age; spouses may be of any age.

Financial data Students in this program receive full payment of tuition fees, the average cost of campus housing, required fees, and applicable course fees at

state-supported colleges and universities in Mississippi. Funds may not be used to pay for books, food, school supplies, materials, dues, or fees for extracurricular activities.

Duration Up to 8 semesters.

Number awarded Varies each year.

Deadline Applications may be submitted at any time.

[1034]
MISSOURI PUBLIC SURVIVOR GRANT PROGRAM

Missouri Department of Higher Education
Attn: Missouri Student Assistance Resource
  Services (MOSTARS)
3515 Amazonas Drive
Jefferson City, MO 65109-5717
(573) 751-3940   Toll-free: (800) 473-6757
Fax: (573) 751-6635
Web: www.mocbhe.gov/Mostars/pssgp.htm

Summary To provide financial assistance for college to spouses and children of disabled and deceased Missouri public employees and public safety officers.

Eligibility This program is open to dependent children and spouses of 1) Missouri Department of Transportation employees who were killed or permanently disabled while engaged in the construction or maintenance of highways, roads, and bridges; and 2) Missouri public safety officers who were killed or permanently disabled in the line of duty. Applicants must be Missouri residents enrolled or accepted for enrollment as a full-time undergraduate student at a participating Missouri college or university; children must be younger than 24 years of age. Students pursuing a degree or certificate in theology or divinity are not eligible. U.S. citizenship or permanent resident status is required.

Financial data The maximum annual grant is the lesser of 1) the actual tuition charged at the school where the recipient is enrolled, or 2) the amount of tuition charged to a Missouri undergraduate resident enrolled full time in the same class level and in the same academic major as an applicant at the University of Missouri at Columbia.

Duration 1 year; may be renewed.

Number awarded Varies each year.

Deadline There is no application deadline, but early submission of the completed application is encouraged.

[1035]
NATIONAL AMPUTEE GOLF ASSOCIATION SCHOLARSHIP

National Amputee Golf Association
Attn: Executive Director
11 Walnut Hill Road
Amherst, NH 03031
(603) 672-6444   Toll-free: (800) 633-NAGA
Fax: (603) 672-2987   E-mail: info@nagagolf.org
Web: www.nagagolf.org/scholarship.htm

Summary To provide financial assistance for college to members of the National Amputee Golf Association and their dependents.

Eligibility This program is open to amputee members in good standing in the association and their dependents. Applicants must submit information on their scholastic background (GPA in high school and college, courses of study); type of amputation and cause (if applicable), a cover letter describing their plans for the future; and documentation of financial need. They need not be competitive golfers. Selection is based on academic record, financial need, involvement in extracurricular or community activities, and area of study.

Financial data The stipend is up to $1,000 per year, depending on need.

Duration Up to 4 years, provided the recipient maintains at least half-time enrollment and a GPA of 2.0 or higher and continues to demonstrate financial need.

Number awarded 1 or more each year.

Deadline July of each year.

[1036]
NATIONAL GUARD ASSOCIATION OF INDIANA EDUCATIONAL GRANTS

National Guard Association of Indiana
Attn: Educational Grant Committee
2002 South Holt Road, Building 9
Indianapolis, IN 46241-4839
(317) 247-3196   Toll-free: (800) 219-2173
Fax: (317) 247-3575   E-mail: director@ngai.net
Web: www.ngai.net/benefits.htm

Summary To provide financial assistance for college to members of the National Guard Association of Indiana (NGAI) and their dependents.

Eligibility This program is open to NGAI members who are currently serving in the Indiana National Guard and their dependents. Children and widow(er)s of former Guard members killed or permanently disabled while on duty with the Indiana National Guard are also eligible. Applicants must submit 2 letters of recommendation, a copy of high school or college transcripts, SAT or ACT scores (if taken), a letter of acceptance from a college or university (if not currently attending college), and an essay on the educational program they intend to pursue and the goals they wish to attain. Selection is based on academic achievement, commitment and desire to

achieve, extracurricular activities, accomplishments, goals, and financial need.
Financial data The stipend is $500.
Duration 1 year; recipients may reapply.
Number awarded A limited number are awarded each year.
Deadline February of each year.

[1037]
NATIONAL KIDNEY FOUNDATION OF CONNECTICUT SCHOLARSHIP PROGRAM

National Kidney Foundation of Connecticut
2139 Silas Deane Highway
Rocky Hill, CT 06067
(860) 257-3770   Fax: (860) 257-3429
E-mail: info@kidneyct.org
Web: www.kidneyct.org/how.html

Summary To provide financial assistance for college to residents of Connecticut who have kidney or urological problems or their dependents.
Eligibility This program is open to dialysis and kidney transplant patients in Connecticut and their dependents, as well as people with Childhood Nephrotic Syndrome. Applicants may be entering college as freshmen, continuing students, or older students returning to school. They must have a GPA of 2.5 or higher. Selection is based on academic performance, financial need, and history of community service.
Financial data Stipends up to $1,000 per year are available.
Duration 1 year; may be renewed.
Number awarded Varies each year.
Deadline June of each year.

[1038]
NATIONAL KIDNEY FOUNDATION OF MASSACHUSETTS, RHODE ISLAND, NEW HAMPSHIRE, AND VERMONT ACADEMIC AWARDS

National Kidney Foundation of Massachusetts,
   Rhode Island, New Hampshire, and Vermont, Inc.
Attn: Academic Awards Committee
129 Morgan Drive
Norwood, MA 02062
(781) 278-0222   Toll-free: (800) 542-4001
Fax: (781) 278-0333
E-mail: sdean@kidneyhealth.org
Web: www.kidneyhealth.org

Summary To provide financial assistance for college to high school seniors and graduates from selected Northeastern states who have kidney disease or to their family members.
Eligibility This program is open to students from Massachusetts, Rhode Island, New Hampshire, and Vermont who are high school seniors or graduates pursuing postsecondary education. Applicants must have active and current kidney disease or be an immediate relative (parent, sibling, child, legal guardian) of a person with active and current kidney disease. The kidney disease must have a significant impact on the applicant's life. A kidney condition that is not progressive or does not impede the person's lifestyle in any way will not be considered. Applicants must submit a 1-page essay describing how the presence of kidney disease in their family has affected their life and career goals, discussing the major they plan to pursue, and including how their experience may have affected their decisions regarding this plan of study and/or particular school. Selection is based on academic achievement and financial need.
Financial data The stipend is $700 per year, paid in 2 installments at the beginning of each semester.
Duration 1 year.
Number awarded 13 each year.
Deadline March of each year.

[1039]
NCFOP FOUNDATION SCHOLARSHIPS

North Carolina Fraternal Order of Police Foundation, Inc.
4801 East Oak Island Drive
Oak Island, NC 28465
(910) 278-4324   E-mail: ncfop@aol.com
Web: ncfop.com/foundation.htm

Summary To provide financial assistance for college to families of disabled or deceased law enforcement officers in North Carolina.
Eligibility This program is open to North Carolina residents who are enrolled in an appropriate postsecondary institution, including colleges and vocational schools. Applicants must be the child or spouse of a North Carolina law enforcement officer killed or disabled in the line of duty.
Financial data A stipend is awarded (amount not specified).
Duration 1 year.
Number awarded Varies each year; recently, 3 of these scholarships were awarded.

[1040]
NEBRASKA WAIVER OF TUITION FOR VETERANS' DEPENDENTS

Department of Veterans' Affairs
State Office Building
301 Centennial Mall South, Sixth Floor
P.O. Box 95083
Lincoln, NE 68509-5083
(402) 471-2458 Fax: (402) 471-2491
E-mail: dparker@mail.state.ne.us
Web: www.vets.state.ne.us

Summary To provide financial assistance for college to dependents of deceased and disabled veterans and military personnel in Nebraska.

Eligibility Eligible are spouses, widow(er)s, and children who are residents of Nebraska and whose parent, stepparent, or spouse was a member of the U.S. armed forces 1) died of a service-connected disability; 2) died subsequent to discharge as a result of injury or illness sustained while in service; 3) is permanently and totally disabled as a result of military service; or 4) is classified as missing in action or as a prisoner of war during armed hostilities after August 4, 1964. Applicants must be attending or planning to attend a branch of the University of Nebraska, a state college, or a community college in Nebraska.

Financial data Tuition is waived at public institutions in Nebraska.

Duration The waiver is valid for 1 degree, diploma, or certificate from a community college and 1 baccalaureate degree.

Additional Information Applications may be submitted through 1 of the recognized veterans' organizations or any county service officer.

Number awarded Varies each year.

[1041]
NEW HORIZONS SCHOLARSHIPS

New Horizons Scholars Program
55 Second Street, 15th Floor
San Francisco, CA 94105-3491
Toll-free: (866) 3-HORIZON
Web: www.hsf.net/DOC-PDF/NewHorizons.pdf

Summary To provide financial assistance for college to Hispanic and African American high school seniors who are infected with Hepatitis C or who are dependents of someone with Hepatitis C.

Eligibility This program is open to high school seniors planning to enroll full time at a 4-year college or university in the following fall. Applicants must be of African American heritage or of Hispanic heritage (each parent half Hispanic or 1 parent fully Hispanic) and have a high school GPA of 3.0 or higher. Along with their application, they must submit 1) verification by a physician that they have Hepatitis C or are the dependent of a person with Hepatitis C; 2) transcripts; 3) a letter of recommendation; 4) documentation of financial need; and 5) a personal statement that addresses the following topics: heritage and family background, personal and academic achievements, academic plans and career goals, efforts toward making a difference in the community, and financial need.

Financial data A stipend is awarded (amount not specified).

Duration 1 year.

Additional Information This program began in 2003 as the result of a partnership of the Thurgood Marshall Scholarship Fund and the Hispanic Scholarship Fund, with support from the Roche Foundation.

Number awarded 1 or more each year.

Deadline February of each year.

[1042]
NORTH CAROLINA BAR ASSOCIATION SCHOLARSHIPS

North Carolina Bar Association
Attn: Young Lawyers Division Scholarship
  Committee
8000 Weston Parkway
P.O. Box 3688
Cary, NC 27519-3688
(919) 677-0561 Toll-free: (800) 662-7407
Fax: (919) 677-0761 E-mail: jtfount@ncbar.org
Web: www.ncbar.org

Summary To provide financial assistance for college or graduate school to the children of disabled or deceased law enforcement officers in North Carolina.

Eligibility This program is open to the natural or adopted children of North Carolina law enforcement officers who were permanently disabled or killed in the line of duty. Applicants must be younger than 27 years of age and enrolled in or accepted at an accredited institution of higher learning (including community colleges, trade schools, colleges, universities, and graduate programs) in North Carolina. Selection is based on academic performance and financial need.

Financial data The stipend depends on the availability of funds but normally does not exceed $1,000 per year.

Duration Up to 4 years.

Number awarded Varies each year; recently, 4 new and 14 renewal scholarships were awarded.

Deadline March of each year.

[1043]
NORTH CAROLINA NATIONAL GUARD ASSOCIATION SPECIAL POPULATION SCHOLARSHIP

North Carolina National Guard Association
Attn: Educational Foundation, Inc.
7410 Chapel Hill Road
Raleigh, NC 27607-5047
(919) 851-3390
Toll-free: (800) 821-6159 (within NC)
Fax: (919) 859-4990   E-mail: ncnga@bellsouth.net
Web: www.ncnga.org/education/index.asp

Summary To provide financial assistance for college to members and dependents of members of the North Carolina National Guard Association who have a disability.

Eligibility This program is open to active and associate members of the association as well as the spouses, children, grandchildren, and legal dependents of active, retired, or deceased members. Applicants must be learning disabled and/or physically disabled. They may be high school seniors, high school graduates, or currently-enrolled college students. Selection is based on financial need, academic achievement, citizenship, leadership, and other application information.

Financial data Stipends are $950, $750, or $350.

Duration 1 year; may be renewed.

Number awarded Varies each year.

Deadline January of each year for high school graduates and college students; February of each year for high school seniors.

[1044]
NORTH CAROLINA SCHOLARSHIPS FOR CHILDREN OF WAR VETERANS

Division of Veterans Affairs
Albemarle Building
325 North Salisbury Street, Suite 1065
Raleigh, NC 27603-5941
(919) 733-3851   Fax: (919) 733-2834
E-mail: Charlie.Smith@ncmail.net
Web: www.doa.state.nc.us/doa/vets/va.htm

Summary To provide financial assistance for college to the children of disabled and other classes of North Carolina veterans.

Eligibility Eligible applicants come from 5 categories: Class I-A: the veteran parent died in wartime service or as a result of a service-connected condition incurred in wartime service; Class I-B: the veteran parent is rated by the U.S. Department of Veterans Affairs (VA) as 100% disabled as a result of wartime service and currently or at the time of death drawing compensation for such disability; Class II: the veteran parent is rated by the VA as much as 20 but less than 100% disabled due to wartime service, or was awarded a Purple Heart medal for wounds received, and currently or at the time of death drawing compensation for such disability; Class III: the veteran parent is currently or was at the time of death receiving a VA pension for total and permanent disability, or the veteran parent is deceased but does not qualify under any other provisions, or the veteran parent served in a combat zone or waters adjacent to a combat zone and received a campaign badge or medal but does not qualify under any other provisions; Class IV: the veteran parent was a prisoner of war or missing in action. For all classes, the veteran parent must have been a legal resident of North Carolina at the time of entrance into the armed forces or the child must have been born in North Carolina and lived in the state continuously since birth.

Financial data Students in Classes I-A, II, III, and IV receive $4,500 per academic year if they attend a private college or junior college; if attending a public postsecondary institution, they receive free tuition, a room allowance, a board allowance, and exemption from certain mandatory fees. Students in Class I-B receive $1,500 per academic year if they attend a private college or junior college; if attending a public postsecondary institution, they receive free tuition and exemption from certain mandatory fees.

Duration 4 academic years.

Number awarded An unlimited number of awards are made under Classes I-A, I-B, and IV. Classes II and III are limited to 100 awards each year in each class.

Deadline April of each year.

[1045]
NORTH CAROLINA SHERIFFS' ASSOCIATION UNDERGRADUATE CRIMINAL JUSTICE SCHOLARSHIPS

North Carolina State Education Assistance Authority
Attn: Scholarship and Grant Services
10 T.W. Alexander Drive
P.O. Box 14103
Research Triangle Park, NC 27709-4103
(919) 549-8614   Toll-free: (800) 700-1775
Fax: (919) 549-8481
E-mail: information@ncseaa.edu
Web: www.ncseaa.edu

Summary To provide financial assistance for college to children of deceased or disabled North Carolina law enforcement officers who are majoring in criminal justice in college.

Eligibility Eligible for this program are North Carolina residents studying criminal justice at any of the 10 state institutions offering that major: Appalachian State University, East Carolina University, Elizabeth City State University, Fayetteville State University, North Carolina Central University, North Carolina State University, the University of North Carolina at Pembroke, the University of North Carolina at Charlotte, the University of North Carolina at Wilmington, and Western Carolina University. First priority in selection is given to children of law enforcement officers killed in the line of duty; second pri-

ority is given to children of sheriffs or deputy sheriffs who are deceased, retired (regular or disability), or currently active in law enforcement in North Carolina; third priority is given to other resident criminal justice students meeting their institution's academic and financial need criteria.

Financial data The stipend is $2,000 per year.

Duration 1 year; nonrenewable.

Additional Information Funding for this program is provided by the North Carolina Sheriffs' Association. Recipients are selected by the financial aid office at the university they plan to attend or are currently attending; after selection, students obtain a letter of endorsement from the sheriff of the county in North Carolina where they reside.

Number awarded 10 each year.

[1046]
NORTH DAKOTA EDUCATIONAL ASSISTANCE FOR DEPENDENTS OF VETERANS

Department of Veterans Affairs
1411 32nd Street South
P.O. Box 9003
Fargo, ND 58106-9003
(701) 239-7165   Toll-free: (866) 634-8387
Fax: (701) 239-7166
Web: www.state.nd.us

Summary To provide financial assistance for college to the spouses, widow(er)s, and children of disabled and other North Dakota veterans and military personnel.

Eligibility This program is open to the spouses, widow(er)s, and dependent children of veterans who are totally disabled as a result of service-connected causes, or who were killed in action, or who have died as a result of wounds or service-connected disabilities, or who were identified as prisoners of war or missing in action. Veteran parents must have been born in and lived in North Dakota until entrance into the armed forces (or must have resided in the state for at least 6 months prior to entrance into military service) and must have served during wartime.

Financial data Eligible dependents receive free tuition and are exempt from fees at any state-supported institution of higher education, technical school, or vocational school.

Duration Up to 36 months or 8 academic semesters.

Number awarded Varies each year.

[1047]
OHIO LEGION AUXILIARY PAST PRESIDENTS' PARLEY NURSES' SCHOLARSHIP

American Legion Auxiliary
Attn: Department of Ohio
1100 Brandywine Boulevard, Building D
P.O. Box 2760
Zanesville, OH 43702-2760
(740) 452-8245   Fax: (740) 452-2620
E-mail: ala_pam@rrohio.com

Summary To provide financial assistance for nursing education to Ohio residents who are dependents or descendants of veterans.

Eligibility The wives, children, stepchildren, grandchildren, adopted children, or great-grandchildren of veterans may apply for this scholarship if they are interested in nursing education, are sponsored by a unit of the American Legion Auxiliary, and are residents of Ohio. The qualifying veteran must be disabled, deceased, or in financial need. Selection is based on character, scholastic standing, qualifications for the nursing profession, and financial need.

Financial data Scholarships are either $500 or $300. Funds are paid directly to the recipients upon proof of enrollment.

Duration 1 year.

Number awarded Varies each year; recently, 17 of these scholarships were awarded (15 at $300 and 2 at $500).

Deadline May of each year.

[1048]
OHIO WAR ORPHANS SCHOLARSHIP

Ohio Board of Regents
Attn: State Grants and Scholarships
57 East Main Street, Fourth Floor
P.O. Box 182452
Columbus, OH 43218-2452
(614) 466-7420   Toll-free: (888) 833-1133
Fax: (614) 752-5903
E-mail: sminturn@regents.state.oh.us
Web: www.regents.state.oh.us

Summary To provide financial assistance for undergraduate education to the children of deceased or disabled Ohio veterans.

Eligibility To be eligible for these scholarships, students must be between 16 and 21 years of age at the time of application; must have been residents of Ohio for the past year or, if the parent was not a resident of Ohio at the time of enlistment, for the year immediately preceding application and any other 4 of the last 10 years; and must be enrolled for full-time undergraduate study at an eligible Ohio college or university. At least 1 parent must have been a member of the U.S. armed forces, including the organized Reserves and Ohio National Guard, for a period of 90 days or more (or dis-

charged because of a disability incurred after less than 90 days of service) who served during World War I, World War II, the Korean conflict, the Vietnam era, or the Persian Gulf War, and who, as a result of that service, either was killed or became at least 60% service-connected disabled. Also eligible are children of veterans who have a permanent and total non-service connected disability and are receiving disability benefits from the U.S. Department of Veterans Affairs. Children of veteran parents who served in the organized Reserves or Ohio National Guard are also eligible if the parent was killed or became permanently and totally disabled while at a scheduled training assembly.

Financial data At Ohio public colleges and universities, the program provides full payment of tuition. At Ohio private colleges and universities, the stipend is equivalent to the average amounts paid to students attending public institutions, currently $4,710 per year.

Duration 1 year; may be renewed up to 4 additional years.

Additional Information Eligible institutions are Ohio state-assisted colleges and universities and Ohio institutions approved by the Board of Regents. This program was established in 1957.

Number awarded Varies, depending upon the funds available. If sufficient funds are available, all eligible applicants are given a scholarship. Recently, 861 students received benefits from this program.

Deadline June of each year.

[1049]
OREGON DECEASED OR DISABLED PUBLIC SAFETY OFFICER GRANT PROGRAM

Oregon Student Assistance Commission
Attn: Grants and Scholarships Division
1500 Valley River Drive, Suite 100
Eugene, OR 97401-2130
(541) 687-7395
Toll-free: (800) 452-8807, ext. 7395
Fax: (541) 687-7419
Web: www.ossc.state.or.us

Summary To provide financial assistance for college to the children of disabled or deceased Oregon peace officers.

Eligibility This program is open to the natural, adopted, or stepchildren of Oregon public safety officers (fire fighters, state fire marshals, chief deputy fire marshals, deputy state fire marshals, police chiefs, police officers, sheriffs, deputy sheriffs, county adult parole and probation officers, correction officers, and investigators of the Criminal Justice Division of the Department of Justice) who, in the line of duty, were killed or disabled. Applicants must be enrolled or planning to enroll as a full-time undergraduate student at a public or private college or university in Oregon. Children of deceased officers are also eligible for graduate study. Financial need must be demonstrated.

Financial data At a public 2- or 4-year college or university, the amount of the award is equal to the cost of tuition and fees. At an eligible private college, the award amount is equal to the cost of tuition and fees at the University of Oregon.

Duration 1 year; may be renewed for up to 3 additional years of undergraduate study, if the student maintains satisfactory academic progress and demonstrates continued financial need. Children of deceased public safety officers may receive support for 12 quarters of graduate study.

Number awarded Varies each year.

[1050]
OREGON LEGION AUXILIARY DEPARTMENT NURSES SCHOLARSHIP

American Legion Auxiliary
Attn: Department of Oregon
30450 S.W. Parkway Avenue
P.O. Box 1730
Wilsonville, OR 97070-1730
(503) 682-3162   Fax: (503) 685-5008
E-mail: pcalhoun@pcez.com

Summary To provide financial assistance for nursing education to the wives, widows, and children of Oregon veterans.

Eligibility Eligible for these scholarships are the wives of veterans with disabilities, the widows of deceased veterans, and the sons and daughters of veterans who are Oregon residents. Applicants must have been accepted by an accredited hospital or university school of nursing in Oregon. Selection is based on ability, aptitude, character, determination, seriousness of purpose, and financial need.

Financial data The stipend is $1,500.

Duration 1 year; may be renewed.

Number awarded 1 each year.

Deadline May of each year.

[1051]
OREGON LEGION AUXILIARY DEPARTMENT SCHOLARSHIPS

American Legion Auxiliary
Attn: Department of Oregon
30450 S.W. Parkway Avenue
P.O. Box 1730
Wilsonville, OR 97070-1730
(503) 682-3162   Fax: (503) 685-5008
E-mail: pcalhoun@pcez.com

Summary To provide financial assistance for college to the dependents of Oregon veterans.

Eligibility To be eligible for these scholarships, an applicant must be the wife of a veteran with a disability, the widow of a deceased veteran, or the child of a veteran or current military service member. Oregon resi-

dency is required. Selection is based on ability, aptitude, character, seriousness of purpose, and financial need.

Financial data The stipend is $1,000. It must be used for education other than high school: college, university, business school, vocational school, or any other accredited postsecondary school in the state of Oregon.

Duration The awards are offered each year. They are nonrenewable.

Number awarded 3 each year; 1 of these is to be used for vocational or business school.

Deadline March of each year.

[1052]
OREGON OCCUPATIONAL SAFETY AND HEALTH DIVISION WORKERS MEMORIAL SCHOLARSHIPS

Oregon Student Assistance Commission
Attn: Grants and Scholarships Division
1500 Valley River Drive, Suite 100
Eugene, OR 97401-2146
(541) 687-7395
Toll-free: (800) 452-8807, ext. 7395
Fax: (541) 687-7419
Web: www.osac.state.or.us

Summary To provide financial assistance for undergraduate or graduate education to the children and spouses of disabled or deceased workers in Oregon.

Eligibility This program is open to residents of Oregon who are U.S. citizens or permanent residents. Applicants must be high school seniors or graduates who 1) are dependents or spouses of an Oregon worker who has suffered permanent total disability on the job; or 2) are receiving, or have received, fatality benefits as dependents or spouses of a worker fatally injured in Oregon. Selection is based on financial need and an essay of up to 500 words on "How has the injury or death of your parent or spouse affected or influenced your decision to further your education?"

Financial data Scholarship amounts vary, depending upon the needs of the recipient.

Duration 1 year.

Number awarded Varies each year.

Deadline February of each year.

[1053]
PENNSYLVANIA EDUCATIONAL GRATUITY FOR VETERANS' DEPENDENTS

Bureau for Veterans Affairs
Fort Indiantown Gap
Annville, PA 17003-5002
(717) 865-8910
Toll-free: (800) 54 PA VET (within PA)
Fax: (717) 865-8589   E-mail: jdavison@state.pa.us
Web: sites.state.pa.us

Summary To provide financial assistance for college to the children of disabled or deceased Pennsylvania veterans.

Eligibility Children of honorably discharged veterans who are rated totally and permanently disabled as a result of wartime service or who have died of such a disability are eligible if they are between 16 and 23 years of age, have lived in Pennsylvania for at least 5 years immediately preceding the date of application, can demonstrate financial need, and have been accepted or are currently enrolled in a Pennsylvania state or state-aided secondary or postsecondary educational institution.

Financial data The stipend is $500 per semester ($1,000 per year). The money is paid directly to the recipient's school and is to be applied to the costs of tuition, board, room, books, supplies, and/or matriculation fees.

Duration The allowance is paid for up to 4 academic years or for the duration of the course of study, whichever is less.

Number awarded Varies each year.

[1054]
PENNSYLVANIA LEGION AUXILIARY SCHOLARSHIP FOR DEPENDENTS OF DISABLED OR DECEASED VETERANS

American Legion Auxiliary
Attn: Department of Pennsylvania
P.O. Box 2643
Harrisburg, PA 17105-2643
(717) 763-7545   Fax: (717) 763-0617
E-mail: paalad@hotmail.com

Summary To provide financial assistance for college to the children of disabled or deceased wartime veterans who are Pennsylvania residents.

Eligibility To be eligible for this scholarship, applicants must be the children of totally disabled or deceased veterans of World War I, World War II, Korea, Vietnam, Grenada/Lebanon, Panama, or the Persian Gulf, residents and high school graduates in Pennsylvania, and in financial need.

Financial data The value of this scholarship is $600 per year, of which $300 is payable at the beginning of the school year and $300 on the following January 1, provided the student stays in school and maintains the required standards.

Duration Up to 4 years.

Additional Information This scholarship may be used only at a college in Pennsylvania.
Number awarded 1 each year.
Deadline March of each year.

[1055]
PENNSYLVANIA NATIONAL GUARD SCHOLARSHIP FUND

Pennsylvania National Guard Associations
c/o Department of Military and Veterans Affairs
Building 9-109
Fort Indiantown Gap
Annville, PA 17003-5002
(717) 865-9631   Toll-free: (800) 997-8885
Fax: (717) 612-9588 E-mail: pngas@voicenet.com
Web: www.users.voicenet.com

Summary To provide financial assistance for undergraduate education to Pennsylvania National Guard members and the children of disabled or deceased members.

Eligibility This program is open to active members of the Pennsylvania Army or Air National Guard. Children of members of the Guard who died or were permanently disabled while on Guard duty are also eligible. Applicants must be entering their first year of higher education as a full-time student or presently attending a college or vocational school as a full-time student. As part of the selection process, they must submit an essay that outlines their military and civilian plans for the future. Other selection criteria include academic achievement, leadership abilities, and contributions to citizenship. Graduate students are not eligible.

Financial data Stipends are $1,000 or $400.

Duration 1 year.

Additional Information The sponsoring organization includes the National Guard Association of Pennsylvania and the Pennsylvania National Guard Enlisted Association. This program began in 1977. It includes the following named awards: the Murtha Fellowship, the BG (Ret) Richard E. Thorn Memorial Scholarship, the USAA Scholarship (sponsored by the USAA Insurance Corporation), and the Armed Forces Insurance Scholarship (sponsored by the Armed Forces Insurance Company). Information is also available from BG (Ret) Joseph Watchilla, Executive Director, 401 East Crestwood Drive, Camp Hill, PA 17011, (717) 865-9631, Fax: (717) 612-9588.

Number awarded 24 each year: 4 at $1,000 and 20 at $400.

Deadline June of each year.

[1056]
PHILIPPIANS FOUNDATION SCHOLARSHIPS

Philippians Foundation
P.O. Box 157
Hickory, NC 28603
(828) 328-3529

Summary To provide financial assistance for college to North Carolina residents whose parents are stricken with Amyotrophic Lateral Sclerosis (ALS).

Eligibility This program is open to students who have been a resident of North Carolina for at least 1 year and who are the dependent of a parent or legal guardian stricken with ALS. Applicants must be enrolling at an accredited college, university, or nursing school.

Financial data The stipend is $1,000 per year.

Duration Up to 4 years.

Number awarded 1 each year.

Deadline August of each year.

[1057]
PINNACOL FOUNDATION SCHOLARSHIP PROGRAM

Pinnacol Foundation
Attn: Mary LaLone
7501 East Lowry Boulevard
Denver, CO 80230
(303) 361-4775
Toll-free: (800) 873-7248, ext. 4775
Fax: (303) 361-5775
E-mail: mary.lalone@pinnacol.com
Web: www.pinnacol.com/foundation

Summary To provide financial assistance for college to Colorado residents whose parent was killed or permanently disabled in a work-related accident.

Eligibility This program is open to the natural, adopted, step-, or fully dependent children of workers killed or permanently injured in a compensable work-related accident during the course and scope of employment with a Colorado-based employer and entitled to receive benefits under the Colorado Workers' Compensation Act. Applicants must be between 16 and 25 years of age and attending or planning to attend a college or technical school. Selection is based on academic achievement and aptitude, community service, and financial need.

Financial data The stipend depends on the need of the recipient.

Duration 1 year; may be renewed.

Additional Information Pinnacol Assurance, a workers' compensation insurance carrier, established this program in 2001. Students are eligible regardless of the insurance carrier for their parent's accident.

Number awarded Varies each year; recently, 24 students (13 new and 11 renewal) received $63,000 in support through this program.

Deadline March of each year.

[1058]
SAD SACKS NURSING SCHOLARSHIP

AMVETS-Department of Illinois
2200 South Sixth Street
Springfield, IL 62703
(217) 528-4713
Toll-free: (800) 638-VETS (within IL)
Fax: (217) 528-9896
Web: www.amvets.com/scholarship.htm

Summary To provide financial assistance for nursing education to Illinois residents, especially dependents of disabled or deceased veterans.

Eligibility This program is open to seniors at high schools in Illinois who have been accepted to an approved nursing program and students already enrolled in an approved school of nursing in Illinois. Priority is given to dependents of deceased or disabled veterans. Selection is based on academic record, character, interest and activity record, and financial need. Preference is given to students in the following order: third-year students, second-year students, and first-year students.

Financial data The stipend is $500.

Duration 1 year.

Number awarded 1 each year.

Deadline February of each year.

[1059]
SALLIE MAE 911 EDUCATION FUND SCHOLARSHIP PROGRAM

Sallie Mae 911 Education Fund
c/o The Community Foundation for the National Capital Region
1201 15th Street, N.W., Suite 420
Washington, DC 20005-2842
(202) 955-5890   Toll-free: (800) 441-4043
Web: www.thesalliemaefund.org

Summary To provide financial assistance for college to children of those killed or disabled in the terrorist attacks of September 11, 2001.

Eligibility This program is open to the children of the victims of the September 11, 2001 terrorist attacks, including children of people killed in airplanes or buildings as well as police, fire safety, or medical personnel killed or disabled as a result of the attacks. Applicants must be enrolled or planning to enroll full time as an undergraduate student at a public or private 2-year or 4-year college or university.

Financial data The stipend is $2,500 per year.

Duration 1 year; may be renewed up to 3 additional years.

Number awarded Varies each year; recently, 6 of these scholarships were awarded.

Deadline May of each year.

[1060]
SOUTH CAROLINA EDUCATION ASSISTANCE FOR CHILDREN OF CERTAIN WAR VETERANS

South Carolina Office of Veterans Affairs
1205 Pendleton Street, Room 477
Columbia, SC 29201-3789
(803) 734-0200   Fax: (803) 734-0197
E-mail: va@govoepp.state.sc.us
Web: www.govoepp.state.sc.us/vetaff.htm

Summary To provide free college tuition to the children of disabled and other South Carolina veterans.

Eligibility This program is open to the children of wartime veterans who were legal residents of South Carolina both at the time of entry into military or naval service and during service, or who have been residents of South Carolina for at least 1 year. Veteran parents must 1) be permanently and totally disabled from any cause, service connected or not; 2) have been a prisoner of war; 3) have been killed in action; 4) have died from other causes while in service; 5) have died of a disease or disability resulting from service; 6) be currently missing in action; 7) have received the Medal of Honor or Purple Heart Medal; or 8) be now deceased but qualified under categories 1 or 2 above. The veteran's child must be 26 years of age or younger and working on an undergraduate degree.

Financial data Children who qualify are eligible for free tuition at any South Carolina state-supported college, university, or postsecondary technical education institution. The waiver applies to tuition only. The costs of room and board, certain fees, and books are not covered.

Duration Students are eligible to receive this support as long as they are younger than 26 years of age and working on an undergraduate degree.

Number awarded Varies each year.

[1061]
SURVIVORS' AND DEPENDENTS' EDUCATIONAL ASSISTANCE PROGRAM

Department of Veterans Affairs
810 Vermont Avenue, N.W.
Washington, DC 20420
(202) 418-4343   Toll-free: (888) GI-BILL1
Web: www.gibill.va.gov

Summary To provide financial assistance for undergraduate or graduate study to children and spouses of deceased and disabled veterans, MIAs, and POWs.

Eligibility Eligible for this assistance are spouses and children of 1) veterans who died or are permanently and totally disabled as the result of a disability arising from active service in the armed forces; 2) veterans who died from any cause while rated permanently and totally disabled from a service-connected disability; 3) servicemembers listed for more than 90 days as currently missing in action or captured in the line of duty by a hos-

tile force; and 4) servicemembers listed for more than 90 days as presently detained or interned by a foreign government or power. Children must be between 18 and 26 years of age, although extensions may be granted. Spouses and children over 14 years of age with physical or mental disabilities are also eligible.

Financial data Monthly stipends from this program are $695 for full-time study at an academic institution, $522 for three-quarter time, or $347 for half-time. For farm cooperative work, the monthly stipends are $561 for full-time, $421 for three-quarter time, or $281 for half-time. For an apprenticeship or on-the-job training, the monthly stipend is $506 for the first 6 months, $378 for the second 6 months, $251 for the third 6 months, and $127 for the remainder of the program.

Duration Up to 45 months (or the equivalent in part-time training). Spouses must complete their training within 10 years of the date they are first found eligible.

Additional Information Benefits may be used to work on associate, bachelor, or graduate degrees at colleges and universities, including independent study, cooperative training, and study abroad programs. Courses leading to a certificate or diploma from business, technical, or vocational schools may also be taken. Other eligible programs include apprenticeships, on-job training programs, farm cooperative courses, correspondence courses (for spouses only), secondary school programs (for recipients who are not high school graduates), tutorial assistance, remedial deficiency and refresher training, or work-study (for recipients who are enrolled at least three-quarter time). Eligible children who are handicapped by a physical or mental disability that prevents pursuit of an educational program may receive special restorative training that includes language retraining, lip reading, auditory training, Braille reading and writing, and similar programs. Eligible spouses and children over 14 years of age who are handicapped by a physical or mental disability that prevents pursuit of an educational program may receive specialized vocational training that includes specialized courses, alone or in combination with other courses, leading to a vocational objective that is suitable for the person and required by reason of physical or mental handicap. Ineligible courses include bartending or personality development courses; correspondence courses by dependent or surviving children; non-accredited independent study courses; any course given by radio; self-improvement courses, such as reading, speaking, woodworking, basic seamanship, and English as a second language; audited courses; any course that is avocational or recreational in character; courses not leading to an educational, professional, or vocational objective; courses taken and successfully completed previously; courses taken by a federal government employee and paid for under the Government Employees' Training Act; and courses taken while in receipt of benefits for the same program from the Office of Workers' Compensation Programs.

Number awarded Varies each year.

Deadline Applications may be submitted at any time.

[1062]
SUSAN G. KOMEN BREAST CANCER FOUNDATION COLLEGE SCHOLARSHIP AWARDS

Susan G. Komen Breast Cancer Foundation
Attn: Grants Specialist
5005 LBJ Freeway, Suite 250
Dallas, TX 75244
(972) 855-1600   Fax: (972) 855-1605
E-mail: djackson@komen.org
Web: www.komen.org

Summary To provide financial assistance for college to high school seniors who lost a parent to breast cancer.

Eligibility This program is open to students who lost a parent to breast cancer and would otherwise find attending college to be a significant financial burden or impossible. Applicants must be sponsored by a local affiliate of the foundation submit an application and essay, and participate in an interview with representatives of the foundation's headquarters. Selection is based on scholastic achievement, community service and participation, and demonstrated leadership potential.

Financial data A stipend is awarded (amount not specified). Funds may be used for tuition, books, fees, and on-campus room and board.

Duration 4 years.

Number awarded 5 each year.

[1063]
TENNESSEE DEPENDENT CHILDREN SCHOLARSHIP

Tennessee Student Assistance Corporation
Parkway Towers
404 James Robertson Parkway, Suite 1950
Nashville, TN 37243-0820
(615) 741-1346   Toll-free: (800) 342-1663
Fax: (615) 741-6101   E-mail: tsac@mail.state.tn.us
Web: www.state.tn.us/tsac

Summary To provide financial assistance for college to the dependent children of disabled or deceased Tennessee law enforcement officers, fire fighters, or emergency medical service technicians.

Eligibility This program is open to Tennessee residents who are the dependent children of a Tennessee law enforcement officer, fire fighter, or emergency medical service technician who was killed or totally and permanently disabled in the line of duty. Applicants must be enrolled or accepted for enrollment as a full-time undergraduate student at a college or university in Tennessee.

Financial data The award covers tuition and fees, books, supplies, and room and board, minus any other financial aid for which the student is eligible.

Duration 1 year; may be renewed.

Additional Information This program was established in 1990.

Deadline July of each year.

[1064]
TEXAS CHILDREN OF DISABLED OR DECEASED FIREMEN, PEACE OFFICERS, GAME WARDENS, AND EMPLOYEES OF CORRECTIONAL INSTITUTIONS EXEMPTION PROGRAM

Texas Higher Education Coordinating Board
Attn: Grants and Special Programs
1200 East Anderson Lane
P.O. Box 12788, Capitol Station
Austin, TX 78711-2788
(512) 427-6101   Toll-free: (800) 242-3062
Fax: (512) 427-6127
E-mail: grantinfo@thecb.state.tx.us
Web: www.collegefortexans.com

Summary To provide educational assistance to the children of disabled or deceased Texas fire fighters, peace officers, game wardens, and employees of correctional institutions.

Eligibility Eligible are children of disabled or deceased Texas paid or volunteer fire fighters, peace officers, custodial employees of the Department of Corrections, or game wardens whose disability or death occurred in the line of duty. Applicants must be under 21 years of age.

Financial data Eligible students are exempted from the payment of all dues, fees, and tuition charges at publicly-supported colleges and universities in Texas.

Duration Support is provided for up to 120 semester credit hours of undergraduate study or until the recipient reaches 26 years of age.

Number awarded Varies each year; recently, 136 students received support through this program.

[1065]
THIRD MARINE DIVISION ASSOCIATION MEMORIAL SCHOLARSHIP FUND

Third Marine Division Association, Inc.
c/o Bert Barton
360 Rexford Drive, Apartment 54
Hermitage, PA 16148-2612
(724) 983-0542   E-mail: ThrdMarDiv@aol.com
Web: www.caltrap.com

Summary To provide financial assistance for college to the dependents of certain military personnel who served in the Third Marine Division during the Vietnam War.

Eligibility This program is open to dependent children of 1) Third Marine Division members who lost their lives while serving in Vietnam; 2) deceased 100% service-connected disabled veterans of any period of Division service, provided the veteran's death resulted from his service-connected disability; 3) certified association members, living or deceased, whose membership extended for at least 2 years prior to death, if deceased, or date of application, if living; and 4) Third Marine Division members who lost their lives while serving in Desert Shield or Desert Storm. All applicants must be between the ages of 17 and 24 and must demonstrate financial need.

Financial data Awards range from $400 to $2,400, depending upon need.

Duration 1 year; may be renewed for up to 3 additional years for undergraduate study.

Additional Information This program was established in 1969 to serve the first category of applicants; it was expanded in 1988 to serve the second and third categories and in 1991 to serve the fourth category. Information is also available from LtCol. R.E. (Dick) Jones, P.O. Box 634, Inverness, FL 34451-0634, (352) 726-2767.

Number awarded 20 to 25 each year.

Deadline April of each year.

[1066]
TIM & TOM GULLIKSON FOUNDATION COLLEGE SCHOLARSHIPS

Tim & Tom Gullikson Foundation
Attn: Executive Director
175 North Main Street
Branford, CT 06405
Toll-free: (888) GULLIKSON
Web: www.gullikson.com

Summary To provide financial assistance for college to patients/survivors and/or children of patients or survivors of brain tumors.

Eligibility This program is open to high school seniors, high school graduates, and currently enrolled or returning college students. Applicants must be brain tumor patients/survivors and/or children of brain tumor patients or survivors. Special consideration is given to applicants who have a connection to the tennis community. Financial need is considered in the selection process.

Financial data The sponsor awards a maximum of $25,000 in scholarships annually. The amounts of the individual scholarships are not specified. Funds are paid directly to the recipient's school and may be used for tuition, fees, books, room, and board.

Duration 1 year. Recipients may reapply up to 3 additional years; however, the total money awarded to each recipient cannot exceed $20,000.

Number awarded Varies each year.

Deadline March of each year.

[1067]
TROY BARBOZA EDUCATION FUND

Hawai'i Community Foundation
Attn: Scholarship Department
1164 Bishop Street, Suite 800
Honolulu, HI 96813
(808) 537-6333   Toll-free: (888) 731-3863
Fax: (808) 521-6286
E-mail: scholarships@hcf-hawaii.org
Web: www.hawaiicommunityfoundation.org

Summary To provide financial assistance for college to disabled public employees in Hawaii or their dependents.

Eligibility This program is open to 1) disabled public employees in Hawaii who were injured in the line of duty or 2) dependents or other immediate family members of public employees in Hawaii who were disabled or killed in the line of duty. The public employee must work or have worked in a job where lives are risked for the protection and safety of others. The injury must have left the employee incapacitated or incapable or continuing in his or her profession and must have occurred after October 22, 1977. Also eligible are private citizens who have performed a heroic act for the protection and welfare of others.

Financial data The amount awarded varies, depending upon the needs of the recipient and the funds available.

Duration 1 year.

Number awarded 1 or more each year.

Deadline February of each year.

[1068]
UNCF LIBERTY SCHOLARSHIPS

United Negro College Fund
Attn: Director, Educational Services
8260 Willow Oaks Corporate Drive
P.O. Box 10444
Fairfax, VA 22031-8044
(703) 205-3466   Toll-free: (866) 671-7237
Fax: (703) 205-3574
Web: www.uncf.org/LibertyScholar/index.asp

Summary To provide financial assistance to students enrolled or accepted at a member institution of the United Negro College Fund (UNCF) whose parent or guardian was killed or permanently disabled on September 11, 2001.

Eligibility Eligible to apply for these scholarships are the dependents of parents/guardians who died or were permanently disabled during the tragedies on September 11, 2001. Applicants must be accepted or enrolled full time at a UNCF college or university.

Financial data Scholarships cover the cost of tuition, fees, room, board, books, and supplies at any of the 39 UNCF institutions.

Duration 1 year; may be renewed if the recipient maintains satisfactory academic standards.

Number awarded Varies each year.

[1069]
UTAH HEMOPHILIA FOUNDATION SCHOLARSHIPS

Utah Hemophilia Foundation
880 East 3375 South
Salt Lake City, UT 84106
(801) 484-0325   Toll-free: (866) 504-4366
Fax: (801) 484-4177
E-mail: info@hemophiliautah.org
Web: www.hemophiliautah.org

Summary To provide financial assistance for college to residents of Utah with bleeding disorders and their caregivers.

Eligibility This program is open to people in Utah with bleeding disorders and to caregivers of people with bleeding disorders. Applicants must be attending or planning to attend a college or university.

Financial data Stipends are $1,500 or $500.

Duration 1 year.

Additional Information This program includes the Choice Source Therapeutics Scholarships (sponsored by Choice Source Therapeutics) and the Chris Townsend Memorial Scholarship.

Number awarded Varies each year, Recently, 7 of these scholarships were awarded: 5 at $1,500 and 2 at $500.

[1070]
VIRGINIA PUBLIC SAFETY FOUNDATION SCHOLARSHIPS

Virginia Public Safety Foundation, Inc.
P.O. Box 1355
Richmond, VA 23218
(804) 282-0148   Fax: (804) 282-2127
E-mail: vpsf@earthlink.net
Web: www.vpsf.org/what.htm

Summary To provide financial assistance for college to the children of current and selected former Virginia public safety officers.

Eligibility Eligible to apply for support are the children of all active-duty Virginia public safety officers and those officers forced to retire because of an injury incurred in the line of duty. "Public safety" officers are defined as state and local police, sheriffs, their deputies, corrections and jail officers, fire fighters, agents of the Alcoholic Beverage Control Department, and volunteer members of a fire company or rescue squad. Applicants may be high school seniors or currently enrolled in college. Selection is based on merit (academic record, character, personal and career goals, extracurricular activities, and

school service). Financial need is not considered in the selection process.

Financial data The stipend is at least $1,000 per year.

Duration 1 year; nonrenewable.

Additional Information This program was originally created in 1987 by the Virginia Police Foundation, which subsequently merged with the Virginia Public Safety Foundation. To date, $200,000 in scholarships has been awarded. Recipients may attend school in any state.

Number awarded Varies each year; recently 29 were awarded.

Deadline February of each year.

[1071]
VIRGINIA WAR ORPHANS EDUCATION PROGRAM

Virginia Department of Veterans' Affairs
270 Franklin Road, S.W., Room 503
Roanoke, VA 24011-2215
(540) 857-7104   Fax: (540) 857-7573
Web: www.vdva.vipnet.org

Summary To provide educational assistance to the children of disabled and other Virginia veterans or service personnel.

Eligibility To be eligible, applicants must meet the following requirements: 1) be between 16 and 25 years of age; 2) be accepted at a state-supported secondary or postsecondary educational institution in Virginia; 3) have at least 1 parent who served in the U.S. armed forces and is permanently and totally disabled due to an injury or disease incurred in a time of war or other period of armed conflict, has died as a result of injury or disease incurred in a time of war or other period of armed conflict, or is listed as a prisoner of war or missing in action; 4) be the dependent of a parent who was a resident of Virginia at the time of entry into active military service or for at least 5 consecutive years immediately prior to the date of application or death.

Financial data Eligible individuals receive free tuition and are exempted from any fees charged by state-supported schools in Virginia.

Duration Entitlement extends to a maximum of 48 months.

Additional Information Individuals entitled to this benefit may use it to pursue any vocational, technical, undergraduate, or graduate program of instruction. Generally, programs listed in the academic catalogs of state-supported institutions are acceptable, provided they have a clearly defined educational objective (such as a certificate, diploma, or degree).

Number awarded Varies; generally more than 150 each year.

[1072]
WASHINGTON LEGION AUXILIARY DEPARTMENT GIFT SCHOLARSHIPS

American Legion Auxiliary
Attn: Department of Washington
3600 Ruddell Road S.E.
P.O. Box 5867
Lacey, WA 98509-5867
(360) 456-5995   Fax: (360) 491-7442
E-mail: alawash@qwest.net
Web: www.walegion-aux.org/scholarships.htm

Summary To provide financial assistance for college to the children of disabled or deceased veterans in Washington.

Eligibility This program is open to residents of Washington who are the children of disabled or deceased veterans. Applicants cannot have attended an institution of higher learning. They must submit a 300 word essay on "My Desire to Further My Education." Selection is based on character, leadership, scholarship, financial need, and desire for education.

Financial data The stipend is $500.

Duration 1 year.

Additional Information Information is also available from Janet Sperry, 1983 Roeder Lane, Everson, WA 98257. Applications must be submitted to the education chair of the local American Legion Auxiliary.

Number awarded 4 each year: 3 to children of disabled or deceased veterans and 1 to Washington's candidate for an American Legion Auxiliary National President's Scholarship.

Deadline March of each year.

[1073]
WILLIAM L. WOOLARD EDUCATIONAL GRANT PROGRAM

North Carolina Lions Foundation
Camp Dogwood Drive
P.O. Box 39
Sherrills Ford, NC 28673
(828) 478-2135   Toll free: (800) 662-7401
Fax: (828) 478-4419   E-mail: nclions@nclf.org
Web: nclf.org/Edgrant.htm

Summary To provide financial assistance for college to sighted children of blind or visually impaired parents in North Carolina.

Eligibility This program is open to residents of North Carolina who are sighted children of blind or visually impaired parents. Applicants must be working on or planning to work on an undergraduate degree or certificate. Family income may not exceed $40,000 for families with 1 dependent child, increasing by $10,000 for each additional dependent child. Selection is based on the financial need of the family and the academic record and character of the applicant.

Financial data The stipend is $1,500. Funds are paid directly to the college, community college, or trade/technical school selected by the recipient.
Duration 1 year; may be renewed up to 4 additional years provided the recipient maintains full-time enrollment and a GPA of 2.0 or higher.
Number awarded 1 or more each year.
Deadline March of each year.

[1074]
WYOMING EDUCATION BENEFITS FOR NATIONAL GUARD FAMILY MEMBERS

Wyoming Veterans' Affairs Commission
LTC Hardy V. Ratcliff National Guard Armory
5905 CY Avenue, Room 101
Casper, WY 82604
(307) 265-7372   Toll-free: (800) 833-5987
Fax: (307) 265-7392   E-mail: wvac@trib.com
Web: www.state.wy.us

Summary To provide financial assistance for college to dependents of deceased and disabled members of the Wyoming National Guard.
Eligibility This program is open to children and spouses of Wyoming National Guard members who have died or sustained permanent total disability from duty as a Guard member while on state active duty or another authorized training duty. Applicants must be attending or planning to attend the University of Wyoming or a junior college or vocational training institution in the state.
Financial data Payment of tuition and fees is provided by this program.
Additional Information Applications may be obtained from the institution the applicant is attending or planning to attend.
Number awarded Varies each year.
Deadline Applications may be submitted at any time, but they should be received 2 or 3 weeks before the beginning of the semester.

[1075]
11 SEPTEMBER MEMORIAL SCHOLARSHIP

Association of Investment Professionals
Attn: 11 September Memorial Scholarship Fund
P.O. Box 3668
Charlottesville, VA 22903-0668
(434) 951-5344   Toll-free: (800) 237-8132
E-mail: rich.wyler@aimr.org
Web: www.aimr.org

Summary To provide financial assistance for selected majors in college to individuals disabled in the September 11 terrorist attacks or to the relatives of individuals injured or killed in the attacks.
Eligibility College scholarships are offered to those who meet the following 2 criteria: 1) they were permanently disabled in the attacks, or were the spouses, domestic partners, or dependents of anyone killed or permanently disabled in the attacks, and 2) they will be pursuing a college-level education in finance, economics, or related fields. Applicants may be residents of any state or country.
Financial data Annual stipends range up to $25,000.
Duration 1 year; renewable up to 3 additional years.
Additional Information Association for Investment Management and Research (AIMR) lost at least 56 of its members and Chartered Financial Analyst candidates in the terrorist attacks of 11 September.
Deadline Applications may be submitted at any time.

[1076]
11TH ARMORED CAVALRY VETERANS OF VIETNAM AND CAMBODIA SCHOLARSHIP

11th Armored Cavalry Veterans of Vietnam and Cambodia
c/o John Sorich
5037 France Avenue South
Minneapolis, MN 55410
(612) 929-1472   Fax: (612) 929-1472
E-mail: johnnydiamond@mindspring.com
Web: www.11thcavnam.com/scholar.html

Summary To provide financial assistance to members of the 11th Armored Cavalry Veterans of Vietnam and Cambodia (ACVVC) and to their dependents.
Eligibility This program is open to 11th ACVVC members and to their dependents. In addition, dependents of deceased troopers who served with the 11th Armored Cavalry in Vietnam or Cambodia may apply (a copy of the father's obituary must be supplied). Affiliation with the cavalry must be documented. Applicants must submit an essay on why they would be a worthy recipient of this scholarship. Selection is based on the essay, grades, and financial need. Priority is given to children of members who are disabled, were killed in action, or died of wounds.
Financial data The total stipend is $3,000; funds are paid directly to the recipient's school, in 2 equal installments.
Duration 1 year; nonrenewable.
Additional Information Recipients must use the awarded money within 20 months of being notified.
Number awarded Varies each year; recently, 20 of these scholarships were awarded.
Deadline May of each year.

Fellowships/Grants

[1077]
ALABAMA G.I. DEPENDENTS' SCHOLARSHIP PROGRAM

Alabama Department of Veterans Affairs
770 Washington Avenue, Suite 530
P.O. Box 1509
Montgomery, AL 36102-1509
(334) 242-5077 Fax: (334) 242-5102
E-mail: wmoore@va.state.al.us
Web: www.va.state.al.us/scholarship.htm

Summary To provide educational benefits to the dependents of disabled, deceased, and other Alabama veterans.

Eligibility Eligible are spouses, children, stepchildren, and unremarried widow(er)s of veterans who served honorably for 90 days or more and 1) are currently rated as 20% or more service-connected disabled or were so rated at time of death; 2) were a former prisoner of war; 3) have been declared missing in action; 4) died as the result of a service-connected disability; or 5) died while on active military duty in the line of duty. The veteran must have been a permanent civilian resident of Alabama for at least 1 year prior to entering active military service; veterans who were not Alabama residents at the time of entering active military service may also qualify if they have a 100% disability and were permanent residents of Alabama for at least 5 years prior to filing the application for this program or prior to death, if deceased. Children and stepchildren must be under the age of 26, but spouses and unremarried widow(er)s may be of any age.

Financial data Eligible dependents may attend any Alabama institution of higher learning or enroll in a prescribed course of study at any Alabama state-supported trade school without payment of any tuition, book fees, or laboratory charges.

Duration This is an entitlement program for 4 years of full-time undergraduate or graduate study or part-time equivalent. Spouses and unremarried widow(er)s whose veteran spouse is rated between 20 and 90% disabled, or 100% disabled but not permanently so, may attend only 2 standard academic years.

Additional Information Benefits for children, spouses, and unremarried widow(er)s are available in addition to federal government benefits. Assistance is not provided for noncredit courses, placement testing, GED preparation, continuing educational courses, pre-technical courses, or state board examinations.

Number awarded Varies each year.

Deadline Applications may be submitted at any time.

[1078]
EDWARD T. CONROY MEMORIAL SCHOLARSHIP PROGRAM

Maryland Higher Education Commission
Attn: Office of Student Financial Assistance
839 Bestgate Road, Suite 400
Annapolis, MD 21401-3013
(410) 260-4565 Toll-free: (800) 974-1024
Fax: (410) 974-5376 TTY: (800) 735-2258
E-mail: osfamail@mhec.state.md.us
Web: www.mhec.state.md.us/SSA/CONROY.htm

Summary To provide financial assistance for college or graduate school to specified categories of veterans, public safety employees, and their children in Maryland.

Eligibility This program is open to undergraduate and graduate students in the following categories: 1) children and unremarried surviving spouses of state or local public safety employees or volunteers who died in the line of duty; 2) children of armed forces members whose death or 100% disability was directly caused by military service; 3) POW/MIA veterans of the Vietnam Conflict and their children; 4) children and surviving spouses of victims of the September 11, 2001 terrorist attacks who died in the World Trade Center in New York City, the Pentagon in Virginia, or United Airlines Flight 93 in Pennsylvania; 5) veterans who have, as a direct result of military service, a disability of 25% or greater and have exhausted or are no longer eligible for federal veterans' educational benefits; and 6) state or local public safety officers or volunteers who were 100% disabled in the line of duty. The parent, veteran, POW, or public safety officer or volunteer must have been a resident of Maryland at the time of death or when declared disabled. Financial need is not considered.

Financial data The amount of the award is equal to tuition and fees at a Maryland postsecondary institution, to a maximum of $14,200 for children and spouses of the September 11 terrorist attacks or $6,178 for all other recipients.

Duration Up to 5 years of full-time study or 8 years of part-time study.

Additional Information Recipients must enroll at a 2-year or 4-year Maryland college or university as a full-time or part-time degree-seeking undergraduate or graduate student or attend a private career school.

Number awarded Varies each year.

Deadline July of each year.

[1079]
GEORGIA COUNCIL OF THE BLIND SCHOLARSHIPS

Georgia Council of the Blind
c/o Janet Clary, Scholarship Committee Chair
318 Walden Glen Lane
Evans, GA 30809

Summary To provide financial assistance for college

or graduate school to students in Georgia who have visual impairments or parents with visual impairments.
Eligibility This program is open to residents of Georgia who are either 1) visually impaired or legally blind or 2) the sighted children of parents who are visually impaired or legally blind. Applicants must be enrolled or accepted for enrollment at a vocational/technical school, a 2-year or 4-year college, or a master's or doctoral program. All fields of study are eligible. Selection is based on academic transcripts, 2 letters of recommendation, a 1-page typed statement of the applicant's educational goals, an audio cassette recording of the applicant reading the goals statement, extracurricular activities, and financial need.
Financial data Stipends up to $1,000 per year are available.
Duration 1 year; recipients may reapply.
Additional Information This program began in 1988.
Number awarded 1 or more each year.
Deadline June of each year.

[1080]
HORIZON SCHOLARSHIPS

Maine Employers' Mutual Insurance Company
Attn: MEMIC Education Fund
261 Commercial Street
P.O. Box 11409
Portland, ME 04104
(207) 791-3300   Toll-free: (800) 660-1306
Fax: (207) 791-3335
E-mail: mbourque@memic.com
Web: www.memic.com

Summary To provide financial assistance for college or graduate school to Maine residents whose parent or spouse was killed or permanently disabled in a work-related accident.
Eligibility This program is open to Maine residents who are the child or spouse of a worker killed or permanently disabled as the result of a work-related injury. The worker must have been insured through the sponsor at the time of the workplace injury. Applicants must be attending or planning to attend an accredited college or university as an undergraduate or graduate student. They must submit a personal statement of 500 words or less on their aspirations and how their educational plans relate to them. Selection is based on financial need, academic performance, community involvement, and other life experiences.
Financial data Stipends range up to $5,000, depending on the need of the recipient. Funds are paid directly to the recipient's institution.
Duration 1 year; may be renewed.
Additional Information The Maine Employers' Mutual Insurance Company (MEMIC) was established in 1993 as the result of reforms in Maine's workers' compensation laws. It is currently the largest workers' compensation insurance company in the state.
Number awarded Varies each year; recently, 3 of these scholarships were awarded.
Deadline April of each year.

[1081]
ILLINOIS GRANT PROGRAM FOR DEPENDENTS OF POLICE OR FIRE OFFICERS

Illinois Student Assistance Commission
Attn: Scholarship and Grant Services
1755 Lake Cook Road
Deerfield, IL 60015-5209
(847) 948-8550   Toll-free: (800) 899-ISAC
Fax: (847) 831-8549
TDD: (847) 831-8326, ext. 2822
E-mail: cssupport@isac.org
Web: www.isac1.org/ilaid/polfirgt.html

Summary To provide financial assistance for college to the children or spouses of disabled or deceased Illinois police or fire officers.
Eligibility This program is open to the spouses and children of Illinois police and fire officers who were at least 90% disabled or killed in the line of duty. Applicants must be enrolled on at least a half-time basis in either undergraduate or graduate study at an approved Illinois public or private 2-year or 4-year college, university, or hospital school. They need not be Illinois residents at the time of application.
Financial data The grants provide funds for tuition and mandatory fees.
Duration Up to 8 academic semesters or 12 academic quarters of study.
Number awarded Varies each year.

[1082]
INDIANA CHILD OF VETERAN AND PUBLIC SAFETY OFFICER SUPPLEMENTAL GRANT PROGRAM

State Student Assistance Commission of Indiana
ISTA Center Building
150 West Market Street, Suite 500
Indianapolis, IN 46204-2811
(317) 232-2350
Toll-free: (888) 528-4719 (within IN)
Fax: (317) 232-3260
E-mail: grants@ssaci.state.in.us
Web: www.in.gov/ssaci/programs/cvo.html

Summary To provide financial assistance for undergraduate or graduate education to students in Indiana who are 1) the children of disabled or other veterans, and 2) the children and spouses of certain deceased or disabled public safety officers.

Eligibility The veterans portion of this program is open to Indiana residents who are the natural or adopted children of veterans who served in the active-duty U.S. armed forces during a period of wartime. Applicants may be of any age; parents must have lived in Indiana for at least 3 years during their lifetime. The veteran parent must also 1) have a service-connected disability as determined by the U.S. Department of Veterans Affairs or the Department of Defense; 2) have received a Purple Heart Medal; or 3) have been a resident of Indiana at the time of entry into the service and declared a POW or MIA after January 1, 1960. Students at the Indiana Soldiers' and Sailors' Children's Home are also eligible. The public safety officer portion of this program is open to 1) the children and spouses of police officers, fire fighters, and emergency medical technicians killed in the line of duty, and 2) the children and spouses of Indiana state policy troopers permanently and totally disabled in the line of duty. Children must be younger than 23 years of age and enrolled full time in an undergraduate or graduate degree program. Spouses must be enrolled in an undergraduate program and must have been married to the covered public safety officer at the time of death or disability.

Financial data Qualified applicants receive a 100% remission of tuition and all mandatory fees for undergraduate or graduate work at state-supported postsecondary schools and universities in Indiana.

Duration Up to 124 semester hours of study.

Additional Information The veterans portion of this program is administered by the Indiana Department of Veterans' Affairs, 302 West Washington Street, Room E-120, Indianapolis, IN 46204-2738, (317) 232-3910, (800) 400-4520, Fax: (317) 232-7721, E-mail: jkiser@dva.state.in.us, Web site: www.in.gov/veteran.

Number awarded Varies each year.

Deadline Applications must be submitted at least 30 days before the start of the college term.

[1083]
JAMES DOYLE CASE MEMORIAL SCHOLARSHIPS

Mississippi Council of the Blind
2501 North West Street
Jackson, MS 39216
(601) 982-1718
Toll-free: (888) 346-5622 (within MS)
E-mail: mcb@netdoor.com

Summary To provide funding for college to legally blind residents of Mississippi and their children.

Eligibility This program is open to residents of Mississippi who are legally blind or the children of at least 1 legally blind parent. Applicants must be enrolled or accepted for enrollment in an undergraduate or graduate program and carrying or planning to carry at least 12 academic hours. Selection is based on a transcript from the last school or college attended, college entrance examination score, 2 letters of recommendation, and a 300-word biographical essay on the applicant's educational and employment goals. Membership in the sponsoring organization is not required.

Financial data The stipend is $1,000 per year.

Duration 1 year.

Additional Information Information is also available from Rebecca Floyd, President, 131 Red Fox Lane, Madison, MS 39110.

Number awarded 2 each year.

Deadline March of each year.

[1084]
JEAN SPINELLI MEMORIAL SCHOLARSHIP

Vermont Student Assistance Corporation
Champlain Mill
Attn: Scholarship Programs
P.O. Box 2000
Winooski, VT 05404-2601
(802) 654-3798   Toll-free: (800) 642-3177
Fax: (802) 654-3765   TDD: (802) 654-3766
TDD: (800) 281-3341 (within VT)
E-mail: info@vsac.org
Web: www.vsac.org

Summary To provide financial assistance to Vermont residents who are upper-division or graduate students and cancer survivors or caregivers to someone with cancer.

Eligibility This scholarship is available to residents of Vermont who are juniors or seniors in college or currently enrolled in graduate school. Applicants must be a cancer survivor or be (or have been) the primary caregiver to someone afflicted with cancer. They must be able to demonstrate 1) the spirit to live a productive, meaningful life while afflicted with cancer, or 2) selfless devoted care-giving to a friend or family member afflicted with cancer. Selection is based on required essays, a letter of recommendation, and financial need.

Financial data The stipend is $500.

Duration 1 year; recipients may reapply.

Number awarded 1 each year.

Deadline June of each year.

[1085]
KATHERN F. GRUBER SCHOLARSHIPS

Blinded Veterans Association
477 H Street, N.W.
Washington, DC 20001-2694
(202) 371-8880   Toll-free: (800) 669-7079
Fax: (202) 371-8258   E-mail: bva@bva.org
Web: www.bva.org/services.html

Summary To provide financial assistance for undergraduate or graduate study to spouses and children of blinded veterans.

Eligibility This program is open to dependent children and spouses of blinded veterans of the U.S. armed

forces. The veteran need not be a member of the Blinded Veterans Association. The veteran's blindness may be either service connected or nonservice connected, but it must meet the following definition: central visual acuity of 20/200 or less in the better eye with corrective glasses, or central visual acuity of more than 20/200 if there is a field defect in which the peripheral field has contracted to such an extent that the widest diameter of visual field subtends an angular distance no greater than 20 degrees in the better eye. The applicant must have been accepted or be currently enrolled as a full-time student in an undergraduate or graduate program at an accredited institution of higher learning. Selection is based on high school and/or college transcripts, 3 letters of recommendation, and a 300-word essay on the applicant's career goals and aspirations.

Financial data The stipends are $2,000 or $1,000 and are intended to be used to cover the student's expenses, including tuition, other academic fees, books, dormitory fees, and cafeteria fees. Funds are paid directly to the recipient's school.

Duration 1 year; recipients may reapply.

Additional Information Scholarships may be used for only 1 degree (vocational, bachelor's, or graduate) or nongraduate certificate (e.g., nursing, secretarial).

Number awarded 16 each year: 8 at $2,000 and 8 at $1,000.

Deadline April of each year.

[1086]
KIDS' CHANCE OF INDIANA SCHOLARSHIP PROGRAM

Kids' Chance of Indiana, Inc.
6612 East 75th Street, Suite 105
Indianapolis, IN 46250
Toll-free: (877) 261-8977
Web: www.kidschancein.org

Summary To provide financial assistance for college or graduate school to Indiana residents whose parent was killed or permanently disabled in a work-related accident.

Eligibility This program is open to Indiana residents between 16 and 25 years of age who are the children of workers fatally or catastrophically injured as a result of a work-related accident or occupational disease. The death or injury must be compensable by the Workers' Compensation Board of the state of Indiana and must have resulted in a substantial decline in the family's income that is likely to impede the student's pursuit of his or her educational objectives. Applicants must be attending or planning to attend a trade/vocational school, junior/community college, undergraduate college or university, or graduate school. Financial need is considered in the selection process.

Financial data Stipends range from $500 to $3,000 per year. Funds may be used for tuition and fees, books, room and board, and utilities.

Duration 1 year; may be renewed.

Additional Information Recipients may attend a public or private educational institution in any state. Information is also available from Marg Hamilton, Scholarship Application Coordinator, (317) 570-9502, Fax: (317) 570-9572.

Number awarded Varies each year.

[1087]
KIDS' CHANCE OF SOUTH CAROLINA SCHOLARSHIPS

Kids' Chance of South Carolina
1135 Dixie Red Road
Leesville, SC 29070
(803) 532-0608   Fax: (803) 532-9892
Web: www.kidschancesc.org

Summary To provide financial assistance for college or graduate school to South Carolina residents whose parent was killed or permanently disabled in a work-related accident.

Eligibility This program is open to South Carolina residents between 16 and 25 years of age who are the children of workers fatally or catastrophically injured as a result of a work-related accident or occupational disease. Applicants must be attending or planning to attend a trade school, vocational school, community or junior college, undergraduate college or university, or graduate school. The work-related injury or occupational disease from which their parent suffers or died must be compensable by the Workers' Compensation Board of South Carolina and must have resulted in a substantial decline in the family's income that is likely to interfere with the student's pursuit of his or her educational objectives.

Financial data Stipends range from $500 to $3,000 per year. Funds may be used for tuition and fees, books, room and board, and utilities.

Duration 1 year; may be renewed.

Additional Information Recipients may attend school in any state.

Number awarded Varies each year.

[1088]
MAINE VETERANS DEPENDENTS EDUCATIONAL BENEFITS

Bureau of Maine Veterans' Services
117 State House Station
Augusta, ME 04333-0117
(207) 626-4464
Toll-free: (800) 345-0116 (within ME)
Fax: (207) 626-4471
E-mail: mvs@me.ngb.army.mil
Web: www.state.me.us/va/defense/vb.htm

Summary To provide financial assistance for undergraduate or graduate education to dependents of disabled and other Maine veterans.

Eligibility Applicants for these benefits must be children (high school seniors or graduates under 25 years of age), non-divorced spouses, or unremarried widow(er)s of veterans who meet 1 or more of the following requirements: 1) living and determined to have a total permanent disability resulting from a service-connected disability; 2) killed in action; 3) died from a service-connected disability; 4) died while totally and permanently disabled due to a service-connected disability but whose death was not related to the service-connected disability; or 5) a member of the armed forces on active duty who has been listed for more than 90 days as missing in action, captured, forcibly detained, or interned in the line of duty by a foreign government or power. The veteran parent must have been a resident of Maine at the time of entry into service or a resident of Maine for 5 years preceding application for these benefits. Children may be seeking no higher than a bachelor's degree. Spouses, widows, and widowers may work on an advanced degree if they already have a bachelor's degree at the time of enrollment into this program.

Financial data Recipients are entitled to free tuition at institutions of higher education supported by the state of Maine.

Duration Benefits extend for a maximum of 8 semesters. Recipients have 6 consecutive academic years to complete their education.

Additional Information College preparatory schooling and correspondence courses do not qualify under this program.

Number awarded Varies each year.

[1089]
MARGARET FUNDS SCHOLARSHIPS

Woman's Missionary Union
Attn: WMU Foundation
P.O. Box 11346
Birmingham, AL 35202-1346
(205) 408-5525   Toll-free: (877) 482-4483
Fax: (205) 408-5508
E-mail: wmufoundation@wmu.org
Web: www.wmufoundation.com

Summary To provide financial assistance for undergraduate or graduate study to the dependent children of appointed missionaries and missionary associates, provided both parents are under North American Mission Board (NAMB) appointment.

Eligibility Students who are dependents of NAMB missionaries and were born prior to or during missionary service are eligible, provided 1) the missionaries or missionary associates are on active status with NAMB and have served a minimum of 4 years or 2) the missionary or missionary associate died or became totally disabled while in missionary service. Missionaries and missionary associates who are placed on reserve status and have served on active status for at least 10 years are also eligible, as are missionaries and missionary associates who have served at least 10 years with NAMB and have resigned to serve in another church or denominational work-related vocation. Married students may not apply.

Financial data Benefits are based on credit hours and years of mission service completed. For undergraduates, stipends range from $21 per credit hour (for 4 years of mission service completed) to $42 per credit hour (for 10 or more years of mission service completed). For graduate students, benefits are paid according to the following: 1) balance of unused undergraduate scholarship; 2) for seminary study, up to 50% of undergraduate benefits. For students who attend technical or professional schools not associated with accredited colleges, payment is made on total hours of training. For missionary or missionary associates retired or placed on reserve status, benefits are based on financial need. All benefits are paid in 4 equal installments to the recipient's college or seminary and cannot exceed the cost of the training.

Duration 1 academic term; may be renewed.

Additional Information This program includes several named awards with additional requirements. Students who are graduating college seniors, have maintained at least a 3.0 GPA in college, and have demonstrated scholarship, leadership, and character while in college are eligible to apply for the Elizabeth Lowndes Award of $400. The Julia C. Pugh Scholarship stipulates that the recipient must have significant financial need and not qualify for regular scholarships. The Mattie J.C. Russell Scholarship is limited to the children of home missionaries. The Mary B. Rhodes Medical Scholarship is for medical students who are the children of foreign missionaries. Endowment Fund Scholarships of $400 are given to former Margaret Fund students appointed as missionaries and $200 scholarships are given to former students of Baptist mission boards appointed as regular missionaries, missionary associates, missionary journeymen, or US-2 missionaries. Undergraduates must begin their studies within 5 years and complete them within 10 years; graduate students must begin within 3 years and complete within 5 years.

Number awarded Varies each year.

[1090]
NORTH CAROLINA BAR ASSOCIATION SCHOLARSHIPS

North Carolina Bar Association
Attn: Young Lawyers Division Scholarship
    Committee
8000 Weston Parkway
P.O. Box 3688
Cary, NC 27519-3688
(919) 677-0561   Toll-free: (800) 662-7407
Fax: (919) 677-0761   E-mail: jtfount@ncbar.org
Web: www.ncbar.org

Summary To provide financial assistance for college or graduate school to the children of disabled or deceased law enforcement officers in North Carolina.

Eligibility This program is open to the natural or adopted children of North Carolina law enforcement officers who were permanently disabled or killed in the line of duty. Applicants must be younger than 27 years of age and enrolled in or accepted at an accredited institution of higher learning (including community colleges, trade schools, colleges, universities, and graduate programs) in North Carolina. Selection is based on academic performance and financial need.

Financial data The stipend depends on the availability of funds but normally does not exceed $1,000 per year.

Duration Up to 4 years.

Number awarded Varies each year; recently, 4 new and 14 renewal scholarships were awarded.

Deadline March of each year.

[1091]
OREGON OCCUPATIONAL SAFETY AND HEALTH DIVISION WORKERS MEMORIAL SCHOLARSHIPS

Oregon Student Assistance Commission
Attn: Grants and Scholarships Division
1500 Valley River Drive, Suite 100
Eugene, OR 97401-2146
(541) 687-7395
Toll-free: (800) 452-8807, ext. 7395
Fax: (541) 687-7419
Web: www.osac.state.or.us

Summary To provide financial assistance for undergraduate or graduate education to the children and spouses of disabled or deceased workers in Oregon.

Eligibility This program is open to residents of Oregon who are U.S. citizens or permanent residents. Applicants must be high school seniors or graduates who 1) are dependents or spouses of an Oregon worker who has suffered permanent total disability on the job; or 2) are receiving, or have received, fatality benefits as dependents or spouses of a worker fatally injured in Oregon. Selection is based on financial need and an essay of up to 500 words on "How has the injury or death of your parent or spouse affected or influenced your decision to further your education?"

Financial data Scholarship amounts vary, depending upon the needs of the recipient.

Duration 1 year.

Number awarded Varies each year.

Deadline February of each year.

[1092]
PARENT PUBLIC POLICY FELLOWSHIP PROGRAM

Joseph P. Kennedy, Jr. Foundation
Attn: Eunice Kennedy Shriver, Executive Vice President
1010 Wayne Avenue
Silver Spring, MD 20910
(301) 365-4766   Fax: (301) 608-3444
E-mail: info@jpkf.org
Web: www.jpkf.org

Summary To provide a public policy fellowship opportunity in Washington, D.C. to the parents of persons with mental retardation.

Eligibility This program is open to the parents of persons with mental retardation or other developmental disabilities who live in the United States. They must be interested in participating in an intensive public policy fellowship in Washington, D.C. Applicants should have experience in state-level advocacy for persons with mental retardation and other developmental disabilities and their families; vocational rehabilitation, education, child care, law, community organizing, or development of community supports and services; or development of family training or family support services. Salaried experience in the field is not a requirement. To apply, interested individual should submit a 2- to 4-page letter stating their interests and accomplishments to date, a resume or summary of their involvement in the field, and at least 3 letters of support.

Financial data The program provides a stipend and a relocation allowance.

Duration 1 year, beginning in January.

Additional Information During the fellowship year, participants learn how legislation is initiated, developed, and passed by Congress. They work on the staff of a congressional committee or a federal department. The expectation is that fellows will become future leaders in the field of disabilities and return home, after their year in Washington, to make significant contributions to policy and program development in their home state.

Number awarded 1 each year.

Deadline August of each year.

[1093]
SURVIVORS' AND DEPENDENTS' EDUCATIONAL ASSISTANCE PROGRAM

Department of Veterans Affairs
810 Vermont Avenue, N.W.
Washington, DC 20420
(202) 418-4343   Toll-free: (888) GI-BILL1
Web: www.gibill.va.gov

Summary To provide financial assistance for undergraduate or graduate study to children and spouses of deceased and disabled veterans, MIAs, and POWs.

Eligibility Eligible for this assistance are spouses and children of 1) veterans who died or are permanently and totally disabled as the result of a disability arising from active service in the armed forces; 2) veterans who died from any cause while rated permanently and totally disabled from a service-connected disability; 3) servicemembers listed for more than 90 days as currently missing in action or captured in the line of duty by a hostile force; and 4) servicemembers listed for more than 90 days as presently detained or interned by a foreign government or power. Children must be between 18 and 26 years of age, although extensions may be granted. Spouses and children over 14 years of age with physical or mental disabilities are also eligible.

Financial data Monthly stipends from this program are $695 for full-time study at an academic institution, $522 for three-quarter time, or $347 for half-time. For farm cooperative work, the monthly stipends are $561 for full-time, $421 for three-quarter time, or $281 for half-time. For an apprenticeship or on-the-job training, the monthly stipend is $506 for the first 6 months, $378 for the second 6 months, $251 for the third 6 months, and $127 for the remainder of the program.

Duration Up to 45 months (or the equivalent in part-time training). Spouses must complete their training within 10 years of the date they are first found eligible.

Additional Information Benefits may be used to work on associate, bachelor, or graduate degrees at colleges and universities, including independent study, cooperative training, and study abroad programs. Courses leading to a certificate or diploma from business, technical, or vocational schools may also be taken. Other eligible programs include apprenticeships, on-job training programs, farm cooperative courses, correspondence courses (for spouses only), secondary school programs (for recipients who are not high school graduates), tutorial assistance, remedial deficiency and refresher training, or work-study (for recipients who are enrolled at least three-quarter time). Eligible children who are handicapped by a physical or mental disability that prevents pursuit of an educational program may receive special restorative training that includes language retraining, lip reading, auditory training, Braille reading and writing, and similar programs. Eligible spouses and children over 14 years of age who are handicapped by a physical or mental disability that prevents pursuit of an educational program may receive specialized vocational training that includes specialized courses, alone or in combination with other courses, leading to a vocational objective that is suitable for the person and required by reason of physical or mental handicap. Ineligible courses include bartending or personality development courses; correspondence courses by dependent or surviving children; non-accredited independent study courses; any course given by radio; self-improvement courses, such as reading, speaking, woodworking, basic seamanship, and English as a second language; audited courses; any course that is avocational or recreational in character; courses not leading to an educational, professional, or vocational objective; courses taken and successfully completed previously; courses taken by a federal government employee and paid for under the Government Employees' Training Act; and courses taken while in receipt of benefits for the same program from the Office of Workers' Compensation Programs.

Number awarded Varies each year.

Deadline Applications may be submitted at any time.

[1094]
VIRGINIA WAR ORPHANS EDUCATION PROGRAM

Virginia Department of Veterans' Affairs
270 Franklin Road, S.W., Room 503
Roanoke, VA 24011-2215
(540) 857-7104   Fax: (540) 857-7573
Web: www.vdva.vipnet.org

Summary To provide educational assistance to the children of disabled and other Virginia veterans or service personnel.

Eligibility To be eligible, applicants must meet the following requirements: 1) be between 16 and 25 years of age; 2) be accepted at a state-supported secondary or postsecondary educational institution in Virginia; 3) have at least 1 parent who served in the U.S. armed forces and is permanently and totally disabled due to an injury or disease incurred in a time of war or other period of armed conflict, has died as a result of injury or disease incurred in a time of war or other period of armed conflict, or is listed as a prisoner of war or missing in action; 4) be the dependent of a parent who was a resident of Virginia at the time of entry into active military service or for at least 5 consecutive years immediately prior to the date of application or death.

Financial data Eligible individuals receive free tuition and are exempted from any fees charged by state-supported schools in Virginia.

Duration Entitlement extends to a maximum of 48 months.

Additional Information Individuals entitled to this benefit may use it to pursue any vocational, technical, undergraduate, or graduate program of instruction. Generally, programs listed in the academic catalogs of state-supported institutions are acceptable, provided they have a clearly defined educational objective (such as a certificate, diploma, or degree).

Number awarded Varies; generally more than 150 each year.

Loans

[1095]
DISABLED AMERICAN VETERANS AUXILIARY NATIONAL EDUCATION LOAN FUND

Disabled American Veterans Auxiliary
Attn: National Education Loan Fund Director
3725 Alexandria Pike
Cold Spring, KY 41076
(606) 441-7300   Fax: (606) 442-2095

Summary To provide loans for college to women who are members of the Disabled American Veterans Auxiliary or to their children or grandchildren.

Eligibility This loan fund is open to women who are paid life members of the auxiliary and to their children and grandchildren. Applicants may be enrolled in a college, university, or vocational school. They must demonstrate academic achievement and financial need.

Financial data A maximum of $1,500 per year is loaned, payable to the school. The loan is to be repaid within 7 years in installments of at least $75 per month upon graduation or leaving school. No interest is charged.

Duration The loan is renewable each year for up to 4 consecutive years, provided the student maintains full-time status and a GPA of 2.0 or higher.

Number awarded Varies; generally, 15 each year.

Deadline February of each year.

[1096]
EDUCATIONAL LOANS FOR SPOUSES OF VETERANS

Department of Veterans Affairs
810 Vermont Avenue, N.W.
Washington, DC 20420
(202) 418-4343   Toll-free: (800) 827-1000
Web: www.va.gov

Summary To provide loans for college to spouses of veterans or military personnel whose deaths or permanent and total disabilities were service connected.

Eligibility Veterans' spouses whose 10-year period of eligibility for Veterans Dependents' Educational Assistance Benefits has passed may apply for these loans. They must be spouses of 1) veterans who died or are permanently and totally disabled as the result of a disability arising from active service in the armed forces; 2) veterans who died from any cause while rated permanently and totally disabled from a service-connected disability; 3) servicemembers currently missing in action or captured in the line of duty by a hostile force; and 4) servicemembers presently detained or interned in the line of duty by a foreign government or power. Applicants must be engaged in a full-time course of study leading to a college degree or a professional or vocational objective that requires at least 6 months to complete. The loan program is based on financial need.

Financial data Eligible spouses may borrow up to $2,500 per academic year.

Duration After the expiration of the 10 years during which eligible spouses may receive Veterans Dependents' Educational Assistance Benefits, they have an additional 2 years in which they may apply for these loans.

Number awarded Varies each year.

Deadline Applications may be submitted at any time.

[1097]
LOANS FOR ACCESSIBILITY

Corporation for Independent Living
30 Jordan Lane
Wethersfield, CT 06109-1258
(860) 563-6011, ext. 221   Fax: (860) 563-2562
E-mail: cil@cilhomes.com
Web: www.cilhomes.com

Summary To provide below-market interest rate loans to low- or moderate-income people with physical disabilities and others to modify their existing housing in Connecticut.

Eligibility Eligible to participate in this program are Connecticut residents who have a physical disability (including people in wheelchairs, the deaf or hearing impaired, the blind or visually impaired, and people who have multiple sclerosis, cerebral palsy, traumatic brain injury, or any other physical disability), own their homes, and have total household income at or below 150% of median income. Also eligible are homeowner parents of a child with a physical disability and landlords of a person with a physical disability whose total household income is at or below 100% of the median. Loan funds may be used to purchase and install fixtures and improvements required to improve accessibility and/or usability of a residential dwelling in Connecticut.

Financial data Loan amounts range from $1,000 to $20,000 at an annual interest rate of up to 7% repayable within a maximum term of 30 years.

Additional Information Funding for this program is provided by the Connecticut Department of Economic and Community Development.

Number awarded Varies each year.

Deadline Applications may be submitted at any time.

FAMILIES OF DISABLED: LOANS

[1098]
MARYLAND ASSISTIVE TECHNOLOGY GUARANTEED LOAN PROGRAM

Maryland Technology Assistance Program
Attn: Project Director
2301 Argonne Drive, Room T-17
Baltimore, MD 21218-1696
(410) 554-9233   Toll-free: (800) 832-4827
Fax: (410) 554-9237   TTY: (410) 554-9233
TTY: (800) 832-4827   E-mail: loans@mdtap.org
Web: www.mdtap.org

Summary To provide low-interest loans to disabled Maryland residents who need to obtain assistive devices.

Eligibility This program is open to anyone who wishes to borrow money to buy assistive technology for a Maryland resident with a disability. People with disabilities, family members, and friends are all eligible to apply. The equipment may include any device that helps a person with a disability live more independently and productively. Funds are also available to pay for training to use equipment, insurance, extended warranties, and maintenance plans. Loans are made only to credit-worthy borrowers, but the criteria for credit-worthiness are less stringent than those at banks.

Financial data The amount loaned varies, depending upon the needs of the recipient, from $500 to $30,000. Interest rates vary but are generally below the prime rate. For borrowers who qualify for loans without guarantees, the rates are higher.

Number awarded Varies each year.

Deadline Applications may be submitted at any time.

[1099]
NEBRASKA HOMECHOICE MORTGAGE LOAN PROGRAM

Nebraska Assistive Technology Partnership
5143 South 48th Street, Suite C
Lincoln, NE 68516-2204
(402) 471-0734   Toll-free: (888) 806-6287
Fax: (402) 471-6052   E-mail: atp@atp.state.ne.us
Web: www.nde.state.ne.us/ATP

Summary To make loans to Nebraska residents with disabilities and their families who are interested in purchasing a home.

Eligibility This program is open to Nebraska residents who 1) are disabled as defined by the Americans with Disabilities Act of 1990 or handicapped as defined by the Fair Housing Amendments Act of 1988, and 2) live in a low- (below 50% of local median income) to moderate-income (below 100% of local median income) household. Loans are available to people with disabilities or who have family members with disabilities living with them. Applicants must be seeking to purchase a single-family home.

Financial data Loans available to borrowers provide the following benefits: lower down payment requirements (depending on income, this ranges from $250 up to 2% of the sale price or appraised value of the home); qualifying and underwriting standards that look at personal budgets and do not rely solely on debt-to-income ratios; use of nontraditional credit histories; and support from other agencies to help a borrower be a successful homeowner.

Additional Information This program was developed by Fannie Mae and the Nebraska Home Of Your Own Coalition, (888) 806-6287.

Number awarded Varies each year.

Deadline Applications may be submitted at any time.

[1100]
VA HOME LOAN GUARANTIES

Department of Veterans Affairs
810 Vermont Avenue, N.W.
Washington, DC 20420
(202) 418-4343   Toll-free: (800) 827-1000
Web: www.va.gov

Summary To assist disabled and other veterans, certain military personnel, and their unremarried surviving spouses in the purchase of residences.

Eligibility Veterans who are eligible for this program include those who served on active duty at any time since September 16, 1940 and were discharged or separated under other than dishonorable conditions. Unless discharged earlier for a service-connected disability, veterans must have served on active duty continuously for 90 days, if any part of their service occurred during World War II, the Korean conflict, or the Vietnam era; veterans who served in peacetime between those wars, or who served as an enlistee prior to September 8, 1980 or as an officer prior to October 17, 1981, must have performed at least 181 days of continuous active duty; veterans separated from enlisted service that began after September 7, 1980, or service as an officer that began after October 16, 1981, must have completed 24 months of continuous active duty unless discharged earlier under specified conditions. Service personnel who have not served at least 181 continuous days in active-duty status are eligible if not discharged, while their service continues without a break. Veterans, including members of the Reserves or National Guard, who served at least 90 days of active duty during the Persian Gulf War are also eligible. Members of the Selected Reserve are eligible if they have completed at least 6 years in the Reserves or National Guard or were discharged because of a service-connected disability. Unremarried surviving spouses of veterans who served after September 16, 1940 and who died as a result of service-connected disabilities, and spouses of service personnel on active duty who are officially listed as missing in action or prisoners of war and who have been in such status for more than 90 days are also eligible. Eligibility also extends to U.S. citizens who served in the armed forces of a U.S. ally

in World War II and members of organizations with recognized contributions to the U.S. World War II effort.

Financial data The Department of Veterans Affairs (VA) does not lend money; the actual loan must come from a commercial lender. The loan may be for any amount, and the VA will guarantee payment on loans for the purchase of homes, farm homes, condominium units, or refinancing of existing loans up to 50% of loans up to $45,000 (or up to $22,500), from 40 to 50% on loans from $45,001 to $56,250 (or $22,500), to 40% on loans from $56,251 to $144,000 (or up to $36,000) and to 25% on loans over $144,000 (up to $60,000). On manufactured homes and/or lot loans, the amount of guaranty is 40% of the loan, not to exceed $20,000. Interest rates vary with market conditions but are fixed for the life of the loan, which may be as long as 30 years and 32 days. No down payments are prescribed by VA. A funding fee must be paid to VA, although it may be included in the loan amount; the amount of the fee varies, depending on the type of loan and whether the borrower is a veteran or a reservist, but ranges from 0.5% to 3% of the amount of the loan. The funding fee is waived for disabled veterans and unremarried surviving spouses of veterans who died as a result of service.

Additional Information In addition to the purchase of a new home, VA Loans may be used to buy a residential condominium; to build a home; to repair, alter, or improve a home; to refinance an existing home loan; to buy a manufactured home with or without a lot; to buy and improve a manufactured home lot; to install a solar heating and/or cooling system or other weatherization improvements; to purchase and improve simultaneously a home with energy conserving measures; to refinance an existing VA Loan to reduce the interest rate; or to refinance a manufactured home loan to acquire a lot. Mortgages guaranteed by VA usually offer an interest rate lower than conventional mortgage rates, require no down payment, provide a long repayment period, allow the VA to appraise the property and inspect it to ensure that it conforms to the plans and specifications, and permit early prepayment without premium or penalty. The VA does not have legal authority to act as an architect, supervise construction of the home, guarantee that the home is free of defects, or act as an attorney if the veteran encounters legal difficulties in buying or constructing a home. Veterans must certify that they intend to live in the home they are buying or building with a VA Loan. Veterans who wish to refinance or improve a home must certify that they are actually in residence at the time of application.

Number awarded Varies each year.

Deadline Applications may be submitted at any time.

Grants-in-Aid

[1101]
ADA RELIEF FUND GRANTS

American Dental Association
Attn: ADA Endowment and Assistance Fund
211 East Chicago Avenue, Suite 820
Chicago, IL 60611-2678
(312) 440-2567   Fax: (312) 440-2822
Web: www.ada.org

Summary To provide relief grants to dentists and their dependents who, because of accidental injury, a medical condition, or advanced age, are not self-supporting.

Eligibility This program is open to dentists, their spouses, and their children under 18 years of age. Dependents of deceased dentists are also eligible. Membership in the American Dental Association (ADA) is not required and members receive no special consideration in awarding of grants. Applicants must be seeking assistance because an accidental injury, advanced age, physically-debilitating illness, or medically-related condition prevents them from gainful employment and results in an inability to be wholly self-sustaining. They must apply through their component or constituent dental society, which forwards the application to the trustees of this fund.

Financial data The amount of the grant depends on the particular circumstances of each applicant, including financial need, age and physical condition, opportunity for assistance from immediate family members, financial assets, and all other relevant factors.

Duration Initial grants are for 6 months. Renewal grants are for an additional 12 months. Emergency grants are 1-time awards.

Additional Information The ADA has been making relief grants to needy dentists since 1906.

Number awarded Varies each year.

Deadline Applications may be submitted at any time.

[1102]
AIR FORCE AID SOCIETY RESPITE CARE

Air Force Aid Society
Attn: Financial Assistance Department
1745 Jefferson Davis Highway, Suite 202
Arlington, VA 22202-3410
(703) 607-3072, ext. 51   Toll-free: (800) 429-9475
Web: www.afas.org/body_respite.htm

Summary To provide financial assistance to Air Force personnel and their families who have a family member with special needs.

Eligibility This program is open to active-duty Air Force members and their families who are responsible for 24 hour a day care for an ill or disabled family member (child, spouse, or parent) living in the household. Applicants must be referred by the Exceptional Family Member Program (EFMP) or the Family Advocacy Office. Selection is based on need, both financial need and the need of the family for respite time.

Financial data Assistance is provided as a grant that depends on the need of the family.

Number awarded Varies each year.

Deadline Applications may be submitted at any time.

[1103]
ALABAMA AD VALOREM TAX EXEMPTION FOR SPECIALLY ADAPTED HOUSES

Alabama Department of Revenue
Attn: Property Tax Division
Gordon Persons Building
50 North Ripley Street, Room 4126
P.O. Box 327210
Montgomery, AL 36132-7210
(334) 242-1525
Web: www.ador.state.al.us

Summary To provide a property tax exemption to the owners of specially adapted housing (housing adapted for disabled veterans) in Alabama.

Eligibility The home of any veteran which is or was acquired pursuant to the provisions of Public Law 702, 80th Congress (specially adapted housing grant for veterans) as amended (38 USC) will be exempted from ad valorem taxation if the house is owned and occupied by the veteran or the veteran's unremarried widow(er).

Financial data Qualifying houses are exempt from all ad valorem taxation.

Duration This exemption continues as long as the qualifying veteran or the unremarried widow(er) resides in the house.

Number awarded Varies each year.

[1104]
ALABAMA MILITARY RETIREE INCOME TAX EXEMPTION

Alabama Department of Revenue
Attn: Income Tax Division
Gordon Persons Building
50 North Ripley Street, Room 4212
P.O. Box 327410
Montgomery, AL 36132-7410
(334) 242-1105   Fax: (334) 242-0064
E-mail: erohelpdesk@revenue.state.al.us
Web: www.ador.state.al.us

Summary To exempt a portion of the income of veterans and their survivors from taxation in Alabama.

Eligibility Eligible are Alabama recipients of regular military retired pay or military survivors benefits. Recipients of benefits paid by the U.S. Department of Veterans Affairs (including disability retirement payments) are also eligible for this exemption.

Financial data All income received as military retired pay, veterans' disability payment, or military survivors benefits is exempt from state, county, or municipal income taxation.

Duration The exemption continues as long as the recipient resides in Alabama.

[1105]
ALZHEIMER'S FAMILY RELIEF PROGRAM

American Health Assistance Foundation
Attn: AFRP Manager
22512 Gateway Center Drive
Clarksburg, MD 20871
(301) 948-3244   Toll-free: (800) 437-AHAF
Fax: (301) 258-9454   E-mail: jwilson@ahaf.org
Web: www.ahaf.org/afrp/afrp_body.htm

Summary To provide funding to Alzheimer's Disease patients and their families for emergency needs.

Eligibility This program is open to patients who have been diagnosed by a physician as suffering from Alzheimer's Disease, probable Alzheimer's Disease, or dementia of the Alzheimer's type. Their caregivers are also eligible to apply. Liquid assets (including cash, checking and savings accounts, money market accounts, stocks, bonds, and mutual funds) of the patient (or patient and caregiver if the patient is the caregiver's dependent) may not exceed $10,000. Liquid assets do not include the patient's car or house, but all of the assets are taken into account in determining the urgency of need. Applications are accepted for such expenses as short-term nursing care, home health care, respite care, adult day care, medications, medical or personal hygiene supplies, transportation, and other expenses related to care for the patient with Alzheimer's Disease. Patients residing in a nursing home are not eligible. First-time applicants receive priority consideration.

Financial data Grants up to $500 are available, depending on the need of the recipient.

Duration Grants may be renewed.

Number awarded Varies each year, depending on the availability of funds. Since this program was created in 1988, it has provided more than $1.9 million in emergency financial assistance to Alzheimer's patients and caregivers in need.

Deadline Applications may be submitted at any time; grants are awarded on a first-come, first-served basis.

[1106]
ARKANSAS DISABLED VETERANS PROPERTY TAX EXEMPTION

Arkansas Assessment Coordination Department
1614 West Third Street
Little Rock, AR 72201-1815
(501) 324-9240　　　　Fax: (501) 324-9242
E-mail: dasbury@acd.state.ar.us
Web: www.accessarkansas.org/acd

Summary To exempt from taxation the property owned by veterans with disabilities, surviving spouses, and minor dependent children in Arkansas.

Eligibility To qualify, the disabled veteran must have been awarded a special monthly compensation from the Department of Veterans Affairs for the loss of, or the loss of use of 1 or more limbs, or total blindness in 1 or both eyes, or a 100% total and permanent service-connected disability. This exemption also extends to the veteran's unremarried surviving spouse and the veteran's minor children.

Financial data Qualifying veterans (or their unremarried widows or dependent children) are exempt from payment of all state taxes on their homestead and personal property.

Duration This exemption continues as long as the qualifying veteran (or dependent) resides in Arkansas.

Number awarded Varies each year.

Deadline Applications may be submitted at any time.

[1107]
ARKANSAS INCOME TAX CREDIT FOR PHENYLKETONURIA DISORDER

Arkansas Department of Finance and Administration
Attn: Revenue Division, Individual Income Tax Section
Joel Ledbetter Building, Room 110
1800 Seventh Street
P.O. Box 3628
Little Rock, AR 72203-3628
(501) 682-7225　　　　Fax: (501) 682-7691
E-mail: Individual.Income@rev.state.ar.us
Web: www.state.ar.us/dfa

Summary To provide a state income tax credit for taxpayers in Arkansas who have a child with phenylketonuria (PKU) disorder.

Eligibility This income tax credit is available to Arkansas individuals and families with a dependent child or children with PKU. Taxpayers must have expenses incurred for the purchase of medically necessary foods and low protein modified food products.

Financial data The maximum state income tax credit is $2,400.

Duration The certificate that qualifies the taxpayer for this credit (AR1113) must be attached to the taxpayer's individual income tax return annually. Any unused credit amount may be carried forward for an additional 2 years.

Additional Information The Arkansas legislature established this credit in 1999.

Number awarded Varies each year.

[1108]
ARKANSAS INCOME TAX CREDITS FOR DEVELOPMENTALLY DISABLED INDIVIDUALS

Arkansas Department of Finance and Administration
Attn: Revenue Division, Individual Income Tax Section
Joel Ledbetter Building, Room 110
1800 Seventh Street
P.O. Box 3628
Little Rock, AR 72203-3628
(501) 682-7225　　　　Fax: (501) 682-7691
E-mail: Individual.Income@rev.state.ar.us
Web: www.state.ar.us/dfa

Summary To provide a state income tax credit for taxpayers in Arkansas who support, maintain, and care for a developmentally disabled individual in their home.

Eligibility In order to qualify and take advantage of this credit, the taxpayer must meet the following conditions: 1) the individual must be the natural or adopted child of the taxpayer or a dependent; 2) the individual must depend on the taxpayer for more than 50% of his/her maintenance, support, and care in the taxpayer's home; 3) the individual must be mentally or physically deficient to the extent that he or she is incapable of managing himself/herself or his/her affairs and must be eligible for admission to an Arkansas Human Development Center; 4) the individual may not have resided in any of the Arkansas Human Development Centers more than 6 months of the tax year; and 5) the individual must be unable to engage in any substantial gainful activity by reason of any medically determinable physical or mental impairment that can be expected to result in death or has lasted or can be expected to last for a continuous period of not less than 12 months. A physical or mental impairment is an impairment that results in anatomical, physiological, or psychological abnormalities that are demonstrable by medically acceptable clinical or laboratory diagnostic techniques. A developmental disability means a disability that is attributable to mental retardation, cerebral palsy, epilepsy, Down's Syndrome, or autism, or is attributable to any other condition of an individual found to be closely related to mental retardation and originates before the person reaches the age of 22 years.

Financial data The annual state income tax credit is $500.

Duration The certificate that qualifies the taxpayer for this credit (AR1000RC5) must be attached to the taxpayer's individual income tax return the first time the credit is taken and renewed every 5 years.

Number awarded Varies each year.

[1109]
ARKANSAS INCOME TAX CREDITS FOR DISABLED INDIVIDUALS

Arkansas Department of Finance and Administration
Attn: Revenue Division, Individual Income Tax Section
Joel Ledbetter Building, Room 110
1800 Seventh Street
P.O. Box 3628
Little Rock, AR 72203-3628
(501) 682-7225   Fax: (501) 682-7691
E-mail: Individual.Income@rev.state.ar.us
Web: www.state.ar.us/dfa

Summary To provide a state income tax credit for taxpayers in Arkansas who support, maintain, and care for a totally and permanently disabled individual in their home.

Eligibility In order to qualify and take advantage of this credit, the Arkansas taxpayer must meet the following conditions: the qualifying individual must be the natural or adopted child of the taxpayer or a dependent; the taxpayer must maintain, support, and care for the totally and permanently disabled dependent in his/her home; totally and permanently disabled means and includes any person who is unable to engage in any substantial gainful activity by reason of any medically determinable physical or mental impairment that can be expected to result in death or has lasted or can be expected to last for a continuous period of not less than 12 months. A physical or mental impairment is an impairment that results in anatomical, physiological, or psychological abnormalities that are demonstrable by medically acceptable clinical or laboratory diagnostic techniques.

Financial data The annual state income tax credit is $500.

Duration The certificate that qualifies the taxpayer for this credit (AR1000DC) must be 1) renewed and certified yearly and 2) attached to the Arkansas tax return when it is filed for individual income tax.

Number awarded Varies each year.

[1110]
ARKANSAS INCOME TAX EXEMPTIONS FOR RETIREMENT AND DISABILITY PAY

Arkansas Department of Finance and Administration
Attn: Revenue Division, Individual Income Tax Section
Joel Ledbetter Building, Room 110
1800 Seventh Street
P.O. Box 3628
Little Rock, AR 72203-3628
(501) 682-7225   Fax: (501) 682-7691
E-mail: Individual.Income@rev.state.ar.us
Web: www.state.ar.us/dfa

Summary To exempt a portion of the income from retirement or disability plans from state income taxes in Arkansas.

Eligibility Eligible are residents of Arkansas receiving income from retirement or disability plans. Surviving spouses also qualify for the exemption.

Financial data Exempt from state income taxation is the first $6,000 in disability pay, retired pay, or survivors benefits. Any resident who receives both military retirement or disability pay and other retirement or disability benefits is entitled to only a single $6,000 deduction. Surviving spouses are also limited to a single $6,000 exemption. Military retirees may adjust their figures if the payment includes survivor's benefit payments; the amount of adjustment must be listed on the income statement, and supporting documentation must be submitted with the return.

Duration The exemption continues as long as the recipient resides in Arkansas.

[1111]
ARTISTS' FELLOWSHIP AID PROGRAM

Artists' Fellowship, Inc.
c/o Salmagundi Club
47 Fifth Avenue
New York, NY 10003
(646) 230-9833

Summary To provide emergency financial aid to artists and their families who are in financial distress because of physical and/or mental disabilities.

Eligibility Professional painters, graphic artists, or sculptors (or members of their families) who are in financial distress because of disability or age, which has interrupted or ended a self-supporting income, are eligible to apply for this assistance.

Financial data The amount awarded varies, depending upon the needs of the recipient. Grants generally range from $900 to $8,000. More than $50,000 is distributed each year.

Duration This is a 1-time grant, presented in response to an emergency situation.

Additional Information No restrictions apply to the use of the money, and aid is given with no expectation of repayment. Applicants need not be members of the foundation. This is not a scholarship fund or grant-giving foundation to aid promising young artists. Only emergency aid to artists with disabilities is available.

Number awarded Generally more than 20 each year.

Deadline Applications may be submitted at any time.

[1112]
CALIFORNIA DISABLED VETERAN EXEMPTION FROM THE IN LIEU TAX FEE FOR A MANUFACTURED HOME OR MOBILEHOME

Department of Housing and Community
  Development
Attn: Registration and Titling
1800 Third Street
P.O. Box 2111
Sacramento, CA 95812-2111
(916) 323-9224   Toll-free: (800) 952-8356
Web: www.hcd.ca.gov

Summary To provide a special property tax exemption to disabled California veterans and/or their spouses who own and occupy a mobile home.

Eligibility This program is open to disabled veterans and/or their spouses in California who have a manufactured home or mobilehome as their principal place of residence. Veterans must be disabled as a result of injury or disease incurred in military service and have been a resident of California 1) at the time of entry into the service and be blind, or have lost the use of 1 or more limbs, or be totally disabled; 2) on November 7, 1972 and be blind in both eyes, or have lost the use of 2 or more limbs; or 3) on January 1, 1975 and be totally disabled. The spouses and unmarried surviving spouses of those disabled veterans are also eligible.

Financial data The exemption applies to the first $20,000 of the assessed market value of the manufactured home or mobilehome. Veterans and/or spouses whose income falls below a specified level are entitled to an additional $10,000 exemption. The amount of the exemption is 100% if the home is owned by a veteran only, a veteran and spouse, or a spouse only; 50% if owned by a veteran and another person other than a spouse or by a spouse and another person other than the veteran; 67% if owned by a veteran, the spouse, and another person; 34% if owned by a veteran and 2 other people other than a spouse or by a spouse and 2 other people; 50% if owned by a veteran, the spouse, and 2 other people; or 25% if owned by a veteran and 3 other people or by a spouse and 3 other people.

Duration The exemption is available annually as long as the applicant meets all requirements.

Number awarded Varies each year.

[1113]
COAL MINERS BLACK LUNG BENEFITS

Department of Labor
Employment Standards Administration
Office of Workers' Compensation Programs
Attn: Division of Coal Mine Workers' Compensation
200 Constitution Avenue, N.W., Room C3520
Washington, DC 20210
(202) 219-6795   Toll-free: (800) 347-2502
TDD: (800) 326-2577
Web: www.dol.gov/esa/public/owcp_org.htm

Summary To provide monthly benefits to coal miners who are disabled because of pneumoconiosis (black lung disease) and to their surviving dependents.

Eligibility Present and former coal miners (including certain transportation and construction workers who were exposed to coal mine dust) and their surviving dependents, including surviving spouses, orphaned children, and totally dependent parents, brothers, and sisters, may file claims if they are totally disabled.

Financial data Benefit amounts vary; recently; the basic monthly benefit was $534 for a single totally disabled miner or surviving spouse, $801 per month for a claimant with 1 dependent, $935 per month for a claimant with 2 dependents, or $1,069 per month for a claimant with 3 or more dependents. Benefit payments are reduced by the amounts received for pneumoconiosis under state workers' compensation awards and by excess earnings.

Duration Benefits are paid as long as the miner is unable to work in the mines or until the miner dies.

Number awarded Varies; approximately 50,000 miners and eligible surviving dependents currently receive nearly $400 million per year in benefits from this program.

[1114]
CONNECTICUT PERSONAL PROPERTY TAX EXEMPTION FOR DISABLED VETERANS

Office of Policy and Management
Attn: Intergovernmental Policy Division
450 Capitol Avenue
Hartford, CT 06106-1308
(860) 418-6322
Toll-free: (800) 286-2214 (within CT)
Fax: (860) 418-6493   TDD: (860) 418-6456
E-mail: ronald.madrid@po.state.ct.us
Web: www.opm.state.ct.us/igp/grants/addvet.htm

Summary To exempt disabled veterans and their surviving spouses who are residents of Connecticut from a portion of their personal property taxes.

Eligibility Eligible to apply for this exemption are Connecticut veterans who are rated as disabled by the U.S. Department of Veterans Affairs (VA). Unremarried surviving spouses of qualified veterans are also eligible. An additional exemption may be available to veterans and spouses whose total adjusted gross income is less than

$25,400 if unmarried or $31,100 if married. If the veteran is rated as 100% disabled by the U.S. Department of Veterans Affairs (VA), the maximum income levels are $18,000 if unmarried or $21,000 if married.

Financial data The amount of the exemption depends on the level of the VA disability rating: for 10 to 25%, it is $1,500; for more than 25 to 50%, $2,000; for more than 50 to 75%, $2,500; for more than 75% and for veterans older than 65 years of age with any level of disability, $3,000. Municipalities may elect to provide an additional exemption, equal to twice the amount provided, to veterans and spouses whose income is less than the qualifying level. For veterans and spouses who do not meet the income requirement, the additional exemption from participating municipalities is equal to 50% of the basic state exemption.

Duration 1 year; exemptions continue as long as the eligible resident lives in Connecticut.

Number awarded Varies each year; recently, a total of 208,538 veterans received property tax exemptions through this and other programs in Connecticut.

Deadline Applications for the additional municipality exemption must be submitted to the assessor's office of the town or residence by September of every other year.

[1115]
CONNECTICUT REAL ESTATE TAX EXEMPTION FOR DISABLED VETERANS

Office of Policy and Management
Attn: Intergovernmental Policy Division
450 Capitol Avenue
Hartford, CT 00106-1308
(860) 418-6322
Toll-free: (800) 286-2214 (within CT)
Fax: (860) 418-6493   TDD: (860) 418-6456
E-mail: ronald.madrid@po.state.ct.us
Web: www.opm.state.ct.us/igp/grants/addvet.htm

Summary To exempt Connecticut veterans with disabilities and their surviving spouses from the payment of a portion of their local property taxes.

Eligibility There are 2 categories of Connecticut veterans who qualify for exemptions from their dwelling house and the lot on which it is located: 1) those with major service-connected disabilities (paraplegia or osteochondritis resulting in permanent loss of the use of both legs or permanent paralysis of both legs and lower parts of the body; hemiplegia with permanent paralysis of 1 leg and 1 arm or either side of the body resulting from injury to the spinal cord, skeletal structure, or brain, or from disease of the spinal cord not resulting from syphilis; total blindness; amputation of both arms, both legs, both hands or both feet, or the combination of a hand and a foot; sustained through enemy action or resulting from an accident occurring or disease contracted in such active service) and 2) those with less severe disabilities (loss of use of 1 arm or 1 leg because of service-connected injuries). Surviving unremarried spouses of eligible deceased veterans are entitled to the same exemption as would have been granted to the veteran, as long as they continue to be the legal owner/occupier of the exempted residence. An additional exemption is available to veterans and spouses whose total adjusted gross income is less than $25,400 if unmarried or $31,100 if married. If the veteran is rated as 100% disabled by the U.S. Department of Veterans Affairs (VA), the maximum income levels are $18,000 if unmarried or $21,000 if married.

Financial data Veterans in the first category receive an exemption from local property taxation of $10,000 of assessed valuation. Veterans in the second category receive exemptions of $5,000 of assessed valuation. For veterans whose income is less than the specified levels, additional exemptions of $20,000 for the first category or $10,000 for the second category are available from municipalities that choose to participate. For veterans whose income exceeds the specified levels, the additional exemption from participating municipalities is $5,000 for the first category or $2,500 for the second category. Connecticut municipalities may also elect to exempt from taxation specially adapted housing acquired or modified by a veteran under the provisions of Section 801 of Title 38 of the United States Code.

Duration 1 year; exemptions continue as long as the eligible resident (or surviving spouse) owns/occupies the primary residence and lives in Connecticut.

Number awarded Varies each year; recently, a total of 208,538 veterans received property tax exemptions through this and other programs in Connecticut.

Deadline Applications for the additional municipality exemption must be submitted to the assessor's office of the town or residence by September of every other year.

[1116]
DEPENDENCY AND INDEMNITY COMPENSATION (DIC)

Department of Veterans Affairs
810 Vermont Avenue, N.W.
Washington, DC 20420
(202) 418-4343   Toll-free: (800) 827-1000
Web: www.va.gov

Summary To provide financial support for the spouses, children, and/or parents of deceased veterans who died of disabilities or other causes.

Eligibility This program is open to surviving spouses, unmarried children under 18, helpless children, those between 18 and 23 if attending a VA-approved school, and low-income parents of servicemembers or veterans who died from 1) a disease or injury incurred or aggravated in the line of duty while on active duty or active duty for training; 2) an injury incurred or aggravated in the line of duty while on inactive-duty training; or 3) a disability otherwise compensable under laws adminis-

tered by the Department of Veterans Affairs. Death cannot be the result of willful misconduct. Dependents of veterans who died from nonservice-connected causes are also eligible if at the time of death the veteran 1) had been continuously rated totally service-connected disabled for a period of 10 or more years immediately preceding death; 2) was so rated for at least 5 years from the date of discharge from military service; or 3) was a former prisoner of war who died after September 30, 1999 and who was continuously rated totally disabled for a period of at least 1 year immediately preceding death. If death occurred after service, the veteran's discharge must have been under conditions other than dishonorable. Surviving spouses must have been married to the veteran 1 year or more (or for any period of time if a child was born of the union), must have lived with the veteran continuously from the time of marriage until the veteran's death, and may not have remarried.

Financial data Surviving spouses of veterans who died after January 1, 1993 receive a flat rate of $948 per month, regardless of pay grade. An additional payment of $204 per month is provided to spouses if the veteran had been 100% disabled for at least 8 years prior to death and the survivor had been married to the veteran for those 8 years. The monthly amount of DIC paid to a surviving spouse of a veteran who was receiving benefits as of 1992 is based on the deceased veteran's highest military pay grade. Monthly payments range from $948 for E-1 to $1,080 for E-9, from $1,001 for W-1 to $1,134 for W-4, and from $1,001 for O-1 to $2,021 for O-10. An additional payment of $237 per month is provided for each dependent child, $237 per month if the recipient requires the aid and attendance of another person, or $113 per month if the recipient is housebound. The monthly rates of DIC for parents depend upon the income of the parents and whether there is only 1 parent, 2 parents not living together, or 2 parents together or remarried with spouse. The income limit for 2 parents together or remarried and with spouse is $14,817, that for 1 parent or 2 parents not together is $11,024. Surviving spouses and parents receiving DIC may be granted a special allowance for aid and attendance if they are patients in a nursing home or require the regular aid and attendance of another person. Surviving spouses qualified for DIC who are not so disabled as to require the regular aid and attendance of another person but who are permanently housebound may be granted an additional monthly allowance.

Duration Monthly payments continue for the life of the surviving spouse (provided remarriage does not occur) or parent, and until unmarried children reach the age of 18 (or 23 if disabled or attending a VA-approved school).

Number awarded Varies each year.

Deadline Applications are accepted at any time.

[1117]
FEDERAL INCOME TAX CREDIT FOR ADOPTION EXPENSES

Internal Revenue Service
c/o Western Area Distribution Center
Rancho Cordova, CA 95743-0001
Toll-free: (800) TAX-FORM   Fax: (703) 368-9694
Web: www.irs.gov

Summary To provide a credit against federal income taxes to people who adopt children, especially special needs children.

Eligibility This credit is available to people who, during the preceding year, adopted a U.S. citizen who was either a child under 18 years of age or a disabled person unable to care for himself or herself. Different rules apply for adopting a child classified as having special needs. To qualify as a special needs child, the state in which the adoptee resides must have determined that the child cannot or should not be returned to his or her parents' home and probably will not be adopted unless assistance is provided to the adoptive parents. Factors used by states to make that determination include: 1) the child's ethnic background and age; 2) whether the child is a member of a minority or sibling group; and 3) whether the child has a medical condition or a physical, mental, or emotional handicap. This credit is not available to taxpayers whose modified adjusted gross income is greater than $190,000.

Financial data Taxpayers may utilize qualified adoption expenses as a credit against their federal income taxes, to a maximum of $10,160. Taxpayers who adopt a special needs child are entitled to the full credit of $10,160, regardless of their actual adoption expenses. The amount of the credit is reduced for taxpayers whose modified adjusted gross income is greater than $150,000 but less than $190,000.

Duration This credit is available for each qualifying child that is adopted.

Additional Information The address above is for taxpayers in the western states; for taxpayers in the central states, the address is c/o Central Area Distribution Center, P.O. Box 8903, Bloomington, IL 61702-8903; for taxpayers in the eastern states, the address if c/o Eastern Area Distribution Center, P.O. Box 85074, Richmond, VA 23261-5074.

Number awarded Varies each year.

Deadline This credit is taken on the qualifying taxpayers' federal income tax return, which is due in April of each year.

[1118]
FEDERAL INCOME TAX DEDUCTION FOR CHILD AND DEPENDENT CARE EXPENSES

Internal Revenue Service
c/o Western Area Distribution Center
Rancho Cordova, CA 95743-0001
Toll-free: (800) TAX-FORM   Fax: (703) 368-9694
Web: www.irs.gov

Summary To provide a federal income tax credit for a portion of the expenses of caring for a child or disabled dependent.

Eligibility Eligible for this credit are U.S. citizens or residents who have earned income and who live with a qualifying dependent who is 1) under the age of 13; 2) a spouse who is physically or mentally unable to care for himself or herself; or 3) another dependent who is physically or mentally unable to care for himself or herself and for whom the taxpayer can claim an exemption. Qualifying expenses include amounts paid for household services and care of the dependent while the taxpayer worked or looked for work.

Financial data A percentage of the qualifying expenses in excess of $3,000 for 1 dependent or $6,000 for 2 or more dependents is applied as a credit against taxes; the percentage depends on the adjusted gross income of the taxpayer, ranging from 35% for incomes less than $15,000 to 20% for incomes greater than $43,000. The maximum credit is $1,050 for the care of 1 qualifying person or $2,100 for the care of 2 or more qualifying persons.

Duration 1 year; taxpayers must reapply each year.

Additional Information The address above is for taxpayers in the western states; for taxpayers in the central states, the address is c/o Central Area Distribution Center, P.O. Box 8903, Bloomington, IL 61702-8903; for taxpayers in the eastern states, the address if c/o Eastern Area Distribution Center, P.O. Box 85074, Richmond, VA 23261-5074.

Number awarded Varies each year.

Deadline This credit is applied to the qualifying tax filers' federal income tax return, which is due in April of each year.

[1119]
FLORIDA HOMESTEAD EXEMPTION FOR DISABLED VETERANS

Florida Department of Veterans' Affairs
Mary Grizzle Building, Room 311-K
11351 Ulmerton Road
Largo, FL 33778-1630
(727) 518-3202   Fax: (727) 518-3217
E-mail: cohenm@vba.va.gov
Web: www.floridavets.org/benefits/hmsted.html

Summary To exempt the real estate owned by disabled veterans and their surviving spouses in Florida from taxation.

Eligibility An exemption is available to the following classes of Florida residents: 1) honorably discharged veterans who have a service-connected permanent and total disability; 2) the spouses or surviving spouses of such veterans; 3) veterans who are paraplegic, are hemiplegic, are permanently and totally disabled, must use a wheelchair for mobility, or are legally blind and have a gross annual household income less than the adjusted maximum; and 4) veterans with service-connected disabilities of 10% or more. Applicants must reside in the property for which they are applying for an exemption.

Financial data Veterans who are permanently and totally disabled, their surviving unremarried spouses, and veterans with specified disabilities and income less than the qualifying limit are entitled to exemption of all real estate taxes on property they use and own as a homestead. Veterans with disabilities of at least 10% are entitled to a $5,000 property tax exemption.

Duration The exemption is available as long as the veteran or surviving spouse resides in Florida.

Number awarded Varies each year.

[1120]
FORWARD FACE DEVELOPMENT GRANTS

Forward Face
Attn: Scholarship Committee
317 East 34th Street, Suite 901A
New York, NY 10016
(212) 684-5860   Fax: (212) 684-5864
E-mail: camille@forwardface.org
Web: www.forwardface.org

Summary To provide financial assistance for developmental activities to parents of young people with craniofacial conditions.

Eligibility Eligible to apply for this program are parents of children who are 12 years of age or younger and have a craniofacial condition. Applicants must be interested in participating in such programs as music lessons, arts and crafts workshops, or other educational activities. Selection is based on essays by the parents (or by children themselves if they are of appropriate age) on how the child's craniofacial condition has affected the family, how the condition has affected the child's educational experience, and the personal qualities and abilities that make the child the best candidate for this grant.

Financial data The grant is $500.

Duration 1 year; nonrenewable.

Number awarded 2 each year.

Deadline January of each year.

[1121]
GEORGIA HOMESTEAD TAX EXEMPTION FOR DISABLED VETERANS

Georgia Department of Revenue
Attn: Property Tax Division
4245 International Parkway, Suite A
Hapeville, GA 30354-3918
(404) 968-0707   Fax: (404) 968-0778
E-mail: griggers@gw.rev.state.ga.us
Web: www2.state.ga.us

Summary To exempt from property taxation a portion of the value of homesteads owned by disabled veterans in Georgia and their families.

Eligibility This program is open to residents of Georgia who qualify as a 100% disabled veteran under any of several provisions of state law. Surviving spouses and minor children are also eligible. Applicants must actually occupy a homestead and use it as their legal residence for all purposes.

Financial data The first $43,000 of assessed valuation of the homestead owned by disabled veterans or their family members is exempt from property taxes for state, county, municipal, and school purposes.

Duration The exemption remains in effect as long as the veteran or family member owns and resides in the homestead.

Number awarded Varies each year.

Deadline The deadline for filing the exemption the first time is the end of May in most Georgia counties. In counties with installment billings, the deadline is at the end of April; in counties with a population of 81,300 to 89,000, the due date is at the end of February.

[1122]
GRANTS FOR ACCESSIBILITY

Corporation for Independent Living
30 Jordan Lane
Wethersfield, CT 06109-1258
(860) 563-6011, ext. 221   Fax: (860) 563-2562
E-mail: cil@cilhomes.com
Web: www.cilhomes.com

Summary To provide grants to low- or moderate-income people with physical disabilities and need to modify their existing housing in Connecticut.

Eligibility Eligible to participate in this program are Connecticut residents who have a physical disability (including people in wheelchairs, the deaf or hearing impaired, the blind or visually impaired, and people who have multiple sclerosis, cerebral palsy, traumatic brain injury, or any other physical disability), own their homes, and have a total household income at or below 80% of median income. Also eligible are homeowner parents of a child who is physically disabled and tenants who have the landlord's written consent to make accessibility renovations. Grant funds may be used to purchase and install fixtures and improvements required to improve accessibility and/or usability of a residential dwelling in Connecticut.

Financial data Grants range from $1,000 to $20,000. Initially, a full lien is placed against the recipient's home. Total lien amounts are reduced automatically by 10% every year. At the end of 10 years, the grant is forgiven in full and the lien is removed.

Additional Information Funding for this program is provided by the Connecticut Department of Economic and Community Development.

Number awarded Varies each year.

Deadline Applications may be submitted at any time.

[1123]
HAWAII PROPERTY TAX EXEMPTIONS FOR DISABLED VETERANS

Office of Veterans Services
Attn: Veterans Services Coordinator
459 Patterson Road
E-Wing, Room 1-A103
Honolulu, HI 96819-1522
(808) 433-0426   Fax: (808) 433-0385
E-mail: ovs@dod.state.hi.us
Web: www.dod.state.hi.us/ovs/benefits.html

Summary To exempt the homes of disabled veterans and surviving spouses in Hawaii from real estate taxation.

Eligibility This program is open to totally disabled veterans in Hawaii and their surviving spouses.

Financial data The real property owned and occupied as a home is exempt from taxation.

Duration The exemption applies as long as the disabled veteran or his/her widow(er) resides in Hawaii.

[1124]
IDAHO FAMILY SUPPORT PROGRAM

Idaho Department of Health and Welfare
Attn: Division of Community Rehabilitation
Statehouse Mall
Boise, ID 83720-5450
(208) 334-5531   Toll-free: (800) 926-2588

Summary To provide financial assistance to eligible family members in Idaho who agree to carry out a planned program of home-based care and training for other family members who are developmentally disabled.

Eligibility Individuals for whom assistance may be granted must have a developmental disability that appeared before the age of 22 and that is attributable to an impairment (such as mental retardation, cerebral palsy, epilepsy, autism, or similar condition) that results in substantial functional limitations in 3 or more areas of major life activity (such as self-care, learning, mobility, self-direction, or economic self-sufficiency). Family members to whom assistance is granted must reside

within the state of Idaho, express willingness for the family member with a developmental disability to reside at home, submit an in-home assistance application for the family member with a developmental disability, obtain the agreed-upon services and equipment, and account for the funds expended for the agreed-upon services and equipment.

Financial data Up to $250 per month per person is provided (this limit may be waived in cases of extraordinary need). In general, the amount of the grant is determined by the need of the individual with a developmental disability for services, rather than the family's income or eligibility for any other programs. The funds may be used for respite care, specialized evaluations, adaptive equipment, therapies, transportation, specialized clothing, housing modifications, and similar or related costs.

Duration The program continues until the family or individual requests termination, or the individual with a developmental disability dies, or the eligibility criteria are no longer met.

Additional Information This program was developed through the Idaho State Council on Developmental Disabilities. Assistance funds may not be used for the payment of educational or educationally-related services that should be the responsibility of local public schools.

Number awarded Varies each year.

Deadline Applications may be submitted at any time.

[1125]
IDAHO INCOME TAX DEDUCTION FOR RETIREMENT BENEFITS

Idaho State Tax Commission
Attn: Public Information Office
800 Park Boulevard, Plaza IV
P.O. Box 36
Boise, ID 83722-0410
(208) 334-7660   Toll-free: (800) 972-7660
TDD: (800) 377-3529
Web: www.state.id.us/tax/home.html

Summary To deduct the retirement and disability income of certain residents from state income tax in Idaho.

Eligibility Eligible for this deduction are full-year residents of Idaho who are age 65 or older, or disabled and age 62 and older, and who are receiving the following annuities and benefits: 1) retirement annuities paid by the United States to a retired civil service employee or the unremarried widow of the employee; 2) retirement benefits paid from the firemen's retirement fund of the state of Idaho to a retired fireman or the unremarried widow of a retired fireman; 3) retirement benefits paid from the policeman's retirement fund of a city within Idaho to a retired policeman or the unremarried widow of a retired policeman; or 4) retirement benefits paid by the United States to a retired member of the U.S. military service or the unremarried widow of those veterans.

Financial data The amount of retirement or disability benefits may be deducted from taxable state income in Idaho, to a maximum deduction of $31,338 for married couples or $20,892 for single persons.

Duration 1 year; must reapply each year.

Number awarded Varies each year.

Deadline April of each year.

[1126]
IDAHO INCOME TAX EXEMPTION FOR MAINTAINING A HOME FOR THE DEVELOPMENTALLY DISABLED

Idaho State Tax Commission
Attn: Public Information Office
800 Park Boulevard, Plaza IV
P.O. Box 36
Boise, ID 83722-0410
(208) 334-7660   Toll-free: (800) 972-7660
TDD: (800) 377-3529
Web: www.state.id.us/tax/home.html

Summary To exempt from state taxation a portion of the income of residents of Idaho who maintain a home for a family member, including themselves and their spouses, who is developmentally disabled.

Eligibility Individuals in Idaho who maintain a household that includes a developmentally disabled person (of any age) are eligible for this program if they provide at least half of the support of the developmentally disabled family member. The taxpayer and spouse may be included as a member of the family. Developmental disability is defined as a chronic disability that 1) is attributable to an impairment such as mental retardation, cerebral palsy, epilepsy, autism, or related condition; 2) results in substantial functional limitation in 3 or more of the following areas of life activity: self-care, receptive and expressive language, learning, mobility, self-direction, capacity for independent living, or economic self-sufficiency; and 3) reflects the need for a combination and sequence of special, interdisciplinary or generic care, treatment, or other services that are of lifelong or extended duration and individually planned and coordinated.

Financial data The amount of the deduction is $1,000 for each developmentally disabled family member, up to a maximum of $3,000.

Duration Application for the deduction must be submitted each year.

Additional Information This deduction also applies to taxpayers maintaining a home for a family member who is age 65 or older. Taxpayers who do not claim the $1,000 deduction may be able to claim a tax credit of $100 for each member of the family who is developmentally disabled or elderly, to a maximum of 3 members.

Number awarded Varies each year.

Deadline April of each year.

[1127]
IDAHO VETERANS TEMPORARY EMERGENCY GRANT PROGRAM

Idaho Division of Veterans Services
Attn: Office of Veterans Advocacy
805 West Franklin Street, Room 201
Boise, ID 83702-5560
(208) 334-1245   Fax: (208) 334-4753
Web: www.idvs.state.id.us/idvsserv.html

Summary To provide emergency assistance to disabled veterans, wartime veterans, and their families in Idaho.

Eligibility Eligible for these grants are disabled veterans, wartime veterans, and surviving dependents who are residents of Idaho. Applicants must be in need of assistance for food, fuel, shelter, and other necessities of daily living.

Financial data The maximum amount available under this program is $1,000, issued in small incremental grants.

Duration The limit of $1,000 applies for the lifetime of each veteran or his/her family.

Additional Information This program was established by the Idaho legislature in lieu of granting a wartime bonus to Idaho veterans.

Number awarded Varies each year.

[1128]
ILLINOIS HOUSING TAX EXEMPTION

Illinois Department of Veterans' Affairs
833 South Spring Street
P.O. Box 19432
Springfield, IL 62794-9432
(217) 782-6641
Toll-free: (800) 437-9824 (within IL)
Fax: (217) 782-4161   TDD: (217) 524-4645
E-mail: webmail@dva.state.il.us
Web: www.state.il.us/agency/dva

Summary To provide an exemption on the assessed value of specially adapted housing to Illinois veterans with disabilities and their spouses.

Eligibility Specially adapted housing units for disabled veterans that have been purchased or constructed with federal funds are eligible for this exemption. The exemption is extended to the veteran, the spouse, or the unremarried surviving spouse.

Financial data Under this program, an exemption is allowed on the assessed value of eligible real property, up to a maximum of $47,500 of assessed valuation.

Duration 1 year; renewable as long as the veteran, or spouse, or unremarried surviving spouse resides in the specially adapted housing in Illinois.

Number awarded Varies each year.

Deadline Applications for the exemption may be submitted at any time.

[1129]
IMPROVED DEATH PENSION FOR SURVIVORS

Department of Veterans Affairs
810 Vermont Avenue, N.W.
Washington, DC 20420
(202) 418-4343   Toll-free: (800) 827-1000
Web: www.va.gov

Summary To provide pensions to disabled and other spouses and children of deceased veterans with wartime service.

Eligibility This program is open to surviving spouses and unmarried children of veterans who were discharged under conditions other than dishonorable and who had at least 90 days of active military service, at least 1 day of which was during a period of war, or a service-connected disability. If the veteran died in service but not in the line of duty, benefits may be payable if the veteran had completed at least 2 years of honorable service. Spouses may not have remarried and children must be under 18 years of age, or 23 if attending a VA-approved school. Children who became incapable of self-support because of a disability before age 18 may be eligible for a pension as long as the condition exists, unless the child marries or the child's income exceeds the applicable limit.

Financial data The pension program provides the following annual rates, payable monthly: surviving spouse without dependent children, $6,497; surviving spouse with 1 dependent child, $8,507; surviving spouse in need of regular aid and attendance without dependent children, $10,387; surviving spouse in need of regular aid and attendance with 1 dependent child, $12,393; surviving spouse permanently housebound without dependent children, $7,942; surviving spouse permanently housebound with 1 dependent child, $9,948; increase for each additional dependent child, $1,653. Surviving children who are living alone receive $1,586 annually. The payment is reduced by the annual income from other sources, such as Social Security.

Duration For surviving spouse: until remarriage. For surviving unmarried child: until the age of 18, or 23 if attending a VA-approved school. For surviving child with disability: as long as the condition exists or until marriage.

Additional Information Pensions are not payable to those whose estates are so large that it is reasonable for them to look to the estates for maintenance.

Number awarded Varies each year.

Deadline Applications may be submitted at any time.

[1130]
INDIANA PROPERTY TAX DEDUCTIONS FOR DISABLED VETERANS

Department of Local Government Finance
Indiana Government Center North, Room 1058
100 North Senate Avenue
Indianapolis, IN 46201
(317) 232-3777   Fax: (317) 232-8779
E-mail: taxboard@tcb.state.in.us
Web: www.in.gov/dlgf

Summary To exempt disabled Indiana veterans and their spouses from a portion of their property taxes.

Eligibility This program is open to the following categories of veterans who are residents of Indiana: 1) served honorably at least 90 days and are either totally disabled (the disability does not need to be service-connected) or are at least 62 years old and have at least a 10% service-connected disability; 2) served honorably during wartime and have at least a 10% service connected disability; or 3) served during World War I and are disabled. A statutory disability rating for pulmonary tuberculosis does not qualify. A disability incurred during Initial Active Duty for Training (IADT) with the National Guard or Reserves is eligible only if the disability occurred from an event during the period of active duty and that duty was performed during wartime. Surviving spouses of those 3 categories of veterans are also eligible.

Financial data Property tax deductions are $6,000 for veterans and spouses in the first category (only if the assessed value of the real property owned by the veteran or spouse does not exceed $113,000), $12,000 in the second category, or $9,000 in the third category (only if the assessed value of the real property owned by the veteran does not exceed $163,000; there is no limit on the value of the property owned by a surviving spouse).

Duration 1 year; may be renewed as long as the eligible veteran or surviving unremarried spouse owns and occupies the primary residence in Indiana.

Number awarded Varies each year.

Deadline Applications must be submitted no later than May of each year.

[1131]
IOWA PENSION/RETIREMENT INCOME EXCLUSION

Iowa Department of Revenue
Attn: Taxpayer Services
Hoover State Office Building
1305 East Walnut
P.O. Box 10457
Des Moines, IA 50306-0457
(515) 281-3114
Toll-free: (800) 367-3388 (within IA)
Fax: (515) 242-6487   E-mail: idrf@idrf.state.ia.us
Web: www.state.ia.us/tax

Summary To exempt a portion of the income received by military and other retirees in Iowa from state taxation.

Eligibility This exemption applies to the retirement income of residents of Iowa who are 1) 55 years of age or older, 2) disabled, or 3) a surviving spouse or a survivor having an insurable interest in an individual who would have qualified from the exclusion on the basis of age or disability.

Financial data For joint filers, the exclusion is the lesser of $12,000 or the taxable amount of the retirement income; for all other statuses of filers, each eligible taxpayer can claim as an exemption the lesser of $6,000 or the taxable amount of the retirement income.

Duration The exemption continues as long as the recipient remains a resident of Iowa for state income tax purposes.

Number awarded Varies each year.

[1132]
KANSAS DISABLED ACCESS INCOME TAX CREDIT

Kansas Department of Revenue
Attn: Taxpayer Assistance Center
Robert B. Docking State Office Building
915 S.W. Harrison Street
Topeka, KS 66612-1712
(785) 368-8222   Toll-free: (877) 526-7738
Fax: (785) 291-3614   TTY: (785) 296-6461
Web: www.ksrevenue.org

Summary To provide an income tax credit to individual and business taxpayers in Kansas who incur certain expenditures to make their property accessible to people with disabilities.

Eligibility This credit is available to state income taxpayers in Kansas who make buildings or facilities accessible and usable by persons with disabilities in conformity with the Americans with Disabilities Act of 1990. The credit applies to the taxpayer's principal dwelling or the principal dwelling of a lineal ascendant or descendant, including construction of a small barrier-free living unit attached to the principal dwelling. The only expenditures that qualify for this credit are those that are specifically intended to 1) make an existing facility accessible to people with disabilities; 2) remove existing architec-

tural barriers; or 3) modify or adapt an existing facility or piece of equipment in order to employ people with disabilities.

Financial data For individuals, the amount of the credit depends on adjusted gross income and the amount of the expenditure, ranging from 100% of the expenditure for incomes less than $25,000, to 50% for incomes greater than $45,000 but less than $55,000; persons with incomes greater than $55,000 do not qualify for the credit; the maximum individual credit is $9,000. For businesses, the credit is 50% of the amount of the expenditure, to a maximum of $10,000.

Duration This is a 1-time credit.

Number awarded Varies each year.

Deadline Claims are filed with the state income tax return, due in April.

[1133]
LONGSHORE AND HARBOR WORKERS' COMPENSATION PROGRAM

Department of Labor
Employment Standards Administration
Office of Workers' Compensation Programs
Attn: Division of Longshore and Harbor Workers'
  Compensation
200 Constitution Avenue, N.W., Room C4315
Washington, DC 20210
(202) 693-0038   Fax: (202) 693-1380
TDD: (800) 326-2577
Web: www.dol.gov/esa/public/owcp_org.htm

Summary To provide benefits to maritime workers disabled or killed during the course of employment and to their spouses.

Eligibility This program is open to longshoremen, harbor workers, and other maritime workers who are injured during the course of employment; by extension, various other classes of private industry workers (including workers engaged in the extraction of natural resources on the outer continental shelf, employees of defense contractors overseas, and employees at post exchanges on military bases) are also eligible if they become disabled for work-related causes. In addition, survivor benefits are provided if the work-related injury causes the employee's death.

Financial data The compensation for disability is 66 2/3% of the employee's average weekly wage, with a minimum of 50% of the national average weekly wage (NAWW) and a maximum of 200% of the NAWW. In a recent year, the Department of Labor calculated the NAWW as $466.91, so the minimum weekly disability payment was $233.46 and the maximum was $933.82. Death benefits are equivalent to the average weekly wage of the deceased employee, with a minimum equivalent to 100% of the NAWW and a maximum equivalent to 200% of the NAWW.

Duration Benefits are paid as long as the worker remains disabled; death benefits are paid for the life of the qualified survivor.

Additional Information This program also provides medical benefits and rehabilitation services to qualifying longshoremen, harbor workers, and other workers.

Number awarded Varies; nearly 15,000 maritime workers recently received compensation and medical benefits through this program.

[1134]
MAINE TAX EXEMPTION FOR SPECIALLY ADAPTED HOUSING UNITS

Maine Revenue Services
Attn: Property Tax Division
P.O. Box 9106
Augusta, ME 04332-9106
(207) 287-2011   Fax: (207) 287-6396
E-mail: prop.tax@maine.gove
Web: www.maine.gov

Summary To exempt the specially adapted housing units of Maine veterans with disabilities or their surviving spouses from taxation.

Eligibility Veterans who served in the U.S. armed forces during any federally-recognized war period, are legal residents of Maine, are paraplegic veterans within the meaning of U.S. statutes, and have received a grant from the U.S. government for specially adapted housing are eligible. The exemption also applies to property held in joint tenancy with the veteran's spouse and to the specially adapted housing of unremarried widow(er)s of eligible veterans.

Financial data Estates of paraplegic veterans are exempt up to $47,500 of just valuation for a specially adapted housing unit.

Duration The exemption is valid for the lifetime of the paraplegic veteran or unremarried widow(er).

Number awarded Varies each year.

Deadline When an eligible person first submits an application, the proof of entitlement must reach the assessors of the local municipality prior to the end of March. Once eligibility has been established, notification need not be repeated in subsequent years.

[1135]
MAINE TAX EXEMPTIONS FOR VETERANS

Maine Revenue Services
Attn: Property Tax Division
P.O. Box 9106
Augusta, ME 04332-9106
(207) 287-2011   Fax: (207) 287-6396
E-mail: prop.tax@maine.gove
Web: www.maine.gov

Summary To exempt the estates of disabled Maine

veterans and selected family members from property taxation.

Eligibility Eligible for this program are veterans who served in wartime during World War I, World War II, the Korean campaign, the Vietnam war, or the Persian Gulf war, are legal residents of Maine, and are either older than 62 years or are receiving a pension or compensation from the U.S. government for total disability (whether service connected or not). Vietnam veterans must have served 180 days on active duty unless discharged earlier for a service-connected disability. The exemption also includes 1) property held in joint tenancy with the veterans' spouses, and 2) property of unremarried widow(er)s, minor children, and mothers of deceased veterans if those dependents are receiving a pension or compensation from the U.S. government.

Financial data Estates of disabled veterans and eligible dependents, including both real and personal property, are exempt up to $5,000 of just valuation. For veterans and dependents who served in wartime prior to World War II, the estates up to $7,000 are exempt.

Duration Veterans, spouses, unremarried widow(er)s, and mothers are eligible for this exemption throughout their lifetimes; minor children of veterans are eligible until they reach the age of 18.

Number awarded Varies each year.

Deadline When an eligible person first submits an application, the proof of entitlement must reach the assessors of the local municipality prior to the end of March. Once eligibility has been established, notification need not be repeated in subsequent years.

[1136]
MARYLAND INCOME TAX ADJUSTMENTS FOR ADOPTING SPECIAL NEEDS CHILDREN

Comptroller of Maryland
Attn: Revenue Administration Division
80 Calvert Street
Annapolis, MD 21411
(410) 260-7980
Toll-free: (800) MD-TAXES (within MD)
Fax: (410) 974-3456   TDD: (410) 260-7157
E-mail: taxhelp@comp.state.md.us
Web: individuals.marylandtaxes.com

Summary To reduce the reportable taxable income of Maryland residents who adopt special needs (particularly disabled) children.

Eligibility Residents of Maryland who adopt disabled and other special needs children through a public or nonprofit adoption agency are eligible for this program.

Financial data Eligible parents are permitted to reduce their reportable taxable income to cover the amount expended for filing fees, attorney's fees, and travel costs incurred in connection with the adoption of a qualifying child, up to a maximum of $6,000 (up to $5,000 for parents who adopt a child without special needs).

Duration This is a 1-time deduction.

[1137]
MARYLAND INCOME TAX EXEMPTION FOR DISABLED AND ELDERLY RESIDENTS

Comptroller of Maryland
Attn: Revenue Administration Division
80 Calvert Street
Annapolis, MD 21411
(410) 260-7980
Toll-free: (800) MD-TAXES (within MD)
Fax: (410) 974-3456   TDD: (410) 260-7157
E-mail: taxhelp@comp.state.md.us
Web: individuals.marylandtaxes.com

Summary To exempt a portion of the income of disabled and elderly residents (and selected spouses) from state income taxation in Maryland.

Eligibility Eligible are Maryland residents who receive income from a pension, annuity, or endowment from an employee retirement system and who are at least 65 years of age or classified as totally disabled; spouses of disabled persons also qualify. The disability must be a mental or physical impairment that prevents the person from engaging in gainful activity and that is expected to be of long, continuing, or indefinite duration (or to result in death).

Financial data Persons with disabilities, who have a spouse who is totally disabled, or who are aged 65 or older may exclude from state income taxation up to $18,500 of income received as a pension, annuity, or endowment.

Duration The exemption continues as long as the recipient resides in Maryland.

[1138]
MARYLAND REAL PROPERTY TAX EXEMPTION FOR BLIND PERSONS

State Department of Assessments and Taxation
Attn: Tax Credit Program
301 West Preston Street, Room 900
Baltimore, MD 21201-2395
(410) 767-1184
Toll-free: (888) 246-5941 (within MD)
TTY: (800) 735-2258
E-mail: taxcredits@dat.state.md.us
Web: www.dat.state.md.us

Summary To exempt the homes of blind people and their surviving spouses from a portion of property taxation in Maryland.

Eligibility This program is open to Maryland residents who are legally blind. Also eligible are their surviving spouses.

Financial data The first $6,000 of assessment on the dwelling houses owned by qualifying blind people is exempt from real property taxes in Maryland.

Duration This exemption continues as long as the qualifying blind person resides in Maryland and owns his or her home.

[1139]
MARYLAND REAL PROPERTY TAX EXEMPTION FOR DISABLED VETERANS

State Department of Assessments and Taxation
Attn: Tax Credit Program
301 West Preston Street, Room 900
Baltimore, MD 21201-2395
(410) 767-1184
Toll-free: (888) 246-5941 (within MD)
TTY: (800) 735-2258
E-mail: taxcredits@dat.state.md.us
Web: www.dat.state.md.us

Summary To exempt the homes of disabled veterans and their spouses from property taxation in Maryland.

Eligibility This program is open to Maryland residents who are veterans with a 100% service-connected permanent disability and their surviving spouses.

Financial data The dwelling houses owned by qualifying disabled veterans and their spouses are exempt from real property taxes in Maryland.

Duration This exemption continues as long as the qualifying disabled veterans or spouses reside in Maryland and own their home.

[1140]
MASSACHUSETTS PROPERTY TAX EXEMPTION

Department of Veterans' Services
239 Causeway Street, Suite 100
Boston, MA 02114
(617) 727-3578   Toll-free: (888) 844-2383
Fax: (617) 727-5903
E-mail: mdvs@vet.state.ma.us
Web: www.state.ma.us/veterans

Summary To provide a property tax exemption to disabled and other veterans (and their families) in Massachusetts.

Eligibility This program is open to veterans who are residents of Massachusetts, were residents for at least 6 months prior to entering the service, have been residents for at least 5 consecutive years, and are occupying property as their domicile. The program is open to several categories of qualified veterans and their families: 1) veterans who have a disability rating of 10% or more as a result of wartime service; veterans who served in the Spanish war, the Philippine insurrection, or the Chinese Relief Expedition; veterans who have been awarded the Purple Heart; unremarried surviving spouses of veterans who served in the armed forces between April 6, 1917 and November 11, 1918 and whose estate is worth less than $20,000; and mothers and fathers of military personnel who lost their lives in wartime service; 2) veterans who have a loss or permanent loss of use of 1 foot at or above the ankle; have a loss or permanent loss of use of 1 hand at or above the wrist; have a loss or permanent loss of sight of 1 eye; or have been awarded the Medal of Honor, the Distinguished Service Cross, the Navy Cross, or the Air Force Cross; 3) veterans who have a loss or permanent loss of use of both feet at or above the ankle, a loss or permanent loss of use of both hands at or above the wrist, a loss or permanent loss of use of 1 foot at or above the ankle and 1 hand at or above the wrist, or a loss or permanent loss of use of both eyes; 4) veterans who have a permanent and total disability as a result of a service-connected injury and have received assistance from the U.S. Department of Veterans Affairs in acquiring "special adapted housing;" 5) unremarried surviving spouses of veterans who died in combat as members of the armed forces in military action at the islands of Quemoy and Matsu in the Pacific; 6) veterans who have a disability rating of 100% as a result of injury in wartime service and in the line of duty and who are incapable of working; and 7) paraplegic veterans with service-related injuries. Surviving spouses (including those who have remarried) of all veterans in the second, third, fourth, sixth, and seventh categories are also eligible for these exemptions.

Financial data The annual exemption is $250 or $2,000 of assessed taxable value of property for the first and fifth categories; $425 or $4,000 of assessed taxable value of property for the second category; $775 or $8,000 of assessed taxable value of property for the third category; $950 or $10,000 of assessed taxable value of property for the fourth category; or $600 or $6,000 of assessed taxable value of property for the sixth category. Veterans and spouses in the seventh category are exempt from all property taxes on their domiciles.

Duration The exemptions are provided each year that the veteran or unremarried surviving spouse lives in Massachusetts and owns the property as a domicile.

Additional Information Applications are available from local assessor's offices.

Number awarded Varies each year.

[1141]
MICHIGAN HOMESTEAD PROPERTY TAX CREDIT FOR VETERANS AND BLIND PEOPLE

Michigan Department of Treasury
Attn: Homestead Exemption
Treasury Building
430 West Allegan Street
Lansing, MI 48922
(517) 373-3200   Toll-free: (800) 487-7000
TTY: (517) 636-4999
E-mail: treasPtd2@michigan.gov
Web: www.michigan.gov/treasury

Summary To provide a property tax credit to veterans,

military personnel, their spouses, blind people, and their surviving spouses in Michigan.

Eligibility Eligible to apply are residents of Michigan who are 1) blind and own their homestead; 2) a veteran with a service-connected disability or his/her surviving spouse; 3) a surviving spouse of a veteran deceased in service; 4) a veteran of wars before World War I, a pensioned veteran, a surviving spouse of those veterans, or an active military member whose household income is less than $7,500; or 5) a surviving spouse of a non-disabled or non-pensioned veteran of the Korean War, World War II, and World War I whose household income is less than $7,500. All applicants must own or rent a home in Michigan, have been a Michigan resident for at least 6 months during the year in which application is made, and fall within qualifying income levels (up to $82,650 in household income).

Financial data The maximum credit is $1,200. The exact amount varies. For homeowners, the credit depends on the state equalized value of the homestead and on an allowance for filing category. For renters, 20% of the rent is considered property tax eligible for credit.

Duration 1 year; eligibility must be established each year.

Number awarded Varies each year.

Deadline December of each year.

[1142]
MICHIGAN VETERANS TRUST FUND EMERGENCY GRANTS

Department of Military and Veterans Affairs
Attn: Michigan Veterans Trust Fund
2500 South Washington Avenue
Lansing, MI 48913-5101
(517) 483-5469   E-mail: paocmn@michigan.gov
Web: www.michigan.gov/dmva

Summary To provide temporary financial assistance to disabled and other Michigan veterans and their families, if they are facing personal emergencies.

Eligibility Eligible for this assistance are veterans and their families residing in Michigan who are temporarily unable to provide the basic necessities of life. Support is not provided for long-term problems or chronic financial difficulties. The qualifying veteran must have been discharged under honorable conditions with at least 180 days of active wartime service or have been separated as a result of a physical or mental disability incurred in the line of duty.

Financial data No statutory limit exists on the amount of assistance that may be provided; a local board in each Michigan county determines if the applicant is genuinely needy and the amount of assistance to be awarded.

Duration This assistance is provided to meet temporary needs only.

Number awarded Varies each year.

Deadline Applications may be submitted at any time.

[1143]
MINNESOTA STATE SOLDIERS ASSISTANCE FUND

Minnesota Department of Veterans Affairs
Veterans Service Building
20 West 12th Street, Second Floor
St. Paul, MN 55155-2079
(651) 296-6728   Fax: (651) 296-3954
E-mail: paula.plum@mdva.state.mn.us
Web: www.mdva.state.mn.us

Summary To provide emergency financial assistance to disabled veterans and their families in Minnesota.

Eligibility This program is open to veterans who are temporarily disabled (from service-connected or other causes) to the extent that normal employment is not possible. Their dependents and survivors are also eligible. Applicants must also meet income and asset guidelines and must be residents of Minnesota.

Financial data Limited emergency assistance is available. The funds may be used to pay for food and shelter, utility bills, and emergency medical treatment (including optical and dental benefits).

Duration This is a short-term program, with benefits payable up to 6 months only. If the veteran's disability is expected to be long term in nature or permanent, the department may continue to provide assistance while application is made for long-term benefits, such as Social Security disability or retirement benefits.

Number awarded Varies each year.

Deadline Applications may be submitted at any time.

[1144]
MISSISSIPPI LAW ENFORCEMENT OFFICERS AND FIREMEN SCHOLARSHIP PROGRAM

Mississippi Office of Student Financial Aid
3825 Ridgewood Road
Jackson, MS 39211-6453
(601) 432-6997
Toll-free: (800) 327-2980 (within MS)
Fax: (601) 432-6527   E-mail: sfa@ihl.state.ms.us
Web: www.ihl.state.ms.us

Summary To provide financial assistance for college to the spouses and children of disabled or deceased Mississippi law enforcement officers and fire fighters.

Eligibility Children and spouses of full-time law enforcement officers and fire fighters who became permanently and totally disabled or who died in the line of duty are eligible to apply if they are high school seniors or graduates interested in attending a state-supported postsecondary institution in Mississippi on a full-time basis. Children may be natural, adopted, or stepchildren up to 23 years of age; spouses may be of any age.

Financial data Students in this program receive full payment of tuition fees, the average cost of campus housing, required fees, and applicable course fees at state-supported colleges and universities in Mississippi.

Funds may not be used to pay for books, food, school supplies, materials, dues, or fees for extracurricular activities.
Duration Up to 8 semesters.
Number awarded Varies each year.
Deadline Applications may be submitted at any time.

[1145]
MISSISSIPPI TAX EXEMPTION FOR THE BLIND

Mississippi State Tax Commission
Attn: Individual Income Tax Division
P.O. Box 1033
Jackson, MS 39215-1033
(601) 923-7089   Fax: (601) 923-7039
Web: www.mstc.state.ms.us

Summary To exempt a portion of the income of blind people and their spouses from state income tax liability in Mississippi.
Eligibility Eligible for this exemption are residents of Mississippi who have been declared legally blind and their spouses.
Financial data The exemption is $1,500.
Duration The exemption continues as long as the blind person resides in Mississippi.
Number awarded Varies each year.
Deadline The exemption must be requested on the resident's state income tax return, which is due in April.

[1146]
MISSOURI SENIOR CITIZEN, DISABLED VETERAN, AND DISABLED PERSON PROPERTY TAX CREDIT CLAIM

Missouri Department of Revenue
Attn: Division of Taxation and Collection
301 West High Street, Room 330
P.O. Box 2800
Jefferson City, MO 65105-2800
(573) 751-3505   Toll-free: (800) 877-6881
TDD: (800) 735-2966
E-mail: PropertyTaxCredit@mail.state.mo.us
Web: www.state.mo.us/dor/tax

Summary To provide a property tax credit to low-income disabled veterans, senior citizens, and other persons with disabilities or their spouses in Missouri.
Eligibility This program is open to residents of Missouri (or their spouses) who are low-income (up to $27,000 per year for married filing combined or $25,000 per year for all other claimants) and have paid property tax or rent on their homestead during the tax year. Applicants must be 1) 65 years of age or older, 2) classified by the U.S. Department of Veterans Affairs as a 100% service-connected disabled veteran, 3) 60 years of age or older and receiving surviving spouse Society Security benefits, or 4) 100% disabled.

Financial data The tax credit depends on the claimant's income and amount paid in property taxes or rent, up to a maximum of $750 per year.
Duration The tax credit is available annually.
Number awarded Varies each year.
Deadline Eligible veterans, people with disabilities, and senior citizens may claim this credit when they file their state income tax return, in April of each year.

[1147]
MONTANA HANDICAPPED DEPENDENT CHILDREN TAX EXEMPTION

Montana Department of Revenue
Attn: Individual Income Tax
125 North Roberts, Third Floor
P.O. Box 5805
Helena, MT 59604-5805
(406) 444-6900   Fax: (406) 444-1505
TDD: (406) 444-2830
Web: www.state.mt.us/revenue

Summary To provide a state income tax exemption to the parents of disabled children in Montana.
Eligibility Eligible are all persons considered Montana residents for purposes of state income taxation who have a disabled child claimed as a regular dependent. The child must be certified by a physician as at least 50% permanently disabled.
Financial data Parents may claim an additional exemption of $1,740 for each child with a disability reported as a dependent.
Duration The exemption continues as long as the recipient resides in Montana with a dependent child with a disability.

[1148]
MONTANA INCOME TAX EXEMPTION FOR THE BLIND

Montana Department of Revenue
Attn: Individual Income Tax
125 North Roberts, Third Floor
P.O. Box 5805
Helena, MT 59604-5805
(406) 444-6900   Fax: (406) 444-1505
TDD: (406) 444-2830
Web: www.state.mt.us/revenue

Summary To provide a state income tax exemption to blind residents of Montana and their spouses.
Eligibility Eligible are all persons considered Montana residents for purposes of state income taxation who are blind or whose spouse is blind.
Financial data Blind people and their spouses may claim an additional exemption of $1,740 from their income for state taxation purposes.
Duration The exemption continues as long as the recipient resides in Montana.

[1149]
MONTANA REAL PROPERTY TAX RELIEF

Montana Veterans Affairs Division
1900 Williams Street
P.O. Box 5715
Helena, MT 59604
(406) 324-3741   Fax: (406) 324-3145
E-mail: jjacobsen@state.mt.us
Web: www.state.mt.us

Summary To exempt from taxation the real property of disabled or deceased veterans and their widow(er)s in Montana.

Eligibility This exemption applies to residential property in Montana that is owned and occupied by an honorably discharged veteran who is rated as 100% disabled or is being paid at the 100% disabled rate by the U.S. Department of Veterans Affairs (USDVA). Also eligible are unmarried spouses of veterans who own and occupy a residence in Montana. Spouses must obtain documentation from the USDVA that the veteran was rated as 100% disabled or was being paid at the 100% disabled rate at the time of death, or that the veteran died while on active duty.

Financial data Eligible veterans or spouses are entitled to real property tax relief that depends on their income. Single veterans with an income of $30,000 or less are exempt from all property taxes; if their income is $30,001 to $33,000, they pay 20% of the regular tax; those with income from $33,000 to $36,000 pay 30% of the regular tax; and those with income from $36,001 to $39,000 pay 50% of the regular tax. Married veterans with an income of $36,000 or less are exempt from all property taxes; if their income is $36,001 to $39,000, they pay 20% of the regular tax; those with income from $39,001 to $42,000 pay 30% of the regular tax; and those with income from $42,001 to $45,000 pay 50% of the regular tax. Surviving spouses with an income of $25,000 or less are exempt from all property taxes; if their income is $25,001 to $28,000, they pay 20% of the regular tax; those with income from $28,001 to $31,000 pay 30% of the regular tax; and those with income from $31,000 to $34,000 pay 50% of the regular tax.

Duration The exemption continues as long as the residence in Montana is owned and occupied by the disabled veteran, or, if deceased, by the veteran's unremarried spouse.

Number awarded Varies each year.

[1150]
NATIONAL VACCINE INJURY COMPENSATION PROGRAM

Health Resources and Services Administration
Bureau of Health Professions
Attn: Division of Vaccine Injury Compensation
5600 Fishers Lane, Room 16C-17
Rockville, MD 20857
(301) 443-2703   Toll-free: (800) 338-2382
Fax: (301) 443-3354   E-mail: jceresa@hrsa.gov
Web: www.hrsa.gov/bhpr/vicp

Summary To provide a no-fault system to compensate those who became injured or died as a result of adverse vaccine or toxoid reactions for vaccines administered after October 1, 1988.

Eligibility The vaccines and toxoids covered under the compensation law are: diphtheria and tetanus toxoids and pertussis vaccine (DTP); measles, mumps, and rubella (MMR); oral poliovirus vaccine (OPV) and inactivated poliovirus vaccine (IPV); hepatitis B vaccine; haemophilus influenza type b vaccine; varicella vaccine; rotavirus vaccine; and pneumococcal conjugate vaccines. No petition may be filed under this program if a civil action is pending for damages related to the vaccine injury or if damages were awarded by a court or in a settlement of a civil action against the vaccine manufacturer or administrator. Applicants must file a petition with the U.S. Court of Federal Claims. In the case of an injury, the effects must have continued at least 6 months after vaccine administration and the claim must be filed within 36 months after the first symptoms appeared. In the case of a death, the claim must be filed within 24 months of the death and within 48 months after the onset of the vaccine-related injury from which the death occurred. Medical documentation must be provided. The court will make a decision based on the individual's health status prior to administering the vaccine, the type of vaccine and the date given, and the date of onset and extent of injury occurring after receiving the vaccine.

Financial data For vaccine-related injury, the program provides reasonable compensation for past and future unreimbursable medical, custodial care, and/or rehabilitation costs; $250,000 maximum for actual and projected pain and suffering and/or emotional distress; lost earnings; and reasonable attorneys' fees and costs. For vaccine-related death, the program provides $250,000 compensation to the estate of the deceased and reasonable attorneys' fees and costs.

Duration Benefits can be awarded for the lifetime of the recipient.

Additional Information This program, established in 1988, is jointly administered by the U.S. Department of Health and Human Services, the U.S. Court of Federal Claims, and the U.S. Department of Justice. Information on the rules of the court, including requirements for filing a petition, is available from U.S. Court of Federal Claims, Attn: Clerk, 717 Madison Place, N.W., Washington, DC 20005, (202) 219-9657. The deadline has passed for fil-

ing claims for conditions that resulted from a vaccine administered prior to October 1, 1988 (the effective date of the National Childhood Vaccine Injury Act).

Number awarded Varies each year.

Deadline In the case of a disability/injury, the residual effects or complications must have continued for at least 6 months after the vaccine was administered before a petition can be filed. In addition, in the case of a disability/injury, the claim must be filed within 36 months after the first symptoms appear. In the case of death, the claim must be filed within 24 months of the death and within 48 months after the appearance of the first symptoms of the disability/injury from which the death occurred.

[1151]
NEVADA DISABLED VETERAN'S TAX EXEMPTION

Nevada Office of Veterans' Services
Attn: Executive Director
1201 Terminal Way, Room 108
Reno, NV 89520
(775) 688-1653   Fax: (775) 688-1656
Web: www.state.nv.us/veterans/benefits.html

Summary To exempt from taxation in Nevada a portion of the property owned by disabled veterans or their surviving spouses.

Eligibility This program is open to veterans who are residents of Nevada and have incurred a service-connected disability of 60% or more. Applicants must have received an honorable separation from military service. The widow(er) of a disabled veteran, who was eligible at the time of death, may also be eligible for this benefit.

Financial data Veterans and widow(er)s are entitled to exempt from taxation the portion of their property's assessed value that depends on the extent of the disability. For disabilities from 60 to 79%, the exemption is on the first $10,000 assessed valuation; for disabilities from 80 to 99%, the exemption is on the first $15,000 assessed valuation; for disabilities of 100%, the exemption is on the first $20,000 assessed valuation.

Duration Disabled veterans and their widow(er)s are entitled to this exemption as long as they live in Nevada.

Additional Information Disabled veterans and widow(er)s are able to split their exemption between vehicle taxes and/or property taxes. Further information is available at local county assessors' offices.

Number awarded Varies each year.

[1152]
NEW HAMPSHIRE PROPERTY TAX EXEMPTION FOR CERTAIN DISABLED SERVICEMEN

New Hampshire Department of Revenue
    Administration
45 Chenell Drive
P.O. Box 457
Concord, NH 03302-0457
(603) 271-2687   TDD: (800) 735-2964

Summary To exempt from taxation certain property owned by New Hampshire disabled veterans or their surviving spouses.

Eligibility Eligible for this exemption are New Hampshire residents who are honorably discharged veterans with a total and permanent service-connected disability that involves double amputation of the upper or lower extremities or any combination thereof, paraplegia, or blindness of both eyes with visual acuity of 5/200 or less. Applicants or their surviving spouses must own a specially adapted homestead that has been acquired with the assistance of the U.S. Department of Veterans Affairs.

Financial data Qualifying disabled veterans and surviving spouses are exempt from all taxation on such specially adapted homestead.

Duration 1 year; once the credit has been approved, it is automatically renewed as long as the qualifying person owns the same residence in New Hampshire.

Number awarded Varies each year.

Deadline The original application for a permanent tax credit must be submitted by April.

[1153]
NEW HAMPSHIRE REAL ESTATE EXEMPTION FOR IMPROVEMENTS TO ASSIST PERSONS WITH DISABILITIES

New Hampshire Department of Revenue
    Administration
45 Chenell Drive
P.O. Box 457
Concord, NH 03302-0457
(603) 271-2687   TDD: (800) 735-2964

Summary To exempt from real estate taxes improvements to assist disabled residents of New Hampshire.

Eligibility This program is open to residents of New Hampshire who own residential real estate where they reside and to which they have made improvements to assist a person with a disability who also resides on such real estate.

Financial data The value of such improvements is deducted from the assessed value of the residential real estate.

Duration 1 year; this exemption will be continued as long as the recipient meets the eligibility requirements.

Number awarded Varies each year.

[1154]
NEW HAMPSHIRE SERVICE-CONNECTED TOTAL DISABILITY TAX CREDIT

New Hampshire Department of Revenue
  Administration
45 Chenell Drive
P.O. Box 457
Concord, NH 03302-0457
(603) 271-2687   TDD: (800) 735-2964

Summary To provide property tax credits in New Hampshire to disabled veterans or their surviving spouses.

Eligibility Eligible for this tax credit are New Hampshire residents who are honorably discharged veterans and who 1) have a total and permanent service-connected disability, or 2) are a double amputee or paraplegic because of a service-connected disability. Unremarried surviving spouses of qualified veterans are also eligible.

Financial data Qualifying disabled veterans and surviving spouses receive an annual credit of $700 for property taxes on residential property. In addition, individual towns in New Hampshire may adopt a local option to double the dollar amount credited to disabled veterans, from $700 to $1,400.

Duration 1 year; once the credit has been approved, it is automatically renewed for as long as the qualifying person owns the same residence in New Hampshire.

Number awarded Varies each year.

Deadline The original application for a permanent tax credit must be submitted by April.

[1155]
NEW JERSEY PROPERTY TAX EXEMPTION FOR DISABLED VETERANS OR SURVIVING SPOUSES

New Jersey Division of Taxation
Attn: Office of Information and Publications
50 Barrack Street
P.O. Box 281
Trenton, NJ 08695-0281
(609) 292-6400
Toll-free: (800) 323-4400 (within selected states)
TTY: (800) 286-6613 (within selected states)
E-mail: taxation@tax.state.nj.us
Web: www.state.nj.us/treasury/taxation

Summary To provide a real estate tax exemption to New Jersey veterans with disabilities and certain surviving widow(er)s.

Eligibility This exemption is available to New Jersey residents who have been honorably discharged with active wartime service in the U.S. armed forces and have been certified by the U.S. Department of Veterans Affairs as totally and permanently disabled as a result of wartime service-connected conditions. Unremarried surviving spouses of eligible disabled veterans or of certain wartime servicepersons who died on active duty are also entitled to this exemption. Applicants must be the full owner of and a permanent resident in the dwelling house for which the exemption is claimed.

Financial data A 100% exemption from locally-levied real estate taxes is provided.

Duration 1 year; the exemption continues as long as the eligible veteran remains a resident of New Jersey.

Additional Information This program is administered by the local tax assessor or collector. Veterans who are denied exemptions have the right to appeal the decision to their county and state governments.

Number awarded Varies each year.

Deadline Applications may be submitted at any time.

[1156]
NEW JERSEY VETERANS AND SPOUSES CATASTROPHIC ENTITLEMENTS

New Jersey Department of Military and Veterans
  Affairs
Attn: Division of Veterans Programs
101 Eggert Crossing Road
P.O. Box 340
Trenton, NJ 08625-0340
(609) 530-7045
Toll-free: (800) 624-0508 (within NJ)
Fax: (609) 530-7075
Web: www.state.nj.us

Summary To supplement the compensation benefits paid by the U.S. Department of Veterans Affairs (VA) to disabled New Jersey veterans or their surviving spouses.

Eligibility Eligible for this benefit are veterans who are receiving VA compensation benefits for 100% disability ratings and who have the following disabilities: loss of sight; amputation of both hands, both feet, or 1 hand and 1 foot; hemiplegia and permanent paralysis of 1 leg and 1 arm on either side of the body; paraplegia and permanent paralysis of both legs and lowers parts of the body; osteochondritis and permanent loss of use of both legs; multiple sclerosis and the loss of use of both feet or both legs; and quadriplegia. Service must have been during wartime and the veteran must have been a resident of New Jersey at the time of entry into the military and be so currently. Surviving spouses of disabled veterans are also eligible.

Financial data Eligible veterans or survivors receive $750 a year, paid in monthly installments.

Duration This benefit is payable for the life of the veteran or spouse.

Number awarded Varies each year.

[1157]
NEW MEXICO DISABLED VETERAN PROPERTY TAX EXEMPTION

New Mexico Department of Veterans' Services
P.O. Box 2324
Santa Fe, NM 87504-2324
(505) 827-6300   Fax: (505) 827-6372
E-mail: nmdvs@state.nm.us
Web: www.state.nm.us

Summary To exempt disabled veterans and their spouses from payment of property taxes in New Mexico.

Eligibility This exemption is available to veterans who are rated 100% service-connected disabled by the U.S. Department of Veterans Affairs, are residents of New Mexico, and own a primary residence in the state. Also eligible are qualifying veterans' unremarried surviving spouses, if they are New Mexico residents and continue to own the residence.

Financial data Veterans and surviving spouses are exempt from payment of property taxes in New Mexico.

Duration 1 year; continues until the qualifying veteran or spouse no longer live in the residence.

Number awarded Varies each year.

[1158]
NEW MEXICO INCOME TAX DEDUCTION FOR THE ADOPTION OF A SPECIAL NEEDS CHILD

New Mexico Taxation and Revenue Department
Attn: Tax Information and Policy Office
1100 South St. Francis Drive
P.O. Box 630
Santa Fe, NM 87504-0630
(505) 827-2523
Web: www.state.nm.us/tax

Summary To provide income tax exemptions to residents of New Mexico who adopt a special needs child.

Eligibility Residents of New Mexico who have adopted a child defined as "difficult to place" on or after January 1 of the tax year are eligible to claim a deduction for that child (and each special needs adopted child) who is under 18 years of age. The classification of children as "difficult to place" may be based on a physical or mental handicap or emotional disturbance that is at least moderately disabling. A copy of the certification issued by the New Mexico Human Services Department must be attached to the resident's tax form for each child for whom a deduction is claimed.

Financial data The deduction is $1,250 if the resident is married and filing separately or $2,500 if single, head of household, or married and filing jointly.

Duration The deduction continues as long as the qualifying resident remains in the state.

Number awarded Varies each year.

Deadline The qualifying resident claims the deduction on the New Mexico state income tax return, which is due in April.

[1159]
NEW YORK ALTERNATIVE PROPERTY TAX EXEMPTIONS FOR VETERANS

New York State Division of Veterans' Affairs
5 Empire State Plaza, Suite 2836
Albany, NY 12223-1551
(518) 474-6114
Toll-free: (888) VETS-NYS (within NY)
Fax: (518) 473-0379
E-mail: info@veterans.state.ny.us
Web: www.veterans.state.ny.us

Summary To provide wartime veterans and their spouses who are residents of New York with a partial exemption from property taxes.

Eligibility This program is open to veterans who served during the Spanish-American War, the Mexican Border Period, World War I, World War II, the Korean War, Vietnam, or the Persian Gulf Conflict, or who received the expeditionary medal for service in Lebanon, Grenada, or Panama. Applicants must have been discharged under honorable conditions; additional benefits are available to those who served in a combat zone and to those who have a service-connected disability. The legal title to the property must be in the name of the veteran or the spouse of the veteran or both, or the unremarried surviving spouse of the veteran. The property must be used exclusively for residential purposes. This program is only available in counties, cities, towns, and villages in New York that have opted to participate.

Financial data This program provides an exemption of 15% of the assessed valuation of the property, to a basic maximum of $12,000 per year; local governments may opt for a reduced maximum of $9,000 or $6,000, or for an increased maximum of $15,000, $18,000, $21,000, $24,000, or $27,000. For combat-zone veterans, an additional 10% of the assessed valuation is exempt, to a basic maximum of $8,000 per year; local governments may opt for a reduced maximum of $6,000 or $4,000, or for an increased maximum of $10,000, $12,000, $14,000, $16,000, or $18,000. For disabled veterans, the exemption is the percentage of assessed value equal to half of the service-connected disability rating, to a basic maximum of $40,000 per year; local governments may opt for a reduced maximum of $30,000 or $20,000, or for an increased maximum of $50,000, $60,000, $70,000, $80,000, or $90,000. At its option, New York City may use the following increased maximum exemptions: war veteran, $45,000; combat-zone veteran, $30,000; disabled veteran, $150,000.

Duration This exemption is available annually.

Number awarded Varies each year.

Deadline Applications must be filed with the local assessor by "taxable status date;" in most towns, that is the end of February.

[1160]
NEW YORK "ELIGIBLE FUNDS" PROPERTY TAX EXEMPTIONS FOR VETERANS

New York State Division of Veterans' Affairs
5 Empire State Plaza, Suite 2836
Albany, NY 12223-1551
(518) 474-6114
Toll-free: (888) VETS-NYS (within NY)
Fax: (518) 473-0379
E-mail: info@veterans.state.ny.us
Web: www.veterans.state.ny.us

Summary To provide a partial exemption from property taxes for veterans and their surviving spouses who are residents of New York.

Eligibility This program is open to veterans who have purchased properties in New York with pension, bonus, or insurance money (referred to as "eligible funds"). Specially adapted homes of paraplegics, or the homes of their widowed spouses, are also covered.

Financial data This exemption reduces the property's assessed value to the extent that "eligible funds" were used in the purchase, generally to a maximum of $5,000. It is applicable to general municipal taxes but not to school taxes or special district levies.

Duration This exemption is available annually.

Number awarded Varies each year.

Deadline Applications must be filed with the local assessor by "taxable status date;" in most towns, that is the end of February.

[1161]
NEW YORK STATE BLIND ANNUITY

New York State Division of Veterans' Affairs
5 Empire State Plaza, Suite 2836
Albany, NY 12223-1551
(518) 474-6114
Toll-free: (888) VETS-NYS (within NY)
Fax: (518) 473-0379
E-mail: info@veterans.state.ny.us
Web: www.veterans.state.ny.us

Summary To provide an annuity to blind wartime veterans and their surviving spouses in New York.

Eligibility This benefit is available to veterans who served on active duty during World War I, World War II, the Korean War, the Vietnam Conflict, or the Persian Gulf, and to veterans who received an expeditionary medal for service in Lebanon, Grenada, or Panama. Applicants must 1) meet the New York State standards of blindness; 2) have received an honorable or general discharge, or a discharge other than for dishonorable service; and 3) be now, and continue to be, residents of and continuously domiciled in New York State. The annuity is also payable to unremarried spouses of deceased veterans who were receiving annuity payments (or were eligible to do so) at the time of their death, and are residents of and continuously domiciled in New York State.

Financial data The annuity is $1,000 per year.

Number awarded Varies each year.

[1162]
NORTH DAKOTA INCOME TAX ADJUSTMENTS FOR ADOPTING CHILDREN WITH DISABILITIES

Office of State Tax Commissioner
State Capitol Building
600 East Boulevard Avenue, Department 127
Bismarck, ND 58505-0599
(701) 328-2770   Toll-free: (800) 638-2901
Fax: (701) 328-3700   TTY: (800) 366-6888
E-mail: taxinfo@state.nd.us
Web: www.ndtaxdepartment.com

Summary To provide an income tax deduction to North Dakota residents who adopt children with disabilities.

Eligibility For the purposes of this program, disabled children are defined as being under the age of 21 and having irreversible mental retardation, blindness, or other disabilities covered under Title XVI of the U.S. Social Security Act. To qualify, the parent must have adopted a child meeting these requirements and supported the child during the taxable year.

Financial data The reportable taxable income of eligible North Dakota residents is reduced by $750 for each qualifying adopted child. In addition, on a 1-time basis, eligible parents are permitted to reduce their reportable taxable income up to $1,000 to cover the amount expended for filing fees, attorney's fees, and travel costs incurred in connection with the adoption of a qualifying child.

Duration The $750 reduction continues until the qualifying child reaches the age of 21 years.

Number awarded Varies each year.

Deadline The deduction is claimed when filing the state income tax return by April of each year.

[1163]
NORTH DAKOTA PROPERTY TAX EXEMPTION FOR THE BLIND

Office of State Tax Commissioner
State Capitol Building
600 East Boulevard Avenue, Department 127
Bismarck, ND 58505-0599
(701) 328-2770　　　Toll-free: (800) 638-2901
Fax: (701) 328-3700　　　TTY: (800) 366-6888
E-mail: taxinfo@state.nd.us
Web: www.ndtaxdepartment.com

Summary To provide partial tax exemption in North Dakota to blind persons and their spouses.

Eligibility Blind persons are defined as those who are totally blind, who have visual acuity of not more than 20/200 in the better eye with correction, or whose vision is limited in field so that the widest diameter subtends an angle no greater than 20 degrees. Eligible for this exemption is property that is owned by a blind person, by the spouse of a blind person, or jointly by a blind person and a spouse. The property that is exempt includes the entire building classified as residential, and owned and occupied as a residence by a person who qualifies, as long as the building contains no more than 2 apartments or rental units that are leased.

Financial data The exemption applies to all or any part of fixtures, building, and improvements upon any nonfarmland up to a taxable valuation of $5,000.

Duration The exemption continues as long as the blind person resides in the home in North Dakota.

Number awarded Varies each year.

[1164]
NORTH DAKOTA PROPERTY TAX EXEMPTION FOR THE DISABLED

Office of State Tax Commissioner
State Capitol Building
600 East Boulevard Avenue, Department 127
Bismarck, ND 58505-0599
(701) 328-2770　　　Toll-free: (800) 638-2901
Fax: (701) 328-3700　　　TTY: (800) 366-6888
E-mail: taxinfo@state.nd.us
Web: www.ndtaxdepartment.com

Summary To provide partial tax exemption in North Dakota to persons permanently confined to the use of a wheelchair and their spouses.

Eligibility Persons permanently confined to the use of a wheelchair are those who cannot walk with the assistance of crutches or any other device and will never be able to do so; this must be certified by a physician selected by a local governing board. The property must be owned and occupied as a homestead according to state law. The homestead may be owned by the spouse or jointly owned by the disabled person and spouse provided both reside on the homestead. Qualified residents and, if deceased, their unremarried surviving spouses are entitled to this exemption. Income is not considered in determining eligibility for the exemption.

Financial data The maximum benefit may not exceed $3,600 taxable value, because a homestead is limited to $80,000 market value.

Duration The exemption continues as long as the homestead in North Dakota is owned by the disabled person and/or the spouse.

Additional Information The exemption does not apply to special assessments levied upon the homestead.

Number awarded Varies each year.

[1165]
NORTH DAKOTA PROPERTY TAX EXEMPTIONS FOR DISABLED VETERANS

Office of State Tax Commissioner
State Capitol Building
600 East Boulevard Avenue, Department 127
Bismarck, ND 58505-0599
(701) 328-2770　　　Toll-free: (800) 638-2901
Fax: (701) 328-3700　　　TTY: (800) 366-6888
E-mail: taxinfo@state.nd.us
Web: www.ndtaxdepartment.com

Summary To provide disabled North Dakota veterans and their spouses or widow(er)s with property tax exemptions.

Eligibility Veterans with disabilities who qualify for tax exemptions fall into 2 categories: 1) paraplegics, including those whose disability is not service-connected, regardless of income, and 2) honorably discharged veterans with more than a 50% service-connected disability whose income is less than $14,000. The property must be owned and occupied as a homestead according to state law. Spouses and unremarried widow(er)s are also eligible.

Financial data The maximum benefit may not exceed $3,600 taxable value, because a homestead is limited to $80,000 market value.

Duration 1 year; renewable as long as qualified individuals continue to reside in North Dakota and live in their homes.

Number awarded Varies each year.

Deadline Applications may be submitted to the county auditor at any time.

[1166]
OHIO EMERGENCY RELIEF AID

Governor's Office of Veterans' Affairs
77 South High Street, 30th Floor
Columbus, OH 43215-6117
(614) 644-0892　　　Fax: (614) 466-9354
Web: www.state.oh.us/gova

Summary To provide emergency aid to Ohio war vet-

erans or their dependents who, because of disability or disaster, are in financial need.

Eligibility Eligible to apply for this aid are disabled and other veterans, their spouses, widow(er)s, children, or parents who require emergency financial relief because of sickness, accident, or destitution. The veteran must have served during World War I, World War II, the Korean conflict, or the Vietnam era. All applicants must be Ohio residents.

Financial data The amount granted varies, depending on the needs of the recipient.

Duration These are emergency funds only and are not designed to be a recurring source of income.

Additional Information These grants are made by the various county veterans services offices in Ohio.

Number awarded Varies each year.

Deadline Applications may be submitted at any time.

[1167]
OKLAHOMA FINANCIAL ASSISTANCE PROGRAM

Oklahoma Department of Veterans Affairs
Veterans Memorial Building
2311 North Central Avenue
Oklahoma City, OK 73150
(405) 521-3684   Fax: (405) 521-6533
E-mail: scylmer@odva.state.ok.us
Web: www.odva.state.ok.us

Summary To provide emergency aid to Oklahoma veterans and their families who, because of disability or disaster, are in financial need.

Eligibility This program is open to veterans with at least 90 days of wartime service and an honorable discharge who are current residents of Oklahoma and have resided in Oklahoma for at least 1 year immediately preceding the date of application. Applicants must be seeking funds for rent or mortgage payments, food, and/or utilities as the result of a loss from a disaster such as flood, storm, or fire, or from an injury or illness that has interrupted the veteran's ability to work and caused him or her to become delinquent in the above payments. Widow(er)s and minor children may also qualify for the benefit.

Financial data The amount of the grant depends on the need of the recipient.

Duration The grant is available only on a 1-time basis.

Additional Information No financial assistance will be granted when regular monetary benefits are being received from other state agencies. The funds cannot be used for old debts, car payments, or medical expenses.

Number awarded Varies each year.

Deadline Applications must be submitted to the local post or chapter of a veterans services organization for initial approval or disapproval. They may be submitted at any time during the year.

[1168]
OKLAHOMA INCOME TAX EXEMPTION FOR THE BLIND

Oklahoma Tax Commission
Attn: Income Tax
2501 North Lincoln Boulevard
Oklahoma City, OK 73194-0009
(405) 521-3160
Toll-free: (800) 522-8165 (within OK)
Fax: (405) 522-0063
E-mail: otcmaster@oktax.state.ok.us
Web: www.oktax.state.ok.us

Summary To exempt a portion of the income of blind people and their spouses in Oklahoma from state taxation.

Eligibility This exemption is available to residents of Oklahoma and their spouses who are legally blind.

Financial data Each qualifying resident is entitled to claim an additional exemption of $1,000.

Duration The exemption is available as long as the recipient resides in Oklahoma.

[1169]
OREGON PROPERTY TAX EXEMPTION FOR VETERANS WITH DISABILITIES AND THEIR SPOUSES

Oregon Department of Revenue
Attn: Property Tax Division
Revenue Building
955 Center Street, N.E.
Salem, OR 97310-2551
(503) 378-4988
Toll-free: (800) 356-4222 (within OR)
TDD: (800) 886-7204 (within OR)
Web: www.dor.state.or.us

Summary To exempt disabled Oregon veterans and their spouses from a portion of their property taxes.

Eligibility Qualifying veterans are those who received a discharge or release under honorable conditions after service of either 1) 90 consecutive days during World War I, World War II, or the Korean conflict; or 2) 210 consecutive days after January 31, 1955. Eligible individuals must meet 1 of these conditions: 1) a war veteran who is officially certified by the U.S. Department of Veterans Affairs (VA) or any branch of the U.S. armed forces as having disabilities of 40% or more; 2) a war veteran who is certified each year by a licensed physician as being 40% or more disabled and has total gross income that is less than $8,778 with no dependents, $11,497 with 1 dependent, or an amount that increases by $1,496 for each additional dependent; or 3) a war veteran's surviving spouse who has not remarried, even if the veteran's spouse was not disabled or did not take advantage of the exemption if disabled. Recipients of this exemption must own and live on the property in Oregon.

Financial data The exemption is $9,860 of the homestead property's real market value.

Duration 1 year; may be renewed as long as the eligible veteran or surviving unremarried spouse owns and occupies the primary residence.

Number awarded Varies each year.

Deadline This exemption is not automatic. Applications must be submitted by March of each year.

[1170]
OREGON PROPERTY TAX EXEMPTION FOR VETERANS WITH SERVICE-CONNECTED DISABILITIES AND THEIR SPOUSES

Oregon Department of Revenue
Attn: Property Tax Division
Revenue Building
955 Center Street, N.E.
Salem, OR 97310-2551
(503) 378-4988
Toll-free: (800) 356-4222 (within OR)
TDD: (800) 886-7204 (within OR)
Web: www.dor.state.or.us

Summary To exempt disabled Oregon veterans and their spouses from a portion of their property taxes.

Eligibility Qualifying veterans are those who received a discharge or release under honorable conditions after service of either 1) 90 consecutive days during World War I, World War II, or the Korean conflict; or 2) 210 consecutive days after January 31, 1955. Eligible individuals must meet 1 of these conditions: 1) a war veteran who has been certified within the last 3 years by the U.S. Department of Veterans Affairs (VA) or any branch of the U.S. armed forces as having service-connected disabilities of 40% or more; or 2) a surviving spouse of a war veteran who died because of service-connected injury or illness or who received at least 1 year of this exemption. Recipients of this exemption must own and live on the property in Oregon.

Financial data The exemption is $13,130 of the homestead property's real market value.

Duration 1 year; may be renewed as long as the eligible veterans or surviving spouse owns and occupies the primary residence.

Number awarded Varies each year.

Deadline This exemption is not automatic. Applications must be submitted by March of each year.

[1171]
PARENT-INFANT/PRESCHOOL SERVICES FINANCIAL AID PROGRAM

Alexander Graham Bell Association for the Deaf
Attn: Financial Aid Coordinator
3417 Volta Place, N.W.
Washington, DC 20007-2778
(202) 337-5220 Fax: (202) 337-8314
TTY: (202) 337-5221
E-mail: financialaid@agbell.org
Web: www.agbell.org

Summary To provide financial aid to the parents of infants and preschool children with moderate to profound hearing loss who need assistance to cover expenses associated with early intervention services.

Eligibility Applicants must be parents or guardians of children less than 6 years of age who have been diagnosed as having a moderate to profound hearing loss (55 dB or greater loss in the speech frequencies of 500, 1000, and 2000 Hz). The parent or guardian must be committed to an oral approach for education of their child, including the development of the child's listening, speech, oral communication, and cognitive skills. The family must be able to demonstrate financial need.

Financial data The amount awarded depends on the needs of the child; most awards range from $300 to $1,000 per year.

Duration 1 year; may be renewed upon reapplication, but preference is given to new applicants who are just enrolling their child in preschool.

Number awarded Varies each year.

Deadline Applications must be requested between June and August of each year.

[1172]
PENNSYLVANIA REAL ESTATE TAX EXEMPTION

Bureau for Veterans Affairs
Fort Indiantown Gap
Annville, PA 17003-5002
(717) 865-8907
Toll-free: (800) 54 PA VET (within PA)
Fax: (717) 865-8589 E-mail: jdavison@state.pa.us
Web: sites.state.pa.us

Summary To exempt Pennsylvania veterans with disabilities and their unremarried surviving spouses from all state real estate taxes.

Eligibility Eligible to apply for this exemption are honorably discharged veterans who are residents of Pennsylvania and who are blind, paraplegic, or 100% disabled from a service-connected disability sustained during wartime military service. The dwelling must be owned by the veteran solely or jointly with a spouse, and the need for the exemption must be determined by the State Veterans' Commission. Upon the death of the veteran, the tax exemption passes on to the veteran's unremarried surviving spouse.

Financial data This program exempts the principal residence (and the land on which it stands) from all real estate taxes.
Duration The exemption continues as long as the eligible veteran or unremarried widow resides in Pennsylvania.
Number awarded Varies each year.

[1173]
PENNSYLVANIA VETERANS EMERGENCY ASSISTANCE

Bureau for Veterans Affairs
Fort Indiantown Gap
Annville, PA 17003-5002
(717) 865-8905
Toll-free: (800) 54 PA VET (within PA)
Fax: (717) 865-8589   E-mail: jdavison@state.pa.us
Web: sites.state.pa.us

Summary To provide financial aid on an emergency and temporary basis to Pennsylvania veterans (or their dependents) who are disabled, sick, or without means.
Eligibility Eligible to apply for this assistance are honorably discharged veterans who served in the U.S. armed forces during wartime and are now disabled, sick, or in financial need. Widow(er)s or orphan children of recently deceased veterans are also eligible if the veteran would have qualified prior to death. Applicants must have been residents of Pennsylvania for 1 year prior to the date of application.
Financial data Financial aid for the necessities of life (food, dairy, shelter, fuel, and clothing) is provided; the amount varies, depending upon the needs of the recipient.
Duration Aid is provided on a temporary basis only, not to exceed 3 months in a 12-month period.
Number awarded Varies each year.
Deadline Applications may be submitted at any time, but the factors that caused the emergency must have occurred within 180 days prior to the application.

[1174]
RAILROAD RETIREMENT DISABILITY ANNUITY

Railroad Retirement Board
Attn: Office of Public Affairs
844 North Rush Street
Chicago, IL 60611-2092
(312) 751-4777   Fax: (312) 751-7154
Web: www.rrb.gov

Summary To provide an annuity to railroad workers with disabilities and their families.
Eligibility The Railroad Retirement Board provides annuities for 2 types of disabilities. Eligible for total disability are regular employees of companies covered by the Railroad Retirement Act (railroads engaged in interstate commerce and certain of their subsidiaries, railroad associations, and national railway labor organizations) who are totally disabled for all regular work and have at least 10 years of creditable railroad service; credit for a month of railroad service is given for every month in which an employee had some compensated service for at least 1 day, but the required 120 service months need not be consecutive. The other type of disability, occupational disability, is available to employees who have at least 20 years of service, or who are aged 60 or older and have at least 10 years of service, and are permanently disabled from their regular railroad occupation. Survivor benefits are available to widows, widowers, unmarried children, and, in certain cases, parents, remarried widow(er)s, grandchildren, and surviving divorced spouses. For widow(er)s of workers with disabilities, annuities are payable at the age of 60; widow(er)s who are permanently and totally disabled are eligible if they are between the ages of 50 and 59 and the disability began within 7 years after the employee's death; widow(er)s of any age are eligible if they are caring for a child of the deceased employee under the age of 18 or a child with a disability of any age who became disabled before age 22. Unmarried children (or grandchildren if both parents are deceased) are eligible for survivor benefits if they are under the age of 18, or still enrolled full time in an elementary or secondary school, or disabled if they became totally and permanently disabled before age 22. Parents over the age of 60 who were dependent on the employee for at least half of the parent's support also qualify for survivor benefits. Surviving divorced spouses qualify if they were married to the employee for at least 10 years and are 60 or older (50 or older if disabled), or if they are still caring for a child of the employee under the age of 16 or disabled. Remarried widow(er)s retain eligibility if they remarry after age 60 (after age 50 if disabled).
Financial data Benefits are based on months of service and earnings credits. Recently, the average monthly annuity paid to employees over 65 years of age with disabilities was $1,410, for those under 65 years of age with disabilities it was $1,884, for spouses and divorced spouses it was $595, for disabled widows and widowers it was $976, for widowed mothers and fathers it was $1,261, for remarried widows and widowers it was $646, for divorced widows and widowers it was $646, and for children it was $742.
Duration Disability annuities are paid until the employee dies or recovers from the disability; survivor annuities are paid until death or, in the case of able-bodied children, until age 18 or graduation from high school.
Additional Information Employees who are disabled from their regular railroad occupation may work in another job and earn up to $400 per month or $4,800 per year without loss of any railroad retirement disability benefits. A 5-month waiting period beginning with the month after the month of the onset of disability is required before disability annuity payments can begin.

Number awarded Varies each year; recently, the number of employees over 65 years of age with disabilities receiving benefits was 36,100, under 65 years of age with disabilities was 46,200, and disabled widows and widowers was 5,236.

[1175]
REIMBURSEMENT OF BURIAL EXPENSES

Department of Veterans Affairs
810 Vermont Avenue, N.W.
Washington, DC 20420
(202) 418-4343   Toll-free: (800) 827-1000
Web: www.va.gov

Summary To provide reimbursement of burial expenses for wartime and certain peacetime veterans.

Eligibility Survivors are eligible for reimbursement if the veteran, at the time of death, was entitled to receive a pension or compensation or would have been entitled to compensation but for receipt of military pay. Eligibility is also established if the veteran died while hospitalized or domiciled in a U.S. Department of Veterans Affairs (VA) facility or other facility at VA expense. The veteran must have been discharged under conditions other than dishonorable.

Financial data Up to $300 is provided for the veteran's burial expenses. The costs of transporting the remains may be allowed if the veteran died while hospitalized or domiciled in a VA hospital or domiciliary or at VA's expense or died in transit at VA's expense to or from a medical facility. Up to $300 is also paid as a plot or interment allowance (in addition to the $300 basic burial allowance) when the veteran is not buried in a national cemetery or other cemetery under the jurisdiction of the U.S. government. For veterans who died of service-connected causes, the payment is $2,000.

Duration For service-connected deaths, the claim may be filed at any time. For other deaths, the claim must be filed within 2 years after permanent burial or cremation.

Number awarded Varies each year.

Deadline Applications may be submitted at any time.

[1176]
RESTORED ENTITLEMENT PROGRAM FOR SURVIVORS (REPS)

Department of Veterans Affairs
810 Vermont Avenue, N.W.
Washington, DC 20420
(202) 418-4343   Toll-free: (800) 827-1000
Web: www.va.gov

Summary To provide benefits to survivors of certain deceased veterans.

Eligibility Survivors of deceased veterans who died of service-connected causes incurred or aggravated prior to August 13, 1981 are eligible for these benefits.

Financial data The benefits are similar to the benefits for students and surviving spouses with children between the ages of 16 and 18 that were eliminated from the Social Security Act. The exact amount of the benefits is based on information provided by the Social Security Administration.

Additional Information The benefits are payable in addition to any other benefits to which the family may be entitled.

Number awarded Varies each year.

Deadline Applications may be submitted at any time.

[1177]
SALLIE MAE 911 EDUCATION FUND LOAN RELIEF PROGRAM

Sallie Mae 911 Education Fund
c/o The Community Foundation for the National
  Capital Region
Attn: Kenny Emson
1201 15th Street, N.W., Suite 420
Washington, DC 20005-2842
(202) 955-5890   Toll-free: (800) 441-4043
Web: www.salliemae.com

Summary To enable spouses, same-sex partners, and co-borrowers of those killed or totally and permanently disabled in the terrorist attacks of September 11, 2001 to pay off the student loans that are owned or serviced by Sallie Mae.

Eligibility The following individuals are eligible for this program: 1) spouses of those killed or declared totally and permanently disabled in the terrorist attacks of September 11, 2001 who are the borrowers on a) an eligible student loan owned or serviced by Sallie Mae; or b) a Sallie Mae spousal consolidated FFELP student loan; 2) same-sex partners of those killed or declared totally and permanently disabled in the attacks who are the borrowers on an eligible student loan owned or serviced by Sallie Mae; 3) co-borrowers of those killed or declared totally and permanently disabled in the attacks who are the borrowers on an eligible student loan owned or serviced by Sallie Mae; 4) individuals who were totally and permanently disabled in the terrorist attacks and hold a private education student loan owned or serviced by Sallie Mae; and 5) estate administrators or similar individuals who were killed in the attack and who held a private education student loan owned or serviced by Sallie Mae.

Financial data This fund will pay off the student loans of eligible applicants that are owned or serviced by Sallie Mae.

Duration All eligible applicants will receive a check for the amount of their eligible student loan owned or serviced by Sallie Mae from the Community Foundation for the National Capital Region within approximately 60 days from the date the application was received.

Additional Information Individuals who either lost their lives or were totally and permanently disabled in the

terrorist attacks and held Sallie Mae FFELP student loans will have their loans discharged in the FFELP program and therefore are not included in this loan relief program.

Deadline Applications for loan relief may be submitted at any time.

[1178]
SOCIAL SECURITY DISABILITY INSURANCE (SSDI) BENEFITS

Social Security Administration
6401 Security Boulevard
Baltimore, MD 21235-0001
(410) 594-1234   Toll-free: (800) 772-1213
TTY: (800) 325-0778
Web: www.ssa.gov

Summary To provide monthly benefits to workers and their families if the worker becomes disabled or blind.

Eligibility This program defines disabled people as those who are unable to do any kind of work for which they are suited and whose disability has lasted or is expected to last for at least a year or to result in death. Blind people qualify if their vision cannot be corrected to better than 20/200 in their better eye or if their visual field is 20 degrees or less, even with corrective lens. Family members who are eligible include 1) unmarried children, including adopted children and, in some cases, stepchildren and grandchildren who are under 18 years of age (19 if still in high school full time); 2) unmarried children, over 18 years of age, if they have a disability that started before age 22; and 3) spouses who are 62 years of age or older, or of any age if caring for a child of the disabled worker who is under 16 years of age or disabled. For deceased workers, disabled widow(er)s 50 years of age or older are also eligible. Applicants must also have worked long enough and recently enough under Social Security in order to qualify. Workers who become disabled before the age of 24 need 6 credits in the 3-year period ending when the disability begins; workers who become disabled between the ages of 24 and 31 must have credit for having worked half the time between the age of 21 and the date of disability; workers 31 years of age or older at the time of disability must have earned as many total credits as needed for retirement (from 20 credits if disabled at age 31 through 42 to 40 credits if disabled at age 62 or older) and must have earned at least 20 of the credits in the 10 years immediately before becoming disabled. An exception applies to blind workers who need no recent credit but may have earned the required credit any time after 1936.

Financial data The amount of the monthly benefit depends on several factors, including the worker's age at the time of disability, the number of dependents, and the amount of earnings on which Social Security taxes have been paid. Recently, the average monthly benefit for disabled workers was $839; for spouses of disabled workers it was $214; and for children of disabled workers it was $246.

Duration For a disabled or blind person, whether a worker, widow, widower, surviving divorced spouse, or person over the age of 18 who became disabled before the age of 22, monthly benefits continue until the person is no longer disabled or dies. For a dependent spouse, benefits are paid until the worker is no longer disabled or dies. For a dependent child, the benefits continue until the child marries or reaches the age of 18 (19 if still enrolled as a full-time high school student).

Additional Information Disabled workers may test their ability to return to work for a trial work period of up to 9 months, during which time they receive full SSDI benefits. At the end of that period, a decision is made as to whether or not they are able to engage in substantial gainful activity. Persons who find that they cannot continue substantial gainful employment continue to receive SSDI benefits without interruption. Persons who can engage in substantial gainful activity receive benefits for an additional 3 months after which payments cease. Several factors are considered to determine if the person can engage in substantial gainful employment, but the most important is income.

Number awarded Varies; recently, approximately 5.7 million persons were receiving SSDI monthly benefits. Annual benefits paid were approximately $4.8 billion. Another 1.7 million dependents (including 150,000 spouses and 1,550,000 children) were receiving $400 million in annual benefits.

[1179]
SOUTH CAROLINA DISABLED PERSON PROPERTY TAX EXEMPTION

South Carolina Department of Revenue
Attn: Property Division
301 Gervais Street
P.O. Box 125
Columbia, SC 29214
(803) 898-5480   Fax: (803) 898-5822
Web: www.sctax.org

Summary To exempt the home of disabled residents of South Carolina and their unremarried widow(er)s from property taxation.

Eligibility Eligible for this exemption are residents of South Carolina who are defined as paraplegic or hemiplegic and own a dwelling house that is their domicile. Surviving spouses are also eligible as long as they do not remarry, reside in the dwelling, and obtain the fee or life estate in the dwelling.

Financial data The exemption applies to all taxes on 1 house and a lot (not to exceed 1 acre).

Duration The exemption extends as long as the person with a disability resides in the house, or as long as the surviving spouse remains unremarried and resides in the house.

Number awarded Varies each year.

Deadline Applications may be submitted at any time.

[1180]
SOUTH CAROLINA DISABLED VETERANS PROPERTY TAX EXEMPTION

South Carolina Department of Revenue
Attn: Property Division
301 Gervais Street
P.O. Box 125
Columbia, SC 29214
(803) 898-5480   Fax: (803) 898-5822
Web: www.sctax.org

Summary To exempt the residence of disabled South Carolina veterans, their unremarried widow(er)s, and others from property taxation.

Eligibility Eligible for this exemption are veterans in South Carolina who are 100% permanently and totally disabled from service-connected causes. The exemption is also available to unremarried widow(er)s of 1) disabled veterans who have died; 2) servicemembers killed in the line of duty; and 3) law enforcement officers killed in the line of duty. Surviving spouses must have owned the lot and dwelling house in fee or for life, or jointly with the spouse. They remain eligible if they dispose of the exempt dwelling and acquire another residence in South Carolina for use as a residence with a value no greater than 150% of the fair market value of the exempt dwelling, but no subsequent house of a surviving spouse is eligible for exemption.

Financial data The exemption applies to all taxes on 1 house and a lot (not to exceed 1 acre).

Duration The exemption extends as long as the veteran resides in the house, or as long as the spouse of a deceased veteran, servicemember, or law enforcement officer remains unremarried and resides in the original house or a single new dwelling.

Number awarded Varies each year.

Deadline Applications may be submitted at any time.

[1181]
SOUTH CAROLINA INCOME TAX EXEMPTION FOR THE ADOPTION OF A SPECIAL NEEDS CHILD

South Carolina Department of Revenue
301 Gervais Street
P.O. Box 125
Columbia, SC 29214
(803) 898-5000   Toll-free: (800) 763-1295
Fax: (803) 898-5822
Web: www.sctax.org

Summary To provide income tax exemptions to residents of South Carolina who adopt a special needs child.

Eligibility South Carolina residents who adopt a special needs child and provide the child's chief financial support are eligible for this exemption. For the purposes of the program, "special needs" is defined as a child with disabilities (physical, mental, or emotional), ethnic minority status, sibling group membership, medical condition, or age status that makes unassisted adoption unlikely. The child must be under the age of 21 or be incapable of self-support because of mental or physical disabilities to qualify for the program.

Financial data Eligible parents receive a $2,000 per year state income tax exemption.

Duration This exemption continues as long as the dependent is under 21 years of age, unless the child is regularly enrolled in an accredited school or college or is incapable of self-support because of mental or physical disabilities.

Additional Information The entire deduction is allowed for a taxable year, even if the special needs child does not survive for the entire year. The program was started in 1985.

Number awarded Varies each year.

Deadline The exemption is filed on the parent's state income tax form each year, due in April

[1182]
SOUTH CAROLINA SPECIALLY ADAPTED HOUSING TAX EXEMPTION

South Carolina Office of Veterans Affairs
1205 Pendleton Street, Room 477
Columbia, SC 29201-3789
(803) 734-0200   Fax: (803) 734-0197
E-mail: va@govoepp.state.sc.us
Web: www.govoepp.state.sc.us/vetaff.htm

Summary To provide for the exemption of taxes on specially adapted housing in South Carolina that was acquired from the U.S. Department of Veterans Affairs (VA).

Eligibility Veterans having service-connected disabilities resulting in the loss or loss of use of lower extremities (requiring braces, crutches, or wheelchairs for locomotion) as well as blinded veterans who have loss of use of a lower extremity qualify for specially adapted housing from the VA. Disabled veterans who are residents of South Carolina and who have acquired such housing with financial assistance from the VA are eligible for this exemption; if the eligible veteran is deceased, the spouse, dependent children, or dependent parents are eligible for the exemption.

Financial data The exemption extends to state, county, and municipal taxes on any real estate acquired as specially adapted housing.

Duration The exemption continues as long as an eligible veteran or a qualified dependent owns and occupies the property.

Number awarded Varies each year.

Deadline Applications may be submitted at any time.

[1183]
SOUTH DAKOTA PROPERTY TAX EXEMPTION FOR VETERANS AND THEIR WIDOWS OR WIDOWERS

South Dakota Department of Revenue
Attn: Property Tax Division
445 East Capitol Avenue
Pierre, SD 57501-3185
(605) 773-5120   Toll-free: (800) 829-9188
Fax: (605) 773-6729
E-mail: PropTaxIn@state.sd.us
Web: www.state.sd.us

Summary To exempt from property taxation the homes of disabled veterans in South Dakota and their widow(er)s.

Eligibility This program applies to dwellings or parts of multiple family dwellings in South Dakota that are specifically designed for use by paraplegics as wheelchair homes and that are owned and occupied by veterans who have lost or lost the use of both lower extremities. The unremarried widow or widower of such a veteran is also eligible. The dwelling must be owned and occupied by the veteran for 1 full calendar year before the exemption becomes effective. For purposes of this program, the term "dwelling" generally includes the real estate up to 1 acre on which the building is located.

Financial data Qualified dwellings are exempt from property taxation in South Dakota.

Duration The exemption applies as long as the dwelling is owned and occupied by the disabled veteran or widow(er).

Number awarded Varies each year.

[1184]
SOUTH DAKOTA PROPERTY TAX REFUND FOR SENIOR CITIZENS AND CITIZENS WITH DISABILITIES

South Dakota Department of Revenue
Attn: Tax Refund Office
445 East Capitol Avenue
Pierre, SD 57501-3100
(605) 773-3311   Toll-free: (800) 829-9188
Fax: (605) 773-5129
Web: www.state.sd.us

Summary To provide a partial refund of property taxes to elderly and disabled residents (including disabled veterans) and their surviving spouses in South Dakota.

Eligibility This program is open to residents of South Dakota who either have a qualified disability or are 65 years of age or older. Applicants must live alone and have a yearly income of less than $9,750 or live in a household whose members' combined income is less than $12,750. They must have owned the house in which they are now living for at least 3 years or, if they have owned the house for fewer than 3 years, have been residents of South Dakota for 5 years or longer. Veterans must have a disability of 60% or greater. Other people with disabilities must have been qualified to receive Social Security disability benefits or Supplemental Security Income disability benefits. Widows and widowers are eligible even if they do not meet the requirements as long as their spouse received a property tax refund in the year before death and the widow or widower has continued to live in the same house and has remained unmarried.

Financial data Qualified residents are entitled to a refund of a portion of the property taxes they paid during the preceding calendar year.

Duration Residents of South Dakota are entitled to this refund annually.

Additional Information This program has been in effect since 1974. South Dakotans are not entitled to both a sales tax refund and a property tax refund in the same year. The state will calculate both refunds and pay the amount that is greater.

Number awarded Varies each year.

Deadline June of each year.

[1185]
TENNESSEE PROPERTY TAX RELIEF FOR DISABLED VETERANS AND THEIR SPOUSES

Tennessee Comptroller of the Treasury
Attn: Property Tax Relief Program
James K. Polk State Office Building
505 Deaderick Street, Room 1600
Nashville, TN 37243-0278
(615) 747-8871   Fax: (615) 532-3866
E-mail: Kim.Darden@state.tn.us
Web: www.comptroller.state.tn.us/pa/patxrvet.htm

Summary To provide property tax relief for veterans with disabilities and their spouses in Tennessee.

Eligibility This exemption is offered to veterans or their surviving unremarried spouses who are residents of Tennessee and own and live in their home in the state. The veteran must have served in the U.S. armed forces and 1) have acquired, as a result of such service, a disability from paraplegia, or permanent paralysis of both legs and lower part of the body resulting from traumatic injury, or disease to the spinal cord or brain, or from total blindness, or from loss or loss of use of both legs or arms from any service-connected cause; 2) have been rated by the U.S. Department of Veterans Affairs (VA) as 100% permanently disabled as a result of service as a prisoner of war for at least 5 months; or 3) have been rated by the VA as 100% permanently and totally disabled from any other service-connected combat-related cause. Veterans who experience total blindness are also eligible. The relief does not extend to any person who was dishonorably discharged from any of the armed services.

Financial data The amount of the relief depends on the property assessment and the tax rate in the city or county where the beneficiary lives.

Duration 1 year; may be renewed as long as the eligible veteran or surviving unremarried spouse owns and occupies the primary residence.
Number awarded Varies each year.

[1186]
TEXAS PROPERTY TAX EXEMPTION FOR DISABLED VETERANS AND THEIR FAMILIES

Texas Veterans Commission
P.O. Box 12277
Austin, TX 78711-2277
(512) 463-5538 Fax: (512) 475-2395
E-mail: info@tvc.state.tx.us
Web: www.tvc.state.tx.us

Summary To extend property tax exemptions on the appraised value of their property to disabled and other Texas veterans and their surviving family members.

Eligibility Eligible veterans must be Texas residents rated at least 10% service-connected disabled. Surviving spouses and children of eligible veterans are also covered by this program.

Financial data For veterans in Texas whose disability is rated as 10 through 30%, the first $5,000 of the appraised property value is exempt from taxation; veterans rated as 31 through 50% disabled are exempt from the first $7,500 of appraised value; those with a 51 through 70% disability are exempt from the first $10,000 of appraised value; the exemption applies to the first $12,000 of appraised value for veterans with disabilities rated as 71% or more. A veteran whose disability is 10% or more and who is 65 years or older is entitled to exemption of the first $12,000 of appraised property value. A veteran whose disability consists of the loss of use of 1 or more limbs, total blindness in 1 or both eyes, or paraplegia is exempt from the first $12,000 of the appraised value. The unremarried surviving spouse of a deceased veteran who, at the time of death had a compensable disability and was entitled to an exemption, is entitled to the same exemption. The surviving spouse of a person who died on active duty is entitled to exemption of the first $5,000 of appraised value of the spouse's property. A surviving child of a person who dies on active duty is entitled to exemption of the first $5,000 of appraised value of the child's property as long as the child is unmarried and under 21 years of age.

Duration 1 year; may be renewed as long as the eligible veteran (or unremarried surviving spouse or child) owns and occupies the primary residence in Texas.

Additional Information This program is administered at the local level by the various taxing authorities.

Number awarded Varies each year.
Deadline April of each year.

[1187]
UTAH PROPERTY TAX EXEMPTION FOR DISABLED VETERANS

Utah Office of Veterans Affairs
Attn: Director
550 Foothill Boulevard, Room 206
Salt Lake City, UT 84108
(801) 326-2372
Toll-free: (800) 894-9497 (within UT)
Fax: (801) 326-2369 E-mail: tschow@utah.gov
Web: www.ut.ngb.army.mil/veterans/exempt.htm

Summary To exempt a portion of the property of disabled veterans and their families in Utah from taxation.

Eligibility This program is available to residents of Utah who are disabled veterans or their unremarried widow(er)s or minor orphans. The disability must be at least 10% and incurred as the result of injuries in the line of duty.

Financial data The exemption is equivalent to the disability rating of the veteran.

Duration This benefit is available as long as the disabled veteran or family members reside in Utah.

Deadline Tax exemption applications must be filed with the county government of residence by August of each year.

[1188]
VERMONT PROPERTY TAX EXEMPTION FOR DISABLED VETERANS

Office of Veterans Affairs
118 State Street
Drawer 20
Montpelier, VT 05620-4401
(802) 828-3379 Toll-free: (888) 666-9844
Fax: (802) 828-5932
E-mail: llefevre@va.state.vt.us
Web: www.va.state.vt.us

Summary To exempt disabled Vermont veterans and their dependents from the payment of at least a portion of the state's property tax.

Eligibility Entitled to a property tax exemption are veterans of any war (or their spouses, widow(er)s, or children) who are receiving wartime disability compensation for at least a 50% disability, wartime death compensation, wartime dependence and indemnity compensation, or pension for disability paid through any military department or the Department of Veterans Affairs. Unremarried widow(er)s of previously qualified veterans are also entitled to the exemption whether or not they are receiving government compensation or a pension.

Financial data Up to $10,000 of the assessed value of real and personal property belonging to eligible veterans or their unremarried widow(er)s is exempt from taxation; individual towns may increase the exemption to as much as $20,000.

Duration 1 year; may be renewed as long as the eligible veteran or widow(er) continues to be the owner/occupant of the residence and lives in Vermont.
Additional Information Only 1 exemption may be allowed on a property.
Number awarded Varies each year.
Deadline April of each year.

[1189]
WEST VIRGINIA SENIOR CITIZEN OR DISABILITY INCOME TAX DEDUCTION

West Virginia State Tax Department
Attn: Taxpayer Services Division
P.O. Box 3784
Charleston, WV 25337-3784
(304) 558-3333
Toll-free: (800) 982-8297 (within WV)
Fax: (304) 558-3269   TDD: (800) 282-9833
Web: www.state.wv.us/taxdiv

Summary To provide income tax exemptions for West Virginia residents with disabilities and their surviving spouses.
Eligibility Residents of West Virginia who are totally and permanently disabled (or 65 years of age or older) are eligible for this income tax exemption. Surviving spouses of eligible residents are also entitled to the exemption.
Financial data Up to $8,000 of income is exempt from taxation.
Duration The exemption continues as long as the eligible resident (or his/her spouse) remains a resident of West Virginia.

[1190]
WISCONSIN VETERANS' SUBSISTENCE AID GRANTS

Wisconsin Department of Veterans Affairs
30 West Mifflin Street
P.O. Box 7843
Madison, WI 53707-7843
(608) 266-1311   Toll-free: (800) WIS-VETS
Fax: (608) 267-0403
E-mail: wdvaweb@dva.state.wi.us
Web: dva.state.wi.us/Ben_subsistencegrants.asp

Summary To provide temporary, emergency financial aid to disabled and other Wisconsin veterans or their dependents.
Eligibility This program is open to veterans (must have served on active duty for at least 2 consecutive years or for at least 90 days during specified wartime periods) who are current residents of Wisconsin and were also residents of Wisconsin either at the time of entry into service or for 5 consecutive years after completing service on active duty. Unremarried widow(er)s and minor or dependent children are also eligible if the deceased veteran's spouse or parent would have been eligible if still living, and if the surviving dependent is also a Wisconsin resident. Applicants must have suffered a loss of income because of illness, disability, or death and be seeking temporary, emergency financial aid.
Financial data The grant equals the amount of lost income or whatever is necessary to pay basic subsistence costs, whichever is less. Basic subsistence costs include essentials such as food, rent or mortgage payments, utilities, and basic transportation costs, although in some cases health insurance premiums, child support payments, property taxes, homeowners insurance, prescribed medications, and other items are covered. In cases of natural disaster, aid may be given to replace such essential items as clothing, food, and utensils.
Duration Assistance is provided on a temporary basis only, up to a maximum of 3 months of subsistence aid within a 12-month period. If the disability or other factor causing loss of income continues beyond that time, the applicant must rely on help from the permanent programs sponsored by the U.S. Department of Veterans Affairs, Social Security, or other agencies.
Additional Information The grant does not normally cover credit card, car, or other debt payments, life insurance premiums, car repairs, long distance phone calls, or religious or entertainment expenses.
Number awarded Varies each year.
Deadline Applications may be submitted at any time.

Awards

[1191]
WENDY F. MILLER PARENT OF THE YEAR NATIONAL RECOGNITION AWARD

Autism Society of America
Attn: Awards and Scholarships
7910 Woodmont Avenue, Suite 300
Bethesda, MD 20814-3015
(301) 657-0881   Toll-free: (800) 3-AUTISM
Fax: (301) 657-0869
E-mail: info@autism-society.org
Web: www.autism-society.org

Summary To recognize and reward parents of people with autism who have made outstanding contributions to the work of the Autism Society of America (ASA).
Eligibility Any member of the society may nominate any other member for this award as long as the nominee is the parent of a person with autism. Selection is based on a demonstration of unusual dedication or effort towards furthering the cause of autism, such as raising community awareness, involvement in advocacy, or another significant accomplishment contributing to progress in achieving the goals of the society.

Financial data The awardee receives complimentary registration to the annual conference, a special commemorative plaque, and a cash award of $1,000.
Duration The award is presented annually.
Number awarded 1 each year.
Deadline February of each year.

Annotated Bibliography of General Financial Aid Directories

- *General Financial Aid Directories*
- *Subject/Activity Directories*
- *Directories for Special Groups*
- *Contests and Awards*
- *Internships*
- *Nothing Over $4.95*
- *Cyberspace Sites*

General Directories

[1192]

The A's & B's of Academic Scholarships. Annual.

Do you have a "B" average or better? Are your SAT/ACT scores 900/21 or better? If so, you might be able to qualify for a college-based merit scholarship. This paperback lists the major awards offered by 1,200 colleges to students in the top third of their class who have combined SAT scores of 900 or more. Most entries provide information—in tabular form—on number of awards, value range, class standing, study fields, renewability, restrictions, and application date. A short section (generally 4 pages) identifies some noninstitution-based awards. A companion annual paperback issued by Octameron Associates is *Don't Miss Out: The Ambitious Student's Guide to Scholarships and Loans* ($10.00), which outlines strategies for seeking financial aid for college students and provides brief information on a number of funding programs.

Price: $10, paper.

Available from: Octameron Associates, P.O. Box 2748, Alexandria, VA 22301. Telephone: (703) 836-5480.

Web site: www.octameron.com

[1193]

Chronicle Financial Aid Guide. Annual.

When it comes to general financial aid directories, this is one of the better ones. It provides authoritative, clear descriptions of more than 1,800 loans, scholarships, competitions, contests, and internships offered nationally or regionally by approximately 700 private and public organizations to high school and undergraduate students. The financial aid sponsors include private organizations, clubs, foundations, sororities and fraternities, federal and state governments, and national and international labor unions. The programs are indexed by subject and sponsor.

Price: $24.98, paper.

Available from: Chronicle Guidance Publications, Box 1190, Moravia, NY 13118-1190. Telephone: (315) 497-0330; toll-free: (800) 900-0454.

Web site: www.chronicleguidance.com

[1194]

College Student's Guide to Merit and Other No-Need Funding. By Gail A. Schlachter and R. David Weber. Published every even-numbered year.

It's a myth that only the neediest get financial aid. In fact, there are 1,400 college aid programs, open only to college students and students returning to college, that never consider income in the selection process. How do you find out about those programs? Use the *College Student's Guide to Merit and Other No-Need Funding*. This is the only directory to concentrate solely on no-need funding for college students. Here's information on all the financial aid programs that award money—not on the basis of need but on academic record, career plans, creative activities, writing ability, research skills, religious or ethnic background, military or organizational activities, or just pure luck in random drawings. Plus, you can access the listings in the directory by discipline, specific subject, sponsoring organization, program title, where you live, where your school of choice is located, and even deadline date.

Price: $32, hardcover.

Available from: Reference Service Press, 5000 Windplay Drive, Suite 4, El Dorado Hills, CA 95762. Telephone: (916) 939-9620.

Web site: www.rspfunding.com

[1195]

Foundation Grants to Individuals. Published every odd-numbered year.

While most foundation grants are for agencies and institutions, some funding opportunities (including a number of scholarships and loans) have been set up specifically for individual applicants. You can find out about these opportunities in the Foundation Center's *Foundation Grants to Individuals,* which is available in print, as a CD-ROM, and as a monthly Internet subscription. The current edition identifies more than 4,300 foundations that annually make grants of at least $2,000 to individuals. The work is organized by type of grant awarded (e.g., scholarships, general welfare, medical assistance) and subdivided by eligibility requirements and means of access (including some "Grants to Foreign Individuals" and "Grants to Employees of Specific Companies"). Collectively, these grants total nearly $100 million each year. However, most of these programs are limited geographically and will related only to very small segments of the population.

Price: $65, paper; $75, CD-ROM; $9.95/month, online.

Available from: Foundation Center, 79 Fifth Avenue, New York, NY 10003-3076. Telephone: (212) 620-4230. Toll-free: (800) 424-9836.

Web site: www.fdncenter.org

[1196]

High School Senior's Guide to Merit and Other No-Need Funding. By Gail A. Schlachter and R. David Weber. Published every even-numbered year.

Do you think you or your parents make too much money for you to qualify for financial aid? Not true! This unique guide identifies and describes more than 1,000 merit scholarships and other no-need funding programs set aside just for high school seniors. These programs never consider income level when making awards for college. Here's your chance to get college aid based solely on your academic record, writing or artistic ability, high school club membership, speech-making skills, religious or ethnic background, parents' military or organizational activities, and even pure luck in random draw-

ings. These no-need programs are grouped by discipline (humanities, sciences, social sciences, and any subject area) and indexed by sponsor, program title, geographic restrictions, specific subject coverage, and deadline date.

Price: $29.95, hardcover.

Available from: Reference Service Press, 5000 Windplay Drive, Suite 4, El Dorado Hills, CA 95762. Telephone: (916) 939-9620.

Web site: www.rspfunding.com

[1197]
Kaplan Scholarships. By Gail A. Schlachter, R. David Weber, and the Staff of Reference Service Press. Annual.

Based on Reference Service Press's award-winning financial aid database and jointly published by Kaplan and Simon & Schuster, this directory identifies more than 3,000 scholarships, grants, and awards that can be used to support study in any discipline in two-year colleges, vocational and technical institutes, four-year colleges, and universities in the United States. A definite plus: no single-school or loan programs are included. All listings offer $1,000 or more per year.

Price: $27, paper.

Available from: Simon & Schuster, Attn: Order Department, 100 Front Street, Riverside, NJ 08075. Toll-free: (800) 445-6991.

Web site: www.SimonSays.com

[1198]
Peterson's Scholarship Almanac. Annual.

Despite the claim of this scaled-down version of *Peterson's Scholarships, Grants & Prizes* ($29.95, annual) that it covers the 500 "largest, most generous student award programs," a number of the listings are under $250 or are available to only 1 or 2 recipients. On the plus side, many of the major programs are described here, the information is quite current, and the price is right. Both private and state-sponsored programs are included. Most entries provide a program summary and specific information on academic/career areas supported, amount awarded, eligibility requirements, application requirements, deadline, number awarded, and contact information. At $12.95, this is a good buy.

Price: $12.95, paper.

Available from: Peterson's Guides, 2000 Lenox Drive, P.O. Box 67005, Lawrenceville, NJ 08648. Telephone: (609) 896-1800; toll-free: (800) 338-3282, ext. 660.

Web site: www.petersons.com

[1199]
The Scholarship Handbook. Annual.

Described here are more than 3,000 funding opportunities, including private, federal, and state scholarships, fellowships, grants, internships, and loans. This is one of the best general financial aid directories, along with *Peterson's Guide to Scholarships, Grants & Prizes* and *Kaplan Scholarships* (both described above).

Price: $25.95, paper.

Available from: College Board Publications, Box 886, New York, NY 19191-0886. Telephone: (212) 713-8000; toll-free: (800) 323-7155

Web site: www.collegeboard.org

[1200]
Scholarships, Fellowships, and Loans. Annual.

Although this directory is too expensive for most students (or their parents) to consider buying, it should not be overlooked; many larger libraries have the title in their reference collection. Described here are 4,000+ scholarships, fellowships, and loans available to undergraduates, graduate students, and postdoctorates in the United States and Canada. Each entry identifies qualifications, funds, purposes, application process, and background. The Vocational Goals Index in the front of the volume summarizes, in chart form, the characteristics of each award (e.g., level of study, subject of study, geographic restrictions, citizenship requirements).

Price: $199, hardcover.

Available from: Gale Group, 27500 Drake Road, Farmington Hills, MI 48331-3535. Telephone: (248) 699-4253; toll free: (800) 877-4253.

Web site: www.galegroup.com

Subject/Activity Directories

[1201]
Directory of Research Grants. Annual.

In the latest edition, more than 4,000 grants, contracts, fellowships, and loan programs for research, training, and innovative effort sponsored by 600 organizations are described. The emphasis is on U.S. programs, although some sponsored by other countries are included. Entries are arranged by program title. Annotations include requirements, restrictions, financial data (but not for all entries), name and addresses, and application procedures. The programs are indexed by subject. The information presented in this publication is also available online (through Dialog) as GRANTS, on CD-ROM with monthly supplements, as an Internet subscription (www.grantselect.com), and in a number of derivative publications, including *Directory of Grants in the Humanities* and *Directory of Biomedical and Health Care Grants*.

Price: $135, paper.

Available from: Oryx Press, 88 Post Road West, Westport, CT 06881. Telephone: (203) 226-3571. Toll-free: (800) 225-5800.

Web site: www.greenwood.com

[1202]
Financial Aid for Research and Creative Activities Abroad. By Gail A. Schlachter and R. David Weber. Published every even-numbered year.

This directory will help Americans tap into the millions of dollars available for research, lectureships, exchange programs, work assignments, conference attendance, professional development, and creative projects abroad. The 1,300 listings cover every major field of interest, are tenable in practically every country in the world, are sponsored by more than 500 different private and public organizations and agencies, and are open to all segments of the population, from high school students to professionals and postdoctorates. A companion volume (described below) identifies funding opportunities for study and training abroad.

Price: $45, hardcover.

Available from: Reference Service Press, 5000 Windplay Drive, Suite 4, El Dorado Hills, CA 95762. Telephone: (916) 939-9620.

Web site: www.rspfunding.com

[1203]
Financial Aid for Study and Training Abroad. By Gail A. Schlachter and R. David Weber. Published every even-numbered year.

If you want to go abroad to study and you need money to do so, this is the directory for you. Described here are more than 1,100 scholarships, fellowships, loans, and grants that Americans can use to support structured or unstructured study abroad, including money for formal academic classes, training courses, degree-granting programs, independent study, seminars, workshops, and student internships. Detailed information is provided for each program: address, telephone number (including fax, toll-free, and e-mail), purpose, eligibility, amount awarded, number awarded, duration, special features, limitations, and deadline date. There's also a currency conversion table and an annotated bibliography of key resources that anyone (interested in study abroad or not) can use to find additional funding opportunities.

Price: $39.50, hardcover.

Available from: Reference Service Press, 5000 Windplay Drive, Suite 4, El Dorado Hills, CA 95762. Telephone: (916) 939-9620.

Web site: www.rspfunding.com

[1204]
How to Pay for Your Degree in Agriculture & Related Fields. Published every even-numbered year.
How to Pay for Your Degree in Business & Related Fields. Published every even-numbered year.
How to Pay for Your Degree in Education & Related Fields. Published every even-numbered year.
How to Pay for Your Degree in Engineering. Published every even-numbered year.
How to Pay for Your Degree in Journalism & Related Fields. Published every even-numbered year.

Majoring in one of these fields? Now you can have information—right at your finger tips—on the billions of dollars available to support students working on one of these undergraduate or graduate degrees. *How to Pay for Your Degree in Agriculture & Related Fields* identifies funding for students majoring in agricultural science, animal science, apiculture, ranching, cooperative extension, dairy science, agricultural economics, crops or soils science, enology/viticulture, horticulture, or other related fields. *How to Pay for Your Degree in Business & Related Fields* describes billions of dollars available to support students working on a degree in such business-related fields as finance, banking, accounting, industrial relations, sales, economics, marketing, and personnel administration. *How to Pay for Your Degree in Education & Related Fields* covers funding for students preparing for a career in preschool education, K-12 education, adult education, special education, guidance, educational administration, and the specialty fields of art education, music education, physical education, etc. *How to Pay for Your Degree in Engineering* provides detailed information on more than 650 funding programs set aside specifically to support study, research, and other activities for both undergraduate and graduate engineering students. *How to Pay for Your Degree in Journalism & Related Fields* covers hundreds of grants, scholarships, fellowships, loans, and awards set aside for students working on a degree in journalism, communications, broadcasting, and similar areas.

Price: $30 for each title, comb binding.

Available from: Reference Service Press, 5000 Windplay Drive, Suite 4, El Dorado Hills, CA 95762. Telephone: (916) 939-9620.

Web site: www.rspfunding.com

[1205]
How to Pay for Your Law Degree. Published every even-numbered year.

Millions of dollars are available specifically to support students who are interested in working on a law degree (J.D., LL.M., etc.) Use this directory to find out about these programs; in one place, you'll find the following information for more than 500 fellowships, competitions, and other financial opportunities aimed primarily or exclusively at students in law school: purpose, eligibility, monetary award, duration, special features, limitations, number awarded, and deadline date.

Price: $30, comb binding.

Available from: Reference Service Press, 5000 Windplay Drive, Suite 4, El Dorado Hills, CA 95762. Telephone: (916) 939-9620.

Web site: www.rspfunding.com

[1206]
Money for Graduate Students in the Arts & Humanities. Published every odd-numbered year.

Money for Graduate Students in the Biological & Health Sciences. Published every odd-numbered year.
Money for Graduate Students in the Physical & Earth Sciences. Published every odd-numbered year.
Money for Graduate Students in the Social & Behavioral Sciences. Published every odd-numbered year.

Each of these four titles, which are sold separately, describe funding sources available to support study and research on the graduate school level in a specific discipline. *Money for Graduate Students in the Biological & Health Sciences* covers 1,100 fellowships, grants, and awards for graduate study and research in botany, dentistry, genetics, horticulture, medicine, nursing, nutrition, pharmacology, rehabilitation, veterinary sciences, zoology, etc. *Money for Graduate Students in the Arts & Humanities* describes nearly 1,000 funding opportunities for graduate work in architecture, art, dance, design, filmmaking, history, languages, literature, music, performing arts, philosophy, religion, sculpture, and the rest of the humanities. *Money for Graduate Students in the Physical & Earth Sciences* identifies more than 1,000 graduate funding opportunities in atmospheric sciences, aviation, chemistry, computer sciences, engineering, geology, mathematics, physics, space sciences, technology, and the other related sciences. *Money for Graduate Students in the Social & Behavioral Sciences* covers nearly 1,100 fellowships, loans, grants, and awards for graduate work in accounting, advertising, anthropology and ethnology, business administration, demography and statistics, economics, library and information science, marketing, political science, psychology, sociology, and the other social sciences.

Price: *Money for Graduate Students in the Biological & Health Sciences,* $42.50; *Money for Graduate Students in the Arts & Humanities,* $40; *Money for Graduate Students in the Physical & Earth Sciences,* $35; *Money for Graduate Students in the Social & Behavioral Sciences,* $42.50.

Available from: Reference Service Press, 5000 Windplay Drive, Suite 4, El Dorado Hills, CA 95762. Telephone: (916) 939-9620.

Web site: www.rspfunding.com

[1207]
RSP Funding for Nurses and Nursing Students. By Gail A. Schlachter and R. David Weber. Published every even-numbered year.

In all, more than 600 scholarships, fellowships, loans, and grants available to nursing students and nurses to support study, professional activities, and research are described in detail in this biennial directory. Each program description is prepared from current material supplied by the sponsoring organization. Entries are grouped by intended recipient. Using the indexes, you can search for these funding opportunities by title, sponsor, residency, tenability, subject, and deadline date.

Price: $30, comb binding.

Available from: Reference Service Press, 5000 Windplay Drive, Suite 4, El Dorado Hills, CA 95762. Telephone: (916) 939-9620.

Web site: www.rspfunding.com

Directories for Special Groups

[1208]
Directory of Financial Aids for Women. By Gail Ann Schlachter. Published every odd-numbered year.

Are you a woman looking for financial aid? Or, do you know women who need funding for school, research, creative projects, travel, or other activities? If so, take a look at the *Directory of Financial Aids for Women.* Here, in one place, are descriptions of more than 1,700 funding programs, representing billions of dollars in financial aid set aside just for women. Each of these programs can be accessed by program title, sponsoring organization, geographic coverage, deadline date, and subject. There's also a state-by-state list of state agencies responsible for student aid and a list of key sources that identify additional financial aid opportunities.

Price: $45, hardcover.

Available from: Reference Service Press, 5000 Windplay Drive, Suite 4, El Dorado Hills, CA 95762. Telephone: (916) 939-9620.

Web site: www.rspfunding.com

[1209]
Financial Aid for African Americans. Published every odd-numbered year.
Financial Aid for Asian Americans. Published every odd-numbered year.
Financial Aid for Hispanic Americans. Published every odd-numbered year.
Financial Aid for Native Americans. Published every odd-numbered year.

Each of these four titles, which are sold separately, describe scholarships, fellowships, loans, grants, awards, and internships set aside for specific ethnic groups. *Financial Aid for African Americans* covers 1,400 funding opportunities available to Black and African Americans at any level, from high school seniors through postdoctorates. *Financial Aid for Asian Americans* describes nearly 1,000 funding opportunities available to undergraduates, graduate students, professionals, and postdoctorates of Chinese, Japanese, Korean, Vietnamese, Filipino, and other Asian ancestry. *Financial Aid for Hispanic Americans* provides detailed information on nearly 1,300 sources of funding for Americans of Mexican, Puerto Rican, Central American, or other Latin American heritage. *Financial Aid for Native Americans* identifies more than 1,500 fellowships and other financial aid programs open to American Indians, Native Alaskans, and Native Hawaiians. All four directories are organized by type of funding and indexed by program title,

sponsoring organization, residency requirements, where the money can be spent, subject coverage, and deadline date.

Price: *Financial Aid for African Americans,* $40; *Financial Aid for Asian Americans,* $37.50; *Financial Aid for Hispanic Americans,* $40; *Financial Aid for Native Americans,* $40.

Available from: Reference Service Press, 5000 Windplay Drive, Suite 4, El Dorado Hills, CA 95762. Telephone: (916) 939-9620.

Web site: www.rspfunding.com

[1210]
Financial Aid for the Disabled and Their Families. By Gail Ann Schlachter and R. David Weber. Published every even-numbered year.

There are more than 1,100 funding opportunities available to meet the individual needs of America's largest minority: 43 million persons with disabilities and their children or parents. To find out about this funding, use *Financial Aid for the Disabled and Their Families.* All disabilities are covered, including visual impairments, hearing impairments, orthopedic disabilities, learning disabilities, and multiple disabilities. The following information is provided for each entry: program title, sponsoring organization address and telephone numbers, purpose, eligibility, financial data, duration, special features, limitations, number awarded, and deadline date. To meet the needs of students with visual impairments, information on programs just for them is also available in a large print report ($30) and on an IBM- or Mac-compatible disk ($50).

Price: $40, hardcover.
Available from: Reference Service Press, 5000 Windplay Drive, Suite 4, El Dorado Hills, CA 95762. Telephone: (916) 939-9620.

Web site: www.rspfunding.com

[1211]
Financial Aid for Veterans, Military Personnel, and Their Dependents. By Gail A. Schlachter and R. David Weber. Published every even-numbered year.

Veterans, military personnel, and their dependents (spouses, children, grandchildren, and dependent parents) make up more than one third of America's population today. Each year, public and private agencies set aside billions of dollars in financial aid for these groups. This directory identifies, in one source, the federal, state, and privately-funded scholarships, fellowships, loans, grants/grants-in-aid, awards, and internships aimed specifically at individuals with ties to the military. More than 1,100 programs are described in the latest edition. These opportunities are open to applicants at all levels (from high school through postdoctoral) for education, research, travel, training, career development, or emergency situations. The detailed entries are indexed by title, sponsoring organization, geographic coverage, subject, and deadline dates.

Price: $40, hardcover.
Available from: Reference Service Press, 5000 Windplay Drive, Suite 4, El Dorado Hills, CA 95762. Telephone: (916) 939-9620.

Web site: www.rspfunding.com

Contests and Awards

[1212]
Awards, Honors, and Prizes. Annual.

While this massive, 2-volume set is not the kind of publication you're likely to buy for your own financial aid library, you will definitely want to look at it at a library. It contains the most extensive and up-to-date listings of awards, honors, and prizes available anywhere. It covers all subject areas, all areas of the world, and all types of awards, except scholarships, fellowships, prizes received only as a result of entering contests, and local or regional awards.

Price: Volume 1 (United States): $220, hardcover; Volume 2 (Foreign): $245, hardcover.

Available from: Gale Group, P.O. Box 9187, Farmington Hills, MI 48333-9187. Telephone: (248) 699-GALE; toll-free: (800) 877-GALE.

Web site: www.galegroup.com

Internships

[1213]
The Best 109 Internships. Annual.

Unlike Peterson's *Internships* directory (described below), this listing is selective rather than comprehensive. It describes in detail the "top" 100 or so paid and unpaid internships in America. Information was gathered through questionnaires, interviews with interns, and on-site visits. Each program entry (generally 3 pages) provides information on: application process, selection process, compensation (from nothing to $1,200 or more per week), quality of the work experience, locations, duration, prerequisites, and sources of additional information. The internship profiles are arranged alphabetically by employer. An appendix groups internships by several interesting categories: highest compensation, most selective, etc.

Price: $21, paper.
Available from: Random House, 4000 Hahn Road, Westminster, MD 21157. Telephone: (212) 751-2600; toll-free: (800) 733-3000.

Web site: www.randomhouse.com/princetonreview

[1214]
Peterson's Internships. Annual.

Work experience gained through an internship can provide an advantage in a student's job search. Plus,

internships can provide cash for college (in stipends, subsequent scholarships, or both). One of the best ways to find out about internship opportunities is with a copy of the latest edition of this directory, which identifies more than 1,300 organizations offering more than 35,000 paid and unpaid on-the-job training opportunities in such fields as architecture, business, communications, and sciences. Program entries describe length and duration of the position, pay, desired qualifications, duties, training involved, availability of college credit, and application contacts, procedures, and deadlines. International internships are also included, as well as information for interns working abroad and non-U.S. citizens applying for U.S. internships.

Price: $26.95, paper.

Available from: Peterson's Guides, 2000 Lenox Drive, P.O. Box 67005, Lawrenceville, NJ 08648. Telephone: (609) 896-1800; toll-free: (800) 338-3282, ext. 660.

Web site: www.petersons.com

Nothing Over $4.95

[1215]

College Countdown. Annual.

Getting into the right college is one of the most important challenges you'll ever face. Are you doing the right things at the right times? This checklist identifies exactly what high school students need to do to get ready to apply for college and for college aid.

Price: $4.50, paper.

Available from: Reference Service Press, 5000 Windplay Drive, Suite 4, El Dorado Hills, CA 95762. Telephone: (916) 939-9620.

Web site: www.rspfunding.com

[1216]

Creating Options: Financial Aid for Individuals with Disabilities. Annual.

Although this pamphlet is issued annually, some of its contents (particularly its guide to resources) hasn't been updated in several years. Nevertheless, this free guide provides a useful overview of the financial aid process and includes very brief descriptions of approximately 40 funding sources or specific funding programs for persons with disabilities.

Price: Free, paper or online.

Available from: HEATH Resource Center, Graduate School of Education and Human Development, George Washington University, 2121 K Street, N.W., Suite 220, Washington, DC 20037. Telephone: (202) 973-0904; (800) 54-HEATH.

Web site: www.heath.gwu.edu

[1217]

Financial Assistance for Library and Information Studies. Annual.

This tabular summary of fellowships, scholarships, grants-in-aid, loans, and other funding for library education is issued annually (usually in November) by the American Library Association. It lists awards from state library agencies, national and state library associations, local libraries, and academic institutions offering undergraduate and graduate programs in library education in the United States and Canada. For each entry, the following information is given: granting body, level of program, type of assistance, number available, academic or other requirements, application deadline, and contact address. Scholarships of less than $200 are not included.

Price: $4, paper.

Available from: American Library Association, 50 East Huron Street, Chicago, IL 60611. Telephone: (312) 280-4277, ext. 4282; (800) 545-2433, ext. 4282.

Web site: www.ala.org

[1218]

Free Application for Federal Student Aid. Annual.

If you are going to be in college next year, you need to fill out the Free Application for Federal Student Aid (FAFSA). By filling out this form, you can start the application process for any of these federal programs: Federal Pell Grants, Federal Supplemental Educational Opportunity Grants, Federal Subsidized and Unsubsidized Stafford Loans, Stafford/Ford Federal Direct Subsidized and Unsubsidized Loans, Federal Perkins Loans, Federal Work-Study, Title VII, and Public Health Act Programs. Fill out this form even if you are not interested in getting (or don't think you can qualify for) federal aid; many privately-sponsored programs require students to have submitted FAFSA before applying for their funding. Help in completing the FAFSA is available online. The address is: www.ed.gov/prog_info/SFA/FAFSA. Students can speed up the FAFSA application process by downloading a free Windows-based program for IBM-compatible computers called FAFSA Express; using it can cut weeks off the application process and eliminate the mistakes and problems that sometimes arise when filling out the paper FAFSA form.

Price: Free, paper or downloadable Windows-based program for IBM-compatible computers.

Available from: To receive a copy, call (800) 4-FED-AID or download FAFSA Express at the following web site:

Web site: www.ed.gov/offices/OPE/express.html

[1219]

Fulbright and Related Grants for Graduate Study and Research Abroad. Annual.

The Fulbright Student Program is designed to give recent B.S./B.A. graduates, master's degree and doctoral candidates, young professionals, and artists oppor-

tunities for personal development and international experience. This annual pamphlet, available without charge from the Institute of International Education, lists Institute-administered Fulbright fellowships and grants available to U.S. graduate students for study and research abroad. The arrangement is by country in which the recipient will study or conduct research. Entries specify recommended fields of study or investigation, language requirements, duration, selection procedures, financial data, application process, special features, and limitations. A similar publication for more advanced applicants is *Fulbright Scholar Program,* also available without charge from IIE.

Price: Free, paper.

Available from: Institute of International Education, 809 United Nations Plaza, New York, NY 10017-3580. Telephone: (212) 883-8200; toll-free: (800) 445-0433.

Web site: www.iie.org

[1220]
Need a Lift? To Educational Opportunities, Careers, Loans, Scholarships, Employment. Prep. by the American Legion Educational and Scholarship Program. Annual.

What started as just a listing of financial aid offered by American Legion affiliates around the country has grown to become a sizeable general financial aid listing (each edition is generally 150 pages or more). While American Legion educational assistance on the national and state level is still covered, much more is now presented in each annual issue: information on calculating financial need, a chart describing the major federal programs, some information on funding for veterans and their dependents, and short descriptions of some other types of financial aid. There is even a list of postsecondary schools nationwide, which gives phone numbers, enrollment by gender, SAT scores, tuition costs, costs for room and board, deadlines for admissions and financial aid, and what financial aid forms are required. All this for $3. Quite a bargain.

Price: $3, paper.

Available from: American Legion, Attn: Emblem Sales, P.O. Box 1050, Indianapolis, IN 46206-1050. Telephone: (317) 630-1207; toll-free: (888) 453-4466.

Web site: www.legion.org

[1221]
Social Science Research Council Fellowships and Grants for Training and Research. Annual.

The Social Science Research Council is an autonomous, nongovernmental, not-for-profit international association devoted to "the advancement of interdisciplinary research in the social sciences." This annual pamphlet, distributed without charge by the Social Science Research Council, provides a listing and short description of grants that the council sponsors either independently or with the American Council of Learned Societies. These programs (dissertation fellowships and advanced research grants) apply to the social sciences and humanities in both the United States and, selectively, abroad. They are open to American and foreign citizens on the advanced graduate or postgraduate levels.

Price: Free, paper.

Available from: Social Science Research Council, 810 Seventh Avenue, New York, NY 10019. Telephone: (212) 377-2700.

Web site: www.ssrc.org

[1222]
The Student Guide: Financial Aid from the U.S. Department of Education. Annual.

Of the more than $80 billion in student aid currently available, one half of it (approximately $40 billion) will be supplied by the federal government. And, most of the federal funds will be channeled through a handful of programs: Pell Grants, Subsidized and Unsubsidized Stafford Loans, PLUS Loans, Federal Supplemental Educational Opportunity Grants, Federal Work-Study, and Federal Perkins Loans. Get information about these programs straight from the source, in this free booklet issued by the U.S. Department of Education. For each program, official information is provided on purpose, financial support offered, application procedures, eligibility, recipient responsibilities, and notification process. The *Guide* is available in print or can be downloaded from the Department of Education's web site.

Price: Free, paper.

Available from: U.S. Department of Education, c/o Federal Student Information Aid Center, P.O. Box 84, Washington, DC 20044. Telephone: (800) 4-FED-AID.

Web site: www.ed.gov/prog_info/SFA/StudentGuide

[1223]
Surfing for Scholarships in Cyberspace. Annual

Use your computer to search for scholarships in cyberspace. This guide will point you in the right direction, by identifying the best Internet sites undergraduate and graduate students can use to find money. Best of all, almost all these sites can be searched online without any charge. Reference Service Press also publishes a companion booklet, *Scholarship Search Strategies,* which outlines the best ways to identify and apply for this financial aid ($4.50, updated annually).

Price: $4.95, paper.

Available from: Reference Service Press, 5000 Windplay Drive, Suite 4, El Dorado Hills, CA 95762. Telephone: (916) 939-9620.

Web site: www.rspfunding.com

Cyberspace Sites

[1224]
CollegeBoard Scholarship Search.

This is a free web version of the College Board's *Scholarship Handbook.* Described here are scholarships, fellowships, loans, internships, and other types of financial aid programs sponsored by 2,000+ federal, state, and private sources. The search interface is relatively easy to use, but the database is limited in scope and only updated annually.

Available on the Internet at: www.collegeboard.org

[1225]
fastWEB: Financial Aid Search Through the Web.

FastWEB advertises itself as "The Internet's largest free scholarship search." It contains concise descriptions of financial aid offered by 3,000+ sponsoring organizations. If you take the time to fill out their multi-page questionnaire online (this can take up to 20 minutes, depending upon connection speed), fastWEB will set up a mailbox for you and deliver a list of scholarships based on the information you supplied.

Available on the Internet at: www.fastWeb.com

[1226]
Fundsnet

Fundsnet has been online since 1996. It is an information-rich site (although somewhat randomly organized) covering grants for individuals, financial aid for students, and grants for organizations. Be sure to check the site list, or you could miss out on a number of site offerings. Each entry on the site is linked to further information from the sponsoring organization on the web, and most of these links are annotated.

Available on the Internet at:
www.fundsnetservices.com

[1227]
FundSource

FundSource was initiated by the National Science Foundation and developed by the American Psychological Association as a service to the "Decade of Behavior." This site is designed to help behavioral and social scientists who are interested in finding research funding. There is no charge to search the database, which provides short descriptions, contact information, and web links to appropriate research funding offered by private and public sources.

Available on the Internet at:
www.decadeofbehavior.org/fundsource

[1228]
InternshipPrograms

InternshipPrograms. com is perhaps the most extensive listing of internship opportunities available in cyberspace today, although internship seekers will also find the Rising Star Internships site useful (www.rsinternships.com). More than 2,000 internships offering more than 200,000 positions are described in considerable detail (more than can be found in traditional print directories). The database can be browsed within categories (e.g., law) by company or by region. Only opportunities in the United States are covered; for information on internships abroad, try idealist.org (www.idealist.org) and the Online Study Abroad Directory (described below).

Available on the Internet at: www.wetfeet.com

[1229]
MACH25.

CollegeNET offers a guide to colleges and universities in the United States (and selected other countries). Its scholarship database provides information on 8,000 private and school-based financial aid programs offered by 1,500 sponsors. It is updated annually. The database is similar to fastWEB, but not as easy to use. You can view the results of your search in brief or detailed formats, save individual awards in your profile, and generate letters to request additional information. You may get more "hits" with your MACH25 search than with either fastWEB or SRN, but your search results will probably be less precise; so, be prepared to sift through a number of irrelevant "leads" to find ones that exactly match your requirements.

Available on the Internet at:
www.collegenet.com/mach25

[1230]
Online Study Abroad Directory.

This site, maintained by the International Study and Travel Center at the University of Minnesota, contains three searchable databases that will be of interest to students looking for money to support activities abroad: the Work & Intern Database; the Volunteer Database, which identifies approximately 150 opportunities in developing countries and eastern Europe (some of which pay travel and/or per diem); and the Scholarships Database, which identifies 200 scholarships intended for Americans looking to study or conduct research abroad.

Available on the Internet at: www.istc.umn.edu

[1231]
Peterson's Scholarship Search

This free Internet search service identifies scholarships, awards, and prizes available to support undergraduate and graduate study. To conduct a free financial aid search, students must first register and supply a password to enter or reenter the service. After register-

ing, students answer a few questions and then wait for a minute or two for the results. Very brief information for each match is presented on a form, which covers sponsor, type of award, deadline, number awarded, renewability, what's required in the application process, and contact. Some programs also include award descriptions, but many do not. Much of this information is the same that Peterson's sells in four print directories: *Peterson's Scholarships, Grants & Prizes* ($29.95), *Getting Money for Graduate School* ($16.95), *Peterson's Scholarship Almanac* ($12.95), and *Peterson's Complete Guide to Financial Aid* ($49.95).

Available on the Internet at: www.petersons.com

[1232]
SRN Express.

Sponsored by Scholarship Resource Network (SRN), this web site can be accessed by students directly, without charge. Students have to register (and give out their phone number), but in return they get a chance to search a scholarship database which lists primarily private-sector aid (8,000 programs). Single-school awards are not included. This same database is also available at a web site hosted by SallieMae: www.wiredscholar.com.

Available on the Internet at: www.srnexpress.com

[1233]
Union-Sponsored Scholarships and Aid.

Unions have an outstanding record of providing assistance to members and their families. Find out about union-sponsored scholarships and awards on the AFL-CIO web site, in a section called "Help with College Costs." In all, more than $4 million in funding is described. Even so, these listings just scratch the surface of scholarships offered by many of the 60,000 international, national, regional, state, and local unions. So, be sure to check directly with unions in your area as well, to find out what is being offered. And, do this even if you are not a union member; not all awards require applicants to belong to a union.

Available on the Internet at: www.aflcio.org

Indexes

Program Title Index •
Sponsoring Organization Index •
Residency Index •
Tenability Index •
Subject Index •
Calendar Index •

Program Title Index

If you know the name of a particular funding program and want to find out where it is covered in the directory, use the Program Title Index. Here, program titles are arranged alphabetically, word by word. To assist you in your search, every program is listed by all its known names or abbreviations. In addition, we've used a two-character alphabetical code (within parentheses) to help you determine if the program falls within your scope of interest. The first character (capitalized) in the code identifies availability group: V = Visual Disabilities; H = Hearing Disabilities; O = Orthopedic and Developmental Disabilities; C = Communication and Other Disabilities; D = Disabilities in General; F = Families of the Disabled. The second character (lower cased) identifies program type: s = scholarships; f = fellowships/grants; l = loans; g = grants-in-aid; a = awards. Here's how the code works: if a program is followed by (H–f) 241, the program is described in the Hearing Disabilities chapter under fellowships/grants, in entry 241. If the same program title is followed by another entry number—for example, (F–g) 1080—the program is also described in the Families of the Disabled chapter, under grants-in-aid, in entry 1080. Remember: the numbers cited here refer to program entry numbers, not to page numbers in the book.

AAAS/NIH Science Policy Fellowships, (D–f) 619
AAAS/NSF Fellowship Program, (D–f) 620
AAAS/NTI Fellowships in Global Security, (D–f) 621
AAPD Leadership Awards. See Paul G. Hearne/AAPD Leadership Awards, entry (D–a) 951
Abbene Scholarship. See Hydrocephalus Association Scholarships, entries (C–s) 102, (C–f) 464
ABC Talent Development Scholarship–Grant Program, (D–f) 622
Ability Loan Program, (D–l) 751
Abraham Nemeth Commitment to Excellence Scholarship, (V–s) 1
Abt Scholarship Awards. See Alexander Graham Bell Association College Scholarship Awards, entries (H–s) 264, (H–f) 280
Academy of Natural Sciences Research Experiences for Undergraduates Fellowships, (D–f) 623
ADA Relief Fund Grants, (D–g) 801, (F–g) 1101
ADHD Scholarship Contest. See CONCERTA "I See Success" ADHD Scholarship Contest, entry (C–s) 378
Adler Science Math Scholarship. See Charles Adler Science Math Scholarship, entry (F–s) 971
ADVANCE Fellows Awards, (D–f) 624
Aerospace Illinois Space Grant Consortium Program, (D–s) 511, (D–f) 625

African American Studies Program Visiting Scholars, (D–f) 626
Agency for Healthcare Research and Quality Health Services Research Grants. See AHRQ Health Services Research Grants, entry (D–f) 627
Agency for Healthcare Research and Quality Independent Scientist Award. See AHRQ Independent Scientist Award, entry (D–f) 628
Agency for Healthcare Research and Quality Mentored Clinical Scientist Development Award. See AHRQ Mentored Clinical Scientist Development Award, entry (D–f) 629
Agency for Healthcare Research and Quality Small Research Grant Program. See AHRQ Small Research Grant Program, entry (D–f) 630
AGMA Emergency Relief Fund, (C–g) 474
AGSD Scholarship, (C–s) 357
AHRQ Health Services Research Grants, (D–f) 627
AHRQ Independent Scientist Award, (D–f) 628
AHRQ Mentored Clinical Scientist Development Award, (D–f) 629
AHRQ Small Research Grant Program, (D–f) 630
AIMR 11 September Memorial Scholarship Fund, (D–s) 512, (F–s) 957
Air Force Aid Society Respite Care, (F–g) 1102

V–Visual	H–Hearing	O–Orthopedic/Developmental	C–Communication/Other	D–Disabilities in General	F–Families
s–scholarships		f–fellowships/grants	l–loans	g–grants-in-aid	a–awards

PROGRAM TITLE INDEX

Air Force Officers' Wives' Club of Washington, D.C. Scholarships, (C–s) 358, (C–f) 454
Air Line Pilots Association Scholarship Program, (F–s) 958
Alabama Ad Valorem Tax Exemption for Specially Adapted Houses, (D–g) 802, (F–g) 1103
Alabama Council of the Blind Scholarship Fund, (V–s) 2
Alabama County Homestead Exemptions, (V–g) 188, (D–g) 803
Alabama G.I. Dependents' Scholarship Program, (F–s) 959, (F–f) 1077
Alabama Military Retiree Income Tax Exemption, (D–g) 804, (F–g) 1104
Alabama Principal Residence Exemption, (D–g) 805
Alabama Scholarships for Dependents of Blind Parents, (F–s) 960
Alabama State Homestead Exemptions, (V–g) 189, (D–g) 806
Alan B., '32, and Florence B., '35, Crammatte Fellowship, (H–f) 279
Alaska Property Tax Exemption, (D–g) 807
Albritton, Jr. Scholarship. See Geological Society of America General Research Grants Program, entry (D–f) 664
Alexander Graham Bell Association College Scholarship Awards, (H–s) 264, (H–f) 280
Alexander Sisson Award. See Geological Society of America General Research Grants Program, entry (D–f) 664
Allan Murphy Memorial Scholarship. See American Meteorological Society Undergraduate Scholarships, entry (D–s) 513
Allan V. Cox Award. See Geological Society of America General Research Grants Program, entry (D–f) 664
Allie Raney Hunt Memorial Scholarship Award. See Alexander Graham Bell Association College Scholarship Awards, entries (H–s) 264, (H–f) 280
Alma Murphey Memorial Scholarship, (V–f) 121
Alpha Sigma Pi Fraternity Fellowship, (H–f) 281
Alternatives in Motion Grants, (O–g) 320
Alzheimer's Family Relief Program, (C–g) 475, (F–g) 1105
Aman Memorial Scholarship. See Delbert K. Aman Memorial Scholarship, entry (V–s) 22
American Association for the Advancement of Science/National Institutes of Health Science Policy Fellowships. See AAAS/NIH Science Policy Fellowships, entry (D–f) 619
American Association for the Advancement of Science/National Science Foundation Fellowship Program. See AAAS/NSF Fellowship Program, entry (D–f) 620
American Association for the Advancement of Science/Nuclear Threat Initiative Fellowships in Global Security. See AAAS/NTI Fellowships in Global Security, entry (D–f) 621

American Association of People with Disabilities Leadership Awards. See Paul G. Hearne/AAPD Leadership Awards, entry (D–a) 951
American Cancer Society Scholarship, (C–s) 359
American Council of the Blind of Colorado Scholarships, (V–s) 3
American Council of the Blind of Maryland Scholarship, (V–s) 4
American Council of the Blind of Minnesota Scholarships, (V–s) 5
American Council of the Blind of Oregon Grant-in-Aid, (V–s) 6, (V–g) 190
American Council of the Blind of Oregon Grant-in-Aid. See American Council of the Blind of Oregon Grant-in-Aid, entries (V–s) 6, (V–g) 190
American Council of the Blind of Texas Scholarships, (V–s) 7
American Guild of Musical Artists Emergency Relief Fund. See AGMA Emergency Relief Fund, entry (C–g) 474
American Meteorological Society Graduate Fellowship in the History of Science, (D–f) 631
American Meteorological Society Undergraduate Scholarships, (D–s) 513
American Meteorological Society 75th Anniversary Scholarship. See American Meteorological Society Undergraduate Scholarships, entry (D–s) 513
American Printing House InSights. See APH InSights, entry (V–a) 259
Americans with Disabilities Abilities Scholarship Program. See Bank of America ADA Abilities Scholarship Program, entry (D–s) 515
Amgen Grants, (C–g) 476
Amgen Scholarship, (C–s) 360, (C–f) 455
AMS 75th Anniversary Scholarship. See American Meteorological Society Undergraduate Scholarships, entry (D–s) 513
Amtrak Disabled Travelers Discount, (D–g) 808
Anderson Memorial Scholarship. See Gladys C. Anderson Memorial Scholarship, entry (V–s) 43
Andrew Craig Memorial Scholarship, (C–s) 361
Andrew W. Mellon Postdoctoral Research Fellowship at Omohundro Institute, (D–f) 632
Ann M. Martin Scholarship. See Eden Services Charles H. Hoens, Jr. Scholars Program, entry (C–s) 384
Anna Plapinger Endowment Award. See Henry and Anna Plapinger Endowment Award, entry (H–s) 269
Anne and Matt Harbison Scholarship, (C–s) 362
Anne Ford Scholarship, (C–s) 363
Anthony Abbene Scholarship. See Hydrocephalus Association Scholarships, entries (C–s) 402, (C–f) 464
Antoinette Lierman Medlin Scholarships. See Geological Society of America General Research Grants Program, entry (D–f) 664
APH InSights, (V–a) 259
Arctic Research Opportunities, (D–f) 633

V–Visual	H–Hearing	O–Orthopedic/Developmental	C–Communication/Other	D–Disabilities in General	F–Families
s–scholarships		f–fellowships/grants	l–loans	g–grants-in-aid	a–awards

PROGRAM TITLE INDEX

Arena Memorial Scholarship Fund. *See* John Arena Memorial Scholarship Fund, entry (C–s) 409
Arizona Council of the Blind Scholarship Program, (V–s) 8, (V–f) 122
Arizona Income Tax Exemption for the Blind, (V–g) 191
Arizona Kidney Foundation Assistance Programs, (C–g) 477
Arizona Loans for Assistive Technology, (D–l) 752
Arkansas Disabled Veterans Property Tax Exemption, (V–g) 192, (O–g) 321, (D–g) 809, (F–g) 1106
Arkansas Governor's Commission on People with Disabilities Fellowships, (D–f) 634
Arkansas Governor's Commission on People with Disabilities Scholarships, (D–s) 514
Arkansas Income Tax Credit for Phenylketonuria Disorder, (F–g) 1107
Arkansas Income Tax Credits for Developmentally Disabled Individuals, (F–g) 1108
Arkansas Income Tax Credits for Disabled Individuals, (F–g) 1109
Arkansas Income Tax Exemptions for Military Compensation and Disability Pay, (D–g) 810
Arkansas Income Tax Exemptions for Retirement and Disability Pay, (D–g) 811, (F–g) 1110
Arkansas Law Enforcement Officers' Dependents' Scholarships, (F–s) 961
Arkansas Sales Tax Exemption for Adaptive Medical Equipment, (D–g) 812
Arkansas Space Grant Consortium Collaborative Research Grants, (D–f) 635
Arkansas Space Grant Consortium Research Infrastructure Grants, (D–f) 636
Arkansas Technology Revolving Loan Fund, (D–l) 753
Armed Forces Insurance Scholarship. *See* Pennsylvania National Guard Scholarship Fund, entry (F–s) 1055
Armstrong Foundation Scholarships. *See* ELA Foundation Scholarships, entry (D–f) 659
Arnold Education Grant Program. *See* General Henry H. Arnold Education Grant Program, entry (F–s) 988
Arnold Sadler Memorial Scholarship, (V–s) 9, (V–f) 123
Arthur B. Kane Memorial Scholarships, (C–s) 364
Arthur D. Howard Research Grants. *See* Geological Society of America General Research Grants Program, entry (D–f) 664
Arthur E. Copeland Scholarship for Males, (V–s) 10, (V–f) 124
Artists' Fellowship Aid Program, (D–g) 813, (F–g) 1111
Arts and Sciences Awards, (H–s) 265
Ash Charitable Foundation Grants. *See* Mary Kay Ash Charitable Foundation Grants, entry (C–g) 492
Assistance for Surviving Children of Naval Personnel Deceased after Retirement (CDR), (F–s) 962
Assistive Technology Loan Fund Authority Loans. *See* ATLFA Loans, entry (D–l) 757
Assistive Technology Loan Guarantee Program, (D–l) 754

Assistive Technology of Minnesota Financial Loan Program, (D–l) 755
Assistive Technology of Ohio Low Interest Loan Program, (D–l) 756
Association for Glycogen Storage Disease Scholarship. *See* AGSD Scholarship, entry (C–s) 357
Association for Investment Management and Research 11 September Memorial Scholarship Fund. *See* AIMR 11 September Memorial Scholarship Fund, entries (D–s) 512, (F–s) 957
Association of Blind Citizens Assistive Technology Fund, (V–g) 193
Association of Blind Citizens Scholarship, (V–s) 11
AstraZeneca Scholarship, (C–s) 365
Astronomy and Astrophysics Postdoctoral Fellowships, (D–f) 637
ATLFA Loans, (D–l) 757
ATTAIN-a-Loan, (D–l) 758
Automobile Assistance for Disabled Veterans, (V–g) 194, (O–g) 322
AvonCares Program for Medically Underserved Women, (C–g) 478
Award of Excellence Asthma Scholarships, (C–s) 366
AZ AER Consumer Grant, (V–g) 195
AZ AER Professional Mini Grant, (V–f) 125
AZ AER Student Merit Scholarship, (V–s) 12

Bailes Award. *See* Monica Bailes Award, entry (C–s) 426
Bailes Award. *See* Patient Advocate Foundation Scholarships for Survivors, entries (C–s) 434, (C–f) 467
Baker Special Assistance Program. *See* Lenox Baker Special Assistance Program, entry (D–g) 865
Bank of America ADA Abilities Scholarship Program, (D–s) 515
Banta College-to-Work Scholarship, (C–s) 367
Barboza Education Fund. *See* Troy Barboza Education Fund, entries (D–s) 600, (F–s) 1067
Barr United Amputee Assistance Fund, (O–g) 323
Barty Scholarship Awards Program. *See* Evelyn Barty Scholarship Awards Program, entries (O–s) 303, (F–s) 981
Baum Undergraduate Scholarship. *See* American Meteorological Society Undergraduate Scholarships, entry (D–s) 513
Bay State Council of the Blind Scholarship, (V–s) 13
Beacon Brighter Tomorrows Scholarship, (F–s) 963
Beck Fellowship. *See* Stan Beck Fellowship, entries (D–s) 586, (D–f) 736
BEF Lung Transplant Grant Program, (C–g) 479
Bellows Fund Grants. *See* Elsie S. Bellows Fund Grants, entry (D–g) 834
Bennet of Maine Scholarship. *See* Richard Bennet of Maine Scholarship, entry (V–s) 102

V–Visual   H–Hearing   O–Orthopedic/Developmental   C–Communication/Other   D–Disabilities in General   F–Families
s–scholarships   f–fellowships/grants   l–loans   g–grants-in-aid   a–awards

Bernbaum Scholarship. *See* Willard Bernbaum Scholarship, entry (C–f) 473
Beth Carew Memorial Scholarships, (C–s) 368
Beverly Prows Memorial Scholarship, (V–s) 14, (V–f) 126
BG (Ret) Richard E. Thorn Memorial Scholarship. *See* Pennsylvania National Guard Scholarship Fund, entry (F–s) 1055
Bidstrup Scholarship Fund. *See* Peter and Bruce Bidstrup Scholarship Fund, entry (C–s) 435
Bill McAdam Scholarship Fund, (C–s) 369, (F–s) 964
Billow Memorial Education Fund. *See* Ruth Billow Memorial Education Fund, entries (V–s) 107, (V–f) 176
Birzer Hall of Fame Scholarship. *See* Debe Birzer Hall of Fame Scholarship, entry (C–s) 381
Biunno Scholarship for Law Students with Disabilities, (D–f) 638
Blackhorse Association Scholarships, (F–s) 965
Blanche Fischer Foundation Grants, (O–s) 300, (O–f) 314, (O–g) 324
Blechschmidt Award. *See* Geological Society of America General Research Grants Program, entry (D–f) 664
Blind Educator of the Year Award, (V–a) 260
Boomer Esiason Foundation Lung Transplant Grant Program. *See* BEF Lung Transplant Grant Program, entry (C–g) 479
Boomer Esiason Foundation Scholarship Program, (C–s) 370, (C–f) 456
Boyce R. Williams, '32, Fellowship. *See* GUAA Graduate Fellowship Fund, entry (H–f) 284
Brian Csikos Memorial Scholarship, (C–s) 371
Brian McCartney Memorial Scholarship, (H–s) 266, (C–s) 372
B.R.I.D.G.E. Endowment Fund Scholarships. *See* Building Rural Initiative for Disabled through Group Effort (B.R.I.D.G.E.) Endowment Fund Scholarships, entry (D–s) 517
Bridge to Tomorrow Grant Program, (F–s) 966
Bristol–Myers Grants, (C–g) 480
Bristol–Myers Squibb Oncology/Immunology Scholarship, (C–s) 373, (C–f) 457
Brooks Stand–Up Comedy Competition Scholarship. *See* Norman G. Brooks Stand–Up Comedy Competition Scholarship, entry (D–a) 949
Brother Scholarship. *See* Millie Brother Scholarship, entry (F–s) 1032
Bruce Bidstrup Scholarship Fund. *See* Peter and Bruce Bidstrup Scholarship Fund, entry (C–s) 435
Bruce L. "Biff" Reed Award. *See* Geological Society of America General Research Grants Program, entry (D–f) 664
Brudnick Scholarship Award. *See* Ina Brudnick Scholarship Award, entry (C–s) 405
Buffett Foundation Scholarship Program, (D–s) 516
Building Rural Initiative for Disabled through Group Effort (B.R.I.D.G.E.) Endowment Fund Scholarships, (D–s) 517

Bunch Memorial Scholarship. *See* Susan Bunch Memorial Scholarship, entries (C–s) 447, (C–f) 471
Burson Memorial Scholarship. *See* Dr. S. Bradley Burson Memorial Scholarship, entries (V–s) 27, (V–f) 130
Byrd Fellowship Program, (D–f) 639

Cahall Memorial Scholarship Fund. *See* John Cahall Memorial Scholarship Fund, entry (V–s) 59
Cal–Vet Loan Program, (D–l) 759
Calhoun Scholarships. *See* Hermione Grant Calhoun Scholarships, entries (V–s) 50, (V–f) 147
California Association for Postsecondary Education and Disability Conference Scholarship. *See* California Association for Postsecondary Education and Disability Scholarships, entries (D–s) 518, (D–f) 640
California Association for Postsecondary Education and Disability General Excellence Scholarship. *See* CAPED General Excellence Scholarship, entries (D–s) 521, (D–f) 642
California Association for Postsecondary Education and Disability Past Presidents' Scholarship. *See* California Association for Postsecondary Education and Disability Scholarships, entries (D–s) 518, (D–f) 640
California Association for Postsecondary Education and Disability Scholarships, (D–s) 518, (D–f) 640
California Council of the Blind Loans, (V–l) 184
California Council of the Blind Scholarships, (V–s) 15, (V–f) 127
California Disabled Veteran Exemption from the In Lieu Tax Fee for a Manufactured Home or Mobilehome, (V–g) 196, (O–g) 325, (D–g) 814, (F–g) 1112
California Fee Waiver Program for Children of Veterans, (F–s) 967
California Fee Waiver Program for Dependents of Deceased or Disabled National Guard Members, (F–s) 968
California Fee Waiver Program for Dependents of Totally Disabled Veterans, (F–s) 969
California Law Enforcement Personnel Dependents Grant Program, (F–s) 970
California Property Tax Postponement for Senior Citizens, Blind, or Disabled Citizens, (V–g) 197, (D–g) 815
California Real Estate Endowment Fund Scholarship Program, (D–s) 519
California Space Grant Graduate Student Program, (D–f) 641
California Young Cancer Survivor Scholarship Program, (C–s) 374
California–Hawaii Elks Major Project Undergraduate Scholarship for Students with Disabilities, (D–s) 520
Callward Memorial Scholarship. *See* Floyd Callward Memorial Scholarship, entries (V–s) 35, (V–f) 134
Calvin Dawson Memorial Scholarship, (C–s) 375
Cancer Care Financial Assistance, (C–g) 481

PROGRAM TITLE INDEX

Cancer Survivors' Scholarship, (C–s) 376, (C–f) 458
Cannon Memorial Scholarship. *See* Kellie Cannon Memorial Scholarship, entry (V–s) 63
CAPED General Excellence Scholarship, (D–s) 521, (D–f) 642
CARE Program, (C–g) 482
CARE+PLUS Program, (C–g) 483
Carew Memorial Scholarships. *See* Beth Carew Memorial Scholarships, entry (C–s) 368
Cargill Scholarship. *See* Floyd R. Cargill Scholarship, entries (V–s) 37, (V–f) 136
Carlock Scholarship. *See* James R. Carlock Scholarship, entries (V–s) 55, (V–f) 151
Carsel Memorial Scholarship. *See* Karen D. Carsel Memorial Scholarship, entry (V–f) 156
Carver Scholars Program, (D–s) 522
Case Memorial Scholarships. *See* James Doyle Case Memorial Scholarships, entries (V–s) 54, (V–f) 150, (F–s) 1005, (F–f) 1083
CDR Program. *See* Assistance for Surviving Children of Naval Personnel Deceased after Retirement (CDR), entry (F–s) 962
Central Intelligence Agency Undergraduate Scholarship Program, (D–s) 523, (D–l) 760
Century Scholarship, (D–f) 643
ChairScholars Foundation National Scholarships, (O–s) 301
Challenged Athletes Grants, (D–g) 816
Charles Adler Science Math Scholarship, (F–s) 971
Charles E. Leonard Memorial Scholarship Fund, (V–s) 16, (F–s) 972
Charles H. Hoens, Jr. Scholars Program. *See* Eden Services Charles H. Hoens, Jr. Scholars Program, entry (C–s) 384
Charron Memorial Scholarship. *See* Sr. Harriet Charron Memorial Scholarship, entry (V–s) 111
Cheryl Grimmel Award, (C–s) 377
Cheryl Grimmel Award. *See* Patient Advocate Foundation Scholarships for Survivors, entries (C–s) 434, (C–f) 467
Chief Master Sergeants of the Air Force Scholarships, (D–s) 524, (F–s) 973
Child Scholarship. *See* Kevin Child Scholarship, entry (C–s) 413
Children of Women Vietnam Veterans Allowance, (D–g) 817
Choice Source Therapeutics Scholarships. *See* Utah Hemophilia Foundation Scholarships, entries (C–s) 451, (F–s) 1069
Chris Townsend Memorial Scholarship. *See* Utah Hemophilia Foundation Scholarships, entries (C–s) 451, (F–s) 1069
Christian A. Herter Memorial Scholarship, (D–s) 525
Christian Record Services Scholarships, (V–s) 17
Christopher Reeve Acting Scholarship, (D–a) 943
Christopher Reeve Paralysis Foundation Fellowships, (D–f) 644

Cindy Kolb Memorial Scholarship, (D–s) 526
Claude C. Albritton, Jr. Scholarship. *See* Geological Society of America General Research Grants Program, entry (D–f) 664
Clothing Allowance for Disabled Veterans, (D–g) 818
CMSAF Richard D. Kisling Scholarship. *See* Chief Master Sergeants of the Air Force Scholarships, entries (D–s) 524, (F–s) 973
Coal Miners Black Lung Benefits, (C–g) 484, (F–g) 1113
College–Bound Award of Lighthouse International, (V–s) 18
Colorado Dependents Tuition Assistance Program, (F–s) 974
Colorado Pension Subtraction, (D–g) 819
Colorado Property Tax Rebate, (D–g) 820
Colorado Rent Rebate, (D–g) 821
CONCERTA "I See Success" ADHD Scholarship Contest, (C–s) 378
Congressional Fellowships, (D–f) 645
Conley Memorial Scholarship. *See* Mike Conley Memorial Scholarships, entry (C–s) 424
Conlon Memorial Scholarship. *See* Sara Conlon Memorial Scholarship, entry (D–s) 582
Connecticut Disabled Tax Relief Program, (D–g) 822
Connecticut Elderly and Disabled Homeowners Tax Relief Program, (D–g) 823
Connecticut Elderly and Disabled Renters Rebate Program, (D–g) 824
Connecticut Personal Property Tax Exemption for Disabled Veterans, (D–g) 825, (F–g) 1114
Connecticut Real Estate Tax Exemption for Disabled Veterans, (D–g) 826, (F–g) 1115
Connecticut Soldiers', Sailors' and Marines' Fund, (D–g) 827
Connecticut Space Grant College Consortium Graduate Student Fellowships, (D–f) 646
Connecticut Space Grant College Consortium Student Project Grants, (D–s) 527
Connecticut Space Grant College Consortium Travel Grants, (D–s) 528, (D–f) 647
Connecticut Space Grant College Consortium Undergraduate Student Fellowships, (D–s) 529
Connecticut Tax Relief Program for Blind People, (V–g) 198
Connecticut Tech Act Project Assistive Technology Loan Program. *See* CTTAP Assistive Technology Loan Program, entry (D–l) 761
Connolly Scholar–Athlete Award. *See* Hal Connolly Scholar–Athlete Award, entry (D–s) 539
Conroy Memorial Scholarship Program. *See* Edward T. Conroy Memorial Scholarship Program, entries (D–s) 533, (D–f) 658, (F–s) 978, (F–f) 1078
Copeland Scholarship for Females. *See* Helen Copeland Scholarship for Females, entries (V–s) 48, (V–f) 145
Copeland Scholarship for Males. *See* Arthur E. Copeland Scholarship for Males, entries (V–s) 10, (V–f) 124

V–Visual H–Hearing O–Orthopedic/Developmental C–Communication/Other D–Disabilities in General F–Families
s–scholarships f–fellowships/grants l–loans g–grants–in–aid a–awards

PROGRAM TITLE INDEX

Cordano Fellowship. *See* GUAA Graduate Fellowship Fund, entry (H–f) 284

Corey Memorial Scholarships. *See* William G. Corey Memorial Scholarship, entries (V–s) 117, (V–f) 183

Courter Sharing a Brighter Tomorrow Hemophilia Scholarships. *See* Soozie Courter Sharing a Brighter Tomorrow Hemophilia Scholarships, entries (C–s) 444, (C–f) 469

Covad Broadband Entrepreneur Award, (D–g) 828

Cox Award. *See* Geological Society of America General Research Grants Program, entry (D–f) 664

Craig Memorial Scholarship. *See* Andrew Craig Memorial Scholarship, entry (C–s) 361

Crammatte Fellowship. *See* Alan B., '32, and Florence B., '35, Crammatte Fellowship, entry (H–f) 279

Creon Family Scholarship Program, (C–s) 379

Csikos Memorial Scholarship. *See* Brian Csikos Memorial Scholarship, entry (C–s) 371

CTTAP Assistive Technology Loan Program, (D–l) 761

Cultural Anthropology Grants for High Risk Exploratory Research, (D–f) 648

Cultural Anthropology Research Experience for Graduates Supplements, (D–f) 649

Cystic Fibrosis Scholarships, (C–s) 380

DaimlerChrysler Automobility Program, (D–g) 829

DakotaLink Low Interest Loan Program, (D–l) 762

Dale M. Schoettler Scholarship for Visually Impaired Students, (V–s) 19, (V–f) 128

Dannels Memorial Scholarship. *See* Robert A. Dannels Memorial Scholarship, entry (D–f) 729

David H. Newmeyer Post–Secondary Scholarship for Visually Impaired Students, (V–s) 20

David Newmeyer Scholarship, (V–s) 21

David Peikoff, '29, Fellowship. *See* GUAA Graduate Fellowship Fund, entry (H–f) 284

David Von Hagen Scholarship Award. *See* Alexander Graham Bell Association College Scholarship Awards, entries (H–s) 264, (H–f) 280

Davidow Memorial Scholarship. *See* Dr. Mae Davidow Memorial Scholarship, entry (V–s) 25

Dawson Memorial Scholarship. *See* Calvin Dawson Memorial Scholarship, entry (C–s) 375

DCU Access Loans, (D–l) 763

DCU Mobility Vehicle Loans, (D–l) 764

Debbie Fox Foundation Grants–in–Aid. *See* National Craniofacial Association Travel Grants–in–Aid, entry (O–g) 335

Debe Birzer Hall of Fame Scholarship, (C–s) 381

Defense Policy Fellowships, (D–f) 650

Delaware Income Tax Deduction for Blind and Elderly Persons, (V–g) 199

Delaware Income Tax Exclusion for Disabled and Elderly Persons, (D–g) 830

Delaware Pension Benefits for Paraplegic Veterans, (O–g) 326

Delaware Space Grant Consortium Graduate Student Fellowships. *See* NASA–DESGC Graduate Student Fellowships, entry (D–f) 697

Delaware Space Grant Consortium Undergraduate Tuition Scholarships. *See* DESGC Undergraduate Tuition Scholarships, entry (D–s) 530

Delbert K. Aman Memorial Scholarship, (V–s) 22

Delson Memorial Scholarship. *See* Eric Delson Memorial Scholarship, entries (C–s) 387, (C–f) 462

Delta Gamma Foundation Florence Margaret Harvey Memorial Scholarship, (V–s) 23, (V–f) 129

Dennis R. Kelly Memorial Scholarship. *See* Robert J. and Dennis R. Kelly Memorial Scholarship, entry (C–s) 439

Dependency and Indemnity Compensation (DIC), (F–g) 1116

Des Moines Chapter Scholarships, (V–s) 24

DesChamps Scholarship Award. *See* EAGA Scholarship Award, entries (O–s) 302, (F–s) 977

DESGC Graduate Student Fellowships. *See* NASA–DESGC Graduate Student Fellowships, entry (D–f) 697

DESGC Undergraduate Tuition Scholarships, (D–s) 530

DIC. *See* Dependency and Indemnity Compensation (DIC), entry (F–g) 1116

DiCaprio Scholarship. *See* Dr. Nicholas S. DiCaprio Scholarship, entry (V–s) 26

Dickman Memorial Scholarship Awards. *See* Alexander Graham Bell Association College Scholarship Awards, entries (H–s) 264, (H–f) 280

Digital Federal Credit Union Access Loans. *See* DCU Access Loans, entry (D–l) 763

Digital Federal Credit Union Mobility Vehicle Loans. *See* DCU Mobility Vehicle Loans, entry (D–l) 764

Dillman Memorial Scholarship. *See* Rudolph Dillman Memorial Scholarship, entries (V–s) 106, (V–f) 175

Dillon Alaska Research Award. *See* Geological Society of America General Research Grants Program, entry (D–f) 664

Diplomacy Fellowships, (D–f) 651

Disabled American Veterans Auxiliary National Education Loan Fund, (F–l) 1095

Disabled American Veterans Disaster Relief Fund, (D–g) 831

Disabled Children's Relief Fund Grants, (D–g) 832

Disabled Investigators Developing Independent Research Careers Research Supplements, (D–f) 652

Disabled Workers Committee Scholarship, (F–s) 975

Disney Young Performer's Scholarship, (D–a) 944

DiStefano Annual Scholarship. *See* SBAA Educational Scholarship Fund, entries (O–s) 312, (O–f) 316

District of Columbia Space Grant Consortium Awards, (D–s) 531, (D–f) 653

Diversity Coalition Fellowships, (C–f) 459, (D–f) 654

V–Visual   H–Hearing   O–Orthopedic/Developmental   C–Communication/Other   D–Disabilities in General   F–Families
s–scholarships   f–fellowships/grants   l–loans   g–grants–in–aid   a–awards

PROGRAM TITLE INDEX

Doctoral Dissertation Improvement Grants in the Directorate for Biological Sciences, (D–f) 655

Doctoral Dissertation Research Improvement Grants in the Directorate for Social, Behavioral, and Economic Sciences, (D–f) 656

Dole Scholarship Fund for Disabled Students. *See* Robert Dole Scholarship Fund for Disabled Students, entries (O–s) 311, (C–s) 437

Donald D. Hammill Foundation Research Scholarships, (D–f) 657

Donnelly Awards, (C–s) 382

Doris B. Orman, '25, Fellowship, (H–f) 282

Dorothy Ferrell Scholarship Award. *See* William and Dorothy Ferrell Scholarship Award, entries (V–s) 116, (V–f) 182

Dorothy Weigner Award, (C–f) 460

Dostie Memorial College Scholarship. *See* Eric Dostie Memorial College Scholarship, entries (C–s) 388, (F–s) 980

Dower Scholarship. *See* John and Rhoda Dower Scholarship, entries (V–s) 58, (V–f) 155

Dr. George F. Howard III Scholarship. *See* Epilepsy Foundation of Massachusetts & Rhode Island Scholarships, entries (C–s) 385, (C–f) 461

Dr. Mae Davidow Memorial Scholarship, (V–s) 25

Dr. Nicholas S. DiCaprio Scholarship, (V–s) 26

Dr. Pedro Grau Undergraduate Scholarship. *See* American Meteorological Society Undergraduate Scholarships, entry (D–s) 513

Dr. S. Bradley Burson Memorial Scholarship, (V–s) 27, (V–f) 130

Drake Memorial Scholarship. *See* Gerald Drake Memorial Scholarship, entries (V–s) 42, (V–f) 140

Dramatists Guild Fund Grants, (D–l) 765

Dugdale/van Eys Scholarship Award, (C–s) 383, (F–s) 976

EAGA Scholarship Award, (O–s) 302, (F–s) 977

Eagles Memorial Foundation Medical Assistance, (D–g) 833

Earl and Eugenia Quirk Scholarship, (D–s) 532

Eastern Amputee Golf Association Scholarship Award. *See* EAGA Scholarship Award, entries (O–s) 302, (F–s) 977

Edelman Scholarship. *See* Max Edelman Scholarship, entry (V–s) 73

Eden Services Charles H. Hoens, Jr. Scholars Program, (C–s) 384

Educational Loans for Spouses of Veterans, (F–l) 1096

Educational Loans to Assist Retraining of Certain Disabled Individuals, (D–l) 766

Educator of Tomorrow Award, (V–s) 28, (V–f) 131

Edward T. Conroy Memorial Scholarship Program, (D–s) 533, (D–f) 658, (F–s) 978, (F–f) 1078

ELA Foundation Scholarships, (D–f) 659

Elizabeth Lowndes Award. *See* Margaret Funds Scholarships, entries (F–s) 1026, (F–f) 1089

Elks National Foundation Emergency Educational Fund Grants, (F–s) 979

Ellen Beach Mack Scholarship, (V–s) 29, (V–f) 132

Elsie Bell Grosvenor Scholarship Awards. *See* Alexander Graham Bell Association College Scholarship Awards, entries (H–s) 264, (H–f) 280

Elsie S. Bellows Fund Grants, (D–g) 834

Emerson Foulke Memorial Scholarship, (V–s) 30

ENABLE Loan Program, (D–l) 767

Environmental Fellowships, (D–f) 660

Epilepsy Foundation of Kansas and Western Missouri Medication Assistance, (C–g) 485

Epilepsy Foundation of Massachusetts & Rhode Island Scholarships, (C–s) 385, (C–f) 461

Epilepsy Foundation of New Jersey Scholarship Program, (C–s) 386

Equipment Loan Fund for the Disabled, (D–l) 768

Eric C. Marder Memorial Scholarship Program. *See* Immune Deficiency Foundation Scholarship, entry (C–s) 404

Eric Delson Memorial Scholarship, (C–s) 387, (C–f) 462

Eric Dostie Memorial College Scholarship, (C–s) 388, (F–s) 980

Esiason Foundation Lung Transplant Grant Program. *See* BEF Lung Transplant Grant Program, entry (C–g) 479

Esiason Foundation Scholarship Program. *See* Boomer Esiason Foundation Scholarship Program, entries (C–s) 370, (C–f) 456

Ethan and Allan Murphy Memorial Scholarship. *See* American Meteorological Society Undergraduate Scholarships, entry (D–s) 513

Ethel Louise Armstrong Foundation Scholarships. *See* ELA Foundation Scholarships, entry (D–f) 659

Ethnic Missions Scholarship Program, (H–s) 267

E.U. Parker Scholarship, (V–s) 31, (V–f) 133

Eugenia Quirk Scholarship. *See* Earl and Eugenia Quirk Scholarship, entry (D–s) 532

Eunice Fiorito Memorial Scholarship, (V–s) 32

Evelyn Barty Scholarship Awards Program, (O–s) 303, (F–s) 981

FAAST Alternative Financing Program, (D–l) 769

Facilitation Awards for Scientists and Engineers with Disabilities, (D–s) 534, (D–f) 661

Faculty Early Career Development Program, (D–f) 662

Fahnestock Memorial Award. *See* Geological Society of America General Research Grants Program, entry (D–f) 664

Families of Freedom Scholarship Fund, (D–s) 535, (F–s) 982

Federal Income Tax Credit for Adoption Expenses, (F–g) 1117

V–Visual   H–Hearing   O–Orthopedic/Developmental   C–Communication/Other   D–Disabilities in General   F–Families
s–scholarships   f–fellowships/grants   l–loans   g–grants-in-aid   a–awards

Federal Income Tax Credit for the Elderly or the Disabled, (D–g) 835
Federal Income Tax Deduction for Child and Dependent Care Expenses, (F–g) 1118
Federal Income Tax Deduction for the Blind and Elderly, (V–g) 200
Feibelman Jr. (PS) Scholarship Award. *See* Alexander Graham Bell Association College Scholarship Awards, entries (H–s) 264, (H–f) 280
Ferdinand Torres Scholarship, (V–s) 33
Ferguson Achievement Scholarship. *See* Jennica Ferguson Achievement Scholarship, entry (V–s) 56
Ferguson Memorial Scholarship. *See* Jennica Ferguson Memorial Scholarship, entries (V–s) 57, (V–f) 152
Ferguson Memorial Scholarship. *See* National Federation of the Blind of Ohio Scholarships, entries (V–s) 86, (V–f) 166
Ferrell Scholarship Award. *See* William and Dorothy Ferrell Scholarship Award, entries (V–s) 116, (V–f) 182
Fiorito Memorial Scholarship. *See* Eunice Fiorito Memorial Scholarship, entry (V–s) 32
First Cavalry Division Association Scholarships, (F–s) 983
First Hand Grants, (D–g) 836
First Marine Division Association Scholarships, (F–s) 984
Fischer Foundation Grants. *See* Blanche Fischer Foundation Grants, entries (O–s) 300, (O–f) 314, (O–g) 324
Fischer Scholarship. *See* Joann Fischer Scholarship, entry (V–f) 154
Florence B., '35, Crammatte Fellowship. *See* Alan B., '32, and Florence B., '35, Crammatte Fellowship, entry (H–f) 279
Florence Margaret Harvey Memorial Scholarship. *See* Delta Gamma Foundation Florence Margaret Harvey Memorial Scholarship, entries (V–s) 23, (V–f) 129
Florida Alliance for Assistive Services and Technology Alternative Financing Program. *See* FAAST Alternative Financing Program, entry (D–l) 769
Florida Council of the Blind Scholarships, (V–s) 34
Florida Division College Scholarships, (C–s) 389
Florida Homestead Exemption for Disabled Veterans, (V–g) 201, (O–g) 327, (D–g) 837, (F–g) 1119
Florida Scholarships for Children of Deceased or Disabled Veterans, (F–s) 985
Florida Space Grant Consortium Fellowship Program, (D–f) 663
Florida Space Grant Consortium Undergraduate Space Research Participation Program, (D–s) 536
Floyd Callward Memorial Scholarship, (V–s) 35, (V–f) 134
Floyd Qualls Memorial Scholarships, (V–s) 36, (V–f) 135
Floyd R. Cargill Scholarship, (V–s) 37, (V–f) 136
Ford Mobility Motoring Program, (O–g) 328
Ford Scholarship. *See* Anne Ford Scholarship, entry (C–s) 363
Forward Face Development Grants, (F–g) 1120
Forward Face Scholarships, (O–s) 304

Foulke Memorial Scholarship. *See* Emerson Foulke Memorial Scholarship, entry (V–s) 30
Four-Year SBAA Educational Scholarship Fund, (O–s) 305
Fox Foundation Grants-in-Aid. *See* National Craniofacial Association Travel Grants-in-Aid, entry (O–g) 335
Francis P. Matthews and John E. Swift Educational Trust Scholarships, (F–s) 986
Franklin and Henrietta Dickman Memorial Scholarship Awards. *See* Alexander Graham Bell Association College Scholarship Awards, entries (H–s) 264, (H–f) 280
Fraternal Order of Eagles Memorial Foundation Medical Assistance. *See* Eagles Memorial Foundation Medical Assistance, entry (D–g) 833
Fred Scheigert Scholarships, (V–s) 38, (V–f) 137
Free Tuition for Dependents of Disabled or Deceased South Dakota National Guard Members, (F–s) 987
Freedom Scientific Technology Scholarship Award Program, (V–s) 39, (V–f) 138, (V–g) 202
Friends-in-Art Scholarship, (V–s) 40
Froncillo Scholarship. *See* EAGA Scholarship Award, entries (O–s) 302, (F–s) 977
Fudge Scholarship. *See* Hydrocephalus Association Scholarships, entries (C–s) 402, (C–f) 464
Fund for Writers and Editors with AIDS, (C–g) 486

Gallaudet University Alumni Association Graduate Fellowship Fund. *See* GUAA Graduate Fellowship Fund, entry (H–f) 284
Gallaudet University President's Fellowship Program, (H–f) 283
General Henry H. Arnold Education Grant Program, (F–s) 988
Gentry Fellowship. *See* Diplomacy Fellowships, entry (D–f) 651
Geological Society of America General Research Grants Program, (D–f) 664
Geological Society of America Undergraduate Student Research Grants, (D–s) 537
George F. Howard III Scholarship. *See* Epilepsy Foundation of Massachusetts & Rhode Island Scholarships, entries (C–s) 385, (C–f) 461
George Hauser/Novartis Scholarship. *See* Epilepsy Foundation of Massachusetts & Rhode Island Scholarships, entries (C–s) 385, (C–f) 461
Georgia Council of the Blind Scholarships, (V–s) 41, (V–f) 139, (F–s) 989, (F–f) 1079
Georgia Homestead Tax Exemption for Disabled Veterans, (D–g) 838, (F–g) 1121
Georgia Income Tax Deduction for the Blind, (V–g) 203
Georgia Income Tax Exemption for Disabled Persons, (D–g) 839
Georgia Law Enforcement Personnel Dependents Grant, (F–s) 990

| V–Visual | H–Hearing | O–Orthopedic/Developmental | C–Communication/Other | D–Disabilities in General | F–Families |
| s–scholarships | | f–fellowships/grants | l–loans | g–grants-in-aid | a–awards |

PROGRAM TITLE INDEX

Georgia Public Safety Memorial Grant, (F–s) 991
Georgia Space Grant Consortium Fellowships, (D–s) 538, (D–f) 665
Gerald Drake Memorial Scholarship, (V–s) 42, (V–f) 140
Gerald S. Fudge Scholarship. See Hydrocephalus Association Scholarships, entries (C–s) 402, (C–f) 464
Geraldine R. Dodge Foundation Fellowship, (D–f) 666
Gile Memorial Scholarship. See Gregory W. Gile Memorial Scholarship, entries (C–s) 393, (C–g) 487
Gillette Scholarships. See R.L. Gillette Scholarships, entry (V–s) 103
Girard Scholarship. See James A. Girard Scholarship, entry (C–s) 406
GiveTech Grants, (O–g) 329
Gladys C. Anderson Memorial Scholarship, (V–s) 43
GlaxoSmithKline Scholarship, (C–s) 390
GM Mobility Reimbursement Program, (H–g) 291, (O–g) 330
GOALI Faculty in Industry Awards, (D–f) 667
GOALI Postdoctoral Industrial Fellowships, (D–f) 668
Gottlieb Foundation Emergency Grants, (D–g) 840
Graduate Award of Lighthouse International, (V–f) 141
Grant M. Mack Memorial Scholarships. See NIB Grant M. Mack Memorial Scholarship, entries (V–s) 94, (V–f) 170
Grant Opportunities for Academic Liaison with Industry Faculty in Industry Awards. See GOALI Faculty in Industry Awards, entry (D–f) 667
Grant Opportunities for Academic Liaison with Industry Postdoctoral Industrial Fellowships. See GOALI Postdoctoral Industrial Fellowships, entry (D–f) 668
Grant Program for Students with Disabilities in Graduate Science Degree Programs, (D–f) 669
Grants for Accessibility, (D–g) 841, (F–g) 1122
Grau Undergraduate Scholarship. See American Meteorological Society Undergraduate Scholarships, entry (D–s) 513
Great Lakes Division College Scholarship, (C–s) 391
Great Lakes Hemophilia Foundation Education and Training Assistance Scholarships, (C–s) 392, (F–s) 992
Gregg Foundation Grants. See Harry Alan Gregg Foundation Grants, entries (D–s) 540, (D–g) 843
Gregory W. Gile Memorial Scholarship, (C–s) 393, (C–g) 487
Gretchen L. Blechschmidt Award. See Geological Society of America General Research Grants Program, entry (D–f) 664
Greyhound Services for Customers with Disabilities, (D–g) 842
Grimmel Award. See Cheryl Grimmel Award, entry (C–s) 377
Grimmel Award. See Patient Advocate Foundation Scholarships for Survivors, entries (C–s) 434, (C–f) 467
Grosvenor Scholarship Awards. See Alexander Graham Bell Association College Scholarship Awards, entries (H–s) 264, (H–f) 280

Gruber Scholarships. See Kathern F. Gruber Scholarships, entries (F–s) 1008, (F–f) 1085
GUAA Graduate Fellowship Fund, (H–f) 284
Guillermo Salazar Rodriguez Scholarship. See American Meteorological Society Undergraduate Scholarships, entry (D–s) 513
Gullikson Foundation College Scholarships. See Tim & Tom Gullikson Foundation College Scholarships, entries (C–s) 450, (F–s) 1066
Guthrie PKU Scholarship. See Robert Guthrie PKU Scholarship, entry (C–s) 438

Haas Scholarship. See Hemophilia Health Services Memorial Scholarships, entries (C–s) 398, (C–f) 463
Hagemeyer Scholarship. See American Meteorological Society Undergraduate Scholarships, entry (D–s) 513
Hal Connolly Scholar–Athlete Award, (D–s) 539
Hamilton Scholarship. See Walter Hamilton Scholarship, entries (C–s) 452, (C–f) 472
Hammill Foundation Research Scholarships. See Donald D. Hammill Foundation Research Scholarships, entry (D–f) 657
Hank Hofstetter Opportunity Grants, (V–s) 44
Hank LeBonne Scholarship, (V–s) 45, (V–f) 142
Hanks, Jr. Scholarship in Meteorology. See American Meteorological Society Undergraduate Scholarships, entry (D–s) 513
Harbison Scholarship. See Anne and Matt Harbison Scholarship, entry (C–s) 362
Harold T. Stearns Fellowship Award. See Geological Society of America General Research Grants Program, entry (D–f) 664
Harriet Charron Memorial Scholarship. See Sr. Harriet Charron Memorial Scholarship, entry (V–s) 111
Harriett G. Jenkins Predoctoral Fellowship Program, (D–f) 670
Harry Alan Gregg Foundation Grants, (D–s) 540, (D–g) 843
Harry Ludwig Memorial Scholarship, (V–s) 46, (V–f) 143
Harvey Memorial Scholarship. See Delta Gamma Foundation Florence Margaret Harvey Memorial Scholarship, entries (V–s) 23, (V–f) 129
Hauser/Novartis Scholarship. See Epilepsy Foundation of Massachusetts & Rhode Island Scholarships, entries (C–s) 385, (C–f) 461
Hawaii Assistive Technology Loan Program, (D–l) 770
Hawai'i Children's Cancer Foundation Scholarships, (C–s) 394
Hawaii Grants for Special Housing for Disabled Veterans, (D–g) 844
Hawaii Income Tax Exclusion for Patients with Hansen's Disease, (C–g) 488
Hawaii Income Tax Exemption for Disabled Residents, (V–g) 204, (H–g) 292, (D–g) 845

V–Visual	H–Hearing	O–Orthopedic/Developmental	C–Communication/Other	D–Disabilities in General	F–Families
s–scholarships		f–fellowships/grants	l–loans	g–grants-in-aid	a–awards

Hawaii Property Tax Exemptions for Disabled Veterans, (D–g) 846, (F–g) 1123
Hazel ten Broek Merit Scholarship, (V–s) 47, (V–f) 144
Hearing Impaired Church Multiplication Team Scholarships, (H–s) 268, (H–f) 285
Hearne/AAPD Leadership Awards. See Paul G. Hearne/AAPD Leadership Awards, entry (D–a) 951
Hebner Memorial Scholarship. See John Hebner Memorial Scholarship, entry (V–s) 60
Helen Copeland Scholarship for Females, (V–s) 48, (V–f) 145
Helen Hagemeyer Scholarship. See American Meteorological Society Undergraduate Scholarships, entry (D–s) 513
Hemophilia Education Fund, (C–s) 395, (F–s) 993
Hemophilia Federation of America Scholarship Program, (C–s) 396
Hemophilia Foundation of Michigan Academic Scholarships, (C–s) 397, (F–s) 994
Hemophilia Foundation of Michigan Emergency Financial Assistance Program, (C–g) 489
Hemophilia Health Services Memorial Scholarships, (C–s) 398, (C–f) 463
Hemophilia of Iowa Scholarship, (C–s) 399, (F–s) 995
Hemophilia Resources of America Scholarships, (C–s) 400, (F–s) 996
Henrietta Dickman Memorial Scholarship Awards. See Alexander Graham Bell Association College Scholarship Awards, entries (H–s) 264, (H–f) 280
Henry and Anna Plapinger Endowment Award, (H–s) 269
Henry H. Arnold Education Grant Program. See General Henry H. Arnold Education Grant Program, entry (F–s) 988
Henry Syle Memorial Fellowship for Seminary Studies, (H–f) 286
Hentges Scholarship, (V–s) 49, (V–f) 146
Herb Schlaughenhoupt, Jr. Memorial Scholarship, (C–s) 401, (F–s) 997
Herbert P. Feibelman Jr. (PS) Scholarship Award. See Alexander Graham Bell Association College Scholarship Awards, entries (H–s) 264, (H–f) 280
Hermione Grant Calhoun Scholarships, (V–s) 50, (V–f) 147
Herron Memorial Scholarship. See Theresa C. Herron Memorial Scholarship, entry (V–g) 258
Herter Memorial Scholarship. See Christian A. Herter Memorial Scholarship, entry (D–s) 525
Hinda Honigman Award for the Blind, (V–a) 261
Hirshberg Fund, (C–g) 490
Hobson Scholarship. See Hemophilia Health Services Memorial Scholarships, entries (C–s) 398, (C–f) 463
Hoens, Jr. Scholars Program. See Eden Services Charles H. Hoens, Jr. Scholars Program, entry (C–s) 384
Hofstetter Opportunity Grants. See Hank Hofstetter Opportunity Grants, entry (V–s) 44
Home Improvements and Structural Alterations for Disabled Veterans, (D–g) 847

Homeland Security Fellowships, (D–f) 671
Honigman Award for the Blind. See Hinda Honigman Award for the Blind, entry (V–a) 261
Hope Scholarship. See American Meteorological Society Undergraduate Scholarships, entry (D–s) 513
Horizon Scholarships, (F–s) 998, (F–f) 1080
How I Live with Managed Asthma Poster Contest, (C–a) 507
Howard Brown Rickard Scholarships, (V–s) 51, (V–f) 148
Howard E. May Memorial Scholarship, (V–s) 52
Howard H. Hanks, Jr. Scholarship in Meteorology. See American Meteorological Society Undergraduate Scholarships, entry (D–s) 513
Howard III Scholarship. See Epilepsy Foundation of Massachusetts & Rhode Island Scholarships, entries (C–s) 385, (C–f) 461
Howard Research Grants. See Geological Society of America General Research Grants Program, entry (D–f) 664
Howard T. Orville Scholarship in Meteorology. See American Meteorological Society Undergraduate Scholarships, entry (D–s) 513
Huber Learning through Listening Awards. See Marion Huber Learning through Listening Awards, entry (C–s) 417
Hughes, '18 Fellowship. See Regina Olson Hughes, '18, Fellowship, entry (H–f) 289
Hunt Memorial Scholarship Award. See Alexander Graham Bell Association College Scholarship Awards, entries (H–s) 264, (H–f) 280
Hydrocephalus Association Scholarships, (C–s) 402, (C–f) 464
Hylton and Ron Niederman Scholarship. See Mike Hylton & Ron Niederman Scholarship, entries (C–s) 425, (F–s) 1031

"I See Success" ADHD Scholarship Contest. See CONCERTA "I See Success" ADHD Scholarship Contest, entry (C–s) 378
IADES Fellowship Award, (H–f) 287
Idaho Assistive Technology Low Interest Loan Program, (D–l) 771
Idaho Circuit Breaker Property Tax Reduction, (V–g) 205, (D–g) 848
Idaho Family Support Program, (F–g) 1124
Idaho Income Tax Deduction for Retirement Benefits, (D–g) 849, (F–g) 1125
Idaho Income Tax Deduction for the Blind and Their Widow(er)s, (V–g) 206
Idaho Income Tax Exemption for Maintaining a Home for the Developmentally Disabled, (C–g) 491, (F–g) 1126
Idaho Minority and "At Risk" Student Scholarship, (D–s) 541

PROGRAM TITLE INDEX

Idaho Public Safety Officer Dependent Scholarship, (F–s) 999
Idaho Space Grant Consortium Graduate Fellowships, (D–s) 542, (D–f) 672
Idaho Space Grant Consortium Research Initiation Grants, (D–f) 673
Idaho Space Grant Consortium Scholarship Program, (D–s) 543
Idaho Space Grant Consortium Travel Stipends, (D–f) 674
Idaho Veterans Temporary Emergency Grant Program, (D–g) 850, (F–g) 1127
I.H. McLendon Memorial Scholarship, (C–s) 403
Illinois Grant Program for Dependents of Correctional Officers, (F–s) 1000
Illinois Grant Program for Dependents of Police or Fire Officers, (F–s) 1001, (F–f) 1081
Illinois Grants for Specially Adapted Housing, (V–g) 207, (O–g) 331
Illinois Honorary Scholarships, (F–s) 1002
Illinois Housing Tax Exemption, (D–g) 851, (F–g) 1128
Illinois Income Tax Exemption for the Blind, (V–g) 208
Illinois Income Tax Subtraction for Government Retirees, (D–g) 852
Illinois MIA/POW Scholarship, (D–s) 544, (F–s) 1003
IMA Diversity Scholarship Program, (V–s) 53, (V–f) 149, (H–s) 270, (H–f) 288, (O–s) 306, (O–f) 315
Immune Deficiency Foundation Scholarship, (C–s) 404
Improved Death Pension for Survivors, (D–g) 853, (F–g) 1129
Improved Disability Pension Program for Veterans, (D–g) 854
Ina Brudnick Scholarship Award, (C–s) 405
Indiana Child of Veteran and Public Safety Officer Supplemental Grant Program, (F–s) 1004, (F–f) 1082
Indiana Disability Retirement Income Tax Deduction, (D–g) 855
Indiana Income Tax Exemption for the Blind, (V–g) 209
Indiana Property Tax Deduction for Blind or Disabled Persons, (V–g) 210, (D–g) 856
Indiana Property Tax Deductions for Disabled Veterans, (D–g) 857, (F–g) 1130
Indiana Space Grant Consortium Graduate Fellowships, (D–f) 675
Indiana Space Grant Consortium Undergraduate Scholarships, (D–s) 545
Individuals with Disabilities in Postdoctoral Training Research Supplements, (D–f) 676
Industry Undergraduate Scholarships, (D–s) 546
Industry-Based Graduate Research Assistantships and Cooperative Fellowships in the Mathematical Sciences, (D–f) 677
Industry/Government Graduate Fellowships, (D–f) 678
Information Technology Research Grants, (D–f) 679
Institute of Management Accountants Diversity Scholarship Program. See IMA Diversity Scholarship Program, entries (V–s) 53, (V–f) 149, (H–s) 270, (H–f) 288, (O–s) 306, (O–f) 315
International Alumnae of Delta Epsilon Sorority Scholarship. See IADES Fellowship Award, entry (H–f) 287
International Art Show by Artists with Disabilities, (D–a) 945
Iowa Able Loan Program, (D–l) 772
Iowa Pension/Retirement Income Exclusion, (D–g) 858, (F–g) 1131
Iowa Property Tax Credit for Disabled and Elderly Residents, (D–g) 859
Isenberg Fund Scholarship. See Leslie Isenberg Fund Scholarship, entry (D–f) 683

J. Hoover Mackin Research Grants. See Geological Society of America General Research Grants Program, entry (D–f) 664
Jackson Scholarship Award for Ethnic Minority Gifted/Talented Students with Disabilities. See Stanley E. Jackson Scholarship Award for Ethnic Minority Gifted/Talented Students with Disabilities, entry (D–s) 587
Jackson Scholarship Award for Ethnic Minority Students with Disabilities. See Stanley E. Jackson Scholarship Award for Ethnic Minority Students with Disabilities, entry (D–s) 588
Jackson Scholarship Award for Gifted/Talented Disabled Students. See Stanley E. Jackson Scholarship Award for Gifted/Talented Students with Disabilities, entry (D–s) 589
Jackson Scholarship Award for Students with Disabilities. See Stanley E. Jackson Scholarship Award for Students with Disabilities, entry (D–s) 590
Jacobsen Scholarship. See Sally S. Jacobsen Scholarship, entries (V–s) 108, (V–f) 177
James A. Girard Scholarship, (C–s) 406
James Doyle Case Memorial Scholarships, (V–s) 54, (V–f) 150, (F–s) 1005, (F–f) 1083
James Lyons Scholarship. See Epilepsy Foundation of Massachusetts & Rhode Island Scholarships, entries (C–s) 385, (C–f) 461
James N. Orman, '23, Fellowship. See GUAA Graduate Fellowship Fund, entry (H–f) 284
James R. Carlock Scholarship, (V–s) 55, (V–f) 151
Jay's World College Scholarship Program, (C–s) 407
Jean Kelsch, '51, Cordano Fellowship. See GUAA Graduate Fellowship Fund, entry (H–f) 284
Jean Spinelli Memorial Scholarship, (C–s) 408, (C–f) 465, (F–s) 1006, (F–f) 1084
Jenkins Predoctoral Fellowship Program. See Harriett G. Jenkins Predoctoral Fellowship Program, entry (D–f) 670
Jennica Ferguson Achievement Scholarship, (V–s) 56

V–Visual   H–Hearing   O–Orthopedic/Developmental   C–Communication/Other   D–Disabilities in General   F–Families
s–scholarships   f–fellowships/grants   l–loans   g–grants-in-aid   a–awards

PROGRAM TITLE INDEX

Jennica Ferguson Memorial Scholarship, (V–s) 57, (V–f) 152

Jennica Ferguson Memorial Scholarship. *See* National Federation of the Blind of Ohio Scholarships, entries (V–s) 86, (V–f) 166

Jernigan Scholarship. *See* Kenneth Jernigan Scholarship, entries (V–s) 64, (V–f) 157

Jewish Braille Institute of America Scholarship, (V–f) 153

JFK Rehab/EAGA Scholarship. *See* EAGA Scholarship Award, entries (O–s) 302, (F–s) 977

Jim Stineback Scholarship. *See* Hemophilia Health Services Memorial Scholarships, entries (C–s) 398, (C–f) 463

Joann Fischer Scholarship, (V–f) 154

John A. Trundle, 1885, Fellowship. *See* GUAA Graduate Fellowship Fund, entry (H–f) 284

John and Rhoda Dower Scholarship, (V–s) 58, (V–f) 155

John Arena Memorial Scholarship Fund, (C–s) 409

John Cahall Memorial Scholarship Fund, (V–s) 59

John E. Swift Educational Trust Scholarships. *See* Francis P. Matthews and John E. Swift Educational Trust Scholarships, entry (F–s) 986

John Hebner Memorial Scholarship, (V–s) 60

John Montagne Fund Award. *See* Geological Society of America General Research Grants Program, entry (D–f) 664

John R. Hope Scholarship. *See* American Meteorological Society Undergraduate Scholarships, entry (D–s) 513

John T. Dillon Alaska Research Award. *See* Geological Society of America General Research Grants Program, entry (D–f) 664

John T. McCraw Scholarship, (V–s) 61

John Van Landingham Scholarship. *See* Arizona Council of the Blind Scholarship Program, entries (V–s) 8, (V–f) 122

John Youtsey Memorial Scholarship Fund, (C–s) 410, (F–s) 1007

Johnson Memorial Scholarship. *See* Association of Blind Citizens Scholarship, entry (V–s) 66

Johnson Memorial Scholarship. *See* LaVyrl Johnson Memorial Scholarship, entries (V–s) 11, (V–f) 159

Johnson Scholarship Program. *See* Theodore R. and Vivian M. Johnson Scholarship Program, entry (D–s) 599

Jonathan May Memorial Scholarships, (V–s) 62

Joseph DiStefano Annual Scholarship. *See* SBAA Educational Scholarship Fund, entries (O–s) 312, (O–f) 316

Joyce Walsh Junior Disability Award, (D–a) 946

Julia C. Pugh Scholarship. *See* Margaret Funds Scholarships, entries (F–s) 1026, (F–f) 1089

Juvenile Arthritis Scholarships, (C–s) 411

Kane Memorial Scholarships. *See* Arthur B. Kane Memorial Scholarships, entry (C–s) 364

Kansas Assistive Technology Cooperative Flexible Term Loan Program. *See* KATCO Flexible Term Loan Program, entry (D–l) 773

Kansas Disabled Access Income Tax Credit, (D–g) 860, (F–g) 1132

Kansas Homestead Tax Refund, (V–g) 211, (D–g) 861

Kansas Intangibles Tax Senior Citizen or Disability Exemption, (V–g) 212, (D–g) 862

Kansas Space Grant Consortium Program, (D–s) 547, (D–f) 680

Kansas State Deaf–Blind Fund, (V–g) 213, (H–g) 293, (D–g) 863

Karen D. Carsel Memorial Scholarship, (V–f) 156

KATCO Flexible Term Loan Program, (D–l) 773

Katherine Vaz Scholarship, (H–s) 271

Kathern F. Gruber Scholarships, (F–s) 1008, (F–f) 1085

Kellie Cannon Memorial Scholarship, (V–s) 63

Kelly Memorial Scholarship. *See* Robert J. and Dennis R. Kelly Memorial Scholarship, entry (C–s) 439

Kenneth Jernigan Scholarship, (V–s) 64, (V–f) 157

Kentucky Assistive Technology Loans, (D–l) 774

Kentucky Deceased or Disabled Law Enforcement Officer and Fire Fighter Dependent Tuition Waiver, (F–s) 1009

Kentucky Homestead Exemption for the Disabled, (D–g) 864

Kentucky Space Grant Consortium Research Grants, (D–f) 681

Kentucky Veterans Tuition Waiver Program, (F–s) 1010

Kermit B. Nash Academic Scholarship, (C–s) 412

Kevin Child Scholarship, (C–s) 413

Kids' Chance of Arizona Scholarships, (F–s) 1011

Kids' Chance of Arkansas Scholarships, (F–s) 1012

Kids' Chance of Indiana Scholarship Program, (F–s) 1013, (F–f) 1086

Kids' Chance of Iowa Scholarships, (F–s) 1014

Kids' Chance of Louisiana Scholarships, (F–s) 1015

Kids' Chance of Maryland Scholarships, (F–s) 1016

Kids' Chance of Mississippi Scholarship Fund, (F–s) 1017

Kids' Chance of Missouri Scholarships, (F–s) 1018

Kids' Chance of Pennsylvania Scholarships, (F–s) 1019

Kids' Chance of South Carolina Scholarships, (F–s) 1020, (F–f) 1087

Kids' Chance of West Virginia Scholarships, (F–s) 1021

Kids' Chance Scholarship Fund, (F–s) 1022

Kids' Chance Scholarships, (F–s) 1023

Killian Memorial Scholarship. *See* Kuchler–Killian Memorial Scholarship, entries (V–s) 65, (V–f) 158

Kim D. Wallace Adaptive Equipment Loan Program. *See* mPower Adaptive Equipment Loan Program, entry (D–l) 781

Kisling Scholarship. *See* Chief Master Sergeants of the Air Force Scholarships, entries (D–s) 524, (F–s) 973

Kolb Memorial Scholarship. *See* Cindy Kolb Memorial Scholarship, entry (D–s) 526

V–Visual   H–Hearing   O–Orthopedic/Developmental   C–Communication/Other   D–Disabilities in General   F–Families
s–scholarships   f–fellowships/grants   l–loans   g–grants-in-aid   a–awards

PROGRAM TITLE INDEX

Komen Breast Cancer Foundation College Scholarship Awards. *See* Susan G. Komen Breast Cancer Foundation College Scholarship Awards, entry (F–s) 1062

Kuchler–Killian Memorial Scholarship, (V–s) 65, (V–f) 158

Larry Smock Scholarship, (C–s) 414
LaSPACE Fellowships, (D–f) 682
LATAN Assistive Technology Loan Program, (D–l) 775
LaVyrl Johnson Memorial Scholarship, (V–s) 66, (V–f) 159
Lawrence Marcelino Memorial Scholarship, (V–s) 67, (V–f) 160
Leaders in Furthering Education Presidential Unsung Hero Award. *See* LIFE Presidential Unsung Hero Award, entry (D–a) 947
LeBonne Scholarship. *See* Hank LeBonne Scholarship, entries (V–s) 45, (V–f) 142
Lenox Baker Special Assistance Program, (D–g) 865
Leonard Memorial Scholarship Fund. *See* Charles E. Leonard Memorial Scholarship Fund, entries (V–s) 16, (F–s) 972
Leslie Isenberg Fund Scholarship, (D–f) 683
Lester Walls III Scholarship, (D–s) 548, (D–f) 684
LIFE Presidential Unsung Hero Award, (D–a) 947
Lighthouse Undergraduate Award for Returning Students, (V–s) 68
Lilly Reintegration Scholarships, (C–s) 415, (C–f) 466
Limbs for Life Prothesis Fund, (O–g) 332
Linwood Walker Scholarship, (V–f) 101
Lions Clubs Support Services for the Blind and Visually Impaired, (V–s) 69, (V–f) 162, (V–g) 214
Lipman Research Award. *See* Geological Society of America General Research Grants Program, entry (D–f) 664
Little People of America Scholarships, (C–s) 416
Llewellyn Miller Fund, (D–g) 866
Loans for Accessibility, (D–l) 776, (F–l) 1097
Longshore and Harbor Workers' Compensation Program, (D–g) 867, (F–g) 1133
Louise C. Nacca Memorial Scholarship, (D–s) 549
Louise Rude Scholarship, (V–s) 70
Louisiana Assistive Technology Access Network Assistive Technology Loan Program. *See* LATAN Assistive Technology Loan Program, entry (D–l) 775
Louisiana Space Consortium Fellowships. *See* LaSPACE Fellowships, entry (D–f) 682
Louisiana Veterans State Aid Program, (F–s) 1024
Lowndes Award. *See* Margaret Funds Scholarships, entries (F–s) 1026, (F–f) 1089
Lucille A. Abt Scholarship Awards. *See* Alexander Graham Bell Association College Scholarship Awards, entries (H–s) 264, (H–f) 280
Ludwig Memorial Scholarship. *See* Harry Ludwig Memorial Scholarship, entries (V–s) 46, (V–f) 143

Lynn M. Smith Memorial Scholarship, (D–s) 550
Lyons Scholarship. *See* Epilepsy Foundation of Massachusetts & Rhode Island Scholarships, entries (C–s) 385, (C–f) 461

Mack Memorial Scholarships. *See* NIB Grant M. Mack Memorial Scholarship, entries (V–s) 94, (V–f) 170
Mack Scholarship. *See* Ellen Beach Mack Scholarship, entries (V–s) 29, (V–f) 132
Mackin Research Grants. *See* Geological Society of America General Research Grants Program, entry (D–f) 664
Mae Davidow Memorial Scholarship. *See* Dr. Mae Davidow Memorial Scholarship, entry (V–s) 25
Main Memorial Scholarship. *See* Mary Main Memorial Scholarship, entry (V–s) 71
Maine Income Tax Deduction for the Blind, (V–g) 215
Maine Property Tax Exemption for the Blind, (V–g) 216
Maine Tax Exemption for Specially Adapted Housing Units, (O–g) 333, (F–g) 1134
Maine Tax Exemptions for Veterans, (D–g) 868, (F–g) 1135
Maine Veterans Dependents Educational Benefits, (F–s) 1025, (F–f) 1088
Making a Difference Award, (C–a) 508
Making Homes Accessible (MHA) Loan Program, (D–l) 777
The Many Colors of ADHD Calendar Contest, (C–a) 509
Marcelino Memorial Scholarship. *See* Lawrence Marcelino Memorial Scholarship, entries (V–s) 67, (V–f) 160
Marchello Scholarship. *See* Stephen T. Marchello Scholarship, entry (C–s) 446
Marder Memorial Scholarship Program. *See* Immune Deficiency Foundation Scholarship, entry (C–s) 404
Margaret Funds Scholarships, (F–s) 1026, (F–f) 1089
Marilyn Yetso Memorial Scholarship, (F–s) 1027
Marion Huber Learning through Listening Awards, (C–s) 417
Mark J. Schroeder Scholarship in Meteorology, (D–s) 551
Mark Reames Memorial Scholarships, (C–s) 418, (F–s) 1028
Mark Richard Music Memorial Scholarship, (C–s) 419
Martin Scholarship. *See* Eden Services Charles H. Hoens, Jr. Scholars Program, entry (C–s) 384
Mary B. Rhodes Medical Scholarship. *See* Margaret Funds Scholarships, entries (F–s) 1026, (F–f) 1089
Mary E. Switzer Memorial Fellowships. *See* Research Fellowships of the National Institute on Disability and Rehabilitation Research, entry (D–f) 724
Mary Kay Ash Charitable Foundation Grants, (C–g) 492
Mary Main Memorial Scholarship, (V–s) 71
Mary P. Oenslager Scholastic Achievement Awards, (V–a) 262

V–Visual   H–Hearing   O–Orthopedic/Developmental   C–Communication/Other   D–Disabilities in General   F–Families
s–scholarships   f–fellowships/grants   l–loans   g–grants-in-aid   a–awards

PROGRAM TITLE INDEX

Maryland Assistive Technology Guaranteed Loan Program, (D–l) 778, (F–l) 1098
Maryland Income Tax Adjustments for Adopting Special Needs Children, (F–g) 1136
Maryland Income Tax Exemption for Blind and Elderly Residents, (V–g) 217
Maryland Income Tax Exemption for Disabled and Elderly Residents, (D–g) 869, (F–g) 1137
Maryland Income Tax Exemption for Readers for Blind Residents, (V–g) 218
Maryland Legion Scholarships, (F–s) 1029
Maryland Real Property Tax Exemption for Blind Persons, (V–g) 219, (F–g) 1138
Maryland Real Property Tax Exemption for Disabled Veterans, (D–g) 870, (F–g) 1139
Maryland Renters' Tax Credits, (D–g) 871
Maryland Space Scholars Program, (D–s) 552
Massachusetts Housing Finance Agency Home Improvement Loan Program. See MHFA Home Improvement Loan Program, entry (O–l) 318
Massachusetts Income Tax Exemption for Blind People, (V–g) 220
Massachusetts Property Tax Exemption, (V–g) 221, (D–g) 872, (F–g) 1140
Massachusetts Rehabilitation Commission or Commission for the Blind Tuition Waiver Program, (V–s) 72, (D–s) 553
Massachusetts Space Grant Consortium Graduate Fellowships, (D–f) 685
Massachusetts Space Grant Consortium Undergraduate Research Opportunity Program, (D–s) 554
Massachusetts Veterans Annuity Program, (D–g) 873
MassAdvantage Purchase and Rehabilitation Loans, (O–l) 317
Mathematical Sciences Postdoctoral Research Fellowships, (D–f) 686
Mathematical Sciences University–Industry Postdoctoral Research Fellowships, (D–f) 687
Mathematical Sciences University–Industry Senior Research Fellowships, (D–f) 688
Matt Harbison Scholarship. See Anne and Matt Harbison Scholarship, entry (C–s) 362
Matt Stauffer Memorial Scholarships, (C–s) 420
Matthews and John E. Swift Educational Trust Scholarships. See Francis P. Matthews and John E. Swift Educational Trust Scholarships, entry (F–s) 986
Mattie J.C. Russell Scholarship. See Margaret Funds Scholarships, entries (F–s) 1026, (F–f) 1089
Maude Winkler Scholarship Awards. See Alexander Graham Bell Association College Scholarship Awards, entries (H–s) 264, (H–f) 280
Max Edelman Scholarship, (V–s) 73
May Memorial Scholarship. See California Association for Postsecondary Education and Disability Scholarships, entries (D–s) 518, (D–f) 640

May Memorial Scholarship. See Howard E. May Memorial Scholarship, entry (V–s) 52
May Memorial Scholarships. See Jonathan May Memorial Scholarships, entry (V–s) 62
Mays Mission for the Handicapped Scholarship, (O–s) 307, (C–s) 421
McAdam Scholarship Fund. See Bill McAdam Scholarship Fund, entries (C–s) 369, (F–s) 964
McCartney Memorial Scholarship. See Brian McCartney Memorial Scholarship, entries (H–s) 266, (C–s) 372
McCraw Scholarship. See John T. McCraw Scholarship, entry (V–s) 61
McDermott Scholarship. See Epilepsy Foundation of Massachusetts & Rhode Island Scholarships, entries (C–s) 385, (C–f) 461
McLendon Memorial Scholarship. See I.H. McLendon Memorial Scholarship, entry (C–s) 403
McQuiston Memorial Scholarship. See Award of Excellence Asthma Scholarships, entry (C–s) 366
Medicare DME Program, (D–g) 874
Medlin Scholarships. See Geological Society of America General Research Grants Program, entry (D–f) 664
Mellon Postdoctoral Research Fellowship at Omohundro Institute. See Andrew W. Mellon Postdoctoral Research Fellowship at Omohundro Institute, entry (D–f) 632
Melva T. Owen Memorial Scholarship, (V–s) 74, (V–f) 163
MHA Loan Program. See Making Homes Accessible (MHA) Loan Program, entry (D–l) 777
MHFA Home Improvement Loan Program, (O–l) 318
Michigan Assistive Technology Loan Fund, (D–l) 779
Michigan Elks Association Charitable Grant Fund Scholarship, (D–g) 875
Michigan Homestead Property Tax Credit for Veterans and Blind People, (V–g) 222, (D–g) 876, (F–g) 1141
Michigan Income Tax Exemption for People with Disabilities, (V–g) 223, (H–g) 294, (O–g) 334, (D–g) 877
Michigan Space Grant Consortium Fellowships, (D–s) 555, (D–f) 689
Michigan Space Grant Consortium Research Seed Grants, (D–f) 690
Michigan Veterans Trust Fund Emergency Grants, (D–g) 878, (F–g) 1142
Michigan Veterans Trust Fund Tuition Grants, (F–s) 1030
Mid–South Division College Scholarships, (C–s) 422
Midwest Division Youth Scholarship Program, (C–s) 423
Mike Conley Memorial Scholarships, (C–s) 424
Mike Hylton & Ron Niederman Scholarship, (C–s) 425, (F–s) 1031
Miller Fund. See Llewellyn Miller Fund, entry (D–g) 866
Miller Parent of the Year National Recognition Award. See Wendy F. Miller Parent of the Year National Recognition Award, entry (F–a) 1191
Millie Brother Scholarship, (F–s) 1032
Minnesota Space Grant Consortium Scholarships and Fellowships, (D–s) 556, (D–f) 691

V–Visual H–Hearing O–Orthopedic/Developmental C–Communication/Other D–Disabilities in General F–Families
s–scholarships f–fellowships/grants l–loans g–grants-in-aid a–awards

PROGRAM TITLE INDEX

Minnesota State Soldiers Assistance Fund, (D–g) 879, (F–g) 1143
Minnesota Veterans Educational Assistance, (D–s) 557
Minnie Pearl Scholarship Program, (H–s) 272
Miss Deaf America Pageant Awards, (H–a) 298
Mississippi Ad Valorem Tax Exemption for Disabled Veterans, (D–g) 880
Mississippi Homestead Tax Exemption for the Disabled, (V–g) 224, (D–g) 881
Mississippi Law Enforcement Officers and Firemen Scholarship Program, (F–s) 1033, (F–g) 1144
Mississippi Space Grant Consortium Campus Activities, (D–s) 558, (D–f) 692
Mississippi Tax Exemption for the Blind, (V–g) 225, (F–g) 1145
Missouri Blind Pension, (V–g) 226
Missouri Council of the Blind Special Service Program, (V–g) 227
Missouri Public Survivor Grant Program, (F–s) 1034
Missouri Senior Citizen, Disabled Veteran, and Disabled Person Property Tax Credit Claim, (D–g) 882, (F–g) 1146
Missouri Supplemental Aid to the Blind, (V–g) 228
Missouri Vocational Special Need Association Student Scholarship. See MVSNA Student Scholarship, entry (D–s) 560
Monica Bailes Award, (C–s) 426
Monica Bailes Award. See Patient Advocate Foundation Scholarships for Survivors, entries (C–s) 434, (C–f) 467
Montagne Fund Award. See Geological Society of America General Research Grants Program, entry (D–f) 664
Montalban/Nosotros Acting Scholarship. See Ricardo Montalban/Nosotros Acting Scholarship, entry (D–a) 955
Montana Assistive Technology Loan Program, (D–l) 780
Montana Disability Income Exclusion, (D–g) 883
Montana Handicapped Dependent Children Tax Exemption, (F–g) 1147
Montana Income Tax Exemption for the Blind, (V–g) 229, (F–g) 1148
Montana Real Property Tax Relief, (D–g) 884, (F–g) 1149
Montana Space Grant Consortium Graduate Fellowships, (D–f) 693
Montana Space Grant Consortium Research Initiation Grants, (D–f) 694
Montana Space Grant Consortium Undergraduate Scholarships, (D–s) 559
Morris L. Ziskind Memorial Scholarship. See Hydrocephalus Association Scholarships, entries (C–s) 402, (C–f) 464
mPower Adaptive Equipment Loan Program, (D–l) 781
Mullin Memorial Scholarship. See Palmer–Mullin Memorial Scholarship, entry (V–s) 100
Murphey Memorial Scholarship. See Alma Murphey Memorial Scholarship, entry (V–f) 121

Murphy Memorial Scholarship. See American Meteorological Society Undergraduate Scholarships, entry (D–s) 513
Murtha Fellowship. See Pennsylvania National Guard Scholarship Fund, entry (F–s) 1055
Muscular Dystrophy Association Direct Services, (C–g) 493
Music Memorial Scholarship. See Mark Richard Music Memorial Scholarship, entry (C–s) 419
Musicians Foundation Financial Assistance, (D–g) 885
MVSNA Student Scholarship, (D–s) 560

Nacca Memorial Scholarship. See Louise C. Nacca Memorial Scholarship, entry (D–s) 549
NASA Earth System Science Fellowship Program, (D–f) 695
NASA Graduate Student Researchers Program, (D–f) 696
NASA–DESGC Graduate Student Fellowships, (D–f) 697
Nash Academic Scholarship. See Kermit B. Nash Academic Scholarship, entry (C–s) 412
National Aeronautics and Space Administration Graduate Student Fellowships in Earth System Science. See NASA Earth System Science Fellowship Program, entry (D–f) 695
National Aeronautics and Space Administration Graduate Student Researchers Program. See NASA Graduate Student Researchers Program, entry (D–f) 696
National Aeronautics and Space Administration–DESGC Graduate Student Fellowships. See NASA–DESGC Graduate Student Fellowships, entry (D–f) 697
National Amputee Golf Association Scholarship, (O–s) 308, (F–s) 1035
National Association of Vocational Education Special Needs Personnel/Piney Mountain Press Student Award. See NAVESNP/Piney Mountain Press Student Award, entry (D–s) 561
National Bass Championship for the Physically Challenged, (D–a) 948
National Craniofacial Association Travel Grants in Aid, (O–g) 335
National Defense Science and Engineering Graduate Fellowship Program, (D–f) 698
National Federation of the Blind Computer Science Scholarship, (V–s) 75, (V–f) 164
National Federation of the Blind Loans for Assistive Technology, (V–l) 185
National Federation of the Blind of Alabama Scholarship Program, (V–s) 76
National Federation of the Blind of Arkansas Scholarship, (V–s) 77
National Federation of the Blind of California Scholarships, (V–s) 78, (V–f) 165
National Federation of the Blind of Colorado Scholarship, (V–s) 79

V–Visual	H–Hearing	O–Orthopedic/Developmental	C–Communication/Other	D–Disabilities in General	F–Families
s–scholarships		f–fellowships/grants	l–loans	g–grants-in-aid	a–awards

National Federation of the Blind of Florida Scholarships, (V–s) 80
National Federation of the Blind of Idaho Scholarships, (V–s) 81
National Federation of the Blind of Illinois Scholarship, (V–s) 82
National Federation of the Blind of Indiana Scholarship, (V–s) 83
National Federation of the Blind of Nebraska Scholarship, (V–s) 84
National Federation of the Blind of New Mexico Scholarship Program, (V–s) 85
National Federation of the Blind of Ohio Scholarships, (V–s) 86, (V–f) 166
National Federation of the Blind of Oregon Scholarships, (V–s) 87, (V–f) 167
National Federation of the Blind of Texas Scholarships, (V–s) 88
National Federation of the Blind of Utah Scholarships, (V–s) 89, (V–f) 168
National Federation of the Blind of Vermont Scholarships, (V–s) 90
National Federation of the Blind of Wisconsin Scholarship, (V–s) 91
National Federation of the Blind Scholarships, (V–s) 92, (V–f) 169
National Foundation for Ectodermal Dysplasias Memorial Scholarship Program. See NFED Memorial Scholarship Program, entry (O–s) 309
National Foundation for Ectodermal Dysplasias Treatment Fund. See NFED Treatment Fund, entry (O–g) 341
National Fraternal Society of the Deaf Scholarships, (H–s) 273
National Guard Association of Indiana Educational Grants, (F–s) 1036
National Industries for the Blind Grant M. Mack Memorial Scholarships. See NIB Grant M. Mack Memorial Scholarship, entries (V–s) 94, (V–f) 170
National Institute of Arthritis and Musculoskeletal and Skin Diseases Small Grant Program for New Investigators. See NIAMS Small Grant Program for New Investigators, entry (D–f) 704
National Institutes of Health Undergraduate Scholarship Program, (D–l) 782
National Kidney Foundation of Arkansas Emergency Grants, (C–g) 494
National Kidney Foundation of Colorado, Idaho, Montana and Wyoming Patient Emergency Assistance Grants, (C–g) 495
National Kidney Foundation of Connecticut Patient Emergency Assistance Fund, (C–g) 496
National Kidney Foundation of Connecticut Scholarship Program, (C–s) 427, (F–s) 1037
National Kidney Foundation of Indiana Emergency Financial Aid, (C–g) 497

National Kidney Foundation of Iowa Patient Special Needs Fund, (C–g) 498
National Kidney Foundation of Kentucky Emergency Financial Assistance, (C–g) 499
National Kidney Foundation of Massachusetts, Rhode Island, New Hampshire, and Vermont Academic Awards, (C–s) 428, (F–s) 1038
National Kidney Foundation of Middle Tennessee Emergency Financial Assistance, (C–g) 500
National Kidney Foundation of the Virginias Patient Assistance Grants, (C–g) 501
National Research Service Award Predoctoral Fellowship Awards for Students with Disabilities. See Predoctoral Fellowship Awards for Students with Disabilities, entry (D–f) 721
National Science Foundation Director's Award for Distinguished Teaching Scholars. See NSF Director's Award for Distinguished Teaching Scholars, entry (D–f) 706
National Science Foundation Research Opportunity Awards, (D–f) 699
National Science Foundation Scholar-in-Residence at NIH Program. See NSF Scholar-in-Residence at NIH Program, entry (D–f) 707
National Science Foundation Small Business Innovation Research Grants. See NSF Small Business Innovation Research Grants, entry (D–f) 708
National Science Foundation Standard and Continuing Grants. See NSF Standard and Continuing Grants, entry (D–f) 709
National Transplant Assistance Fund Grants, (O–g) 336, (C–g) 502
National Vaccine Injury Compensation Program, (D–g) 886, (F–g) 1150
NAVESNP/Piney Mountain Press Student Award, (D–s) 561
NCFOP Foundation Scholarships, (F–s) 1039
Nebraska HomeChoice Mortgage Loan Program, (D–l) 783, (F–l) 1099
Nebraska Space Grant Statewide Scholarship Competition, (D–s) 562, (D–f) 700
Nebraska Waiver of Tuition for Veterans' Dependents, (F–s) 1040
Nelson Music Award for the Disabled and Visually Impaired. See Vivian Menees Nelson Music Award for the Disabled and Visually Impaired, entries (V–a) 263, (D–a) 956
Nemeth Commitment to Excellence Scholarship. See Abraham Nemeth Commitment to Excellence Scholarship, entry (V–s) 1
Nevada Assistive Technology Loan Fund, (D–l) 784
Nevada Council of the Blind Scholarship, (V–s) 93
Nevada Disabled Veteran's Tax Exemption, (D–g) 887, (F–g) 1151
Nevada Space Grant Consortium Graduate Fellowship Program, (D–f) 701

V–Visual	H–Hearing	O–Orthopedic/Developmental	C–Communication/Other	D–Disabilities in General	F–Families
s–scholarships		f–fellowships/grants	l–loans	g–grants-in-aid	a–awards

PROGRAM TITLE INDEX

Nevada Space Grant Consortium Undergraduate Scholarship Program, (D–s) 563
New England Chapter Scholarships, (C–s) 429
New Hampshire Charitable Foundation Statewide Student Aid Program, (D–s) 564, (D–f) 702, (D–l) 785
New Hampshire Guaranteed Collateral Loan Fund, (D–l) 786
New Hampshire Property Tax Exemption for Certain Disabled Servicemen, (V–g) 230, (O–g) 337, (F–g) 1152
New Hampshire Real Estate Exemption for Improvements to Assist Persons with Disabilities, (F–g) 1153
New Hampshire Real Estate Exemption for the Blind, (V–g) 231
New Hampshire Real Estate Exemption for the Disabled, (D–g) 888
New Hampshire Service–Connected Total Disability Tax Credit, (O–g) 338, (D–g) 889, (F–g) 1154
New Hampshire Space Grant Consortium Project Support, (D–s) 565, (D–f) 703
New Horizons Scholarships, (C–s) 430, (F–s) 1041
New Jersey Homestead Rebate, (V–g) 232, (D–g) 890
New Jersey Income Tax Exclusions for Persons with Disabilities, (D–g) 891
New Jersey Income Tax Exemptions for the Blind and Disabled, (V–g) 233, (D–g) 892
New Jersey Partial Exemption from Realty Transfer Fee for Senior Citizens or Disabled Persons, (V–g) 234, (D–g) 893
New Jersey Pension Exclusion, (D–g) 894
New Jersey Property Tax Deduction, (V–g) 235, (D–g) 895
New Jersey Property Tax Exemption for Disabled Veterans or Surviving Spouses, (D–g) 896, (F–g) 1155
New Jersey Property Tax Reimbursement, (D–g) 897
New Jersey Utilities Association Scholarships, (D–s) 566
New Jersey Veterans and Spouses Catastrophic Entitlements, (V–g) 236, (O–g) 339, (F–g) 1156
New Mexico Disabled Veteran Property Tax Exemption, (D–g) 898, (F–g) 1157
New Mexico Income Tax Deduction for the Adoption of a Special Needs Child, (F–g) 1158
New Mexico Tax Exemption for the Blind and Elderly, (V–g) 237
New Mexico Technology Assistance Program Financial Loan Program. See NMTAP Financial Loan Program, entry (D–l) 787
New York Alternative Property Tax Exemptions for Veterans, (D–g) 899, (F–g) 1159
New York "Eligible Funds" Property Tax Exemptions for Veterans, (O–g) 340, (F–g) 1160
New York State Blind Annuity, (V–g) 238, (F–g) 1161
New York State Disability Income Exclusion, (D–g) 900
Newmeyer Post–Secondary Scholarship for Visually Impaired Students. See David H. Newmeyer Post–Secondary Scholarship for Visually Impaired Students, entry (V–s) 20

Newmeyer Scholarship. See David Newmeyer Scholarship, entry (V–s) 21
NFED Memorial Scholarship Program, (O–s) 309
NFED Treatment Fund, (O–g) 341
NIAMS Small Grant Program for New Investigators, (D–f) 704
NIB Grant M. Mack Memorial Scholarship, (V–s) 94, (V–f) 170
Nicholas S. DiCaprio Scholarship. See Dr. Nicholas S. DiCaprio Scholarship, entry (V–s) 26
Niederman Scholarship. See Mike Hylton & Ron Niederman Scholarship, entries (C–s) 425, (F–s) 1031
NMTAP Financial Loan Program, (D–l) 787
Nora Webb–McKinney Scholarship, (V–s) 95, (V–f) 171
Norman G. Brooks Stand–Up Comedy Competition Scholarship, (D–a) 949
North Carolina Bar Association Scholarships, (F–s) 1042, (F–f) 1090
North Carolina Council of the Blind Scholarship, (V–s) 96
North Carolina Fraternal Order of Police Foundation Scholarships. See NCFOP Foundation Scholarships, entry (F–s) 1039
North Carolina Income Tax Exemption for the Aged and Blind, (V–g) 239
North Carolina National Guard Association Special Population Scholarship, (O–s) 310, (C–s) 431, (F–s) 1043
North Carolina Property Tax Relief for Disabled Veterans, (D–g) 901
North Carolina Property Tax Relief for Elderly and Permanently Disabled Persons, (D–g) 902
North Carolina Scholarships for Children of War Veterans, (F–s) 1044
North Carolina Sheriffs' Association Undergraduate Criminal Justice Scholarships, (F–s) 1045
North Dakota Assistive Technology Financial Loan Program, (D–l) 788
North Dakota Association of the Blind Scholarships, (V–s) 97, (V–f) 172
North Dakota Educational Assistance for Dependents of Veterans, (F–s) 1046
North Dakota Income Tax Adjustments for Adopting Children with Disabilities, (F–g) 1162
North Dakota Property Tax Credit for Senior Citizens or Disabled Persons, (D–g) 903
North Dakota Property Tax Exemption for the Blind, (V–g) 240, (F–g) 1163
North Dakota Property Tax Exemption for the Disabled, (O–g) 342, (F–g) 1164
North Dakota Property Tax Exemptions for Disabled Veterans, (O–g) 343, (D–g) 904, (F–g) 1165
North Dakota Space Grant Program Fellowships, (D–s) 567, (D–f) 705
North Dakota Space Grant Program Scholarships, (D–s) 568

| V–Visual | H–Hearing | O–Orthopedic/Developmental | C–Communication/Other | D–Disabilities in General | F–Families |
| s–scholarships | | f–fellowships/grants | l–loans | g–grants-in-aid | a–awards |

PROGRAM TITLE INDEX

Northeastern Amputee Class Scholarship. *See* EAGA Scholarship Award, entries (O–s) 302, (F–s) 977
Nosotros Acting Scholarship. *See* Ricardo Montalban/Nosotros Acting Scholarship, entry (D–a) 955
Novartis Oncology Scholarship, (C–s) 432
NRSA Predoctoral Fellowship Awards for Students with Disabilities. *See* Predoctoral Fellowship Awards for Students with Disabilities, entry (D–f) 721
NSF Director's Award for Distinguished Teaching Scholars, (D–f) 706
NSF Scholar–in–Residence at NIH Program, (D–f) 707
NSF Small Business Innovation Research Grants, (D–f) 708
NSF Standard and Continuing Grants, (D–f) 709
Nurses House Financial Assistance, (D–g) 905
Nutrition Action Fellowship, (D–f) 710

O'Daniel Memorial Scholarship. *See* Shannon O'Daniel Memorial Scholarship, entry (C–s) 443
Oenslager Scholastic Achievement Awards. *See* Mary P. Oenslager Scholastic Achievement Awards, entry (V–a) 262
Office of Naval Research Historically Black Engineering Colleges Future Engineering Faculty Fellowship Program, (D–f) 711
Ohio Emergency Relief Aid, (D–g) 906, (F–g) 1166
Ohio Income Tax Deduction for Disability Benefits, (D–g) 907
Ohio Legion Auxiliary Past Presidents' Parley Nurses' Scholarship, (F–s) 1047
Ohio Scholarships for Young Cancer Survivors, (C–s) 433
Ohio Space Grant Consortium Community College Scholarship, (D–s) 569
Ohio Space Grant Consortium Doctoral Fellowship, (D–f) 712
Ohio Space Grant Consortium Junior Scholarships, (D–s) 570
Ohio Space Grant Consortium Master's Fellowship, (D–f) 713
Ohio Space Grant Consortium Senior Scholarship, (D–s) 571
Ohio War Orphans Scholarship, (F–s) 1048
Oklahoma Disability Deduction, (D–g) 908
Oklahoma Financial Assistance Program, (D–g) 909, (F–g) 1167
Oklahoma Income Tax Exemption for the Blind, (V–g) 241, (F–g) 1168
Oklahoma Space Grant Consortium Education Program. *See* OSGC Education Program, entries (D–s) 573, (D–f) 715
Oklahoma Space Grant Consortium Research Program. *See* OSGC Research Program, entry (D–f) 716

Old Dominion Foundation Fellowship. *See* GUAA Graduate Fellowship Fund, entry (H–f) 284
Omohundro Institute Postdoctoral NEH Fellowship, (D–f) 714
Opportunities for the Blind Grants, (V–s) 98, (V–g) 242
Optimist International Communication Contest for the Deaf and Hard of Hearing, (H–a) 299
Oral Hearing–Impaired Section Scholarship Award. *See* Alexander Graham Bell Association College Scholarship Awards, entries (H–s) 264, (H–f) 280
Oregon Council of the Blind Scholarships, (V–s) 99
Oregon Deceased or Disabled Public Safety Officer Grant Program, (F–s) 1049
Oregon Income Tax Deduction for the Blind, (V–g) 243
Oregon Income Tax Deduction for the Severely Disabled, (O–g) 344
Oregon Legion Auxiliary Department Nurses Scholarship, (F–s) 1050
Oregon Legion Auxiliary Department Scholarships, (F–s) 1051
Oregon Lions Patient Care Program, (V–g) 244, (H–g) 295
Oregon Occupational Safety and Health Division Workers Memorial Scholarships, (F–s) 1052, (F–f) 1091
Oregon Property Tax Deferral for Disabled and Senior Citizens, (V–g) 245, (D–g) 910
Oregon Property Tax Exemption for Veterans with Disabilities and Their Spouses, (D–g) 911, (F–g) 1169
Oregon Property Tax Exemption for Veterans with Service–Connected Disabilities and Their Spouses, (D–g) 912, (F–g) 1170
Oregon Space Grant Undergraduate Scholar Program, (D–s) 572
Oregon Veterans Home Loan Program, (D–l) 789
Orman, '23, Fellowship. *See* GUAA Graduate Fellowship Fund, entry (H–f) 284
Orman, '25, Fellowship. *See* Doris B. Orman, '25, Fellowship, entry (H–f) 282
Orville Scholarship in Meteorology. *See* American Meteorological Society Undergraduate Scholarships, entry (D–s) 513
OSGC Education Program, (D–s) 573, (D–f) 715
OSGC Research Program, (D–f) 716
Otto Sussman Trust Grants, (D–g) 913
Outstanding Individual with Autism of the Year Award, (C–a) 510
Outstanding Secondary Special Populations Career and Technical Education Student Award, (D–s) 574
Owen Memorial Scholarship. *See* Melva T. Owen Memorial Scholarship, entries (V–s) 74, (V–f) 163

PAAD Program. *See* Pharmaceutical Assistance to the Aged and Disabled (PAAD) Program, entry (D–g) 917
Palmer–Mullin Memorial Scholarship, (V–s) 100
Panasonic Young Soloists Award, (D–a) 950

V–Visual   H–Hearing   O–Orthopedic/Developmental   C–Communication/Other   D–Disabilities in General   F–Families
s–scholarships   f–fellowships/grants   l–loans   g–grants-in-aid   a–awards

PROGRAM TITLE INDEX

Pangere Foundation Scholarships. *See* Ross N. and Patricia Pangere Foundation Scholarships, entries (V–s) 105, (V–f) 174
Parent Public Policy Fellowship Program, (F–f) 1092
Parent–Infant/Preschool Services Financial Aid Program, (H–g) 296, (F–g) 1171
Parker Scholarship. *See* E.U. Parker Scholarship, entries (V–s) 31, (V–f) 133
Parker–Gentry Fellowship. *See* Diplomacy Fellowships, entry (D–f) 651
Patient Advocate Foundation Scholarships for Survivors, (C–s) 434, (C–f) 467
Patient Aid Program, (C–g) 503
Patricia Pangere Foundation Scholarships. *See* Ross N. and Patricia Pangere Foundation Scholarships, entries (V–s) 105, (V–f) 174
Paul DesChamps Scholarship Award. *See* EAGA Scholarship Award, entries (O–s) 302, (F–s) 977
Paul G. Hearne/AAPD Leadership Awards, (D–a) 951
Paul W. Ruckes Scholarship, (V–s) 101, (V–f) 173
PAVESNP Life/Work Challenge Awards, (D–a) 952
Peace Officers Research Association of California Scholarships. *See* PORAC Scholarships, entry (D–s) 577
Pearl Scholarship Program. *See* Minnie Pearl Scholarship Program, entry (H–s) 272
Pearle Vision Foundation Individual Grant, (V–g) 246
Pedro Grau Undergraduate Scholarship. *See* American Meteorological Society Undergraduate Scholarships, entry (D–s) 513
Peikoff, '29, Fellowship. *See* GUAA Graduate Fellowship Fund, entry (H–f) 284
Pennsylvania Assistive Technology Financing Program, (D–l) 790
Pennsylvania Association of Vocational Education Special Needs Personnel Life/Work Challenge Awards. *See* PAVESNP Life/Work Challenge Awards, entry (D–a) 952
Pennsylvania Blind Veterans Pension, (V–g) 247
Pennsylvania Educational Gratuity for Veterans' Dependents, (F–s) 1053
Pennsylvania Legion Auxiliary Scholarship for Dependents of Disabled or Deceased Veterans, (F–s) 1054
Pennsylvania National Guard Scholarship Fund, (F–s) 1055
Pennsylvania Paralyzed Veterans Pension, (O–g) 345
Pennsylvania Property Tax and Rent Rebate Program, (D–g) 914
Pennsylvania Real Estate Tax Exemption, (V–g) 248, (O–g) 346, (D–g) 915, (F–g) 1172
Pennsylvania Space Grant Consortium Fellowships, (D–f) 717
Pennsylvania Space Grant Consortium Scholarships, (D–s) 575
Pennsylvania Veterans Emergency Assistance, (D–g) 916, (F–g) 1173
Peter and Bruce Bidstrup Scholarship Fund, (C–s) 435

Pfizer Epilepsy Scholarship Award, (C–s) 436, (C–f) 468
Pharmaceutical Assistance to the Aged and Disabled (PAAD) Program, (D–g) 917
Philippians Foundation Scholarships, (F–s) 1056
Pike Prize, (D–a) 953
Pike Prize for Service to People with Disabilities. *See* Pike Prize, entry (D–a) 953
Pinnacol Foundation Scholarship Program, (F–s) 1057
Pistilli Scholarships. *See* P.O. Pistilli Scholarships, entry (D–s) 576
Plapinger Endowment Award. *See* Henry and Anna Plapinger Endowment Award, entry (H–s) 269
Playwright Discovery Award, (D–a) 954
P.O. Pistilli Scholarships, (D–s) 576
PORAC Scholarships, (D–s) 577
Post Baccalaureate and Post–Master's Degree Students with Disabilities Research Supplements, (D–f) 718
Postdoctoral Research Fellowships in Biological Informatics, (D–f) 719
Postdoctoral Research Fellowships in Microbial Biology, (D–f) 720
Predoctoral Fellowship Awards for Students with Disabilities, (D–f) 721
Prentice Memorial Personal Advancement Award. *See* Sally Prentice Memorial Personal Advancement Award, entry (V–g) 249
Prequalification Pilot Loan Program, (D–l) 791
Professional Development Assistance for Artists with Disabilities, (D–g) 918
Professional Development Fellowships for Doctoral Candidates in Art History, (D–f) 722
Professional Development Fellowships for Master of Fine Arts Candidates, (D–f) 723
Prows Memorial Scholarship. *See* Beverly Prows Memorial Scholarship, entries (V–s) 14, (V–f) 126
Pugh Scholarship. *See* Margaret Funds Scholarships, entries (F–s) 1026, (F–f) 1089

Quality of Life Patient Grants, (C–g) 504
Qualls Memorial Scholarships. *See* Floyd Qualls Memorial Scholarships, entries (V–s) 36, (V–f) 135
Quirk Scholarship. *See* Earl and Eugenia Quirk Scholarship, entry (D–s) 532

Railroad Retirement Disability Annuity, (D–g) 919, (F–g) 1174
Ray Froncillo Scholarship. *See* EAGA Scholarship Award, entries (O–s) 302, (F–s) 977
Reames Memorial Scholarship. *See* Mark Reames Memorial Scholarships, entries (C–s) 418, (F–s) 1028
Reed Award. *See* Geological Society of America General Research Grants Program, entry (D–f) 664

V–Visual   H–Hearing   O–Orthopedic/Developmental   C–Communication/Other   D–Disabilities in General   F–Families
s–scholarships   f–fellowships/grants   l–loans   g–grants-in-aid   a–awards

Reeve Acting Scholarship. *See* Christopher Reeve Acting Scholarship, entry (D–a) 943

Reggie Johnson Memorial Scholarship. *See* Association of Blind Citizens Scholarship, entry (V–s) 11

Regina Olson Hughes, '18, Fellowship, (H–f) 289

Reimbursement of Burial Expenses, (F–g) 1175

REPS. *See* Restored Entitlement Program for Survivors (REPS), entry (F–g) 1176

Research Fellowships of the National Institute on Disability and Rehabilitation Research, (D–f) 724

Research in Undergraduate Institutions Faculty Research Projects. *See* RUI Faculty Research Projects, entry (D–f) 732

Research Supplements for Graduate Students with Disabilities, (D–f) 725

Research Supplements for Undergraduate Students with Disabilities, (D–s) 578

Restored Entitlement Program for Survivors (REPS), (F–g) 1176

Revelle Fellowship in Global Stewardship. *See* Roger Revelle Fellowship in Global Stewardship, entry (D–f) 731

Rhoda Dower Scholarship. *See* John and Rhoda Dower Scholarship, entries (V–s) 58, (V–f) 155

Rhode Island Educational Benefits for Disabled American Veterans, (D–s) 579

Rhode Island Space Grant Graduate Fellowship Program, (D–f) 726

Rhode Island Space Grant Undergraduate Scholarship Program, (D–s) 580

Rhodes Medical Scholarship. *See* Margaret Funds Scholarships, entries (F–s) 1026, (F–f) 1089

Ricardo Montalban/Nosotros Acting Scholarship, (D–a) 955

Richard and Helen Hagemeyer Scholarship. *See* American Meteorological Society Undergraduate Scholarships, entry (D–s) 513

Richard Bennet of Maine Scholarship, (V–s) 102

Richard D. Kisling Scholarship. *See* Chief Master Sergeants of the Air Force Scholarships, entries (D–s) 524, (F–s) 973

Richard E. Thorn Memorial Scholarship. *See* Pennsylvania National Guard Scholarship Fund, entry (F–s) 1055

Richardson Memorial Scholarship. *See* Hemophilia Resources of America Scholarships, entries (C–s) 400, (F–s) 996

Rickard Scholarships. *See* Howard Brown Rickard Scholarships, entries (V–s) 51, (V–f) 148

Ricky Hobson Scholarship. *See* Hemophilia Health Services Memorial Scholarships, entries (C–s) 398, (C–f) 463

Ridge Inter–Disciplinary Global Experiments 2000 Initiative Postdoctoral Fellowships. *See* RIDGE 2000 Postdoctoral Fellowship Program, entry (D–f) 727

RIDGE 2000 Postdoctoral Fellowship Program, (D–f) 727

Risk Policy Fellowships in Health, Safety and the Environment, (D–f) 728

R.L. Gillette Scholarships, (V–s) 103

Robert A. Dannels Memorial Scholarship, (D–f) 729

Robert Dole Scholarship Fund for Disabled Students, (O–s) 311, (C–s) 437

Robert Guthrie PKU Scholarship, (C–s) 438

Robert H. Weitbrecht Scholarship Awards. *See* Alexander Graham Bell Association College Scholarship Awards, entries (H–s) 264, (H–f) 280

Robert J. and Dennis R. Kelly Memorial Scholarship, (C–s) 439

Robert K. Fahnestock Memorial Award. *See* Geological Society of America General Research Grants Program, entry (D–f) 664

Robert M. Stanley Memorial Scholarship, (V–s) 104

Robin Romano Memorial Scholarship, (C–s) 440

Rocky Mountain Division College Scholarship Program, (C–s) 441

Rocky Mountain NASA Space Grant Consortium Graduate Research Fellowships, (D–f) 730

Rocky Mountain NASA Space Grant Consortium Undergraduate Scholarships, (D–s) 581

Rodriguez Scholarship. *See* American Meteorological Society Undergraduate Scholarships, entry (D–s) 513

Roger Revelle Fellowship in Global Stewardship, (D–f) 731

Romano Memorial Scholarship. *See* Robin Romano Memorial Scholarship, entry (C–s) 440

Ron Niederman Scholarship. *See* Mike Hylton & Ron Niederman Scholarship, entries (C–s) 425, (F–s) 1031

Ross N. and Patricia Pangere Foundation Scholarships, (V–s) 105, (V–f) 174

Roy Foundation Grants. *See* Travis Roy Foundation Grants, entry (O–g) 356

Roy J. Shlemon Scholarship Awards. *See* Geological Society of America General Research Grants Program, entry (D–f) 664

Ruckes Scholarship. *See* Paul W. Ruckes Scholarship, entries (V–s) 101, (V–f) 173

Rude Scholarship. *See* Louise Rude Scholarship, entry (V–s) 70

Rudolph Dillman Memorial Scholarship, (V–s) 106, (V–f) 175

RUI Faculty Research Projects, (D–f) 732

Russell Scholarship. *See* Margaret Funds Scholarships, entries (F–s) 1026, (F–f) 1089

Ruth Billow Memorial Education Fund, (V–s) 107, (V–f) 176

S. Bradley Burson Memorial Scholarship. *See* Dr. S. Bradley Burson Memorial Scholarship, entries (V–s) 27, (V–f) 130

Sad Sacks Nursing Scholarship, (F–s) 1058

V–Visual **H–Hearing** **O–Orthopedic/Developmental** **C–Communication/Other** **D–Disabilities in General** **F–Families**
s–scholarships **f–fellowships/grants** **l–loans** **g–grants-in-aid** **a–awards**

PROGRAM TITLE INDEX

Sadler Memorial Scholarship. *See* Arnold Sadler Memorial Scholarship, entries (V–s) 9, (V–f) 123

Sallie Mae 911 Education Fund Loan Relief Program, (D–g) 920, (F–g) 1177

Sallie Mae 911 Education Fund Scholarship Program, (F–s) 1059

Sally Prentice Memorial Personal Advancement Award, (V–g) 249

Sally S. Jacobsen Scholarship, (V–s) 108, (V–f) 177

Sam Scholarships. *See* Sybil Fong Sam Scholarships, entry (C–s) 448

Sanofi Grants, (C–g) 505

Sara Conlon Memorial Scholarship, (D–s) 582

Saturn Mobility Program for Persons with Disabilities, (O–g) 347

SBAA Educational Scholarship Fund, (O–s) 312, (O–f) 316

SBAC Scholarship, (O–s) 313

Scheigert Scholarships. *See* Fred Scheigert Scholarships, entries (V–s) 38, (V–f) 137

Schlaughenhoupt, Jr. Memorial Scholarship. *See* Herb Schlaughenhoupt, Jr. Memorial Scholarship, entries (C–s) 401, (F–s) 997

Schoettler Scholarship for Visually Impaired Students. *See* Dale M. Schoettler Scholarship for Visually Impaired Students, entries (V–s) 19, (V–f) 128

Scholarship Trust for the Deaf and Near Deaf, (H–s) 274, (H–g) 297

School-Age Financial Aid Awards, (H–s) 275

Schroeder Scholarship in Meteorology. *See* Mark J. Schroeder Scholarship in Meteorology, entry (D–s) 551

Scott Tarbell Scholarships, (C–s) 442

Scripps Fellowships in Environmental Journalism. *See* Ted Scripps Fellowships in Environmental Journalism, entry (D–f) 740

Second Century Fund Awards. *See* Alexander Graham Bell Association College Scholarship Awards, entries (H–s) 264, (H–f) 280

Senior Gold Prescription Discount Program, (D–g) 921

Sertoma Scholarships for Hearing-Impaired Students, (H–s) 276

Shannon McDermott Scholarship. *See* Epilepsy Foundation of Massachusetts & Rhode Island Scholarships, entries (C–s) 385, (C–f) 461

Shannon O'Daniel Memorial Scholarship, (C–s) 443

Sheldon M. Wolff, M.D. Fellowship in International Health. *See* Diplomacy Fellowships, entry (D–f) 651

Shlemon Scholarship Awards. *See* Geological Society of America General Research Grants Program, entry (D–f) 664

Show Me Loans, (D–l) 792

Sigma Alpha Iota Scholarship for the Visually Impaired, (V–s) 109, (V–f) 178

Singers' Assistance, (D–g) 922

Sisson Award. *See* Geological Society of America General Research Grants Program, entry (D–f) 664

Smith Memorial Scholarship. *See* Lynn M. Smith Memorial Scholarship, entry (D–s) 550

Smock Scholarship. *See* Larry Smock Scholarship, entry (C–s) 414

Social Security Disability Insurance (SSDI) Benefits, (V–g) 250, (D–g) 923, (F–g) 1178

Soozie Courter Sharing a Brighter Tomorrow Hemophilia Scholarships, (C–s) 444, (C–f) 469

South Carolina Disabled Person Property Tax Exemption, (O–g) 348, (F–g) 1179

South Carolina Disabled Veterans Property Tax Exemption, (D–g) 924, (F–g) 1180

South Carolina Education Assistance for Children of Certain War Veterans, (F–s) 1060

South Carolina Homestead Exemption Program, (V–g) 251, (D–g) 925

South Carolina Income Tax Exemption for the Adoption of a Special Needs Child, (F–g) 1181

South Carolina Permanent Disability Retirement Income Tax Exclusion, (D–g) 926

South Carolina Space Grant Consortium Graduate Fellowships, (D–f) 733

South Carolina Space Grant Consortium Research Grants, (D–f) 734

South Carolina Space Grant Consortium Undergraduate Scholarship Program, (D–s) 583

South Carolina Specially Adapted Housing Tax Exemption, (V–g) 252, (O–g) 349, (F–g) 1182

South Carolina Tax Exemption for Compensation, Pension, Disability Retirement Pay, and Veterans Administration Payments, (D–g) 927

South Dakota Free Tuition for Veterans and Others Who Performed War Service, (D–s) 584

South Dakota Free Tuition for Visually Impaired Persons, (V–s) 110, (V–f) 179

South Dakota Property Tax Exemption for Veterans and Their Widows or Widowers, (O–g) 350, (F–g) 1183

South Dakota Property Tax Refund for Senior Citizens and Citizens with Disabilities, (D–g) 928, (F–g) 1184

South Dakota Sales Tax Refund for Senior Citizens and Citizens with Disabilities, (D–g) 929

Southeast Division College Scholarships, (C–s) 445, (C–f) 470

Special People in Need Grants. *See* S.P.I.N. Grants, entry (D–f) 735

Special People in Need Scholarships. *See* S.P.I.N. Scholarships, entry (D–s) 585

Specially Adapted Homes for Disabled Veterans, (V–l) 186, (V–g) 253, (O–l) 319, (O–g) 351

S.P.I.N. Grants, (D–f) 735

S.P.I.N. Scholarships, (D–s) 585

Spina Bifida Allowance for Children of Vietnam Veterans, (O–g) 352

Spina Bifida Association of America Educational Scholarship. *See* SBAA Educational Scholarship Fund, entries (O–s) 312, (O–f) 316

V–Visual H–Hearing O–Orthopedic/Developmental C–Communication/Other D–Disabilities in General F–Families
s–scholarships f–fellowships/grants l–loans g–grants-in-aid a–awards

Spina Bifida Association of Connecticut Scholarship. *See* SBAC Scholarship, entry (O–s) 313

Spinelli Memorial Scholarship. *See* Jean Spinelli Memorial Scholarship, entries (C–s) 408, (C–f) 465, (F–s) 1006, (F–f) 1084

Sr. Harriet Charron Memorial Scholarship, (V–s) 111

SSDI Benefits. *See* Social Security Disability Insurance (SSDI) Benefits, entries (V–g) 250, (D–g) 923, (F–g) 1178

Stan Beck Fellowship, (D–s) 586, (D–f) 736

Stanley E. Jackson Scholarship Award for Ethnic Minority Gifted/Talented Students with Disabilities, (D–s) 587

Stanley E. Jackson Scholarship Award for Ethnic Minority Students with Disabilities, (D–s) 588

Stanley E. Jackson Scholarship Award for Gifted/Talented Students with Disabilities, (D–s) 589

Stanley E. Jackson Scholarship Award for Students with Disabilities, (D–s) 590

Stanley Memorial Scholarship. *See* Robert M. Stanley Memorial Scholarship, entry (V–s) 104

State Vocational Rehabilitation Services Program, (D–s) 591, (D–f) 737

Stauffer Memorial Scholarships. *See* Matt Stauffer Memorial Scholarships, entry (C–s) 420

Stearns Fellowship Award. *See* Geological Society of America General Research Grants Program, entry (D–f) 664

Stein Memorial Space Grant Scholarship. *See* Pennsylvania Space Grant Consortium Scholarships, entry (D–s) 575

Stephen T. Marchello Scholarship, (C–s) 446

Stineback Scholarship. *See* Hemophilia Health Services Memorial Scholarships, entries (C–s) 398, (C–f) 463

Stokoe Scholarship. *See* William C. Stokoe Scholarship, entry (H–f) 290

Stratton/Tipton Scholarship for Adult Returning Students, (D–s) 592

Stratton/Tipton Scholarship for High School Seniors, (D–s) 593

Supplemental and Emergency Grant Program for Individuals, (D–g) 930

Supplemental Security Income (SSI), (V–g) 254, (D–g) 931

Supplements for Established Investigators Who Become Disabled, (D–f) 738

Supreme Emblem Club of the United States of America Grant–in–Aid Awards, (D–s) 594

Survivors' and Dependents' Educational Assistance Program, (D–s) 595, (D–f) 739, (F–s) 1061, (F–f) 1093

Susan Bunch Memorial Scholarship, (C–s) 447, (C–f) 471

Susan G. Komen Breast Cancer Foundation College Scholarship Awards, (F–s) 1062

Sussman Trust Grants. *See* Otto Sussman Trust Grants, entry (D–g) 913

Swift Educational Trust Scholarships. *See* Francis P. Matthews and John E. Swift Educational Trust Scholarships, entry (F–s) 986

Switzer Memorial Fellowships. *See* Research Fellowships of the National Institute on Disability and Rehabilitation Research, entry (D–f) 724

Sybil Fong Sam Scholarships, (C–s) 448

Syle Memorial Fellowship for Seminary Studies. *See* Henry Syle Memorial Fellowship for Seminary Studies, entry (H–f) 286

Sylvia Stein Memorial Space Grant Scholarship. *See* Pennsylvania Space Grant Consortium Scholarships, entry (D–s) 575

Tanner McQuiston Memorial Scholarship. *See* Award of Excellence Asthma Scholarships, entry (C–s) 366

Tarbell Scholarships. *See* Scott Tarbell Scholarships, entry (C–s) 442

TechConnect Low Interest Loan Program, (D–l) 793

Ted Scripps Fellowships in Environmental Journalism, (D–f) 740

ten Broek Merit Scholarship. *See* Hazel ten Broek Merit Scholarship, entries (V–s) 47, (V–f) 144

Tennessee Dependent Children Scholarship, (F–s) 1063

Tennessee Income Tax Exemption for Blind Residents, (V–g) 255

Tennessee Income Tax Exemption for Quadriplegics, (O–g) 353

Tennessee Property Tax Relief for Disabled and Elderly Homeowners, (D–g) 932

Tennessee Property Tax Relief for Disabled Veterans and Their Spouses, (V–g) 256, (O–g) 354, (D–g) 933, (F–g) 1185

Terry Zahn Scholarships, (C–s) 449

Texas Blind/Deaf Student Exemption Program, (V–s) 112, (H–s) 277

Texas Children of Disabled or Deceased Firemen, Peace Officers, Game Wardens, and Employees of Correctional Institutions Exemption Program, (F–s) 1064

Texas Exemption for Peace Officers Disabled in the Line of Duty, (D–s) 596

Texas Property Tax Exemption for Disabled Veterans and their Families, (V–g) 257, (O–g) 355, (D–g) 934, (F–g) 1186

Texas Space Grant Consortium Graduate Fellowships, (D–f) 741

Texas Space Grant Consortium Undergraduate Scholarships, (D–s) 597

Texas Veterans Home Improvement Program, (D–l) 794

Texas Veterans Housing Assistance Program, (D–l) 795

Texas 4–H Courageous Heart Scholarships, (D–s) 598

Theodore R. and Vivian M. Johnson Scholarship Program, (D–s) 599

Theresa C. Herron Memorial Scholarship, (V–g) 258

Third Marine Division Association Memorial Scholarship Fund, (F–s) 1065

V–Visual	H–Hearing	O–Orthopedic/Developmental	C–Communication/Other	D–Disabilities in General	F–Families
s–scholarships		f–fellowships/grants	l–loans	g–grants-in-aid	a–awards

PROGRAM TITLE INDEX

Thorn Memorial Scholarship. *See* Pennsylvania National Guard Scholarship Fund, entry (F–s) 1055

Tim Haas Scholarship. *See* Hemophilia Health Services Memorial Scholarships, entries (C–s) 398, (C–f) 463

Tim & Tom Gullikson Foundation College Scholarships, (C–s) 450, (F–s) 1066

TIP Grants. *See* Wisconsin Talent Incentive Program (TIP) Grants, entry (D–s) 613

Todd M. Richardson Memorial Scholarship. *See* Hemophilia Resources of America Scholarships, entries (C–s) 400, (F–s) 996

Torres Scholarship. *See* Ferdinand Torres Scholarship, entry (V–s) 33

Townsend Memorial Scholarship. *See* Utah Hemophilia Foundation Scholarships, entries (C–s) 451, (F–s) 1069

Transportation Loan Guarantee Program, (D–l) 796

Travis Roy Foundation Grants, (O–g) 356

Troy Barboza Education Fund, (D–s) 600, (F–s) 1067

Trundle, 1885, Fellowship. *See* GUAA Graduate Fellowship Fund, entry (H–f) 284

ULS Assistive Technology Loan Program, (D–l) 797

UNCF Liberty Scholarships, (F–s) 1068

Undergraduate Awards of Lighthouse International, (V–s) 113

University Legal Services Assistive Technology Loan Program. *See* ULS Assistive Technology Loan Program, entry (D–l) 797

USA Funds Access to Education Scholarships, (D–s) 601, (D–f) 742

USAA Scholarship. *See* Pennsylvania National Guard Scholarship Fund, entry (F–s) 1055

Utah Assistive Technology Foundation Loan Program, (D–l) 798

Utah Elks Association Handicapped Student Scholarship Award, (D–s) 602

Utah Hemophilia Foundation Scholarships, (C–s) 451, (F–s) 1069

Utah Property Tax Exemption for Disabled Veterans, (D–g) 935, (F–g) 1187

VA Home Loan Guaranties, (D–l) 799, (F–l) 1100

van Eys Scholarship Award. *See* Dugdale/van Eys Scholarship Award, entries (C–s) 383, (F–s) 976

Van Landingham Scholarship. *See* Arizona Council of the Blind Scholarship Program, entries (V–s) 8, (V–f) 122

Vaz Scholarship. *See* Katherine Vaz Scholarship, entry (H–s) 271

Vermont Adaptive Equipment Revolving Loan Fund, (D–l) 800

Vermont Property Tax Exemption for Disabled Veterans, (D–g) 936, (F–g) 1188

Vermont Space Grant Undergraduate Scholarships, (D–s) 603

Veterans Disability Compensation, (D–g) 937

VFW Ladies Auxiliary Cancer Aid Grants, (C–g) 506

Virginia Public Safety Foundation Scholarships, (F–s) 1070

Virginia Space Grant Aerospace Graduate Research Fellowships, (D–f) 743

Virginia Space Grant Aerospace Undergraduate Research Scholarships, (D–s) 604

Virginia Space Grant Community College Scholarship Program, (D–s) 605

Virginia Space Grant Teacher Education Scholarship Program, (D–s) 606

Virginia War Orphans Education Program, (F–s) 1071, (F–f) 1094

Vivian M. Johnson Scholarship Program. *See* Theodore R. and Vivian M. Johnson Scholarship Program, entry (D–s) 599

Vivian Menees Nelson Music Award for the Disabled and Visually Impaired, (V–a) 263, (D–a) 956

Vocational Rehabilitation for Disabled Veterans, (D–s) 607, (D–f) 744, (D–g) 938

Volta Scholarship Award. *See* Alexander Graham Bell Association College Scholarship Awards, entries (H–s) 264, (H–f) 280

Von Hagen Scholarship Award. *See* Alexander Graham Bell Association College Scholarship Awards, entries (H–s) 264, (H–f) 280

Waldo T., '49 and Jean Kelsch, '51, Cordano Fellowship. *See* GUAA Graduate Fellowship Fund, entry (H–f) 284

Walker Scholarship. *See* Linwood Walker Scholarship, entry (V–f) 161

Wallace Adaptive Equipment Loan Program. *See* mPower Adaptive Equipment Loan Program, entry (D–l) 781

Walls III Scholarship. *See* Lester Walls III Scholarship, entries (D–s) 548, (D–f) 684

Walsh Junior Awards for the Handicapped. *See* Joyce Walsh Junior Disability Award, entry (D–a) 946

Walter Hamilton Scholarship, (C–s) 452, (C–f) 472

Walter Young Memorial Scholarship, (V–s) 114, (V–f) 180

Washington Council of the Blind Scholarships, (V–s) 115, (V–f) 181

Washington Legion Auxiliary Department Gift Scholarships, (F–s) 1072

Washington State Trial Lawyers Association Presidents' Scholarship. *See* WSTLA Presidents' Scholarship, entry (D–s) 615

Webb–McKinney Scholarship. *See* Nora Webb–McKinney Scholarship, entries (V–s) 95, (V–f) 171

Weigner Award. *See* Dorothy Weigner Award, entry (C–f) 460

V–Visual   H–Hearing   O–Orthopedic/Developmental   C–Communication/Other   D–Disabilities in General   F–Families
s–scholarships   f–fellowships/grants   l–loans   g–grants-in-aid   a–awards

PROGRAM TITLE INDEX

Weitbrecht Scholarship Awards. *See* Alexander Graham Bell Association College Scholarship Awards, entries (H–s) 264, (H–f) 280
Wendy F. Miller Parent of the Year National Recognition Award, (F–a) 1191
Werner A. Baum Undergraduate Scholarship. *See* American Meteorological Society Undergraduate Scholarships, entry (D–s) 513
West Virginia Homestead Exemption, (D–g) 939
West Virginia Senior Citizen or Disability Income Tax Deduction, (D–g) 940, (F–g) 1189
West Virginia Space Grant Consortium Graduate Fellowship Program, (D–f) 745
West Virginia Space Grant Consortium Research Capability Enhancement Mini–Grants, (D–f) 746
West Virginia Space Grant Consortium Research Initiation Grants, (D–f) 747
West Virginia Space Grant Consortium Undergraduate NASA Space Grant Fellowships, (D–s) 608
West Virginia Space Grant Consortium Undergraduate Scholarship Program, (D–s) 609
Willard Bernbaum Scholarship, (C–f) 473
William and Dorothy Ferrell Scholarship Award, (V–s) 116, (V–f) 182
William C. Stokoe Scholarship, (H–f) 290
William G. Corey Memorial Scholarship, (V–s) 117, (V–f) 183
William L. Woolard Educational Grant Program, (F–s) 1073
William May Memorial Scholarship. *See* California Association for Postsecondary Education and Disability Scholarships, entries (D–s) 518, (D–f) 640
Williams, '32, Fellowship. *See* GUAA Graduate Fellowship Fund, entry (H–f) 284
Wilma H. Wright Memorial Scholarship, (V–s) 118
Winkler Scholarship Awards. *See* Alexander Graham Bell Association College Scholarship Awards, entries (H–s) 264, (H–f) 280
Wisconsin Council of the Blind Loans, (V–l) 187
Wisconsin Council of the Blind Scholarships, (V–s) 119
Wisconsin Disability Income Exclusion, (D–g) 941
Wisconsin Hearing and Visually Handicapped Student Grant Program, (V–s) 120, (H–s) 278
Wisconsin Part–Time Study Grants for Veterans and Their Dependents, (D–s) 610, (D–f) 748
Wisconsin Space Grant Consortium Graduate Fellowships, (D–f) 749
Wisconsin Space Grant Consortium Research Infrastructure Program, (D–f) 750
Wisconsin Space Grant Consortium Undergraduate Research Awards, (D–s) 611
Wisconsin Space Grant Consortium Undergraduate Scholarships, (D–s) 612
Wisconsin Talent Incentive Program (TIP) Grants, (D–s) 613
Wisconsin Tuition and Fee Reimbursement Grants, (D–s) 614
Wisconsin Veterans' Subsistence Aid Grants, (D–g) 942, (F–g) 1190
Wolff, M.D. Fellowship in International Health. *See* Diplomacy Fellowships, entry (D–f) 651
Woolard Educational Grant Program. *See* William L. Woolard Educational Grant Program, entry (F–s) 1073
Wright Memorial Scholarship. *See* Wilma H. Wright Memorial Scholarship, entry (V–s) 118
WSTLA Presidents' Scholarship, (D–s) 615
Wyoming Education Benefits for National Guard Family Members, (F–s) 1074
Wyoming Space Grant Consortium Undergraduate Research Fellowships, (D–s) 616

Yellow Ribbon Scholarship, (D–s) 617
Yetso Memorial Scholarship. *See* Marilyn Yetso Memorial Scholarship, entry (F–s) 1027
Young Memorial Scholarship. *See* Walter Young Memorial Scholarship, entries (V–s) 114, (V–f) 180
Youth Opportunity Scholarships, (C–s) 453
Youtsey Memorial Scholarship Fund. *See* John Youtsey Memorial Scholarship Fund, entries (C–s) 410, (F–s) 1007

Zahn Scholarships. *See* Terry Zahn Scholarships, entry (C–s) 449
Ziskind Memorial Scholarship. *See* Hydrocephalus Association Scholarships, entries (C–s) 402, (C–f) 464

11 September Memorial Scholarship, (D–s) 618, (F–s) 1075
11th Armored Cavalry Veterans of Vietnam and Cambodia Scholarship, (F–s) 1076

| V–Visual | H–Hearing | O–Orthopedic/Developmental | C–Communication/Other | D–Disabilities in General | F–Families |
| s–scholarships | | f–fellowships/grants | l–loans | g–grants-in-aid | a–awards |

Sponsoring Organization Index

The Sponsoring Organization Index makes it easy to identify agencies that offer financial aid to persons with disabilities and members of their families. In this index, sponsoring organizations are listed alphabetically, word by word. In addition, we've used a two-character alphabetical code (within parentheses) to help you identify which programs sponsored by these organizations fall within your scope of interest. The first character (capitalized) in the code identifies availability group: V = Visual Disabilities; H = Hearing Disabilities; O = Orthopedic and Developmental Disabilities; C = Communication and Other Disabilities; D = Disabilities in General; F = Families of the Disabled. The second character (lower cased) identifies program type: s = scholarships; f = fellowships/grants; l = loans; g = grants-in-aid; a = awards; and sb = state benefits. Here's how the code works: if the name of a sponsoring organization is followed by (D-f) 260, a program sponsored by that organization is described in the Disabilities in General chapter, under fellowships/grants, in entry 260. If that sponsoring organization's name is followed by another entry number—for example, (F-a) 1070—the same or a different program sponsored by that organization is described in the Families of the Disabled chapter, under awards, in entry 1070. Remember: the numbers cited here refer to program entry numbers, not to page numbers in the book.

Abbott Northwestern Hospital. Sister Kenny Auxiliary, (D-a) 945
ABC Entertainment, (D-f) 622
The Abilities Fund, (D-g) 828
Able Trust, (D-g) 930
Academy of Natural Sciences of Philadelphia, (D-f) 623
Adolph and Esther Gottlieb Foundation, Inc., (D-g) 840
Aerospace Illinois Space Grant Consortium, (D-s) 511, (D-f) 625
AHF, Inc., (C-s) 368
Air Force Aid Society, (F-s) 988, (F-g) 1102
Air Force Officers' Wives' Club of Washington, D.C., (C-s) 358, (C-f) 454
Air Force Sergeants Association, (D-s) 524, (F-s) 973
Air Line Pilots Association, (F-s) 958
Airmen Memorial Foundation, (D-s) 524, (F-s) 973
Alabama Council of the Blind, (V-s) 2
Alabama Department of Rehabilitation Services, (D-l) 751, (F-s) 960
Alabama Department of Revenue, (V-g) 188-189, (D-g) 802-806, (F-g) 1103-1104
Alabama Department of Veterans Affairs, (F-s) 959, (F-f) 1077
Alabama Law Foundation, (F-s) 1022

Alabama State Bar. Workers' Compensation Section, (F-s) 1022
Alaska Independent Blind, (V-s) 70
Alaska. Office of the State Assessor, (D-g) 807
Alexander Graham Bell Association for the Deaf, (H-s) 264-265, 275, (H-f) 280, (H-g) 296, (F-g) 1171
Alliance Bank, (D-l) 773
Alpha One, (D-l) 781
Alternatives in Motion, (O-g) 320
American Academy of Allergy, Asthma & Immunology, (C-s) 366, (C-a) 507
American Academy of Pediatrics, (C-a) 507
American Action Fund for Blind Children and Adults, (V-s) 84, (V-f) 157
American Association for the Advancement of Science, (D-f) 619-621, 645, 650-651, 660, 671, 728, 731
American Association of Museums, (C-f) 459, (D-f) 654
American Association of People with Disabilities, (D-l) 763-764, (D-a) 951
American Cancer Society, (C-s) 434, (C-f) 467
American Cancer Society. California Division, (C-s) 374
American Cancer Society. Florida Division, (C-s) 389
American Cancer Society. Great Lakes Division, (C-s) 391

V-Visual   H-Hearing   O-Orthopedic/Developmental   C-Communication/Other   D-Disabilities in General   F-Families
s-scholarships   f-fellowships/grants   l-loans   g-grants-in-aid   a-awards   sb-state benefits

American Cancer Society. Mid–Atlantic Division, (C–s) 449
American Cancer Society. Mid–South Division, (C–s) 422
American Cancer Society. Midwest Division, (C–s) 423
American Cancer Society. Ohio Division, (C–s) 433
American Cancer Society. Rocky Mountain Division, (C–s) 441
American Cancer Society. Southeast Division, (C–s) 445, (C–f) 470
American Council of the Blind, (V–s) 3–4, 9, 13, 22, 25–27, 32, 36, 39, 60, 63, 94, 99, 102, 105, 117, (V–f) 121, 123, 130, 135, 138, 170, 174, 183, (V–g) 202
American Council of the Blind of Colorado, (V–s) 3
American Council of the Blind of Indiana, (V–s) 44
American Council of the Blind of Maine, (V–s) 102
American Council of the Blind of Maryland, (V–s) 4
American Council of the Blind of Minnesota, (V–s) 5
American Council of the Blind of Ohio, (V–s) 21, 73, 95, (V–f) 154, 161, 171
American Council of the Blind of Oregon, (V–s) 6, (V–g) 190
American Council of the Blind of South Carolina, (V–s) 29, (V–f) 132
American Council of the Blind of Texas, (V–s) 7
American Dental Association. ADA Endowment and Assistance Fund, (D–l) 766, (D–g) 801, (F–g) 1101
American Diabetes Association, (C–s) 382
American Foundation for the Blind, (V–s) 23, 33, 39, 43, 101, 103, 106, (V–f) 129, 138, 156, 173, 175, (V–g) 202
American Guild of Musical Artists, (C–g) 474
American Health Assistance Foundation, (C–g) 475, (F–g) 1105
American Legion. Connecticut Department, (D–g) 827
American Legion. Maryland Department, (F–s) 971, 1029
American Legion. Ohio Auxiliary, (F–s) 1047
American Legion. Oregon Auxiliary, (F–s) 1050–1051
American Legion. Pennsylvania Auxiliary, (F–s) 1054
American Legion. Washington Auxiliary, (F–s) 1072
American Library Association. Association of Specialized and Cooperative Library Agencies, (D–f) 643
American Meteorological Society, (D–s) 513, 546, 551, (D–f) 631, 678
American Nuclear Society, (D–f) 729
American Printing House for the Blind, Inc., (V–a) 259
American Red Cross, (C–s) 395, 404, (F–s) 993
American Savings Bank, (D–l) 770
American Society for Engineering Education, (D–f) 698
American Society of Journalists and Authors, (D–g) 866
American Speech–Language–Hearing Foundation, (D–f) 683
Amgen Inc., (C–s) 360, 434, (C–f) 455, 467, (C–g) 476
AmSouth Bank, (D–l) 769
Amtrak, (D–g) 808
AMVETS. Department of Illinois, (F–s) 1058
Andrew W. Mellon Foundation, (D–f) 632
Arizona Community Foundation, (D–l) 752

Arizona Council of the Blind, (V–s) 8, (V–f) 122
Arizona Department of Revenue, (V–g) 191
Arizona Kidney Foundation, (C–s) 435, (C–g) 477
Arizona MultiBank Community Development Corporation, (D–l) 752
Arizona Technology Access Program, (D–l) 752
Arkansas Assessment Coordination Department, (V–g) 192, (O–g) 321, (D–g) 809, (F–g) 1106
Arkansas Department of Finance and Administration, (D–g) 810–812, (F–g) 1107–1110
Arkansas Department of Higher Education, (F–s) 961
Arkansas Governor's Commission on People with Disabilities, (D–s) 514, (D–f) 634
Arkansas Rehabilitation Services, (D–l) 753
Arkansas Space Grant Consortium, (D–f) 635–636
Armed Forces Insurance Company, (F–s) 1055
Arthritis Foundation. Southern New England Chapter, (C–s) 411
Artists' Fellowship, Inc., (D–g) 813, (F–g) 1111
Assistive Technology Loan Fund Authority, (D–l) 757
Assistive Technology of Minnesota, (D–l) 755
Assistive Technology of Ohio, (D–l) 756
Assistive Technology Resource Centers of Hawaii, (D–l) 770
Assistive Technology Through Action in INdiana, (D–l) 758
Association for Computing Machinery, (D–s) 576
Association for Education and Rehabilitation of the Blind and Visually Impaired, (V–s) 116, (V–f) 182
Association for Education and Rehabilitation of the Blind and Visually Impaired of Ohio, (V–s) 20
Association for Enterprise Opportunity, (D–g) 828
Association for Glycogen Storage Disease, (C–s) 357
Association for Investment Management and Research, (D–s) 512, (F–s) 957
Association for the Education and Rehabilitation of the Blind and Visually Impaired. Arizona Chapter, (V–s) 12, (V–f) 125, (V–g) 195
Association of Blind Citizens, (V–s) 11, (V–g) 193
Association of Investment Professionals, (D–s) 618, (F–s) 1075
Asthma and Allergy Foundation of America. New England Chapter, (C–s) 429
AstraZeneca, (C–s) 434, (C–f) 467
AstraZeneca Pharmaceuticals, L.P., (C–s) 365
Autism Society of America, (C–s) 384, (C–a) 510, (F–a) 1191
Aventis Behring, (C–s) 364, 404, (C–g) 504
Avon Products, Inc., (C–g) 478

Bank of America, (D–l) 784
Bank of America Foundation, (D–s) 515
Bank of New Hampshire, (D–l) 786
Banta Corporation, (C–s) 367
Baptist General Convention of Texas, (H–s) 267

V–Visual   H–Hearing   O–Orthopedic/Developmental   C–Communication/Other   D–Disabilities in General   F–Families
s–scholarships   f–fellowships/grants   l–loans   g–grants-in-aid   a–awards   sb–state benefits

SPONSORING ORGANIZATION INDEX

Barr Foundation, (O–g) 323
Baxter Health Care Corporation, (C–s) 404
Bay State Council of the Blind, (V–s) 13
Bayer Corporation, (C–s) 404
Beacon Mutual Insurance Company, (F–s) 963
Billie Jean King WTT Charities, Inc., (C–s) 382
Billy Barty Foundation, (O–s) 303, (F–s) 981
Blackhorse Association, (F–s) 965
Blanche Fischer Foundation, (O–s) 300, (O–f) 314, (O–g) 324
Blinded Veterans Association, (F–s) 1008, (F–f) 1085
Bodman Foundation, (D–a) 951
Bone Marrow Foundation, (C–g) 503
Boomer Esiason Foundation, (C–s) 370, (C–f) 456, (C–g) 479
Boston University School of Law, (D–a) 953
Braille Institute of America, (V–s) 39, (V–f) 138, (V–g) 202
Braille Revival League of Missouri, (V–f) 121
Bristol Myers–Squib Oncology, (C–s) 434, (C–f) 467
Bristol–Myers Squibb Company, (C–g) 480
Bristol–Myers Squibb Oncology, (C–s) 373, (C–f) 457
Buffett Foundation, (D–s) 516

California Assistive Technology System, (D–l) 754, 796
California Association for Postsecondary Education and Disability, (V–s) 114, (V–f) 180, (C–s) 447, (C–f) 471, (D–s) 518, 521, 526, 550, (D–f) 640, 642
California Community Colleges, (D–s) 519
California Council of the Blind, (V–s) 15, (V–f) 127, (V–l) 184
California. Department of Housing and Community Development, (V–g) 196, (O–g) 325, (D–g) 814, (F–g) 1112
California Department of Rehabilitation, (D–l) 754, 796
California Department of Veterans Affairs, (D–l) 759, (F–s) 967–969
California Governor's Committee on Employment of People with Disabilities, (D–s) 539, (D–a) 943–944, 949, 955
California Space Grant Consortium, (D–f) 641
California. State Controller's Office, (V–g) 197, (D–g) 815
California State University. Office of the Chancellor, (V–s) 19, (V–f) 128
California Student Aid Commission, (F–s) 970
California–Hawaii Elks Association, (D–s) 520
Canadian National Institute for the Blind, (V–s) 39, (V–f) 138, (V–g) 202
Cancer Care, Inc., (C–g) 476, 478, 480–481, 490, 492, 505
Cancer Survivors' Fund, (C–s) 376, (C–f) 458
The Center for Reintegration, Inc., (C–s) 415, (C–f) 466
The Center for Scholarship Administration, Inc., (D–s) 515
Center for Science in the Public Interest, (D–f) 710
Centers for Independent Living, (D–l) 779, 793

Cerebral Palsy of New Jersey, (D–s) 549
ChairScholars Foundation, Inc., (O–s) 301
Challenged Athletes Foundation, (D–g) 816
CHARO Community Development Corporation, (D–g) 828
Children of Deaf Adults, (F–s) 1032
Choice Source Therapeutics, (C–s) 451, (F–s) 1069
Christian Record Services, (V–s) 17
Christopher Reeve Paralysis Foundation, (D–f) 644
City First Bank of DC, (D–l) 797
Coalition of Citizens with Disabilities in Illinois, (D–l) 793
CODA International, (F–s) 1032
College Art Association of America, (D–f) 666, 722–723
Colorado Commission on Higher Education, (F–s) 974
Colorado Department of Revenue, (D–g) 819–821
Community Business Network, (D–g) 828
Comptroller of Maryland, (V–g) 217–218, (D–g) 869, (F–g) 1136–1137
Connecticut Department of Economic and Community Development, (D–l) 776, (D–g) 841, (F–l) 1097, (F–g) 1122
Connecticut Department of Social Services. Bureau of Rehabilitation Services, (D–l) 761
Connecticut Department of Veterans' Affairs, (D–g) 827
Connecticut. Office of Policy and Management, (V–g) 198, (D–g) 822–826, (F–g) 1114–1115
Connecticut Space Grant College Consortium, (D–s) 527–529, (D–f) 646–647
ConvaTec, (C–s) 405
Corporation for Independent Living, (D–l) 776, (D–g) 841, (F–l) 1097, (F–g) 1122
Council for Exceptional Children, (D–s) 582, 587–590
Council of Citizens with Low Vision International, (V–s) 38, (V–f) 137
Covad Communications Group, Inc., (D–g) 828
Crohn's and Colitis Foundation of America, (C–s) 405
Cystic Fibrosis Foundation, (C–f) 473
Cystic Fibrosis Scholarship Foundation, (C–s) 380

DaimlerChrysler Corporation, (D–g) 829
DakotaLink, (D–l) 762
Delaware Commission of Veterans Affairs, (O–g) 326
Delaware Community Foundation, (C–s) 453
Delaware Council of the Blind and Visually Impaired, (V–s) 59
Delaware. Division of Revenue, (V–g) 199, (D–g) 830
Delaware Valley Space Grant College Consortium, (D–s) 530, (D–f) 697
Delta Gamma Foundation, (V–s) 23, 107, 118, (V–f) 129, 176
Design Automation Conference, (D–s) 576
Detroit Entrepreneurship Institute, Inc., (D–g) 828
Digital Federal Credit Union, (D–l) 763–764
Disabled American Veterans, (D–g) 831
Disabled American Veterans Auxiliary, (F–l) 1095

V–Visual   H–Hearing   O–Orthopedic/Developmental   C–Communication/Other   D–Disabilities in General   F–Families
s–scholarships   f–fellowships/grants   l–loans   g–grants-in-aid   a–awards   sb–state benefits

Disabled Children's Relief Fund, (D–g) 832
Disabled Workers Committee, (F–s) 975
District of Columbia Space Grant Consortium, (D–s) 531, (D–f) 653
Donald D. Hammill Foundation, (D–f) 657
Dramatists Guild Fund, Inc., (D–l) 765

EAR Foundation, (H–s) 272
Eastern Amputee Golf Association, (O–s) 302, (F–s) 977
Eli Lilly and Company, (C–s) 415, (C–f) 466
Elks National Foundation, (F–s) 979
Entomological Society of America, (D–s) 586, (D–f) 736
Epilepsy Foundation, (C–a) 508
Epilepsy Foundation of Idaho, (C–s) 393, 419, (C–g) 487
Epilepsy Foundation of Kansas and Western Missouri, (C–g) 485
Epilepsy Foundation of Kentuckiana, (C–s) 443
Epilepsy Foundation of Massachusetts & Rhode Island, (C–s) 385, (C–f) 461
Epilepsy Foundation of New Jersey, (C–s) 386
Epilepsy Foundation of Vermont, (C–s) 406
Eric Delson Memorial Scholarship Program, (C–s) 387, (C–f) 462
Essex County Bar Association, (D–f) 638
Ethel Louise Armstrong Foundation, (D–f) 659

FACES: The National Craniofacial Association, (O–g) 335
Factor Support Network Pharmacy, (C–s) 425, (F–s) 1031
Fannie Mae, (D–l) 783, (F–l) 1099
FFF Enterprise, Inc., (C–s) 404
Fifth Third Bank, (D–l) 756, 758, 774
Financial Health Credit Union, (D–l) 779
First Cavalry Division Association, (F–s) 983
First Hand Foundation, (D–g) 836
First Marine Division Association, (F–s) 984
First National Bank, (D–l) 788
First Security Bank of Missoula, (D–l) 780
First Union National Bank, (D–l) 790
Firstar Bank, (D–l) 755
Florida Alliance for Assistive Services and Technology, Inc., (D–l) 769
Florida Council of the Blind, (V–s) 34
Florida Department of Education, (F–s) 985
Florida Department of Veterans' Affairs, (V–g) 201, (O–g) 327, (D–g) 837, (F–g) 1119
Florida Space Grant Consortium, (D–s) 536, (D–f) 663
Ford Motor Company, (O–g) 328
Forward Face, (O–s) 304, (F–g) 1120
Foundation for Science and Disability, Inc., (D–f) 669
Fraternal Order of Eagles, (D–g) 833
Freedom Scientific Inc., (V–s) 39, (V–f) 138, (V–g) 202
Friends–in–Art, (V–s) 40

Gallaudet University, (H–f) 283
Gallaudet University Alumni Association, (H–f) 279, 281–282, 284, 286, 289
General Conference of Seventh–Day Adventists, (V–s) 17
General Motors, (H–g) 291, (O–g) 330
Geological Society of America, (D–s) 537, (D–f) 664
Georgia Council of the Blind, (V–s) 41, (V–f) 139, (F–s) 989, (F–f) 1079
Georgia Department of Revenue, (V–g) 203, (D–g) 838–839, (F–g) 1121
Georgia Space Grant Consortium, (D–s) 538, (D–f) 665
Georgia Student Finance Commission, (F–s) 990–991
Geraldine R. Dodge Foundation, (D–f) 666, 722–723
GiveTech.org, (O–g) 329
GlaxoSmithKline, (C–s) 390, 434, (C–f) 467, (C–a) 508
Great Lakes Hemophilia Foundation, (C–s) 392, (F–s) 992
Greater Kanawha Valley Foundation, (F–s) 1021
Greyhound Lines, Inc., (D–g) 842

Harry Alan Gregg Foundation, (D–s) 540, (D–g) 843
Hartford Foundation for Public Giving, (C–s) 403
Hawai'i Community Foundation, (C–s) 394, (D–s) 600, (F–s) 1067
Hawaii. Department of Taxation, (V–g) 204, (H–g) 292, (C–g) 488, (D–g) 845
Hawaii. Office of Veterans Services, (D–g) 844, 846, (F–g) 1123
Hemophilia Association of New Jersey, (C–s) 371, 439, 452, (C–f) 472
Hemophilia Federation of America, (C–s) 396
Hemophilia Foundation of Greater Florida, (C–s) 375
Hemophilia Foundation of Michigan, (C–s) 369, 397, (C–g) 489, (F–s) 964, 994
Hemophilia Health Services, (C–s) 398, 442, (C–f) 463
Hemophilia of Georgia, (C–s) 410, (F–s) 1007
Hemophilia of Iowa, Inc., (C–s) 399, (F–s) 995
Hemophilia Resources of America, (C–s) 400, (F–s) 996
Hemophilia Society of Colorado, (C–s) 418, 424, (F–s) 1028
Hispanic Scholarship Fund, (C–s) 430, (F–s) 1041
Hydrocephalus Association, (C–s) 402, (C–f) 464

Idaho Assistive Technology Project, (D–l) 771
Idaho Community Foundation, (D–l) 771
Idaho Department of Health and Welfare, (F–g) 1124
Idaho Division of Veterans Services, (D–g) 850, (F–g) 1127
Idaho Space Grant Consortium, (D–s) 542–543, (D–f) 672–674
Idaho State Board of Education, (D–s) 541, (F–s) 999
Idaho State Council on Developmental Disabilities, (F–g) 1124

V–Visual   H–Hearing   O–Orthopedic/Developmental   C–Communication/Other   D–Disabilities in General   F–Families
s–scholarships   f–fellowships/grants   l–loans   g–grants-in-aid   a–awards   sb–state benefits

Idaho State Tax Commission, (V–g) 205–206, (C–g) 491, (D–g) 848–849, (F–g) 1125–1126
Illinois Assistive Technology Project, (D–l) 793
Illinois Council of the Blind, (V–s) 37, (V–f) 136
Illinois Department of Human Services. Office of Rehabilitation Services, (D–l) 793
Illinois Department of Revenue, (V–g) 208, (D–g) 852
Illinois Department of Veterans' Affairs, (V–g) 207, (O–g) 331, (D–s) 544, (D–g) 851, (F–s) 1002–1003, (F–g) 1128
Illinois Network of Centers for Independent Living, (D–l) 793
Illinois Student Assistance Commission, (F–s) 1000–1001, (F–f) 1081
Immune Deficiency Foundation, (C–s) 404
Indiana. Department of Local Government Finance, (V–g) 210, (D–g) 856–857, (F–g) 1130
Indiana Department of Revenue, (V–g) 209, (D–g) 855
Indiana Space Grant Consortium, (D–s) 545, (D–f) 675
Institute of Electrical and Electronics Engineers. Circuits and Systems Society, (D–s) 576
Institute of Management Accountants, (V–s) 53, (V–f) 149, (H–s) 270, (H–f) 288, (O–s) 306, (O–f) 315
International Alumnae of Delta Epsilon Sorority, (H–f) 287
Iowa Able Foundation, (D–l) 772
Iowa COMPASS, (D–l) 772
Iowa Council of the United Blind. Des Moines Chapter, (V–s) 24
Iowa Department of Revenue, (D–g) 858–859, (F–g) 1131
Iowa Program for Assistive Technology, (D–l) 772

Jack Kent Cooke Foundation, (F–s) 966
Jay's World Childhood Cancer Foundation, (C–s) 407
Jewish Braille Institute of America, Inc., (V–f) 153
Jewish Deaf Congress, (H–s) 269
Joseph P. Kennedy, Jr. Foundation, (F–f) 1092

Kansas Assistive Technology Cooperative, (D–l) 773
Kansas Department of Revenue, (V–g) 211–212, (D–g) 860–862, (F–g) 1132
Kansas Federation of Business & Professional Women's Clubs, Inc., (C–s) 381
Kansas Space Grant Consortium, (D–s) 547, (D–f) 680
Kansas State Department of Education. Kansas Project for Children and Young Adults Who Are Deaf–Blind, (V–g) 213, (H–g) 293, (D–g) 863
Kentucky Assistive Technology Loan Corporation, (D–l) 774
Kentucky Association of Vocational Education Special Needs Personnel, (D–s) 592–593
Kentucky Department of Veterans Affairs, (F–s) 1010
Kentucky Fire Commission, (F–s) 1009
Kentucky Hemophilia Foundation, (C–s) 401, (F–s) 997

Kentucky Housing Corporation, (D–l) 774
Kentucky Revenue Cabinet, (D–g) 864
Kentucky Space Grant Consortium, (D–f) 681
KeyBank, (D–l) 771
Kids' Chance, Inc., (F–s) 1023
Kids' Chance Inc. of Missouri, (F–s) 1018
Kids' Chance of Arizona, (F–s) 1011
Kids' Chance of Arkansas, (F–s) 1012
Kids' Chance of Indiana, Inc., (F–s) 1013, (F–f) 1086
Kids' Chance of Iowa, (F–s) 1014
Kids' Chance of Louisiana, (F–s) 1015
Kids' Chance of Maryland, Inc., (F–s) 1016
Kids' Chance of Pennsylvania, (F–s) 1019
Kids' Chance of South Carolina, (F–s) 1020, (F–f) 1087
Kids' Chance of West Virginia, Inc., (F–s) 1021
Knights of Columbus, (F–s) 986
Kurzweil Foundation, (V–s) 3–4, 9, 13, 22, 25–28, 31–32, 36, 45, 50–51, 57, 63–65, 74–75, 92, 94, 99, 102, 105, 108, 117, (V–f) 121, 123, 130–131, 133, 135, 142, 147–148, 152, 157–158, 163–164, 169–170, 174, 177, 183

LA Kelley Communications, (C–s) 388, (F–s) 980
Landscape Architecture Foundation, (D–s) 548, (D–f) 684
Leaders in Furthering Education, (D–a) 947
Learning Disabilities Association of California, (C–s) 409
Lighthouse International, (V–s) 18, 68, 113, (V–f) 141
Limbs for Life Foundation, (O–g) 332
Lions Clubs International, (V–s) 69, (V–f) 162, (V–g) 214
Little People of America, (C–s) 416
Louisiana Assistive Technology Access Network, (D–l) 775
Louisiana Bar Foundation, (F–s) 1015
Louisiana Department of Veterans Affairs, (F–s) 1024
Louisiana Space Consortium, (D–f) 682
Luso–American Education Foundation, (H–s) 271

Maine. Bureau of Maine Veterans' Services, (F–s) 1025, (F–f) 1088
Maine Employers' Mutual Insurance Company, (F–s) 998, (F–f) 1080
Maine. Finance Authority, (D–l) 781
Maine Revenue Services, (V–g) 215–216, (O–g) 333, (D–g) 868, (F–g) 1134–1135
Mary Kay Ash Charitable Foundation, (C–g) 492
Maryland Higher Education Commission, (D–s) 533, (D–f) 658, (F–s) 978, (F–f) 1078
Maryland Space Grant Consortium, (D–s) 552
Maryland. State Department of Assessments and Taxation, (V–g) 219, (D–g) 870–871, (F–g) 1138–1139
Maryland Technology Assistance Program, (D–l) 778, (F–l) 1098

V–Visual   H–Hearing   O–Orthopedic/Developmental   C–Communication/Other   D–Disabilities in General   F–Families
s–scholarships   f–fellowships/grants   l–loans   g–grants-in-aid   a–awards   sb–state benefits

SPONSORING ORGANIZATION INDEX

Massachusetts Department of Revenue, (V–g) 220
Massachusetts. Department of Veterans' Services, (V–g) 221, (D–g) 872–873, (F–g) 1140
Massachusetts Housing Finance Agency, (O–l) 317–318
Massachusetts Office of Student Financial Assistance, (V–s) 72, (D–s) 525, 553
Massachusetts Space Grant Consortium, (D–s) 554, (D–f) 685
Mays Mission for the Handicapped, (O–s) 307, (C–s) 421
McNeil Consumer & Specialty Pharmaceuticals, (C–s) 378
Michigan Association for Deaf, Hearing and Speech Services, (H–s) 266, (C–s) 372
Michigan. Department of Military and Veterans Affairs, (D–g) 878, (F–s) 1030, (F–g) 1142
Michigan Department of Treasury, (V–g) 222–223, (H–g) 294, (O–g) 334, (D–g) 876–877, (F–g) 1141
Michigan Disability Rights Coalition, (D–l) 779
Michigan Elks Association, (D–g) 875
Michigan Space Grant Consortium, (D–s) 555, (D–f) 689–690
Milbank Foundation for Rehabilitation, (D–a) 951
Milton & Sally Avery Arts Foundation, (D–f) 722–723
Minnesota Department of Veterans Affairs, (D–s) 557, (D–g) 879, (F–g) 1143
Minnesota Space Grant Consortium, (D–s) 556, (D–f) 691
Mississippi Bar Foundation, (F–s) 1017
Mississippi Council of the Blind, (V–s) 54, (V–f) 150, (F–s) 1005, (F–f) 1083
Mississippi Office of Student Financial Aid, (F–s) 1033, (F–g) 1144
Mississippi Space Grant Consortium, (D–s) 558, (D–f) 692
Mississippi State Tax Commission, (V–g) 224–225, (D–g) 881, (F–g) 1145
Mississippi State Veterans Affairs Board, (D–g) 880
Missouri Assistive Technology, (D–l) 792
Missouri Council of the Blind, (V–g) 227
Missouri Department of Higher Education, (F–s) 1034
Missouri Department of Revenue, (D–g) 882, (F–g) 1146
Missouri Department of Social Services, (V–g) 226, 228
Missouri Vocational Special Need Association, (D–s) 560
Mitsubishi Electric America Foundation, (D–a) 951
Montana Department of Revenue, (V–g) 229, (D–g) 883, (F–g) 1147–1148
Montana Space Grant Consortium, (D–s) 559, (D–f) 693–694
Montana Veterans Affairs Division, (D–g) 884, (F–g) 1149
Muscular Dystrophy Association, (C–g) 493
Musicians Foundation, Inc., (D–g) 885

National Amputee Golf Association, (O–s) 308, (F–s) 1035
National Association of the Deaf, (H–f) 290, (H–a) 298
National Association of Vocational Education Special Needs Personnel, (D–s) 561
National Center for Learning Disabilities, (C–s) 363

National Federation of Music Clubs, (V–a) 261, 263, (D–a) 946, 956
National Federation of the Blind, (V–s) 28, 31, 39, 45, 50–51, 57, 64–65, 74–75, 92, 108, (V–f) 131, 133, 138, 142, 147–148, 152, 157–158, 163–164, 169, 177, (V–l) 185, (V–g) 202, (V–a) 260
National Federation of the Blind of Alabama, (V–s) 76
National Federation of the Blind of Arizona, (V–s) 55, (V–f) 151
National Federation of the Blind of Arkansas, (V–s) 77
National Federation of the Blind of California, (V–s) 42, 66–67, 78, (V–f) 140, 159–160, 165
National Federation of the Blind of Colorado, (V–s) 79
National Federation of the Blind of Connecticut, (V–s) 52, 62, 71, (V–g) 249
National Federation of the Blind of Florida, (V–s) 80
National Federation of the Blind of Idaho, (V–s) 81
National Federation of the Blind of Illinois, (V–s) 82
National Federation of the Blind of Indiana, (V–s) 83
National Federation of the Blind of Kentucky, (V–s) 30
National Federation of the Blind of Maine, (V–s) 111
National Federation of the Blind of Maryland, (V–s) 61
National Federation of the Blind of Michigan, (V–s) 1, 56, 100
National Federation of the Blind of Missouri, (V–s) 49, 58, (V–f) 146, 155
National Federation of the Blind of Nebraska, (V–s) 84
National Federation of the Blind of New Hampshire, (V–s) 35, (V–f) 134, (V–g) 258
National Federation of the Blind of New Mexico, (V–s) 85
National Federation of the Blind of North Carolina, (V–s) 104
National Federation of the Blind of Ohio, (V–s) 86, (V–f) 166
National Federation of the Blind of Oregon, (V–s) 87, (V–f) 167
National Federation of the Blind of Texas, (V–s) 88
National Federation of the Blind of Utah, (V–s) 89, (V–f) 168
National Federation of the Blind of Vermont, (V–s) 90
National Federation of the Blind of Washington, (V–s) 14, 47, (V–f) 126, 144
National Federation of the Blind of Wisconsin, (V–s) 91
National FFA Organization, (D–s) 517
National Foundation for Ectodermal Dysplasias, (O–s) 309, (O–g) 341
National Fraternal Society of the Deaf, (H–s) 273
National Gaucher Foundation, Inc., (C–g) 482–483
National Guard Association of Indiana, (F–s) 1036
National Hemophilia Foundation, (C–s) 413
National Industries for the Blind, (V–s) 94, (V–f) 170
National Kidney Foundation of Arkansas, (C–g) 494
National Kidney Foundation of Colorado, Idaho, Montana and Wyoming, Inc., (C–g) 495
National Kidney Foundation of Connecticut, (C–s) 427, (C–g) 496, (F–s) 1037

V–Visual   H–Hearing   O–Orthopedic/Developmental   C–Communication/Other   D–Disabilities in General   F–Families
s–scholarships   f–fellowships/grants   l–loans   g–grants-in-aid   a–awards   sb–state benefits

SPONSORING ORGANIZATION INDEX

National Kidney Foundation of Indiana, Inc., (C–s) 414, (C–g) 497
National Kidney Foundation of Iowa, Inc., (C–g) 498
National Kidney Foundation of Kentucky, Inc., (C–g) 499
National Kidney Foundation of Massachusetts, Rhode Island, New Hampshire, and Vermont, Inc., (C–s) 428, (F–s) 1038
National Kidney Foundation of Middle Tennessee, Inc., (C–g) 500
National Kidney Foundation of the Virginias, Inc., (C–g) 501
National PKU News, (C–s) 438
National Railroad Passenger Corporation, (D–g) 808
National Science Foundation, (D–f) 620, 624, 679, 709
National Science Foundation. Directorate for Biological Sciences, (D–f) 655, 719–720
National Science Foundation. Directorate for Education and Human Resources, (D–s) 534, (D–f) 661–662, 699, 706, 732
National Science Foundation. Directorate for Engineering, (D–f) 667–668, 707–708
National Science Foundation. Directorate for Geosciences, (D–f) 727
National Science Foundation. Directorate for Mathematical and Physical Sciences, (D–f) 637, 677, 686–688, 707
National Science Foundation. Directorate for Social, Behavioral, and Economic Sciences, (D–f) 648–649, 656
National Science Foundation. Office of Polar Programs, (D–f) 633
National Tourism Foundation, (D–s) 617
National Transplant Assistance Fund, (O–g) 336, (C–g) 502
Navy–Marine Corps Relief Society, (F–s) 962
Nebraska Assistive Technology Partnership, (D–l) 777, 783, (F–l) 1099
Nebraska Association of Blind Students, (V–s) 84
Nebraska. Department of Economic Development, (D–l) 777
Nebraska. Department of Veterans' Affairs, (F–s) 1040
Nebraska Home Of Your Own Coalition, (D–l) 783, (F–l) 1099
Nebraska Space Grant Consortium, (D–s) 562, (D–f) 700
Nevada Community Enrichment Program, (D–l) 784
Nevada Council of the Blind, (V–s) 93
Nevada Division of Rehabilitation, (D–l) 784
Nevada Office of Veterans' Services, (D–g) 887, (F–g) 1151
Nevada Space Grant Consortium, (D–s) 563, (D–f) 701
New Hampshire Charitable Foundation, (D–s) 564, (D–f) 702, (D–l) 785
New Hampshire Department of Revenue Administration, (V–g) 230–231, (O–g) 337–338, (D–g) 888–889, (F–g) 1152–1154

New Hampshire Space Grant Consortium, (D–s) 565, (D–f) 703
New Jersey Department of Health and Senior Services, (D–g) 917, 921
New Jersey Department of Military and Veterans Affairs, (V–g) 236, (O–g) 339, (F–g) 1156
New Jersey Division of Taxation, (V–g) 232–235, (D–g) 890–897, (F–g) 1155
New Jersey Utilities Association, (D–s) 566
New Mexico Community Development Loan Fund, (D–g) 828
New Mexico Department of Veterans' Services, (D–g) 898, (F–g) 1157
New Mexico Taxation and Revenue Department, (V–g) 237, (F–g) 1158
New Mexico Technology Assistance Program, (D–l) 787
New York State Department of Taxation and Finance, (D–g) 900
New York State Division of Veterans' Affairs, (V–g) 238, (O–g) 340, (D–g) 899, (F–g) 1159–1161
New York State Office of Children and Family Services, (D–l) 768
Nina Mason Pulliam Charitable Trust, (D–l) 752
North Carolina A&T State University, (D–f) 711
North Carolina Bar Association, (F–s) 1042, (F–f) 1090
North Carolina Council of the Blind, (V–s) 96
North Carolina Department of Revenue, (V–g) 239, (D–g) 901–902
North Carolina. Division of Veterans Affairs, (F–s) 1044
North Carolina Fraternal Order of Police Foundation, Inc., (F–s) 1039
North Carolina Lions Foundation, (F–s) 1073
North Carolina National Guard Association, (O–s) 310, (C–s) 431, (F–s) 1043
North Carolina Sheriffs' Association, (F–s) 1045
North Carolina State Education Assistance Authority, (F–s) 1045
North Dakota Association for the Disabled, (D–l) 788
North Dakota Association of the Blind, (V–s) 97, (V–f) 172
North Dakota. Department of Veterans Affairs, (F–s) 1046
North Dakota Interagency Program for Assistive Technology, (D–l) 788
North Dakota. Office of State Tax Commissioner, (V–g) 240, (O–g) 342–343, (D–g) 903–904, (F–g) 1162–1165
North Dakota Space Grant Program, (D–s) 567–568, (D–f) 705
Novartis Oncology, (C–s) 432, 434, (C–f) 467
Nuclear Threat Initiative, (D–f) 621
Nurses House, Inc., (D–g) 905

Ohio Aerospace Institute, (D–s) 569–571, (D–f) 712–713
Ohio Arts Council, (D–g) 918
Ohio Board of Regents, (F–s) 1048
Ohio Department of Taxation, (D–g) 907

V–Visual   H–Hearing   O–Orthopedic/Developmental   C–Communication/Other   D–Disabilities in General   F–Families
s–scholarships   f–fellowships/grants   l–loans   g–grants-in-aid   a–awards   sb–state benefits

SPONSORING ORGANIZATION INDEX

Ohio. Governor's Office of Veteran's Affairs, (D–g) 906, (F–g) 1166
Ohio Space Grant Consortium, (D–s) 569–571, (D–f) 712–713
Ohio State University. Byrd Polar Research Center, (D–f) 639
Oklahoma Department of Veterans Affairs, (D–g) 909, (F–g) 1167
Oklahoma NASA Space Grant Consortium, (D–s) 573, (D–f) 715–716
Oklahoma Tax Commission, (V–g) 241, (D–g) 908, (F–g) 1168
Omohundro Institute of Early American History and Culture, (D–f) 632, 714
Opportunities for the Blind, Inc., (V–s) 98, (V–g) 242
Optimist International, (H–a) 299
Oregon Community Foundation, (V–s) 46, (V–f) 143
Oregon Council of the Blind, (V–s) 99
Oregon Council of the Blind, Inc., (V–s) 6, (V–g) 190
Oregon Department of Revenue, (V–g) 243, 245, (O–g) 344, (D–g) 910–912, (F–g) 1169–1170
Oregon Department of Veterans' Affairs, (D–l) 789
Oregon Lions Sight & Hearing Foundation, (V–g) 244, (H–g) 295
Oregon Space Grant, (D–s) 572
Oregon Student Assistance Commission, (V–s) 46, (V–f) 143, (F–s) 1049, 1052, (F–f) 1091
Oticon, (H–s) 276
Otto Sussman Trust, (D–g) 913

P. Buckley Moss Society, (C–s) 362
Panasonic Consumer Electronics Company, (D–a) 950
Patient Advocate Foundation, (C–s) 359–360, 365, 373, 377, 390, 426, 432, 434, (C–f) 455, 457, 467
Peace Officers Research Association of California, (D–s) 577
Pearle Vision Foundation, (V–g) 246
PEN American Center, (C–g) 486
Pennsylvania Assistive Technology Foundation, (D–l) 790
Pennsylvania Association of Vocational Education Special Needs Personnel, (D–a) 952
Pennsylvania. Bureau for Veterans Affairs, (V–g) 247–248, (O–g) 345–346, (D–g) 915–916, (F–s) 1053, (F–g) 1172–1173
Pennsylvania Council of the Blind, (V–s) 25
Pennsylvania Department of Community and Economic Development, (D–l) 790
Pennsylvania Department of Revenue, (D–g) 914
Pennsylvania National Guard Associations, (F–s) 1055
Pennsylvania Space Grant Consortium, (D–s) 575, (D–f) 717
People's Bank, (D–l) 761
Pfizer Inc., (C–s) 436, (C–f) 468
Philippians Foundation, (F–s) 1056

Phonic Ear, (H–s) 276
Piney Mountain Press, (D–s) 561
Pinnacol Foundation, (F–s) 1057
PKU of Illinois, (C–s) 361

Recording for the Blind and Dyslexic, (V–s) 39, (V–f) 138, (V–g) 202, (V–a) 262, (C–s) 417
Renaissance Entrepreneurship Center, (D–g) 828
Rhode Island. Division of Veterans' Affairs, (D–s) 579
Rhode Island Foundation, (F–s) 963
Rhode Island Space Grant, (D–s) 580, (D–f) 726
Robin Romano Memorial Fund, (C–s) 440
Roche Foundation, (C–s) 430, (F–s) 1041
Rocky Mountain NASA Space Grant Consortium, (D–s) 581, (D–f) 730
Roy J. Carver Charitable Trust, (D–s) 522

Sallie Mae 911 Education Fund, (D–g) 920, (F–s) 1059, (F–g) 1177
Saturn Corporation, (O–g) 347
Scholarship America, (C–s) 395, (D–s) 512, 535, 564, 601, (D–f) 702, 742, (D–l) 785, (F–s) 957, 982, 993
Scholarship Program Administrators, (C–s) 398, 442, (C–f) 463
Security Bank of Springfield, (D–l) 793
Self–Employment Loan Fund, (D–g) 828
Sertoma International, (H–s) 276
Seth Sprague Educational and Charitable Foundation, (D–a) 951
Shire US Inc., (C–a) 509
Sickle Cell Disease Association of America, (C–s) 412
Sickle Cell Disease Association of America. Connecticut Chapter, (C–s) 403, 448
Sigma Alpha Iota Philanthropies, Inc., (V–s) 109, (V–f) 178
Sister Kenny Rehabilitation Institute, (D–a) 945
Society of Singers, (D–g) 922
Solvay Pharmaceuticals, Inc., (C–s) 379
South Carolina Comptroller General, (V–g) 251, (D–g) 925
South Carolina Department of Revenue, (O–g) 348, (D–g) 924, 926, (F–g) 1179–1181
South Carolina Office of Veterans Affairs, (V–g) 252, (O–g) 349, (D–g) 927, (F–s) 1060, (F–g) 1182
South Carolina Space Grant Consortium, (D–s) 583, (D–f) 733–734
South Dakota Association of the Blind, (V–s) 22
South Dakota Board of Regents, (V–s) 110, (V–f) 179, (D–s) 584, (F–s) 987
South Dakota Department of Revenue, (O–g) 350, (D–g) 928–929, (F–g) 1183–1184
Southern Baptist Convention. North American Mission Board, (H–s) 268, (H–f) 285
Southern Disability Foundation, Inc., (D–l) 751

V–Visual   H–Hearing   O–Orthopedic/Developmental   C–Communication/Other   D–Disabilities in General   F–Families
s–scholarships   f–fellowships/grants   l–loans   g–grants-in-aid   a–awards   sb–state benefits

SPONSORING ORGANIZATION INDEX

SouthTrust Bank of Alabama, N.A., (D–l) 751
Special People in Need, (D–s) 585, (D–f) 735
Spina Bifida Association of America, (O–s) 305, 312, (O–f) 316
Spina Bifida Association of Connecticut, Inc., (O–s) 313
Starkey, (H–s) 276
Start Up, (D–g) 828
State Student Assistance Commission of Indiana, (F–s) 1004, (F–f) 1082
State University System of Florida, (D–s) 599
Statewide Independent Living Council, (D–l) 793
Stephen T. Marchello Scholarship Foundation, (C–s) 446
SunTrust Bank, (D–l) 757
Supreme Emblem Club of the United States of America, (D–s) 594
Susan G. Komen Breast Cancer Foundation, (F–s) 1062

Tennessee Comptroller of the Treasury, (V–g) 256, (O–g) 354, (D–g) 932–933, (F–g) 1185
Tennessee Department of Revenue, (V–g) 255, (O–g) 353
Tennessee Hemophilia and Bleeding Disorders Foundation, (C–s) 383, (F–s) 976
Tennessee Student Assistance Corporation, (F–s) 1063
Terra Foundation for the Arts, (D–f) 722–723
Texas Higher Education Coordinating Board, (V–s) 112, (H–s) 277, (D–s) 596, (F–s) 1064
Texas Space Grant Consortium, (D–s) 597, (D–f) 741
Texas Veterans Commission, (V–g) 257, (O–g) 355, (D–g) 934, (F–g) 1186
Texas Veterans Land Board, (D–l) 794–795
Texas 4-H Foundation, (D–s) 598
Third Marine Division Association, Inc., (F–s) 1065
Thurgood Marshall Scholarship Fund, (C–s) 430, (F–s) 1041
Tim & Tom Gullikson Foundation, (C–s) 450, (F–s) 1066
Travelers Protective Association of America, (H–s) 274, (H–g) 297
Travis Roy Foundation, (O–g) 356
Turning P.O.I.N.T., (D–a) 948

UCP Michigan, (D–l) 779
Ulman Cancer Fund for Young Adults, (C–s) 420, (F–s) 1027
Union Planters Bank, (D–l) 775
United Amputee Services Association, Inc., (O–g) 323
United Cerebral Palsy, (D–g) 834
United Cerebral Palsy of North Carolina, Inc., (D–g) 865
United Negro College Fund, (O–s) 311, (C–s) 437, (F–s) 1068
United Negro College Fund Special Programs Corporation, (D–f) 670

United States Association of Blind Athletes, (V–s) 10, 48, (V–f) 124, 145
University Legal Services, (D–l) 797
University of Colorado at Boulder. Center for Environmental Journalism, (D–f) 740
University of Houston. African American Studies Program, (D–f) 626
University of New Hampshire. Institute on Disability, (D–l) 786
U.S. Agency for Healthcare Research and Quality, (D–f) 627–630
U.S. Agency for International Development, (D–f) 651
U.S. Air Force. Office of Scientific Research, (D–f) 698
U.S. Army. Research Office, (D–f) 650, 698
U.S. Bank, (D–l) 772
U.S. Centers for Medicare & Medicaid Services, (D–g) 874
U.S. Central Intelligence Agency, (D–s) 523, (D–l) 760
U.S. Court of Federal Claims, (D–g) 886, (F–g) 1150
U.S. Department of Agriculture, (D–f) 728
U.S. Department of Defense, (D–f) 650, 698
U.S. Department of Education. Office of Special Education and Rehabilitative Services, (D–s) 591, (D–f) 724, 737, (D–l) 752, 761
U.S. Department of Homeland Defense, (D–f) 671
U.S. Department of Justice, (D–g) 886, (F–g) 1150
U.S. Department of Labor. Employment Standards Administration, (C–g) 484, (D–g) 867, (F–g) 1113, 1133
U.S. Department of State, (D–f) 651
U.S. Department of Veterans Affairs, (V–l) 186, (V–g) 194, 253, (O–l) 319, (O–g) 322, 351–352, (D–s) 595, 607, (D–f) 739, 744, (D–l) 799, (D–g) 817–818, 847, 853–854, 937–938, (F–s) 1061, (F–f) 1093, (F–l) 1096, 1100, (F–g) 1116, 1129, 1175–1176
U.S. Environmental Protection Agency, (D–f) 660, 728
U.S. Food and Drug Administration, (D–f) 728
U.S. Health Resources and Services Administration, (D–g) 886, (F–g) 1150
U.S. Internal Revenue Service, (V–g) 200, (D–g) 835, (F–g) 1117–1118
U.S. National Aeronautics and Space Administration, (D–g) 511, 527–531, 536, 538, 542–543, 545, 547, 552, 554–556, 558–559, 562–563, 565, 567–573, 575, 580–581, 583, 597, 603–606, 608–609, 611–612, 616, (D–f) 625, 635–636, 641, 646–647, 653, 663, 665, 670, 672–675, 680–682, 685, 689–697, 700–701, 703, 705, 712–713, 715–717, 726, 730, 733–734, 741, 743, 745–747, 749–750
U.S. National Endowment for the Arts, (D–f) 722–723
U.S. National Endowment for the Humanities, (D–f) 714, 722–723
U.S. National Institutes of Health, (D–s) 578, (D–f) 619, 652, 676, 707, 718, 721, 725, 738, (D–l) 782
U.S. National Institutes of Health. Fogarty International Center, (D–f) 651

V–Visual H–Hearing O–Orthopedic/Developmental C–Communication/Other D–Disabilities in General F–Families
s–scholarships f–fellowships/grants l–loans g–grants-in-aid a–awards sb–state benefits

SPONSORING ORGANIZATION INDEX

U.S. National Institutes of Health. National Institute of Arthritis and Musculoskeletal and Skin Diseases, (D–f) 704
U.S. Navy. Office of Naval Research, (D–f) 650, 698, 711
U.S. Railroad Retirement Board, (D–g) 919, (F–g) 1174
U.S. Small Business Administration, (D–l) 791
U.S. Social Security Administration, (V–g) 250, 254, (D–g) 923, 931, (F–g) 1178
USA Funds, (D–s) 601, (D–f) 742
USAA Insurance Corporation, (F–s) 1055
Utah Assistive Technology Foundation, (D–l) 798
Utah Elks Association, (D–s) 602
Utah Hemophilia Foundation, (C–s) 451, (F–s) 1069
Utah Office of Veterans Affairs, (D–g) 935, (F–g) 1187

Vermont Assistive Technology Project, (D–l) 800
Vermont Association for the Blind and Visually Impaired, (V–s) 16, (F–s) 972
Vermont Development Credit Union, (D–l) 800
Vermont. Office of Veterans Affairs, (D–g) 936, (F–g) 1188
Vermont Space Grant Consortium, (D–s) 603
Vermont State Housing Authority, (D–l) 767
Vermont Student Assistance Corporation, (V–s) 16, (C–s) 408, (C–f) 465, (F–s) 972, 1006, (F–f) 1084
Vermont Studio Center, (C–f) 460, (D–f) 644
Very Special Arts, (D–a) 950
Veterans of Foreign Wars. Ladies Auxiliary, (C–g) 506
Virginia Department of Veterans' Affairs, (F–s) 1071, (F–f) 1094
Virginia Public Safety Foundation, Inc., (F–s) 1070
Virginia Space Grant Consortium, (D–s) 604–606, (D–f) 743
Visually Impaired Data Processors International, (V–s) 63
Vocational Foundation of Nebraska, (D–s) 574
VSA Arts, (D–a) 954
VSA Arts of Wisconsin, (D–s) 532

Washington Council of the Blind, (V–s) 115, (V–f) 181
Washington State Trial Lawyers Association, (D–s) 615
Wells Fargo Bank, (D–l) 762, 787
West Virginia Space Grant Consortium, (D–s) 608–609, (D–f) 745–747
West Virginia State Tax Department, (D–g) 939–940, (F–g) 1189
Wisconsin Council of the Blind, (V–s) 119, (V–l) 187
Wisconsin Department of Revenue, (D–g) 941
Wisconsin Department of Veterans Affairs, (D–s) 610, 614, (D–f) 748, (D–g) 942, (F–g) 1190
Wisconsin Foundation for Independent Colleges, Inc., (C–s) 367
Wisconsin Higher Educational Aids Board, (V–s) 120, (H–s) 278, (D–s) 613

Wisconsin Space Grant Consortium, (D–s) 611–612, (D–f) 749–750
Woman's Missionary Union, (F–s) 1026, (F–f) 1089
Women's Opportunities Resource Center, (D–g) 828
Women's Self–Employment Project, (D–g) 828
World Team Tennis, Inc., (C–s) 382
Wyeth Pharmaceuticals, (C–s) 444, (C–f) 469
Wyoming Space Grant, (D–s) 616
Wyoming Veterans' Affairs Commission, (F–s) 1074

Zions Bank, (D–l) 771, 798
ZLB Bioplasma Inc., (C–s) 404

11th Armored Cavalry Veterans of Vietnam and Cambodia, (F–s) 1076

V–Visual   H–Hearing   O–Orthopedic/Developmental   C–Communication/Other   D–Disabilities in General   F–Families
s–scholarships   f–fellowships/grants   l–loans   g–grants-in-aid   a–awards   sb–state benefits

Residency Index

Some programs listed in this book are restricted to residents of a particular city, county, state, or region. Others are open to applicants wherever they may live. The Residency Index will help you pinpoint programs available only to residents in your area as well as programs that have no residency restrictions at all (these are listed under the term "United States"). To use this index, look up the geographic areas that apply to you (always check the listings under "United States"), jot down the entry numbers listed after the availability groups and program types that apply to you, and use those numbers to find the program descriptions in the directory. To help you in your search, we've provided some "see also" references in each index entry. Remember: the numbers cited here refer to program entry numbers, not to page numbers in the book.

Alabama
    Visual disabilities: **Scholarships,** 2, 76; **Grants-in-aid,** 188–189
    Communication and other disabilities: **Scholarships,** 422
    Disabilities in general: **Loans,** 751; **Grants-in-aid,** 802–806
    Families of the disabled: **Scholarships,** 959–960, 1022; **Fellowships/Grants,** 1077; **Grants-in-aid,** 1103–1104
    See also United States
Alaska
    Visual disabilities: **Scholarships,** 70
    Disabilities in general: **Grants-in-aid,** 807
    See also United States
Arizona
    Visual disabilities: **Scholarships,** 8, 12, 55; **Fellowships/Grants,** 122, 125, 151; **Grants-in-aid,** 191, 195
    Communication and other disabilities: **Scholarships,** 435; **Grants-in-aid,** 477
    Disabilities in general: **Scholarships,** 515, 601; **Fellowships/Grants,** 742; **Loans,** 752; **Grants-in-aid,** 828
    Families of the disabled: **Scholarships,** 1011
    See also United States
Arkansas
    Visual disabilities: **Scholarships,** 77; **Grants-in-aid,** 192
    Orthopedic and developmental disabilities: **Grants-in-aid,** 321
    Communication and other disabilities: **Scholarships,** 422; **Grants-in-aid,** 494

    Disabilities in general: **Scholarships,** 514–515; **Fellowships/Grants,** 634–636; **Loans,** 753; **Grants-in-aid,** 809–812
    Families of the disabled: **Scholarships,** 961, 1012; **Grants-in-aid,** 1106–1110
    See also United States

Bronx County, New York. See New York, New York
Bronx, New York. See New York, New York
Brooklyn, New York. See New York, New York

California
    Visual disabilities: **Scholarships,** 15, 19, 42, 66–67, 78, 114; **Fellowships/Grants,** 127–128, 140, 159–160, 165, 180; **Loans,** 184; **Grants-in-aid,** 196–197
    Orthopedic and developmental disabilities: **Grants-in-aid,** 325
    Communication and other disabilities: **Scholarships,** 374, 409, 447; **Fellowships/Grants,** 471
    Disabilities in general: **Scholarships,** 515, 518–521, 526, 539, 550, 577; **Fellowships/Grants,** 640, 642; **Loans,** 754, 759, 796; **Grants-in-aid,** 814–815, 828; **Awards,** 943–944, 949, 955
    Families of the disabled: **Scholarships,** 967–970; **Grants-in-aid,** 1112
    See also United States
Canada
    Visual disabilities: **Scholarships,** 17, 39, 107, 118;

471

Fellowships/Grants, 138, 176; **Grants-in-aid,** 202
Hearing disabilities: **Scholarships,** 276; **Awards,** 299
Orthopedic and developmental disabilities: **Grants-in-aid,** 356
Disabilities in general: **Scholarships,** 617; **Fellowships/Grants,** 643, 664; **Grants-in-aid,** 833
See also Foreign countries

Caribbean
Hearing disabilities: **Awards,** 299
See also Foreign countries

Central America
Disabilities in general: **Fellowships/Grants,** 664
See also Foreign countries

Chicago, Illinois
Disabilities in general: **Fellowships/Grants,** 622
See also Illinois

Colorado
Visual disabilities: **Scholarships,** 3, 79
Communication and other disabilities: **Scholarships,** 418, 424, 441, 446; **Grants-in-aid,** 495
Disabilities in general: **Scholarships,** 581; **Fellowships/Grants,** 730; **Grants-in-aid,** 819–821
Families of the disabled: **Scholarships,** 974, 1028, 1057
See also United States

Connecticut
Visual disabilities: **Scholarships,** 18, 52, 62, 68, 71, 113; **Fellowships/Grants,** 141; **Grants-in-aid,** 198, 249
Orthopedic and developmental disabilities: **Scholarships,** 302, 313
Communication and other disabilities: **Scholarships,** 403, 411, 427, 448; **Grants-in-aid,** 481, 496
Disabilities in general: **Scholarships,** 527–529; **Fellowships/Grants,** 646–647; **Loans,** 761, 776; **Grants-in-aid,** 822–827, 841
Families of the disabled: **Scholarships,** 975, 977, 1037; **Loans,** 1097; **Grants-in-aid,** 1114–1115, 1122
See also New England states; United States

Delaware
Visual disabilities: **Scholarships,** 18, 59, 68, 113; **Fellowships/Grants,** 141; **Grants-in-aid,** 199
Orthopedic and developmental disabilities: **Scholarships,** 302; **Grants-in-aid,** 326
Communication and other disabilities: **Scholarships,** 449, 453
Disabilities in general: **Grants-in-aid,** 830
Families of the disabled: **Scholarships,** 977
See also United States

District of Columbia. *See* Washington, D.C.

Durham, North Carolina
Disabilities in general: **Fellowships/Grants,** 622
See also North Carolina

Essex County, New Jersey
Disabilities in general: **Fellowships/Grants,** 638
See also New Jersey

Florida
Visual disabilities: **Scholarships,** 34, 80; **Grants-in-aid,** 201
Orthopedic and developmental disabilities: **Grants-in-aid,** 327
Communication and other disabilities: **Scholarships,** 375, 389
Disabilities in general: **Scholarships,** 515, 536, 599; **Fellowships/Grants,** 663; **Loans,** 769; **Grants-in-aid,** 837, 930
Families of the disabled: **Scholarships,** 985; **Grants-in-aid,** 1119
See also United States

Foreign countries
Communication and other disabilities: **Scholarships,** 438
Disabilities in general: **Scholarships,** 512, 618; **Fellowships/Grants,** 655–656; **Grants-in-aid,** 836; **Awards,** 945
Families of the disabled: **Scholarships,** 957, 1075

Georgia
Visual disabilities: **Scholarships,** 41; **Fellowships/Grants,** 139; **Grants-in-aid,** 203
Communication and other disabilities: **Scholarships,** 410, 445; **Fellowships/Grants,** 470
Disabilities in general: **Scholarships,** 515, 538; **Fellowships/Grants,** 665; **Grants-in-aid,** 838–839
Families of the disabled: **Scholarships,** 989–991, 1007, 1023; **Fellowships/Grants,** 1079; **Grants-in-aid,** 1121
See also United States

Guam
Disabilities in general: **Scholarships,** 601; **Fellowships/Grants,** 742
See also United States

Harbor City, California. *See* Los Angeles, California

Hartford, Connecticut
Communication and other disabilities: **Scholarships,** 382
See also Connecticut

Hawaii
    Visual disabilities: **Grants-in-aid,** 204
    Hearing disabilities: **Grants-in-aid,** 292
    Communication and other disabilities: **Scholarships,** 394; **Grants-in-aid,** 488
    Disabilities in general: **Scholarships,** 520, 600–601; **Fellowships/Grants,** 742; **Loans,** 770; **Grants-in-aid,** 844–846
    Families of the disabled: **Scholarships,** 1067; **Grants-in-aid,** 1123
    See also United States
Hollywood, California. See Los Angeles, California
Houston, Texas
    Disabilities in general: **Fellowships/Grants,** 622
    See also Texas

Idaho
    Visual disabilities: **Scholarships,** 81; **Grants-in-aid,** 205 206
    Communication and other disabilities: **Scholarships,** 393, 419, 441; **Grants-in-aid,** 487, 491, 495
    Disabilities in general: **Scholarships,** 515, 541–543; **Fellowships/Grants,** 672–674; **Loans,** 771; **Grants-in-aid,** 848–850
    Families of the disabled: **Scholarships,** 999; **Grants-in-aid,** 1124–1127
    See also United States
Illinois
    Visual disabilities: **Scholarships,** 37, 82; **Fellowships/Grants,** 136; **Grants-in-aid,** 207–208
    Orthopedic and developmental disabilities: **Grants-in-aid,** 331
    Communication and other disabilities: **Scholarships,** 361
    Disabilities in general: **Scholarships,** 511, 515, 544; **Fellowships/Grants,** 625; **Loans,** 793; **Grants-in-aid,** 828, 851–852
    Families of the disabled: **Scholarships,** 1000–1003, 1058; **Fellowships/Grants,** 1081; **Grants-in-aid,** 1128
    See also United States
Indiana
    Visual disabilities: **Scholarships,** 44, 83; **Grants-in-aid,** 209–210
    Communication and other disabilities: **Scholarships,** 391, 414; **Grants-in-aid,** 497
    Disabilities in general: **Scholarships,** 545, 601; **Fellowships/Grants,** 675, 742; **Loans,** 758; **Grants-in-aid,** 855–857
    Families of the disabled: **Scholarships,** 1004, 1013, 1036; **Fellowships/Grants,** 1082, 1086; **Grants-in-aid,** 1130
    See also United States
Iowa
    Visual disabilities: **Scholarships,** 24
    Communication and other disabilities: **Scholarships,** 399, 423; **Grants-in-aid,** 498
    Disabilities in general: **Scholarships,** 515, 522; **Loans,** 772; **Grants-in-aid,** 858–859
    Families of the disabled: **Scholarships,** 995, 1014; **Grants-in-aid,** 1131
    See also United States

Kansas
    Visual disabilities: **Grants-in-aid,** 211–213
    Hearing disabilities: **Grants-in-aid,** 293
    Communication and other disabilities: **Scholarships,** 381; **Grants-in-aid,** 485
    Disabilities in general: **Scholarships,** 515, 547, 601; **Fellowships/Grants,** 680, 742; **Loans,** 773; **Grants-in-aid,** 860–863
    Families of the disabled: **Grants-in-aid,** 1132
    See also United States
Kansas City, Missouri
    Communication and other disabilities: **Scholarships,** 382
    See also Missouri
Kentucky
    Visual disabilities: **Scholarships,** 30
    Communication and other disabilities: **Scholarships,** 401, 422, 443; **Grants-in-aid,** 499
    Disabilities in general: **Scholarships,** 592–593; **Fellowships/Grants,** 681; **Loans,** 774; **Grants-in-aid,** 864
    Families of the disabled: **Scholarships,** 997, 1009–1010
    See also United States
Kings County, New York. See New York, New York

Latin America. See Caribbean; Central America; Mexico
Los Angeles, California
    Disabilities in general: **Fellowships/Grants,** 622
    See also California
Louisiana
    Communication and other disabilities: **Scholarships,** 422
    Disabilities in general: **Fellowships/Grants,** 682; **Loans,** 775
    Families of the disabled: **Scholarships,** 1015, 1024
    See also United States

Maine
    Visual disabilities: **Scholarships,** 18, 68, 102, 111, 113; **Fellowships/Grants,** 141; **Grants-in-aid,** 215–216
    Orthopedic and developmental disabilities: **Scholarships,** 302; **Grants-in-aid,** 333

Disabilities in general: **Loans,** 781; **Grants-in-aid,** 868
Families of the disabled: **Scholarships,** 977, 998, 1025; **Fellowships/Grants,** 1080, 1088; **Grants-in-aid,** 1134–1135
See also New England states; United States
Manhattan, New York. See New York, New York
Maryland
Visual disabilities: **Scholarships,** 4, 18, 61, 68, 113; **Fellowships/Grants,** 141; **Grants-in-aid,** 217–219
Orthopedic and developmental disabilities: **Scholarships,** 302
Communication and other disabilities: **Scholarships,** 449
Disabilities in general: **Scholarships,** 515, 533, 552, 601; **Fellowships/Grants,** 658, 742; **Loans,** 778; **Grants-in-aid,** 869–871
Families of the disabled: **Scholarships,** 971, 977–978, 1016, 1029; **Fellowships/Grants,** 1078; **Loans,** 1098; **Grants-in-aid,** 1136–1139
See also United States
Massachusetts
Visual disabilities: **Scholarships,** 13, 18, 68, 72, 113; **Fellowships/Grants,** 141; **Grants-in-aid,** 220–221
Orthopedic and developmental disabilities: **Scholarships,** 302; **Loans,** 317–318
Communication and other disabilities: **Scholarships,** 385, 428; **Fellowships/Grants,** 461
Disabilities in general: **Scholarships,** 525, 553–554; **Fellowships/Grants,** 685; **Grants-in-aid,** 828, 872–873
Families of the disabled: **Scholarships,** 977, 1038; **Grants-in-aid,** 1140
See also New England states; United States
Mexico
Disabilities in general: **Fellowships/Grants,** 664
See also Foreign countries
Michigan
Visual disabilities: **Scholarships,** 1, 56, 100; **Grants-in-aid,** 222–223
Hearing disabilities: **Scholarships,** 266; **Grants-in-aid,** 294
Orthopedic and developmental disabilities: **Grants-in-aid,** 334
Communication and other disabilities: **Scholarships,** 372, 391, 397; **Grants-in-aid,** 489
Disabilities in general: **Scholarships,** 555; **Fellowships/Grants,** 689–690; **Loans,** 779; **Grants-in-aid,** 828, 875–878
Families of the disabled: **Scholarships,** 994, 1030; **Grants-in-aid,** 1141–1142
See also United States
Minneapolis, Minnesota
Disabilities in general: **Fellowships/Grants,** 622
See also Minnesota
Minnesota
Visual disabilities: **Scholarships,** 5

Communication and other disabilities: **Scholarships,** 423
Disabilities in general: **Scholarships,** 556–557; **Fellowships/Grants,** 691; **Loans,** 755; **Grants-in-aid,** 879
Families of the disabled: **Grants-in-aid,** 1143
See also United States
Mississippi
Visual disabilities: **Scholarships,** 54; **Fellowships/Grants,** 150; **Grants-in-aid,** 224–225
Communication and other disabilities: **Scholarships,** 422
Disabilities in general: **Scholarships,** 558, 601; **Fellowships/Grants,** 692, 742; **Grants-in-aid,** 880–881
Families of the disabled: **Scholarships,** 1005, 1017, 1033; **Fellowships/Grants,** 1083; **Grants-in-aid,** 1144–1145
See also United States
Missouri
Visual disabilities: **Scholarships,** 49, 58; **Fellowships/Grants,** 146, 155; **Grants-in-aid,** 226–228
Communication and other disabilities: **Grants-in-aid,** 485
Disabilities in general: **Scholarships,** 515, 560; **Loans,** 792; **Grants-in-aid,** 882
Families of the disabled: **Scholarships,** 1018, 1034; **Grants-in-aid,** 1146
See also United States
Montana
Visual disabilities: **Grants-in-aid,** 229
Communication and other disabilities: **Grants-in-aid,** 495
Disabilities in general: **Scholarships,** 559; **Fellowships/Grants,** 693–694; **Loans,** 780; **Grants-in-aid,** 883–884
Families of the disabled: **Grants-in-aid,** 1147–1149
See also United States

Nebraska
Visual disabilities: **Scholarships,** 84
Disabilities in general: **Scholarships,** 516, 562, 574; **Fellowships/Grants,** 700; **Loans,** 777, 783
Families of the disabled: **Scholarships,** 1040; **Loans,** 1099
See also United States
Nevada
Visual disabilities: **Scholarships,** 93
Disabilities in general: **Scholarships,** 515, 601; **Fellowships/Grants,** 742; **Loans,** 784; **Grants-in-aid,** 887
Families of the disabled: **Grants-in-aid,** 1151
See also United States

New England states
    Communication and other disabilities: **Scholarships,** 429
    See also United States
New Hampshire
    Visual disabilities: **Scholarships,** 18, 35, 68, 113; **Fellowships/Grants,** 134, 141; **Grants-in-aid,** 230–231, 258
    Orthopedic and developmental disabilities: **Scholarships,** 302; **Grants-in-aid,** 337–338
    Communication and other disabilities: **Scholarships,** 428
    Disabilities in general: **Scholarships,** 540, 564–565; **Fellowships/Grants,** 702–703; **Loans,** 785–786; **Grants-in-aid,** 843, 888–889
    Families of the disabled: **Scholarships,** 977, 1038; **Grants-in-aid,** 1152–1154
    See also New England states; United States
New Jersey
    Visual disabilities: **Scholarships,** 18, 68, 113; **Fellowships/Grants,** 141; **Grants-in-aid,** 232–236
    Orthopedic and developmental disabilities: **Scholarships,** 302; **Grants-in-aid,** 339
    Communication and other disabilities: **Scholarships,** 371, 386, 439, 452; **Fellowships/Grants,** 472; **Grants-in-aid,** 481
    Disabilities in general: **Scholarships,** 549, 566; **Fellowships/Grants,** 638; **Grants-in-aid,** 890–897, 913, 917, 921
    Families of the disabled: **Scholarships,** 977; **Grants-in-aid,** 1155–1156
    See also United States
New Mexico
    Visual disabilities: **Scholarships,** 85; **Grants-in-aid,** 237
    Disabilities in general: **Scholarships,** 515; **Loans,** 787; **Grants-in-aid,** 828, 898
    Families of the disabled: **Grants-in-aid,** 1157–1158
    See also United States
New York
    Visual disabilities: **Scholarships,** 18, 68, 113; **Fellowships/Grants,** 141; **Grants-in-aid,** 238
    Orthopedic and developmental disabilities: **Scholarships,** 302; **Grants-in-aid,** 340
    Communication and other disabilities: **Grants-in-aid,** 481
    Disabilities in general: **Loans,** 768; **Grants-in-aid,** 899–900, 913
    Families of the disabled: **Scholarships,** 977; **Grants-in-aid,** 1159–1161
    See also United States
New York County, New York. *See* New York, New York
New York, New York
    Visual disabilities: **Scholarships,** 33
    Disabilities in general: **Fellowships/Grants,** 622
    See also New York

Newport Beach, California
    Communication and other disabilities: **Scholarships,** 382
    See also California
North Carolina
    Visual disabilities: **Scholarships,** 96, 104; **Grants-in-aid,** 239
    Orthopedic and developmental disabilities: **Scholarships,** 310
    Communication and other disabilities: **Scholarships,** 431, 445; **Fellowships/Grants,** 470
    Disabilities in general: **Scholarships,** 515; **Grants-in-aid,** 865, 901–902
    Families of the disabled: **Scholarships,** 1039, 1042–1045, 1056, 1073; **Fellowships/Grants,** 1090
    See also United States
North Dakota
    Visual disabilities: **Scholarships,** 97; **Fellowships/Grants,** 172; **Grants-in-aid,** 240
    Orthopedic and developmental disabilities: **Grants-in-aid,** 342–343
    Communication and other disabilities: **Scholarships,** 441
    Disabilities in general: **Scholarships,** 567–568; **Fellowships/Grants,** 705; **Loans,** 788; **Grants-in-aid,** 903–904
    Families of the disabled: **Scholarships,** 1046; **Grants-in-aid,** 1162–1165
    See also United States

Ohio
    Visual disabilities: **Scholarships,** 20–21, 73, 86, 95; **Fellowships/Grants,** 154, 161, 166, 171
    Communication and other disabilities: **Scholarships,** 433
    Disabilities in general: **Scholarships,** 569–571; **Fellowships/Grants,** 712–713; **Loans,** 756; **Grants-in-aid,** 906–907, 918
    Families of the disabled: **Scholarships,** 1047–1048; **Grants-in-aid,** 1166
    See also United States
Oklahoma
    Visual disabilities: **Grants-in-aid,** 241
    Disabilities in general: **Scholarships,** 515; **Fellowships/Grants,** 716; **Grants-in-aid,** 908–909, 913
    Families of the disabled: **Grants-in-aid,** 1167–1168
    See also United States
Oregon
    Visual disabilities: **Scholarships,** 6, 46, 87, 99; **Fellowships/Grants,** 143, 167; **Grants-in-aid,** 190, 243–245
    Hearing disabilities: **Grants-in-aid,** 295

Orthopedic and developmental disabilities:
Scholarships, 300; **Fellowships/Grants,** 314;
Grants-in-aid, 324, 344
Disabilities in general: **Scholarships,** 515, 572;
Loans, 789; **Grants-in-aid,** 910–912
Families of the disabled: **Scholarships,** 1049–1052;
Fellowships/Grants, 1091; **Grants-in-aid,** 1169–1170
See also United States

Pacific Islands
Disabilities in general: **Scholarships,** 601;
Fellowships/Grants, 742
See also Foreign countries
Pennsylvania
Visual disabilities: **Scholarships,** 18, 68, 113, 117;
Fellowships/Grants, 141, 183; **Grants-in-aid,** 247–248
Orthopedic and developmental disabilities:
Scholarships, 302; **Grants-in-aid,** 345–346
Disabilities in general: **Scholarships,** 575;
Fellowships/Grants, 717; **Loans,** 790; **Grants-in-aid,** 828, 913–916; **Awards,** 952
Families of the disabled: **Scholarships,** 977, 1019, 1053–1055; **Grants-in-aid,** 1172–1173
See also United States
Philadelphia, Pennsylvania
Communication and other disabilities: **Scholarships,** 382
See also Pennsylvania
Puerto Rico
Disabilities in general: **Scholarships,** 601;
Fellowships/Grants, 742
See also Caribbean; United States

Queens County, New York. See New York, New York
Queens, New York. See New York, New York

Raleigh, North Carolina
Disabilities in general: **Fellowships/Grants,** 622
See also North Carolina
Rhode Island
Visual disabilities: **Scholarships,** 18, 68, 113;
Fellowships/Grants, 141
Orthopedic and developmental disabilities:
Scholarships, 302
Communication and other disabilities: **Scholarships,** 385, 411, 428; **Fellowships/Grants,** 461
Disabilities in general: **Scholarships,** 579–580;
Fellowships/Grants, 726
Families of the disabled: **Scholarships,** 977, 1038
See also New England states; United States
Richmond County, New York. See New York, New York

Sacramento, California
Communication and other disabilities: **Scholarships,** 382
See also California
San Pedro, California. See Los Angeles, California
Schenectady, New York
Communication and other disabilities: **Scholarships,** 382
See also New York
South Carolina
Visual disabilities: **Scholarships,** 29;
Fellowships/Grants, 132; **Grants-in-aid,** 251–252
Orthopedic and developmental disabilities: **Grants-in-aid,** 348–349
Communication and other disabilities: **Scholarships,** 445; **Fellowships/Grants,** 470
Disabilities in general: **Scholarships,** 515, 583;
Fellowships/Grants, 733–734; **Grants-in-aid,** 865, 924–927
Families of the disabled: **Scholarships,** 1020, 1060;
Fellowships/Grants, 1087; **Grants-in-aid,** 1179–1182
See also United States
South Dakota
Visual disabilities: **Scholarships,** 22, 110;
Fellowships/Grants, 179
Orthopedic and developmental disabilities: **Grants-in-aid,** 350
Communication and other disabilities: **Scholarships,** 423
Disabilities in general: **Scholarships,** 584; **Loans,** 762; **Grants-in-aid,** 928–929
Families of the disabled: **Scholarships,** 987;
Grants-in-aid, 1183–1184
See also United States
Springfield, Missouri
Communication and other disabilities: **Scholarships,** 382
See also Missouri
St. Louis, Missouri
Communication and other disabilities: **Scholarships,** 382
See also Missouri
Staten Island, New York. See New York, New York

Tennessee
Visual disabilities: **Grants-in-aid,** 255–256
Orthopedic and developmental disabilities: **Grants-in-aid,** 353–354
Communication and other disabilities: **Scholarships,** 383, 422; **Grants-in-aid,** 500
Disabilities in general: **Scholarships,** 515; **Grants-in-aid,** 828, 932–933
Families of the disabled: **Scholarships,** 976, 1063;
Grants-in-aid, 1185
See also United States

RESIDENCY INDEX

Texas
  Visual disabilities: **Scholarships,** 7, 88, 112; **Grants-in-aid,** 257
  Hearing disabilities: **Scholarships,** 267, 277
  Orthopedic and developmental disabilities: **Grants-in-aid,** 355
  Communication and other disabilities: **Scholarships,** 376; **Fellowships/Grants,** 458
  Disabilities in general: **Scholarships,** 515, 596, 598; **Loans,** 794–795; **Grants-in-aid,** 934
  Families of the disabled: **Scholarships,** 1064; **Grants-in-aid,** 1186
  See also United States

United States
  Visual disabilities: **Scholarships,** 9–11, 17, 21–23, 25–28, 31–33, 36, 38–40, 43, 45, 48, 50–53, 55, 57, 60, 62–65, 69, 71, 73–75, 92, 94–95, 98, 101, 103, 105–109, 116, 118; **Fellowships/Grants,** 121, 123–124, 129–131, 133, 135, 137–138, 142, 145, 147–149, 151–154, 156–158, 161–164, 169–171, 173–178, 182; **Loans,** 185–186; **Grants-in-aid,** 193–194, 200, 202, 214, 242, 246, 250, 253–254; **Awards,** 259–263
  Hearing disabilities: **Scholarships,** 264–265, 268–276; **Fellowships/Grants,** 279–290; **Grants-in-aid,** 291, 296–297; **Awards,** 298–299
  Orthopedic and developmental disabilities: **Scholarships,** 301–309, 311–312; **Fellowships/Grants,** 315–316; **Loans,** 319; **Grants-in-aid,** 320, 322–323, 328–330, 332, 335–336, 341, 347, 351–352, 356
  Communication and other disabilities: **Scholarships,** 357, 359–360, 362–366, 368–370, 373, 377–380, 382, 384, 387–388, 390, 395–396, 398, 400, 402, 404–405, 407, 412–413, 415–417, 420–421, 425–426, 430, 432, 434, 436–438, 440, 442, 444, 446, 450; **Fellowships/Grants,** 455–457, 459–460, 462–464, 466–469, 473; **Grants-in-aid,** 474–476, 478–480, 482–484, 486, 490, 492–493, 502–506; **Awards,** 507–510
  Disabilities in general: **Scholarships,** 512–513, 517, 523–524, 530, 534–535, 537, 546, 548, 551, 561, 563, 573, 576, 578, 582, 585–591, 594–595, 597, 601, 607, 617–618; **Fellowships/Grants,** 619–621, 623–624, 626–633, 637, 639, 641, 643–645, 648–652, 654–657, 659–662, 664, 666–671, 676–679, 683–684, 686–688, 695–699, 701, 704, 706–711, 714–715, 718–725, 727–729, 731–732, 735–742, 744; **Loans,** 760, 763–766, 782, 791, 799; **Grants-in-aid,** 801, 808, 813, 816–818, 829, 831–836, 840, 842, 847, 853–854, 866–867, 874, 885–886, 905, 919–920, 922–923, 931, 937–938; **Awards,** 945–948, 950–951, 953–954, 956
  Families of the disabled: **Scholarships,** 957–958, 962–966, 973, 977, 979–984, 986, 988, 993, 996, 1008, 1021, 1026–1027, 1031–1032, 1035, 1041, 1059, 1061–1062, 1065–1066, 1068, 1075–1076; **Fellowships/Grants,** 1085, 1089, 1092–1093; **Loans,** 1095–1096, 1100; **Grants-in-aid,** 1101–1102, 1105, 1111, 1113, 1116–1118, 1120, 1129, 1133, 1150, 1171, 1174–1178; **Awards,** 1191

Utah
  Visual disabilities: **Scholarships,** 89; **Fellowships/Grants,** 168
  Communication and other disabilities: **Scholarships,** 441, 451
  Disabilities in general: **Scholarships,** 581, 602; **Fellowships/Grants,** 730; **Loans,** 798; **Grants-in-aid,** 935
  Families of the disabled: **Scholarships,** 1069; **Grants-in-aid,** 1187
  See also United States

Vermont
  Visual disabilities: **Scholarships,** 16, 18, 68, 90, 113; **Fellowships/Grants,** 141
  Orthopedic and developmental disabilities: **Scholarships,** 302
  Communication and other disabilities: **Scholarships,** 406, 408, 428; **Fellowships/Grants,** 465
  Disabilities in general: **Scholarships,** 603; **Loans,** 767, 800; **Grants-in-aid,** 936
  Families of the disabled: **Scholarships,** 972, 977, 1006, 1038; **Fellowships/Grants,** 1084; **Grants-in-aid,** 1188
  See also New England states; United States

Virgin Islands
  Disabilities in general: **Scholarships,** 583, 601; **Fellowships/Grants,** 733–734, 742
  See also Caribbean; United States

Virginia
  Visual disabilities: **Scholarships,** 18, 68, 113; **Fellowships/Grants,** 141
  Orthopedic and developmental disabilities: **Scholarships,** 302
  Communication and other disabilities: **Scholarships,** 449; **Grants-in-aid,** 501
  Disabilities in general: **Scholarships,** 515, 604–606; **Fellowships/Grants,** 743; **Loans,** 757
  Families of the disabled: **Scholarships,** 977, 1070–1071; **Fellowships/Grants,** 1094
  See also United States

Washington
  Visual disabilities: **Scholarships,** 14, 47, 115; **Fellowships/Grants,** 126, 144, 181
  Disabilities in general: **Scholarships,** 515, 615
  Families of the disabled: **Scholarships,** 1072
  See also United States

Washington, D.C.
   Visual disabilities: **Scholarships,** 18, 68, 113;
     Fellowships/Grants, 141
   Orthopedic and developmental disabilities:
     Scholarships, 302
   Communication and other disabilities: **Scholarships,** 358, 449; **Fellowships/Grants,** 454
   Disabilities in general: **Scholarships,** 515, 531;
     Fellowships/Grants, 622, 653; **Loans,** 797
   Families of the disabled: **Scholarships,** 977
   See also United States

West Virginia
   Orthopedic and developmental disabilities:
     Scholarships, 302
   Communication and other disabilities: **Scholarships,** 449; **Grants-in-aid,** 501
   Disabilities in general: **Scholarships,** 608–609;
     Fellowships/Grants, 745–747; **Grants-in-aid,** 939–940
   Families of the disabled: **Scholarships,** 977, 1021;
     Grants-in-aid, 1189
   See also United States

Westchester County, New York
   Communication and other disabilities: **Scholarships,** 382
   See also New York

Wilmington, California. *See* Los Angeles, California

Wilmington, Delaware
   Communication and other disabilities: **Scholarships,** 382
   See also Delaware

Wisconsin
   Visual disabilities: **Scholarships,** 91, 119–120;
     Loans, 187
   Hearing disabilities: **Scholarships,** 278
   Communication and other disabilities: **Scholarships,** 367, 392, 423
   Disabilities in general: **Scholarships,** 532, 610–614;
     Fellowships/Grants, 748–750; **Grants-in-aid,** 941–942
   Families of the disabled: **Scholarships,** 992;
     Grants-in-aid, 1190
   See also United States

Wyoming
   Communication and other disabilities: **Scholarships,** 441; **Grants-in-aid,** 495
   Disabilities in general: **Scholarships,** 601, 616;
     Fellowships/Grants, 742
   Families of the disabled: **Scholarships,** 1074
   See also United States

Tenability Index

Some programs listed in this book can be used only in specific cities, counties, states, or regions. Others may be used anywhere in the United States (or even abroad). The Tenability Index will help you locate funding that is restricted to a specific area as well as funding that has no tenability restrictions (these are listed under the term "United States"). To use this index, look up the geographic areas where you'd like to go (always check the listings under "United States"), jot down the entry numbers listed after the availability groups and program types that relate to you, and use those numbers to find the program descriptions in the directory. To help you in your search, we've provided some "see also" references in each index entry. Remember: the numbers cited here refer to program entry numbers, not to page numbers in the book.

Alabama
    Visual disabilities: **Scholarships,** 2; **Grants-in-aid,** 188–190
    Disabilities in general: **Loans,** 751; **Grants-in-aid,** 802–806
    Families of the disabled: **Scholarships,** 959–960, 1022; **Fellowships/Grants,** 1077; **Grants-in-aid,** 1103–1104
    See also United States
Alaska
    Visual disabilities: **Scholarships,** 70
    Disabilities in general: **Grants-in-aid,** 807
    See also United States
Arctic region
    Disabilities in general: **Fellowships/Grants,** 633
    See also Foreign countries
Arizona
    Visual disabilities: **Scholarships,** 8, 12, 55; **Fellowships/Grants,** 122, 125, 151; **Grants-in-aid,** 191, 195
    Communication and other disabilities: **Scholarships,** 435; **Grants-in-aid,** 477
    Disabilities in general: **Loans,** 752; **Grants-in-aid,** 828
    See also United States
Arkansas
    Visual disabilities: **Grants-in-aid,** 192
    Orthopedic and developmental disabilities: **Grants-in-aid,** 321
    Communication and other disabilities: **Grants-in-aid,** 494
    Disabilities in general: **Scholarships,** 514; **Fellowships/Grants,** 634–636; **Loans,** 753; **Grants-in-aid,** 809–812
    Families of the disabled: **Scholarships,** 961; **Grants-in-aid,** 1106–1110
    See also United States
Arlington, Virginia
    Disabilities in general: **Fellowships/Grants,** 620
    See also Virginia

Bethesda, Maryland
    Disabilities in general: **Fellowships/Grants,** 619, 707; **Loans,** 782
    See also Maryland
Bethlehem, Pennsylvania
    Disabilities in general: **Scholarships,** 530; **Fellowships/Grants,** 697
    See also Pennsylvania
Boulder, Colorado
    Disabilities in general: **Fellowships/Grants,** 740
    See also Colorado

California
    Visual disabilities: **Scholarships,** 15, 19, 42, 66–67, 78, 114; **Fellowships/Grants,** 127–128, 140, 159–160, 165, 180; **Loans,** 184; **Grants-in-aid,** 196–197
    Orthopedic and developmental disabilities: **Grants-in-aid,** 325
    Communication and other disabilities: **Scholarships,** 374, 447; **Fellowships/Grants,** 471
    Disabilities in general: **Scholarships,** 518–519, 521, 526, 539, 550; **Fellowships/Grants,** 640–642;

Loans, 754, 759, 796; **Grants-in-aid,** 814–815, 828; **Awards,** 943–944, 949, 955
    Families of the disabled: **Scholarships,** 967–970; **Grants-in-aid,** 1112
    See also United States
Canada
    Visual disabilities: **Scholarships,** 17, 39, 107, 118; **Fellowships/Grants,** 138, 176; **Grants-in-aid,** 202
    Hearing disabilities: **Scholarships,** 276; **Awards,** 299
    Orthopedic and developmental disabilities: **Grants-in-aid,** 356
    Disabilities in general: **Scholarships,** 617; **Fellowships/Grants,** 643, 664; **Grants-in-aid,** 833
    See also Foreign countries
Caribbean
    Hearing disabilities: **Awards,** 299
    See also Foreign countries
Central America
    Disabilities in general: **Fellowships/Grants,** 664
    See also Foreign countries
Chicago, Illinois
    Communication and other disabilities: **Scholarships,** 367
    See also Illinois
Cleveland, Ohio
    Disabilities in general: **Fellowships/Grants,** 670, 696
    See also Ohio
Colorado
    Visual disabilities: **Scholarships,** 79
    Communication and other disabilities: **Grants-in-aid,** 495
    Disabilities in general: **Grants-in-aid,** 819–821
    Families of the disabled: **Scholarships,** 974
    See also United States
Columbus, Ohio
    Disabilities in general: **Fellowships/Grants,** 639
    See also Ohio
Connecticut
    Visual disabilities: **Scholarships,** 18, 52, 62, 68, 71, 113; **Fellowships/Grants,** 141; **Grants-in-aid,** 198, 249
    Orthopedic and developmental disabilities: **Scholarships,** 302
    Communication and other disabilities: **Scholarships,** 427; **Grants-in-aid,** 481, 496
    Disabilities in general: **Scholarships,** 527, 529; **Fellowships/Grants,** 646; **Loans,** 761, 776; **Grants-in-aid,** 822–827, 841
    Families of the disabled: **Scholarships,** 977, 1037; **Loans,** 1097; **Grants-in-aid,** 1114–1115, 1122
    See also United States

Delaware
    Visual disabilities: **Scholarships,** 18, 68, 113; **Fellowships/Grants,** 141; **Grants-in-aid,** 199
    Orthopedic and developmental disabilities: **Scholarships,** 302; **Grants-in-aid,** 326
    Communication and other disabilities: **Scholarships,** 453
    Disabilities in general: **Grants-in-aid,** 830
    Families of the disabled: **Scholarships,** 977
    See also United States
Denver, Colorado
    Disabilities in general: **Scholarships,** 581; **Fellowships/Grants,** 730
    See also Colorado
District of Columbia. *See* Washington, D.C.
Dover, Delaware
    Disabilities in general: **Scholarships,** 530; **Fellowships/Grants,** 697
    See also Delaware

Edwards, California
    Disabilities in general: **Fellowships/Grants,** 670, 696
    See also California

Florida
    Visual disabilities: **Scholarships,** 34, 80; **Grants-in-aid,** 201
    Orthopedic and developmental disabilities: **Grants-in-aid,** 327
    Communication and other disabilities: **Scholarships,** 389
    Disabilities in general: **Scholarships,** 536, 599; **Fellowships/Grants,** 663; **Loans,** 769; **Grants-in-aid,** 837, 930
    Families of the disabled: **Scholarships,** 985; **Grants-in-aid,** 1119
    See also United States
Foreign countries
    Communication and other disabilities: **Scholarships,** 438
    Disabilities in general: **Scholarships,** 512, 595, 618; **Fellowships/Grants,** 624, 637, 650–651, 686, 696, 719–720, 727, 739; **Grants-in-aid,** 836
    Families of the disabled: **Scholarships,** 957, 1061, 1075; **Fellowships/Grants,** 1093
Fort Worth, Texas
    Hearing disabilities: **Scholarships,** 268; **Fellowships/Grants,** 285
    See also Texas

Georgetown, Delaware
    Disabilities in general: **Scholarships,** 530; **Fellowships/Grants,** 697

See also Delaware
Georgia
Visual disabilities: **Scholarships,** 41;
Fellowships/Grants, 139; **Grants-in-aid,** 203
Disabilities in general: **Scholarships,** 538;
Fellowships/Grants, 665; **Grants-in-aid,** 838–839
Families of the disabled: **Scholarships,** 989–991;
Fellowships/Grants, 1079; **Grants-in-aid,** 1121
See also United States
Gettysburg, Pennsylvania
Disabilities in general: **Scholarships,** 530;
Fellowships/Grants, 697
See also Pennsylvania
Greenbelt, Maryland
Disabilities in general: **Fellowships/Grants,** 670, 696
See also Maryland

Hampton, Virginia
Disabilities in general: **Fellowships/Grants,** 670, 696
See also Virginia
Hawaii
Visual disabilities: **Grants-in-aid,** 204
Hearing disabilities: **Grants-in-aid,** 292
Communication and other disabilities: **Scholarships,** 394; **Grants-in-aid,** 488
Disabilities in general: **Scholarships,** 600; **Loans,** 770; **Grants-in-aid,** 844–846
Families of the disabled: **Scholarships,** 1067; **Grants-in-aid,** 1123
See also United States
Houston, Texas
Disabilities in general: **Fellowships/Grants,** 626, 670, 696
See also Texas
Huntsville, Alabama
Disabilities in general: **Fellowships/Grants,** 696
See also Alabama

Idaho
Visual disabilities: **Scholarships,** 115;
Fellowships/Grants, 181; **Grants-in-aid,** 205–206
Communication and other disabilities: **Scholarships,** 393, 419; **Grants-in-aid,** 487, 491, 495
Disabilities in general: **Scholarships,** 541–543;
Fellowships/Grants, 672–674; **Loans,** 771;
Grants-in-aid, 848–850
Families of the disabled: **Scholarships,** 999;
Grants-in-aid, 1124–1127
See also United States
Illinois
Visual disabilities: **Scholarships,** 37, 82;
Fellowships/Grants, 136; **Grants-in-aid,** 207–208
Orthopedic and developmental disabilities: **Grants-in-aid,** 331

Disabilities in general: **Scholarships,** 511, 544;
Fellowships/Grants, 625; **Loans,** 793; **Grants-in-aid,** 828, 851–852
Families of the disabled: **Scholarships,** 1000–1003, 1058; **Fellowships/Grants,** 1081; **Grants-in-aid,** 1128
See also United States
Indiana
Visual disabilities: **Scholarships,** 44, 83; **Grants-in-aid,** 209–210
Communication and other disabilities: **Scholarships,** 391
Disabilities in general: **Scholarships,** 545;
Fellowships/Grants, 675; **Loans,** 758; **Grants-in-aid,** 855–857
Families of the disabled: **Scholarships,** 1004;
Fellowships/Grants, 1082; **Grants-in-aid,** 1130
See also United States
Iowa
Communication and other disabilities: **Grants-in-aid,** 498
Disabilities in general: **Scholarships,** 522; **Loans,** 772; **Grants-in-aid,** 858–859
Families of the disabled: **Grants-in-aid,** 1131
See also United States

Johnson, Vermont
Communication and other disabilities:
Fellowships/Grants, 460
Disabilities in general: **Fellowships/Grants,** 644
See also Vermont

Kansas
Visual disabilities: **Grants-in-aid,** 211–213
Hearing disabilities: **Grants-in-aid,** 293
Communication and other disabilities: **Scholarships,** 381; **Grants-in-aid,** 485
Disabilities in general: **Scholarships,** 547;
Fellowships/Grants, 680; **Loans,** 773; **Grants-in-aid,** 860–863
Families of the disabled: **Grants-in-aid,** 1132
See also United States
Kansas City, Missouri
Hearing disabilities: **Scholarships,** 268;
Fellowships/Grants, 285
See also Missouri
Kennedy Space Center, Florida
Disabilities in general: **Fellowships/Grants,** 670, 696
See also Florida
Kentucky
Communication and other disabilities: **Grants-in-aid,** 499
Disabilities in general: **Scholarships,** 592–593;
Fellowships/Grants, 681; **Loans,** 774; **Grants-in-aid,** 864

Families of the disabled: **Scholarships,** 1009–1010
See also United States

Lancaster, Pennsylvania
    Disabilities in general: **Scholarships,** 530;
        Fellowships/Grants, 697
    See also Pennsylvania
Latin America. *See* Caribbean; Central America; Mexico
Louisiana
    Disabilities in general: **Fellowships/Grants,** 682;
        Loans, 775
    Families of the disabled: **Scholarships,** 1015, 1024
    See also United States
Louisville, Kentucky
    Hearing disabilities: **Scholarships,** 268;
        Fellowships/Grants, 285
    See also Kentucky

Maine
    Visual disabilities: **Scholarships,** 18, 68, 113;
        Fellowships/Grants, 141; **Grants-in-aid,** 215–216
    Orthopedic and developmental disabilities:
        Scholarships, 302; **Grants-in-aid,** 333
    Disabilities in general: **Loans,** 781; **Grants-in-aid,** 868
    Families of the disabled: **Scholarships,** 977, 1025;
        Fellowships/Grants, 1088; **Grants-in-aid,** 1134–1135
    See also United States
Marshall Space Flight Center, Alabama
    Disabilities in general: **Fellowships/Grants,** 670
    See also Alabama
Maryland
    Visual disabilities: **Scholarships,** 18, 61, 68, 113;
        Fellowships/Grants, 141; **Grants-in-aid,** 217–219
    Orthopedic and developmental disabilities:
        Scholarships, 302
    Disabilities in general: **Scholarships,** 533, 552;
        Fellowships/Grants, 658; **Loans,** 778; **Grants-in-aid,** 869–871
    Families of the disabled: **Scholarships,** 971, 977–978, 1029; **Fellowships/Grants,** 1078; **Loans,** 1098; **Grants-in-aid,** 1136–1139
    See also United States
Massachusetts
    Visual disabilities: **Scholarships,** 13, 18, 68, 72, 113;
        Fellowships/Grants, 141; **Grants-in-aid,** 220–221
    Orthopedic and developmental disabilities:
        Scholarships, 302; **Loans,** 317–318
    Disabilities in general: **Scholarships,** 553–554;
        Fellowships/Grants, 685; **Grants-in-aid,** 828, 872–873
    Families of the disabled: **Scholarships,** 977;
        Grants-in-aid, 1140
    See also United States

Menasha, Wisconsin
    Communication and other disabilities: **Scholarships,** 367
    See also Wisconsin
Mexico
    Disabilities in general: **Fellowships/Grants,** 664
    See also Foreign countries
Michigan
    Visual disabilities: **Scholarships,** 1, 56, 100; **Grants-in-aid,** 222–223
    Hearing disabilities: **Grants-in-aid,** 294
    Orthopedic and developmental disabilities: **Grants-in-aid,** 334
    Communication and other disabilities: **Scholarships,** 391; **Grants-in-aid,** 489
    Disabilities in general: **Scholarships,** 555;
        Fellowships/Grants, 689–690; **Loans,** 779;
        Grants-in-aid, 828, 876–878
    Families of the disabled: **Scholarships,** 1030;
        Grants-in-aid, 1141–1142
    See also United States
Mill Valley, California
    Hearing disabilities: **Scholarships,** 268;
        Fellowships/Grants, 285
    See also California
Minnesota
    Disabilities in general: **Scholarships,** 556–557;
        Fellowships/Grants, 691; **Loans,** 755; **Grants-in-aid,** 879
    Families of the disabled: **Grants-in-aid,** 1143
    See also United States
Mississippi
    Visual disabilities: **Grants-in-aid,** 224–225
    Disabilities in general: **Scholarships,** 558;
        Fellowships/Grants, 692; **Grants-in-aid,** 880–881
    Families of the disabled: **Scholarships,** 1033;
        Grants-in-aid, 1144–1145
    See also United States
Missouri
    Visual disabilities: **Grants-in-aid,** 226–228
    Communication and other disabilities: **Grants-in-aid,** 485
    Disabilities in general: **Scholarships,** 560; **Loans,** 792; **Grants-in-aid,** 882
    Families of the disabled: **Scholarships,** 1034;
        Grants-in-aid, 1146
    See also United States
Moffett Field, California
    Disabilities in general: **Fellowships/Grants,** 670, 696
    See also California
Montana
    Visual disabilities: **Grants-in-aid,** 229
    Communication and other disabilities: **Grants-in-aid,** 495
    Disabilities in general: **Scholarships,** 559;
        Fellowships/Grants, 693–694; **Loans,** 780;
        Grants-in-aid, 883–884
    Families of the disabled: **Grants-in-aid,** 1147–1149

See also United States

Nebraska
    Visual disabilities: **Scholarships,** 84
    Disabilities in general: **Scholarships,** 516, 562, 574;
        Fellowships/Grants, 700; **Loans,** 777, 783
    Families of the disabled: **Scholarships,** 1040;
        Loans, 1099
    See also United States
Nevada
    Visual disabilities: **Scholarships,** 93
    Disabilities in general: **Scholarships,** 563;
        Fellowships/Grants, 701; **Loans,** 784; **Grants-in-aid,** 887
    Families of the disabled: **Grants-in-aid,** 1151
    See also United States
New Castle, Delaware
    Disabilities in general: **Scholarships,** 530;
        Fellowships/Grants, 697
    See also Delaware
New Hampshire
    Visual disabilities: **Scholarships,** 18, 35, 68, 113;
        Fellowships/Grants, 134, 141; **Grants-in-aid,** 230–231, 258
    Orthopedic and developmental disabilities:
        Scholarships, 302; **Grants-in-aid,** 337–338
    Disabilities in general: **Scholarships,** 540, 564–565;
        Fellowships/Grants, 702–703; **Loans,** 785–786;
        Grants-in-aid, 843, 888–889
    Families of the disabled: **Scholarships,** 977;
        Grants-in-aid, 1152–1154
    See also United States
New Jersey
    Visual disabilities: **Scholarships,** 18, 68, 113;
        Fellowships/Grants, 141; **Grants-in-aid,** 232–236
    Orthopedic and developmental disabilities:
        Scholarships, 302; **Grants-in-aid,** 339
    Communication and other disabilities: **Grants-in-aid,** 481
    Disabilities in general: **Fellowships/Grants,** 638, 666; **Grants-in-aid,** 890–897, 913, 917, 921
    Families of the disabled: **Scholarships,** 977;
        Grants-in-aid, 1155–1156
    See also United States
New Mexico
    Visual disabilities: **Scholarships,** 85; **Grants-in-aid,** 237
    Disabilities in general: **Loans,** 787; **Grants-in-aid,** 828, 898
    Families of the disabled: **Grants-in-aid,** 1157–1158
    See also United States
New Orleans, Louisiana
    Hearing disabilities: **Scholarships,** 268;
        Fellowships/Grants, 285
    See also Louisiana

New York
    Visual disabilities: **Scholarships,** 18, 68, 113;
        Fellowships/Grants, 141; **Grants-in-aid,** 238
    Orthopedic and developmental disabilities:
        Scholarships, 302; **Grants-in-aid,** 340
    Communication and other disabilities: **Grants-in-aid,** 481
    Disabilities in general: **Loans,** 768; **Grants-in-aid,** 899–900
    Families of the disabled: **Scholarships,** 977;
        Grants-in-aid, 1159–1161
    See also United States
Newark, Delaware
    Disabilities in general: **Scholarships,** 530;
        Fellowships/Grants, 697
    See also Delaware
North Carolina
    Visual disabilities: **Scholarships,** 104; **Grants-in-aid,** 239
    Orthopedic and developmental disabilities:
        Scholarships, 310
    Communication and other disabilities: **Scholarships,** 431
    Disabilities in general: **Grants-in-aid,** 865, 901–902
    Families of the disabled: **Scholarships,** 1042–1045;
        Fellowships/Grants, 1090
    See also United States
North Dakota
    Visual disabilities: **Scholarships,** 97;
        Fellowships/Grants, 172; **Grants-in-aid,** 240
    Orthopedic and developmental disabilities: **Grants-in-aid,** 342–343
    Disabilities in general: **Scholarships,** 567–568;
        Fellowships/Grants, 705; **Loans,** 788; **Grants-in-aid,** 903–904
    Families of the disabled: **Scholarships,** 1046;
        Grants-in-aid, 1162–1165
    See also United States

Ohio
    Visual disabilities: **Scholarships,** 21, 73, 95;
        Fellowships/Grants, 154, 161, 171
    Disabilities in general: **Scholarships,** 569–571;
        Fellowships/Grants, 712–713; **Loans,** 756;
        Grants-in-aid, 906–907, 918
    Families of the disabled: **Scholarships,** 1047–1048;
        Grants-in-aid, 1166
    See also United States
Oklahoma
    Visual disabilities: **Grants-in-aid,** 241
    Disabilities in general: **Scholarships,** 573;
        Fellowships/Grants, 715–716; **Grants-in-aid,** 908–909, 913
    Families of the disabled: **Grants-in-aid,** 1167–1168
    See also United States

Oregon
  Visual disabilities: **Scholarships,** 6, 46, 87, 115; **Fellowships/Grants,** 143, 167, 181; **Grants-in-aid,** 190, 243–245
  Hearing disabilities: **Grants-in-aid,** 295
  Orthopedic and developmental disabilities: **Scholarships,** 300; **Fellowships/Grants,** 314; **Grants-in-aid,** 324, 344
  Disabilities in general: **Scholarships,** 572; **Loans,** 789; **Grants-in-aid,** 910–912
  Families of the disabled: **Scholarships,** 1049–1052; **Fellowships/Grants,** 1091; **Grants-in-aid,** 1169–1170
  See also United States

Pasadena, California
  Disabilities in general: **Fellowships/Grants,** 696
  See also California
Pennsylvania
  Visual disabilities: **Scholarships,** 18, 68, 113; **Fellowships/Grants,** 141; **Grants-in-aid,** 247–248
  Orthopedic and developmental disabilities: **Scholarships,** 302; **Grants-in-aid,** 345–346
  Disabilities in general: **Scholarships,** 575; **Fellowships/Grants,** 717; **Loans,** 790; **Grants-in-aid,** 828, 913–916; **Awards,** 952
  Families of the disabled: **Scholarships,** 977, 1053–1055; **Grants-in-aid,** 1172–1173
  See also United States
Philadelphia, Pennsylvania
  Disabilities in general: **Fellowships/Grants,** 623
  See also Pennsylvania

Rhode Island
  Visual disabilities: **Scholarships,** 18, 68, 113; **Fellowships/Grants,** 141
  Orthopedic and developmental disabilities: **Scholarships,** 302
  Disabilities in general: **Scholarships,** 579–580; **Fellowships/Grants,** 726
  Families of the disabled: **Scholarships,** 977
  See also United States

South Carolina
  Visual disabilities: **Grants-in-aid,** 251–252
  Orthopedic and developmental disabilities: **Grants-in-aid,** 348–349
  Disabilities in general: **Scholarships,** 583; **Fellowships/Grants,** 733–734; **Grants-in-aid,** 865, 924–927
  Families of the disabled: **Scholarships,** 1060; **Grants-in-aid,** 1179–1182
  See also United States

South Dakota
  Visual disabilities: **Scholarships,** 22, 110; **Fellowships/Grants,** 179
  Orthopedic and developmental disabilities: **Grants-in-aid,** 350
  Disabilities in general: **Scholarships,** 584; **Loans,** 762; **Grants-in-aid,** 928–929
  Families of the disabled: **Scholarships,** 987; **Grants-in-aid,** 1183–1184
  See also United States
Stennis Space Center, Mississippi
  Disabilities in general: **Fellowships/Grants,** 670, 696
  See also Mississippi
Swarthmore, Pennsylvania
  Disabilities in general: **Scholarships,** 530; **Fellowships/Grants,** 697
  See also Pennsylvania

Tennessee
  Visual disabilities: **Grants-in-aid,** 255–256
  Orthopedic and developmental disabilities: **Grants-in-aid,** 353–354
  Communication and other disabilities: **Scholarships,** 383; **Grants-in-aid,** 500
  Disabilities in general: **Grants-in-aid,** 828, 932–933
  Families of the disabled: **Scholarships,** 976, 1063; **Grants-in-aid,** 1185
  See also United States
Texas
  Visual disabilities: **Scholarships,** 112; **Grants-in-aid,** 257
  Hearing disabilities: **Scholarships,** 267, 277
  Orthopedic and developmental disabilities: **Grants-in-aid,** 355
  Disabilities in general: **Scholarships,** 596–598; **Fellowships/Grants,** 741; **Loans,** 794–795; **Grants-in-aid,** 934
  Families of the disabled: **Scholarships,** 1064; **Grants-in-aid,** 1186
  See also United States

United States
  Visual disabilities: **Scholarships,** 3–5, 7, 9–11, 13–14, 16–17, 20–33, 35–36, 38–40, 43, 45, 47–55, 57–60, 62–65, 69–71, 73–77, 81, 84, 86, 88–92, 94–96, 98–99, 101–103, 105–109, 111, 116–118; **Fellowships/Grants,** 121, 123–124, 126, 129–135, 137–138, 142, 144–158, 161–164, 166, 168–171, 173–178, 182–183; **Loans,** 185–186; **Grants-in-aid,** 193–194, 200, 202, 214, 242, 246, 250, 253–254; **Awards,** 259–263
  Hearing disabilities: **Scholarships,** 264–266, 268–276; **Fellowships/Grants,** 279–282, 284–290; **Grants-in-aid,** 291, 296–297; **Awards,** 298–299

Orthopedic and developmental disabilities:
Scholarships, 301–309, 311–313;
Fellowships/Grants, 315–316; **Loans,** 319;
Grants-in-aid, 320, 322–323, 328–330, 332, 335–336, 341, 347, 351–352, 356
Communication and other disabilities: **Scholarships,** 357–366, 368–373, 375–380, 382, 384–388, 390, 392–393, 395–426, 428–430, 432–434, 436–446, 448–453; **Fellowships/Grants,** 454–459, 461–470, 472–473; **Grants-in-aid,** 474–476, 478–480, 482–484, 486–487, 490, 492–493, 497, 502–506; **Awards,** 507–510
Disabilities in general: **Scholarships,** 512–515, 517, 520, 523–525, 528, 532, 534–535, 537, 546, 548–549, 551, 561, 564, 566, 576–578, 582, 585–591, 593–595, 601–602, 607, 617–618; **Fellowships/Grants,** 622, 624, 627–631, 633, 638–639, 643, 647–649, 652, 654–657, 659, 661–662, 664, 666–670, 676–679, 683–684, 686–688, 695–696, 698–699, 702, 704, 706–709, 711, 718–725, 727, 729, 732, 735–739, 742, 744; **Loans,** 760, 763–766, 782, 785, 791, 799; **Grants-in-aid,** 801, 808, 813, 816–818, 829, 831–836, 840, 842, 847, 853–854, 866–867, 874–875, 885–886, 905, 919–920, 922–923, 931, 937–938; **Awards,** 945–948, 950–951, 953–954, 956
Families of the disabled: **Scholarships,** 957–958, 962–966, 972–973, 975, 977, 979–984, 986, 988, 992–998, 1005–1008, 1011–1014, 1016–1021, 1023, 1025–1028, 1031–1032, 1035–1036, 1038–1039, 1041, 1056–1057, 1059, 1061–1062, 1065–1066, 1068–1070, 1073, 1075–1076;
Fellowships/Grants, 1080, 1083–1089, 1093; **Loans,** 1095–1096, 1100; **Grants-in-aid,** 1101–1102, 1105, 1111, 1113, 1116–1118, 1120, 1129, 1133, 1150, 1171, 1174–1178; **Awards,** 1191
Utah
Disabilities in general: **Scholarships,** 581; **Fellowships/Grants,** 730; **Loans,** 798; **Grants-in-aid,** 935
Families of the disabled: **Grants-in-aid,** 1187
See also United States

Vermont
Visual disabilities: **Scholarships,** 16, 18, 68, 90, 113; **Fellowships/Grants,** 141
Orthopedic and developmental disabilities: **Scholarships,** 302
Disabilities in general: **Scholarships,** 603, **Loans,** 767, 800; **Grants-in-aid,** 936
Families of the disabled: **Scholarships,** 972, 977; **Grants-in-aid,** 1188
See also United States
Villanova, Pennsylvania
Disabilities in general: **Scholarships,** 530; **Fellowships/Grants,** 697

See also Pennsylvania
Virgin Islands
Disabilities in general: **Scholarships,** 583; **Fellowships/Grants,** 733–734
See also Caribbean; United States
Virginia
Visual disabilities: **Scholarships,** 18, 68, 113; **Fellowships/Grants,** 141
Orthopedic and developmental disabilities: **Scholarships,** 302
Communication and other disabilities: **Grants-in-aid,** 501
Disabilities in general: **Scholarships,** 604–606; **Fellowships/Grants,** 743; **Loans,** 757
Families of the disabled: **Scholarships,** 977, 1071; **Fellowships/Grants,** 1094
See also United States

Wake Forest, North Carolina
Hearing disabilities: **Scholarships,** 268; **Fellowships/Grants,** 285
See also North Carolina
Washington
Visual disabilities: **Scholarships,** 115; **Fellowships/Grants,** 181
Disabilities in general: **Scholarships,** 615
Families of the disabled: **Scholarships,** 1072
See also United States
Washington, D.C.
Visual disabilities: **Scholarships,** 18, 68, 113; **Fellowships/Grants,** 141
Hearing disabilities: **Fellowships/Grants,** 283
Orthopedic and developmental disabilities: **Scholarships,** 302
Disabilities in general: **Scholarships,** 523, 531; **Fellowships/Grants,** 621, 645, 650–651, 653, 660, 671, 710, 728, 731; **Loans,** 760, 797; **Awards,** 954
Families of the disabled: **Scholarships,** 977; **Fellowships/Grants,** 1092
See also United States
West Virginia
Orthopedic and developmental disabilities: **Scholarships,** 302
Communication and other disabilities: **Grants-in-aid,** 501
Disabilities in general: **Scholarships,** 608–609; **Fellowships/Grants,** 745–747; **Grants-in-aid,** 939–940
Families of the disabled: **Scholarships,** 977; **Grants-in-aid,** 1189
See also United States
Williamsburg, Virginia
Disabilities in general: **Fellowships/Grants,** 632, 714
See also Virginia

Wilmington, Delaware
    Disabilities in general: **Scholarships,** 530; **Fellowships/Grants,** 697
    See also Delaware
Wisconsin
    Visual disabilities: **Scholarships,** 119–120; **Loans,** 187
    Hearing disabilities: **Scholarships,** 278
    Communication and other disabilities: **Scholarships,** 367, 392
    Disabilities in general: **Scholarships,** 610–614; **Fellowships/Grants,** 748–750; **Grants-in-aid,** 941–942
    Families of the disabled: **Scholarships,** 992; **Grants-in-aid,** 1190
    See also United States
Wyoming
    Communication and other disabilities: **Grants-in-aid,** 495
    Disabilities in general: **Scholarships,** 616
    Families of the disabled: **Scholarships,** 1074
    See also United States

Subject Index

There are nearly 150 different subject areas indexed here. Use this index when you want to identify either 1) available funding programs by subject or 2) directories listing funding in a particular subject area. To help you pinpoint your search, we've also included hundreds of "see" and "see also" references. In addition to looking for terms that represent your specific subject interest, be sure to check the "General programs" entry; hundreds of programs are listed there that can be used to support study, research, or other activities in *any* subject area (although the programs may be restricted in other ways). Remember: the numbers cited in this index refer to program entry numbers, not to page numbers in the book.

Accounting
    Visual disabilities: **Scholarships,** 53; **Fellowships/Grants,** 149
    Hearing disabilities: **Scholarships,** 270; **Fellowships/Grants,** 288
    Orthopedic and developmental disabilities: **Scholarships,** 306; **Fellowships/Grants,** 315
    Communication and other disabilities: **Scholarships,** 367
    Disabilities in general: **Scholarships,** 512, 566
    Families of the disabled: **Scholarships,** 957
    See also Finance; General programs
Acting. See Performing arts
Administration. See Business administration; Management; Personnel administration; Public administration
Adoption
    Families of the disabled: **Grants-in-aid,** 1117, 1136, 1158, 1162, 1181
    See also General programs
Aeronautical engineering. See Engineering, aeronautical
Aeronautics
    Disabilities in general: **Scholarships,** 536, 555; **Fellowships/Grants,** 663, 670, 689–690, 750
    See also Aviation; Engineering, aeronautical; General programs; Physical sciences
Aerospace engineering. See Engineering, aerospace
Aerospace sciences. See Space sciences
African American studies
    Disabilities in general: **Fellowships/Grants,** 626
    See also General programs
African history. See History, African
Agricultural engineering. See Engineering, agricultural

Agriculture and agricultural sciences
    Disabilities in general: **Scholarships,** 517, 598; **Fellowships/Grants,** 750
    See also Biological sciences; General programs
American history. See History, American
Anthropology
    Disabilities in general: **Scholarships,** 556; **Fellowships/Grants,** 633, 648–649, 656, 691
    See also General programs; Social sciences
Applied arts. See Arts and crafts
Aquatic sciences. See Oceanography
Archaeology
    Disabilities in general: **Fellowships/Grants,** 633, 656
    See also General programs; History; Social sciences
Architectural engineering. See Engineering, architectural
Architecture
    Visual disabilities: **Scholarships,** 51; **Fellowships/Grants,** 148
    Disabilities in general: **Scholarships,** 556, 811–812; **Fellowships/Grants,** 691, 749–750
    See also Fine arts; General programs
Architecture, naval. See Naval architecture
Arithmetic. See Mathematics
Armed services. See Military affairs
Art
    Visual disabilities: **Scholarships,** 40, 90; **Awards,** 259
    Hearing disabilities: **Fellowships/Grants,** 202, 209
    Communication and other disabilities: **Fellowships/Grants,** 460; **Awards,** 507, 509
    Disabilities in general: **Scholarships,** 556; **Fellowships/Grants,** 644, 691; **Grants-in-aid,** 813, 840, 918
    Families of the disabled: **Grants-in-aid,** 1111

See also General programs; names of specific art forms
Art history. *See* History, art
Arthritis
Disabilities in general: **Fellowships/Grants,** 704
See also Disabilities; General programs; Health and health care; Medical sciences
Arts and crafts
Visual disabilities: **Awards,** 259
Disabilities in general: **Awards,** 945
See also Art; General programs; names of specific crafts
Asthma
Communication and other disabilities: **Awards,** 507
See also Disabilities; General programs; Medical sciences
Astronautics
Disabilities in general: **Scholarships,** 536; **Fellowships/Grants,** 663, 750
See also General programs; Space sciences
Astronomy
Disabilities in general: **Scholarships,** 552, 556, 559, 565, 570–571, 583; **Fellowships/Grants,** 635–637, 663, 670, 691, 693, 696–697, 703, 712–713, 741
See also General programs; Physical sciences
Athletics
Disabilities in general: **Awards,** 948
See also General programs; names of specific sports
Atmospheric sciences
Disabilities in general: **Scholarships,** 513, 536, 546, 551, 556, 565; **Fellowships/Grants,** 631, 633, 663, 678, 691, 695, 703, 750
See also General programs; Physical sciences
Attorneys. *See* Law, general
Autism
Families of the disabled: **Awards,** 1191
See also Disabilities; General programs
Automation. *See* Computer sciences; Information science; Technology
Avian science. *See* Ornithology
Aviation
Disabilities in general: **Scholarships,** 562; **Fellowships/Grants,** 700
See also General programs; Space sciences

Behavioral sciences
Disabilities in general: **Scholarships,** 563, 578; **Fellowships/Grants,** 619, 652, 655, 676, 698, 701, 721, 725, 738, 750; **Loans,** 782
See also General programs; Social sciences; names of special behavioral sciences
Biochemistry
Disabilities in general: **Scholarships,** 556; **Fellowships/Grants,** 635–636, 691, 720
See also Biological sciences; Chemistry; General programs

Biological sciences
Visual disabilities: **Scholarships,** 27, 101; **Fellowships/Grants,** 130, 173
Disabilities in general: **Scholarships,** 536, 545, 552, 556, 559, 563, 565–566, 570–571, 597; **Fellowships/Grants,** 619–621, 623, 633, 635–636, 645, 650–651, 655, 660, 663, 670–671, 675, 690–691, 693, 695–696, 698, 701, 703, 707–708, 712–713, 719–720, 728, 731, 741
See also General programs; Sciences; names of specific biological sciences
Biomedical engineering. *See* Engineering, biomedical
Biomedical sciences
Disabilities in general: **Scholarships,** 578; **Fellowships/Grants,** 619, 621, 652, 676, 721, 725, 738; **Loans,** 782
See also Biological sciences; General programs; Medical sciences
Black American studies. *See* African American studies
Blindness. *See* Visual impairments
Botany
Disabilities in general: **Scholarships,** 556; **Fellowships/Grants,** 623, 691
See also Biological sciences; General programs
Brain research. *See* Neuroscience
Burial allowance. *See* Death benefits
Business administration
Visual disabilities: **Scholarships,** 7, 94; **Fellowships/Grants,** 170
Hearing disabilities: **Fellowships/Grants,** 279
Disabilities in general: **Scholarships,** 512, 515, 519, 563, 566, 611–612; **Fellowships/Grants,** 701, 749–750; **Loans,** 791
Families of the disabled: **Scholarships,** 957, 1068
See also Entrepreneurship; General programs; Management
Business enterprises. *See* Entrepreneurship

Canadian history. *See* History, Canadian
Caribbean history. *See* History, Caribbean
Chemical engineering. *See* Engineering, chemical
Chemistry
Visual disabilities: **Scholarships,** 27; **Fellowships/Grants,** 130
Disabilities in general: **Scholarships,** 552, 556, 559, 566, 570–571, 597; **Fellowships/Grants,** 635–636, 670, 678, 691, 693, 695, 698, 712–713, 727
See also Engineering, chemical; General programs; Physical sciences
Choruses. *See* Voice
Civil engineering. *See* Engineering, civil
Clothing
Disabilities in general: **Grants-in-aid,** 818
See also General programs
Colleges and universities. *See* Education, higher
Commerce. *See* Business administration

Communications
    Disabilities in general: **Scholarships,** 563; **Fellowships/Grants,** 701
    See also General programs; Humanities
Community colleges. See Education, higher
Computer engineering. See Engineering, computer
Computer sciences
    Visual disabilities: **Scholarships,** 63, 75, 101; **Fellowships/Grants,** 164, 173
    Communication and other disabilities: **Scholarships,** 367, 442
    Disabilities in general: **Scholarships,** 515, 538, 552, 556, 559, 563, 565, 569–571, 576; **Fellowships/Grants,** 635–636, 665, 669–670, 678, 691, 693, 698, 701, 703, 712–713, 741
    See also General programs; Information science; Libraries and librarianship; Mathematics; Technology
Computers. See Computer sciences
Conservation. See Environmental sciences
Construction. See Housing
Consumer affairs
    Disabilities in general: **Fellowships/Grants,** 710
    See also General programs
Counseling
    Visual disabilities: **Scholarships,** 95; **Fellowships/Grants,** 171
    See also Behavioral sciences; General programs; Psychology
Crafts. See Arts and crafts
Criminal justice
    Disabilities in general: **Scholarships,** 577
    Families of the disabled: **Scholarships,** 1045
    See also General programs; Law, general

Data entry. See Computer sciences
Deafness. See Hearing impairments
Death benefits
    Disabilities in general: **Grants-in-aid,** 853
    Families of the disabled: **Grants-in-aid,** 1129, 1175
    See also General programs
Defense. See Military affairs
Demography. See Population studies
Dentistry
    Disabilities in general: **Loans,** 766; **Grants-in-aid,** 801
    Families of the disabled: **Grants-in-aid,** 1101
    See also General programs; Health and health care; Medical sciences
Dietetics. See Nutrition
Disabilities
    Visual disabilities: **Scholarships,** 9; **Fellowships/Grants,** 123
    Communication and other disabilities: **Awards,** 509

Disabilities in general: **Scholarships,** 548; **Fellowships/Grants,** 657, 684, 724; **Loans,** 776; **Grants-in-aid,** 841
    Families of the disabled: **Loans,** 1097; **Grants-in-aid,** 1122
    See also General programs; Rehabilitation; names of specific disabilities
Disabilities, hearing. See Hearing impairments
Disabilities, visual. See Visual impairments
Documentaries. See Filmmaking
Drama. See Plays

Earth sciences
    Disabilities in general: **Scholarships,** 545, 556, 565, 575, 606; **Fellowships/Grants,** 633, 635–636, 675, 691, 695–696, 698, 703, 717, 734, 750
    See also General programs; Natural sciences; names of specific earth sciences
Eastern European history. See History, European
Ecology. See Environmental sciences
Economic development
    Disabilities in general: **Fellowships/Grants,** 651
    See also Economics; General programs
Economic planning. See Economics
Economics
    Disabilities in general: **Scholarships,** 512, 556, 563, 618; **Fellowships/Grants,** 633, 656, 691, 701
    Families of the disabled: **Scholarships,** 957, 1075
    See also General programs; Social sciences
Education
    Visual disabilities: **Scholarships,** 23, 108; **Fellowships/Grants,** 129, 161, 177; **Awards,** 260
    Disabilities in general: **Scholarships,** 542–543, 556, 563, 583, 606; **Fellowships/Grants,** 672, 691, 701, 706
    See also General programs; specific types and levels of education
Education, elementary
    Visual disabilities: **Scholarships,** 28; **Fellowships/Grants,** 131
    See also Education; General programs
Education, higher
    Visual disabilities: **Scholarships,** 28; **Fellowships/Grants,** 131
    See also Education; General programs
Education, secondary
    Visual disabilities: **Scholarships,** 28; **Fellowships/Grants,** 131
    See also Education; General programs
Education, special
    Visual disabilities: **Scholarships,** 9, 95, 106–108, 116, 118; **Fellowships/Grants,** 123, 171, 175–177, 182
    Disabilities in general: **Scholarships,** 582
    See also Disabilities; Education; General programs
Electrical engineering. See Engineering, electrical

Electronic engineering. *See* Engineering, electronic
Electronics
    Disabilities in general: **Scholarships,** 569; **Fellowships/Grants,** 708
    See also Engineering, electronic; General programs; Physics
Elementary education. *See* Education, elementary
Employment
    Disabilities in general: **Scholarships,** 607; **Fellowships/Grants,** 744; **Grants-in-aid,** 930, 938
    See also General programs
Engineering
    Visual disabilities: **Scholarships,** 16, 27, 51, 101; **Fellowships/Grants,** 130, 148, 173
    Disabilities in general: **Scholarships,** 534, 546, 552, 558, 563, 566, 569, 580–581, 583, 608–609, 611–612; **Fellowships/Grants,** 619–620, 624, 635–636, 645, 650–651, 656, 661–662, 667–671, 678–679, 692, 699, 701, 706, 708–709, 726, 728, 730–732, 749
    Families of the disabled: **Scholarships,** 972
    See also General programs; Physical sciences; names of specific types of engineering
Engineering, aeronautical
    Disabilities in general: **Scholarships,** 556, 570–571; **Fellowships/Grants,** 691, 698, 712–713
    See also Aeronautics; Engineering; General programs
Engineering, aerospace
    Disabilities in general: **Scholarships,** 511, 527–531, 536, 538, 542–543, 547, 554–556, 558–559, 565, 567–568, 570–573, 575, 580–581, 583, 597, 603–605, 608–609, 611–612, 616; **Fellowships/Grants,** 625, 646–647, 653, 663, 665, 672–674, 680–682, 685, 689–694, 697, 703, 705, 711–713, 715–717, 726, 730, 733–734, 741, 743, 745–747, 749–750
    See also Engineering; General programs; Space sciences
Engineering, agricultural
    Disabilities in general: **Scholarships,** 556; **Fellowships/Grants,** 691
    See also Agriculture and agricultural sciences; Engineering; General programs
Engineering, architectural
    Disabilities in general: **Scholarships,** 556; **Fellowships/Grants,** 691
    See also Architecture; Engineering; General programs
Engineering, biomedical
    Disabilities in general: **Scholarships,** 556; **Fellowships/Grants,** 670, 691, 707
    See also Biomedical sciences; Engineering; General programs
Engineering, chemical
    Disabilities in general: **Scholarships,** 556, 559, 570–571, 597; **Fellowships/Grants,** 691, 693, 697–698, 711–713
    See also Chemistry; Engineering; General programs
Engineering, civil
    Disabilities in general: **Scholarships,** 556, 559, 570–571; **Fellowships/Grants,** 691, 693, 711–713
    See also Engineering; General programs
Engineering, computer
    Disabilities in general: **Scholarships,** 556, 570–571, 576; **Fellowships/Grants,** 691, 712–713, 741
    See also Computer sciences; Engineering; General programs
Engineering, electrical
    Visual disabilities: **Scholarships,** 16
    Communication and other disabilities: **Scholarships,** 367
    Disabilities in general: **Scholarships,** 556, 559, 570–571, 576, 597; **Fellowships/Grants,** 691, 693, 698, 711–713, 741
    Families of the disabled: **Scholarships,** 972
    See also Engineering; General programs
Engineering, electronic
    Disabilities in general: **Scholarships,** 556; **Fellowships/Grants,** 691
    See also Electronics; Engineering; General programs
Engineering, environmental
    Disabilities in general: **Scholarships,** 556; **Fellowships/Grants,** 660, 691
    See also Engineering; Environmental sciences; General programs
Engineering, industrial
    Communication and other disabilities: **Scholarships,** 367
    Disabilities in general: **Scholarships,** 556, 570–571, 597; **Fellowships/Grants,** 691, 712–713
    See also Engineering; General programs
Engineering, manufacturing
    Disabilities in general: **Scholarships,** 570–571; **Fellowships/Grants,** 711–713
    See also Engineering; General programs
Engineering, materials
    Disabilities in general: **Scholarships,** 556, 570–571; **Fellowships/Grants,** 691, 698, 712–713, 741
    See also Engineering; General programs; Materials sciences
Engineering, mechanical
    Communication and other disabilities: **Scholarships,** 367
    Disabilities in general: **Scholarships,** 556, 559, 570–571, 597; **Fellowships/Grants,** 691, 693, 697–698, 711–713
    See also Engineering; General programs
Engineering, mining
    Disabilities in general: **Scholarships,** 556; **Fellowships/Grants,** 691
    See also Engineering; General programs
Engineering, nuclear
    Disabilities in general: **Scholarships,** 556; **Fellowships/Grants,** 691, 729
    See also Engineering; General programs

SUBJECT INDEX

Engineering, ocean
    Disabilities in general: **Fellowships/Grants,** 698, 711
    See also Engineering; General programs; Oceanography
Engineering, petroleum
    Disabilities in general: **Scholarships,** 556, 570–571; **Fellowships/Grants,** 691, 712–713
    See also Engineering; General programs
Engineering, systems
    Disabilities in general: **Scholarships,** 570–571; **Fellowships/Grants,** 712–713
    See also Engineering; General programs
Engineering technology
    Disabilities in general: **Scholarships,** 556; **Fellowships/Grants,** 635–636, 691
    See also Engineering; General programs
English history. See History, English
Entrepreneurship
    Disabilities in general: **Loans,** 791; **Grants-in-aid,** 828, 930
    See also Business administration; General programs
Environmental engineering. See Engineering, environmental
Environmental sciences
    Disabilities in general: **Scholarships,** 556, 566, 583, 606; **Fellowships/Grants,** 651, 655, 660, 670, 678, 691, 695, 728, 731, 740
    See also General programs; Sciences
Epilepsy
    Communication and other disabilities: **Awards,** 508
    See also Disabilities; General programs; Health and health care; Medical sciences
Equipment
    Visual disabilities: **Scholarships,** 6, 69, 98; **Fellowships/Grants,** 162; **Loans,** 184–185; **Grants-in-aid,** 190, 193–194, 213–214, 242, 246, 254
    Hearing disabilities: **Scholarships,** 274; **Grants-in-aid,** 291, 293, 297
    Orthopedic and developmental disabilities: **Grants-in-aid,** 320, 322, 328–330, 332, 347, 356
    Communication and other disabilities: **Grants-in-aid,** 493, 503
    Disabilities in general: **Scholarships,** 534, 540; **Fellowships/Grants,** 661; **Loans,** 751–758, 761–764, 768–775, 778–781, 784, 786–788, 790, 792–793, 796–798, 800; **Grants-in-aid,** 812, 829, 832, 834, 836, 843, 863, 865, 874, 931, 937
    Families of the disabled: **Loans,** 1098
    See also General programs
Ethics
    Disabilities in general: **Scholarships,** 512
    Families of the disabled: **Scholarships,** 957
    See also General programs; Humanities
European history. See History, European
Evolution
    Disabilities in general: **Fellowships/Grants,** 655
    See also Biological sciences; General programs; Sciences
Eye problems. See Visual impairments

Fabric. See Clothing
Farming. See Agriculture and agricultural sciences
Fiber. See Textiles
Filmmaking
    Disabilities in general: **Fellowships/Grants,** 622
    See also General programs
Finance
    Visual disabilities: **Scholarships,** 53; **Fellowships/Grants,** 149
    Hearing disabilities: **Scholarships,** 270; **Fellowships/Grants,** 288
    Orthopedic and developmental disabilities: **Scholarships,** 306; **Fellowships/Grants,** 315
    Disabilities in general: **Scholarships,** 512, 515, 618
    Families of the disabled: **Scholarships,** 957, 1075
    See also Accounting; Economics; General programs
Fine arts
    Hearing disabilities: **Scholarships,** 265
    Disabilities in general: **Scholarships,** 632, 583; **Grants-in-aid,** 840; **Awards,** 945
    See also General programs; Humanities; names of specific fine arts
Flight science. See Aviation
Flying. See Aviation
Food. See Nutrition
Food service industry
    Visual disabilities: **Scholarships,** 7
    Disabilities in general: **Scholarships,** 617
    See also General programs
Foreign affairs. See International affairs
Foreign language. See Language and linguistics
Fossils. See Paleontology

General programs
    Visual disabilities: **Scholarships,** 1–8, 10–22, 24–26, 29–39, 41–42, 44–50, 52, 54–62, 64–74, 76–93, 96–99, 102, 104–105, 107, 110–115, 117–120; **Fellowships/Grants,** 121–122, 124–128, 132–147, 150–152, 154–160, 162–163, 165–169, 172, 174, 176, 179–181, 183; **Loans,** 187; **Grants-in-aid,** 190, 195, 202, 211, 213–214, 226–228, 236, 238, 242, 244, 246–247, 249–250, 254, 258; **Awards,** 262
    Hearing disabilities: **Scholarships,** 264, 266–267, 271–278; **Fellowships/Grants,** 280–281, 283–284, 287, 290; **Grants-in-aid,** 293, 295–297; **Awards,** 298–299
    Orthopedic and developmental disabilities: **Scholarships,** 300–305, 307–313; **Fellowships/Grants,** 314, 316; **Grants-in-aid,** 323–324, 326, 335–336, 339, 341, 345, 352

Communication and other disabilities: **Scholarships,** 357–441, 443–453; **Fellowships/Grants,** 454–458, 461–473; **Grants-in-aid,** 474–485, 487, 489–490, 492–506; **Awards,** 510
Disabilities in general: **Scholarships,** 514, 516, 518, 520–526, 533, 535, 539–541, 544, 549–550, 553, 557, 560–561, 564, 574, 577, 579, 584–585, 587–596, 598–602, 607, 610, 613–616; **Fellowships/Grants,** 634, 640, 642, 658–659, 702, 735, 737, 739, 742, 744, 748; **Loans,** 760, 785; **Grants-in-aid,** 808, 816–817, 821, 824, 827, 831–832, 836, 842–843, 850, 854–855, 861, 863, 867, 873, 875, 878–879, 885–886, 906, 909, 913, 916–917, 919–923, 929–931, 937–938, 942; **Awards,** 947, 951–953
Families of the disabled: **Scholarships,** 958–970, 972–1044, 1046, 1048–1049, 1051–1057, 1059–1067, 1069–1074, 1076; **Fellowships/Grants,** 1077–1091, 1093–1094; **Loans,** 1095–1096; **Grants-in-aid,** 1102, 1105, 1113, 1116, 1120, 1124, 1127, 1133, 1142–1144, 1150, 1156, 1161, 1166–1167, 1171, 1173–1174, 1176–1178, 1190

Genetics
Disabilities in general: **Fellowships/Grants,** 720
See also General programs; Medical sciences

Geography
Disabilities in general: **Scholarships,** 556, 570–571; **Fellowships/Grants,** 633, 656, 691, 697
See also General programs; Social sciences

Geology
Disabilities in general: **Scholarships,** 537, 552, 556, 559, 570–571, 597; **Fellowships/Grants,** 664, 691, 693, 695, 712–713, 727
See also Earth sciences; General programs; Physical sciences

Geosciences. See Earth sciences
Government. See Political science and politics; Public administration
Grade school. See Education, elementary

Graphic arts
Visual disabilities: **Awards,** 259
Communication and other disabilities: **Scholarships,** 367; **Fellowships/Grants,** 460
Disabilities in general: **Fellowships/Grants,** 644; **Grants-in-aid,** 813, 840; **Awards,** 945
Families of the disabled: **Grants-in-aid,** 1111
See also Art; General programs

Guidance. See Counseling

Handicapped. See Disabilities
Health and health care
Visual disabilities: **Fellowships/Grants,** 161
Disabilities in general: **Scholarships,** 556; **Fellowships/Grants,** 619, 627–630, 651, 691, 710, 718; **Grants-in-aid,** 833, 942

Families of the disabled: **Grants-in-aid,** 1190
See also General programs; Medical sciences

Hearing impairments
Hearing disabilities: **Fellowships/Grants,** 290
Disabilities in general: **Fellowships/Grants,** 683
See also Disabilities; General programs; Rehabilitation

High schools. See Education, secondary
Higher education. See Education, higher

History
Disabilities in general: **Scholarships,** 556; **Fellowships/Grants,** 633, 691
See also Archaeology; General programs; Humanities; Social sciences; specific types of history

History, African
Disabilities in general: **Fellowships/Grants,** 632, 714
See also General programs; History

History, American
Disabilities in general: **Fellowships/Grants,** 632, 714
See also General programs; History

History, art
Disabilities in general: **Fellowships/Grants,** 666, 722–723
See also Art; General programs; History

History, Canadian
Disabilities in general: **Fellowships/Grants,** 632, 714
See also General programs; History

History, Caribbean
Disabilities in general: **Fellowships/Grants,** 632, 714
See also General programs

History, English
Disabilities in general: **Fellowships/Grants,** 632, 714
See also General programs; History

History, European
Disabilities in general: **Fellowships/Grants,** 632, 714
See also General programs; History

History, Latin American
Disabilities in general: **Fellowships/Grants,** 632, 714
See also General programs; History

History, science
Disabilities in general: **Fellowships/Grants,** 631
See also General programs; History; Sciences

History, South American. See History, Latin American
Hospitality industry. See Hotel and motel industry
Hospitals. See Health and health care

Hotel and motel industry
Disabilities in general: **Scholarships,** 617
See also General programs

Housing
Visual disabilities: **Loans,** 186; **Grants-in-aid,** 207, 253
Orthopedic and developmental disabilities: **Loans,** 317–319; **Grants-in-aid,** 331, 351
Disabilities in general: **Scholarships,** 540; **Loans,** 759, 767, 776–777, 783, 789, 794–795, 799; **Grants-in-aid,** 841, 843–844, 847, 942
Families of the disabled: **Loans,** 1097, 1099–1100; **Grants-in-aid,** 1122, 1190
See also General programs; Property tax benefits

Human resources. *See* Personnel administration
Humanities
    Hearing disabilities: **Fellowships/Grants,** 282
    Disabilities in general: **Fellowships/Grants,** 626
    See also General programs; names of specific humanities
Hydrology
    Disabilities in general: **Scholarships,** 513, 546, 551; **Fellowships/Grants,** 631, 678, 695
    See also Earth sciences; General programs

Income tax benefits
    Visual disabilities: **Grants-in-aid,** 191, 199–200, 203–204, 206, 208–209, 212, 215, 217–218, 220, 223, 225, 229, 233, 235, 237, 239, 241, 243, 255
    Hearing disabilities: **Grants-in-aid,** 292, 294
    Orthopedic and developmental disabilities: **Grants-in-aid,** 334, 344, 353
    Communication and other disabilities: **Grants-in-aid,** 488, 491
    Disabilities in general: **Grants-in-aid,** 804, 810–811, 819, 830, 835, 839, 845, 849, 852, 858, 860, 862, 869, 877, 883, 891–892, 894–895, 900, 907–908, 926–927, 940–941
    Families of the disabled: **Grants-in-aid,** 1104, 1107–1110, 1117–1118, 1125–1126, 1131–1132, 1136–1137, 1145, 1147–1148, 1158, 1162, 1168, 1181, 1189
    See also General programs
Industrial engineering. *See* Engineering, industrial
Information science
    Visual disabilities: **Scholarships,** 53; **Fellowships/Grants,** 149
    Hearing disabilities: **Scholarships,** 270; **Fellowships/Grants,** 288
    Orthopedic and developmental disabilities: **Scholarships,** 306; **Fellowships/Grants,** 315
    Communication and other disabilities: **Scholarships,** 367
    Disabilities in general: **Fellowships/Grants,** 679, 695, 708, 719
    See also Computer sciences; General programs; Libraries and librarianship
International affairs
    Disabilities in general: **Scholarships,** 563; **Fellowships/Grants,** 651, 701
    See also General programs; Political science and politics
International relations. *See* International affairs
Internet design and development
    Disabilities in general: **Grants-in-aid,** 828
    See also General programs; Graphic arts; Technology

Jewish studies
    Visual disabilities: **Fellowships/Grants,** 153

    See also General programs; Religion and religious activities
Jobs. *See* Employment
Journalism
    Disabilities in general: **Scholarships,** 583; **Fellowships/Grants,** 740
    See also Communications; General programs; Writers and writing; names of specific types of journalism
Junior colleges. *See* Education, higher
Jurisprudence. *See* Law, general

Landscape architecture
    Disabilities in general: **Scholarships,** 548; **Fellowships/Grants,** 684
    See also Botany; General programs
Language and linguistics
    Disabilities in general: **Fellowships/Grants,** 633, 656
    See also General programs; Humanities; names of specific languages
Latin American history. *See* History, Latin American
Law enforcement. *See* Criminal justice
Law, general
    Visual disabilities: **Scholarships,** 9, 51, 100; **Fellowships/Grants,** 123, 148
    Disabilities in general: **Scholarships,** 536, 563, 611–612; **Fellowships/Grants,** 633, 638, 656, 663, 701, 749–750
    See also Criminal justice; General programs; Social sciences; names of legal specialties
Lawyers. *See* Law, general
Leadership
    Hearing disabilities: **Fellowships/Grants,** 282
    See also General programs; Management
Legal studies and services. *See* Law, general
Librarians. *See* Libraries and librarianship
Libraries and librarianship
    Disabilities in general: **Fellowships/Grants,** 643
    See also General programs; Information science; Social sciences
Life sciences. *See* Biological sciences
Linguistics. *See* Language and linguistics
Literature
    Visual disabilities: **Scholarships,** 103
    See also General programs; Humanities; Writers and writing; specific types of literature

Magazines. *See* Journalism; Literature
Management
    Visual disabilities: **Scholarships,** 53, 94; **Fellowships/Grants,** 149, 170
    Hearing disabilities: **Scholarships,** 270; **Fellowships/Grants,** 288
    Orthopedic and developmental disabilities: **Scholarships,** 306; **Fellowships/Grants,** 315

Communication and other disabilities: **Scholarships,** 367
Disabilities in general: **Fellowships/Grants,** 656
See also General programs; Social sciences
Manufacturing engineering. See Engineering, manufacturing
Marine sciences
Disabilities in general: **Fellowships/Grants,** 697
See also General programs; Sciences; names of specific marine sciences
Marketing
Communication and other disabilities: **Scholarships,** 367
See also General programs
Mass communications. See Communications
Materials engineering. See Engineering, materials
Materials sciences
Disabilities in general: **Scholarships,** 556, 570–571; **Fellowships/Grants,** 635–636, 670, 691, 697–698, 708, 712–713, 741
See also General programs; Physical sciences
Mathematics
Communication and other disabilities: **Scholarships,** 442
Disabilities in general: **Scholarships,** 538, 542–543, 555–556, 558, 569–571, 580, 597, 603, 606; **Fellowships/Grants,** 635–636, 665, 669–670, 672, 677–678, 686–692, 698–699, 706, 712–713, 719, 726
Families of the disabled: **Scholarships,** 971
See also Computer sciences; General programs; Physical sciences; Statistics
Mechanical engineering. See Engineering, mechanical
Media. See Communications; names of specific media
Media specialists. See Libraries and librarianship
Medical sciences
Visual disabilities: **Scholarships,** 51; **Fellowships/Grants,** 148
Communication and other disabilities: **Scholarships,** 434; **Fellowships/Grants,** 467
Disabilities in general: **Scholarships,** 536, 556, 581, 611–612; **Fellowships/Grants,** 619, 635–636, 663, 669, 691, 704, 707, 730, 741, 749–750
See also General programs; Health and health care; Sciences; names of specific diseases; names of medical specialties
Mental retardation
Families of the disabled: **Fellowships/Grants,** 1092
See also General programs; Medical sciences
Meteorology
Disabilities in general: **Scholarships,** 513, 551, 556; **Fellowships/Grants,** 631, 670, 691
See also Atmospheric sciences; General programs
Microcomputers. See Computer sciences
Military affairs
Disabilities in general: **Fellowships/Grants,** 650
See also General programs
Mining engineering. See Engineering, mining

Missionary work. See Religion and religious activities
Motel industry. See Hotel and motel industry
Museums
Communication and other disabilities: **Fellowships/Grants,** 459
Disabilities in general: **Fellowships/Grants,** 654
See also General programs; Libraries and librarianship
Music
Visual disabilities: **Scholarships,** 40, 43, 103, 109; **Fellowships/Grants,** 178; **Awards,** 261, 263
Disabilities in general: **Grants-in-aid,** 885; **Awards,** 946, 950, 956
See also Fine arts; General programs; Humanities; Performing arts

Natural sciences
Visual disabilities: **Scholarships,** 51; **Fellowships/Grants,** 148
Disabilities in general: **Scholarships,** 563; **Fellowships/Grants,** 701
See also General programs; Sciences; names of specific sciences
Naval architecture
Disabilities in general: **Fellowships/Grants,** 698
See also Architecture; General programs
Neuroscience
Disabilities in general: **Fellowships/Grants,** 656
See also General programs; Medical sciences
Newspapers. See Journalism
Nonfiction
Communication and other disabilities: **Awards,** 509
Disabilities in general: **Grants-in-aid,** 866
See also General programs; Writers and writing
Nuclear engineering. See Engineering, nuclear
Nuclear science
Disabilities in general: **Fellowships/Grants,** 729
See also General programs; Physical sciences
Nurses and nursing, general
Disabilities in general: **Fellowships/Grants,** 750; **Grants-in-aid,** 905
Families of the disabled: **Scholarships,** 1047, 1050, 1058
See also General programs; Health and health care; Medical sciences; names of specific nursing specialties
Nutrition
Disabilities in general: **Scholarships,** 556; **Fellowships/Grants,** 691, 710
See also General programs; Medical sciences

Ocean engineering. See Engineering, ocean
Oceanography
Disabilities in general: **Scholarships,** 513, 546, 551,

556, 565; **Fellowships/Grants,** 631, 633, 678, 691, 695, 698, 703, 727
See also General programs; Marine sciences
Opera. See Music; Voice
Optics
Disabilities in general: **Fellowships/Grants,** 698
See also General programs; Physics
Oratory
Hearing disabilities: **Awards,** 299
See also General programs
Orchestras. See Music
Ornithology
Disabilities in general: **Fellowships/Grants,** 623
See also General programs; Zoology

Painting. See Art
Paleontology
Disabilities in general: **Fellowships/Grants,** 623
See also Archaeology; General programs; Geology; General programs
Performing arts
Hearing disabilities: **Scholarships,** 265
Disabilities in general: **Scholarships,** 532; **Awards,** 943–944, 949, 955
See also General programs; names of specific performing arts
Personnel administration
Communication and other disabilities: **Scholarships,** 367
See also General programs; Management
Petroleum engineering. See Engineering, petroleum
Philology. See Language and linguistics
Photography
Communication and other disabilities: **Fellowships/Grants,** 460
Disabilities in general: **Fellowships/Grants,** 644; **Awards,** 945
See also Fine arts; General programs
Physical sciences
Visual disabilities: **Scholarships,** 90, 101; **Fellowships/Grants,** 173
Disabilities in general: **Scholarships,** 545, 556, 563; **Fellowships/Grants,** 619–620, 645, 650–651, 660, 670–671, 675, 691, 701, 707, 728, 731
See also General programs; Sciences; names of specific physical sciences
Physics
Visual disabilities: **Scholarships,** 27; **Fellowships/Grants,** 130
Disabilities in general: **Scholarships,** 552, 556, 559, 565, 570–571, 597, 603; **Fellowships/Grants,** 635–637, 663, 670, 678, 691, 693, 695–698, 703, 712–713, 727, 733, 741
See also General programs; Mathematics; Physical sciences

Physiology
Disabilities in general: **Fellowships/Grants,** 720, 741
See also General programs; Medical sciences
Plays
Visual disabilities: **Scholarships,** 40
Disabilities in general: **Fellowships/Grants,** 622; **Loans,** 765; **Awards,** 954
See also General programs; Literature; Performing arts; Writers and writing
Poetry
Communication and other disabilities: **Awards,** 509
Disabilities in general: **Fellowships/Grants,** 644
See also General programs; Literature; Writers and writing
Poisons. See Toxicology
Polar studies
Disabilities in general: **Fellowships/Grants,** 639
See also General programs
Police science. See Criminal justice
Political science and politics
Visual disabilities: **Scholarships,** 100
Disabilities in general: **Scholarships,** 556; **Fellowships/Grants,** 633, 656, 691
See also General programs; Public administration; Social sciences
Population studies
Disabilities in general: **Fellowships/Grants,** 651
See also General programs; Social sciences
Posters. See Graphic arts
Pottery
Visual disabilities: **Awards,** 259
See also Arts and crafts; General programs
Presidents, U.S. See History, American
Press. See Journalism
Print journalism. See Journalism
Prints. See Art; Graphic arts
Property tax benefits
Visual disabilities: **Grants-in-aid,** 188–189, 192, 196–198, 201, 205, 210, 210, 219, 221–222, 224, 230–232, 234–235, 240, 245, 248, 251–252, 256–257
Orthopedic and developmental disabilities: **Grants-in-aid,** 321, 325, 327, 333, 337–338, 340, 342–343, 346, 348–350, 354–355
Disabilities in general: **Grants-in-aid,** 802–803, 805–807, 809, 814–815, 820, 822–823, 825–826, 837–838, 846, 848, 851, 856–857, 859, 864, 868, 870–872, 876, 880–882, 884, 887–890, 893, 895–899, 901–904, 910–912, 914–915, 924–925, 928, 932–936, 939
Families of the disabled: **Grants-in-aid,** 1103, 1106, 1112, 1114–1115, 1119, 1121, 1123, 1128, 1130, 1134–1135, 1138–1141, 1146, 1149, 1151–1155, 1157, 1159–1160, 1163–1165, 1169–1170, 1172, 1179–1180, 1182–1188
See also General programs; Housing

Psychology
    Disabilities in general: **Scholarships,** 556; **Fellowships/Grants,** 633, 635–636, 691
    See also Behavioral sciences; Counseling; General programs; Social sciences
Public administration
    Visual disabilities: **Scholarships,** 100; **Fellowships/Grants,** 161
    Disabilities in general: **Scholarships,** 556, 563; **Fellowships/Grants,** 619–621, 645, 650, 691, 701, 710
    Families of the disabled: **Fellowships/Grants,** 1092
    See also General programs; Management; Political science and politics; Social sciences
Public affairs. See Public administration
Public health
    Disabilities in general: **Fellowships/Grants,** 621
    See also General programs; Health and health care
Public policy. See Public administration
Public sector. See Public administration
Public speaking. See Oratory

Real estate
    Disabilities in general: **Scholarships,** 519
    See also General programs
Reentry programs
    Visual disabilities: **Scholarships,** 68
    Disabilities in general: **Fellowships/Grants,** 662
    See also General programs
Rehabilitation
    Visual disabilities: **Scholarships,** 9, 23, 95, 106, 116; **Fellowships/Grants,** 123, 129, 171, 175, 182
    Disabilities in general: **Fellowships/Grants,** 724
    See also General programs; Health and health care; specific types of therapy
Religion and religious activities
    Visual disabilities: **Scholarships,** 43; **Fellowships/Grants,** 153
    Hearing disabilities: **Scholarships,** 267–269; **Fellowships/Grants,** 285–286
    See also General programs; Humanities
Restaurants. See Food service industry
Retardation. See Mental retardation
Risk management
    Disabilities in general: **Fellowships/Grants,** 633
    See also Business administration; Finance; General programs

Schools. See Education
Science, history. See History, science
Sciences
    Hearing disabilities: **Scholarships,** 265
    Disabilities in general: **Scholarships,** 534, 542–543, 546, 558, 569, 580–581, 583, 586, 606, 608–609, 611–612; **Fellowships/Grants,** 624, 661–662, 667–669, 672, 679, 692, 699, 706, 708–709, 726, 730, 732, 736, 749
    Families of the disabled: **Scholarships,** 971
    See also General programs; names of specific sciences
Sculpture
    Communication and other disabilities: **Fellowships/Grants,** 460
    Disabilities in general: **Fellowships/Grants,** 644; **Grants-in-aid,** 813, 840; **Awards,** 945
    Families of the disabled: **Grants-in-aid,** 1111
    See also Fine arts; General programs
Secondary education. See Education, secondary
Sight impairments. See Visual impairments
Singing. See Voice
Social sciences
    Hearing disabilities: **Fellowships/Grants,** 290
    Disabilities in general: **Scholarships,** 556, 578; **Fellowships/Grants,** 620, 626, 645, 650–652, 660, 671, 691, 725, 728, 731; **Loans,** 782
    See also General programs; names of specific social sciences
Sociology
    Disabilities in general: **Scholarships,** 563; **Fellowships/Grants,** 633, 656, 701
    See also General programs; Social sciences
Songs. See Music
South American history. See History, Latin American
Space sciences
    Disabilities in general: **Scholarships,** 511, 527–531, 536, 538, 542–543, 545, 547, 552, 554–556, 558–559, 562–563, 565, 567–568, 570–573, 575, 580–581, 583, 597, 603–606, 608–609, 611–612, 616; **Fellowships/Grants,** 625, 635–636, 641, 646–647, 653, 663, 665, 670, 672–675, 680–682, 685, 689–697, 700–701, 703, 705, 712–713, 715–717, 726, 730, 733–734, 741, 743, 745–747, 749–750
    See also General programs; Physical sciences
Special education. See Education, special
Speech impairments
    Disabilities in general: **Fellowships/Grants,** 683
    See also Disabilities; General programs
Speeches. See Oratory
Sports. See Athletics
Stage design. See Performing arts
Statistics
    Disabilities in general: **Fellowships/Grants,** 656, 719
    See also General programs; Mathematics
Systems engineering. See Engineering, systems

Teaching. See Education
Technology
    Visual disabilities: **Loans,** 185; **Grants-in-aid,** 193
    Disabilities in general: **Scholarships,** 534, 555, 569, 581, 606; **Fellowships/Grants,** 656, 661, 689–690,

706, 708, 730; **Loans,** 751–758, 761–764, 769–775, 778–781, 784, 786–788, 790, 792–793, 797–798, 800; **Grants-in-aid,** 834
  Families of the disabled: **Loans,** 1098
  See also Computer sciences; General programs; Sciences
Textiles
  Visual disabilities: **Awards,** 259
  See also Arts and crafts; General programs
Theater. *See* Performing arts; Plays
Theology. *See* Religion and religious activities
Tourism
  Disabilities in general: **Scholarships,** 617
  See also General programs
Toxicology
  Disabilities in general: **Fellowships/Grants,** 698
  See also General programs; Medical sciences
Travel and tourism. *See* Tourism

Universities. *See* Education, higher
Unrestricted programs. *See* General programs

Veterans. *See* Military affairs
Video. *See* Filmmaking
Visual arts. *See* Art
Visual impairments
  Visual disabilities: **Scholarships,** 16, 23, 50, 95, 106–107, 116, 118; **Fellowships/Grants,** 129, 147, 171, 175–176, 182
  Families of the disabled: **Scholarships,** 972
  See also Disabilities; General programs; Health and health care
Voice
  Visual disabilities: **Awards,** 261
  Disabilities in general: **Awards,** 946, 950
  See also General programs; Music; Performing arts

Web design. *See* Internet design and development
Western European history. *See* History, European
Work. *See* Employment
World literature. *See* Literature
Writers and writing
  Visual disabilities: **Scholarships,** 40
  Hearing disabilities: **Scholarships,** 271
  Communication and other disabilities: **Grants-in-aid,** 486; **Awards,** 509
  Disabilities in general: **Fellowships/Grants,** 622, 644, 714; **Loans,** 765; **Grants-in-aid,** 866; **Awards,** 954
  See also General programs; Literature; specific types of writing

Zoology
  Disabilities in general: **Scholarships,** 556; **Fellowships/Grants,** 691
  See also General programs; Sciences; names of specific zoological subfields

Calendar Index

Since most financial aid programs have specific deadline dates, some may have already closed by the time you begin to look for funding. You can use the Calendar Index to identify which programs are still open. To do that, go to the type of program and recipient categories that apply to you, think about when you'll be able to complete your application forms, go to the appropriate months, jot down the entry numbers listed there, and use those numbers to find the program descriptions in the directory. Keep in mind that the numbers cited here refer to program entry numbers, not to page numbers in the book. Note: not all sponsoring organizations supplied deadline information to us, so not all programs are listed in this index.

Scholarships

Visual disabilities:
January: 34, 76, 85, 118
February: 3–4, 9, 13, 22, 25–27, 32, 36, 46, 49, 53, 58, 60, 63, 94, 98–99, 102, 105, 117
March: 8, 17–18, 28, 31, 39, 45, 50–51, 54, 57, 59, 64–65, 68, 74–75, 82, 89, 91–92, 97, 108, 113
April: 7, 11–12, 16, 23–24, 33, 38, 40, 43, 70, 80, 93, 96, 101, 103–104, 106, 109, 111, 116
May: 2, 20, 42, 55, 61, 66–67, 78, 86, 88, 98
June: 5, 15, 37, 41, 69
July: 21, 30, 73, 77, 95, 115
August: 14, 47, 90, 98, 114
September: 10, 29, 35, 48, 52, 62, 71, 79, 84, 119
October: 1, 56, 98, 100
Any time: 6, 44, 107

Hearing disabilities:
February: 265–266, 270, 272, 274
March: 275
April: 276
June: 273
December: 264
Any time: 268

Orthopedic and developmental disabilities:
January: 304, 310
February: 301, 305–306, 310, 312
April: 309
June: 302, 307
July: 308, 313
October: 303, 307, 311
Any time: 300

Communication and other disabilities:
January: 367, 381, 395, 401, 429, 431
February: 358, 372, 384, 388, 414–415, 417, 430–431, 433, 436
March: 362, 364, 380, 393, 402, 404, 416, 419, 423, 428, 446, 448–450
April: 359–360, 365, 368, 371, 373–375, 377, 389–392, 397–398, 400, 403, 407, 411, 425–426, 432, 434, 439, 442–443, 452
May: 369, 376, 379, 383, 386, 399
June: 357, 385, 387, 394, 408–409, 413, 418, 421, 424, 427
July: 401
August: 447
October: 361, 405, 421, 437–438
November: 378, 382
December: 363, 366, 396

Disabilities in general:
January: 514, 536–537, 539, 549, 576, 582–583, 587–590
February: 513, 515, 517, 530, 542–543, 545–546, 551, 570–571, 598, 600, 603–606, 611–612, 616
March: 520, 524–525, 532, 548, 556, 559, 563, 574, 577, 592–594, 597, 615
April: 516, 519, 522, 560, 562, 564, 585, 601, 617
May: 512, 527–529, 599
July: 533
August: 518, 521, 526, 550, 552, 586
October: 523, 527, 529, 561, 572
November: 555

Scholarships (Continued)

December: 554
Any time: 534–535, 540, 578, 595, 607, 610, 614, 618

Families of the disabled:
January: 993, 997, 1043
February: 962, 980, 1021, 1036, 1041, 1043, 1052, 1058, 1067, 1070
March: 958, 965, 971, 973, 975, 985, 1005, 1029, 1038, 1042, 1051, 1054, 1057, 1066, 1072–1073
April: 961, 972, 986, 988, 992, 994, 996, 998, 1017–1019, 1022, 1031, 1044, 1065
May: 957, 963–964, 976, 983, 995, 1012, 1015, 1032, 1047, 1050, 1059, 1076
June: 961, 977, 989, 1006, 1028, 1037, 1048, 1055
July: 961, 978, 990–991, 997, 1035, 1063
August: 1056
October: 979, 981, 1018
November: 961
December: 979
Any time: 959, 970, 982, 1033–1034, 1061, 1074–1075

Fellowships

Visual disabilities:
February: 121, 123, 130, 135, 143, 146, 149, 155, 170, 174, 183
March: 122, 131, 133, 138, 141–142, 147–148, 150, 152, 157–158, 163–164, 168–169, 172, 177
April: 129, 137, 156, 173, 175, 178, 182
May: 140, 151, 159–160, 165–166
June: 127, 136, 139
July: 154, 161, 171, 181
August: 126, 144, 180
September: 124, 132, 134, 145
Any time: 153, 176

Hearing disabilities:
February: 288
March: 290
April: 279, 281–282, 284, 286, 289
May: 283
August: 287
December: 280
Any time: 285

Orthopedic and developmental disabilities:
February: 315–316
Any time: 314

Communication and other disabilities:
February: 454, 466, 468
March: 464
April: 455, 457, 463, 467, 472
May: 458
June: 460–462, 465
August: 471
Any time: 459

Disabilities in general:
January: 619–621, 629, 634, 645, 649–651, 660, 663–664, 666, 670–671, 673, 696, 698, 708, 722–723, 728–729, 731
February: 623, 631, 633, 672, 675, 678–679, 697, 704, 712–713, 717, 727, 733, 740–741, 743, 749–750
March: 630, 684, 691, 693, 695, 701, 711
April: 638–639, 643, 681, 700, 702, 721, 735, 742
May: 629, 646–647, 659, 734
June: 624, 657, 683, 704, 708
July: 630, 658, 662
August: 633, 640, 642, 727, 736
September: 629, 644, 720
October: 632, 637, 646, 682, 686, 704, 714, 724
November: 630, 655, 669, 677, 679, 687–690, 706, 719, 721
December: 622, 626, 679, 685
Any time: 627, 648, 652, 654, 661, 674, 676, 699, 707, 710, 718, 725, 738–739, 744, 748

Families of the disabled:
February: 1091
March: 1083, 1090
April: 1080, 1085
June: 1079, 1084
July: 1078
August: 1092
Any time: 1077, 1093

Loans

Visual disabilities:
Any time: 184, 186–187

Orthopedic and developmental disabilities:
Any time: 317–319

Disabilities in general:
February: 782
April: 785
October: 760
Any time: 751–759, 761–781, 783–784, 786–800

Families of the disabled:
February: 1095
Any time: 1096–1100

Grants-in-aid

Visual disabilities:
January: 213, 246
February: 242
March: 202, 216, 224
April: 200, 205–206, 211, 215, 225, 230, 232, 235, 237, 243, 245–246, 257
May: 210, 242
June: 193
July: 246, 251
August: 242
September: 193, 198, 249, 258
October: 242, 246
December: 193, 197, 222
Any time: 190, 192, 194, 207, 227, 244, 247, 252–253

Hearing disabilities:
January: 293
February: 297
August: 296
Any time: 291, 295

Orthopedic and developmental disabilities:
February: 340
March: 333, 341
April: 337–338, 344, 355
June: 341
September: 341
December: 341
Any time: 320–324, 328–332, 335–336, 343, 345, 347–349, 351–352, 356

Communication and other disabilities:
March: 487
April: 491
Any time: 474–476, 478–483, 485–486, 489–490, 492–506

Disabilities in general:
January: 863, 903
February: 838, 899
March: 868, 881, 911–912
April: 835, 838, 848–849, 860–861, 882, 889–890, 895, 908, 910, 934, 936
May: 823, 838, 856–857, 859, 897, 902
June: 914, 928–929
July: 925
August: 871, 935
September: 822, 824–826, 832, 859, 939
November: 816
December: 815, 859, 876
Any time: 801, 807, 809, 813, 817–818, 827, 831, 834, 836, 840–841, 843, 847, 851, 853, 854, 865–866, 874, 878–879, 885–886, 896, 904–906, 909, 913, 916–918, 920–922, 924, 927, 930, 937–938, 942

Families of the disabled:
January: 1120
February: 1121, 1159–1160
March: 1134–1135, 1169–1170
April: 1117–1118, 1121, 1125–1126, 1132, 1145–1146, 1152, 1154, 1158, 1162, 1181, 1186, 1188
May: 1121, 1130
June: 1184
August: 1171, 1187
September: 1114–1115
December: 1141
Any time: 1101–1102, 1105–1106, 1111, 1116, 1122, 1124, 1128–1129, 1142–1144, 1150, 1155, 1165–1167, 1173, 1175–1177, 1179–1180, 1182, 1190

Awards

Visual disabilities:
January: 261, 263
February: 262
April: 259
May: 260

Hearing disabilities:
September: 299

Communication and other disabilities:
January: 509
February: 510
June: 508

December: 507

Disabilities in general:
January: 946, 956
February: 945, 952
April: 948, 954
June: 949
August: 953
September: 943–944, 951, 955
October: 950

Families of the disabled:
February: 1191